D1607476

Encyclopedia of Local History

About the Series
The American Association for State and Local History Book Series addresses issues critical to the field of state and local history through interpretive, intellectual, scholarly, and educational texts. To submit a proposal or manuscript to the series, please request proposal guidelines from AASLH headquarters: AASLH Editorial Board, 1717 Church St., Nashville, Tennessee 37203. Telephone: (615) 320-3203. Website: www.aaslh.org.

About the Organization
The American Association for State and Local History (AASLH) is a national history membership association headquartered in Nashville, Tennessee. AASLH provides leadership and support for its members who preserve and interpret state and local history in order to make the past more meaningful to all Americans. AASLH members are leaders in preserving, researching, and interpreting traces of the American past to connect the people, thoughts, and events of yesterday with the creative memories and abiding concerns of people, communities, and our nation today. In addition to sponsorship of this book series, AASLH publishes *History News* magazine, a newsletter, technical leaflets and reports, and other materials; confers prizes and awards in recognition of outstanding achievement in the field; supports a broad education program and other activities designed to help members work more effectively; and advocates on behalf of the discipline of history. To join AASLH, go to www.aaslh.org or contact Membership Services, AASLH, 1717 Church St., Nashville, TN 37203.

Encyclopedia
of
Local History

Third Edition

Edited by
AMY H. WILSON

ROWMAN & LITTLEFIELD
Lanham • Boulder • New York • London

Published by Rowman & Littlefield
A wholly owned subsidiary of The Rowman & Littlefield Publishing Group, Inc.
4501 Forbes Boulevard, Suite 200, Lanham, Maryland 20706
www.rowman.com

Unit A, Whitacre Mews, 26-34 Stannary Street, London SE11 4AB

British Library Cataloguing in Publication Information Available

Library of Congress Cataloging-in-Publication Data

Names: Wilson, Amy H., 1965-
Title: Encyclopedia of local history / edited by Amy H. Wilson.
Description: Third edition. | Lanham : Rowman & Littlefield, [2017] | Series:
    American Association for State and Local History book series | Includes
    bibliographical references.
Identifiers: LCCN 2016041416 (print) | LCCN 2016042983 (ebook) | ISBN
    9781442278776 (cloth) | ISBN 9781442278783 (ebook)
Subjects: LCSH: United States—History, Local—Research—Encyclopedias. |
    United States—Historiography—Encyclopedias.
Classification: LCC E180 .E52 2017 (print) | LCC E180 (ebook) | DDC
    973.03—dc23
LC record available at https://lccn.loc.gov/2016041416

∞™ The paper used in this publication meets the minimum requirements of American
National Standard for Information Sciences—Permanence of Paper for Printed Library
Materials, ANSI/NISO Z39.48-1992.

Printed in the United States of America

CONTENTS

LIST OF PHOTOS

List of Photos

List of Photos

INTRODUCTION

This third edition of the *Encyclopedia of Local History* reflects the expansive scope of the field of local history. Highlighted here is the ever-growing variety of subjects that most local historians face daily and the many resources available for their work. As wide-ranging as the topics herein are, this book is not meant to be comprehensive, but rather to encourage local historians to think about their work in a broader context and to expose them to the innovative work of their colleagues. Throughout this edition we see how local, state, and regional history institutions are increasingly mindful of inclusion, diversity, multiplicity, relevance, and shared authority. This volume provides a snapshot of the current state of local history.

I coedited the last edition with Carol Kammen and, as a founding editor of this series, her influence can still be seen throughout. Although Carol chose to take a less prominent role in this third edition of the Encyclopedia, I have leaned on her heavily for her expertise and advice. She provided encouragement as well as content, including her overview of local history in the United States. As a member of my editorial advisory board, she made many wonderful suggestions and tracked down quite a few authors. I am grateful for her generosity and mentorship.

The third edition continues the benchmarking begun in the second edition with the historical biographies of all the states in the United States, the territory of Guam, and all the Canadian provinces. Importantly, these pieces show how we have viewed our own history over time and, updated for this edition, we can note progress in some places and how others have maintained the status quo. A broader, international perspective can enhance our understanding of local and state history, so continued in this volume you will find updated sketches of local history in England, Scotland, Ireland, Wales, New Zealand, Australia, and Canada.

Introduction

Lacking an index, this volume features an internal set of connections made from essay to essay that should help the reader negotiate from one subject to another. Throughout, there are asterisks (*) that indicate cross-references to other encyclopedia entries.

Found within this book are some remarkable articles. Do not miss "building bridges through local history," George McDaniel's thought-provoking piece that looks for ways in which the use of history can bring healing to divided communities. Tim Grove's essay on historical thinking charges local history institutions with educating their public on the historian's process—that history is often a moving target and not simply cut and dried.

Many essays focus on how the use of technology has enhanced the work of the local historian. There are entries on digitization and doing digital history projects, the use of apps by local history organizations, and how institutions are using Historypin, as well as other social media, to foster community engagement. There is also a look at online encyclopedias by example of what Texas is doing.

You will find excellent new entries on historic resorts; analyzing primary sources; evaluation of programming; interpreting and researching gardens at historic sites; the interesting local history one can glean from post office records; and how local history organizations are incorporating STEM education into their programming and the benefits of doing so. Check out the new entries on interpreting slavery, interpreting LGBT history, architectural history, and vernacular architecture. Catherine Hughes contributes an essay on museum theater, spotlighting examples of this highly engaging form of programming to which museums are increasingly turning. Benjamin Filene looks at history museums and identity. Carol Kammen challenges local historians to see themselves as public intellectuals.

Most essays were commissioned and the task was taken up by exceedingly generous people to whom all I can say is thank you. Everyone wrote against the burden of word count, although many of the essayists could have said much more if offered more space.

The editorial advisory board became active partners in this project, people to whom I went for essays and ideas. Carol Kammen was instrumental in bringing in authors to provide updated essays on each of the states in addition to contributing her own essays. Jim Folts of the New York State Archives provided suggestions for new entries and contributed the appendix on religious organizations along with a number of technical essays regarding government records. Max van Balgooy of Engaging Places, LLC contributed wonderful essays on vision and mission statements of local history organizations, the values of history, and the challenges facing house museums in the twenty-first century. In addition to providing several of the photos found throughout the book, he helped track down authors as well. Anne Ackerson of the Council of State Archivists contributed essays and ideas, helped find authors, and made sure state archives and state archivists were well represented in this volume; see Appendix E. Tim Grove of the Smithsonian National Air and Space Museum suggested ideas for new content and contributed several essays on subjects ranging from shared authority and historical relevance to many of the technology-related opportunities for museums.

Many others have been very helpful. I especially thank Bob Beatty and John Dichtl of AASLH, Linda Norris of the Uncataloged Museum, Bob Kibbee of the History Center in Tompkins County (NY), Dee Harris at the National Archives at Kansas City, and the many people who provided photographs of historical markers for this volume.

As Carol Kammen says, the *Encyclopedia of Local History* is less "encyclopedia" and more "a compendium of useful information, interesting scholarship, and other good stuff." As you dip into this book, the cross-references encourage exploration. As one topic leads to another, the reader can discover some true gems and maybe even a few surprises. Happy reading!

AMY H. WILSON

$\mathcal{A}$

abstract. An abstract is a summary of a document, such as an abstract of judgment or abstract of title to real property.

accessioning. See deaccession.

account books. Financial records kept by individuals, shops, and companies. These are often difficult to use because of the cryptic nature of the entries, because frequently too little information is provided, and because often the currency is not specified. Nevertheless, a store account book can help create a picture of credit offered in a neighborhood, especially in times of economic depression, or of the importation of goods from beyond the community, or of the nature of barter and credit in a locality. Company records are likely to be more extensive than what is found in a simple account book; if these have survived they will be a challenge to use and might require knowledge of accounting. Personal financial accounts, sometimes kept in diaries along with other entries, are useful in recreating the life of an individual and sometimes show how a segment of the community managed financial matters. Account books have been used by a number of colonial historians to understand particular industries, such as the tobacco economy of the Chesapeake or the economy of Southern plantations.

See AASLH Technical Leaflet #140 by Robert J. Wilson III, "Early American Account Books: Interpretation, Cata-loguing, and Use." See Barbara Dubis Merino and Gary J. Previts, *A History of Accounting in America* (1979).

adoption. To voluntarily take a child of other parents as one's own child. Adoption laws vary by state. Attitudes and customs concerning adoption have changed over time from a private arrangement (in the past often kept secret), to supervised adoption from public homes or other institutions, to an act regulated by the state. Adoption is a complex process with many cultural ramifications. *Wikipedia* provides an excellent overview with notes and bibliography: https://en.wikipedia.org/wiki/Adoption. An even more exhaustive treatment is *The Adoption History Project*: http://pages.uoregon.edu/adoption/index.html.

Local historians will primarily be concerned with helping family historians and genealogists locate information about specific adoptions. Records can be difficult to locate and may be restricted. For a good overview and guide to appropriate state courts, see the chapter "Court Records" by Sandra Hargreaves Luebking et al. in *The Source: A Guidebook to American Genealogy* (2010). Also see E. Wayne Carp, *Family Matters: Secrecy and Disclosure in the History of Adoption* (1998), and more recently by the same author, *Adoption in America: Historical Perspectives* (2002).

ROBERT KIBBEE
HISTORY CENTER IN
TOMPKINS COUNTY (NY)

advent. In the ecclesiastical calendar, Advent begins the fourth Sunday preceding Christmas.

adventists. In the United States, an Adventist is one who believes in the second coming of Christ and the imminent end of the world or era.

See Appendix B.

advertisements. These are of various types; they might appear in newspapers or they might be posters, broadsides, or on products. Advertising has changed over time from ads that inform about a product to advertisements that make claims about the user of the product. Ads are sometimes overlooked by local historians, but they offer interesting commentary about a community. Advertisements in newspapers can date changes; for example, in 1849 a number of people offered houses and farms for sale in order to go west to the goldfields. Medical ads can reveal contemporary concerns, such as those that appeared at the end of the nineteenth century that were placed by Lydia Pinkham, in which she suggested that her tonic was good for women students who might suffer from undue stress caused by too much study. "Advertisements and classified sections can illuminate aspects of black community life that may not be readily apparent from other sources, such as runaway ads for slaves and indentured servants." Advertisements also give evidence of the introduction of new technologies or ingredients, or signal fashion changes such as ads for wallpaper. In addition, advertisements can give detailed information about the contents of a home, farm, or business.

Advertisements document economic, cultural, and technological change in a community. In *Saltwater Foodways: New Englanders and Their Food, at Sea and Ashore, in the Nineteenth Century* (1995) Sandra Oliver documents the arrival of spices brought by sea to New England communities. Automobile advertisements signal a change in technology that led to a number of other physical, economic, and social changes in local communities. See Beth Bailey, *From the Front Porch to the Back Seat: Courtship in Twentieth-Century America* (1989), and of course see Dolores Hayden, *The Grand Domestic Revolution* (1989) where advertisements often heralded the changing technology of care of a house. Real estate promotions also reveal desired features and show how the modern house evolved.

CAROL KAMMEN
TOMPKINS COUNTY (NY) HISTORIAN

affinity. An affinity relationship is one created by marriage, but not through blood; for example, sister-in-law, stepchild.

African American genealogy. See genealogy, African American.

African American history. The forced migration of approximately a half million Africans into Britain's North American colonies began in 1619 and continued up to the Civil War. Slavery took shape gradually during the 1600s, primarily to supply the colonies' agricultural labor force. While slavery was practiced in all thirteen colonies, Southern economies relied more heavily on labor-intensive cash crops, and so developed a stronger commitment to maintaining an enslaved labor force. As black Americans, slave and free, adapted their various African languages, religions, and cultural practices to their oppressed status in American society, white America developed a racist ideology that defined blacks as an inferior race in order to justify their enslavement. After the Revolution the northern states took steps toward emancipation, but free blacks, North and South, were still denied the basic rights, privileges, and protections enjoyed by white American citizens.

With northern emancipation well under way by the early nineteenth century, slavery became the South's "peculiar institution." American slavery was brutal and dehumanizing. Blacks were not permitted to read or write; families were separated by sale; white masters sexually exploited black women; and the constant threat of violence hung over all aspects of slaves' lives. Nonetheless, enslaved blacks developed an important sense of community and identity, with family ties and religion serving particularly central roles. African Americans consistently resisted their enslavement from the 1600s on, often by attempting to escape. While most escape attempts resulted in recapture, tens of thousands of African Americans succeeded in liberating themselves during the nineteenth century alone. In addition to running away, slaves broke tools, slowed their pace of work, stole property, and at times resorted to direct attacks against their masters. While small-scale acts

of poisoning, arson, and personal violence were more common, hundreds of slave rebellions were planned or perpetrated over the 250 years of American slavery. None of these rebellions were ultimately successful, but they indicate African Americans' sustained opposition to their enslavement.

This ongoing pressure from the slaves themselves was an essential counterpoint to the work of northern abolitionists. Abolition was a controversial issue that generated little support among whites, but an increasingly vocal movement played a crucial role in U.S. society after the 1830s. While a small number of sympathetic whites provided an essential biracial component to abolitionism, free northern African Americans—many of them former slaves—remained the driving force behind the movement to abolish slavery and to attain full citizenship rights. One might say that the first African American civil rights movement took shape during the early 1800s.

That movement appeared to have achieved its goals during the Civil War era. Between 1865 and 1870 slavery was abolished, African Americans' citizenship rights were protected under the constitution, and black males were guaranteed the right to vote. By 1880, however, white-supremacist governments had reclaimed power in the South, and through violence, economic coercion, and legal trickery, quickly stripped southern blacks of their rights and imposed the system of Jim Crow segregation that defined southern race relations up to the 1960s.

This erosion of black rights in the South was all the more important because, even as late as 1900, 90 percent of

African Americans lived in that section. Under the system of sharecropping, blacks with little educational opportunity and few rights or options continued to provide the labor that supported the southern agricultural economy. The major political parties showed little interest in protecting African Americans' rights, so black activists worked for their economic, political, and civil rights largely through their own organizations.

The twentieth century brought both dramatic changes and disturbing continuities in the experiences of African Americans. One of the most striking developments has been the "Great Migration." In 1900, 90 percent of African Americans lived in the rural South. By 1960, over half of all African Americans lived in urban areas outside the South. While blacks in non-Southern cities generally found greater educational and employment opportunities and greater protections of their citizenship rights, they also found continued discrimination, especially in housing, where restrictive policies limited most blacks to racially defined ghettos. In many respects the ghetto helped stimulate thriving community institutions and a growing black middle class. Urban African American writers, artists, and performers also began having a larger impact on American popular culture than ever before. But the limited opportunities of the ghetto helped to create problems in underemployment, crime, and poverty that continue to plague inner cities.

In the South, sharecropping, segregation, and white supremacy enforced by violence continued to define the experiences of most African Americans through World War II. After the war, mechanized agriculture displaced many black sharecroppers who increasingly moved to northern, western, and southern cities to find employment. In addition, the modern civil rights movement began to challenge the racial order that had been in place since Reconstruction. By the mid-1960s the federal government finally began using its authority, through Supreme Court decisions and congressional legislation, to protect African Americans' constitutional rights. The system of legal segregation was gradually dismantled and black voting rights expanded markedly.

The gains of the civil rights movement in the South, however, were counterbalanced by the continued oppression of blacks in northern and western ghettos. Police brutality, discrimination in housing and education, and unemployment gave rise to a series of urban riots during the mid-1960s, illustrating blacks' frustration. The cry of "Black Power" swept out of the South, giving rise to movements for greater solidarity and community control among urban blacks. An emphasis on the distinctive elements of black American culture expressed itself in hairstyles, clothing, arts, and political activism, primarily geared toward the full empowerment of black Americans, both in their own communities and in American society as a whole.

There have been mixed results from the turmoil of the 1960s. Federal government protections have allowed an unprecedented degree of African American participation in politics, and educational and employment opportunities have expanded. But these advances have been uneven. While the black middle class has grown dramatically, a black underclass rooted in urban ghettos has also grown since the 1970s. Employment and educational opportunities are limited, and patterns of segregation in housing have changed little since the 1970s. In the 2010s, allegations of racial profiling and police violence against African Americans gave rise to renewed activism in black communities. This situation has caused some analysts to suggest that black Americans in the early twenty-first century faced their most severe crisis since the end of slavery. America remains a racially divided nation, and African Americans, perhaps more than ever before, are divided internally along class lines. Moreover, increasing immigration from Africa and the Caribbean has reshaped black America's ethnic and linguistic makeup and complicated the notion of African American identity.

The first generation of historians interested in African American history was comprised of free blacks in the Northern states between the 1840s and 1870s. Their early works called attention to the long history of African Americans' contributions to American society, and emphasized their rights to full citizenship. Black men's patriotic military service in the Revolution and the Civil War was especially accentuated. This project took on great importance since popular white-authored histories excluded any mention of African Americans and, even after blacks' rights were protected by constitutional amendments during Reconstruction, racial discrimination and violence continued to restrict black opportunities

in education, employment, political participation, and all realms of public life. Key works from this period include William C. Nell, *The Colored Patriots of the Revolution* ([1855] 1968); William Wells Brown, *The Black Man* ([1863] 1968) and *The Negro in the American Rebellion* ([1867] 1968); and William Still, *The Underground Railroad* ([1872] 1968).

Between the 1880s and the 1910s African American historians expanded and professionalized their work. George Washington Williams' two-volume *History of the Negro Race in America from 1619 to 1880* ([1882] 1968) was the first comprehensive scholarly treatment of the African American past. By the early twentieth century, organizations like Philadelphia's American Negro Historical Society (1897) and New York's Negro Society for Historical Research (1911) were systematically collecting documents and artifacts related to black history. W. E. B. Du Bois became the first African American to receive a PhD in history (Harvard, 1895), and numerous works were written attempting to describe African Americans' role in the nation.

A real turning point came in 1915 with Du Bois's publication of his ambitious study, *The Negro* ([1915] 1975). But it was Carter G. Woodson, another Harvard PhD, who became the dominant force in black history for the first half of the century. Beginning with his founding of the Association for the Study of Negro History and Life (1915) and *Journal of Negro History* (1916), Woodson and his many protégés began a thorough scholarly exploration of the historical experiences of black Americans.

Woodson's *The Negro in Our History* ([1922] 1972) and *The Mis-Education of the Negro* ([1933] 1977) were important critiques of the exclusion or distortion of black history in mainstream works by white historians. Woodson's followers made outstanding contributions that slowly began to awaken the historical profession to the legitimacy of studying the African American past. Works by Lorenzo Greene, A. A. Taylor, Charles H. Wesley, and Rayford Logan investigated various aspects of the black past with academic rigor that white historians had to respect. Greene's *The Negro in Colonial New England, 1620–1776* ([1942] 1968), for example, is still considered by many the best single-volume work on that topic. Another key work from this period was Du Bois's *Black Reconstruction in America, 1863–1880* ([1935] 1969), which challenged the existing racist scholarship on that subject. Du Bois's interpretations are now considered far more accurate than those of the white supremacists whose interpretations held sway through the 1950s.

While African Americans had been producing important studies of the African American past since the mid-nineteenth century, the mainstream historical profession has only begun a systematic exploration of the field since World War II. Before that time white historians considered African American history a marginal and unimportant subject about which there was little of value to say and nothing that would add to the understanding of U.S. history. The "Woodson school" was beginning to turn some heads, but it was two black scholars not closely associated with Woodson who had the greatest impact on the mainstream profession.

John Hope Franklin (Harvard PhD, 1941) and Benjamin Quarles (Wisconsin PhD, 1940) departed from previous black historians by emphasizing the integration of African American history with broader patterns of the American past. Franklin's *From Slavery to Freedom: A History of Negro Americans* (1947) was immediately recognized as a thorough and objective survey of African American history, and influenced many scholars to take the subject seriously as an important aspect of the American past. The book is now in its ninth edition (2011) and continues to be assigned in college-level survey courses, though the first decade of the twenty-first century witnessed the publication of numerous high-quality African American history textbooks. Quarles, like Franklin, devoted much of his career to advancing the idea that African American history is an integral part of American history. This objective is reflected in the title of his best-known book, *The Negro in the Making of America* ([1964] 1987). Quarles and Franklin were instrumental in opening the mainstream historical profession to black scholars. Franklin, in particular, compiled an impressive list of "firsts" in publishing, presenting papers, joining and chairing university departments, and leading major historical associations.

During the 1950s and 1960s, white historians, stimulated in part by World War II's assault on racism in Europe and by a reinvigorated civil rights movement, joined black scholars in re-evaluating American slavery, studying the development of black urban ghettos and the system of racial segregation, and generally assessing the important role African Americans have played in U.S. history. Two books, Kenneth Stammp's *The Peculiar Institution* (1956) and Stanley Elkins's *Slavery* (1959), represent early examples of white scholars' attempts to challenge the racist interpretations of slavery that had dominated the field. Other important early works include C. Vann Woodward's *The Strange Career of Jim Crow* (1955), which examined the emergence of legal segregation in the post–Civil War South; Gilbert Osofsky's *Harlem: The Making of a Ghetto* (1966), which dealt with urbanization as a major aspect of Northern blacks' experiences; and Winthrop Jordan's *White Over Black* (1968), which explored the history of racism and race relations during the colonial era. While this acceptance of African American history by the profession is important, most works from this period portrayed blacks as the passive victims of white racism, and their conclusions have been revised by more recent studies.

During the 1970s, in the wake of the civil rights and black power movements, both university history departments and major publishing houses began to devote more attention to black history. An explosion of works was published by white and black historians, black studies departments were formed in many universities, and history departments began to offer courses in African American history. Much attention was devoted to treating blacks as active creators of their history rather than as passive victims of whites. This became a special focus for scholars interested in slavery and blacks' resistance to their enslavement. Much of this scholarship focused on enslaved blacks' worldview and culture, arguing that even under slavery black Americans developed their own institutions and were not completely controlled by white slaveholders. John Blassingame's *The Slave Community* (1972) departed from earlier studies by using the recollections of former slaves in order to describe slave culture, and Albert Raboteau probed the distinctive spiritual lives of enslaved African Americans in his *Slave Religion* (1978). Perhaps the most ambitious, and controversial, reassessment of slavery during this era was Eugene Genovese's *Roll, Jordan, Roll* (1974), which argued that slavery involved a compromise between the needs and demands of both the slaveholders and the enslaved. Lawrence Levine's influential *Black Culture and Black Consciousness* (1977) extended the community/culture analysis into the twentieth century, examining black folk culture in order to understand the attitudes and actions of the black masses in slavery and in freedom.

Since the 1970s, scholarship on African American history has continued to accelerate, giving us unprecedented opportunities for appreciating the role black Americans, their culture, and their institutions have played in the nation and in local communities. The vast complexities and varieties of African Americans' historical experiences make African American history one of the most exciting and active areas of historical study. Scholarship since the 1990s especially has deepened our understanding of the African American past and its interconnectedness with broader patterns in U.S. and world history. Historians have delved into ever more specialized areas of research dealing with family life, gender, migration, literature, local and regional histories, and particular time periods and issues. Public historians and others have devoted increasing attention to the presentation of African American history in monuments, textbooks, museums, historic sites, and public commemorations. The following recent works provide a starting point for understanding the major themes in the black American experience. Most of these works contain bibliographies or footnotes indicating sources on more specialized topics.

Some to note are Darlene Clark Hine et al., *The African American Odyssey*, 4th ed. (2010); John Hope Franklin and Evelyn Brooks Higginbotham, *From Slavery to Freedom: A History of African Americans*, 9th ed. (2011); Ira Berlin, *The Making of African America: The Four Great Migrations* (2010); James Oliver Horton and Lois E. Horton, eds., *Slavery and Public History: The Tough Stuff of American History* (2006).

Perhaps the most comprehensive single-volume guide to researching African American history is Evelyn Brooks Higginbotham et al., eds., *The Harvard Guide to African American History* (2001). Basic encyclopedias of the African American experience include Jack Salzman, David Lionel Smith, and Cornell West, eds., *Encyclopedia of African American Culture and History*, 5 vols. (1996); Henry Louis Gates and Evelyn Brooks Higginbotham, eds., *The African American National Biography*, 8 vols. (2008); Jessie Carney Smith and Carrell Horton, eds., *Historical Statistics of Black America*, 2 vols. (1995); Darlene Clark Hine, Elsa Barkley Brown, and Rosalyn Terborg-Penn, eds., *Black Women in America: An Historical Encyclopedia*, 2 vols. (1993).

In some areas of the country, especially near large cities, one can find important repositories of documents relating to African American history. Some of the most extensive collections are found at the Schomburg Center for Research in Black Culture in New York, the *Amistad Research Center at Tulane University in New Orleans, the *Moorland-Spingarn Research Center at Howard University in Washington, D.C., and the Charles L. Blockson Afro-American Historical Collection at Temple University in Philadelphia.

In addition, there are numerous Internet resources relating to the study of African American history. One must always use caution in relying on Internet information; there is no control over the reliability of these sources. Generally speaking, sites related to universities are the most reliable for scholarly information. A few useful sites, all of which provide links to other Internet sources on black history, include the "American Memory" electronic exhibits from the *Library of Congress, which contain selected collections pertinent to African American topics: https://memory.loc.gov/ammem/aaohtml/aohome.html. Another site addressing an extensive range of black history topics can be found at the BlackPast: Remembered and Reclaimed website: http://www.blackpast.org. The Smithsonian Institution's National Museum of African American History and Culture, which opened in fall 2016, also has an interesting set of online materials: https://nmaahc.si.edu. The Association for the Study of African American Life and History (ASALH) is a preeminent organization for the study of black history: https://asalh100.org. Finally, for those interested especially in genealogy, AfriGeneas http://www.afrigeneas.com, and the Afro-American Historical and Genealogical Society, http://www.aahgs.org, each provide resources for researching African American family histories.

Communities with significant African American populations often have resources related to local black history. Local or regional African American newspapers began appearing in large numbers after the Civil War. Many contain a wealth of information on political debates, meetings of organizations and clubs, marriages and social events, church activities, black businesses, and more. Even the *advertisements and classified sections can illuminate aspects of black community life that may not be readily apparent from other sources. These papers are often available on microfilm at university libraries and at local or state historical societies. Increasingly they are being made available in online, searchable databases through subscription services like Accessible Archives and ProQuest; university or local libraries often provide access to these databases. Information on conducting local and genealogical research, with sections identifying resources in every state, can be found in James M. Rose, *Black Genesis: A Resource Book for African American Genealogy*, 2nd ed. (2003).

Census and *city directory data can also suggest patterns of black population change in a community. Before the 1920s or so, many city directories noted race in their entries, which can help develop a sense of racially defined residence patterns. Property deeds can also be useful in this regard. General county or local histories, especially those published before the 1960s, rarely contain much information on African Americans, but they can provide at least a few names or events as a starting point for an investigation of other sources. Many states were included in government-sponsored WPA writing projects during the 1930s, and at times produced volumes giving brief but useful overviews of the black presence in the state. Also, theses and dissertations from nearby colleges can be important sources for understanding historical patterns in local African American communities. Churches, fraternal orders, community centers, NAACP branches, and other black community institutions might have records they would be willing to share. And, of course, *oral history is crucial. Black history has long been transmitted through stories passed from generation to generation, and the memories of older local residents are irreplaceable sources for understanding patterns of everyday life in a community. If trust is established, individuals might be willing to share both their stories and the miscellaneous information (photos, clippings, programs, etc.) contained in scrapbooks or shoeboxes in the attic.

Any effort to conduct local historical research must strive to understand how the local story relates to broader patterns and a larger historical context. In addition to the general works listed above, much of the published scholarship on African American history in the early twenty-first century has focused on the black presence in specific communities and regions. A few examples include Randal Maurice Jelks, *African Americans in the Furniture City: The Struggle for Civil Rights in Grand Rapids* (2006); Bruce A. Glasrud and James M. Smallwood, eds., *The African American Experience in Texas: An Anthology* (2007); Jeffrey A. Crow et al., *History of African Americans in North Carolina*, revised 2nd ed. (2002); Mark J. Sammons and Valerie Cunningham, *Black Portsmouth: Three Centuries of African American Heritage* (2004).

Researchers of black communities must always keep in mind the diversity of people's experiences, even in a small town. Also, it is necessary to make connections between local events and developments and the broader patterns of African American history in order to understand the way a particular community reflects changes and continuities in American and African American society.

MITCH KACHUN
WESTERN MICHIGAN UNIVERSITY

See biographical dictionaries building bridges through local history; census, United States; diversity and inclusion in museums; emancipation celebrations; genealogy, African American; HeritageQuest; slave schedules; slavery interpretation at museums and historic sites.

African immigrants in North America, sources for. See Appendix A.

African Methodist Episcopal (AME) church, sources for. See Appendix B.

African Methodist Episcopal Zion (AMEZ) church, sources for. See Appendix B.

agricultural and mechanical colleges. The Morrill Land-Grant College Act of 1862 created land-grant institutions to teach agriculture, engineering, and military science, as well as the traditional liberal arts. Some money went to existing schools, but the measure is known for having created a number of new public universities. Congress passed a second Morrill Land-Grant College Act in 1890 that provided annual appropriations of federal aid to the fledgling schools and, as a by-product, brought into existence a number of segregated land-grant colleges for African American students in the South.

See Roger L. Williams, *The Origins of Federal Support for Higher Education: George W. Atherton and the Land-Grant College Movement* (1991) and Laurence R. Veysey, *The Emergence of the American University* (1965).

ROGER L. WILLIAMS
PENNSYLVANIA STATE UNIVERSITY,
RETIRED

agricultural history, problems documenting. A historian must try to incorporate multiple disciplines when studying the agricultural history of a local community. America began as a place of desert, plains, forests, and valleys; everywhere that people lived, cultivation of the land occurred. This essay will include insights gleaned from the remarkable *Rethinking Home* by Joseph Amato, and from the recent trilogy of books I have written about Napa.

Agricultural history begins with the land and the indigenous, even if they were migratory and the dwellings impermanent. Recent scholarship has allowed us to understand the multiple ways by which indigenous peoples cultivated plants. Here in Napa, the indigenous were removed in 1850, but are no less worthy of historical attention than others who came later. Fortunately, a park naturalist created a native plant garden at the Bale Mill State Park where I was able to learn about the uses of native plants by the Mey'ankmah, the tribe who lived here.

Each local historian must grapple with those who labor on the land. Here, Mexicans and Mexican Americans have returned to the lands that were once part of Mexico, and though they exclusively harvest the monoculture crop of grapes, they also teach in the schools and hunger for an inclusive portrait of their nineteenth-century ancestors as well as their own history of migration and immigration. The records of the Mexican settlers here—the Californios—are only recently being translated from the Spanish. Their reign was brief, about 1821 to 1848, but their influence remains in the names of streets and neighborhoods and the consequences of the dishonoring of land claims after the Treaty of Guadalupe Hidalgo. The writer of local agricultural history must absorb the particularities of region, of class, and race dislocations that form the modern situation.

All historians use evidence, but the language of crop reports must be transformed to bins and barrels of foodstuffs, of money changing hands, of workers advertised for, hired, and often fired. Records of minutes from the local Farm Bureau during World War II provided me with information about the labor of German POWs, of state hospital inmates, and of Jamaican and Mexican braceros in the local orchards and vineyards.

Writing agricultural history demands that we think about the ecology that gave rise to the particular agriculture of a region. Water and access to it, plumbing and engineering, are key to analysis. Who worked the land? Where did they live, if not on the farms they owned? How did the nature of "hired help" change, and thus the relations of worker to farmer? How were agricultural products transported? What did the river look like when it was full of steamships; what did the train sound like when it carried cargo?

The agricultural historian must try to imagine the smells and sounds of a time when the world was vastly different. Agricultural history is the history of tools, of pesticides, or the decision to abandon them, the history of buildings—barns, silos, underground caverns for canned fruits and bottled wines. Agricultural history considers the role of animals both wild and domestic. It asks about social conditions and organizations: who founded the local 4-H? The Grange?

How do we acquire the records to answer these questions? Information and artifacts are not necessarily in the public domain. We must always ask, whose story? We need demographic data in order to present a reasonably accurate picture of family farms and who lived on them, and we need oral information from those who remain on the land. Agricultural history is not just the story of successful farms, but of farms that changed and survived, farms that deteriorated, farms that were plowed under. There is a great deal of pain associated with the demise of family farms, as well as guilt by the offspring when they trade their parents' land for a secure retirement income for themselves. These disappearances need to be carefully documented.

LAUREN COODLEY
NAPA COLLEGE, RETIRED

See American Indian history.

Alabama, local history in. Lacking a robust historical society with the capac-ity to collect and publish in the nineteenth century, historical efforts in Alabama were sporadic until the creation of the Alabama Department of Archives and History (ADAH) in 1901. Founding director Thomas M. Owen rapidly expanded collections that included state and local government records, private manuscripts, published reference materials, and artifacts.

Early state histories include Albert James Pickett's *History of Alabama* (1851) and Willis Brewer's *Alabama* (1872), which contains county profiles. In 1921, Thomas Owen's second major contribution to Alabama history was published posthumously. His four-volume *History of Alabama and Dictionary of Alabama Biography* remains an indispensable resource on state and

Unveiling ceremony for the E. L. Posey Parking Lot historical marker in Montgomery, Alabama. The parking lot served the black community as a transportation center during the Montgomery Bus Boycott. CREDIT: ALABAMA DEPARTMENT OF ARCHIVES AND HISTORY.

local topics through the early twentieth century.

Additional major syntheses came in 1934 with A. B. Moore's *History of Alabama* and in 1994 with the publication of *Alabama: The History of a Deep South State* by William Warren Rogers, Sr., Leah Rawls Atkins, Robert Ward, and Wayne Flynt. More recent additions to the canon include Harvey H. Jackson's reader-friendly *Inside Alabama* (2003) and Wayne Flynt's *Alabama in the Twentieth Century* (2004). A Bicentennial history of the state by Edwin C. Bridges is scheduled for publication in 2016.

Important serial sources for local history include the *Alabama Official and Statistical Register* (1903–1979) and the *Alabama Historical Quarterly* (1930–1982), both published by the ADAH; the *Alabama Review* (1948–), published by the Alabama Historical Association; and *Alabama Heritage* magazine (1986–), published jointly by the University of Alabama, the University of Alabama at Birmingham, and the ADAH. Numerous journals of local historical societies are also available at the ADAH and university and public libraries.

The scope and availability of Alabama resources have proliferated in the digital era. *Alabama Mosaic* (www.alabamamosaic.org) is an online repository of images from the collections of archives and libraries throughout the state. Launched in 2008, the *Encyclopedia of Alabama* (www.encyclopediaofalabama.org) offers profiles of all sixty-seven counties and many municipalities among its expansive content. Full-text searches of Owen, the *Official and Statistical Register*, and the *Alabama*

Historical Quarterly are available online at www.archives.alabama.gov. Access to local collections improved dramatically in 2010 with the completion of the *Alabama Repositories Directory* (www.archives.alabama.gov/hrb/search.cfm).

Local historical and genealogical societies support a wide array of programs, ranging from pilgrimages and cemetery preservation to repositories and museums. Local "Friends" organizations also partner with the Alabama Historical Commission to support the preservation of structures and sites that have community and statewide significance.

Regional organizations such as the Tennessee Valley Historical Society, the Black Belt African American Genealogical & Historical Society, and the Historic Chattahoochee Commission work across county (and sometimes state) boundaries to promote local histories connected by geography, economy, or transportation.

Founded in 1947, the Alabama Historical Association supports local history through its historical marker program. The Association's twice-yearly meetings move around the state and offer extensive programming on the history of the host communities. Other statewide organizations with local interests include the Alabama Trust for Historic Preservation and the Alabama Genealogical Society.

Since 1979, the Alabama Historical Association has sponsored an award recognizing outstanding achievement by a local historical society; in 2008 the award was named for James Ray Kuykendall, a DeKalb County pharmacist and lifelong advocate for local history efforts.

The Alabama Course of Study requires a dedicated course on Alabama studies during the fourth grade. Standards for all other grades except eighth and ninth also require the inclusion of community or state history or government within a broader curriculum. Many of the organizations named above support the enrichment of Alabama history education through the provision of resource materials or professional development opportunities for teachers.

The public's engagement with the past was significantly enhanced in 2014 with the opening of the Museum of Alabama at the ADAH. Exhibits covering prehistory to the near-present provide an overview of Alabama history and point visitors to local museums for further exploration of history at the regional and community levels.

In 2013, the state legislature created the Alabama Bicentennial Commission to coordinate commemorative programs during an anticipated three-year period of activities culminating with the bicentennial of statehood in December 2019. Examples of Commission products include professional development programs for educators, templated promotional materials for adoption by local governments and historical societies, historical markers, publications, cultural resource surveys, and public celebrations. Calendars and links to resources can be found at www.alabama200.org.

These efforts toward collaboration and historical programming are taking place during a time of diminishing public resources. Amid a larger crisis in state government budgets, appropriations to state-affiliated organizations have declined precipitously since 2008, and cut-backs are subsequently felt in the reduction of services to local organizations. In 2015, an informal network called Alabama History Advocacy began working in conjunction with allied nonprofits to raise awareness among governing officials of the value of history.

STEVE MURRAY
ALABAMA DEPARTMENT OF
ARCHIVES AND HISTORY

See United States, local history in.

Alaska, local history in. Alaska's human history extends back more than 15,000 years, known through investigations of some of the oldest archaeological sites in North America. Europeans completing the map of the world in the 1700s acquired items from Alaska's indigenous people to tell about the distant place. The Russian colonizers exhibited cultural items at Sitka, their capital in the North Pacific in the 1800s. After the United States acquired Alaska and steamships brought tourists in the 1880s, residents of Sitka organized the Society of Alaskan Natural History and Ethnology and built a museum. Sheldon Jackson, missionary, then U.S. General Agent for Education in Alaska, donated the core of the society's exceptional ethnographic collection. Alaska's first museum is now named the Sheldon Jackson Museum and owned by the State of Alaska. Congress created an Alaska Historical Library and Museum in June 1900 and directed the governor to collect papers and periodicals of the District of Alaska and materials of historical interest. The collection opened to the public in 1920. The U.S. Forest Service used the Civilian Conservation Corps program in Alaska in the late 1930s to establish totem parks in a number of southeast Alaska communities to preserve the poles, art, and clan houses of the area's native people.

Alaska changed dramatically with World War II, when residents fought for statehood, which happened in 1959. During the 1950s residents in several communities organized historical societies, collected and sought places to exhibit the materials. The centennial of the purchase of Alaska, 1967, provided the means to build cultural facilities. The federal and state governments made significant appropriations for Alaskan communities to build museums, libraries, and visitor facilities, and over forty buildings were constructed.

An Alaska State Museum in Juneau was one, giving the collection started in 1900 a permanent home. People from the local societies and museums organized the Alaska Historical Society in 1967 to facilitate communication with each other, pursue training opportunities, and promote state programs to preserve and study Alaska's history.

The State of Alaska separated the Alaska Historical Library from the State Museum in 1966, and established the State Archives in 1970. These programs are merging and in 2016 will be in the new Andrew P. Kashevaroff State Library, Archives and Museum in Juneau. The Alaska Historical Society advocated and the state passed a historic preservation act in 1970, and created the Alaska

Echoes of Independence interpretive sign. CREDIT: ALASKA DIVISION OF PARKS AND OUTDOOR RECREATION.

Historical Commission in 1974. The preservation and research programs were combined in 1986 into the Office of History and Archaeology in the Department of Natural Resources. With oil wealth, the State of Alaska provided significant funds to the University of Alaska for the Museum of the North and to the Municipality of Anchorage for the Anchorage Museum at Rasmuson Center, and has helped many smaller museums around the state.

Congress passed the Alaska Native Claims Settlement Act in 1971, paying the people with land and money, and their corporations have invested in several cultural centers. The Alaska Native Heritage Center opened in Anchorage in 1999, representing all eleven major native groups in its exhibits, events, and educational programs.

Hubert Howe Bancroft published a *History of Alaska, 1730–1885* as part of his thirty-nine-volume history of the American West. It was written in the grand, engaging style of histories of the time; it is unfortunate that the principal researcher, Ivan Petroff, inaccurately translated Russian materials and fabricated some information. Although not the first, Bancroft's book was considered the history of early Alaska until the 1970s. The first history of Alaska, Petr Tikhmenev's *A History of the Russian American Company*, completed in 1863, was not translated into English until the 1930s.

After the United States purchased Alaska in 1867, William Dall, who was in Alaska as a member of the 1865–1868 Western Union Telegraph Expedition, wrote *Alaska and Its Resources* (1870). Half travel narrative and half encyclo-

pedia, it is considered the "first real book about Alaska" addressing history, geography, ethnology, and natural resources. James Wickersham, Alaska's nonvoting delegate to Congress for much of the first third of the twentieth century, compiled *A Bibliography of Alaskan Literature 1724–1924*, which consisted of material about Alaska by European explorers, Russians, early American entrepreneurs, government agents, gold seekers, miners, visitors, and missionaries. Published in 1927, it is still a fundamental reference.

Ernest Gruening, territorial governor from 1939 to 1953 and U.S. senator from Alaska 1959–1969, wrote *The State of Alaska: A Definitive History of America's Northernmost Frontier* (1954). The title is misleading, but the book updated Dall's work. In the 1960s, university and public historians began to write Alaska history in response to the great interest in Alaska after the North Slope oil discovery in 1968. Claus-M. Naske wrote about the campaign for statehood, and *Alaska: A History of the 49th State* (1979) was recently updated and is still used as a college textbook.

Stephen Haycox edited a bibliography of Alaskan material published after Wickersham's compilation, and culminated years of research and writing with *Alaska: An American Colony* (2002). Terrence M. Cole wrote his dissertation on the gold rush town of Nome and many histories since, with *Fighting for the Forty-Ninth Star* (2010) his most recent. Dermot Cole, Fairbanks journalist (and Terrence's twin), wrote a community history of Fairbanks and for the fiftieth anniversary of statehood *North to the Future: The Alaska Story, 1959–*

2009 (2008). For the Alaska Historical Society, historian Frank Norris and librarian Bruce Merrell coordinated *The Alaska 67: A Guide to Alaska's Best History Books* (2007), an annotated guide. The society, for over thirty years, has published a semiannual journal *Alaska History*, the primary place to find current scholarship on the state.

Probably the first history of an Alaskan community was *The Story of Sitka* by journalist Clarence Andrews in 1922. A fraternal organization, the Pioneers of Alaska, published the *Pathfinder of Alaska* magazine during the 1910s and 1920s with features on community histories with "igloos." Of the many who have written about Alaska communities, most notable is R. N. "Bob" DeArmond, who chronicled events in several southeast Alaska towns from the 1930s until 2010. The Juneau–Douglas City Museum created "Digital Bob," a searchable electronic compilation with his weekly local history columns from area newspapers.

The Alaska Commercial Company produced a primer about Alaska in 1870 for schools it operated on the Pribilof Islands as part of its lease from the U.S. government to hunt fur seals. The classic school text is Mariette Shaw Pilgrim's *Alaska: Its History, Resources, Geography and Government* (1939). Through the years, school districts created curriculum materials on communities and Native people for elementary students and an Alaska history unit for middle school students, but little for high school students. In the late 1960s Alaskans, including educators, began to call for a requirement that high school students take a semester class in Alaska history. The primary argument for creation of the Alaska Historical Commission was for preparation of Alaska history materials to be used in secondary schools. The commission published a textbook, *Alaska's Heritage* (1986) by Joan M. Antonson and William S. Hanable that is still used. The Department of Education required teachers to pass a class in Alaska history to be certified to teach in Alaska in 1993. The Department of Education developed Alaska history content standards and a scope and sequence document in the 1990s. The Alaska State School Board in 2004 enacted a requirement that to graduate from an Alaska high school a student take a semester course in Alaska history and cultural studies or meet performance standards adopted in 2005. The Alaska Humanities Forum has been the leader in developing materials to meet the standards, primarily online, for teachers and students.

JOAN M. ANTONSON
DEPUTY STATE HISTORIC
PRESERVATION OFFICER, ALASKA

See United States, local history in.

Albanians in North America, sources for. See Appendix A.

Alberta, local history in. March can be a raw, damp month in Alberta. But that did not dissuade a group of history enthusiasts led by Premier Alexander Rutherford from meeting on March 15, 1907, two years after the formation of the province, to establish the Historical Society of Alberta (HSA). The society remained based in Edmonton until 1958 when its headquarters moved to

Calgary, the beginning of an expansion that saw three more chapters established. The society is a registered nonprofit organization run largely by volunteers. Its quarterly journal, *Alberta Historical Review* (now *Alberta History*), was established in 1953. Hugh Dempsey, author of twenty local history books, remains the journal's chief editor. The society also boasts a quarterly newsletter, *History Now*. The HSA created the Alberta Records Publications Board that has published over fifty titles concentrating on broad stories such as *William Stewart Herron: Father of the Petroleum Industry in Alberta*, and *A New Day for Women: Life & Writings of Emily Spencer Kerby*. In addition, each HSA chapter publishes its own local history titles.

Established in 1895, Banff National Park Natural History Museum is the province's oldest. In 1911 Calgary supported a museum and in 1914 the University of Alberta had a geology collection. The Father Lacombe Museum in St. Albert opened in 1928. During the province's jubilee year, 1955, the government voted $25,000 per year toward preserving the province's heritage. The next big boost came with 1967, Canada's centenary, when numerous local historical societies and museums sprang up. Many were private initiatives, the largest and most prestigious being the Glenbow Museum in Calgary. Philanthropist Eric Harvie, who began collecting artifacts related to the history of Alberta and western Canada in the 1950s, donated his collection of art, artifacts, and documents to the people of Alberta in 1966. Part of the Glenbow Museum is the Glenbow Archives. This is Canada's largest nongovernmental archival repository, its collections emphasizing the history of southern Alberta and Calgary.

Canada's centenary was also the motivation behind the establishment of the Provincial Museum and Archives of Alberta (PMAA) located in Edmonton. Both the archives and the museum had antecedents. The Provincial Library had been the repository of archival material since its establishment in 1906. When the new PMAA building opened in 1967, the archives was a section within the museum. In 1973 the archives and museum administrations were split and the Provincial Archives of Alberta (PAA) has operated as a separate branch since then. Mandated to acquire, preserve, and make available private and government records of provincial significance, the PAA outgrew its modest wing in the PMAA building, and in 2003 the archives moved to a custom 11,000-square-meter building. The PAA sponsors and hosts workshops, exhibits, and a four-part lecture series every autumn. Talk of a provincial museum took place as early as 1919 but as late as the 1950s there was only a modest display in the legislature. The purpose-built Provincial Museum of Alberta (PMA) was a state-of-the-art building when it opened in 1967. Since then, its thirteen curatorial programs have collected, preserved, and interpreted over one million artifacts and specimens related to Alberta's history as well as 1.5 million archaeological artifacts. Having long outgrown its original home, the Royal Alberta Museum (RAM, formerly the PMA) celebrates its move into a new museum building in

2017. Every year, the RAM hosts three four-part lecture series.

The Alberta Museums Association (AMA), formed in 1971 in response to the growth in the number of museums in the province, has grown to 260 institutional members and over 300 individual members. At first a volunteer-run organization, the AMA evolved into a professional clearinghouse of information on museum practice while at the same time awarding grants and establishing protocols of museum excellence. The 173-member Archives Society of Alberta (ASA) was formed in 1992 by the merger of two other archival organizations.

An early program of the then Provincial Museum of Alberta was the Historic Sites Service (HSS), formed in 1972 and charged with identifying and preserving historic sites of provincial and regional importance. Now a separate branch of government, Historic Sites & Museums boasts twelve seasonal sites and seven year-round major museums and interpretive centers such as the UNESCO world heritage site Head-Smashed-In Buffalo Jump. The latter are members of the AMA. All government organizations operate under the 1973 Alberta Historical Resources Act.

The RAM, HSS, and the Archaeological Society of Alberta, established in 1975, had an Occasional Paper series from 1975 to 1994. HSS and the RAM now collaborate with university and trade presses to bring out titles such as the two-volume centennial history *Alberta Formed—Alberta Transformed* (2006).

There have been many publications dealing with the history of Alberta. In 1924 John Blue wrote his two-volume *Alberta, Past and Present, Historical and Biographical*. Later, University of Alberta librarian Bruce Peel compiled a bibliography of 2,769 prairie titles. The 1973 second edition of his *Bibliography of the Canadian Prairies to 1953* brought the number of titles to 4,408, and today the online edition includes 7,500 digitized books, over 66,000 newspaper issues, 16,000 postcards, and 1,000 maps.

The Alberta Historical Resources Foundation (AHRF) was legislated in 1973 to promote Alberta's cultural heritage. It provides annual funding to the AMA, the ASA, and the HSA as well as Alberta's Main Street Programme that assists municipalities in the revitalization of their historic central districts. It also offers matching grants and technical and advisory assistance for the conservation of historic places and heritage awareness initiatives such as historical interpretive signage, historical research, and publications. AHRF reports to a government-appointed Board of Directors composed of people from around the province.

The Alberta Genealogical Society, a volunteer, nonprofit organization founded in 1973, has eleven branches. Services to its members include online databases, an annual conference, and publications.

Alberta history is studied in grade four, and western Canadian history is studied in grade seven. Courses on post-1867 Canadian history and western Canadian history are offered at all the universities. The University of Alberta alone offers an undergraduate course specifically on Alberta history. Athabasca University offers a course on

Métis history while the other universities offer courses in Canadian native studies.

An online encyclopedia—Alberta Source.ca—is a multimedia website documenting Alberta's natural, cultural, scientific, and technological heritage. Its funding agency is the Heritage Community Foundation. Other online resources include *Our Future Our Past*, a collection of digitized newspapers, local history books, even air photos, and *Peel's Prairie Provinces*, which has digitized the full texts of 7,500 books and over 4.8 million newspaper articles.

Since 2002 the Heritage Community Foundation has encouraged organizations and communities to participate in Doors Open, an international movement to promote an awareness of local history through open house tours of commercial, industrial, and residential properties.

In 2010 the City of Edmonton established a historian laureate position, the first in Canada. Ken Tingley, appointed for a two-year term, established protocols and procedures for the position while making presentations to historical and heritage preservation groups.

JANE ROSS
J. ROSS & ASSOCIATES

See Canada, local history in.

aliens. The number of aliens, that is, resident noncitizens, is listed in the first Federal Census (1790) and appears in each *census thereafter.

almanacs. The most famous of these annually issued books is *The Farmer's Almanack*, which contains a calendar of days, weeks, and months; astronomical data such as the phases of the moon; and various statistics. The first book of this sort was *An Almanac for New England for the Year 1639*, compiled by William Pierce and printed under the supervision of Harvard College. Many people associate Benjamin Franklin with the origins of almanacs because of the popularity of *Poor Richard's Almanac*, which he first issued in 1732. In the nineteenth century there were approximately 2,000 almanacs printed yearly. Those published locally often contain somewhat eccentric information, but there is usually an interesting section of local advertising, announcements of local manufacturers, and other eclectic data. See Robert K. Dodge, *A Topical Index of Early United States Almanacs, 1776–1800* (1997).

See also advertising; herbal; Library of Congress.

alumni records. Many colleges and universities and some private secondary schools keep records about a student's admission, progress through college, and events in later life including awards, honors, jobs, and participation in alumni events. Sometimes there will be pictures or letters. These can be very helpful to the local historian, but are infrequently consulted. Expect restrictions for persons who are still alive; by and large grades will not be available for view without special permission. Write to the alumni office or to the university archives and request by name, class, and date of death.

For some essays about alumni, see Clifford K. Shipton, ed., *New England Life in the 18th Century: Representative*

Biographies from Sibley's Harvard Graduates (1963).

amateur. From the Latin, amateur means "lover of"; an amateur historian is regarded as a lover of the history of a place. The rise of the professional historian, dating from 1884 with the creation of the *American Historical Association, led to a devaluation of the works of amateurs, and there has been some recent discomfort with the word as amateur came to mean the opposite of "professional" or "academic." The premise that amateur works of local history could be as good as any other is the focus of the *Nearby History series.

See Carol Kammen, *On Doing Local History* ([1986] 2014); and *Pursuit of Local History: Readings on Theory and Practice* (1996).

Amateur Historian. This was the original name of the journal published by the Standing Conference for Local History in Great Britain, from 1952 until 1968, when its name was changed to *The Local Historian*.

See England, local history in.

American Antiquarian Society (AAS). The AAS is a learned society founded in 1812 in Worcester, Massachusetts. It is the third-oldest historical society in the United States and dedicated to the collecting and preservation of the single largest collection of printed source material of American history through 1876. Its holdings include over three million books, papers, manuscripts, maps, newspapers, and other printed material, including more than 40,000 local history titles from all fifty states and the Canadian provinces. The American Antiquarian Society publishes scholarly monographs and a quarterly online journal, *Common-place.org*. American Antiquarian Society, 185 Salisbury Street, Worcester, MA 01609-1634; (508) 755-5221; fax (508) 753-3311; www.americanantiquarian.org.

ELLEN S. DUNLAP
AMERICAN ANTIQUARIAN SOCIETY

American Association for State and Local History. The American Association for State and Local History (AASLH) emerged from a late-nineteenth- and early-twentieth-century wave of professionalization across the historical discipline. State historical society leaders primarily from the Midwest and South began to engage with the *American Historical Association (AHA) in the late 1890s, and in 1904 at the AHA's annual meeting in Chicago launched the *Conference of State and Local Historical Societies. The conference continued as a part of the AHA for several years, its members consisting of organizations such as state historical societies, academic history departments, archives, and libraries. With the development of the *Organization of American Historians in 1907 (then called the Mississippi Valley Historical Association), the conference began to wane, and eventually became a two-hour session at the AHA annual meeting. At the same time, the archivists began to separate themselves into their own AHA conference group, while academic members of the AHA stayed within sessions devoted to research. In 1936 the archivists broke away to form the *Society of American Archivists.

At the 1939 AHA meeting in Washington, D.C., the thirty-fifth annual meeting of the state and local historical conference, state historical society and historical commission leaders proposed that membership be expanded to include individuals, that a board representing the United States and Canada be established, and that the organization should begin a publications program. Then chairman Dr. Christopher C. Crittenden, secretary of the North Carolina Historical Commission, appointed a committee of fifteen to map out what the new organization would look like and the functions it would serve. On December 27, 1940, the Conference disbanded and established a new organization: The American Association for State and Local History (AASLH).

From its inception, AASLH brought a wide variety of history professionals and volunteers together to propagate information about preserving and interpreting state and local history. In 1944, the association began an annual awards program that continues to this day. Mary E. Cunningham, editor for the New York State Historical Association, founded in 1947 a quarterly publication for AASLH aimed at educators and general audiences that eventually became *American Heritage* magazine. Relaunched in 1954 with its own commercial publisher, the magazine reached a huge national audience and generated substantial revenues for AASLH (until it separated from the association in 1983). AASLH sought new ways to raise professional standards and expertise, focusing on its annual meeting, publishing technical bulletins and its newsletter as well as the magazine, recognizing excellence with its awards, and seeking to help professional as well as amateur historians.

In 1956, incoming president Clifford L. Lord of the State Historical Society of Wisconsin hired AASLH's first staff member; Clement M. Silvestro became a part-time administrative assistant. In 1957 Silvestro's position was increased to full time, and he was named editor of *History News*, and subsequently director of AASLH. In 1964, William T. Alderson from the Tennessee State Library and Archives took over the position and moved the association to Nashville; Dr. Alderson remained the driving force behind the growth of AASLH for fourteen years. During his tenure, the association grew to have thirty-five staff members, a reflection in part of how AASLH had benefited from the creation of the *National Endowment for the Humanities (NEH) in 1965 and the arrival of the nation's 200th anniversary in 1976. NEH, for example, funded the association's training programs and a major study of how local historical organizations could effectively commemorate the bicentennial. Also with NEH's help, the association launched an ambitious bicentennial publishing project with W. W. Norton & Company for fifty-one state histories. AASLH has continued to maintain a thriving publishing program covering all aspects of the administration of historical organizations, from historic preservation to working with volunteers, from historical interpretation to community engagement.

During the tenure of Director, then President & CEO Terry Davis, 1995–2014, the association achieved financial stability and developed new key programs. The Seminar for Historical Administration, which it had begun cosponsoring with Colonial Willamsburg in the 1960s, was reestablished firmly with the Indiana Historical Society in 2004 and renamed Developing History Leaders @SHA. With support from the Institute for Museum and Library Services, AASLH began offering the *Visitors Count!* program in 2006, for improving historic sites through visitor surveys, and the Standards and Excellence Program for History Organizations (StEPS) in 2009, which helps small and mid-sized organizations, including all-volunteer groups, assess and improve themselves across six core areas.

Having passed its seventy-fifth anniversary in 2015, the association remains a forum for organizations and individuals in the field of state and local history—a place to share models of programs that work. Every fall the AASLH annual meeting welcomes hundreds of participants from all facets of the historical enterprise. The association's thriving *History News* magazine, book series with Rowman & Littlefield Publishing Group, and Technical Leaflet series complement its many continuing education, professional development, and advocacy initiatives. For the next several years the AASLH will be emphasizing diversity and inclusiveness, creative and experimental approaches to persistent challenges, and collaborating with academic colleagues while finding new ways to serve and learn from avocational historians. AASLH is located at 2021 21st Avenue, Nashville, TN 37212; (615) 320-2303; www. aaslh.org.

John Dichtl
American Association for
State and Local History

American Alliance of Museums. For more than one hundred years, the American Alliance of Museums (AAM) has been the only organization representing and serving the entire scope of the broad museum community. AAM's mission is to champion museums and nurture excellence. To do this, AAM brings the field together around ethics, standards, best practices, and advocacy. AAM provides its more than 30,000 individual museum professionals and volunteers, institutions, and corporate partners with year-round professional development opportunities, timely updates on what's happening in the field and among policy makers, and a network for peer-to-peer sharing. AAM is located at 2451 Crystal Drive, Suite 1005, Arlington, VA 22202. Phone: (202) 289-1818; Fax: (202) 289-6578; www.aam-us.org.

Janet Vaughan
American Alliance of Museums

American exceptionalism. This phrase, widely used and much abused, actually has two meanings. The first, which is as old as the nation itself, expresses the belief that the United States is not only unique compared with all other nations and cultures, but morally and socially superior in its distinctiveness. Advocates of American exceptionalism in that sense would point to the virtue of the American yeoman farmer and the remarkably high standard of living achieved in the United States. Some people even called attention to the notion of Americans enjoying a special covenant with the Almighty, thereby achieving the status of a chosen people.

The second, and much more recent usage, commonly found in current scholarship and supported by numerous comparative studies (e.g., of slavery and race relations, of industrialization, and of modes of commemoration) simply contends that every nation-state is distinctive in significant ways and seeks to determine the nature (or configuration) of qualities that make the United States different from other societies. The latter definition continues to have its critics, especially those who believe that industrialization and modernization have increased international (and also national) similarities; but almost no scholar who subscribes to it insists that America is better, only that it is different. They would readily acknowledge the same for France, Russia, Brazil, and Japan. Among the general public, however, there are still individuals who subscribe to the older, chauvinistic view that the American polity and culture are superior. The older meaning remains in common parlance, however—to justify anti-immigration views or reluctance to ratify treaties that might "compromise" American sovereignty.

MICHAEL KAMMEN
AMERICAN HISTORIAN (1936–2013)

American Folklife Preservation Act of 1976. See folklore and folklife.

American Historical Association (AHA). Founded in 1884 and incorporated by Congress in 1889, the AHA promotes historical work and historical thinking across a wide variety of settings. Its activities and publications support the collection and preservation of historical documents and artifacts, disseminate research, and establish guidelines for professional historical practice. In 1905 the AHA initiated an annual *Conference of Historical Societies that spun off in 1940 to form the *American Association for State and Local History.

The largest organization of professional historians in the world, the AHA supports the rights of historians to pursue research, disseminate historical work, and teach in an atmosphere characterized by open critical conversation. The association publishes the *American Historical Review*; *Perspectives on History*; booklets on teaching, research, and professional issues; and a full directory of departments of history. In 2015 the AHA began promoting a Twitter hashtag, #everythinghasahistory, as part of its advocacy program. If "everything has a history," the association maintains, then history and historians ought to play significant roles in public culture. www.historians.org; 400 A Street, SE, Washington, D.C. 20003-3889; e-mail: aha@historians.org.

JAMES GROSSMAN
AMERICAN HISTORICAL ASSOCIATION

American Indian history. Until recently, someone browsing through the literatures on local and American Indian histories could reasonably have concluded that American Indian history is not a history of communities and that the history of American communities does not include American Indians. Assumptions about both the nature of Indian life—tribal, nomadic, primitive—and the options open to Indians confronted by Euro-American expansion—retreat, removal, reservations—precluded serious discussion of either Indian towns or Indians' places within American communities. The situation, however, is quickly changing. Even *William and Mary Quarterly*—the premier national journal on the origins of the United States—now regularly publishes articles that include local American Indian communities and their impact on eighteenth-century American history. This more nuanced understanding of Indian societies and a deeper appreciation for the possibilities inherent in culture contact and territorial expansion have led scholars to reevaluate old assumptions about the American past. For local historians, these developments offer a variety of challenges and opportunities. Scholars focused on the history of a particular area will increasingly be encouraged to include Indian communities within their research projects. At the same time, these scholars will face mounting pressure to acknowledge—and account for—American Indians within both their own communities and their models of local development.

As European explorers fanned out across what was to them "the New World," they encountered peoples so diverse that their very dissimilarity—hundreds of mutually unintelligible languages, tens of thousands of distinct communities—bespoke this world's antiquity. In North America

alone, native communities ranged from the Southwest's nucleated pueblos to mobile bands inhabiting the far north and the deserts; from sedentary villages on the Pacific coast to seasonally occupied towns bordering the Plains; from Mississippians living in hierarchically ranked towns to eastern villages whose people combined sedentism and mobility. Local historians seeking to incorporate the realities of this world into their narratives must acquaint themselves with the general outline of their region's pre-Columbian cultures. Then, archaeological evidence, native traditions, and ethnographic analogy can provide more detail on a specific community.

The arrival of literate Europeans, of course, opens up new vistas for local history. Although European documents must be approached with caution, they allow scholars to investigate aspects of American Indian communities that other sorts of evidence rarely address; when combined with archaeology and oral traditions, local historians will find that some Indian communities have surprisingly accessible pasts. That said, however, postcontact Indian history presents local history with conceptual and methodological challenges.

In the first place, the presence of Europeans did not transform North America's native tribes into a culturally homogenous people; in fact, contact with Europeans only encouraged American Indian diversity. For example, some tribes, responding to opportunities offered by the newcomers, relocated their villages or reconfigured their seasonal activities, while others, reeling from the impact of foreign diseases and European-induced wars, came together in multiethnic communities. Even indirect contact with the newcomers encouraged cultural experimentation and elaboration; the buffalo-hunting, nomadic, Plains peoples—the archetypal image of the American Indian—had been agriculturalists prior to obtaining European horses. For local historians interested in their area's Indian communities, then, the onset of the "historic" era necessitates a heightened awareness of both the distinctiveness of local Indian culture and the fluid nature of postcontact sociocultural patterns.

Moreover, for generations following the Europeans' arrival, the vast majority of Indian communities were, if not free from Euro-American influence, certainly independent of Euro-American control. Local historians studying these communities must, therefore, come to grips with unfamiliar models of social organization and community process. Modern understandings of the nature and scope of "local" and "community" frequently differ profoundly from those of colonial-era Indians. To begin with, "community" could depend as much upon social relations as upon contiguity; an eighteenth-century Creek town, for example, consisted of people who looked to a common square ground for sociospiritual renewal, no matter how far apart they lived. In addition, the "local" area visited by Indian townspeople on a regular basis could cover hundreds of miles; thus, many New England Indians left settled agricultural villages for yearly expeditions to hunting grounds or seacoasts. Finally, many Indians valued what one historian calls "spiritual community," affective bonds transcending vertical (upper and lower

worlds) and horizontal (plants and animals) boundaries. Local Indian history, therefore, encourages an expansive notion of the local.

These challenges notwithstanding, the good news for local historians is that the study of Indian communities prior to the reservation period is both relatively wide open and increasingly seen as important and necessary. Academic historians have acknowledged the importance of examining this level of Indian life, but studies of towns in "Indian Country" are still few and far between. During the past decade, for example, historians of the native South have come to realize that tribal studies are somewhat limiting because even at the time of Indian removal in the 1830s the formation of unified Indians nations was a relatively recent development. These nations were frequently broken up and reformed in combination with other native polities. Thus, a new generation of local historians has begun to shift the comparative parameters from nations to towns and from single tribes to thematic pantribal studies examined at the local level. Local historians, with their knowledge of their areas' history and natural characteristics, have a great deal to contribute to the study of these communities.

To do so, they must examine the (often published) papers of the colonists who oversaw diplomacy and trade, as well as newspapers, traders' records, and travelers' accounts. They must also resign themselves to the fact that Euro-American concerns pervade the documents. Thus, the fur trade receives more play than agriculture, and international diplomacy overshadows intra-town relations. The creative use of *material culture and *oral history can offset the documents' weaknesses and enhance their strengths, as can carefully controlled comparisons to neighboring Indian communities.

Of course, as Euro-American expansion picked up speed, fewer and fewer Indian communities enjoyed the degree of autonomy experienced by their contemporaries in Indian Country. New types of Indian communities, with varying degrees of Euro-American supervision, appeared in areas controlled by non-natives. The Spanish founded mission towns for Indians in the sixteenth century, and French and English versions appeared less than a century later. Reservations, under various guises, date back almost as far, although they became the cornerstone of U.S. Indian policy only in the mid-nineteenth century. Local historians interested in investigating these manifestations of Indian community history will find that the Euro-Americans' focus on converting and "civilizing" the Indian inhabitants translated into a concern with all aspects of Indian life. As a result, even the older missions may have archival resources well beyond those available for an Indian community in Indian Country, and the quality of data available for reservation peoples has led two historians to describe these American Indians as "among the best documented populations in the world."

Local historians who focus on such a community—for example, a mission in the area, or the current reservation of a people who once lived nearby—should be aware that historians and anthropologists have abandoned assump-tions about the inevitability of Indian assimilation and deculturation. Recent scholarship—on subjects including Cherokee basketry, Crow settlement patterns, California mission leadership styles, and Comanche sociality—demonstrates that U.S. Indians have succeeded in articulating distinctive values and identities while simultaneously participating in American culture. Local historians focused on mission and reservation communities will need both to consider the tremendous changes in Indian lifeways and to acknowledge the continuity in crucial aspects of personal and corporate identity and behavior.

Local historians who wish to make sense of the complexities apparent in these Indian communities—to understand, in the words of one historian, "the human decisions that shape the meanings embedded in a census report"—should avail themselves of the knowledge preserved in the Indians' own historical traditions. A number of tribes have developed programs for preserving and disseminating this information. These websites, archives, research projects, speakers, and publications will be quite useful to local historians. Moreover, many Indian cultures have made the collection and transmission of historical knowledge the province of elders trained in techniques of memorization and exposition. Although these men and women can be of tremendous help to historians, non-Indians must be aware that generations of scholarly misappropriation have made Indians leery of sharing their knowledge with outsiders. Interested parties should contact tribal officials to find out the appropriate method for inquiring into that people's oral traditions. Be prepared to explain your project's relevance to the Indian community; to treat interviewees as collaborators, not sources; to respect both their traditions and their silences.

It would be a mistake, however, for local historians to assume that studying American Indians will necessarily take them outside of their own area. Our national narrative of an onrushing frontier that pushed Indians away from Euro-American settlements has been challenged by scholars stressing the fluid nature of frontier regions, the mosaic-like quality of settlement patterns, and the possibilities for social coexistence, cultural interpenetration, and ethnic persistence long after "the frontier . . . passed by." Historians working in the southeast, New England, and the Mississippi Valley have demonstrated that American Indians found a variety of ways to integrate themselves into U.S. communities while maintaining distinct cultural practices, social networks, and group identities; Mestizo communities in the Southwest and Metis communities in the upper Midwest offer additional evidence of the cultural and biological fluidity of American life. The titles of studies from the past two decades focusing on Indians in nineteenth-century New England attest to the emergence of a new narrative: "Unseen Neighbors"; "They Were Here All Along"; "Presence and Persistence"; "Enduring Traditions"; "Behind the Frontier."

Additionally, the last decade has conclusively shown that studying Native local community history can and should be extended into the twentieth century. In doing so, local historians can help us

all come to terms with images of Geronimo driving a Cadillac by showing how Indians could embrace modernity while keeping traditions alive. For instance, one scholar has traced four generations of Dull Knife family history, covering various themes including open conflict with whites, heightened assimilation attempts, and participation in World Wars I and II. Utilizing biography and family history has allowed historians to investigate local community trends and place those trends within larger national narratives. Recent biographies of Clyde Warrior, Carlos Montezuma, and Ada Deer will continue this positive development by tracing the role of individual leaders in the process of community development during the twentieth century. Moreover, many recent twentieth-century local studies are unique in their ability to leave the reservation and find local Indian communities within the urban United States. Local studies of Indian enclaves within urban settings, such as one fine study of Indian communities inside the Chicago metropolis, have the potential to greatly expand the understanding of the large urban Indian population. Several local historians have begun exploring other urban settings with large Indian populations. A simple search of dissertation databases reveals numerous scholars investigating Indian communities inside Chicago, Seattle, and San Francisco. These urban communities frequently coalesced on a pantribal basis and became hotbeds of Indian activism.

When viewed in this light, local history's long-standing tendency to refer to Indians in post-frontier communities as either colorful primitives or as people "who were here but now are gone" obviously requires rethinking. To exclude Indians from local histories that might reasonably include them results in two disturbing problems. To begin with, an approach that denies Indian peoples their rightful place in our collective past inevitably produces bad local history; inaccurate and exclusionary assumptions produce misleading and partial narratives. Of equal importance, the absence of Indians in local history allows the general public to dismiss Indians who share our modern communities as fakes and opportunists; "real" Indians, people assume, lived/live elsewhere.

Local historians who seek to remedy this situation must recall that, for much of the last two hundred years, this country was dominated by a bipartite racial system that had little room for Indians. Moreover, Euro-Americans often had economic and political reasons for insisting that Indians no longer lived in their area. Indians, in consequence, frequently disappeared (for official purposes) into the "colored" category. Yet many of these people continued to view themselves as Indians, and researchers have been remarkably successful in mining the archives for hints about their lives, as seen in the recent works on Pamunkeys and Lumbees. Investigations often begin with a stray reference, one clue to a person's identity or a place's use that can lead to an ever-widening search for the networks and behaviors that allowed individuals to live as Indians in U.S. towns.

In investigating the place of Indians in an area's history, local historians have the opportunity to address a number of important issues. Perhaps the most obvious, local Indian history offers new perspectives on changing racial and ethnic relations, as well as on debates about resource ownership and utilization. More fundamentally, however, local Indian history allows scholars to consider the relationship between the Indians' presence, beliefs, and actions, on the one hand, and the larger community's articulation of social boundaries, behavioral standards, and local self-image, on the other.

Take one example, for instance: The work of local historians has recently assisted in addressing these issues and elaborated upon the distinctive results of slavery and racial thought for native peoples' cultural, ideological, and political lives. Histories centering on the significance of native captivity, the importance of the slave trade, and the existence of racial ideals among Indian polities have appeared in the last decade. These works address the nature and consequences of the slave trade across native polities in the seventeenth, eighteenth, and nineteenth centuries. Other scholarship continues to raise questions about the dynamic and unique role of race in influencing both pre- and post-removal Southern native life. These studies have garnished heightened interest as issues regarding the legitimacy and position of black and white Indians present challenges to numerous contemporary tribes. Nonetheless, analysis of race and captivity remains an open field begging for exploration and thorough study by local historians who sit in the advantageous position of testing these broader narratives on local communities.

Moreover, local indigenous historians have increasingly demonstrated the possibility of using education as a lens for greater understanding of local native communities from the nineteenth century to today. In some instances, education came in the form of notoriously brutal boarding schools that created new inter-tribal community connections. While boarding schools failed in their stated goal of ending tribal identities, they often created a new layer of community for those who attended them. Other education historians focus on native-driven education efforts that reinforced community cohesiveness while strengthening national structures. Using education as a lens, therefore, local historians are given the choice of examining traditional local communities and their impact on national structure or examining nascent local communities and their impact on pantribal identities.

Different, but equally exciting, opportunities await local historians who focus on a single Indian community. Historians who study communities in Indian Country come face to face with our nation's diverse past. Such investigations challenge local historians to rethink cherished notions about community boundaries and processes, while providing researchers with a greater understanding of the situation confronting the initial generations of Euro-Americans in the area. Likewise, reservation and mission communities offer local historians the chance to delve into unfamiliar aspects of their area's distant and/or recent past. Moreover, Indian experiences on reservations and in missions challenge all historians to reconsider their understanding of cross-cultural interaction, identity formation, and community development. Which-

ever area of Indian life local historians elect to investigate, however, they can be confident that their efforts will contribute to the ultimate goal of local history: to describe a locality's distinctive aspects while discussing its connections to more broad-reaching developments.

JEFFREY L. FORTNEY JR.
CENTRAL MICHIGAN UNIVERSITY
JOSHUA PIKER
COLLEGE OF WILLIAM & MARY

See biographical dictionaries frontier thesis; historic preservation; intellectual property rights; Native American Graves Protection and Repatriation Act (NAGPRA); repatriation.

American Library Association (ALA). In 1876, 103 librarians met at a convention of librarians and founded the ALA with the purpose of enabling "librarians to do their present work more easily and at less expense." The ALA includes groups representing public school librarians, along with those involved with technical services, college and research, technical and specialized librarians, and young adult librarians, among others. The organization provides information and professional development and engages in advocacy activities. See their extensive and informative website at www.ala.org.

Amistad Research Center. Amistad Research Center is a manuscripts library for the study of ethnic history, culture, and race relations in the United States. It is the nation's oldest, largest, and most comprehensive independent archives of original manuscripts and primary sources that chronicle the history of African Americans and ethnic minorities. The center holds over 800 manuscript collections that contain more than 15 million original documents dating from 1798 to the present. These collections are supported by 25,000 library volumes; over 1,000 audio and video oral histories; and an art collection of over 300 original paintings, drawings, and sculptures by African American artists dating from the nineteenth century. Amistad, on Tulane University's campus, is at 6823 St. Charles Avenue, New Orleans, LA 70118. It opens to the public from 8:30 a.m. to 4:30 p.m. Monday–Friday and on Saturday from 9:00 a.m. to 1:00 p.m.; (504) 862-3222; www.amistadresearchcenter.org; info@amistadresearchcenter.org.

KARA OLIDGE
AMISTAD RESEARCH CENTER

Anabaptist. The name given to Protestant sects in Europe, many of whom, beginning in the seventeenth century, emigrated to the United States and Canada. Anabaptists believe the church is a society of adult believers and oppose infant baptism. They are known today by various names, including Amish, Mennonites, and Hutterites, each having evolved independently and with separate identities in the New World despite many common concerns.

See Appendix B.

Ancestry.com. Ancestry.com is a commercial genealogical website that provides access to a wide array of databases and information sources through a powerful search interface. Ancestry.com is the flagship website of Ancestry.com LLC. Ancestry.com also owns Ge-nealogy.com, Fold3.com (military records), Archives.com (census and vital records), Newspapers.com (historical newspapers), and supports *RootsWeb.com, the free genealogy site.

Family Tree Maker, the popular personal genealogy software, was produced by Ancestry.com until 2015. The software is now produced by MacKiev under the name Software MacKiev Family Tree Maker 2014 (https://www.mackiev.com).

Ancestry.com's strength is its coverage of *census, immigration, and *military records. It includes indexes and page images of all available U.S. federal censuses 1790–1940 and UK and Canadian censuses from 1841. Many state censuses are now available. Immigration records include records from the ports of New York, Boston, Philadelphia, and others. Particularly valuable for local historians is the Map Center, which contains thousands of historical maps including many landownership maps from the nineteenth-century United States with a searchable index of the names on the maps. Military records include WWI draft records and WWII military records as well as Civil War and Revolutionary War records. Ancestry had made the *Social Security Death Index available for no charge, but searching is now available to subscribers only. Ancestry.com claims sixteen billion records overall.

Ancestry's search algorithms have become increasingly sophisticated. The presentation of the United States census in particular provides effective searching with little effort. With so many databases and features the site can be difficult to navigate, but basic searching is easy and intuitive with plenty of online help.

Ancestry.com also provides many learning tools and reference works. *The Source: A Guidebook to American Genealogy* is presented full text as a wiki, as is *Red Book: American State, County, and Town Sources* and many other resources.

Ancestry, in the form of AncestryDNA (http://dna.ancestry.com) is becoming increasingly known for its DNA testing and database analysis. A separate paid service, AncestryDNA tests your DNA sample using autosomal testing. The lineage restrictions (patrilineal for Y chromosome analysis and matrilineal for mitochondrial analysis) do not apply. Samples are tested against a two-million-sample database for close matches, providing information about possible ethnic backgrounds and, more specifically, close ancestors.

Ancestry has an excellent online tree builder. It's free, requiring only registration, but without a subscription, the functionality is limited. GEDCOM files derived from computer software such as Family Tree Maker can be uploaded and form a basis for your tree, or you can begin inputting data online. Ancestry searches for related records and provides "hints" for individual entries. Used with caution this can be a very effective way to build a tree and add documentation. Trees can be shared and built collaboratively. They can also be searched for shared ancestors.

Ancestry is available through individual subscription. Many public and university libraries also subscribe to the "Library Edition," which offers similar coverage with a slightly different inter-

face from the individual subscription version and no ability to create trees.

ROBERT KIBBEE
HISTORY CENTER IN
TOMPKINS COUNTY (NY)

See genealogical resources online; local history resources online.

Anglicans, sources for. See Episcopalian church, Appendix B.

Annales School. The Annales School is the name given to one of the most influential approaches to historical inquiry developed in the twentieth century. Its founders during the 1920s, Lucien Febvre (1878–1956) and Marc Bloch (1886–1944), along with their most prominent disciple, Fernand Braudel (1902–1985), emphasized social and economic forces as being more consequential than political and diplomatic events, whose mere chronology seemed a superficial approach to understanding the past and its legacy for the present.

These French Annalistes also highlighted the importance of geographical and climatic influences. They insisted upon the need for *histoire totale*, a multidimensional approach to history, by probing unconventional sources in depth and using quantitative methods wherever possible in order to be more precise. In recent decades (since the 1970s), members of the Annales School have also been receptive to new ways of thinking about cultural history, such as the development of literacy and numeracy.

Work done by the Annalistes is important for local historians because its members have created some masterpieces of microhistory as a new, subtle genre, combining neglected primary sources, complex and multifaceted analysis, and engaging narrative. They commonly use a historical crisis or episode as the point of departure for recreating historical context and implications in astonishing depth. Prime examples include Bloch's *The Ile de France: The Country around Paris* ([1913] 1971), and two books by Emmanuel LeRoy Ladurie, *Montaillou: The Promised Land of Error* (1978) and *Carnival in Romans* (1979).

MICHAEL KAMMEN
AMERICAN HISTORIAN (1936–2013)

annuity. An annual payment from an investment or as the result of an agreement. For example, the Iroquois were paid an annuity by the state of New York in exchange for their removal from the land.

Appalachia. Defining Appalachia may, at first glance, seem a rather simple proposition. The Appalachian Mountains sweep from Canada southwestward to Texas. Crafting boundaries that accommodate the cultural variations inherent in such a wide swath of territory has, however, bedeviled even the region's closest and most astute observers. The difficulty in precisely mapping the region's boundaries has not prevented a host of attempts. Most frequently, Appalachia has been defined as encompassing the mountainous territory from northeastern Alabama to the southern half of New York. Precisely which counties within which states are included in this definition has been a source of disagreement. In his 1921 study, for example, the sociologist John

C. Campbell included 254 counties, but no states north of Maryland. Forty-one years later a Ford Foundation study pared the number of counties down to 190, ended the region at Maryland's northern border, and reversed Campbell's inclusion of South Carolina and Maryland. In a 1965 survey for a newly formed federal agency, the Appalachian Regional Commission, the number of counties ballooned to 360, and the northern border extended into New York; political pressures by 1967 had increased the number of counties to 397.

Even the narrowest definition still covers 80,000 square miles, so many scholars have attempted to isolate distinct subregions such as the Blue Ridge, the Cumberland Plateau, and so on. Most of these definitions attempt to combine physical geography with social and cultural factors, such as income level, dialect, folk traditions, and religious affiliation. Until recently, the residents themselves were not asked whether they considered themselves Appalachian. In large part, the problem of defining the area arises from deciding which criteria are essential to fixing *regional identity. Consequently, the researcher should use the term "Appalachia" with caution, and should fully examine how and why the term is relevant and useful to their study.

In the popular imagination the region is, at best, the home of quaintly old-fashioned inhabitants ("yesterday's people") and, at worst, a hillbilly haven. The people are considered uniformly poor, white, and intensely rural. However, these generalizations do not withstand close scrutiny. Unquestionably

37

the region has significant pockets of poverty, racial and ethnic homogeneity, and deep isolation. At the same time, Appalachia has always supported a large and prosperous class of people, had a significant nonwhite population, and been home to important cities. In the period before the Civil War many landowners, like their lowland kin, reaped hefty profits from plantation agriculture, and had significant contacts with cultural and political trends outside the region. Their use of slave labor introduced a sizable group of African Americans into the region, whose numbers were augmented in the post–Civil War period by black migrants searching for work in lumber camps, mines, and on railroad construction crews. The significant presence of Native Americans, particularly the Cherokee in western North Carolina, further complicates the portrait of homogenous whiteness. Nor have the Appalachian people lived solely in remote mountain coves. Major urban centers like Asheville, North Carolina; Knoxville, Tennessee; and Charleston, West Virginia, were and remain important cities. In short, it is very hard to make useful generalizations about Appalachia. In fact, the difficulty in arriving at a unified portrait has prompted one of the region's most thoughtful scholars to argue that "it is futile to look for a 'correct' definition of the region" (David E. Whisnant, *Modernizing the Mountaineer: People, Power, and Planning in Appalachia*, 2nd ed., rev. [1994], 134).

Those interested in learning more about the region should consult John Alexander Williams, *Appalachia: A History* (2002), Richard A. Straw and H.

Tyler Blethen, eds., *High Mountains Rising: Appalachia in Time and Place* (2004), and Rudy Abramson et al., eds., *Encyclopedia of Appalachia* (2006), as well as the links on the Center for Appalachian Studies website maintained by Appalachian State University in Boone, North Carolina: http://www.appstudies.appstate.edu.

GAVIN JAMES CAMPBELL
DOSHISHA UNIVERSITY, KYOTO, JAPAN

See regionalism.

apprentice. See journeyman.

apps. Apps, short for "application software," are a type of computer program. Apps are made available on "smart" devices such as phones and tablets that have the capabilities and internal features of a personal computer. Each app is themed according to content and use, making it easy for users to customize their mobile devices. Since the late 2000s, the number of unique apps has exploded to around 1.5 million as of July 2015. History institutions use apps to connect with visitors, provide them with information or access to institutional resources, or give them an engaging museum experience either inside or outside museum walls.

Apps function on different operating systems developed by tech companies such as Apple, Google, Microsoft, and BlackBerry. Apple's iOS and Google's Android operating systems are the most widely used. Android functions on mobile devices made by Samsung, Nexus, LG, and HTC, while iOS systems function solely on Apple devices.

Most mobile devices come with pre-installed apps such as a web browser, e-mail, calendar, contacts, phone, messages, camera, photos, music, or video. Other apps are downloaded free or purchased on app stores such as the Apple App Store, Google Play, Windows Phone Store, and BlackBerry App World.

Like websites in the 1990s, apps may become a standard piece of museum technology in the twenty-first century. Nearly two-thirds of Americans are smartphone owners, and 19 percent of them are considered "smartphone-dependent" because they lack Internet access or other devices to go online. An average of 30 percent of smartphone users consume educational content on their devices; that percentage jumps to 44 percent among users ages eighteen to twenty-nine (Pew Research Center, 2015). The prevalence of smartphones and their ability to provide educational content suggests apps can be an important way for museums to reach the public.

The 2012 Mobile in Museums Study (Fusion Research + Analytics, American Alliance of Museums, UK Museums Association, 2012) examined how visitors use mobile devices in museum spaces. Of the museums with *American Alliance of Museums memberships, around half-used apps or app technologies. History institutions are catching up with the art world, which adopted app technologies earlier than other cultural institutions. Most of the museums that offer apps are also larger institutions receiving more than 50,000 visitors per year. A 2012 study showed that of the 17,500 museums in the United States, only around 2 percent had an app ("Museums Still Ignoring Mobile, Especially Small Museums," Idea.org, 2012). Currently, QR codes are the easiest and most popularly used mobile feature in history museums, though their success is debatable. The second and third most common apps are for guided tours and audio tours (Mobile in Museums Study).

Museum apps can serve a variety of purposes. They may complement or even replace materials such as maps, brochures, or event schedules. They can provide guided tours of the museum, supplement exhibit text with additional audio or visual features, or give a behind-the-scenes look into museum collections. They can house digital versions of institutional magazines, journals, or textbooks with added media such as audio, video, and hyperlinks. Through all of this content, a museum's app can be an extension of its mission to provide information about the institution and engage visitors with history. Like anything else a museum produces, apps should be based in education and user experience.

Museums should consider what audience they envision the app serving. Three apps from the Smithsonian Institution target different audiences. The National Air and Space Museum's Go Flight app, developed for the Milestones of Flight gallery, includes a map, hour-long guided tours, a schedule of events, videos, and stories curated according to the user's personal interest. Go Flight guides museum visitors but also allows them to take history and science home. To engage young children, the National

Air and Space Museum developed Pilot Pals, a game for ages four to six. The app's simple interface and colorful cartoons make it easy for young learners to use, while its content is based on the history and technologies addressed in the museum's Pioneers of Flight gallery. Pilot Pals invites children to build an airplane or rocket, pilot an aircraft dodging inclement weather, and learn how a machine's gears function. The National Museum of American History developed an educational game app for older children and teens. Ripped Apart: A Civil War Mystery coincided with the 150th anniversary of the end of the Civil War. In this game, players portray a Smithsonian intern exploring Civil War collections, interpreting historical evidence, and creating "*cartes de visites*" with the device's camera. A teacher's guide is also available to support the app ("Changing the Game").

The most sophisticated museum apps are using cutting-edge technologies such as GIS to map out spaces, indoor reference positioning to identify an individual's location within a museum, and augmented reality to overlay digital content on real-world environments. These tools can engage audiences in new ways and provide them with experiences they may not have had elsewhere. Simple app technologies, however, can also break new ground. An *American Association for State and Local History blog post suggested small museums attach QR codes synced with screen-reader apps to read aloud or translate exhibit text for visitors with visual impairments or language barriers (Janice Klein and Chuck Dean, posted April 5, 2016).

Curatescape is an app framework popular among smaller historical institutions. Affordable yet sophisticated, Curatescape uses map layers, multimedia, and GPS to create indoor and outdoor experiences. The Cleveland Historical app, based in Curatescape, guides users to more than 570 historical sites around the city. Users can choose individual sites or tours with themes such as music history and venues, Irish immigration, and iconic architecture. A number of cities from Spokane to Baltimore have used Curatescape to make their histories more accessible.

Careful planning can help museums overcome the challenges associated with app development. Museums without mobile technologies acknowledge that they are held back by limited resources, a lack of dedicated budget, and insufficient staff time. The Mobile in Museums Study suggests museums develop a "mobile strategy" that establishes a vision for the app, facilitates institutional support, and educates stakeholders on the development process. In today's high-tech culture, many funding sources are eager to support institutions in entering the digital age, especially cultural organizations not typically associated with technology. A strong mobile strategy can strengthen a museum's funding proposal. It can also provide plans for interpretation and marketing to sustain the app once it is complete.

Quality content and quality technology go hand in hand. Good wireless Internet in the museum is top priority so that the app is easily accessible. A well-functioning app empty of educational value may not serve the museum's mission, while an app with quality information and multimedia that a user cannot access is impractical.

Historians may also take note from the science and art fields, which have developed a variety of apps that encourage citizen science or creating digital works of art. Apps provide an opportunity for museums to reimagine how they interact with the public and the services they provide.

PAMELA CURTIN
WEST VIRGINIA UNIVERSITY

See digital history.

Arabs in North America, sources for.
See Appendix A.

Arcadia Publishing. Arcadia Publishing Company was founded in 1993 in Dover, New Hampshire by Tempus Publishing, a British company. It became independent in 2004 and moved its headquarters to Mount Pleasant, South Carolina. The company issues more than 900 books a year and has more than 12,000 titles in print in a variety of series, from Images of America; postcard and pictorial histories of American and Canadian towns and villages; baseball teams, railroads, college campuses among many other topics. Arcadia has consolidated its holdings by acquiring several other smaller publishers, including The History Press. Arcadia offers historians and first-time authors a clear format, a quick turnaround time for manuscript to paper copy, and royalties.

Arcadia Publishing has changed the landscape of local history with its accessibility, format, its emphasis on images, and especially because of its recognizable covers that have proved to be pop-

ular with the public. Rows of brown-covered books can be found in major bookstores and in groceries and even gas stations. Theree is no peer review, and only minor stylistic editing; nonetheless, the publishing of local history has acquired a standard and recognizable form. For more information: www. arcadiapublishing.com.

CAROL KAMMEN
TOMPKINS COUNTY (NY) HISTORIAN

See county histories; postcards; United States, local history in.

archaeology, engaging the public with. Archaeological resources are an important part of the local history record for every community. The significance of these resources to our communities is explicitly stated in the preamble to the Historic Preservation Act of 1966, which encourages their preservation as a "living part of our community life in order to give a sense of orientation to the American people" (Public Law 89-665; 16 USC 470). We often underestimate the value of the past in our "backyard" or are put off by difficulties in finding resources that would help define and protect archaeological sites and properties that are important to our communities.

Archaeology is sometimes thought of in terms of either grand discoveries of a pharaoh's tomb or a fictional "Indiana Jones"–style caricature. These depictions of the field of study have a tendency to make archaeological inquiry appear both remote and adventurous. In order to better place archaeology within a local history context it is better to view archaeology as a more democratic study of past ways of life (Stuart and McManamon 1996, 1). Detailed archaeological studies can sometimes make the difference in gaining rightful recognition to historical sites of local and national significance. From experience I have seen the importance of local community leaders, historic site managers, and historians working with archaeologists to illuminate the details of local history. Archaeological studies at the Harriet Tubman Home in Auburn/Fleming, New York, have brought greater accuracy to public interpretation of the site and material remains that visitors can see and relate to (Armstrong 2011; 2015). Engaged public archaeology at the Tubman site, with the archaeologist working cooperatively with the A.M.E. Zion Church (owners of the property), local historians, descendent family members, local government, congressional representative, and the National Park Service, have had positive results with the designation of the property as part of the new Harriet Tubman National Historic Park.

Christopher R. DeCorse provides a good introduction to the field of archaeology in *The Record of the Past*. DeCorse notes that through archaeological study "we learn about the culture of those societies, the shared way of life of a group of people that includes their values, beliefs, and norms" (DeCorse 2000, 5). Archaeological sites include a full suite of historic and prehistoric properties reflecting a wide array of cultural contexts. They include everything from abandoned mills, farms, mining camps, and stage stops in rural settings to foundations and refuse middens associated with domestic residences and industrial complexes in urban settings.

The importance of cemeteries (marked and unmarked) is well recognized. Yet like other sites, even these commemorative places are often defaced or forgotten. The problem resonates in the text of a simple sign on the cemetery at the ghost town of Bodie, a California state historic site, reminding visitors that "this site is still in use."

The visibility of cemeteries, buildings, and standing ruins makes them relatively easy rallying points for preservation and ideal tools for public education. Prehistoric sites are more difficult to deal with because they are less visible, and with the exception of contact-period sites, they lack the associated documentation of historical sites. In many cases these "older" resources in our communities are reflections of past social and economic conditions and, in the case of prehistoric sites, the residue of cultures that are quite different from our own. The cultural separation between "past" and "present" often leads to the destruction of resources of local importance. The ability to protect local archaeological sites is linked to the realization that local sites are of significance and that there are many resources available to assist the process of site protection. Local historians can assist in the evaluation of local resources based on their knowledge of local history, their knowledge of where to find resources, and their ability to educate the public.

Local historians can play an essential part in the illumination and dissemination of information on all types of archaeological sites. Their knowledge of local archives, researchers, and general history makes them key resource persons with respect to archaeological sites. Because early settlers' accounts often document the location of early historic sites and contact-period relations with Native Americans, the local historian often has information about archaeological sites that has not been reported to or recorded by state and federal registers of prehistoric and historic properties. It is therefore important to integrate the local historian into the archaeological sites-management network of communication concerning the local, state, and national levels.

In recent years, archaeologists realized that their goals must include public involvement and education and public interpretation along with the traditional goals of archaeological site protection and scientific excavation. An excellent review of archaeological studies that engage the public and reconstruct the past can be found in John. H. Jameson's *The Reconstructed Past* (2004). LuAnn de Cunzo and John H. Jameson present a public-oriented view of historical archaeology in *Unlocking the Past* (2005). Barbara J. Little's *Historical Archaeology: Why the Past Matters* (2007) does an excellent job of projecting the importance of integrating history and historical archaeology through discussions on how archaeology provides tangible evidence that can engage the public to understand the relationship of the past to the modern world. These studies also encourage local historians to integrate archaeology into their educational programs. The goals of the archaeologist mesh with the basic goals and responsibilities of local historians. Though the goals are shared, formal archaeological-site registers of each state are still not readily available at the local level; hence,

information on archaeological sites has not been made available to the public. Fortunately, detailed findings related to numerous significant archaeological and historical studies are readily available online. Good examples include detailed background information on archaeological sites and historical information related to: Jamestown, Virginia (http://historicjamestowne.org); Thomas Jefferson's Monticello (https://www.monticello.org/site/research-and-collections/monticello-archaeology); and the archaeological study of the recovery and conservation of La Salle's ship *La Belle* off the coast of Texas and the public exhibition of archaeological findings at the Texas State Museum (http://www.thestoryoftexas.com/la belle/the-exhibit).

Below are guides to published materials available online that provide information on archaeological sites and the process of site protection. Mark Leone's *Critical Historical Archaeology* (2010) provides a theoretically rich review of the importance of historical archaeology in rethinking local history. Leone's study includes a series of archaeological studies revolving around Annapolis, Maryland.

Archaeological resources within the community. The first step for the local historian is to link up with knowledgeable people to find out about archaeological resources. Make contacts with the faculty at your local college or university; in most cases they will be quite pleased to know of your interest. They often have students looking for projects and most have access to information that can help you get started. Ask them to put you in touch with the local state historic preservation officer (SHPO) archaeologist or professional archaeological contract firms (lists of firms can be gained through your state SHPO or the Register of Professional Archaeologists at www.rpanet.org.

A wonderful book aimed at protecting local resources is Susan Henry's *Protecting Archaeological Sites on Public Lands.* This volume, published by the *National Park Service, is a practical guide that deals with archaeological resources that are not state or federally owned. It contains important bibliographic materials, a detailed summary of protection strategies, a very good guide to the process of archaeological resource assessment, and an important section called "Sources of Financial Assistance." This volume was written with local communities in mind and includes an address list for state historic preservation offices around the country. Your SHPO will be able to inform you about archaeological resources in your area.

Local historians have a solid working relationship with local historical societies and museums. To gain a better understanding of local archaeology they might also link up with local and regional archaeological societies. For example, groups like the New York State Archaeological Association (nysarchae ology.org/nysaa), and similar groups in states such as Arkansas and Pennsylvania, have a strong avocational archaeology tradition. In many cases the local knowledge of archaeological sites far exceeds information that has been centralized at the state level. There is also a network of local nonprofit historic site preservation organizations, like the Preservation Association of Central New York (pacny.net), that have infor-

mation on protecting historic properties including archaeological sites. The *National Trust for Historic Preservation is a good source of information on local preservation groups (see list of website listings).

Federal law provides for the creation of Certified Local Governments (CLGs), which allow the designation of "local" protected sites status to archaeological sites and historic properties on a community level. Contact your state historic preservation office for details concerning local CLGs in your area or to obtain information on the advantages of creating a process for local designation in your community. A few communities, such as Santa Fe, New Mexico, have well-conceived preservation plans that fully engage the potential of CLG designation to protect local sites (see Elliot 1988).

Many communities, particularly in the western United States, are in close proximity to lands that are managed by state and federal agencies, including state parks, military bases, national parks and national forests, Bureau of Land Management lands, and properties managed by the Army Corp of Engineers. Most of these agencies have archaeologists assigned to the management of archaeological resources. These professional archaeologists can be of considerable assistance to the local historian in communicating knowledge of resources on public lands and in providing direction to assist the protection of archaeological resources on private property. For best results consult the local or regional office of the respective agency.

Archaeological resources within your state. The primary "formal" repositories of information on archaeological sites are at the state level. Under federal law each state is required to keep a register, or list, of archaeological sites and properties. In most cases, the list of archaeological sites is separate and independent from the National Register of Historic Places and includes all reported prehistoric and historic archaeological sites regardless of relative significance.

Many archaeological sites are located in rural, isolated, and unprotected areas, and because there is a history of looting and site destruction, information on sites, including their location, is restricted to professional archaeologists. In a few states, such as Florida and North Carolina, this information is available to the public. In almost every case an inquiry by a serious local historian will be viewed by the SHPO as a professional inquiry, and they will be forthcoming with information to assist that individual in order to enhance local knowledge of archaeological sites. Unfortunately, in many states the SHPO office is understaffed and may not be able to provide direct assistance (site visitation, evaluation of significance, filing for site protection); however, they will provide information to assist in documenting sites. They will also be able to put you in contact with academic and professional archaeologists who can make an evaluation of the site's significance. They can provide information on local community archaeological projects and events such as regional "Archaeology Weeks" and "Historic Preservation Weeks" that are organized in order to involve the public in archaeology and preservation.

National-level resources. The National Park Service's Archaeology Division has primary responsibility for archaeological resources in the United States. They have published a long list of publications that explains federal laws governing archaeological resources. Two key lists of reference materials are the *Catalog of Historic Preservation Publications* and *Federal Historic Preservation Laws* (National Park Service 1990a and 1990b; some key federal publications, pamphlets, and bulletins are included in the bibliography under National Park Service).

The cornerstone of federal preservation law is the National Historic Preservation Act of 1966 and its several amendments. The publication *Held in Trust: Preserving America's Historic Places* (National Park Service 1991) provides an overview of this act. It is important to consider that this act specifically includes archaeological sites among those historically significant to our nation's heritage. The act outlines the mechanism for the establishment of the *National Register of Historic Places. This register provides federal recognition to sites that are significant at the state and local level as well as those that are of national significance. It established an Advisory Council on Historic Preservation that advises the president and the Congress on historic preservation matters, and it establishes a protocol for the Historic Preservation Fund. This fund provides matching grants to states, Certified Local Governments, Native American tribes, and the National Trust for Historic Preservation (see website listings for the National Park Service and the National Trust for Historic Preservation).

Archaeology and the local historian. The protection and preservation of prehistoric and historical resources is dependent upon the careful recording of information on sites and on systems of interpretation that make this information available and usable by scholars, planners, Native American groups, and the broader communities in which the resources are located. As caretakers of the past, local historians can assist planners and developers at the community level to gain a solid grasp of the resources located within the region for which they are responsible.

Local historians can also play a vital role in assisting the scholarly community and local planners in developing resource management strategies that ensure that all significant resources are afforded protection from destruction. Archaeological resources are an important part of our "living" heritage. Local historians have the ability to link the local community with archival and resource information at the local, state, and national levels. It is hoped that local historians will be encouraged to get involved with archaeology and to utilize archaeological resources in interpreting local history.

See Christopher R. DeCorse, *The Record of the Past: An Introduction to Physical Anthropology and Archaeology* (2000); Elizabeth J. Kellar, "The Public Trust" (unpublished master's thesis, Anthropology Department, Syracuse University, 1996); Thomas F. King, *Cultural Resource Laws and Practice* (2008); George E. Stuart and Francis McManamon, *Archaeology and You* (1996); Daniel Haas, "Reaching the Public: Looking at the Past—Looking at the Future," *Common Ground: Archaeology and Ethnography in the Public Interest* 3, no. 1 (1998): 12–13; Susan L. Henry, "Protecting Archeological Sites on Private Lands," National Park Service, Preservation Planning Branch, Interagency Resources Division (1993); William D. Lipe, *Introduction to Save the Past for the Future II: Report of the Working Conference* (1995); *Catalog of Historic Preservation Publications*, Cultural Resource Program, National Park Service (1990); *Held in Trust: Preserving American's Historic Places—The National Historic Preservation Act of 1966, 25th Anniversary Report* (1991); "Archaeology and the Federal Government," *Cultural Resources Management* 17, no. 6 (1994); "The Native American Graves Protection and Repatriation Act, Special Report," *Federal Archaeology* 7, no. 3 (Fall/Winter 1995); *Common Ground: Archaeology and Ethnography in the Public Interest* 3, no. 1 (1998); "Mapping Out a Career in Historical Archaeology," Society for Historical Archaeology (1996); *With Heritage So Rich: A Report of a Special Committee on Historic Preservation*, United States Conference of Mayors (1966). Douglas V. Armstrong, "Harriet Tubman's Farmsteads in Central New York: Archaeological Explorations Relating to an American Icon," in *The Limits of Tyranny: Archaeological Perspectives on the Struggle Against New World Slavery*, ed. James A. Delle (2015); Douglas V. Armstrong, "Excavating Inspiration: Archaeology of the Harriet Tubman Home," in *The Materiality of Freedom: Archaeologies of Post-Emancipation Life*, ed. Jodi Barnes (2011).

Selected websites. *National Park Service Archaeology Program, https://www.nps.gov/archeology: general information and resources on archae-

ology. See also https://www.nps.gov/
orgs/1345/cr-publications.htm for a list
of National Park Service publications;
and the NPS Southeast Archaeological
Center's website at https://www.nps.
gov/seac/index.htm.

Secretary of the Interior's Standards
for Treatment of Historic Properties,
36 CRF 68: https://www.nps.gov/tps/
standards/four-treatments/treatment-
guidelines.pdf.

The *National Trust for Historic
Preservation, https://savingplaces.org:
congressionally chartered, this organization publishes *Preservation* magazine
and has personnel with knowledge of
legal structures and resources. The National Trust has regional field officers
who may be able to come to your community to provide assistance with your
preservation projects and programs.

Register of Professional Archaeologists, http://www.rpanet.org: this is a
group of professional archaeologists
who have demonstrated training and
expertise and who declared their intention to work ethically within the field of
archaeology.

Society for American Archaeology,
www.saa.org: general information presented by the largest professional and
academic archaeology organization in
the United States. See also http://www.
saa.org/publicftp/public/links/websites.
html for links to public information
and resources.

The Society for Historical Archaeology can be contacted at https://sha.org.

DOUGLAS V. ARMSTRONG
SYRACUSE UNIVERSITY

See American Indian history; historic preservation; intellectual property

rights; Native American Graves Protection and Repatriation Act (NAGPRA);
patrimony; repatriation.

architectural history. Today, one can
state with some confidence that architectural history is a diverse, thoroughly
inclusive field whose focus is the global
*built environment in its myriad mani-
festations—from stately mansions to entire neighborhoods, from courthouses to
outbuildings, from highways to bridges,
and everything in between. The methods of architectural history draw from a
range of disciplines including geography,
art history, anthropology, literary theory,
cultural studies, visual culture, *archaeology, urban history, *material culture,
and, to a certain degree, the natural and
physical sciences.

It was not always this way. Up until the late twentieth century—and to
some extent still—architectural history, particularly in the United States,
was marked by celebratory studies of
individual architects and their designs,
and dominated by an assumption that
the stylistic categories established by
art historians in the nineteenth century held scientific, irreducible truths
that lent legitimacy to those buildings
grouped underneath them. The architects were predominantly white, male,
and professionally educated; the buildings typically monumental, institutional, or spiritual; the styles usually of
European origin and identified by their
formal or aesthetic characteristics.

Although no academic discipline
of architectural history existed until
the mid-twentieth century, architectural history scholarship—much of it
performed by architects themselves—

veered toward identifying precedents for architects to follow, attempted to establish architecture as a distinct profession attained through a specialized education, and tried to parse out a particular *American* architecture free from the trappings of Europe. Depending upon taste or clientele, precedent studies were alternatively classical or medieval in origin, and given that the majority of writing was produced by architects based in New England or New York and often directed toward potential clients in those areas, much scholarship examined the built environment of the eastern seaboard.

Perhaps also to define itself as a tight discipline with its own internal sets of concerns, most architectural historians looked to a distant, Western past for which there was substantial existing material. Leafing through twentieth-century publications, one discovers far more scholarship about the architecture of antiquity, the Renaissance, and colonial America, for example, than that of modernism, the process of construction, or the built environment outside of the Western world. This situation was lamented by John Maass in his scathing 1969 critique of the state of architectural historical scholarship in the *Journal of the Society of Architectural Historians*. Surveying the articles that appeared in the journal in a ten-year period from the late 1950s to the late 1960s, Maass noted their Western bent and challenged architectural historians to shift their focus. His lament, at least at that time, had little impact.

For much of the twentieth century, local historians writing about architecture essentially followed the academic lead. Buildings that marked local histories were of the monumental type or featured details that identified them with larger, national styles; narratives focused upon the (typically white and male) settlers, founders, benefactors, and industrialists; and rarely can one find much information about a town's built environment constructed after World War II. Architectural style books, such as Marcus Whiffen's *American Architecture Since 1780: Guide to the Styles* (1969) or Virginia and Lee McAlester's *A Field Guide to American Houses* (1984), sorted American architecture within distinct categories and provided the backbone for local historians who sought to write about architectural resources in the community. It became *de rigueur* for local histories to determine a building's style (whether Greek Revival, Spanish Colonial, Queen Anne, Prairie, or several other regional or derivative examples), as if the mere declaration of a style revealed a shared, immutable meaning. Buildings not easily categorized might be written off as quirky or altogether ignored—the assumption, perhaps, being that buildings without a style might lack a history—or at least might lack any history worthy of note. Architectural history, despite the inclusive 1940 founding principles of the Society of Architectural Historians welcoming a broad range of topics and historians of every stripe, remained caught in something of a time warp.

This landscape had begun to shift before millennium's turn. The expanded array of building types, districts, and sites that found themselves eligible for listing on the *National Register of Historic Places and worthy of protection following the National Historic Preservation Act of 1966 marked an important legislative moment that necessitated the documentation of a broader cross-section of the built environment—much of it previously overlooked. Important, too, for architectural history were the methodologies emerging from a postmodernist (and poststructuralist and postcolonial) discourse beginning in the 1960s that rejected positivist metanarratives and revealed greater complexity—and greater clarity—through interdisciplinarity. Cultural landscape studies and its attendant examination of people, the places they inhabit, and their perceptions of place—rather than a more exclusive analysis of architects and the handful of impressive buildings they designed—brought the "ordinary," yet more common, *built environment of mass housing, retail, industry, and infrastructure to the forefront.

Such developments also have lessened architectural history's focus on single architects, original intent, aesthetics, and vision-oriented approaches toward an investigation of architecture as a collaborative process where interdisciplinary and multi-sensory approaches offer a wider interpretive lens. Today, the *process* of design and construction and the use or function of a building—as well as its political, social, cultural, spiritual, or economic implications—is frequently afforded as much, if not more, attention as the designer's intent, the finished product, or its original function. Rather than an obsession with the mere classification of buildings under stylistic categories, architectural histories are far more concerned with the larger meaning of a style; that is,

the context, physical or otherwise, that may have influenced that style. Rather than a discussion of architectural details for their own sake, scholars are wont to dissect what those aesthetics might suggest about a building's patrons, its systems of power, its locality, or its time. There is a greater recognition, too, that a building's history extends well beyond the moment of invention or the day its doors swung open to the public; indeed, alterations or new occupants may have a profound impact on the manner in which the building has been understood over the years—at times running counter to the perceived meaning of its original design.

There has also been a substantial expansion beyond the field's traditional European-American geography and alleged standards of value, as scholars have helped established a more global architectural history that investigates cultures and countries from their own perspective rather than that of the west. Thinking globally has also had important ramifications for local architectural histories in the United States, for greater attention is now paid to immigrant or ethnic groups whose indigenous traditions and stories—whether architectural or cultural—came to bear on the built environment of the locality. These developments have not only expanded the architectural scope from which local historians might choose, but offer new approaches that highlight the crucial roles that all members of the community have in shaping the built environment.

New web-based technologies have facilitated a shift to a more inclusive set of histories, making information about architecture more accessible to greater numbers of people—and necessarily more collaborative as well. At the same time, such technologies have reduced the expense, labor, and time involved in visiting archival repositories, sifting through documents, and securing photocopies. Internet searches now quickly uncover sources once the province of a privileged few, while an increasing number of *blogs, *apps, QR codes, podcasts, and Wikipedia entries (an online, publicly edited encyclopedia) provide basic—although not always accurate and rarely peer-reviewed—information about an ever-widening assortment of buildings and *landscapes. *Social media sites such as Facebook, Twitter, Reddit, and Pinterest have accelerated the collaborative possibilities for architectural history, permitting users to contribute information and ideas through shared platforms and *crowdsourcing. Recognizing the ability for new technologies to disseminate information in new ways (if not portending the decline of architectural history in print), the Journal of Architectural Historians launched the multimedia platform JSAH Online in 2010 and the Vernacular Architecture Forum's Buildings & Landscapes implored readers, by 2015, to "please have a look at the digital supplement."

Nonetheless, the field still retains the physicality of the building itself as its principal mode of inquiry and, as archival repositories gradually place once-selective material online, the explosion of electronic resources has placed a vast collection of data at the local historian's disposal. Somewhat ironically, local historians, given their commitment to public outreach, now have the opportunity to provide more accurate and detailed information about architectural resources. By gathering the proliferation of data and placing it online, local historians can avoid the typically selective and lengthy peer-review process that characterizes print-oriented academic publishing. Instead, they can move their material more quickly into the public realm and permit the general public to help them keep up to date. Academically oriented institutions and organizations are hardly immune to the electronic proliferation of once difficult-to-access architectural information—from sketches, plans, working drawings, and specifications to *photographs and written descriptions in *diaries and *travel narratives. The challenge for all historians, in part, is to ensure that some level of clarity, oversight, and rigor is retained as this material is released into the public realm.

The Society of Architectural Historians' Archipedia project offers but one prominent example of how an academically oriented organization might manage the proliferation of architectural data without reducing the rigor of the enterprise (http://sah-archipedia. org). Aided by a *National Endowment of the Humanities grant and support from the University of Virginia Press, the peer-reviewed project appeared online in 2012 and includes narrative histories, images, and associated metadata (such as builders, materials, dates of alteration, and precise geospatial coordinates) regarding one hundred of the nation's most representative works of architecture in each state. To jump-start the website, many of the state's building histories were culled from SAH's older, print-only *Buildings of the United States volumes which—while scholarly, informative, and catholic in their approach—lacked widespread accessibility and could not be updated, changed, or corrected without revised editions and major expenditures of time and money. Placing this information online—together with "born digital" content that permits authors to interpret architecture broadly and reconsider the stylistic taxonomies that have long characterized the history of architecture—has the potential to offer an authoritative, web-based alternative both to the slow and inflexible process of print and the often scattershot, non-refereed architectural information that regularly appears online. *Archipedia* may eventually expand the number of entries into the tens of thousands, permit more frequent revisions, and allow historians to more conveniently make connections among buildings that blur state lines.

Similarly, software applications for mobile devices (smartphones, smartwatches, and tablets) are increasingly putting architectural information within immediate reach of anyone who owns such a device—which by the second decade of the twenty-first century is nearly everyone. Mobile platforms such as Curatescape provide opportunities for architectural history to be delivered "on the go," but their subscription costs requiring sponsorship by local agencies (such as historical societies, museums, municipalities, libraries, or universities) ensures that some level of oversight is necessary and that quality should remain high.

Augmented reality apps, meanwhile, have the potential to push architectural history into even newer frontiers. Such apps can compile historical information, photographs, and renderings to craft street scenes and cityscapes that help bring otherwise staid historical information about buildings and people to life. The historical accuracy of augmented reality notwithstanding, the existence of such technologies offers new interpretive possibilities for local historians who may otherwise struggle to bring their work to a large audience.

No doubt the staying power of certain sites and technologies is compromised by their very accessibility; with so much access, quality control will offer challenges and it is perhaps only a matter of time before new technologies render many of the current tools obsolete. What is not compromised, however, is the very existence of electronic, online tools, from which local historians and the practice of architectural history serves to benefit.

See Dianne Harris, "Field Note: Architectural History's Futures," *Journal of the Society of Architectural Historians* 74, no. 2 (June 2015): 147–51; Patricia Morton, "Editorial: SAH at 75," *Journal of the Society of Architectural Historians* 74, no. 1 (March 2015): 5–7; Swati Chattopadhyay, "Architectural History and Spatial Imagination," *Perspectives on History: The Newsmagazine of the American Historical Association* (January 2014), https://www.historians.org/publications-and-directories/perspectives-on-history/january-2014/architectural-history-and-spatial-imagination; Gabrielle Esperdy, "Building Data: Field Notes on the Future of the

Past," *Places* (September 2013); Nancy Stieber, "Editorial: Architecture Between Disciplines," *Journal of the Society of Architectural Historians* 62, no. 2 (June 2003): 166–67; Dell Upton, "Architecture History or Landscape History?" *Journal of Architectural Education* 44, no. 4 (August 1991): 195–99; Elisabeth Blair MacDougall, ed., *The Architectural Historian in America* (1990).

J. PHILIP GRUEN
WASHINGTON STATE UNIVERSITY

See architectural pattern books; Historic American Building Survey; historic preservation; vernacular architecture

architectural pattern books. In the mid-nineteenth century, the American architectural landscape was increasingly shaped by the widespread circulation of pattern books. These were illustrated architectural manuals that defined taste by providing examples of appropriate, fashionable, and "modern" designs. Although illustrated architectural manuals had been available as early as the sixteenth century, and books with construction details for builders and craftsmen became more widespread by the mid-eighteenth century, the practice of using pattern books as sources for house designs really took hold in America by the 1840s. Pattern books became popular during a period of great change in the building trades, and many builders relied on them to keep abreast of current fashions.

The earliest architectural publications in the United States were reprints of English books. Abraham Swan's *The British Architect* (1775) was the first architectural book published in America, although it had appeared in London several decades earlier. Asher Benjamin's *Country Builder's Assistant* (1797), which was the first U. S. handbook that was not based on English or foreign sources, marked the beginning of a long line of progressively more influential architectural publications that continued through the nineteenth and twentieth centuries.

Pattern books evolved through several stages. The first of these were builders' handbooks, which typically included drawings of details or discussions of specific building problems, but offered few designs for complete buildings. These builders' guides, such as Owen Biddle's *Young Carpenter's Assistant* (1805) and John Haviland's *The Builder's Assistant* (1818), attempted to systematize building practice and to synthesize architectural knowledge into something of a science. In the 1830s, stylebooks began to appear. Unlike the builders' guides, stylebooks such as Alexander Jackson Davis's *Rural Residences* (1837) presented models for complete buildings within appropriately landscaped surroundings, and were aimed at a broader audience that included prospective clients as well as builders. Stylebooks typically included plans as well as perspective views of buildings in naturalistic settings; they also stressed the tastefulness of their designs. Andrew Jackson Downing, author of *Cottage Residences* (1842), *Rural Architecture & Landscape Gardening* (1842), and *The Architecture of Country Houses* (1850), was one of the most famous proponents of a tasteful and appropriate domestic environment, arguing that thoughtfully planned dwellings played an important role in forming moral character and shaping behavior. Style and pattern books played an important role in spreading many nineteenth-century architectural styles throughout the country. They also effectively connected the architect's specialized knowledge to a much broader population, diffusing architectural ideas to working-class people who wanted single-family suburban houses at a moderate cost.

Despite the popularity of pattern books in the antebellum period, literal copies of published designs were not particularly common. Most builders borrowed from these books selectively, working within a traditional architectural vocabulary and grafting stylish motifs onto more conservative and often local forms to appeal to the tastes of their clientele. Exact copies of published examples became more widespread only later in the nineteenth century, when complete plans and prefabricated dwellings began to appear.

After the Civil War and through the later nineteenth and early twentieth centuries, books promoting mail-order house plans began to appear, followed eventually by catalogs marketing completely prefabricated houses. Mail-order plan books were simply catalogs of house plans that readers could purchase, and usually included multiple perspective renderings, floor plans, construction cost estimates, and price tables for working drawings. George Palliser's *Model Homes for the People* (1876) spawned the first significant mail-order plan business. In time, the widening reach of railroad lines permitted customers to select building components and entire prefabricated houses from catalogs such as those issued by Sears, Roebuck & Co. and Montgomery Ward and have them shipped directly. Mail-order plans placed new design standards and technologies within the reach of the middle-class consumer.

While mail-order architectural plans and pattern books stimulated the proliferation of common house types such as bungalows across America, they also helped to set standards for middle-class notions of what a home should be. The emphasis was usually on designs that were practical, convenient, efficient, compact, and moderately priced. Pattern books transformed American architecture not only by promoting change and novelty, but also by bringing fashionable designs within reach of an ever-widening audience.

See Daniel D. Reiff, *Houses From Books: Treatises, Pattern Books, and Catalogs in American Architecture, 1738–1950: A History and Guide* (2000); Linda Smeins, *Building an American Identity: Pattern Book Homes and Communities, 1870–1900* (1999); Jan Jennings, "Cheap and Tasteful Dwellings in Popular Architecture," in *Gender, Class, and Shelter*, Perspectives in Vernacular Architecture, vol. 5, ed. Elizabeth Collins Cromley and Carter L. Hudgins (1995); Clifford Edward Clark Jr., *The American Family Home: 1800–1960* (1986); Dell Upton, "Pattern Books and Professionalism: Aspects of the Transformation of Domestic Architecture in America, 1800–1860," *Winterthur Portfolio* 19 (Summer/Autumn 1984): 108–50; Gwenn Wright, *Building the Dream: A Social History of Housing in America* (1983); Catherine W. Bishir, "Jacob W.

Holt: An American Builder," *Winterthur Portfolio* 16, no. 1 (Spring 1981): 1–31; James L. Garvin, "Mail-Order House Plans and American Victorian Architecture," *Winterthur Portfolio* 16, no 4 (Winter 1981): 309–334; Clay Lancaster, "The American Bungalow," in *Common Places: Readings in American Vernacular Architecture*, ed. Dell Upton and John Michael Vlach (1986); Charles B. Wood III, "The Architectural Book in Nineteenth Century America," in *Building By The Book 3: Palladian Studies in America I*, ed. Mario di Valmarana; and Henry-Russell Hitchcock, *American Architectural Books, New Expanded Edition* (1976).

Note: The classic source for pre-1895 pattern books is Hitchcock's bibliography; probably the most useful secondary source for understanding the influence of pattern books is Upton's article. Reiff's book provides a detailed overview as well as an especially useful appendix with sample compilations of plan books. All three are cited above. Following are some key builder's-guide and pattern-book authors to look for, although there are many others: Benjamin, Asher; Bicknell, Amos J.; Biddle, Owen; Davis, Alexander Jackson; Downing, Andrew Jackson; Fowler, Orson Squire; Haviland, John; Lafever, Minard; Palliser, Palliser & Co., Architects; Ranlett, William H.; Sloan, Samuel; Stickley, Gustav; Vaux, Calvert; Wheeler, Gervase; and Woodward, George E. Daniel D. Reiff identified more than seventy-five companies that provided house plans from illustrated catalogs. Some of the most popular of these companies included the Radford Architectural Company, the Aladdin Company, and Sears, Roebuck & Co.

GABRIELLE M. LANIER
JAMES MADISON UNIVERSITY

See architectural history.

archives and local history. Governments, organizations, families, and individuals create and assemble documents in a variety of print or electronic formats in the course of their daily activities. Most of these documents will eventually be discarded as no longer necessary for business, but a relatively small proportion of the records will be preserved because of their historical, legal, or general cultural value. Those records having such enduring value are archival. In some usages, the term "archives" is reserved for institutional records, while family records or an individual's papers are referred to as "papers," "collections," or "manuscripts." Archives can range in size and complexity from a single item to the millions of linear feet of records preserved in the *National Archives. The term "archives" can also refer to the location or agency responsible for the care of the permanent records of an institution. The archives of a local church might be contained in a file drawer under the care of the church officers or of a volunteer historian. Archives have taken on an additional meaning in the digital age. A storage place for backup copies of digital documents, regardless of their importance, is generally referred to as "archives," and the process of backing up these files is referred to as "archiving." Not all of the backed up files would be suitable for preservation in an archives.

Records are often created and used with little or no thought of their long-term value. Federal and state pension records for Civil War service were created to ensure that those who were entitled to receive pensions were paid. A century later, those records are valuable to genealogists and historians who use them to re-create past lives. *Census and tax records, originally compiled by local, state, and federal government for the purposes of collecting revenue and apportioning political representatives, are now used to trace migration patterns or examine the occupational structure of a community.

Records documenting a community may be divided among many types of archival repositories. Some will be in the immediate area, either in the local historical society or the offices of local governments. However, much significant documentation may also be available in state and federal archives, in regional and state historical societies, and specialized collections. Records of a defunct local church may have been transferred to a regional or national church archives. Records of a regional, but state-operated mental hospital may have been transferred to a state archives. Military service and pension records for Revolutionary or Civil War service can be found in both state and national archives. The papers of individuals and nongovernmental organizations may be scattered among different types of archives and manuscript collections. In addition to the collections documenting a locality or region, there are repositories specializing in particular subjects, ranging from the histories of special populations, including women, racial and ethnic minorities, and religious communities, to topics from medicine or physics to the labor movement and reform. The papers of a nineteenth-century woman botanist who was also active in the women's suffrage movement could easily fall within the subject area of the local historical society where she lived and also within the collecting scope of a repository, perhaps far distant, interested in the history of science or in the experience of women.

There is no single source for locating information about archival collections. Efforts to encode finding aids for archival holdings in an accessible online format resulted in the creation of EAD: Encoded Archival Description, which operates with Internet search engines to link keyword searches to archival repositories with relevant content. The National Union Catalog of Manuscript Collections from the *Library of Congress provides a gateway to search 1.5 million descriptions of archival resources in OCLC Worldcat at https://www.loc.gov/coll/nucmc/oclcsearch.html. Many archives and historical societies, particularly in larger institutions, list some or all of their collections in the Online Computer Library Center (OCLC) or the Research Libraries Information Network (RLIN) online catalogs. In addition, there are guides to individual repositories and subjects, many of which are available online.

Unfortunately, many repositories have neither the time nor the staff to contribute information about their holdings to the national guides and library catalogs. Researchers need to use multiple strategies to locate material. The published and online guides are useful but incomplete. Comprehensive research requires individual contacts with libraries, archives, and fellow researchers.

Researchers should expect to work with the reference staff of the archives or historical society. Letters or e-mail messages of inquiry addressed to an archives should be as specific as possible. A brief explanation of your research topic may also be helpful. Often an archivist or librarian can suggest related material. Don't ask for "everything you have on the Civil War" if your subject is limited to life on the home front in a specific locality. Researchers should also be familiar with the secondary literature on their topic. Researchers often locate relevant materials by looking at footnotes and bibliographies in published histories. There is no need for a researcher to spend his or her time, or that of an archives staff, reading through boxes of records if the information required is readily accessible in a printed source. It is often a good idea to call in advance when first visiting an archives to verify their hours and the accessibility of materials. It is wasted expense to travel to a remote city only to find that the material you seek is in a remote storage area and cannot be retrieved for several days or has been loaned to another institution for an exhibit. Check also to see whether the material you need has been microfilmed or published. Many repositories publish their archival resources online as part of large *digitization initiatives; one example is American Memory at the Library of Congress (https://memory. loc.gov/ammem/index.html). It may be possible to obtain copies or digital images of needed items in order to avoid traveling to a collection.

While archives and manuscript collections exist to support research, and most welcome any knowledgeable researcher, archives have a responsibility to ensure the preservation of unique and often fragile records. Archives have to protect the documents in their care from loss or damage. A diary kept by a schoolteacher in 1905 may have little monetary value, but if it is damaged by improper photocopying, or is stolen, it is still irreplaceable and its loss is a loss to history. Archives usually require that a researcher sign in to the reading room, provide identification, and use materials under supervision. Most archives will charge a fee for reproducing images from its collection.

Archives and researchers should be aware of potential *copyright issues involved in the reproduction and use of documents and images. Any plans for publication should be cleared with the archives. A local historical society may own a *diary or a collection of photographs, but the copyright may remain with the original writer or photographer, or their descendants and heirs. It is the responsibility of the archives to inform persons wishing to publish direct copies or extensive quotations that the material may be covered by copyright, and it is the responsibility of the user to investigate the copyright status of any document or image he or she wishes to publish.

CHRISTOPHER DENSMORE
UPDATED BY HEATHER A. WADE, CAE
INDEPENDENT SCHOLAR

See copyright; intellectual property rights; local government records.

Archives of American Art. Founded in Detroit in 1954 by Edgar P. Richardson, then Director of the Detroit Institute of Arts, and Lawrence A. Fleischman, a Detroit executive and active young collector, the initial goal of the archives was to serve as a microfilm repository of papers housed in other institutions. This mission expanded quickly to collecting and preserving original material and, in 1970, the archives joined the Smithsonian Institution, sharing the institution's mandate—the increase and diffusion of knowledge.

The archives today is the world's preeminent and most widely used research center dedicated to collecting, preserving, and providing access to primary sources that document the history of the visual arts in America.

Its vast holdings—more than twenty million letters, diaries, and scrapbooks of artists, dealers, and collectors; manuscripts of critics and scholars; business and financial records of museums, galleries, schools, and associations; photographs of art world figures and events; sketches and sketchbooks; rare printed material; film, audio and video recordings; and the largest collection of *oral histories anywhere on the subject of art—are a vital resource to anyone interested in American culture over the past 200 years.

Founded on the belief that the public needs free and open access to the most valuable research materials, the archives' collections are available to the thousands of researchers who consult original papers at its research facilities or use its reference services remotely every year, and to millions who visit online to consult digitized collections.

The archives' resources serve as reference for countless dissertations, exhibitions, catalogs, articles, and books on American art and artists, and preserve the untold stories that, without a central repository such as the archives, might have otherwise been lost.

Through collecting, preserving, and providing access to its collections, the archives inspires new ways of interpreting the visual arts in America and allows current and future generations to discover the nation's rich artistic and cultural heritage.

Anyone may consult original documents by appointment at the archives' headquarters in Washington, D.C., view more than two million digital files online through the archives website at www.aaa.si.edu, or use the substantial microfilm holdings available through interlibrary loan or at the archives' D.C. headquarters, New York Research Center at 1285 Avenue of the Americas, and affiliated research centers at the Amon Carter Museum, Boston Public Library, de Young American Art Study Center, and the Huntington Library. The website for the Archives of American Art is www.aaa.si.edu.

LIZA KIRWIN
ARCHIVES OF AMERICAN ART

Archives Week and American Archives Month. Usually held in October, this program is for raising public awareness about the values of archivists and the archival community. The advocacy initiative stemmed from a grassroots

American effort that has become recognized and celebrated internationally. Professional associations for archivists and individual states sometimes choose to recognize Archives Week in conjunction with a regionally significant date or event during the month of October.

The Council of State Archivists (CoSA) promotes Archives Week and Archives Month activities by offering planning resources on its website, http://www.statearchivists.org. The Society of American Archivists (SAA), after its governing board identified "Public Awareness" as one of its top three strategic goals in 2005, joined CoSA in developing a unified approach to the advocacy initiative; sample PR kits are available to download from the SAA website at http://www2.archivists.org/initiatives/american-archives-month. SAA's year-round "I Found It in the Archives!" program, initiated in 2010, provides an opportunity to extend the advocacy initiative beyond a calendar week or month.

Archives Week and Archives Month activities can include open houses, speakers, workshops, and exhibits that involve the public, from school-age youngsters to adults, and teach the value of historically important materials. Local historical societies, genealogical societies, and community history centers in public libraries frequently have materials, such as photographs, maps, and even newspaper clippings, which can be used in the annual observance. Many programs organized by professional archivists also have a poster for distribution focusing on the rich resources housed in archival repositories.

There is no shortage of creativity in the activities offered. For example, Portland, Oregon, has initiated a successful "Archives Crawl" (http://www.portlandoregon.gov/archives/article/499788). Philadelphia-area archival repositories have banded together to feature a host of opportunities(https://archivesmonthphilly.com).

Since 2014, #AskAnArchivist Day has been widely celebrated on October 1 with archivists around the country fielding questions about their collections from participants on social media.

The idea for an annual Archives Week program was first promoted in the late 1970s by the International Council on Archives (ICA). The North American impetus came from the New York State Archives and Records Administration, which began in the late 1980s. The *National Archives and Records Administration and the *National Historical Publications and Records Commission have hosted the Annual Washington, D.C., Metropolitan Area Archives Fair since 1996. Participation in Archives Week events had expanded to at least thirty-five states by 2005.

By 2006, the Society of Rocky Mountain Archivists and the states of Arizona, Colorado, North Dakota, Utah, and Wyoming had named the month of October "Archives Month." Similar events, such as Michigan's Family History Month, were also recognized in October.

GEORGE W. BAIN AND HEATHER A. WADE
UPDATED BY ABIGAIL CHRISTIAN
SOCIETY OF AMERICAN ARCHIVISTS

This Gadsden Purchase historical marker is located at a rest stop along Interstate 10 near the Gila River in Arizona. CREDIT: JIM TURNER.

archivist. See Society of American Archivists (SAA).

Arizona, local history in. The name Arizona comes from the Basque phrase Aritz ona (good oak). Spanish communities of extended families immigrated to what they called the Pimeria Alta to support the Catholic missions. Later, some served in four Spanish forts until the United States took possession after the Treaty of Guadalupe Hidalgo (1848) and the Gadsden Purchase (1854). Most of the American settlers in the 1860s were prospectors, and the motto on the territorial seal showed a prospector with the motto, *Ditat Deus*—God Enriches. By the 1870s, Mormon settlers began farming in the northeast, central, and southern part of the state. Cattle ranching thrived in the late 1870s as a large portion of the U.S. Army was stationed in the territory during the clash of cultures between Native Americans and pioneers. Copper was king when the railroad crossed the state in 1881, and with the completion of the Theodore Roosevelt Dam in 1911, cotton and citrus farming became a major part of the economy. Arizona benefited from many New Deal programs during the Great Depression, and its population and economy exploded with the building of military bases and war production plants during World War II. The G.I. Bill brought thousands of veterans to attend college and settle in Arizona after the war, and Del Webb's Sun City, the first seniors-only retirement community in the nation, made Arizona a leading state for retirement. Recently, high-tech manufacturing from computer chips to genetic research are major factors in the state economy, as well as resorts and tourism because of the mild winters.

The Arizona Historical Society (AHS) was established by an Act of the First Territorial Legislature in Prescott, Arizona on November 7, 1864. The institution disappeared from the record but was restarted in 1884, and they dropped the word pioneer from their name in 1971.

In the decades that followed, AHS absorbed the Northern Arizona Pioneers Society in Flagstaff, and the Yuma County Historical Society, and created an AHS division in Phoenix. In 1968, the Arizona legislature enacted a law to provide funds to the Arizona Historical Society to designate at least one Certified Museum in each county, eligible for grant money and professional support. AHS now serves more than seventy local museums in every corner of the state. Contact information for these local museums is available at the AHS web site, and the Museum Association of Arizona and the Central Arizona Museum Association are both valuable resources for serving and networking between local museums.

AHS has an online catalog at http://catalog.azhsarchives.org. The Sharlot Hall Museum in Prescott, founded by State Historian Sharlot Hall, also has a large archive and museum. The Arizona State Library, Archives, and Public Records also collects and preserves historical manuscripts, photographs, and materials pertaining to all localities in Arizona, as do the special collections departments of the University of Arizona, Arizona State University, and Northern Arizona University.

A good number of primary sources and historic texts are available at the University of Arizona's online Southwest Electronic Text Center: http://southwest.library.arizona.edu. Reliable Arizona history books include Thomas Farish's eight-volume *History of Arizona* (1920); Thomas Sheridan, *Arizona: A History* (revised 2012); Marshall Trimble, *Arizona: A Cavalcade of History* (1989); and Jim Turner, *Arizona: A Celebration of the Grand Canyon State* (2011). For Native American culture, Henry Dobyns and Trudy Griffin-

Pierce, *Native Peoples of the Southwest* (2000); and Edward Spicer, *Cycles of Conquest: The Impact of Spain, Mexico, and the U.S. on the Indians of the* Southwest (1967). In Latin American culture, John Kessell, *Spain and the Southwest* (2002); and James Officer, *Hispanic Arizona, 1536–1856* (1987). The nationally acclaimed *Journal of Arizona History* is a peer-reviewed quarterly with fully annotated articles and book reviews, first published in 1960.

Since the 1920s, Arizona's schoolchildren have had the opportunity to learn state history thanks to books by Ida Flood Dodge, *Our Arizona* (1936), and Madeline Ferrin Pare, *Arizona Pageant: A Short History of the 48th State* (1965). In 2009, Kyle McCoy and Jim Turner wrote *The Arizona Story*, an AASLH award-winning fourth-grade textbook.

Since the 1950s, Arizona history has been taught at the fourth-, seventh-, and tenth-grade levels, but is now required only in fourth grade. Since 2001, budget cuts have limited the number of field trips students can make to museums and emphasis on basic skills and test results have limited the amount of history, and specifically Arizona history, taught in the schools. However, a great many social studies teachers are invested in getting their students to participate in *National History Day, and work with Arizona Historical Society educators to win top honors at the national competitions.

New technology has been an invaluable resource in teaching local history at all levels, ranging from public service television documentaries to online materials for teachers, resources for students, electronic texts, historic photographs, and online resource databases. These have made teaching Arizona history much more accessible, and individual teachers and classes are able to network with other students around the state and across the world.

Since a lot of Arizona's tax base centers around the home building industry, for retirement homes, health seekers, military service employees, and large corporations who get tax breaks and hire non-union employees at lower wages, the mortgage bubble hit the state hard. Most state museums were closed and the Arizona Historical Society suffered massive budget cuts. Many of the state museums were eventually turned over to local volunteer groups who now face the problem of raising funds independently. Many of these converted museums are now Arizona Historical Society Certified Museums and are thus eligible for state grants.

The situation is turning around, however, and there are more AHS Certified Museums now than there were in 2008. Very few museums, state or local, have closed their doors. Arizona's is a growing population and as the descendants of the pioneers become fewer, moving away for better jobs in more prosperous states, the growing number of retirees still looking for ways to remain active have taken up the banner of Arizona history and are keeping it flying.

JIM TURNER
ARIZONA HISTORICAL SOCIETY, RETIRED

See United States, local history in.

Arkansas, local history in. Arkansas's first fifty years of statehood did not produce any significant written histories of

This marker notes the site of Civil War skirmishes in Roseville, Arkansas, in 1864. CREDIT: ARKANSAS HISTORIC PRESERVATION PROGRAM.

the state, but that began to change in the 1880s. Joe Hallum published the *Biographical and Pictorial History of Arkansas* in 1887, while lawyer and poet Fay Hempstead came out with *A School History of Arkansas* in 1889, followed by *A Pictorial History of Arkansas: From Earliest Times to the Year 1890* the next year. Around the same time, the Goodspeed Publishing Company of Chicago, Illinois, was producing historical and biographical memoirs of Arkansas counties, which were published in six volumes between 1889 and 1891, with a seventh volume appearing in 1894.

Interest in Arkansas history increased in the twentieth century. John Hugh Reynolds of the University of Arkansas in Fayetteville helped to organize the Arkansas Historical Society, which met occasionally and published four volumes of writings about Arkansas during the next five years. Reynolds was also instrumental in establishing, in 1905, the Arkansas History Commission and State Archives in Little Rock. The commission's first director, Dallas Tabor Herndon, wrote a three-volume *Centennial History of Arkansas* in 1922, following that with the four-volume *Annals of Arkansas* in 1947, while Pulitzer Prize–winning poet John Gould Fletcher produced a single-volume history of the state in 1947, simply titled *Arkansas.* Newspapers also fed the growing interest in state and local history. Fay Williams wrote regular columns for the *Arkansas Democrat,* and Margaret Ross did the same for the *Arkansas Gazette*; their writings are useful resources for later researchers and have been collected into book form.

In 1941, the Arkansas Historical Association was formed in Little Rock and, the following year, began publishing its quarterly journal, the *Arkansas Historical Quarterly*. University of Arkansas professor Walter Lemke led the creation of the Washington County Historical Society, the state's first local historical organization, in 1951. Several other such societies were established soon thereafter, as was the Arkansas Genealogical Society, founded in 1962. In addition to producing journals and books, these societies frequently operate local museums, restore historic sites, erect monuments and markers, and hold meetings and lectures about state and local history. In 1967 the state legislature created the Arkansas Archeological Survey, the nation's first state-wide research and service organization; the Arkansas Archeological Society, founded in 1960, brings together professionals and amateurs to increase the public's awareness of the state's archeological heritage. The nonprofit Historic Preservation Alliance of Arkansas was established in 1981 to protect the state's architectural and cultural resources.

Arkansas is home to many excellent museums. The Arkansas State University Museum, one of the state's oldest, was founded in 1933 and houses an impressive collection of documents and artifacts relating to the history of northeast Arkansas. The Department of Arkansas Heritage (DAH) oversees four museums, including the Mosaic Templars Cultural Center in Little Rock and the Delta Cultural Center in Helena-West Helena, but much of the responsibility for preserving the artifacts of Arkansas history has been placed in the hands of local museums and historical societies. Several cities operate local and regional museums, such as the northwest Arkansas community of Springdale, which maintains the acclaimed Shiloh Museum of Ozark History, while the impressive Grant County Museum in Sheridan is maintained by the county government. The state's role in military history is documented at the Arkansas National Guard Museum, the MacArthur Museum of Military History, and the Jacksonville Museum of Military History. Many colleges and universities also operate off-campus museum sites geared toward local history. For example, Black River Technical College in Pocahontas maintains Project REACH, which has restored local historic structures with an eye toward heritage tourism. Perhaps the most famous university-operated site is the Historic Dyess Colony: Boyhood Home of Johnny Cash, maintained by Arkansas State University as part of the university's Arkansas Heritage Sites operation; it opened to international fanfare in 2014. In addition, the Arkansas Department of Parks and Tourism manages over a dozen sites preserving local history, such as the Arkansas Museum of Natural Resources in Smackover, while the National Park Service maintains Hot Springs National Park, the Fort Smith *National Historic Site, the Little Rock Central High School National Historic Site, Pea Ridge National Military Park, and the Arkansas Post National Memorial.

The Arkansas History Commission houses the largest repository of state documents and also operates two regional facilities: the Southwest Arkansas Regional Archives at Washington and the Northeast Arkansas Regional Archives at Powhatan. Other large archival institutions include the Arkansas Studies Institute in Little Rock and the Special Collections department of the University of Arkansas. Religious groups and their related institutions also house local history records. For example, Hendrix College in Conway holds the archives of the United Methodist Church in Arkansas, while records of the state's Roman Catholic diocese are held at St. John's Center in Little Rock. Several archives and museums now maintain digital collections and online exhibits.

While many of the local historical societies maintain publishing programs, the state's most prominent publisher of state and local history is the University of Arkansas Press, established in 1980. The Little Rock-based publishers August House and Rose Publishing Company, both established in the 1970s, also produced several works of state and local history (though the former was sold in 2004 and now focuses upon children's books). Created in 1997, the Butler Center for Arkansas Studies, a department of the Central Arkansas Library System, maintains a lively publishing program, as well as the *Encyclopedia of Arkansas History & Culture* website (www.encyclopediaofarkansas. net). The *Encyclopedia of Arkansas* went online in May 2006 and, as of mid-2015, contained more than 4,000 entries and 5,400 pieces of media, as well as resources for elementary and secondary teachers. The website of the Arkansas Historic Preservation Program of the Department of Arkansas Heritage provides the nomination forms of the state's properties on the *National Register of Historic Places—a good source of local history. Also, many agencies, most notably the Arkansas Department of Parks and Tourism, now provide mobile websites or smartphone apps.

Act 787 of 1997 mandates that a unit of Arkansas history shall be taught as a social studies subject at each elementary-grade level in every public elementary school in the state, with greater emphasis at the fourth and fifth grades. In addition, at least one semester of Arkansas history shall be taught to all students at the secondary level in every secondary school in the state. Since July 2001, persons cannot obtain a license to teach social studies at the secondary level or obtain a license as an elementary teacher unless they have successfully completed three hours of coursework in Arkansas history. Teachers moving from out of state may obtain a provisional license for one year. After the passage of Act 969 of 2013, two hours of professional development in Arkansas history, for those who teach the subject, is no longer required every year but is offered on a rotating basis, every four years, with other subjects.

STEVEN TESKE, MIKE POLSTON, KAY BLAND, GUY LANCASTER
ENCYCLOPEDIA OF ARKANSAS HISTORY AND CULTURE

See United States, local history in.

Armenians in North America, sources for. See Appendix A.

armory. A place in which weapons and ammunition are stored and where meetings are often held.

Asian American history. American economic, political, and religious ambitions in Asia and Asian migration to America prompted some of the earliest works of Asian American history. Accordingly, trade, missionary labors, colonialism, the U.S. Pacific destiny, and Asian exclusion and assimilation are dominant themes within that foundational literature, and Asian American history is commonly grouped under the rubrics of U.S. diplomatic history and the history of U.S. race relations. Prominent within Asian American historiography are three interpretive strands advanced by anti-Asianists and cultural brokers, liberals, and Asian Americanists.

Central to the debate between anti-Asianists and cultural brokers are the questions over America's place within world history and the nature of U.S. history and society. William Speer, a Presbyterian missionary to China, published his *The Oldest and Newest Empire: China and the United States* (1870). Contemporary concern over Chinese migration or "the Chinese question" motivated Speer to write a book that, he promised, would explain to Americans the true character and capacities of the Chinese by a cultural broker (someone who claims the ability to mediate between cultures). Speer's canvas is large and offers a history of Europe's fascination and encounters with Asia beginning with Marco Polo's late-thirteenth-century account of China. It provides an argument for American expansion because of the republic's location, sitting at the confluence of Europe's civilization and Asia's wealth. The world's oldest empire—China—writes Speer, must give way to its newest empire—the United States—that was destined for "peculiar glory" in the meeting of East and West.

Those Pacific visions by cultural brokers like Speer arose in defense of America's westward expansions across the continent and the ocean that was the highway to Asia's raw materials and manufactures. These were the forerunners of the imperialists of the late nineteenth century who proclaimed America's *manifest destiny in the Pacific and Asia. But they also sought to counter the anti-Asianists' claim that Asian migration to America threatened to tear the nation's economic, political, and moral fabric. Pierton W. Dooner's *Last Days of the Republic* (1879), for instance, presented a case for the exclusion of Chinese workers in a genre called by Dooner "deductive history." The book is set in the future, but reads as a historical account of the demise of the United States brought about by cheap Chinese labor that swamps first California and then the rest of the nation. In 1893, during the noonday of European imperialism, English historian Charles H. Pearson published his *National Life and Character: A Forecast* (1894), in which he predicted a final conflict for global supremacy between whites and nonwhites led by Asians. Nonwhite migration from the tropics to the temperate, white heartlands, warned Pearson, threatened to engulf white civilization and conjured up the specter of the "yellow peril," an idea then prevalent in Europe and America. For both the cultural brokers and anti-

Asianists, especially after the advent of European and U.S. expansions to the tropics, what happened "out there" in the peripheries held growing significance for what happened "here" within the core.

Asians, like whites, offered to interpret Asian culture to whites and to contest the claims of the anti-Asianists. Indeed, to cultural brokers, the acculturation of Asians documented the falsity of the anti-Asianist contention that Asian cultures were at odds with European civilization and that they were unassimilable. Born near Macao in 1828, Yung Wing was schooled by missionaries before leaving for the United States in 1847 to further his education. After graduating from Yale in 1854, Yung returned to China, where he organized the government-sponsored Chinese Educational Mission that sent 120 Chinese youths for studies in the United States from 1872 to 1881. In his autobiography, *My Life in China and America*, published in 1909, Yung endorsed the missionaries' claim that Christianity had the power to transform Chinese culture and that education could lead to the "reformation and regeneration" of China. Yung testified to "a metamorphosis in his inward nature," yet declared his "undying love for China."

In the early twentieth century, "liberals" joined the debate between cultural brokers and anti-Asianists. What distinguishes the liberal writers from their nineteenth-century predecessors is their belief in the progressive view of American history that conceives of the republic as a nation of immigrants who were "pushed" by hard times and persecution and were "pulled" to these shores by the land's bounties and the society's freedoms and opportunities. The saga moves from despair to hope, from poverty to plenty, failure to success as immigrants struggle to make a home for themselves in the United States and achieve the "American dream." Liberals applied the historical template derived from the late-nineteenth-century European migrations to the simultaneous migrations from Asia.

Liberal writings might have marked a departure from previous Asian American histories, but they were also connected with the works of cultural brokers in that both sought to undermine the arguments posed by anti-Asianists and thereby defend not only Asian migrants but the ideals of American society and America's national interests as they saw them. Mary Roberts Coolidge's *Chinese Immigration* ([1909] 1986) is clearly the most important liberal text, because it identified the historical problem as posed by the liberals and offered its explanation. Begun during the debate around the Geary Act of 1892 that extended the decade-long exclusion of Chinese workers, Coolidge's book delineated the processes whereby Asians became or were prevented from becoming Americans—that of inclusion or exclusion—along with their domestic and international ramifications. And despite subsequent compelling evidence that refutes and revises her version of Asian American history, Coolidge's statement of the problem and its explanation remain the standard treatment today.

Called the California thesis, Coolidge's account of the rise and nature of the anti-Chinese movement depends upon conditions peculiar to the time but also to the place. Pivotal was the gold rush that attracted to the state, according to Coolidge, Southerners who held racial prejudices against darker-skinned people, ignorant and greedy frontiersmen who viewed all nonwhites as inferiors, and recent immigrants such as the Irish who resented competition from the Chinese. East Coast Know-Nothing *nativism and xenophobia were additional ingredients exported to the California mix of hatred against the Chinese, who were vilified as scapegoats for the economic decline that followed the initial euphoria of instant wealth and the exhaustion of surface mining. In truth, maintained Coolidge, Chinese workers bolstered California's economy and the anti-Chinese movement tarnished the reputation of the United States abroad and threatened its trade with China and Asia.

Although European immigration proved the rule for some liberals, the "Oriental question" seemed to pose an exception to the melting-pot notion to others. Robert Park, a sociologist like Mary Roberts Coolidge, and several of his colleagues and students at the University of Chicago during the 1920s and 1930s took a special interest in that "question." Park's race-relations cycle of migration, competition, accommodation, and assimilation described the European experience, but failed to account for the receptions of both Africans and Asians because of their "physical marks." Race constituted a barrier to their full participation in American life, Park concluded. Park's Survey of Race Relations that interviewed hun-

dreds of Asians and non-Asians along the West Coast and publications that emanated from the "Chicago school" were enormously influential in reshaping and validating the liberal interpretation of the Asian-American experience. Still prevalent are the ideas drawn from the Chicago school such as Park's race-relations cycle, an approach to race relations that pivots on the white and nonwhite axis, the assumption of assimilation, European immigration's paradigmatic status, the focus upon urban communities, and the notion that minorities are "deviations" from the European "norm."

Asian Americanist writings depart from the liberal tradition in that they center upon the Asian American subject for and of itself. In their view, inaccurate are representations of Asian Americans drawn from European American models and by studies that conceive of Asian Americans as social problems and deviations or that ignore the aspirations and perspectives of the subjects themselves. During the 1920s and 1930s, with the coming of age of a second generation, Asian Americanists began documenting their lives and histories to record the realities of their past and present as they saw them, and to mobilize a sense of community and collective agency. Takashi Tsutsumi, secretary of the Federation of Japanese Labor, published in 1921 his *Hawaii Undo Shi* (*History of Hawai'i Laborers' Movement*). He wrote to inform Japanese sugar-plantation workers about the injustices perpetrated by the sugar planters, and to present the union's version of the 1920 strike that involved 8,300 Filipino and Japanese laborers or about 77 percent of the total plantation workforce on the island of Oahu. Ernest K. Wakukawa's *A History of the Japanese People in Hawaii* (1938) was written in English and addressed the second generation, who, the author observed, often failed to appreciate "the achievements and accomplishments of the pioneers and their forebears." History, he hoped, would help them understand "their own status and problems."

Those Asian Americanist concerns and purposes are evident in contemporary texts such as Ronald Takaki's *Strangers from a Different Shore* (1989) and Sucheng Chan's *Asian Americans: An Interpretive History* (1991) that have become standard surveys of the Asian American experience. But the rise and now predominance of the Asian Americanist interpretation hasn't foreclosed its antecedents, and readers can still find remnants and variants of cultural brokers, anti-Asianists, and liberals in the comparative effusion of writings on Asian Americans today. Although they might comprise distinctive strands, the three varieties of Asian American history overlap and form continuities as well as breaks. Cultural brokers held liberal ideals of America's identity and promise; Asian Americanists claimed the role of cultural brokers between wider society and "their" communities; and anti-Asianists and liberals contended their versions of the past and present were in the best traditions of the republic's founders.

For local historians, the writings by liberals and Asian Americanists should hold the most interest. The sociological studies from the University of Chicago,

for instance, offer exemplary accounts of Asian American communities in places like Seattle, Chicago, San Francisco, Los Angeles, Hawai'i, and Butte, Montana. Key texts include S. Frank Miyamoto's *Social Solidarity among the Japanese of Seattle* (1939), and Paul C. P. Siu's *The Chinese Laundryman: A Study of Social Isolation* (1987). Asian Americanists, like the liberal sociologists, have stressed urban communities, mainly Chinatowns and Japantowns in California and New York. Exceptions include Illsoo Kim, *New Urban Immigrants: The Korean Community in New York* (1981); Robert N. Anderson et al., *Filipinos in Rural Hawaii* (1984); and Bruce La Brack, *The Sikhs of Northern California, 1904–1975* (1988). Asian Americanists have also studied rural communities primarily in Hawai'i and on the West Coast, and local historians and history societies have published significant numbers of works designed principally to document the past and ensure a collective identity in the future. These include Ethnic Studies Oral History Project, *Uchinanchu: A History of Okinawans in Hawaii* (1981); Steven Misawa, ed., *Beginnings: Japanese Americans in San Jose* (1981); Chinese Historical Society of Southern California, *Linking Our Lives: Chinese American Women of Los Angeles* (1984); Ron Chew, ed., *Reflections of Seattle's Chinese Americans: The First 100 Years* (1994); Pepi Nieva, ed., *Filipina: Hawaii's Filipino Women* (1994); and Daisy Chun Rhodes, *Passages to Paradise: Early Korean Immigrant Narratives from Hawaii* (1998).

Exemplary community studies not cited above include Peter Kwong, *Chinatown, N.Y.: Labor and Politics, 1930–*

1950 (1979); Timothy J. Lukes and Gary Y. Okihiro, *Japanese Legacy: Farming and Community Life in California's Santa Clara Valley* (1985); Sandy Lydon, *Chinese Gold: The Chinese in the Monterey Bay Region* (1985); on Philadelphia, Nazli Kibria, *Family Tightrope: The Changing Lives of Vietnamese Americans* (1993); Linda Tamura, *The Hood River Issei: An Oral History of Japanese Settlers in Oregon's Hood River Valley* (1993); Timothy P. Fong, *The First Suburban Chinatown: The Remaking of Monterey Park, California* (1994); on Los Angeles and San Diego, Rick Bonus, *Locating Filipino Americans: Ethnicity and the Cultural Politics of Space* (2000); Yong Chen, *Chinese San Francisco, 1850–1943: A Trans-Pacific Community* (2000); Claire Jean Kim, *Bitter Fruit: The Politics of Black-Korean Conflict in New York City* (2000); Madhulika S. Khandelwal, *Becoming American, Being Indian: An Immigrant Community in New York City* (2002); Jianli Zhao, *Strangers in the City: The Atlanta Chinese, Their Community, and Stories of Their Lives* (2002); Jacalyn D. Harden, *Double Cross: Japanese Americans in Black and White Chicago* (2003); and on San Diego, Linda Trinh Võ, *Mobilizing an Asian American Community* (2004).

GARY Y. OKIHIRO
COLUMBIA UNIVERSITY

Association of Gravestone Studies (AGS). See gravestones.

Association of Living History, Farm and Agricultural Museums (ALFAM). See living history museums.

atlases. See maps and atlases.

attainder, bill of. In English law, a bill of attainder is passed by the legislature that decreed that certain crimes, especially treason, required the forfeiture of all property and civil rights. Such bills are expressly forbidden under the U.S. Constitution.

Australia, local history in. Australian local history had its origins as a documentation and, yes, celebration of European discovery, pioneering, and development in the nineteenth century. The first echoes rested with European settlers who provided personal stories of achievement in what was perceived as the alien and challenging Australian environment and who sought to memorialize pioneer communities. Anglocentric, male, and conservative, the tone and themes they set shaped Australian local histories well into the twentieth century, and were reflected in the foundation and early years of the increasing number of local history societies and activities that emerged following World War II. The growth is attributed to social and economic changes that were threatening to transform or even destroy local communities, and to the arrival of the sesquicentenaries and centenaries of towns and local institutions and an accompanying desire to create commemorative histories.

The growth of interest in local history was flanked by—and partly an expression of—an increasingly assertive interest in Australian history. Until the post–World War II era, the history that was taught in Australian schools and universities was essentially British history and, when Australia was encountered, it was primarily in terms of the British discovery, exploration, and settlement of the country. The 1950s and 1960s saw this emphasis undermined. An increasing number of historians elected to focus on Australian history and the first of many overtly Australian history courses was introduced into Australian universities. These developments occurred in a social and political environment in which the concerns of minorities were bringing about changes in government policies and attitudes, and in which many historians were directing their attention to the new social history and to themes and groups whose histories had previously been ignored. *Oral history has also played its part. From the 1970s through to the present, Australian histories became increasingly concerned with the voices and perspectives of, among others, aboriginal people, women, the working class, and ethnic communities. This push also influenced local and community histories. There are now local histories and local historical societies that at least integrate the experiences of these groups into their publications and activities; and there are others that focus primarily on the experiences of these previously silenced minorities. There are also local histories that reflect more recent developments in historical research and practice. These include local histories that are preoccupied with ideas about place, about environmental history, and about identity and belonging: They explore conceptual and environmental issues in relation to specific geographical localities, they dissect relations between people and place, they unpack the past and present language used to identify and describe place. There are also local histories that have moved away from celebrations of achievement and the identification of common features that mark the Australian experience to acknowledgements of the intersections, tensions, and layers within localities, and there are other local histories that overtly explore the ways in which the local reflects global and transnational trends and developments.

Another change has been increasing activity from professional historians in the research and production of local histories. These include local residents who also happen to be historians; consultant historians contracted to produce a local history; and academic historians focusing on specific localities for research projects. Some local councils have also created and funded positions for a historian of their localities. Somewhat ironically, and with some exceptions, this move by professional historians into local history has not been paralleled by an overt recognition of local history as an academic study. A notable exception is the local, family, and applied history courses taught since the early 1980s by the University of New England (Armidale, NSW). Other training in local history is primarily provided by workshops, publications, and public education programs organized through local historical organizations and their networks including, for example, the Royal Australian Historical Society and the Federation of Australian Historical Societies.

The profile of local history has also been enhanced—and challenged—by the growth of the heritage industry and by government initiatives at national, state, and local levels. Heritage legislation requires local governments to research, document, and assess the heritage value of their localities. This entails commissioning research into aspects of local history, and recognizing the value of local history resources and expertise. For some localities, this has resulted in the funding of significant local studies collections and services in local libraries, in government funding and assistance to local museums that quite often had their origins as the offshoots of local historical societies, and in the commissioning of publications. A locality's history and heritage is also increasingly being seen as a potential economic commodity: a means to sell the locality to tourists, to potential residents, to state and national funding authorities.

And forms of collating and presenting local histories are changing. Exhibitions, walking tours, reenactments, and festivals are increasingly used as means to engage old and new audiences. Similarly, the digital age is playing its part.

Archival and library collections are increasingly online; local history organizations have websites; there are online databases; there are online publications; and there are local history blogs and social networking.

Sense of place in both urban and rural Australia, landscape, indigenous voices, diverse communities, the local and global, heritage tourism, in print, online and on display: these are some of the words that capture the current directions of Australian local history. For additional information see Janis Wilton, "Local Stories, Places and People: Writing History into Localities and Communities" in *Once Upon a Time: Australian Writers on Using History*, ed. Paul Ashton, Anna Clark, and Robert Crawford (2016).

JANIS WILTON
UNIVERSITY OF NEW ENGLAND

Austrians in North America, sources for. See Appendix A.

B

Bancroft Library. In 1905 the University of California purchased the Hubert Howe Bancroft collection of research materials. Bancroft (1832–1918) was a historical entrepreneur based in San Francisco who laid the foundations for state and local history throughout the western part of the United States by commissioning historians and writers to create a thirty-nine-volume history of the West. Since its inception the library has continued to add documentary materials, supplemented by an extensive *oral history program. Their major collections include Western Americana, Latin Americana, History of Science and Technology, Rare Books and Manuscripts, a Pictorial Collection, and University Archives of the University of California. Major research programs include the Mark Twain Papers and Project, and the Oral History Center. The Bancroft Library is located at the University of California at Berkeley, Berkeley, California 94720-6000; (510) 642-6481; bancref@library.berkeley.edu; or consult www.lib.berkeley.edu/libraries/bancroft-library.

See also California, local history in.

Baptists, sources for. See Appendix B.

Basques in North America, sources for. See Appendix A.

Belgians in North America, sources for. See Appendix A.

biographical dictionaries. Internet access to digitized U.S. newspapers, census records, city directories, and local histories has greatly expanded the volume and granularity of biographical data available to researchers, particularly those who are attempting to reconstruct lives previously unremarked. For figures of recognized historical significance, biographical dictionaries remain a useful source of life narratives. Ranging in scope from general (*American National Biography*) to specific (*Black Authors and Illustrators of Books for Children and Young Adults*), the best of these compendia offer concise, well-researched biographical overviews along with bibliographies for further reading. While Wikipedia and other publicly editable sites on the Internet offer relatively easy access to biographical articles, researchers are advised to seek out corroborative or complementary sources, especially where the facts as presented are insufficiently documented or subject to conflicting interpretations. The selective list that follows favors dictionaries with broad historical or multidisciplinary coverage, moving from the most comprehensive to the more narrowly focused. Preference is given to online sources, though information on print correlatives is noted where relevant. (See other articles in this volume for information on ethnic, cultural, or discipline-specific resources.)

Biography and Genealogy Master Index. Though international in scope, this comprehensive database indexes approximately fifteen million biographical sketches in more than 1,700 printed biographical sources, both current and retrospective. A good starting point for biographical research.

Biographical Dictionaries and Related Works: An International Bibliography of Approximately 16,000 Collective Biographies, ed. Robert B. Slocum (1986). Though not a biographical dictionary, this is a relatively comprehensive bibliography of published collective biographies. Those covering persons of local interest are listed under the section headed "United States: Local (States, Cities, and Regions)."

Marquis Biographies Online. Database that includes all biographies appearing in twenty-four Marquis publications since 1985 (e.g., *Who's Who in America, Who's Who of American Women, Who's Who in the East, Who's Who in the West,* etc.), as well as the historical biographies in *Who Was Who in America* (volumes 1607–1985). Coverage is updated and expanded daily.

Who Was Who in America (1897–). This ongoing print set contains brief biographies of figures previously profiled in *Who's Who in America* but who have since died. A *Historical Volume 1607–1896* issued in 1963 (rev. 1967) is supplemented by additional retrospective volumes and annual updates, including periodic name indexes to the entire set.

American Biographical Archive Online. Electronic version of the microfiche set that reproduced entries from nearly 400 major English-language biographical reference works encompassing the United States and Canada, published between 1702 and 1956. Part of DeGruyter's World Biographical Information System (WBIS) Online.

American National Biography Online. Reflective of recent historical scholarship and based on the 1999 Oxford University Press print edition edited by John A. Garraty and Mark C. Carnes, this online source includes signed biographical entries for nearly 19,000 Americans from all areas of endeavor, as well as illustrations, bibliographies, and hyperlinked cross-references. Updated semi-annually.

The National Cyclopaedia of American Biography (1898–1984). A sixty-three-volume set focused on "lives of the founders, builders, and defenders of the republic." Illustrated with portraits, but articles are unsigned and lack supporting bibliographies. Some data was supplied by relatives of those profiled. An index volume published in 1984 provides access to the set. Scattered volumes are publicly available online through various digital repositories.

Encyclopedia of American Biography, eds. John A. Garraty and Jerome L. Sternstein (1996). Focused on Americans who have made significant impacts on American history and culture, the signed entries in this one-volume work have two components: a factual biographical summary followed by an evaluative essay.

Notable American Women: A Biographical Dictionary (1971–2004). This respected five-volume set includes signed scholarly biographies of 2,284 women living from the sixteenth through the twentieth centuries whose influence and achievements were deemed significant in their fields. Online edition is available through Alexander St. Press.

Great American Women of the 19th Century: A Biographical Encyclopedia, ed. Francis E. Willard and Mary A. Livermore (2005). Essentially a reprint of *A Woman of the Century* (1893, rev. 1897), this single-volume work provides brief narrative biographies of women who achieved public prominence in their fields, most illustrated with a portrait of their subject. A new, analytical introduction and a classified index by occupational area are added.

African-American Biographical Database: AABD. Online resource combining the contents of the microform collection *Black Biographical Dictionaries, 1790–1950* and its index, *Black biography, 1790–1950: A Cumulative Index*. Additional content includes biographical portraits drawn from other published reference sources, obituary files, slave narrative collections, and Internet sites.

African-American National Biography: AANB, eds. Henry Louis Gates Jr. and Evelyn Brooks Higginbotham (2008). This eight-volume set contains signed entries for notable African Americans from the sixteenth century through the present. Content is regularly updated online in the *Oxford African American Studies Center*.

Who's Who Among African Americans (1976–). Focused on contemporary biographies, the 2015 edition highlights individuals active across a wide range of endeavors. The geographic and occupation indexes are especially useful. Available online through *Gale Virtual Reference Library*.

The Encyclopedia of Native American Biography, ed. Bruce E. Johansen and Donald A. Grindle Jr. (1997). Presents approximately 600 biographical summaries on historically important American Indians living in the sixteenth through the twentieth centuries.

Encyclopedia of the American Indian in the Twentieth Century, by Alexander Ewen and Jeffrey Wollock (2015). Offers many biographical essays on twentieth-century figures among its topical and historical entries, most supplemented by brief bibliographies.

Who Was Who in Native American History: Indians and Non-Indians from Early Contacts through 1900, by Carl Waldman (1988). This collection of short biographical sketches covers individuals who played significant roles in the pre-twentieth-century history of American Indian peoples in North America.

Distinguished Asian Americans. A Biographical Dictionary, ed. Hyung-Chan Kim (1999). Presents 166 biographical essays on prominent Americans of Asian ancestry, including those identified with India and Pakistan. Each entry concludes with a list of further readings. Appendixes list subjects by professional field and ethnic subgroup.

Jewish Women in America: An Historical Encyclopedia, eds. Paula E. Hyman and Deborah Dash Moore (1997). This two-volume work surveying the history and contributions of Jewish women in the United States. Includes 800 biographical entries on individuals living in the nineteenth and twentieth centuries.

Biographical Dictionary of Hispanic Americans, by Nicholas E. Meyer (2001). Features biographical essays on

250 notable figures, both historical and contemporary, primarily in politics, entertainment, sports, the military, and the arts.

Latinas in the United States: A Historical Encyclopedia, eds. Vicki L. Ruiz and Virginia Sánchez Korro (2006). Most of the 300 signed entries in this three-volume survey are biographies of Latinas from many walks of life: community organizers, ranchers, artists, and more. Sources are listed for each entry. Also available online as part of *Gale Virtual Reference Library.*

Dictionary of Canadian Biography Online/Dictionnaire biographique du Canada (DCB/DBC). Provides access to the printed fifteen-volume *Dictionary of Canadian Biography* (1966–2005) as well as a selection of biographies from unprinted volumes. Available in both English and French. Updated regularly.

People of the Founding Era: A Prosopographical Approach (2013). Compiled from digitized primary sources—largely letters and official papers—*PFE* is an online resource containing biographical information on approximately 25,000 Founding Era individuals, both notable and obscure, born between 1713 and 1815. *PFE*'s structured data facilitate collective biographical analysis for digital humanities scholarship.

FRED MURATORI
CORNELL UNIVERSITY

bird's eye view. The term refers to a landscape seen from above. In nineteenth-century America, prints with bird's eye views of towns and cities were immensely popular. Most of the prints are lithographs, a process that became commercial in America after 1820; lithography was much quicker and cheaper than etching or engraving. These prints, often in color, showed every building and landmark in the urban scene as well as some of the surrounding landscape. The idea of making such prints was not new, but what was distinctively American according to John Reps (*Views and Viewmakers of Urban America* [1984]), was their sheer volume. According to Reps, by the time the fad died in the early twentieth century, there was one bird's-eye view lithograph of as many as 4,480 places, often in more than one version.

Although prominent artists like Fitz Hugh Lane were known to produce these prints, most of the work was done by lesser-known artists who traveled from town to town soliciting enough orders to make a printing run profitable. These itinerant urban viewmakers were welcomed by town *boosters. In some cases, the "towns" depicted were in fact the fantasies of real estate promoters. However, even the most accurate were highly selective. They tended to emphasize commerce and suggest an order and dynamism that did not exist at street level. Key parts of the city, such as scenes of squalor, vice, and congestion, were ignored. Nevertheless, local historians will find these wonderful views a treasure trove of information. Not only do they depict existing structures and their relationship to one another; they often included descriptive text and detailed vignettes of individual buildings. Today, these images have been replaced by aerial views taken from aircraft and now by satellite images accessed through Bing and Google search engines. See also John W. Reps,

Bird's Eye Views: Historic Lithographs of North American Cities (1998).

NORMA PRENDERGAST
CORNELL UNIVERSITY, RETIRED

blogs. Blog, blogger, blogosphere, blogroll, blogsnob, dark blog, milblog, photoblog, plog, splog, vlog—sounds like an alien language rather than a new vocabulary that formed to articulate the world of blogging. The strange term is a composite of web log. A blog is a website in the form of an online journal. The blogger writes new entries on a regular basis and commentary often includes graphics, videos, and links to other websites and blogs. Visitors to the blog can respond by commenting on the entries, linking to them, or e-mailing the blogger.

Since they first appeared in the late 1990s, blogs have had a major impact on many facets of culture—including journalism and politics. They provide a voice for millions of people. Many history organizations maintain blogs. Blogs often focus on a specific topic and bring together a community of people who have an interest in that topic. Thus, in this regard a blog seems an obvious communication tool for organizations wanting to reach their membership.

Though there are many styles of blogs, there are some common characteristics. Blogs tend to feature an informal, conversational tone. Blog readers do not expect an academic or newspaper tone. Their readers value timely information and new information and expect new entries on a regular basis.

Why consider a blog? The *National Trust for Historic Preservation launched a blog in November 2007 as an alternative to an e-newsletter and as a timely resource for its twenty-nine historic sites located across the country. The Smithsonian Traveling Exhibition Service (SITES) started a blog in August 2007. Recognizing their unique ability to share stories and years of expertise, SITES decided that a blog targeted to museum professionals could be a valuable contribution to the museum field. Smaller organizations like the General Lew Wallace Study and Museum in Indiana started a blog in large part because of the ease of updating information and reaching members, prospective visitors, and local residents. The current blog software available is user-friendly and inexpensive, often free. As a complement to e-newsletters or standard hard-copy newsletters, a blog offers an opportunity to hear back from the people who matter most to your organization.

But who is the audience? Most organizations find it difficult to track their blog's readership. They can track what website the reader has just come from, and they can track the number of times a blog has been viewed. Many blog platforms can track how many times a post is shared on social media websites such as Facebook or Twitter. Any reader who comments on the blog also provides clues about the audience. But very few readers take the time to comment. This ability to offer readers the opportunity to comment provides the potential for increased dialogue, but only if readers contribute. Blogs work best when their topic attracts a community of readers who are passionate about the topic and want to discuss it at a deep level. When this happens, it benefits both that community and novices who want to learn more about the topic.

Blogs of cultural organizations focus on many different topics. Some offer behind-the-scenes stories and tips from their staff about exhibition installation and mounting and other related topics. Some promote an annual event, some an ongoing project such as a restoration project. Colonial Williamsburg's blog *Making History: Inspiration for the Modern Revolutionary*, http://making historynow.com, contains almost fifty blog post topics including archaeology, interpreter profiles, and historic music. The Lower East Side Tenement Museum's blog, *Notes from the Tenement*, http://www.tenement.org/blog, highlights stories of immigrants and New York City culture both past and present. The *National Archives features documents from a date in history on *Today's Document*, http://todaysdocu ment.tumblr.com. For example, on May 24, 2016, *Today's Document* featured a Lewis Hine photograph taken on May 24, 1911. The text under the photograph briefly described child labor activism in the United States and linked to a National Archives exhibit on attempts to mend the Constitution. These blogs provide additional web presence and reflect the missions of their organizations.

Like any social media, blogs are not a good idea for every organization. The first requirement of a successful blog is commitment. The organization must be prepared to provide the human resources necessary to maintain the blog and to write entries on a continual basis. A blog that does not show recent activity will lose readers very quickly.

An organization should determine its blog's purpose, content, and scope before starting. Careful strategizing will help put a blog on the path to success. It can also help determine whether a blog is a suitable investment for fulfilling an organization's mission. A blog should be active and engaging, and present quality content.

Another challenge is marketing. If you want people to read your blog, you need to advertise it wherever you can. List the address on your website and in the signature line of staff e-mails, write a press release, and advertise on Listservs and special AASLH Yahoo groups. Share individual posts on social media when they are published. One of the best ways to drive traffic to your blog is to make comments on other blogs—become part of a blog community.

Tim Grove
National Air and Space Museum,
Smithsonian Institution

See radical trust and voice of authority; social media.

boosterism. A civic booster promoting his or her city is a familiar sight. Boosters promote the virtues of their villages, small towns, and big cities to encourage progress, by which they mean economic development and growth. Boosters, in short, sell their locality. While to this day leaders continue to hail the advantages to be found in their city, the heyday of boosterism was in the nineteenth and early twentieth centuries, as community leaders competed with their rivals to attract business.

Who tended to be boosters? The most common image of the booster is

Sinclair Lewis's character Babbit, a shallow, materialistic member of the middle class. His image is only partially correct. In contrast to Lewis's fictional account, perhaps the most famous living booster was small town newspaper editor William Allen White, who parlayed his Midwest boosterism into a career. Historian Daniel Boorstin described the businessman as booster thus: "We might better characterize him as a peculiarly American type of community maker and community leader. His starting belief was in the interfusing of public and private prosperity" (Boorstin 1965, 115–16). Civic boosters were local elites—politicians, business leaders, lawyers, and other people holding positions of prestige who promoted their communities to the outside world. In the process, some scholars argue, they also created an identity for their community, an identity that could be oppressive to those who did not share it. Much of boosterism was about projecting a favorable image that would attract new businesses and workers to an area. A typical booster appeal blended a combination of civic pride, an appeal to a patriotic history, and the promise of future greatness. Boosters hailed progress through technological development and "old-fashioned" values that stressed the centrality of business in the community. Boosters placed great value on the latest in urban conveniences; at the turn of the twentieth century the streetcar and the railroad were the chief symbols of the age. The use of athletic teams as champions, and the related building of arenas and stadiums, has a long history. Boosters, whether bringing a new factory or a new stadium to town, often created controversy by using government funds to subsidize private ventures in the name of the common good.

Boosters represented a stable elite in a mobile population and a volatile economy. During the nineteenth century, boosters were concerned with building communities in a period of intense disruption. In the frontier town of Jacksonville, Illinois, according to a historian of the city, most of the "population at any given time were transient strangers" and only a small core of the residents had a long-term stake in the town's future (Doyle 1978, 3). One outgrowth of boosters' emphasis on progress was a call for tolerance in the name of stability and economic growth, sometimes leading boosters to overlook or ignore the grievances of workers. Boosters of *Middletown in the 1920s urged solidarity and quieted criticism for fear of discouraging new business, calling those who did not share in their civic vision "knockers" (Lynds 1929, 222). Boosters also utilized a variety of methods for spreading their message. They joined middle-class associations, clubs, and lodges such as Rotary, Jaycees, and Lions. Business groups such as local trade associations and chambers of commerce played a large role. Boosters used their influence in local governments to provide incentives for business growth, such as tax breaks and favorable zoning. They shaped local news coverage. Local newspapers could be as much about promotion as news. Boosters had deep roots and influence in the locality.

The message of the booster was intended to lure outsiders to the locality, but it was also supposed to change and control how residents viewed their community, especially in times of controversy or adversity. Occasionally their optimism could prove a hindrance to growth and change. In Dalton, Georgia, boosters held economic interests in local mills because of their wealth and not necessarily because of their expertise in manufacturing textiles. The lack of technical skill meant that the mills began to fall behind. At the turn of the twentieth century, community leaders felt they had to celebrate economic trends, despite a slowing economy, lack of diversification, and the movement of young people to other areas in search of employment. To improve image and life, boosters promoted cultural events—both middlebrow and highbrow—as a method of economic development.

Boosters embraced a linear view of progress. A town's evolution, as they saw it, traced a course from industry and business in its rawest form to a role of leadership in culture and society. Examples of this can be seen throughout the nineteenth and twentieth centuries as towns and cities vied for prominence. This was particularly true of the cities of the Midwest, especially Cincinnati and Chicago, where leaders often hoped to overtake New York City both economically and culturally. Museums, libraries, sports teams, and symphonies acted as proxy champions in the competition. For example, to overcome the city's reputation as the "hog butcher" of the world and to improve middle-class life, Chicago leaders brought highbrow culture to their city after the Civil War. Organizers intended the 1893 Colombian Exposition as more of an announcement that Chicago had arrived as a major city than as a celebration of Christopher Columbus's voyage. Cincinnati, also a center of butchering and industry, joined Chicago in this movement to improve the region's image. The first two decades following the Civil War saw Midwestern cities try to assume a leading place in cultural as well as industrial affairs.

Boosterism in the late twentieth and early twenty-first centuries has taken a different turn. While growing cities, especially those of the Sun Belt, still exhibit boosterism in its purest form, many of the towns and cities that had been once so heavily touted have begun to decline. Small towns, in both image and reality, have declined since World War II. For boosters of such declining centers, the old linear evolutionary model of progress has become questionable. With decline the boosters sought to make use of history to provide examples of past glory and an exploitable past that could point to future growth. Leaders of such towns have embraced *historic preservation and *tourism as the answer to the community's problems.

Boosters interested in historic tourism often emphasize the "apex" of a community's history—the point at which the town was most successful or best dealt with a crisis. Thus, historic districts and local history museums generally emphasize a particular moment, presenting a clear, positive, lesson. Boosters and tourist officials often avoid the ambiguities of change. History as interpreted by local historians and preservation groups is often static, romantic, and one-dimensional, reflecting a neighborhood or theme at a certain time. Not surprisingly, past civic leaders, boosters in their own day, are featured. The historic districts and local history museums do preserve, in a limited way, material culture and history that otherwise would have been lost. Again, image and economic opportunity play a critical role. In 1978, the U.S. Department of Housing and Urban Development and the Massachusetts Department of Community Affairs argued for the economic use of history for community development: "Perhaps the single most important problem facing the New England mill towns is the problem of image. The overwhelming decline and collapse of the textile industry in the North has tarnished the image of these cities, not only in the eyes of the people from the outside but also in the eyes of the citizens themselves" (Hamer 1998, 118–19). Thus the modern historic preservation movement relies on tourism and many of the same techniques that boosters have historically used to promote a better future.

See Richard O. Davies, *Main Street Blues: The Decline of Small-Town America* (1998); Sally Foreman Griffith, *Home Town News: William Allen White & the Emporia Gazette* (1989); David Hamer, *History in Urban Places: The Historic Districts of the United States* (1998); Jon C. Teaford, *Cities of the Heartland: The Rise and Fall of the Industrial Midwest* (1993); Douglas Flamming, *Creating the Modern South: Millhands & Managers in Dalton, Georgia, 1884–1984* (1992); Andrew R. L. Cayton and Peter S. Onuf, *The Midwest and the Nation: Rethinking the History of an American Region* (1990); Thomas Bender, *Community and Social Change in America* ([1978] 1986); Don Harrison Doyle, *The Social Order of a Frontier Community: Jacksonville, Illinois, 1825–1870* (1978); Robert H. Wiebe, *The Search for Order, 1877–1920* (1967); Daniel J. Boorstin, *The Americans: The National Experience* (1965); and Robert S. Lynd and Helen Merrell Lynd, *Middletown: A Study in Modern American Culture* ([1929] 1956); and for discussions of Warren G. Harding as a booster see Phillip Payne, *Dead Last: The Public Memory of Warren G. Harding's Scandalous Legacy* (2009).

PHILLIP PAYNE
ST. BONAVENTURE UNIVERSITY

See cultural heritage tourism; Dun & Bradstreet credit reports; historic preservation.

borders and boundaries. Anyone who practices local history will quickly run up against borders and boundaries. Examining the history of a neighborhood, a community, a city, a township, a county, a river valley, or any other local area requires decisions about what to include and what to exclude. Borders and boundaries both divide and unite; they help to define what makes people unique as well as what they have in common. Because borders and boundaries separate and connect, cross-border topics present a particularly rich and challenging opportunity for local historians.

Borders and boundaries can be viewed simply as survey lines on maps that delineate political subdivisions or mark the ownership of property. Borders and boundaries designate cities and towns, townships and counties and parishes, states and provinces and nations. In addition to circumscribing one place from another, political borders are contact points; they provide the framework that unites townships into counties, counties into states, and states and provinces into nations. Asking why a community or county is bounded in a particular manner can open up interesting and useful avenues of historical inquiry. In the United States, where private property has played a central historical role, we have systematically and elaborately divided the land into metes and bounds; sections, townships, and ranges; lots and blocks, and so on.

In addition to lines on maps, cultural boundaries have influenced how people understand themselves and others and have played an important role in the unfolding story of local history. While on the surface it may appear as though the surveyed lines that mark political subdivisions and property are distinct from cultural boundaries, closer examination reveals that that is not always that case. Cultural boundaries have established a myriad of overlapping and shifting fault lines that divide and distinguish groups of people one from another. Attitudes and values embedded within cultures have played a major role in the creation of historical memory and in the understanding of place—two variables that have powerfully influenced the construction of local identities. People are distinguished by virtue of living in a nation, state, province, county, township, city, or town. Because they reside in a particular place, they define themselves as different from those who do not; yet, what is outside of the boundary also

helps to establish the context for what is within.

Benedict Anderson's *Imagined Communities: Reflections on the Origins and Spread of Nationalism* and Seymour Martin Lipset's *Continental Divide: The Values and Institutions of the United States and Canada* both provide useful explanations of the cultural origins of modern national identities. Read with care; their observations on the cultural construction of national identity can shed light on the local history as well. *Continental Divide* does an especially good job of addressing significant, but sometimes subtle, differences that distinguish people. Historically, Canada and the United States have been divided not only by political borders but also by different historical experiences and memories—experiences and memories that have influenced how they interpreted the past and how they understood themselves and each other. Former Canadian Prime Minister Pierre Trudeau neatly and dramatically encapsulated some the key cultural differences between Canada and the United States when he described the relationship between the two nations as similar to "sleeping with an elephant." Residents of a rural town in New England or a county in the upland south or a neighborhood in New York City or a barrio in Los Angeles or a Chinese enclave in Vancouver, British Columbia, are as much members of imagined communities as they are of physical locations. One of the challenges faced by local historians is to untangle the overlapping and evolving imagined communities to which people belong based on factors such as age, race, class, gender, religion, politics, ethnicity, hobbies, and occupation. The Internet and social media have added to the challenge by creating a rich tapestry of imagined communities separated by virtual, cultural borders.

Bounding of land to validate ownership and facilitate sale offers another example of the historical blending of lines on maps with cultural distinctions. When European colonists surveyed their land and marked it with fences, their fences were cultural symbols of profoundly different attitudes toward land and the ownership of land between themselves and the Native Americans. William Cronon's *Changes in the Land* offers a good introduction to cultural attitudes toward land and private property that distinguished colonists and Native Americans in colonial New England. In 1785, the Confederation Congress passed an ordinance that established the rectangular survey system, which imposed a uniform grid comprised of sections, townships, and ranges on a diverse natural landscape. The rectangular survey reflected cultural attitudes toward the relationship between people and land, as well as deeply held beliefs on the nature of citizenship and the future of the new nation. Over time, the rectangular survey has had a major impact on the cultural geography of most of the United States. *Order Upon the Land: The U.S. Rectangular Land Survey and the Upper Mississippi Country* by Hildegard Johnson would be a good place to begin an inquiry into the local significance of the rectangular survey system. Land in urban areas is also carefully subdivided

into lots and blocks, the complexities of which Kenneth Jackson effectively and insightfully addressed in *Crabgrass Frontier: The Suburbanization of the United States.*

In the end, the plethora of border- and boundary-related topics that present themselves for examination are circumscribed only by the breadth of human experiences. The range of potential topics might include politics, religion, commerce and industry, popular culture, crime, migration, tourism and cultural heritage, sports, goods and services, financial activities, transportation, communication and technical systems, the environment, energy, literature, ideas, race, class, gender, and ethnicity. John Stilgoe's *Outside Lies Magic: Regaining History and Awareness in Everyday Places* offers a good starting point for reimagining nearby history and inspiring curiosity and imagination among local historians.

PHILIP SCARPINO
INDIANA UNIVERSITY-PURDUE
UNIVERSITY, INDIANAPOLIS

See Canada, local history in.

Bosnian Muslims in North America, sources for. See Appendix A.

British Association for Local History (BALH). This is Great Britain's national organization for local history. Its stated mission is "to encourage and assist the study of local history throughout Great Britain as an academic discipline and as a rewarding leisure pursuit for both individuals and groups." This dual aim reflects the strong traditions in Britain of interests and activities shared between academic and grassroots practitioners of local history. BALH was established in its present form in 1982. It operates as a voluntary, charitable body and succeeded the Standing Conference for Local History, a post-1945 offshoot of the National Council of Social Service (NCSS), which promoted local history national meetings, and published a journal The *Amateur Historian (since 1968 The Local Historian) and an influential pamphlet series. This national structure was paralleled locally in many counties by umbrella organizations set up to foster and bring together local historical activity. By the late 1970s British local history was burgeoning. At the grassroots level individual and group interest in locality and family was growing. More formally the subject's importance was being recognized by libraries and museums and providers of adult and higher education from university departments to local authorities. The NCSS, the then parent body, was looking to an independent existence for its growing offspring, and commissioned a review (the Blake report) that recommended the connecting and strengthening of local history through independent organizations bringing together groups and individuals locally, and at county and national levels. BALH was one result of this, as were various new county organizations.

Today BALH publishes a quarterly journal, The Local Historian, with articles (often by local participants), reviews, and debates. A quarterly magazine, Local History News, gives a roundup of developments in local and county societies, archives, museums, libraries, and education, mirroring the state of the subject overall. The BALH also publishes separate titles; a directory of local history websites (with advice on assessing sites for accuracy, authority, objectivity, currency, and coverage) has been a best seller since 2010. There is a BALH website (www.balh.co.uk); an annual Local History Day blending discussion of current topics, awards (nominated by members and recognizing personal contributions, research, and publishing by members, and the best local society newsletter), and an annual lecture by an academic local historian. Elsewhere, BALH organizes visits to specialist sites and archives, brings together local history tutors, collaborates in conferences, and is represented on other bodies including the Historical Association, Royal Historical Society, and the National Archives. Many local history societies are corporate members of BALH, so that its wider membership encompasses a high percentage of local historians, and its work is widely disseminated.

KATE TILLER
UNIVERSITY OF OXFORD, UK

British Columbia, local history in. The singular trait of British Columbia's history is how recently the region was incorporated into the Eurocentric world. Given this fact, it is not surprising that efforts to write and commemorate that history have lagged behind other parts of North America.

The first history of the region appeared in 1887 as one volume in San Francisco publisher Hubert Howe Bancroft's magisterial history of the Pacific slope. British Columbia from the Earliest Times to the Present (1914), coauthored by E. O. S. Scholefield and Frederick Howay, was the first locally produced history of any value. Margaret Ormsby became the first academic historian to pen a provincial history with her *British Columbia: A History* (1958). Numerous provincial histories have appeared more recently, including Jean Barman's *The West Beyond the West* (1991, 2007) and Hugh Johnston, ed., *The Pacific Province* (1996).

Efforts to create historical organizations likewise followed a halting path. A number of nineteenth-century pioneer societies took shape, then vanished, leaving little by way of a legacy. More successful were twin groups—the Native Sons of British Columbia and the Native Daughters of British Columbia—which took root in Victoria, Nanaimo, and Vancouver after the turn of the twentieth century. The Sons and Daughters pushed for the restoration and preservation of a number of historic sites that stand to this day, including the Nanaimo Bastion, the Craigflower House and School, Fort Langley, and the Old Hastings Mill Store.

Meanwhile, in 1922, the British Columbia Historical Association (BCHA) was founded by historically minded individuals organized around Victoria's Natural History Society (1890) and the Art, Historical and Scientific Association of Vancouver (1894). Four years later, a puerile disagreement over the date of BC's founding fractured the BCHA along regional lines. It limped along until 1936, when it was reorganized to permit the affiliation of local societies, breathing new life into it. Regional historical societies stepped into this vacuum, the most notable being the Okanagan Historical Society (OHS). Since its founding in 1925, the OHS has published its annual *Okanagan History*, the longest-running historical journal in the province. In 1983, the BCHA was renamed the BC Historical Federation (BCHF) to better reflect its role as an umbrella organization. Today, the BCHF boasts scores of member societies and affiliate organizations throughout the province.

BC was more fortunate with the early establishment of a provincial archives, in 1908. The untiring, if ill-disciplined, efforts of E. O. S. Scholefield, the institution's second archivist, laid the foundations for a rich collection. The provincial archives languished through the Depression, but then was revitalized and modernized by W. K. Lamb, who went on to become Canada's national archivist. Through systematic collection efforts, the provincial archives amassed the largest collection of historical material in BC. At the same time, municipal archives, museums, and historic sites emerged and multiplied. Currently, the Archives Association of BC (AABC) lists sixty-three full institutional members, along with numerous associate members (most of whom also hold membership in the BCHF).

Historical journals have had a more checkered existence. The BCHA published four issues of *Report and Proceedings* through the 1920s, but the first bona fide historical journal emerged after the association's reorganization in 1936. The *British Columbia Historical Quarterly* ran from 1937 to 1958, though the last issue was actually released in 1961. Eight years later, *BC Studies* was launched as a more rigorous, scholarly journal dedicated to the province's past and present. The *BCHF News* began publication in 1969, and received a name change to *BC History* in 2005. The emergence of local publishers such as Harbour Publishing, Heritage House, and Sono Nis gave a boost to non-academic local historical writing.

Academic history came late to the province, with the establishment of the University of British Columbia in 1915. Through the 1920s and 1930s, the UBC history department encouraged a focus on provincial history, at both undergraduate and graduate levels. Lamb and Ormsby were both graduates of these programs. This early focus lapsed into relative inactivity until it was revived in the 1970s. Over the past decade, of the province's twenty-two academic postsecondary institutions, more than half teach provincial history at the undergraduate level, while graduate studies in it can be pursued at four universities. UBC and the University of Northern British Columbia offer dedicated courses in research methods for local history, while others permit research through provincial history classes.

Historians in BC have taken good advantage of the past decade's electronic revolution. The provincial archives broke ground with its own website, uploading thousands of historical photographs and providing direct access to many records (bcarchives.bc.ca). The province's nearly 200 local sites can be searched through Memory BC, an initiative of the AABC (memorybc.ca). Two valuable websites are the brainchild of archivist David Mattison: the BC History Internet/website (1995–2004—victoria.tc.ca/Resources/bchistory-titlepage) and the BC History Por-

tal (2005–2010—bchistoryportal.tc.ca). The sites no longer are being updated and some links are no longer active, but the pages still connect the researcher to a wealth of other sites and material.

Over the past two decades, BC historiography has undergone a veritable renaissance, particularly in the fields of postcolonial studies, First Nations history, and *environmental history. Adele Perry's *On the Edge of Empire: Gender, Race, and the Making of British Columbia, 1849–71* (2001), Cole Harris's *Making Native Space: Colonialism, Resistance, and Reserves in British Columbia* (2002), and Robert Boyd's *The Coming of the Spirit of Pestilence: Introduced Infectious Diseases and Population Declines among Northwest Coast Indians, 1774–1874* (1999) address the complex forces of colonization. Other notable titles on First Nations are John Lutz, *Makúk: a New History of Aboriginal White Relations* (2008), Keith Carlson, ed., *A Stó:l Coast Salish Historical Atlas*, and K. Carlson, *The Power of Place, the Problem of Time* (2010). Contributions in environmental history include Jeff Oliver, *Landscapes and Social Transformations on the Northwest Coast* (2010), and John Thistle, *Resettling the Range: Animals, Ecologies, and Human Communities in British Columbia* (2015).

The most insightful of this work has demonstrated the importance of place and the local in examining the sweep of global historical forces.

CHAD REIMER
INDEPENDENT SCHOLAR

See Canada, local history in.

broadsides. Broadsides are large sheets of paper printed on one side only, usually for purposes of advertising. Early broadsides were small and were sometimes referred to as handbills; today they are generally called posters.

building bridges through local history. How do local history organizations build bridges in their communities? How can they contribute so that they are seen as not just a nicety but a necessity? How can they move from just surviving to thriving? Across the nation, local history organizations are striving to answer such questions. There are no easy answers, no one template to take off the shelf.

One effective way is for local history organizations to become less insular and to partner with one another and with professional associations and their own communities to answer such questions. Many organizations are recognizing the history they research and present is not "my" history but "our" history. To be sure, there are differences among us in race, gender, social class, economic status, ethnicity, religion, age, or other factors, so our history is indeed different, but living in the same historic place or town, state or nation, we still have a shared history—a history that can bind us together and help us understand one another more fully. Local history can help us empathize with those different from us and also appreciate how we are all similar. By becoming intentionally engaged in this more inclusive history, organizations are being led to become more engaged in public outreach and in the active preservation of a more diverse history, instead of being just a passive recipient of it. They are finding themselves changing their public pro-

grams, school programs, exhibits, and community communications—on site, off site, and online. They are also seeing that the public, key decision makers, and funders are responding with enhanced support.

The second effective way for local history organizations to build bridges and to thrive is to research, interpret, and promote a more holistic history. This means that they research and interpret the positive aspects of the past, to be sure, but combine them with the negative and the tragic. Rather than intentionally "disremembering" negative things about the past and lapsing into a nostalgia that is blind to prejudice, violence, or exploitation, they shed light on them. They help us understand how things happened and why and what their effects were. They help see good people doing bad things, or good people caught up in a bad system, or remaining quiet and doing nothing. They show good people standing up and speaking out, and not always rewarded. By combining these elements they create tension. They unsettle. They tell a richer, more robust story that injects contradictions, nuance, and complexity into our heritage. Like a good playwright, they create experiences that enhance our lives. By such efforts, these local history organizations are helping individuals and communities to feel that their heritage too has relevance and meaning.

In looking back over his years of writing, novelist William Faulkner, who certainly knew tragedy, said that he wrote (and I'm paraphrasing) in order to "uplift our hearts." That's a simple phrase, but spot on. He's not referring to just my heart or your heart, but to our hearts. We "uplift our hearts" by trying to tell the truth, warts and all, about our past. If we just look at one side of history—only at the good or the bad, or only at the elite or the oppressed—we don't uplift our hearts. We are in this life together, and the people of the past were no different. To deny either the evil aspects of history or its good aspects is to defraud our past.

Though we may hear voices to the contrary, I think the public wants history organizations to present this more complete story of the past. Like a good novelist, we need to find ways to tell it. And like a good marketer, find ways to promote it. We should not assume that we know what constitutes "good history" and force it down the public's throat like a health drink. Instead, we need to ask: How can we find ways for people to hear what we say so that bridges may be built and minds opened?

A well-told story is often the way to do this. And for the story to be heard, the person must be prompted to care—to care about the people in the story and to feel connected to them. Now that story may be told by way of text, artifacts, photographs, documents, video, or computer animations, and even places and landscapes may tell a story; and if it is well told, the public will respond and want to see that that history is preserved and told. By such endeavors, we can change the perception that history is seen as something that happened to somebody else somewhere else, to something that happened to me. And we can build an understanding of how that connects us to others, even to those "different" from us. We are not islands. We can help history be seen as some-

thing not peripheral or extraneous, but rather central to the understanding of who we are as individuals, as a community, as a nation, or as human beings.

Why is that important? Because as Martin Luther King Jr. is said to have declared, "He who controls my mind controls my body. He who controls my history controls my mind." With this in mind, how can history museums reach out and build bridges that both connect past, present, and future and connect people of different backgrounds and experiences? To answer that question, history organizations must strategically plan for and recruit leadership among their board, staff, and donors who share this larger vision. This requires leadership that is fearless and that seeks a creative tension between change and continuity in order to promote growth. Too often, historical organizations get so caught in operations that they neglect the care and feeding of good leadership, and do not do the careful planning, so the building of bridges suffers.

For historical organizations to nurture leadership, they need to strive to be seen as places that matter, places where people will feel safe and respected—challenged to be sure, but respected. They become places where the history of people of diverse backgrounds is preserved and featured in engaging exhibits and programs, on site and online. They are places where different components of the public—different ethnicities, religious backgrounds, sexual orientation, immigrant status (whether native born or recent arrival)—may feel that their history is respected, not shut down. Safe places where community leaders, scholars, educators, preservationists, activists, and citizens of differing points of views can come together, discuss issues, get to know one another, break stereotypes, and devise positive solutions. If used proactively, local history may be used both to better understand the past and to chart a course for the future that moves beyond polarization. Such a move is desperately needed in the nation today. If done strategically, this process can attract support of different kinds, including funding.

In Dolores Hayden's excellent book, *Power of Place: Urban Landscapes as Public History,* she tells the story of place-based work in Los Angeles that nurtures leadership and community engagement by lifting up the stories of common people who contributed to the history of the city through their community work. A specific example is the project to recognize publicly the life and service of Biddy Mason, an African American midwife who birthed hundreds of children of different ethnicities and all social classes in nineteenth-century Los Angeles. As an enslaved woman from Mississippi, she trekked with her owner in 1851 in a wagon train to Los Angeles, where she won her freedom in court and made her mark as a highly respected midwife, nurse, mother, landowner, and community and church leader. Among her sayings told from one generation to another was: "If you hold your hand closed, nothing good can come in. The open hand is blessed, for it gives in abundance, even as it receives." In the larger history of Los Angeles, she had been more or less forgotten, and her homestead had become a parking lot.

To remedy this, Hayden, then an urban historian and architect at the University of California–Los Angeles (UCLA), worked with the city government and with Mason's descendants and her church, and brought together scholars from UCLA, community historians, the California Afro-American History Museum, artists, and others. They designed and produced a remarkable set of museum exhibits, educational materials, and public memorials to Mason, including a pocket park named after her and a display along an eighty-one-foot wall that interweaves her life within the timeline of Los Angeles and features photographs, maps, and documents that personalize her history and engage the viewer. Such efforts have in turn inspired similar endeavors in the city.

The point is that there are thousands of Biddy Masons across the nation, whose lives deserve to be remembered and lifted up. When members of under-recognized communities can recognize themselves in public memorials and in their local history institution, a place most Americans view as a voice of authority (see Roy Rosensweig and David Thelen, *Presence of the Past* [1998]), this enhances a sense of belonging. Further, the recognition of such significant figures and events can offer opportunities to enrich local history by adding contradictions, complexity and multidimensional realities to it.

By seeing history as a way to build bridges, we will open up our museums and invite people to contribute their stories about historical places, events, and activities, which could be used for what is now being called "public curation." Museum professionals and historians Bill Adair, Benjamin Filene, and Laura Koloski have teamed up and ably presented this process in their book of essays and interviews, entitled *Letting Go: Sharing Historical Authority in a User-Generated World*. In this "public curation" process, as Filene explains, professional curators or historians are not pushed aside, but rather develop partnerships with the public. Such partnerships call for new skills from historians and a willingness to share authority yet still maintain their professional standards. The result can be a more informed selection of what warrants preservation and why, as well as a richer, more nuanced historical narrative— one that better resonates with diverse audiences, for they can see and hear themselves more clearly. This narrative has the curatorial voice, to be sure, but also that of the people themselves, thereby enhancing the public reckoning of the history being preserved and interpreted.

Historic sites too can become places for "public curation," or "public dialogue," places where people whose ancestors were once entrapped by prejudice and locked in conflict and/ or accommodation with one another can come together and discuss how their shared, albeit different, histories have shaped their lives and how they hope to build on the past to create a brighter future. Such sites may be historical plantations, frontier settlements contested by Native Americans, battlefields, industrial workplaces, or even households where both the homeowners and domestic servants lived. Almost all of these sites have descendants, and

surveys have shown that visitors want to learn about not just the people of the past, but of today, and the descendants' different points of view make for a more personal, complex, and nuanced story. For example, Drayton Hall in South Carolina has videotaped *oral histories with a range of descendants of its former enslaved and slave-owner residents and featured them in tours, conferences, schools, colleges, and public television, in order to add deeply personal dimensions to site interpretation. Partnering with others, it has produced public programs at the local, state, and national levels with personal participation of these descendants, white and black. Middleton Place, Montpelier, Somerset Place, Sotterley, and many other sites have organized family reunions for descendants, white and black together. At Cliveden in Philadelphia, descendants even contributed to the writing of a play dealing with slavery and freedom. Fostering such relationships can also enhance support for the organization not only through the building of goodwill, but also through funding and donation of artifacts, documents, or photographs for collections.

For all of these programs with descendants, the immediate goal has been the development of dialogue, not the finalization of reconciliation or forgiveness since that is a long and deeply personal process. Instead, the organizations have created safe places so that can happen, understanding that everyone is at different places in their journey. One benefit is that descendants themselves learn from one another, both cognitively and experientially. What is required is respect for one another and differing points of view. The main thing is the descendants' participation, so the public can hear from them. The organization should also respect the silences, the things a person wishes not to discuss. Also, it is critical that descendants know that the historical organization will genuinely support their participation and it will not lead to an embarrassing "gotcha" moment. In such ways, site interpretation may be opened up and dialogue encouraged so that not just museum professionals or historians are telling the stories, but also the real people whose ancestors' history is fraught with the good and the bad of our past and whose presence connects us to that history in ways that words alone cannot.

Another question important to the practice of local history is how to enhance the relationship between a historical organization and the local communities that have been the source for the history in its archives, exhibits, or programs. Too often the practice has been for the organization to do research in a community, identify and remove historical resources (documents, artifacts, photographs, oral histories, or even buildings) from that community, preserve them in their collections or archives, use them in an exhibit or book, and return little to nothing to that community. The community members hardly benefit, and the appreciation for that community's history is not lifted up for all the more people to respect. So a key question for historical organizations, when they are seeking local historical resources, is how will that partnership work? How might the community benefit by having its historical

resources used so that heritage tourism, *historic preservation, or school curricula and teacher training may be enhanced? One answer is for the historical organization to interweave into its exhibits, archives, or programs suggestions that encourage its audience to interact with the community at large and to include planning and implementation of such in the initial project and funding proposals.

Mark Twain once declared, "Travel is the enemy of prejudice," and I envision historical organizations producing exhibits and programs and then enabling their public to visit—online, in person, or by virtual reality—those communities, to meet their people, visit their historical places and neighborhoods, go to their churches or restaurants or community centers, and to learn not just cognitively but experientially. In so doing, the organization will deepen its public's connection with the papers read in the archives or with the history featured in the exhibit or program, and thereby help realize Mark Twain's dictum. The historical organization will also help that community to become less isolated and more connected to the larger story of our nation and to receive funding from tourism, perhaps for education and community improvements. Partnerships of this kind can lift one another's boats, a concept that can make funding proposals more attractive.

An ongoing question for local historical organizations is and will continue to be how to find innovative and effective ways to become a part of the lives of young people, so that they too feel connected to the continuum of history. One response, as Stephanie Meeks, president of the *National Trust for Historic Preservation, has explained, is to find ways to reach out to the young and connect to "where they are." They are, as she said, "digital natives." Before asking questions to adults or learning from books, they first turn to the Internet or social media. So we need to (and I think we will) find ways to translate both what we are doing and why into ways that reach them digitally. Virtual reality, videogames, animated films, holograms, augmented reality, avatars, or 3-D printing are all ways by which an organization today may engage the young. One may rest assured that in the future, such will be expanded upon in ways that we today can hardly imagine. In light of funders' increasing appreciation of both technology and the need to reach young audiences, funders will be looking for such ways of engagement.

As we strive to enhance the public reckoning of history, we must always be appreciative of one thing: surprise. All of us—of whatever age, color, gender, or ethnicity—need to be open to surprise. We need to be prepared for surprise, and not be afraid. For if history teaches us anything, it is that the future will bring us surprise.

Whether we be staff, volunteers, or board members, what is the one ingredient needed for success in local history? Courage. Because if we are to mainstream an appreciation for history into the American ethos, we need to build bridges. For that to occur, we need courage and not cynicism, whose call is all too easy to heed. Cynicism can convince us that by not trying, we are being "realistic." As good bridge-

builders know, a bridge, to be effective, cannot serve just one side of a divide. It cannot serve just one segment of the public. Our communities have diverse "publics" to connect, and often those "publics" may not agree or even like one another. And the support of a key staff or board member or donor may not be there to start off with. Also, the other side of a bridge may be just that, the "other side," and it may be seen only dimly or misperceived, and may generate fear of conflict or rejection. Thus the need for us, as individuals and as organizations, to have courage and to put cynicism aside.

To be effective bridge-builders, we need to work together and ameliorate our "disremembering." We need to push one another beyond our comfort zones, whatever our station in the profession or in the public, and create expanding circles that engage people in the research, preservation, and interpretation of history, including its tragic moments, in order to, as William Faulkner said, "uplift our hearts." If we can find ways to do that, we will have secured a strong foundation for local history for the future.

This essay is drawn partly from a paper presented at the symposium, "The Future of the African American Past," sponsored by the National Museum of African American History and Culture and the American Historical Association.

GEORGE W. McDANIEL
McDANIEL CONSULTING, LLC

See censorship; digital history; diversity and inclusion in museums; house museums; house museums in the twenty-first century; LGBT history, interpreting; local historical societies and core purpose; museum theaters; museums, public value of; radical trust and voice of authority; relevance; slavery interpretation at museums and historic sites; values of history.

Buildings of the United States (BUS).
The *Buildings of the United States* published by the Society of Architectural Historians (SAH at www.sah.org) is a growing series of sixty volumes which, when completed, will provide a comprehensive, scholarly overview of and guide to the architectural heritage of the United States. These volumes roughly correspond to the states although in some cases they are further divided by region or by city. For instance, the cities of Boston, Pittsburgh, and Savannah merit their own volume distinct from the rest of their respective states, and Pennsylvania is divided into two volumes with the first covering eastern Pennsylvania and Philadelphia and the second western Pennsylvania and Pittsburgh. Twenty-one have been published.

The BUS series provides a more comprehensive, focused, scholarly, and up-to-date guide to the architectural heritage of the United States from presettlement days to the present than is found in the American Guide Series, which was produced by the Federal Writers Project of the Works Progress Administration between 1935 and 1943. Each volume is written by a team of leading local and national scholars and is generously illustrated with photographs and maps. Every volume covers a complete range of structures that shape the built environment of the state or city

including government buildings, grand residences, agricultural structures, commercial buildings, factories, and parks. Attention is paid to both the high-style and *vernacular architecture that is important, representative of a specific style or type of building, or is of historical or architectural interest. These comprehensive guides are valuable reference resources both for the professional (the architectural historian, the preservationist, etc.) and for the general or traveling public. They are useful in elementary and secondary school classrooms, to community planners and historians, and to the tourist industry.

The information contained in these volumes is becoming even more valuable and accessible with the development of SAH Archipedia, an innovative comprehensive, authoritative, and media-rich online database of American architecture jointly developed by SAH and the University of Virginia Press with support from the National Endowment for the Humanities. This project brings together the entire publication program of the Society of Architectural Historians including SAHARA, the digital image archive developed in collaboration with Artstor, into a unified digital resource. Records are based on entries from the published volumes of the Buildings of the United States series and include building histories, photographs, *maps, and essays. SAH Archipedia, which currently contains records for 13,000 buildings, is available to SAH members and institutional subscribers. The open access counterpart, SAH Archipedia Classic Buildings, which will include records for one hundred most representative buildings in each state, is available to the public at http://sah archipedia.org.

MARGARET N. WEBSTER
INDEPENDENT CONSULTANT

See architectural history.

built environment. The term "built environment" refers to the shape, pattern, function, and appearance of our present surroundings that result from human intervention. The term is often used in opposition to the term *natural environment.* However, the built environment includes designed *landscapes and plantings. The term came into common usage in the 1950s among city and regional planners and was adopted by the *historic preservation community to indicate the broadest possible interpretation of the term *cultural resources.*

W. BROWN MORTON III
INTERNATIONAL ARCHITECTURAL
CONSERVATOR

Bulgarians in North America, sources for. See Appendix A.

Bureau of Land Management. See archaeology; maps and atlases.

Bureau of Reclamation. Congress established the Bureau of Reclamation within the Department of the Interior in 1902 with the strong support of President Theodore Roosevelt. The Bureau of Reclamation's charge was development of water resources in the arid West. Reclamation developed over 180 water projects for irrigation, hydroelectric generation, and municipal and industrial uses. Other significant benefits of Reclamation projects include recreation and flood control.

Reclamation's records include correspondence, manuscript and printed reports, drawings and maps, films, videos, and photographs. Reclamation's original objective was to create new irrigated farms for families in the arid West. Because of that objective, Reclamation was especially interested in the communities and living conditions on and around its projects. Reclamation's early records, especially the photographs, document their efforts. In addition, there are early Reclamation photographs of Western *national parks and projects in the South where swamp and overflow lands were reclaimed.

Reclamation's records and photographs are found in several locations. Older, historic records of Reclamation have been transferred to the *National Archives and Records Administration. The older photographs are in the still-picture collection of the National Archives and Records Administration in College Park, Maryland. Many of those older images are duplicated in the National Archives holdings in Denver, which is the location of the vast majority of Reclamation's written, printed, and image collections that have been transferred permanently to the National Archives and Records Administration. More current records are retained in Reclamation's offices: Washington, D.C.; Denver; regional offices in Salt Lake City; Sacramento; Billings; Boise; and Boulder City, Nevada; and in over twenty area offices in the West.

Burned-Over District. The Burned-Over District is a portion of central

New York that experienced repeated incursions of religious enthusiasms. The region was so identified and written about by Whitney Cross in his book *The Burned-Over District: The Social and Intellectual History of Enthusiastic Religion in Western New York, 1800– 1880* ([1950]1965).

business and industrial history as a local history subject. Business and industry offer great opportunities for historians of any locality. The history of any town or city, no matter how small, is intimately connected to the rise and fall of local businesses. "In American society," Mansel Blackford, Austin Kerr, and Amos Loveday have observed, "with the possible exception of a few utopian communities, towns and cities have been established, have existed and prospered, and have died for economic or business reasons." Blackford, Kerr, and Loveday, along with the *American Association for State and Local History, have provided a valuable resource book for local historians seeking to develop business histories: *Local Businesses: Exploring Their History* (1990).

Some businesses and industries of national (or international) significance are closely linked to a particular locality. The U.S. automobile industry is synonymous with Detroit, Michigan (the "Motor City"), and this industry has played a crucial role in shaping the history of Detroit. Pittsburgh, Pennsylvania, is likewise linked to the steel industry; the rise and decline of steel manufacture in the United States is in many ways the story of Pittsburgh.

California's Silicon Valley and Massachusetts's Route 128 area have re-ceived much scholarly attention recently. These two distinctive localities have produced important innovations in computer technology since World War II in very different ways. Networks of small firms and producers in California created a flexible system for producing technological innovation, while a more rigidly structured system of large integrated firms in Massachusetts had greater difficulty in adapting to changing economic conditions. Textile manufacture in New England and the Philadelphia area also evolved in distinctive ways. While New England firms were large, integrated, and well capitalized from the earliest days, Philadelphia's textile industry grew from a great variety of small, flexible firms (as chronicled by Philip Scranton). The details of each local story, therefore, were important factors in explaining the relative successes of each region. The stories of these industries are crucial to understanding much of the national history of the United States. Smaller, lesser-known industries are also often linked to particular localities. Dalton, Georgia, residents accurately refer to their town as "the carpet capital of the world." The area around High Point, North Carolina, has long been a major center of U.S. furniture production.

Economists and economic geographers call such clusters "regional agglomerations," and the study of these areas has become a major area of research within business history. Indeed, Nobel economics laureate Paul Krugman has argued that "the most striking feature of the geography of economic activity . . . is surely concentration" (*Geography and Trade*, 1993). A number of business historians have argued that many such industries are not simply located in a particular place, but grow out of a complex web of relationships closely connected to the rhythms of particular communities. Thus local history takes on added significance; the study of industrial agglomerations links local business history in important ways to broader fields of study. Former House Speaker Tip O'Neill famously remarked that "all politics is local." In the field of business and industrial history, it now seems that much, if not quite all, history is local. See Philip Scranton, *Proprietary Capitalism: The Textile Manufacture at Philadelphia 1808–1885* (1987) and *Endless Novelty: Specialty Productions and American Industrialization, 1865–1925* (1997).

Connecting local business history to larger trends in economic history forms one entry point into the subject. Tracking the history of local businesses is also a way to trace the evolution of a community over time. *City directories, manuscript *census records (now usefully available online in many cases), local newspapers, advertising, *oral histories with workers and business leaders, and other similar sources can help the local historian develop a history of community life, demographic changes, and the socio-economic structure of a town. Business history is an integral part of community history. For an example of such integration of business/industrial history into a larger community study, see Thomas A. Scott, *Cobb County, Georgia, and the Origins of a Suburban South: A Twentieth Century History* (2003).

Entire towns have been created by businesses in the United States. A wide variety of company towns and mill villages can be found, from textile villages in the southeast (see, for example, Douglas Flamming, *Creating the Modern South: Millhands and Managers in Dalton, Georgia, 1884–1984*, 2000) to mining and lumbering towns in Michigan (Christian Holmes, *Company Towns of Michigan's Upper Peninsula*, 2015) to the cattle towns of the southwest and Midwest (Robert Dykstra, *Cattle Towns*, 2013, revised from 1968 edition).

Business and industrial history is a rich field for investigation by local historians. No matter the local community, business has played an integral role in its development. Local history can illuminate important aspects of business history. Just as significantly, businesses leave behind records—legal documents, marketing materials and advertising, press coverage, and sometimes much more—that can serve as the skeletal structure of a local history study, complementing church records, census materials, and other documentary evidence.

RANDALL PATTON
KENNESAW STATE UNIVERSITY

C

California, local history in. Statewide responsibility for history in California is divided among several public and private agencies and organizations. One of the first acts of the first state legislature, meeting in San Jose in 1849–1850, created the California State Library, and its history division now holds one of the state's largest collections of historical print and manuscript materials. That same session ("the legislature of a thousand drinks") established what later would become the State Archives, which now also is responsible for assisting counties and municipalities in maintaining their public records.

In 1969, the legislature assigned the preexisting (1949) Historical Landmarks Advisory Committee responsibility for administering the provisions of the 1966 National Historic Preservation Act in California. That program now is integrated within the Department of Parks and Recreation as the Office of Historic Preservation. At the same time, with the exception of the *National Park Service, California State Parks operate more historic sites and museums than any organization or agency in America. Each of these sites, in turn, is a key resource within its individual community. State Parks also manage the largest single collection of historical artifacts in California. The Golden State Museum was established within the State Archives in 1989 and has evolved into the semiautonomous

California Museum. The Oakland Museum of California also holds and exhibits a remarkable collection of art, history, and natural history that represents and serves the entire state.

While the state agencies are centered in Sacramento, the private California Historical Society (CHS) is headquartered in San Francisco. Following at least six unsuccessful attempts to establish a state historical organization, beginning in 1852, the most recent incarnation of the California Historical Society dates to 1922. One of the founders, C. Templeton Crocker, grandson of one of "The Big Four" founders of the Central Pacific Railroad, underwrote the organization's budget for years. Crocker's immense personal collection of California books, maps, images, and manuscripts eventually became the foundation of the organization's research collections. The new organization immediately began publishing the *California Historical Society Quarterly*, which continues as *California History*.

The 1922 CHS founders envisioned a group of amateur gentleman scholars dedicated to studying, sharing, and enhancing California historical scholarship—among themselves. It was not until J. S. (Jim) Holliday's two terms as executive director, between 1971 and 1985, that CHS begrudgingly expanded its vision to include public education and invited anyone, anywhere in the state, to share in the California narra-

This plaque decorates the front lawn of the Gamble House, a California Registered Historic Landmark in Pasadena. The 1908 home is recognized as an outstanding example of Arts and Crafts style architecture. CREDIT: MAX A. VAN BALGOOY.

tive and participate in the organization. The traveling exhibit, *Executive Order 9066 (1972)*, was the first exhibit in the country on the internment of 110,000 Japanese Americans during World War II and provided a model for bringing contemporary historical subjects before broad publics that continues to guide the Historical Society. The 2006 Strategic Plan committed CHS to (a) expanding statewide service through a network of local historical societies, (b) increasing public accessibility to its collections, and (c) improving classroom history education throughout the state.

The Huntington Library and Gardens in San Marino and the Bancroft Library at the University of California–Berkeley provide remarkable resources in state and local history. The Bancroft

Library officially dates from 1905, when the University of California acquired Hubert Howe Bancroft's incomparable personal library of books, manuscripts, and oral history transcripts. The Bancroft Library has expanded its scope over the years to become one of the world's major research libraries, but it continues to collect actively and share California's past, including the contemporary Regional Oral History Office.

Founded by railroad magnate Henry E. Huntington in 1919, the Huntington Library from the beginning was intended to be one of the world's great research libraries and art collections, while still representing fully its California origins. Thus, an important research collection on California and the American West shares space with priceless icons of Western civilization. In addition, the Huntington-USC Institute on California and the West, the Autry Institute in Los Angeles, and the Bill Lane Center for the American West at Stanford University support applied scholarship on California history.

Similar to California's microclimates of geology and weather, the state's cultural, historical, demographic, and geopolitical microclimates have nurtured over 600 diverse local and subject-specific historical organizations. Every county has multiple organizations serving specific geographic areas, subjects, or populations. There are literally hundreds of culture-specific institutions, and Silicon Valley has produced a paean to its own history in Mountain View's Computer History Museum. Some of these local institutions are quite large, but most are very small and often volunteer. However, each is treasured equally by the communities it serves.

In addition to the California Historical Society, both the San Diego History Center and the Historical Society of Southern California publish respected scholarly journals, and many other local organizations publish quarterlies and occasional pieces. Heyday Press publishes *News of Native California*, the only state quarterly journal in the country about and by American Indians. In 2011, the University of California Press began publishing *Boom: A Journal of California*, which covers both contemporary and historical subjects.

Although technically not accurate, it is not an overstatement to say that California's printed history begins with the monumental accomplishments of Hubert Howe Bancroft. His methods may not meet today's standards, but his thirty-nine volumes of history of the North American West, from Alaska through Central America, published between 1874 and 1890, is an incomparable accomplishment, and the original sources and interviews that he gathered in the process remain priceless resources for scholars today. Since then, thousands of authors have continued to mine California's past. One contemporary author especially stands out. Kevin Starr's continuing multivolume syntheses, *Americans and the California Dream*, is encyclopedic in scope and brilliant in interpretive nuance. At the same time, the ninth edition of *California: An Interpretive History*, by James J. Rawls and Walton Bean, remains an exceptional interpretive state history text, if for no other reason than its courageous honesty.

Unfortunately, all of this historical activity and scholarship is not represented in the state's K–12 classrooms. Although California history technically is required in fourth grade, there are no standards of adequacy or accountability. History is not one of the core competencies of standardized testing at any level. Further, in an unfortunate but symptomatic moment of governmental dysfunction, the 2009 state legislature suspended implementation of the revised "Social Studies Framework for California Schools" until the 2013–2014 school year. This is especially unfortunate, because those guidelines proclaim that "preparing students for responsible citizenship . . . with a firm grounding in history . . . [students] should have the capacity to make wise choices in their own lives and to understand the swift-moving changes in state, national, and world affairs."

Several organizations are trying desperately, yet so far unsuccessfully, to re-insert history as a core competency. While the California Studies Association takes the battle to the bastions of teacher training, the California History and Social Studies Project, working out of the University of California, is trying to impact classroom teaching directly. The National Center for History Education in the Schools is located at UCLA. But no single group or organization is coordinating strategy or bringing these disparate groups together. Because they localize and personalize what otherwise may appear as abstract historical forces beyond our control, California's state and local history organizations are challenged to become more engaged with the classroom history education process.

DAVID CROSSON
BRYAN AND JORDON CONSULTING, LLC

See Bancroft Library; United States, local history in.

Cambridge Group for the History of Population and Social Structure. The Cambridge Group is an interdisciplinary core of researchers using social scientific approaches to study the past. University of Cambridge scholars E. A. Wrigley and the late Peter Laslett founded the group in 1964. Within a relatively short period Roger Schofield, Richard M. Smith, Jim Oeppen, the late Ros Davies, and the late Richard Wall joined Wrigley and Laslett. These members remained as a core in situ with no permanent defections for four decades, until age began to reduce their numbers. From the start the group has welcomed visiting scholars—both local and foreign—for a seminar, a day, a week, a year. Its continuing influence on colleagues around the world has been as great as any research group of its kind and perhaps longer lasting. Outside of the United Kingdom its impact may have been particularly large in the Anglophone United States.

The Cambridge Group capitalized, quite literally, on the 1960s interest in social theory and in methodology. For years after its inception the group was one of the research centers supported by the British Social Science Research Council (later the Economic and Social Research Council [ESRC]). After the ESRC withdrew funding in 2001, the University of Cambridge Geography

Department provided a new home. Since 2001 the group has been funded in an ad hoc manner by a large number of individual research grants. Since 2012 the group has been a joint research unit shared by the Faculty of History and the Department of Cambridge. Smith and Wrigley remain active and have been joined as emeritus members by John Broad and Bob Bennet. Leadership has passed to a younger group of scholars: Leigh Shaw-Taylor (director), Chris Briggs, Romola Davenport, Amy Erickson, Alice Reid, Paul Warde, and Samantha Williams.

The period of the group's founding was propitious for development of new methods and computer applications useful for study of blocks of data from the past, data that had not commonly been examined earlier and that resulted in new interpretations of English historical events. Borrowing Louis Henry's methods in French family reconstitution, the group broke new ground in population history. The Henry model featured painstaking work linking family members using baptism, marriage, and burial records not unlike the parish registers that served as civil registers in England from the mid-sixteenth to the early nineteenth centuries. In time other records would augment these, and the methodology would be extended and computerized. Whether families could be reconstituted has depended on the quality of the records including their completeness and time span. Although genealogists have often used many of the same records and techniques, the group's social scientists were aggregating data to detect English family structure and its social and economic impact across time as well as comparing such structure and impact to other cultures. Family reconstitution informed Laslett's *The World We Have Lost* (1965) as well as his *Household and Family in Past Time* (edited with Wall, 1972), which included cross-cultural comparisons. Smith extended such inquiries to kinship as well as the Middle Ages in his edited volume *Land, Kinship, and Life Cycle* (1982). These works resulted in a revised history of English social structure in the past—documenting late age of first marriage for both partners, small households, low illegitimacy rates, expected migration of young people, and more. Such studies were emulated in many other countries and had an important influence on a spate of local studies by American historians in the 1970s.

Wrigley's *Introduction to Historical Demography* (1963) served to familiarize others with the field of population studies. Wrigley and Schofield's seminal tome, *The Population History of England, 1541–1871* (1981) captured the demographic contours of England in centuries preceding modern censuses. Moreover, its dedication to the "local population historians of England" recognized the essential role those dedicated amateurs had played in making parish registers usable. Both it and its successor, *English Population History from Family Reconstitution, 1580–1837* (1997) by Wrigley, R. S. Davies, J. E. Oeppen, and Schofield, featuring Oeppen's backward projection programs, depended for much of their data on local researchers.

The group's demographic emphasis has informed both micro and macro histories, both local works and studies of great national events like the Industrial Revolution (for which see Wrigley, *Continuity, Chance & Change*, 1988), all in all a body of work too vast to mention. Demographic work in recent years has focused on the long-run improvements to the urban mortality regime between the seventeenth and early twentieth centuries and on the decline of fertility in the late nineteenth century. A major project on the Occupational Structure of Britain c. 1379–1911 growing initially out of the large-scale collection of evidence in parish registers has been under way since 2003. One key finding is that England was much more industrialized c. 1700 than previously thought and that most of the increase in the share of the male labor force in the secondary sector traditionally associated with the Industrial Revolution took place in the early modern period. Through the work of Max Satchell, who joined the group in 2002, the group's work has undertaken a fundamentally spatial turn with a central role for Geographical Information Systems (GIS) in most projects. Richard Smith's long and successful tenure as director (1994–2011) saw a broadening of the group's research interests, which now encompass agrarian history, welfare systems, occupational structure, women's work, the structure of enterprises, wages, and energy use and consumption.

In addition to publications by group members, visiting scholars and research students have contributed vastly to the literature in population, kinship, and social structure. Several of these works appear in the group's sometime book series, Cambridge Studies in Popula-tion, Economy and Society in Past Time. Also, the group has in the past housed two journals, *Continuity and Change* and *Local Population Studies*, in which many local historians have appeared in print and group members and former members remain in key editorial roles on both journals. While in recent years historical demography and social history have lost popularity to other disciplinary areas like cultural studies, former students who trained at the group or have been visitors there now hold positions worldwide, many in American universities. Additionally, over the group's long life, American research centers and database collections, emulating to some extent those at Cambridge, have burgeoned.

More information on the group and its history can be found on the group's website: www.campop.geog.cam.ac.uk.

SHEILA McISAAC COOPER
UPDATED BY LEIGH SHAW-TAYLOR
CAMBRIDGE GROUP FOR THE HISTORY OF
POPULATION AND SOCIAL STRUCTURE

See demography, GIS in local history.

Canada, Library and Archives. Library and Archives Canada (LAC), is a federal government institution that was created in 2004 through the merger of the National Archives of Canada and the National Library of Canada. LAC is mandated under the *Library and Archives of Canada Act* to preserve the nation's documentary heritage; to be a source of enduring knowledge accessible to all; to contribute to the cultural, social, and economic advancement of Canada; to facilitate cooperation among Canadian communities involved in acquiring, preserving, and diffusing knowledge; and to serve as the continuing memory of the government of Canada. The term "documentary heritage" is used deliberately to encompass both published and unpublished materials, in all types of analog and digital formats.

LAC identifies, acquires, and preserves documentary heritage that has a significance to the nation as a whole. It also works with libraries and archives at the provincial, regional, municipal, and institutional levels to ensure the preservation of documentary heritage material that has more localized importance. In its role as the national archives, LAC identifies and acquires documentary heritage created by the government of Canada, along with that of private individuals, corporations, and associations that capture the stories of important people, themes, and events. In its role as the national library, LAC mainly acquires published material through legal deposit along with gifts. These programs are complemented by select purchases and web harvesting.

LAC's collections, which are the largest in the country, include textual records, photographs, paintings, motion-picture films, television and radio programs, sound recordings, drawings, manuscripts, music, and digital documents. The collections are intended to comprehensively document Canada, from before the arrival of European settlers to the present day. As such, the collections include many documents relating to the country's aboriginal peoples, copies of British and French colonial records, and records from virtually all federal government departments. Private life is captured through the docu-

mentary heritage of companies, associations, nongovernmental organizations, and individuals ranging from prime ministers and those with international profiles, to ordinary Canadians.

LAC's more notable collections include government records documenting the state's interactions with aboriginal peoples; personal papers of Canada's prime ministers; military service files of Canadian men and women; census records; negatives, prints, transparencies, and business records created by the portrait photographer Yusuf Karsh; the world's most extensive collection of Canadian comic books; lithographs, drawings, and prints of early Canada collected by Peter Winkworth; a multilingual collection of editions of *Anne of Green Gables*; musical recordings made in Canada or by Canadians; the Jacob M. Lowy collection of old and rare Hebraica and Judaica; and newspapers and magazines from the colonial period to the present day.

Canada is a bilingual country, and so the items in LAC's collections are predominantly in either English or French. At the same time, many other languages are represented, reflecting the nation's aboriginal peoples, successive waves of immigration, and the multicultural nature of modern Canada.

LAC's collections are built on the items acquired by its predecessor institutions. The first federal archives was created in 1872, five years after the modern nation of Canada was founded. Its small staff focused on copying and collecting records of colonial administrations and those created by private citizens. A separate archives acquired and preserved the records of the new federal government. The entities were merged in 1903, and moved to a permanent home three years later where divisions were dedicated to manuscripts, prints, and library materials. In 1912 the institution became the Public Archives of Canada (PAC), a department within the federal government. The PAC initially focused on identifying and acquiring documents created by private individuals, organizations, and associations. An extensive collection of World War I trophies and art amassed by the PAC is now preserved by the Canadian War Museum. During the twentieth century, ever-increasing autonomy from Britain coupled with an expansion of federal government programs resulted in an almost exponential growth in the volume of federal government records. The PAC responded by initiating records management programs, like disposition, microfilming, and operating a network of centers across the country in which government departments stored their dormant records.

A *Public Records Order* in 1966 formalized the PAC's role in government records management. At the same time, the institution continued to set broad collecting goals. A national map collection was inaugurated in 1967, followed by programs targeting private sector multicultural, economic, social, cultural, and scientific records. The National Film Archives (subsequently expanded to include television and sound) was established in 1976. Eleven years later, the *National Archives of Canada Act* gave the institution a new name and formalized the head's sole jurisdiction over the destruction of government documents.

LAC's library collections rest on the published works collected by the Library of Parliament, which was founded in the mid-nineteenth century, and those that had been acquired by the PAC. The National Library of Canada (NL) was established in 1953. It had been recommended two years earlier in the report of the Royal Commission on National Development in the Arts, Letters, and Sciences, which largely set the blueprint for modern federal cultural programs. Legal deposit regulations were simultaneously enacted that required Canadian publishers to provide two copies of every book to the NL. The regulations, which remain the main mechanism through which LAC acquires published materials, have been successively expanded to encompass serial publications, sound recordings, multimedia kits, microforms, video recordings, CD-ROMs, cartographic materials, and online and digital publications. In addition to works published in Canada, the NL collected ones about Canada or written by Canadians that were published abroad. The NL also produced a national union catalog and a bibliography of works published in Canada, and played important roles in international library and bibliographic associations. A music division was established in 1970 to manage the collections of printed scores and recordings and to acquire manuscript collections of Canadian music and musicians.

Though the NL and PAC were separate and autonomous, William Kaye Lamb, a trained historian, archivist, and librarian headed both institutions from 1953 until his retirement in 1968. From then until the creation of LAC in 2004, the institutions were headed by separate individuals. The head of LAC is officially called the Librarian and Archivist of Canada, reflecting these equivalent responsibilities.

LAC's physical presence has expanded greatly over the years. In 1967, as part of Canada's centennial celebrations, a dedicated building for the PAC and the NL incorporating storage areas, reading rooms, offices, exhibition spaces, and an auditorium was opened on Wellington Street in Ottawa. Its proximity to the Supreme Court and Parliament Hill indicated the importance that the government of the day accorded to the institutions. Most in-person public services still take place at this location. Storage of the ever-expanding collections has been increasingly consolidated. In 1997, the Gatineau Preservation Center was opened about five miles from downtown Ottawa. Its secure, climate-controlled vaults house many of LAC's key collections, while preservation, conservation, and digitization activities are carried out in its state-of-the-art laboratories and workshops. The majority of LAC staff work in an adjacent building. Since 2011, LAC has housed volatile, nitrate-based films and photographic negatives in a specially constructed facility in the far west end of Ottawa. A high-density storage facility, which houses preservation copies of published items and other material that rarely circulates opened in 2013.

LAC and its predecessors have always faced the challenge of making collections accessible throughout Canada. For over a century, LAC and its predecessors published extensive descriptions, catalogs, brochures, slides, microfilms, microfiches, and reference works, and organized traveling exhibitions. Publications were circulated to libraries in Canada and abroad through interlibrary loan and some more locally focused archival collections were housed in those regions. LAC now carries out many of these activities online, often in partnership with other government agencies, universities, memory institutions, and genealogical societies. The digitized documentary heritage material created by these activities includes original records, non-copyright published works, exhibitions, catalogs, descriptions, and finding aids. Most of these are accessible through LAC's website (www.collectionscanada.ca). LAC also makes increasing use of social media to disseminate collections and information about its operations. LAC receives important support from the Friends of Library and Archives Canada, a private association that promotes and encourages public awareness about the institution, attracts gifts and donations of documentary heritage material, and raises funds, most notably to assist with purchases.

Researchers do not have to be Canadian citizens or residents of Canada to consult LAC's collections. While LAC strives to make its collections as accessible as possible, they are subject to Canadian Access to Information, Privacy and Copyright legislation as well as individual donor agreements. LAC's main reference and consultation rooms are located in downtown Ottawa. Researchers are strongly advised to contact the institution well in advance of any visit. LAC may be contacted through the website; by telephone at (613) 996-

5115 or 1-(866) 578-7777 (toll-free in Canada and the United States); by fax at (613) 995-6274; and by mail at 395 Wellington Street, Ottawa, K1A 0N4, Canada.

ANDREW HORRALL
LIBRARY AND ARCHIVES CANADA

See Canada, local history in; National Archives and Records Administration.

Canada, local history in. The earliest local histories in Canada—mostly county or town histories—date from late in the colonial era just prior to Confederation in 1867. The first county history in Upper Canada (now Ontario) was James Croil's *Dundas; or, A Sketch of Canadian History* (1861). Some were intended as background to county "prize essays," solicited and published in the 1850s by provincial boards of agriculture. Similar prizes were offered by King's College in Nova Scotia. The essays were motivated in part by a Victorian sense of the progress achieved by the first generation of pioneers who had transformed the "howling wilderness," but rather than articulating a sense of local particularity they were motivated by a dawning sense of colonial identity as loyal, British, and progressive, frequently asserting a moral superiority to their neighbors to the south.

The late nineteenth century saw renewed interest in the colonies' early years, stimulated in part by celebrations in 1884 to mark the centennial of the arrival of the loyalist refugees of the American Revolution in the Maritimes, Quebec, and Ontario, resulting in the founding of several local and county historical societies.

Entrepreneurs in the United States signed up subscribers for county landownership maps in the 1860s, and for a series of county-by-county "illustrated historical atlases" with extended historical and biographical texts in 1874–1881. While they remain important sources of geographical and historical information, in light of British geographer Brian Harley's insistence that cartographic representations are a reflection of power relations and never a neutral depiction of what was, we must understand their inclusions and exclusions as visual manifestations of Victorian ideals.

Some American entrepreneurs extended their Canadian efforts to voluminous, stand-alone county history books with chapters on the various townships, and biographies or genealogies of subscribers and their families. Such efforts inspired domestic historians to follow suit. Where authors were local, they were frequently retired businessmen or wealthy farmers, or doctors, clergymen, or newspaper editors. Women joined their ranks late in the century, and even created female associations, such as the Women's Canadian Historical Societies of Toronto and Ottawa, but feminization of the genre seems not to have progressed as far as Kammen has observed in the United States.

In the countryside, local history as women's work became associated with the Women's Institutes (founded 1897). In 1925 they added historical research to a wide range of other activities, appointing curators or community archivists to collect documentation to preserve the myth of the pioneer in a period of rural decline, and maintain a scrapbook record of contemporary events. In 1940 the patronage of Lady Tweedsmuir, wife of the governor general, was sought to raise the profile of their work. By 1945 a standardized thematic structure was urged on local institutes, with annual awards for the best Tweedsmuir History from 1947. Some institutes operated local museums and organized centennial parades and pageants.

As the capacity to draw upon oral recollections of the pioneer era dimmed in the early twentieth century, the quality of eastern and central Canadian local histories deteriorated. This was due partly to a democratization of authorship, and a tendency to recycle the contents of earlier works, notably the county atlases. The years after World War II saw a proliferation of such amateur productions, receiving impetus from federal encouragement and funding associated with the national centennial in 1967 and some subsequent provincial centennials. The centennial promotions stimulated a copycat interest that has scarcely let up since, with the 100th or 200th anniversaries of many townships and municipalities providing the occasion for commissioned local histories, sometimes written by professional historians. Many amateur productions continue to be derivative of earlier work. Some of the best break free from a thematic arrangement (churches, schools, social institutions) and draw upon local newspapers to provide observant and often very useful chronological accounts. In doing so, they sometimes break free as well from Whiggish progress as a central theme, or its common flip side, the nostalgia of

an author for the golden age of his or her youth.

In the prairie west, settled most intensively around the turn of the twentieth century, the centenaries of white settlement and the passing of the pioneer generation were again capitalized upon by commercial enterprises. The genre of land ownership maps was revived for Ontario as well as the three prairie provinces in the early 1920s. More recently Friesens, an Altona, Manitoba publisher of high school yearbooks, developed a template for local history books, canvassing rural communities for subscribers and sometimes supplying an author, as its predecessors had done a century earlier in Ontario and the Maritimes. The historical chapters in these works tend to be thematic and to be overwhelmed by the genealogical sketches that follow. Friesens determined that roughly five books would be sold for every early-settler genealogy included. The American firm Arcadia Publishing offers an alternative and less demanding formula in paperback compilations of vintage photographs, complementing its prolific Images of America series with the first of its much smaller Historic Canada series in 1995.

Donald Wright has demonstrated that academic historians laid exclusive claim to professional status by drawing clear boundaries around their own activities. For them local history occupied an inferior position in an epistemological hierarchy. A 1932 paper by D. C. Harvey declared that local historians performed a useful service in gathering facts for professional synthesis by national historians. It was in this context that J. B. Brebner felt compelled to apologize for writing about as confined an area as Atlantic Canada. An academic local history tradition did become established in the interwar years at the University of Western Ontario, in London, but it never achieved much importance outside the local area and has since foundered. It is perhaps symptomatic of the situation of local history in Canada that in the early 1970s historians and social scientists there put forward an elaborate proposal for an interdisciplinary study of southwestern Ontario, but no thought was given to producing a good history of the region and, following refusal of Canada Council funding, little of the work continued independently.

The early twentieth century saw the maturation of nineteenth-century "colony to nation" narratives of national development. This in time prompted a regional backlash that had lasting consequences. While a politicized regionalism grew in the universities of the east and west, the social turn in historical practice was validating the microstudy as a methodology.

The impetus for academic study of urban history was influenced by American, British, and French precedent but it was more attentive to place than most other new fields of historical study. The Canadian Urban History Association, organized at the Annual Congress of the Humanities and Social Sciences in 1971, meets annually at the congress as an affiliated committee of the Canadian Historical Association.

Urban activist Jane Jacobs moved to Toronto in 1968 and the year following her death there in 2006 friends and colleagues organized a weekend of free community walking tours in her memory. By 2016 Jane's Walks were being held in 212 cities in thirty-six countries (janeswalk.org). Also popular is Doors Open day when many buildings normally closed to the public open for viewing. In 2000 Toronto became the first North American city to adopt the idea, which originated in France in 1984. Ontario Heritage Trust began coordinating a province-wide program in 2002, and by 2016 the idea had been taken up in seven other provinces and territories and several American states.

The rural history tradition, so strongly allied with local history in England, has had less academic resonance in Canada and has been partially eclipsed by the new field of *environmental history, but there is an active program at University of Guelph (www.uoguelph.ca/ruralhis tory). A major resource is the Canadian Agriculture Library in Ottawa; its catalog may be searched on cat.cisti.nrc.ca/ screens/opacmenu.html.

Some academics, librarians, and archivists wrote handbooks to assist members of the public in researching and writing local history during the spike in interest following the 1967 Centennial celebrations. The first was probably H. A. Stevenson and F. H. Armstrong, *Approaches to Teaching Local History* (1969). Their idea that local history should be promoted primarily to young people was perpetuated in the looseleaf guide *Discovering Your Community: Activities and Suggestions for Developing Local History Projects for Young People*, in 1984, and updated in 1992 (along with a French-language edition, *Découvre ta communauté*). The volume proposed thematic projects including family history and natural and *built environment. Attempts to obtain support for a guide for Ontario adults were stymied by granting agency policies against funding self-help manuals.

Guidebooks for tracing *genealogy and house history continue to proliferate, evidencing an increasingly personal engagement with the past. Interest in genealogy has achieved the level of popularity where, like local history in the mid-nineteenth century, it has become increasingly commercialized. In the 1990s the activities and functions of the genealogical societies established in the 1960s and 1970s began to be complemented and then eclipsed by commercial firms. The greater transformation arrived with the Internet. While cash-strapped public institutions divert resources to making historical source materials accessible online, their efforts are outstripped by corporations such as ancestry.ca, the Canadian wing of the Utah-based multinational *Ancestry.com.

There are some signs of a reconvergence of popular and academic history. While there has not been a manifesto in Canada challenging marginalized groups to reclaim their own community and neighborhood histories, ethnic and working-class history were among the "limited identities" that were pursued "from the bottom up" by Canadian community groups in the last quarter of the twentieth century. The preservation of vernacular and ethnic structures appeared on the historic preservation agenda in the 1970s, alongside landmark buildings and urban districts.

Projects to record *oral history testimony began in the 1960s and were attractive to activist historians intent upon rescuing the silenced voices of workers, women, and minorities and providing information about neglected aspects of the past. Interview projects were also taken on by local historical societies and museums, often with the financial assistance of federal seniors or provincial student employment programs. The Canadian Oral History Association headquartered at University of Winnipeg was, like so many specialist associations, established in the 1970s. Concordia University's Centre for Oral History and Digital Storytelling, founded in 2006, emphasizes community-university collaboration. The concept of "shared authority" acknowledges the reality of engaged scholarship, as academics are frequently sympathetic to the plight of marginalized groups, but it also challenges them not to sacrifice informed broader perspectives to a particular interest. Nor is it easy to share authority if one's aim is to deconstruct community agendas and narratives.

Interest in the social construction of space, place, and landscape is bringing historians to the local to analyze the varying ways in which places have been understood in past and present generations. A good introduction to the genre is James Opp and John C. Walsh, *Placing Memory and Remembering Place in Canada* (2010). Instructive examples exploring how disparate conceptions of a place have contended and evolved over time are William J. Turkel, *The Archive of Place: Unearthing the Pasts of the Chilcotin Plateau* (2007) and Claire E. Campbell, *Shaped by the West Wind: Nature and History in Georgian Bay* (2005), a book anticipated in some respects by W. R. Wightman's unjustly neglected *Forever on the*

Fringe: Six Studies in the Development of the Manitoulin Island (1982). Articles in the Opp/Walsh volume and in journals give insight into local pastkeepers even if they focus on museums, monument promoters, parades, *pageants, and old boys' reunions rather than on the writers of local history.

In what was for a long time a sparsely populated and largely rural country to which industrialization (the source of much of America's philanthropic wealth) came late, museums are more likely to be operated by government bodies than privately endowed foundations. The same applies to archives. The Public Archives of Canada (now *Library and Archives Canada), founded in 1872, pioneered the concept of "total archives" in which the official record is complemented by accessions from the private and corporate sectors. This model was emulated by the later provincial and territorial archives.

The proliferation of local history publications, heritage conservation, and cultural institutions in the 1970s was not only an outgrowth of the euphoria of the Canadian Centennial celebrations of 1967; it also reflected a more interventionist attitude on the part of government. Nationally this was manifested in the "new nationalism" of the Pierre Trudeau administration. In the fields of history and heritage much government activity took place at the provincial/territorial level, as constitutionally municipalities, education, and property rights fall under provincial jurisdiction. The Heritage Canada Foundation, established in 1973 to "hold in trust for the nation, the buildings and landscapes that are its heritage," now the National Trust for Canada, was set up as an NGO; it would have been difficult for a federal agency to lobby the provinces to enact heritage conservation legislation.

The size of the country and the diminishing population further from the American border has meant that networks of local history societies, archives, and genealogical societies have also tended to organize at the provincial level. Additional details of local and provincial heritage activity should be sought in the provincial and territorial articles in this volume, and in the article on Library and Archives Canada.

The coming to power in the 1990s of neoconservatives avowing a commitment to smaller and less interventionist government saw the emphasis shifted to tourism profits from intangible cultural and citizenship benefits, and the replacement at senior levels of staff possessing discipline-specific knowledge with professional managers. The research functions of museums have eroded in favor of the exhibitions that enhance visitor numbers and revenues. At archives and libraries discipline-specific knowledge gave way to generalist staff and a growing encouragement of keyword searches over relying on detailed staff knowledge of the archive. In the area of heritage conservation, the promotion of preservation as an exercise in sustainability, quality of life, local identity, and civic pride has been an increasingly tough sell against accusations of anti-modernism, NIMBYism, and gentrification, and policies of intensifying land use in older neighborhoods.

In heavily francophone Quebec where provincial history is conceived in national terms, the cultural industries have continued to be important to both citizens and governments, whether separatist or federalist. The production of local histories has benefited from agreements signed since 1979 between municipalities and the Quebec Cultural Affairs Ministry under the *entente de développement culturel*, which began as a program to repurpose heritage buildings. Since 2005 Quebec has celebrated August as Archaeology Month with numerous local events and programs (www.archeoquebec.com). Saskatchewan has designated June.

Despite periodic cutbacks and downsizing, professional employment opportunities in the public sector have grown since the 1970s as many community museums established by volunteers have been taken over by governments (Alberta's Ukrainian Cultural Heritage Village) or subjected to enhanced standards with increased public funding (City of Ottawa's Museums Sustainability Plan). While disciplinary training in history is still viewed in many circles as indispensable, the 1970s and 1980s saw the creation of specialized academic programs to meet growing public sector demand. Museum studies programs in Canada ranging from professional development seminars and certificate programs offered by museum associations to graduate degree programs are listed on the Canadian Museums Association website: www.museums.ca/site/msp. A list of archival studies programs may be found on archivescanada.ca.

*Digitization of historical resources has burgeoned since the 1990s. The AMICUS catalog (http://amicus.col-lectionscanada.gc.ca/aaweb/aalogine.htm) is a searchable union catalog to published materials in the holdings of 1,300 Canadian libraries, including its sponsor Library and Archives Canada. Like Worldcat (www.worldcat.org), access is free. The standard search tool for Canadian academic journal literature, however, is *America: History and Life*, a proprietary database of EBSCO Information Services, available by subscription or to members of subscribing institutions.

Ourroots.ca is a national program to digitize published local histories in both official languages, organized by the Universities of Calgary and Laval and supported by a number of partner institutions. Canadian research libraries also support canadiana.ca, formerly the Canadian Institute for Historical Microreproductions (CIHM), founded in 1978 with an initial federal grant to reproduce on microfiche pre-1900 Canadian monographs. A content catalog for *Genealogy and Local History to 1900* by J. B. Gilchrist and C. D. Collier was published in 1995. Subsequent projects extended the monograph and periodical collections to 1920 and complemented them with pre-1900 annuals, almanacs, and directories. In 1996 Canadiana commenced digital OCR scanning of fiches on selected topics for website access as ECO/Early Canadiana Online. In 2003 work began on federal, provincial, and territorial official publications to 1900. ECO and part of the official publications series are freely searchable on eco.canadiana.ca, while the rest of the latter are accessible by subscription. The website includes only 10 percent of the initial fiche collection, but the remainder is being scanned on behalf of Canadiana by University of Alberta Libraries and made freely available for viewing on the nonprofit Internet Archive (archive. org) where, however, only the metadata is keyword searchable. An explanation of the project may be found on http://canadiana.library.ualberta.ca/index.html. A ten-year project to scan Library and Archives Canada archival microfilms commenced in 2013: http://heritage.canadiana.ca.

The scholarly *Dictionary of Canadian Biography* is available online at www.biographi.ca, and past volumes of the *Champlain Society* (1905), a national record society on the European model, may be accessed on www.champlainsociety.ca. Links to websites of local and specialist archives in Canada may be found at www.archivescanada.ca/car/menu.html.

BRUCE S. ELLIOTT
CARLETON UNIVERSITY, OTTAWA

See Australia, local history in; Canada, Library and Archives; England, local history in; local history resources online; maps and atlases; mug books; New Zealand, local history in; oral history; United States, local history in; and Canadian provincial histories by province name.

candlemas. The feast of the Purification of the Virgin Mary celebrated on February 2. Candlemas plays a role in folklore as it marked what would have been the end of winter in Great Britain; in the United States that day is usually about halfway through winter and is known as Groundhog Day.

Caribbeans in North America, sources for. See Appendix A.

celebrations. Over the past fifty years the nature of community celebrations has changed. At one time, we celebrated Independence Day or town founding day or some significant local holiday with sermons and orations, sometimes with community dinners for a town's elite, or picnics at the fairgrounds or churchyard. Fireworks were primarily individually motivated and were often dangerous. It was a time of preachers, politicians, picnics, and parades.

In some places the parades became more elaborate, the marching punctuated with homemade floats, and around the turn of the twentieth century historical *pageants were introduced. David Glassberg has written of that era when the "Spirit of Pageantry" appeared in a gauzy dress to bless the festivities.

That changed. At midcentury, publicists and others became involved in *"boosting" communities and in attracting visitors to what were originally local events. Ron Powers, in his book *White Town Drowsing* (1986) provides a vivid account of the Mark Twain Celebration planned and mounted in Hannibal, Missouri. Celebrations ceased to be homegrown affairs and became instead, slowly and inexorably, about a town's image, then about a place being able to attract others to it, to enjoy and appreciate but also to take away coffee mugs and T-shirts duly marked with place, date, and event.

States that once had modest offices to attract tourists now have development directors with several-million-dollar budgets to lure the visitor and book concessionaires. Local celebrations are now marketed with an eye to the tourist, to the "heads in the beds," "butts in the seats," and the bottom line; they are often organized not by local volunteers, but by paid events managers, and the measure of success is counted in the number of cars parked and hot dogs sold rather than by scouts marching not so neatly to the music of the local high school band, the smell of hot dogs cooking in the park, and neighbors facing neighbors along Main Street each armed with a small paper flag.

See David Glassberg, *American Historical Pageantry: The Uses of Tradition in the Early 20th Century* (1990); Michael Kammen, *Mystic Chords of Memory* (1991); Ron Powers, *White Town Drowsing* (1986); W. Lloyd Warner, *The Living and the Dead: A Study of the Symbolic Life of Americans* (1959); and the movie *Waiting for Guffman* (1997), available on video.

See also boosterism; emancipation celebrations; and tourism.

cemeteries. See gravestones.

cemetery records. See genealogical resources online.

censorship. Local historians sometimes censor history. Consciously or without premeditated thought, this censorship is important to recognize because it limits the topics that we select; it colors our outlook about doing local history for the community in which we live; it sometimes skews the sort of history that the local public expects and gets from local historical societies and from local historians.

There is censorship that stems from the desire to portray our local past in the best possible light. In such cases, the historian restricts local history topics and bypasses important episodes because they might cause people to think ill of the community or of individuals—or of local history. These are inescapable motives for local historians who are dependent upon the community for additional information and new materials and whose audience is local townspeople. An "unreliable" local historian, that is, one who embarrasses area residents or who makes them uncomfortable, will soon find documents unavailable and people unwilling to cooperate.

Another form of local censorship involves what a historical society is willing to endorse as an exhibit, program, or research topic. Some historical societies, conscious of the need for local support and contributions, are loath to touch subjects that might become controversial; their motive is self-preservation and preserving good community relations. This is censorship that derives from the attitude that local history should be *boosterish of—or good for—the community. Our communities are avid consumers of local history because it provides tourist destinations and because local history provides good copy for publicity about place. It is also expected to make people knowledgeable about and feel good about the place where they live.

A third manifestation of local censorship comes in the form of disappearing documents; the motive is the same, but in this case it is the archivist who exercises a form of censorship. A friend, researching the lives of teenage girls in the nineteenth century, came across the record book of a home for unwed mothers. There was a good deal of information in the book about the girls, their ages, what happened to their babies, and where the mothers went from the home. On a second visit, my friend was told that the book had been lost. In that way, the keeper of the archive was able to censor what was studied and consequently, what was known about the local past.

In addition, some local historians censor the topics they research, concentrating on a few standard topics, neglecting study of local *crime, race relations and conflict, the actions of strikers and bosses, and *political topics of all sorts. These are legitimate subjects to pursue, but they are generally about divisive moments in our past; they do not promote a picture of a unified community or of a harmonious past. They do, however, reflect life, even as we know it today.

The final way in which local historians censor the past is by a preference for beginnings rather than an examination of the development of a community over time. There is a bias for the remote past, for those first to till the land, early institutions, and how the community grew from a rude place to one of enterprise, industry, and culture. A 106-page history of a city not far from my home devotes the first eighty pages to the period before the Civil War. This is surely a distortion: yet it is not an uncommon one, and it is often the way we perceive local history. Nevertheless, this bias for the earliest era to the exclusion of other, more recent topics, cheats us of fully understanding how the present came

about and knowing that we, ourselves, are living in historical times.

Local historians do all of these things for the best of reasons, yet in doing so we shortchange ourselves and our communities. By presenting local history as always positive, we deny the fact that the past was as controversial as we know the present to be.

CAROL KAMMEN
TOMPKINS COUNTY (NY) HISTORIAN

See boosterism; building bridges through local history; county histories.

census, United States. The U.S. census is the first wonder of the statistical world: a decennial census dating from 1790 and continually refined and expanded from that simple count of heads of households to the present multibillion-dollar effort. While the value of the census for understanding trends in the new country was recognized at the outset, realization of its value to historians came late. Joseph Hill, the head of the Census Bureau for the eleventh census, told historians in 1909 that "it would be very difficult to write history either social or economic or indeed political without statistics, and it would be a very defective economic or social history of the United States that ignored the statistics compiled by the United States census" (Joseph A. Hill, "The Historical Value of the Census Records," *Annual Report of the American Historical Association for the Year 1908* vol. 1 [1909]: 199). He went on to extol the even greater utility of the census manuscripts. Although historians were slow to take up Hill's challenge—they were balked by the inaccessibility of much of the material—it is difficult today to imagine a local history that does not use census material: Robert P. Swierenga, "Historians and the Census: The Historiography of Census Research," *The Annals of Iowa* 50 (Fall 1990): 650–73.

As more census content is digitized and made available for personal computers—much of it distributed on the Internet and the World Wide Web—it will become increasingly important for historians to understand and be able to evaluate and use census information.

Many cultures have employed some form of census for administrative purposes, usually for identifying taxable units, or men of fighting age. There are several censuses in the Bible: the misfortunes that befell the Israelites after David's attempted enumeration (2 Samuel 24 and 1 Chronicles 27) reportedly influenced many cases of noncompliance in the early American republic; and it was a version of the Roman census that brought Joseph and Mary to Bethlehem (Luke 2). Rome's periodic enumeration and classification of its citizenry provided the intellectual and historical precedent for all later European efforts, although no comprehensive nationwide census was attempted before the U.S. Census of 1790. At the instigation of the British Board of Trade, the American colonies were frequently, if grudgingly, enumerated, but only as individual units. The accuracy of the results depended on the administrative ability of the governor and the political climate. Thirty-eight pre-Revolutionary censuses have been identified. These provided a tradition of census-taking and developed some expertise, particularly in the northern states. The 1774 census

of Rhode Island, for example, may have been a model for the U.S. Census of 1790. In *American Population before the Federal Census of 1790* (1966), Evarts B. Greene and Virginia D. Harrington thoroughly review colonial census history and content. Only a scattering of these early censuses survive.

More directly, however, the origin of U.S. Census stemmed from the desire of the Continental Congress to apportion the debt incurred from the Revolution fairly among the colonies (Articles of Confederation, Article IX). Early in the Congress one important train of thought was that the basis for apportioning the debt should be the value of land and property in each colony. Methodological and logistic difficulties stymied efforts along these lines, and eventually it was decided to base apportionment on the number of households. Even this proposed "capitation" was never actually carried out, but the concept of proportional taxation based on a census carried over to the Constitutional Convention. There it was ready at hand when the delegates sought a method of apportioning seats in the House of Representatives once the constitutional compromises were struck.

The Constitution calls for a complete enumeration of inhabitants every ten years for the purpose of apportioning the House (article 1, sec. 2), and the first House of Representatives, consisting of sixty-five representatives apportioned by the Constitution itself, immediately authorized a census for that purpose, which was carried out in 1790. Federal district marshals, the only countrywide federal bureaucracy available, hired enumerators to count the heads of households in their judicial districts. There were no standardized forms or training. The post-census check consisted of tacking the results up at two local gathering places in the district and inviting comments.

The manuscripts of the enumerators, the lists, or "schedules" of names, were collected by the marshals, who did the actual tallying for their districts. They then sent the tally sheets directly to the president. From these, clerks in the Secretary of State's office did the final tally and wrote up the report. The report was published and distributed to the states and to Congress. It was also made available to the public. The marshals placed the manuscript schedules in the district courts for safekeeping.

The population totals from the first census were disappointingly low—the first of many perceived undercounts. The Secretary of State, Thomas Jefferson, forwarded the report of the first census, a fifty-six-page summary still missing the totals from South Carolina, to President Washington. After some disagreement about the apportionment formula, and the first presidential veto, 105 congressional seats were reapportioned for the election of the Third Congress according to the results.

There are several excellent histories of the U.S. Census: Carroll D. Wright, assisted by William C. Hunt, *The History and Growth of the United States Census* (1900), remains indispensable. Wright provides the schedules for every census through 1890, along with instructions to enumerators, texts of the census laws, and extensive bibliographies. A briefer, but very useful overview of early census history is Bureau of the Census, *A Century of Population Growth: From the First Census of the United States to the Twelfth, 1790–1900* (1967).

The first census established the procedural and publishing patterns for succeeding censuses. The public result was the summary report. The report of the first census was not ambitious, and only summarized data at the state level, but subsequent reports have grown in importance as more and more detailed information has been collected and summarized at local levels, such as county and town. The presentation of the data also became more sophisticated with more information extensively cross-tabulated. The census report is extremely useful to historians in itself. The report will tell the researcher, for example, how many white females there were in Tompkins County, New York, in 1850 and how many foreign citizens (but not yet how many naturalized females). It will report how many suspender-makers in New York State, but not how many in Tompkins County. The published summary reports are available at large libraries and the contents for all the population censuses from 1790 to 1940 have been indexed by Suzanne Schulze, *Population Information in Nineteenth Century Census Volumes* (1983), and successive volumes.

A complete bibliography of all published census publications to 1945 is Library of Congress, Census Library Project, *Catalog of United States Census Publications, 1790–1945*, prepared by Henry J. Dubester, Chief (1950); now reprinted and augmented with additional information as Kevin L. Cook, *Dubester's U.S. Census Bibliography with SuDocs Class Numbers and Indexes* (1996).

The materials behind the reports are just as valuable, and for local historians, perhaps more so. The unpublished, or manuscript, schedules contain the answers to the census questions collected for each household, or, after 1850, each individual person. The questions themselves varied from census to census, increasing in detail and scope each decade. In the first census, for example, there were only six questions: name of householder, race, free or slave, sex of free white householder and whether white males were above sixteen years of age, or below. By 1880 there were thousands of questions (on many different schedules).

The manuscript schedules will tell the researcher, among other things, that a man named Horace Mack lived in Ithaca in 1850. He was twenty-five years old and had a wife and two daughters (known by inference). He was born in Connecticut, was a publisher by profession, and had real estate worth $750. This household- or individual-level information is available for most states and most censuses from 1790 to 1930. Personal information in later censuses is protected by the "72-year directive," which requires a seventy-two-year wait before the census schedules are made available to the public.

For a state-by-state listing of available census schedules, see *The 1790–1890 Federal Population Censuses: Catalog of National Archives Microfilm* (1993).

The Census to 1850: The same basic pattern established in the first census was maintained for the next four censuses. The marshals remained the executors and their judicial districts were the basic census-collection units, although the reporting was by state and usually, but not necessarily, by county. Census logistics and reporting became the responsibility of the Secretary of State. The questions asked of each household were still few, and differed slightly from census to census, mostly in the way people in the household were grouped by age. The only name asked and recorded was still the head of the household. Questions about social characteristics, such as occupation and naturalization, began to be asked in 1820 and expanded each decade, so the 1840 census asked, in addition to the demographic information, about the number of people engaged in specific occupational categories, number in school, literacy of adults, and the number of insane.

The 1850 Census: The census of 1850 is often called the first modern census. Enumerators for this census were now hired on the basis of merit. They received some training, and, since 1830, provided with standard forms and printed instructions. Although the marshals were still in charge in the field, a temporary office, first established in 1840, coordinated the census effort centrally, now under the Secretary of the Interior. Census geography was regularized: the judicial districts were subdivided along the lines of known civil divisions, such as towns, villages, and wards, for purposes of both enumeration and summarizing data.

In terms of content there was a radical break from the old concept of the household as the basic census unit. From 1850 on, every free individual in the United States was enumerated by name, and his or her demographic and social characteristics were recorded. In addition to the standard questions of age, sex, free or slave (in slave states, separate slave schedules were used), occupational category was also recorded. Earlier censuses had experimented with questions on nativity and naturalization, but the 1850 census asked the state or country of birth. The head of the household provided information on the value of the family real estate. The individual's relationship to the head of the household was not asked but often indicated by the enumerator by indentation or some other means. In total, there were eleven questions.

1860–1920: The next six censuses grew in complexity, but the underlying pattern endured. An important development, after an explosion of questions in many different schedules, was to conduct special censuses, with specially trained enumerators, for many aspects of U.S. life such as manufactures and agriculture. In 1910, these were completely separate from the population censuses and formed the basis for what would become the economic census. The first housing question occurs in 1890, and from that time the census content begins to evolve into the modern census triad of individuals, households, and housing. The Census Office became permanent in 1902, enhancing greatly the professionalism of the census enterprise. A particularly portentous event was the development of an automated counting machine using punch cards to tally the results of the 1890 census. Invented by Herman Hollerith, a Census Office clerk, this machine was a precursor of the modern computer. Hollerith left the Census Office to found what would become International Business Machines.

For a comprehensive guide to the questions asked in each census, along with the instructions to the enumerators, and illustration of the forms used, see Bureau of the Census, *200 Years of U.S. Census Taking: Population and Housing Questions, 1790–1990* (1989). A more compact census-by-census review is "Research in Census Records," in *The Source: A Guidebook of American Genealogy*, ed. Loretto Dennis Szucs and Sandra Hargreaves Luebking (c. 1997).

Census Geography: One problem for historians has been the lack of consistent census-unit boundaries in small areas, so that valid comparisons can be made over time. Many states have changed boundaries or been carved out of earlier territories while counties have proved even more fluid, changing shapes and dividing as population shifted. Wards and then enumeration districts were used to divide cities into manageable units for enumeration, but the lack of a consistent sub-municipal census unit before the tract was adopted in 1940 makes understanding neighborhood dynamics difficult.

Street addresses were not provided on the returns until 1880, so that enumerator routes must be reconstructed from directories. Despite the difficulties, interesting work in understanding local history has featured joining information from census schedules to reconstructed local maps or other geospatial data. See, for example, Michael P. Conzen, "Spatial Data from Nineteenth Century Manuscript Censuses: A Technique for Rural Settlement and Land Use Analysis," *Professional Geographer* 21 (September 1969): 337–42. The standard guide to census geography is William Thorndale and William Dollarhide, *Map Guide to the U.S. Federal Censuses, 1790–1920* (1987).

Historians and the Census—Accessibility: For many years the manuscript census schedules were scarcely used, at least by historians. Although mail requests for information from the schedules are recorded as early as 1850, extensive research was impossible without hands-on access. The establishment of a permanent Census Bureau in 1902 increased accessibility. The older schedules were inventoried and bound. The first census index, the twelve-volume *Heads of Families at the First Census of the United States Taken in the Year 1790,* was published in 1907–1908, but only the most intrepid genealogists made the trip to Washington to consult the fragile, otherwise unindexed schedules of later censuses.

Three important developments brought about a revolution in accessibility. The most important was the founding of the National Archives and the transfer of the extant schedules to them from the Census Bureau in 1942. The Archives applied the newly developed technologies of photostatic reproduction and microfilming to the schedules throughout the 1940s. This allowed for the distribution of the schedules, as well as guaranteeing their survival. Somewhat earlier, the Civil Works Administration had begun indexing schedules for the Census Bureau. Indexing began with the 1900 Census, and eventually resulted in the *Soundex indexes for the 1880, 1900, 1910, and 1920 censuses. These indexes, which are available on microfilm, are still not complete for all censuses. Accelerated Indexing Systems and other commercial genealogical indexing companies began indexing in the 1960s, and have produced printed indexes of the 1800–1860 censuses for most states.

Researchers hoping to consult the original paper schedules for 1900–1920 will discover that microfilming, for all its benefits, turned into a two-edged sword. Once the original census schedules had been microfilmed, they were destroyed by act of Congress with the acquiescence of the Archivist of the United States. And the move from the Census Bureau did not come in time to save the schedules of the 1890 census, which were partially burned in 1921, and then destroyed, possibly unnecessarily, in 1930, before they could be filmed or indexed.

Modern census-taking methods will challenge future historians. The use of mail-back forms, which began with the 1960 Census, completely changes the enumerator-driven model upon which historical census research is based. It is not at all clear what kind of access researchers will have to the forms or how they can be presented coherently. Even more crippling for historians will be the shift from acquiring basic household data through the census to the use of survey instruments such as the American Community Survey. Surveys essentially separate the individual from the data and that makes inferences about social networks on the local level almost impossible. The 2010 Census asked fewer questions than the 1810 Census and so will have very diminished utility for historians when it is opened to the public in 2082.

The enumerations themselves are far from perfect. There are problems with compliance and accuracy. The indexes mirror their problems and add several of their own, but together they offer the local historian a magnificent resource for analyzing and understanding families, governments, and institutions, either captured in time or changing decade by decade.

For a state-by-state listing of census schedules, see *The 1790–1890 Federal Population Censuses: Catalog of National Archives Microfilm* (1993). Szucs, op. cit., 104–8, has an excellent discussion of problems inherent in census data.

Nonpopulation Schedules and Censuses: Immediately after the first census, Thomas Jefferson and many others urged Congress to order census-takers to ask additional questions about social characteristics, agriculture, and the state of manufactures. The third census actually included a separate schedule of manufacturing questions, but this early experiment in economic census-taking was not successful. A sustained effort to gather agricultural information began in 1840 and continued until a separate census of agriculture was undertaken in 1925. Also in 1840, a special census of Revolutionary War veterans was made and separately published.

The 1850 census retained the agricultural schedules and added schedules for slaves, mortality, manufactures, and social statistics. The slave schedules were also used in 1860. Slave names were not recorded, but the schedules have been used successfully for historical research. The mortality schedules asked questions about anyone who died within the previous year and some other vital-statistics questions. The social statistics were an at-tempt to collect information about a wide range of social institutions within the enumerator's district: for example, how many libraries and schools, and taxes collected. These questions were not asked of individuals, but depended on the enumerators' research. Mortality and social-statistics schedules were part of the census through 1880.

In addition, there have been several population censuses that fall outside of the decennial period. In 1885, states were encouraged to take their own censuses, which would be partially paid for with federal money. Only a few states accepted the offer, but these schedules have survived and been microfilmed.

Finally, there was a special census of Union veterans of the Civil War in 1890. These are the only surviving schedules of the 1890 census, except for a scattering of counties.

In 1919, Congress authorized the disposal of the nonpopulation schedules from 1850 to 1880, but the objections of organizations such as the Daughters of the American Revolution (DAR) forced the Census Bureau to offer the volumes to state libraries and historical societies. If they were refused, the DAR Library in Washington held them for safekeeping. The National Archives has since attempted to locate as many as possible for filming.

There is a complete discussion of availability and location of the non-population census schedules through 1890 in Szucs, 128–34. The fate of later schedules is reviewed by Louis Malcomb, "Non-Population Census Schedules: Description, Accessibility and Disposition," *Indiana Libraries* 11, nos. 1 & 2 (1992): 23–34.

State and Local Censuses: Many states conducted their own censuses. Like the federal censuses, both the manuscript schedules and the summary reports are extremely useful. In addition to the states, some cities, such as Boston, conducted censuses. State and local manuscript schedules suffer from limited availability—most are not even microfilmed and many are not held in a central location. New York, for example, took regular censuses from 1825 to 1925. After tallying, the schedules were returned to the county clerks. Very few counties have preserved complete runs of the schedules entrusted to them, without missing years or damage. Indexes for state censuses are very rare, although the occasional county or town may have been indexed by a local group or individual. *Library of Congress, Census Library Project, State Censuses: An Annotated Bibliography of Censuses of Population Taken after the Year 1790 by States and Territories of the United States,* prepared by Henry J. Dubester (1948) is the standard bibliography of the published reports. All the censuses listed in this work have been microfilmed. For state censuses, see *Microfiche Collection of Censuses of Population Taken after the Year 1790 by States and Territories of the United States* (1970).

A very useful companion volume for the schedules has been prepared by Anne S. Lainart, *State Census Records* (1992), who provides information on availability and additional bibliographies, along with extensive annotations. For a briefer overview, see Szucs, op. cit., 134–36.

The Electronic Census: Microfilm technology and indexing of the federal censuses dramatically increased accessibility to census information. An even more dramatic rise in historians' ability to gather and analyze information from previous censuses took place with the advent of the personal computer and high-speed networks. Many printed indexes were entered into machine-readable databases that are readable by personal computers or could be delivered over the Internet. Since the indexes were created mostly for genealogical purposes, they were limited to searches by name, frequently only the head of the household, and couldn't be searched by other attributes such as age, race, and occupation. Nevertheless, several academic researchers and historians have constructed elaborate databases for local geographic units by keying in all the information on the manuscript returns into modern survey or statistical software.

As increasingly accurate scanning equipment and optical character recognition software were developed, it has become possible to develop databases based on the historical schedules with additional content. These can then be enhanced with other sources of information, such as maps, nonpopulation schedules, voting records, tax lists, or any other individualized information.

The last fifteen years have seen the production of databases containing all the records of all the censuses. The schedules have been through several iterations of transcription, each iteration producing records with increasing numbers of attributes. When the records are indexed the result is that searches can be segmented in very powerful ways, and search times are blazingly fast. For example, one can easily produce a list of all the Hungarian-born people in Harrisburg, Pennsylvania, in 1910; this list, exported to a spreadsheet, can be further analyzed. The same list can be produced for all of Pennsylvania and for multiple censuses.

At the same time the records of individuals are now more discoverable than ever, due to the development of sophisticated search interfaces and algorithms. *Ancestry.com, the genealogical information site, followed closely by *FamilySearch, has led the way in putting powerful search engines in front of huge collections of data. Now one can search for an individual by any number of attributes at varying levels of specificity and confidence.

Distribution of census information now takes place over the Internet on the World Wide Web. Databases of census records residing on servers in many different locations can now be searched from personal computers anywhere in the world. Page images of the census schedules can also be distributed along with the data. Access to the images allows researchers to validate the transcription and develop contexts of community and neighborhood.

Ambitious projects are under way that will utilize the newly accessible census information in new and compelling ways. One notable early example is Edward L. Ayers, Anne S. Rubin, and William G. Thomas, *In the *Valley of the Shadow* http://valley.lib.virginia.edu. This project has cross-linked the indexes from 1840 and 1850 censuses for two counties, one in the Virginia's Shenandoah Valley and another in Pennsylvania, and added information

from other manuscript sources such as church records.

The University of Minnesota's National Geographic Information System presents county-level and some tract-level data from summary reports from 1790 to 2015 (www.nhgis.org).

The personal computer, distributed storage, powerful search algorithms, and high-speed Internet have combined to make more census data available more quickly and in more useful formats than ever before.

Robert Kibbee
The History Center in Tompkins County (NY)

See children's history; demography; ethnography; family history; genealogical resources online; genealogy, African American; genealogy, Jewish; household; slave schedules; Soundex.

Central and South Americans in North America, sources for. See Appendix A.

chattel. The word comes from the Latin for cattle and refers to articles of personal property both animate and inanimate.

Chicago Historical Society. See ethics and local history; labor history and the history of communities.

children's history. Children's history is, like its namesake, a relatively young field. Until recent decades, adults were the focus of almost all historical research. Beginning in the 1960s, as historians began to examine the lives of those ordinary Americans who had been at the margins of more traditional histories (such as people of color, workers, and women), children also began to become subjects of historical analysis. Historians in the field explore a number of interrelated issues: the meaning of childhood as a concept, the history of how adults have treated children, and the history of how children themselves have experienced their youth. The field's relative youth offers opportunities for scholars of local history to forge original and exciting paths of research.

While all humans pass through childhood on the way to adulthood, this period of life is both culturally and biologically constituted. The meaning of childhood has varied in the context of particular communities, circumstances, and generations. The experiences and expectations of Italian-American immigrant children of the early twentieth century, for example, differed significantly from those of white children of the colonial period, and of young enslaved African Americans of the eighteenth and nineteenth centuries. The histories of children living on farms and those growing up in large cities have been distinctive. Girls and boys have often played different games, been assigned distinct chores, and been inculcated in gender-specific expectations for their future lives as adults. Over time, factors such as decreased infant mortality, fewer siblings, longer schooling, and rising rates of divorce have affected family life. The secondary literature (see sources suggested below) allows local historians to put their own evidence into the context of national trends. In many cases, the childhood practices of individual towns or regions correspond to broader social norms,

but in some instances, local practices reflect issues specific to one community or region. Even within a study of any single group, local historians are likely to uncover some degree of diversity of adult expectations for children and of children's experience.

The terms we use to describe youthful age cohorts reflect the varied ways in which we measure youth. Today, for example, we might consider seventeen-year-olds to be children; define them more specifically as adolescents or teens; think of them as legal minors; or understand them as young women and young men. Historically, adults and children have also described stages of youth somewhat variably across time and cultural differences. Secondary reading is thus invaluable in determining the relative relevance of current definitions to specific historical contexts.

Within a particular community, the intergenerational transmission of cultural values from adults to children has much to tell us about a given society's ideas and attitudes. Seemingly simple questions can reveal much about the larger culture. When and where were children expected to be silent unless spoken to at the dinner table, to earn money for the family at a young age, or to achieve high levels of education? How, when, and why did such customs shift? And what does children's own peer transmission of games, songs, and codes of friendship tell us about their particular historical moment and the future expectations that shaped their young lives? If the history of childhood offers a unique perspective on local history, it also speaks to larger national concerns, including family life, education, sexuality, leisure, labor, and preparation for adult citizenship.

Before undertaking a children's history project, researchers might consider the resources that are likely to be available. One person might be interested in child care, another might look at Girl Scout troops, a third might explore high school dances. Available source materials for each of these projects will likely differ. Children, especially young children, have left behind few of the documents that historians might normally use as evidence, such as laws or published speeches; in general, the younger the cohort of the children under consideration, the harder it is to uncover their own voices. A project about babies might uncover extensive evidence, including birth records, child-rearing manuals, and evidence of child-care arrangements, but would be unlikely to discover much about the feelings of babies themselves. Studies of older children, on the other hand, may provide better access to evidence of youthful self-representation (sometimes mediated by adults): school yearbooks, youthful fashions, diaries, oral histories, and newspaper descriptions of dances, parties, and youth groups. Historians of twentieth-century childhood generally have better access to a wider range of material than do scholars investigating earlier periods.

The following suggestions for research are not all-inclusive, but they are meant to underscore the variety of documents that local historians can use to write children's history, whether a study of adult ideas about children, an excavation of children's experiences, or both.

Prescriptive literature, such as child-care manuals and educational treatises, illuminates adult ideas about how to raise children. What kinds of child-rearing manuals or precepts were considered valuable among the adults of your study? What did these treatises propose? To what degree were these ideas debated locally, and how did their authors' advice change over time (or in subsequent editions of popular texts)?

Many local newspapers and magazines have written about special events in the lives of children, such as the first day of school, summer recreation, sports events, and dances. How did the local newspaper describe appropriate (and inappropriate) parenting or childhood behavior? Was there a children's column or another venue for local children to participate in the print media, or were children interviewed in local news sources?

Laws governing childhood have varied from locality to locality. What kind of child-labor legislation was proposed or enacted? At what age were girls and boys allowed to marry, leave school, drive a car, or consume alcoholic beverages? When were schools racially segregated or integrated? Under what conditions was corporal punishment or juvenile detention allowed? More broadly, when and why did these laws come into being? Why did they change, what kind of resistance did these changes meet, and how did such changes reflect larger community or national trends?

Educational trends reveal much about communities' economic opportunities and social expectations. When was the first local school built? The first high school? What were the physical conditions of schooling? What kinds of textbooks were used, and what pedagogical methods did teachers emphasize? Which children attended school, and for how long? What do we learn from these facts about children's socioeconomic expectations, and the impact of gender, race, and ethnicity? Which facets of education changed over time, and what do such shifts suggest about the expectations of the larger society? Did the school maintain a newspaper, a yearbook, or prize-winning compositions, any of which might provide insight into student life?

Institutional records, such as the records of orphanages, youth groups, social service providers, and juvenile detention centers, are often fairly accessible. While these collections often focus more on adult perspectives, historians may find children's voices represented here as well. What kinds of programs did churches, synagogues, and mosques run? What kinds of services and activities did local branches of the Boy Scouts, 4-H clubs, or Camp Fire Girls offer? When were these institutional programs founded, reorganized, or shuttered, and why? What did participation in these groups mean for the children who took part in them?

*Oral histories provide valuable firsthand information about childhood, by allowing access to the kinds of personal stories that are often absent from the public record. Some localities have repositories of already extant oral histories; in other cases, researchers may wish to undertake personal interviews.

Municipal records, including lists of births and deaths and records of juvenile crime, are also revealing. How many children were born to a family during a particular period, and what was the prevalence of infant mortality? Were grown children likely to stay or to leave the town in which they grew up? How do the answers to these questions differ by race, gender, ethnic group, or economic class, and what do those differences tell us about the community as a whole?

The *material culture and *folklore of childhood illustrate how children were represented—for example, in photographs and paintings—while offering clues about children's experience. What were the material conditions of children's lives? Did they share a bed, have their own room, have many toys and clothes or only a few? Where and when did they play? What were considered appropriate playthings for particular children, and why? The culture that children themselves propagated is a rich resource for historical study. What toys did young people make for themselves, what songs did they sing, what clubs or sports did they initiate, and what do these artifacts tell us about how children understood their world?

See Joe Austin and Michael Nevin Willard, eds., *Generations of Youth: Youth Cultures and History in Twentieth-Century America* (1998); Karin Calvert, *Children in the House: The Material Culture of Early Childhood, 1600–1900* (1992); Paula S. Fass and Michael Grossberg, *Reinventing Childhood After World War II* (2011); Miriam Forman-Brunell and Leslie Paris, *The Girls' History and Culture Reader* (2011, vols. 1 and 2); N. Ray Hiner and Joseph M. Hawes, eds., *Growing up in America: Children in Historical Perspective* (1985); Steven Mintz, *Huck's Raft: A History of American Childhood* (2004); Grace Palladino, *Teenagers: An American History* (1996); Peter N. Stearns, *Anxious Parents: A History of Modern Childrearing in America* (2003); Elliott West and Paula Petrik, eds., *Small Worlds: Children and Adolescents in America, 1850–1950* (1992); and Elliott West, *Growing Up in Twentieth-Century America: A History and Reference Guide* (1996).

LESLIE PARIS
UNIVERSITY OF BRITISH COLUMBIA

See family history.

Chinese in North America, sources for. Appendix A.

Church of England, sources for. See Episcopal Church, Appendix B.

city. A large or important settlement. The word comes from "see" (from the Latin sedes, meaning "seat") or the seat of a bishop. The term is often used to distinguish an urban area from the surrounding countryside. Legally, a city is distinguished by its size, the fact that it has governmental power derived from the state, that it is incorporated, and that it has legally defined boundaries.

city directories. City directories are one of the local historian's great treasures. They can be a source of simple information regarding a specific person or site, or they can be used for studies that can explore a wide variety of topics.

City directories appeared on the scene very early in the nation's history. It is likely that the first one was published in Baltimore in 1752; directories then appeared in Charleston, South Carolina, in 1782 and 1785. By the nineteenth century many communities had city directories, and they were popular until replaced by the ubiquitous telephone directory. Even after the rise of the "phone book" they have continued in many cities in a variety of forms. The presence of a recent directory may be determined by consulting James A. Ethridge, ed., *Directories of Directories* (1983) but it will only list those in print at the time of its publication. The best places for local historians to locate pertinent local directories would be the local library or historical society.

The information that directories provide the local historian varies. Some simply list name and street address. Most will list occupation—sometimes a simple designation such as "merchant," "chandler," "carpenter," and at other times a descriptive title and even where the subject is employed. Some will list a spouse's name, and, of course, later a telephone number. These directories were (and are) published primarily for business use, so they reflect that bias. They tend to slight nonwhites, ethnic minorities, and unskilled laborers, and often do not list women unless they are business owners. Obviously they list some information that might also be in a U.S. manuscript *census, but city directories are likely to be published annually (unlike the decennial census), and may include additional information helpful in seeking biographical information, data on a building (for an application for historical-site status, for example), or about a neighborhood.

City directories can also be used for more complicated and sophisticated research on localities or communities. For instance, Judith Liu used the city directories to find the location of Chinese laundries in San Diego, and to note the transitory nature of the Chinese population in that city (Judith Liu, "Celestials in the Golden Mountain: The Chinese in One California City, San Diego, 1870–1900," master's thesis, San Diego State University, 1977). Don H. Doyle used the city directories to tabulate the social characteristics of Nashville's economic leaders in *Nashville in the New South* (1985). Stephen R. Thernstrom and Peter R. Knight's "Man in Motion: Some Data and Speculations about Urban Population Mobility in Nineteenth-Century America" in *Anonymous Americans: Explorations in Nineteenth-Century Social History*, ed. Tamara K. Hareven (1971), 17–47 provides a succinct example of the use of directories, along with other sources, to measure in- and out-migration in a locality. Each of these historians also published more extensive studies using city directories and related sources (see Knight's *Plain People of Boston, 1830–1860* [1971]; and Thernstrom's *The Other Bostonians* [1973], which are regarded as models of this kind of methodology).

David Kyvig and Myron Marty give a good, brief introduction to city directories and a bibliography on them in *Nearby History: Exploring the Past Around You* (1982), 72–73 and 85. More detail can be found in Gordon Lewis Remington, "City Directories and their Cousins," in *The Source: A Guidebook of American Genealogy*, ed. Arlene Eakle and Johni Cerny (1984), 387–404. The most extensive essays on problems of using city directories for social history are the essays in the back of the books by Knight and Thernstrom; they are especially helpful in indicating the limits of city directories as a source for local history. Those limitations, however, should not obscure the fact that city directories are one of the most valuable tools available for the local historian. U.S. city directories from 1822–1995 are searchable at *Ancestry.com (subscription required). See also http://microformguides.gale.com/SearchForm.asp and *United States City Directories, 1861–1901*, available on microfilm (1977).

RAYMOND STARR
UPDATED BY ROBERT KIBBEE
HISTORY CENTER IN
TOMPKINS COUNTY (NY)

Civil War federal tax records. Historical data about the wealth of a community and of its individual property holders may be found in tax, land, probate, census, and credit records. However, those records provide only clues as to disposable income. Since 1913 the federal government has levied a tax on personal incomes, and the states began adopting income taxes around the same time. Both federal and state income-tax returns are confidential, and they are destroyed after audit and legal requirements have been satisfied. Fortunately the records of an earlier federal income tax, imposed during and immediately after the Civil War, are in the *National Archives and are available for research.

Before the Civil War, the U.S. government operated on revenue generated mostly by customs duties, land sales, and occasional excise taxes on liquor. During the Civil War years, the federal government had to find massive new revenues to help pay for the huge cost of the war and also to fund the growing national debt and stabilize the currency. In August 1861 Congress authorized a 3 percent tax on incomes over $800 per year. This tax was never implemented; it was supplanted by a revised income tax that was part of an omnibus "internal revenue" act passed in July 1862. This act imposed a plethora of new taxes, some of them still unmatched in their fiscal creativity. Businesses paid monthly duties on a wide range of products, "from ale to zinc." There were monthly taxes on the receipts of canal and ferry boats, and railroad and steamboat lines; on the surpluses of banking and insurance companies; and on auction sales. Proprietors of almost every kind of retail and financial business, as well as professionals like lawyers and physicians, had to pay a yearly license fee. Licenses were also required of hotels, taverns, restaurants, theaters, circuses, billiard halls, and bowling alleys. Every deed, mortgage, contract, stock, bond, pack of playing cards, and bottle of medicine or perfume had to bear an Internal Revenue adhesive stamp. Luxury possessions like carriages, yachts, gold and silver plate, gold watches, pianos, and parlor organs were taxed. Of course, alcoholic beverages and tobacco products were taxed. Even newspaper advertisements were taxed.

The income-tax rates were initially 3 percent on incomes over $600, and 5 percent on incomes over $10,000 per year. In 1864 the rates were increased to 5 percent on incomes over $600, and 10 percent over $5,000. Collection of the income, excise, and direct taxes and duties was the responsibility of a Commissioner of Internal Revenue in the

U.S. Treasury Department. Every state and territory under federal control was divided into one or more collection districts, each with an appointed collector and assessor. Taxpayers were required to submit lengthy, complicated forms listing their incomes and any items or transactions that were subject to tax or duty. Assistant assessors in each community compiled summary lists from the individual tax returns. Both the lists and the taxpayers' returns were forwarded to Washington. The internal revenue taxes remained in force for several years after the Civil War. Most of them, including the income tax but excepting excise taxes on liquor and tobacco, were repealed in 1872, effective July 1873. The individual tax returns were destroyed in 1895, but the summary assessment lists are today in the National Archives (Record Group 58).

The lists are organized by state, then by collection district, then by county, then by year. Annual and monthly lists for each county enumerate the taxes and duties paid in those periods. Like other records containing data on wealth, the Internal Revenue assessment lists from the 1860s must be used with caution. Most individuals paid no income tax, because of the $600 exemption and other deductions. However, the lists do identify the wealthier individuals in a community. The successive returns for 1863, 1864, and 1865 often indicate increasing incomes, the result of wartime prosperity and currency inflation. The listing of taxable items like gold watches and reed organs is an interesting indicator of middle-class aspirations. Assessment lists for a sample community in western New York often list such items for individual taxpayers for only one year; evidently the owners thought they should pay the tax on these prized possessions only once! The assessments on businesses likewise must be used with care, since few Internal Revenue employees were hired to enforce the laws. Another source of bias in the records is the fact that the district collectors, assessors, and assistant assessors were political appointees, not all of whom may have been completely honest.

The Internal Revenue assessment lists for the states and territories for the period 1862–1866 (excluding several Southern states) are available on microfilm and *digitized by *Ancestry. The subsequent assessment lists for income and direct taxes through 1872 (when they were discontinued), and for the remaining excise taxes through the end of the century are available at the National Archives. Overall the nineteenth-century Internal Revenue assessment lists are an abundant source of economic and social data for the community historian.

See Cynthia G. Fox, "Income Tax Records of the Civil War Years," *Prologue: Quarterly of the National Archives* 18, no.4 (Winter 1986): 250–59, reprinted in *Our Family, Our Town: Essays on Family and Local History Sources in the National Archives*, ed. Timothy Walch (1987), 141–46; Kenneth W. Munden and Henry Putney Beers, *The Union: A Guide to Federal Archives Relating to the Civil War* ([1962] 1986), 204–11; Robert B. Matchette and others, comps., *Guide to Federal Records in the National Archives of the United States*, 3 vols. (1995), Record Group 58, "Records of the Internal Revenue Service"; *Guide to Genealogical Research in the National Archives*, 3rd ed. (2000), 334.

James D. Folts
New York State Archives

Civil War nurses. See nurses, civil war.

clan. In the discipline of anthropology, a clan is defined as a genealogically related corporate group whose members reckon descent from a common ancestor. The founding ancestor may be a human being, a supernatural being, or a totem (an entity in the natural world such as an animal, plant, or heavenly body). The founding ancestor's name (eponym) identifies the clan and their descendants and ascendants as a related group. In its simplest manifestation, the clan reckons its line of descent only through persons of one sex. If the clan is matrilineal, then descent is reckoned solely through women. Thus, a woman's husband is not a member of her matriclan, but belongs to his own matrilineal clan. The matrilineal descent group (the matriline) is composed solely of women, their brothers, and the women's children. These persons are viewed as the consanguineal group (people who share the same blood). Following this logic, clan-brothers' children are not members of their fathers' matriclan, but belong to a distinct clan: that of their mothers. Neither of the sexes may marry a person within their own clan, but must marry "out" to persons of a different clan (a practice termed *exogamy*). Male members of a matriclan usually assume the political leadership (as among the Iroquois or the Hopi of North America) although opinions of older women are sought and are important factors in clan decision making.

The organization of a patrilineal clan mirrors that of the matriclan, such that the rules of descent are reversed. Patriclan membership is reckoned only through men and their children. Although sisters are members of the patriline, the children they bear are not: they belong to their fathers' patriline, and clan-exogamy is the rule.

In the United States and Canada, many families have surnames reflecting descent from Gaelic patriclans. Ancient clan names were said to be originally taken from chiefs, who were land-holders, and each clan was distinguished by its unique tartan plaid worn as kilts and other clothing. Clans organized economic, social, and political life. In Scotland, patriclans practiced "fosterage"—the custom of sending offspring to be raised in other clans such as that of their mother's brother. This practice was thought to create strong inter-clan ties. Clan names were not necessarily passed on through lines of descent; they often were adopted by persons who lived and worked on clan lands.

Demographically, throughout the world, patriclan organization is predominant, but matriclans still exist and are widely distributed. For centuries, clan-forms of organization have guided the social and political lives of human groups, and also organized conflicts with other groups. Of interest to local historians is their presence in Native American communities in the past and present.

The term *clan* is loosely used in U.S. society today. It often is employed to describe a family line of women and men reaching back through only two or three generations. This common usage does not follow the identifying rule of a true clan: descent traced through only one sex. Some U.S. "clans" were notorious, such as the outlaw clans of the Western frontier during the eighteenth and nineteenth centuries, or the much publicized feud between the Hatfield and McCoy clans who lived in the mountains of Kentucky and West Virginia. A local historian will find that clan-like associations (in terms of mutual support, responsibilities, and loyalties) often are used in contemporary social clubs, whose members identify themselves fictively as "brothers" or "sisters."

Many of the laws governing marital relationships in Western nations were originally written under the assumption of patriarchal dominance. A trace of patrilineality is retained in U.S. naming practices in that at marriage, a woman takes her husband's surname, and the children of the marriage bear only their father's surname.

LAURIS MCKEE
FRANKLIN AND MARSHALL COLLEGE

class. See social class.

Colorado, local history in. The study and preservation of history in Colorado dates back to the late 1800s when the leading citizens of Denver established the first pioneer association to document their contributions to the state's development. A spate of history volumes followed telling part of the story of Colorado and its communities. Since the 1970s there have been significant additions to the story. On all fronts the

This marker tells the story of Redstone, Colorado, a company town founded in 1901. Credit: History Colorado.

narrative has become more complex, more inclusive, and more nuanced, as voices and regions of the state, once silent, begin to speak out.

The flagship historical organization in Colorado is the Colorado Historical Society, rebranded as History Colorado. After losing its thirty-year home in downtown Denver, in spring of 2012 it moved into a new, state-of-the-art building at Twelfth and Broadway Streets. History Colorado has been presenting cutting-edge interpretive exhibits that document both well-known and new areas of Colorado. However in mid-2015 it had a major shake-up that left the innovative exhibit focus in jeopardy. A new board seemed intent on returning History Colorado's exhibits to an earlier focus that would be more artifact-centered and less interpretive.

The society houses the Office of Archeology and Historic Preservation and the State Historic Fund, which grants historic preservation money to communities. In addition to its main building, History Colorado has branch sites in Denver and around the state. The education staff of History Colorado collaborates with schools to initiate innovative and inclusive programs. History Colorado's extensive Stephen Hart Library is one of the most sought-after research facilities in the state.

Most communities in Colorado have museums dedicated to interpreting local heritage. Denver, the largest city in the state, is not one of them. Some especially notable community museums are the Smithsonian affiliate Littleton Historical Museum, the Museum of Western Colorado in Grand Junction, the Greeley History Museums, and the Longmont Museum and Cultural Center. These are city-funded institutions with professionally trained staffs. Many other museums have small paid and volunteer staffs who struggle with budgetary challenges, while still providing significant historical services to their communities. The museums on the state's Eastern Plains have developed a collaborative association that provides joint marketing and other benefits to its members.

Some museums specialize in Colorado's industrial or economic past. The Leadville-based National Mining Hall of Fame and Museum, and the Western Museum of Mining and Industry near Colorado Springs detail the state's extensive mining history. The Colorado Railroad Museum in Golden interprets the state's rail history.

In southern Colorado the San Luis Museum tells the story of the Hispano heritage of the San Luis Valley. The Southern Ute Cultural Center and Museum in Ignacio and the Ute Mountain Ute Indian Museum in Montrose pass tribal history and traditions to the younger generations and to visitors.

History and historic preservation are well represented by Colorado nonprofits. The Colorado Wyoming Association of Museums (CWAM) is a two-state organization that provides training and resources for the museums in the two states and features a guide to Colorado museums and cultural sites on its website. It also offers specialists on tap for consultations with local museums. Denver-based Colorado Preservation Incorporated holds an annual meeting each February, which brings together preservationists from around the state. Historic Denver has long been a leader in the historic preservation movement in Denver, now running the Molly Brown House Museum.

Colorado has diverse archeological and historical sites. The *National Park Service runs Mesa Verde, the Great Sand Dunes, and Rocky Mountain National Park, which in 2015 celebrated its centennial. Crow Canyon is a southwestern Colorado nonprofit that offers tours and school programs. Many local living history parks around the state highlight people and places dear to the residents. Sites such as Denver's Four Mile Historic Park educate through living history programs, often with trained living historians provide quality living history experiences for visitors.

Colorado's books on state, regional, and local history number in the thousands. Fort Lewis College Emeritus Professor Duane Smith has written over forty books on mining and local history. University of Colorado–Denver Professor Thomas Noel publishes on many Colorado subjects but is increasingly focused on the histories of Denver-area institutions. Patricia Limerick has trained a generation of historians who are now writing refreshingly nuanced histories of Colorado. University Press of Colorado and Fulcrum Publishing specialize in Colorado history topics.

In 2009 the Center for Colorado and the West opened at the Auraria Library in Denver. At the University of Colorado–Boulder, the Center of the American West, presided over by Professor Limerick, produces programs and publications that promote a broadly interdisciplinary approach to Western and Colorado history. The Colorado State Archives has a large repository of documents on state and local government. For those doing virtually any kind of research on Colorado or American

Western history, the Denver Public Library Western History and Genealogy Department is a central repository. Its breadth of collections as well as knowledgeable and helpful staff make this an especially important resource.

The Colorado State Board of Education's standards continue to require that all fourth graders in public schools study Colorado history. Many school districts also offer community history in the third grade. The fourth-grade Colorado history requirement has helped stimulate robust enrollment in the Colorado history courses of the state's colleges and universities. This has encouraged academics to focus on Colorado history as an area of specialty, broadening new scholarship in the field. All public universities in Colorado that offer a master's degree have an option that emphasizes Colorado history.

In a state with a chronic shortage of money for history education, collaboration is becoming standard practice. History Colorado has developed partnerships that share the organization's experience and extensive program materials with museums and schools in the state's many cultural regions.

In Colorado, history continues to draw millions of visitors to the state's historical places. Cultural destinations provide a bigger boost to tax revenues than sports and draw new residents to the state. Coloradoans value their heritage.

REBECCA A. HUNT
UNIVERSITY OF COLORADO–DENVER

See United States, local history in.

commonwealth. A commonwealth is a body of people of an area organized as a community or a state; the archaic term was "commonweal," meaning of the general welfare. In the United States, Massachusetts, Pennsylvania, Virginia, and Kentucky are officially designated commonwealths.

company town. A town where the majority of the housing and commercial area is owned by a single employer or group of employers. The town may or may not be incorporated, and the employer may or may not be a benevolent landlord. Companies built housing for their workers for a variety of reasons: to attract employees, to stabilize the workforce and reduce turnover, to have additional power over workers through threats of eviction, and to turn a profit on the housing. The opposition of unions to company towns has reduced the number of company towns in the United States. The history of company towns is often marked by stresses other towns do not face.

Conference of State and Local Historical Societies. The Conference of State and Local Historical Societies (also known as the Conference of Historical Societies) was an organization of primarily state historical societies in the Midwest and the western part of the United States in the first half of the twentieth century. The group was formed as a subcommittee of the *American Historical Association (AHA), when a call went out from the association's program committee to meet during the 1904 annual meeting of the AHA in Chicago.

The conference was formed in response to the growing number of historical societies in the Midwest and West that differed greatly from the traditional eastern models. Whereas the older, eastern historical societies were private institutions supported by membership and charged with producing publications, the newer historical societies focused on funding, structure, and purpose. Many of the western historical societies were state-supported institutions—often tied to land-grant universities—with a mandate to collect, preserve, and disseminate state history for the masses.

The conference met regularly with the AHA, having its own opportunities to network and air common concerns of collecting and publishing primary resources, working with the local historical societies in their respective states, and finding better ways to forge bonds with the academic, political, public, and amateur communities. Eventually the latter would drift off—more from their disconnect to the AHA than to the conference.

As professionalism grew within state, and to some degree the larger local historical societies, the ranks of the conference grew. However, relations with the AHA continued to grow more distant as the needs of academic historians and the needs of public historians drifted apart—and with that the need to rely on each other. Members of the Conference of Historical Societies started to focus more on services to the public and the collection and administration of local history, especially as the United States entered the Great Depression. Government supported agencies also looked for ways they could serve those needs within the new federal aid pro-

grams—issues of less concern to its parent organization. Eventually the separation of the conference and the AHA grew to the point where the conference members agreed to split themselves off from the AHA in 1940. Meeting now on their own, the group renamed itself the *American Association for State and Local History (AASLH).

HARRY KLINKHAMER
INDEPENDENT PUBLIC HISTORIAN

See American Association of State and Local History; American Historical Association.

Congregational church, sources for. See United Church of Christ, Appendix B.

Connecticut, local history in. Connecticut is the third smallest state in the United States. Despite one's ability to traverse the state in any direction in under two hours, Connecticut is very diverse in its geography, culture, and history. This diversity is either the cause or the result of a history of fierce independence among the state's citizenry. Connecticut has never had a strong overarching authority. More than twenty self-identified Native American tribes occupied the state prior to the Dutch and English outposts that were established in 1633. In 1636, the English took control of the Connecticut River Valley, establishing the Connecticut Colony, and later King Charles II merged this colony with two other colonial claims (Saybrook Colony in 1644 and New Haven Colony in 1662). Despite the consolidation of colonial government, Connecticut has historically been

This marker presents some of the interesting history of West Hartford, Connecticut. CREDIT: CONNECTICUT HISTORICAL SOCIETY.

reluctant to cede local control to regional or statewide authority. Connecticut held two capitals from 1701 until 1874, separating governmental departments and responsibilities between Hartford and New Haven. The state is divided into eight counties that are little more than lines on a map. Local government is firmly established in 169 towns, most of which operate independent school systems and police departments. For many citizens, individual identity is grounded in the town where they live. This sense of localism is apparent in Connecticut's history and cultural landscape.

There are three statewide organizations dedicated to collecting and sharing the state's history including the Connecticut Historical Society (Hartford), the State Library of Connecticut, which houses the Museum of Connecticut History (Hartford), and the Thomas J. Dodd Research Center at the University of Connecticut (Storrs). These organizations, along with the many local historical societies, museums, and historic sites are supported by the Connecticut League of History Organizations and Connecticut Humanities (Middletown).

Connecticut houses nearly four hundred organizations that are dedicated to local or regional history. These organizations range from the large multifaceted Mystic Seaport, to the "history room" in the Suffield Library. Most of these organizations are small, operating with an all-volunteer staff and an annual budget of less than $5,000, but there are a number of organizations with substantial budgets and collections that employ professionally trained staff who operate facilities with regular public hours.

Beyond historical societies dedicated to location-based history, Connecticut is home to a host of ethnic and topical institutions that house historical collections. While some of these organizations do not expressly identify their purpose as historical, they hold and provide access to important collections. Examples of organizations dedicated to identity and history include the Mashantucket Pequot Museum & Research Center (Mashantucket), the museum and archive at the American School for the Deaf (Hartford), and the West Indian Social Club (Hartford). Topical museums in the state include the Vintage Radio and Communication Museum (Windsor), the American Watch and Clock Museum (Bristol), and the Dan-

bury Railway Museum (Danbury). While these organizations' names connote a regional or national significance, they are located in a town that claims to be home to some significant discovery or personality that propelled the topic in question.

Connecticut holds a strong predilection toward historic preservation. Three organizations lead statewide preservation efforts: the State Historic Preservation Office (SHPO), the Connecticut Trust for Historic Preservation (CTHP), and Connecticut Landmarks (CTL). The SHPO is a governmental agency within the Department of Economic and Community Development; it provides technical and grant-making support across the state. The CTHP operates as a public/private partnership and supports local and statewide preservation activities through advocacy, field service, resource development, and grant making. The CTL owns and operates a set of important and critical historic structures and landscapes throughout the state.

Statewide preservation efforts are bolstered by a host of local preservation organizations including the Hartford Preservation Alliance, the New Haven Preservation Trust, and many others. Due to the efforts of these organizations and an active public interest, Connecticut houses some nationally important historic sites such as the Mark Twain House, the Harriet Beecher Stowe House, and Connecticut's Old State House (Hartford); Phillip Johnson's Glass House (New Canaan); the Prudence Crandall Home (Canterbury); and the Noah Webster House (West Hartford).

While the last overarching work about Connecticut's history was published in 1979 as a part of The States and the Nation series, the state's scholarly community is active through a number of organizations that publish and promote history. These include the Association for the Study of Connecticut History, which holds two annual conferences and publishes *Connecticut History Review*; the Connecticut Coordinating Committee for the Promotion of History, which serves as one of the history community's advocacy groups; and the Acorn Club, a group founded in 1899 to "publish books of the enduring value about Connecticut history." In terms of academic archives and libraries, both Yale's Bienecke Rare Books and Manuscript Library and Trinity's Watkinson Library and College Archives supplement the significant archival holdings at the Connecticut Historical Society and the University of Connecticut as academic research collections.

Connecting each of these groups and organizations is the Office of the State Historian, established in 1930 and housed at the University of Connecticut. Dr. Walter Woodward has held this post since 2004. The State Historian publishes, promotes, and shares the state's history with citizens and organizations across Connecticut.

While Connecticut ranks as one of the nation's smallest in terms of geographic size, it surely ranks among the largest in terms of historical resources.

JODY BLANKENSHIP
CONNECTICUT HISTORICAL SOCIETY

See United States, local history in.

copyright. Copyright law governs the rights of authors, publishers, and users of artistic works, such as books, songs, plays, movies, choreography, photographs, paintings, sculpture, sound recordings, and works of architecture. A copyright is a legal right to control the reproduction and dissemination of an artistic work. In many countries, a copyright is considered to be a natural right of the author. In the United States, however, copyrights are granted to promote the public welfare by giving authors and publishers an economic incentive to create and publish new artistic works.

Under the Copyright Act of 1976, the author of an artistic work is granted the exclusive right to reproduce the copyrighted work, to distribute copies of the copyrighted work to the public, to perform or display the copyrighted work publicly, and to prepare derivative works (such as translations or adaptations) based upon the copyrighted work. These exclusive rights, however, are subject to a number of important limitations that are designed to balance the rights of authors against the rights of consumers, and to ensure that copyright does not unreasonably restrict the rights of others to freely express themselves.

First, copyright protection extends only to those elements of a copyrighted work that are original to the author. For example, because facts are not created by the author of a copyrighted work, the copyright does not prevent a second author from copying those facts, even if the first author was the first person to discover or report those facts. Instead, copyright protects only the author's original expression of those facts. Thus, one author can prevent another author from using the same sentences and paragraphs used by the first author (or a close paraphrase of them), but he or she cannot prevent the second author from expressing the same facts in his or her own words.

Second, copyright protection does not extend to any idea, procedure, process, system, method of operation, concept, principle, or discovery that is contained in the copyrighted work, even if those concepts or ideas are original to the first author. Instead, copyright protects only the author's original expression of those ideas. According to the U.S. Supreme Court, this limitation on copyright law (known as the idea/expression dichotomy) is necessary to ensure that the Copyright Act does not violate the rights of free speech and press that are guaranteed by the First Amendment.

Third, copyright protection is subject to a number of express exceptions contained in the statute. For example, libraries and archives are permitted to make copies of copyrighted works under certain circumstances. Schools and churches are permitted to perform or display certain works publicly in the course of classroom teaching activities and religious services, respectively. Certain nondramatic works may be performed publicly if no admission is charged or if the proceeds are used exclusively for educational, religious, or charitable purposes. The act also contains comprehensive, highly detailed and technical provisions governing the retransmission of copyrighted works by hotels and apartments, cable-television systems, and satellite broadcasters.

One of the most important limitations on the exclusive rights of the author is the first sale doctrine. The first sale doctrine permits the lawful owner of an authorized copy of a copyrighted work (including the original) to display that copy publicly, or to lend or sell that copy to anyone else, without the permission of the copyright owner. An exception to the first sale doctrine, however, prohibits the commercial rental or lease of sound recordings and computer programs, in order to prevent consumers from renting those works for the purpose of making unauthorized copies at home.

Finally, copyright protection is subject to the fair use doctrine, which permits a second author to use some original expression from a copyrighted work in creating a new work, where doing so would not unreasonably interfere with the copyright owner's ability to sell or license the copyrighted work. Examples include the use of quotations in a review of a book, and exaggerated imitation in a parody of the original work.

The fair use doctrine was originally developed in judicial opinions, and was later codified in Section 107 of the Copyright Act. Section 107 does not attempt to define fair use, but it lists several potential examples and directs courts to consider four factors in determining whether a use is fair. The first factor is the purpose and character of the use: transformative uses, in which the copied material is used as a small portion of a new work or for a substantially different purpose than the original, are more likely to be fair uses than superseding uses, in which the material is copied without change or comment; and noncommercial or educational uses are more likely to be fair uses than commercial uses. The illustrative purposes listed in the statute include criticism, comment, news reporting, teaching (including multiple copies for classroom use), scholarship, and research. The second factor is the nature of the copyrighted work: Copying material from factual works is more likely to be a fair use than copying material from works of fiction; and copying material from published works is more likely to be a fair use than copying material from unpublished works (especially where the unpublished works have the potential to be published by the copyright owner). The third factor is the amount and qualitative importance of the portion used, in relation to the copyrighted work as a whole. Using a relatively small amount of the copyrighted work is more likely to be a fair use than reproduction of the entire work. The fourth factor is the effect of the use upon the potential market for or value of the copyrighted work. If the defendant's use would substantially diminish the revenue that a copyright holder would expect to receive by acting as a substitute for the original work, the use is less likely to be a fair use.

History. Copyright law evolved in England out of efforts by the Crown to control the use of the printing press by granting a monopoly on publishing to the Stationers' Company, a group of London printers and booksellers who were required to submit their publications for approval by official censors. Shortly after the official monopoly expired, Parliament passed the first copyright statute, the Statute of Anne, in 1710. It granted to authors the exclusive right to publish their works for an initial term of fourteen years, renewable for an additional fourteen years. After that, the work passed into the public domain, meaning that anyone was free to copy or publish it.

In 1789, the U.S. Constitution authorized Congress "[t]o Promote the Progress of Science and useful Arts, by securing for limited Times to Authors and Inventors the exclusive Right to their respective Writings and Discoveries." The first Copyright Act in the United States was enacted by Congress in 1790. Comprehensive revisions were made to the Copyright Act in 1831, 1870, 1909, and 1976. The 1976 act has since been amended several times to accommodate new technologies and international trade considerations. Most importantly, in 1988 the United States enacted several amendments to allow joining the Berne Convention, the most important international agreement concerning copyright protection. Additional amendments were made in 1994 to implement the Agreement on Trade-Related Aspects of Intellectual Property (TRIPs) adopted at the Uruguay Round of the General Agreement on Tariffs and Trade (GATT); and in 1998 to implement the World Intellectual Property Organization (WIPO) Copyright Treaty, and the WIPO Performances and Phonograms Treaty.

In general, works created before January 1, 1978, are governed by the 1909 act (with some important modifications in the 1976 act), while works created on or after January 1, 1978, are governed by the 1976 act, as amended. The current provisions of the Copyright Act can be found in the first eight chapters of Title 17 of the United States Code.

Requirements for Protection. To receive copyright protection, a work must be "original." Courts have construed the word "original" to mean only that a work must have been independently created, and that it contain a minimal amount of creativity. Thus, a work that consists entirely of facts or data, or other public domain material, cannot be protected by copyright unless the preexisting material has been selected, coordinated, or arranged in an original way. The author of such a work may receive a copyright in the original compilation, but the copyright protects only the original aspects of the work and does not affect the copyright status of the preexisting material. Likewise, the author of a derivative work (a work based on one or more preexisting works) may receive a copyright if the preexisting material was used lawfully; but the copyright extends only to the original aspects added by the second author.

Under the 1909 act, copyright protection was divided between federal and state law. State law, or common-law copyright, protected a work prior to publication. To receive a federal copyright, the work had to be published with a copyright notice consisting of the word "Copyright" or the symbol ©, the date of first publication, and the name of the copyright owner. If a work was published without notice, the copyright was forfeited and the work entered the public domain. To reduce the number of inadvertent forfeitures, courts distinguished between a general publication (the distribution of copies to any member of the general public), and a

limited publication (the distribution of copies only to a select group of people for a limited purpose). Only a general publication without notice would place the work in the public domain. While the copyright owner was not strictly required to register the copyright with the Copyright Office, he or she could not renew the copyright or bring an action for infringement until the copyright had been registered and a copy or copies of the work had been deposited with the Copyright Office as required by the act.

Publication ceased to be the dividing line between state and federal protection under the 1976 act. For works created on or after January 1, 1978, federal copyright protection attaches as soon as the work is "fixed in a tangible medium of expression." A work is "fixed" when it is recorded in some permanent form. The act allows copyright to protect works fixed in any medium, now known or later developed, regardless of whether technology is needed to perceive or reproduce it. Common-law copyright can still be used to protect works that have not yet been fixed; but for fixed works, the 1976 act preempts all other state laws that provide rights equivalent to those provided by copyright.

The 1976 act retained the requirement of notice when the work was published; however, it permitted the copyright owner to cure the omission of notice in some circumstances. Despite this provision, however, the notice and registration provisions continued to prevent U.S. membership in the Berne Convention, which prohibits conditioning copyright on any such formalities. In order to join the Berne Convention, the United States eliminated the requirement of notice for all works published on or after March 1, 1989. It also eliminated registration as a prerequisite to filing suit for works created by authors from, and first published in, a foreign nation adhering to the Berne Convention. Registration is still a prerequisite to filing suit for works by U.S. authors or works first published in the United States; and the act retains certain procedural and remedial advantages for those who comply with the notice and registration provisions.

Ownership. A copyright is owned initially by the author or authors of the work. The authors of a work of joint authorship are co-owners of the copyright. The "author," however, is not always the person who created the work. Under U.S. law, a work created by an employee acting within the scope of his or her employment is a "work made for hire," and the copyright is owned initially by his or her employer. A specially commissioned work can also be a "work made for hire" if it falls within one of nine categories listed in the statute (such as a motion picture), and if the parties agree in a signed writing that the work shall be a work made for hire. If these requirements are met, the copyright is owned initially by the commissioning party.

A copyright owner may authorize another person to reproduce, adapt, sell, publicly perform, or publicly display the copyrighted work. Such an authorization is called a license. A license may be restricted in duration or geographically, and it may be either exclusive or nonexclusive. A signed writing is required to grant an exclusive license or to transfer a copyright.

Ownership of a copyright is distinct from ownership of the material object in which the work is fixed. Thus, the sale of an original work of art, such as a painting or sculpture, does not transfer the copyright to the buyer. The copyright is retained by the author, and the buyer (such as a museum or gallery) must obtain permission to reproduce the work. Likewise, the recipient of a letter does not have the right to reproduce the letter; the copyright is retained by the original author.

Duration. Like the Statute of Anne, the Copyright Act of 1790 provided for an initial duration of fourteen years from the date of first publication, and the copyright could be renewed for an additional fourteen years. The Copyright Act of 1831 increased the initial term to twenty-eight years; and the 1909 act increased the renewal term to twenty-eight years, for a maximum duration of fifty-six years.

The 1976 act changed the term of copyright for works of individual or joint authors to the life of the author (or longest surviving author) plus fifty years. For works made for hire, the term was the shorter of seventy-five years from the date of first publication, or one hundred years from the date of creation. Works first published before January 1, 1978, had their copyrights extended to seventy-five years from the date of first publication. Works that had been created prior to January 1, 1978, but that had not been published (and were therefore subject to common-law copyright) were given the same term of protection as new works; but in exchange for being forced to relinquish their common-law protection, which was in theory perpetual, the act provided that such copyrights would not expire before December 31, 2002; and if the work was published before then, they would not expire before December 31, 2027.

In 1998, Congress passed the Sonny Bono Copyright Term Extension Act, which extended the term of all existing and future copyrights by an additional twenty years. (The sole exception was the statutory minimum term for works created before January 1, 1978, that remained unpublished by the end of 2002.) In 2003, the U.S. Supreme Court held that the Term Extension Act did not violate the Copyright Clause of the Constitution, which provides that copyrights can only be granted "for limited times."

The Term Extension Act did not attempt to revive copyrights that had already fallen into the public domain. As a result, works first published in 1922 or earlier are now in the public domain in the United States. Works first published in 1923–1963 and properly renewed, and all works first published in 1964–1977 (for which renewal is automatic), are protected for ninety-five years from the date of first publication. Works created before 1978, and first published in 1978–2002, are protected for the term given to new works, or until December 31, 2047, whichever is greater. Works created before 1978, but not published before the end of 2002, are protected for the term given to new works, as the statutory minimum term for such works has now expired. Works created in 1978 or later are protected

for the life of the author plus seventy years, except that works made for hire are protected for the shorter of ninety-five years from first publication or 120 years from creation. As under the 1976 act, all copyrights run to the end of the calendar year in which they would otherwise expire.

Infringement. When a copyright owner discovers that someone else is reproducing, adapting, selling, publicly performing, or publicly displaying a work without authorization, he or she has three years in which to commence an action for infringement. Such an action must be filed in a federal district court. To prevail, the copyright owner must demonstrate that he or she is the owner of a valid copyright; that the defendant has exercised one of the exclusive rights without authorization; and that the defendant's work is substantially similar to protected expression in the plaintiff's work. If the copyright owner does so, then the defendant bears the burden of proving that he or she falls within one of the statutory exceptions, including fair use.

If infringement is proved, the plaintiff will usually receive an injunction against any further infringing use of the copyrighted work. The court may also order that any infringing copies be impounded and sold or destroyed. The plaintiff is also entitled to recover any actual damages suffered as a result of the infringement, plus any profits earned by the infringer, to the extent they do not overlap. If the plaintiff cannot prove any damages or profits, he or she may elect to recover statutory damages in an amount fixed by the court within the range provided in the statute. The court also has discretion to award both costs and attorneys' fees to the prevailing party. Criminal penalties of up to ten years in prison may also be imposed for intentional infringement, but as a practical matter criminal penalties are rarely enforced except against those who commit large-scale infringement for commercial gain.

TYLER OCHOA
SANTA CLARA UNIVERSITY LAW SCHOOL

corporation. A corporation is a legal entity, usually made up of a group of people but sometimes of an individual. It differs from a company in that it is legally incorporated and, unlike a partnership, it remains a corporation even if the participants change. A corporation may be public or private. Examples of public corporations are municipalities, water districts, and school districts. Private corporations, on the other hand, have no governmental duties. They may be formed as business organizations or for charitable purposes, such as assisting the poor or administering hospitals, asylums, or colleges. The United States, unlike England, does not have ecclesiastical corporations. Churches are incorporated like any private charitable organization.

costume history. Historical societies often harbor mountains of old clothes that loom disconcertingly in back room, attic, or cellar in a state of neglect ranging from abuse to indifference. Everyone knows that something needs to be done, but no one knows where to first grab that sleeping tiger, and the decisive moment is evaded. However, when the costume collection finally is brought

into order, it becomes useful for study as well as for exhibits; the inclusion of clothing enhances other exhibits as well. Very possibly a real treasure will have been uncovered in the process.

There are four basic concerns for a costume collection (please note the resources at the end of this essay):

Physical well-being: As with manuscripts, paintings, drawings, and furniture, clothing requires storage in conditions that prevent or minimize damage from mold and fungus, vermin, dehydration, and acid formation. Temperature and humidity should be maintained at levels more or less comfortable for humans. The floor needs to be clear of obstacles to regular cleaning that will discourage infiltration by pests. Racks and shelves should be sturdy, clean, resistant to corrosion, and free from the off-gassing of deleterious chemicals. There should be room enough for a work table, and aisles large enough to move about in without endangering the objects or workers. The application of accession numbers must be done in an archivally responsible manner, certainly not directly upon a cloth object. Storage boxes and bags must be made from archivally safe materials, and the packing or hanging must be accomplished with the support of the garment uppermost in mind. (A common but injurious instinct is to force pliable garments into as small a space as possible.) Not the least of concerns is the need to handle clothing with gloved, or frequently washed, hands. Wearing clothes or jewelry that might catch on the objects is to be avoided. It is counterproductive to smoke, eat, drink, or use ink in storage, work, or exhibit areas.

Cataloging: If a collection is to be useful, the objects must be retrievable, and data describing each object and giving its storage location must be made available in a catalog. The catalog is worthless if the data are inaccurate or superficial. At the very least, the description must identify specific details that clearly distinguish an object from others like it. In computerized catalogs, it is important to settle upon consistent terminology and to ensure correct spelling to facilitate successful searches. References are available to assist in the challenging task of identifying, dating, and categorizing clothing. Because it is easy to misconstrue the subtleties of fashion cues as dating criteria, it may be advisable to seek help from a specialist.

Acquisition: Even the best-funded clothing collections will experience the pinch of inadequate storage space. The fast track to a storage problem is to uncritically accept every offered donation. The responsible approach is to establish a collection policy stipulating the time period, geographical area, quality level, and object type to be collected. When the time comes to cull irrelevant, redundant, or shabby items that have been in the collection for decades, this frustrating job will be simplified if no more unsuitable objects have been added to the collection recently. A collection committee should be formed to take the responsibility of ensuring the acquisition of only those items that best enhance the collection. This arrangement has the additional advantage of indicating to the donor that the decision to decline an offering was reached thoughtfully by a group, not one person. The bottom line is that it does cost money—if only in terms of volunteer effort and donated storage equipment and materials—to add a newly acquired object to the collection, and still more to remove it.

Use: "Old clothes" have been closely associated in our lives with activities like children's play, Halloween parades, and theatrical productions; thus many persons find it difficult to adjust to regarding those familiar and fascinating objects as museum artifacts. Respect for the ephemeral nature of clothing is extremely important to its survival. Articles of apparel are less able to withstand ordinary handling than most objects—what appears to be sturdy may crumble at an overconfident touch. Beaded work and silks are particularly vulnerable; many a parasol has remained intact until today when the silk cover was split by being opened completely. Many garments have been damaged permanently by fading during prolonged exposure to light. Nevertheless, some objects are retained for their value to the collection although they are too fragile to mount on mannequins, or even to exhibit flat. Discretion is required in selecting examples capable of withstanding handling for extensive study or exhibit. There is no difficulty in deciding whether to allow clothing to be worn, because wearing clothing intended for preservation is inappropriate.

Books: Janet Arnold, *Patterns of Fashion 1: 1660–1860* (1964, 1972); Linda Baumgarten, *What Clothes Reveal: The Language of Clothing in Colonial and Federal America* (2002); James R. Blackaby, Patricia Greeno, and the Nomenclature Committee, *The Revised Nomenclature for Museum Cataloging*

(1995); Stella Blum, ed., *Harper's Bazaar 1867–1898* (1974); Nancy Bradfield, *Costume In Detail—Women's Dress 1730–1930* (1968); Karen Finch and Greta Putnam, *The Care and Preservation of Textiles* (1985); Valerie Hewitt, Heather Vaughan, Lynn Payne, Jose F. Blanco, and Scott Leff, *The Greenwood Encyclopedia of Clothing through American History, 1900 to the Present* (2010); Lawrence R. Pizer, *A Primer for Local Historical Societies: Revised and Expanded from the First Edition by Dorothy Weyer Creigh* (1991); Sally Queen and Vicki Berger, *Clothing and Textile Collections in the United States* (2006); Naomi Tarrant, *Collecting Costume* (1983); Ann Buermann Wass and Michelle Webb Fandrich, *The Greenwood Encyclopedia of Clothing through American History: The Federal Era through Antebellum, 1786–1860* (2010); Susan W. Greene, *Wearable Prints, 1760–1860: History, Materials, and Mechanics* (2014).

Collections: Cornell University, Ithaca, NY; Kent State University, Kent, OH; Genesee Country Village & Museum, Mumford, NY; Old Sturbridge Village, Sturbridge, MA; Colonial Williamsburg, Williamsburg, VA; Metropolitan Museum of Art, New York, NY; National Museum of American History, Smithsonian Institution, Washington, D.C.; Los Angeles County Museum of Art, Los Angeles, CA.

Websites: www.costumesocietyamerica.com; www.costumepage.org; www.costumes.org; www.aaslh.org; www.si.edu/mci/english/learn_more/taking_care/handletex.html.

SUSAN W. GREENE
INDEPENDENT SCHOLAR

Council of State Archivists. See Archives Week and American Archives Month; state archives.

courts and court records. Civil and criminal court records are a promising source of evidence for historians. The academic field of legal history has developed and matured since the 1960s. Family and community historians have long used probate court records, because of their valuable information about family relations and material culture. However, records of other courts generally lie untouched in courthouses across the land. The obstacles to use of court records for historical research are considerable: highly technical legal language; unfamiliar terms in Latin and French; incomplete indexes; poor storage conditions; complex and confusing court organization and jurisdiction. Yet historians will find in court records ample evidence of the role that courts have played in maintaining community order, facilitating commerce, protecting the interests of the unfortunate, and, in many times and places, upholding the rights of the powerful. Records of a particular case—a lawsuit, a murder trial, a divorce or bankruptcy proceeding—may reveal striking details about the relationships and tensions in a family or community.

Each of the fifty states has its own judicial system, and superimposed on the state court systems are the federal courts (discussed below). Today every state has multiple levels of courts: a supreme court that hears final appeals (in Maryland and New York the court of last resort is called the court of appeals), a court that hears initial appeals (called the court of appeals in most states), a trial court of general jurisdiction (larger lawsuits, probate matters, other civil proceedings, and felonies), and municipal courts of limited jurisdiction (smaller lawsuits, misdemeanors). Some states have courts of specialized jurisdiction (for example, family courts that deal with juvenile violators). Court procedure and court organization have changed greatly over the past two centuries. During the nineteenth century, almost all the states simplified the complex system of writs and pleadings inherited from the common-law courts of England. (A modified form of common-law pleading persisted in Illinois until the 1950s.) During the twentieth century most states have simplified the structure of their court systems, reducing the number of courts and the overlapping jurisdiction among trial courts.

Despite the many changes in court organization and court procedure, the basic judicial remedies available in the Anglo-American legal system have endured for centuries. All the American states except one derive their legal and judicial systems from England, usually via models established in the older states. (Louisiana's legal system is modeled on the continental civil law, as codified under Napoleon.) The once-separate English courts of common law and equity, each with its own procedure and governing precedents (case law), have long since been merged into courts of general jurisdiction, both in England and the United States. (The first combination of common-law and equity jurisdiction in one court occurred in several of the American colonies. Today only Delaware has a separate equity court.) However, the remedies developed in the old English courts of common law and equity have been incorporated into the modern state and federal judicial systems.

The common-law courts of England and early America offered a limited number of remedies for a potential litigant: a plaintiff could seek to recover a money debt of one sort or another, or money damages for injury to a person or property, or possession of real or personal property or its monetary value. The usual mode of trial was by jury, and testimony was given orally. The documents produced in a debt case typically included (1) a writ (sealed court order) summoning the defendant to appear; (2) the pleadings filed by the plaintiff and defendant; (3) a judgment roll summarizing the appearances, the pleadings, the result of the trial if one were held, and the court's determination; and (4) a writ of execution ordering the sheriff to collect the money owed by the losing party, or sell his or her property to satisfy the court judgment. (In many cases there never was a judgment, because the parties settled their dispute out of court.) All these documents were loaded with stilted legal formulas developed in the English common-law courts during the Middle Ages, and they usually reveal little about the actual facts of the case.

The bulk of the business of the courts held by county judges and local justices of the peace was debt cases, which though routine can tell quite a lot about a family or community. A review of court docket books (case registers) or filed papers should reveal patterns of litigation—who were the creditors who brought lawsuits, who were the debtors who got into financial trouble? Civil court records can help explain changes in the fortunes of families and businesses, changes that are only alluded to in letters or newspapers. Some scholars have considered the civil courts to be debt-collection machines, favored by well-off merchants and lenders. However, this view is somewhat belied by the fact that many civil judgments were never satisfied. Many delinquent judgment debtors left town before the sheriff arrived to put them in jail for unpaid debts (before the abolition of imprisonment for debt in the early nineteenth century), or to sell their personal or real property to satisfy the judgment. Creditors certainly went to court to try to get their money, however slim their chances. But there could be other motives behind a lawsuit. A judgment placed a lien upon the debtor's real property and thereby advised the public of a bad credit risk. (Credit reporting agencies did not appear until the mid-nineteenth century.) A lawsuit could be a means of harassing an enemy, though the plaintiff had to have grounds for the case. A complaint of "trespass" might really concern a criminal act; for example, an individual might sue for money damages after being beaten up in a brawl. During the later nineteenth and early twentieth centuries the higher state courts were very busy with tort cases—particularly suits for personal injuries sustained in railroad, factory, or automobile accidents. Such cases can illustrate the negative impact of modern technology on a community or a family.

Equity jurisdiction originated in the office of England's chancellor. In the later Middle Ages the chancellor began to dispense discretionary, "equitable" justice in the king's name, in what became known as the court of chancery. That court offered important judicial tools and remedies not available in the common-law courts. Equity jurisdiction came to include supervision of trustees for the property of persons needing judicial protection (widows and orphans, lunatics and drunkards, insolvent corporations); foreclosure of mortgages; other disputes requiring an equitable remedy; and (in America) divorce and probate proceedings (in England those matters were traditionally handled by the church courts). The court of chancery could issue powerful writs (such as subpoena, discovery, and injunction) to assist the other courts in doing justice. Courts of equity used no juries and often obtained evidence in the form of written depositions. Equity court records therefore contain much information about the facts of cases. And because of the nature and scope of equity jurisdiction, the records can be rich sources for social and economic history.

Until the twentieth century criminal procedure was relatively simple, cases were swiftly resolved, and the resulting records were modest in volume. Judges of the civil courts (county or municipal) generally presided over the criminal courts as well (the largest cities had entirely separate criminal courts). Records of a felony case that went to trial consisted of the indictment or presentment, and trial minutes naming the witnesses and jurors and stating the verdict and the sentence (if the defendant were found guilty). Until state and federal appellate court laws were somewhat liberalized around 1900, appeals by convicted criminal defendants were rare. The records of the minor criminal courts, which handled misdemeanors and violations, contain similar information. Despite their laconic nature, criminal court records can provide evidence of the types of crimes and punishments that prevailed in a particular community. The majority of criminal defendants have always been young males—evidence of a community's failure to socialize some of its youths.

The public's vision of the law and the courts is shaped by the sight of law libraries—seemingly endless shelves of reported state and federal cases, legal digests and encyclopedias, and treatises. This huge, elaborate apparatus of reported and analyzed case law is built on the relatively very small number of court cases that raise unsettled points of law. Those questions are normally argued before and decided by appellate courts (though decisions of trial courts occasionally establish useful, though not definitive, legal precedents). The historian may want to learn how to use a law library (it is easier than it may seem), because those dull-looking case reports and the accompanying digests and indexes lead to trial court documents and testimony that were transcribed for appellate court hearings. (Court stenographers make the transcripts only in event of an appeal.) The "record on appeal" and accompanying legal briefs from the appellant and respondent can be a wonderful source of information on the facts of a particular case being appealed, as well as on the legal arguments of the opposing sides.

Records and briefs on appeal are typeset and bound like published books. However, they are prepared in very small numbers (usually just a few dozen copies) and are preserved as sets in only a few large law libraries in each state, or possibly in the state archives. (A copy of the record on appeal may be remitted, or sent back, to the trial court after the appeal is decided.) Printed records and briefs began to appear in federal and some state appellate courts in the early nineteenth century, and were in general use by mid-century. (The predecessor to the record on appeal was a manuscript transcription or summary of trial court proceedings attached to a writ of error or writ of certiorari, the common-law writs by which allegedly erroneous proceedings in a trial court were called up for review by an appellate court.)

Though the federal trial courts have always had a much smaller caseload than the state courts, federal court records can be useful sources for community history. The federal courts have operated since 1789 in both states and territories. Their jurisdiction embraces a wide variety of civil and criminal matters arising under the U.S. Constitution and federal statutes and treaties. Federal court records of particular interest for community history are bankruptcy proceedings (the bankruptcy statute was in effect for several periods during the nineteenth century and continuously since 1898); prosecutions for violation of federal revenue acts (particularly excise taxes on liquor and customs duties); recovery of fugitive slaves (under the acts of 1793 and 1850); admiralty proceedings involving ocean-going vessels, or their cargoes, owners, officers, or crew members (in 1845 admiralty jurisdiction was extended to inland navigable lakes and rivers); and strike- and union-breaking injunctions (particularly during the 1920s). Federal courts have been active in the fight against organized crime. In the nineteenth century, counterfeiting was frequently prosecuted. In the twentieth century, illegal sale of liquor during Prohibition and racketeering activities more recently have kept federal courts busy. The jurisdiction of federal courts expanded significantly when they were authorized to hear appeals from determinations of regulatory agencies such as the Interstate Commerce Commission. The Civil Rights Acts of 1964 and 1965 resulted in thousands of suits in federal courts in the southern states and elsewhere, challenging discriminatory practices that violated those statutes.

Certain areas of federal court jurisdiction are shared with state courts. Under their constitutional "diversity" jurisdiction, federal courts may hear and decide a civil suit by a plaintiff residing in one state against a defendant in another state (businesses have often considered it easier to recover money from out-of-state debtors by suing in a federal court, rather than in a state court). During much of the nineteenth century, violations of federal customs and excise laws could be prosecuted in either a state or federal court. *Naturalization of aliens is a federal function, performed since 1991 by the agency now known as U.S. Citizenship and Immigration Services. However, the higher state trial courts formerly had "concurrent" jurisdiction over naturalization. For over a century state courts performed most naturalizations, and federal courts the rest.

The federal court system is simpler in structure than most state court systems, but it has changed considerably over time. During the nineteenth century there were two federal trial courts, the district courts and the circuit courts. The jurisdiction of the two courts overlapped, with the U.S. district courts having the more limited jurisdiction. In practice, after the 1840s the district courts handled mainly criminal and admiralty cases, and the circuit courts, mostly civil cases. The circuit courts also heard some appeals from the district courts, but most appeals from those courts and all appeals from the circuit courts went directly to the U.S. Supreme Court for final review. In 1891 Congress established circuit courts of appeals as the main appellate courts in the federal court system (since 1948 those courts have been called courts of appeals). The district courts have continued as trial courts (the now-redundant circuit courts were abolished in 1911). Since 1891 appeals heard by the Supreme Court have been limited almost entirely to cases involving significant constitutional questions. Since 1789 every state has had at least one U.S. district court; today some states have as many as four districts. Originally the United States was divided into three circuits, each with a circuit court. More circuits were established as the nation expanded; since 1980 there have been twelve regional circuits of the U.S. Court of Appeals.

Special federal courts create some records relating to local communities and individuals. All claims against the United States for debts or damages were reviewed and decided by the Continental Congress or the U.S. Congress until 1855, when a court of claims was established. (Its present-day successor is the U.S. Claims Court.) During the later nineteenth century the court of claims determined many cases relating to damages inflicted by Confederate forces on Union loyalists in the southern states during the Civil War, and by Indian raids on American settlers in the western states. A Court of Private Land Claims, active between 1891 and 1904, determined numerous land titles deriving from the Mexican government in what became the southwestern states. Federal military courts try officers and enlisted personnel for violations of military law.

Records of state and municipal courts are generally found nearby, in a county courthouse or a city hall; older court records may be in the state archives. Archival records of the federal courts for a particular state are located in one of eleven regional branches of the *National Archives. Except for some naturalization records, relatively few older federal court records have been microfilmed, and they typically occupy over 60 percent of the space in a National Archives regional branch.

BIBLIOGRAPHY

On the history of Anglo-American law, see Charles Rembar, *The Law of the Land: The Evolution of Our Legal System* (1980) (explains origins of juries, pleading, equity, etc.) and John H. Baker, *An Introduction to English Legal History*, 4th ed. (2007) (standard textbook). Surveys of American legal history are Michael Grossberg and Christopher L. Tomlin, eds., *The Cambridge History of Law in America*, 3 vols. (2008) (topical essays); Lawrence M. Friedman, *A History of American Law*, 3rd ed. (2005) and *Crime and Punishment in American History* (1993); Kermit L. Hall and Peter Karsten, *The Magic Mirror: Law in American History*, 2nd ed. (2009); and Peter Hoffer, *Law and People in Colonial America*, rev. ed. (1998). For help in understanding historical court procedure and court documents, see Arlene H. Eakle, "Research in Court Records," in *The Source: A Guidebook of American Genealogy*, rev. ed., ed. Loretto Dennis Szucs and Sandra Hargreaves Luebking (1997), 172–238; William E. Nelson, "Court Records as Sources for Historical Writing," *Law in Colonial Massachusetts 1630–1800* (1984), 499–518; Herbert A. Johnson, "Civil Procedure in John Jay's New York," *American Journal of Legal History* 11 (1967): 69–80; Michael S. Hindus and Douglas L. Jones, "Quantitative Methods or *Quantum Meruit?*: Tactics for Early American Legal History," *Historical Methods Newsletter* 13, no.1 (Winter 1980): 63–74; Peter J. Coleman, *Debtors and Creditors in America: Insolvency, Imprisonment for Debt and Bankruptcy, 1607–1900* (1974). Also useful for understanding old court procedure are contemporary manuals written for lawyers and justices of the peace; and the published legal papers of John Adams, Alexander Hamilton, Aaron Burr, John Marshall, Daniel Webster, and Abraham Lincoln.

On the federal courts and their records, see Jonathan W. White, comp.,

Guide to Research in Federal Judicial History (2010) (excellent overview); Robert A. Carp and others, *The Federal Courts*, 5th ed. (2010) (introductory text); Erwin C. Surrency, *History of the Federal Courts*, 2nd ed. (2002) (organization, jurisdiction, procedure, etc.); Robert B. Matchette and others, comps., *Guide to Federal Records in the National Archives*, 3 vols. (1995); Loretto Dennis Szucs and Sandra Hargreaves Luebking, *The Archives: A Guide to the National Archives Field Branches* (1988); *Guide to Genealogical Research in the National Archives*, 3rd ed. (2000) (chapters on U.S. district court and naturalization records); *Prologue: Quarterly of the National Archives* 21, no. 3 (Fall 1989) (special issue on research uses of federal court records); Peter A. Wonders, comp., *Directory of Manuscript Collections Related to Federal Judges, 1789–1997* (1998).

General guides to published legal research and legal history resources (including both federal- and state-level materials) include Stephen Elias, *Legal Research: How to Find and Understand the Law*, 16th ed. (2012) (intended for nonlawyers); Steven M. Barkan and others, *Fundamentals of Legal Research*, 10th ed. (2015); Morris L. Cohen, *Bibliography of Early American Law*, 6 vols. (1998) (pre-1861 materials only); Kermit L. Hall, *A Comprehensive Bibliography of American Constitutional and Legal History, 1896–1979*, 5 vols., and *Supplement, 1980–1987*, 2 vols. (1984, 1991); Erick B. Low, *A Bibliography on the History of the Organization and Jurisdiction of State Courts* (1980). Reported (published) state and federal court decisions and opinions may be located through the multivolume *American Digest* or (more conveniently) through the *Federal Reporter* and the various regional and state reporters. On legal terms and language, *Black's Law Dictionary*, 10th ed. (2014; 4th and earlier eds. include more obsolete legal terms) and David Mellinkoff, *The Language of the Law* (1963).

Books that suggest approaches for using court records for community history are M. Michelle Jarrett Morris, *Under Household Government: Sex and Family in Puritan* Massachusetts (2013); David E. Narrett, *Inheritance and Family Life in Colonial New York City* (1992); Mary K. Bonsteel Tachau, *Federal Courts in the Early Republic: Kentucky 1789–1816* (1978); Lea VanderVelde, *Redemption Songs: Suing for Freedom before Dred Scott* (2014) (lawsuits in antebellum St. Louis seeking freedom for black slaves); Robert A. Silverman, *Law and Urban Growth: Civil Litigation in the Boston Trial Courts, 1880–1900* (1981); Michael S. Hindus, *Prison and Plantation: Crime, Justice, and Authority in Massachusetts and South Carolina, 1767–1878* (1980); Stephen Mihm, *A Nation of Counterfeiters: Capitalists, Con Men, and the Making of the United States* (2007); Lawrence M. Friedman and Robert V. Percival, *The Roots of Justice: Crime and Punishment in Alameda County, California, 1870–1910* (1981); and Richard M. Brown, "The Archives of Violence," *American Archivist* 41, no. 4 (October 1978): 431–43 (strikes, vigilantes, outlaws, and the records that tell their stories).

JAMES D. FOLTS
NEW YORK STATE ARCHIVES

See local government records.

county historians. For decades, local historical societies and local historians have served their respective communities by recording and preserving the past for present audiences and future generations. Inspired in part by the nation's centennial celebration in 1876, these organizations and individuals, devoted to the preservation of grassroots history, have shared, through written accounts, county atlases, museum exhibitions, oral histories, tours, and special events, the rich stories and events that have shaped their communities over the generations. Through these means, they have proved themselves to be powerful and articulate advocates for the preservation of local community records and material culture as well as history educators committed to reaching a wider public.

While most local historians are connected with a particular community, village, town, or township, there are others whose responsibilities cover the entire county. Some county historians are affiliated with the county historical society; others, however, may claim the self-appointed or honorary title based upon their longevity in and extensive knowledge of their area. Their numerous and varied tasks include gathering stories and recollections of longtime residents, publishing newsletters and books, writing history columns for local newspapers, assisting at the county historical society/museum, serving as a resource for local schools and the media, assisting with family history and genealogical research, and collaborating on historic preservation projects.

In most cases, there is no formal appointment to the post of county histo-

rian. There are, however, two examples of long-established county historian programs in the United States—one implemented by state legislation; the other, a partnership between a state agency and a private historical society.

In 1919, New York Governor Alfred E. Smith signed a bill, known as "The Historian's Law," that made his state the first to establish a formal network of appointed municipal historians. The bill's intent was to designate an individual in every community to serve as a resource for inquiries about local history and to assist the *state historian in preserving historical records and memories. State historian Dr. James Sullivan believed that this network also would promote the preservation of primary sources at the local level and encourage the development of history programs statewide. The first official task of these municipal historians was to gather materials pertaining to New York's communities during World War I, a project that continued well over a decade. Since a few counties previously had appointed historians, those individuals assisted in the war research project, thereby laying the foundation for the next phase of history at the local level.

The New York State Legislature amended the civil code in 1933 to permit the appointment of a historian for every county. The legislation authorized these individuals, designated by the board of county supervisors, to oversee the activities of their respective county's municipal historians and to promote those goals established by the state historian. Under the direction of Dr. Albert Corey, state historian from 1944 to 1963, the county historian program expanded beyond the task of collecting war records and reminiscences. Rather, Corey redirected these historians' attention toward issues that affected their own work, namely, *historic preservation, public records, education, and advocacy. In so doing, he developed an active statewide network of local and county historians and strengthened their ties with the office of the state historian.

Recognizing the need to obtain a greater knowledge about their municipal responsibilities, local and county historians participated in workshops and seminars offered by state government agencies. Since these agencies did not specifically address matters pertaining to history or provide a professional affiliation, the historians formed their own organizations—the County Historians Association (1967) and the Association of Municipal Historians (1979)—to provide more collegial support and in-depth training within the profession. In 1999, these two groups merged to establish the Association of Public Historians of New York State (APHNYS), an organization that remains active in promoting the heritage and history of New York State.

By the early 1980s, the laws of the State of New York continued to include the position of "county historian" under the section "Divisions of History and Public Records." The law specified that each county board of supervisors had the authority to select the county historian, who would serve without compensation, unless the governing board decided otherwise. Once appointed, the historian was expected "to supervise the activities of the local historians in towns and villages within the county in performing the historical work recommended by the state historian, and . . . to prepare and to present to the board of supervisors a report of the important occurrences within the county for each calendar year." They were charged with tasks and responsibilities traditionally associated with being a historian: researching and writing on aspects of local history; interpreting the history of the community through public presentations; encouraging the preservation of historic manuscripts, records, artifacts, and buildings; and organizing local historical *celebrations.

Although there were initially few requirements for holding the position of county historian, the state historian of New York has recommended certain professional standards for individuals occupying that office. Since the position requires greater administrative responsibilities than those at the municipal level, individuals who serve as county historians should possess at least a master's degree with a major concentration in American history or a related field. By law, county authorities are required to provide their historians with sufficient space in a fireproof structure to collect and maintain historical materials. The counties' boards of supervisors are also empowered to raise taxes and spend money for historical purposes, including historical buildings, erecting historical markers, collecting documents, preparing and printing historical materials.

The Local Government Records Law, effective August 1988, updated the 1933 Historian's Law, which had defined the initial tasks of local and county historians. With the increased awareness for preserving local government records, the 1988 law specifically addressed the new records-related activities for local and county historians:

Each local government historian shall promote the establishment and improvement of programs for the management and preservation of local government records with enduring value for historical or other research; encourage the coordinated collection and preservation of non-governmental historical records by libraries, historical societies, and other repositories; and carry out and actively encourage research in such records in order to add to the knowledge, understanding, and appreciation of the community's history.

The State of Indiana launched a local history-oriented program in the early twentieth century that served as a forerunner of a county historians' program organized decades later. In 1915 the Indiana General Assembly authorized the creation of the Indiana Historical Commission to oversee the state's centennial celebration in 1916. In an effort to ensure statewide participation, the commission planned commemorative programs in every county of the state and encouraged greater emphasis on local history through reinvigorated local and county historical societies. Following the state centennial and a two-year lull in activity brought on by World War I, Governor James P. Goodrich summoned the commission members to organize a county-by-county history of Indiana during the Great War. Funding from the General Assembly provided support for this research and retrieval of historical materials, which often devolved to those individuals most familiar with each county's history.

In an effort to improve its communication with the local historical communities statewide, the Indiana Library and Historical Board, the governing agency for the Indiana State Library and the Indiana Historical Bureau, voted in January 1952 to approve the creation of the office of county historian. The bureau, established in 1925 and renamed from the Indiana Historical Commission, oversaw the program. Based upon nominations from the historical community for each county, the Library and Historical Board appointed individuals to serve in these honorary, unsalaried positions. Duties specified for the new county historians included starting or nurturing county historical societies; stimulating attendance at the annual statewide history conference; notifying the State Library of available manuscript collections; keeping track of county records; gathering information for the Gold Star Honor Roll of World War II; and serving as local resource persons for schools and research inquiries. These individuals were deemed "a public-spirited group of men and women who cooperate . . . in preserving Indiana's historical heritage." For various reasons, this local history program gradually disappeared over the years.

The years around the nation's Bicentennial celebration brought renewed interest in and new commitments to strengthen local history programs in Indiana. During 1979, Pamela J. Bennett, director of the Indiana Historical Bureau, and Thomas Krasean, then field representative for the Indiana Historical Society, a private not-for-profit headquartered in Indianapolis, joined their institutions to expand the state's local history program. Originating in a series of "Local History Today" workshops and lectures that reached out to and assisted local historical societies and local history practitioners, Bennett and Krasean reinstituted the county historian program in 1980–1981, a program defunct since the mid-1950s. By resuming this practice, the bureau continued its emphasis on local history throughout the state, while the society, in commemoration of its sesquicentennial in 1980, demonstrated a new commitment to providing history services at the local level. The bureau and the society, intending to improve historical communication and network statewide, produced a handbook for historians that described historical resources and services and offered regular training opportunities regarding working with local communities and their diverse constituents.

As in the original 1950s program, Indiana's county historians receive their three-year appointments jointly from the society and the bureau after being nominated by the local historical community. Each historian is expected to be "well acquainted with the county and its history," to be a clearinghouse for information on local history, and a resource for research inquiries. The county historian encourages coordination and cooperation among the county's historical groups to avoid duplication of efforts; seeks broader public participation in doing history; and promotes the understanding of how history shapes our present and the future. The county historian also serves as the local representative of the society and the bureau, providing information

about potential collections, assisting in identifying potential sites for historical markers, encouraging the expansion of local history activities, and serving as an advocate for historic preservation and access to public records. The Indiana Historical Society currently administers this program within its Local History Services office.

Other states have explored initiatives that address the public's and local governments' interest in county history. In 1965 the General Assembly of Tennessee passed legislation that created a county historian program with responsibilities similar to those of New York and Indiana. In the spring of 1999, representatives in the Pennsylvania legislature discussed the feasibility of authorizing county commissioners to appoint county historians. Critics expressed concern that the position could become a political appointment instead of one properly held by a trained professional historian or someone with extensive experience in local history. This proposal was never implemented, leaving the state's county historical societies to serve as the official representatives for most local history initiatives.

Besides having similar responsibilities of collecting and preserving, educating the larger public, and serving as an information resource, county historian programs share a common (and somewhat disturbing) feature in that appointees usually serve without compensation. This clearly diminishes the importance of the unique skills possessed by historians, perpetuates the belief that *anyone* can do history, and ultimately implies that history, unlike other commodities and services, has no value in contemporary society.

County historians provide valuable services both to the community and the historical profession. As keepers of local memories and records, they help to preserve documents and artifacts that are useful in historical research, nurture an appreciation for history among a broader audience, assist in building collaborations among local historical organizations, serve as advocates for history-related issues at the local level, and explain the relevance of an understanding of the past in making public policy decisions. They also are active in historical advocacy—promoting the preservation of historic sites, structures, and public records—and encouraging membership in local historical organizations.

In the twenty-first century, states and counties, whether through governmental agencies or private historical institutions, continue to commit themselves to preserving the histories of their local communities. Many county historians are active through online local history and genealogy websites, such as findagrave.com, rootsweb.com, or other similar local history/genealogy resources. By supporting the initiatives of local and county historians today, the current generation will be able to leave a rich and detailed record for generations to come, thereby providing present and future generations with a greater appreciation of their history and heritage and helping them to understand the past as they build toward the future.

See Robert W. Arnold III, *Documenting the Community: Suggested Records-Related Activities for Local Government Historians* (1994); *McKinney's Consolidated Laws of New York: Book 3B, Arts and Cultural Affairs Law* (1984); State University of New York, *Historian's Guide: A Handbook for Local Historians* (1982); *Indiana History Bulletin* 57, no. 12 (December 1980): 179–80; *Indiana History Bulletin* 29, no. 2 (February 1952): 31–32.

DAVID G. VANDERSTEL
INDEPENDENT HISTORIAN

See fees, consulting; Indiana, local history in; New York, local history in.

county histories. Although some county histories appeared earlier, the peak decades for publishing of county histories came between 1876 and 1900. Building on an interest in locality that emerged throughout the nation following the Centennial Celebration of the American Revolution in 1876, publishers saw possibilities for making money by issuing county histories, mug books, and compilations of biographies and the memoirs of prominent citizens. In some cases, the books were written locally, but in the main, compilers were sent out to solicit the aid of the public, determine subjects to be included, and even write entries. These books were, for the most part, paid for by subscribers even before they were printed. *Mug books were those books that contained pictures and biographies, inclusion depending upon one's willingness and ability to pay.

P. William Filby, in his *Bibliography of American County Histories* (1985), improved upon and expanded Clarence S. Peterson's *Consolidated Bibliography of County Histories in Fifty States,* published in 1961. Marion J. Kaminkow included county histories in her five-volume work, *United States Local Histories in the Library of Congress: A Bibliography* (1975). Filby states that some 5,000 county histories were published during the peak period. A number of them were reprinted in the 1970s and 1980s, some with extensive name indexes. See, for example, *History of Randolph and Macon Counties, Missouri* ([1884], 1983, with complete name index). Few county histories of the scope and size of the early books have been published since that time.

When county histories were written at other periods, they were often limited in subject matter to the earliest times: see David D. Oliver, *Centennial History of Alpena County, Michigan . . . 1837–1876* (1903), or Rhoda C. Ellison, *Bibb County, Alabama: The First Hundred Years 1818–1918*, published in 1984. This interest in the settling generation has continued.

There are some consistent themes to be found in those nineteenth-century books. Their authors complained in preface after preface that gathering the material and writing were hard work, but they recognized that the work had to be done to preserve a record of the past and so was pleasant despite the strain. They also feared their books would not come up to expectations, that some would think they had gone into "too much detail and that I have put in much that might have been left out" (A. S. Salley Jr., *History of Orangeburg County, South Carolina* [1898]). They also boasted, such as in the preface in *The History of Saline County* [Kansas] (1881) where the author notes that his

book had been "carefully written and compiled." Meanwhile in the *History of Buchanan County and St. Joseph* [Missouri] (1899) the author insisted, "Accuracy our first aim."

Almost without exception, those nineteenth-century county histories were written because the old-timers— the original settlers, or those with memory of the early days—were dying, and there was a need to get the story written down. But these books did more than preserve early history, for they selected which history it was that would be recorded, and they stated their intentions clearly. From *Holt and Atchison Counties* [Kansas] (1882), the preface notes that the book was written because "the energy and bravery of these hardy pioneers and their descendants have made Holt and Atchison Counties what they are." The early settlers had made the wilderness "bud and blossom," something this author wanted to encourage the younger generation to stay around and replicate. The story of those two counties needed to be preserved in order to "hand it down to posterity."

In the *History of Jackson County, Missouri* (1881), the author complains that "oral memory is sometimes at odds and gives conflicting versions of the same events" making it necessary for the historian to take "much care and delicacy to bring harmony to the story." While county histories most often record harmony, our local history was not always harmonious even though the discords are infrequently reported. Rather than a single note to represent the past, groups of chords are best; harmonious or disharmonious, a multitude of chords better represent the human condition.

County histories written within the past fifty years tend to follow two patterns. Some attempt to replicate the older books with short essays about a variety of topics but many others attempt to give a chronological overview of the past.

The biggest change in the publication of county histories should be ascribed to commercial publishers like Arcadia and the History Press (which have now merged), and others, that have published numerous county, city, and town histories within a format that highlights old pictures, full captions, and some chronological balance.

See Richard Wohl and A. Theodore Brown, "The Usable Past: A Study of Historical Traditions in Kansas City," *Huntington Library Quarterly* 23 (May 1960): 237–59, reprinted in Carol Kammen, *The Pursuit of Local History: Readings on Theory and Practice* (1996), 145–63. See also Joseph N. Kane, *The American Counties: Origins of County Names, Dates of Creation and Organization, Area, Population including 1980 Census Figures, Historical Data, and Published Sources* (1983).

CAROL KAMMEN
TOMPKINS COUNTY
(NEW YORK) HISTORIAN

See mug books.

crime, history of. Crime in the United States is a fluid rather than a static subject. Factors as diverse as religion, population density, technological advancements, social class, etc., have changed the notions of crime and the distinguishing characteristics of criminals since the country's founding.

Crime in the colonies was a product of numbers of people settling near each other. Clustered together, the colonists could defend themselves from environmental and native threats and help each other survive when weather and disease conspired to destroy a settlement. However, individuals in the nuclear settlement might reject the beliefs of the majority or endanger the welfare of the community. The three colonial geographical areas appear to have had distinctive ideas about crime. All of them held sacred the right of an individual to his person and his property, but variations in goals of a settlement led to regional variations in criminal statutes and in the application of justice. Several secondary sources offer helpful overviews of colonial philosophies regarding crime.

Settled by Puritans, colonial New England's ideas about crime centered early on religious beliefs and practices. Thus, the Bible, particularly the Ten Commandments, and doctrinal writings and preaching dominated a community's judgment about criminal acts. Heretical views, violation of Sabbath restrictions, and even eccentric behavior were punishable by law. Conformity in thought and behavior, it was believed, led to the survival of the colony and the betterment of the individual; its opposite would lead to earthly chaos and eternal damnation. Accounts about nonconformists like Anne Hutchinson and the "witches" of Salem are easy to find, and state archives and other historical repositories preserve original documents from this period.

The southern colonies with their plantation systems had concepts of crime that were more economically based. Colonists' motives for settling in these areas were to gain material rather than spiritual improvement. Since free labor contributed to the prosperity of isolated properties and the well-being of their inhabitants, laws governing behaviors were determined by individual plantation owners. Slaves, indentured servants, and apprentices owed total allegiance to their owners or sponsors. Punishments for infractions were meted out swiftly and often brutally, and masters did not need the authority of either court or community to discipline their own property. Slave narratives like *The Autobiography of Frederick Douglass* and *The Narrative of Harriet Jacobs* give firsthand accounts of plantation justice.

The middle colonies, with demographically diverse populations, were somewhat more liberal in their views of crime, although slavery, indentured servitude, and apprenticeships were common in all areas well into the nineteenth century. The *Autobiography of Benjamin Franklin* offers a fascinating view of an apprentice's life in the middle colonies during the eighteenth century. The Protestant ethic and the Golden Rule seem to have dominated notions of proper and improper behavior in mercantile settlements. Thus in the 1750s, a notorious New York counterfeiter was hanged for his crimes. Densely populated communities meant a greater number of temptations, increasing possibilities for violating neighbors' rights and rising ability to evade arrest and prosecution.

Early in the nineteenth century, crime might be seen as related to the "haves" and the "have nots." The first half of the nineteenth century was dominated by westward expansion and settlement and Irish and German immigration. Trailblazers and canal builders created pathways to the interior along which "boom towns" were soon strung. While new settlers attempted to recreate the orderly communities they had left, problems caused by transients and opportunists outpaced the citizenry's inclination to finance services and municipal improvements. Community ordinances burgeoned as tensions increased. Criminality was thought to be limited to the "have nots"; to be poor was to be a criminal in the early nineteenth century.

Canals brought not only new settlers, but also workers who were idle during months when the weather prevented construction and water travel. These workers, frequently Irish immigrants, loitered in frontier towns from late fall to early spring. Uneducated and unskilled, they could find few employments. Often, a community's first response to this situation was to create an almshouse to which vagrants and drunks were sentenced because of their inability to pay for housing and sustenance. Almshouses might be thought of as benevolent institutions because they did provide shelter and structured work experiences for the inmates who might not survive on their own. On the other hand, almshouses can also be seen as institutions designed to rid a community of unpleasant, unsightly and unruly derelicts by restricting their freedom. Some communities, like Rochester, New York, have preserved almshouse registers that identify inmates by name, age, and nationality to the second generation. Nationality was very important to communities where births among immigrant populations outnumbered those among native citizens, threatening established political power.

Canals brought another problem. Canal boats were towed by mules or horses driven by young boys. The youngsters had little to do in the off season and no means of support, and so many of them plagued canal-town businesses with pilfering and petty thievery. They spent their idle time with adult canallers, brawling, frequenting bars and brothels, and learning the colorful but lewd language of their elders. State houses of refuge were the earliest institutions established for juvenile delinquents, an attempt to separate young felons from an environment that might turn them into hardened criminals. Inmates farmed, attended an institutional school, and went to mandatory religious services. Those who were judged incorrigible could be sent to a seaport and sentenced to serve a term on an outgoing ocean vessel. State repositories, for example the New York State Archives, may hold registers of house-of-refuge inmates, if they exist. Names, ages, birthplaces, places of arraignment, criminal charges, and nationalities to the second generation may be found in the registers.

Newspapers illustrate the issue of crime during this period, quite often in a colorful way. Murders appear to have been infrequent, but assaults were plentiful. Drunk and disorderly was by far the most common crime, with vagrancy and wife beating coming in close behind. Criminals are listed by name, crime, and disposition of the case. In some cases, editors used sto-

ries of crimes as comic relief, particularly if the criminal was an intoxicated Irishman whose crime was against a countryman. Names of established families rarely appear in crime reports, although there is an occasional mention of anonymous "rowdies" disturbing the peace on a weekend night. Newspapers are also a good source for reports of local government proceedings where new ordinances give clues about behaviors that offended mainstream citizens. Local ordinances regulating alcohol sales, Sabbath activities, and health practices correspond to the increasing problems of rapidly growing communities and a moral-reform movement that paralleled westward settlement.

The social-reform movement shifted attention to crimes committed by the "haves" in the latter half of the nineteenth century. New waves of immigrants, handicapped by ignorance, by lack of skills, and usually by the inability to speak English, crowded into cheap housing in large cities. Slum landlords profited from them. Sweatshop operators exploited them. Politicians bought their votes. Unregulated monopolies, especially the railroads, reaped profits at the expense of those who depended on them, farmers, ranchers, manufacturers, and passengers. The magnitude of apparently legal abuses practiced by "robber barons" resulted in the romanticizing of mere outlaws and lesser offenders. Again, newspapers have probably the best information on local developments of the period, particularly about local ethnic gangs engaged in illegal activities. Biographies of social reformers will detail the conditions in which victims lived.

The moral-reform movement peaked in 1919 when temperance advocates succeeded in outlawing the transportation and sale of alcoholic beverages. With Prohibition, crime became more sophisticated; organized criminal bodies set up networks for importing illegal substances and established "speakeasies." Indeed, many ordinary citizens themselves became accomplices in these activities. Beginning in the latter years of the nineteenth century, American criminals were increasingly romanticized in the press and in popular literature. Biographies of the notorious became as popular as stories of the merely noteworthy. Repeal of the Eighteenth Amendment in 1933 did not wipe out the mob, however; it continued to profit from the sale of illegal—but for many, enticing—substances and the provision of illegal—but for many, pleasurable—activities.

Political unorthodoxy became increasing criminalized, peaking with the notorious McCarthy hearings in the 1950s. Abuse of political power continued to be a major concern throughout the latter half of the twentieth century, with Watergate and Whitewater scandals dominating headlines.

Americans' notions of crime in the last half of the twentieth century have concentrated on acts of omission as well as acts of commission. Abuse of economic, political, and military power and dishonest use of technology have joined the list of misdeeds of the past. The nineteenth-century robber baron has evolved into twentieth-century "white collar" criminal and the corporate criminal. Thefts of individuals' *intellectual property and private identities have joined robbery of material goods as criminal acts. An emphasis on persons' civil rights has mitigated formerly punishable acts like civil disobedience, cohabitation out of wedlock, and other private behaviors that do not violate the rights of others. In fact, some once condemned actions, most notably abortion, have been decriminalized.

The best research sources for questions about local crime in the twentieth century will be local newspapers. In contrast to the last century and the early years of this century, today there is little suppression of scandalous behaviors of the middle and upper classes in the local press. Secondary sources abound and biographies are well detailed and documented.

See Douglas Greenberg, *Crime and Law Enforcement in the Colony of New York, 1691–1776* (1976); Edwin Powers, *Crime and Punishment in Early Massachusetts, 1620–1692* (1966); and Raphael Semmes, *Crime and Punishment in Early Maryland* (1938). In addition, don't miss *Annals of Murder: A Bibliography of Books and Pamphlets on American Murders from Colonial Times to 1900* (1961).

TERESA LEHR
SUNY BROCKPORT, RETIRED

See social purity movement.

Croats in North America, sources for. See Appendix A.

crowdsourcing (and crowdfunding). Crowdsourcing is loosely defined as mining the collective knowledge of a group. Jeff Howe coined the term in a *Wired* magazine article in 2006, and offered this definition: "the act of taking a job traditionally performed by a designated agent (usually an employee) and outsourcing it to an undefined, generally large group of people in the form of an open call" (http://www.wired.com/wired/archive/14.06/ crowds.html). Since there are never enough resources to accomplish the research projects that most history organizations hope to complete, crowdsourcing offers one strategy to address the challenge.

The *Library of Congress experimented with the concept in early 2008 when it posted 3,000 photos from its collections on the photo sharing site Flickr and asked users to contribute information about the photos. The experiment is now regular practice. The library staff can put a collection of historic photos online, ask users to help identify them, and within a few days, Flickr members have identified every single photo and have left a lively comment stream in the process (http://www.flickr.com/photos/library_of_congress/sets/72157623063035332).

The concept of enlisting the contributions of the general public has adherents across the history spectrum with archives and historical societies and preservation groups of various sizes experimenting with it. However, for some people, user-generated content is viewed with healthy skepticism, especially by those responsible for maintaining the trust of an institution's various audiences. Yet faced with diminishing resources, most people agree that the option of soliciting the involvement of online users and thus recognizing the collective potential of historians in the general public is worth considering.

Some organizations have developed wikis, websites built collaboratively by their users. Whether you know the term or not, you are no doubt familiar with the concept. Wikipedia, the online collaborative encyclopedia, is the best example. Anyone can log on and make additions and changes to an entry. The site's standards demand that information be supported by hotlinks to published articles. While some still question the authority of the site's sources, it has become an easy way to find quick overview information about a topic.

The following examples illustrate the concept:

A wiki started by Historic Saranac Lake (HSL), a local history organization founded in 1980, focuses on architectural preservation (http://hsl.wikispot.org). HSL operates a museum and a website in a small community about ten miles west of Lake Placid, in New York's Adirondack Mountains. In late 2008 the organization began this online archive of local history and encouraged the public to make additions. Each day, the staff posts a new historical photo or tidbit of history on their Facebook page with a link to the wiki.

Placeography (http://www.placeography.org/index.php), is a wiki project of the Minnesota Historical Society. Started in 2008, it was inspired by a program at the society's library that taught people how to research house and property history. Since there was no vehicle to share the resulting research, staff with a passion for community organization and personal stories created the wiki. An early research project that made contributions to the wiki was Right on Lake Street, based on an exhibition about an important commercial street in Minneapolis. A group of students from Macalester College interviewed business owners and wrote entries about various building and sites on the street. The staff's goal was to generate 150 entries during the wiki's first year, but with a little promotion the site received more than 1,000 contributions. Though about 90 percent of the entries detail Minnesota history, the wiki also includes entries about sites in six other states, and the staff invites contributions about places anywhere in the world.

Another example of crowdsourcing, again from the Minnesota Historical Society, is the MN 150 exhibition, developed to celebrate the state's sesquicentennial. Museum staff asked the people of Minnesota to nominate people, places, things, or events originating in Minnesota that transformed the state, the United States, or the world. A committee of staff, community members, and subject experts then sorted through more than 2,700 nominations to select top 150 list, and to add ideas (http://discovery.mnhs.Org/MN150/index.php). Though the staff could easily have developed the list without public input, their willingness to be inclusive no doubt made the exhibition a richer and more engaging experience.

A related concept is crowdfunding. Just as crowdsourcing utilizes the wisdom or expertise of the crowd, crowdfunding recognizes the collective financial potential of the crowd, in the form of microdonations. Usually the request focuses on a specific project or cause, and the campaign period is limited to a short time frame. History organizations constantly seek new funding sources,

and many are intrigued with the idea of crowdfunding. Kickstarter and Indiegogo are two popular crowdfunding platforms. Crowdfunding offers an alternative to traditional fundraising. To be successful, it necessitates strategic planning and a defined project that will resonate with a wide audience, demands effective collaboration among organization departments, and requires effort to maintain and build funder relationships. It offers the potential to reach new funders and raise awareness of your institution.

TIM GROVE
NATIONAL AIR AND SPACE MUSEUM,
SMITHSONIAN INSTITUTION

Cubans in North America, sources for. See Appendix A.

culinary history and the local historian. Everyone eats. Where the stories of military, political, artistic, or industrial endeavors may have no relevance to someone's modern daily life, what a general, president, artist, or inventor ate for breakfast does. And most people are going to be intrigued at how earlier people grew or gathered, stored and sold, and cooked and consumed daily meals.

Food history touches on every aspect of human life. Any exploration and new settlement, and all military campaigns and sea voyages, depended absolutely on an assured supply of food, and on fuel, basic equipment, and skill to cook it. When the food supply fails, so does human enterprise. Once the supply is guaranteed, then people express their economic status, power, and taste with their food and how they serve it and with whom they share it.

Even though museums very seldom have historic food—except perhaps hardtack relics or bones or seeds from an archaeological excavation—nonetheless food history is rich in material culture. Farm equipment, fishing vessels, cooking equipment, tableware, linens, artistic depictions of food or meals, photographs, plus cookbooks, advice manuals, manuscript recipes in notebooks or on recipe cards, newspapers, and magazines all illustrate meals that are now mere memories.

Food history is everywhere. Historic homes contain kitchens, food storage areas like cellars, ice houses, smokehouses, and pantries, and dining rooms and sitting rooms where food and beverages were consumed. Museums may have food production intensive exhibits like grist mills, dairies, or grocery stores. Taverns and inns may obviously illustrate food service but even schools, churches, and meeting halls sometimes had kitchens and spaces dedicated to eating. Even vessels, camps, and temporary habitations show food transport, preparation, and consumption whether it's a ship's galley, a chuck wagon, or a field kitchen. Any historical agency can exhibit evidence of historic foodways. Even a one-room school house or blacksmith shop can display a lunch pail.

Food historians sometimes use the term foodways to describe the whole food picture. Cooking and eating are behaviors and performance, a kind of folkway. Foodways takes into account all aspects of people and their food even to the present. Food history examines the foodways of the past. Culinary history focuses on the specific stories of particular dishes; culinary historians do a kind of genealogical research project for recipes to discover how a dish changes over time or leads to the creation of another.

Researching local food history requires a broad-based approach and layering evidence. References to food—raising animals, grains, vegetables, and fruits, cooking, food sharing and sales, meals—in narratives, diaries, and letters, will need amplification with newspaper advertising showing available products and account book entries to show commercial transactions and personal exchanges. Archaeological and architectural evidence, plus inventories, drawings and photographs, and material culture of known provenance all add to the picture. Cookbooks and recipe collections are valuable sources of information but are insufficient unto themselves.

Food triggers memory powerfully. Local history organizations can capitalize on this with *oral history interviews to capture foodways of a particular locality. Inviting membership and the local public to share family recipes by way of a potluck of old family favorites makes for a repeatable event that helps turn up further local food history. Holiday fare is often rich in family or community social history, particularly ethnic traditions. Seasonal food celebrations or festivals may help define a locality's origins, unique products, or ethnic connections whether they be a ramp or blueberry festival, fish boil, or Mardi Gras celebration.

Recreated historic meals based on diary entries or narratives, newspaper accounts, or oral history, or even printed menus are effective for fundraising events and help build community support for a historical organization. When participants are invited to attend in period dress and an effort is made to re-create a historic setting, the event takes on special, even magical, dimensions well within the reach of nearly any local history group.

Suggested Reading
Cleveland Amory, Helen Durpey Bullock, Helen McCulley, et al., *The American Heritage Cookbook and Illustrated History of American Eating and Drinking*, 2 vols. (1964); Louise Conway Belden, *The Festive Tradition: Table Decoration and Deserts in America, 1650–1900*, (1983); Megan Elias, *Food in the United States, 1890 to 1945* (2009); Sandra L. Oliver, *Food in Colonial and Federal America* (2005); Andrew F. Smith, editor in chief, *Encyclopedia of Food and Drink in America*, 2 vols. (2004); and Susan Williams, *Savory Suppers and Fashionable Feasts: Dining in Victorian America* (1985) and *Food in the United States, 1820s to 1890* (2006). See also www.foodhistorynews.com.

SANDRA L. OLIVER
FREELANCE WRITER

See material culture, travel literature.

cultural heritage tourism. The *National Trust for Historic Preservation defines *cultural heritage tourism* as "traveling to experience the places and activities that authentically represent the stories and people of the past and present." Tourism is big business in the United States, contributing $947 billion to the U.S. economy in 2015. Travel and tourism is one of America's largest employers, directly employing more than 8.1 million people (U.S. Travel Association, 2016). In addition to creating new jobs, new businesses, and higher property values, well-managed cultural heritage tourism programs can improve quality of life and build community pride.

According to a 2013 national research study on cultural and heritage travel conducted by Mandala Research, 76 percent of all leisure travelers in the United States participate in cultural and/or heritage activities while traveling, translating to 129.6 million adults each year. Cultural heritage travelers spend more than other kinds of travelers, spending on average $1,319 per trip as compared to $820 per trip for all other U.S. travelers (2013 Cultural & Heritage Traveler Study, Mandala Research, LLC). In addition to the economic benefits, cultural heritage tourism helps to diversify local economies and preserves the unique character of communities.

These characteristics make cultural heritage travelers a very attractive target market for the tourism industry, which has led to the creation of new partnerships between cultural and heritage attractions and the tourism industry. In 1989, the National Trust for Historic Preservation received a challenge grant from the National Endowment for the Arts to work in sixteen pilot regions in four states (Indiana, Tennessee, Texas, and Wisconsin) over a three-year period. The goal of the initiative was to determine what it took to create successful and sustainable heritage tourism programs. While this experience demonstrated that every program is different, five guiding principles emerged from the pilot regions that were important components for success.

Five Principles for Successful and Sustainable Cultural Heritage Tourism

1. *Collaborate*: By its very nature, cultural heritage tourism requires effective partnerships. Much more can be accomplished by working together than by working alone.
2. *Find the Fit Between the Community and Tourism*: Cultural heritage tourism should make a community a better place to live as well as a better place to visit.
3. *Make Sites and Programs Come Alive*: Look for ways to make visitor experiences exciting and interactive by engaging as many of the five senses as possible.
4. *Focus on Quality and Authenticity*: Today's cultural heritage traveler is more sophisticated and will expect a high level of quality and an authentic experience.
5. *Preserve and Protect Resources*: Many cultural, historic, and natural resources are irreplaceable. Once they are gone, they are lost forever.

Developing cultural heritage tourism programs is an incremental process that does not produce changes overnight. The National Trust for Historic Preservation's heritage tourism initiative also identified four steps for starting a new program or effort for taking an existing program or effort to the next level. While many people equate tourism with marketing, responsible cultural heritage tourism programs include a comprehensive effort that encompasses tourism development, marketing, and management.

Four Steps for Cultural Heritage Tourism Development

Step One: Assess the Potential

Evaluate existing and potential attractions, visitor services, organizational capabilities, and marketing.

Step Two: Plan and Organize

Set priorities and measurable goals to maximize your potential, taking full advantage of human and financial resources to showcase your cultural and heritage attractions.

Step Three: Prepare for Visitors; Protect and Manage Your Resources

Implement planning efforts to improve the visitor experience and ensure that increasing visitors will not negatively impact the cultural or heritage resource.

Step Four: Market for Success

Identify target markets and develop a multi-year, many-tiered marketing plan.

The National Trust for Historic Preservation has continued to incorporate these principles and steps into cultural heritage tourism projects since the end of the heritage tourism initiative in 1993, and has consistently found that these principles and steps have stood the test of time. This has continued to hold true even during times of economic uncertainty. In 2011, the National Trust for Historic Preservation received another grant from the National Endowment for the Arts to seek out "survival stories" to demonstrate creative ways that cultural and heritage attractions had found to remain viable in financially challenging times.

While the guiding principles still ring true for both strong and weak economic climates, in tough times cultural and heritage attractions need to place an increased emphasis on tracking results and being prepared to make their case with key decision makers. Many attractions are finding that technology and social networking are not only good ways to reach out to new audiences; they also offer cost-effective alternatives to other approaches. Lack of funding has forced many attractions to reevaluate their offerings, allowing them to identify audiences with the greatest potential and focusing programs and marketing efforts to reach that target audience. Recognizing that visitors are also feeling the economic pinch, some attractions are emphasizing value in order to attract audiences that may have less disposable income than they did previously. Taking advantage of anniversaries and celebrations is another way that attractions have found to enhance their visibility. Cultural heritage sites are also reaching out to the local community in new ways, working to establish a deeper connection with locals who may have the ability and interest to do more than just a one-time visit or tour.

Cultural heritage tourism is here to stay, and savvy managers of cultural and heritage tourism attractions are finding ways to remain grounded in the basic principles while adapting the visitor experience to meet the needs and interests of cultural heritage travelers. To learn more about cultural heritage tourism, visit www.culturalheritagetourism.org.

Amy Webb
National Trust for
Historic Preservation

See tourism.

Cultural Resource Geographic Information Systems (CRGIS). The Cultural Resource Geographic Information Systems facility is the only program in the *National Park Service (NPS) dedicated to developing and fostering the use of *Geographic Information Systems (GIS) and Global Positioning Systems (GPS) technologies in documenting, analyzing, and managing cultural resources. Working closely with parks, partners, and other NPS programs such as the *Historic American Buildings Survey (HABS), the *Historic American Engineering Record (HAER) and the *Historic American Landscapes Survey (HALS), CRGIS records the nation's heritage using a variety of tools. Begun in the 1990s in response to the congressionally mandated survey of Civil War battlefields to help locate, define, and document these resources, CRGIS has expanded into providing a wide array of technical services and training as well as applying these technologies more expansively in cultural resource management.

Within historic preservation, accurate locational data remains a critical element in our understanding of cultural landscapes, building traditions, settlement patterns, and past life ways. However, relying completely on traditional survey and documentation efforts limits our options. CRGIS explores the use of GIS and GPS to better manage and protect cultural resources. Combining these technologies with traditional documentation methods expands the use of documentation for wider audiences. As we continue to broaden our definitions of cultural resources, we must also entertain new ways to record these resource types.

CRGIS works on projects that illustrate how GIS and GPS technologies can better illustrate cultural resources, provide better access to sites, and allow users to engage in dynamic analysis. Projects range from focusing on engineering features to historic buildings to large *landscapes and traditional cultural properties, enhancing the stories told by the resources with technology. CRGIS also works to use GIS and GPS following disasters such as hurricanes or floods to identify and evaluate affected properties, determine their historic significance, and document the resources in the event of other disasters. CRGIS employs all forms of technologies related to geographically representing cultural resources, providing better visualization, analysis, and resource protection tools.

Sharing and disseminating locational information is important to understanding the context within which resources acquire significance and remains critically important in quickly responding to emergencies. Under Office of Management and Budget (OMB) Circular A-16, the NPS is designated the lead federal agency for the cultural resource data theme throughout the federal government, tasked with providing standards, guidelines, and methods of sharing information. CRGIS collaborates with other federal, state, and tribal agencies to develop tools and standards to facilitate this data sharing, developing cultural resource spatial data transfer standards.

Providing cultural resource–oriented GIS and GPS training is a key component of the CRGIS program. CRGIS offers an array of training experiences ranging from classroom hands-on introduction to GIS and GPS field schools providing a basis for designing and carrying out GPS survey and performing analysis with GIS data using cultural resource applications as the base.

CRGIS continues to explore the range and depth of possibilities that GIS and GPS technologies offer cultural resource specialists as they work to find new ways to more accurately record, manage, and promote cultural resources.

For more information about the CRGIS program and to contact the Cultural Resource GIS Facility, visit the website at https://www.nps.gov/crgis.

DEIDRE MCCARTHY
NATIONAL PARK SERVICE

See GIS; Historic American Buildings Survey; Historic American Engineering Record; Historic American Landscapes Survey; National Park Service.

cultural tradition. See folklore and folklife.

Cyndi's list. See genealogical resources online; local history resources online.

Czechs and Slovaks in North America, sources for. See Appendix A.

$\mathcal{D}$

Danes in North America, sources for. See Appendix A.

databases. See local history resources online.

Daughters of the American Revolution Library, Archives, Museum, and Office of the Historian General, National Society (NSDAR). The National Society Daughters of the American Revolution (NSDAR) is a membership-based, genealogy-driven organization founded in 1890 by and for women; it serves a historical, educational, and patriotic mission. The DAR owns and administers one of the largest properties to be owned exclusively by women; the headquarters encompasses a city block and includes Constitution Hall and Memorial Continental Hall in Washington, D.C., both Registered National Historic Landmarks. At the NSDAR headquarters, local history researchers, regardless of gender or membership status, may access local history information in the library, archives, museum, and the Office of the Historian General.

The library's core collection and its online catalog are organized geographically; the strength of its holdings rests in family history, Native American history, regional history, American women's history, and American Revolutionary history. Special collections include the more than 500-volume library of the National Huguenot Society, the approximately 1,200 publications of the Works Progress Administration's *Historical Records Survey*, 300,000 files containing genealogical information relative to American Revolutionary participants and their families, and a 2,000-volume collection of Native American historical and genealogical information. The library offers electronic access to its membership application records through its automated Genealogical Research System. Records that supplement the membership applications are also available through the Library Search Service, in which library staff search the membership records manually and provide copies of needed documents to patrons. Manuscript collections at the library, usually involving unpublished family or local research notes and compilations, may be searched through the library catalog. The library is open Monday–Friday from 8:30 a.m. to 4:00 p.m. and Saturday from 9:00 a.m. to 5:00 p.m.

The NSDAR's closed institutional archives holds founding records of all DAR chapters, and architectural records of DAR-owned properties worldwide. These records may be accessed by first obtaining written permission of the Office of the President General. The Office of the Historian General is open from 8:30 a.m. to 4:00 p.m., Monday through Friday.

The permanent collections of the NSDAR Museum include more than

30,000 pieces of furniture and *decorative arts, most of which predate the Industrial Revolution, many donated by members of the organization and have family and regionally significant provenance; the holdings also depict family history and women's history. Visitors may access exhibited items in two galleries and thirty-one regional "period rooms." The period rooms are accessible whenever the building is open; guided tours are offered from 10:00 a.m. to 2:30 p.m. Monday through Friday, and 9:00 a.m. to 4:30 p.m. on Saturday. Museum gallery hours run from Monday through Friday, 8:30 a.m. to 4:00 p.m., and Saturday from 9:00 a.m. to 5:00 p.m.

The NSDAR's Office of the Historian General maintains records of monuments and markers placed by DAR chapters worldwide. Additionally, this office administers the Americana Collection, a trove of more than 4,000 colonial-American, Revolutionary, and early Federal manuscripts, including diaries, letters, court records, birth records, military records, household inventories, and other documents and imprints. Visitors may access these materials from 8:30 a.m. to 4:00 p.m., Monday through Friday.

Contact the NSDAR at 1776 D Street NW, Washington, D.C. 20006-5392; (202) 628-1776; www.dar.org.

HEATHER A. WADE, CAE
INDEPENDENT SCHOLAR

See WPA Historical Records Survey.

deaccessioning. Deaccessioning is the formal, legal process by which museums and history organizations remove objects from their permanent collections. When an institution accepts objects for its permanent collection, a process called accessioning is used to record critical information about the source of the item and the terms of the gift. From time to time, institutions will remove accessioned items from their permanent collections for reasons such as poor condition, redundancy, failure to support the mission, *repatriation, or their inability to care for them.

Because collecting organizations hold objects in trust for the benefit of the public, professional standards have been developed to guide institutions through the deaccessioning process in an attempt to make deaccessioning a transparent activity. As a result, various ethical and professional guidelines governing the deaccessioning process should always be included within an institution's written collections management policy.

Once an item has been deaccessioned from a museum's collection, it can be disposed of in a variety of ways, including transferring the item to another museum or history organization, repatriating it in the case of stolen material, or selling it. In addition to an organization's governing board making responsible choices regarding the content of collections and the act of accessioning, the guidelines of the *American Alliance of Museums (AAM) and the *American Association for State and Local History (AASLH) stipulate that the proceeds from the sale of deaccessioned material not be used to provide financial support for museum operations. Instead, the ethical standard to be followed requires that funds are to

169

be used for the purchase of new collections or for the preservation of existing collections. A 2016 white paper from AAM (http://aam-us.org/docs/default-source/default-document-library/direct-care-of-collections-ethics-guidelines-and-recommendations-pdf.pdf?sfvrsn=8) provides additional guidance on the definition of "direct care" and includes information specifically for history museums and historic sites.

In recent years, deaccessioning has attracted broad attention and generated substantial public controversy as cash-strapped institutions have looked to deaccessioning collections to provide much-needed operating income. A common argument questions whether an institution's overall fiscal and programmatic health should be held hostage to its collections. Others believe that when an institution deaccessions to pay its debts, it has diminished its public trust obligations in favor of short-term gain. Because AASLH and AAM provide only guidelines regarding ethical deaccessioning, each institution must make its own decisions about creating and implementing a deaccessioning policy that meets the prevailing standards of the profession.

The Active Collections Project (http://www.activecollections.org) proposes new models for thinking about history museum collections, proposing that "We believe we need to change the conversation from caring for artifacts to caring about people." One of many ways to move toward that change is for the field to develop basic, streamlined procedures for deaccessioning.

For more information on policies and procedures, see American Association for State and Local History: www.aaslh.org; American Alliance of Museums: www.aam-us.org.

Linda Norris
The Uncataloged Museu
Anne W. Ackerson
Council of State Archivists

See museum ethics; Native American Graves Protection and Repatriation Act (NAGPRA).

decorative arts. The term usually means all aesthetic objects that are not architecture or fine art, such as furniture, textiles, metalwork, and ceramics, but may extend to toys, jewelry, costumes, bookbinding, and wallpaper. These objects can be studied in a number of ways: as articles to be collected by connoisseurs, as part of the history of art, the history of technology, or social history. In museums they may be grouped by period, style, region of origin, material, or function. For the most thorough survey of decorative arts worldwide see Pat Kirkham and Susan Weber, eds., *History of Design: Decorative Arts and Material Culture, 1400–2000* (2013), which presents design from six parts of the world: East Asia, India, the Islamic World, Africa, Europe, and the Americas. For a good overview of scholarship trends in American decorative arts up to 1989 see Kenneth L. Ames and Gerald W. R. Ward, eds., *Decorative Arts and Household Furnishings in America, 1650–1920: An Annotated Bibliography* (1989). While useful, this book includes no Native American references and few Canadian or Mexican American works. For Canadian works, see Donald B. Webster, ed., *The Book of Canadian An-*

tiques (1974). For materials up to 1860, Rosemary Troy Krill, *Early American Decorative Arts: 1620–1860* (revised and enhanced, 2010) provides an overview directed toward museum interpreters. Its initial chapters place the decorative arts in context, while later chapters examine objects by type.

As the focus in history museums continues to move away from the objects themselves and toward how objects can be used to tell myriad stories about people of all classes, including servants, children, women, and other previously invisible subjects, the canon of important works and creators has broken down, as has the emphasis on the material culture of the ruling class. From early on, provenance has been significant because the mere fact that an object was owned by a prominent person conferred value on that object. Now the interest has shifted to the consumers themselves, no matter what their class or status in the community. A good examination of this theme can be found in Ann Smart Martin, *Makers and Users: American Decorative Arts 1630–1820* (1999).

Typological histories that trace the evolution of particular forms have been important sources of information. The study of vernacular materials, regional variations, and patterns of change and diffusion has always been useful. Scholars are now moving beyond tracing the diffusion of certain forms, such as dining-room sideboards, to ask why there are shifts in taste and regional variations in forms. Increasingly they are studying the interaction of cultural and production centers with social and geographic margins.

The study of decorative arts is often multidisciplinary and increasingly difficult to distinguish from an interest in *material culture. Folklorists have offered new insights about visual thinking, and historians have learned the value of contextual studies from social scientists and anthropologists. Scholars have pointed out that objects have multiple contexts—social, cultural, political, ideological, and technological—all of which can shed light on a work's meaning and significance. The decorative arts are shaped not only by aesthetics, availability of materials, and craftsmanship, but also by trade disputes, price fixing, fuel supplies, or labor shortages.

Much work is being done on the ideology of material goods. Scholars have begun to examine why certain objects are sometimes desirable and sometimes out of fashion. Other researchers look for patterns of consumption and use that may have been too obvious to record at the time. As in other fields, scholars are currently paying more attention to ethnicity and class, often bringing a Marxist or feminist perspective to the task. For example, the interest in quilts that was stimulated by the Bicentennial has led to a broader discussion of women's issues.

This is an exciting time for those interested in the decorative arts, and local historians in particular can make substantial contributions to our understanding of the past. While eighteenth-century primary sources may be scarce, there is much material for nineteenth- and twentieth-century objects. *Photographs and trade catalogs are just two important sources. See E. Richard McKinstry, *Trade Catalogs at*

Winterthur: A Guide to the Literature of Merchandising, 1750–1980 (1984) and William Seale, *The Tasteful Interlude: American Interiors through the Camera's Eye, 1860–1917*, 2nd ed. (1981). For suggestions on research strategies, see Kenneth Ames et al., *Material Culture: A Research Guide* (1985).

The recent proliferation of Internet sites that provide access to scholarly articles and good images has made the study of decorative arts easier for those far from specialized libraries. It is often possible to access reference works remotely through state library systems with just a local library card. One reference available this way is the *Grove Encyclopedia of the Decorative Arts*, which is part of Oxford Art Online. The University of Wisconsin–Madison maintains its Digital Library of Decorative Arts and Material Culture (deco rativearts.library.wisc.edu) with links to images and other online resources. Some of the best decorative arts publications have all or some of their articles online, including *American Furniture* and *American Ceramics*, both published annually by the Chipstone Foundation (chipstone.org). The AHRC Centre for the Study of the Domestic Interior maintains a searchable Domestic Interiors Database with images and textual sources relating to western Europe and North America (csdi.rca.ac.uk/didb/in dex.php).

Museums are increasingly placing their collections online. Currently, some of the best museum websites for the decorative arts are the Victoria and Albert Museum (vam.ac.uk), the Metropolitan Museum of Art (metmuseum. org), and the Museum of Fine Arts,

Boston (mfa.org). It is always advisable to check the websites of local and regional museums as well, because collections are constantly being added (and removed). On many museum sites, decorative arts objects are scattered among different departments, so searching for "furniture," "silver," or "embroidery" under American Art might produce results on a site that at first seems to lack these collections.

BONNIE STACY
MARTHA'S VINEYARD MUSEUM

See material culture.

decree. A court judgment; judicial decision.

deed, title. Legal document that shows ownership, used to transfer property from one person to another.

Delaware, local history in. Delawareans have long been proud of a rich history that reaches back more than 350 years. The state, one of the original thirteen colonies, traces its development to the 1600s when the first permanent European settlement was established in 1638 with the landing of a Swedish contingent led by Dutchman Peter Minuet. The Swedes proved ineffective managers and New Sweden was short-lived; the colony passed through Dutch and then English authority in quick succession. But the roots of human habitation existed centuries earlier, with the Lenni Lenape and other native peoples living in the lands around the Delmarva peninsula for thousands of years.

Delaware residents are cognizant of their home state's unique persona

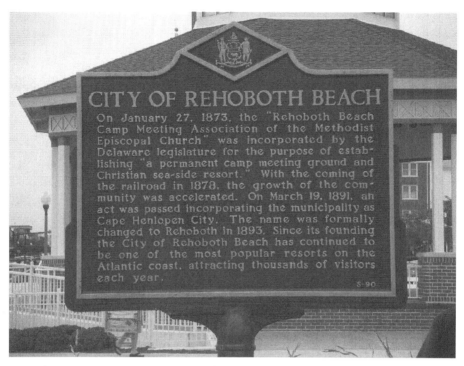

This Delaware state marker describes the origins of the City of Rehoboth Beach. CREDIT: WIKIPEDIA, PUBLIC DOMAIN.

as the "First State" because it was the first to ratify the new Constitution of the United States in 1781. Delawareans annually celebrate unique holidays such as Separation Day in New Castle, which commemorates the colony of Delaware breaking away from Pennsylvania, and Return Day, where Delaware politicians, victorious and otherwise, gathered in the community of Georgetown to literally bury the hatchet, shake hands, and "return" to civil discourse. Delaware is composed of three counties—New Castle, Kent, and Sussex—but it displays two distinct cultural temperaments delineated by residents living above and below the Chesapeake and Delaware Canal, which cuts through the lower half of New Castle County. The compact nature of the state, which began as the "Three Lower Counties" of Pennsylvania before becoming the colony of Delaware in 1776, belies its stubborn tendency to view culture and community through the lens of a definite upstate-downstate contrast. New Castle County includes the city of Wilmington, which is the largest metropolitan area in Delaware and historically the state's economic and industrial center. Kent and Sussex Counties, in contrast, have been largely rural and agricultural, a situation that has only begun to change within the last forty years.

Efforts to officially recognize and preserve the state's history began in the nineteenth century. One of the first private agencies to be established was the Historical Society of Delaware (today the Delaware Historical Society), which began in Wilmington in 1864. As of 2011, this organization remains the largest private repository of Delaware history in the state and publishes the periodic scholarly journal *Delaware History*. The state of Delaware began playing a more official role in preservation in 1905, when, recognizing the importance of preserving state records for future generations, the Delaware General Assembly created the Delaware Public Archives. As the largest and oldest university in this small state, the University of Delaware also plays an important role in preserving historic resources. Programs within the university such as the Center for Historic Architecture & Design (CHAD) have enabled the inventory and documentation of historic structures throughout the state. Within Morris Library's Special Collections Department, the Delaware Collection holds a wealth of materials related to state and local history with a particular strength in political papers and memorabilia.

Given the independent character of the state's people and communities, many preservation efforts have tended to develop on the local level, usually prompted by concern for a specific building or issue. For example, in 1895, the Friends of Old Drawyers Church organized to save a Georgian-style brick church structure built in 1773. In 1934, the New Castle Historical Society was formed to save the Amstel House, built in the 1730s and one of that city's oldest structures. These informal groups tended to subsequently become more

organized collecting entities, so small repositories of historical materials can be found throughout the state.

Delaware remained predominantly rural until after World War II, and the postwar boom in suburban neighborhoods, land development, and changing demographics is reflected in a second wave of historical interest in the latter part of the twentieth century. Specialized institutions such as Winterthur (1951) and Hagley Museum & Library (1953) developed during this period, organizations that specifically documented interests and history springing from the du Pont family, the dominant catalyst for most of Delaware's industrial, economic, and social infrastructure.

Historical societies and preservation agencies also continued to develop throughout the state, creating a plethora of small institutions, some of which struggle to remain viable. The Lewes Historical Society was founded in 1962, in response to growing concerns about the fate of eighteenth-century buildings in a rapidly changing resort community. The trend of small agencies has continued to exist with organizations such as the Middletown Historical Society established in 1985, and Claymont Historical Society in 2000. The State of Delaware has also continued to invest in preservation of historical resources, opening an $18 million state-of-the-art facility for historical resources and document preservation in January 2001.

Elementary and secondary school students in Delaware learn about their state's history beginning in fourth grade, with more in-depth explorations of local history in the later grades.

Students in sixth through eighth grade concentrate on pre-industrial Delaware to 1877, while those in high school (ninth through twelfth grades) focus on Reconstruction through contemporary history. Delaware state standards for history were first established as part of the Delaware Department of Education's Social Studies Curriculum Framework in 1995.

Among publications that address Delaware history, one of the earliest is *Original Settlements on the Delaware* by Benjamin Ferris (1846). Another nineteenth-century work that documents the state's history in a systematic manner is the two-volume *History of Delaware: 1609–1888*, by J. Thomas Scharf (1888). Among more recent publications is Carol Hoffecker's *Readings in Delaware History* (1973). For most Delaware scholars, John A. Munroe's *History of Delaware* (2nd ed., 1984) is generally recognized as the standard history of the state.

STEPHANIE PRZYBYLEK
CREATIVE ANIMAL FINE AND
DECORATIVE ARTS

demography. Demography is the statistically based study of population. It is as old as the initial counting of a distinct group of people in the distant past, perhaps for purposes of taxation or defense. It is as new as the last census or unemployment rate. An interdisciplinary study, demography draws from and is important to many academic areas—anthropology, biology, economics, geography, history, mathematics, medicine, political science, and sociology, among others. Demographers from related disciplines, like the social sciences, often share data, use similar quantitative techniques, and frequently explore related if not identical issues. The field has burgeoned in the last fifty years. Steady advances in computing, in techniques for statistical analysis, and in the availability of data have made demographic analyses pervasive. They inform our lives in ways of which we are often unaware. Nonetheless, now as in the past the value of population studies depends on demographers' knowing whom to count, how to count, and how to frame valid research questions. In other words, investigators need to have reliable data, quantitative skills, and an appropriate research plan.

Reliable data are the foundations of any demographic study. For a project's validity a researcher must evaluate all data rigorously for accuracy, adequacy, and appropriateness. All demographers necessarily use data collected in the past (if only the very recent past), but historical demographers routinely delve into earlier periods, when standards were often less exacting, handwriting subject to easy misreading, and documents frequently in a pitiful state from fire, flood, rodents, and other calamities. If a historian collects raw data, the need to make it usable, to "massage" it, will generally be great. Some local historians, especially those working in the more recent past, may consult large, computerized databases or parts thereof like the federal census (or that of another nation or entity). Decennial censuses may contain successively greater amounts of raw data. That material also usually requires refining although digests of massaged data appear in the Statistical Abstracts of the United

States, among other works. Modern civic authorities have collected a host of census-type materials and have joined central repositories like governments and libraries worldwide in placing their records online (although a built-in delay in availability for reasons of privacy is frequently the case). Many of these data sources reach back several centuries. The Church of Jesus Christ of Latter-day Saints, for one, has photocopied local demographic material from past centuries and across the world. Originally collected for genealogical research, these records are available to historians among others in the church's libraries around the country. Collecting demographic information from good photocopies is much like having the original documents. However, a demographer should take care if using someone else's genealogical linking.

Whatever the demographic question being examined, there must be an adequate amount of data. Demographers often do not perform statistical procedures on limited data, knowing that the results may be spurious. Researchers working with more modern sources generally have enough data, often more than enough, in which case a well-drawn random sample can make the data more manageable. Mathematical formulas can help to determine a desirable sample size, and randomness assumes that every datum in the original set has an equal chance of selection. Some large databases available for general use have ready-drawn samples available. Moreover, historians frequently share data. While record survival is often a problem with primary sources, demographers may also find that a more re-

cent database has disappeared on aging equipment. Making copies of data and updating them regularly are important.

While many demographers working with more modern data may have to consider narrowing a study, often by sampling, some historians may find it difficult to locate sufficient earlier data for adequate analysis. These historians may begin with an important but very limited data source, then search for other sources to which the first can be linked. Material often surfaces in repositories like county courthouses, local archives, state libraries, and church headquarters, as well as other smaller archives. That material may include civil or parish registers, tax records, welfare rolls, ship manifests, enlistment accounts, town censuses, cemetery records, and the like. Such documents frequently chronicle key points in the life-cycle such as birth, marriage, death, and migration—events that gave demography its original contours—as well as other population information including economic, disease, and occupational activity. Like other local history, locally focused demography may originate with or become part of mega-studies, some of which change long-held historical assumptions (see Cambridge Group for the History of Population and Social Structure).

Even with modern technology, difficult data problems persist in demographic analysis. What seems like a relatively simple operation may be quite complex, like linking by using the variable of name. A person named a single time without further characterization in one source may be difficult to link to one of multiple namesakes that occur in a second source. Other common problems that interfere with linking by name include lack of standardized spelling of names, aliases resulting from Anglicization of names, and clerical error. These problems are more frequent in documents that predate social security and other government registration; they are at times and places where illiteracy has been common. Computer programs, like those that list possible variant spellings, may help, but there is much that they cannot do. Even what may appear to be simple linkage requires critical thinking.

Valid record-linkage as well as subsequent analysis requires a clear definition of the variable. Lack of such clarity may well distort a study. In some cases in order to make data more manageable and understandable, demographers create subcategories of the variable. For example, a variable such as cause of death could be divided into subcategories such as pulmonary disease, accidents, or maternal mortality into which individual values such as pneumonia, drowning, or postpartum bleeding could fit. Every cause of death in the database should fit into one of the subcategories and yet each subcategory should be mutually exclusive under normal circumstances. Definition is often a difficult task because terms are imprecise (Midwest, flu), long forgotten (gripping of the guts), and deliberately redefined (manic-depressive). Moreover, boundaries change (U.S.S.R., political districts) and categories expand (race). In some cases definition is not just an analytical but a creative act. A local historian might wish to compare mortality rates in neighborhoods where

neighborhoods are not official entities. That historian must then define a variable, neighborhood, that would include all the neighborhood units being investigated as categories, mapping the units verbally if not visually.

Demographers need statistical skills to analyze and summarize data. Percentages, proportions, ratios, measures of central tendency, and other more demanding procedures such as bivariate and multivariate analyses help make sense of data. Social data fall into levels determined by the statistical flexibility that each level can accommodate. Statistical tests used on a lower level of data may be used on each succeeding level. The lowest level of social data, nominal data, consists of variables such as name, location, or occupation. Such data, which cannot be averaged, may be measured by simple statistical procedures such as proportions, percentages, or ratios as well as some bivariate analyses. The next level of data, ordinal, consists of rank-ordered variables (first to last, best to worst) and may be summarized in medians and used in rank-order correlation tests as well. The two highest levels of data—equal interval and ratio—may be considered as one. Both have equal intervals between values, such as miles or dollars. In addition to procedures used on lower levels of data, equal-interval variables withstand multivariate analysis and measures of central tendency (means, medians, modes, and standard deviation, for example). At every level there are other statistical procedures not discussed here that may be appropriate. One must remember, however, that where a statistic indicates correlation between variables, the correlation may not be meaningful. Moreover, some correlations may suggest causality, but correlation does not necessarily indicate causality.

Governments and the public make decisions based on the ability of demographers, notably epidemiologists and pollsters among others, to analyze past data statistically and to infer future behavior and events from that analysis. Statistical inference is also sometimes employed in backward projection, like that used to produce credible estimates of English population from the mid-sixteenth century to the advent of the modern census. Statistical inference necessitates a command of probability theory as well as appropriate statistical methods.

Demography is a valuable tool for historians—local and otherwise. Historians who may not have the requisite mathematical skills for demographic analysis can seek help in many places. Among others, institutions such as libraries and universities have staff that can assist in selecting statistical textbooks or statistical packages designed for demographic applications on the computer. A wealth of other pertinent information is readily available online. Good data and statistical skill are necessary to but not sufficient for a good demographic study. That study will require a carefully constructed and appropriate research plan as well.

SHEILA MCISAAC COOPER
INDIANA UNIVERSITY, RETIRED

See Cambridge Group for the History of Population and Social Structure; census, United States; FamilySearch; mortality schedules.

devise. Refers to a gift of land or buildings made through a last will and testament. Usually personal property that is not real estate is called a "bequest" or a "legacy."

diaries. Diaries, offspring of the invention of the pendulum clock in the early seventeenth century, are records consisting of chronologically structured entries, at least some of which must be dated. Although diaries and journals are often used synonymously, according to some scholars, diaries differ from journals; diary entries may include content on more random, informal, and unguarded everyday occurrences, while journals are a medium for deeper reflection that reveal interests in specific subjects or preoccupations with certain themes. Generally themeless, the diary is a method of documenting the passage of time focused on the immediate observations of its author. Diarists represent an extremely diverse demographic; as Paul C. Rosenblatt notes in *Bitter, Bitter Tears: Nineteenth-Century Diarists and Twentieth Century Grief Theories* (1983), the common traits of people who keep diaries may be limited to (1) an ability to write; (2) the means to support the diary-writing habit; and (3) sufficient energy and time to keep a diary. People write diaries for many reasons: to seek order and method; for companionship; to keep accounts; to express unspeakable emotions; to leave evidence of one's life; or simply out of habit.

See Thomas Mallon, *A Book of One's Own: People and Their Diaries* (1984), in which he studies diarists who can be characterized as "Chroniclers," "Travelers," "Pilgrims," "Creators," "Apologists," "Confessors," and "Prisoners."

The contents of diaries can be as diverse as their authors, most of whom never anticipated a public life for the diaries. Such obstacles as cryptic entries, inaccurate spellings, marginalia, and coded information present a challenge to local historians who use diaries. Researchers may expect to find descriptions of daily activities or special occasions, weather reports, observations of human behavior, and descriptions of feelings. In *Emerson and the Art of the Diary*, Lawrence Rosenwald writes, "[I]n a diary, every entry can be compared with the world outside it" (1988, 7). Local history researchers may apply the vast variety of information found in diaries in countless ways.

Both Rosenblatt, *Bitter, Bitter Tears* and Jennifer Sinor, *The Extraordinary Work of Ordinary Writing: Annie Ray's Diary* (2002) explore differences between published and unpublished diaries. Editing a diary for publication alters the document; the process attempts to answer questions posed by the historian and may ignore the intent of the diarist. Aspects of the document such as doodles, the appearance and quality of the paper on which the diary was kept, idiosyncrasies in spelling and punctuation, or the use of margins or line breaks may be lost when the diary is published.

Viviane Serfaty, "Online Diaries: Towards a Structural Approach," *Journal of American Studies* 38 (2004), assesses the contemporary phenomena of self-representational writing using the newest technologies designed to disseminate information to a broad audience. The traditional text-only method of writing diaries yields to the accumulation of illustrations, audio files, hyperlinking, and the inclusion of sponsors' advertisements; online diarists often belong to *blog circles. In the online format, a diarist becomes preoccupied with his or her audience and with the technology; online diarists split their commentary between observations of the Internet and self-reflection.

To locate diaries, see Laura Arksey, Nancy Preis, and Marcia Reed, *American Diaries: An Annotated Bibliography of Published American Diaries and Journals* (1987) in two volumes, I: 1492–1844, II: 1845–1980, a guide to more than 5,000 published diaries and journals, with indexes arranged by name, subject, and geographical place. Unpublished diaries may be located in private homes, estate sales, used book stores, museums, libraries, and archives. Those that have been documented in cultural repositories may be included in finding aids or union catalogs such as the National Union Catalog of Manuscript Collections (http://www.loc.gov/coll/nucmc).

HEATHER A. WADE, CAE
INDEPENDENT SCHOLAR

See blogs.

dictionaries of biography. See biographical dictionaries.

Dictionary of Americanisms. Mitford Matthews was the lexicographer who compiled *A Dictionary of Americanisms on Historical Principles* (1951). This massive work documents American words and phrases, their meanings, and the first and some subsequent uses. For the phrase "all-American," for example, the entry, listing the first date of published use and the book or magazine where the usage appeared, reads:

1888 Outing Nov. 166/2 The All-American team . . . is composed of men picked from the ranks of the representative ball teams of America. 1920 Outing Nov. 84/3 The little cripple, none other than Eddie Dillon, sometime All American, caught the ball and ran with it through the entire opposing eleven for another touchdown. 1949 Atlantic March 24/1 You can't be an All-American on a losing team.

See manifest destiny; regionalisms; slang.

digital history. Roy Rosenzweig, for whom the Center for History and New Media at George Mason University is named, is arguably the father of digital history as we know it today. In the 1990s, when experimenting with CD-ROM technology and comparing it with the merits of the fledgling Internet, he theorized about the potentials and pitfalls associated with digital tools used by and for historians. Along with colleagues at the American Social History Project (creator of "Who Built America?" and "The Lost Museum") and the UVA Scholars' Lab (creator of "The Valley of the Shadow"), he imagined a world of unprecedented access to historical knowledge, democratization of content and knowledge production, and preservation and distribution of scarce historical resources. He also warned about classes of access that would define a new system of digital "haves" and "have-nots," new problems with verifying historical accuracy and policing misinformation, and historical resources lost to the rapid pace of changing media and effacing the

old in favor of the new. Almost thirty years after Rosenzweig first began writing about the topic, we live in a world where digital history has hardly lived up to the utopian visions of its early boosters, nor has it plunged the practice of history into the chaotic state feared by its detractors. Instead, it is the new normal, a balance of challenges and opportunities to be embraced by historians of all stripes.

Definitions of digital history vary depending on whom you ask. For some, digital history is a scholarly methodology. For others, it is a presentation tool. Yet others spend time debating the philosophical relationship between digital history, public history, and digital humanities. (The Humanities and Technology Camp or THATCamp for short has been a great place to engage in insightful un-conferences on the topic for almost a decade; see THATCamp. org.) However you define it, digital history need not intimidate local historians. It is merely a toolkit, and results depend only on selecting the right tool for the job.

For the purposes of interested local historians, I recommend dividing digital history into sets of tools for research, preservation, and presentation. Some of the most innovative digital history sites combine all three. (For inspiration, see http://mallhistory.org, http://digital-harlem.org, clevelandhistorical.org and americanyawp.com.)

Digital research tools are ever evolving and vary in computational skills prerequisites. Researchers interested in sifting through large data sets (such as census tracts, large-scale government surveys, or collections of digitized newspapers) in order to find statistical patterns would benefit from learning a scripting language. (For a debate on the relative merits of various scripting languages, see http://www.infoworld.com/article/2620515/application-development/from-php-to-perl—whats-hot—what-s-not-in-scripting-languages.html.)

For more traditional researchers, citation managers and digital organizers for note-taking and collaboration are both important and easy to use. Depending on your hardware of choice, there are many applications available, but ones that work especially well across platforms include Google docs and Zotero. Wikis and *blogs also provide excellent opportunities for groups of scholars to work together to develop content and test out ideas.

For researchers, another important digital history skill is the navigation of online databases, both closed and open access. Subscription services such as *Ancestry.com and Newspapers.com are quite familiar to local historians and genealogists, but reference librarians and archivists can introduce you to a wide array of research databases and digital finding aids accessible within particular computer networks. Even when using free and open databases, such as those operated by the U.S. government, be careful to consider multiple access points. For example, you may find different results if you search for the same keyword on American Memory and the Library of Congress websites.

These research databases provide a solid example of the "preservation" aspect of digital history. In the digital world, preservation is exemplified through redundancy and migration. It's not enough merely to digitize a historical document. The preservation-minded historian or archivist must make more than one copy in the highest fidelity available (TIF files for images or WAV files for audio, for example), preserve at least one on a separate, safe server protected from the elements (human and natural), and then create lower-fidelity access copies for researchers to view on access databases (JPGs for images, or MP3s for audio, for example). It is also important to note that the traditional experience of "authenticity" shifts with the access of digital and digitized resources. Experience and medium are important to consider. For example, a PDF of a single article from a newspaper extracted from microfilm does not preserve the experience of the reader finding that article buried on page 16 between an ad for hair tonic and a recipe for apple cobbler. A more recent example would be the text file extracted from a writer's 1991 Word Perfect file that had been preserved on a floppy disk and now exists on multiple servers in the cloud.

Digital historians (and others working with digital information) are developing new metadata tools and conventions to address these issues of durability and accessibility. Interested in enabling comparisons by researchers across file types and data locations, a consortium of scholars developed the Text Encoding Initative (TEI) for the XML markup languages starting in 1994. TEI for XML is machine readable and enables the construction of sophisticated databases of people, places, and events as well as standardized nomenclature for complex phenomena present in oral history interviews (environmental noise or laughter, for example). For more on TEI, please see http://www.tei-c .org/index.xml.

The world of digital history provides a plethora of opportunities for sharing research and historical materials with a wide range of audiences. At this stage in your work, some of your considerations will be philosophical while others will be practical. As in all public history endeavors, you need to think about your audience first. Do they prefer to access the Internet through computers or mobile devices? Do they simply want help finding a physical location, or do they want a virtual experience? If you are hoping to appeal to educators and students, how can you best connect your work to state history standards? Have you obtained all necessary licenses for displaying images and artifacts in a publicly accessible digital format? You need also to consider duration. If you are looking to find your audience on a short-term targeted basis, you might be best meeting them in their social media environment of choice, whether that be Twitter, Facebook, Pinterest, Instagram, or even Snapchat. These venues are also excellent spaces for specific flavors of history work. For example, Pinterest can provide a structure for a crowd-sourced informal archive. Photo sharing sites such as Flickr and Instagram are great places to connect with history enthusiasts around particular topics. Connections over social media have inspired successful spin-off sites like *HistoryPin. For durability and exposure, historical organizations are increasingly finding a need to be in multiple places at the same time including anchor sites on the web and mobile-responsive sites and applications.

In considering your project resources, it's also important to consider the relative merits of proprietary tools versus open-source options. Proprietary tools such as Google Cultural Institute benefit from name recognition and a wide audience draw. However, your content is hosted under a for-profit umbrella and subject to the preferences of the parent company. Other programs, such as Esri's ArcGIS software, provide a suite of sophisticated tools, but they sometimes come along with a steep price tag and high learning curve. Open-source programs, such as the tools created by the Center for History and New Media (including Omeka and its slate of university-sponsored plug-ins) are theoretically "free" but they require some sophisticated programming skills to customize, and feature updates wax and wane with the interest and attention of the active developer community. Often geographically defuse and varying in interest and time commitment, open-source developers are known to work on multiple projects at once and are not tied to working on something specific even if it is a fantastic product that you just discovered for the first time! Grant-funding tends to play a significant role in which projects advance and when, as well.

However, for small historical organizations with relatively small budgets, there is a lot to recommend Omeka and its cousins, Curatescape and Neatline. Numerous examples of websites that combine robust archives, rich historical interpretation, and advanced search tools for researchers can be found by Googling these three programs.

These tools are also ideal for projects that involve students. In the spring of 2015 I taught a digital history course for master's-level students at Georgia State University (GSU). I wanted my students to gain experience collaborating on a digital history project. I also wanted them to have an opportunity to produce individual digital exhibits to showcase their research. Loosely modeling my endeavor on the Greenwich Village History project at New York University (gvh.aphdigital.org), I selected a topic of lasting relevance to the greater Atlanta community. Since 2006, work on the Atlanta Beltline (www.beltline.org) has been ongoing. The project was conceived as a way to integrate Atlanta's historic twenty-two-mile rail corridor with new parks, trails, transit, and housing (both affordable and market-driven). I wanted to delve with my students into the historic aspects of that rail corridor, so we created the Atlanta Rail Corridor Archive project (atlrailcorridorarchive.org).

The project includes an Omeka-based website that is hosted on an off-site server supported by GSU. The site showcases items from repositories around the city of Atlanta and the United States, gathered and posted by students in HIST 8885, Theory and Practice of Digital History, a course in the Heritage Preservation Program at GSU. Students also created narrative exhibits that investigate themes relevant to the history of the rail corridor including communities, neighborhoods, educational institutions, businesses, and the changing uses of the natural and *built environment. Students helped to craft a permissions form to distribute to repositories for rights to re-post content on the Atlanta Rail Corridor Archive site and use that content in their exhibits. Only content for which we received permission, or that is in the public domain, could be used on the site. Students learned the fundamentals of the Dublin Corps metadata schema through posting digital objects on the site. During the second half of the semester, they honed their topics and created exhibits using Omeka's exhibit builder tool and a customizable theme that enabled them to more finely tune colors, fonts, and other aspects of the look and feel. Some used the Neatline plug-in or ArcGIS to produce annotated maps and interactive historical documents. You can view a selection of these exhibits here: atlrailcorridorarchive.org/exhibits. Through creating their exhibits, students learned about digital navigation, and some discovered the limits of "off-the-shelf" creative tools, finding themselves inspired to learn even more.

In conclusion, don't be afraid of digital history. Just think realistically about your project goals, time commitment, budget, and risk tolerance. With good background information, you can choose the right tool for the job.

Adina Langer
Kennesaw State University

See Valley of the Shadow, the.

digitization. Digitization refers to the process of creating digital replica from analog sources, as well as providing a means to access those digital files. Common examples are scans of documents or images, photographs of artifacts, and digitized video and audio files. The digital versions of analog items, as well as materials that are born digital, are commonly referred to as "digital assets." Many cultural organizations have been working on a degree of digitization for the past few decades. Now that we live in a digital age, in which most of the public expects to discover some degree of information through an online search, communities have been working to make their historical materials available online, but often with no consistent strategy. In order to create accessible digital collections that bring lasting value, organizations must begin to see digital collections as a necessary deliverable—indeed at the center of each historical society's mission—rather than a "nice to have" addition to the physical collection.

Creating and implementing a digitization strategy is becoming a priority for any organization seeking to increase membership or engagement, drive more foot traffic to exhibits and events, and expand fundraising potential. While strategies will vary depending on an organization's size, personnel, and budget, as well as the scope of its holdings, each must assess its collections and digital efforts in order to create a specific strategy for digitization that relates to its three main aspects: preservation, access, and use.

Preservation

Preservation has always been a driving impetus to digitize. Creating a digital replica of physical items provides a "backup" should anything happen to the original material. When consider-

ing digital preservation needs, assuring quality imaging is critical. Many organizations have opted to purchase a scanner, create lower resolution files, such as JPGs, and quickly get some images online. While this has the immediate benefit of making some materials digitally available, it fails to meet minimum digital preservation standards. In the long run, this approach will likely necessitate future digitization at a higher resolution when lower resolution digital assets are no longer readable. The best practice is to create higher-resolution archival preservation copies, typically in the form of TIFs, and then web-friendly derivatives of those files, such as JPGs or PDFs, to view online or through a local management system. Creating as high a resolution as possible for archival preservation copies does, however, have implications for the time it takes to create each digital asset (higher resolutions take longer to scan and render) and for storage costs (since larger files require more storage space).

Both the *National Archives and Records Administration and the *Library of Congress publish guidelines for the resolution for each type of historical item (http://www.archives.gov/preservation/technical/guidelines.html; https://www.loc.gov/preservation/care/scan.html). The resolution for a negative will differ from that of a document and from that of a photographed artifact, for example. The key is to examine the current digital standards and your capacity—through machines and labor resources and budget for outsourcing—and strive to meet current standards or else establish as high a resolution as possible and then apply that resolution *consistently* across your digital collection. Creating multiple formats from high-resolution images will assure the highest likelihood for lasting preservation of physical items in the form of digital assets.

Organizations can create their digital collections in-house with the help of staff and volunteers or outsource the imaging to a vendor, or do some of both. Selection of a method will depend not only on budgets and timelines, but also on the kinds of materials that must be digitized. Often a good flatbed scanner can be used to capture most photograph and document collections, but some collections will require the use of overhead or cradle scanners. Whatever the methodology, it is important to include a quality control review in any digitization plan. During the imaging process, it is imperative that each digital asset is reviewed to make sure that nothing is blurry, cut off, or skewed. If you are going to invest in a digital collection, make sure that the results are of the highest quality possible in every way.

Access

An organization's digitization plan must consider not only imaging standards, but also how to manage and share their digital assets. To make a digital collection truly accessible, people must be able to find and navigate the digital records. This requires:

1. A robust collection management system that contains the digital assets, as well as searchable information, or metadata, that describes each asset.
2. The adoption of a metadata plan that allows the organization to easily manage their digital collections while providing a way for the general public to explore the materials online.
3. A person, group, or vendor to write the descriptive information and catalog or index the records so that a diverse array of people can find them. This is the most involved step in the digitization process, but without it, we simply have a haystack of digital needles.
4. An online space for visitors to search this information, find linkages among the items, and easily view or read the digitized original item.

There are several collection and digital asset management systems available for cultural heritage institutions. When selecting a system, it is best to consider (1) the costs to maintain and support the system in addition to up-front costs (many systems have a considerable technology need that will require additional funding, for example); (2) whether a local or web-based system best supports your workflow; and (3) whether the system can handle the kinds of collections you maintain. In general, organizations should look for a solution that will allow them to manage all of their collections in a single program and that has an integrated digital asset management system so that they can connect metadata to images without having to construct and maintain an outside path to the digital assets.

The metadata, or descriptive information such as item names and descriptions and people and subject tags, is the key to making digital historical collections discoverable and informative for the online visitor. There are various professional metadata standards for different types of collections. Museum collections, for example, often utilize Nomenclature and Dublin Core, whereas bibliographic library collections tend to be managed according to a MARC system. (See Paul Bourcier, et al., eds., *Nomenclature 4.0 for Museum Cataloging: Robert G. Chenhall's System for Classifying Cultural Objects*, 4th ed.; descriptions of various metadata standards by the Library of Congress at https://www.loc.gov/standards and by the American Library Association at http://www.ala.org/tools/atoz/metadata/metadata.) Twenty-first-century digital collections must consider not only professional metadata standards, but also how online visitors search and behave. Simply making a management system's information available online does not provide a widely accessible digital collection. When selecting a digital management system and adopting a metadata plan, organizations are advised to consider what is also best for public consumption of digital collections, not only their management needs.

Use

In the past, the cultural heritage world has looked at preservation and access as the two pillars of digitization. But the third—use—is just as important for a strong digitization strategy. When creating digital collections, cultural heritage organizations greatly benefit by implementing strategies that consider public audiences and potential funding sources. Forming connections between online exhibits and social media outreach and on-site events strengthen the value of a digital collection and underscore the *relevancy of the organization in the community. Working to understand what online audiences would draw value from a particular digital collection will inform the metadata plan for that digitization effort.

Once an organization has established a digital collection, it is important to continue to care for it, just as we would the physical materials. This requires establishing a budget line, creating a plan for ongoing maintenance, monitoring usage and feedback, regularly backing up the information and digital images, and making sure that the web can still read and deliver the digital assets.

KRISTEN GWINN-BECKER
HISTORYIT

digitized source materials. See genealogy resources online; local history resources online.

diocese. An ecclesiastical administrative unit under the jurisdiction of a bishop.

District of Columbia, local history in. Washingtonians are fiercely proud of their local history. While outsiders and temporary residents often mistakenly assume that D.C. history involves only Congress, the president, and the workings of the federal government, D.C. has a rich, two-century local history. It

One of the graphic historical markers along the Adams Morgan Heritage Trail in Washington, D.C. CREDIT: HISTORICAL SOCIETY OF WASHINGTON, D.C.

is preserved and shared by an array of public and private entities, as well as individual history enthusiasts.

The first body organized to focus on D.C. history was the Association of Oldest Inhabitants of the District of Columbia, founded in 1865 to celebrate the city's "old" families. A more scholarly group came together in 1894 as the Columbia Historical Society. The thirty-six white men and women founders were mainly scientists and scholars working in the federal service and putting down roots. They wrote and delivered papers, often reminiscences as well as research. These papers were bound and published as the *Records of the Columbia Historical Society*. Members also collected photos, manuscripts, and ephemera. In 1956 the Historical

Society opened a library at the former home of brewer Christian Heurich in the Dupont Circle neighborhood.

In its early decades, the interests of the Columbia Historical Society reflected the composition of its white, professional, prosperous membership. Much of the history told in the earliest *Records* was theirs. Soon, however, the *Records* began publishing on city institutions, especially both divisions of the segregated school system. Through the 1950s, local black Washington's social history was more readily available in oral tradition, area churches, and the collections of Howard University's *Moorland-Spingarn Research Center. The D.C. Public Library's Washingtoniana materials covered the broad spectrum of local interests, reflecting its operation as one of the city's few nonsegregated public centers.

The civil rights and home rule movements of the 1960s and 1970s, which helped Washingtonians gain limited self-government for the first time in a century, spurred new interest in local D.C. history. In 1975 the D.C. School Board added D.C. history to the public school curriculum, and dozens of historians led by School Superintendent Vincent E. Reed and historian Kathryn Schneider Smith collaborated to write the first local history textbook. *The City of Magnificent Intentions* was published in 1983, and a revised edition continues to be used in D.C. public schools, where the subject is required in third and twelfth grades. Scholarly research on city history proliferated in the 1970s and 1980s, particularly in the urban studies department at the University of the District of Columbia (a new

institution that opened in 1977) and George Washington University's Center for Washington Area Studies, which opened in 1980. That year also saw the arrival of the Humanities Council of Washington, D.C., an affiliate of the *National Endowment for the Humanities, offering grants and programs for local Washington history.

While not all of these initiatives proved sustainable, the broader interest in local history helped catalyze changes within the Columbia Historical Society. In the early 1970s, it welcomed its first black members. In 1989 the group changed its name to the Historical Society of Washington, D.C., retired *Records of the Columbia Historical Society*, and unveiled *Washington History*, still the only scholarly journal devoted exclusively to the history of the nation's capital.

In the twenty-first century, local D.C. history is ever more accessible thanks to public and private efforts and the impact of the new field of public history. Peppered throughout the city are eighteen deeply researched, self-guided walking tours produced by the nonprofit Cultural Tourism DC, founded in 1999 to drive tourist traffic to historic neighborhoods and cultural destinations located off the National Mall. The city's Historic Preservation Office produces important studies of architectural history, and the Smithsonian Institution museums, especially the Anacostia Community Museum, often find local inspiration for interpretive projects. The Association for the Study of African American Life and History, founded by Carter G. Woodson, does the same. The Jewish Historical Society of Greater Washington and the Catholic Historical Society are two leaders in collecting and presenting materials on the city's religious history.

Washington does not have a museum dedicated solely to D.C. history—an abortive attempt to launch the City Museum of Washington, D.C., failed in 2003—but local history speaks in the city's small museums such as the Frederick Douglass Historic Site, Lincoln's Cottage, and Sumner School Museum and Archives. Urban and suburban groups, including the Cleveland Park Historical Society, the Arlington (Virginia) Historical Society, and the Prince George's County (Maryland) Historical Society, enrich the understanding of Washington as the heart of its metropolitan area. The Historical Society of Washington's Kiplinger Research Library and the Washingtoniana Collection at the Martin Luther King Jr., Public Library remain the primary research destinations, complemented by special collections at area universities. Because Washington was (and remains) subject to congressional oversight, much of its official story is recorded in U.S. government archives, and the city's agency archives have moved between the *National Archives and their current locally controlled repository. The recent development of websites and blogs use new technologies to document the city's past and share it with new audiences.

CHRIS MYERS ASCH AND
JANE FREUNDEL LEVEY
HISTORICAL SOCIETY
OF WASHINGTON, D.C.

See United States, local history in.

diversity and inclusion in museums. The United States is a mix of cultures and races and this diversity is increasing in the third millennium. Further, diversity sensitivity extends beyond cultural concerns when gender, sexual orientation, and range of ability and age are included. Museums will need to design culturally and linguistically appropriate programs and strategies targeted to the particular needs of their heterogeneous workforce and audiences. Museums must be prepared and willing to serve their diverse audiences if they wish to continue to have the support of the community. A critical step in meeting the diverse needs of the community is a diverse staff that reflects its community and understands the larger societal realities.

The Pew Research Center (2014) published telling stories about the changing U.S. demographics and the Andrew W. Mellon Foundation (2015) reported on U.S. art museums' changing demographics. By 2060, the racial majority (white) will become the minority at 43 percent and in the interceding years, the slow change will become increasingly apparent in ads and political campaigns. Millennials (born in the early 1980s to the late 1990s) are the most "racially and ethnically diverse generation ever," and more than "four-in-ten are non-white, many the U.S.-born children of Hispanic and Asian immigrants who began arriving a half a century ago" (Paul Taylor, *The Next America*, 2014).

But will the arts and culture sector be as responsive to the changing demographic? The Mellon research reveals that in art museums, African Americans comprise only 4 percent of the curators, conservators, educators, and leaders (the positions most associated with the intellectual and educational mission of museums); and Latinos are represented at 3 percent. In these jobs, 84 percent are white, which is significantly out of step with the diversity of American culture (62 percent white). Interestingly, women make up about 60 percent of art museum staff nationwide and are increasingly leaders in their institutions, demonstrating a swifter path to leadership for gender equality than minority representation. Another finding of the Mellon report is that promotion protocols will not diversify museum leadership until there is diversity in the educational pipeline. While this study focused on art museums, more studies will likely present similar results; having this baseline of research will only help the field change policy and opportunity to attract diversity (Roger Schonfeld and Mariet Westermann, *The Andrew W. Mellon Foundation Art Museum Staff Demographic Survey*, 2015).

A first step for any museum administrator is to be a part of the development of a diversity and inclusion policy (may also be known as a statement). Drawing from examples in academia and the corporate world, this kind of policy is written by a diverse team of staff members, trustees, and stakeholders. Reviewing other policies is helpful to the process, and be sure to include in the policy the museum's values and goals for diversity. The final policy will need to be vetted by the organization and board to ensure awareness and compliance (Elizabeth Wolfenden, "How to Write a Diversity Statement for an Employer," *Houston Chronicle*).

From *Museum Administration 2.0* by Hugh H. Genoways and Lynne M. Ireland, revised by Cinnamon Catlin-Legutko. Copyright 2016. Reprinted with permission of Rowman & Littlefield Publishers.

See building bridges through local history; mission statements; vision statement.

DNA analysis. See genealogy, African American; genealogy, Jewish.

docent. A *docent* is generally defined as a tour guide at a museum, and most docents are volunteers. The word comes from the Latin docere, to teach, but other terms include guide and interpreter. During the last several decades, the role of the docent has changed considerably. It's not enough anymore to simply be a deliverer of facts—to know that that chair was owned by Captain So and So and donated to the museum by Captain So and So's great-granddaughter, Miss Such and Such.

Docents are the public face of the museum or history organization. As such, they should be welcoming to all, flexible, knowledgeable, and committed to creating engaging experiences for visitors. However, they should always keep the organization's mission at the forefront of their work and place personal likes and dislikes aside. They serve as a bridge between visitors' knowledge and the learning that happens during a tour or site visit. They are not solely fact-bearers, but catalysts for learning.

To be effective catalysts, docents must know their stuff by having an understanding of the material and be able to assess their audience (Are they young people? Local visitors? From out of town? What kinds of interests and perspectives do they bring to the museum or historic site?). Each of those elements will affect, to some degree, the conversation with visitors.

Docents have a right to expect that they will receive information, training in both content and tour delivery, and regular evaluation and interaction with staff or volunteer docent chairs. Organizations have a right to expect that docents will participate in ongoing training, interact with all visitors respectfully, and follow the rules of the institution.

For more information see National Docent Symposium Council, *The Docent Handbook* (2001); Larry Beck and Ted Cable, *Interpretation for the 21st Century: Fifteen Principles for Interpreting Nature and Culture* (2002); and Barbara Abramoff Levy, Sandy Mackenzie Lloyd, and Susan Schreiber, *Great Tours!: Thematic Tours and Guide Training for Historic Sites* (2002).

LINDA NORRIS
THE UNCATALOGED MUSEUM

See mission statement; volunteers.

documentary editing. *Documentary editing* is the current, accepted term for what was once called *historical editing*: the methods and standards developed by the editors of comprehensive editions of the papers of Founding Fathers and other significant figures and organizations in American history in the decades following World War II. The name distinguished this technique from the more traditional approach of textual editors, who consciously applied critical judgment and scholarly experience to produce new, editorially emended texts for their audiences. Such ideal, nonhistorical text did not serve the needs of political, intellectual, and social history. Here other editorial methods were required, and they emerged in a series of editions of American statesmen's papers published in the 1950s and 1960s.

Until the late 1970s, such editors were generally known as "historical editors" and their series, "historical editions." The terminology changed when "historical editors" belatedly opened a dialogue with literary scholars who had inaugurated a similar program for reliable editions of the published works and correspondence of well-known American authors. Representatives of both groups formed the Association for Documentary Editing in 1978; this group has worked to establish and maintain professional standards ever since. While documentary editors have borrowed many of the methods and insights of modern, critical editors of literary texts, they are distinguished from that field of endeavor by their insistence that the editorial text that they produce will preserve, as far as possible, the nature of their sources as documentary evidence.

Most simply stated, documentary editors usually prepare modern editions from source materials that can themselves be described as documents—artifacts inscribed on paper or a similar medium, or recorded by audiovisual means, whose unique physical characteristics and original nature give them special evidentiary value. The significance of such sources demands that their editors provide editorial texts that themselves communicate as much of the sources' evidentiary value as possible. Documentary editing generally means a far more limited level of editorial intervention than occurs when the same sources are edited critically. The documentary editor's goal is not to supply the words or phrases of a vanished archetype but rather to preserve the nuances of a source that has survived the ravages of time.

These are, of course, precisely the materials that historical societies and their members will need to publish in some form—the contents of family letters or *diaries, organizational archives, *oral history memoirs, and the like. Most of the traditional methods of these scholarly projects are directly related to the needs of such smaller-scale undertakings. The hallmarks of those "projects" were:

1. collection in some surrogate image form (originally photostats, then Xeroxes and microfilms, and now digital images) of all materials that are candidates for publication in the "papers of X" or the "works of Y";
2. recognized criteria for selecting the most appropriate "source text" from various versions of a given letter, drawing, or other document;
3. objective criteria for transcribing or translating that source text from its original form (handwritten, typewritten, audio-recorded, etc.) into an editorial text (nowadays usually a machine-readable product of word processing) and for proofreading that transcription before its publication; and

4. preparation of an appropriate non-textual editorial apparatus (often combining notes, glossary, maps, biographical directory, and indexing) that will not only provide the user with the original document's context but also ensure convenient access to the intellectual content of the edition.

Modern technology has eased the task of documentary editing enormously and improved its potential. No longer must an editor choose among a variety of symbols to represent inscriptional details such as crossed-out text, raised letters, or underlining. Even the simplest word-processing system can reproduce formatting that, in traditional typeset printing, meant extra time and extra costs. Digital imaging enables editors to provide online supplements to editorial texts, images of sources whose visual information would be impossible to "translate" into anything on a printed page.

For local history organizations, the most convenient reference tool is *A Guide to Documentary Editing*, a publication of the Association for Documentary Editing (ADE) now in its third edition (2008). This volume traces the process of documentary editing from the collection of document images through the choices and formats available for paper or digital publication. Sections that discuss creating a "virtual archive" of documentary images are of little interest to a local history society or individual bent on making available a readable and accessible version of a group of family letters or journal. Those that trace the history of symbols used to represent details in the text are less relevant than they once were. However, the *Guide*'s treatment of basic issues in documentary editing are as important for a small historical society or family historian as for large-scale editorial projects. These include identifying the "best" candidate for a source text; planning textual method; and assigning responsibility for transcription of a source. Similarly, the *Guide*'s survey of methods of editorial additions like annotation and indexes among dozens of different editions over the decades will help any would-be editors avoid mistakes and find the "best practice" to meet challenges in their texts.

The third edition of the *Guide* originally featured an "electronic component" that made it possible for purchasers to access a machine-readable version on the University of Virginia Press website. In 2013, the press and the ADE agreed to make this electronic edition of the *Guide* universally available at no cost, and users can access this free online text at http://gde.upress.virginia.edu.

This feature is of special interest to historical societies and individual local historians; it means that the book can easily be downloaded for future reference—or distribution. You may also wish to consult Katherine Scott Sturdevant's *Organizing & Preserving Your Heirloom Documents* (2002). Addressing the needs of individual owners of family records, Professor Sturdevant's book includes substantial material on the preservation of such documents as well as their transcription and publication.

Just as valuable is the website of the Association for Documentary Editing (documentaryediting.org). Its most helpful feature may be the directory of member editions and projects. Anyone can identify projects whose source texts, chronological era, or other features make them relevant to a prospective editor in the same field. The page's links to each project's website provide instant access for the interested observer: http://www.documentaryediting.org/wordpress/?page_id=363.

MARY-JO KLINE
INDEPENDENT SCHOLAR

See digital history; digitization.

donation visits. In lieu of an adequate salary, or sometimes, of any salary, donation visits or donation parties were held to which parishioners brought gifts of food and sometimes money to a minister's family. These parties were frequently put on in the fall, after the crops were in, and before winter. Daniel L. Cady in his *Rhymes of Vermont Rural Life* (1919) commented on the irony of donations:

It's funny how our ancestors
Would gather at the minister's
And eat him out of house and home
And call it "A Donation."

dowry. Property that a wife brought to a marriage; also called a marriage portion. A "dower Negro" was a slave brought by a wife to a marriage. A woman's "dower right" in her husband's estate after his death was an allotted percentage to compensate her for what she brought to the marriage.

MARY BETH NORTON
CORNELL UNIVERSITY

due process

due process. The right of due process is the right to legal protection through the courts. In other words, it prevents individuals or governments from depriving citizens of their legal rights without adjudication in the courts of the land.

Dun & Bradstreet credit reports. These represent a valuable but under-used resource for the local historian. Because they document the economic ups and downs of a locality, they provide a window into the dynamics of community relationships. Interactions between business elites, salaried employees, and laboring people can be made vivid using these records.

The R. G. Dun and Company Credit Ledgers constitute one of the most extensive and important aggregations of business records in the United States. Located at Harvard University's Baker Library, the collection contains about 2,580 volumes that encompass 249 linear feet of shelf space. Although the volumes span the period 1840 to 1895, the bulk of the material pertains to the 1850s, 1860s, and 1870s. The ledgers are not digitized, but for more information go to www.library.hbs.edu/hc/collections/dun.

In 1841, Lewis Tappan established the Mercantile Agency in New York City to gather credit information on merchants in the United States and Canada doing business in the New York City area. By the late 1850s, the firm had been taken over by Robert Graham Dun and the business—by then the dominant player in the field—continued as R. G. Dun and Company until merging with the Bradstreet Company, forming Dun and Bradstreet, in 1933.

At one time during the nineteenth century, R. G. Dun and Company had as many as 2,000 local agents throughout the country who reported semiannually (more often if circumstances required) on businesses in their area. These reports were sent to the central office in New York City where they were recorded in ledgers arranged by state and then by county or city. This information was sold to individuals and business firms.

Although the main focus was financial, the reports often contain information of a personal nature regarding the owners and top officials in the concerns under scrutiny. The agents typically reported on the individual entrepreneur's background, marital status, church membership, involvement in civic affairs, reputation in the community, and previous business experience. It was not unusual for the agents to give their own subjective opinion of the business acumen and credit worthiness of the subject. In the case of this author, a report in the 1880s indicated that it was my grandmother, rather than my grandfather, who was the real "brains of the operation."

As these reports were relied upon by individuals and institutions contemplating the loan of money, they needed to have a high degree of accuracy. The R. G. Dun and Company Credit Ledgers present their subjects "warts and all" and therefore are a valuable source for anyone interested in getting the true history of a place. They are a good corrective to the optimistic *boosterism usually found in nineteenth-century newspapers and pronouncements of local governments and other public bodies.

The fact that the records are arranged by state and within each state by county or city makes them very useful for the local historian. This arrangement facilitates the examination of the major business entities within a locality. The presence of a name index in most volumes is another valuable feature.

There are some drawbacks to the Dun and Company records. The individuals and businesses reported upon tended to be the largest and most successful in an area, those making purchases outside the community and/or applying for credit. Thus, smaller enterprises do not always show up. The records are sometimes incomplete, and they can be difficult to read because of illegible handwriting and extensive abbreviation. Permission to publish any material from the records must be obtained from the Baker Library and Dun and Bradstreet. Perhaps the greatest difficulty for local historians is the fact that the Credit Ledgers are available only at the Baker Library at Harvard University.

If these impediments are too great, the local historian can explore the possibility of using financial records closer to home. Local banks, credit bureaus, chambers of commerce, better business bureaus, and other business-oriented concerns, including local businesses themselves, may be willing to allow the use of their historical records. Although such records are usually jealously guarded, the local historian may get access by assuring the firm that the records will be used in an evenhanded way for noncompetitive, noncommercial purposes. If the attempt is successful it will return dividends in a more well-rounded, informative historical analysis.

For more information, see James H. Madison, "The Credit Reports of R. G. Dun & Co. as Historical Sources," *Historical Methods Newsletter* (September 1975); and James H. Madison, "The Evolution of Commercial Credit Reporting Agencies in Nineteenth-Century America," *Business History Review* 48, no. 2 (summer 1974). Baker Library at Harvard can be located at http://library.hbs.edu, which contains a list of the volumes available by date, and state and county.

G. David Brumberg
Cornell University Library, retired

See business and industrial history as a local history subject.

Dutch in North America, sources for. See Appendix A.

E

East Asians in North America, sources for. See Appendix A.

economic history, local. See business and industrial history; Dun & Bradstreet credit reports; post office records.

Ellisisland.org. See genealogy resources online.

emancipation celebrations. African American emancipation celebrations commemorate events connected with blacks' struggle to end slavery in the United States. This commemorative tradition began in 1808, when Congress prohibited further importation of enslaved Africans into the United States. Enthusiasm for this particular commemoration died out by the 1820s, but the commemorative tradition revived when Great Britain abolished slavery in its West Indian colonies on August 1, 1834. Free black Americans and white abolitionists saw this as a portent of American emancipation and held massive annual August 1 celebrations in dozens of northern communities that included parades, religious observances, speeches, music, feasting, and assorted amusements.

When U.S. slavery ended in the 1860s, northern and southern African Americans commemorated various dates associated with that event. Some continued to celebrate on August 1, while others, especially the freed persons in the South, commemorated Lincoln's Emancipation Proclamation, which went into effect on January 1, 1863. Still others celebrated various dates that had local or regional significance, often connected with the date when Union troops liberated the area or when the news of emancipation arrived.

During the nineteenth century, emancipation celebrations served many functions. They celebrated freedom, helped spread knowledge of African American history, facilitated political and social networking, and provided an annual gathering of blacks from small communities around a region who normally may not have had much opportunity to interact. Special excursion rates on trains made attendance more affordable, and black churches, veterans' groups, and fraternal lodges were often among the organizers. While women were usually excluded from prominent public roles in these events, they were central to behind-the-scenes organizing and fundraising activities.

During the early twentieth century, emancipation celebrations' significance gradually declined and they were discontinued in many areas, continuing mainly in the South. As blacks migrated out of the South between the 1910s and 1960s, they carried their traditions with them. The most resilient of African American commemorations of emancipation has been the once-marginal and regional "Juneteenth" tradition, which was initiated by Texas blacks in commemoration of the June 19, 1865 date when Union troops liberated slaves in that state. This tradition has been rediscovered and is now celebrated in many communities in all parts of the country. By 2016, at least forty-three states had designated Juneteenth an official holiday, though most do not close government offices. In addition, hundreds of communities large and small across the United States observe Juneteenth regardless of official governmental recognition, and several organizations are promoting the celebration, with one attempting to establish "Juneteenth National Freedom Day" as an official national holiday. Other states and regions, however, observe different dates. In 2007 the governor of Tennessee proclaimed August 8 Emancipation Day in Tennessee, honoring the date in 1865 when then-President Andrew Johnson is said to have freed his own slaves. In the same year, Congress formally established April 16 as a permanent public holiday in Washington, D.C., in observance of the date in 1862 when slavery was abolished in the district.

In investigating the role these events played in local communities, past and present, local black or white newspapers, as well as prominent black papers from major cities, often provide excellent information. Newspaper accounts provide a sense of who the local leaders were, and suggest the extent of interaction among African Americans from across a given region. Some key questions to consider when researching emancipation celebrations: What dates were commemorated by African Americans in your community? When

and why did these observances begin and how long did they continue? To what extent was there interaction with other black communities around the area? How were churches, fraternal organizations, literary societies, veterans' organizations, or other institutions involved? For scholarly discussion of emancipation celebrations, see Mitch Kachun, *Festivals of Freedom: Memory and Meaning in African American Emancipation Celebrations, 1808–1915* (2003); Kachun, "Celebrating Freedom: Juneteenth and the Emancipation Festival Tradition," in *Remixing the Civil War: Meditations on the Sesquicentennial*, ed. Thomas J. Brown (2011); Kathleen Ann Clark, *Defining Moments: African American Commemoration and Political Culture in the South, 1863–1913* (2005); and William Wiggins, *O Freedom! Afro-American Emancipation Celebrations* (1987).

Mitch Kachun
Western Michigan University

See African American history.

eminent domain. The right of the government to seize property for the good of the majority of citizens.

England, local history in. The impulse to record and write about particular places has run deep and long in English history. As early as the late fifteenth century descriptive accounts were appearing, in the form of itineraries. Preeminent among these was the work of John Leland (1506–1552), who from 1533 was charged by Henry VIII with recording evidence from the libraries of monasteries and colleges, then being dismantled. As he toured England and Wales Leland made notes, later written up in a mixture of historical evidence and contemporary description. Leland noted castles, markets, towns, cities, churches and principal buildings, houses of great men, street plans, building materials, bridges, rivers and watercourses, and land use. Happily, Leland's itineraries are available in a twentieth-century printed edition (L. Toulmin Smith, ed., *The Itinerary of John Leland in or about the years 1535–1543*, 5 vols., [1907]). The historical value of itineraries is enhanced by comparing the descriptions provided by the succession of later curious and observant visitors who wrote in this genre, from Daniel Defoe in the 1720s to J. B. Priestley in the 1930s and beyond.

It was in the late sixteenth century that more formal histories of specific localities began to be written and published, starting with county histories. Counties were first recorded in maps; Christopher Saxton's famous series dates from 1574 to 1576. In 1576 the first county history, Lambarde on Kent, appeared. In 1586 William Camden's *Britannia* was published, an account arranged in chapters by county of the history and topography of the lands of the former Roman province, for which it was titled. Camden initially published in Latin and wrote in the idiom of post-Renaissance classical learning. Many characteristics of the antiquarian writing, which was to dominate published local history until the twentieth century, were apparent. He recorded major archaeological features but interpreted them speculatively. Such assertions tended to gain weight by repetition as antiquarian local histories multiplied. Typically such histories were written by and for the county gentry (including the rising new men of the period in search of patrimony) and emphasized the history of their patch, its antiquity and importance. Content includes the descent of manors, pedigrees and heraldry, monuments, the church and its fabric and incumbents, religious houses, hospitals and chantries, and sometimes archaeological sites.

Antiquarian historians subsequently extended their interest from county to parish and town level. Well-educated clergy with historical and archaeological interests, time, and access to local documents were prominent among them. The very first parish history appeared in 1695. *Parochial Antiquities Attempted in the History of Ambrosden, Burcester, and other adjacent parts in the Counties of Oxford and Bucks* was written by White Kennett, vicar of Ambrosden, and later Bishop of Peterborough. A national organization, the Society of Antiquaries, received its Royal Charter in 1751.

In the nineteenth century local studies appealed to an increasingly large range of people, including middle-class readers and participants. This was reflected in the establishment of numbers of local groups and organizations, some still in being. They often spanned archaeology, architecture, and local and natural history and energetically visited, recorded, excavated, and collected specimens, artifacts, and archives. It has been characteristic of some antiquarians to accumulate great amounts of material, but never to fully analyze or publish it, and so their manuscripts notes were sometimes part of the collections. However, the efforts of nineteenth- and twentieth-century local organizations often led to the regular publication of journals and other historical and archaeological records. Their collections have also formed the basis of museums and archives, sometimes independently but in the twentieth century mostly incorporated into public provision. The twentieth century has seen the increasing availability of a widening range of original documents, through the National Archives (formerly the Public Record Office), and most significantly through local authority (usually county) record offices and local studies libraries. They have transformed the lot of the English local historian. An invaluable county-by-county guide to the development of local history and principal publications is provided by C. R. J. Currie and C. P. Lewis, eds., *English County Histories* (1994).

In many ways the culmination of the antiquarian tradition is the Victoria County History (VCH). Founded in 1899, with the ambitious self-confidence of a late Victorian national project, it aims to publish consistently researched histories of every parish and town in England. The VCH began on a subscription basis, and its early volumes reveal elements of an antiquarian, county history lineage. They used predominantly central records, with a strong emphasis on the medieval, and covered manorial descents, landholding, and ecclesiastical institutions in particular detail. Since the 1930s the VCH has been headquartered at the University of London's Institute of Historical Research. Its later volumes show

developments that reflect wider changes in English local history in the twentieth century. Thus parish histories now draw on local documents such as parish and probate records, on landscape and *oral history, cover periods up to and including the twentieth century, and take in economic and social history, farming and industry, religious nonconformity, settlement, population, and local government.

The practice of local history in England is today very different from that of the still largely antiquarian concerns of the early twentieth century. It deals in questions and themes, uses a range of sources transformed by public archive provision and changes in attitude to what is relevant, employs more systematic methods, has access to transforming tools when it comes to capturing and analyzing the mass of detailed information that characterizes local research, and involves many more people with different interests and experience. There are strong links between local research and many aspects of general and national history. *Landscape history, *demography, economic history, social history, *political history, cultural studies and anthropology, *religious history, and personal history are all examples of this. Interdisciplinary work is a welcome consequence. How has this come about?

These changes have, in part, followed from the professionalization of the study of history since the later nineteenth century. This generated new approaches to local evidence, now valued as a way of exploring many emergent themes, political, economic, and social. So patterns of landholding, the linguistic origins of local names, and customary organization of agriculture were the stuff of nineteenth-century enquiries into the origins of national identity, of institutions and democracy. Rural change and the processes of modernization, like enclosure, generated much debate from the 1880s. Contemporary debates into, for example, the relief of poverty were paralleled by detailed investigations into the historic experiences of small-scale, parish welfare provision. The interweaving of local and "mainstream" historical developments continued into the twentieth century. Local studies played a major part in economic history, and the exploration of the genesis and growth of the industrial revolution. The French *Annales School was influential from the 1920s, bringing a marriage of history and social science, and a new concentration on social and cultural life, mentality, and attitudes. In this the holistic approach of local history and its microcosmic nature were valued. However, when it comes to a distinct local history agenda and method, neither a continuation of deeply-rooted antiquarianism nor an adjunct of "outside" interests, it is to the period from the late 1940s that we should look.

This new local history was initially associated particularly with the Leicester school and the work of Britain's first university department of English Local History at the University of Leicester. Established in the late 1940s, its leading figures—Finberg, Hoskins, Thirsk, Everitt, Phythian Adams, Dyer, Snell—have also been those of the subject nationally. Finberg set a specific agenda for English local history, to trace the origin,

growth, decline, and fall of community. This rooted study firmly in the locality, while also fostering comparative studies. Its products dealt across periods, but seldom beyond 1918 by when the traditional community was generally thought to have died. It concentrated most on rural and small town experience. Research methods incorporated the evidence of landscape and buildings with traditional documentary sources to a then unprecedented degree. This transformation of method owed most to W. G. Hoskins (1908–1992), his seminal work *The Making of the English Landscape* (1955), and to the many new students both academic and lay who followed him into this new historical landscape. A growing culture of local history societies, university and adult education outreach classes, full- and part-time study opportunities including certificate and diploma, master's and research degree programs, local history teaching in schools, and individual enthusiasm were all part of this momentum.

In the half century since these redefinitions of local history, other perspectives have been added to both academic and grassroots studies. From the 1960s to the 1980s interactions between social and local history again became strong through shared themes like family, community, and demography. The Open University offered courses in "applied historical studies," which were "explorations of the past undertaken for the explicit purpose of advancing social scientific enquiry," and local volunteers contributed data from parish registers to Cambridge University's national project on population and social structure. The History Workshop movement, begun at Ruskin College, Oxford, was a leading example of history from below, bringing to the fore the experiences of those previously excluded by class, gender, or color from the consideration of historians. Specific and local experiences, recent periods, oral testimony, and people themselves as sources and researchers of the histories of their own places and families were of the essence. By the 1990s the theoretical certainties of the academic models and methods that had underpinned some earlier work (in applied social history, quantification, *demography, historical geography, or Marxist history) were increasingly under fire. The development of cultural history has valued the qualitative dimensions of past experience, and has emphasized local evidence as key to understanding it. The evidence of documents, landscapes, and buildings alike have been seen in new ways. English local history has inevitably shown the influence of these trends, especially in its academic reaches, although in many parts of its broad church it has continued to exhibit a determined empiricism and skepticism about the relevance of theory. The lively debates in the pages of *The Local Historian* during 2010–2011 bear witness to this.

Post-millennium, English local history faces challenges to adapt and develop. As it increasingly takes on the considered study of the local history of the twentieth century, the Leicester school agenda, for all its earlier strengths, serves less well for a post-1918, largely urban world. Family history and individual memory are now powerful drivers of large-scale inter-

est, but in a local history initially seen through a personal prism, with the past approached retrogressively from a recent viewpoint. Local history is increasingly mediated through public history, an alliance of historians, archivists, curators, heritage providers, and the public, which can make both for the understanding and the misunderstanding and over-simplification of history. Online resources provide unprecedented access to evidence, ways of storing and analyzing it, and means of communicating. They also pose questions of quantity and quality. In schools following the National Curriculum, a compulsory local history investigation is included in primary schools and the opportunity (reduced from 2014) for project work in examined courses at secondary level. For adults, elements of the structures that supported the postwar local history boom remain but pressures on funding are reducing courses and archive and library services while the professional career demands of academe have lessened some links with lay local historians. English local history remains a broad church, with elements of the neo-antiquarian, empirical, and theoretical. It is eclectic and espouses no single body of evidence and no exclusive, prescribed methodology. At its best it offers ways of asking key historical questions, gaining insights, avoiding imposed generalizations, producing original and new knowledge, and having fun and satisfaction along the way. It continues to be an important part both of historical studies and of popular historical understanding and participation in England.

KATE TILLER
UNIVERSITY OF OXFORD, UK

See *Amateur Historian*; Australia, local history in; British Association for Local History; Cambridge Group for the History of Population and Social Structure; Canada, local history in; Ireland, local history in; New Zealand, local history in; Scotland, local history in; United States, local history in; Wales, local history in.

English in North America, sources for. See Appendix A.

environmental history. Two major literary works published right before and after World War II articulate themes that play a central role in understanding and interpreting the local environmental experience. *The Grapes of Wrath*, John Steinbeck's Pulitzer Prize–winning novel, sympathetically chronicles the plight of tenant farmers like the Joads displaced from their homes in Oklahoma by drought and greedy absentee landlords who cared more for profit than people or the land. Shortly after the Joads abandoned their farm and hit the road for California, Grandpa Joad died. Seeking to understand the first of what would be many tragic events, "Reverend" Casy explains "Grampa an' the old place, they was jus' the same thing. . . . He died the minute you took 'im off the place." With these words, and throughout the novel, Steinbeck addresses the connection between people and place, which is one of the key themes in understanding both the human experience and local environmental history. Steinbeck's characters also highlight the role of memory in assigning meaning and significance to place.

Ten years later, in 1949, Oxford University Press posthumously published *A Sand County Almanac and Sketches Here and There* by Aldo Leopold—forester, father of wildlife biology, pioneering ecologist, and one of the most important environmental philosophers of the twentieth century. Part I of *A Sand County Almanac* recounts the experiences of Leopold and his family on an abandoned farm that he bought in Wisconsin in the mid-1930s. Leopold's narrative combines a keen sense of the interdependent, reciprocal relationship between natural and human history with a subtle and effective treatment of evolution and ecology—two watershed concepts in modern environmental understanding. Anyone interested in local environmental history would do well to start with Part I of *A Sand County Almanac* especially "Good Oak" and "Burr Oak."

Environmental history did not exist as a field until after the mid-1960s, and it emerged as a direct result of the post-WWII environmental movement. Americans had long been interested in nature, and there had been powerful and sustained conservation movements in this country in the early twentieth century and again in the 1930s. In the mid-1920s, the Izaak Walton League of America (IWLA) developed a strong following that included dozens of active chapters in the Midwest. Concerned about water pollution, drainage of wetlands, and other practices that threatened opportunities for fishing and hunting, the IWLA organized a successful nationwide campaign to establish the Upper Mississippi River Wildlife and Fish Refuge.

The post-WWII environmental movement was different from the earlier conservation movements; it drew its scientific and philosophical inspiration from the science of ecology, popularized by writers such as Aldo Leopold, Rachel Carson, and Barry Commoner. As was the case with evolution in the nineteenth century, ecology brought with it a sea change in the ways that people saw and understood the world around them. In the 1960s, the word "environment" first came into general use, often as a shorthand description of the natural world as a complex, interdependent life support system of which people were a part. One powerful "lesson" that many took from their understanding of ecology was the idea that people who make war on nature ultimately make war on themselves.

The passion and urgency and excitement of the environmental movement created a constituency that from the mid-1960s through the mid-1970s prompted several sessions of Congress and two presidents (Lyndon Johnson and Richard Nixon) to lend their support to one of the most important periods of federal-level environment-related legislation and executive action in the history of the United States. A partial list includes the Wilderness Act (1964); the National Historic Preservation Act, which was aimed at preserving the *built environment (1966); the National Environmental Policy Act, which created the Environmental Protection Agency (1969); and the Endangered Species Act (1973). This unprecedented level of action by the federal government, driven by a popular constituency, had profound influences at the local level.

In addition to providing a constituency for federal-level actions on behalf of the environment, the environmental movement jump-started historians' interest in examining the interplay between people and the natural world. Scholars such as William Cronon, Thomas Dunlap, Susan Flader, Samuel Hays, Carolyn Merchant, Roderick Nash, Richard White, and Donald Worster began to develop a body of literature that quickly took shape as a distinct field of study. Within recent years a number of monographs have looked at local and regional environmental topics, but one of the most successful at developing a useful and understandable model for the interaction between people and nature is Richard White's *Organic Machine*. Writing about the Columbia River, White describes the modern, re-engineered river and its valley as an "organic machine," in which nature and technology, human and natural systems have been thoroughly intertwined and organized for the material benefit of people. The organic machine, which is a cyborg-like human creation composed of natural and artificial parts, is representative of the places that most of us inhabit in the early twenty-first century.

In many ways, local environmental history is the story of the creation of place over time, as people acting on attitudes and values embedded in their cultures intentionally and unintentionally altered their surroundings. As scholars such as William Cronon have shown (*Changes in the Land* [1983]), Native Americans, largely through the use of fire, shaped the environment that Europeans found when they arrived in what they called the "New World." One of the great historical stories since European contact has been the dramatic making and remaking of the face of the land, a process that accelerated rapidly in the late nineteenth and twentieth centuries. Over the course of the twentieth century, fewer and fewer Americans have lived in environments that are "natural." Cities, suburbs, small towns, farms, river valleys, lake shores—all have environmental histories worth exploring. One way to begin thinking about local environmental history is to look at your local surroundings and ask: How did they get that way? This question directs attention to the evolving interplay between people and place and to the attitudes and values that underlie people's actions.

While there are plenty of things people did not create and cannot control, generally speaking the contemporary environment both locally and beyond is a human artifact; it is an example of human *material culture. Archaeologist James Deetz has defined material culture as "that portion of man's physical environment purposely transformed by him according to culturally dictated plans" (Warren Leon and Roy Rosenzweig, eds., *History Museums in the United States: A Critical Assessment*, 294). Local museums and historical societies routinely interpret the past using material culture. Employing a definition of material culture that embraces the humanized environment allows these institutions to include the creation of place over time in the presentation of local history.

Increasingly, those who research and write local history should pay attention to the fact that our nearby surroundings are part of an interdependent and interconnected global environment that is as much a human creation as a natural system. Cities and towns along navigable rivers, for example, have a local history that is a product of a particular place, but at the same time they are also part of the story of the development of a worldwide, maritime navigation system that facilitates commerce as well as the movement of exotic species over the surface of the earth. Local historians should be aware of the debates over global issues like climate change and the increasing support among scholars for the idea that the earth may have entered a new geological epoch, the Anthropocene, in which human action is the most significant force in driving change in global environmental systems. In the modern world, local environmental history does not exist in isolation.

Environmental history offers exciting interpretive opportunities for local historians, but it presents challenges as well. All of us make sense of the past through the prism of our own culture. Topics like the environment, on which there are likely to be strong and conflicting opinions, make it disarmingly easy to slip into measuring people from the past against the knowledge and standards of the present. As is the case with other historical subjects, it is important to try to understand past interaction with the environment in the context of its own time. While there were people in the past who were stupid or greedy or deliberately destructive, most acted in ways that they believed would produce personal or social benefits. All too often, the expected benefits came packaged with significant unintended and unanticipated consequences. Indeed, in trying to understand cause and effect in the evolving relationship between people and the environment, unintended and unanticipated outcomes are at least as important as what they deliberately set out to accomplish. It is also worth remembering that not everyone has had the same environmental experience. Historically, people's relationships with the environment have been influenced by variables such as race, class, gender, and employment.

Examined imaginatively, almost any local topic can shed light on the creation of place over time and can contribute to an understanding of the intertwined accounts of human and natural history. Conner Prairie Interactive History Park and Old Sturbridge Village, outdoor museums in Indiana and Massachusetts, both feature country stores—their shelves stocked with products common to antebellum life. Each of those products could be the starting point for an environmental history. Together they can shed light on a developing economy, which linked those local places to a worldwide trading network that converted the products of nature into products for people.

Many additional topics have a local environmental history, while simultaneously being part of broader processes in a highly interconnected and interdependent world. Lyme disease, which is named for the Connecticut town where it was first isolated and discovered, is a relatively recently identified affliction spread by tiny ticks. Viewed as environmental history, Lyme disease becomes a chapter in a saga involving the unintended and unanticipated consequences of changes in agricultural practices, reforestation, recovery of deer and other wildlife populations, suburban growth, and shifting attitudes toward animals and hunting. So, too, do forest fires, which as historian Stephen Pyne has shown, have increasingly become "artifacts" of fire suppression policies and human settlement patterns as much as natural phenomena.

Every local area has multiple and overlapping topics waiting to be researched and interpreted by historians prepared to understand the past through an environmental lens. Writing in *A Sand County Almanac*, Aldo Leopold said that "many historical events, hitherto explained solely in terms of human enterprise, were actually biotic interactions between people and land." Leopold's words still suggest a model and a direction of travel for anyone interested in pursuing local environmental history.

PHILIP SCARPINO
INDIANA UNIVERSITY–PURDUE
UNIVERSITY, INDIANAPOLIS

See landscape; living history museums; parks.

ephemera. Handwritten or printed papers not meant for posterity, but that have survived and are now available for historical purposes.

episcopal. This word comes from the Latin *episcopus*, meaning of or pertaining to bishops. Its use denotes a church hierarchy in which a bishop is at the head, such as is found in the *Methodist Episcopal Church. For Episcopalian, see *Protestant Episcopal Church.

Episcopal Church, sources for. See Appendix B.

epitaphs. Inscriptions on gravestones or monuments commemorating the deceased.

See gravestones.

equity. In law, equity refers to natural law or ethics, referring to moral principles, rather than the legal system. A second use of the word equity refers to the amount that remains after all liens and mortgages are deducted from the value of a property.

escheat. A term that comes from feudal law and refers to those circumstances where there is no heir to a property and so the estate reverts to the lord of the manor, or in the United States, to the state.

esquire. An honorific term used primarily in addressing envelopes to a person entitled to respect but not fitting into a higher classification. Today in the United States it is added at the end of the person's name in addressing correspondence to those who have been admitted to practice law, but who hold no higher title, such as legislator, high executive office, or judge. In old England, it referred to a person who ranked above a gentleman, but who had not been knighted, and to officers of the law such as barristers (but not solicitors), sheriffs, and justices of the peace. Women of appropriate rank are addressed as esquire. Use of the term is frequently omitted, and as frequently applied as a compliment to any person.

estate. This term refers to all property—either real or personal—and is not a legal definition. However, in the law there are a number of kinds of estates that are defined by the conditions under which the owner holds the property such as an estate in severalty (property held by one person) or estate in common (property held by two or more people).

Estonians in North America, sources for. See Appendix A.

ethics and local history. Two types of ethics concern the conscientious local historian. There are the corporate ethics of the broader historical profession, the accepted norms of the majority of people who work in institutions dealing with the preservation or presentation of local history. The local historian also has recourse to another type of ethics, a tool kit that is part of her or his everyday community life: personal ethics.

The corporate ethics of the local history practitioner are formally set out in codes of ethics, such as the *American Alliance of Museums' (AAM) very detailed 2000 text "Code of Ethics for Museums," the *National Council on Public History's "Code of Ethics and Professional Conduct," and the formal statements of principle and practice laid out by a wide variety of history-related professional organizations. Interested readers might see Theodore J. Karamanski, ed., *Ethics and Public History: An Anthology* (1990), the *American

Association for State and Local History's "Statement of Professional Standards and Ethics," http://www.aaslh.org/ethics.htm, NCPH "Code of Ethics and Professional Conduct, http://ncph.org/cms/about/bylaws-and-ethics, and AAM "Code of Ethics for Museums," http://www.aam-us.org/museumresources/ethics/coe.cfm.

The corporate ethics of the local historian are sometimes a reflection of professional training, perhaps in a public history graduate program. For those without the benefit of such training, professional development can provide exposure to the same norms of practice. Through reading publications like *History News* and participating in historical conferences, both regional and national, local historians learn the language, attitudes, and values of the larger historical profession. Codes of ethics and professional acculturation ensure that the hard-won experiences of senior practitioners are passed on to the rising generation of local historians. Unfortunately, after a flurry of activity in the late 1980s, the systematic discussion of historical ethics has waned, leaving practitioners with an attenuated set of professional ethics.

The strength and weakness of a corporate approach to ethics is that it reflects the experience of past professionals. Yet in the past generation, history as practiced on the local level in the United States and Canada has changed a great deal. The number and type of historical museums exploded in the 1970s and 1980s. Even with this expansion, the day is past when local historical museums or local history reading rooms in community libraries constitute the majority of institutions requiring the participation of the local historian. Today the story of our communities is also preserved and presented by local landmark commissions, Main Street organizations, *living history sites, consulting firms, genealogical societies, and reenactment groups. Each of these organizations brings its own approach to the past, be it buildings, families, neighborhoods, or battlefields. The means by which history can be presented by local groups has also changed the face of local history. Video and audio productions are no longer the province of a handful of expensive professionals. Desktop publishing has made local history dissemination easier, and websites bring local stories to an international audience. The exhibit in the historical society, once the principal mode of disseminating local history to the public, has been joined by tools unimagined in 1949 when the *American Association for State and Local History was created. When these new means of presenting our stories are added to the ever-widening range of stories historians are interested in exploring on a local level—from labor history to technology, from popular culture to gender and sexual orientation—the potential for venturing onto new ground is manifest. An ethical awareness based simply on an understanding of the norms of the profession is inadequate to the task of being an effective community history leader.

Unlike fellow historians working in the university or in state and federal agencies, local historians often work in an environment in which they are the only history professional, or in many cases the local historian is a volunteer without the benefit of graduate training. Also, the local historian is by definition rooted in a community. While an academician may pronounce with impunity on the foibles of people of the past, the local historian lives and works in a milieu where history's judgments have a more intimate and immediate impact. These and other distinctions between local history and the larger profession make it imperative that the local historian have an internalized, personal code of ethics that goes beyond the received wisdom of people who have operated museums or conducted oral histories in the past, but which instead grows out of reflection on the basic questions of the historical enterprise. Ethics for the local historian is not simply about following codes, but is the case-by-case making of moral choices.

Much of the background for making such choices is personal and reflects values deeply held and character formed through the years. Experience plays a role as well. There is no substitute for knowing the community in which you work, its personalities and cultural fault lines. In dealing with controversial topics, for example, the lessons learned from past difficulties or the well-publicized debacle of the *Enola Gay* exhibit, can serve to reduce the possibility for conflict by bringing stakeholders in the community into the planning process. To be able to anticipate ethical challenges before they become dilemmas goes a long way toward defusing the potential for compromising deeply held values. Experience, however, cannot always help us anticipate and defuse ethical challenges. The danger of asserting ethical principles that grow more out

of our individual conceptions of history than any existing codes of ethics or canons of practice is that the local historian risks standing alone. This is sometimes inevitable, and the price of doing the "right thing" by your light can sometimes be a pink slip or the cold shoulder of your neighbors. For a particularly good case study concerning local historians and controversial topics, see Robert R. Weyeneth, "History, He Wrote: Murder, Politics, and the Challenges of Public History in a Community with a Secret," *Public Historian* 16, no. 2 (Spring 1994): 51–74.

Particularly vexing are issues that pit personal values against clear professional responsibilities. There is little in the existing codes of ethics of public history that would guide the local historian in dealing with controversial topics. Admonishments from the *American Historical Association of the importance of "integrity" or from the *National Council on Public History to "represent the past in all of its complexity" are useful yardsticks, but they do not provide direct guidance to a historian working within a community where the past is intimate and immediate. In doing a history of a Midwestern community, I was once confronted with the challenge of narrating a petty political-corruption case, suppressed at the time, that led to the dismissal of an important local official. The incident was important in that it led to a change in leadership. The details of the case were not widely known at the time and therefore were not part of public discussion when it occurred. The individual involved had cooperated with my research. I liked and respected him as a person. My decision was to reveal the incident but not to narrate it in great detail, and to try to place the end of the official's career in balance with his accomplishments. I felt very much caught between my responsibility to tell the whole truth, personal sympathies, and a recognition that my narrative was going to be the "official" record of a community and the evaluation of an individual's life. Certainly an investigative journalist would have afforded the incident much more print space, and another historian would have been perfectly within the ethical bounds of the profession to do so as well. My decision grew out of a web of personal considerations from religious values, long-shaped attitudes toward political institutions, frequent positive association with people in government service, and my relationship with the individual in question. Each of these were values that influenced the way I presented the past, although I sought to ensure that they did not override my overarching obligation to historical truth. While the assertion of personal ethics in local history is perhaps inevitable given the intimate nature of the work, it clearly puts the practitioner on a slippery slope. See the National Council on Public History, "Ethical Guidelines for the Historian," *Ethics and Public History* (76–77) and American Historical Association, "Statement on Standards of Professional Conduct," http://www.historians.org/pubs/free/professionalstandards.cfm.

Historical ethics, like personal ethics, in the end reflect the type of human relations we seek to cultivate. Most existing codes offer guidance on our relationship with employers, colleagues, and the community. Strangely, professional historians have been much less explicit about the vital relationship between the historian and the people of the past. The local historian is especially engaged in the question of what a museum or historical society owes to the past. The *Oral History Association offers very thoughtful guidelines regarding the mutual rights of the historian and the living informant. The American Alliance of Museums' *Museum Ethics* concerns the curator's responsibilities to the present, even the future. What of the dead? Do we have a responsibility to the people of the past? This is discussed in the Oral History Association, "Goals and Guidelines of the Oral History Association," http://chnm.gmu.edu/digitalhistory/links/cached/chapter6/6_23e_evaluation.htm.

More than in any other field of history the local practitioner has felt the tug of the past at their sleeve. In the nineteenth and early twentieth centuries, local history was sometimes disparaged as, in Albert Bushnell Hart's words, the "worship of ancestors." Writing about deceased family members or others they knew, many early local historians were motivated by their bonds to the people of the past. During the last two generations local history has been consciously professionalized, with an increasing number of local historians having received at least some advanced training in the subject. As the *filiopietistic approach to the past has been gradually eroded, the local historian is left with the same ambiguous relationship with the dead as the academic historian. We read their mail. We save it for posterity. We use it to help our contemporaries better understand the communities in which they live and to appreciate our own humanity.

Their words and possessions are a treasured part of our "heritage." Local historians have a relationship based upon intimate association with those who left us historic houses we now operate as museums, dresses that we now exhibit as artifacts, and letters we now store as documents. But human relationships are based on reciprocity. What do we, as historians, owe to those who have given us so much? One might consult David J. Russo, *Families and Communities: A New View of American History* (1974).

Certainly we owe the people of the past our memory. The act of remembering is what local historians are doing when they arrange manuscripts, craft exhibits, and author histories. The corridors of memory are the space in which the dead are reanimated to suit the needs of the present. But utility alone cannot dictate how we use the memory of the past. Our debt to the people of the past includes the responsibility to remember them as part of a whole world that is past. The contextual integrity of the past as it was lived balances the need to remember the past to suit present needs.

The dead are vulnerable to our probing. While laws govern the disposition of the physical body, the way a person is remembered is constantly being reevaluated. Are there questions we should not pose? Are there issues we should not explore? Should the veil of privacy be drawn over aspects of past lives? New scientific techniques expand the range of questions for which we can

seek answers. Because we have the ability to find the answers, should we ask the questions? Thomas Jefferson has been subjected to a posthumous paternity test, Zachary Taylor to forensic examination almost 150 years after his death. Yet in these cases the new technologies were used to answer questions long raised in the past. More recently historical societies possessing materials related to Abraham Lincoln have been approached to allow genetic testing to determine if the martyred president had Marfan syndrome (a condition unknown in Lincoln's time and unconnected to any aspect of his public career). Supporters of testing contend that knowledge that Lincoln had this disease would be heartening to people who currently suffer from Marfan syndrome (an inherited connective tissue disorder). In 1999, the Chicago Historical Society, which holds a large number of blood-stained items from the president's assassination, had to ask itself if Lincoln's DNA was as open to investigation as was his official correspondence. Such issues transcend the established bounds of historical ethics, and point to the need for further professional dialogue. This issue is discussed by Glen W. Davidson, "Abraham Lincoln and the DNA Controversy," *Journal of the Abraham Lincoln Association* 17, no. 1 (1996): 2–26 and Lorie Andrews, Nancy Buenger, Theodore J. Karamanski, Russell Lewis, et al., "Ethical Guidelines for Biohistory," *Science* 304 (April 2004): 215–16.

Historical museums have always been the physical embodiment of the bifurcated nature of history, embodying the things left by the past as well as the interpretation of those things into a narrative or exhibit. History was lived; history is remembered. Through preservation, curators of history perform their responsibility to the people of the past. Only through the unity and integrity of the historical record can the past live again as history. In interpretation the local historian can assume many roles, from prosecutor to defender of the dead. But whatever stance he or she may take, the subject is due full and unbiased interpretation of the historical record. Such a plane of objectivity is a noble fiction, but one toward which it is essential that all historians consciously strive. Local historians must fight against the trend, increasingly a problem in the academic sector, for authors to preface their interpretations with statements of their gender, ethnic, racial, religious, or class perspectives (biases) as if such a statement is an absolution from traditional aspirations to objectivity, or at least fairness.

The local historian who works with a society or museum takes on additional responsibilities. Open access to historical society collections (unless those collections have legal restrictions) is expected for all researchers. It is understandable that local historians will develop a strong, personal identification with their history, particularly if they are in the process of writing their own volume. Nonetheless, documents in a historical society collection should not be confused with personal property, nor should the history of a community be seen as a proprietary possession. Research results, of course, are private until published, but research materials should be made available to fellow historians.

The local historian works on the grassroots level and has a responsibility to protect the full range of historical resources within their community, including documents, districts, buildings, and artifacts. The local historian's responsibilities include building historical consciousness in the schools, businesses, voluntary organizations, and government of their community. Most important of all, the local historian makes the results of historical research available to the community. While the act of writing local history can sometimes be a solitary pursuit, the mission of a conscientious local historian is to be an advocate for history within the community.

The good historian is the result of the fusion of personal ethics and professional ethics. Just as the local historian presents the story of a town in the context of its region and nation, historical ethics encourage us to build outward from the self. Our goal is a series of just relationships that unite the individual historian and the community, the living and the dead. The local historian is responsible to the people of the past, the community in which they work, and the larger enterprise of history. It is a wonderful and exciting prospect to be in a place you know and mediate between the past and the present, but our work comes with a perplexing range of challenges. If we thoughtfully confront the complexity of our jobs, we give ourselves a chance to ethically meet those challenges.

THEODORE J. KARAMANSKI
LOYOLA UNIVERSITY–CHICAGO

See museum ethics; museums and the matter of ethics.

Ethnic Heritage Studies Act. Passed in 1972 by the U.S. Congress, it amends the Elementary and Secondary Education Act of 1965. The Ethnic Heritage Studies Act recognized the multicultural nature of American society and promoted a greater understanding of the components of the population. Grants were made to plan, develop, establish, and operate ethnic heritage studies programs that were charged with creating curriculum materials, disseminating knowledge throughout the school system, training, and promoting research into the history, culture, or traditions of America's ethnic groups.

ethnicity. The very creation of communities in U.S. history often had an ethnic component. Clusters of immigrants moved together from various locations in a homeland to places of residence in the United States that promised good land for farming or jobs needed for adjustment and survival. Thus, it was Silesian Poles who settled Panna Maria, Texas, in 1854. In a similar way, families of Dutch immigrants located in Carver County, Minnesota, in the 1870s. Historian Jon Gjerde, in his *The Minds of the West: Ethnocultural Evolution in the Rural Middle West, 1830–1917* (1997), reveals that over 2,000 Norwegians moved from Fortun, a parish in western Norway, to Dane County, Wisconsin, around the same time. If the immigrant arrivals did not initiate a settlement, they often transformed it. Dubuque, Iowa, populated by English and Irish arrivals in the 1830s and 1840s, was heav-

ily German by the middle of the nineteenth century. After 1880, Cambridge, Minnesota changed from a town of native-born Americans to one consisting mostly of Swedish newcomers.

Although cities invariably contained several ethnic and racial groups, specific urban neighborhoods housed particular concentrations of some groups. During the early twentieth century, Jews and Italians dominated life on the Lower East Side of Manhattan. Poles concentrated on the South Side of Pittsburgh. The Bohemian Flats neighborhood of Minneapolis, clutching a narrow strip of land alongside the Mississippi River, was essentially a village of Czechs, Slovaks, and Swedes. In the 1930s and 1940s, East Harlem was attracting newcomers from Puerto Rico. By the 1930s, as George Sanchez demonstrates in *Becoming Mexican American: Ethnicity, Culture, and Identity in Chicano Los Angeles* (1993), the Belvedere section of Los Angeles was home to over 30,000 Mexicans who were attracted by low rents and inexpensive housing. At the same time, the Boyle Heights area of the city was home to 10,000 Jews who found it a short commute to their jobs in the downtown area. In the 1960s and 1970s Asian Indians—according to Arthur and Usha Helweg, *An Immigrant Success Story: East Indians in America* (1990) began to establish residences in the Flushing, Queens area of New York City because it was near their point of entry—Kennedy airport.

Newcomers inevitably relied on ethnic contacts to shape the economic life of their locale and of their group. Local economic conditions often attracted settlers in the first place. Thus, German Mennonites brought their skills in wheat farming to Kansas in the nineteenth century when land was available to them. In the same century, Chinese laborers were attracted to silver mines in California and coal mines in Utah. Early in the twentieth century the construction of interurban lines by the Pacific Electric Railway brought unskilled Mexicans to Los Angeles, many of whom settled in the Watts area. In New York City in the 1980s and 1990s, West Indian women found most of their jobs in service work in private homes or public hospitals. Sometimes the reverse was true: the existence of a large supply of immigrant workers attracted industry. Thus cigar manufacturers located in Detroit in the 1920s due to the presence of thousands of Polish women who would work for relatively low wages.

Ethnic colonies not only seized portions of local labor markets, but also rapidly created countless numbers of neighborhood businesses. Small shops lived off ties forged by migration and ethnic settlement. German Catholics who opened a general store in Dyersville, Iowa, in 1858 became so successful that they expanded into the buying of grain and stocks. In 1915, the Chinese community of Locke, California, supported six restaurants and nine grocery stores. Jews on the Lower East Side around the same time patronized over 140 groceries and 130 kosher butchers. In San Antonio, Mexican vendors carried tamales and enchiladas in buckets and sold them in the streets. Donna Gabaccia, in her book *We Are What We Eat: Ethnic Food and the Making of Americans* (1998), revealed that many ethnic enterprises eventually expanded

to meet the demands of a mass market. An Italian-Swiss immigrant opened a cafe in 1828 that became Delmonico's, a famous New York restaurant. Domingo Ghirardelli began grinding imported chocolate in the nineteenth century and was soon selling goods throughout San Francisco. Germans mobilized to form the California Wine Association in 1894 to promote their product; the formation of the Italian Wine Makers Association soon followed. In recent years Koreans in the New York area have used ethnic ties to recruit workers from their homeland and open over 9,000 shops of all kinds.

Perhaps one of the most dramatic examples of ethnic enterprise influencing a local economy took place in the 1970s and 1980s in Miami. In the book *City on Edge: The Transformation of Miami* (1993), Alejandro Portes and Alex Stepick explain how Cuban entrepreneurs reshaped the economy of South Florida. Building on ethnic connections between Cubans in Miami and Spanish-speaking companies in Latin America, these immigrants came to dominate local business. By 1979, over half of all construction companies in Dade County were Cuban-owned. When these entrepreneurs were no longer able to hire other Cubans because of the group's upward mobility, they turned to Nicaraguans, and, consequently, provided an economic base for another ethnic settlement. Iranian entrepreneurs were able to build retail and manufacturing facilities in Los Angeles in the 1980s by hiring spouses and other relatives for relatively low wages.

The ethnic character of local America could lead to conflict as well as financial

Ethnography

success. Tensions between Irish Catholics and native-born Protestants were strong in Philadelphia in the 1840s. Natives resented the fact that the Irish worked for low wages and competed for jobs. The Catholic newcomers were resentful of the practice of reading a Protestant version of the Bible in the public schools. The riots in the Kensington section of the city in 1844 resulted from this tension. In Grass Valley, California, in the 1850s, Cornish miners in search of gold competed with German and Irish men and fought with them in taverns on Saturday nights. During World War I, German Americans were often looked upon with suspicion, and the teaching of the German language was ended in many public schools. And in the 1940s, in Los Angeles, servicemen attacked young Mexican males whom they held in contempt because of their ethnic background and the unusual "zoot suits" they wore.

Politics, however, offered an arena in which ethnic hostility could be resolved in less violent ways. Throughout much of American history, local politics was ethnic politics. In the nineteenth century there was a strong correlation between nationality and party. Irish Catholics tended to find a home in the Democratic Party apart from many Protestant groups like the Scandinavians who joined the Republicans. John Allswang, in his book *A House for All Peoples: Ethnic Politics in Chicago* (1971), explained how ethnic and religious differences made Prohibition a major issue in the city, one that often determined the results of mayoral elections. Anton Cermak, a Czech, actually mobilized Germans, Czechs, and Poles who opposed Prohibition and re

sented the anti-immigrant views of the Republican candidate to win the mayor's office in 1931. From 1930 to 1960, Italians living on "the Hill" in St. Louis could find jobs by contacting a local political boss like Lou Berra (Yogi's father). And in the 1980s Cubans not only came to play a major role in the economy of Miami, but transformed South Florida into a bastion of conservative Republican power.

Additional information on the importance of ethnic identity in local history can be found in the many entries of the *Harvard Encyclopedia of American Ethnic Groups* (1980). Valuable archival and newspaper collections regarding ethnic settlements can be found at the *Immigration History Research Center of the University of Minnesota, the Balch Institute archives now held by the *Pennsylvania Historical Society in Philadelphia, the Asian-American Studies Center at the University of California in Los Angeles, and the YIVO Institute for Jewish Research in New York.

JOHN BODNAR
INDIANA UNIVERSITY

See Appendix A.

Ethnography. This term refers to an analytic, written description of human social life within a specific cultural group, tribe, or a subgroup of people living in a large society who define themselves ethnically, religiously, or culturally, as distinct from other human groups. Ethnographers seek to record the lifeways of a "group" that is defined by its shared beliefs, practices, customs, moral standards, and corresponding behaviors. Local historians working in complex

214

communities where many subgroups coexist may choose to describe a single group that is self-defined, for example, by ethnicity, beliefs, political orientation, or any shared cultural traits its members claim to possess and/or practice. In contrast, an ethnographer may choose to investigate the ways in which different groups are socially linked by discovering certain broader standards and values, social, moral, or legal, that are common to the community as a whole and facilitate its integration.

LAURIS MCKEE
FRANKLIN AND MARSHALL COLLEGE

ethnohistory and local history. The methodologies of the local historian and the ethnohistorian may converge or differ depending on their approach to research. Both approaches require selecting a defined period of the human past as their object of study, but the focus differs somewhat. The local historian, after selecting a specific time period in the history of a human community, may focus only on public life, and thus concentrate primarily on records such as *census tallies, newspaper reports of public events, *diaries, and the actions of selected individuals within the public arena to determine how community life was influenced and shaped.

Ethnohistorical methodology turns more attention to the conventions underlying social exchanges. The challenge is to reconstruct the explicit and implicit cultural rules (mores) that influence interpersonal life and, thus, how persons and groups comport themselves. Analyses of material culture and documentary data (such as letters, literature, laws, stated customary behav-

ior, etc.) are employed in both types of research, but the ethnohistorian's interest is in discovering commonly shared beliefs and behaviors that shape cultural lifeways (both public and private).

Some examples of specific anthropological methods can be useful to local historians interested in cultural phenomena. The journal *Ethnohistory* is a good source for gaining access to the range of research strategies and breadth of inquiry that one can use in a research project. A few examples given below are from studies by ethnohistorians and anthropologists whose work focuses on North American subcultures. Of course the more multiethnic the community, the more problematic is research that attempts a community-wide analysis. Class conflicts, inter-ethnic competition, etc., disrupt social unity in complex communities. Thus, cultural studies in North American society generally are done in small towns or else they focus on small groups that cohere due to ethnic identity or shared religious convictions.

William H. Lyon circumvented this problem by studying a cultural stereotype: North American Indians. See his article "Navajos in the American Historical Imagination, 1868–1900," *Ethnohistory* 45, no. 2 (Spring 1988): 237–76. Lyon studies documents and photographs of Navajos from the late 1900s and contrasted attitudes among the Southwestern whites who lived in proximity to the Indian groups: persons who lived near the Navajo tended to be assimilationists and admirers of the Navajo way of life. Other whites who had no association with tribal members called for the demise of Navajo culture and demanded the Indians become "civilized." They particularly deplored the Navajo practice of polygyny (multiple wives), considering it scandalous and immoral.

Virtually all cultural groups invent or inherit ceremonies that give shape and direction to their society's lifeways. In analyzing archival materials and archaeological data from early missions in northern California, Russell K. Skowronek found that despite sixty years of intense Christian missionizing, the Ohlone Indians still conserved most of their original cosmology. The Franciscan missionaries were dismayed that the Ohlone shamans continued to practice healing rituals and traditions of dance, whose symbolic content gave direction and shape to cultural life. For example, the Indian tradition of burning all the material belongings of the dead was deemed barbaric and wasteful by missionaries.

Lauris McKee
Franklin and Marshall College

evaluation. How do you define success? What is it you want your visitors to know, feel, and do as a result of an experience with your organization? What do they want to know, feel, and do when they visit? What do you know about the people already visiting your institution? Why do they come? Who is not coming and why?

Understanding the needs and interests of your current and potential audience and what they think about your organization is critical to its sustainability. You can have the best historical research and the finest collection related to your mission, but if the stories you share are not relevant and engaging for

your audiences, the future of your institution will be in jeopardy. Asking visitors and/or potential visitors what they think of your institution also shows that you care about them.

Evaluation is the *systematic* collection of information about programs and operations—from the *user's perspective*—that examines the successes and shortcomings of operations and programs *against what you wanted to achieve.*

There are three key elements included in the statement above. *Systematic* refers to a system used to collect data that ensures the data is valid and reliable. Reliability is about measuring something consistently. The questions you ask visitors must be planned in advance and every visitor must be asked the same question. It also means using random sample selection to select the visitors you will survey. If you are not able to ask questions of every single visitor, you need to collect information from a representative sample of your visitors. Choose a number and a location to select the visitor you will survey. For example, select every third visitor who walks past a specific doorway. If you follow this protocol, at the end of the day, the demographics such as age, sex, number of visits, and education will be representative of the entire group of visitors that comes to your institution. Validity is about measuring what you intend to measure. For example, if you are observing visitors in an exhibit and tracking how much time they are spending with your interactives, and some of the interactives are not working, then you are not measuring what you intend to measure.

The *user's perspective* may seem obvious, but when you are evaluating your services and programs you need to ensure that the people you are surveying or interviewing are people not associated with your museum and are actually using or experiencing the programs and services that you are offering.

Against what you wanted to achieve is the most important element of an evaluation. Being intentional about the outcomes of your programs and exhibits helps you decide what types of questions you want to ask and the best methodology you should use for asking those questions. Before you go out and survey or interview visitors, you must clarify what you want your visitors to know, feel, and do as a result of their interaction with your programs and exhibits. These outcomes are the baseline against which you measure the success of your offerings. For example, if you want visitors to feel more confident in being able to analyze a *primary document, then that outcome needs to be measured in your surveys. Determining what you want to achieve before you collect information ensures that the data you collect is not just nice-to-know information but is actionable.

There are three types of evaluation you can use to help you make informed decisions about your programs and exhibits. *Front-end* evaluation is very useful for testing your outcomes and strategies to achieve those outcomes with your target audience. This type of evaluation can also uncover what your audience already knows about the topic so that you can make connections between what they know and the story you are sharing. This is typically done with either surveys or interviews where you share a list of outcomes for an upcoming project and the techniques (exhibit, film, tour, etc.) you are considering for achieving those outcomes. After you complete the evaluation, the information can be used to revise and clarify both your outcomes and strategies for achieving them.

Formative evaluation is useful for testing prototypes of your exhibits and programs with your target audiences. This allows you to test out labels, signage, small sections of an exhibit, and interpretive techniques with your target audience. This allows you to test many different versions of the same label or exhibit section to see which is most effective in achieving your outcomes. In addition, if you and your staff have been debating different ways to write a label or different ways to engage families, formative evaluation can help you decide which version is most effective. For example, if you are designing a new family program, offer version "A" of a segment of the program to two or three groups of families for a period of several days. While you are doing the program, have a volunteer or staff member observe the families and then interview them after the program to see what they think about the experience and whether it meets the outcomes you intended it to achieve. Then offer version "B" of the program, conduct observations and interviews, and compare the results.

Summative evaluation is done after the program and exhibit have been implemented; the information gathered in this process can help you learn lessons about how to design future exhibits and programs.

There are many different methods you can use to collect information about your visitors, potential visitors, and their opinions of their experiences. The best methods combine quantitative data (anything that can be expressed with a number, such as number of visitors with children or how many visitors rated the experience excellent) with qualitative data (describes why people think what they think and usually involves open-ended questions). Some of the methods most commonly used are observation studies, on-site surveys, interviews, focus groups, and online surveys. For a more detailed description of the pros and cons of different methods see *The Small Museum Toolkit: Reaching and Responding to The Audience*, 59–66. The chapter titled "In Lieu of Mind Reading" also has several examples of evaluations conducted by *small museums and historic sites on very limited budgets.

Evaluation is not the last step in the planning process—it is a planning tool. It is one of the best ways to involve your target audiences in the design of your programs and exhibits and determine if the experiences you have designed are achieving your outcomes and meeting their needs. Predicting how people will behave in an upcoming exhibit or program is very difficult. Human beings are not logical. The only way to know if the experience you are creating will be meaningful, relevant, and memorable is to test it out with your visitors. Involving staff, board, volunteers, community members, and stakeholders in the planning and implementation of an evaluation can also help bring everyone together around a common goal. In fact, evaluation is not only a process, it is a way of thinking about everything you do.

For further reading, see Cinnamon Catlin-Legutko and Stacy Klingler, *The Small Museum Toolkit: Reaching and Responding to the Audience*, vol. 4 (2012).

CONNY C. GRAFT
CONNY GRAFT RESEARCH
AND EVALUATION

See exhibits and local history; mission statement; museums, small; museums and families; relevance; vision.

exhibits and local history. Many, if not most, local history organizations produce exhibits. Exhibits are a way of combining, in some fashion, objects, images, text, interactives, and media in an installation. Exhibits differ from displays (of say, glassware or wedding gowns) in that they have a theme; a big idea that allows the visitor to connect some topic from the past to their own lives today.

What's an Interpretive Exhibit?

Interpretive exhibits are those that seek to create meaning for the visitor. The principles articulated by Freeman Tilden (*Interpreting Our Heritage*, 1957) in writing about historic and natural interpretation decades ago still hold true for exhibit interpretation. Among his principles:

- Information as such, is not interpretation. Interpretation is revelation based on information.
- The chief aim of interpretation is provocation, not instruction.

Exhibits at local history organizations generally fall into three categories:

- Permanent or long-term: on exhibit for five or more years. Often these unchanging exhibits are cited as a reason for a lack of return visits.
- Short-term or temporary exhibits: usually mounted for less than a year and usually based on materials from either the organization's own collections or community lenders.
- Traveling exhibits: these are exhibits developed by another organization that travel to a number of sites. In particular, the Museum on Main Street Project (www.museumonmainstreet.org) of the Smithsonian Institution and state humanities councils have brought quality interpretive exhibits to many small museums across the country.

What's the Exhibit Development Process?

The development of exhibits can be more clearly thought of as a production of a play or film rather than the writing of a book. It requires an understanding of a number of different elements. Even in small museums, a team can be the most effective way of developing the exhibit. Here's a very simple list of steps than can be infinitely expanded depending on your resources.

- Begin with an idea. The idea can spring from objects or archival materials in your collection, the history of your community, or visitor feedback.
- Write a "big idea" statement (from Beverly Serrell's invaluable book, *Exhibit Labels: An Interpretive Approach* [1996]) that has a subject, a verb, and a consequence.
- Develop an outline that includes key areas of emphasis along with objects and images.

- Ask colleagues or friends to review the outline. Make changes.
- Consider developing simple interactive elements that museum visitors of all ages enjoy.
- Create a floor plan and wall elevations of the space for the exhibit and begin to place your elements. Even if done in simple sketch form, this allows you to understand how the visitor will respond.
- Consider which objects need special care or special mounting methods.
- Write final exhibit text, working in a hierarchal fashion, with a main introductory label, key labels for each section, and object labels.
- Install the exhibit.
- Solicit visitor feedback to ensure improvements for the next time.

Fabricating Exhibits

Most small historical organizations have to rely on small budgets or volunteers for exhibit construction, but today, computers have made it much easier to produce a professional-looking exhibition. Exhibit labels can be produced and printed in-house, large, high-resolution photographs can be printed on a large-format printer, probably available in your community, and ideas abound online. Volunteer carpenters and painters can build exhibit cases and paint walls. Volunteer seamstresses can create appropriate mounts for textiles and even construct mannequins.

Resources

Exhibit Files (www.exhibitfiles.org) is an enormous resource featuring both exhibit reviews and case studies. Although many of the exhibits featured are at larger institutions, the reviews and case studies provide many ideas that are scalable to smaller organizations. The *American Association for State and Local History (www.aaslh.org) provides regular features on exhibits in *History News*; their technical leaflets include topics such as "Exhibit Makeovers: Do It Yourself Exhibit Planning," "Families First: Rethinking Exhibits to Engage all Ages," and "Telling a Story in 100 Words: Effective Label Copy."

LINDA NORRIS
THE UNCATALOGED MUSEUM

See American Association of State and Local History; evaluation; museums and families; museums, small.

F

Facebook. See social media.

failure and local history. Cycles of "boom and bust" are as characteristic of the American experience as the familiar "rags to riches" story. Although most people would rather perpetuate success stories and most local historical activities celebrate "the winners," personal, organizational, and regional failures should not be forgotten when recounting the history of a locality. By including the saga of the unsuccessful, the local historian provides a more complex and realistic perspective on the past.

In the nineteenth century, many communities that ultimately failed were founded on *utopian principles. The list is long and varied, including the Shakers, Fourierists, the New Harmony Community (in Pennsylvania and Indiana), the Oneida Community, and many others. While the social and economic programs of these particular groups did not stand the test of time, it is important that their stories be told so that the history of social reform and "alternative lifestyles" is fully recorded.

The failure of utopian social movements affected a relatively small number of communities, but economic downturns shaped the histories of many cities, towns, and villages. Most places have experienced agricultural and/or business growth and then decline. In some cases the economic downturns were overcome relatively quickly; in others, problems persisted for long periods. The "faded glory" of many upstate New York towns, as well as towns and cities in the Midwestern "Rust Belt," testifies to the tenacity of "hard times." Sometimes a community simply disappeared. The American West is not the only area where "*ghost towns" dot the countryside. U.S. history is replete with "panics" and "depressions," as well as lost opportunities and schemes that did not come to fruition. In some cases success for one area meant failure for another. The Erie Canal led to the creation of great cities at Syracuse, Rochester, and Buffalo; it caused a loss of population and economic dominance for Geneva and Canandaigua, New York. By analyzing these larger movements and explaining their local impact, the local historian makes the history of the community understandable.

Large economic trends affect whole communities; personal failures are also reflected in history. The presence of poorhouses, almshouses, and orphan asylums in most nineteenth-century towns and cities were symbolic of very personal tragedies. City and county jails and state and federal penitentiaries are all indications of social ills that are still very much with us. For women, the existence of prostitution and welfare dependency represents personal difficulties that our communities have handled in different ways over time.

The sources for documenting personal and institutional failures may be difficult to find. One good source is old newspapers. Others include old bank records, labor union records, bankruptcy records, and *court records. This is an area where *oral history interviews can also be important.

As difficult as they may be, the stories of lost dreams and unfulfilled promises constitute a vital element in the histories of all communities. In retelling these stories, the local historian paints a fuller and more realistic portrait of the past while allowing for a better perspective on current problems faced by the locality. By dealing with failure as well as success, the local historian helps the community more fully appreciate their collective past, which should assist them in facing their collective future.

G. DAVID BRUMBERG
CORNELL UNIVERSITY LIBRARY, RETIRED

fakelore, folklorism, and intangible heritage. The term fakelore was devised by Richard Dorson (1916–1981), folklorist at Indiana University, to describe commercial, cleverly packaged, uncritical, and random collections of stories presented as genuine folklore, such as those about Paul Bunyan, Joe Magarac, and Pecos Bill. He also railed against inauthentic presentations that distorted folk traditions, such as folk singers and folk festivals. Dorson worried about jingoistic uses of folklore during the 1940s when Disney and governmental propagandists created commercial exaggerations of "national" folklore to unite the country. Dorson wrote, "fakelore is the presentation of spurious and synthetic writings under the claim that they are genuine folklore. These productions are not collected in the field but are rewritten from earlier literary and journalistic sources in an endless chain of regurgitation, or they may even be made out of whole cloth." See "Fakelore," in Richard M. Dorson, *American Folklore & the Historian* (1971).

Critics of Dorson's usage suggested the idea of "invented tradition," the term used by Eric Hobsbawn and Terence Ranger, to interpret adaptations of tradition more objectively as a part of the cultural process. Rather than dismissing heritage productions, scholars proposed analyzing the image of the "folk" or "heritage" in popular culture that communities use for boosting their image, creating an identity, or carrying a sense of tradition. This process of heritage construction is also referred to in the scholarly literature, especially in Europe, as "folklorism" or "folklorismus." In the twenty-first century, scholars have referred to the "folkloresque" following from the theories of Russian philosopher Mikhail Bakhtin of the "carnivalesque," and have hypothesized that distortions of folklore have political and social functions of mocking and protesting the massification of society and dominance of commercial culture. In many academic circles, issues of the presentation of folklore and folklife in the public sector have become part of the discourse of heritage studies concerned for the meaning of cultural and historical preservation and exhibition to and by the public. In addition to concern for the agency of heritage organizations to affect localized culture and traditions, historical societies and cultural agencies, in addition to academic folklorists, have been also in dialogue internationally with UNESCO and other international monitoring organizations about identification of tangible "World Heritage Sites" and guidelines for safeguarding what UNESCO designates as authentic "Intangible Cultural Heritage," or traditional knowledge and folklore.

See Michael Dylan Foster and Lisa Gilman, eds., *UNESCO on the Ground: Local Perspectives on Intangible Cultural Heritage* (2015); William Woys Weaver, *As American as Shoofly Pie: The Foodlore and Fakelore of Pennsylvania Dutch Cuisine* (2013); Trevor J. Blank and Robert Glenn Howard, eds., *Tradition in the Twenty-First Century: Locating the Role of the Past in the Present* (2013); Celeste Ray, ed., *Southern Heritage on Display: Public Ritual and Ethnic Diversity within Southern Regionalism* (2003); Guntis Šmidchens, "Folklorism Revisited," *Journal of Folklore Research* 36 (1999): 51–70; Regina Bendix, *In Search of Authenticity* (1998); Venetia J. Newall, "The Adaptation of Folklore and Tradition (Folklorismus)," *Folklore* 98 (1987): 131–51; Hermann Bausinger, "Toward a Critique of Folklorism Criticism," in *German Volkskunde: A Decade of Theoretical Confrontation, Debate, and Reorientation* (1986), 113–23; and Vilmos Voigt, "Folklore and 'Folklorism' Today," in *Folklore Studies in the Twentieth Century*, ed. Venetia J. Newall (1978), 419–24.

Simon J. Bronner
Pennsylvania State
University–Harrisburg

families and museums. See museums and families.

family. Local historians may find that a variety of family forms coexist in contemporary societies. Generally, we think of a family as finding its origins in marriage between one man and one woman, a union that results in the nuclear form. However, in both the present and the past, several types of families have existed that are structurally similar to, or conversely, quite distinct from a conventional nuclear family. Among these types are single parents with children, same-sex couples with children, grandparents raising their grandchildren, and foster parents raising children. In order to record a community's family life appropriately, all extant variations in family form should be recognized and taken into account.

Local historians are aware of the complexity of contemporary family ties that socially link people in small communities. But surprisingly often in U.S. societies, genealogical memory is shallow: people may have little or no recall of the names of their ascendants beyond the grandparental level, or of their collateral relatives.

Bilateral descent is the basic principle of affiliation in nuclear families. In a bilateral family, two unrelated kin groups become united as co-relatives when their offspring marry. The children that issue from that marriage are legitimate, *consanguineal* relatives of both families (as they, conceptually, share the "blood" of both parents' families of birth (see Schneider 1968 for a controversial analysis of "blood relationship" in the United States). Cousin-marriage poses a special case in which a bilateral/biological relationship already exists between the partners, and as such, is prohibited in some states, but permitted in others. Another aspect of bilaterality that occasionally reaches family courts concerns the children of an unmarried couple. These children, depending on state laws, might be classed as illegitimate, but they are conceptually and decidedly the consanguineal kin of each of their parents and their parents' kin.

A marriage creates a multifamily complex of relationships, but each ego ultimately chooses particular persons within that complex with whom she or he will build close, affectionate ties. In anthropology, this group of relatives is known as a person's "kindred." Each person in a family is the center of her or his own kindred: those people with whom the person (ego) has close ties of affection and mutual interest. Members of ego's kindred share implicit, reciprocal rights, responsibilities, and obligations. We think of the kindred as a group of relatives who comprise ego's close family circle within the bilateral family.

The extended bilateral family is much larger than an ego's kindred; it theoretically includes *all* of ego's legitimate, living relations, acquired through birth and/or marriage. American families limit mutual obligations by limiting the number of kin they actively recognize. Relationships with more distant relatives and the relatives of their relatives (e.g., a great-uncle's children's children) may never be activated.

A kinship chart is helpful when analyzing the structure of either a kindred or an extended multigenerational family. One begins with a single person (ego), and his or her nuclear family of birth (parents and siblings), and the new nuclear family ego forms at marriage. One then records all generational lines of ascent and descent for each of ego's parents and their siblings' spouses and children and their ascendants, and similarly, records ego's own children's nuclear families. In short, all kin types are recorded when possible. For aid in plotting kin relationships, see Ernest Schusky, *Manual for Kinship Analysis* (1965).

In sum, a bilateral family can produce an enormous array of kinspersons and the larger the family, the greater the likelihood that genealogical distance instantiates emotional distance (as, for example, between ego and a fourth cousin, or ego and a great-great-uncle). Close kin ties entail mutual responsibilities. In contemporary American social ideals, the sense of responsibility and affection is supposed to be strong between parents and children, and between siblings as well. But conventional standards are somewhat vague concerning ego's relationships to cousins or even to nieces and nephews. Affective ties tend to grow weaker as genealogical distance between family members increases, and in our mobile society, geographical distance from family members is a factor as well.

Expectations of mutual support within historic nuclear or extended families can be gleaned from a variety of documentary evidence. Stories in the popular press may implicitly define conventional family roles, obligations, and values. Court cases throw light on legal rights and obligations of family members, including those of bilateral kin (siblings, aunts, uncles, and in-laws).

All family forms exist within particular economic conditions and constraints that exert pressure on family organization, and one can argue that the contemporary predominance of the nuclear family (rather than the extended family) is related to rapid urbanization and the decline of family farms dating from the beginning of the past century. Nuclear family units tend to predominate in a society that requires mobility. It is relatively easy for a corporation to uproot and move nuclear families in response to job requirements. Contrast this with the difficulty posed for large, extended landholding farm families to simply pack up and move elsewhere.

Suggested references include Mirra Komarovsky, *Blue Collar Marriage* (1967), David Schneider, *American Kinship: A Cultural Account* (1968), and Kath Weston, *Families We Choose: Lesbians, Gays, Kinship* (2007).

LAURIS MCKEE
FRANKLIN AND MARSHALL COLLEGE

family history. Family history is a new field that has attracted scholars in the last three decades. Out of the *New Social History of the 1960s, historians interested in family life formed part of a larger effort to reconstruct the private lives of everyday people. For them, "history from the bottom up" also meant probing the daily interactions of family members to understand the impact of family life on the individual and to understand the ways in which families resisted or supported the prescriptions of the larger society. Yet, the new family historians of the 1970s, 1980s, and 1990s did not break entirely fresh ground. Prior to their interest in family

as a legitimate area of academic study, two other groups—antiquarians and behavioral scientists—pioneered both the historical materials and the theoretical context for the work.

Although the purpose of antiquarian and genealogical research differs in large part from that of family historians, it was the by-product of that diligent research that attracted historians. Indeed, the recovery work of antiquarians and genealogists developed and preserved vast collections of documentary materials—now available to family historians. Wills, deeds, town records, *census reports, *cemetery inscriptions, and a host of other *material culture artifacts as well as documents were the grist for their personal histories. Indeed many of the research methods such as collecting personal statistics from government documents such as the federal census or town records or searching out material artifacts such as *photographs and personal documents were techniques developed by genealogists and antiquarians. While historians searched out the personal writings and published works of the highborn, political or military notables, antiquarians and genealogists mined more humble strata. The results of their painstaking explorations (and off-handed rummaging) often found their way into local archives and have become valuable today. In addition, many government documents such as the federal census manuscript schedules were microfilmed to meet the demand of their work. In the process of their work, these independent scholars created some truly remarkable repositories, such as the Family History Library in Salt Lake City. For a new look at genealogists and their history see Francois Weil, *Family Trees: A History of Genealogy in America* (2013).

While genealogists and antiquarians scoured the countryside for documents and artifacts, the behavioral scientists—sociologists, psychologists, and anthropologists—established theoretical models for understanding the structure and complexities of family relationships. To most of these researchers, the family provided a fundamental unit that seemed universal to most, if not all, human experience. To understand the construction of the individual, behavioral scientists examined the way in which that person's life came to be encapsulated, organized, and shaped by the internal authority of the family. Moreover, social scientists theorized that the external forces working on the family could be resisted or reinforced depending on how the family unit responded to larger societal pressures. Initially, the theoretical work of social scientists became important to social historians when they began to focus on larger social groups delineated by religion, *ethnicity, economics, or skin color. Naturally, when interest in the family developed, this same theoretical base informed family historians.

The field of family history did not emerge with one seminal work or a particular school of historians; rather, the earliest family historians simply chose families as the best subject group for their interests in other social forces. Bernard Bailyn's *Education in the Formation of American Society* (1960) and Edmund Morgan's *The Puritan Family* (1966) were not self-conscious attempts to create a new field. However, by 1970 John Demos recognized the emergence of family history as a new field in the foreword of his work, *A Little Commonwealth: Family Life in Plymouth Colony* (1970). In his assessment, Demos noted that the appearance of works that could be categorized as "family history" proliferated, but, on the whole, the current body of scholarship lacked a solid set of "guiding themes and questions." All the same, Demos predicted that family history was an important new development in social history. He also observed that one of the most useful methods for exploring family life was through the study of local history. By confining his work to materials "indigenous" to Plymouth Colony, Demos hoped to construct as accurate a picture of family structure and relationships as possible.

By the early 1980s, more historians were actively working in the field, and, in the process, refining the direction that family history moved in the last decade of the twentieth century. More than just a method of recapturing the social experience of everyday people, the study of the family provides social historians an ideal "place" to explore the construction of race, class, and gender. A more inclusive approach for studying gender and relationships between generations and across ethnic lines, current methodology in family history attempts to weave the conventional "impressionistic" evidence with the quantitative evidence of social history. By Jacquelyn Dowd Hall and others, *Like a Family* (1987) combined the interests of family, social, and economic historians to reconstruct the Southern cotton-mill communities. As *Like a Family* demonstrates, the family unit was the primary point of intersection between private and public life. Clearly, it is the place, metaphorically as well as physically, where human/social reproduction and production are linked. Since individual identity is generally formed in the context of family, the construction of race and class identity must also be part of that process. From this perspective, the evolution of American society is irrevocably linked to the influences both emanating from and acting upon the family units that make up the larger community.

Aside from the advantages, family historians have also recognized there are also inherent problems. How can those working in the field create a standardized definition beyond a single individual historian's work? Once scholars began to look at the family unit as a valuable category for analysis, they also began to understand the endless permutation of family models. Despite the fact that most cultures recognize some type of family arrangement, the forms and functions vary widely and are not always comparable. Even in the American context, the concept of family differed over time and across distinct cultural/sectional divides; this variation makes nonsense of descriptors like "traditional" or "modern."

In seventeenth-century New England, the social identity of family generally encompassed all who lived under one roof under the authority of the male head, but in practice many New England families were nuclear. In contrast, Native Americans' families typically included individuals beyond the "*household" members, and "households" were not necessarily defined by Anglo-patri-archal standards. Iroquois families, for instance, defined kin along *matrilineal lines and, though individual families may have shared distinct hearths within the family dwelling, Iroquois longhouses contained large extended-family units linked by a senior female relative. Should historians define a longhouse as a group of families or as one unit? In the slave quarters of Southern plantations, African Americans attempted to maintain nuclear families around conjugal couples, but were often forced to rely on a broader definition of kinship due to the realities of slave life. Sale, work in the fields, and separation between neighboring plantations meant slave families functioned very differently from their white neighbors. How does a historian winnow out what a particular group desired as family patterns from what they were forced to accept?

In the nineteenth and into the twentieth centuries, as the market revolution helped to define a new U.S. middle class, Americans more fully adopted a nuclear family model. The "cult of domesticity" dictated that women remain in the home as caretakers, men become breadwinners, and conjugal couples with children form the appropriate family archetype. Again, there were obvious concessions to the exigencies of the industrial workplace. Despite the impact of hegemonic U.S. cultural ideals on immigrant families, alternative family structures persisted. Families who relied on factory labor for their subsistence often took in boarders and perhaps incorporated them into their family structures as more than just paying guests. Middle-class families often incorporated domestic staff into their lives as more than just household laborers.

In the West, the last half of the century was a time of enormous change for native people as assimilation became a national policy after 1880. The Dawes General Allotment Act encouraged native people to become individual landowners through the break-up of reservations into family-run farms. Indian leaders argued loudly against the Dawes Act, pointing out that under their communal land-ownership system everyone was protected. As individuals, all Indian people would not have the benefit of access to land for cultivation or pasture. Despite great pressure, many tribal groups resisted and continued to operate in communal systems.

Other Americans developed new models of family and community life in clear protest to the prevailing industrial/nuclear trend. The Shakers rejected family altogether and opted for celibate separation of the sexes. Free love communities rejected "traditional" marriage and practiced plural or universal marriage. Some groups even abolished particular parent/child relationships and imagined a communal kind of parenting. The Mormons practiced their own version of plural marriage and also tinkered with mainstream American family structure.

Clearly, throughout the nineteenth century, American notions of what constituted "family"—or what it should be—remained unsettled. They seem to remain unsettled. The language of recent political debates over "family values" underscores that confusion. Certainly, the "ideal" family by mainstream American definition is the nuclear parent/children unit. Yet, the evidence points overwhelmingly to the fact that this is an ideal, and the reality is that many families in twentieth- and twenty-first-century United States are not typically "ideal." Indeed, much of the interest in family history has been a direct result of the puzzling political rhetoric that invokes "traditional" family values with no clear indication of whose "tradition" and from what era these values emanate. Even if there were agreement as to what "traditional" values are, there exists a great disparity between the "ideal" and the reality of family life. The development of civil union and gay marriage rights in the most recent past has generated a new debate over what constitutes family. The legal construction of gay families—with or without children—and their place in American society has launched a whole new round of discussion on the concept of family and cultural and legal challenges to the "ideal."

As a result, family historians often find—willingly or not—that a political dimension exists in their work. (See, for instance, Naomi Cahn and June Carbone, *Red Families v. Blue Families: Legal Polarization and the Creation of Culture* [2010].) Often, political and social critics demand that historians provide definitive and concrete models that can inform their contemporary dialogue—with little understanding of the difficulty in developing broad generalizations. The shifting landscape of family patterns against the economic and social trends of any given period makes such particular observations extremely difficult. Instead, historians often find that there is great variation across time and space that militates against broad general models. As historian Stephanie Coontz noted, "What we [family historians] need to do is approach families as organic parts of a total yet ever-changing network of social interactions in which equilibrium is never achieved" (*The Social Origins of Private Life* [1988], 16). Family should be understood in the historical context as a vehicle for governing and organizing individual behavior within the unit and as an interactive part of a much larger set of changing historical and cultural imperatives. This kind of cultural and historical relativity seems to lend itself well to another related field: local history. Coontz's own work demonstrates how fruitful such collaboration can be.

While Coontz produced a comprehensive study of the history of the American family, *The Social Origins of Private Life and The Way We Never Were* (1992), many of the works she drew upon for her study were local and community studies. Thus, for her larger synthesis, scholars of local or regional history provided the raw material in their particular histories of small places and minor groups. In short, both fields, local and family history, have much to offer each other.

In the twenty-first century, family history is now an important part of many college and university curriculums. A growing number of sessions at national conferences have been devoted to family history as well as several scholarly meetings held at Carleton University in Ottawa, Ontario, that focused entirely on the family. The National Council on Family Relations in Minneapolis, Minnesota, publishes a *Journal of Family*

History. Recently, there has been an expansion of interest and work in the field that has resulted in new publications on both American and a growing genre of international family history. See Stephanie Coontz, *American Families: A Multicultural Reader* (1998, 2008); Susan M. Ross, *American Families Past and Present: Social Perspectives on Transformations* (2006); Rosalind Edwards, *Researching Families and Communities: Social and Generational Change* (2008); Marilyn Coleman and Lawrence H. Ganong, *The Social History of the American Family: An Encyclopedia* (2014). For international family history, see Charles Nickie et al., *Families in Transition: Social Change, Family Formation, and Kin Relationships* (2008); Rukmalie Jayakody et al., *International Family Change: Ideational Perspectives* (2008).

SUSAN OUELLETTE
ST. MICHAEL'S COLLEGE, VERMONT

See American Indian history; Cambridge Group for the History of Population and Social Structure; census, United States; children's history; genealogy, an archivist's view; women's history at local history sites, interpreting.

Family History Library. See FamilySearch.

FamilySearch. FamilySearch is one of the largest and most comprehensive genealogical resources online (www.familysearch.org). FamilySearch is provided at no charge by the Church of Jesus Christ of Latter-day Saints (Mormons). Since it provides many of the same resources as *Ancestry and even uses the Ancestry interface for the U.S. Census and other sources, it is a very popular alternative to the subscription-only Ancestry.com.

The hidden strength of FamilySearch is the host of volunteers who over the years have transcribed and indexed millions of records. It includes the valuable *International Genealogical Index (IGI), which is a key starting point for carrying out genealogical research overseas. IGI forms the basis for an astounding collection of international, mostly European, records. These records and many others have been made available online through a sophisticated search engine that was redesigned in 2011 to search the entire range of material in many different databases, while also allowing the ability to narrow and filter search results for productive searching. FamilySearch is in the midst of a very aggressive record transcription project, which adds millions of searchable records to the site every year.

FamilySearch also provides access to the catalog of the Family History Library at Salt Lake City and features many training guides and programs for genealogists. Their research wiki is particularly helpful for genealogical researchers just beginning to expand their research to overseas sources. The library has many resources for local historians and the catalog can be searched by geography as well as by surname.

FamilySearch hosts an online family tree service, which is built on some earlier attempts at a "worldwide" family tree. Although not as user-friendly as the Ancestry.com online tree it is a useful repository of earlier genealogical work.

FamilySearch is a very well-designed site with staggering, if not always completely digested, content. It is certainly a good beginning point for local historians and genealogists alike.

ROBERT KIBBEE
THE HISTORY CENTER IN TOMPKINS
COUNTY (NY)

See genealogical resources online.

Farm Security Administration photographs. The Farm Security Administration (FSA) was created in the Department of Agriculture in 1937 to succeed the New Deal Resettlement Administration (RA). Its purpose was to assist farmers, but one of its most notable legacies is a series of photographs documenting American life. Under the direction of Roy Emerson Stryker, head of the special photo section of the RA and the FSA from 1935 to 1942, over 77,000 black-and-white photographs were produced by a number of outstanding photographers including Dorothea Lange, Gordon Parks, and Walker Evans. Early on, these photographs documented rural life and the negative impact of the Great Depression, farm mechanization, and the Dust Bowl. In 1942, the photography unit was moved to the Office of War Information and recorded the mobilization for World War II.

The collection is housed in the Prints and Photography Division of the Library of Congress. These world-famous photographs can be accessed through the websites http://hdl.loc.gov/loc.pnp/pp.fsaowi (FSA/OWI black and white photos) and http://hdl.loc.gov/loc.pnp/pp.fsac (FSA/OWI color photos). There were 164,000 black and white photographs, of which 160,000 are available, along with 1,600 color photos by less well-known photographers. A number of these images have been published in books on photography and in books of photographs from several states. See also Penelope Dixon, "Photographers of the Farm Security Administration: An Annotated Bibliography, 1930–1980," in *Garland Reference Library of the Humanities*, vol. 373.

NORMA PRENDERGAST
CORNELL UNIVERSITY, RETIRED

See photography.

federal involvement with place-names. See place-names.

Federation of State Humanities Councils. The Federation of State Humanities Councils, founded in 1977, is the membership association of the fifty-six state and territorial councils. The federation advocates with Congress on behalf of the councils and the *National Endowment for the Humanities and promotes the work of the councils through the federation's website and social media channels. The federation enters into collaborations with other national organizations, which potentially offer additional funding, programming resources, or connection to new networks and partners for councils. Contact information: Federation of State Humanities Councils, 1600 Wilson Blvd, Suite 902, Arlington, VA 22209; (703) 908-9700; www.statehumanities.org.

ESTHER MACKINTOSH
FEDERATION OF STATE
HUMANITIES COUNCILS

fee simple. Property held in fee simple or fee absolute is owned uncondition-

ally and will descend to the owner's heirs even if he or she dies intestate. It is distinguished from an entailed estate where there are limitations on who may inherit and under what circumstance.

fees, consulting. Like anyone else offering services, a history consultant has to determine how much to charge a client for a specific project. First, you need to come up with your baseline consulting fees—the amounts you charge for each hour of work and for any expenses you incur. Next, you need to develop a scope of work for the project that clearly states what work you will perform. Then you can price the project according to the scope and your fees.

A history consultant should ask three questions when setting fees: (1) What are my true costs? (2) How much profit do I want/need to make? (3) What will the market(s) I work in bear?

When computing a budget or a bid for a prospective or existing client, it makes sense to divide your costs into labor and expenses. Labor cost is the number of hours you expect a project to take you, multiplied by your labor rate, which is a cost per hour. A labor rate should include the wage you would pay yourself, plus the cost of overhead you need to sustain your business, plus profit. (Profit is discussed in the next section.)

Wage: If consulting were a full-time job for you, how much would you need to earn per hour to meet your living expenses and other needs (such as saving for retirement, putting your kids through college, or paying your mortgage)? How many hours can you reasonably expect to be working and billing to clients during the course of a year? That equation will help you figure out your hourly wage. If the project will involve other employees, their wages are what you pay each of them on an hourly basis (whether or not they are salaried).

Overhead: If you are a full-time consultant, your overhead should include the cost of office space (even if it is in your own home), general supplies and equipment, health insurance, and administrative costs (such as invoicing clients, balancing your books, or doing taxes, even if you do these things yourself). You can figure out your overhead on an annual basis and then divide it by the hours you expect to be doing billable work during the year. Add that to the figure you came up with for your wage.

Part-time consultants who have other paid employment should still include overhead as a factor in their labor rate. Even if you use your university office and already have your health care covered, you should treat consulting as an independent, self-sustaining business and set your rates accordingly. You may be tempted to undercut full-time consultants' rates by omitting overhead, but doing so misleads clients about the real costs of consulting. If you suddenly had to rely on consulting for your primary income, you might have difficulty retaining clients who had grown to expect very low labor costs. And you won't be able to sustain your business if you continue to charge rates without overhead.

Some clients may require that your overhead and profit be calculated according to specified formulas—this is the case for some state and federal agencies.

Expenses: Consultants should charge their clients the full cost of any direct expenses specific to a project. These include travel, copying or imaging, research fees charged by the facilities you'll be using, special supplies or equipment (such as DVDs, rental of a GPS unit, etc.), and subcontractors. Do careful research and be fair to both yourself and your client. For example, a plane ticket bought well in advance will be less expensive and thus will benefit your client. But if the client insists that you travel *tomorrow*, then the ticket will be expensive and that should be factored into your budget.

Profit: History consultants are often not comfortable with the thought of making a profit on their work. After all, we became historians to advance knowledge, not to get rich, right? But if consulting is your business, you should approach it like a business. Adding a profit factor to your labor rates can do several things for you: create some capital to invest in your business, provide a financial cushion in case your workload declines or a project goes over budget, and allow you to reward yourself and pay bonuses to employees for good performance. The amount of profit is up to you and what the market will bear. But once you set a profit factor (say 5 or 10 percent added to the total of your wage plus overhead), you should manage your business to achieve that factor. Don't allow projects to go over budget thinking that the profit factor will soak up the overage. You'll drive yourself out of business that way.

Markets: A market is a discrete sector of the business opportunities available to you. You might determine your markets by client type (museums, federal agencies, lawyers, state historic preservation officers) or by project type (building surveys, National Register nominations, expert witness work, book-length histories). Your expertise may be more valuable in some markets than in others. You should recognize this and set your labor rate accordingly. Conversely, some markets might be more competitive than others or might have limited funding, driving down the rates clients are willing to pay. You will need to consider using lower rates for such markets, or perhaps choose to stay out of them altogether.

You might also need to consider region as a market factor. Clients in more prosperous states or in urban areas are probably less price-sensitive than clients in less prosperous or more rural areas. Conversely, more populous areas may mean more competitors in your market, which could drive prices down.

Figuring out what a particular market will bear is not easy. History consultants don't have an industry-wide professional organization that collects and reports standard rates by market sector or region. If you bid on a job but don't get it, you can ask for a debriefing to see how you rated on various factors, such as price, expertise, experience, and work plan. The client may or may not be willing to provide this information. Federal agencies disclose the amount of a winning contract, so you can at least determine how you stacked up on price. They also provide the name of the successful bidder, so you can evaluate your expertise and experience in comparison to that person or firm.

In addition, you can seek advice from other consultants and conduct informational interviews of potential clients. Ultimately, you will want to develop appropriate rate sheets for the different markets in which you work. That will make it easier to respond quickly to inquiries from potential clients or to develop bids for specific projects.

Scopes of Work and Cost Estimates: Once you have developed rate sheets, you're ready to bid on work. Developing a scope of work (SOW) and a bid (or cost estimate) is an iterative process. To price a specific job properly, you need to identify the tasks involved in completing that job and then determine how much each task will cost. To stay within a client's available funds or cost comfort zone, you might need to reduce the scope of work, thus lowering the price.

Fixed Price or Time and Materials? Most competitively bid projects are fixed price; that is, you bid a specific amount for the job, and if you win the contract, it is for that amount. If your actual costs are greater, you will either eat into your profit or lose money on the project. Time and materials contracts are those where you are paid for the actual number of hours you have worked, plus actual expenses. These are better for situations where the scope of work is not well defined and the project is ongoing rather than finite. But a time and materials contract might have a "not to exceed" limit (a cost ceiling), and you could run into problems (eating profit or running at a loss) if you do not complete the contracted work within the cost limit.

Scope of Work (SOW): Competitively bid projects are generally announced as requests for proposals (RFPs) that include a description of the work to be performed. This is the starting point for your SOW, and you should make sure that your SOW includes all of the work described in the RFP. RFPs usually list a contact person to whom you can address questions if aspects of the project description are unclear.

Noncompetitive projects—where you are the only contractor being considered for the job—do not usually have a formal description of work. You will need to talk with the client about his or her needs and timeline, and then you can use that information to develop an SOW.

An SOW should demonstrate that you understand what the client needs and are qualified to perform the work. Most RFPs will require information about your capabilities and prior experience. They might also ask you to identify the project staff and provide résumés. A basic SOW might include the following (whether or not the RFP asks for it): project overview, capabilities, project staff, work plan, deliverables, schedule, prior experience, references, and résumés.

It's a good idea to break your work plan into discrete tasks that you can describe clearly and price definitively. Some RFPs define the tasks for you and require you to price each one separately. Otherwise, it's up to you to determine the appropriate tasks. A typical project's tasks might include project management, secondary source research, field research, draft report, and final report.

Some RFPs lay out the entire schedule for you, while others have only a project end date, leaving it up to you to figure out the intermediate deadlines. The schedule for a noncompetitive project can be negotiated with the client, but you should be realistic about how quickly you can accomplish the work.

Price: Once you have figured out the tasks necessary to complete the project, you can develop a cost estimate for each task. Spreadsheet software can facilitate the process. Include a line for each separate expense item that is part of the task (labor cost, photocopying/scanning, supplies, transportation, lodging, meals, etc.) and then add them up to develop a price for that task.

Labor cost, as explained above, is your hourly labor rate multiplied by the number of hours needed to complete the task. Determining the number of hours (level of effort) is challenging, although it gets easier with experience performing similar tasks.

If you know approximately how much a client has to spend on a project (which is not often the case), you can adjust your scope accordingly so the total price falls within the client's budget. Otherwise, you have to judge for yourself whether you have overscoped the project (made it too big and expensive for the client to afford). Again, experience will help. Keep in mind that if you want to lower the price, you have to reduce the level of effort or the direct expenses going into the project, and you need to adjust your scope of work accordingly.

EMILY GREENWALD
HISTORICAL RESEARCH ASSOCIATES, INC.

fiction. See historical fiction.

field services. Field services is an intentional activity generally offered by a statewide history organization intended to develop the capacity of local or regional history organizations. The work is commonly referred to as outreach. Field services is one of the oldest public history professions, and was originally developed by Reuben Gold Thwaites at the State Historical Society of Wisconsin in 1896. The Minnesota Historical Society employed the first full-time, permanent field services professional (Richard Sackett) in 1945. The primary work was to encourage organizing local history groups and to advise local history organizations on methods of preserving and disseminating history. In the early days this often meant locating and transcribing original documents in preparation for publication and distribution.

Presently, the majority of states provide field services programs, most often located in a state historical society, state historical agency, state museum association, regional conservation center, or other similar nonprofit or government agency. The primary work centers on improved collections care and management, more appropriate interpretation of history, and greater capacity to meet nonprofit regulations and expectations of transparency in serving local communities.

The growth in providing field services came when capacity development emerged as a profession due in part to the United Nations providing capacity development to developing nations (often those emerging from colonialism) and the growth in U.S. government services and programs. Following the New Deal, U.S. programs and services were often provided by parallel state and local agencies, which could often be inconsistent in providing services and programs. The federal government then began to provide technical assistance in the form of information, training, and grants to increase consistency at the state level, which then replicated the activity for local governments.

In the decade leading to the national Bicentennial of the American Revolution in 1976, many state history agencies and nonprofits created field services programs to complement the many new and emerging local history organizations. The decade of the 1970s also saw federal government developments in creating greater transparency and accountability in nonprofits, leading to a major revision of the Internal Revenue Service's Form 990 for nonprofits in 1979. State history field services programs adapted with the times to fold in guidance on nonprofit governance, reporting, and regulation.

The practice of field services attempts to achieve three things. First, field services professionals seek to have paid staff and volunteers of local history organizations know that they are all colleagues working together as equals. Second, field services professionals seek what matters most to those they serve to solve issues of immediate concern. And finally, field services professionals tailor their advice to time and place so that the local history organization can perform well for their constituents with their available resources.

Field services programs provide many kinds of offerings, and the menu of offerings differs by state depending on local needs. The hallmark of services is to provide on-site consultations.

Services may also include technical assistance, training in workshops or conferences or through a specialized presentation for the local history organization, *historical markers, data collection about local history to be used in communicating *value to stakeholders, newsletters (printed and/or electronic), conservation training and assistance, awards programs or other recognition, strategic planning, grants programs or assistance in writing grants, and many other services. Generally these services are free of charge to local history organizations, though some services may bear charges in keeping with costs to provide them.

Field services professionals often come to the profession after serving in local history organizations. Generally they possess college degrees in history; nonprofit, public, or business administration; museum science; public history; conservation; anthropology; and other related fields. Field services professionals continue their training through the Field Services Alliance (FSA), an affinity group of the *American Association for State and Local History.

For further reading see Tom McKay, "20th Anniversary History of Field Services Alliance," 2008 (http://download. aaslh.org/FSA+documents/FSAHistory. pdf); David M. Grabitske and David J. Nichols III, "Materially Strengthened: the Minnesota Historical Society and Providing Field Services," *Studies in Midwestern History* 2, no. 5 (2016); and Field Services Alliance Records, 1988–present (http://community.aaslh.org/ fsa-annual-records).

DAVID GRABITSKE
MINNESOTA HISTORICAL SOCIETY

See individual state entries by state name.

Field Services Alliance. Field Services Alliance (FSA) is the professional association of Field Services workers. FSA began with a meeting in Chicago in the summer of 1988, and completed its organization at the 1988 *American Association for State and Local History (AASLH) Conference and Annual Meeting in Rochester, New York. Though convened by AASLH, FSA was autonomous for much of its early history, but always met in conjunction with AASLH. In 2009 the membership of FSA voted to become an affinity group of AASLH. FSA maintains the profession's code of *ethics and a manual on the operation of field services programs. FSA holds two national meetings annually: the annual meeting ahead of the AASLH conference and the spring training hosted by one of FSA's members.

DAVID GRABITSKE
MINNESOTA HISTORICAL SOCIETY

See field services.

filiopietism. A term for a child's debt to a parent, particularly to a father, and the child's proper regard for that parent. The word, when used to describe local history, refers to the way that nineteenth-century local historians honored and wrote about the founders of a community—in deferential, non-questioning terms. While this might be an ideal way of parenting—and even that is suspect—it is not a good way of researching or writing history, for it cuts off questioning the past and seeking answers in favor of accepting the information given. Filiopietistic history is that which accepts an older idea that the only actors in history were the healthy, wealthy, and wise—unlike the trends of recent decades in which females, males who failed, those who left a place, and people of various ethnicities and races are also part of the local story.

See ethics and local history.

Filipinos in North America, sources for. See Appendix A.

financial and business history. See business and industrial history; Dun & Bradstreet credit reports; post office records.

Find-a-Grave. See genealogical resources online.

Finns in North America, sources for. See Appendix A.

Flickr. See crowdsourcing and crowdfunding; photography.

Florida, local history in. Established in 1856, the Florida Historical Society (FHS) is dedicated to preserving Florida's past through the collection and archival maintenance of historical documents and photographs, the publication of scholarly research on Florida history, and educating the public about Florida history through a variety of public history projects and programs. The FHS is the oldest existing cultural organization in the state, and the only statewide historical society. While operations ceased during the Civil War, the FHS was reestablished in 1902, and

incorporated in 1905. FHS headquarters are in the Library of Florida History in Cocoa Village, in a building that was originally a U.S. Post Office built in 1939 as a WPA project.

The FHS operates the Florida Historical Society Press, which publishes a diverse selection of books, maintains the archival collection at the Library of Florida History in Cocoa Village, manages the Brevard Museum of History and Natural Science and the Florida Historical Society Archaeological Institute (FHSAI) in Cocoa, and oversees the Historic Rossetter House Museum and Gardens in Eau Gallie. The Florida Historical Society publishes scholarly research in the *Florida Historical Quarterly* and host a variety of public events. The FHS Annual Meeting and Symposium is held each May at different locations around the state, and features academic paper presentations, panel discussions, tours of local historic sites, an awards luncheon, a gala banquet, and a picnic.

Florida Frontiers: The Weekly Radio Magazine of the Florida Historical Society airs on public radio stations throughout the state and is archived on the FHS website at www.myfloridahistory. org. *Florida Frontiers* helps to fulfill the society's mission of collecting and disseminating information about the history of Florida in ways that inform contemporary issues. Since its premiere in January 2009, *Florida Frontiers* reaches, educates, and engages a wide audience not previously accessed by the society.

The Florida Historical Society Presents: Florida Frontiers is a public television series based on the *Florida Frontiers* radio program. The half-hour documentary

This *King Philipstown / Osceola* marker in Seminole County, Florida, marks the site of both pre-historic and historic Native American settlements. CREDIT: SANFORD HISTORICAL SOCIETY.

series debuted in January 2016, covering a wide variety of issues relating to the history and culture of the state.

Through *Florida Frontiers* and other educational outreach programs, the FHS supports the efforts of hundreds of city, county, and other local historical societies and organizations around the state. Established in 1883, the St. Augustine Historical Society is the oldest local historical society in Florida, operating the Oldest House Museum Complex and maintaining an extensive archive at their Research Library. Florida has dozens of other active local historical societies including the Pensacola Historical Society, the Jacksonville Historical Society, and the Marco Island Historical Society.

State and local history can be explored at a wide variety of cultural institutions throughout the Sunshine State including the Museum of Florida History in Tallahassee, operated by the Florida Department of State, Division of Cultural Affairs; the Orange County Regional History Center in Orlando, operated by the Historical Society of Central Florida and the Orange County Board of County Commissioners; the Historical Museum of Southern Florida in Miami, operated by HistoryMiami; and the Brevard Museum of History and Natural Science, operated by the Florida Historical Society.

The primary publishers of books about Florida history are the University Press of Florida, the Florida Historical

Society Press, and Pineapple Press. The University of Alabama Press, the University of Georgia Press, and the University Press of Nebraska are among others that have also published outstanding books on Florida history and culture. Arcadia Publishing, Inc. and the History Press each have many titles focusing on local history in communities throughout Florida.

Books providing an overview of Florida history include *The History of Florida*, ed. Michael Gannon (2013), *Florida: A Short History*, by Michael Gannon (2003), and *A History of Florida*, 3rd ed., by Charlton W. Tebeau and William Marina (1981). Other books offering important insight into the history and culture of Florida include *The Everglades: River of Grass*, by Marjory Stoneman Douglas (1947, 2007), *Palmetto Country*, by Stetson Kennedy (1942, 2009), and *Land of Sunshine State of Dreams: A Social History of Modern Florida*, by Gary R. Mormino (2008). Although it is a work of fiction, the novel *A Land Remembered*, by Patrick D. Smith (1996) is a popular description of Florida history that is often incorporated into public school curricula.

Under the Florida Department of Education's Sunshine State Standards, fourth graders must be exposed to Florida history. The teacher guidelines state that fourth graders must be able to analyze primary and secondary resources to identify significant individuals and events throughout Florida history; synthesize information related to Florida history through print and electronic media; compare Native American tribes in Florida; identify explorers who came to Florida and the motivations for their expeditions; describe causes and effects of European colonization on the Native American tribes of Florida; identify the significance of St. Augustine as the oldest permanent European settlement in the United States; explain the purpose of and daily life on missions such as San Luis; identify the significance of Fort Mose as the first free African American community in the United States; identify the effects of Spanish rule in Florida; identify nations (Spain, France, England) that controlled Florida before it became a U.S. territory; explain how the Seminole tribe formed and the purpose for their migration; explain how Florida (Adams-Onis Treaty) became a U.S. territory; identify the causes and effects of the Seminole Wars; explain the effects of technological advances on Florida; describe pioneer life in Florida; describe Florida's involvement in the Civil War; summarize challenges Floridians faced during Reconstruction; describe the economic development of Florida's major industries; summarize contributions immigrant groups made to Florida; and describe the contributions of significant individuals to Florida.

The Florida Historical Society is working to have Florida history included in all levels of education, in addition to fourth grade. The society's educational projects and programs reflect how Florida history has had a significant impact on global, national, and regional history. For example, Florida is the site of a large prehistoric mortuary pond that is one of the most important archaeological discoveries in the world (the Windover Dig), the home of the oldest continuous European settlement in North America (St. Augustine), the oldest incorporated African American municipality in the United States (Eatonville), and the place where every American manned space flight was launched (the Kennedy Space Center). With its various public history initiatives, the FHS strives to demonstrate how the state's diverse history is relevant to contemporary society.

BEN BROTEMARKLE
FLORIDA HISTORICAL SOCIETY

See United States, local history in.

folklore and folklife. The materials of folklore and folklife are expressions of cultural tradition. Typically transmitted by word of mouth, custom, imitation, and demonstration, enactments of legends, crafts, or games are socially shared and hence people can draw identities from them. Among the common social identities that folklore and folklife represent for people are family, ethnicity, religion, occupation, class, gender, region, age, and, significantly, community. The ties of folklore and folklife to community are apparent from the ways that tradition is used to signify, and adapt to, the place in which folklore is performed and persists through time. Insofar as such tradition is usually associated with cultural practices within communities, it reveals locality in the way it depicts the people who inherit and transmit their experiences, values, symbols, and concerns, and references the places that act as settings shaping identities. Its significance in local historical work is in its special evidence of

localized knowledge and variable cultural practice through time.

"Folklore" was a term coined by Englishman W. J. Thoms in 1846 to replace use of "popular antiquities" and "popular literature" for forms of cultural traditions. He had been inspired by use of Volkskunde ("knowledge of the people") presented by Jacob and Wilhelm Grimm in the early nineteenth century in what is now Germany. They collected ancient tales that shared similar plots from contemporary storytellers who included in their performances details of local sites and practices. The repetition and variation characteristic of oral tradition among ordinary people, they argued, formed valuable cultural evidence that could be used to trace international diffusion of ideas and at the same time the development of local and national traditions. Sir Walter Scott's collection of Scottish ballads and folk songs, also in the early nineteenth century, drew similar attention to an overlooked artistic tradition among ordinary people who comment through their lore the meaning of historical events and the character of their values and beliefs. The antiquarian and literary interests of many early "folklorists" in the British Isles identified folklore by its comparable, and relatively stable, textual forms—the lyrics of ballads, the plots of tales, the rules of games. Indicative of the local collecting enterprise was a massive "county folklore" series of books (published by "The Folklore Society," established in 1878) recording examples of oral traditions throughout England. In addition to showcasing artistry in oral performances, the collections also uncovered valuable references to groups and events that were regionally significant but not typically covered in documentary records. In these collections are found lasting themes connecting folklore and local history of finding traditions that illuminated the diverse, often unrecorded heritage of a nation at its roots, providing reminders of creativity in everyday life by ordinary people, and raising questions about the sources and spread of ideas in culture.

If the British folklorists tended to emphasize the "lore," others, particularly in Scandinavia and Germany, focused more on different communities of "folk," many of which had similarly been overlooked. The materials included social and material practices that bound a community, including crafts, housebuilding, and cooking. The significant context was social—the groups among whom the practices were functioning—and geographical—the landscapes and environments in which people adapted their traditions. For focus on everyday lives, the term "folklife" began circulating in the nineteenth century as a counterpart to folklore. Folklife scholars developed presentations of the social and physical contexts of ordinary groups in "folk" museums such as Skansen in Sweden. Organizers displayed traditional buildings, crafts, and landscapes representing deeply rooted, regional cultures of the nation. In showing the aesthetic patterns displayed and adaptations to the environment that such structures revealed, they hoped to discern the core and borders of cultures, the symbols by which social identities were communicated, and the relations of humans to their surroundings. They implied that such communities and their structures carried with them a pride in the ancient legacies, and often a shared racial stock, that aligned a nation-state with its culture.

To many Europeans, the United States appeared too new as a nation and too socially and physically diverse as a settlement to register significant findings for folklore and folklife research. As the United States underwent rapid social change in the nineteenth century, several writers took the lead in presenting literature and local historical chronicles that recorded and interpreted an emergent folklore in America. Notables such as Nathaniel Hawthorne, Washington Irving, and James Fenimore Cooper helped create an American literature based on their representation of local place legends, comic anecdotes of ethnic and rustic characters, folk-hero tales, and customs of "pioneer" practices. In cities such as Philadelphia and New York that were rapidly growing with newcomers, many immigrants, and industrializing, antiquarians took note of endangered traditions, even if they appeared to be of short duration compared with the "antiquities" of Europe and Asia. John Fanning Watson, for instance, published *Annals of Philadelphia and Pennsylvania in the Olden Time* (1830), he claimed, "to awaken the public to the utility of bringing out their traditions and ancient family records." He collected this material with questionnaires given to the elder residents who recalled the everyday practices of the past, and in the process, he recorded beliefs, crafts, foodways, and local legends. Before "folklore" was even coined, he called this material "traditionary lore," and went on to compile similar tomes for New York City, bringing out the cultural depth of American communities. He explained that the traditions taken from ordinary individuals' traditions gave insight into their perceptions (embedded in narratives) of what happened in the past—what they thought of as history—and he presaged a wider view of heritage, including everyday life and cultural expressions, extending the understanding of local historical legacies.

Although the United States was relatively new as a nation, many observers proclaimed that a rich and varied store of folklore indeed thrived there for abundant reasons: (1) the spread and extent of small settlements and ethnic-religious communities gave rise to a variety of local traditions and the transplantation of others; (2) the varied landscape, distinctive flora and fauna, and new encounters with the environment as settlers moved west inspired the narration of natural surroundings in the form of place-names, beliefs, customs, and legends; (3) terrain and conditions unfamiliar to settlers forced adaptation of Old World material traditions in the form of foodways, architecture, clothing, and crafts; (4) isolation of some settlement pockets on mountains, in valleys, on islands, and along shores fostered the persistence of traditions; (5) encounters of settlers with American Indians and the mixing of races, classes, and ethnic groups encouraged cultural exchanges; and (6) the creation and maintenance of a new republic with constituent regions and states resulted in national/state/regional rituals and performances, some of which became embedded into culture as they were accepted as traditions.

In 1888, an organization consisting mainly of writers, clergy, professors, museum professionals, and local historians formed the American Folklore Society "for the collection of the fast-vanishing remains of Folk-Lore in America." In the proclamation of the society's founder, William Wells Newell, is specific reference to local historical work when he called the "remains of a tradition which was once the inheritance of every speaker of the English tongue" as essential to the historian of American life as "the dust of letters and pamphlets" in local historical societies. He emphasized the direct experience of local traditions as they are spoken, sung, performed, and demonstrated, taken from people in their homes and communities as a necessary supplement to the analysis of human legacies. In its early years, the society had an orbit of chapters devoted to local research in Philadelphia, Berkeley, Boston, and Hampton (an organization working particularly on African American lore), among others. In the twentieth century, regional and state societies formed and continued the spirit of local studies, including a few directly associated with historical societies such as the New York Folklore Society and Pennsylvania Folklore Society. This "fieldwork" orientation toward the interpretation of culture through the collection of living traditions, at the heart of the work of these organizations, is still part of the folkloristic enterprise. A revision of Newell's vision, however, for contemporary research is the embracing of folk as representing a communicative process used by people acting in groups. In this view, folk is not a level of society, but a type of learning and expression used by all people; it can be useful to reveal social needs and identities enacted in different settings. Further, the distinctions between the scope of folklore and folklife have arguably become less noticeable in the twenty-first century as cultural and historical investigators typically take into account material and social traditions.

Revisions of historical research to interpret the influence of everyday life, community events, and social movements on the American past have had the effect of engaging more historians in folkloristic methods of *ethnographic fieldwork, comparative textual analysis, and cultural mapping. In the common discussion of history as "*heritage," and "legacy," for example, is a reference to the significance of traditions and the role of community in passing and adapting those traditions. Folklore, it is often stressed, is not false information or primitive practice; it is socially truthful because it reveals perceptions, ideas, beliefs, and biases—sometimes summarized as worldview—that helps answer questions about the meaning of local and national experiences. As historians have been engaged by folklore's revelation of community traditions, so folklorists have been attracted by the social orientations of local history that record families, neighborhoods, rituals, legends, and customs. Indeed, several classics of folklore collection come from rigorous research projects in local settings: Richard Dorson's *Land of the Millrats* (1981); David Steven Cohen's *The Ramapo Mountain People* (1974);

Lynwood Montell's *Saga of Coe Ridge* (1970); Richard Dorson's *Bloodstoppers and Bearwalkers: Folk Traditions of the Upper Peninsula* (1952); and Harry M. Hyatt's *Folk-Lore from Adams County, Illinois* (1935).

"A New Triangulation of Local Studies" of documents, oral traditions, and artifacts articulated in 1956 by New York State Historical Association director Louis C. Jones exemplified a growing vision of folklore studies in rewriting local histories: "What I want to see is a new kind of local history that considers not alone the political and institutional development of a community [but that] which really tells us how Everyman lived, the details of his work day, how he courted, loved, married, raised his family, accepted his responsibility in the social patterns of his time, and what he thought about these experiences." By the time of the Bicentennial of America's independence, a trend had been established in observances for local historical societies to highlight the everyday life, indeed folk arts, of their community's past. Folklore and folklife added to the historical record allowed for representation of plural groups, reflection on changing cultural experience in everyday life, and recognition of ordinary individuals and vernacular practices in the story of the community. In the twenty-first century, these groups expanded from traditional immigrant groups to refugees, new religions, migrant workers, retirees, and student populations.

Since the late twentieth century, many historical societies have taken up a call to folklore and folklife research to reveal cultural traditions of America's diverse communities. State and regional organizations commonly call for conserving "cultural" resources that contribute to local pride and sometimes heritage *tourism. Economic development through festival promotion and folk arts marketing, diversified audiences for community programming, and outreach to youth in schools with folklore and folklife relating to the local area are often the results. These considerations have been part of governmental involvement in cultural-resource management that has brought many folklorists into public programming, and many have had prominent roles in state historical and arts agencies. America's first official state folklorist, Henry Shoemaker, began work in 1948 for the Pennsylvania Historical and Museum Commission, and by 1990, over forty states established such positions. In addition to academic institutions, regional and state societies, and research centers devoted to local and regional folklife studies, many agencies at the municipal and county level have also employed folklorists to guide local cultural research, organize archives, prepare publications, and mount exhibitions. The American Folklife Center in the Library of Congress, a national agency established by the Folklife Preservation Act of 1976, offers archives, publications, and technical assistance to encourage grassroots efforts. In 1998, the center launched an ambitious "Local Legacies" project to gather examples of community traditions from every locality in America. The Smithsonian Institution, which has a Center for Folklife Cultural Heritage, meanwhile has sponsored institutes for community investi-

gators in folklore and folklife research. Universities regularly offer courses and workshops in folklore research (several, including Indiana University, Pennsylvania State University, University of North Carolina, University of California–Berkeley, University of Oregon, and Western Kentucky University offer graduate degrees in it), and several have sponsored massive encyclopedias of regional history and culture that have featured folklore and folklife sections (e.g., *Encyclopedia of Southern Culture; Encyclopedia of Appalachia; Encyclopedia of New England Culture*).

With the advent of the twenty-first century and the digital age, challenges and opportunities continue for enhancing the role of folklore and folklife research within local history work. Among the challenges is taking into account newly formed communities with a variety of languages and traditions as part of local heritage. Folklorists have been instrumental in establishing exhibitions and documentary projects for local agencies on groups such as Vietnamese, Hmong, Ethiopian, Sudanese, Yemenite, Haitian, Bosnian, and Chicanos in the recent American experience. Other migrations of traditional groups such as the Amish and Hasidim to new localities require revisions of local history that should involve assessment of cultural traditions in the life of the community. The changing physical structure of communities invites questions that link folklorists in local historical settings to subjects such as patterns of suburbanization, retirement and recreational developments, and temporary settlements. More than recording the past, the ties of folklore and folklife to local history raise pressing issues of sustainability of traditional communities in the wake of changes to their natural, technological, and social environments. There is opportunity for local historical work that examines at the grassroots level emergent social and environmental movements of great national impact. Indeed, the field experience of folklorists may inform local agencies that move outside their old headquarters to establish outposts within a variety of communities and offer cultural historical programming and services for cultural conservation. Archives and exhibitions are changing to accommodate new forms of information; technology, ranging from digital cameras to computers, allows for expansion and systematization of the material being recorded, enhancing access to records of what ordinary people said, sang, and made, as well as what they wrote.

See Simon J. Bronner, *Folklore: The Basics* (2016); *Explaining Traditions* (2011); *Encyclopedia of American Folklife* (2006); *Following Tradition: Folklore in the Discourse of American Culture* (1998); and *American Folklore Studies: An Intellectual History* (1986). Also, William Clements, ed., *The Greenwood Encyclopedia of World Folklore and Folklife* (2006); Jan Harold Brunvand, *The Study of American Folklore: An Introduction*, 4th ed. (1998); and *American Folklore: An Encyclopedia* (1996); Charlie T. McCormick and Kim Kennedy White, eds., *Folklore: An Encyclopedia of Beliefs, Customs, Tales, Music, and Art* (2011). A major proponent of historical American folklore was Richard M. Dorson; see his *Handbook of American Folklore* (1983),

America in Legend: Folklore from the Colonial Period to the Present (1973), *American Folklore and the Historian* (1971), *Buying the Wind: Regional Folklore in the United States* (1964), *American Folklore* (1959), *Bloodstoppers and Bearwalkers: Folk Traditions of the Upper Peninsula* (1952). Also, C. Kurt Dewhurst, Charlie Seamann, and Patricia Hall, eds., *Folklife and Museums* (2016); Martha C. Sims and Martine Stephens, *Living Folklore: An Introduction to the Study of People and Their Traditions* (2005); Robert Georges and Michael Owen Jones, *Folkloristics: An Introduction* (1995); Mary Hufford, ed., *Conserving Culture: A New Discourse on Heritage* (1994); Patricia A. Hall, "A Case for Folklife and the Local Historical Society," in *American Material Culture and Folklife*, ed. Simon J. Bronner, 205–14 (1992); Burt Feintuch, ed., *The Conservation of Culture: Folklorists and the Public Sector* (1988); Bruce Jackson, *Fieldwork* (1987); and Austin Fife, "Folklore and Local History," *Utah Historical Quarterly* 31 (1963): 315–23. Still useful is William Wells Newell, "On the Field and Work of a Journal of American Folk-Lore," *Journal of American Folklore* 1 (1888): 3–7. Also, Barre Toelken, *The Dynamics of Folklore* (1996); Don Yoder, *Discovering American Folklife: Studies in Ethnic, Religious, and Regional Culture* (1990); and Elliott Oring, ed., *Folk Groups and Folklore Genres: An Introduction* (1986).

SIMON J. BRONNER
PENNSYLVANIA STATE
UNIVERSITY, HARRISBURG

food. See culinary history and the local historian; material culture.

foodways. See culinary history and the local historian; living history museums.

free boarders. In many communities, laws were passed to give hogs and other domestic animals free rein to forage for food, in which case they were declared to be free boarders. Other communities restricted animals to a common land or to an owner's care and thus denied them the right to be free boarders.

Freedmen's Bureau. See genealogy, African American.

Freedom of Information Act. James Madison once observed that "a popular government, without popular information, or the means of acquiring it, is but a Prologue to a Farce or a Tragedy—or perhaps both." For most of our history, however, Americans had no way of obtaining essential information about the workings of government agencies or the kinds of information those agencies had in their files. All of that finally changed—for the better, Madison would surely have agreed—with congressional enactment of the Freedom of Information Act (FOIA) in 1966 and the Privacy Act in 1974. The FOIA had major amendments in 1974, 1996, and 2007, and the principles it embodies—government openness and accountability—remain firmly in place despite different interpretations of them. (The Privacy Act continues to govern access to federal records or information about individuals but is not the subject of this essay.)

The FOIA declares that records maintained by federal government agencies are available to the public, with limited exceptions. Before 1966 the burden was on the individual to establish a right to examine such records (a right, incidentally, having no statutory basis and no remedy at law if denied). As the House Committee on Government Operations noted: "With the passage of the FOIA, the burden of proof shifted from the individual to the government. Those seeking information are no longer required to show a need for information. Instead, the 'need to know' standard has been replaced by a 'right to know' doctrine." In 1978 the Supreme Court declared: "The basic purpose of FOIA is to ensure an informed citizenry, vital to the functioning of a democratic society, needed to check against corruption and to hold the governors accountable to the governed" (*NLRB v. Robbins Tire & Rubber Co.*, 437 U.S. 214, 242 [1978]).

The FOIA provides that "any person"—not only citizens but also permanent resident aliens and foreign nationals (with limited exceptions)—may obtain access to the records of federal agencies except where there is a compelling need to maintain confidentiality. The act covers cabinet-level departments (such as the Defense Department), executive branch agencies (such as the Federal Bureau of Investigation), independent regulatory commissions (such as the Environmental Protection Agency), and federally controlled corporations (such as the Tennessee Valley Authority). The FOIA does not apply to Congress, the federal judiciary, or the president and his advisory staff. Although the act is applicable only to federal agencies, all the states and some local governments have passed similar freedom of information statutes establishing a right of access to their records.

In Canada the Access to Information Act (ATIA) establishes a right of access to federal government records (with exemptions considerably more numerous than those in the U.S. FOIA).

Under the terms of the FOIA, most federal records are available to the public, but certain categories of information are exempt from disclosure. The most frequently invoked exemption is classified documents, such as those relating to military plans and diplomatic communications, which, if released, "reasonably could be expected to cause damage to the national security." Other exemptions are provided for internal government memoranda during the decision-making process; personnel files or medical records whose disclosure would result in an unwarranted invasion of personal privacy; documents whose release would interfere with law enforcement investigations; and records whose disclosure is barred by a specific federal statute.

The FOIA exemptions are discretionary and successive administrations have interpreted them narrowly or broadly. In 1986 the Reagan administration toughened the standards for the release of government records, particularly those having to do with criminal investigations. In 1993 President Bill Clinton urged all federal agencies to observe the "spirit" as well as the "letter" of the FOIA. The Clinton administration sought to achieve "maximum responsible disclosure of government information," and it established a new "foreseeable harm" standard for responding to FOIA requests; a record should be disclosed if doing so posed no significant risk. After the terrorist attacks of 2001, the administration of President George W. Bush issued directives tending to limit disclosure of records under the FOIA. The Attorney General would now defend an agency if denial of a FOIA request had a "sound legal basis," a far less stringent standard than "foreseeable harm." Agencies were directed to withhold "sensitive but unclassified information" despite the lack of a clear definition of such information. However, President Bush signed the OPEN Government Act of 2007, which amends the FOIA to require better agency compliance with the law and to establish a new Office of Government Information Services in the National Archives and Records Administration. That office assists persons in making FOIA requests and offers mediation services to resolve disputes between requesters and agencies holding the requested records. In 2009 the administration of President Obama issued directives emphasizing the FOIA's presumption that records should be available, and encouraging agencies to "take affirmative steps to make information public," even without specific FOIA requests.

The Electronic Freedom of Information Act amendments of 1996 (E-FOIA), strongly promote electronic access to federal government records. The original FOIA required agencies to make basic documents available proactively: final decisions and opinions in administrative proceedings; policy statements and interpretations; and administrative staff manuals. The E-FOIA amendments in addition require agencies to make previously requested records available without a FOIA request if the agency determines that the records "have become or are likely to become the subject of subsequent requests for substantially the same records." Agencies must make such records, and an index to them, available in agency reading rooms and online. E-FOIA also required agencies to prepare indexes to and descriptions of all major information systems and to make them available in a reading room and online by March 31, 1997. Some federal agencies have not yet achieved that ambitious goal.

FOIA and the E-FOIA amendments are of most use to community historians who need access to relatively recent federal government records. Pursuant to records retention and disposition schedules, older agency records are destroyed or transferred to the National Archives (usually after a minimum of thirty years in agency custody). Two basic guides to using the FOIA to obtain access to or copies of records are available in print and online: *Your Right to Federal Records: Questions and Answers on the Freedom of Information Act and Privacy Act* (2006) and *A Citizen's Guide on Using the Freedom of Information Act and the Privacy Act of 1974 to Request Government Records* (2012). A greater challenge in preparing a FOIA request is identifying the specific records of interest and the agency that holds them. A historian may begin the search by consulting the *United States Government Manual* (2011). (These publications are available online.) Federal agencies generally have FOIA websites, accessible through an Internet search engine, that provide instructions for making FOIA requests. Many recent and cur-

rent documents, and some older ones, have been posted in agency "electronic reading rooms" as required by the E-FOIA. For example, the Federal Bureau of Investigation has posted thousands of documents (many heavily redacted), some dating back to the 1930s, in its "electronic reading room," http://vault.fbi.gov.

In signing the E-FOIA amendments in 1996, President Clinton asserted: "The Freedom of Information Act has played a unique role in strengthening our democratic form of government. The statute was enacted based upon the fundamental principle that an informed citizenry is essential to the democratic process and that the more the American people know about their government the better they will be governed." James Madison would have agreed, for as the "Father of the Constitution" once said: "Knowledge will forever govern ignorance, and a people who mean to be their own Governors must arm themselves with the power which knowledge gives."

RICHARD POLENBERG
REVISED AND UPDATED
BY JAMES D. FOLTS
NEW YORK STATE ARCHIVES

freehold. A freehold refers to land, buildings, or other immovable property that are held in fee simple. The property may be held through a lease rather than owned outright, but the lease must be for ninety-nine years and be renewable in perpetuity. The term also refers to oil and gas leases.

French in North America, sources for. See Appendix A.

Friends, Society of, sources for. See Society of Friends, Appendix B.

frontier thesis. In 1893 at the World's Columbian Exposition in Chicago, historian Frederick Jackson Turner presented his famous essay, "The Significance of the Frontier in American History." His ground-breaking theory was a watershed moment in the conceptualization of American history. Replacing the popular "germ theory," which viewed the American colonies as a composite of transplanted English institutions and modes of living, Turner argued instead that Europeans discarded their traditional lifestyles in the untamed frontier. For Turner, the frontier was the elastic term referring to the unsettled land lying on the edge of inhabited towns and villages that, as the number of colonists increased, continually moved farther and farther west. This process of westward migration left its mark on American development and led to the appearance of a uniquely American democracy and character. According to Turner, the harsh living conditions of the frontier created unique opportunities for Europeans, culminating in self-sufficiency, individualism, inventiveness, and independence among pioneers.

Over the course of nearly 120 years, Turner's frontier thesis has endured both praise and censure from several generations of historians. In the early 1990s, new Western historians presented a revision of the frontier thesis, interpreting the West as a specific place, rather than a process, and highlighting the abuses and exploitation that occurred throughout American history. According to these and many contemporary Western historians, the Turner thesis has lost its relevance. Although Turner's thesis has fallen out of favor with more recent historians, his theory continues to stimulate debate and exploration. Turner remains one of the most influential and gifted American historians. For the text of the frontier thesis, see Frederick Jackson Turner, *Rereading Frederick Jackson Turner: "The Significance of the Frontier" and Other Essays* with commentary by John Mack Faragher (1994). For the lasting influence of the frontier thesis, see Wilbur Jacob's *On Turner's Trail: 100 Years of Writing Western History* (1994) and Alan Bogue's *Frederick Jackson Turner: Strange Roads Going Down* (1998).

NATALIE PANTHER
GILCREASE MUSEUM

See western history and local historians.

fundraising. See crowdsourcing and crowdfunding; culinary history.

G

gardens. The earliest gardens, or, more broadly, human-manipulated landscapes, date back to our most ancient ancestors. The first time a human being collected a few seeds and sowed them, selected a plant to nurture, or fenced off a small plot to keep out browsing animals was the onset of gardening. There is much ancient evidence of gardens of various types, and references appear in such divergent sources as the Gilgamesh Epic, Egyptian tomb paintings, Chinese poetry, and Roman villa descriptions.

The approaches to gardening have been as diverse as the cultures that pursued them, from country to country, region to region, even between closely connected groups. But some cultures have exerted greater, more far-reaching, and more durable influence, which in itself is fascinating to track. There are not, however, firm demarcations between the decline of one style and the start of the next, and there is much chronological, cultural, and geographical overlap. Some of today's landscapes even simultaneously reflect all styles that have come before.

Generally books on the history of gardens focus primarily on the evolution of landscapes in the Middle East and Europe, though many do include gardens in such countries as China and Japan. The evolution and contributions of gardening in other parts of the world, such as Central and South Africa, and Central and South America, usually get short shrift, as do the Native cultures of North America. The gulf between history and prehistory is as apparent in the study of gardens as it is in other concentrations in the field, with the greatest attention being paid to *landscapes that have been documented in word and image.

The history of gardens is also subject to another divide—between places for beauty and pleasure, and plots for subsistence and agricultural profit. This is sometimes viewed as a division between classes. Very often the gardens of the wealthy, which were predominantly for pleasure, have come to exemplify historical design trends, and present the archetypes still referred to today. Yet the gardens of the less-than-wealthy are no less rich in information as relates to both beautiful and functional landscapes. In certain periods there was not so sharp a line between ornamentals and edibles, the two being grown in concert, a trend that has reemerged in modern times.

There are also distinctions made between gardens, farms, and landscapes. Farms are predominantly agricultural, though "a farm" as demarcated by private property lines might include an ornamental section. A garden, per se, is most often either purely ornamental or a plot of edibles smaller than a farm. Landscape is a more general, flexible term, referring to a designed space (often by a professional), a location that encompasses various types of spaces, a park setting, the natural topography of a place, or some combination.

A third division, somewhat oversimplified, exists between two broad geographic categories: Western gardens (evolving primarily in Spain, Italy, France, and England) and Eastern gardens (China and Japan being the two most referenced countries), developing simultaneously and separately for centuries, and along rather different lines, though with commonalities. Gardens in both West and East have impacted garden design in the Western world. Twentieth-century garden design has also found inspiration in the work of practitioners in additional countries, such as Brazil, Mexico, the United States, and Thailand.

Influential styles are most often identified by a geographical/cultural source (such as Italian or French), by a time period (such as Medieval or Renaissance), or by a descriptive name (such as gardenesque). The various styles exhibit identifiable characteristics, some of which can be tracked as the styles have been adopted by other cultures over time and customized to suit taste and local conditions.

The Western world often hails Persian "Paradise" gardens, or Islamic gardens, as the primary starting point for designed garden spaces. These landscapes were initiated in the Middle East and North Africa, and peaked in Spain under Moorish rule. Exemplified by wall-enclosed spaces, features with moving water, a symmetrical layout, fragrant plants, fruit, and flowers, Persian-style gardens have continued to influence landscape design over the

centuries. Two outstanding exemplars are the gardens of the Alhambra and the Generalife. Other significant garden styles emerged in Italy, France, and England, with noteworthy horticultural contributions by the Dutch.

Natural topography and climate have played key roles in the development of types of gardens—Persian gardens countered an arid climate and relatively featureless terrain; Italy's hilly Mediterranean settings fostered terraces, containers, and dry-climate plants; England's gently rolling terrain and mild climate engendered lawns, wooded groves, and exuberant flower borders; and the level plains and cool, moist climate of Northern France effected the expansive water features, tight geometry, and elaborate plantings of such landscapes as the Gardens of Versailles.

Eastern gardens were stimulated by both natural landscapes and philosophies, including Taoist and Buddhist ideas. For example, Chinese gardens reverence natural surroundings and reveal the harmony of creation, not only connecting designed spaces to the wider landscape, but also representing nature in symbolic form within the garden. Japanese gardens are usually highly stylized, and range in size and setting from expansive stroll gardens of the emperor, to temple meditation gardens, to miniaturized courtyard landscapes.

Similarities between gardens and various art forms can provide a window to cultural identity, as well as offer reference for the many gardens that are no longer extant. For example, Persian carpets, Chinese scroll paintings, English landscape painting, and even poetry, all offer clues to garden layouts, specific plants, and design philosophies.

If one tackles the history of gardens in the United States, it is a somewhat different track than a history of gardens in, say, England, though the latter country has traditionally been the source of much information for American gardeners. Early colonists were focused on survival and establishing functional landscapes rather than aesthetics, so agricultural pursuits were of primary importance, including the production of cash crops like tobacco. So landscapes would have contained crops, orchards, and edible gardens, some of the latter perhaps qualifying as "kitchen gardens" that incorporated herbs and perhaps a few flowers. In the late seventeenth and early eighteenth centuries, accounts of gardens that were more than utilitarian began to appear.

The time lag necessary for information and trends to reach the colonies from Europe created an asynchronous situation, so a fashion in European gardens might not reach America until decades after it blossomed across the Atlantic. Colonists were meanwhile adapting to their North American natural surroundings, as well as pursuing their own ideas. Thus by the time there were enough sufficiently wealthy landowners to create gardens for pleasure, and news of European garden style had made its way to the colonies, the era of formal French gardens had passed and the fashion for English gardens, which began in the mid-eighteenth century, had taken hold. Because much of the land in the Atlantic region is rolling and not steeply inclined, that region was the site of early examples of English

landscape design in America, including the estates of George Washington and Thomas Jefferson.

In the mid-nineteenth century, with increased international travel, trade, and communications, and an eager search under way for new plants, both native and cultivated, edible and aesthetic, a paradigm shift occurred. The post-English-style passion was for gardens with much greater plant diversity, presented in a mix of styles, often with a more intensely planted area around the house and the semblance of a "wild" area farther out. Some of the results were decried as vulgar and overdone, but others managed to combine the elements harmoniously and impose a sense of order on the variety.

After the fashion for exuberance and eclecticism and keen focus on growing plants as an end in itself (often viewed as a facet of Victorianism, though it is not limited to that era), the next big shift was toward designing gardens as spaces for outdoor living, where house and landscape are linked together. This was not an entirely new idea since landscape styles of the past, such as Italian gardens, had allied the two, but twentieth-century gardens made the connection using a wide range of styles. Mid-twentieth-century gardens are also particularly noted for their aesthetic of simplicity, minimal materials, and modern forms.

There are myriad other aspects of garden history in the United States, including the Rural Cemetery Movement of the early nineteenth century, the evolution of designed public spaces (the work of Frederick Law Olmsted provides early examples, but the emphasis on creating such places, particularly in urban settings, continued post-Olmsted even to today), the enthusiastic promotion of gardens and gardening by garden clubs across the country, the City Beautiful movement of the late nineteenth and early twentieth centuries, the establishment and proliferation of botanical gardens and arboreta, the Victory Gardens of World War II, the advent of xeriscape and water-wise gardening in the latter twentieth century, and the Farm-to-Table Movement. A list of noteworthy contributors to the history of gardens would be ridiculously long, ranging from Gertrude Jekyll, Capability Brown, Andrew Jackson Downing, and Beatrix Farrand, to Roberto Burle Marx, Thomas Church, Isamu Noguchi, Charles Jenks, and Dan Kiley. This short list focuses on designers, but every garden-related organization—plant societies, botanical gardens, and so on—has its own account of momentous events and tally of luminary figures that have contributed to garden history.

In the latter half of the twentieth century and continuing in the twenty-first, all garden styles that have come before have played a role. And professional designers, now considered artists in their own right, have created and continue to create noteworthy landscapes in the United States and abroad. Cultivators and developers of plants have exponentially increased the material available. Thus avid amateur gardeners have had at their disposal a wealth of design ideas, plants, and research resources, which they incorporate in uncountable local gardens.

JENNY ANDREWS
MIDDLE TENNESSEE STATE UNIVERSITY

See gardens, interpreting at local historic sites; gardens and landscapes, researching historic; horticulture.

gardens, interpreting at local historic sites. Built structures typically dominate historic sites, receiving the lion's share of both interpretation and budget allocations. Yet gardens have the potential to communicate equally important and compelling insights into the past. Historic landscapes, whether functional or decorative, agricultural or horticultural, can reflect such aspects of local and regional character as commerce, transportation, fashion, manners, class structure, education, ethnicities, lifeways, diet, and even *health care. Some interesting questions to ask are what plants were being grown, what were people eating, what techniques and tools were in use, where were plants and design ideas coming from, and how were people arranging and utilizing their outdoor spaces.

The landscape is a key part of stage-setting for the visitor experience. It is frequently the first thing people encounter upon arrival at a historic site, and the last thing they see when they leave. From a logistical perspective, the landscape can direct pedestrian traffic flow and give visitors something to observe between stations, and garden spaces can themselves be primary destination points. More than that, the landscape can be the connective tissue of a site, acting as the bridge between separate elements, making the property one cohesive entity.

While historic landscapes do cost money to research, construct, and maintain, they can also bring financial boons. Because a garden is ever-changing, from season to season, from year to year, it encourages repeat visitation, something all public venues are keen to garner. For many visitors one viewing of a house museum is enough, but the landscape can be different from one month to the next. Such seasonality can present opportunities for marketing initiatives, educational activities, and events.

Of fundamental importance, landscapes at historic sites have the capacity for reinforcing and augmenting the historical narrative. People in the past were not sealed in their houses; they interacted with their landscapes in many ways, for both pleasure and survival. They labored on it, socialized in it, grew vegetables and fruit, planted flowers to reflect their personalities, designed gardens to exhibit taste, cut blossoms to bring indoors, and shared favorite plants with neighbors.

How authentic should, indeed can, a garden or landscape be? If much of the original landscape remains, and if there is ample primary source material for research and verification, that is a best-case scenario, but that is rarely the case. Not every location has had a record-keeper like Thomas Jefferson. And even a relatively intact garden will likely need adjustments—plants die, walls fall down, visitor amenities need to be added. Research into the specific property is paramount, and studying appropriate period gardens, locally, regionally, and nationally, is also effective. Fortunately there are a host of experts with applicable specialties (even in single types of plants, like daffodils) who can be prevailed upon for assis-

tance. But there will necessarily be gaps in knowledge. And there is always the chance of new information coming to light—a ledger, a letter, a sketch—that might prompt alterations later.

There are three main categories of historic landscapes: restoration, re-creation, and adaptation. These are on a continuum, the first usually considered the most authentic since it takes its cues from extant garden elements and solid primary source material, though the other two can be effective and informative as well. A re-creation is often site-specific and based on research data, even though nothing, or very little, might be extant. An example of an adaptation would be a garden that is, in general, appropriate for the period and region (in other words, a "reasonable facsimile") and suits the parameters of the site, but is not necessarily based on information about the particular location.

Given the changeability of gardens and the usual dearth of information about them, it can be difficult to accurately fix and re-create a landscape at a defined moment in time. This should not discourage diligent research and striving for accuracy. It might ultimately be decided to embrace the changes that occurred over time or under a sequence of owners, rather than limiting the garden to one owner or period; this can even offer additional educational entry points. Whatever the landscape plan, the interpretation should endeavor to be honest, pointing out the historical accuracies while also admitting where the garden diverges from authenticity.

The "pretty factor" is not without merit and can be a valuable part of making a site attractive, including for rental activities. But a few hastily planted flats of flowers from the local nursery might not make an appropriate, illustrative setting for a historic property. Such palliatives can in fact look wholly out of place, dispelling the sense of stepping back in time and, more critically, offering nothing in the way of interpretation. Staff, board members, and *volunteers should invest the same dedication to the outdoors as they do the indoors, granting the landscape and its interpretation an equal amount of homework and preparation as the historic buildings. They should also set landscape goals, budgets, and schedules. A garden can have its own interpretive plan while also fitting into the interpretive mission for the entire site.

Just as with historic buildings, there are a number of information vectors possible, including brochures, signs, the website, guided tours, and docents. A more recent arrival is the use of *apps. Different demographics, even different individuals, will be more engaged by some approaches than others, so interpretation can require a mix of methods. Since there is typically more space outdoors than indoors, there is the option of using larger signs, with multiple layers of information. Attention should be given to height and number of signs, however, to avoid blocking views and "junking up" the landscape. The choice of interpretation methods depends on a number of factors, though often the budget is a priority.

While it is important to communicate the basic facts of a property (that is what visitors are expecting), there are a host of topics and angles related to gardens that can be both apropos and creative, and provide a "hook." Topics particularly relevant to modern audiences include edibles, organic gardening, heirloom plants, herbal medicine, and water usage. It is also critical to relate to a broad demographic mix, and not overlook the presence of many types of people in the historic landscape, such as African Americans, women, immigrants, and Native Americans.

JENNY ANDREWS
MIDDLE TENNESSEE STATE UNIVERSITY

See gardens; gardens and landscapes, researching historic; horticulture.

gardens and landscapes, researching historic. While even the sturdiest buildings can seem tenuous in the face of development pressures and neglect, landscapes are yet more ephemeral because they involve living things, and are vulnerable to such outdoor factors as weather and predation. Even a current garden when denied care can quickly be overtaken by weeds or natural succession, or devastated by insects or browsing deer.

The first step in researching a landscape is to physically investigate the site and ascertain what is present. Some elements might be relatively intact. Others will be visible only as vestiges—a row of trees indicating a fence line, an overgrown pile of rocks that was once a stone wall, bricks that outlined a flower bed now covered over with soil. It is important to create an accurate site survey, take reference photos, and even press samples of plants on the property.

Some existing plants might in fact be original to the site, such as long-lived trees and shrubs. Perhaps less well known is the longevity of certain herbaceous plants, particularly those with such underground structures as bulbs, corms, and tubers. Peonies, irises, daffodils, grape hyacinths, and daylilies are all capable of persisting in a landscape with little or no care. Plant experts can even determine the identities of specific varieties, which were developed and entered into trade in a definable year or period. This can assist in determining how long a plant might have been at a site and where it might have come from, such as a particular nursery in business at the time. Take stock of the landscape at different seasons, since some plants, like daffodils, will be apparent only at certain times of the year.

*Archaeology is also a critical research method for discovering the history of a landscape, though it can be expensive. The layout of gardens can be revealed, such as walkways, walls, fence posts, and structures. Remarkably, information on plants can be determined by archaeological methods since some plant material, such as pollen, seeds, and phytoliths, is actually persistent and can be used for determination of species. Sometimes larger samples are preserved well enough for identification; at Colonial Williamsburg, leaves of variegated boxwood were discovered at the bottom of a well.

Many of the same *primary sources used for researching other aspects of history can be used for landscapes as well, though mentions of landscape elements can be scarce. Letters, diaries, and journals might reference camellias or lilacs in bloom, picking a bouquet of zinnias to take to a sick friend, crop maintenance issues, or a dessert of fresh peaches or strawberries. Old recipes and local recipe books can also be good references. Travelogues can present detailed accounts of select sites or even whole regions.

Plant lists, ledgers, and receipts are guides to specific plants being purchased, grown, and sold. Contemporary newspaper ads and nursery catalogs also point to plants and varieties available at a certain time. Probate documents might mention gardens, as well as farming and gardening tools. Deeds can refer to gardens, agricultural fields, fences, walls, and significant trees. In many towns and cities there were local garden, horticultural, and agricultural organizations; the minutes of their meetings and newsletters are other possible sources for information regarding plants, methods, problems, trends, and even what certain members were growing.

Visual resources include *maps and landscape plans, the latter being as invaluable as architectural ones, whether crudely or professionally drawn. Sketches, prints, paintings, and photographs of a site can also be revealing, even if the primary subject is a house or person. In a portrait painting, peeking over the shoulder might be a home and its garden; even if romanticized, this mini-landscape can offer evidence. Occasionally items related to gardens can be found in scrapbooks, a popular pastime in the late 1800s. Or a nineteenth-century lady or budding botanist might have pressed samples from the garden, labeled and preserved them. Poet Emily Dickinson created such a herbarium of leaves and flowers, pressing them in books such as her Bible, and collecting them in an album.

Though today there is a wealth of information accessible in books, magazines, newspapers, and on the Internet, in times past there were far fewer sources. A personal garden library might consist of only a handful of volumes, which had relatively wide availability. In the nineteenth century such a collection might include books by J. C. Loudon, Bernard McMahon, and Andrew Jackson Downing. Even far from his home turf of New York's Hudson Valley, Downing's *A Treatise on the Theory and Practice of Landscape Gardening* (1841) was popular inspiration for garden design. As time went on, there were a greater number of resources published, yet each period has classic volumes that can prove enlightening for understanding and deducing period landscapes.

JENNY ANDREWS
MIDDLE TENNESSEE STATE UNIVERSITY

See gardens; horticulture; landscapes.

gazetteer. A gazetteer is a list of place-names, usually organized alphabetically, with locations provided for each place or geographic feature. Often the place will be located within a hierarchy (district, state, county, township, for example) and may be further located using some grid system, either latitude and longitude, or one related to a particular map set. A gazetteer is designed to be used with a map. Reference to the map provides a visual placement of the town in relationship to a number of surrounding towns. Many gazetteers also provide social and physical information. It is not unusual to find descriptions of surrounding terrain, elevation, how well the town is served by roads or rail, area of the town, and population statistics, such as total population, literacy rate, etc. A gazetteer directed at the business community may identify the town's principal industries.

Finding the appropriate gazetteer may take a little research. There is no comprehensive list of gazetteers, although *Index of Atlases and Gazetteers in the Harold B. Lee Library*, 2015, is a good compilation for local historians and available online: http://net.lib.byu.edu/~scishare/Index%20of%20Atlases%20and%20Gazetteers.htm.

Another strategy is to use the online catalog of an accessible large research library using the keyword "gazetteer." For more general coverage, WorldCat, available at most public and academic libraries, combines the records of many thousands of libraries all over the world into one searchable catalog online. Gazetteers found there can be ordered through interlibrary services.

Gazetteers of some sort have been produced since antiquity. Gazetteers for U.S. states began to be published early in the nineteenth century; these early works are extremely valuable in locating places and in constructing the historical geography of a place. A good example is J. H. French's *Gazetteer of the State of New York* (1860). This is available online from the Internet Archive: https://archive.org/details/gazetteerofstate04fren, and many other sites.

There are quite a number of online gazetteers that cover different time periods and geographical areas and provide different kinds of functionality, beyond the format of a traditional printed gazetteer. Those primarily concerned with locating places, without any social information, are called "name servers." The most important of these is the Geographic Names Information System (GNIS) geonames.usgs.gov. Online mapping services such as Google Maps (http://maps.google.com) and community identifiers such as e-Podunk (http://www.epodunk.com) provide much of the functionality of gazetteers with newer, friendlier interfaces.

genealogical resources online. The development of the World Wide Web has revolutionized genealogical research and made millions of records easily accessible to even casual researchers. Development is continuous and new websites with new content and access appear almost daily. At the same time established sites continue to expand their offerings. The core of most sites is a database or databases of resources. Databases provide structured information through carefully designed records. This allows indexing and very fast and multifaceted search capabilities. Although these sites are designed for genealogical research, many offer resources that are applicable to other areas of local historical research. See also *local history resources online for other sites. Some sites are free; others require a subscription.

Among the free sites, the largest and most comprehensive is *FamilySearch (www.familysearch.org), which is provided by the Church of Jesus Christ of Latter-day Saints (Mormons). The hidden strength of FamilySearch is the host of volunteers who over the years have transcribed and indexed millions of records. These records and many

others have been made available online through a sophisticated search engine. *FamilySearch also provides access to the Catalog of the Family History Library at Salt Lake City and features many training guides and programs for genealogists.

*Ancestry.com (www.ancestry.com) is the premier commercial site for genealogical records, providing access to thousands of databases through a single search interface. Ancestry.com is particularly strong in *census records, immigration records and *military records. It also has a good collection of *maps and atlases and some important reference works. The Ancestry "family" includes Fold3.com (military records), Archives.com (archival materials), and Newspapers.com (historical newspapers—all require separate subscription). Ancestry.com is complemented by another commercial site, *HeritageQuest Online, which features U.S. Census records and page-image access to thousands of family histories, local histories, and other books, as well as an index to genealogical periodicals (PERSI). Ancestry is available by subscription and at many libraries; HeritageQuest is specifically designed for libraries and can often be accessed remotely by library card holders. FamilySearch is free.

Ancestry.com and FamilySearch both offer ways to share one's personal genealogies. A site that attempts to provide shared linkages is Geni (www.geni.com). Using the basic free service at Geni.com, users create their own trees and invite their relatives to join their family tree, which Geni then compares to other trees. Matching trees are then merged into the single world family tree, which currently contains nearly 50 million living users and their ancestors.

Other general sites are Genealogy. com and Mocavo (www.findmypast. com/mocavo-info), recently purchased by Findmypast, a UK company specializing in UK and Irish records and now joined with Mocavo in a single search interface: www.findmypast.com. Although Mocavo was touted as a free genealogy site, it never really was and all these sites are now subscription-only.

An invaluable reference site is Cyndi's List (www.cyndislist.com), a comprehensive, categorized, and cross-referenced list of tens of thousands of links to other genealogical websites. The site is free. It's particularly helpful with finding links to ethnic or international genealogical sites (e.g., Slovenian genealogy) or sites that have specialized content (DNA genealogy).

A number of sites are volunteer-driven and each has its own particular focus. RootsWeb (www.rootsweb. ancestry.com) is a volunteer site that depends on individual submissions of data, such as cemetery transcriptions and local tax lists. These are then made accessible to researchers through several different kinds of search engines. RootsWeb is best known for its extensive tools for surname research, in particular around 30,000 surname mailing lists and 130,000 message boards, which allow researchers working on particular families or topics to communicate with each other. It also has its own system for connecting submitted genealogies called WorldConnect. RootsWeb was acquired by Ancestry.com but remains a free site with an emphasis on sharing resources and connecting researchers.

Another volunteer site is the *US GenWeb Project (www.usgenweb.org). This again is an all-volunteer site, but organized by geographical hierarchy (state-county). The county sites host databases of local information and maintain message boards on which researchers can contact each other. A related project is US GenWeb Archives, which provides access to a variety of user-submitted documents and records.

There are a number of very useful government sites. The most important is the *National Archives and Record Administration site, NARA (www.archives.gov/research). This provides access to a wide variety of government records, including military records.

Another government-provided database is the *Social Security Death Index (SSDI). This database is searchable from a number of genealogical websites, each providing its own search interface. SSDI contains partial Social Security records for most people who died after 1965. The record contains basic information. The full application form, which has valuable additional information (such as mother's maiden name) can be ordered for a fee.

There are many specialized databases that index records from a single source or on special topics. One of the best known is the very popular Ellis Island database (www.ellisisland.org) of immigration records of passengers passing through Ellis Island in New York Harbor. There are also extremely useful sites based on race or ethnicity. Two of the most active are Afrigeneas (http://afrigeneas.com) for African American genealogy and JewishGen, for Jewish genealogy. JewishGen provides access to 20 million records, has many search tools specialized for Jewish family research, and is absolutely free. The site is affiliated with the Museum of Jewish Heritage.

Cemetery indexes are also useful. The path-breaking Find-a-Grave (http://findagrave.com) maintains a database of 150 million graves, many with photographs and attached genealogies. It was recently purchased by Ancestry.com. The very similar BillionGraves (https://billiongraves.com) is more closely associated and integrated with FamilySearch. Both sites are free but heavily encrusted with ads and links to subscription sites.

Genealogical resources online provide revolutionary access to millions, perhaps billions, of records for individuals, and so are a direct help in family historians and local historians researching individuals, but many genealogical websites have resources that can be used for other aspects of local history. Even genealogical resources, such as census and immigration records, allow historians to analyze the relationships between people in a particular historical setting. Other resources on these websites, such as maps, gazetteers, and land records provide the basis for local historical geography. The many newspaper-related sites can be used to research the economic and social environment of the local area in a way never possible before. As shown by sites such as *The Valley of the Shadow, creative local historians can use these resources to provide new and exciting ways to present their local histories to an increasingly web-aware audience.

ROBERT KIBBEE
THE HISTORY CENTER IN TOMPKINS
COUNTY (NY)

See digital history; genealogy, African American; genealogy, Jewish; Immigration History Research Center; mortality schedules.

genealogy, African American. African American interest in genealogy has been frustrated by limited access to records and the immense obstacles presented by slavery and to a lesser degree by segregation and Jim Crow laws. With the appearance of Alex Haley's book, *Roots: The Saga of an American Family* (1976) and the subsequent TV mini-series, African Americans, indeed, all Americans, took an increased interest in genealogy and family history. Haley showed, although in a somewhat fictionalized account, that it was possible to use many different resources to uncover information about black families in slavery and even earlier, perhaps even finding connections to specific African places and peoples. More recently Harvard Professor Henry Louis Gates Jr. has reignited interest with a series of publications (*Colored People: A Memoir* [1994]; *In Search of our Roots* [2009]), television productions (*African American Lives* I and II, *Finding Your Roots*), websites (*The Root*: http://www.theroot.com) and resource collections (*The African American National Biography* [2008]). Gates has popularized the use of DNA analysis to connect families and to link to specific ethnic groups in Africa.

African American genealogy has been enabled as never before by the Internet and the World Wide Web. These technologies have allowed many governmental, religious, and private groups to publish resources not previously available or very difficult to access. Many of the newly available resources, such as *census records, are useful to all American genealogical researchers, but many, such as the records of the Freedmen's Bureau (freedmensbureau.com) are of specific interest to African Americans. The web also provides new avenues of communication through African American research groups and sites with extensive message boards such as Afrigeneas.com.

For beginner and even experienced researchers, a very useful book is Tony Burroughs, *Black Roots: A Beginner's Guide to Tracing the African American Family Tree* (2007). This book would also be useful as a general guide for local historians incorporating African American family histories into their work. There are many web-based resources for beginners. Burroughs has also written the section on African American genealogical resources for *The Source: A Guidebook to American Genealogy*, 3rd ed. (2007) which is offered free online to the public by *Ancestry.com: www.ancestry.com/wiki. Cyndi's List (www.cyndislist.com) provides a portal to other online resources and has a very well-organized collection of links for African American researchers. *Top 10 Sites for African American Genealogy* (about.com) provides a more selective list. There are several useful online tutorials: http://www.lowcountryafricana.com/beginning-genealogy. The Newberry Library provides an easily accessible online bibliography: Jack Simpson and Matt Rutherford, *Bibliography of African American Family History at the Newberry Library* (2005): www.newberry.org/sites/default/files/textpage-attachments/af-amer-bib.pdf. The um-

brella organization for African American Genealogists is the Afro-American Historical and Genealogical Society, Inc.: www.aahgs.org.

Experienced African American genealogists suggest that the best strategy for beginning genealogists and local historians using African American material is to gain a thorough understanding of *African American history in order to develop appropriate research strategies for their own families and place their family histories in a broader context. Recommended reading includes Herbert G. Gutman, *The Black Family in Slavery and Freedom, 1750–1925* (1976); John Hope Franklin and Alfred Moss, *From Slavery to Freedom: A History of African Americans* (2001); Joe William Trotter, *The African American Experience* (2001); Darlene Clark Hine et al., *The African American Odyssey* (2000), and many others. There are several published and online bibliographies of African American history. An online bibliographic essay by Wilma King strikes a good balance between inclusivity and selection while providing some context: *Bibliographic Essay on African American History* (n.d.): https://www.nps.gov/parkhistory/resedu/king.pdf.

For additional cultural context and some genealogical help, there are several institutes devoted to African American history and culture: The Schomburg Center for Research in Black Culture at the New York Public Library (www.nypl.org/locations/schomburg), the W. E. B. Du Bois Institute for African and African American Research at Harvard University, and the *Amistad Research Center at Tulane (www.amistadresearchcenter.org) are among the best known. There are several online sub-scription sources that are available at large academic libraries. ProQuest, for example, offers Black Studies Center with several useful indexes to periodicals and newspapers as well as the full text of dissertations. Oxford African American Studies Center offers the full text of many specialized African American encyclopedias and other reference sources.

Once a historical background has been gained there are several sites devoted to African American genealogy. The best known is Afrigeneas (www.afrigeneas.com). Christine's Genealogy Website (ccharity.com) is more informal, but useful for tips and tricks and opportunities to communicate with fellow researchers, although mailing lists such as AFRICANAMER-GEN-L from *RootsWeb.com is also active. The USF Africana Heritage Project is an all-volunteer research project and website sponsored by the Africana Studies department at the University of South Florida: www.africanaheritage.com. This is an excellent site for researching slave records, as is Low Country Africana: www.mylcafricana.com.

The standard genealogical databases such as Ancestry.com, *HeritageQuest, and *FamilySearch are also critical for African American genealogists. Among the most important general resources available is the U.S. Census. Several hundred thousand African Americans were or became free citizens before the Emancipation Proclamation, and so were recorded in the censuses from 1790 to 1860. The enslaved population was counted but not individually identified in censuses from 1790 to 1840 and

in Slave Schedules in 1850 and 1860. From 1870 on, all African Americans were recorded, but searching the schedules for African American ancestors may require some additional expertise. The census is available online through Ancestry.com (subscription required) and free through FamilySearch. HeritageQuest is available in most libraries. Burrough's *Black Roots* is a very good print guide to using the census; his chapter in *The Source* is online through Ancestry's wiki. Several sites, such as Low Country Africana, offer tutorials geared toward finding census records of African Americans.

The *National Archives and Records Administration (NARA) is often overlooked, perhaps because it is daunting to navigate the online site. NARA's catalogs are designed to lead researchers to archival record groups, not records of individuals, although it is possible to find these also. NARA has made special efforts to attract African American genealogists. An entire issue of the NARA newsletter, *Prologue*, has been devoted to African American research: www.archives.gov/publications/prologue/1997/summer/index.html, although it was produced before extensive online access to records was available. NARA is particularly good for military records, which can be critical for documenting an African American ancestor.

One very rich source of African American records available through NARA is the Freedmen's Bureau: www.archives.gov/research/african-americans/freedmens-bureau, the informal name for The Bureau of Refugees, Freedmen, and Abandoned Lands, which was established after the Civil War to supervise all activities relating to freedmen and refugees. See the magisterial overview of the bureau by W. E. B Dubois himself (from a series of articles in the *Atlantic*) for background: http://history.eserver.org/freedmens-bureau.txt. The records are for the most part only available on microfilm, although some sites have transcribed local records: freedmansbureau.com. Related are the Freedman's Bank records. These are available through HeritageQuest and other sites.

An enslaved ancestor—and very few blacks arrived as free people on American shores before 1865—can be very difficult to find and document. A good print guide is David H. Streets, *Slave Genealogy: A Research Guide with Case Studies* (1986), although this was written before the Internet was available. Several online sites already mentioned offer limited guidance. Census records can be used by interpolating from 1870 back to the 1860 and 1850 Slave Schedules, but at this point, since slaves are not identified by names, the schedules can only suggest matches. Assuming the slave ancestor took the name of his or her most recent owner is one approach, but estimates of how often that was the case vary from 70 percent to a more sober and realistic 15 percent. Plantation records offer another possibility. Kenneth Stampp, whose book *Peculiar Institution: Slavery in the Ante-Bellum South* (1964) exploded the myth of the benign plantation, assembled tens of thousands of documents from plantations. They are available on microfilm as *Records of Ante-Bellum Southern Plantations*, now with an index: Jean Cooper, *Index to Records of Ante-Bellum*

Southern Plantations: Locations, Plantations, Surnames and Collections (2009). This "Stampp Collection" is available in large academic libraries and the Family History Library. Local libraries may have selections.

Slaves themselves produced history and family history through narratives, often oral, but occasionally written. See, for example, *North American Slave Narratives*: http://docsouth.unc.edu/neh, a collection of the full texts of several thousand published narratives. The 2,300 transcribed oral narratives from the Federal Writers Project, *Born in Slavery: Slave Narratives from the Federal Writers' Project, 1936–1938* are now available online from the *Library of Congress: http://memory.loc.gov/ammem/snhtml/snhome.html.

African Americans, faced with the seemingly unbridgeable chasm of slavery between their documentable ancestors and families that seem to be related, have turned to DNA testing to establish links to those families—usually suggested through common surnames—that are otherwise untraceable. American genealogists in general frequently use DNA testing for this purpose and many family websites provide information on how to test and how to interpret results.

Another goal of DNA testing—one that is specific to African Americans—is to find a link to their African heritage and specific ethnic or tribal groups in Africa. This effort has been popularized by Henry Louis Gates Jr.: *In Search of Our Roots: How Nineteen Extraordinary African Americans Reclaimed Their Past* and *American Lives*. An article in Wikipedia has a good overview with links:

en.wikipedia.org/wiki/Genealogical_ DNA_test. African Ancestry (www.afri canancestry.com) is an example of one of several services offering DNA testing specifically for African Americans.

This is a golden age for African American genealogists. Print and online help can get one started easily and communication through mailing lists and social media bring together supportive communities of researchers. More and more resources are becoming available and are more accessible than ever. This trend will only increase. Finally, new technologies, such as DNA testing, are still in their infancy and may well revolutionize genealogical research as they mature.

ROBERT KIBBEE
THE HISTORY CENTER
IN TOMPKINS COUNTY (NY)

See African American history; Amistad Research Center; building bridges through local history; *Roots: The Saga of an American Family*; slave schedules; slavery interpretation at museums and historic sites.

genealogy, an archivist's view. They come in little packs, or in busloads. They're there in the mornings waiting semi-patiently for the doors to open. They're there to be gently shooed out when you close up at night. They make more visits, ask more questions, write more letters (and e-mails), they visit your website more often than any other part of your constituency. They are genealogists.

Genealogical researchers need records—records of their ancestors and kin—where they lived, who they were connected to, and what they did. Any organization that holds those records (or might hold those records) will be a magnet to people whose ancestors once lived in the area, however briefly.

The major difference between genealogists and local historians is that local historians are primarily concerned with groups—organizations, schools, churches, societies; while genealogists are concerned with individuals and families. And, while a historian can turn to another subject or locale if the records are too scant to support a research project, the genealogist works with whatever resources are available. If their ancestors were in county X, research in county Y won't do.

Genealogical research can be challenging and rewarding. Genealogy, when done well, is a research-intensive interest/pastime/obsession. Gathering any substantial amount of genealogical and biographical information about one's ancestors often involves a significant investment in time, money, and effort. This research can, and often does, extend over many years. For that research to be useful, the results must be carefully documented, and citations to sources used need to be included in any finished product. Because of the time and expense involved, genealogists tend to be (but are not always) at the older end of the population spectrum. Most are now computer literate. And beginners will always outnumber experienced researchers.

The first step in genealogical investigation should be to put down, in some organized fashion, what is known about one's ancestors and their families. The second step is to gather whatever information can be obtained from relatives. There is a good chance someone in the family has already done some of this work and this research should be appreciated.

Today, the third step (and often the first or second step) is to explore the wealth of information (and actual records) available in online resources, both commercial and non-commercial. Much information (and misinformation) is available to the researcher, but "serious" genealogical research still involves tracking down and using a wide range of actual records, many still in the offices (or homes) in which they were created; but many in archival repositories—libraries, archives, historical societies, genealogical societies, etc.

At some point, though, the actual "research" begins. Exactly what records may be of help will vary according to what particular information is missing, what time period, and exactly where one's ancestors lived. There are numerous genealogical guides (see the suggestions below) that give detailed descriptions of what records and other resources are available and where they can be consulted. Some key genealogical records may be held by the federal government, such as records of the U.S. *Censuses, passenger lists, and military and pension records for service in the country's various wars. The originals of these are generally found in research libraries, although many may also be available on microfilm, or online. Some resources will be found in county repositories, such as courthouse records: *vital records (civil records of birth, marriage, divorce, and death), probate records (i.e., records concerned with

the settling of an estate), land records, tax rolls, and *court records (including *naturalization or citizenship records). Others are more likely to be housed at the local level, such as newspapers, church and cemetery records, manuscript records of all types (letters, journals, organizational records, etc., including materials gathered by previous historians and genealogists). It is with these resources that a local historical organization can be most useful.

The best response of a historical agency is to have the record resources in its custody well cataloged, organized, and available. It is often helpful to work with other record-holding agencies, such as the local courthouse, libraries, and archival agencies. The more a historical society knows about area records, the more helpful it can be to genealogical researchers, for being able to refer researchers to other resources is a valuable service.

The *Family History Library of the Church of Jesus Christ of Latter-day Saints (Mormons) in Salt Lake City is a special resource. Because of the importance in Mormon theology of gathering family history, the Family History Library (FHL) has acquired, primarily by microfilming, genealogical source records from around the world. A network of local libraries, called Family History Library Centers, allows researchers who cannot get to Salt Lake City an opportunity to borrow records and use them locally. Some local libraries have also been designated borrowing libraries as well. Access to significant portions of the FHL collections is available through their website, www.fami lysearch.org.

The Family History Library is but one of many important repositories. Many public libraries have genealogy/local history collections and in some cities there are large and useful collections. Every state has at least one major resource institution, such as a state historical society, state archives, or state library with important materials.

There are, in addition, resources available on the Internet. Many organizations serving genealogists have a website and many more soon will. Some of these sites are little more than advertising, but more and more are making resources available in this novel way. See in particular www.familysearch.org, the site created by the Church of the Latter-day Saints. A great deal can be accomplished on the Internet, but certainly not everything.

The literature on genealogy is vast, but a first-rate introductory book is (despite its unfortunate title) *The Complete Idiot's Guide to Genealogy*, by Kay Ingalls and Christine Rose (3rd ed., 2012). An excellent guide to state and county records is Ancestry's *Red Book: American State, County & Town Sources*, ed. Alice Eichholz (3rd. ed., 2004). For more in-depth discussion of a wide range of genealogical resources, see *The Source: A Guidebook of American Genealogy*, ed. Loretto Dennis Szucs and Sandra Hargreaves Luebking (3rd ed., 2006); *Professional Genealogy: A Manual for Researchers, Writers, Editors, Lecturers, and Librarians* (2000). In addition to these, many societies offer classes in genealogical research, and some have regular programs about various aspects of the field. Some large societies hold substantial seminars or multiday conferences, where genealogists meet and learn. The largest gatherings are annual conferences sponsored by the National Genealogical Society (www.ngsgenealogy.org) and the Federation of Genealogical Societies (www.fgs.org).

Institutes, such as those held annually at the *National Archives (Genealogical Institute on Federal Records [formerly the National Institute on Genealogical Research], www.gen-fed.org) and the Institute of Genealogy and Historical Research (formerly at Samford University in Alabama), hosted 2017– by the Georgia Genealogical Society (www.gagensociety.org) offer concentrated education in specific aspects of genealogical research.

In addition to the many researchers primarily interested in their own ancestors, there are a few who go beyond that to research entire communities or particular groups. Some gather and publish genealogical resource materials; others teach people how to "do" genealogy. Still others provide support to genealogical societies, local libraries, and even local historical societies. They help process material, and they respond to inquiries. Genealogists, wherever they may live today, can be an important source of support to any local historical society. And, because of their numbers, they can be a political force as well, providing backing in the never-ending battles for funding and support.

JAMES L. HANSEN
WISCONSIN HISTORICAL
SOCIETY, RETIRED

See Ancestry.com; family history; FamilySearch; genealogical resources online; local history resources online.

genealogy, Jewish. There has been growing interest in Jewish genealogy over the past decades, but that interest has exponentially accelerated with the availability of computers, the Internet, and DNA analysis. This genealogical interest has three principal goals: tracing the individual's forebears; locating the individual's living relatives; and understanding the lives and development of the family.

There was little interest in genealogy among the early Jewish immigrants to the United States. The American ethos of a democratic country where a person succeeded on the basis of ability reduced the importance of family connections. Like other U.S. immigrants, most Jews came to the United States because of the promise of better economic conditions. Unlike their fellow immigrants, most Jews were not well-integrated into the societies of the countries they left, so no outpouring of nostalgia drove an interest in genealogy. If there was nostalgia, it was for a community that no longer existed because war, oppression, or mass migration had devastated it. For whatever reason, it was common for the immigrant generation to tell their children little or nothing about the old country, including genealogical information related to it.

The return to genealogy is really a return to roots in more than one sense. Jewish genealogy reaches back to the Bible. Genesis carefully traces the family relationships between its characters. This tradition has been carried on in rabbinic circles as some families have produced large numbers of rabbis over the centuries. Any rabbi who writes a book will normally include as a preface his genealogy, which may be complete, or males-only, or rabbis-only, and often attempts to connect the author to one of the great leaders of the past, such as Rashi or the Baal Shem Tov.

Most American, English, French, South African, Australian, and Canadian Jews are descended from the great wave of immigrants leaving between 1880 and 1920 from the Russian and Austro-Hungarian Empires. A smaller, but significant, number came from Germany and neighboring lands after the failed revolutions of 1848. A much smaller group are Sephardic Jews, descended from those who left the Iberian peninsula during the fifteenth century who settled in London, Amsterdam, Rouen, around the Mediterranean, and as far east as Iraq and India, and some who remained in Iberia or went to its colonies in the New World as Roman Catholics. Some are refugees from the devastated Europe of World War II. In the 1990s, Jews began arriving from the former Soviet Union, often seeking the descendants of relatives who left the Russian Empire a century ago.

The first task of the person seeking his genealogy is to gather an *oral history of his family. Just as "one peek is worth a thousand finesses" in bridge, genealogy is much simplified by being told what to look for and where to look. Most helpful is knowing the town of origin in Europe, which is sometimes more easily discovered in conversation than by examining the records.

Family oral history should be done first because it is a transitory asset. Barring fire or other disaster, the records will be equally available in the future. But the persons who carry the oral history age every day. Death will silence them completely; mental deterioration may scramble their memories irretrievably; and macular degeneration or glaucoma may render them unable to identify the persons in their family photo albums.

Oral history also puts flesh on the skeletal records. Genealogy is more than who begat whom. It is the way families lived and interacted. Stories about holiday celebrations, business partnerships, shared vacations, cousins' clubs, and the like are unlikely to appear in official records or in yellowed newspaper columns, but they are available from older relatives. Though oral history seems a slender reed upon which to build anything, as memories play tricks after only a few years, the experience of most genealogists is that family stories are remarkably accurate and, even when they are deficient in some details, useful if carefully investigated.

Social history is sometimes useful in genealogical pursuits. For instance, Jewish naming traditions can be helpful.

Most eastern European Jews followed a uniform naming system. No child was named for a living person. Children were named to honor a deceased relative. The first boy was named for the father's father; the second boy for the mother's father; the first girl for the mother's mother; the second girl for the father's mother. The fact that my oldest uncle was named for my grandmother's father tells me that my grandfather's dad was still alive when Uncle Sol was born. The fact that the second son was also not named for him tells me that he was still alive. The third son was named

for him, which tells me that he died 1909–1912, between the births of sons #2 and #3.

A person's Jewish given name (Mikhael), denotes that the person is the son or daughter of their father (ben Yaakov). So if the genealogist finds a person's tombstone, that stone also states the name of the person's father (and occasionally, the name of the father's father).

Cemeteries are useful places for Jewish genealogy. Cremation among Jews was nonexistent until recent times, and Jewish law required quick burial, within no more than twenty-four hours of death. So the initial grave location was almost always near where the person died. The stone, in addition to the name information referred to above, always contained the exact date of death, and often the age of the decedent. As cemeteries, or areas within cemeteries, were often associated with particular synagogues and families often belonged to the same synagogue, neighboring stones will often provide information about potential relatives. If the decedent had been a kohain or a levite, that will be noted on the stone, either in writing or with hands showing the priestly blessing for a kohain, or by a pitcher of water depicting a levite.

A cemetery can sometimes provide a clue about the European origin of the deceased. Many cemeteries sold blocks of graves to *landsmanschaften*, organizations of persons who came from the same town and who banded together for various communal purposes, such as life or burial insurance. Being buried in such a plot was no guarantee of origin in that community, but it can be a valuable lead.

A generation's work in social history has also helped the Jewish genealogist flesh out a family. We now have studies of birth-control methods used by immigrant women at the turn of the twentieth century; patterns of work among men, women, and children; and recreational habits. While we cannot be sure that our ancestors fit the common mold, we can relate the results of those studies and speculate about whether our ancestors were more likely to have conformed.

Simultaneously with collecting oral history and reading social history, one needs to collect records. Oral history needs to be documented, and one often discovers whole branches of a family by an informed look at vital records.

The common conception of the stable Jewish family could not be further from the truth. As early as the 1850s, Russian Jewish communities had a high rate of divorce unequaled anywhere in Europe, ranging from 15 percent in some towns to 45 percent in others. These figures do not include de facto divorces where the husband emigrated and simply remarried in the new country without having formally divorced the wife left behind in the old country. Also, mortality was high among young men, and even higher among young women. This left many young widows and widowers shopping for new mates and finding them; so the concept of "my children, your children, and our children" was possibly more prevalent in 1895 than in 1995. Records can make sense of these shifting family affiliations.

Most records are local. They are kept by the city or county and only occasionally gathered into statewide or province-wide archives. They are seldom kept nationally. Sometimes older records are kept by religious groups, and most Jewish genealogists find significant numbers of intermarriages and conversions, both into and out of Judaism. There is little uniformity in the records or the methods of search or the local rules of access.

For instance, in the Russian Empire, the Russian Orthodox Church and the Roman Catholic Church had been keeping their usual baptismal and marriage records for some time. In the 1830s, the government mandated that all religions keep records of births, marriages, deaths, and divorces, and send those records every month, one copy to the provincial government and another to the district government. In the case of the Jewish community, those records were kept in duplicate form, both in Russian and in Hebrew. (The records were kept in a different format in that part of the empire comprising the Kingdom of Poland, and different forms were used for each religious group.)

In addition, the government took periodic censuses.

In the Russian system, each person was assigned a status and a location. Most Jews were registered as "townspersons," as opposed to peasants or nobility or clergy, but about 10 percent of them were registered in one of several classes of merchants. They were also assigned to a town. These registrations were patriarchal and hereditary. A wife took her husband's registration; children took their father's. These registrations could be changed, but that took money, something in rather short supply in the Jewish community. So my maternal grandfather's family was listed in the records as "townspeople of Vitebsk," despite the fact that they had in fact resided in Nezhin Ukraine from at least 1852 when the first surviving Jewish metrical records appear. The locational registration may tell the researcher something about history, but nothing about residence at the time the record was made.

Likewise, the census is often not helpful. One reason is that in the nineteenth century, there were few taken (1858, then 1897). Another is that their principal use was for taxation and the draft, which did not encourage the populace to provide accurate results. A third is that Jews were late to adopt surnames. This generally occurred after Napoleonic times. The result is that it is difficult to correlate pre-Napoleonic census records that listed a person as David son of Yankel, with post-Napoleonic families. But the biggest problem is that most of the census records have disappeared, some ordered destroyed after the statistics were extracted, some suffering the ravages of war or poor storage.

This is also often true of the metrical records produced by the Jewish community. Of the metrical records produced by Nezhin Ukraine 1852–1918, we have a relatively complete set: fewer than ten years are missing in each category of records. On the other hand, for Chernigov, the provincial capital relatively close to Nezhin and a city of about the same size, we have barely twenty years of records in each category.

In the search for records, hours are long, and it is easy to become discouraged.

Into this breach has come the computer and the Internet.

An informal Jewish genealogy chat group called JewishGen is located at www.jewishgen.org, providing Frequently Asked Questions (FAQs) and Infofiles that take the novice through approaches to particular genealogical problems, and providing a daily forum for asking people around the world for their expertise, for their help, or whether they are related. JewishGen also maintains online the Family Tree of the Jewish People (FTJP), to which any person can submit his family tree for publication and correlation with others. By 2009, 3,900 researchers had submitted at least one family tree each, and it is likely that FTJP contains more than 1,000,000 names.

JewishGen has also encouraged the compilation of databases. Jewish Online Worldwide Burial Records asks volunteers to survey their local cemeteries and place data online. Jewish Records Indexing Poland indexes many Polish records. Other databases index Russian business directories and a government survey of officers of Russian religious institutions. The Jewish Genealogy Family Finder helps group persons researching the same town or the same surname.

Perhaps the most significant aspect of JewishGen is the help participants offer each other. I can easily look up a California obituary for a person in Florida while someone in Philadelphia takes photos of my ancestors' *gravestones there. JewishGen also provides an online *gazetteer for locating places with historical Jewish populations, many that no longer exist.

A second major contribution of the computer and the Internet for persons with U.S. families is the *Social Security Death Index. This database lists dates of birth and death for individuals for whom a death benefit was paid from the mid-1960s to the present, about 90,000,000 individuals. It also provides the key to getting further information about individuals by obtaining copies of their social security applications, which have extensive personal information, from the federal government.

There are sites on the Internet such as zabasearch and intellius that allow one to locate people in the United States and learn their approximate birth year and persons to whom they may be closely related.

Some states and provinces are beginning to put their indexes to some vital records on the Internet as searchable databases. Thus, the amount of actual research one can do without leaving home has greatly expanded.

Private parties and organizations have taken advantage of the Internet. A number of Jewish cemeteries have posted to their websites searchable databases of their "residents." The Ellis Island Foundation and the City of Hamburg have posted databases of immigration and emigration respectively. Volunteers index newspaper obituaries and death notices at obituaries.rootsweb.com. There is a www.rootsweb.com chat group for most cities. Enterprising individuals and genealogical societies have indexed genealogical records, and posted those indexes. Most noteworthy for Jewish genealogy is the Italian Genealogical Group, which has posted New York and New Jersey nat-uralizations and vital records indexes at www.italiangen.org. Stephen Morse has developed programs that more efficiently and more comprehensively survey a number of online databases from stevemorse.org.

Of great importance has been the development of genealogy sites containing large numbers of documents available by subscription. Some are specifically Jewish; others are general genealogy sites. The largest of the latter is www.ancestry.com. Some specialize in particular documents, such as city directories; others are omnivorous.

Genealogy is important in Mormon Church doctrine. Because of this, the Church of Jesus Christ of Latter-day Saints tries to accumulate microfilms of every vital record it can find, as well as any index available, and maintains *Family History Centers in most major U.S. cities. For the cost of mailing, any of the church's microfilms can be sent to your local FHC within a couple of weeks for temporary use. For double that cost, the microfilm can be kept there permanently. So it is not necessary to travel to major records centers because the Mormon Church is willing to bring the records to you. See www.familysearch.org.

With the disintegration of the former Soviet Union, the Mormon Church is becoming even more helpful to Jewish genealogists. Teams of Mormon microfilmers criss-cross Poland, Ukraine, and Belarus filming vital records. While these records are difficult to use because there are no indexes, volunteer groups have created indexes for Poland and Lithuania so that entire communities can be reconstructed.

Jewish genealogy has also benefited from increased publications and support groups. *Avotaynu*, an excellent quarterly journal, has expanded to publish monographs, both practical and scholarly. There are Jewish genealogical societies that meet regularly in about seventy different cities, and an international association of Jewish genealogical societies that ties them together. There are special-interest groups that concentrate on particular areas (Galicia, Kielce-Radom, Belarus), and groups that band together to raise money and share knowledge about particular towns.

A major untapped resource for genealogy in Latin America and continental Europe is the notarial record. The notary is not to be confused with the Anglo-American notary public, whose function is to certify that signatures are genuine. The notary in countries that follow the system of Roman law is a legal officer necessary to many private contracts. While the details vary from country to country, a notary typically must bless marriage, divorce, and adoption settlements, the transfer of land, inheritances, and major contracts such as partnerships, concession agreements, loan agreements where land is the security, transfers of intellectual property, etc. The notary's function is to draft these agreements, giving one executed copy to each party and retaining a copy himself. The notary's copies are bound in a notarial book.

Thousands of notarial books lie largely unused in archives around the world. Documents are bound in them chronologically. There is seldom an index allowing the reader to expeditiously find documents signed by a single individual.

Because these documents touch on so many aspects of life, they are an important genealogical resource. But they are unlikely to be much used until they are either indexed or digitized in a way that will permit the parties to be identified quickly.

The genealogist's search for records becomes like a detective story. With practice, one learns what data is likely to be present in what records, and how available the records might be. As a general rule, federal government records are housed at the *National Archives, regional archives, or the originating agency; state records, at a state library or archives, department of health, department of vital records, or department of motor vehicles. Found closer to home are local records, such as those at a marriage license bureau, department of health, department of vital records, register of wills, register of deeds, register of voters, orphan's court, probate court, city or county archives, business license bureau, or school board. There are also newspapers that can be located at the *Library of Congress, local university or public libraries, genealogical or historical societies or online; and maps, at the Library of Congress, U.S. Geological Survey, or local tax assessor.

The United States is decentralized (as is most of the rest of the world; even strongly centralized countries tend to keep genealogical records locally), so the agency that designs the forms decides what questions to ask and may change the questions over time. For example, in less than two years of existence, there were three different forms for World War I draft registration, each asking somewhat different questions. (Only one of them asked the city in which the registrant was born.)

Also, jurisdictions differ in the privacy they accord records and the degree of indexing provided. In Massachusetts, all *vital records (with a few exceptions, such as adopted persons' original birth certificates) are open to the public and are indexed alphabetically in five-year indexes. In Maryland, there are annual indexes that are arranged chronologically but separated by first letter and first vowel of surname, but death records are not open to the public for twenty years, while the wait for marriage and birth records is one hundred years. For this reason, it is useful to consult a variety of sources for each item of data sought.

Below is a list of the sorts of facts a genealogist might like to know and the sorts of records that might contain valuable information.

Date of birth: census (year), birth certificate, marriage certificate, death certificate, immigration manifest, *naturalization petition, social security death index, social security application, voter registration, driver's license, draft registration, alien registration, passport application, business license application, obituary, gravestone.

City of birth: census (state), marriage certificate, death certificate, immigration manifest, naturalization petition, social security application, draft registration, alien registration, passport application, obituary.

Date of marriage: marriage certificate, naturalization petition, alien registration, obituary.

City of marriage: alien registration.

Date of death: death certificate, social security death index, gravestone, obituary, probate records.

City of death: social security death index (hint), obituary, probate records.

Place of burial: death certificate, funeral-home records, obituary, probate records.

Family relationships: census, birth certificate, marriage certificate, death certificate, immigration manifest, naturalization petition, social security application, draft registration, alien registration, passport application, obituary, gravestone, probate records.

Physical description: naturalization declaration of intent, driver's license, draft registration, alien registration, passport application.

World War II poses an enormous problem for genealogists researching persons who were in Europe during the decade framing that war. World War II caused unbelievable carnage and record displacement of people. It is estimated that more than 35 million people died. Of the 6 million Jews who died, Yad Vashem is still trying to memorialize details of the deaths of a third of them. Family members ended up in different ghettos or camps or partisan groups.

Resettlement after the war was also divisive. One family member might go to Canada, another to Israel, with neither knowing that the other had survived. Reunions of family members each of whom thought that he was the last surviving member of his family occurred frequently in the 1990s and the 2000s. One quotation from the French Memorial to the Martyrs of the Deportation is apt: "They were sent to the ends of the earth and they did not return."

Trying to trace a family through this carnage defies the normal methods.

The Germans have a reputation for excellent recordkeeping, and that was true of World War II. If a person was deported from Drancy to Auschwitz, there is a record of that. If a person was ever in a concentration camp, there is a record. In Nezhin Ukraine, I was shown a two-page typed list in German entitled "Persons to be Killed" containing information on persons with Jewish-sounding names, mostly over age sixty. But for persons taken as a group into the forest and shot, there is no record. For persons sent to a death camp, or for persons sent to a concentration camp who on arrival were deemed incapable of working and so were quickly gassed, there is no record. Likewise for Jews in hiding who were discovered and immediately shot.

Beginning in 1955, Yad Vashem in Jerusalem encouraged people who knew of victims to submit Pages of Testimony. These range from a simple name to a detailed description of the time, place, and manner of death.

After the war, the allies set up through the International Committee of the Red Cross the International Tracing Service. Located in Arolsen, Germany, its job is to collect information about persons who died or survived the war. Complaints about the secrecy of its functioning and the time required to obtain answers have led to a decision to digitize its files and make them available to Yad Vashem and designated repositories in the allied countries, such as the United States Holocaust Memorial Museum in Washington, D.C. This will take some years; there are nearly 50 million re-

cords and more are arriving. Also, it requires some expertise to extract useful information from those records.

Survivors of more than 1,000 communities banded together after the war to create Yizkor (memorial) books of their individual communities. Written mostly in Yiddish or Hebrew, these books try to re-create in writing communities as they existed before World War II. Though written independently and of varying quality, these books share a structure. First, there is a history of the Jewish participation in the town. Maps show the locations of synagogues and Jewish schools, as well as Jewish residential areas. The second section presents memories of the authors' families, complete with names and family relationships. Third are memories of families for whom there are no surviving authors. Then there is often a necrology, a list of all people from the town who were killed in the Holocaust. The book usually closes with the names and addresses of the town's survivors.

Some countries and organizations have compiled lists of victims, such as the German *Gedenkbuch* or a comparable volume for France, Belgium, or the Netherlands. Some lists are by region or city.

Most recently, Jewish genealogy has benefited from the development of DNA testing. Because of the paucity of records, it is difficult to trace many Jewish families before 1850. DNA testing has helped fill this gap in several ways.

Most chromosomes inherited by children are a combination of the chromosomes of their parents. But only males have a Y chromosome. This means that a boy's Y chromosome is the same as his father's except for possible muta-tions. Mutations are uncommon events that occur randomly, but average rates of mutation have been established. Sci-ence has developed tests that compare twelve, twenty-five, and thirty-seven points on a man's Y chromosome. The more those points are identical to some other man, the more likely it is that they have a common male ancestor. Two persons who match at twelve points have a 90 percent likelihood of a com-mon male ancestor within twenty-four generations; for a match at thirty-seven points, the common ancestor is 90 per-cent likely within five generations.

Jewish tradition divides all Jews into three classes: kohanim, the priestly class, supposedly all descended from the first High Priest, Aron, Moses's brother, who belonged to the tribe of Levi; lev-ites, supposedly descended from all other descendants of Jacob's son Levi; and Israelites, all other Jews. Who be-longs to which group is passed along in the oral tradition. Kohanim and levites usually note that fact on their tomb-stones.

DNA testing has indicated that most Jewish men who claim to be kohanim seem to be descended from a common male ancestor who differs from the an-cestor of most other Jews.

More specifically, DNA testing allows one to either confirm or negate that two families with the same surname are re-lated. Matches on Y-chromosome tests will provide evidence of relation. Since eastern European Jews only adopted surnames in the nineteenth century, Y-chromosome tests also permit persons with different surnames to discover that they are descended from the same man.

The Y-chromosome test has a signifi-cant defect. It only operates through an unbroken male line. If there is a female in the line you wish to test, it is useless. It will report whether I am related to someone through my paternal grand-father, but not through my paternal grandmother, or through either of my maternal grandparents. To fill that gap, science has now developed a "cousin" or Family Finder test. It purports to de-tect whether a person is related to you up to the relationship of fifth cousin. Put another way, you share a relative who is a great-great-great-great-grand-parent or closer, regardless of whether that relationship passes through males or females, and regardless of whether you are male or female. As this test is quite new, its ramifications are yet to be explored.

It should be obvious that the benefit of DNA tests expands with the size of the library of DNA samples that the testing organization holds, because of the greater likelihood of matches when comparing your test to a larger number of persons previously tested. This "net-work effect" gives a great advantage to www.familytreeDNA.com, as it has the largest collection of Jewish tests.

A key guide is Sallyann Amdur Sack and Gary Mokotoff, *Avotaynu Guide to Jewish Genealogy* (2004) because it cov-ers every aspect of Jewish genealogy ex-cept DNA testing, and each chapter is followed by an extensive bibliography.

Other useful work includes:

Names: Alexander Beider, *A Dic-tionary of Jewish Surnames from the Kingdom of Poland* (1996); Beider, *A Dictionary of Jewish Surnames from the Russian Empire* (rev. ed. 2009); Beider,

A Dictionary of Ashkenazic Given Names (2008); Beider, *A Dictionary of Jewish Surnames from Galicia* (2004); Guilherme Faiguenboim, Paulo Valdares & Anna Rosa Campagnano, *Dictionary of Sephardic Surnames* (2d ed. 2009); Lars Menk, *A Dictionary of German-Jewish Surnames* (2005).

Journal articles: *Avotaynu: The International Review of Jewish Genealogy.*

*Gazeteer: Gary Mokotoff, Sallyann Sack, and Alexander Sharon, *Where Once We Walked: A Guide to the Jewish Communities Destroyed in the Holocaust* (rev. ed. 2002).

Guides to records: Aleksander Kronik and Sallyann Sack, *Some Archival Sources for Ukrainian-Jewish Genealogy* (1998); Susan Wynne, *Finding Your Jewish Roots in Galicia* (1997); Miriam Weiner, *Jewish Roots in Poland: Pages from the Past and Archival Inventories* (1997); Harold Rhode and Sallyann Sack, *Jewish Vital Records, Revision Lists and Other Jewish Holdings in the Lithuanian Archives* (1996); Dorit Sallis and Marek Webb, *Jewish Documentary Sources in Russia, Ukraine and Belarus: A Preliminary List* (1996); Sallyann Sack, *A Guide to Jewish Genealogical Resources in Israel* (rev. ed., 1995); Dmitri Elyashevich, *Documentlnye Materialy po Istorii Evreev v Arkhivakh SNG i Stran Baltii* (in Russian, 1994); Arthur Kurzweil and Miriam Weiner, *The Encyclopedia of Jewish Genealogy*, vol. 1: *Sources in the U.S. and Canada* (1991); Miriam Weiner, *Jewish Roots in Ukraine and Moldova* (1999); and Estelle Guzik, *Genealogical Resources in the New York Metropolitan Area* (1989).

Social history: Raphael Patai, *The Jews of Hungary: History, Culture, Psychology* (1996); Masha Greenbaum, *The Jews of Lithuania: A History of a Remarkable Community 1316–1945* (1995); Chae-Ran Freeze, *Jewish Marriage and Divorce in Imperial Russia* (2001); and Irving Howe, *World of Our Fathers* (1976).

Holocaust research: Gary Mokotoff, *How to Document Victims and Locate Survivors of the Holocaust* (1995) with portions online at www.avotaynu.com/holocaust.

Genealogies: Chaim Freedman, *Eliyahu's Branches: The Descendants of the Vilna Gaon and his Family* (1997); David Zubatsky and Irwin Berent, *Sourcebook for Jewish Genealogies and Family Histories* (1996); and Neil Rosenstein, *The Unbroken Chain*, 2 vols. (1990).

For children: Ira Wolfman, *Do People Grow on Family Trees? Genealogy for Kids and Other Beginners* (1991).

HERBERT LAZEROW
UNIVERSITY OF SAN DIEGO

See genealogical resources online.

Genealogy.com. See genealogy resources online.

generation. In general, a generation is reckoned to be thirty-three years.

Geni.com. See genealogical resources online.

GenWeb. See genealogical resources online; U.S. GenWeb Project.

Geographic Information Systems (GIS). See GIS in local history; Cultural Resource Geographic Information Systems (CRGIS).

geological surface maps. See maps and atlases.

Georgia, local history in. The Georgia Historical Society, chartered by the state in 1839, is a private nonprofit membership association that maintains an archive, carries out programs for the public, manages a historical marker program, and prints a newsletter. Since 1917 it has also published the highly regarded *Georgia Historical Quarterly*. The state's directory of historical and cultural organizations places their number at more than 600 in 2015, many volunteer-staffed. The state's

Department of Natural Resources supports and interprets eighteen sites that include battlefields, plantations, farms, homes, birthplaces, agricultural and industrial sites, and waterways.

There are eight sites of cultural and historical significance administered by federal agencies including the Civil War-era Union Prison at Andersonville, FDR's "Little White House" in Warm Springs, President Jimmy Carter's home in Plains, and Macon's Kolomoki Mounds of the Woodland period.

Georgia does not operate an official state history museum but it does offer a superb collection of local and

This historical marker in Roswell, Georgia marks the childhood home of Mittie Bulloch, the mother of President Theodore Roosevelt, Jr. CREDIT: AMY H. WILSON.

regional museums, historic districts, and archives. The state's capital, Atlanta, includes a branch of the National Archives that serves the Southeast region of the United States; here are the records of important civil rights litigation in Alabama, Florida, Georgia, Mississippi, North Carolina, South Carolina, and Tennessee, as well as the records associated with the trial of Leo Frank (1915). The State of Georgia Archives, formerly in the Secretary of State's office, in 2013 became a unit of the Board of Regents of the University System of Georgia. Its holdings are extensive with some digital access. The Jimmy Carter Presidential Library in Atlanta houses the president's papers and a new exhibition hall. It regularly conducts educational programs for teachers and the general public (not to be confused with the Carter Center with whom it shares land). The land the Carter Library sits on was General Sherman's field headquarters in 1864.

The Atlanta History Center in the city's Buckhead district occupies a thirty-three-acre campus with exhibition space, three historic homes (including the Margaret Mitchell House in midtown), an archive, research library, and exhibit galleries that make it one of the largest museums in the nation. In 2014 it acquired from the city of Atlanta the historic cyclorama of the Battle of Atlanta with the historic locomotive "the Texas." On the west end of the city is a cluster of historically black colleges and universities that compose the Atlanta University Center (AUC). The AUC is home to historically significant buildings and people (Benjamin Mayes, Martin Luther King Jr.,

W. E. B. Dubois). The AU Center's impressive Robert W. Woodruff Library holds records that are integral to the region's history. In downtown Atlanta is the Auburn Avenue Research Library on African American Culture and History, which opened its doors in 1994. Emory University and Georgia State University libraries, both in Atlanta, are repositories for the papers of Flannery O'Connor, Andrew Young, Johnny Mercer, Alice Walker, Salmon Rushdie, and others. The most significant collections of Georgiana—papers, rare books, documents, newspapers, maps, and political archives—are the Hargrett Rare Book and Manuscript Library and the Richard B. Russell library, both of the University of Georgia.

In 1969 the state created the Historic Preservation Office (today Historic Preservation Division) as part of the Department of Natural Resources (DNR), which also has responsibility for managing the nomination of candidates for the *National Register of Historic Places. In 1980 the legislature encouraged the formation of local *historic preservation commissions of which there are more than ninety-two in 2015. The state also facilitated creation of the nonprofit Georgia African American Historic Preservation Network (GAAHPN) in 1984 and in 2000 funded a full-time administrative position within Georgia's Historic Preservation Division. (GAAHPN's mission is that of providing technical assistance to community partners while promoting diversity in historic preservation and heritage tourism.) DNR is home to the State Archaeologist as well as the Council on American Indian Concerns, which protects burial sites and historical artifacts.

There is a vibrant state historic preservation trust (the Georgia Trust), and at the University of Georgia (Athens), the Savannah College of Art and Design, and Georgia State University (Atlanta) there are degree-granting programs in historic preservation. Two universities (Georgia State and the University of West Georgia) offer degree-granting programs in public history. Georgia State University's folk life program specializes in regional folklore and material culture.

Statewide, Georgia is home to regional and local history museums that are actively engaged in (and supported by) their communities. These include the Tubman Museum of Macon, the Columbus Museum, the Savannah History Museum, the William Breman Jewish Heritage Museum of Atlanta, the Museum of Aviation in Warner Robins, the National Civil War Naval Museum of Port Columbus, and the Augusta Museum of History. The Morris Museum of Art in Augusta includes the works of Southern artists in a variety of mediums dating to the late eighteenth century. Among the most significant historic house museums are Woodrow Wilson's, Mittie Bulloch's (Theodore Roosevelt's mother), Tom Watson's, Martin Luther King Jr.'s, Jimmy Carter's, and FDR's (in Warm Springs). Because of Georgia's important role in the civil rights movement, new museums of conscience are appearing. The Ralph Mark Gilbert Civil Rights Museum in Savannah is one such development, as is the Albany Civil Rights Institute. The newest is the Atlanta-based National Center for Civil and Human Rights (2014).

The first school textbook on Georgia history appeared in 1884 but not until 1985 did the General Assembly mandate the statewide teaching of Georgia Studies in the eighth grade. Three different textbooks (one of which is a digital version) are available to teachers, and each uses a multidisciplinary approach emphasizing history, geography, economics, and civics. All of the state's public universities offer courses in Georgia history. The Georgia Association of Historians is the state's professional historical organization; many K–12 teachers of history belong to the Georgia Council for the Social Studies. Three organizations specialize in workshops and programs for teachers (and students) that utilize historical study: the State YMCA of Georgia, the Georgia Council for Economic Education, and Georgia Humanities.

As the largest landmass east of the Mississippi, the immense size and diversity of Georgia presents challenges to its historians. Its coastal region has a distinctive heritage rooted in Sea Island cotton, slavery, and transatlantic trade that made Savannah (remarkably well preserved and interpreted) an international port city. The "wiregrass" region in the southern part of the state is characterized by sandy soil and along its border with Florida, skirts North America's largest swamp (the Okefenokee). A fertile "black belt" that at one time was the world's leading cotton producer traverses the state's midsection (today this region in Georgia is the nation's leading producer of pecans and peanuts). The rolling hills, valleys, and mountains of north Georgia form part of Appalachia. This remarkable geologic and cultural diversity includes an urban dimension as well, with almost half the population of the state today living in metropolitan Atlanta in the northwest corner of Georgia, while the other half is dispersed over a vast countryside that includes a handful of mid-sized cities and a scattering of small municipalities in thinly populated counties (of which Georgia has very many: 159). Inevitably, the politics of the state since the 1920s has revolved around this urban-rural divide, with a 1962 U.S. Supreme Court decision (*Baker v. Carr*) finally ending the "county unit" system that gave rural districts a weighted electoral advantage in statewide as well as U.S. congressional district elections.

Founded as the last of the thirteen original colonies, Georgia's role in the American Revolution was limited. After 1793, the invention of the cotton gin made short-staple cotton a highly profitable upcountry crop; its cultivation spread rapidly, as did the institution of slavery upon which cotton wealth depended. The grab for land led to the removal of the Cherokee in a "trail of tears." The Civil War (and Sherman's infamous march) devastated Georgia's commercial infrastructure with long-term consequences; the arrival of the boll weevil in 1915 (not eradicated until the 1990s) further delayed the state's recovery, while the Great Depression made a bad situation worse. Not until the agricultural and electrification programs of the New Deal, the post-WWII GI Bill and Great Society, and the new era heralded by the civil rights movement of the 1960s did many Georgians experience the social, economic, and educational opportunities associated with progress.

Georgia's historians have chronicled these events, though not until a relatively recent period did they take a decidedly more inclusive approach. Yale historian Ulrich Bonnell Phillips (1877–1934) was a native of Georgia and his scholarship reflected a pro-confederacy and racist perspective, as did the work of Georgia's preeminent historian of his day, E. Merton Coulter (1890–1981) of the University of Georgia. A more modern approach begins with A. Phinizy Spalding (1930–1994), a native of Atlanta and a distinguished faculty member of the University of Georgia. With fellow faculty member Kenneth E. Coleman, he edited a classic collection of essays that is still widely used, *A History of Georgia* (1977, 1991). The three most important in-print historical treatments of the state are those by James Cobb with coauthors Christopher C. Meyers and David Williams, and Buddy Sullivan.

The Georgia Humanities Council and the University of Georgia Press co-publish books on Georgia themes. These include the leading one-volume narrative history of the state by James C. Cobb, *Georgia Odyssey* (1997, 2008); a thoroughly revised version of the old WPA guide, *The New Georgia Guide*, ed. Thomas Dyer (1996); a compendium of articles on *The Civil War in Georgia* (2011), ed. John Inscoe; a volume of contributed essays on *African American Life in the Georgia Low Country* (2010), ed. Philip Morgan, and *Courthouses of Georgia*, with text by George Justice. Mercer University Press in Macon annually publishes books on Georgia historical topics and figures while Arcadia Publishers has a strong list of local historical topics and places.

The premier public resource for Georgia history and culture is the award-winning *New Georgia Encyclopedia* (NGE—www.georgiaencyclopedia.org), an exclusively online project of Georgia Humanities in partnership with the University System of Georgia/ GALILEO (the state's virtual library and NGE's host), the University of Georgia Press, and the Office of the Governor. Its entry on "Georgia History: Overview" by James Cobb and John Inscoe is an up-to-date summary. The NGE is widely used in schools and colleges, by tourists, media, and the general public; it consists of 2,100 digitally born article entries on all aspects of the state, each signed with a bibliography. GALILEO also hosts the *Digital Library of Georgia*, specializing in primary source material in state and local history and, with the NGE, serves as an invaluable digital gateway to the history and present state of Georgia, its people, and places.

JAMIL S. ZAINALDIN
GEORGIA HUMANITIES COUNCIL

See United States, local history in.

germ theory. See frontier thesis; health care as local history topic.

Germans in North America, sources for. See Appendix A.

GIS (Geographic Information Systems) in local history. GIS is computer software designed to analyze and display social, political, or economic data in a geographic framework. The displays take several forms, but are commonly digitally produced maps. One very common display is the choropleth or thematic map, which shades geographic units according to some social variable. An example might be a map in which the percent of children below poverty level, grouped into five classes (0–20 percent, 21–40 percent, etc.) by county for 1940 is shown by coloring each county with a different color or color intensity according to the class. GIS software joins social variables from one source, such as the U.S. *Census with boundary files from another source, and allows users to choose classification techniques and intervals as well as color and labeling schemes. Historians can make use of this technology when historical data is available—data from earlier censuses and boundary files from earlier time periods. Basic GIS analysis can be done online using interactive mapping sites such as *Social Explorer* (www.socialexplorer.com) and *NHGIS National Historical GIS* (www.nhgis.org) simply by choosing variables, geographies, and time periods.

Another display example is of information referenced by a point. For example, a map in which houses built before 1860 are identified by one marker, houses built after 1860 by a different marker. These markers can be generated from databases of geo-referenced addresses—each house is located by latitude and longitude.

The real power of GIS comes when the point layer is superimposed on the county or polygon layer and one can see whether pre-1860 houses tend to cluster in counties with higher rates of child poverty.

Other kinds of spatial relationships can be analyzed and visualized with GIS software, which has become extremely powerful and continues to be developed. There are several commercial companies, including ESRI with its ArcGIS products, MapInfo from Pitney Bowes, and Manifold, a Windows-based GIS, each with its own set of features and strengths.

GIS is a powerful tool for local historians, either for quantitative analyses of local areas, or for displaying historical information for the public, either in printed maps or on websites. Although the software has become easier to use, the challenging conceptual bases of GIS analysis and the numerous pitfalls of digital mapping means most historians will require technical help to achieve the best results. Those ready to jump in or intrigued by the possibilities should consult Ian N. Gregory and Paul S. Ell, *Historical GIS: Technologies, Methodologies, and Scholarship* (2007), and Amy Hillier and Anne Kelly Knowles, eds., *Placing History: How Maps, Spatial Data, and GIS Are Changing Historical Scholarship* (2008).

ROBERT KIBBEE
THE HISTORY CENTER IN TOMPKINS COUNTY (NY)

See Cultural Resource Geographic Information Systems; local government records; maps and atlases.

godparent. A godparent is one asked by parents to sponsor a child at the time of baptism. Customs vary as to the godparent's responsibilities thereafter.

Google Maps. See gazetteer; maps and atlases.

Google Scholar. See local history resources online.

government. See local government records.

grassroots history. An early use of the term *grassroots* dates to 1876 when the Black Hills were described as having gold everywhere, "even in the 'grass roots'" (see Richard I. Dodge, *The Black Hills* [1876]). Later uses of the term imply getting down to basics.

In 1940, Constance McLaughlin Green wrote an essay entitled "The Value of Local History" (in Caroline F. Ware, *The Cultural Approach to History* [reprinted in Carol Kammen, *Pursuit of Local History* (1996, 90–99)]) wherein she wrote that, to understand the importance of American history, one had to look locally. "There lie the grass roots of American civilization," she noted. The term, thereafter, has meant the history closest to the people.

Theodore Blegan begins his book *Grassroots History* (1947) with the comment that "the pivot of history is not the uncommon, but the usual, and the true makers of history are 'the people, yes.'" He insists that the essence of history should be to grapple with the "need to understand the small, everyday elements, the basic elements, in the large movements"—that grassroots history recognizes the importance of the simple, "however complex and subtle the problem of understanding the simple may be."

gravestones. Many becoming as fragile as paper documents, gravestones can offer insights into biographical, artistic, cultural, and social trends in addition to a community's history.

Genealogists use gravestones to trace individuals. Dates inscribed on stones verify other documentary evidence and clusters of stones in family plots may lead to other relatives. Epitaphs, like one composed in 1771: "Here lies as silent clay/Miss Arabella Young/Who on the 21st of May/ Began to hold her tongue," sometimes reveal amusing personality traits.

Symbols on the stones may denote military service, occupations, fraternal and religious affiliations, and professions. Researchers can reconstruct the identities of early stone carvers.

Tombstones have reflected changing styles of ornament. The death's head, common before the American Revolution, reflects the austerity of Puritanism. The winged-soul image that followed demonstrates a more liberal artistic taste, paralleling the optimism of the new country. Greek and Egyptian motifs duplicate the early-nineteenth-century interest in classical designs. Voluptuous statuary and funereal symbols like the tree stump, the severed flower bud, and the lamb characterize the Victorian period. Modern stones, some with amusing decoration, such as a set of golf clubs, a sailboat, or a gun, reflect the person they memorialize.

During the late nineteenth and early twentieth centuries it was common for distinctive cultural groups to reserve cemetery sections for their own members. Stones in these areas often use language and symbols that distinguished the culture; for example, the Star of David, portrait medallions, Eastern and other variations of the cross. The popu-larity of buying monuments for pets and incorporating images of celebrities on tombstones reflects changes in American culture.

Burial plots have always been separated according to social classes. In larger cemeteries, barren paupers' grounds are distant from landscaped plots reserved for the affluent. Even in small town and country settings, plain stones memorializing African Americans sit on the fringes of old burying grounds. Hedgerows and iron railings separate prominent families from each other and from other social classes. And, of course, impressive mausoleums and fine sculpture define the resting places of more prosperous residents.

One problem with using very early gravestones as historical documents concerns the accuracy of dates and spelling. Verifying data with other documents can assure accuracy.

Finding particular tombstones can present problems as well. While large cemeteries may have carefully kept records, it is often difficult to find the person(s) responsible for graveyards in smaller communities. Fortunately, a Works Progress Administration project during the Great Depression encouraged municipalities to inventory cemeteries. Inventories, if they exist, may be found in local libraries and/or historical societies. However, monuments mentioned in them may no longer exist.

Due to natural and human factors, gravestones are disappearing as historical documents. Alternating freezing and thawing splits slate and sandstone, shearing off sections of a gravestone's face. Acid rain erodes the carvings on more porous stones. Careless mowing of burial plots chips away at the bases of tombstones. Researchers sometimes apply damaging substances to capture a rubbing or a photograph. Graveyards have been perennial haunts of pranksters who think that tipping over a monument is a daring deed. And the late-twentieth-century development of the memorial park, with its unadorned markers, has little research appeal.

*Volunteers can raise consciousness by leading tours, sponsoring photographic publications, and giving illustrated lectures. The Association for Gravestone Studies (AGS), begun in 1977, is an organization devoted to "furthering the study and preservation of gravestones." Broadening its focus from New England graveyards to a national and finally an international scope, the AGS holds annual conferences and publishes a quarterly newsletter and an annual journal, *Markers*. It also advises interested groups and individuals about gravestone preservation, research, and education. Information may be obtained from the Association of Gravestone Studies, Greenfield Corporate Center, 101 Munson Street, Greenfield, MA 01301; (413) 772-0836; or www.gravestonestudies.org.

One place to discover "noteworthy" (and a few notorious) gravesites is www.findagrave.com. The researcher can search by names of persons, by burial sites, and by "claims to fame." This website also has a valuable bibliography of publications about regional gravesites and can lead a researcher to other resting places of local celebrities.

See M. Ruth Little, *Sticks & Stones: Three Centuries of North Carolina Gravemarkers* (1998); Theodore Chase and Laurel K. Gabel, *Gravestone Chronicles I* (1997); David C. Sloane, *The Last Great Necessity: Cemeteries in American History* (1991); Francis Y. Duval and Ivan B. Rigby, *Early American Gravestone Art in Photographs* (1978); and Harriett Merrifield Forbes, *Gravestones of Early New England and the Men Who Made Them 1653–1800* (1927).

TERESA K. LEHR
COLLEGE AT BROCKPORT,
SUNY, RETIRED

Great Awakening. Between 1726 and 1756, the Great Awakening consisted of a series of religious revivals, spurred by the preaching of George Whitefield, Theodorus Frelinghuysen, Jonathan Edwards, Samuel Davies, and others, that swept from Maine to Georgia.

Greeks in North America, sources for. See Appendix A.

Guam, local history in. The indigenous people of Guam, the Chamorros, first settled the island some 4,500 years ago. In this traditionally matrilineal society, core values of Chamorro culture reflected kinship and interdependence over individualism, with a focus on the extended family group or *clan. Like other Micronesian societies, Chamorros practiced ancestral worship and embraced a cosmology based on associations of spirits with natural phenomena, land, sea, and sky. These values can be seen today in practices of sharing resources and reciprocity, hospitality, the emphasis on familial ties and obligations, respect for elders and authority, caring for the natural environment, and spiritual devotion. Migration and intermarriage between Chamorros and Spanish, Mexican, and Philippine natives through the eighteenth and nineteenth centuries have resulted in an ethnically mixed population. And while many of the traditional cultural beliefs and practices of Chamorros have been lost, altered, or adapted, the Chamorro language and the sense of Chamorro identity have endured despite the influences of colonialism.

The United States acquired Guam in 1898 following the Spanish-American War. The U.S. Navy administered the island until the beginning of World War II. America's primary interest in Guam was the establishment of a military base. The civil and political rights of the Chamorro people were secondary.

In 1941, Chamorros withstood thirty-one months of Japanese occupation until American troops forcefully recaptured the island in 1944. In the early postwar years, Guam was rebuilt largely by imported labor. The signing of the Organic Act in 1950 and the removal of travel restrictions to the territory in the 1960s allowed the island to experience small-scale development. Over time, especially within the last forty years, Guam has evolved into a multi-ethnic, urban society.

With the passage of the Organic Act, a civilian government was established on the island and Chamorros were granted U.S. citizenship, though not allowed to vote for their own governor until tewnty years later. Throughout this period, Chamorros adapted to American-imposed models of health, education, politics, economics, and justice while struggling for equality and self-determination under U.S. rule.

Today, Guam remains an unincorporated U.S. territory with a continued military presence that occupies approximately one-third of the island. Plans are now under way for a major military expansion. In light of Guam's colonial history and the profound political, social, and cultural impacts the military buildup will have for Guam, efforts to preserve and promote knowledge of Chamorro history, culture, and language are on the rise, although with limited resources.

In the summer of 2016, Guam hosted the twelfth Festival of Pacific Arts, a major regional celebration of indigenous arts and culture that is held every four years to bring together twenty-seven Pacific nations and territories to share their contemporary and traditional artistic and cultural practices. A new museum, the Guam and Chamorro Educational Facility, is also under construction and will serve as a main venue for the festival. The new Guam Museum will also be a major educational facility for learning, preserving, and interpreting Chamorro and Guam history, culture, the arts, and natural environment.

The Guam Museum was initially established in 1932 by Naval Gov. Edmund S. Root at the Plaza De España and was run by the American Legion Mid Pacific Post I for the first four years. In 1936, the naval government took over the museum, which included an ancient Chamorro collection curated by Chamorro educator and community leader Agueda Johnston. The original Guam Museum was destroyed during the U.S. bombardment of the island during WWII, and throughout the postwar period no permanent museum was ever built. Tony Palomo, former senator and local historian, directed the Guam Museum from 1995 to 2007, operating a small gallery space at the Micronesia Mall.

Guam also has a small number of galleries and cultural centers, including the Isla Center for the Arts at the University of Guam, which was established in 1994 as a center for the arts of the larger Micronesian region and beyond. In 2014, Sagan Kotturan Chamoru, the Chamoru Cultural Immersion Center, opened to preserve and promote Chamorro heritage and language, and is run by a group of artists and community members.

The Guam Council on the Arts and Humanities Agency (CAHA) was established in 1967 by the late Dr. Pedro Sanchez under the University of Guam and was called the Insular Arts Council (IAC). The agency, which is now under the Department of Chamorro Affairs, remains dedicated to the development of programs in music, visual arts, cultural heritage, literature, and arts education.

The Guam Historic Resources Division, also known as the State Historic Preservation Office (SHPO), was founded in 1974 under the Department of Commerce and later moved to the Parks and Recreation Division in 1976. Originally, the office was dedicated to field archeology rather than regulatory work. In 1983, the office shifted in order to follow federal guidelines for the preservation of cultural sites.

Local libraries such as the Nieves M. Flores Memorial Library and the Robert Taitano Micronesian Area Research Center at the University of Guam have possession of historical photographs, document collections, and artifacts. Public access to these collections through exhibitions is quite limited.

In the 1990s, the government also published the Chamorro Heritage Books series, with seven books covering the cultural, historical, political, and economic lives of the Chamorros from the ancient period through the colonial eras. The series is written in English from the Chamorro perspective and was led by Dr. Katherine Aguon, a longtime educator.

There are a number of community-based organizations that are also working to provide cultural and historical resources to the public. The Guam Humanities Council is one such organization. Established in 1991, the council is an independent nonprofit organization committed to providing support and opportunities for the people of Guam to engage in the humanities in their daily lives. The council's mission is dedicated to preserving the island's diverse cultures and histories, promoting indigenous Chamorro cultural identity as essential to Guam's unique way of life, and addressing important contemporary issues facing our island. The council has curated and presented several interpretive exhibitions and projects on a wide range of topics focused on Guam and Micronesia.

Guampedia, Guam's online encyclopedia, founded by the Guam Humanities Council, is a community project to create a comprehensive online encyclopedic resource about local history and culture and contemporary Guam.

The Guam Preservation Trust (GPT) was created in 1990 as a nonprofit, public corporation governed by a board of directors. It is dedicated to preserving Guam's historic sites and culture, as well as educating the public about heritage issues.

Various other organizations focus primarily on the preservation of Chamorro language and the interpretation of Chamorro performance art, chant, and dance as a way to protect and perpetuate Chamorro culture and identity.

Pa'a Taotao Tano' is a leading organization to meet this goal. Established in 1998 by Master of Chamorro Dance, Frank Rabon, the organization is the result of earlier projects, which focused on Chamorro dance and interpretation. Carlos P. Taitano, who held the position of consultant and historian for Pa'a Taotao Tano' since its inception, produced the "History of Guam in Songs and Dances" in 1948 and the play "Guahu Taotao Tano" in 1983. These projects led the way to the estab-

lishment of Pa'a Taotao Tano, which is currently the umbrella organization for several other cultural performance groups on island.

Historic Inalahan Foundation was founded in March 2007, and highlights cultural folkways, arts, crafts, and Chamorro values of the early 1900s through living history demonstrations and historic buildings at the Gef Pa'go Cultural Village. The organization also works to preserve and revitalize the Inalahan Historic District through capital improvements, economic stimulation, and the adaptive reuse of historic structures.

KIMBERLEE KIHLENG
AND MONAEKA FLORES
GUAM HUMANITIES COUNCIL

See United States, local history in.

Gypsies in North America, sources for. See Appendix A.

H

H-Local. H-Local was established by Tom Costa in 1994 under the H-Net umbrella of electronic mailing lists for historians. Costa, who was teaching a local history methods class at then Clinch Valley College in Wise, Virginia (now University of Virginia's College at Wise), had learned about H-Net through his explorations of online materials and communities for scholars, and e-mailed H-Net's founder Richard Jensen to offer his services in establishing an electronic list for local history and historians.

His first co-moderators (called editors in H-Net parlance) were Ken Aitken, Prairie History Librarian at Regina Public Library in Regina, Saskatchewan, and Joe Arpad, a local historian in San Francisco. Arpad soon dropped out, citing other concerns and Costa and Aitken were joined by Randy Patton of Kennesaw State University. Later, Mary Mannix, then Library Director of Maryland's Howard County Historical Society, joined as editor.

Costa was particularly interested in the relationship between professional academic historians and local history organizations, museums, and archivists. Mannix wanted the list to serve as a support system for librarians, archivists, curators, and other local history professionals working alone. To facilitate discussion across the range of interests, the editors of H-Local cross-posted from H-Pub and various state history

e-mail lists such as VA-Hist, NJ-Hist, and GA-Hist. It was a moderated list; therefore, the editors screened postings before distribution, and tended to avoid posting narrow questions of interest only to persons of one locality.

The list provided valuable service by posting announcements of museum exhibits and other items of interest to the public and public historians. H-Local provided several early museum reviews, but its value during its early years lay in the wide-ranging discussions of theoretical and methodological issues in local and public history.

Early topics of particular interest included discussions of oral history versus documentary sources, a long thread on the relationship between sports history, memorabilia, and collecting that eventually branched into women's history. Other discussions centered on the limitations of a focus on politics and political boundaries, the connection between bowling alleys and a local sense of community, and the importance of obituaries (and differences between men's and women's obits) in historical and genealogical studies.

There were postings from archivists and special collections librarians describing highlights of their collections and introducing the list to new collections. While most subscribers were North American, there was a scattering of international posters who offered interesting perspectives on the way local history was understood, particularly in a discussion of the British tradition of local history.

Matthew Gilmore is the current editor of H-Local, which has played an important role in broadening the lines of communication within the local history community, bringing practitioners together through virtual connections.

The virtual world of H-Net's local history community has expanded with geographic particularization. Numerous state-level lists/networks were created throughout the 2000s (H-Connecticut, H-Florida, H-Kentucky, H-Louisiana, H-Maryland, H-NC (North Carolina), H-New-Jersey, H-NewMexico, H-Pennsylvania, H-SC (South Carolina), H-Texas, and several regional ones (H-Appalachia, H-Midwest, H-NewEngland, H-South, H-West). While each network has its niche audience, a critical mass for networks has been an issue. Those networks for Midwestern states were recently collapsed into H-Midwest.

In response to the changing digital world, H-Net moved to a new content platform in April of 2014, moving off of listserv technology. The new platform offers new technological opportunities, still being explored.

Tom Costa
Updated by Matthew Gilmore
Editor H-DC, H-Local

H-Public. H-Public is a listserv, or electronic mailing list, created to facilitate communication among public historians. Its first incarnation, PUBLHIST, was launched in 1993 by John Hurley, then a graduate student at Harvard University. In 1995, Hurley allied the list with the *National Council on Pub-

lic History (NCPH), an Indianapolis-based organization seeking to establish its presence in the then new realm of the Internet. Another important connection was made in 1998 when PUBLHIST joined with H-Net, then a network of ninety discussion lists on topics in the humanities and social sciences (as of 2016, there were more than 180 H-Net lists). Under its new name H-Public, the list was required by H-Net to become somewhat more formalized, governed by an advisory board chosen by NCPH and moderated by its editors rather than consisting of direct postings by subscribers. While some subscribers expressed concern that this might curtail the openness of the list, others recognized the benefits the H-Net affiliation could provide through increased exposure for NCPH and for public history, as well as the ability to archive digital conversations securely for the long term.

The move from an open to moderated list mirrored a common progression among listservs, as electronic communication shifted from an exciting novelty promising new modes of scholarly and professional communication to a more everyday feature of working and educational life, often delivering far more material than subscribers can hope to read. With the advent of more interactive and visually engaging "Web 2.0" platforms in the first decade of the twenty-first century, listservs like H-Public came to seem somewhat antiquated to many. After a lengthy planning and transition process, H-Net created a more dynamic and flexible online venue in 2014 and H-Public became part of the new H-Net Commons. At the same time, however,

NCPH was expanding its own capabilities for digital communication and publication. The 2012 advent of the *Public History Commons and the History@ Work blog (both later absorbed into a more multifunctional NCPH website) as well as the expansion of the organization's social media presence have meant that many of the former functions of H-Public (for example, job postings) now appear within NCPH's own sites and feeds. The listserv is now primarily an electronic bulletin board for announcements relating to an expanding field, with occasional professional queries and discussion. It is currently overseen by editor Debbie Ann Doyle and the NCPH Digital Media Group.

In 2016, H-Public had more than 2,300 subscribers, largely from the United States but with substantial minorities in Canada, the United Kingdom, Europe, and Australia, as well as some in Asia and other parts of the world. While the list is open to anyone with an interest in "doing history" in the public realm, postings have always tended to reflect the specifically *professional* interests of those who are employed (or seeking employment) in public history—for example, those working in government, museums, consulting, public interpretation, and similar areas. Although the original vision of H-Public as a lively and central online meeting place for public historians has changed as the Internet itself has developed, the listserv remains one node in an evolving network of digital communication and conversation about the practice of history in public.

CATHY STANTON
DIGITAL MEDIA EDITOR, NCPH

See National Council on Public History.

habeas corpus. The term is Latin for "you have the body." It refers to a legal writ used to free an individual from illegal confinement, a guarantee that a prisoner is given due process of law. In the United States, it is the constitutional guarantee against false imprisonment.

Haitians in North America, sources for. See Appendix A.

hamlet. The word hamlet appears in a number of early languages. The Old French is *hamelet*, the German is *heim*, the Dutch is *heem*, and the Old English is *ham*, all meaning home. A hamlet is a cluster of residential, incidental, and possibly agricultural buildings without a municipal designation. Sometimes a hamlet is called an unincorporated *village.

Hawai'i, local history in. Local history in the Hawaiian Islands does not have a single meaning. The Hawaiian word *mo'olelo* translates as "history, story, tale, folktale, account," reflecting a personal, interpretive, and selective side of doing and telling history. The Native Hawaiian oral tradition begins to appear in written form during the missionary period, with local histories soon following. Early written histories and *primary sources, particularly newspapers, maintain a dynamic and diverse local heritage. There is even a history of locals, with a unique language, pidgin or Hawai'i Creole English, ethnic heritage, and cultural identity coming out of the immigrant plantation experience.

The Waikīkī Heritage Trail in Honolulu, Hawai'i, features surfboard-shaped historical markers like this one telling the story of "The Beaches of Waikīkī." CREDIT: HONOLULU MAYOR'S OFFICE OF CULTURE AND THE ARTS.

Each such local history has its own traditions, historical societies, museums, archives, and oral histories.

The first *mo'olelo Hawai'i* (Hawaiian history) was written at Lahainaluna School in 1835–1836 by some of its older students, such as David Malo, then forty-two years old. The school was founded in 1831 as a Protestant missionary school and is the oldest post-secondary school west of the Rocky Mountains. Malo (*Hawaiian Antiquities*) was one of a trio of outstanding Hawaiian historians of the time. The other two were Samuel M. Kamakau (*Ruling Chiefs of Hawai'i*) and John I'i (*Fragments of Hawaiian History*). The work of these early historians of the Hawaiian Kingdom were then and now recognized as an authoritative canon.

However, the works were less formal histories than edited compilations of writings from Hawaiian language newspapers, printed from 1834 to 1940, when local writers filled 125,000 pages in nearly one hundred different newspapers, just 1 percent of which has been translated into English. An argument has been made, by M. Puakea Nogelmeier in *Mai Pa'a I Ka Leo: Historical Voice in Hawaiian Primary Materials, Looking Forward and Listening Back* (2010), that this editing was highly selective, even distorted, and did not represent the back-and-forth, oral-like nature of the originals. Still, these are most certainly the books that started our local history. For another assessment of how newspapers recorded events as well as actively affected local history from 1834 to 1976, see *Shaping History: The Role of Newspapers in Hawai'i* (1996) by Helen Geracimos Chapin.

Early writers of general histories of Hawai'i include Abraham Fornander, who wrote a history in 1878–1885 along with his more noted *Collection of Hawaiian Antiquities and Folk-lore*; Martha Warren Beckwith, who wrote in the 1930s and 1940s; Ralph S. Kuykendall, whose three-part history came out in 1938, 1953, and 1967; and Gavan Daws, *Shoal of Time: A History of the Hawaiian Islands* (1968). More recent histories reflect the contested nature of this history; for example, *Land and Power in Hawaii* (1990) by George Cooper and Gavan Daws, *Native Land and Foreign Desires* (1992) by Lilikala Kame'eleihiwa, and *Dismembering Lāhui: A History of the Hawaiian Nation to 1887* (2002) by Jonathan K. Osorio.

Working in Hawaii: A Labor History (1985) by Edward Beechert remains a good overview of local economic history. The history of encounter and exchange, often devastating to Kanaka Maoli (Native Hawaiians), is reflected in *Ma'i Lepera: Disease and Displacement in Nineteenth Century Hawai'i* (2013), a social history of leprosy (Hansen's Disease) in Hawai'i, by Kerri Inglis. For precontact Hawaiian cultural history, see *Feathered Gods and Fishhooks: An Introduction to Hawaiian Archaeology and Prehistory* (1985) by Patrick Vinton Kirch and *'Ōlelo No'eau: Hawaiian Proverbs and Poetical Sayings* (1983) by Mary Kawena Pukui, a collection of Hawaiian sayings organized by topics, themes, and places.

Several major archival collections are in Honolulu on the island of O'ahu. The Hawaiian Historical Society, established in 1892 to preserve historical materials and publish scholarly work on Hawaiian history, has its library at Hawaiian Mission Houses Historic Site and Archives, with collections of the Hawaiian Mission Children's Society and Hawaiian Evangelical Association Archives. Their major focus is on the missionaries, who created a written language version of Hawaiian that was used to translate the Bible and other books. By the mid-to-late 1800s, Hawaiians had become one of the most literate people on earth. The Hawaiian Historical Society has published papers and books since 1892 and its *Hawaiian Journal of History* has been a preeminent source of local history since 1967. The oldest museum in Hawai'i, Bernice Pauahi Bishop Museum, founded in

1889, has the largest collection of Polynesian artifacts, manuscripts, ethnographic notes and personal papers, Hawaiian language newspapers, historical photographs (over one million images from 1840s to present), audiotapes, oral histories, art, genealogies, documents, maps, and over 700 titles of moving images; summarized in *Hawai'i Looking Back: An Illustrated History of the Islands* (2000) by Glen Grant, Bennett Hymer, and Bishop Museum Archives. In 2009, Bishop Museum completed a significant restoration of its Hawaiian Hall to showcase and interpret this collection, with artifact and digital displays providing a powerful introduction to local history. The Hawai'i Museums Association, founded in 1968, provides professional development for its statewide member museums, historical societies, and archives. The University of Hawai'i has impressive Hawaiian Studies departments at all of its campuses and a Hawaiian and Pacific Collection of archival materials housed at Hamilton Library. The Hawai'i State Archives, established by statute in 1905, collects government records from the monarchy through contemporary legislative sessions.

Particular resources of local history can be found on other Hawaiian Islands, mostly associated with missionary history and labor history related to Hawai'i's nineteenth- and early-twentieth-century sugar and pineapple plantations. On the island of Hawai'i, Lyman Museum and Mission House, originally a station for New England missionaries who ran the Hilo Boarding School there, became a museum

and archives in 1931; the Kona Historical Society, founded in 1976, preserves two historical sites as community educational resources: the nineteenth-century Greenwell Store and twentieth-century Uchida Coffee Farm, with archived collections on ranching and coffee growing. On Maui, the Maui Historical Society was founded in 1951 at Bailey House Museum, built in 1833 as part of a school for Hawaiian girls, and operates an Archive Resource Center. On Kaua'i, the Kaua'i Historical Society was founded in 1914; Kaua'i Museum in 1960; and Grove Farm Homestead in 1978, preserving records of the sugar plantations from 1864–1878. On Moloka'i, Moloka'i Museum and Cultural Center was founded in 1980, in association with the R. W. Meyer Sugar Mill historic site; and Kalaupapa National Historical Park, founded in 1980, has collections related to the Kalaupapa Hansen's Disease (formerly called leprosy) Settlement. On Lana'i, the Lana'i Culture and Heritage Center was founded in 2007 to house local artifacts and archival collections.

An important part of Hawai'i local history comes from the collection, transcription, and public presentation of oral histories. The Center for Oral History at the University of Hawai'i houses thousands of *oral histories, prints a newsletter with select transcribed oral histories edited into narrative form, and published *Hanahana: An Oral History Anthology of Hawai'i's Working People* (1984) and *Talking Hawai'i's Story: Oral Histories of an Island People* (2009), both edited by Warren S. Nishimoto, Michi Kodama-Nishimoto, and Cynthia

Oshiro. The Center for Biographical Research combines life stories and oral histories into context-rich publications and documentaries, including *Biography Hawai'i*, a film series featuring significant figures at turning points in local history, such as nineteenth-century political gadfly Joseph Nāwahī and Kumu Hula Maiki Aiu Lake, who redefined traditional protocols for passing down hula's teaching lineage to fit the modern world. *Nā Kua'āina: Living Hawaiian Culture* (2007) by Davianna Pomaika'i McGregor uses oral histories to look at local Hawaiian communities that have managed to maintain some traditional cultural practices due to their relative isolation. For life stories of women in Hawai'i, from a wide variety of backgrounds and time periods, see *Notable Women of Hawaii* (1984) edited by Barbara Bennett Peterson and *Women's Voices in Hawaii* (1991) by Joyce Chapman Lebra. A number of community histories reflect place-based local histories; two good examples are *Mō'ili'ili: The Life of a Community* (2005) edited by Laura Ruby and *Kailua: In the Wisps of the Malanai Breeze* (2009) published by the Kailua Historical Society. A more controversial story can be seen *in Ē Luku Wale Ē* (2015) by Mark Hamasaki and Kapulani Landgraf, a pictorial history of the decades-long construction of H-3 Freeway in Hālawa valley and associated activism/protest, a story oft-repeated when core community or cultural values confront particular development and public transportation projects.

Certainly World War II was a major turning point in local history; Hawai'i served as the American home front for the War in the Pacific against Japan. Major exhibitions, archival collections, historic sites, oral histories, and K–12 educational resources can be found at the World War II Valor in the Pacific National Monument at Pearl Harbor, including those associated with the USS *Arizona* Memorial Museum (founded in 1980), USS *Bowfin* Submarine Museum and Park (1978), Battleship *Missouri* Memorial (1998), and Pacific Aviation Museum (2006). Local history during this period can be found in *The First Strange Place: The Alchemy of Race and Sex in World War II Hawaii* (1992) by Beth Bailey and David Farber, *Hawaii Goes to War: Life in Hawaii From Pearl Harbor to Peace* (1980) by DeSoto Brown, and in the documentary *First Battle: The Battle for Equality in Wartime Hawai'i* (2006) by Tom Coffman. The period leading up to this can be seen in *Local Story: The Massie-Kahahawai Case and the Culture of History* (2014) by John P. Rosa, a story also told by David E. Stannard in *Honor Killing: How the Infamous Massie Affair Transformed Hawai'i* (2005).

A Hawaiian cultural renaissance took place in the 1960s and 1970s, discussed in *Hawaiki Rising: Hōkūle'a, Nainoa Thompson, and the Hawaiian Renaissance* (2015) by Sam Low. This movement is sometimes called the Second Hawaiian Renaissance, since King David Kalakaua in 1887 had tried so hard to restore traditional Hawaiian practices of hula, chants, sports, and royal rituals, albeit limited by the "bayonet constitution." Hawaiian local history was greatly affected by the 1978 Constitutional Convention, providing that Hawaiian history, culture, and language be taught in public schools and establishing Hawaiian and English as official state languages, an interesting parallel to a decision in 1859 that English serve as a second official language to Hawaiian for the Hawaiian Kingdom. 'Aha Pūnana Leo in 1983 used the Māori *language-nest* model to create Hawaiian language-immersion charter schools. Educational history between the monarchy period and Hawaiian Renaissance was much less inclusive, with English-only schools aimed at discrediting Asian immigrant languages, Hawaiian, and local pidgin in K–12 classrooms; see *Americanization, Acculturation, and Ethnic Identity* (1994) by Eileen Tamura.

The local history of Hawai'i is complex, with continuities alongside competing stories and resistance. The telling of this local history moves from precontact through the Hawaiian monarchy, republic, territory, and state of Hawai'i, the stories of which are as diverse as they are incomplete—Mai pa'a i ka leo ("do not hold back the voice").

ROBERT G. BUSS
HAWAI'I COUNCIL FOR THE HUMANITIES

See United States, local history in.

health care, as local history topic. The subject of health care has become increasingly complicated in the past two centuries. Early Americans believed in simple theories of diseases and their treatments, casual methods of educating physicians, and simple solutions to the problems of health care financing and delivery. However, the end of the nineteenth century experienced an explosion of knowledge about microbes and how they affect the human body, which brought about a multifaceted revolution in medical science that has mushroomed into the complex systems of today.

In the early years, physicians attributed disease to one of two causes. The first, an imbalance of fluids in the body, led to the heroic remedies of bleeding and purging. The second, the miasmic theory, held that contagion originated in the noxious odors from stagnant pools and untreated sewage spread disease in crowded urban centers.

Until Elizabeth Blackwell earned the first medical degree awarded a woman in 1849, the profession was exclusively male. A man could assume the title of "doctor" by merely attending a two-year series of lectures at one of the medical colleges associated with Eastern universities. Or he could call himself "doctor" by taking a few courses at a local school of medicine and apprenticing to a local physician for a few years. Many of the schools of medicine were located in small but growing communities; their durations were short, and they sometimes were transient. Records of these establishments are rare, but the schools' existence can be established by searching announcements in local newspapers or listings in *city directories.

In the late 1800s, the germ theory of disease gained adherents and surgical methods improved. Other theories proliferated, for example, magnetic, electric, and clairvoyant doctors can be found among names of local physicians. Originally, medical training distinguished between two specialties: medicine and surgery, the former being the most prestigious because of its greater rate of success. As knowledge about the human body grew and as technology became more sophisticated, however, curricula in colleges of medicine became more involved and lengthy. Medical libraries at universities with schools of medicine often have excellent archival collections that trace the evolution of an institution's medical curricula.

The belief that miasmas caused disease led to public health ordinances requiring individuals and businesses to clean up their properties, particularly during epidemics. Minutes of local government bodies show increasing attempts to control the spread of disease by regulating the environment. In the early twentieth century, municipalities appointed city health officers, monitored drinking water sources, and established milk stations that distributed uncontaminated milk for infants. Later, visiting, district, and industrial nurses educated citizens; free clinics examined children in schools; immunization clinics became routine. Newspaper articles document these public health advancements.

The public's growing awareness of a community's health during the last half of the nineteenth century enhanced medical practitioners' prestige. From mid-century on, professional societies, formed to influence health care legislation at both the state and community levels, gave physicians prominence and power. Academies of medicine, designed to isolate the profession from pretenders—quacks and patent medicine purveyors—established libraries and scheduled lecture series to keep local physicians abreast of new discoveries and to share observations with one another. Publication of the highly critical Flexner Report in 1910 eventually led to a standardization of medical practice.

Toward the end of the Great Depression in the late 1930s, medical associations identified increasing government intervention as a new threat to their autonomy. Thereafter, malpractice insurance, hospital and medical school policies, and an educated public further eroded physicians' unquestioned authority. Medical societies and academies of medicine in midsized to large cities have preserved many of the documents that help tell this story.

As settlements turned into villages and towns and the number of physicians increased, the rich and the upper middle class could afford the services of private practitioners in their own homes. The impoverished sick and the working poor, on the other hand, were a serious problem in the close environments of industrial cities. Benevolent societies, overseers of the poor, city officials, pest houses, and almshouse infirmaries were early attempts to isolate the sick poor. The third quarter of the nineteenth century saw a shift in attitudes toward hospitals, which had originally been established for the destitute. Physicians recognized that their private patients might also benefit from a hospital stay. Accordingly, hospitals added luxurious private rooms to accommodate the wealthy. Gradually, clinics and dispensaries allowed the working class to receive treatment. The establishment of hospital insurance during the Great Depression finally made hospital stays possible for every economic level in a community.

Hospitals in large cities, established by physicians and local businessmen, became demonstration laboratories, giving students clinical experience. Immigration and westward expansion prompted religious groups and charitable organizations to create hospitals in newly formed communities. Church collections, benevolent subscriptions, public festivals, and community contributions supported hospitals, activities well documented in local newspapers. Records, photographs, and relics, collected and preserved for institutional anniversaries, are frequently available to researchers. Much of this information may be available on the Internet as well.

As the twentieth century progressed and communities became more dependent on hospitals for health care, individual physicians established small private hospitals in outlying towns. From the mid-twentieth century on, federal aid for local health care, particularly from the Commonwealth Fund and the Hill-Burton Act, encouraged small communities to build, equip, and staff their own hospitals. Newspaper accounts document these movements. Records for private hospitals are rare. Community hospitals, on the other hand, have been required to keep good records. Hospital public relations personnel may have a sense of where to find information, but lack of time and human resources makes historical research in such institutions difficult.

Training for nurses was formalized after the Civil War when the earliest hospitals established schools of nursing. As an understanding of the causes of disease grew, training for nurses became more complex. At first, hospitals relied on student nurses' services.

Two-year programs expanded to three years as the twentieth century opened. Early in the twentieth century, hospital-trained nurses succeeded in professionalizing the field, thereby excluding women who had gained their nursing skills at the bedsides of family members and neighbors. An increasingly complex curriculum gradually shifted hospital nursing chores from the students to graduate nurses. Nursing shortages, notably during the world wars, contributed to the training of adjunct nursing personnel: practical nurses, nurses' aides, nurse cadets, and others. During the second half of the twentieth century, increased specialization and technological advances led to four-year, registered nursing programs at community colleges and baccalaureate degrees in nursing awarded by four-year colleges and universities.

Hospital-based schools of nursing closed during the last half of the twentieth century. No longer did nurses identify themselves with a particular school by wearing a distinctive uniform and cap. Nurses' alumni associations and military organizations have proudly preserved their documents and material culture.

A recent development in local health care has been the establishment of urgent care sites where minor medical emergencies are treated, and immediate diagnoses of more serious health crises are given. These facilities have reduced some of the frustration faced by both staffs and patients in the overcrowded emergency departments of major hospitals.

During its first two centuries, hospital care has evolved from a benevolent model to a business model, and health insurance has become a dominant factor in Americans' health care. See Paul Starr, *The Social Transformation of American Medicine* (1982); Susan Reverby, *Ordered to Care* (1987); Susan Malkan, *Daring to Care* (2007).

TERESA LEHR
COLLEGE AT BROCKPORT,
SUNY, RETIRED

See nurses, Civil War.

herbal. A book with descriptions of plants, giving their medicinal uses. The first herbals were written in ancient Greece around the fourth century B.C. Because the reader needed to correctly identify the plants in order to use them medicinally, most herbals were illustrated. The credit for the first herbal of indigenous drugs designed for the former British North American colonies goes to Samuel Stearns, a colonial physician. His landmark work entitled, simply, *The American Herbal* was published in Walpole, New Hampshire, in 1801 and focused on the organic and inorganic materia medica indigenous to both North and South America.

heritage. Heritage is an elusive and frequently misunderstood word concept that has meant diverse things to different people in varied times and places. Although it came into very common usage during the last quarter of the twentieth century (excessively invoked at times, often to the point of cliché), it had assorted predecessors, such as the word "patrimony," which has cognates in all cultures where romance languages

are used, such as *patrimoine* in French and *patrimonio* in Portuguese.

At the end of the nineteenth century and early in the twentieth, when colonialism reached its peak, many observers in Europe and the United States assumed that some of the world's people (such as themselves) had a history, whereas others in less "developed" societies had seemingly timeless cultures that existed beyond the boundaries of history. Nevertheless, both types of societies had "heritages" even though that particular word was not yet widely used. The concept itself, however, certainly was. But heritage is not a broader or a more inclusive notion than history or culture. Rather, it is a different kind of concept, more value laden, that can selectively draw upon or cut across the other two.

In recent decades, as heritage has been increasingly invoked for purposes of commercial promotion and cultural *tourism, many professional scholars have felt that the word concept has been degraded, particularly when used casually, confusingly, or interchangeably with history. Hence, David Lowenthal (a historical geographer) wrote the following in 1996: "Heritage is not a testable or even a reasonably plausible account of some past, but a declaration of faith in that past. Critics castigate heritage as a travesty of history. But heritage is not history, even when it mimics history. It uses historical traces and tells historical tales, but these tales and traces are stitched into fables that are open neither to critical analysis nor to comparative scrutiny." That is a harsh judgment, yet understandable given the many abuses during immediately preceding decades.

Heritage may be appropriately perceived and understood in many contexts: national, regional (e.g., Southern or Yankee heritage), ethnic, racial, and religious (denominational, sectarian, or even a particular parish with a strong sense of tradition and identity). It is also suitably used in connection with ceremonies and rituals, cuisine, *folklore, festivals, and distinctive styles of dress. There are, of course, numerous combinations of these categories and subcategories that are described and understood as heritage, such as the blues and jazz being vital in the African American heritage.

It should be acknowledged, however, that heritage is invoked intensively in a positive, even celebratory manner. It is applied to those aspects of life that people affirm and wish to remember—quite often uncritically. Groups are entitled to take pride in their heritage, but not in the ersatz versions that have been invented for commercial purposes or to validate a sense of superior identity. Above all, people should not blithely assume that pride in heritage is the same thing as historical information and understanding. Ideally, an enthusiastic interest in the former may stimulate an increased desire and appetite for the latter.

It also needs to be recognized that important institutions and organizations exist whose legitimate purpose is to preserve historical knowledge and to promote a sense of heritage. Examples include state and local historical societies, the *National Park Service, the *National Trust for Historic Preservation, Historic New England (formerly Society for the Preservation of New England Antiquities), and the Association for the Preservation of Virginia Antiquities.

History and heritage are less like fraternal twins than they are like second cousins: related but not intimately so. Ideally, they ought to be collaborative friends rather than conflicted foes, as Lowenthal discerned to be the case so often in the later twentieth century.

See David Lowenthal, *Possessed by the Past: The Heritage Crusade and the Spoils of History* (1996); and Michael Kammen, "History is Our Heritage: The Past in Contemporary American Culture," in Kammen, *In the Past Lane: Historical Perspectives on American Culture* (1997), 213–25.

MICHAEL KAMMEN
AMERICAN HISTORIAN (1936–2013)

heritage tourism. See cultural heritage tourism; tourism.

HeritageQuest Online. HeritageQuest Online is a commercial website from ProQuest that provides a portal to a limited but useful variety of historical resources. It is an amalgamation of an earlier ProQuest genealogy website and HeritageQuest, once an independent provider of genealogical materials for libraries. The contents are particularly useful for genealogists, but local historians can certainly benefit from many of them. From 2015 HeritageQuest Online reproduces the interface design and resources from *Ancestry.com. HeritageQuest provides page image access to thousands of genealogical books and an index to many genealogical periodicals (PERSI). There is also access to Freedman's Bank records, which are helpful in researching *African American families. Another resource is an index to Revolutionary War soldiers. HeritageQuest Online replicates a select group of resources from Ancestry.com and packages them for libraries. Access to HeritageQuest is through a local library, not by individual subscription.

ROBERT KIBBEE
THE HISTORY CENTER IN TOMPKINS
COUNTY (NY)

See genealogical resources online.

historian, a or an. There are two schools of thought concerning the use of "a" or "an" preceding historical, historian, history, and other words that are derived from Greek, which had no letter "h." According to a learned and charming article by Wendell Tripp, entitled "How to Disenvowel a Charging Historian" (*Wisconsin Magazine of History* [Spring 1970]), the h sound that we hear today was represented by a symbol called a *spiritus asper* (s.a.). Thus, the Greek word would have been preceded by "a." The s.a., however, gave way to our modern h; consequently many people use "an" believing it the correct article.

This is something about which people will probably always disagree. For the sake of sanity and unity in this volume, we have elected to follow the Greeks and use "a." So: a historian might wrestle with a historical problem when writing a history of her hometown.

Those wishing to avoid the problem altogether might consider Wendell Tripp's solution, which is to insert an adjective. Thus, he suggests we praise a

good history written by a careful historian who considers a thorny historical problem part of a day's work.

Historic American Buildings Survey (HABS). In an effort to preserve our nation's architectural legacy, in 1934 the *National Park Service (NPS) formed a unique alliance between the public and private sectors through a tripartite agreement with the *Library of Congress (LoC) and the American Institute of Architects (AIA). The Historic American Buildings Survey (HABS) was thus established to create a public archive of measured drawings, historical reports, and large-format black-and-white photographs of important and/or representative examples of our built environment. Under the terms of the agreement, the AIA provides advice and support through the lens of private-sector architectural practice and education, the LoC maintains the collection under state-of-the art conditions and provides public accessibility, and the NPS (HABS) develops guidelines, field tests new technologies and techniques, and produces standard-setting documentation. Since its inception, the program has been motivated by the need to mitigate the effects of rapidly vanishing historic resources upon America's built environment as well as upon its history and culture. While creating a lasting record for future generations, the rich HABS archive of period-specific architectural details also aids in rehabilitation and interpretation.

The significance of the HABS program resides in the broad scope of the collection and its public accessibility, as well as in the establishment of national standards for recording historic architecture. As was stated in the 1933 proposal for the creation of HABS, the collection represents "a complete resume of the builder's art," from the monumental and high style to the vernacular and utilitarian. Priority is also given to endangered structures for which no record would otherwise exist. The HABS records are available to the public copyright-free and online through the Prints and Photographs Division of the Library of Congress. The collection is a resource for architectural historians, restoration architects, preservationists, scholars, and those of all ages interested in American history and architecture. Together with the *Secretary of the Interior's Standards and Guidelines for Architectural and Engineering Documentation*, HABS guidelines establish uniform criteria and methodology for the production of architectural documentation.

The documentation is produced by a combination of HABS staff working with sponsors, by students, and by professionals either in compliance to Section 106 mitigation or through donations to the collection. HABS works in cooperation with groups in both the public and private sectors to help underpin preservation efforts including rehabilitation, community development, advocacy, and historical interpretation. In the 1950s, HABS began the summer program whereby students and young professionals gain practical field experience as part of a summer recording team. Student participation is also encouraged through the Charles E. Peterson Prize, an annual competition for the best set of drawings to HABS standards. Students and architecture professionals

can participate in the annual Leicester B. Holland Prize, which recognizes the best single-sheet measured drawing of a historic site, structure, or landscape prepared to program standards.

For more information about the HABS program, or to access the HABS Guidelines for Drawings, History, or Photography, visit the website at http://www.nps.gov/history/hdp.

The HABS, HAER, and HALS Collection is available through the Library of Congress, Prints and Photographs Division, Madison Building, First Street & Independence Avenue, SE, Washington, D.C.; or at http://www.loc.gov/pictures/collection/hh.

The HABS, HAER, and HALS programs can be followed on Facebook at: http://www.Facebook.com/HeritageDocumentationPrograms.

CATHERINE LAVOIE
NATIONAL PARK SERVICE

See Historic American Engineering Record; Historic American Landscapes Survey; Library of Congress; National Park Service.

The Historic American Engineering Record (HAER). The *National Park Service (NPS), the American Society of Civil Engineers (ASCE), and the *Library of Congress (LOC) established the Historic American Engineering Record (HAER) in 1969 to create a permanent documentary record of the nation's engineering and industrial legacy. The agreement was later ratified by four other engineering societies: the American Society of Mechanical Engineers, the Institute of Electrical and Electronic Engineers, the American

Institute of Chemical Engineers, and the American Institute of Mining, Metallurgical, and Petroleum Engineers. The NPS administers the HAER program with funds appropriated by Congress and supplemented by donations from outside sources. The NPS sets qualitative standards and organizes and staffs recording projects. The Library of Congress curates the records, makes them available free of charge for study both at the library and on its Prints and Photographs website, and provides reproductions to the public via downloadable files. The engineering societies offer professional counsel through their History and Heritage Committees and national memberships.

Since its inception HAER documentation has followed the basic format of *Historic American Buildings Survey (HABS) documentation, the program after which it was modeled, with one important difference: HAER often documents process, such as how machinery worked, bridge components fit together, or a plant functioned to produce a good or service. The formal documentation consists of measured and interpretive drawings, historical reports, and large-format photographs. All HAER documentation, as well as that from companion HABS and *Historic American Landscapes Survey (HALS) programs, shares four characteristics: it explains and/or illustrates the site's significance; is accurate and verifiable; is stored on archival media tested for a 500-year lifespan that is also reproducible; and is clear and concise. Guidelines for meeting these standards, formally the *Secretary of the Interior's Standards for Architectural and Engineering Documen-*

tation, are available online at the HAER website.

Drawings can include plans, elevations, sections, axonometrics, schematics, or interpretive illustrations that depict the evolution of the site. The written report uses fieldwork and primary and secondary sources to develop a physical description of the resource and trace changes over time. In addition, it includes contextual information to convey the significance of the site or structure and an explanation of the process in use. Finally, large-format photographs depict the current condition of the site or structure and the landscape on which it is located.

Not only does HAER documentation provide a comprehensive view of a resource for posterity, but it also serves as baseline documentation for rehabilitation and restoration projects. Documentation is also used as the basis for interpretive materials and to illustrate all types of publications. Not surprisingly, the HABS/HAER/HALS collection is among the most heavily used at the Library of Congress's Division of Prints and Photographs.

HAER documentation comes from a variety of sources. In addition to staff working with sponsors, HAER runs twelve-week summer projects that train students in doing fieldwork, preparing measured drawings, and researching and writing historical reports. HAER documentation is also produced under the provisions of the amended National Historic Preservation Act of 1966, which requires that historic sites or structures threatened with adverse action (demolition or alteration) from federally funded initiatives and listed or eligible for listing in the *National Register of Historic Places be documented to HABS/HAER/HALS standards. The mitigation program is administered by the NPS regional offices. Finally, HAER accepts donations of documentation that meets the program's standards. *Every* historic site that is of national, regional, or local significance has a place in the HABS/HAER/HALS collections at the Library of Congress.

For more information about the HAER program, or to access the HAER Guidelines for Drawings, History, or Photographs, visit the website at http://www.nps.gov/history/hdp.

The HABS, HAER, and HALS Collection is available through the Library of Congress, Prints and Photographs Division, Madison Building, First Street & Independence Avenue, SE, Washington, D.C.; or at http://loc.gov/pictures/collection/hh/.

The HABS, HAER, and HALS programs can be followed on Facebook at: http://www.Facebook.com/HeritageDocumentationPrograms.

RICHARD O'CONNOR
NATIONAL PARK SERVICE

See Historic American Buildings Survey; Historic American Landscapes Survey; Library of Congress; National Park Service; National Register of Historic Places.

The Historic American Landscapes Survey (HALS). In an effort to preserve, protect, and interpret America's significant and threatened historic landscapes, the American Society of Landscape Architects (ASLA), the *National Park Service (NPS) and the *Library of Congress (LOC) cooperated to establish the Historic American Landscapes Survey (HALS) program.

HALS is modeled on two existing historic resource documentation programs: the *Historic American Buildings Survey (HABS) and the *Historic American Engineering Record (HAER). Since its establishment in 1934, HABS has documented over 28,000 structures and made these records publicly available through the Library of Congress. HAER, established in 1969, has recorded over 7,500 engineering and industrial sites to date. Today's growing interest in historic landscape research, planning and stewardship, underscores the value of a similar program devoted to historic landscape documentation.

Recognizing the value of landscape documentation, the National Park Service established HALS as a permanent federal program in October 2000. HALS will build on HABS and HAER documentation traditions, while expanding the range of stories that can be told about human relationships with the land. HALS will document the dynamics of landscapes, as HABS and HAER have documented unique building and engineering structures and systems.

Teams of students and interested professionals in landscape architecture, architecture, planning, horticulture, and related disciplines conduct fieldwork for HALS as short-term projects. Guided by HALS documentation specialists, the participants record significant historic landscapes nationwide through measured and interpretive drawings, large-format photography, written narratives and other documentation techniques. The results not only document significant landscapes, but instill a greater understanding of the relationship between land and history for the participant and the related community. Promoting this critical ethic among future stewards and design professionals mirrors ASLA's own stated purpose: "The advance of knowledge, education, and skill in the art of landscape architecture." Through its existing documentation programs, HABS and HAER have educated thousands of professionals over the past eighty years; the intent is the same for HALS.

For more information about the HALS program, or to access the HALS Guidelines for Drawings, History, or Photographs, visit the website at http://www.nps.gov/history/hdp/.

The HABS, HAER, and HALS Collection is available through the Library of Congress, Prints and Photographs Division, Madison Building, First Street & Independence Avenue, SE, Washington, D.C.; or at http://loc.gov/pictures/collection/hh.

The HABS, HAER, and HALS programs can be followed on Facebook at: http://www.Facebook.com/Heritage DocumentationPrograms.

PAUL DOLINSKY
NATIONAL PARK SERVICE

See Historic American Buildings Survey; Historic American Engineering Record; Library of Congress; National Park Service.

historic monuments. See memorials and monuments.

historic preservation. Historic preservation is concerned with the rec-ognition and protection of historic resources and the planning necessary to accomplish those objectives. Historic preservation includes methods of education and presentation of what has been identified, recorded, and interpreted. Although the term "historic preservation" did not become popular until the mid-twentieth century, the process of conserving historic resources dates much earlier. The earliest effort in the United States was the preservation of George Washington's home, Mount Vernon, in the 1850s.

During the nineteenth century, memorialization was a key theme of historic preservation efforts. Following the Civil War, Americans marked and preserved places important to both sides. They placed markers on graves, monuments on battlefields, and monuments to the women of the home front. They saved trench lines, and shell holes and cannonballs in the walls into which they had been shot. Meanwhile, pioneer struggles were represented in historical monuments and sites preserved in the later nineteenth century. Even as the remaining struggles were carried on to force the Indians onto reservations, historic sites important to *Indian history began to be saved.

The U.S. Centennial brought a surge in interest in preserving the nation's history. In 1873 a committee formed to restore Independence Hall in Philadelphia. The Centennial Exposition in 1876 featured a replica of "An Old-Time New England Farm House" as an ode to the early days of the republic. Other preservation activities of 1876 illustrate the breadth of interest in preservation, for properties as distant and disparate as the Old South Meeting House in Boston and the old mission church of San Luis Obispo, California, were saved then from demolition and ruin.

In the late nineteenth century, states began acquiring historic properties at a rate of about one a year, and the acceleration grew by the early 1900s into a major move of state governments into historic preservation. The first statewide preservation organization was the Association for the Preservation of Virginia Antiquities, created in 1889. In 1895 Allison Owens suggested a landmarks preservation society for New Orleans and Andrew H. Green outlined the idea of a nationwide preservation organization, subsequently developed as the American Scenic and Historic Preservation Society. The 1890s also brought the founding of the Daughters of the American Revolution and the National Society of Colonial Dames of America, eventually taking on hundreds of preservation projects over the next century.

In each of the first four decades of the twentieth century, the rate of acquisition of historic sites by the states doubled, often linked to natural conservation through state park services. The themes represented by state historic sites continued to be those of the grandeur and the hardship of settlement and pioneering westward, the memorialization of Native Americans, of George Washington and the Revolution, of the Civil War, and of battles won and lost, including those of the local and regional governments.

Direct federal involvement in historic preservation was one of the great achievements of preservationists in the twentieth century. The Antiquities Act of 1906 authorized the president to protect archaeological and historical sites on federally owned or federally controlled land—the first time a preservation principle was made national law. Congress followed this by creating the *National Park Service in 1916, the Historic Sites Act of 1935, and chartering the *National Trust for Historic Preservation in 1947.

The development of automobile *tourism in the 1920s and 1930s contributed to the interest in the establishment of state historic sites. Automobile tourism is the force behind state highway marker programs, which in turn became the framework of a limited kind of historic sites survey program. The creation of state and national highways—U.S. Routes 1, 17, 40, 66—led to the study of old roads themselves, and the identification of historic transportation structures, beginning with West Virginia establishing the Wheeling Suspension Bridge as a historic site in 1924.

In 1933, the National Park Service, along with the Library of Congress and the American Institute of Architects, established the *Historic American Buildings Survey (HABS), the country's first federal historic preservation program. One of the less-known, but very important, actions of the Franklin Roosevelt administration was the Historic Sites Act of 1935, which strengthened HABS, created the National Historic Sites Survey to identify National Historic Landmarks, and enlarged the National Park Service involvement in historic parks.

In the second half of the twentieth century, both academic studies and specialized organizations helped preservationists focus on ever-wider aspects of the historical record. In 1964 the National Trust helped broaden the definition of preservation when it acquired the Gothic Revival Lyndhurst at Tarrytown, New York (1837 and later), and Frank Lloyd Wright's 1940 Pope-Leighey House. A few years later, the listing of Wright's masterpiece, Fallingwater, near Ohiopyle, Pennsylvania, as a National Historic Landmark and the acceptance by the National Trust of Philip Johnson's 1949 Glass House at New Canaan, Connecticut, as a historic house museum, further enlarged the scope of concern for "high architecture."

Simultaneously, there was a growing interest in collecting data about more ordinary sites and structures. Preservation groups with an antiquarian bent had begun recording *vernacular data early in the century, an outstanding effort being that of the Society for the Preservation of New England Antiquities (now Historic New England), founded in 1910.

In the two decades after World War II, there was a marked acceleration in the creation of local historic district programs throughout the United States. By the mid-1960s there were dozens of historic districts, located in many regions of the country, with strong local review powers. They were the harbingers of the many hundreds of such districts to come.

Massive building projects, begun as part of the National Interstate and Defense Highway System in 1954, and the Urban Renewal Program of the early 1960s had drastic effects on cities. Resulting destruction of downtown areas, including historic properties, caused alarm throughout the country and brought public awareness to the cause of historic preservation. This led to the passage of the National Historic Preservation Act of 1966.

The National Historic Preservation Act of 1966 radically changed the role of historic preservation in American culture. The act established a State Historic Preservation Office in each state to facilitate historic preservation and support local preservation efforts through grants and technical assistance. The act instructed the Secretary of the Interior to enlarge the National Register of Historic Places to include properties of state and local significance, through programs to be developed with the states and territories; to provide for protection of the listed properties against threats resulting from federal programs; and to provide financial assistance for both "survey and planning" and "acquisition and development" of such properties.

Additionally, the act made *archaeology a cornerstone of preservation by requiring that an archaeologist be on the staff of every state historic preservation officer, and that the survey work to be carried out included identifying archaeological sites. Hundreds of thousands of archaeological sites were recorded in the 1960s through the 1990s and archaeologists made a major contribution to all preservationists in teaching methods of "thinking anthropologically" about historic sites and patterns of use, methods that fit well with "the *new social history."

The National Historic Preservation Act of 1966 was one of several dramatically important congressional acts of the period 1966–1975, of which the other most important were perhaps the 1966 Department of Transportation (DOT) Act, which included an absolute prohibition ("section 4f") of any DOT funding of a transportation project that required the taking of historic sites or structures; and the National Environmental Policy Act (NEPA) of 1969, which established a series of levels of review of federal projects for their potential effects on the environment. In 1973 the president proclaimed the first observance of National Historic Preservation Week, an observance celebrated every year since then.

Importantly, the tax-benefit programs after 1976 greatly increased private investment in the rehabilitation of old office buildings, factories, and other commercial properties. Other developments of the 1980s and 1990s included understanding the "cultural landscape," and included folklife elements in the sites and structures around which they occurred, something called "cultural conservation."

Thus, in the twenty-first century, all the multitude of activities of historic preservation continue, important enrichments of the identification, preservation, protection, interpretation, celebration, and enhancement of local history. Simply put, the most important characteristic in historic preservation— as in local history—is its continued growth in intellectual vitality.

For further reading, see Robert E. Stipe, ed., *A Richer Heritage: Historic Preservation in the Twenty-First Century* (2003); Thomas F. King, *Federal Planning and Historic Places: The Section 106 Process* (2000); Norman Tyler, *Historic Preservation: An Introduction to its History, Principles, and Practice* (1999); William Murtagh, *Keeping Time: The History and Theory of Preservation in America*, 3rd ed. (2006); *The National Parks and Cultural Conservation* (1987); Charles B. Hosmer Jr., *Preservation Comes of Age: From Williamsburg to the National Trust, 1926–1949* (1981); Philip D. Spiess II, "A Chronology of Significant Preservation Events in the United States, 1966–1978" (offset, 1979); Charles B. Hosmer Jr., "Introduction," in *Material Culture and the Study of American Life*, ed. Ian M. G. Quimby (1978); *A Guide to State Historic Preservation Programs* (1976); Charles E. Peterson, "Historic Preservation U.S.A.: Some Significant Dates," *Magazine Antiques*, February 1966; and Charles B. Hosmer Jr., *Presence of the Past: A History of the Preservation Movement in the United States Before Williamsburg* (1965).

See Historic American Buildings Survey; Historic American Engineering Record; Historic American Landscapes Survey; historical markers; National Trust for Historic Preservation; Virginia, local history in.

historic resorts. See resorts, historic.

historical editing. See documentary editing.

historical fiction. Not all historians are enthusiastic about historical fiction. Some absolutely disdain it while the others embrace it as interesting, as an alternative way of expanding the audience for history, and as a means of telling historical truths that cannot necessarily be documented in the sources.

historical fiction

There have been times when historical fiction was our most popular literary form. George Dekker writes in *The American Historical Romance* (1987), that "nothing has sold as well as historical fiction." He points to Sir Walter Scott and his Waverley books (c. 1814) as the origin of the historical romance in which the novel develops a historical consciousness by "multiplying the variety of natural and social forces that impinged on its characters' behavior." Dekker claims too, that the development of the historical novel forced professional historians to rethink their research methods and extend the "range of interests and motives surveyed in their accounts of historical causation." Historians might not all agree, although it would be hard to ignore the popularity some historical fiction has with the public.

Ernest E. Leisy, who studied and categorized historical fiction, points out that there have been three periods when Americans have turned to this genre. The first was the era following 1813 when the nation was creating its own identity. In *The Spy* (1821) James F. Cooper followed the pattern established by Scott in his portrayal of a family divided by partisan interests during the American Revolutionary War.

The second period came at the end of the nineteenth and the beginning of the twentieth centuries, coinciding with the appearance of the local color and regional novels. His third phase includes the decades between the 1930s and 1950s, with Margaret Mitchell's *Gone with the Wind* the star attraction. Dekker cites that book as the most famous and best-selling twentieth-century American historical romance;

he judged Edith Wharton's *The Age of Innocence* and William Faulkner's *Absalom, Absalom!* "the greatest" of all time.

Leisy defends historical fiction as being more than escapist literature, because it "satisfied the need of the human mind for a story." He saw it full of suspense and drama, broadening the reader by presenting people more fully than the historian could do. He wrote that historical fiction "attracts us to the past" as it satisfied the reader with "color, pageantry, and the love of excitement." More importantly, he believed that historical fiction led to a belief in "national homogeneity."

Historical fiction has attracted writers of various abilities and entertained readers with authentic detail. Consider the enthusiastic reaction to Charles Frasier's *Cold Mountain* (1997), which was full of the author's precise knowledge and often arcane and interesting vocabulary.

Historical fiction has also taken a prominent place in our schools. This might be seen as a good thing because these books for children are interesting and generally well written; they are full of small and telling details and their attractive illustrations add to a child's understanding of a different era or time. These books might also be viewed as a failure on the part of historians to produce books and pamphlets that are useful to classroom teachers.

In 1991, recognizing that many novelists have profoundly deepened our understanding of the past, the Society of American Historians (SAH) created a biannual prize named the James Fenimore Cooper Prize for Historical Fiction. The winners to date have been:

The novelist John Hersey observed that "the superior novel of contemporary events will in time come to be regarded as a historical novel." See George Dekker, *The American Historical Romance* (1987); A. T. Dickinson Jr., *American Historical Fiction,* 2nd ed. (1963), which contains an annotated bibliography of books from colonial to contemporary times; Robert A. Lively, *Fiction Fights the Civil War* (1957); and Ernest E. Leisy, *The American Historical Novel* (1950). There are also a number of websites devoted to best sellers and historical fiction over time.

CAROL KAMMEN
TOMKINS COUNTY (NY) HISTORIAN

historical markers. Historical markers have been a staple on the American landscape since the late nineteenth and early twentieth centuries when historical organizations and patriotic societies installed metal plaques on buildings and geological landmarks. These organizations were founded, for the most part, by white, middle- or upper- class men and women who had become increasingly alarmed by the mass immigration and working-class activism of the late nineteenth century. They were the same people who had sought to preserve "American values" by forming such organizations as the Association for the Preservation of Virginia Antiquities and the Society for the Preservation of New England Antiquities. Not surprisingly, their markers commemorated early settlers, political or military leaders, or the Indians whom their ancestors had driven from their lands.

State and local governments eventually became involved with historical marking, too, though often to the same ends as—and even in partnership with—their patrician counterparts. The Pennsylvania Historical Commission, for example, worked with historical groups to install bronze plaques commemorating such traditional topics as the Sullivan Campaign against the Iroquois (1779), and the New York State Education Department launched a program to celebrate the Sesquicentennial of the American Revolution. Increasingly, states began casting double-faced metal signs installed on poles, and as momentum grew, Virginia took things to a new level by publishing *Key to Inscriptions on Virginia Highway Historical Markers* (1929). North Carolina, West Virginia, and other Southern states expanded their programs, too (often with a particular focus on Civil War topics).

States continued to expand their historical marker programs in the 1930s, as Texas alone installed over 1,000 markers commemorating the Texas

Revolution. Predictably, marker installations slowed during World War II. New York even turned over marker responsibilities to local authorities in 1939. After the war, however, state-sponsored programs entered into what were arguably their golden years, thanks to the love Americans had for their automobiles and the roads they built to accommodate them. States sensed that they could promote tourism by, in effect, using historical markers to transform their highways (and eventually city streets) into outdoor museums. S. K. Stevens recognized a strategic opportunity to build political support for the newly authorized Pennsylvania Historical and Museum Commission by partnering with local historical groups and installing more than 1,000 new markers during the late 1940s and early 1950s. Georgia, which had placed a few WPA-sponsored markers in the 1930s, expanded its historical marker efforts with the authorization of the Georgia Historical Commission in 1951. Other states and provinces created new programs: Tennessee in 1950, for example, Michigan in 1955, and Ontario in 1956. Still, markers continued to commemorate traditional history—with some occasional Cold War flair. The three most popular topics for marker commemoration in Ontario were community founding, churches, and politicians.

Beginning in the 1960s, however, marker programs began to change, in part as a result of the Historic Preservation Act of 1966. Some states, Michigan and New Mexico, for example, turned over responsibilities for their programs to newly created state historic preservation offices. Marker designations promoted historic preservation activities but were rarely accompanied by the legal protections of the separately administered *National Register of Historic Places (which installed its own plaques). As a result of the growing professionalization of state historical agencies, meanwhile, markers in many places reflected scholarly trends and commemorated newer kinds of history (generally with better written, more coherent texts). By the opening decade of the new century, Ohio markers recognized such topics as "The Fight for an Eight Hour Day" and "The Ohio AFL-CIO"; Pennsylvania historians worked with Philadelphia's African American community to install sixty-six new black history markers; Indiana, Vermont, and numerous other states dedicated more and more women's history markers; and Alabama unveiled a unique 1993 marker honoring Civil Rights activist Rosa Parks on one side and country singer Hank Williams on the other.

To be sure, historical markers tell us as much about the people who install them as they do the history they actually commemorate. In this sense, markers permanently document the public's changing understanding of the past—and, as artifacts, they become as historic as they are historical. As James Loewen has famously shown, markers even demonstrate the age-old ways in which people have manipulated public opinion for inappropriate political or commercial purposes (*Lies Across America: What Our Historic Sites Get Wrong*, 1999). Given the fact that so many people truly do value the markers in their neighborhoods or the ones they pass on their roads, however, it would be a mistake to overstate the case for a conspiracy of some kind, just as it would be unfortunate to declare historical markers an obsolete holdover from a hopelessly distant past.

No one should ever overlook the really useful purposes that a marker can serve. Simply stated, historical markers are educational resources that supply large, diverse audiences with important information. A good historical marker can in fact change the way in which people understand their environment. A marker can turn a building in a rundown neighborhood from a liability into an asset when people come to understand that a famous artist or writer once lived there, for example, just as a marker can make a recently built shopping center more than yet another commercial development when people realize that the land it occupies was once an airfield from which Amelia Earhart flew. Granted, markers merely note that someone significant was associated with a specific place; or that some important event happened there; or that some nearby building or site holds some historical value. That's why an individual marker's obvious shortcoming is that it may not communicate a good sense of historical context. This presents today's historians with a challenge—but hardly an insurmountable one. For example, it is now very possible to build websites (such as www.explorepahistory.com) that group markers into stories to fully interpret a state's ethnic and immigration history or its industrial heritage. Even without cutting-edge technology, historical groups can build public programs around marker dedications.

Or educators can use markers to create lesson plans or programs that take students out of their classrooms and into the streets. All it takes is a little imagination and some determination.

ROBERT WEIBLE
NEW YORK STATE HISTORIAN, RETIRED

historical societies. See local historical societies and core purpose.

historical thinking. *Historical thinking* is a term that describes a set of skills that historians use to study evidence from the past and to make sense of that evidence, drawing conclusions and shaping our understanding of history. But anyone, whether or not she or he is a historian, will understand the past better if they learn a little about historical thinking. Plus historical thinking skills can be applied to many aspects of daily life and help people make more informed decisions.

Five key elements of historical thinking are:

1. *Multiple perspectives.* There are always several ways to look at a story. Is one more valid or accurate than another?
2. *Analysis of primary sources.* Think critically about their validity. Is one source more valid than others because of when it was written or who wrote it?
3. *Sourcing.* The whys related to a source—consider a source's origins to make sense of it. Is one source more credible than another?
4. *Context.* What else happened at the time to impact the story? Context helps answer "why" questions.

5. *Claim/evidence connection.* Historical arguments are based on evidence. Historians who make a conclusion must base it on evidence that backs up their conclusion.

Sam Wineburg, a professor at Stanford University, writes: "Historical thinking, in its deepest forms, is neither a natural process nor something that springs automatically from psychological development. Its achievement actually goes against the grain of how we ordinarily think, one of the reasons why it is much easier to learn names, dates, and stories than it is to change the basic mental structures we use to grasp the meaning of the past. The odds of achieving mature historical understanding are stacked against us in a world in which Disney and MTV call the shots." (*Historical Thinking and Other Unnatural Acts: Charting the Future of Teaching the Past* [2001], 7.)

Certainly many people can learn to do research, whether *family history, house history, or community history, but professional historians are trained to undertake specific analysis and critical thinking. They ask a lot of questions. They go beyond the who, what, when, and how and ask why. What was the motivation behind an event or decision? What evidence confirms the answer? How solid is that evidence?

In *Who Owns History? Rethinking the Past in a Changing World* (2003), historian Eric Foner compares the basic differences between a historian's understanding of his work and the broader public's. "Historians view the constant search for new perspectives as the lifeblood of historical understanding. Outside the academy, however, the act of reinterpretation is often viewed with suspicion, and 'revisionist' is invoked as a term of abuse." He adds, "History always has been and always will be regularly rewritten, in response to new questions, new information, new methodologies, and new political, social, and cultural imperatives. But the most difficult truth for those outside of professional historians to accept is that there often exists more than one legitimate way of recounting past events."

Rush Limbaugh once said, "History is real simple. You know what history is? It's what happened." Historians know it is not so simple, but complex. History is not often discussed in black/white terms, but in gray. Historians often do not know all of the answers, because the evidence may be incomplete or the sources might not be credible. Historians will often argue over causes of historical events or what might have happened if different actions had shaped the outcome. For example: What caused World War I or the Great Depression? Did President Roosevelt know the Japanese were planning to attack Pearl Harbor? Who fired the first shot at the Battle of Lexington?

What is the role of history organizations when it comes to educating the public about the past? Should they deal in content only or do they have a responsibility to teach historical thinking skills to the degree possible? Most exhibitions and programs highlight the interpretations and conclusions of the research and curatorial staff. If history professionals are frustrated that society in general does not understand that history interpretations change with new evidence and perspectives, a way to solve this is to educate the public in historical thinking. In exhibitions, include a series of panels that give visitors some of the evidence and help them understand how historians analyze it. Incorporate questioning strategies: Why did professional historians draw the conclusions they did? How do we know what we know? What do you think? Encourage them to make comparisons, look at the evidence with a critical eye, and draw their own conclusions to compare with those of historians.

TIM GROVE
NATIONAL AIR AND SPACE MUSEUM,
SMITHSONIAN INSTITUTION

See historicism; local historian as public intellectual.

Historical Records Survey. See WPA Historical Records Survey.

historicism. The term refers to particular beliefs about the nature of history and historiography. It implies that history should be conceived as a professional discipline and conducted as a rigorous science that requires objective research based on primary sources. Historicism rejects value judgments and metaphysical speculations. Instead, it insists that the historian should use rational methods and rigorously examine and evaluate his or her sources. Historicism is primarily identified with a worldview dominant in the nineteenth-century German academic world. For example, while historicism theoretically opens up all spheres of human activity to historical study, in fact, it has tended to focus on Europeans and the political life of nations.

Historicism has come under attack in recent years from a number of sides. Because historians are products of their culture, critics have pointed out that absolute objectivity is impossible. Others have suggested that since history is usually written as a narrative, the historian perforce fills in gaps, guesses at intention, surmises about cause and effect, and generally engages in what scientists call "smoothing the data" in order to form a comprehensible narrative. These critics suggest that history is thus more akin to literature than to science. Still others have argued that language itself is a cultural construct and in fact bears little or no relation to "reality." The New Historicists, including Stephen Greenblatt, while sharing these ideas about language, rejected the notion that the texts forming the basis of history were unconnected to reality. Instead, they argued that these texts were shaped by the same forces that shaped society at large, but cautioned that they therefore had, like works of literature, multiple meanings.

Such attacks question the very notion that history can be written at all. Therefore, contemporary historians have taken account of these criticisms by varying their approaches and using more sophisticated methods. A benefit of this criticism has been to greatly diversify the scope of historical studies—a situation that has favored those engaged in small-scale histories, such as local historians. For a clear overview of the problem, see Georg G. Iggers, *Historiography in the Twentieth Century: From Scientific Objectivity to the Postmodern Challenge* (1997).

NORMA PRENDERGAST
CORNELL UNIVERSITY, RETIRED

See historical thinking.

historiography. Historiography is the accumulation of historical writing and knowledge about a particular subject from previous generations. It is a review of that which has been previously written about a subject. In 1938 Carl Becker and Harry Elmer Barnes agreed on a succinct definition: historiography is the "the study of the history of historical study" (Becker, "What Is Historiography?" in *Detachment and the Writing of History* (1957), 65–78). Donald R. Kelley is the leading modern authority on historiography. See his edited volume, *Versions of History from Antiquity to the Enlightenment* (1991). Historiography often involves revisionism—correcting misperceptions based upon new information or fresh interpretations. At the secondary school level, see James W. Loewen, *Lies My Teacher Told Me: Everything Your American History Textbook Got Wrong* (2007). For revised perspectives in U.S. scholarship, see Eric Foner, ed., *The New American History* (1990).

MICHAEL KAMMEN
AMERICAN HISTORIAN (1936–2013)

History@Work. See public history commons.

History Day. See National History Day.

history museums and identity. History museums used to chronicle events that happened outside the daily experiences of visitors: stories of great men and great ideas from the past. The mode was instructional. Like many institutions that found their footing in the late nineteenth and early twentieth centuries, museums disseminated concepts and encouraged behaviors that reinforced visions of a stable and enduring nation supported by a dedicated citizenry. In the 1960s, museums began to expand the cast of characters that they featured, showcasing ordinary people to tell history "from the bottom up." Interpretive authority, though—the right to decide who and what "counts" as history and what it means—remained firmly in the hands of the professional historians. In the last two decades or so, this model has begun, tentatively, to be recast. History museums are focusing less on presenting a single unified narrative than on creating environments in which visitors can feel resonances between the past and their lives, tell their own stories, and reinforce their sense of community belonging. In this model, history becomes not external to visitors but internal, a personal past. The trend suggests a powerful new role for museums—as sites for facilitating the formation of individual and collective identities.

This shift from unity to multiplicity has transformed history museums. In charting the impact on the field, one can identify two complementary approaches, both of which surfaced around the early 1990s and both of which remain in evidence to this day.

One posited museums as sites for individual exploration of identity. The other, related but distinct, centered on museums as places for reinforcing community identity.

The first approach focused on creating opportunities for museum visitors to make connections between history and their own lives, shaped by individual backgrounds and interests. This approach drove the path-breaking work of the Minnesota Historical Society (MHS) in the early 1990s. Given the opportunity to reinvent its exhibition program with the opening in 1992 of a new History Center building, assistant director for museums Barbara Franco and her staff determined to start with where visitors *are*, not where historians might wish them to be. Instead of the usual chronological survey of the state's history, MHS focused on creating opportunities for visitors to explore their personal pasts—to reflect on their own lives and to connect with family memories.

The philosophy behind this approach was encapsulated by a maxim oft-repeated among MHS staff: visitors should "see themselves" in the exhibition. Such self-recognition might happen directly (a Swedish American learns about her Swedish ancestors) or indirectly (a twenty-first-century mother empathizes with the grief of a nineteenth-century mother who has lost her son). Regardless, through a series of emotional encounters and connections with the past, the museum becomes a site where visitors shape their identities.

This impulse to use history to encourage personal identification with the past continues to drive prominent work in museums. For its exhibition *Teen Chicago* (2005), the Chicago History Museum engaged an advisory council of fifteen teens who conducted oral interviews and helped shape the show's design. Ellis Island famously allows site visitors to search for their ancestors through computerized passenger records. Inspired visitors can memorialize their connection to the site by paying to inscribe their ancestors' names on the "American Immigrant Wall of Honor."

The Lower East Side Tenement Museum in New York City takes a similar "stand in their shoes" approach to encourage empathy, as visitors tour an actual tenement building, home to nearly 7,000 immigrants in the late nineteenth and early twentieth centuries. Exploring period room recreations, visitors learn about the Levine family, whose tiny apartment is serving as garment workshop; the Gumpertzes, whose father has abandoned the family during the Panic of 1873; and the Moores, an Irish family coping with the death of a child. Instead of seeing immigration history as remote and impersonal, the museum encourages visitors to identify with these long-ago residents as workers, parents, and children who faced human concerns not so foreign to our own.

The recent explosion of efforts to invite visitor feedback and contributions to exhibitions is a legacy of the "seeing themselves in the gallery" approach. Increasingly, museum visitors are being encouraged to engage with historical content, make personal connections to it, and then express the meanings they have uncovered. The Oakland Museum's installation *The Story of California*

315

(opened 2010), for instance, offers multiple opportunities for visitors to share their thoughts on the history they encounter. After they learn about the Great Depression, they fill out Post-it notes with suggestions for addressing the country's contemporary economic crisis. On a world map, they can mark their family's country origin. The Levine Museum of the New South is but one institution that has added a video "talk back" booth to its galleries in recent years. The update of its *Cotton Fields to Skyscrapers* exhibition (opened 2011) invites visitors to record personal reactions to the exhibition (to be viewed by subsequent visitors) and, as well, to pose for pictures in front of backdrops representing their favorite exhibit sections.

Such participatory techniques are shaped by the ethos of the web, where everyone can be commentator and curator. As museums today work to translate the appeal of such online activities into their galleries, they are not only capitalizing on current trends but also drawing on over two decades' worth of efforts to make the museum a place for personal exploration and self-understanding.

If "seeing themselves in the gallery" captured one vision for how museums could become venues for exploring identity, another approach was encapsulated by a different catchphrase: "the dialogic museum." Coined in 1989 by John Kuo Wei Tchen, co-founder of the Chinatown History Museum, the phrase signaled a belief that museums should be central to building *community* identity. Although not at odds with the focus on individual explorations—

indeed the two approaches were being advanced concurrently, often by the same adherents—the dialogic museum placed a greater emphasis on collective conversation and shared identities, a decisive turn outward for museums. Tchen urged that museums need to be in conversation with their constituents and to become places where people gather to share insights, explore dilemmas, and build a shared sense of self. In this vision, exhibitions become a "vehicle for dialogue." (Tchen, "Creating a Dialogic Museum," in *The Politics of Public Culture*, ed. Ivan Karp, Christine Mullen Kreamer, and Steven D. Lavine, 1992.)

The most enduring result of Tchen's vision was a rising interest in engaging contemporary communities already self-defined by race, ethnicity, or geography. The notion of a dialogic museum offered professionals a model (and a language) for how they could work with constituents to solidify and express a sense of collective identity. The 1990s and 2000s saw an explosion of museums dedicated to identity-based communities. This proliferation of identity-focused museums suggests that such institutions have filled a real need. For starters, they brought long-overdue public recognition to the history of minority communities. To their backers, these museums literally put these communities on the map, giving them respect and prominence that no number of plaques and proclamations could begin to achieve. More concretely, the process of creating these institutions brought new focus to researching, collecting, and preserving the history of these under-documented groups.

The *New York Times* (December 12, 2004) called the approach at the National Museum of the American Indian (NMAI) "nonhegemonic curating." NMAI's exhibitions discomfited critics by treating past and present as part of one seamless tradition (displaying spearheads and arrowheads from 9000 B.C. together with those from the twentieth century, for example). More than just academic conventions were at stake here, though. Implicitly, these ethnically specific institutions challenged the notion of a single American identity. To establish separate Latino or Arab American or Asian museums suggested that these people's experiences were distinct from those of "mainstream" Americans and from each other. In one sense, even a cursory consideration of historical and contemporary reality makes that claim seem only obvious: different ethnic and racial groups experienced different settlement patterns, carried different cultural traditions (not to mention different languages), faced different legal and economic obstacles, etc. To codify these variations in separate museums, though, implies that these differences preclude melding into a unified culture, a fracturing of the notion of national identity that had held sway earlier in the century.

Even as observers worried that ethnically specific museums fractured identity, they simultaneously criticized them for artificially hardening it. While museums of *American Indian or Latino or *African American history need not suggest a single definition of these identities, they do depend on the notion that there *is* such a thing as Indian or Latino or African American identity

and imply an overarching understanding of these terms and their boundaries. Even as these museums celebrated difference, critics feared, they essentialized it, falling back on generalizations about identity that elided internal diversity, conflict, and change.

In short, in trying to bring institutional and spatial form to the historical experiences of oppressed minorities, the new museums cast identity as both too diffuse and too solid. As the heirs to Tchen's dialogic museum, they picked up on his vision of cultural connectedness, but they failed to actualize his call for cross-cultural dialogue and fluidity. Certainly there are exceptions, both in aspiration and in practice; some ethnically identified museums have worked explicitly to broaden their reach beyond a single group. Perhaps conscious of the criticisms that the NMAI faced, the National Museum of African American History and Culture (not yet open as of this writing) has strived to position itself not as a monocultural island but as a bridge-builder: the museum, says its vision statement, aspires to be "a place where all Americans can learn about the richness and diversity of the African American experience, . . . [a] place that transcends the boundaries of race and culture that divide us, and becomes a lens into a story that unites us all." In a similar vein, the mission statement of the Japanese American National Museum states, "We share the stories of Japanese Americans because we honor our nation's diversity. . . . We strive . . . to provide a voice for Japanese Americans and a forum that enables all people to explore their own heritage and culture."

While some ethnically focused museums have strived to allow room for cultural fluidity in their depictions, other museums in recent years have taken a different approach to the challenge of representing identity: they have turned their focus to the process of identity-formation itself, exploring the interstices where identity blurs and even threatens to dissolve. For instance, the traveling exhibition *Race: Are We So Different?* (opened in 2007, developed by the Science Museum of Minnesota for the American Anthropological Association) begins with the fact that there is no scientific basis for racial distinctions. Such categories, the exhibit explains, "are human-made," "recent invention[s], only a few hundred years old." The exhibition, then, becomes an exploration of the historical and cultural processes by which racial differences have been constructed. The controversial 2010–2011 exhibition *Hide/Seek: Difference and Desire in American Portraiture* at the *National Portrait Gallery likewise explored the contingency of identity. By highlighting the preponderance of themes of sexual difference (particularly about gay life) in modernism, it invited visitors to consider how our conceptions of art and artists shift when we look at their work through different identity lenses.

The Lower East Side Tenement Museum (LESTM) also came to focus on destabilizing categories of identity. Opened in 1992, the museum had set out to use the stories from its tenement building (occupied from the 1860s to the 1930s) to "promote tolerance" in the present day. But as descendants of Eastern European immigrants heard rich tales of their ancestors, some responded by voicing disparaging, even racist viewpoints about more recent immigrants. In response, the LESTM began to work on creating dialogues about difference, inviting visitors to link the stories they had heard on their tenement tour to contemporary issues such as "Who is American?" In these "Kitchen Conversations," people could hear perspectives different from their own and rethink assumptions about others that they had formed at a distance. The visit to the museum became less about personal legacies than about mutual understanding.

Indeed, many museums have come to feel that their job is less to reinforce visitors' identities than to destabilize them. The International Coalition of Sites of Conscience, for instance, facilitates dialogues designed to have participants "recognize and reflect on their own assumptions." At these often fraught sites of tragedy or conflict, facilitators "encourage people to have a dialogue with themselves, to question themselves, as a starting point for having any encounter with others." The process aims to "help people see something different in the familiar" (Tchen and Liz Sevcenko, "'The Dialogic Museum' Revisited" in *Letting Go?: Sharing Historical Authority in a User-Generated World*, ed. Bill Adair, Benjamin Filene, and Laura Koloski [2011]).

Before visitors can come to full understandings of identity, they need to understand how identity-formation works. Here is an opportunity for "general" history museums—those founded to tell the story of a nation, region, state, city, or town—to again find a role for themselves in identity-formation. If identity is not singular but multiple and interdependent, it may be best understood in the moments of encounter that simultaneously define identity and reveal its instability.

One's sense of self depends on others; one's sense of other depends on one's sense of self. As such, the emphasis on the fluidity of identity does not inherently imply a fractured society. Even as recent approaches in museums destabilize identity, they offer a vision of collectivity—a unity based on an ongoing process of self-definition. Museums become sites where publics of diverse outlooks and backgrounds congregate to explore their sense of identity. This is a role for which bricks-and-mortar museums are particularly well suited. The museum serves as a safe place where people can intersect and drift away, converse and ponder in silence, agree and disagree—act, in short, like a disparate, often ungainly but distinctly civic body.

In this unexpected sense, museums circle back and again become sites to enable a collective civic identity. Whereas a century ago that identity was thought to be singular and best shaped by social engineers and experts, today identity-formation is seen as a fluid process continually navigated and negotiated by individuals, communities, and cultures. The idea endures, though, that museums play a role in shaping identity. The museum remains a public space where people can gather, envision a world, and find their place within it, together.

For further reading see John Kuo Wei Tchen, "Creating a Dialogic Museum," in *The Politics of Public Culture*, ed. Ivan Karp, Christine Mullen Kreamer, and Steven D. Lavine (1992); James Clifford, *Routes: Travel and Translation in the Late Twentieth Century* (1997); Robert R. Archibald, *A Place to Remember: Using History to Build Community* (1999); Ellen Hirzy, ed., *Mastering Civic Engagement: A Challenge to Museums* (2002); Robert R. Archibald, *The New Town Square: Museums and Communities in Transition* (2004); Sojin Kim, "All Roads Lead to Boyle Heights," in *Common Ground: The Japanese American National Museum and the Culture of Collaborations*, ed. Akemi Kikumura-Yano, Lane Ryo Hirabayashi, and James A. Hirabayashi (2005); Pam Korza, Barbara Schaffer Bacon, and Andrea Assaf, *Civic Dialogue, Arts & Culture: Findings from Animating Democracy* (2005); Steven Conn, "Heritage vs. History at the National Museum of the American Indian," *Public Historian* 28 (Spring 2006); Daniel J Walkowitz and Lisa Maya Knauer, eds., *Contested Histories in Public Space: Memory, Race, and Nation* (2009); Steven Conn, *Do Museums Still Need Objects?* (2010); Philipp Schorch, "Humanising Contact Zones," in *Narratives of Community: Museums and Ethnicity*, ed. Olivia Guntarik (2010); Liz Sevcenko, "Sites of Conscience: New Approaches to Conflicted Memory," *Museum International* 62 (2010); Daniel T. Rodgers, *Age of Fracture* (2011); John Kuo Wei Tchen and Liz Sevcenko, "'The Dialogic Museum' Revisited," in *Letting Go?: Sharing Historical Authority in a User-Generated World*, ed. Bill Adair, Benjamin Filene, and Laura Koloski (2011); and Benjamin Filene, "Passionate Histories: 'Outsider' History-Makers and What

They Teach Us," *Public Historian* 34 (February 2012).

This essay is drawn from a longer chapter by Benjamin Filene in *The Oxford Handbook of Public History*, ed. Paula Hamilton and James B. Gardner (2017) and used by permission of Oxford University Press.

BENJAMIN FILENE
UNIVERSITY OF NORTH CAROLINA,
GREENSBORO

See building bridges through local history; diversity and inclusion in museums; historical thinking; LGBT history, interpreting radical trust and voice of authority.

History News and Dispatch. On December 27, 1940, eighty-nine men and women representing forty-eight organizations gathered in New York to create the *American Association for State and Local History (AASLH). Included in their number were historical society executives, academic historians, archivists, librarians, and local historians, nearly all of them members of the *American Historical Association's Conference of State and Local Historical Societies. The new association published its first bimonthly newsletter, *State and Local History News*, six months later. The eight-page newsletter shared with its membership news from the field of state and local history along with association business. Interesting to note from those early newsletters is the association's support of and partnerships with the *WPA Historical Records Survey and the *National Park Service. Since that first issue the newsletter has changed its title, its print

style and length, its frequency, and its city of publication several times. Now published from the AASLH permanent headquarters in Nashville, Tennessee, the newsletter known at one time as *History News*, then *History News Dispatch*, is called *Dispatch*. *Dispatch* is published monthly and moved to an electronic newsletter format in 2010. The association's magazine is *History News*. Published quarterly, *History News* also includes a Technical Leaflet. *History News* exists to foster publication, scholarly research, and an open forum for discussion of best practices, applicable theories, and professional experiences pertinent to the field of state and local history. The magazine publishes manuscripts dealing with all aspects of public history including current trends, timely issues, and best practices for professional development and the overall improvement of the history field. The address is History News, AASLH, 1717 Church Street, Nashville, TN 37203; (605) 320-3203; www.aaslh.org.

BOB BEATTY
AMERICAN ASSOCIATION FOR STATE
AND LOCAL HISTORY

History News Network (HNN). Founded in 2001, HHN (www.histo rynewsnetwork.org) is a nonprofit organization whose mission is "to help put current events into historical perspective." Headquartered in Seattle, Washington, HNN promotes the relevance of history through articles and commentaries by professional historians who provide historical context for current events, address and debunk myths, expose those who misrepresent the past, and help the general public in understanding the complexity as well as the relevance of history for contemporary society.

Richard Shenkman is the founder, publisher, and editor-in-chief of History News Network. He is a writer, historian, journalist, and producer as well as the author of several books including the best-selling *Legends, Lies & Cherished Myths of American History* (1988). An advisory board of well-known academic historians, including Joyce Appleby, Walter Nugent, Gil Troy, Liz Cohen, James Banner, Leonard Steinhorn, and Lewis Gould provide editorial direction for HNN.

Shenkman and his co-founders established HNN because they believed that public understanding and opinions of current and past events have been shaped by misinformed media and biased talk show hosts who have failed to address issues in-depth or within a historical context. HNN believes that historians have a responsibility beyond their academically oriented profession to use their expertise to provide the public with valuable and factual insights into contemporary issues and discussions about the past.

HNN maintains a website and distributes a regular electronic newsletter that focuses on commentary on breaking news and historians' writings from all fields of history. The HNN website offers a rich assortment of materials pertaining to history including:

- News about historians and history topics;
- Sections on current events from home and abroad with op eds written by historians;
- Features devoted to special topics;

- A section on "D.C. News," offering insight into current history- and humanities-related policy issues in the nation's capital;
- "Roundup," a compilation of excerpts from mainstream media that address historical controversies, analysis of key historical anniversaries, research findings, and reviews of movies, exhibitions, and documentaries;
- Book reviews written specifically for HNN;
- *Blogs that offer readers the opportunity to exchange ideas with historians; and
- The "Teacher's Lounge," which provides a compilation of resources for history teachers.

History News Network reports that its website receives 300,000 unique visitors and over 7 million hits per month. Its motto is a derivation of a quote from Eugene O'Neil's *Long Day's Journey into Night:* "Because the past is the present, and the future, too."

DAVID G. VANDERSTEL
INDEPENDENT HISTORIAN

See local historian as public intellectual; National Coalition for History; relevance; values of history.

Historypin. Historypin is a user-generated online platform that provides users with digital tools with which they can create projects that foster community engagement, encourage communication and collaboration across generational and cultural lines, and give users a place where they can exchange stories of their local communities. Running a

Historypin

"Historypin project" encourages the sharing of photos, documents, sounds, moving images, stories, descriptive narrative text, and oral histories relating to the history of a local area, which users can curate, digitize, and share to the website. Once content is added to Historypin, or "pinned," any user can add to it and engage with it. To emphasize the importance of the relationship of history to location, content is pinned directly on a map, which allows users to build social connections through a shared sense of place and history. Content can also be added to collections, which are clusters of pinned content centered on a certain theme, topic, or event. Historypin users have used collections as a space to share content that they have curated for their community projects.

We believe that one way the health and progress of communities can be measured is by the strength and inclusiveness of their local social networks. The weakening of social networks, as has happened over many parts of the United States and United Kingdom, can disproportionately affect groups most vulnerable to exclusion, such as seniors and minority ethnic groups. In partnering with cultural heritage institutions, civic organizations, and community groups, Historypin aims to encourage people to build communities based on local history because of its capability to reduce social isolation and provide a way for marginalized individuals to represent themselves within local culture.

Another major goal of our organization that we can help carry out through partnerships is to provide communities all over the world with resources and services for community engagement. In projects that we have contributed to in the past, 70 percent of people met new people and 38 percent became involved in other activities in their communities. We hope that partnering with these groups will aid in the development of projects that make use of local history and archiving as a means to start new conversations and create local connections.

Communities all over the world with an interest in local history have pinned content to Historypin, including approximately 60,000 individuals and community groups as well as 2,500 libraries, archives, and museums and over seventy-five countries. The Queens Library in Queens, New York, for example, created a project that centered on increasing community participation and celebrating the heritage of Queens and the diversity of its neighborhoods. The Queens Library staff, assisted by two City University of New York (CUNY) Service Corps interns, spearheaded this collaborative project by working with local branch libraries to run a series of community events that brought together community groups in their local library to share and capture local stories. At one Hip Hop History event, Queens residents were invited to share their knowledge of hip hop history and culture in South Jamaica. They brought photos, event posters, and stories that were eventually digitized. The event was a great example of how Historypin projects can help to encourage intergenerational conversations; around 40 percent of participants surveyed met someone new from a different generation or culture. *Queens: Neighborhood Stories* resulted in a digital archive of over 800 photos and stories, now viewable on Historypin.

Local community and history organizations are at the core of our user base, and the focus of our projects over the years has increasingly been to develop tools and services that will allow these groups to better run Historypin projects in their local areas. This involves striking the right balance between digital engagement and more traditional methods, and all of our projects have been learning experiences in this sense and have contributed to the overall improvement of the engagement methods we promote.

Our experience working with the Bernal Heights History Group on the Year of the Bay project, for example, a partnership between Historypin and Stanford University's Center for Spatial and Textual Analysis in the Humanities, illustrated how applying digital tools in a very traditional environment could, with a balanced approach, help enable participation and knowledge sharing. One of the aims of Year of the Bay was to provide a platform where "knowledge communities"—local museums, archives, enthusiasts, and community groups—could share expert knowledge with a broader audience. The Bernal Heights History group, a small gathering of mostly older local history enthusiasts who meet once a month to discuss the history of San Francisco's so-named quiet and suburban-like neighborhood, participated in "mystery solving" events with Historypin, where members discussed never-before-seen images of their neighbor-

hood and posited what or where certain archival photos might have been taken. This close-knit history group—representative of many like it around the country—relies on more traditional methods of engagement such as regular in-person meetings and a simple Facebook page. A primarily digitally led engagement approach revealed how digital literacy barriers, as well as a lack of resources and time, will limit participation. However, after multiple iterations, bringing in Historypin as a means to discuss and focus on community stories and mysteries revealed the true value in Historypin as a catalyst for discussing meaningful places, enhancing what this community loved to do on a regular basis. Tapping into this group's expert knowledge also connected them with archival photos from a local library collection, with Historypin as a tool through which to enrich the data associated with these photographs. While these are some of the fun and engaging activities that groups might also use our tools for, the Bernal Heights experience underlined the importance of identifying and understanding your audience before carrying out engagement, a rule we abide by in order to inform the digital tools we create and for whom, and recognizing the value in balancing digital with the more traditional methods of engagement.

We continue to use these past experiences to deepen and expand Historypin activities in local communities in an effort to increase the social connections and well-being of groups that are most affected by and at risk of social isolation and exclusion, while also giving priority to those whose stories are not traditionally valued. To this end, we have developed a model of digital and local community archiving and story-telling, which is slightly altered based on the needs of the organization involved in the partnership. This model, which includes user-centric design and a focus on measuring activities and outcomes, has shown benefits in terms of local connectedness between residents, intergenerational relationships, and community engagement.

We value projects such as those mentioned above, which harness local history to build stronger communities. During the process, history is recorded, new connections are made, and communities become stronger. For further information visit www.historypin.org.

KERRI YOUNG AND KIERRA VERDUN
HISTORYPIN

See digital history; digitization; maps and atlases; social media.

History Relevance Campaign. See relevance; values of history.

history workshops. See England, local history in; local history workshops.

horticulture and local history. Liberty Hyde Bailey, Cornell University, provided the most succinct—and still useful—definition of horticulture in the *Cyclopedia of American Horticulture* (1900): "*hortus* a garden, originally an enclosure; *cultura*, to care for or to cultivate." He then elaborates: "Horticulture is the growing of flowers, fruits and vegetables, and of plants for ornament and fancy." As Bailey notes, there had been little interest in this specialized form of agriculture before the turn of the nineteenth century. By the turn of the twentieth century, however, the efforts of countless nurserymen and landscape designers merited the 2,016-page *Cyclopedia* in four volumes, counting more than 216 contributors under Bailey's and associate editor Wilhelm Miller's guidance.

Early in the nineteenth century, horticulture emerged in the form of garden nurseries, small-scale enterprises with the purpose of supplying local farms and gardens. Iconic among these were the wilderness nurseries, with brush enclosures to keep deer out, established by John Chapman, "Johnny Appleseed," in the 1790s. His peripatetic planting provided apple seedlings for pioneer farms in Ohio and Indiana. Dried apples, apple cider, and apple vinegar were essential to the diet of settlers moving west following the American Revolution. John Means explores Chapman's enterprise as both creative business venture and personal quest in *Johnny Appleseed: The Man, the Myth, The American Society* (2011).

By contrast, Robert Prince, at Flushing on Long Island, New York, established what would become a highly successful commercial nursery in the 1730s. Prince was known both in the colonies and in Britain. Following the Battle of Brooklyn, British General Howe cordoned off the nursery and posted armed guards. The Prince Linnean Botanic Garden would persist until the American Civil War. Among its employees in 1837 was a recent immigrant from Belfast, Ireland, Patrick Barry. He left Prince for Rochester, New York, where in 1840 he met George Ellwanger and joined in partnership with him. Together they created Mount Hope Nurseries, which would earn the sobriquet "the greatest nursery in the world" by the end of the American Civil War. Barry brought with him back wages from Prince in the form of plants and trees that became rootstock for the Rochester enterprise (Ellen and Paul Grebinger, *Pioneers of American Landscape Design*, ed. Charles A. Birnbaum and Robin Karson [2000]).

A narrative of horticultural change in America through means of in-depth case studies, for example, America's first invasive species, the Hessian Fly, is provided in Philip Pauley's *Fruits and Plains* (2007). Here, however, time and change are marked by local events in the life and times of key contributors to the growth of horticultural industries. From the 1820s until the moment in 1869, at Promontory, Utah, when a transcontinental railroad was created in the joining of the Union Pacific and Central Pacific roads, garden nurseries morphed into regionally, even nationally, important nursery enterprises.

Boston became an early center with the formation of the Massachusetts Horticultural Society in 1829. Among its luminaries were Marshall P. Wilder and Charles Hovey. Wilder was an early adopter and disseminator of European pear varieties, and instrumental in facilitating the formation of the American Pomological Society (APS) at mid-century (John H. Sheppard, "Memoir of Marshall P. Wilder," 1867). The APS medal for outstanding contributions in fruit breeding and growing is given in his name. Charles Hovey developed the early commercially viable Hovey Seedling strawberry and created the *Magazine of Horticulture*, which became a national medium for communication among budding horticulturists. In Newburg, New York, a nursery family, in particular brothers Andrew Jackson Downing and Charles Downing, emerged as leading contributors to both American landscape design and to fruit culture. Before his untimely death in the explosion of a Hudson riverboat in 1852 at the age of thirty-seven, A. J. Downing had already published *A Treatise on the Theory and Practice of Landscape Gardening* (1841), regarded at the time as revolutionary and to this day as a foundational work in landscape architecture. His *Fruits and Fruit Trees of America* (1845) was carried forward into the later nineteenth century in revised editions by his brother Charles, recognized as a leading pomologist in his own right. In addition, A. J. Downing established *The Horticulturist and Journal of Rural Art and Rural Taste* as a competitor with Hovey's *Magazine*, and a leading arbiter in matters of rural architecture and garden design. Among its contributing authors was Patrick Barry. As a prolific writer, author of *The Fruit Garden* (1851), and editor of the *Genesee Farmer*, Barry became an obvious choice as editor of the *Horticulturist* after A. J. Downing's tragic death. James Vick, who would become perhaps the most famous seedsman specializing in floriculture in the nineteenth century, had purchased Downing's journal and brought it to Rochester. By the end of the Civil War, Rochester was among the nation's leading nursery centers, owing to its favorable location on the Erie Canal and rail lines, at the leading edge of

America's expansion into the "Great West" as William Cronon characterizes Chicago and beyond in *Nature's Metropolis* (1992).

There were other notable contributors to the growth of horticultural enterprise before the Civil War. At the foundation was John Bartram's Botanical Garden, established on the Schuylkill River at Philadelphia in 1728 and carried forward by his sons. Bartram was an avid collector and disseminator of native American plant species and received seeds of vegetables, fruits, and flowers from his Quaker correspondent, Peter Collinson, in England as noted in U. P. Hedrick, *A History of Horticulture in America to 1860*. His botanic garden and house are on the *National Register of Historic Places. Among nurserymen there were the W. T. & E. Smith Nurseries and T. C. Maxwell & Brothers, who established Geneva, New York, by 1850 as a nursery center that would rival Rochester by the later nineteenth century (Paul Grebinger and Ellen Grebinger, *To Dress and Keep the Earth*, 1993). And among market gardeners there was Peter Henderson, who established himself in Jersey City, New Jersey, supplying produce and flowers for metropolitan New York. His *Gardening for Profit* (1866) and *Practical Floriculture* (1868) became foundation texts in the literature of horticulture. *Gardening for Profit* played a significant role in the post–Civil War expansion of market gardening in the American South (Alfred Henderson in *One Hundred Years of American Commerce*, 1895). However, the geographical center of the United States had shifted west, and with it the story of American horticulture.

In June and July 1870 Marshall P. Wilder, Patrick Barry, George Ellwanger, and Charles Downing traveled via the transcontinental railroad to California for a reconnaissance survey of horticultural progress in the Golden Gated Main. Eureka! Their report, published in four installments (September through December 1870) in *Tilton's Journal*, was the herald of horticultural transformation in America. Gold Rush 1849, statehood 1850, and by the summer of 1870 California was clearly the fruitful garden of the world. Those who were drawn by gold fever often turned their hands to supplying the needs of forty-niners. For example, on their arrival Wilder et al. were greeted by, among others, Colonel James Lloyd La Fayette Warren, president of the Fruit Growers Society. His roots were in Boston where he had been proprietor of Warren's Floral Saloon in 1844. He then removed to California to manage the Sweden Mining Company, but quickly realized that provisioning mining camps was more profitable. Warren turned to raising food crops and is recognized as the "Father of California Agriculture." The Mount Hope Nurseries contributed to the florescence of the original California orchards; they were the first capable of packing seedling trees for the long journey via the Isthmus of Panama. However, what Wilder and his companions saw growing in this western Eden astonished even them: optimum growing conditions; vast acreage under cultivation; fruits of enormous size (cherries three-and-one-half inches in diameter); trees growing twice as fast as any in their experience; exotic varieties of flowers; and vineyards producing enormous quantities of grapes originating in Europe. And, on their return via train there were two specially designed railroad cars carrying ten tons each of pears for eastern markets. These were from the orchards of Charles Reed, whom they had visited in Sacramento, and who was recognized in his obituary of 1896 as a pioneer fruit grower who "shipped the first load of pears east from 'Golden State'" (Paul Grebinger, "Horticulture at the Summit," MS, n.d.).

The population of the United States nearly doubled between 1840 and 1860. The Homestead Act of 1862 provided 160 acres of public land to settlers willing to move west. The Timber Culture Act of 1873 granted 160 acres of land if the settler would plant trees on forty acres for ten years. The flow of population westward led to the expansion of commercial nurseries there and new business opportunities elsewhere, especially following the Panic of 1873. For example, Charles A. Green of Rochester "made the old farm pay" via catalogs and orders through the U.S. Mail (Paul Grebinger, "How We Made the Old Farm Pay," MS, n.d.). The First Horticultural Census of the United States in 1890 recorded 4,500 nurseries.

At the same time the U.S. Congress passed the Morrill Act, or Land Grant College Act of 1862. It provided grants of land to states in order to create colleges of agriculture and the mechanic arts. Now breeding and improving plants and trees would become a matter of science and centered in state-funded universities. Patrick Barry foresaw these changes and became an early advocate for, and served as Chair of the Board of Control at the founding of the New

York State Agricultural Experiment Station in 1880–1881 (P. J. Chapman and E. H. Glass, *The First 100 Years of the New York State Agricultural Experiment Station*, 1991). He understood that systematic experiments in plant breeding were necessary to keep eastern growers competitive with horticulture as it was advancing on the Pacific Coast. It is ironic, therefore, that the last great intuitive plant breeder, Luther Burbank, following his success in breeding and sale of rights to his Burbank Seedling potato, moved from Massachusetts to California in 1875, establishing his gardens and his international reputation at Santa Rosa (Jane E. Smith, *The Garden of Invention*, 2009). Also in 1875, it was obvious to nurserymen that they needed a professional organization, the American Association of Nurserymen, through which to set standards for their industry (Richard P. White, *A Century of Service*, 1975).

By the early twentieth century, early nursery centers were in decline. Mount Hope Nurseries donated land to the City of Rochester, which became Highland Park, the central feature of a Frederick Law Olmstead–designed park system. Other nursery lands became attractive for urban housing, both in Rochester and Geneva. The automobile abetted the suburbanization of America. In response, in the early twentieth century, the American Association of Nurserymen encouraged advertising campaigns such as "a house is not a home, until it is planted" and "the outdoor living room" in order to promote the sale of landscape plants. Scientific plant-breeding efforts intensified, as for example, apples at the New York

Agricultural Experiment Station. New varieties such as Cortland, Empire, and Jonagold replaced heritage apples. In 1901 Samuel D. Willard, a well-known pomologist and fruit grower in Geneva, New York, superintended the New York State horticultural exhibition at the Pan-American Exposition in Buffalo. He was able to display 345 varieties of apples grown in the state. You are not likely to find the three most popular cultivars of that era in the produce section of supermarkets today—Baldwin, Rhode Island Greening, and Northern Spy. More flavorful, firmer textured, sweeter apples with more attractive colors are in demand among consumers. Rose floriculture was a specialty of both the Mount Hope Nurseries and W. T. Smith Geneva Nurseries. By the 1950s rose production, like fruits and vegetables, had moved to more favorable growing environments south and west. Today we get our nursery stock via national distributors, through catalogs, online, and from the garden department in stores such as Lowes and Home Depot. And, just down the road in your hometown is an iteration of the early-nineteenth-century garden nursery, where vegetable, flower, and tree seedlings are available for your home garden.

PAUL GREBINGER
ROCHESTER INSTITUTE OF TECHNOLOGY

See agricultural and mechanical colleges; gardens; gardens and landscapes, researching historic; landscapes.

house museums. Historic house museums range from humble to grand, from those of one specific period to others with the accumulated layers of continued occupancy. They are connected to a single individual or representative of a group of people or significant architecture. They may be furnished or unfurnished. Guided by docents, *volunteers, or professionals, or by self-activated electronic devices or passive text panels, visitors to historic house museums achieve a unique connection to the past.

House museums are the most common type of history museum and are often underfunded and dependent on volunteer staff. Nevertheless, historic house museums can provide spaces for discussing *social history, *economic history, *political history, and *material culture.

From the beginning of the historic house museum as an entity, a pattern emerged. A group of like-minded citizens organized to purchase and preserve a building of particular architectural interest or one associated with a historic event or personality. The first historic house museums were established in the 1850s. These structures were chosen for their association with American heroes and usually dated from the American Revolution and the early national period. The state of New York purchased and preserved the Hasbrouck House in Newburgh, New York, as the site of George Washington's headquarters from April 1782 to August 1783. In 1856, the Mount Vernon Ladies' Association formed to preserve Washington's home on the banks of the Potomac River. Mount Vernon underwent its first restoration beginning in 1859. Also in 1856, the state of Tennessee purchased the Hermitage, home of President Andrew Jackson, hero of the Battle of New Orleans in 1815 and seventh president of the United States. In 1888 the Association for the Preservation of Virginia Antiquities became the first state organization formed to preserve historic structures. The APVA (now Preservation Virginia) has expanded its holdings from Jamestown Island, site of the first permanent English settlement in North America, to six properties reflecting the history of the commonwealth. The Society for the Preservation of New England Antiquities (now Historic New England) was founded in 1910 and today manages thirty-seven properties in New England that document the architectural and social history of that region. The decade of the 1920s witnessed the formation of the Thomas Jefferson Memorial Foundation, which operates Monticello, and the beginning of John D. Rockefeller's partnership with the Reverend W. A. R. Goodwin that resulted in the creation of Colonial Williamsburg.

Historic house museums offer three-dimensional educational spaces where, through multiple layers of interpretation, visitors learn about the occupants, their tastes, and their times. The most successful historic house museums incorporate contemporary scholarship and primary source materials to achieve authenticity of furnishings and accuracy of interpretation. Whereas earlier furnishings more often reflected modern tastes in decoration and focused on the owners, today's historic house museums reflect research using probate inventories, looking at contemporary paintings and prints, and conducting microscopic paint analyses. For house museums that have been open

for several generations, changes can be dramatic and unexpected. When paint analysis at Mount Vernon and Gunston Hall resulted in certain rooms being painted bright green or blue, the colors forced a reevaluation of ideas about taste. Research into contemporary paintings and prints suggested that oriental carpets, which so often graced the floors of historic houses, were, in fact, more indicative of twentieth-century interior design than eighteenth-century taste.

Interpretation in historic house museums generally celebrated individuals, almost always white men, who achieved wealth and status or who made significant contributions to the establishment of the United States. Women, immigrants, Indians, and enslaved Africans rarely appeared in the interpretation. In the last quarter of the twentieth century, however, curators and historians have developed more inclusive interpretations of their historic houses both to present a more representative history and to attract a more diverse audience. The Bicentennial in 1976 combined patriotic interest in American history and a growing awareness of the loss of the historical *built environment to urban renewal. As Americans' greater mobility and discretionary income resulted in increased *tourism and generated revenue for localities, historic house museums advertise their unique attraction more aggressively to visitors through signage on nearby highways, colorful brochures, informative websites, and social media. To attract local audiences on a continuing basis to basically static furnished rooms, staff of historic house museums have developed programs, such as dressing the rooms for summer or decorating the house for Christmas, or used first-person interpretation or other theatrical devices to focus on the people who inhabited the building.

Many historic house museums recently have responded to a growing interest in the lives of underrepresented Americans, such as workers, enslaved people, or immigrants, by expanding or refocusing their interpretation beyond the traditional emphasis on the structure and the material culture displayed. The Wickham House, an 1812 National Historic Landmark now part of the Valentine Museum, Richmond, Virginia, in many ways reflects the changing attitudes toward historic house museums throughout the twentieth century. Founded as the Valentine Museum in 1892, by 1928 the museum had purchased three row houses adjoining the Wickham House and renovated the interiors of those houses for gallery and storage space. The Wickham House then underwent a two-year restoration that resulted in a series of rooms that reflected periods of the decorative arts available to Richmonders from the late 1700s through the 1870s. Although known as the Wickham-Valentine House, for the first and last owners, the history of the house as a residence to four owners was ignored in favor of an interpretation that treated the furnishings as curios. In 1985 the museum staff refocused the interpretation of the house as a neoclassical structure and home to John Wickham, a prominent Richmond attorney, his family, and his slaves. Architectural research resulted in an extensive historic structures report and paint research revealed the extent and complexity of the original wall paintings. The new interpretation emphasized that the Wickham House was home to thirty-one people by 1820, the Wickhams as well as their enslaved workers, and explored how the use of the spaces reflected the division between public and private spaces, work and leisure spaces. Monticello now interprets Thomas Jefferson's home more fully by including information about the enslaved *African Americans who lived and worked on the mountain. Whitney Plantation in Louisiana and McLeod Plantation Historic Site near Charleston, South Carolina, both provide extensive interpretation of American slavery and the lives of the enslaved. And the Royall House and Slave Quarters in Medford, Massachusetts, is a rare example of a site that explores the history of slavery in New England.

Historic house museums may represent significant architectural features that can produce unique interpretive challenges. The Wickham House remained open throughout the restoration and the interpreters were given daily updates on research into the Wickham family and their slaves who inhabited the house. A rare survival of Jacobean architecture is located in Isle of Wight County, Virginia. Although built and owned by several generations of Allens, the house is known as Bacon's Castle for its brief association with Nathaniel Bacon, who in 1676 led a rebellion against Governor Sir William Berkeley. Bacon forced Arthur Allen, son of the house's builder, to flee the house for supporting Berkeley. Interested in the unique architectural elements, the Association for the Preservation of Virginia Antiquities opened Bacon's Castle as a historic house in 1983 and began a research and restoration project that has refurnished the house according to Allen family inventories dating between 1711 and 1755. The docent must tread carefully to make clear to the visitor (1) the history of the Allen family, (2) the architectural significance of the house, (3) why the house is named for Bacon, and (4) why the furnishings reflect the material culture of wealthy Virginians in the early eighteenth century.

Local history and popular culture combine for a particular interpretive challenge in the Molly Brown House, owned by Historic Denver, Inc. Maggie Brown, popularized on stage and in film as the "Unsinkable Molly Brown," purchased the three-story structure in 1894 with her husband J. J. Brown. Although the docents clearly explain that the Browns spent little time in the house, and, in fact, rented it as a single-family dwelling and then as a boarding house, they acknowledge the association of the house with Maggie Brown's successful escape from the sinking White Star liner Titanic. By the end of the tour, visitors are aware that Maggie was never known as Molly and that the house reflects the lifestyle of Denver's upper middle class at the turn of the twentieth century.

Some historic house museums exist as architectural remnants of the *built environment. Both Hampton, owned by the State of South Carolina, and Drayton Hall, owned by the *National Trust for Historic Preservation, are examples of preserved historic houses that remain unfurnished by intent. Built between 1738 and 1742 by John Drayton and occupied continuously by the fam-

ily until 1974, Drayton Hall had neither electricity nor plumbing. Changes to the house over time were minimal and the Trust consciously chose to present the house as a unique architectural survival. Hampton, home to the Rutledge family of South Carolina, was restored by its last owner, the writer Archibald Rutledge, who, at his death, left the house to the state. Rather than attempt to furnish the house, the state of South Carolina determined to open the house as an architectural restoration in progress.

Preservation, restoration, and interpretation of historic houses today draws from a large body of resources and experiences gathered by curators and interpreters. The most successful historic house museums blend contemporary scholarship and primary research disseminated by interpreters trained and encouraged not only in historical research methodologies, but also in public presentation to diverse audiences. The variety of historic house museums offers visitors connections to lifestyles of both extraordinary and ordinary Americans. Whereas earlier houses stressed grandeur and conspicuous consumption, visitors today may see restored homes of workers, immigrants, enslaved people, and Native Americans. Historic house museums document the literary heritage of America, as well as its political, social, and economic history.

See Patricia West, *Domesticating History: The Political Origins of America's House Museums* (1999); William J. Murtagh, *Keeping Time: The History and Theory of Preservation in America* (1997); Sherry Butcher-Younghans,

Historic House Museums: A Practical Handbook for Their Care, Preservation, and Management (1993); Thomas J. Schlereth, *Cultural History & Material Culture: Everyday Life, Landscapes, Museums* (1992); Peggy Coats, "Survey of Historic House Museums," *History News* 45, no. 1 (1990): 26–28; and Laurence Vail Coleman, *Historic House Museums* (1933).

Barbara C. Batson
Library of Virginia

See slavery interpretation at museums and historic sites; museum theater; Virginia, local history in.

house museums in the twenty-first century. "Historic house museums" are often defined as significant houses that are open to the public as museums, but it can include a broader category of places where people lived, such as forts, farms, tenements, camp sites, lighthouses, factories, shops, and villages, and is part of the much larger class of historic sites, such as schools, churches, offices, libraries, cemeteries, and battlefields. Unlike most museums, the building and surrounding landscape are among the most important artifacts in the collections and the interpretation emphasizes placing the collections, people, and events in spatial and temporal context.

Historic house museums were first established in the mid-nineteenth century in the United States but it was not until the late twentieth century that they became prolific. Much of this growth is due to the establishment of the *National Register of Historic Places, the passage of the National Historic Preservation Act of 1966, and the popularity of the Civil War Centennial and the nation's Bicentennial, which prompted increased interest in America's history and efforts to protect its physical legacy.

Historic house museums and historic sites are the most common form of museum in the United States and among the most popular with the American public. The specific number of historic house museums in the United States at the beginning of the twenty-first century is unknown; however, it has been estimated to be 8,000–16,000 (about 1–2 percent of places recognized as historic landmarks on state or national registers) and a 2005 survey by the *American Alliance of Museums showed that historic sites and historic house museums represent about 10 percent of the museums in the United States (which includes aquaria, art galleries, natural history museums, and science centers).

According to the Travel Industry Association in 2015, while business travel has slowed, leisure travel is increasing. Most of these tourists want to learn more about the places they visit and include a cultural or historical activity while traveling, such as touring historic house museums. As a result, historic house museums also play a significant role in *tourism and the hospitality business, often outpacing recreation and sports. Heritage travelers spend more money and stay longer at destinations than the average U.S. traveler. Compared to the average trip in the United States, historical/cultural trips are more likely to be seven nights or longer and include air travel, a rental car, and a hotel stay. Historical/cultural travelers are also more likely to extend their stay to experience history and culture at their destination. In fact, four in ten added extra time to their trip specifically because of a historical/cultural activity.

As small businesses, historic house museums are often major contributors to the local economy as well. They usually hire local skilled labor, provide skills that are easily transferable, and emphasize local spending. Furthermore, historic house museums have little environmental impact and result in nearly no pollution compared to other enterprises. Preservation of historic buildings is a cost-competitive alternative to new construction and is more likely to use local contractors and suppliers and result in higher customer and community satisfaction.

Historic house museums also face an uncertain future in the twenty-first century. The National Endowment for the Arts' decennial survey shows that visitation to historic sites has fallen from 37 percent in 1982 to 24 percent in 2012 (by comparison, 21 percent of Americans visited art museums in 2012). Declining tax revenues prompted most states to reduce or close admission to their historic parks, defer maintenance, and lay off staff, a situation so serious that the *National Trust for Historic Preservation included state parks and state-owned historic sites to its list of 11 Most Endangered Places in 2010 and sites imperiled by state actions in 2011. The Pennsylvania Historical and Museum Commission, which oversees forty historic sites and museums, was forced to cut its budget and staff by 50 percent since 2009.

Sites operated by private nonprofit organizations face similar challenges. A 2005 survey by the American Alliance of Museums showed that historic sites and historic house museums have median annual operating expenses of $287,204 and three full-time paid staff and forty volunteers—a level far below most museums. Indeed, about half (primarily large and mid-sized organizations) are experiencing annual financial deficits.

These challenges prompted Richard Moe, president of the National Trust, to publish a provocative article, "Are There Too Many Historic House Museums?" in 2002 and a decade later his successor, Stephanie Meeks, concluded that "the house museum is a fundamentally unsustainable model." Placed in the context of the larger arts and culture organizations, this experience is also shared by poets, novelists, opera companies, theaters, symphonies, jazz concerts, and arts festivals (making photographs and videos seem to be the only activities that are moving upward).

In response, several national and regional organizations such as the Heritage Philadelphia Program, National Trust for Historic Preservation, and the *American Association for State and Local History began to focus on the financial sustainability of historic house museums through their conferences and publications. National symposia at Kykuit in 2002 and 2007 convened leaders in historic house museums, historic preservation, funding agencies, and national organizations that resulted in a series of findings and recommendations. Among the findings were that serving the needs of the local community (not the tourist audience) is the most valuable and most sustainable goal for most historic house museums; many standards and practices followed at historic sites are borrowed from museums and often deter creativity and sustainability; and responsible stewardship achieves a sustainable balance between the needs of the buildings, landscapes, collections, and the visiting public.

At the same time, local and regional newspapers reported on the record-breaking crowds at Mt. Vernon, Lindenwald, and Valley Forge following major restoration or construction projects as well as the trend of declining attendance and financial shortfalls. Most significant was the December 31, 2006 article "Homes Sell, and History Goes Private" by Tracie Rozhon in the *New York Times* that brought national attention to the serious challenges facing historic house museums, mentioning such places as Robert E. Lee's boyhood home, Samuel Morse's home "Locust Grove," Old Sturbridge Village, and Colonial Williamsburg. These reports seemed to signal that if these hallowed sites are threatened or if success was possible only through magical high-tech exhibits, stunning visitor centers, or painstaking restoration (and the mega-millions needed to complete them), other more modest sites faced a doubtful future.

In response, national and regional associations have encouraged two major approaches: rethinking current operations to focus both on financial sustainability and contemporary relevance or seeking an entirely different use of their historic house than a museum.

To explore these alternatives, some organizations have adopted new types and forms of strategic planning and budgeting. Plans are shortening their time horizon from five to ten years to three to five years and incorporating vision statements along with revised missions and metrics to balance short-term flexibility and long-term focus. Budgets, on the other hand, are looking further into the future by moving from one-year to multi-year forecasts and more frequently including diverse sources of earned income. To more effectively make decisions and garner support, some organizations are significantly expanding their pool of stakeholders, consulting outside perspectives, and relying on market and visitor research. Finally, partnerships, collaborations, and mergers are being taken more seriously to accomplish major goals in an era of diminished resources. These strategies, however, question assumptions and past practices and are thus difficult to implement without strong leadership and support.

Multigenerational families, growing ethnic and cultural diversity, an aging population, new patterns of travel, and changing ways of communication are prompting the examination of the visitor experience to ensure it is appropriate and relevant for everyone. Coupled with continuing discoveries by scholars and high expectations by visitors, historic house museums often find themselves evaluating and revising their activities, programs, and interpretation to maintain their vitality.

The research of David Thelen and Roy Rosensweig presented in *Presence of the Past* showed that Americans considered museums to be the most trustworthy source of information, more than movies, books, and professors, so anecdotes and unsubstantiated facts can quickly undermine a site's credibility. Increasingly sophisticated, visitors are challenging stories popular at historic house museums about the diminutive size of past residents, the absence of closets in colonial houses due to a tax on "rooms," and a long-lost tunnel that allowed the family to escape during attacks. There's usually a hint of truth that allows these legends to gain traction. However, even superficial research into the source of these stories often shows they are unfounded or exaggerated.

Numerous other studies show that a mere recounting of historic names and dates is insufficient to engage most visitors. Missing is the "so what?" and "why is this important?" aspect of interpretation. *Relevance, meaning, and significance resonate when connected to the visitor's experiences, *values, and emotions. The Lower East Side Tenement Museum and President Lincoln's Cottage are among the leading house museums that have broadened their interpretation to tackle contemporary issues and public policies; balanced perspectives by including traditionally overlooked groups, such as women and immigrants; or placed their site in a larger context by interpreting the surrounding *landscape and community or by linking it to national and regional events. These approaches seem to be most effective in attracting support and making an impact on the public.

In 2009, the American Association for State and Local History with sup-port from the *Institute of Museum and Library Services and dozens of historical organizations consolidated many of these strategies into the "Standards and Excellence Program for History Organizations" (StEPs). Using nationally recognized standards and graduated levels of performance (e.g., basic, good, better), participating organizations conduct self-assessments in six areas—*mission, *vision, and governance; audience; interpretation; collections; historic structures and landscapes; and management—and develop strategies for improvement based on specific measures. StEPs has provided a useful planning and evaluation framework for small and mid-sized historic house museums.

Some organizations have discovered that they can no longer adequately support a museum but still want to preserve the house. Easements have long been used as a successful approach to protect those elements of the buildings and landscapes that are most significant while allowing the property to shift to private ownership. Some organizations, such as Historic New England and Indiana Landmarks, have successfully incorporated entirely new uses such as long-term residential, neighborhood recreation, and animal welfare. Interest in alternative uses and systematic decision-making processes grew sufficiently that it prompted Donna Harris to write *New Solutions for House Museums* and Donovan Rypkema to produce a *Feasibility Assessment Manual for Reusing Historic Buildings*, both published in 2007.

Historic house museums will continually evolve to meet the needs and interests of each generation. The economic downturn at the opening of the twenty-first century not only intensified the debate about the sustainability of historic sites but also about their relevance and contribution to American society. By the end of the century, historic house museums will still be with us but for whom and why they exist will have substantially changed.

MAX A. VAN BALGOOY
ENGAGING PLACES LLC

See cultural heritage tourism; evaluation; historic preservation; house museums; gardens, interpreting at local history sites; women's history at local history sites, interpreting.

household. "Household" refers to people living in a single dwelling unit such as a house or apartment. This informal usage usually assumes some sort of familial relationship between the people living in the unit. Households are an essential unit of modern social analysis and historical research. See, for example, Richard Netting et al., *Households: Comparative and Historical Studies of the Domestic Group* (1984). Local historians are more likely to see the term used in publications of government statistical agencies, in particular the Census Bureau, all of which use more formal definitions. The Census Bureau differentiates between family and nonfamily households. Nonfamily households are most often people living alone, or a group of unrelated people sharing the housing unit. Nonfamily households are contrasted with group quarters, such as dormitories and prisons, which are not considered households. One person in a household is designated a "householder" and relationships are referenced to this person. The Census Bureau defines a *household* as "an occupied housing unit" and a *family household* as "a household in which there is at least one person present who is related to the householder by birth, marriage, or adoption" (http://www.census.gov/hhes/families/about). In censuses through 1970 the term "head of household" was used. Only the head of the household was named until 1850. Relationships were not uniformly and explicitly stated for others in the household until 1880. Definitions of household and research using household data are challenged by issues such as transiency (particularly for economically disadvantaged groups), non-Western cultural norms, extended multigenerational families, and same-sex relationships.

ROBERT KIBBEE
THE HISTORY CENTER IN TOMPKINS
COUNTY (NY)

See census, United States; family.

humanities councils. See state humanities councils.

Hungarians in North America, sources for. See Appendix A.

Huntington library. See California, local history in.

I

ICOM. See museums, public value of.

Idaho, local history in. In 1881, eighteen years after the establishment of Idaho Territory, a group of men met in downtown Boise to establish the Historical Society of Idaho Pioneers in order to "discover and preserve" Idaho's history. As "the only organization in our Territory of a scientific and literary character" in the words of the Boise newspaper, the society received financial assistance from the territorial legislature, a rather remarkable funding accomplishment for the time.

In 1907, seventeen years after statehood, the legislature confirmed its commitment to preserving history by creating the Idaho State Historical Society as a state agency. Under the leadership of early Idaho entrepreneur and historian John Hailey—its first secretary/director—the society launched a significant effort to collect artifacts and archival/manuscript materials. The society found a home in the state capitol, and generations of Idaho schoolchildren made annual pilgrimages to the statehouse museum until 1950, when the society constructed its own facility. A new State Historical Museum opens in 2017 with a goal of bringing a level of national excellence with exhibits that will inspire Idahoans' sense of pride in their state while serving an essential educational role for students of all ages.

Travelers can find this Idaho historical marker along state highway 21, northeast of Lowman, in south central Idaho. TRICIA CANADAY, IDAHO STATE HISTORICAL SOCIETY.

During the society's first fifty years, the legislature or governor appointed its secretary/director. This patronage system resulted in a new administrator being appointed after nearly every change in political leadership. At a time when the secretary constituted 50 percent of the staff, such turnover hardly fostered professional standards.

In 1956, Governor Robert Smylie led an effort to dramatically revamp the agency, and brought in the society's first professionally trained director, H. J. "Jerry" Swinney. Smylie also ceased the practice of political appointment of directors, in favor of their hiring by the board of trustees.

Prior to Swinney's arrival, under the leadership of Merle Wells who served the society as a volunteer, consultant, and staff member for half a century, the legislature in 1947 established the Idaho State Archives under the society's auspices. This legislation provided the foundation for extensive expansion of the society's services, which were further enhanced when federal funding became available in 1970 for a state historic preservation program.

Today, the Idaho State Historical Society, consisting of the State Historical Museum, State Archives and Records Center, State Historic Preservation Office, and the Historic Sites Program, offers essential services while engaging Idahoans by building on shared experiences, demonstrating the relevance of history. As an example, a century after its establishment as a state agency, the State Historical Society provided a key leadership role in the biggest historic preservation project in Idaho history, the restoration and expansion of the

state capitol—the building that had housed the society's first museum. The society's rich collections provided documentation for restoration efforts; the society's curatorial staff restored and interpreted key artifacts from the state's history that now are on permanent exhibit in the statehouse; and the society developed an expansive interpretive exhibit on the role of state government in Idahoan's lives.

The collections gathered by the Historical Society of Idaho Pioneers constituted Idaho's first historical museum. But other people led early museum efforts. Henry Talkington, historian and professor, began gathering artifacts for a museum at the Lewiston State Normal School in 1902. In 1910, the Franklin Pioneer Association began acquiring artifacts for a Relic Hall in Idaho's oldest city. While the Talkington Museum at today's Lewis-Clark State College no longer exists, the Franklin Museum continues as a collaborative effort of the Pioneer Association and the State Historical Society.

Sister Alfreda Elsensohn established the Historical Museum at St. Gertrude's Monastery in Cottonwood in 1931 as another of Idaho's pioneer museums. Today, the state's most prestigious museum recognition—the Sister Alfreda Award for Outstanding Museum Service—goes to one museum annually, along with a cash award, presented jointly by the State Historical Society, Idaho Heritage Trust, and Idaho Humanities Council.

In the 1950s and 1960s, aided by Swinney and Wells, local historical societies and museums proliferated as the State Historical Society encouraged the development of partner organizations. The number of local historical organizations again grew substantially following the national Bicentennial of 1976. Today, nearly all of Idaho's forty-four counties have historical societies, and the state boasts more than one hundred museums. The Idaho Association of Museums, established in 1977, is an active organization of museum professionals and volunteers that hosts regular workshops and conferences, and in other ways provides "self-help" to Idaho's museums.

Idaho Heritage Trust, established as a lasting legacy of the statehood centennial of 1990, is another key component of the heritage community. With funds generated from the sales of state license plates, the trust supports the preservation of historic buildings, sites, and collections through a program of grants and technical assistance.

Following the tradition of Swinney, the State Historical Society today recognizes not only the value but also the necessity of creating strong partners. Through a grant program and professional outreach—and working in collaboration with organizations like the Heritage Trust and Humanities Council—the society fosters the best possible professional standards at partner organizations, and recognizes outstanding efforts with its annual Esto Perpetua Awards program.

In addition to the rich manuscript, photographic, and archival collections maintained at the Idaho State Archives and Records Center, most of the state's colleges and universities also house special collections that are frequented by scholars from throughout the nation.

And some of Idaho's local historical societies and public libraries retain outstanding historical collections.

This accessibility of research materials in a diversity of repositories has encouraged a rich tradition of publication on the state's history. Carlos Schwantes, *In Mountain Shadows: A History of Idaho* (1991) and Adam Sowards, ed., *Idaho's Place: A New History of the Gem State* (2014), are the most significant recent books encompassing the state's history. Local and regional authors and scholars continue to generate an outstanding body of literature on individuals and topics germane to Idaho history, many of which have been recognized through the Idaho Library Association's "Outstanding Book on Idaho" awards program.

Many local historical societies also publish local history journals. The State Historical Society began publication of *Idaho Yesterdays* in 1957, which is today an online journal.

Idaho history is generally taught in the fourth grade. The Idaho Department of Education's content standards require that, by the end of that grade, students have an understanding of Idaho history. The State Historical Society's education program works with educators throughout the state to help students meet these standards, and also coordinates the annual *National History Day program in Idaho, which attracts entries from thousands of fourth-to-twelfth-grade students who compete for thousands of dollars in scholarships and awards.

One hundred and thirty-five years after the formation of Idaho's first historical organization, the "state" of state and local history in Idaho is strong. Idaho has demonstrated that, through both difficult and robust financial times, it has a talented pool of volunteers and professionals willing to work for the preservation of the state's history and culture.

Keith C. Petersen
Idaho State Historical
Society (retired)

See United States, local history in.

Illinois, local history in. The Antiquarian and Historical Society of Illinois was established on December 8, 1827, for the "promotion of elegant and useful learning." Its members included the leading political and legal figures in Illinois, which, in large part, was the reason for its demise several years later. Members were too busy attending to the business of the state or their respective professions to record Illinois history properly. The Chicago Historical Society (now the Chicago History Museum) was founded in 1856 and serves as the premier institution for collecting the history of the Windy City. Growing interest in preserving state and local history led to the creation of the Illinois State Historical Library and Natural History Museum (now the Illinois State Museum) in 1877. Amos H. Worthen, the state geologist and first director, failed to establish the library portion, neces-

This Illinois state marker is located in Rock Islands, near Somanauk, the ancestral home of the Sauk and Fox Indians, along the Rock and Mississippi Rivers. Credit: William Fury

sitating new legislation in 1889 that established the Illinois State Historical Library as a separate organization. Ten years later, the Illinois State Historical Society was created and made a department of the library in 1903. On July 1, 1985, the Illinois Historic Preservation Agency came into being by executive order. It merged the Illinois State Historical Library with the Historic Sites and Preservation Services units from the Department of Natural Resources. In 1996, the Illinois State Historical Society ceased being a department of the library. The Illinois State Historical Library changed its name in 2004 to the Abraham Lincoln Presidential Library, reflecting its affiliation with the new Abraham Lincoln Presidential Museum. The library's mission remains the same: to collect, preserve, and interpret the history of Illinois.

Henry Brown's *A History of Illinois* (1844) was the first history, but the writings of former governors John Reynolds and Thomas Ford provided more useful information. *A Complete History of Illinois from 1673 to 1873*, by Alexander Davidson and Bernard Stuvé appeared in 1874, followed by John Moses, *Illinois, Historical and Statistical* (1889). In 1918, the Illinois Centennial Commission funded six volumes to cover the period from the French and British occupation up to 1918. In 1968, the Illinois Sesquicentennial Commission funded two supplemental volumes covering Illinois history from 1865 to 1928. Roger Biles, *Illinois: A History of the Land and Its People* (2005), is the most recent one-volume history. The Illinois Historical Collections series (thirty-eight volumes from 1903

to 1973) offers documentary sources from prehistoric settlement at Cahokia through the nineteenth century. Local and county histories proliferated in the late nineteenth century. The more significant titles can be found in John Hoffmann, ed., *A Guide to the History of Illinois* (1991). *The Encyclopedia of Chicago* (2004) is a necessary reference work.

The position of state historian was created in 1943 with Paul M. Angle appointed to the title. Illinois statutes permit but do not require any county, municipality, or township to establish a position of local historian, usually without compensation. Many public libraries house local or regional history collections, often with a staff member designated as the local historian. The Sangamon Valley Collection at the Lincoln Public Library in Springfield and the Joiner Room at the Sycamore Public Library are examples. The Illinois Association of Museums is largely comprised of local and county historical societies and house museums, providing a clearinghouse of information on local history as well as an annual conference. The Illinois Heritage Association is a private organization providing a similar service, though no conference. Two state historical conferences and journals provide avenues for interaction among academic and independent scholars. The Illinois Board of Education requires state history to be taught in the fourth grade and for high school students to pass before graduation an American history and government course that covers the state constitution. Once a course offering at public universities, the study of Illinois history has largely disappeared, with community colleges providing the few remaining opportunities.

Family history remains the most popular research topic throughout the state. Noteworthy collections and programs are at the Newberry Library and the Abraham Lincoln Presidential Library.

A series of community studies associated with Abraham Lincoln enlisted the talents of Benjamin P. Thomas on New Salem, Paul M. Angle on Springfield, and William E. Baringer on Vandalia. More recent authors of note are Don Doyle on Jacksonville, John Mack Faragher on Sugar Creek, and William Cronon on Chicago.

THOMAS F. SCHWARTZ
HERBERT HOOVER
PRESIDENTIAL LIBRARY

See United States, local history in.

imagined communities. See borders and boundaries.

Immigration History Research Center. Founded in 1965, the Immigration History Research Center (IHRC) is an interdisciplinary research center in the University of Minnesota's College of Liberal Arts. Its mission is to discover new ways of understanding immigration in the past and present. Along with its partner, the IHRC Archives (University of Minnesota Libraries), it is the oldest and largest institution devoted to preserving and understanding immigrant and refugee life in North America.

The IHRC promotes interdisciplinary research on migration, race, and ethnicity in the United States and the

world through monthly seminars like its Global Race, Ethnicity, and Migration series, conferences, and symposia. Recent events include an international conference on the fiftieth anniversary of the 1965 Immigration Act, a symposium marking forty years of Lao migration to the United States with the Lao American Writers Summit, a conference and exhibit on Arab American history and culture with the Arab American National Museum, and a conference and exhibit with the Immigration History Research Center Archives on immigration from and to Finland over the past 150 years.

The IHRC also connects U.S. immigration history research to contemporary immigrant and refugee communities. The IHRC's *Immigrant Stories* project works with recent immigrants and refugees to collect, share, and preserve their own unique stories. Using the latest digital technology and specially developed curricula, we help immigrants create digital stories—short personal videos with images, text, music, and audio—and share and preserve them for future generations through the IHRC Archives, the Minnesota Digital Library, and the Digital Public Library of America. With support from the *National Endowment for the Humanities, the IHRC is currently designing and building a new website application that will allow anyone anywhere to create their own immigrant stories to preserve and share. Plus, we're partnering with several organizations nationally to expand the *Immigrant Stories* project across the nation.

The IHRC advances public dialogue about immigration with innovative research and timely programs that draw audiences from around the corner and around the world. Recent events include a symposium on the future of immigration policy, panel discussions on the history of refugee resettlement in Minnesota, and walking tours of immigrant neighborhoods in Minneapolis and St. Paul.

The IHRC supports teaching and learning at all levels through specially designed curricula, teaching resources for the classroom, and teacher training. The IHRC provides research support to University of Minnesota graduate students and other student researchers from around the world, and IHRC staff are in college and community classrooms every year. It also helps to develop archives documenting immigrant and refugee experiences for future generations.

The IHRC is located on the west bank campus of the University of Minnesota in Andersen Library, home of the Special Collections of the University of Minnesota Libraries: 311 Elmer L. Andersen Library, 222-21st Ave S., Minneapolis, MN 55455; (612) 625-4800; ihrc@umn.edu.

ERIKA LEE
IMMIGRATION HISTORY
RESEARCH CENTER

See digital history; genealogical resources online; Appendix A.

immigration records. See genealogical resources online.

indenture. The term refers to a contract or deed between two individuals. The word comes from the ancient practice of tearing or cutting a contract in two using a jagged (indented) line. Fitting the two pieces back together was proof that it was a true contract. Most often, indenture refers to a contract between a master and an apprentice in which both parties have obligations and responsibilities to one another. The contract usually is in force for a set period of time.

Indian history. See American Indian history.

Indiana, local history in. Just fourteen years after Indiana became the nineteenth state in the Union, some leading figures of the Hoosier State formed an organization to collect "all materials calculated to shed light on the natural, civil, and political history of Indiana." These efforts suffered through growing pains over the years, with one observer noting that the group's existence had been quiet enough "as to suggest death." Contemporary historical organizations in the state are still burdened with the challenges of limited resources faced by their forebears, but with a much stronger base of brick-and-mortar facilities, both private and state funded.

On December 11, 1830, a "large and respectable meeting" was held at the Marion County Courthouse that included Indiana Supreme Court judges and more than half the members of the state legislature to consider forming a historical society for Indiana. A constitution for the organization, today's Indiana Historical Society (IHS), was adopted thanks in no small part to the efforts of John H. Farnham, an attorney who played a pivotal role in the IHS's early history, including starting its

The Polly Strong Slavery Case marker in Corydon, Indiana, was dedicated on April 20, 2016. CREDIT: INDIANA HISTORICAL BUREAU.

collection of documents on the history of Indiana and the Old Northwest, available today in the IHS's William Henry Smith Memorial Library. Unfortunately, Farnham died in 1833, and the organization languished in obscurity for some years. In 1886 three amateur historians—Jacob P. Dunn Jr., William H. English, and Daniel Wait Howe—revitalized the society and began its longstanding publishing program, which has issued a number of important documentary editions, biographies, and monographs. The financial support of Indianapolis businessman Eli Lilly in the 1960s and 1970s enabled the IHS, a private, nonprofit membership organization, to expand its operations, with offices in an extension to the Indiana State Library and Historical Building. In 1999 the IHS moved into a new, approximately 165,000-square-foot headquarters building along the Central Canal in downtown Indianapolis. Renovations completed in 2009 enhanced the IHS's public spaces, including new hands-on exhibitions.

In addition to the private IHS, Indiana's historical memory is preserved by such institutions as the state-sponsored Indiana State Museum (ISM), which had its beginnings during the Civil War when Indiana State Librarian R. Deloss Brown began collecting minerals and other curios. The ISM moved from its home in the old Indianapolis City Hall to a new building in White River State Park in May 2002. Established in 1825, the Indiana State Library (ISL) has an extensive genealogy collection as well as books and manuscripts on the state's heritage. The Indiana State Archives division of the Indiana Commission on Public Records protects and provides access to the records of state government. Indexes for more than 2.5 million searchable records can now be accessed through the institution's Indiana State Digital Archive (http://www.indiana digitalarchives.org).

Since a 2001 renovation to the ISL, the state archives had been located in a former warehouse without climate controls and prone to roof leaks. After years of advocacy by researchers, archivists, and genealogists for improved facilities, the Indiana General Assembly in April 2015 approved a budget bill that included $25 million for a new state archives building. Several sites in downtown Indianapolis are under consideration for the new building.

The celebration of the state's centennial in 1916 sparked renewed interest in Indiana's past, and also saw the first notable state commitment of funds to the history of Indiana with an appropriation of $25,000 and the creation of the nine-member Indiana Historical Commission (today's Indiana Historical Bureau). The commission, aided by thousands of *volunteers, sponsored historical *pageants throughout the state, sparked the creation of Indiana's state park system, published the first four volumes in the *Indiana Historical Collections*, and helped inspire interest in an improved statewide road system. The centennial spirit inspired many

counties and communities to begin their own historical institutions. As of 2010, there were more than two hundred groups in Indiana calling themselves historical societies, with a majority of them operating museums open to the public.

In 1981 the bureau and the society created the County Historian Program to improve historical communication in the state by naming local experts to serve as historians for each of Indiana's ninety-two counties. The two organizations also worked together to form and support the Indiana Junior Historical Society, which since 1938 has offered programs and clubs for students in elementary grades through high school. Indiana history is taught in the fourth grade, as mandated by the Indiana Department of Education.

The first published histories of the state came from the pens of former journalists and amateur historians. John B. Dillon, known as the "Father of Indiana History" and an early state librarian, published *History of Indiana*, which went through four printings between 1843 and 1859. Other former reporters added to Indiana's written history, with Dunn producing such books as *Indiana: A Redemption from Slavery* (1905) and the two-volume *Indiana and Indianans: A History of Aboriginal and Territorial Indiana and the Century of Statehood* (1919). John Bartlow Martin, a reporter for the *Indianapolis Times* and a nationally known freelance writer, produced what historian Arthur Schlesinger Jr. called the "best book on Indiana" with his *Indiana: An Interpretation*, published in 1947. The most comprehensive contemporary work on the state's history is *Hoosiers: A New History of Indiana*, written by James H. Madison, an emeritus Indiana University history professor, co-published in 2014 by IU Press and the IHS Press.

In addition to books, two historical journals have been mainstays for publishing the work of the state's academic and popular historians. George S. Cottman, a printer by trade who wrote about the state's history for a variety of Indiana newspapers, launched *The Indiana Quarterly Magazine of History* (today the *Indiana Magazine of History*) in 1905 with the assistance of William E. Henry, state librarian. The historical journal became a benefit for IHS members and has been under the operation of IU's history department since 1913. In hopes of attracting new members, in 1989 the IHS began publication of a new popular history magazine, *Traces of Indiana and Midwestern History*, which is issued on a quarterly basis.

RAY BOOMHOWER
INDIANA HISTORICAL SOCIETY

See United States, local history in.

Indochinese in North America, sources for. See Appendix A.

inflation and local history. Inflation refers to an economic situation in which the purchasing power of a central currency declines. There are several different ways of looking at inflation, but for local historians, purchasing power is usually the central issue and most questions of inflation revolve around comparing the value of goods and services from one historical period to the present. The degree of inflation is measured by the decline of the ability of a currency to purchase a standard set of goods and services. Often this is indexed to a standard year. For the United States this index is the Consumer Price Index (CPI). Other indexes can be used to measure inflation in certain sectors of the economy, such as the Producer Price Index (PPI). The adjusted value of the currency may be used to calculate other indicators that would highlight inflation-influenced economic variables, such as real median household income. Any of these indexes could be useful in analyzing local historical economic conditions.

The value of a dollar over time has been calculated and published in Scott Derks, *The Value of a Dollar: Prices and Incomes in the United States, 1860–2009*, (2009); and Susan B. Carter, *Historical Statistics of the United States* (2006), http://hsus.cambridge.org/HSUSWeb. Discussions of purchasing power are complicated by changes in technology (horses to airplanes) as well as monetary policy (gold standard versus fiat currency). The introductions to these works should be consulted for guidance in interpreting the tables. The Bureau of Labor Statistics provides an inflation calculator at http://www.bls.gov/data/inflation_calculator.htm.

ROBERT KIBBEE
THE HISTORY CENTER IN TOMPKINS
COUNTY (NY)

Institute of Museum and Library Services (IMLS). IMLS is the federal agency that supports learning experiences, strong communities, and broad access to content in the nation's 123,000 libraries and 35,000 museums. Through grant making, policy development, and research it inspires innovation, lifelong learning, and cultural and civic engagement.

IMLS helps libraries and museums stay relevant and meet changing societal needs. Each year, it supports thousands of institutions that are focused on the needs of their communities.

IMLS brings together the best thinking in library and museum services and creates opportunities to improve practice nationwide. The agency is known for its trusted grant review process and its capacity to draw on expertise from throughout the nation. IMLS serves as a catalyst for leveraging private and public partnerships to advance library and museum service. For more information visit www.imls.gov.

Janelle Brevard
Institute of Museum
and Library Services

insurance maps. See maps and atlases.

intellectual property rights. Property is anything that can be possessed and disposed of in a legal manner. We usually think of property as either "real" property, or realty such as land and buildings, or as tangible property, all that we personally own of value that is not realty. Intellectual property is another kind of property, an *intangible* personal property represented by knowledge, lore, and various forms of personal expression. The best-known Western legal right of intellectual property is copyright, legal protections for individually created works of literature, drama, architecture, choreography, art, music, digital products, motion pictures, and sound recordings. These rights of original authorship apply to any thoughts or concepts that can be expressed in tangible form, for example in writing, film, or art, or recording of any type (although facts and words or things commonly known cannot usually be copyrighted). Such works are protected by law from unapproved use, modification, reproduction, distribution, performance, or display. These legal rights are outlined in the U.S. Copyright Act of 1976 (as currently revised) and last from the creation of the work to the author's death plus seventy years. While patent and trademark rights are similar, less commonly known intellectual property rights are identified in the Visual Artists Rights Act of 1990, which protects an artist's right of attribution to a work of art and the integrity of the art from unauthorized change.

It is important that museums, historical societies, and researchers are knowledgeable about intellectual property rights laws since the transfer of ownership of an object does not, unless otherwise specified in writing by the owner, also transfer the rights of copyright or artist's rights. In other words, a museum can own an object but not the rights to modify, copy, and distribute it, and perhaps even display it. This means that a specific clause transferring such rights must be a part of any gift or other acquisition form with a clause of indemnification that protects the museum if a donor or seller does not in fact have those rights. Institutions that acquire artifacts or archival materials anonymously or from third parties should attempt to verify, whenever possible, whether those materials are still protected by copyright, using collective rights organizations or similar resources. There are "fair use" provisions that can allow limited legal use of copyrighted materials for educational and other purposes without the author's approval, but such use must be carefully examined on a case-by-case basis. These and other issues, such as the duration of copyright, depend in part on when a work was first created since the length of copyright protection has changed over the years. Materials created prior to 1923 are in the public domain, and not protected by copyright.

Less well-known principles apply to intellectual property represented by the traditional knowledge of native peoples. Such "esoteric" knowledge is usually acquired by special training, is owned as property by an individual or group, and may also be sacred or *patrimonial. Contemporary legal battles over patents of traditional medicinal knowledge and recent requests that the U.S. Patent and Trademark Office protect tribal symbols illustrate this issue. Many Native American governments are now restricting research access to and use of traditional knowledge, including *oral histories, songs, traditional designs, and other information, often by legal contracts with outsiders for any access or use. Some communities insist on retaining their ownership, including copyright, of any research data. The right to use such information, especially if acquired prior to federal human subject rights laws, may be disputed. New policies, such as the Protocols for Native American Archival Materials, establish guidelines for community consultation and the *repatriation of information (e.g., documents, photos, and recordings), and mirror similar policies and laws in other countries. These perspectives have also been reinforced by the 2010 U.S. adoption of the UN Declaration on the Rights of Indigenous Peoples. Accordingly, institutions should review the status of archival materials they have derived from native sources. For many native peoples this is, like repatriation through the Native American Graves Protection and Repatriation Act (25 USC 3001-13), an important human rights and legal issue, and thus should be handled openly, sensitively, and expeditiously. It can also be expected that native peoples in other parts of the world will begin to request information about institutional holdings related to them and wish to explore copying or repatriation of such materials.

JAMES D. NASON
UNIVERSITY OF WASHINGTON

See copyright; Native American Graves Protection and Repatriation Act (NAGPRA).

internal revenue records. See Civil War federal tax records.

International Genealogical Index (IGI). The International Genealogical Index is a database of records of life events for deceased persons abstracted from a variety of sources. Despite the name it was not developed as a genealogical tool but as a way to check that the deceased person had not already been baptized and put through temple ordinances—the process by which they were converted after death to the Church of Jesus Christ of Latter-day Saints (LDS). Originally birth, baptism/christening, and marriage information made up most of the content; now the variety of information included has expanded beyond the original guidelines. The IGI is international in scope, although records are primarily from North America, Europe, and South America. Begun as a computerized database in the 1960s and published in several editions on microfiche, from 1999 researchers have been able to gain access to the over 400 million records of the IGI through an online search engine hosted by the LDS at www.FamilySearch.org. Records come from two sources: Individual members of the LDS, motivated by the desire to ensure that their ancestors have been baptized into the Mormon faith, can submit records of their own families. These records must be used with caution. About half the records have been transcribed from microfilm of primary sources such as parish registers by LDS volunteers for the same purpose. Transcription and submission are not without controversy. Some Jewish groups have objected to the process leading to baptism in the LDS and the Roman Catholic Church has directed local parishes not to allow LDS volunteers to transcribe their records. The IGI is an important tool for genealogical resource, but there are limitations arising from the original purpose of the database. Each entry is essentially an index record to a microfilmed document, so the complete research process involves retrieving the original document. For a good overview of the process see www.ancestor-search.info/SRC-IGI.htm. The data collected from the IGI online should be traced back to the original source and verified there. FamilySe-

arch has now incorporated IGI records so thoroughly into its search environment that the IGI exists as an independent resource only in an older interface, which still remains accessible from the main FamilySearch site. For a view of the post-IGI FamilySearch, see Robert Raymond, "Life after the IGI" (course syllabus), https://www.familysearch.org/learn/wiki/en/Life_After_the_IGI.

ROBERT KIBBEE
THE HISTORY CENTER IN TOMPKINS COUNTY (NY)

See FamilySearch; genealogical resources online.

intestate. The legal condition of dying without making a will and thus allowing the laws of a particular state to dispose of one's assets. Dying intestate also means that the next of kin will have to apply to probate court to settle the estate.

inventories. "The archaeological historian," noted Ivor Noel Hume in his essay *"Material Culture with the Dirt on It," "sees a side of life that rarely finds its way onto paper and is rarely manifested in objects of museum quality. He becomes the custodian of the commonplace, the treasurer of trivia, but from it can emerge the features of hitherto faceless masses, without whom there could be no social history, nor any 'material culture.'" In her book, *The Age of Homespun,* Laurel Thatcher Ulrich has revealed stories inherent in objects from the past, found above the ground. She added that other stories "are surviving in tax lists, . . . probate records, . . . merchants' accounts." Indeed, lists of objects may expand upon the tale of the single object separated from its natural context. Most often such lists or inventories are made upon the death of the owner, freezing a conceptual "slice" of the environment of an individual or *household. Even the daily life of a community can be illumined by a series of related inventories.

Counties and other local governments usually have archives that include wills and probate or intestacy inventories. For examples of research making good use of this kind of resource, see Jayne Nylander's *Our Own Snug Fireside* (1993) and Historic New England's (formerly SPNEA) *Bed Hangings* (1961). In 1987, the annual proceedings of the Dublin Seminar for New England Folklife focused on the topic, "Early American Probate Inventories," which resulted in *Early American Probate Inventories*, ed. Peter Benes (1961), a publication rich in advice for the novice researcher. If there is any question about the relevance of material culture to the study of history, refer to *Material Culture and the Study of American Life* (1978), ed. Ian M. G. Quimby. The Internet offers access to past and recent scholarly writing on the subject.

Conclusions based on inventory findings must be made with appropriate caution. Inventories that look "complete" or "incomplete" may not be so; it is advisable to take the opportunity to review as many examples as possible to develop a sense for that which is ordinary or extraordinary. With the changes brought about by improved transportation and the Industrial Revolution came an increase in ownership by more persons of small things like chairs, teacups, dresses, and books. Re-

flecting this, inventories of this period tended to be more detailed than earlier examples, particularly with regard to clothing. There are four ways in which inventories might confuse or mislead the unwary.

Unintentional errors and miscommunications. Even today, it is unreasonable to expect everyone to have a high level of organizational skill. It might be assumed that the ablest or most responsible persons available for the job were asked to perform the task of taking and recording an inventory, but in more sparsely populated communities, the "ablest" might have left something to be desired. In the nineteenth century or earlier, literacy and numeracy were far from universal. Occasionally inventories exhibit conceptual and graphic chaos. Often the unfamiliar style of period handwriting is, in itself, a major obstacle to gaining accurate information; the elegant script of a lawyer may be as difficult to decipher as the scratchy hand of a farmer.

Appropriately excluded information. Some inventories are remarkably brief, or at least seem to lack the sort of contents the researcher expected to find, which does not necessarily indicate a job done poorly. The obvious explanation would be that the possessions were, indeed, few. If the owner was sharing a household as a grandparent, newcomer, or partner, the list might be short. A wife's belongings might be excluded. Perhaps an important heirloom, like a rifle, was passed on to the next generation in advance of the occasion for the inventory. In some cases, belongings already may have been moved on to settle debts. Humble items crafted of available materials, like brooms or breadboards, may have been considered expendable and without significance where even a seemingly worthless broken plate was evaluated.

Inappropriately excluded information. There is no way of knowing what was left off a list surreptitiously. In the case of inventories made upon a person's death, the only assurance of accuracy is that these lists typically were made by two men who were well known in the community, and the community was probably intimate enough to have a fairly good idea of how well they did the job. Except in the rare case of blatant collusion or fraud, it seems likely that most inventories were honestly prepared.

Different standard of reporting. Cultural practices influenced what was selected to be listed. The religious traditions of the owner or the inventory taker—even his or her degree of conservatism—should be kept in mind as the list is evaluated. In the eighteenth century a man's estate typically included all his wife's possessions except, perhaps, small personal items like needles. Eventually, a wife's belongings ceased to be listed as a matter of course on her husband's inventories. Women's rights to ownership began a slow process of upgrading in the nineteenth century. Widows came to be acknowledged as beings in need of sustenance apart from the public dole and were finally guaranteed a portion of the husband's estate. However, these developments may not be assumed to have been consistent within a time period or a region.

SUSAN W. GREENE
INDEPENDENT SCHOLAR

Iowa, local history in. Iowa's greatest contribution to the discipline of state and local history is Dr. Benjamin Shambaugh, who concurrently held the positions of chairman of the political science department at the University of Iowa and superintendent of the State Historical Society of Iowa at the beginning of the twentieth century. In this dual role he pioneered what he called "applied history," writing books and monographs on the history of significant social and political issues and biographies of Iowa political luminaries. Until the Depression cut off his funding, he hosted Commonwealth Conferences where nationally recognized authorities debated social and economic issues. For his innovative work, he has been called "the father of public history." Today the Historical Society's Benjamin F. Shambaugh Award recognizes the best book on Iowa history published each year.

Another Shambaugh legacy at the Historical Society was the creation of the scholarly *Iowa Journal of History and Politics.* Today that function continues with *The Annals of Iowa*, published four times a year with articles and book reviews of works with Iowa significance. The society's journal of popular history, *The Palimpsest,* another Shambaugh achievement beginning in 1920, was renamed *Iowa Heritage Illustrated* in 1996 and, like the *Annals*, is published from the society's offices in Iowa City. Capturing the intimate detail of daily life, the Historical Society maintains extensive microfilm files of Iowa's newspapers, from small-town weeklies to the award-winning *Des Moines Register*, a resource used extensively by historians and genealogists. The State Historical

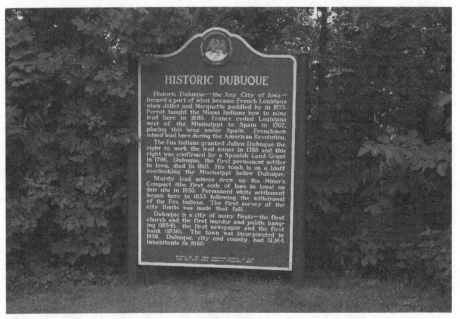

"Historic Dubuque" marker placed by the State Historical Society of Iowa. CREDIT: STATE HISTORICAL SOCIETY OF IOWA.

Society has begun *digitizing representative newspapers from the early 1900s selected for their ethnic and political diversity. Thanks to the visionary leadership of Iowa labor leaders, the society also houses one of the nation's largest collections of *oral histories from the state's labor unions.

Through the last half of the previous century, the nonprofit Iowa State University (ISU) Press was the preeminent publisher of Iowa history manuscripts. Like so many others in the print media, the digital world brought severe economic pressures and ISU Press closed, a major blow to Iowa authors seeking an outlet for their manuscripts. To meet current needs, the University of Iowa Press has recently begun publishing books in its Iowa and Midwest Experience series. In 1974, the state welcomed the one-volume *History of Iowa* by University of Northern Iowa professor emeritus Leland Sage, which was primarily a primer on Iowa politics. In 1978, Joseph Wall of Grinnell College authored *Iowa: A Bicentennial History*, the state's contribution to the *American Association of State and Local History (AASLH) state history series. The most recent survey is Dorothy Schwieder's *Iowa: The Middle Land*. Ineligible for the Shambaugh Award because she was serving at the time on the Historical Society board of trustees, Schwieder received a special commendation from Gov. Terry Branstad for her masterful integration of rural, ethnic, and women's history into a narrative flow. Her death in 2015 was mourned throughout the state by Iowa historians and the public. In 1996 Marvin

Bergman collected seventeen scholarly articles in *Iowa History Reader* that move chronologically through topics from Native American tribal relations to the contemporary abortion controversy and the Iowa political caucus.

Schwieder partnered with Thomas Morain and Lynn Nielsen in writing the three-hundred-page *Iowa Past to Present*, an upper-elementary-level textbook now going into its fourth edition. Nielsen also passed away in 2015. Iowa Public Television maintains an extensive Iowa history website called "Pathways" as a classroom resource. Iowa law specifies that Iowa history be included in the curriculum but it does not specify for how much time or at what level. While the Department of Education has established standards, Iowa local school districts retain considerable control over curriculum. The department has begun the process of certifying standards for what schools should teach in the area of Iowa studies.

Current scholarship in Iowa history explores diverse fields. In 2001, a consortium of historians and civil rights activists compiled and published a collection of twenty essays on various dimensions of the experiences of blacks in the Hawkeye state, *Outside In: African-American History in Iowa, 1838–2000*. With a special appropriation from the legislature, copies of the work were distributed statewide and sparked a renewed appreciation of the role of race in the Iowa experience. Iowa historians have made significant contributions to the new *social history in the areas of rural life, women's history, labor, coal mining, children, and community development.

*African American history continues to attract scholarship and professional attention in the state. The Iowa Freedom Trail Grant collected information on Iowa abolitionists and the *Underground Railroad while the State Historical Society partnered with the *National Park Service to add several buildings associated with Underground Railroad to the *National Register of Historic Places. The John Brown Freedom Trail marked the route of the controversial abolitionist on his last trip through Iowa on his way to Harper's Ferry. Dr. Lowell Soike completed two detailed volumes on Iowa's role in the struggle against slavery in the 1850s: *Necessary Courage: Iowa's Underground Railroads in the Struggle against Slavery* and *Busy in the Cause: Iowa and the Free State Struggle in the West, 1851–1860*.

Native Americans have also attracted the attention of historians and archeologists. Several new sites relating to prehistoric lifeways in western Iowa have been added to the National Register. The nonprofit Loess Hills Archaeological Interpretive Center opened to focus on significant prehistoric resources in the area. Fort Atkinson in northeastern Iowa also received a National Register nomination as did the Patterson Trading Post that served the Meskwaki tribe in the 1830s and 1840s. In 2011 the Meskwaki tribe opened its own museum on its settlement near Tama.

Iowa boasts several other outstanding ethnic museums of national stature. The Vesterheim ("Western Home") Museum in Decorah tells the story of Norwegian migration and adaptation to America. The Danish-American Museum in Elk Horn and the National

Czech and Slovak Museum and Library in Cedar Rapids are the leading interpretive centers of their respective traditions. The German-American Heritage Center in Davenport draws on rich local resources while the African American Museum of Iowa in Cedar Rapids weaves its own vital threads into the diverse cultural fabric of the state. The State Historical Museum just west of the capitol in Des Moines houses an impressive collection of artifacts of natural, political, and social history. The world-class National Mississippi River Museum and Aquarium in Dubuque attracts visitors fascinated by the history, ecology, and economic vitality of the "Mother of Waters." Re-creating operating farming operations from the past three hundred years, *Living History Farms in Des Moines has earned the title as "the best outdoor agriculture museum in the world." In 1979, Pope John Paul II celebrated mass on the front yard of the farms to an audience of over 379,000, often cited as the largest single gathering in Iowa history. The Herbert Hoover *Presidential Library and Museum located at West Branch on Interstate 80 connects the thirty-first president with his Quaker roots in Iowa.

Iowans created the State Historical Society of Iowa in 1857, following its admission into the United States on December 28, 1846. In 1996, Iowa celebrated its 150th anniversary as the twenty-ninth state of the Union. Planning for the observance became a model of grassroots participation. The legislature granted the Sesquicentennial Committee a monopoly on the sale of vanity license plates. With the money, the committee, in addition to its own statewide projects, granted funding to a coalition of planners in each of the ninety-nine counties, generating creative and enthusiastic local efforts.

Iowa history entered a new phase in 2015 with the introduction of three online courses offered free to the public. (A MOOC is a Mass-enrollment, Open enrollment Online Course.) Katy Swalwell, an assistant professor in the ISU School of Education, offered a course aimed at classroom teachers on the history of civil rights in the state. In preparation for the Iowa presidential caucuses that kick off the official selection of delegates to the national conventions, ISU political science professor Steffen Schmidt offered an online primer on the Iowa caucus system and its history and process. Dr. Tom Morain at Graceland University developed a MOOC on Iowa's territory days.

Tom Morain
Graceland University

See United States, local history in.

Ireland, local history in. The history and local history of Ireland have been, more than most, unfinished and contentious business. It is unsurprising that a search for national identity, rather than recognizing variations in local experience, has often dominated historical perspectives. The vexed relationship with Great Britain over seven hundred years has produced an emphasis, in the words of David Dickson, on "the collective experience of victimhood" while often neglecting historical and cultural differences and nonpolitical aspects of experience. Yet there have also been features in the development of Irish local history that parallel those found in *England, *Scotland, and *Wales.

In the seventeenth century, narrative histories in both Irish and English, together with collecting, mapping, and descriptions by both natives and settlers, suggest an emerging interest in particular places and how they had developed, although not as yet in the form of specific local histories. The following century saw the emergence of enthusiastic antiquarianism, with local enquiries, by both Catholics and Protestants, largely gentry and clergy, interested in ancient monuments, documents, Irish literature, language, and folklore. The county was an early focus of documentary and topographical collecting and publication. The resulting volumes were in a conventional and recognizably British mold, with county histories of eighteen of the thirty-two Irish counties published between 1820 and 1921. At the national level new standards in the investigation of Irish places were set by the detailed surveys undertaken by the British Ordnance Survey between 1824 and 1846. Although used for valuation and taxation purposes this recording, in *maps and written memoirs, of boundaries, jurisdictions, local names, and features produced a key source for Irish local historians.

The county, an English import between the twelfth and early seventeenth centuries, has proved a surprisingly persistent unit of historical writing and local identity. Indeed, county allegiances were, and remain, a feature of that most nationalist of cultural activities, the Gaelic Athletic Association (GAA, established 1884), whose bottom-up organization rests on teams from townlands (of which there are 62,000), parishes, and counties. However, studies of the parish, manor, and estate, which feature among antiquarian local histories elsewhere in the British Isles, were seldom found. County studies continue to be produced, from modern academic monographs pursuing particular themes to the eclectic potpourri of Willi Nolan's series of nineteen county histories, published between 1991 and 2008.

In the nineteenth century, divergent rather than shared historical concerns became increasingly apparent. History was seen through very different lenses, of unionism, nationalism, romantic Irishness, or shared, nonsectarian heritage. Cultural nationalism, first developed in the Young Ireland movement in the 1840s, and out of which the GAA and Gaelic League (1893) grew, valued the particular and the local, but as part of a transcendent and independent national identity. The violent struggles of 1916–1922 and the establishment of the Irish Free State meant that, more than ever, recent conflict and political perspectives influenced the direction of national and local historical studies, directly or indirectly. So when, as in Great Britain, community studies sparked by ethnography and social anthropology began to gain momentum in the 1920s and 1930s, and scholars investigated the Blasket and Aran Islands on the rural west coast, their findings were valued as emblematic of a truly Irish past rather than describing culturally distinct communities. The 1930s saw the establishment of the Irish Folklore Commission (1935), and the publication of the *Harvard Irish Survey*, a major social anthropological study of communities in County Clare by Arensberg and Kimball.

Such projects leave rich archives for modern microhistories. However, Irish local history is less fortunate in the availability of some key research materials. Another very practical and continuing consequence of Ireland's troubles has been the loss of evidence, most drastically of documents, from medieval to modern, in the destruction of the Four Courts in Dublin in 1922.

Among some Irish academic historians, responding to the early twentieth century has required a "new history," intent on replacing unsubstantiated myths through a dispassionate examination of evidence. This agenda generated numbers of local monographs, on subjects including famine, British and Irish politics, union, the Catholic Church, emigration, land, the 1916 rising, and the following "Troubles." The power of local history in such areas is apparent in, for example, Peter Hart's study of *The IRA and its Enemies: Violence and Community in Cork 1916–1923* (1998). Hart tackles probably the most violent of all Irish counties and reconstitutes, through painstaking linkage of varied sources, the individual, family, and neighborhood circumstances and personalities that underlay the events and historical experiences of violence and community, and the viewpoints of participants, observers, and victims. He uses gripping reconstructions of single events or groups, suggesting sectarian and other motives beyond (in the words of Roy Foster, a leading current historian of Ireland) any "simple dualities of the nationalist impulse to separatism." Hart's work also shows how controversial local studies can be, prompting heated debate about its evidence

(including anonymous interviews), its method, its conclusions, and whether the differing roles of academic history and *public history, allegedly driven by other motives, can ever be compatible. It is an issue of which in the 2010s, a decade of centenaries and anniversaries, Irish local historians are acutely aware. It is also true that since the 1970s the dominant grand narrative of political and religious history eventually grew less prominent. Economic, social, and cultural history, and history from below, make their appearance, as reflected in the journal *Irish Economic and Social History* (established 1974). Raymond Gillespie, of National University of Ireland–Maynooth, has argued for an Irish local history based on "community" and on the experience of "ordinary people" in relationship to their various communities, units more real than the traditional county or parish. His suggested themes for study include *landscape and topography, population, land tenure, *religion, *folklore, and customs. The Maynooth Studies in Local History, first published in 1995 and by 2014 reaching 116 titles, represent the work of Maynooth's MA students in local history. They are complemented by seventeen Maynooth Research Guides for Irish local history.

As in English local history, links with *archaeology, geography, anthropology, and folklore studies have been increasingly productive since the 1950s. E. Estyn Evans, a geographer, championed going beyond the documents to include fieldwork and participant observation of rural and working life, and was one of the instigators of the Ulster Folk and Transport Museum. Landscape history, a vehicle for a holistic view of the whole island, across periods and employing elements of archaeology, documentary evidence, buildings, and topographical and cultural studies, is comprehensively on show in the *Atlas of the Irish Rural Landscape*, published in 1997 (revised edition, 2011). Irish local history has been overwhelmingly rural, working at county or townland level. This reflects the distinctive Irish experience. As Tony Judt has written, Ireland in 1945 was still largely rural and pre-industrial, transformed to a service-based economy in a single generation, and "virtually bypassing the industrial stage in which Britain or Belgium had been caught for nearly a century." More urban studies are now appearing.

Today, local history in Ireland is being researched and written by professional historians, geographers, anthropologists, and sociologists in universities, and by a wide range of lay practitioners. In terms of grassroots local history, an all-Ireland survey published in 2001 (*The Local History Project Co-operating North and South*) estimated the number of local history societies at between three hundred and five hundred, many affiliated to the Federation of Ulster Local Studies (established 1974) or the Federation of Local History Societies (established 1981). There was an upsurge of activity in the 1970s and 1980s with three main spurs—the threat of development; national and local anniversaries (ranging from the Famine and the risings of 1798 and 1803, to silver, gold, or centenary events for schools, churches, and clubs, to the millennium itself); and projects linked to employment schemes and community develop-

ment projects. In the latter, local history has been used to help bridge sectarian divides, as in 1989 when the Department of Education in Northern Ireland introduced "education for mutual understanding" and "cultural heritage" into schools. Outside formal education, local history was supported in the 1990s by a Cross Border History Collective in counties Cavan, Leitrim, Fermanagh, and Sligo, "to reconcile identities, create relationships and celebrate unique ways of life and cultural traditions" (J. Holmes, "Ireland" [2009]; see below). In 2010 the Oral History Network of Ireland was established. Irish local history now manifests familiar motivations and patterns of grassroots, local society activities, alongside connections with mainstream academic history and education. Yet, as so often in the past, Irish local history remains unavoidably prone to other uses, now more likely to be community building across borders, rather than reinforcing conflicting national identities.

See *The Local History Project Co-operating North and South* (2001); D. Dickson, *County Histories, National Narratives and Missing Pieces: A Report from Ireland* (2009); J. Holmes, "Ireland," in *Historiography of Local and Regional History* (Open University, 2009).

KATE TILLER
UNIVERSITY OF OXFORD, UK

See England, local history in.

Irish in North America, sources for.
See Appendix A.

Italians in North America, sources for.
See Appendix A.

J

Japanese in North America, sources for. See Appendix A.

Jews in North America, sources for. See Appendix A.

journeyman. As distinguished from an apprentice, foreman, or master, a journeyman is a worker who has learned a handicraft or a trade. An apprentice is one who is still learning; a foreman is one who directs others in work; a master is one who has learned a trade, become a journeyman, and teaches others.

judicial records. See courts and court records.

K

Kansas, local history in. Kansans and would-be Kansans recognized the significance of the times in which they lived, and took documentation of their history seriously, writing about and preserving it from an early date. Although the nature of the settlement process and a deeply ingrained, conservative attitude toward private property rights has meant that Kansas has less publicly owned land than any other state in the Union, one of the nation's most progressive state preservation laws was passed in the 1970s. It reflected a general attachment to the historic, and Kansans seem especially enamored with their territorial and early statehood history—Bleeding Kansas, homesteading, and cattle town heritage being perhaps the most popular.

That early history was indeed compelling, but it is only part of the story. The land now called Kansas was occupied, crossed, and explored for hundreds of years before the modern political entity was created in 1854. It became part of the United States with the Louisiana Purchase in 1803 and was home to many removed tribes of *American Indians after 1830. Pressures for expansion at mid-century led to the passage of the Kansas-Nebraska Act in 1854. Because this enabling legislation repealed the Missouri Compromise ban on slavery and turned the decision in this critical area over to settlers ("popular sovereignty"), the "Kansas Question" took center stage nationally. The epithet "Bleeding Kansas" characterized conditions on the ground and the emotionally charged debate that divided the nation and put it on a faster track to civil war. Kansas entered the Union as the thirty-fourth state on January 29, 1861, as the nation split, North and South, slave and free. The newly minted state did its part and more in defense of the Union during the war and was poised for growth after. Encouraged and enabled by the Pacific Railroad and Homestead acts, an era of rapid growth and expansion commenced, and the state was settled up by 1890. By that time 105 counties had been created and the population approached 1.5 million. Rapid growth meant good things for some, bad for others, and Kansas was a focal point of three major reform efforts—Prohibitionism, Populism, and Progressivism.

A preoccupation with history and Kansas's place in it emerged immediately, and the first efforts to establish a state historical society predated statehood. From modest beginnings in 1875, when it was established by the Kansas Editors' and Publishers' Association and housed in a couple of rooms in the statehouse, the present Kansas Historical Society evolved into a state agency and a private foundation that employs about one hundred full- and part-time staff and operates a multimillion-dollar archive and museum complex. In addi-

Sunflowers decorate this Kansas historical marker in Wichita that tells the story of the Chisholm Trail. CREDIT: KANSAS HISTORICAL SOCIETY.

tion to the state archives and museum, the society maintains and interprets numerous historic sites. It also administers state historic preservation and archeology programs and develops a variety of educational materials and programs for elementary and secondary schools and teachers.

The society enjoys a long history of quality publications, including *Kansas History: A Journal of the Central Plains*, a peer-reviewed, quarterly journal that carries on a tradition dating back to the *Transactions*, first published in 1880, and its successor the *Kansas Historical Quarterly*, 1931–1977. But even 130-year-old traditions change. Shrinking state agency budgets in the wake of the financial crisis of 2008 and the rush toward privatization and small government following

the 2010 gubernatorial and legislative elections led to a sharp increase in fees and openness to new public and private partnerships. In the area of publications, the private society (now known as the Kansas Historical Foundation) entered into a partnership with Kansas State University. The journal's editorial office moved to Manhattan in 2012, and within two years all facets of production, from manuscript selection to printing, resided in the K-State's Department of History. The society's foundation remains the publisher and distributes the journal to its membership.

In the face of a new reality, the society continues to serve a vast and varied constituency and to support local historical and cultural institutions in all of the state's 105 counties. Each year tens of thousands of people visit the Kansas Museum of History, attend special events at the Topeka complex, and conduct research at the State Archives. Literally millions more patrons take advantage of the agency's ever-expanding presence on the World Wide Web, which has been second to very few for well over a decade. Officially launched in January 2004, TerritorialKansasOnline.org was the agency's first major digitization project. It was accomplished in cooperation with the Kansas Collection at the University of Kansas and remains a valuable online resource, although now subsumed by Kansas Memory.org, which provides access to the society's diverse and growing digital collections: photographs, books, *maps, *diaries and letters, state government records, museum and archaeological artifacts, and video and audio files. In partnership with the *Library of Congress and Ancestry, among others, the archives continues to greatly expand its online offerings.

Kansas Memory and many other educational programs are designed, in part, to serve teachers and students with select sources correlated to Kansas and U.S. history teaching standards. As a requirement of graduation, Kansas law stipulates that students must take a course in state history between the seventh and twelfth grades; the state history assessments include Kansas history. Most schools now offer Kansas history as a semester course in the seventh grade, and the society's *The Kansas Journey* (1999) text is widely used at the middle-school level.

Numerous towns and counties throughout this quintessential plains state maintain local historical, genealogical, and preservation societies. Some of these are quite active, supporting paid, professional staff and maintaining significant research collections, and many have published local histories of considerable interest to the history buff and the professional historian.

Books claiming to be histories of Kansas were published in the mid-1850s, beginning with Edward Everett Hale's *Kanzas and Nebraska* (1854); but they were in reality little more than promotional tracts or partisan polemics. In 1954 the eminent University of Kansas historian James C. Malin took stock of one hundred years of publishing history about Kansas and produced an important five-part series entitled "Notes on the Writing of General Histories of Kansas" for the *Kansas Historical Quarterly*. A. T. Andreas and William G. Cutler's two-volume *History of the State of Kansas* (1883) remains an invaluable reference, as does William E. Connelley's five-volume work, *A Standard History of Kansas and Kansans* (1918–1928). Among the more recent single-volume treatments of note are William Frank Zornow, *Kansas: A History of the Jayhawk State* (1957); Kenneth S. Davis, *Kansas: A Bicentennial History* (1976); Robert W. Richmond, *Kansas: A Land of Contrasts*, 4th ed. (1999); James R. Shortridge, *Peopling the Plains: Who Settled Where in Frontier Kansas* (1995) and *Cities on the Plains: The Evolution of Urban Kansas* (2004); and Craig Miner, *Kansas: The History of the Sunflower State, 1854–2000* (2002). Although dated, *Kansas History: An Annotated Bibliography*, ed. Homer E. Socolofsky and Virgil W. Dean (1992), is a useful reference tool.

VIRGIL W. DEAN
KANSAS STATE UNIVERSITY

See United States, local history in.

Kentucky, local history in. The late Dr. Thomas D. Clark, the historian for whom the Kentucky Historical Society's headquarters is named, outlined how local history is linked to our nation's past. Dr. Clark believed that local history performs a "sacred mission" by connecting people with "an intimate sense of time and place and of being part of a community." Throughout Kentucky's nearly 225-year history, residents of the Bluegrass State—who have innately understood this sacred mission—have valued and preserved their history.

From organizations that are transforming how people find meaning in their collective history to groundbreaking digital initiatives and the efforts to create new state social studies standards, Kentucky is reshaping the use of

This historical marker honors Muhammad Ali's childhood home in Louisville, Kentucky.
CREDIT: KENTUCKY HISTORICAL SOCIETY.

local history. Together, these sites are making it clear that the study of history is relevant to modern Kentuckians.

Among the agencies that are transforming the role of history in the state is the Kentucky Historical Society (KHS). Founded in 1836, KHS is working to become a forum where meaningful conversations take place and important issues are confronted. The KHS campus includes the Thomas D. Clark Center for Kentucky History (opened in 1999), Kentucky's Old State Capitol, and the Kentucky Military History Museum at the State Arsenal, which recently underwent a $2.5 million renovation. Along with outreach efforts and public programs, this integrated campus allows KHS to reach its mission of educating and engaging the public through Kentucky's history in order to confront the challenges of the future.

KHS helps people understand, cherish, and share Kentucky's stories through a broad range of publications, programs, and services. In many instances, conversations begin in the pages of *The Register of the Kentucky Historical Society*, a quarterly, peer-reviewed journal. Recent issues, like one examining important episodes from the twentieth century, have encouraged KHS and others to reassess what types of collections they build. Another volume, a microhistory of the city of Henderson, engaged new scholars and created a sense of community as articles from that issue evolved into public programs.

Today, scholars and researchers from around the world can access these articles online via Project MUSE and JS-TOR. In addition, KHS has broadened its digital reach through the *Civil War*

Governors of Kentucky Digital Documentary Edition, a groundbreaking project that connects scholars to a wealth of previously underutilized *primary sources. This project has truly redefined what we know about the Civil War in Kentucky and will aid local history organizations by connecting these collections to their communities. The agency also realizes that people come to local history from multiple avenues, including family history. Therefore, *Kentucky Ancestors Online*, a website that provides articles and professional development for genealogists, has reshaped the way KHS assists family history researchers.

In addition to telling Kentucky's stories, KHS also collects them. The society houses more than 8,000 *oral histories, which are part of a statewide oral history collection of more than 30,000 interviews found in repositories across the commonwealth. These statewide oral histories are shared with the broader public though *Pass the Word*, an extensive digital library. Furthermore, the Bluegrass State's status as a recognized leader in the field of oral history is cemented, in part, thanks to the Kentucky Oral History Commission (KOHC), the only state-supported commission in the United States that seeks to preserve and promote oral histories. Administered by KHS, this commission will celebrate its fortieth anniversary next year (2017).

KHS also works with communities, students, and teachers to highlight the relevance of history and to broaden its use and impact. The KHS *historical marker program now has more than 2,300 markers located across the commonwealth, connecting Kentuckians and travelers to local history.

ExploreKYHistory, a mobile phone application that includes tours based on those historical markers, has propelled the historical marker program into the twenty-first century by connecting communities with collections and historic images. The KHS HistoryMobile, a tractor-trailer–based mobile exhibit that visits schools, brings the importance of individual choices in history to Kentuckians' doorsteps. And, each year •National History Day programs and the Kentucky Junior Historical Society inspire hundreds of students by engaging them with programs related to historical inquiry.

While the Kentucky Historical Society plays an important role in showcasing the relevance of our past, local history is anchored across the commonwealth by dozens of museums and smaller historical societies. From the Mississippi River to the mountains in eastern Kentucky, more than four hundred organizations preserve and interpret Kentucky's diverse and important stories.

These organizations focus on a variety of interpretive themes, from the quintessential Kentucky stories of bluegrass music and the horse, bourbon, and coal industries, to history museums that examine specific regions of the state. Civil War battlefields, house museums, folk art centers, religious sites, sports museums, •National Park Service and state historic sites, and more spark conversations and create rich and transformative experiences. In the Lexington area alone, visitors can tour museums that interpret famous Kentuckians (the Mary Todd Lincoln House and Ashland, The Henry Clay Estate), the horse industry (the Museum of the Horse at the Kentucky Horse Park), art collections (the University of Kentucky Museum of Art and the Headley-Whitney Museum), aviation (the Aviation Museum of Kentucky located at Blue Grass Airport), a Civil War recruiting ground for African Americans (Camp Nelson), house museums about Kentucky families (Waveland and the John Hunt Morgan House), a children's museum (the Explorium), and more. Several innovative partnerships have grown out of these sites, including the Henry Clay Center for Statesmanship. This leadership program, now managed by Transylvania University, educates high school and college students from across the country on statesmanship and compromise.

Other Kentucky museums are developing similar initiatives. Shaker Village at Pleasant Hill, located near Harrodsburg, has created a suite of visitor-centered experiences coupled with the rich history of the site that has transformed their business model. In Ashland in Eastern Kentucky, the Highlands Discovery Center interprets the rise of aerospace technology that is part of Kentucky's story. This site is creating museum experiences for young people tied to this technology that helps them understand that these innovations are part of their past and their future. The Behringer-Crawford Museum, northern Kentucky's history museum, combines immersive on-site experiences with a variety of programming and events to engage its audiences. These sites—and many more—have built momentum to provide experiences for visitors that highlight the modern *relevance of history.

Many of these organizations have re-invented themselves during economic downturns to create bold and vibrant spaces that engage visitors and tackle tough, sometimes controversial, topics. These efforts, and state commemorations like the Abraham Lincoln Bicentennial and the Civil War Sesquicentennial, have made heritage *tourism a significant part of the Bluegrass State's economy. The success of many of these organizations has been helped thanks to other state agencies, including the Kentucky Heritage Council (state historic preservation office) and the Kentucky Arts Council, and the public-private partnership of the Kentucky Humanities Council.

It is, of course, important for these sites to be grounded in extensive research in primary sources. Fortunately, the state has preserved many documents and manuscripts that unlock Kentucky's great stories, all of which have aided local history.

The Kentucky Department for Libraries and Archives collects state and county records and helps libraries across the state preserve their local history. The University of Kentucky houses a wide range of manuscripts, publications, videos, historic newspapers, photographs, and images. Many of these collections have been *digitized, greatly broadening their use. The University of Louisville, Eastern Kentucky University, and Western Kentucky University, which sponsors the Kentucky Museum, all preserve manuscripts and other impressive collections. In addition, the state's independent colleges and universities and many public libraries across the state preserve photographs, oral histories, and archives that further our understanding of what it means to be a Kentuckian. The public libraries in Kenton, Boone, and McCracken Counties are leading the way in making local history materials more accessible both on site and online.

History organizations in Louisville have always been innovative, vibrant places. One of the first was the Filson Historical Society, which was founded in 1884. Housed in the historic Ferguson Mansion in downtown Louisville, the Filson has amassed an excellent collection that primarily pertains to Louisville and the Ohio River Valley. This organization quickly embraced the providing of online resources for researchers, and they continue to publish *Ohio Valley History*, a scholarly journal that engages the public in meaningful ways. The Filson has also supported statewide initiatives, including the Lewis and Clark Bicentennial and the Civil War Sesquicentennial. Soon, the completion of a multimillion-dollar expansion will increase their efforts to preserve and promote the region's history. Other Louisville sites of note include the Kentucky Derby Museum, the Frazier History Museum, the national headquarters of the Sons of the American Revolution, the Louisville Slugger Museum, Farmington (home of the Speed Family), Locust Grove (home of George Rogers Clark), the Portland Museum, the Louisville Science Center, the Lincoln Memorial at Waterfront Park, the Muhammad Ali Center, and more.

Scholarly publications about state and local history abound, and writers have embraced innumerable topics about Kentucky history. The University Press of Kentucky has maintained a long-term commitment to the scholarly interpretation of the state's past and has published many important titles. Among these is *The Kentucky African American Encyclopedia* (2015), the first of its kind published in the United States. This publication has broadened our understanding of the African American experience in the Bluegrass State.

Legislative support also has aided local history. In 2015, the General Assembly passed the Kentucky Local History Trust Fund, which enables Kentuckians to make voluntary donations on their state income tax returns to provide grants to museums and local history organizations. The state legislature also encourages all fourth-grade students to study Kentucky history. This content, coupled with proposed new social studies standards that require the use of inquiry-based skills, will help create college- and career-ready students across the state.

*Public history programs have also helped Kentucky's local history infrastructure. For nearly forty years the Folk Studies Program at Western Kentucky University has engaged local communities around their living traditions and history. More recently, the University of Kentucky established a graduate program in historic preservation, and both Northern Kentucky University and the University of Louisville offer master's degrees in public history. The documentation and presentation of local and state history has benefited from the intellectual energy created and sustained by all of these programs.

The state of local history remains strong in Kentucky. Despite shifting trends and economic uncertainty, organizations across the commonwealth are following, as Dr. Clark termed it, the "sacred mission" of local history. Much of this was evident when the *American Association for State and Local History (AASLH) held their annual conference in Louisville in September 2015. As nearly one thousand museum professionals gathered to examine "The Power of Possibility" (the conference theme), conference organizers showcased Kentucky's rich history and vibrant institutions. Today, Kentuckians realize that in order to understand what is possible for our future, we must fully comprehend our past. And, in the words of Dr. Thomas D. Clark, we do this work "so all Kentuckians may discover their roots in time and place."

KENT WHITWORTH
AND STUART SANDERS
KENTUCKY HISTORICAL SOCIETY

See United States, local history in.

kindred. The nuclear family traces its descent from both parents; this is called a kindred system. How a family defines itself determines from whom it can expect aid and favors and to whom it has responsibilities. There are a number of ways of defining who is one's kindred.

See clan; family; household.

Koreans in North America, sources for. See Appendix A.

L

labor history and the history of communities.

Throughout history, earning one's daily bread has been a defining characteristic of human existence. Today, Americans spend one-third of their productive adult lives working. In the nineteenth and eighteenth centuries, it was half or more. How its inhabitants have traditionally earned their livelihoods determines not only the relative wealth of a community, but its institutions, social structure, politics, and even the physical conditions of its environment. The availability of work is an important factor in the birth and growth of communities; its absence explains their decline and demise.

These insights are, of course, commonplace to most students of history today. Nevertheless, it was only in the 1970s that professional labor historians started turning their attention from the study of institutional and political labor history to the roots of workers' history in community sources. In this "social history" approach, workers were studied as complex human beings whose behavior in the workplace can be explained by examining their roles as members of communities, voters, racial minorities, women, and immigrants, not just as union members. Historians also identified workers' culture as an essential explanation of their behavior and their role in the community. Gender, racial and ethnic identity, religious beliefs, culinary traditions, leisure, sports, and civic organizations are only some of the competing and often overlapping factors historians have turned their attention to, in their quest for understanding workers' culture. Communities are obviously an important focus of studies of workers' culture, because that is where it is so often manifested and nurtured. Readers can find a classic explanation of the *social history approach in David Brody, "The Old Labor History and the New: In Search of an American Working Class," *Labor History* 20 (1979): 111–26, and in David Montgomery's "To Study the People: The American Working Class," *Labor History* 21 (1980): 485–512. More recently, the introduction by Donna T. Haverty-Stacke and Daniel J. Walkowitz to *Rethinking U.S. Labor History* (2010) pointed out that labor scholarship is placing less stress on the study of communities and more on questions of culture, identity, and the transnational dimension of the working-class experience. Yet, this does not translate into a disregard for local communities. Studies of workers' culture and identity—especially of migrants—are still often grounded and better understood in the framework of the local experience; and many of the studies of transnationalism analyze the influence of changes at the supra-national level on local communities.

Local sources for the study of workers as community members are abundant.

Account books of mills and craftsmen, payroll records, labor contracts, city and county histories, business correspondence, local newspapers, and city directories are some of the sources contained in the public library and in the historical society. Individual workers seldom had the time to personally document their lives, but historians can sometimes locate oral history interviews, diaries, correspondence, letters to the editors of newspapers, testimonies to police, and government-collected surveys, which convey more of the personal, subjective workers' worldview. Now, to these traditional sources one would want to add websites and *social media platforms, a sometimes fleeting and ever-changing source of personal/local perspective and information. Excellent methodological suggestions on how to conduct research on local communities with a focus on workers and their organizations can be found in older but still relevant works such as Jeremy Brecher's *History from Below: How to Uncover and Tell the Story of Your Community, Association, or Union* (1986); and in Dennis Harison's *Working History: A Manual for Researching and Writing Labor History in Cleveland, Ohio* (1984).

The bulk of the nation's most important international labor unions have found homes for their archives. A large percentage of the records of 700 AFL-CIO city or regional central bodies, however, still require placement. More significantly, most of the records of over 60,000 local affiliates of American unions—many of which prove rich resources for the social and political history of the communities of which they are a part—have not yet been placed

in a historical repository. The trend toward merger among American labor unions in the last decade, moreover, has resulted in the elimination of many long-lived locals and, sadly, the resulting loss of their records. See Daniel J. Leab and Philip P. Mason, eds., *Labor History Archives in the United States: A Guide for Researching and Teaching* (1992).

The State Historical Society of Wisconsin at Madison housed the first major labor history collection in the United States. Built by Professor John R. Commons and his colleagues at the University of Wisconsin and in the society, this premier collection served as the basis for John R. Commons et al., *Documentary History of American Industrial Society*, 11 vols. (1910–1911, republished 1958 in 10 vols.). The society has continued its collecting in this area to the present time. Other state historical societies such as those of Illinois and Ohio and the Western Reserve Historical Society have joined in preserving labor history. Historical societies in major industrial cities frequently acquire major labor collections. Most prominent in this regard is the Chicago Historical Society, but there are also significant labor collections in the Buffalo and Erie County Historical Society, in the Rochester Historical Society in New York, and in many others around the nation.

Beyond these repositories, the bulk of major international labor union records are either housed in specialized repositories such as the George Meany Labor Archives in Silver Spring, Maryland, or as part of the archival programs of colleges and universities. There are major labor manuscript collections in institutions of higher education in California, Georgia, Illinois, Maryland, Ohio, Michigan, New Jersey, New York, Pennsylvania, Texas, and Washington.

Statewide surveys of local labor union records have been conducted in Wisconsin, Illinois, and New York, and efforts to preserve important local records have been made in these states. Much more still needs to be done if important local history is not to be lost.

Local union records typically consist of union meeting minutes, officers' correspondence, grievance records, local publications, photographs, and memorabilia, in addition to blogs and websites. They can provide valuable documentation regarding local working conditions and, frequently, local politics. Community historical repositories must begin to view the preservation of such documentation as the necessary complement to the preservation of other forms of community economic and business records.

Membership minute books form the core of most local union records. They are treasured by succeeding generations of union officers and may extend from the founding of the local through the present. It is not uncommon to find local minutes dating from the late nineteenth century. Such records are, of course, particularly fertile resources for local historians and genealogists. Other forms of membership records may also be particularly valuable for genealogical research.

When preserved, the correspondence of local union officials offers useful insight on the relations of these organizations with their national bodies, their

lobbying activities, organizing activities, and support for community social agencies. Local unions also frequently maintain documentation relating to the local impact of work stoppages.

Newsletters offer personal details about the lives of the local members, insights into accidents, and work stoppages, or other incidents of importance that are frequently published by locals. They proudly chronicle the activities of local members serving their nation in time of war and the participation of the membership in local charitable activities.

Formal printed histories were often commissioned for important local union anniversaries. These are typically well illustrated, detailing the history of the locals and the biographies of its officers. They also frequently contain shop-floor pictures of union members at work and detailed descriptions of community businesses that employ union labor.

Local unions frequently keep collective-bargaining agreements with local employers long after the plant or company has ceased to be a factor in the local community. They offer important insights into the hours, wages, and working condition of the unionized worker in the community.

Photographs of local events such as Labor Day marches and picnics are almost always preserved by local officers, as are photographs of members engaged in a wide variety of activities from picketing to team sports.

The fraternal roots of craft unions are evident in the wide variety of ritual memorabilia they used in connection with union activities. Common were elaborate officer insignias, ritual handbooks, and artifacts such as Labor Day sashes, and a wide variety of membership pins and badges. Most locals had a banner emblazoned with the seal of the national union, the name and number of the local union, and an official local seal. Such items add substantial graphic interest to community history displays, in addition to providing a sense of the image of themselves that unions wished to portray to the members and the public.

Beyond the important documentation and artifacts that can be obtained through local labor unions, records that were never before thought of as specifically pertaining to "labor" turn out to be very rich sources on the lives of working people. These include *diaries, letters, local newspapers, *city directories, parish registers, old *county histories, *census records, fire insurance *maps, and minutes of various organizations' meetings, just to mention a few of the available sources in local historical societies, public libraries, and museums.

Diaries and letters may tell us of the hard work and low wages of women in early textile mills, of their aspirations and often difficult choices, and how a farm girl could find the strength and motivation to join a strike. Census records may reveal the age at which children started working, what foreign country the immigrants in the community came from, in what neighborhoods people with given occupations lived, or whether married women worked outside the home. In addition, some local and state historical societies have sponsored oral history projects that contain a wealth of insights into people's perceptions of their working lives. Finally,

old photographs sometimes have great documentary value. They might reveal that blacks and whites worked side by side in a particular shop where racial segregation had been assumed. Or photographs of the annual Labor Day parade may depict all sorts of groups marching behind their banners, not just labor activists, thus showing community-wide support for the meaning of the celebration.

Recently, the decline of the labor movement, especially in the United States, has prompted many historians to analyze its causes and implications, spurring studies of deindustrialization and unemployment centered in specific geographical locations. Such studies of economic decline are just as important to the history of local communities, many of which were devastated by the flight of industry offshore. But there is another dimension that is attracting scholarly attention. Globalization may have wiped out manufacturing jobs, but people are engaged in other types of work and in new organizational forms that deserve study and understanding. A case in point is Jobs with Justice (JWJ), a national network of community-based coalitions of local labor unions and activists in faith-based, environmental, and civic groups. JWJ acts as a bridge between the institutions of organized labor and the grassroots global justice activists, by explaining how globalization impacts individuals and communities and by mobilizing around these issues. The literature that analyzes the impact of globalization on workers and mobilization such as the one conducted by JWJ is vast, rich, and growing fast. Such studies are truly significant and meaningful if they are grounded in the way in which broad change impacts local communities. Their study remains, for the foreseeable future, as vital as it has been in the past decades.

PATRIZIA SIONE
AND RICHARD STRASSBERG
CORNELL UNIVERSITY

land management. See maps and atlases.

land survey records. See maps and atlases.

land warrant. A document issued by a local U.S. government land office to the purchaser of public land. It usually states the amount of land and describes the land and its boundaries.

landscape. Landscapes are products of the mind's eye, scenes composed through the act of framing disparate elements of the environment together into an intellectually and emotionally coherent whole. In documenting and interpreting landscapes, local historians often examine three things: the interaction of nature and culture in a particular site, the relationship of the site to the larger world, and the diverse ways that local residents and outsiders have thought about the site as a place.

Landscapes reflect how successive generations of local residents adapted to their natural surroundings and, more often than not, remade those surroundings in accordance with their economic goals and cultural ideals. Before European contact, native peoples regularly burned forests to create more edge to improve the hunting of game, and built roads and irrigation canals to facilitate agriculture and trade. European settlers replaced native plants with regular rows of whatever commodities farmers deemed most valuable at the time, and agricultural landscapes still offer perhaps the most obvious evidence of the interaction of nature and culture. Historians can uncover evidence of how past local residents reshaped the water as well as the land, whether through digging canals for transportation and power, damming rivers for electricity and irrigation, or draining wetlands for new housing developments. Even landscapes considered "wild" bear evidence of the human hand, such as the carefully constructed natural look of New York's Central Park, a reflection of the mid-nineteenth-century romantic ideals of its designers, Frederick Law Olmsted and Calvert Vaux, or the uninhabited "wilderness" landscapes created in the West by the establishment of national parks and removal of Indians to reservations.

Cultural landscapes include buildings as well, such as meetinghouses and churches, storefronts and factories, apartments and private homes. Their construction reflects the influence not only of economics and their natural setting, but also of prevailing social relations and ideologies. The impressive Greek Revival facade of the big house on a Southern plantation contributes to a landscape of power and domination, just as the vine-covered suburban cottage based on a design from an Andrew Jackson Downing *pattern book contributes to one of middle-class Christian nurturance. Over the past one hundred years, many designed landscapes have been explicitly historical, such as the town commons developed by village improvement societies in New England at the turn of the century to emphasize the colonial character of where they lived. Local historians cannot limit their interpretation of landscapes to only physical descriptions of land and buildings; indeed, social characteristics not always evident to the eye, such as inhabitants' ethnicity and race, often contribute the most to the distinctive character of a landscape. Whether urban neighborhood or rural village, landscapes can be characterized not only by the architecture of the buildings but also by the habits of the people who lived in them.

Local historians also investigate how particular landscapes relate to one another within regions and in the wider world. The mansions of Pittsburgh's steel barons cannot be understood apart from the coal fields of southwestern Pennsylvania or the iron ore mines of Michigan's Upper Peninsula. The landscape of abandoned textile mills in New England is the result of the industry's move to the Carolinas, China, and Bangladesh. Many towns owe their look and feel to federal government actions, such as the grid Congress imposed over much of the nation with the Northwest Ordinance of 1787 to facilitate the sale of western lands, a regular pattern still visible from the air. Across America, landscapes have been shaped indelibly by federal land grants to the railroads, and after World War II by the building of a national interstate highway system for automobiles. The rise of the automobile in turn facilitated the growth of national retail chains using a standardized architecture easily recognizable from the roadside. More subtly, landscapes have been shaped by Federal Housing Administration mortgage policies in the 1930s through 1950s that favored the construction of new single-family suburban homes in areas restricted to whites over the renovation of older, more densely settled African American urban neighborhoods. Analysis of the relationship of landscapes to one another, and to national land-use policies and trends, helps the local historian understand the position of the local landscape in the larger world.

Finally, local historians investigate how local residents and outsiders, past and present, have themselves interpreted the land. Views of the land exist in *maps, paintings, and *photographs; in promotional literature aimed at tourists, and *travelers' accounts written by them; in memoirs, newspaper articles, and stories about places handed down in the community. If landscapes exist in the eye of the beholder, and different observers have different perceptions of the environment, then local historians of landscape need to explore how particular views of the land become the prevailing ones in a particular time, and gained physical expression through land-use legislation. When some residents see a field as vacant awaiting development while others see it as full of native plants requiring protection, which side wins out and why? Local historians can also explore, through public programs, the diverse environmental perceptions of contemporary local residents, the special places in the community, and the memories and environmental values residents attach to them.

Understanding landscapes is essential to the task of local history. It is literally what makes local history local—about a place. Beyond researching the history of past landscapes, local historians often seek to document and preserve landscapes deemed significant by contemporary communities. Landscape preservation brings historians together with archaeologists, conservation biologists, landscape architects, and regional planners. Local historians can also organize public programs that represent local residents' experience of place, collecting memories and photographs. While such programs may be of interest to outsiders, they are of far more importance to local residents. Such programs create environmental value by helping local residents to see the specialness of otherwise ordinary places in their community and to make informed decisions about the future of their environment.

More and more in the twenty-first century, those decisions will be shaped by the reality of increasing global temperatures and, depending on the locale, desertification, violent storms, and sea level rise. In an era of rapid climate change, when familiar natural environments are altering faster than native flora and fauna can adapt to or that humans can comprehend, the efforts of local historians to develop public programs that promote an understanding of landscape history can help communities to maintain a sense of historical continuity and identity amid change.

The best introduction to the study of cultural landscapes, with examples of landscape analysis from different regions and diverse ethnic groups, are

anthologies by Donald Meinig, ed., *Interpretation of Ordinary Landscapes* (1979); Michael Conzen, ed., *The Making of the American Landscape* (1990); Paul Groth and Todd Bressi, eds., *Understanding Ordinary Landscapes* (1997); Arnold R. Alanen and Robert Z. Melnick, eds., *Preserving Cultural Landscapes in America* (2000); Paul Shackel, ed., *Myth, Memory, and the Making of the American Landscape* (2001); Kenneth Foote, *Shadowed Ground: America's Landscapes of Violence and Tragedy* (2003); Paul Groth and Chris Wilson, eds., *Everyday America: Cultural Landscape Studies After JB Jackson* (2003); Richard H. Schein, ed., *Landscape and Race in the United States* (2006); and Richard Longstreth, ed., *Cultural Landscapes: Balancing Nature and Culture in Heritage Practice* (2008). These works include superb bibliographies of basic works in landscape studies.

Also near the top of any list of exemplary landscape studies are the essays of John Brinckerhoff Jackson and his former student John R. Stilgoe. Jackson's essays range from New England to the Southwest, and have been collected in a number of volumes, including *Landscape in Sight: Looking at America*, ed. Helen L. Horowitz (1997). Jackson's *American Space: The Centennial Years* (1972) offers a fascinating portrait of American landscapes in the decade after the Civil War. Among Stilgoe's works are *Common Landscape of America, 1580–1845* (1982); *Metropolitan Corridor: Railroads and the American Scene* (1983); *Borderland: Origins of the American Suburb, 1820–1939* (1988); *Outside Lies Magic: Regaining History and Awareness in Everyday Places* (1998);

Landscape and Images (2005); and *What is Landscape?* (2015).

Local historians seeking to incorporate landscape history in public programming will be inspired by Dolores Hayden, *The Power of Place: Urban Landscapes as Public History* (1995) and by Ned Kaufman, *Place, Race, and Story: Essays on the Past and Future of Historic Preservation* (2009).

Finally, the *National Trust for Historic Preservation, the Alliance for Historical Landscape Preservation (www.ahlp.org) and the *National Park Service (NPS) have published several guidelines for local communities seeking to document and preserve historically significant cultural landscapes. Among many useful NPS publications are National Register Bulletin no. 18, *How to Identify and Evaluate Designed Historical Landscapes* (1987); National Register Bulletin no. 30, *How to Identify, Evaluate, and Register Rural Historical Landscapes* (1988). These resources are available online at www.cr.nps.gov/nr, while Preservation Brief no. 36, *Protecting Cultural Landscapes: Planning, Treatment, and Management of Historic Landscapes* (1994) is at (http://www.cr.nps.gov/hps/tps/briefs/brief36.htm). See also the website of the NPS Historic Landscapes Initiative (www.nps.gov/hps/hli), and the Olmsted Center for Landscape Preservation (http://www.nps.gov/oclp).

DAVID GLASSBERG
UNIVERSITY OF MASSACHUSETTS–
AMHERST

See environmental history; gardens and landscapes, researching historic; Historic American Landscapes Survey; parks.

Latter-Day Saints, sources for. See Church of Jesus Christ of Latter-day Saints, Appendix B.

Latvians in North America, sources for. See Appendix A.

lease/leasehold. A document spelling out an agreement between a landlord and a tenant. The agreement usually specifies a set period of time. Leasehold refers to a property held under a lease agreement.

legal history. See courts and court records.

Leicester School. See England, local history in.

LGBT history, interpreting. The subject of Lesbian Gay Bisexual Transgender (LGBT) history offers a perfect opportunity for museums to inhabit their roles as sites of conscience, education, and dialogue. Yet for many institutions, interpreting the queer past means moving into new terrain. The four most compelling reasons for museums to undertake interpretation in the history of same-sex love and desire are (1) the role of museums as sites of public dialogue, (2) the responsibility of historical organizations to strive for a full and accurate presentation of the American past, (3) LGBT historical interpretation is likely to diversify and expand both audiences and collections, and (4) the powerful experience museums can offer by restoring visibility to a group of people who have been consistently marginalized or erased in the larger culture.

Public attitudes about same-sex relationships have changed drastically in recent years. At the same time, LGBT struggles for acceptance continue. There are deep differences in opinion based on age, religion, and geographic region. To some, the political gains of the LGBT community represent losses for sexual morality, and these citizens are fighting back, as demonstrated by recent debates in state legislatures. Even those who profess acceptance of expressions of variant sexuality may be more comfortable with same-sex affection as represented by marriage than by other, more "queer" demonstrations of desire (such as nonmonogamous arrangements or leather fetishism). And acceptance of same-sex love and desire does not necessarily equal ease with the concept of gender crossing, as many transgender people will attest.

The rapidly changing cultural landscape begs for a wider historical perspective in which to understand the context and precursors of current debates. Museums provide a perfect setting for such exploration; they have become, in the words of Robert R. Archibald, "The New Town Square." The museum, he says, "is a place to discuss what we have done well, where we have fallen short, and how we can do better. It is a place for coming together and appreciating how we differ and examining how very much we share" (Archibald, *The New Town Square: Museums and Communities in Transition* [2004], 78). Graham Black concurs, offering an ideal vision of museums that understand "the museum visit as a conversation between the collections, the users and the museum rather than viewing

users as empty vessels to be filled with didactic content" (Black, *Transforming Museums in the Twenty-first Century* [2011], 143).

The idea of museums as sites of public dialogue is not a new concept for anyone working in this profession. Rather than simply imparting knowledge, museums now facilitate a process by which visitors participate in the construction of meaning. This meaning making quite often involves a conversation among visitors and between museum staff and the wider community. In this way, museums have become sites of intellectual exchange during a time when other physical spaces of public interaction have diminished.

To truly embrace their identity as town squares, however, museums must face the possibility of controversy. As thoughtful and meaningful intellectual exchange becomes rarer in American culture, some institutions have come to equate public debate about an exhibit with public relations failure rather than as a successful execution of the mission to create community dialogue. Yet if everyone agrees from the outset, a dialogue has not been achieved. As an example, one of the most thought-provoking exhibits of the 1990s, Fred Wilson's Mining the Museum, generated mixed reactions on the part of its 55,000 visitors at the same time that it greatly influenced the museum field and the way that museum professionals view collections. The exhibit was revolutionary precisely because it sparked discussion and demanded that audience members consider questions of race and power in society. In doing so, it illustrated the potential of museums to foster meaningful conversation with their visitors.

But LGBT history is no longer the lightning rod that it once was, at least in many parts of the country. Many institutions interpreting the LGBT past received overwhelming support from their constituencies. This is particularly true of efforts undertaken in the past five years. Historic New England (Beauport) changed its interpretation at one of its historic *house museums to acknowledge the homosexuality of Henry Davis Sleeper, a prominent turn-of-the-twentieth-century interior designer, and received only positive feedback. Similarly, when the Jane Addams Hull-House Museum introduced visitors to the fact that American icon Jane Addams shared her life with a woman, the majority of visitor responses expressed a desire for more information.

The federally funded Rosie the Riveter/National World War II Home Front National Historical Park received only positive responses when it issued a call for firsthand LGBT stories of World War II. Even the tiny Morrison County (MN) Historical Society was able to include the story of a transgender county resident in its What It's Like . . . in Morrison County exhibit without outcry. Such examples suggest a public acknowledgment of the reality of sexual and gender variance and a desire to learn more, regardless of one's particular stand on current events. Museums represent a safe place in which the public can gain knowledge and consider the issues.

In recent decades, the awareness of museums' role as conveyors of cultural

*values and, by extension, relations of power, has led cultural organizations to expand their interpretive focus in an effort to reveal and interrogate standard social hierarchies. LGBT historical interpretation falls under this larger professional effort. It provides a means of telling a fuller story of the American past, introducing questions of power in society, and conveying welcome to a segment of society that has traditionally experienced exclusion.

In 2008, Reach Advisors conducted a survey of visitors to outdoor history museums and found that 95 percent of respondents thought it important for the sites to include stories of different races and cultures in their interpretation. Even more revealing, a full 69 percent of respondents said it was "extremely important" to do so. The experiences of gays and lesbians, of bisexuals, and of transgender people are part of the multicultural fabric of the United States. If museums are to truly engage with a holistic telling of the American past, LGBT history must be included in the narrative.

Growth in Visitation and Collections
With regard to collections, chances are that the outreach involved in interpreting the history of same-sex desire will lead to donations of LGBT-related material to the collection, which in turn will ensure that these items are preserved for future generations. In truth, some examples of interpretation in this area actually began primarily as collecting efforts. The Brooklyn Historical Society began planning its exhibit AIDS/Brooklyn after executive

director David Kahn noted that people who had lost loved ones to AIDS sometimes chose to destroy all material that reminded them of that loss. Out of fear that future generations would not understand the AIDS crisis, the society began preserving the *material culture of AIDS and opened its AIDS exhibit in 1993.

Collecting is often an integral part of interpreting LGBT history, and this can be an added benefit to organizations that lack substantial holdings in this area. However, Stacia Kuceyeski, director of outreach at the Ohio History Connection (formerly the Ohio Historical Society) and staff liaison to the Gay Ohio History Initiative (GOHI), argues that collecting is not enough on its own. GOHI's initial purpose was to collect and preserve the material culture of Ohio's LGBT communities; it did not have an immediate plan to present the materials to the public. In retrospect, however, Kuceyeski realized that the momentum generated by the project might have been better sustained had GOHI's strategic plan included the display of some of the items collected.

The Power of Revealing Lost History

Discussing LGBT history can be part of a larger mission of inclusivity. It can allow museums to reach new audiences and educate the public about the larger society in which they live. In addition to these benefits, there is also the simple power of providing a group of people with a past. Unlike ethnic minorities, queer people generally do not grow up among others like them. Many identify as LGBT only as adults or near-adults, and the act of adopting this identity quite often means abandoning other communities to which they have formerly belonged (such as families of origin, hometowns, and religious denominations). For people who have experienced this kind of displacement, history can heal. Unmoored people can find a sense of belonging in learning about the experiences of others like them who have come before.

Independent curator Gregory Hinton founded the Out West programming effort. Begun at the Autry National Center of the American West, Out West has now spread to museums and libraries throughout the mountain states and as far east as Indiana. It has combined a variety of efforts—exhibits, collecting, public presentations, special tours—in the service of interpreting the experiences of lesbian, gay, bisexual, transgender, and TwoSpirit people in the American West. For Hinton, a gay Wyoming native, Out West is an act of reclamation and healing:

"Born in rural western towns, many of us feel forced to leave our families behind and move to the city in search of safety, community, and companionship. . . . I wanted to come home to the West, but I wanted to come home as who I am. The dignity a museum, a library or a university lends to our community by preserving and sharing LGBT western history and culture is reassuring, esteeming, and therefore immeasurable" (Hinton, "Out West," keynote address, LGBTQ Alliance Luncheon presented at the American Alliance of Museums, Seattle, 2014).

Other observers agree, noting the power of LGBT history to provide validation to LGBT communities. One visitor to Becoming Visible: The Legacy of Stonewall (1994) at the New York Public Library cried as he walked through the exhibition, saying that the show made him feel he had "a place, a legitimate place, in the fabric of this country" (David W. Dunlap, "Library's Gay Show is an Eye-Opener, Even for Its Subjects," *New York Times*, September 6, 1994). Aren't we striving to make all our visitors welcome and feel they have a place in our country's history?

Incorporating LGBT experiences into museum interpretation holds the potential to embody museums' higher purposes. LGBT historical interpretation can foster public dialogue, enrich the full telling of U.S. history, expand audiences and collections, and provide a sense of belonging to a group whose contributions to the nation have been largely unrecognized.

SUSAN FERENTINOS

Adapted by Amy H. Wilson from Susan Ferentinos, *Interpreting LGBT History at Museums and Historic Sites* (2015).

See building bridges through local history; diversity and inclusion in museums; history museums and identity; relevance.

Library and Archives Canada. See Canada, Library and Archives.

Library of Congress. The Library of Congress has one of the world's premier collections of U.S. and foreign genealogical and local history publications. The library's collection began as early as 1815 when Congress purchased Thomas Jefferson's personal library. In August 1935, a "Reading Room for American Local History and Genealogy" was opened. Over the years the collection has greatly expanded. The library currently has more than 60,000 genealogies and more than 100,000 U.S. local histories.

In addition, the Library of Congress possesses related material of great significance such as archival resources, biographies, church histories, city directories, folklore collections, as well as geographical and historical works. Important resources can be found in the special collections of manuscripts, *maps and atlases, microforms, newspapers, *photographs, rare books, and electronic databases, housed in various areas of the Library.

The Library of Congress provides many resources and services via the Internet, all of which are described or available from the Library's home page at http://www.loc.gov.

Online Catalogs

The Library of Congress Online Catalog (http://catalog.loc.gov) contains approximately 18 million records representing books, serials, computer files, manuscripts, cartographic materials, music, sound recordings, and visual materials. The online catalog also displays searching aids for users, such as cross-references and scope notes. Many items from the library's special collections are accessible to users but are not represented in the online catalog. In addition, some individual items within collections (microforms, manuscripts, photographs, etc.) are not listed separately in the online catalog, but are represented by collection-level catalog records. In many such cases, the reading room holding the items or collections will have specialized catalogs or finding aids for identifying specific materials.

The Prints and Photographs Online Catalog (http://www.loc.gov/pictures) contains catalog records and many digital images representing a rich cross-section of still pictures held by the Prints & Photographs Division and other units of the library. The catalog provides access through group or item records to about 95 percent of the division's holdings. Many of the records are accompanied by one or more digital images. In some collections, only thumbnail images display to those searching outside the Library of Congress because of rights restrictions.

Digital Collections

The Library of Congress has provided access to a growing resource of digitized historical documents, photographs, sound recordings, moving pictures, books, pamphlets, maps, as well as "born digital" materials such as websites, and other collection materials from the Library of Congress's vast holdings. The library's digital collections (https://www.loc.gov/collections) consist of one of the largest bodies of noncommercial high-quality content on the Internet that document U.S. history and culture. Collections of interest to local historians include *American Life*

Histories: Manuscripts from the Federal Writers' Project, 1936 to 1940; *California as I Saw It: First-Person Narratives of California's Early Years, 1849–1900*; *Pioneering the Upper Midwest: Books from Michigan, Minnesota, and Wisconsin, ca. 1820–1910*; and *The Capital and the Bay: Narratives of Washington and the Chesapeake Bay Region, ca. 1600–1925*.

Research Centers

Although collections of interest to local historians are found throughout the library's many reading rooms and collections, Local History & Genealogy Reference Service (http://www.loc.gov/rr/genealogy) reference specialists in the Main Reading Room orient researchers to resources available to pursue local historical research at the library. The website includes online research orientations and published guides to the local history and genealogical collections of the Library of Congress. The library's collection of printed material is complemented by subscription databases available in each reading room. These include many titles that may also be available in large public or university libraries. Examples include ProQuest (*Ancestry Library Edition, ProQuest Historical Newspapers*, and *HeritageQuest Online*).

Researchers are able to send their inquiries to the library via Ask a Librarian (http://www.loc.gov/rr/askalib), the electronic reference service. If the Ask a Librarian link is selected from the Local History & Genealogy Reference Services web page, the question will go directly to the local history reference staff. Although the library staff cannot undertake original research in local history or genealogy, reference librarians will assist researchers with developing search strategies and providing research guidance in using the collections.

The library's historic Main Reading Room (http://www.loc.gov/rr/main), through its catalogs, 56,000 volumes of print reference works, and a wide variety of online databases, is the primary entrance to the library's general collections. It is the principal reading room for work in the social sciences and humanities. Here one may research the history of medicine, or look up biographical details about pioneer doctors or even the history of a particular hospital. Similar research material is available about other professions and religion.

The Microform Reading Room (http://www.loc.gov/rr/microform), located in the Microform and Electronic Resources Center, has a collection of directories from selected cities and towns, dating from the colonial period to as recently as 1960. This microform collection is complemented by the New York City telephone directories from 1878 to 1959, plus those of selected towns in surrounding areas of New York and New Jersey. Other important microform collections include

- Slave narratives, which are interviews with former slaves recorded between 1936 and 1938 by the Federal Writers Project. (Copies of the original transcripts are in the Manuscript Division.)
- The Barbour Collection, which indexes vital records transcribed from pre-1850 records for most Connecticut towns.

- Massachusetts Vital Records to 1850, and for some towns until around the beginning of the twentieth century.

These microforms are supplemented by the library's extensive collection of unclassified city directories in paper. All book material cataloged by the library is searchable in the library's online catalog.

In the Manuscript Reading Room (http://www.loc.gov/rr/mss) the researcher will find a wealth of material, including the Draper Manuscripts, the American loyalists collection, and, for German Americans, microfilm of the Hamburg ship passenger lists from 1850 to 1873. The Alaskan Russian Church Records, 1772 to 1936, may also be helpful to researchers.

The Geography and Map Reading Room (http://www.loc.gov/rr/geogmap) has material that can help researchers identify geographic locations. County atlases from 1825 onward show land ownership; some 1,500 county land-ownership maps date from the early nineteenth century; and ward maps are essential for obtaining ward numbers needed to undertake census research in major cities. U.S. Geological Survey Topographical Quadrangles from the 1880s are helpful in locating cemeteries as well as boundary lines described on plats and deeds. Fire insurance maps from 1867 to the present in the Sanborn collection indicate the size, shape, and construction of dwellings in 12,000 cities and towns.

The Newspaper and Current Periodical Reading Room (http://www.loc.gov/rr/news) houses a large collection of U.S. and foreign newspapers on microfilm and in hard copy. Through the *Chronicling America* website (chroniclingamerica.loc.gov) users may access millions of digitized newspaper pages from many different states between 1836–1922. The site also contains a U.S. newspaper directory to find information about American newspapers published from 1690 to the present. The Reading Room's reference collection has a number of helpful indexes to newspapers, and abstracts of marriage records, death notices, obituaries, and other data from a wide variety of local newspapers.

The Rare Book and Special Collections Reading Room (http://www.loc.gov/rr/rarebook) includes material such as the Confederate States Imprints, *almanacs, printed documents of the Colonial Congress and the colonial governments of New England, and the Charles H. Banks material on early Pilgrim families in Massachusetts. Also available are a large number of local histories, published and unpublished genealogies, pre-1861 city directories, and the library's collection of works published prior to 1801.

The Library of Congress provides book loans, periodical article photocopies, and newspaper microfilm loans when this material is not readily available from other sources. Not everything in the collection can be lent or copied. Many items in microfilm and microfiche formats are available for loan. Although the library does not circulate original copies of items published before 1801, genealogies, heraldries, or U.S. local histories, these materials will circulate if they have been micro-

filmed. Periodicals, whether bound or unbound, are noncirculating, but the library's Collections Access, Loan and Management (CALM) Division makes every effort to send gratis photocopies of individual articles when requested on interlibrary loan. The library's duplication service can supply photocopies for a fee if there are no copyright restrictions.

Using the Library

The Library of Congress is open to researchers over age sixteen with a library reader identification card that can be obtained easily with photo identification such as a driver's license or passport. In preparing to do research at the library, a few key points will increase the chances for a successful experience.

- Before arrival, search the library's website and the online catalog for books and materials of interest. This will help determine which library collections are accessible from remote locations and those that can be made available only within the Library of Congress.
- Define the research aims. With limited time in the world's largest library, well-defined research questions will help avoid tangential wanderings.
- Involve the library's experienced reference staff in your search. Researchers who do not ask for guidance and suggestions from the reference librarians may never know what they missed.

While the library is rich in collections of manuscripts, microfilms, newspapers, photographs, maps, and published material, it is not an archive or repository for unpublished or primary source county, state, or church records. Researchers seeking county records will need to visit the courthouse or a library in the county of interest, the state archives, the Family History Library in Salt Lake City, or one of its Family History Centers, all of which might have either the original county records or microform copies.

JAMES SWEANY
LIBRARY OF CONGRESS

See FamilySearch; Farm Security Administration photographs; genealogical resources online; Historic American Buildings Survey (HABS); Historic American Engineering Record (HAER); Historic American Landscapes Survey (HALS); radical trust and voice of authority.

Lithuanians in North America, sources for. See Appendix A.

living history museums. Living history is a technique of museum presentation and interpretation that attempts to create and animate a historical context or environment. Living history exhibits engage museum visitors through live interpretation and demonstrations as well as by providing sensory experiences that represent, evoke, and even try to re-create past life. Living history techniques have been embraced by many museums, particularly outdoor museums and historic sites. The majority of living history sites and museums focus on pre-industrial rural life on farms and in small villages or on military history in restored and recreated forts. With their high entertainment

value, living history techniques have been adopted by many historic sites and outdoor museums. Many of these institutions are more recently founded and more closely tied to tourist visitation and admission revenues than are typical traditional museums.

The Association for Living History, Farm, and Agricultural Museums (ALHFAM) brings together over 1,000 museum institutions, professionals, and practitioners who are engaged in living history. Embracing a range of definitions of living history practice, ALHFAM is at the forefront of the growth and professionalization of the use of living history techniques in museum programs. Such efforts most often include interpreters performing historical work and trades, domestic activities including historic *foodways, as well as agriculture (gardens, crops, and livestock), and military interpretation. Living history sites most often depict pre-industrial periods and settings.

Sites and museums that fully embrace living history strive to create a total historical context and environment. They select a date or period of presentation and attempt an authentic restoration of buildings, landscapes, furnishings, and costumes, eliminating or minimizing intrusions that "are not period." In living history farm museums, these restorations sometimes include back-bred livestock and heirloom crop varieties that reflect and even preserve the genetic characteristics of the past. At the same time, certain amounts of modern intrusion and anachronism remain inevitable.

Most living historical programs are presented by interpreters dressed in period costume, who speak to visitors in one of two styles or voices, known as "first" and "third person." Using techniques of improvisational theater based on research, first-person interpreters speak as individuals of the past, conversing as if visitors were time travelers to the interpreter's place in history. In first-person interpretation, the time is the "period" of the presentation; visitors are enticed into the historical time frame, and questions are limited accordingly. Third-person interpreters describe the past from the time frame of the visitor, normally not attempting to impersonate a historical character. This offers third-person interpreters greater freedom to respond to visitors and explain the past in the context of the present. Some living history museums and sites selectively employ both techniques, providing general third-person interpretation with first-person "impressions" offered as historical vignettes. Some use third-person guides to introduce visitors to first-person interpreters, assisting visitors in making the transition between present time and "period." Others employ a "modified third-person" technique that allows interpreters who are based in present time to embrace the historical period, describing "things we do" in the historical context.

The achievement and sustainability of high-quality living history presentations is challenging and expensive, requiring significant ongoing commitments to staffing, training, site preservation and maintenance, and supporting research. Particularly through the post-WWII decades, the popularity of the living history farms movement and

of military reenactments led to a proliferation of pre-industrial farms, villages, and forts that sometimes seem to mimic each other while they ignore other periods and themes of history, such as the urban and industrial past and the histories of immigrants and ethnic minorities. In more recent decades, many institutions with living history programs have been challenged by declining attendance and revenue. Changes in tourism patterns since the U.S. Bicentennial and the recessions of the subsequent decades appear to have challenged the growth of the living history field, as well as those of outdoor history museums and historic house museums.

At the same time, living history sites are often looked to as drivers of *cultural heritage tourism. A nostalgically attractive living history site may both appeal to visitors and inadvertently idealize the realities of past life and work. Similarly, the enthusiastic zeal for past life espoused by some living history interpreters may inadvertently skew the educational value of their sites.

Despite these pitfalls, living history can offer exciting, multisensory museum experiences that can captivate the interest of visitors and staff alike. The power of living history lies in its merging of educational interpretation and entertainment value, as well as in the immediacy of its engagement of museum visitors, often stimulating their interest in ways that static exhibits cannot.

A partial list of museums that conduct significant living history programs includes the following: Fort Ross (California); Bent's Old Fort and the White House Ranch (Colorado); Mystic Seaport (Connecticut); Conner Prairie and

Historic Fort Wayne (Indiana); Living History Farms (Iowa); Homeplace 1850 (Kentucky); Washburn-Norlands Living History Center (Maine); Old Sturbridge Village and Plimoth Plantation (Massachusetts); Fort Michilimackinac and the Henry Ford Museum & Greenfield Village (Michigan); Fort Snelling and the Oliver Kelley Farm (Minnesota); the Farmers' Museum, the Genesee Country Museum, and Philipsburg Manor (New York); Old Salem (North Carolina); Pennsbury Manor (Pennsylvania); Colonial Williamsburg, Jamestown Settlement, the Museum of Frontier American Culture, and the Yorktown Victory Center (Virginia); Old World Wisconsin; the Ronald V. Jensen Living Historical Farm (Utah); the Ukrainian Heritage Village (Alberta); the Fortress of Louisbourg (Nova Scotia); Black Creek Pioneer Village, Old Fort William, and Ontario's Sainte-Marie Among the Hurons and Upper Canada Village. This list is not exhaustive.

See Association for Living Historical Farms and Agricultural Museums (http://www.alhfam.org); Jay Anderson, *A Living History Reader*, Vol. I: *Museums* (1990), and Jay Anderson, ed., *Time Machines: The World of Living History* (1984); Warren Leon and Margaret Piatt, "Living History Museums," in *History Museums in the United States: A Critical Assessment*, ed. Warren Leon and Roy Rosenzweig (1989), 64–97; and "National Trust for Historic Preservation," *Forum Journal* (special issue, *America's Historic Sites At a Crossroads*, Spring 2016).

DAVID A. DONATH
BILLINGS FARM AND MUSEUM

See culinary history; gardens; gardens, interpreting at local history sites; museum theater.

local government records. County and municipal records document business processes and decisions, define prerogatives, track expenditures, defend the actions of local governments, and record the routine of government. "Record" means any book, paper, map, photograph, or other information-recording device, regardless of physical form or characteristic, that is made, produced, executed, or received by any local government or local government officer pursuant to law or in the transaction of public business. Records may occur in any format or in many formats. Counties, boroughs, parishes in Louisiana, towns, townships, cities, and villages—also known as general purpose local governments—create records on a daily basis. Approximately 5 percent of those records will be archival, with permanent research value for legal, historical, or other purposes, and on rare occasions, because of some identification with a famous person or event, some intrinsic value as well. Information contained in local records sometimes may be highly detailed and include important historical or genealogical information incidental to their original purposes.

While counties are generically similar to one another, they are particular and unique in their histories and structures. No two of them conduct their public business identically. Counties are often surrogates for federal or state programs, with funds passing to and through them to carry out a federal or state agenda.

There are far more municipalities in the United States than there are counties, and while they may be structured in similar fashions, they too are unique in the way they apply themselves to the public business, a condition that may vary even more from state to state. Functions of local government that are the responsibility of municipalities in one state may not be so in another. In some states, for example, public education may be a function of county or city governments, while in others school districts may be independent or quasi-independent special-purpose local governments.

Records provide an evolutionary trail through the growth and development of local governments, illustrating the development and history of governments as they became broader purveyors of public services, taking on roles—especially since the Great Depression of the 1930s and since World War II—unforeseen when they were established originally. Records are generated following such functions of local government as public health, public safety, public education, ownership or use of real property, social services, collection and expenditure of revenues, or public works. Because of the particular characteristics of county or municipal government, records for similar functions can vary widely in their creation, scope, content, organization, accessibility, and physical form, as well as the range of dates that such records may cover. Records from the early years of very old communities are different in almost every respect from contemporary records.

Not all public records may be available for public use. Some records are confidential and cannot be made available to the public, as may be the case with adoption or divorce records. Other records may be excluded from public use even under the various "sunshine laws" regarding *freedom of information, because they regard ongoing contract negotiations or confidential personnel matters. The uneven and frequently unsystematic acquisition and deployment of computer and other information technologies may also make access to records difficult, particularly when legacy software and obsolete hardware have not been replaced or information systematically converted to the next generation of technology. Finally, by no means do all local governments possess articulated programs of records and information management and archival administration, so that, while current records may be well maintained and accessible, older records or archival records may be lost, badly damaged, or stored haphazardly and without controls in scattered sites.

Many important records are the responsibility of municipal or county clerks or registrars. The best-known responsibility of the county clerk is as register of land documents, the recording and indexing of deeds, mortgages, mortgage satisfactions, and similar records. Municipal clerks are often the clerks of their respective legislative bodies and may also serve as registers of deeds and of vital statistics, keepers of minutes and as the administrative interface with the general public. All clerks may serve as agents for various state functions or as official receivers of documents for recording or filing. Some are marriage officers and registrars for marriage records.

Land-use records. Found in county and municipal governments, they may include the usual deeds and mortgages, but also records relating to environmental management, toxic spills or waste dumps, landfill openings and closures, site-plan and zoning reviews and decisions, environmental quality review records, official maps, subdivision documentation, and tax records. Building safety records can include building permits, code enforcement and inspection reports, and building condemnation and demolition records. The materials found in these records may include surveys, maps, blueprints, photographs, specifications, and detailed plans. Although often voluminous, such records contain valuable information on siting, design, construction, occupancy, use, and alterations to the *built environment. Tax records such as assessment rolls contain information on the owner, occupant, or user of property; assessed value; dates when constructed or modified; changes in property ownership; boundaries; neighboring properties; and lot or building dimensions. Early tax records may also reflect local responsibilities regarding militia or volunteer fire department service by adult male property owners and indicate special assessments and include lists of those eligible for militia duty or already serving. Environmental health records most often relate to community sanitation, sewage disposal systems, water supply, and lead paint and asbestos abatement. Many land-use–related records are created and maintained in electronic formats such as Geographic Information Systems, systems of computer software with the capability to manage, analyze, and display geographic data in a highly sophisticated manner.

Administrative records. Administrative records contain a wealth of material on the origins and operations of local government. Both general- and special-purpose local governments keep minutes of their governing bodies, boards, commissions, and panels. Minutes document hiring and firing, actions of governing bodies—including, where applicable, passage of local laws, resolutions, and ordinances; accounts of hearings, discussion and approval of contracts and expenditures; and all the business of local legislative bodies and their subsidiary and specialized lesser boards. Minutes from smaller local government entities may be quite detailed and personalized or simply a general account of the proceedings of meetings. Minutes may be subjective in content and can reveal, however unintentionally, a portrait of a given board, time, or community. Minutes can be an important source of community history and contain biographical or other genealogical information. Administrative records also include the documentation of expenditures and revenues, payrolls, oaths of office, personnel files, correspondence, plans, reports, and a wealth of other information about the daily operation of local government.

Vital records. Important information may also be found where municipal or county clerks are registrars of births, deaths, or marriages. In some states, vital records of this sort are considered state records, and local officials who keep them act as agents of state government. In states where public education was or is a function of general-purpose local governments, school attendance registers, annual reports, and similar materials may be filed with a county or municipal clerk. These are important records for legal, historical, or genealogical purposes: a researcher, for example, of the post–World War I Spanish influenza epidemic may find significant raw data in death certificates. In some states, access to these records is broader and more open than in others. In many states, access to these records is restricted to some degree. Access to some school records may be restricted under the Federal Education Rights and Privacy Act (FERPA).

Public safety records. The activities and functions of sheriff's departments, police and fire departments, building code inspectors, and similar agencies are documented by public records, some of which may be unavailable to researchers for legal reasons. Records in this category can document trends in crime, public protection, fire prevention and arson investigation, ambulance and paramedic activity, and the deployment of related resources. These records contain demographic information and a range of historical data. Early records of a city or county jail may include admission registers of prisoners detailing even the contents of their pockets, while police blotters contain descriptions of arrests and related information on a very local level.

Social-program records. Such records are often seen as "welfare records." They provide a long-term portrait of a given community and its care for its poor or disabled citizens. Early records may include Poor Rolls listing indigent citizens and the records of local alms-houses supported by local government. Rolls often note reasons for indigence such as "lunatic," "widow," or "crippled," and reflect both the state of the community and the values it associated with poverty, mental illness, and the use of public resources to support individuals unable to support themselves. Modern records comprise the full panoply of social service programs, may not be fully available to the public, and are often enormously voluminous.

Public works records. Public works records document the construction and maintenance of the public infrastructure: buildings, roads, bridges, and the like. Records may contain legal research on rights of way and eminent domain, surveys, maps, drawings, elevations, plans, contracts, specifications, agreements, environmental impact statements and reviews, and a considerable range of related materials. Documents regarding locally or nationally famous architects, engineers, or planners who were contracted for specific projects may be found as well as significant information of purely local importance regarding the layout of communities, parks, streets, and highways, and the construction of firehouses, court buildings, monuments, city halls, and other structures.

Court records. The structure of court systems varies greatly from state to state and has evolved and changed from the very beginning of this nation. Court records reflect the entire range of judicial jurisdiction and function, with case files that deal with petty and capital criminal cases and civil litigation from the most minor of contested issues to cases of national significance. Probate or surrogate courts settle wills and safeguard the estates of minors or the incapacitated. A huge amount of social, legal, and other information can be found in court records, although statutes or judges may seal certain cases, by type or specifically. Court records are voluminous, and the records of modern courts increasingly so, reflecting the litigious nature of society and other trends.

Public health records. Many county and municipal governments have in the past operated or are now operating hospitals, clinics, treatment programs of various sorts, laboratories, medical examiners' and coroners' offices, boards of health and health departments, departments of mental hygiene, and other health-related facilities and programs. Records from municipal or county facilities can include registers of patients or inmates, provide environmental or epidemiological data, and illustrate the history and development of local *health care and the factors that drove the creation of corresponding treatment efforts. Such records may be voluminous and also are likely to restrict the public access to them for legal or other reasons.

Miscellaneous local records. Early records in this broad category may include registers of cattle brands or earmarks, lists of those obligated to maintain public roads, registers of the manumission of slaves, registers of those in medical, legal, or other professions, election records, and cemetery maps and registers.

County and municipal records are as myriad as the histories and the influences continually shaping the governments that create them. They are created for relatively mundane purposes

and usually without an eye to future use beyond their administrative employment. They are an essential historical resource for academic and avocational users, and use of local records is on the increase nationally. Records in large local governments can be particularly voluminous and there may be records whose use is restricted by statute or regulation. In states without strong state regulatory or other oversight of local records, records may be relatively more difficult to access and utilize than in states that provide technical assistance and guidance to local officials in the management of their records. Local governments, many of which may lack even a municipal building, are often not equipped physically to offer ready use of their records. The challenges in local governments presented by the costs, uses, understanding, and balkanization of information technologies are unresolved and likely to remain so for decades, hindering both administration and research. Local records, especially those of general-purpose local governments, are a vital and highly significant administrative and research resource. As with any public records, access to and use of local government records is essential to an open society. Local government records provide the most intimate and candid picture of the community in which they were created. No portrait of a community can be complete without them.

ROBERT W. ARNOLD III
NEW YORK STATE ARCHIVES, RETIRED

See courts and court records; environmental history; vital records and vital statistics.

local government research topics.
Each local government is unique and
parochial, reflecting the particular history, needs, composition, issues, personalities, stresses, tensions, and challenges that shaped it. While all cities
may share some generic similarities, no
two are quite the same, which is also
true of all other types of general- and
special-purpose local governments. No
two are precisely identical. Local governments mirror their communities
and are created and changed according
to the needs of prominent citizens, important interests, state or federal statutes, and the sentiments of voters and
taxpayers. Local government is intimate
and immediate, the level of government
with which most citizens have at least
some familiarity, contact, and comfort.

General-purpose local governments
include counties, boroughs, parishes in
Louisiana, towns and townships, cities, and villages. General-purpose local
governments serve a broad spectrum of
public needs, providing services ranging from police protection to hospital
care. The menu of services can differ
widely from place to place, contingent
upon tax bases, traditions, population
size and demographics, and urban,
suburban, exurban, or rural location.
The tradition of governance in New
England, for instance, is mainly municipal, based on towns and cities. In
other parts of the country, counties are
strong and pervasive regional forces,
sometimes controlling public education
and dispensing social services.

Special-purpose local governments
usually are formed to provide a single
service or a band of services addressing
a single need. School districts provide
education. Fire districts provide fire
safety and, sometimes, paramedic and
ambulance services. Other types of special-purpose local governments—for
instance, public benefit corporations,
or special districts—focus on a particular community requirement. The extent and fullness of specialized services
offered depends on the same factors as
those that influence the extent of services offered by general-purpose local
governments.

Whatever the reason for the formation of a local government, whether
general or special purpose, each is
unique to its community, often the
product of a very long evolution—at
the town limits of Plymouth, Massachusetts, are signs tersely stating "founded
1620." Albany, New York, dates from
1624; Santa Fe, New Mexico, from circa
1609. These places, respectively, represented English-Separatist, Dutch, and
Spanish colonial administration and
stem originally from different cultures,
administrative practices, and traditions,
since modified by the centuries that
have passed. All local governments,
like the communities they govern, were
shaped as their histories unfolded, as
specific challenges raised stresses and
issues, and as their prosperity waxed
and waned. Local governments formed
prior to the American Civil War, or in
frontier communities, may be more
likely to have recorded their information as a sort of series of unique transactions. They may have been more ru-
dimentary and idiosyncratic in the sorts
of records created and the methods they
used to create those documents. With
the passage of time and the emergence
of various information technologies,

local government tends to have become increasingly systematic, creating records that are more detailed, comprehensive, and voluminous.

Until the Great Depression of the 1930s and World War II, the connection between local governments and state or federal levels of government was a relatively weak one. The connections that exist today were forged largely and are maintained by the pass-through of revenues or grant funds from one level to another, vertically and horizontally, combined occasionally with a less parochial political worldview permissive of resource or information sharing and the need for audit and control. In response to depression, world war, and their aftermath, general-purpose local governments began to widen the selection of services, particularly social services, that they provided for their citizens. Additionally, in the past half-century, local governments have become surrogates for the delivery of an increasing number of state and federal initiatives and therefore also mirror local responses to the larger issues with which the nation and the states attempt to deal.

Researching a local government can provide insight into trends in public administration and in the expansion and contraction of local governments at a given point in time. Study of the growth of social programs—aid to families with dependent children, for example, or institutional care for the community's infirm or elderly citizens—can lead from the colonial or nineteenth-century "overseers of the poor" or "comforters of the sick" (titles of actual offices in New England and New York) to municipal or county poorhouses, almshouses,

"Homes for the Incurable," and orphan asylums, and on to contemporary public hospitals, health clinics, and nursing homes for the aged. Such a study could illustrate on a purely local level the evolution of health care, public charity, and care for the elderly and the prevailing national, regional, and local attitudes toward those issues.

The transportation, communications, and industrial revolutions of the nineteenth century helped to create the cities of the United States. As cities grew rapidly, municipal leaders battled to keep pace with the needs of burgeoning populations. Cities gradually became more closely governed, under city councils and strong mayors. The nature of leadership, of just who composed the governing class, where they came from, and what they wrought, can be gleaned from a study of local government. The evolution of local government in large part depends on the impetus of civic groups or political factions—progressive or conservative, to one degree or another—and the leaders who emerge from their ranks. The egos of such leaders—who may be elected, appointed, or neither—play a strong role in the evolution of local government. A major role may also be played by other powerful interests and the minutes of a governing body may indicate the influence that a major employer may have on a town, or a taxpayers' group or neighborhood association on some city. In communities with a strong academic presence, such as a city with colleges or universities, town-and-gown issues may occupy an ongoing and significant place on the municipal agenda. An important regional flavor can often be detected, or at times also a close resemblance to what seems to be the regional, state, or national zeitgeist. Studying elections and which political parties, factions, or people are in or out of office thereby can be a barometer for political trends and styles and philosophies of governance.

As populations grew, so did the needs for potable water, adequate sewer systems, and all the other essentials and amenities of community life. Local government is as reactive as any other level of government, and its uphill struggle to provide for its citizens while living within its revenues—or its potential to bond or borrow—is probably the real story revealed in local government and its records. Examining the public works—including the architecture of public buildings—of a local government is often revealing of its past and present prosperity, or lack of it. The great city halls and county buildings of rich or once-rich communities are testimony to the worldviews once espoused by their citizens. In the second half of the twentieth century, the role of the *automobile is prominent, evidenced by paved streets and highways, traffic circles, stoplights, one-way streets, the rise of more remote residential neighborhoods, suburbs, and exurbs, police cars, municipal parking lots, parking meters, parking enforcement and assigned parking spaces, and arterial highways. The minutes of town or village meetings and the maps of highway superintendents will illustrate over the years the ever-growing importance of the internal combustion engine in American life.

Public records, produced routinely and for prosaic purposes, are an in-valuable and underutilized resource in historical, legal, and genealogical inquiry. Such records, too, are essential to demographic research, architectural preservation, historical *archaeology, and social and community planning, in preparing environmental-impact statements, and otherwise in understanding the effects of human actions on a certain area of occupation over time.

Local governments are not always equipped to accommodate researchers, especially when those governments are small, part-time, without a municipal building, or in the midst of particularly busy seasons, such as when tax bills are being prepared or collected, or in schools at the beginning or end of the academic year. Where this is the case, the public records may be spottier, a result of the absence of systematic continuity as officials may have failed to pass records and experience to their successors. The political environment of local government is often personal, and officials who fail to win reelection are not always graceful about transitioning their offices to those who replace them. Local officials, however, generally are well motivated and deeply rooted in the communities they serve. Usually they will be intimately acquainted with their current records, but may be less conversant with older ones. Not all local governments will enjoy the same high standard of administrative housekeeping and may lack even elementary programs for the management of their records while others may be highly sophisticated and employ up-to-date information technologies. Local officials cannot make some records available to researchers due to statutory or regulatory protections of the information therein or because of confidentiality requirements that frequently differ from state to state.

The study of local government per se has not been a prominent activity, although the use of local government records for historical, legal, and genealogical inquiry seems to be on the increase. Comprehending the structure of local government and its evolution is necessary for the researcher wishing to use local government records. To understand a community, the way it has been governed or has governed itself must be known. Local governments are small brushstrokes—sometimes most significant brushstrokes—on the national canvas. To underestimate the importance of local government in the pursuit of historical inquiry is to neglect a very large and important body of evidence of very diverse sorts.

ROBERT W. ARNOLD III
NEW YORK STATE ARCHIVES, RETIRED

See Freedom of Information Act; local government records.

Local Historian, The. See England, local history in.

local historian as public intellectual. In 1835 Ralph Waldo Emerson delivered an oration on the anniversary of the bicentennial of his town. "The History of Concord" is part of his great opus and widely available online. Emerson was a preacher, transcendentalist, lecturer, poet, essayist, romantic-localist, and travel writer. He was the—perhaps I should write *The*—public intellectual of his day who engaged in writing about

large topics, most of which still engage us today. But it is often forgotten that Emerson was also a local historian.

It is my contention that public and local historians are also public intellectuals, though not always recognized as such by our audiences or even by ourselves. It would seem presumptuous to stand up at a public meeting and say, "Well hi, I'm a public intellectual." That would not go over well.

However, in not claiming ownership of our status as being public intellectuals, we ignore an important feature of our role as investigators of our local history and we miss the opportunity to use our local knowledge for public enlightenment. As historians we raise questions worthy of our attention and of our audience. We are, after all, motivated by seeking an understanding of the past—not for commercial, and certainly not for personal, gain.

So what is this thing called a public historian? I have gathered some definitions. A public historian is first and foremost, a teacher of his or her community. Check! A public historian is a translator of academic interests to a general public. Check! A public historian is a speaker and writer about community topics and about our discipline. Check again, perhaps even twice! Emerson was a public historian. So have been Gore Vidal, Wendell Berry, Susan Sontag, Noam Chomsky, Edward Said, and most recently Ta-Nehisi Coates.

These are the things we do, especially when we think carefully and respectfully of our privileged place within a community. We are expected to explain, to teach, to translate, to raise questions—even those that make people uncomfortable. We are respecters of the past and also participants in contemporary life—something that the great French historian Marc Bloch thought important and that separates us from the charge of being antiquarians. I would argue that over the past thirty years we have made great strides in living our roles as public intellectuals by raising topics of importance to the people we live among, broadening our topics and our audience.

There are some cautions, however, as we stretch for audience. Polls and some recent political speakers show that Americans are woefully ignorant about the past. There seems to be an indifference to fact. There has been a move from the Jeffersonian and Emersonian belief in the burden of the past to a superficial passion for youthful memory. In some ways we have gone from a history of shared and broad significance to trivialization and fragmentation.

We need to remember that history is not story. This does not mean we should not tell history well and in an engaging fashion, using the storyteller's ability to engage the public. What it means is that history is not shaped by literary convention, with a beginning, middle, and end. Rather, history sometimes takes its own shape and the end might be in the future, as yet unformed. One historical society director recently said that in his organization, he was replacing the traditional lecture series with storytelling. He wanted to present, he commented, "The history they didn't teach in school. A little bit goofy and a little bit funny." I understand why he said this, but I think it demeans not only history and history teachers, but perhaps even his public.

The StoryCorps approach is inclusive and heartwarming, but without analysis and context we are left with vignettes. It would not be enough for Marc Bloch.

We have sometimes allowed ourselves to think that a cultural exhibit covers a subject. In our world, Hopi pots and Hungarian lace are lovely to look at and important to know about, but they are not enough to convey the subject of government-Indian relations in regard to land and culture or to explore the sometimes awkward welcome we have offered immigrants to this country. These cultural exhibits (which I always enjoy looking at) mask the greater and tougher questions of how we treat others, of how we all fit into a stew of people who are Americans. That is the bigger and more important subject.

So what questions should inform our work as public intellectuals? Below are some that concern me but I will not attempt to answer them. You will have others, I am sure. Each of us will have different ways of approaching these large issues, will have different evidence, and often arrive at different conclusions. Such is the practice of history.

I think it is very important that we ask how we became modern—whatever that means at the moment. We are obviously always evolving, both personally and as societies, but the question for me is how did we get to *this* place, right here, right now. The route is not straight or complete, but it is important.

Geography of place is important. What advantages does one place have, and have those advantages changed over time? What pulled people to a place and what pushed them out? And what have we done to our environment?

I think community evolution is important: how and when our communities took on the roles they have today. When did the poormaster evolve into the social service department? What are our responsibilities to each other as well as to ourselves as we attempt to create a just and better society for all? I like to ask why public participation in voting is so sadly lacking.

The idea of the family as a crucial unit of society is important to me. I think we should look at how families have been defined and how that definition has changed over time. What does being a member of a family mean and how has that also evolved? What are the consequences of our changing roles within a family (however it is structured)? What has been the consequence of a declining birth rate among some Americans and a high birth rate among others? What do these changes mean to the needs of families and communities?

Significantly, I think it is important that we look at history itself: how we have told the community's past and how we are telling it today. And what does that say about us? We should examine how we construct a historical question or narrative. How can we involve the public in that very construction because they are, as are we, living through history? What do we leave to the future that our times might be better understood?

I am interested in how our population has diversified and how we have opened up the democratic experience. This is true not only for suffrage, but also for education, business, mobility, and countless other factors. How has our sense of who we are as a community, as a people, changed over time? Whom do we include?

We need to think about our national myths. Are we all equally free? Is our democracy working? Is there fairness under the law? For any of these, the answer is certainly not always, and not for everyone. Other myths involve the idea of how we have amalgamated into one people. Yet, have we really? Are we a melting pot, a salad bowl, or do we sit at separate tables in the cafeteria and talk to our own? To paraphrase Martin Luther King, Jr., the arc of justice needs to further bend. We need to ask what we can learn from the past, without being, in Emersonian terms, beholden to the past but rather energized by our history.

Emerson's history will no longer satisfy. He honored his own ancestors excessively. He mythologized Concord. He called it a favorite and fortunate place. He talked of the merit of its famous people and the high character of its old stories. He wrote, "[In Concord] I find no ridiculous laws, no eavesdropping legislators, no hanging of witches, no ghosts, no whipping of Quakers, no unnatural crimes." He wrote Concord's history as if it was nothing but heroic.

But this approach is no longer good enough for us. Our histories have to be more complex because our world is complex and we reflect that in the questions we ask. We have broadened our topics and let in light. We have acted as the public intellectual, searching, preserving, researching while conscious of the bias in our documents and in ourselves. We have imposed order, and we have provided an immortality to events, places, and people of the past. We translate the documents of the past, pay attention to what scholars have to offer, and bring knowledge to our communities.

It is our job to ask the large questions of the day, going beyond the beauty of artifacts, beyond the heroism of ancestors. We have to also look at the condition of those who might be called the common people, who did not make it to prominence but whose histories accumulate to create our own. There is really no one else to ask these questions. Others *use* history, but we *explore* it to find out what is there and tell it in our hometowns so that others might know as well.

In this fractured time of boutique politics, ethnic and class divisions, inequality of condition and opportunity, and the gross misuse of history for partisan goals—of positions taken without sound historical bases—local history provides us with a place of quietude where we can find common ground and shared language. It's a base from which to investigate, to debate, to listen, and to learn. And it is the right place to ask the important questions of our time. Local history is our common space, and we need to use it, preserve it, and treat it well.

We need to justify what we do and we must just do it well. There is no one else. The local historian is qualified and trusted. Unlike some, we have not lost our audience. We are not an eddy of history; for many people we are the mainstream. If we do not ask the hard moral questions about the past, if we do not inhabit the role of public intellectual, who over time will do that for our age? What could be more worthy of our attention?

Reprinted from *History News* (Winter 2016).

Carol Kammen
Tompkins County (NY) Historian

See building bridges through local history; historical thinking; public history; values of history.

local historical societies and core purpose. As Tip O'Neill, the late Speaker of the House, famously said of politics: it's all local. So too is history. The sweeping historical narrative of the United States is ultimately—always—played out every day in town halls and church basements, and around water coolers and kitchen tables in American communities large and small.

Despite the seeming homogenization of American culture, a rich tapestry of socioeconomic, ethnic, and political variations exists that is often deeply rooted in a place. States, regions, and localities continue to respond differently, sometimes uniquely, to a whole host of national issues: New York's economic meltdown is not California's; Vermont's commitment to environmentalism remains true to its independent and often contrarian past; New Mexico and Arizona have front-row seats on a host of immigration issues that other states do not. Seeing and understanding these differences adds texture and complexity to the national historical narrative, which otherwise makes the United States look far too monolithic.

Adding layers of texture and complexity to the national story is why local history and local historical societies matter. But rather than encase the past in amber or revere some romanticized notions of nation-building as many historical societies are wont to do, the real work of these organizations lies in providing critical connective tissue that helps people understand how life today is shaped by the past and why that's important. In fact, a truly healthy historical society has only one foot rooted in the past; the other foot is firmly in the present and it's pointed toward the future. It understands that its real mission underlying the massive weight of collections and historic properties (which so often take precedent) is teaching history literacy and assuming accountability for it being done well.

That's right. It's not about the wedding dress exhibit or the precisely restored Victorian parlor or recreating a turn-of-the-twentieth-century ice cream social—these activities are only conduits for examining the human story, for connecting the dots over the continuum of time and making meaning out of it all. If the connecting and meaning pieces are missing, then what do you really have? A warehouse of old stuff. A historic building that's more mausoleum than "living history." A nice event that people attend, but don't think twice about.

The expectations are great for what historical societies can do and the impact they could make as a result. They become even greater when one considers the host of external and internal challenges most history-based institutions face today. As one historic site curator wrote in an editorial for her local paper:

The work of history museums, including historic sites, must be reliable, transparent and unbi-ased, or they lose the point for which they exist. But perhaps it is the point of historic sites that is most in jeopardy. Their goal cannot simply be to sustain themselves as an entertainment venue for yet another generation. If that is all historic sites are, why bother? The fact is, at their best, historic sites are so much more: They are quite literally the stuff of history. They make the past tangible; they embody art, beauty, the human spirit, the human experience. (Deborah Emmons-Andarawis, "Wrong Way to Promote History Museums," Albany Times Union, *June 5, 2011)*

Compounding this challenge is the seeming diminution of history literacy among children and adults, which does not bode well for the long-term health of historical societies. Despite the argument academics, researchers, and classroom educators make about the importance of social studies education, its presence in the life of the elementary, middle school, and secondary student seems to have been eclipsed by other subjects, most notably math and science. One high school teacher lamented the state of social studies education in this Internet post:

With [the focus] on reading and math skills leading to a "teach to the test" mentality, history has been getting short shrift in schools these days. Already, in the past few decades, the study of history has been shuffled into the shelter of social studies making it now one of a myriad of social sciences studied in one small period each day. In my state, public school social studies classes often have upwards of 40 students/class, which makes learning very difficult. The study of history does not seem to hold a place of importance any more.

This is sad to me because I see the study of history as very important in creating knowledgeable and engaged citizens for our nation. By teaching us to analyze the social, political, and economic threads of the past, the study of history gives us the skills to analyze those threads in the present. (Post by jilllessa, a tenth-grade teacher, in answer to the question why is the study of history important. E-Notes, April 2008, http://www.enotes.com/history/discuss/why-study-history-important-2651)

This is a tall order for many local historical societies that face the challenge every day of too few resources, but especially for those that struggle to be open to the public more than an afternoon or two a week, or lack training to develop "reliable, transparent and unbiased" programming, or wither under the shroud of backward-looking board or staff leadership. The result is that almost every historical society works, to greater or lesser degrees, with a mindset of scarcity imposed, yes, in part by many competing external realities, but more often hardened by rigid, dated, or simply small-bore thinking.

So, how does the local historical society (an organization based on a nineteenth-century model, we must remember) avert encasing its own self in amber? How should it, does it, reenvision itself for the twenty-first century?

First and foremost, let's get one thing absolutely clear: the best work of any historical society comes from great ideas, and the best ideas are scalable to place, budget, and time. Ideas come from all sorts of unexpected places within and outside of the museum field and the larger nonprofit sector, from other countries, from books and magazines, and from the blogosphere, YouTube, and a host of other Internet-based sources. Unfortunately, the silos that exist between small and large historical societies, and among museums of various disciplines, often prevent them from

grabbing and adapting great ideas. We have a lot to learn from each other, so it's necessary to keep small thinking at bay by permanently retiring the worn-out mantras of "we've never done it that way before" or "we did it that way once and it failed so we'll never do it again," and "we're too small/poor/rural for that." (Feel free to add your institution's own well-worn mantras here.)

Secondly, it's past time to replace the words *collect*, *preserve*, and *interpret* in the main body of the mission statement with words that embody the real reasons people and their communities need historical societies. The most successful historical societies understand that their research, education, collections, and conservation and preservation activities are first and foremost meant to deepen connection with external audiences, many of whom will never visit.

The reenvisioned core purpose can be summed up with a new trinity of externally focused actions supporting big, overarching ideas that speak to creating community impact and external value (with credit to the Ohio History Connection's 2008–2011 strategic plan for some powerful language):

- **Connection:** Empower and facilitate individuals, families, and groups to connect with each other and explore how ideas, people, actions, and the tangible evidence of the past shape contemporary life.
- **Civic Engagement:** Bring people and communities together to engage in meaningful activities and constructive dialogue that use a shared understanding of the past in ways that build a shared commitment to the future.

- **Collaboration:** Develop diverse partnerships to make more of what one has individually in order to multiply the benefits for all.

Lastly, embracing and making real a re-envisioned core purpose can be as satisfying as throwing open the windows of a room after a long winter. The rush of fresh organizational oxygen brings the work of the historical society into clearer focus. It can energize board and staff to tackle the complementary challenges so many historical societies face: difficulty finding board members, board leaders, and volunteers; attracting and retaining talented staff, and expanding the base of support.

Go ahead, open the windows.

ANNE W. ACKERSON
COUNCIL OF STATE ARCHIVISTS

See building bridges through local history; local historian as public intellectual; mission statements; museums, public value of; values of history; vision.

Local History. See England, local history in.

local history resources online. A collection of information stored electronically and available online, usually accessed through the web, is generally referred to as a database or digital collection. Many of the most powerful and largest databases and digital collections are produced by commercial firms and require subscription for access. Libraries, especially large city public libraries, university research libraries, or state libraries, often provide access for their patrons. Reference librarians are famil-

iar with the intricacies of access and are often trained and highly experienced in the use of databases.

Just like printed books, online databases and digital collections come in a variety of forms and content. New ones are produced every day by commercial firms, historical societies, archives, museums, and occasionally even individuals. Databases or collections can be the equivalent of a print index describing and listing books and articles, or they can consist of the sources themselves in scanned (digitized) and searchable form, referred to as full text.

America: History & Life (subscription required) is an essential for historical research; it's a continually updated index to books, articles, and dissertations, covering all aspects of the North American past, including local history and state history. It offers a variety of sophisticated search options. For precise, focused local history searching, try using the "advanced search" with the name of a town or county as a subject (use the dropdown menu) and a range of dates in the historical period boxes on the lower part of the screen.

Google Scholar (http://scholar.google.com) is a freely available index to scholarly articles on all topics. *Google Books* (http://books.google.com) is a massive and continually growing collection of scanned books and periodicals. Many older titles (pre-1923), which are now in the public domain, can be viewed in their entirety and the full text searched. In both Google Scholar and Google Books, the "advanced search" will provide options for narrowing the focus and getting more precise results. In the case of Google Books, it's desirable and possible to restrict the results by time period in the advanced search, found under the "My Library" option.

Genealogy databases often overlap with local history. *HeritageQuest Online (subscription required) has two useful components: Books, a collection of searchable full-text books, relating to biography, family history, town and county history, and PERSI, a comprehensive bibliography of articles from North American genealogy and local history periodicals since 1800. The search interface is simple and friendly. *Ancestry.com (subscription required) has many resources for local historians: census records, land ownership records, and many reference tools. Cyndi's List (http://www.cyndislist.com), which is free, collects and categorizes websites; it's primarily aimed at genealogists but local historians will find it useful too, especially because the categories are frequently updated.

Newspapers are an invaluable source for local history, and they are increasingly being scanned and made available online. Two important full-text databases are America's Historical Newspapers (subscription required), which includes issues from the earliest American newspapers back to the seventeenth century, and Proquest Historical Newspapers (subscription required), which contains full page scans of major U.S. newspapers, such as the *New York Times* and the *Wall Street Journal*. In recent years, organizations and individuals have begun digitizing issues of newspapers and making them publicly available on the web. Examples of such initiatives include Chronicling America: Historic American Newspapers,

Small Town Newspapers, and Google News Archive (a mixture of freely available and subscription). More of these collections will no doubt appear in the future. Individuals, societies, or organizations sometimes scan a few issues of a particular newspaper and post them on the web. Try using a search engine, such as Google, with the name of the newspaper in quotations to locate scanned issues of a particular publication.

Other types of *primary sources— *diaries, government records, *maps, photographs, contemporary books and articles, manuscripts, etc.—are also increasingly being digitized and made available online. Although their focus is more broadly the nation, many of these digital collections include gems for the local history researcher. Some representative examples include the *Library of Congress's American Memory (http://memory.loc.gov/ammem/index.html); the Making of America (http://quod.lib.umich.edu/m/moagrp) and (http://digital.library.cornell.edu/m/moa), and American Journeys: eyewitness accounts of early American exploration and settlement (http://www.americanjourneys.org). The *Valley of the Shadow (http://valley.lib.virginia.edu) is an innovative site that compares one Northern and one Southern county at opposite ends of the Shenandoah Valley during the Civil War using a variety of original sources to examine local economics and political culture.

Increasingly, regional, state, and county historical societies, university libraries, organizations, state libraries, and even individuals are creating modest bibliographic databases and digitizing smaller collections of primary sources. The websites of local/regional historical and/or genealogy societies often serve as portals to area collections and resources and can sometimes be one of the first places to list and describe new projects. Check them periodically.

Databases, digital collections, websites, and search engines are subject to change at any time. Keeping current with what is available and discovering additional resources is an ongoing process.

VIRGINIA COLE
CORNELL UNIVERSITY

See Ancestry.com; genealogy, an archivist's view; genealogy resources online; Heritage Quest.

local history workshops. Local history workshops (sometimes called research groups) grew up in the United Kingdom in the 1960s. They took two main forms. One was a movement that emerged from the post–WWII adult education program. This consisted of local history study groups (LHSG), provided with professional tutorial assistance by adult education agencies such as the Workers' Educational Association (WEA), various university departments of extramural studies (or adult education), and other bodies. Such groups undertook a joint study of an aspect of the history of their own locality, and many wrote up and published their findings in some form or other (sometimes in book or booklet format, sometimes in other forms such as an exhibition or radio program, etc.). Many useful studies were produced: for example, Bernard Jennings's *History of Nidderdale* (Yorkshire) in 1967. Training and other forms of support were

provided, and adult education agencies often helped with the costs involved in such group work. A training manual for such group work was published, *Group Projects in Local History* (ed. Alan Rogers, 1977); this included general chapters on "working with groups" and "group writing" as well as more detailed examples of local history projects ranging from medieval landscapes to twentieth-century history. This movement was particularly strong in local population studies where groups transcribed parish registers and other records and analyzed them, and a regular journal (*Local Population Studies, LPS*) for such groups was published.

It is important to distinguish these LHSGs from the other local history, and especially family history, groups (LHGs, FHGs) that formed at this time, in which all the members were pursuing their own studies and meeting to share experiences. The members of LHSGs combined on a single project to share their work. The value of this approach was not only that the groups could cover more ground and more sources than could be handled by a single local historian in the same time, but also that they encouraged creative work from a number of persons who may not have done such work alone. They showed that different group members brought to their combined study their individual and different knowledge, experience, and skills. And in them, knowledge was shared among the group and throughout the community rather than belonging to an individual expert. But much depended on the leadership and, in the case of publication, the editorial skills available to the group. Several of these LHSGs did not produce published work, but their educational value was still high. Some of these research groups resulted in longer-lasting local history societies.

This movement spread into the United States in the early 1980s, most notably in the East Tennessee "Hard Times Remembered" project. But it largely died out in the United Kingdom as funding for adult education changed and local history courses in adult education became certificated. The emphasis is now once again on the education of individuals who are expert on the history of their region or on some local history theme. Even population history groups are now rarer. A research report in 1993 by Joan Unwin of Sheffield University attempted to provide evidence of the social and educational value of study groups such as these—not just in local history but also creative-writing groups and natural history groups.

Recently, however, there has been something of a revival of a number of LHSGs in many parts of the United Kingdom in a new form. This is the result of three parallel strands—the Millennium, which stirred interest at the community level in local history, new funding available from the National Lottery Heritage Fund for community activities, and the spread of the Internet. Village groups have been formed to collect historical material relating to local communities or to make surveys of older sites in the locality, and (as well as exhibitions and publications) the findings have been disseminated on websites devoted to particular local communities. This process is spreading. Some groups have been able to obtain professional monitoring and mentoring from friendly academics but many are unsupervised—with the result that the quality of the work is variable; some of the more remarkable myths of local history are reappearing. For an example of high-quality work, see www.langham-village.com.

The second form of workshops was the History Workshop movement. This started at Ruskin College, Oxford, the former trade union study center, again in the 1960s. Students at the college engaged in research into topics that drew on their own working-class experiences and expertise in regular seminars, and several publications resulted from their work. Once or more each year, a large and very informal two- or three-day meeting of social (mostly socialist and later feminist) historians (many of them former students of Ruskin College) gathered to discuss a large number of pioneering studies, not all but several of them on themes of local history. These workshops widened interest among historians more generally in areas of radical social history, focusing on gender, ethnicity, the very poor, disadvantaged groups, marginal and often overlooked groups of workers such as quarry workers, children, immigrants, etc. There was often a political agenda in these debates. Reports of these meetings were produced, and from 1976, an annual journal entitled *History Workshop* was published. From 1980, the annual History Workshop more often than not moved out of Oxford to other parts of the country; it became more closely tied to the formal education system, especially in the polytechnics, and more professional in its membership.

These workshops tended to have more local history papers in them than the Oxford History Workshops. In addition, "Local History Workshops" were held briefly, from time to time, in various other venues. The movement has declined, largely because of the death of its primary inspiration, Dr. Raphael Samuel.

ALAN ROGERS
UNIVERSITY OF NOTTINGHAM

See England, local history in.

Louisiana, local history in. Louisiana is a history-conscious state. The diverse culture as well as the fact that Louisiana has been the setting of significant events—from the Louisiana Purchase through Katrina—accounts for a sense of connectedness to the past. The study of history is supported by both historical organizations and the schools.

The Louisiana Historical Society was chartered by an act of the state legislature in 1836. Historian and jurist Charles Gayarre was the first president. The society has always been a volunteer organization that has encouraged the study, writing, and promulgation of Louisiana history. In 1860 the legislature placed in the society's possession the French Superior Council Records from 1718–1766 and the Spanish Judicial Records from 1766–1803. In 1907 the society actively supported the legislation for the creation of a state museum in New Orleans to house the colonial documents in addition to works of art and artifacts that the society acquired over time. Between 1901 and 1961 the society published *Louisiana Historical Quarterly*, a journal commit-

ted to research and writing of articles on Louisiana history by both amateur and professional historians. Today the Louisiana Historical Society sponsors lectures, historical tours, a Creole Family Symposium, and an annual banquet commemorating the Battle of New Orleans. The LHS is currently supporting the *digitization process of the colonial documents at the State Museum so that they will be available to scholars on the Internet.

The Louisiana Historical Association was originally founded as a Confederate veteran's organization in New Orleans in 1889. In 1891 they dedicated Memorial Hall on Camp Street, a Romanesque-style building that became a repository for Confederate records, writings, and artifacts. This latter became the Confederate Museum, and today is the Civil War Museum. However, the character and identity of the LHA changed dramatically when in 1958 academic historians from Louisiana colleges turned it into an organization of professional historians. Since 1961, the Louisiana Historical Association has published *Louisiana History*, a journal of scholarly articles written mainly by professional historians. The organization is run out of the University of Louisiana at Lafayette. In 2012 the LHA will hold their annual conference in New Orleans as part of a series of events celebrating the bicentennial of Louisiana statehood. The Louisiana Historical Association and the Louisiana Historical Society plan on having a joint session on the respective histories of both organizations.

January 8, 2015, was the bicentennial of the Battle of New Orleans. The Louisiana Historical Society led the centen-

This historical marker, at the corner of Press and Royal Streets in New Orleans, Louisiana, marks the site where Homer Adolph Plessy was arrested, instigating what became the landmark U.S. Supreme Court case, Plessy v. Ferguson. CREDIT: BRIAN SWANNER.

nial celebration of 1915 and thought it important to play a role in the commemoration of 2015. In October the historical society hosted an all-day workshop geared for teachers but open to the public. Howard Hunter, president of the historical society, gave the keynote on how the battle was memorialized in 1915 and 1965; Ron Chapman, author of *But for a Piece of Wood* spoke on the military causes of the American victory; Jason Wiese of the Historic New Orleans Collection gave a lecture on the British experience leading up to the battle; and Carolyn Kolb of Tulane University treated the audience to examples of music in New Orleans during the period.

Louisiana history is required in public schools in grades three and eight.

Nevertheless, Louisiana has the highest percentage of children in nonpublic schools in the nation and it's safe to say that a number of children are exposed to a paucity of Louisiana history. All secondary history teachers in both public and private schools are required to take Louisiana history. Unfortunately, there is a shortage of teachers in the public sector with a degree in history (most have a certification in that opaque discipline, social studies). However, there have been some gains. The Louisiana Endowment for the Humanities obtained federal grants for teacher summer institutes in the teaching of American history for school districts in New Orleans, Lake Charles, Shreveport, and Monroe. Other school districts in Algiers and Hammond have also participated in the Teaching American History federal grant program. The Louisiana Endowment for the Humanities has also launched KnowLa, the digital *Encyclopedia of Louisiana History and Culture.* All students will have free access to what looks to be a dynamic educational tool for all Louisiana schools.

Histories of Louisiana have been written almost since its inception. The first history was written by jurist Francois Xavier Martin in 1827, and Charles Gayarre completed a four-volume history between 1848 and 1866. Joe Gray Taylor's *Louisiana: A Bicentennial History* (1976) and Bennet Wall and Light Cummins's *Louisiana: A History* (1990) are the most accessible for a general readership, and in both cases the scholarship of the authors has the benefit of perspective.

G. HOWARD HUNTER
LOUISIANA HISTORICAL SOCIETY

See United States, local history in.

Lutheran church, sources for. See Appendix B.

$\mathcal{M}$

Macedonians in North America, sources for. See Appendix A.

Maine, local history in. Though Maine only separated from Massachusetts in 1820, and became a state as a result of the Missouri Compromise, it has been inhabited for some 12,000 years by native peoples. The French first settled at St. Croix in 1604, establishing the colony of Acadia and the English, briefly, at Popham in 1607. By 1639 the Province and County of Maine was established at York, though by the 1750s the province was swallowed by the Bay Colony. Wars between the English, French, and native people led to the destruction of all English towns (except the York, Kittery, Wells area) and by 1755 the English began expelling the French from Acadia and establishing truck houses for the Indians.

Interest in the history of Maine commenced at an early date. In 1795 James Sullivan, a native of Berwick, attorney and governor of Massachusetts, produced his fascinating *The History of the District of Maine* (reprinted by the Maine State Museum in 1970). The great geographer Moses Greenleaf followed with *Statistical View of the District of Maine* (1816) and *A Survey of the State of Maine* (1829). Between these books, and only two years after Maine became a state, forty-nine prominent men incorporated the Maine Historical Society (MHS), the third such society in the nation. The object of the group was "to collect, preserve . . . whatever in their opinion, may tend to explain and illustrate any department of civil, ecclesiastical and natural history, especially in this state and the United States." Meeting in the Portland State House (Augusta was selected as the new capital 1827), the society chose Gov. Albion K. Parris as president and Rev. Edward Payson as librarian, and started its peripatetic life as a private organization sanctioned by the state. In the 1830s the organization moved from Portland to Bowdoin College (1794) and back to Portland in the 1880s.

Through the vision of Anne Longfellow Pierce (who deeded the Wadsworth-Longfellow House to the society), a companion library was opened in 1907 (expanded 2009). In its long history, MHS has built a holding of over several million manuscript pages, including the J. S. H. Fogg Collection of 5,000 significant documents including all the signers of the Declaration of Independence as well as the Benedict Arnold Letter book of 1775 donated by Col. Aaron Burr in 1831. During the nineteenth and twentieth centuries, the society published the notable collections of the MHS and Documentary History Series, the Province and Court Records, and the journal *Maine History*. Since the 1960s MHS has made major changes in both outreach, facilities, and professional personnel, adding a gallery for visual objects that had been collected in the course of three centuries and the award-winning Maine Memory Network, an online museum and archive of collections from historical organizations across the state.

Interest in state and local history flourished in Maine colleges beginning with Bowdoin and its extraordinary library, Colby (1813), Bates (1855), University of Maine (1862), and a variety of others. The University of Southern Maine has an important ethnic Diversity Collection and the University of New England houses the Maine Women Writers Collection, both founded in the twentieth century. However, private historians working on their own propelled scholarship. William D. Williamson wrote the excellent *The History of the State of Maine* in 1832, and the remarkable George Folsom (a critic of Williamson and Sullivan) produced the influential *History of Saco and Biddeford* (1830), a model of many town histories to follow. William Willis produced his first *History of Portland* in 1833 and the revised classic in 1863. In 1920 Fr. Thomas Albert gave voice to Acadians in his much-quoted *Histoire du Madawaska*.

The proliferation of town histories and Civil War regimentals was soon matched by organizations, including the Bangor Historical Society (1864), founded by John E. Godfrey and others to "acquire facts and materials in relation to this part of the State and particularly as it relates to the valley of the Penobscot"; the York Institute (1866), founded by photographer John Johnson and others to promote the study of natural and civic history in Saco

and York Counties and the Pejepscot Historical Society (1888) founded by sixteen citizens in the Brunswick, Topsham, Harpswell region. This growth is discussed in *Maine Bibliographies*, by Elizabeth Ring (1973). At the dawn of the twentieth century interest in family history led societies including MHS to include more genealogy and indeed, the first ethnic budding occurred with such publications as *Catholic History* (begun 1913). The WPA had a major impact on the state with a number of town histories and cataloging projects accomplished under the Historical Records Survey (1937–1941) and publications by Maine Studies (1938–1941) under the Federal Emergency Relief Act.

The State of Maine founded the Maine State Library in Augusta in 1839 and in 1907 appointed the celebrated historian Henry S. Burrage to the office of State Historian, a position held since 2003 by Earle G. Shettleworth. In 1919 the Maine State Museum was begun and in 1965 Maine State Archives appeared (previously all archiving was by department) and in 1971 all three departments were housed in Augusta's Maine Cultural Building. In that same year the legislature took a major step in creating the Maine Historic Preservation Commission, whose director is the State Historic Preservation Officer. The commission is responsible for the identification, evaluation, and protection of Maine's significant cultural resources. During the 1960s as a result of the preservation movement, under the former League of Historical Societies and Museums and other groups, the study and understanding of Maine's history rose to new heights and led to important practitioners including Laurel Thatcher Ulrich, Alan Taylor, William Bunting, and a variety of others.

As Elizabeth Ring, the first instructor of Maine history at the University of Maine at Orono wrote in 1973, "many areas of historical investigation still remain to be explored."

WILLIAM DAVID BARRY
MAINE HISTORICAL SOCIETY

See United States, local history in.

manifest destiny. As defined by Mitford M. Mathews in his *Dictionary of Americanisms on Historical Principles* (1951), this term has been used by those who believed that it was the destiny—or the right—of the United States to govern the entire Western Hemisphere, as in "our manifest destiny to overspread the continent." Julius W. Pratt, in an article in the *American Historical Review* (XXXII [1927], 798) entitled "The Origin of 'Manifest Destiny,'" traced its first use in the House of Representatives to Robert C. Winthrop of Massachusetts on January 3, 1846, when Winthrop stated "the right of our manifest destiny to spread over this whole continent." But the term was not original to Winthrop. Pratt found it used in the *New York Morning News* on December 27, 1845, in an editorial entitled "The True Title," in which editor John L. O'Sullivan stated that it was the "right of our manifest destiny to overspread and possess the whole of the continent." O'Sullivan was editor of both the *Morning News* and the *Democratic Review*. He had written in a *Democratic Review* editorial, on July 9, 1845, that it was the "fulfillment of our destiny to overspread this entire North America." While the December use of the term was in association with the debate over Oregon, O'Sullivan first used the concept of "manifest destiny" in a discussion of the annexation of Texas.

CAROL KAMMEN
TOMPKINS COUNTY (NY) HISTORIAN

See American exceptionalism; Dictionary of Americanisms.

Manitoba, local history in. Many Manitobans know a great deal about the history of their local community and about the limited groups that they regard as important. They are not especially knowledgeable about their province's history nor, according to a recent survey, are they especially interested in it.

The first agency to address public awareness of the past, the Historical and Scientific Society of Manitoba, was founded in 1879, nine years after Manitoba became the first new province of Canada. For the next decade, during the initial era of large-scale western settlement, it was a key research institution and its library, scientific papers, and expeditions were widely known. It gave up many of these activities in the following generation, becoming the Manitoba Historical Society and serving as an educational agency, sponsor of lectures, and lobbyist for historical plaques. It fulfills similar roles today, though it has added a magazine and two museums to its list of responsibilities.

Provincial historical awareness and research have been bolstered by the exceptional contributions of government agencies, whether local, provincial, or national, which made local history a priority from about 1970. These include Library and Archives Canada (MB Regional Service Centre), Archives of Manitoba (the first provincial archivist was appointed in 1952), Manitoba Vital Statistics, City of Winnipeg Archives, Manitoba Legislative Library (the first provincial librarian was appointed in 1884), Winnipeg Millennium Library (Local History Room), Manitoba Museum, and Winnipeg Art Gallery. The extraordinary Hudson's Bay Company collection (1670–), opened to the public in 1975, has been included in UNESCO's "Memory of the World" registry. The universities have archival branches that collect materials for the broader community as well as those pertaining to the institution, and scholarly departments that encourage local study. Municipal and school records are sometimes held in formal archival collections but are often available through specific municipalities. Other important sources include church archives (e.g., United Church Archives, Archives of the Anglican Diocese of Rupert's Land, Mennonite Heritage Centre, and others) and files held by fraternal and other nonprofit organizations. Lists of community-based resources are available from the Association for Manitoba Archives and the Association of Manitoba Museums. Manitoba historical records can also be found in corporate archives though public access is not always readily available.

The work of the provincial historical society has been supplemented by a number of voluntary community historical organizations, including those of ethnic and religious groups (Métis,

French Canadian, Ukrainian, Jewish, among others), occupational and hobby groups (antiques and collectibles, aviation, firefighting, hydro, military, railways, telephones, and others), and research interest groups (archaeology, genealogy, heritage buildings, living history, naturalists, and others). There are active local historical societies and heritage associations around Manitoba, and vibrant archives in some schools and community museums.

Public campaigns have enlisted the support of federal, provincial, and local governments to ensure that major landmarks are preserved. The record of Manitobans' preservation of buildings and sites includes some wonderful successes, such as the fur trade posts of Lower Fort Garry, Fort Prince of Wales (Churchill), and York Factory. Some communities have advocacy groups that promote sites of special interest (e.g., Heritage Winnipeg, Brandon Municipal Heritage Committee).

The writing of provincial history began in the mid-nineteenth century with the publication of fur traders' and travelers' observations. Papers have been published periodically since that time, beginning in the *Transactions of the Historical and Scientific Society of Manitoba* and, since 1980, in the society's journal, *Manitoba History*. The first historians to present narratives based on archival research include George Bryce, Margaret McWilliams, and Chester Martin. Professor W. L. Morton became the dean of Manitoba historians in the mid-twentieth century and among his books is a fine local history, *Third Crossing: A History of the First Quarter Century of the Town and District of Gladstone in the*

Province of Manitoba (1946), cowritten with Margaret Morton Fahrni. The various ethnic, religious, and other societies have also published newsletters, books, and documentary collections. Local history received a boost with the celebration of Canada's centennial in 1967 and Manitoba's centennial in 1970. Since that time, numerous local histories have been published, many by an Altona, Manitoba, printing corporation, Friesens, which also advises groups on the preparation of such volumes. *A Guide to the Study of Manitoba Local History* (1981) by Gerald Friesen and Barry Potyondi contains some useful material. Two recent collections of essays, one on political history (Barry Ferguson and Robert Wardhaugh, eds., *Manitoba Premiers of the 19th and 20th Centuries* [2010]), the other on provincial parties and government (Paul G. Thomas and Curtis Brown, eds., *Manitoba Politics and Government* [2010]), survey many aspects of the Manitoba story. The *Encyclopedia of Manitoba* contains almost 2,000 entries that cover many more.

The provincial school system requires classes to study the local community, including its history, in grade four. The compulsory Canadian history course in grade eleven contains materials on Manitoba provincial and prairie regional history. Heritage Fairs aimed at schoolchildren foster interest in local history. Courses in the universities also address local topics.

There is a growing collection of materials relating to Manitoba history on the Internet. The Manitoba Historical Society has digitized all its older publications (*Transactions, Manitoba Pageant, Manitoba History*) and those of the Manitoba Record Society, and is developing web-only finding aids and collections such as biographies of noteworthy Manitobans and an interactive map of historic sites throughout the province. Digitized newspapers are an excellent source of primary information; the entire run of the *Manitoba Free Press* (now *Winnipeg Free Press*), from 1874 to the present, is available online, along with select issues of the *Winnipeg Tribune* and *Brandon Sun* and smaller community papers. The Manitoba Library Consortium's *Manitobia* website is an excellent repository of historical materials. The Manitoba Digital Alliance is scanning all local history books published in Manitoba and has put over 200 text-searchable versions online with more to come. National online resources with material specific to Manitoba include Library and Archives Canada (e.g., fire insurance maps, military personnel files), Automated Genealogy (1901, 1906, and 1911 Manitoba census transcriptions), Manitoba Vital Statistics, and Henderson's Directories of Winnipeg.

GERALD FRIESEN AND GORDON
GOLDSBOROUGH
UNIVERSITY OF MANITOBA

See Canada, local history in.

manuscript. Any document written by hand such as a letter, diary, report. Manuscript also refers to the unpublished text of a book prior to publication; its abbreviation is "MS" or "MSS," in the plural.

maps and atlases. Maps and related geographical resources are essential to local history. Historical events take place in geographical contexts: administrative contexts such as towns, villages, cities, and counties, or topographies such as plains, lakes, or mountains. Many aspects of the geographical context can be represented with maps. Maps show, for example, the boundaries of the local area of study and related administrative boundaries. They represent features, such as topography, transportation networks, settlement patterns, geology, and many others, which the local historian will need to understand to write a coherent history of a place. Maps frequently represent changes a place undergoes over time, for example boundary changes, road and railroad building, housing construction, and geologic changes such as landslides and floods.

Maps represent features by projecting the rounded surface of some part of the earth onto a flat surface, then shrinking the representation of the earth on the surface to provide a suitable scale for what is being studied. Projection and scale allow features on the map to be shown with correct geographical relationships to each other. Some sort of coordinate system (usually latitude and longitude) allows one to locate features on the map. Geographical relationships allow historians to frame salient historical relationships. Maps also provide a set of symbols for particular features, so that the features can be correctly identified and shown on the map with appropriate labels.

The decisions that go into creating a map are arbitrary, so some knowledge of map production is required to use maps effectively. An excellent guide for local historians is Melinda Kashuba, *Walk-*ing with Your Ancestors: A Genealogist's Guide to Using Maps and Geography* (2005), in particular chapter 4, "The Secrets of Map Reading." More extensive technical help is available from A. John Kimerling et al., *Map Use: Reading, Analysis and Interpretation* (2011).

Maps are an important resource for local historians, but they need to be used with care. Every map is created for a purpose. Often the purpose is explicit, but frequently there may be a hidden agenda, or simply a set of assumptions that need to be examined before drawing historical conclusions. A useful antidote to our tendency to accept maps uncritically is Mark Mononier, *How to Lie with Maps* (1996).

Maps are dense with information, but even so, historians will need to supplement the information a map supplies with other resources. *Gazetteers and *city directories, land survey records (see below), and *census records can be useful adjuncts to maps. Frequently research will require several different kinds of maps; an excellent overview of the many types of maps a local historian is likely to consult is Carol Mehr Schiffman, "Geographic Tools: Maps Atlases and Gazetteers," in Kory Leland Meyerink, *Printed Sources: A Guide to Published Genealogical Records* (1998), 95–145. Schiffman appends a state-by-state bibliography of major cartographic resources.

Mapmakers have depicted the natural and human landscape of America on maps and charts since the Age of Discovery and the colonial era. The Revolution put the job of describing the new country into the hands of an increasingly skilled group of American cartographers. The westward movement after the American Revolution provided an additional impetus to produce more and increasingly accurate maps. Large numbers of individual farms and other landholdings, the growth of towns, villages, and cities, and the expansion of the transportation network of canals, roads, and railroads led to a rapid increase in the number and types of maps. Cartographers began producing accurate, comprehensive state maps and atlases in the early nineteenth century. By midcentury, commercial map publishers were regularly producing a wide variety of maps including, beginning in the 1850s, large-scale county wall maps, many showing landownership.

Immediately after the Civil War, entrepreneurial publishers produced thousands of county atlases. Originally these were constructed from the unwieldy county wall maps that still decorate many a historical society, but later they were designed as atlases from the inception. The county atlases included detailed maps of all the towns and villages in the county with the landowners shown right on the map. The atlases appealed to the vanity of subscribers who could pay to have their houses and farms illustrated on separate pages and they appealed to civic pride by including illustrations of local landmarks. They were immensely popular. The phenomenon is described in Michael P. Conzen, "The County Land Ownership Map in America: Its Commercial Development and Transformation, 1814–1939," *Imago Mundi* 36 (1984). The *Library of Congress has microfilmed all available county landownership atlases. The film can usually be borrowed through a lo-

cal library. *Ancestry.com has digitally cleaned and indexed approximately 2,100 of these atlases. They can be searched by town, village, and even the name of the landowner, although this feature must be used with caution. The maps can be difficult to find in Ancestry (www.ancestry.com): search "All Databases" for "land ownership." Ancestry.com is a subscription service, but there is usually some local access through a public or university library. Both the microfilmed or photocopied versions and the digital copies of these atlases pale in comparison with the originals, which were often beautifully rendered in pastels in much larger formats than the copies. Even so, it's possible to appreciate an almost whimsical folk art strain of many details along with the earnest small town *boosterism that pervades the maps. And, of course they are very useful to local historians trying to understand the cultural geography of the late nineteenth century.

After the Revolutionary War the states of the new United States surrendered their claims to the lands west of them. These lands and all western lands later acquired by the federal government became part of the public domain and were governed by the Land Ordinance of 1785. This and the Northwest Ordinance of 1787 provided for the systematic survey of public domain lands through a rectangular survey system designed to facilitate the transfer of federal lands to private citizens. The rectangular survey evolved into the U.S. Public Land Survey (PLS), which is also known as the Township and Range System. The survey ensured that every parcel of land could be located easily for sale or public use. Many of the states that were not surveyed under the PLS used a similar system for their own public lands. New York State, for example, provided bounty lands for Revolutionary War veterans using a similar system, so even eastern local historians should have some familiarity with the PLS, and it is critical for understanding the historical geography of the states that were formed from the public domain. E. Wade Hone, *Land and Property Research in the United States* (1997) provides a thorough introduction to the PLS, and Kashuba, *Walking with Your Ancestors* (2005) has a very accessible description of the system. Among many sources of online description is the Bureau of Land Management (BLM): http://www.nationalatlas.gov/articles/ boundaries/a_plss.html. The Government Land Office (GLO) provides a search engine for over 5 million land patents covering over a billion acres and beginning in 1810: http://www. glorecords.blm.gov. A service from Montana State University allows one to enter the patent description for land in many western states and returns the location on a Google Map: http://www. esg.montana.edu/gl/trs-data.html. The PLS delineates the geography of thirty states, providing a grid for roads, administrative boundaries, the placement of schools and churches, and much else.

Urban centers, both large and small, benefited from the publication of insurance maps, specifically the Sanborn Fire Insurance Atlases ("Sanborn Maps"). The Sanborn and Perris Company began publishing these maps after the Civil War and the Sanborn Company continues to produce them for large urban areas. Fire insurance maps are often the most detailed and accurate maps of urban neighborhoods available for the late nineteenth and early twentieth centuries and are a significant resource for local historians. The maps are large-scale lithographed street plans at a scale of fifty feet to one inch on twenty-one-by-twenty-five-inch sheets of paper. They provide a consistent interface and symbol set, which makes them very easy to consult across time and place. They were updated and reissued at intervals—about every seven years—so they provide an unparalleled series of snapshots of growth (and decline) for thousands of cities and towns. There were several competing companies and occasionally local entrepreneurs or county engineers produced similar maps. These can be much more difficult to locate, but extremely valuable for local historians. Your municipal archives or planning departments may be hoarding these very useful resources.

Although the fire insurance maps are called urban maps, 12,000 cities, towns, and villages were mapped—any place that had some measure of industry. The Bureau of the Census gave its entire inventory to the Library of Congress, supplementing the Library of Congress's own collection, which had been acquired through *copyright deposit. The library then microfilmed the maps. Regional collections of the microfilm are available in large research libraries. The ProQuest Corporation digitized the film and made the images available through an online database. Access to their collection is available at a handful of libraries. Subscriptions are expensive and use is highly restricted.

The digitized maps are less useful than the originals, since they lack the color that was used to code construction materials. Even so this is an extraordinary resource. Many states and municipalities are now making their own collections of Sanborns available to the public online at no charge. See, for example, North Carolina's collection: http://www.lib.unc.edu/dc/ncmaps/sanborn.html. An ambitious plan by the Library of Congress to provide full color *digitizations of its collection of 700,000 maps was discontinued over copyright issues, but there is an online index to the library's holdings: http://www.loc.gov/rr/geogmap/sanborn. The site also has W. W. Ristow's excellent history of fire insurance maps.

Also in the nineteenth century, entrepreneurial lithographers produced panoramic maps, also known as *bird's-eye views, of many urban communities. For a checklist see J. W. Reps, *Views and Viewmakers of Urban America* (1985). Quality varied but the best were beautifully done with high production values. The views are valuable snapshots of the *built environment in the nineteenth and early twentieth centuries. Many of these views are now online.

Two other important categories of urban maps are ward maps and census maps, both of which help local historians understand urban geography. Wards are local geographic units that many cities use to organize city services as well as voting and political representation, so maps of the wards are critical for locating people and businesses. A frequently consulted collection of ward maps is Michael H. Shelley, *Ward Maps of United States Cities* (1975) with

an accompanying microfiche set of the maps themselves. Often, however, locating ward maps for smaller municipalities can be difficult and may require a thorough search of the archives.

With the advent of online census records indexed by name, access to microfilm of census schedules through enumeration districts is less necessary than formerly. Nevertheless, since many state censuses are likely to remain unindexed for the foreseeable future, understanding enumeration district (ED) geography is still important for local historians using census records. A useful tool for finding EDs from a known street address and then linking to the correct film roll—and sometimes directly to the Ancestry.com images of the census schedules—is the "One Step" ED locater: http://stevemorse.org/census/intro.html.

The establishment of the U.S. Geological Survey (USGS) and the creation of many state geological surveys also occurred in the late nineteenth century. These federal and state agencies over the past century have produced thousands of geological, hydrological, soil survey, transportation, and many other maps that are useful resources for local historians. The fifteen-minute topographical series begun by the USGS in the 1880s provides an important historical record of America on the cusp of extraordinary changes in the *landscape through highway and railroad building, reservoirs and river channelization, and urban expansion. All these maps are now online from the USGS store: http://nationalmap.gov/historical. Maps from the much more detailed modern (post-1940) series of 7.5 minute topographical quadrangles are available for download from the same site.

Users will find many historical maps of states and local communities, including a range of maps from colonial times to insurance maps, digitized and available for viewing on the Internet. The most important collection is the David Rumsey Historical Map Collection: http://www.davidrumsey.com. This contains over 150,000 historical maps. Another important collection of digital maps is the Library of Congress's American Memory Collection: http://memory.loc.gov/ammem. These scanned images of maps along with the vast numbers of maps created through the use of geographic information systems dramatically increase the cartographic resources available for local historians.

*Geographic Information Systems (GIS) and digital mapping allows historians to create maps themselves for elucidating their own work or presenting aspects of the local historical geography to the public. There is enormous potential in these systems that remains largely untapped. A review of some applications: *Placing History: How Maps, Spatial Data, and GIS Are Changing Historical Scholarship*, ed. Anne Kelly Knowles (2008). At the same time the availability of online mapping services such as Google Maps (maps.google.com) and Bing Maps (www.bing/maps) allow public participation in historical mapping projects. *Historypin (www.historypin.com), for example, uses Google Maps to archive thousands of user-submitted historical photos "pinned" to a location. In conjunction with the Google Maps street-view

feature, this allows "then and now" comparisons. Museums and historical societies are using Historypin to create themed presentations of their photographic holdings.

Maps, both government and commercially published, may be found in a variety of institutions, including libraries, archival repositories, government records offices, historical societies, and private collections. Many libraries and archival repositories have cataloged their maps online into national bibliographic databases such as OCLC's WorldCat, as well as their own local online catalogs. These databases for maps of local communities are a useful tool for local historians in search of significant historical information about their community. Many collections of digital maps are uncataloged, however, and will require some careful sleuthing to uncover. Still, large-scale *digitization has given historians unparalleled access to maps and access continues to expand as more collections are converted and viewing interfaces improve.

ROBERT KIBBEE
THE HISTORY CENTER
IN TOMPKINS COUNTY (NY)

See Canada, local history in.

Maryland, local history in. Founded in 1844, the Maryland Historical Society (MdHS) is the state's oldest continuously operating cultural institution. In keeping with the founders' commitment to preserve the remnants of Maryland's past, MdHS remains the premier institution for state history. With over 350,000 objects and 7 million books and documents, this institution now

This historical marker tells some of the Civil War history of Rockville, Maryland. CREDIT: MAX A. VAN BALGOOY.

serves upward of 100,000 people per year through its museum, library, press, and educational programs.

In January 1844, the founders gathered in the Maryland Colonization Society rooms of the Baltimore City post office, selected John Spear Smith as its first president, appointed officers, and formed committees to draft a constitution, write a membership circular, and find a suitable meeting place. They proposed collecting the "remnants of the state's history" and preserving their heritage through research, writing, and publications. By the end of the first year, there were 150 members. The society's undeniable early success inspired plans for a permanent home. They had already outgrown the post office rooms and increasing numbers of donated

documents and artifacts overflowed the fireproof safe at the Franklin Street Bank. The new committee planned a grand building for Baltimore's new cultural institution, including space for an art gallery. One of America's foremost architects, Robert Carey Long, designed the Athenaeum, a four-story "Italian palazzo" with fireproof closets.

The Maryland Historical Society publishes a quarterly journal and selected books. MdHS publications bring into print the freshest and brightest new research on Maryland's past. The highly acclaimed *Maryland Historical Magazine*, continuously published for more than one hundred years, is a peer-reviewed quarterly. The society publishes books that bring forth rich episodes of Maryland's history in a readable style that engages both scholarly and general audiences. The Friends of the Press is an independent charitable organization committed to providing financial support for new publications. The MdHS offers education programs that highlight the society's collections, provide deeper context to exhibitions, and allow a forum for discussion and learning in a variety of formats and fields. Adult programs are offered year round and vary in topic and format to meet the interests and educational needs of different adult learners. Lectures, workshops, symposia, and music and theater presentations allow adults to interact with MdHS collections and the topics important in the state's history. Programs developed by the Francis Scott Key Society take patrons into historic homes around Maryland and provide another fun learning opportunity for adults interested in the past.

The Maryland State Archives (MSA) (predecessor of the Hall of Records), was created as an independent agency in 1935, charged with the collection, custody, and preservation of the official records, documents, and publications of the state (Chapter 18, Acts of 1935). The Maryland Tercentenary Commission made a modern and centralized archive a key feature of the commemoration of the state's 300th anniversary and a Hall of Records Commission, created in 1935, served as management and took on an advisory role in 1984. The Hall of Records was incorporated into the Maryland Department of General Services in 1970 (Chapter 97, Acts of 1970). In 1984, it was renamed the State Archives and became an independent agency within the office of the governor (Chapter 286, Acts of 1984). See also *Maryland Manual On-Line* for information on the archives' origins and functions.

The MSA serves as the central depository for government records of permanent value. Its holdings date from Maryland's founding in 1634, and include colonial and state executive, legislative, and judicial records; county probate, land, and court records; church records; business records; state publications and reports; and special collections of private papers, *maps, photographs, and newspapers. These records are kept in a humidity- and temperature-controlled environment and any necessary preservation measures are conducted in the archives' conservation laboratory.

For much of Maryland, local government typically is county government. Twenty-three counties and Baltimore City make up the twenty-four main local jurisdictions found in Maryland. Baltimore City, although a municipality, has been considered on a par with county jurisdictions since the adoption of the Maryland Constitution of 1851. Most of the counties have local historical societies and historical organizations.

Lois Green Carr was recognized for her important work on social and economic conditions of the Colonial Chesapeake area. See *County Government in Maryland, 1689–1709* (1987); *Maryland's Revolution of Government 1689–1692* (with David William Jordan (1974) and *Robert Cole's World: Agricultural Society in Early Maryland* (1991).

PATRICIA DOCKMAN ANDERSON
MARYLAND HISTORICAL SOCIETY

See United States, local history in.

Massachusetts, local history in. The early founding of the Massachusetts Bay Colony in 1630, and an even earlier European presence along the New England coast, means that the local history of Massachusetts extends back four centuries. Massachusetts has been both smaller—Plymouth, or New Plymouth, was a separate colony from 1620 until 1691—and larger—Maine remained a district of Massachusetts until 1820—than the present-day Commonwealth.

The history of Massachusetts begins with a 150-year colonial period leading up to the American Revolution during which Boston, although still a small town, was the metropolis of New England—the political, business, and cultural capital of a colony made up largely of agricultural communities and small seaports facing out upon the Atlantic. Many Bay State political, cultural, and educational institutions trace back to the colonial and early national period and citizens of the Commonwealth are rightly proud of the role Massachusetts played in the coming of the Revolution. Boston was not the only center. Salem, settled in 1626, had become a world-famous port (and the sixth largest city in the country) by 1790. Salem was famous for its China trade, which included tea and ceramics, along with exporting codfish to Europe and the West Indies, and importing sugar and molasses from the West Indies. Beginning with the War of 1812 shipping declined and this continued throughout the nineteenth century with Boston and New York taking more and more of the business.

The plaque on this boulder in Edgartown, Massachusetts, marks the homestead of Reverend Joseph Thaxter, the first chaplain of the American Revolution. CREDIT: BONNIE STACY.

Massachusetts was profoundly changed by developments that began in the first half of the nineteenth century: rapid industrial growth, especially the development of the textile and shoe industries, followed by large-scale immigration, first from Ireland and later from Canada and eastern and southern Europe. Boston remained a cultural and literary center—the Athens of America—and Massachusetts continued to play an important role in national affairs as the birthplace and nursery for social and educational reforms including the antislavery movement. At the same time, the Commonwealth saw a gradual decline in the importance of agriculture and traditional maritime trades. There was out-migration from the countryside both westward and also within Massachusetts to rapidly developing mill towns and urban centers.

After a long period of industrial decline during the middle decades of the twentieth century, Massachusetts shifted to an economy based on technology, finance, higher education, and medicine. Today, the Commonwealth is a compact, densely populated state that retains some characteristics dating back to its founding period—open town meeting government at the local level, for example—but also is the home of an ethnically diverse population that includes a large number of recent immigrants.

The Massachusetts Historical Society, founded in 1791, is the oldest historical organization in the United States, its mission not directly state and local history—but to collect, preserve, and disseminate materials for the study of the history of the nation, although its early publications, beginning in 1792, contain much useful statistical and topographical information on colonial Massachusetts.

The Essex Historical Society, founded in 1821 and now part of the Peabody Essex Museum in Salem, Massachusetts, was the first historical organization devoted to the history of a county; the long settlement and high population density of Massachusetts means that there is almost no unincorporated land within the Commonwealth, and the county system of government has all but disappeared except for court and property recordkeeping. Local historical materials, for the most part, are scattered in the 351 cities and towns that make up the Bay State.

Massachusetts lacks a statewide network for local history organizations, a gap filled by the New England Museum Association (NEMA) based in Massachusetts, which offers programs and workshops in Massachusetts and throughout the region. NEMA provides the best contact information for local historical organizations. The close connection between local and family history (genealogy) means that the library and online services of the New England Historic Genealogical Society (NEHGS) in Boston also are very important for the study of Bay State local history. The NEHGS also has played a key role in the systematic publication of Massachusetts vital records prior to 1850. The Massachusetts State Archives holds valuable manuscript records and maps for the study of state and local history both from the colonial and national period. For more than one hundred years, beginning in 1857 and continuing on a regular basis from 1865, Massachusetts has had its own decennial census that provides extremely detailed statistical information about the towns and counties of the Commonwealth.

The Commonwealth of Massachusetts has no requirement for local history education except as covered in the *Massachusetts History and Social Science Curriculum Framework* (2003) where guidelines call for third graders to learn about the history and geography of Massachusetts from 1620 onward through the history of their own cities and towns and about famous people and events in Massachusetts history. Students may study local history in the context of national history in their U.S. History I and II: 1763–2001 courses offered in grades eight through twelve, particularly when examining "the historical and intellectual origins of the United States during the Revolutionary and Constitutional eras" and later "the causes and consequences of the Industrial Revolution." A prime example of the latter is the Tsongas Industrial History Center at Lowell National Historical Park, where students learn about the textile industry through both in-classroom programs and field trips.

Historical writing about Massachusetts begins with the founding of the Massachusetts Bay Colony. In fact, Governor John Winthrop began a manuscript, "History of New-England," in the form of a journal before he departed from England in 1630, although it was not published until the end of the eighteenth century. Thomas Hutchinson, a reviled royal governor, but a meticulous historian, prepared a *History of the Colony and Province of Massachu-*setts Bay* (1767). In the centuries since, many of America's foremost historians have written studies of aspects of Massachusetts state and local history including Samuel Eliot Morison's *Maritime History of Massachusetts* (1921; reprinted 1979); Bernard Bailyn, *New England Merchants of the 17th Century* (1955; reprinted 1979); Robert Gross, *The Minutemen and Their World* (1976; republished 2001), Oscar Handlin, *Boston's Immigrant: A Study in Acculturation* (1941; reprinted 1991) and Sam Bass Warner Jr., *Streetcar Suburbs: The Process of Growth in Boston, 1870–1900* (1962).

The starting place for a survey of the history and bibliography of local history in Massachusetts (and for all of New England) is "Reassessing the Local History of New England," a seminal article by David D. Hall and Alan Taylor, which appeared in *New England: A Bibliography of Its History* (1989). Hall and Taylor trace the development of local Massachusetts history from its beginnings through the golden age of nineteenth-century town histories to the "advent and triumph" of academic community studies culminating in 1970 with three landmark publications: *A Little Commonwealth: Family Life in Plymouth Colony* by John Demos; Philip J. Greven Jr.'s *Four Generations: Population, Land, and Family in Colonial Andover, Massachusetts*; and Kenneth A. Lockridge's *A New England Town: The First Hundred Years, Dedham, Massachusetts, 1636–1736.*

Jeremiah Colburn's pioneering *Bibliography of the Local History of Massachusetts* (1871) shows that the earliest published Massachusetts town histories date from the 1820s and were flourishing by the 1860s—there already were sixty published by 1870. His work was supplemented by Charles A. Flagg's *A Guide to Massachusetts Local History: Being a Bibliographic Index to the Literature of the Towns, Cities and Counties of the State* (1907), but only truly superseded a century later with the publication of John Haskell's inaugural volume for the Committee for a New England Bibliography (CNEB), *Massachusetts: A Bibliography of Its History* (1976) containing 13,520 entries for Massachusetts state and local history. Roger Parks added 5,965 entries for Massachusetts in his *New England: Additions to the Six State Bibliographies* (1989) with even more entries in additional CNEB supplements published since.

Many of the most useful books for the study of Massachusetts history date from a previous generation and are increasingly out of date in both the time span covered and sources cited. The standard history of the Bay State, the five-volume *Commonwealth History of Massachusetts*, edited by Albert Bushnell Hart (1927–1930) is an artifact of an early era of historical research. *Massachusetts: A Concise History* by Richard D. Brown and Jack Tager (2000) remains the best one-volume history and *A Guide to the History of Massachusetts* (1988) is another fine but increasingly outdated resource. *The Historical Atlas of Massachusetts*, edited by Jack Tager and Richard W. Wilkie (1991) also is very valuable, but now is more than twenty years old. Over the years, the *Historical Journal of Massachusetts* (formerly the *Historical Journal of Western Massachusetts*) has published much

useful material for Massachusetts local history, as have the *Essex Institute Historical Collections, Old Time New England* published by the Society for the Preservation of New England Antiquities, now Historic New England, the *New England Historical and Genealogical Register*, and the publications of the Colonial Society of Massachusetts.

PETER DRUMMEY
UPDATED BY KENNETH C. TURINO
HISTORIC NEW ENGLAND

See United States, local history in.

material culture. The term *material culture* can be used in a variety of contexts in related, but distinct, ways. At the most basic level, material culture refers to physical things, which alternatively can be called artifacts, objects, or even stuff. Material culture can range in size from a whole neighborhood to an individual building to the furniture, fixtures, and finishes found inside to the clothing and accessories worn by the people who inhabit the space. Modifications to the body, including hairstyles and tattoos, also fall into the category, as do foods, *landscapes, and even soundscapes. What stands out about material culture is that it is tangible—physically present—and it is understood through the senses, often visually or tactilely, but also through taste, smell, and sound.

The "things" that form the *material* of material culture are important in the context of local history because they embody *culture*, or the ideas, values, and beliefs of the people who come in contact with them. Exploring the use of the two-part term at a deeper level, the latter word becomes as important as the first. In fact, a standard definition of material culture emphasizes the relationship between objects and people by stating that the physical things under consideration are made, modified, or used by human beings. While this seems to exclude natural forms such a rocks, plants, or animals, it still allows for their inclusion if they have been manipulated by processes such as landscape design or selective breeding controlled by people.

Historians, as well as those working in other disciplines such as art history, cultural geography, anthropology, and folk culture, are interested in material culture because they want to understand the interaction between human beings and the physical world. While it is tempting to say that objects *represent* or *symbolize* the ideas and values of a given group at a given time—for example, a smartphone represents, or symbolizes, our current need for immediate access to information—people who study material culture often emphasize the role of objects in shaping our reality as well as being shaped by it. In a simplistic but contemporary example, the installation of sidewalks where there once were none can encourage individuals to walk between nearby destinations rather than driving an automobile—in this case, the physical has the potential to play an active role in how we behave.

A final meaning of the term material culture, sometimes lengthened to *material culture studies*, refers to a way of studying the past, or the present, and using evidence. Often historians draw much of their information from the written word. When examining primary sources, such as manuscripts,

the focus is on the text, rather than the paper or ink. Using a material culture approach, the physical nature of the object becomes an additional form of evidence, as does its context. Is the paper handmade from rags, or is it industrially produced from a wood pulp mixture? Is it a reused scrap or part of a bound journal? Was it tucked between the pages of a book for safekeeping, or was it filed with the county clerk? And, most importantly, what does all this tell us about the people who created it, read it, and saved it? A simple analogy between reading text and *reading* objects has generally been rejected by those who study material culture, but objects are seen as a nonverbal form of communication that conveys information and contributes to analysis.

While a material culture approach can be applied to a written document, those who study material culture typically deal with other kinds of artifacts. Particularly in a museum context, material culture as a field grew out of the study of existing collections of decorative arts, often high style urban masterpieces, and household furnishings. From those beginnings, it evolved to encourage the study of vernacular, or commonplace, objects as keys to understanding the lives of the less affluent. Often touted as a more democratic and truthful type of evidence than written documents, material culture became a way to study those who could not write or were not inclined to leave behind numerous documents for later historians to study. Today popular culture and mass-produced items are gaining increasing attention in a field where nothing, including art and the high-style objects that served as an initial inspiration, is off limits.

One of the seminal works in the developing field of material culture studies was an article published by Jules D. Prown in the journal *Winterthur Portfolio* in 1982 entitled "Mind in Matter: An Introduction to Material Culture Theory and Method." In this work, Prown outlined what has come to be known as the Prownian method, consisting of careful observation and description, deduction, and speculation about meaning followed by a program of research using additional forms of evidence. Prown's methodology has continued to inform students of material culture and is used in the more recent volume *American Artifacts: Essays in Material Culture* (2000) to analyze objects ranging from a parlor stove to an Amish quilt to a cigarette lighter.

While Prown received his training in the history of art, other scholars have brought different disciplinary perspectives to the study of American material culture. Archaeologist James Deetz's *In Small Things Forgotten* (1977) and folklorist Henry Glassie's *Folk Housing in Middle Virginia* (1975) helped to shape the field, and both made clear the importance of fieldwork to the study of material culture. Deetz expanded his book in 1996 to include a greater emphasis on the lives of African Americans in early America, an important topic that material culture seems especially well suited to inform. Glassie developed an increasingly international perspective; his later volume *Material Culture* (1999) brings together research done in Bangladesh, Ireland, Turkey, as well as the United States. Glassie is joined

in this global approach by British anthropologist Daniel Miller whose books such as *Material Cultures: Why Some Things Matter* (1998), *Stuff* (2010), and *Blue Jeans* (2012) highlight his work in the Caribbean, Asia, and Europe, and focus on the role of ethnography in the study of material culture.

Today, material culture proves to be a multidisciplinary field that can shed light on both the distant past and the not-so-distant present. Working from the perspective of historians, a Harvard-affiliated team composed of Laurel Thatcher Ulrich, Ivan Gaskell, Sara Schechner, and Sarah Anne Carter undertook the Tangible Things project to explore how museums collect, catalog, and exhibit objects and what we can learn from those collections. Their book *Tangible Things: Making History through Objects* (2015) and the accompanying Tangible Things website and MOOC specifically aim to look beyond the moment of origin, highlighting one of the features of current material culture scholarship by examining the meaning of objects as they move globally through time and space.

Material culture continues to be a field that seeks to understand the human experience through the interaction of people and objects, the latter ranging significantly in manufacture, physical qualities, temporality, and cultural origin. Increasingly interest is on more contemporary meanings involving the continued employment of older artifacts or the utilization of newer consumer goods. There is a heightened awareness of objects used in unintended ways, objects that cross cultural boundaries, and objects whose meanings vary depending on context. Practitioners have used material culture to engage contemporary debates on sustainability, human diversity, economic development, and social justice. Yet the focus of material culture remains on the relationship between the tangible and the intangible, the physical thing and the behaviors, thoughts, and values it facilitates and embodies.

CYNTHIA FALK
COOPERSTOWN GRADUATE PROGRAM

See culinary history and the local historian; decorative arts.

matrilineal. A society where descent is traced through the female line and membership defines an individual's primary social relationships and responsibilities within the natural and supernatural world. Matrilineal is not the same as matriarchy, which is where women rule. The Hopi of northeastern Arizona live in a matrilineal society.

See clan; patrilineal.

medicine, history of. See health care as local history topic.

memorials and monuments. These related word concepts first appear in Middle English and were commonly used by Shakespeare's time. Usages are briefer for *memorial*, principally defined as "preserving the memory of a person or thing, as a statue, a festival, etc." Examples of the word *monument* are more variable and versatile, ranging from a sepulcher to "anything that by its survival commemorates a person, action, period, or event" but also "a structure or edifice intended to commemorate

a notable person, action, or event." A distinction could be made with memorials being deliberate creations whereas some phenomena might simply be survivals retrospectively regarded as monuments, such as the ancient Indian ceremonial complex known as the Ocmulgee National Monument in Georgia. Owing to the particularities of persons, places, and events, both words are germane to the topography encountered by local historians.

At first glance the words seem to be interchangeable in American usage. The Washington Monument and the Lincoln Memorial on the Mall in Washington fulfill the same function: gratitude and glorification of national icons. It is tempting to speculate that in local contexts and usage the words overlap but do not entirely coincide. Perhaps so-called memorials are more likely to invoke sacrifice or the remembrance of causes whereas monuments are more likely to signify that something notable was accomplished here. Many memorials have more to do with death or loss, and with tragedy rather than triumph. Yet the Oregon Trail Memorial, erected in 1931 by the citizens of Kemmerer, Wyoming (Lincoln County), signifies the perseverance of pioneers—glory rather than gloom. Sites such as the Gettysburg National Military Park include monuments as well as memorials. Hence the difficulty of making a distinction.

When certain local history sites become contested, however, *both* designations may come into play in polarized ways. One person's memorial might be another's monument. On May 4, 1886, bombs were thrown into a crowd at

Haymarket Square in Chicago, resulting in the deaths of eight policemen. Three years later the Haymarket Riot Police Memorial was erected on that site: John Gelert's statue of an officer standing guard on a pedestal. Because it was vandalized numerous times on account of anarchist objections to the injustice of executing innocent men as retribution, in 1972 that memorial had to be relocated to the lobby of the central police headquarters and in 1976 to even greater security at the Chicago police academy. Meanwhile, sympathizers with the rights of labor erected the Haymarket Martyrs Monument at Forest Home Cemetery just outside Chicago. Thus the very same event has both a memorial and a monument, each one devoted to an opposing view of the same traumatic episode.

Over time there has been a gradual democratization of American memorials, though we cannot be too precise about the chronology of that process. Consider the many generals and admirals from the American Revolution, Mexican War, and Civil War memorialized in places like Washington, Richmond, and New York's Central Park. That pattern was gradually followed by the generic depiction of symbolic fighting men, Rebels as well as Yankees standing at parade rest on their pedestals in town squares and village cemeteries. Then came the listing of names on World War I and II memorials, usually with no reference to rank, only age at death if anything. That became completely normative with the realization of Maya Lin's memorial to Vietnam veterans in Washington (1982), which since then has spawned almost five hundred Viet-

nam memorials scattered in communities all across the United States—90 percent of them highly derivative from Maya Lin's minimalist prototype of an inscribed wall. We see a similar though less numerous pattern with the Marine Corps Memorial overlooking the Potomac River (1954), a template for reminders of what happened on Iwo Jima in places like Salem, Ohio.

For some communities there is the problem of what to do about memorials that no longer seem appropriate because of changing values, especially when they are situated in highly visible places, such as the Memorial to Confederate Dead located close to the Texas State Capitol in Austin, and the 1874 "Liberty Monument" in New Orleans (celebrating the restoration of white control there). If those were relocated to less conspicuous sites, would we also have to move the Monument to the Union Dead on Boston Common? I think not, but the problem of what to do with inappropriate monuments and memorials that remain in prominent venues is unresolved in many places. See Sanford Levinson, *Written in Stone: Public Monuments in Changing Societies* (1998).

Since the 1980s there has been a marked increase in the production of event-related memorials, especially to honor victims, ranging from Holocaust memorials in diverse American cities, coast to coast, to the Salem Village Witchcraft Memorial in Danvers, Massachusetts (1992) and the Oklahoma City Memorial dedicated in 2000. For some communities the concept of a "living memorial" has seemed like a more fruitful way to commemorate the tragic loss of life—a trend that emerged most visibly following World War II. Omaha, Nebraska, opted for a Memorial Park in 1948 and refurbished it fifty years later. Other cities chose to erect memorial auditoriums to serve civic needs.

The terrorist attacks on September 11, 2001, have accelerated the production of memorials all across the United States, from Palos Hills, Illinois to Lake Charles, Louisiana, to Albuquerque, New Mexico. In many instances such communities have obtained some fragment from what remained of the Twin Towers, like pieces of the True Cross to justify consecration of a local memorial. For communities not fortunate enough to obtain a physical relic, the designs have tended to follow Maya Lin's logic of minimalism. But Naperville, Illinois, and Green Bay, Wisconsin, felt perfectly entitled to remember the national loss as locally meaningful. As one mayor remarked: "9/11 didn't just happen in New York, it happened to America."

In November 2010 a park in Irvine, California, was dedicated as the first U.S. memorial to American troops who have died in Iraq and Afghanistan, indicative of an ongoing spirit of competition to be the first community to recognize a particular phenomenon or cause.

See Erika Doss, *Memorial Mania: Public Feeling in America* (2010); Patrick Hagopian, *The Vietnam War in American Memory: Veterans, Memorials, and the Politics of Healing* (2009); and the American Battle Monuments Commission website, www.abmc.gov, lists all American war memorials.

MICHAEL KAMMEN
AMERICAN HISTORIAN, (1936–2013)

Mennonites, sources for. See Appendix B.

Methodists, sources for. See Appendix B.

Mexicans in North America. See Appendix A.

miasmic theory. See health care as local history topic.

Michigan, local history in. Michigan's recorded history begins with the seventeenth-century letters, documents, and reports of French missionaries, explorers, officials, and businessmen. Montreal and Quebec registries of baptisms and marriages document the region's earliest settlers. Efforts to make this material more accessible to English speakers began in the nineteenth century with the translation of the *Jesuit Relations* and continue in recent publications by Mackinac State Historic Parks and the Michigan State University Press.

Between 1754 and 1815, the land that became Michigan was claimed by France, Great Britain, and the United States. Although this land was ceded to the United States under the Treaty of Paris of 1783, the British did not leave Detroit and Mackinac until 1796. Through the fur trade and proximity, Great Britain retained an interest in Michigan and reoccupied both Detroit and Mackinac Island during the War of 1812. Anyone researching this early period will find information housed in archives in Great Britain, France, Canada, and the United States.

Michigan's early American settlers were primarily Yankees from New

This Michigan historical marker was placed in 2013 to commemorate the DeTour Reef Light Station near DeTour Village. CREDIT: MICHIGAN HISTORY CENTER.

England and New York. They brought with them a commitment to preserving and studying local history. The Historical Society of Michigan formed in 1828, almost a decade before Michigan achieved statehood. (Michigan adopted and began operating under its first state constitution in 1835, but it was not accepted into the Union until January 26, 1837, due to a conflict with Ohio over ownership of the "Toledo Strip.")

Though centered in Detroit, the society had members and collections from Mackinac and the settled regions of southern Michigan. It met intermittently and reorganized several times over the years. Its collections were placed in the Detroit Public Library in 1886.

One of the society's leaders, Henry Roe Schoolcraft, spent twenty years as an Indian agent, first at Sault Ste. Ma-

rie and then on Mackinac Island. Interviewing hundreds of Indians who visited the agency, he created a record of the life and customs of the Anishinaabe people of the Great Lakes region (primarily Ojibway, Odawa and Potawatomi). His more than twenty books and scores of monographs and articles remain invaluable to historians.

In 1873, the Michigan legislature authorized the incorporation of state, county, and municipal historical, biographical, and geological societies. The next year several county societies sent delegates to a meeting in the state capital, Lansing, to organize a state pioneer society. Membership was open to anyone over the age of forty who had resided in the state for twenty-five years.

In 1876, the Pioneer Society of the State of Michigan appointed a Committee of Historians to publish its current materials and solicit others in order to record the "early history of the State, given by the pioneers themselves." The forty volumes of the *Michigan Pioneer and Historical Collections*, ranging from transcribed (and translated) government documents to republished newspaper accounts, biographies, and *obituaries, and personal memories, are filled with details of early life in Michigan.

The era of the *Pioneer and Historical Collections* also saw the publication of county histories and, in 1884, the first of Silas Farmer's editions of *The History of Detroit and Wayne County*. These works, county atlases and records of the state mid-decade census enumerations created between 1854 and 1904, provide rich resources for nineteenth-century Michigan local history.

The state appropriated funds for the publication of the *Pioneer and Historical Collections* until 1911, when the governor vetoed the appropriation. Two years later, the state created the Michigan Historical Commission.

The private organization changed its name to the Historical Society of Michigan in 1913. It shared executive direction with the commission until 1948, when the two organizations went their separate ways. The historical society focused on conferences and support of local history organizations; the state retained responsibility for the archival and museum collections of the state, historic preservation, and archaeology. In 1959, Henry Brown, Director of the Detroit Historical Museum, began the annual Local History Conference, which continues under the direction of the Historical Society of Michigan.

In 1917, the commission and the society began publishing *Michigan History*, a quarterly academic journal. The state converted that journal to a bimonthly popular format magazine in 1978. In compliance with an executive order, *Michigan History* magazine was transferred to the Historical Society of Michigan in October 2009. Since 1986, the Clarke Historical Library at Central Michigan University has been the home of the *Michigan Historical Review*, a scholarly journal published twice yearly.

A visible record of Michigan state and local history is found in the more than 1,700 Michigan Historical Markers that dot the state. The program, established in 1955, is funded by local sponsors and administered through the Michigan Historical Center.

During the twentieth century, Michigan university archives and libraries, as well as public libraries, assembled rich collections of *primary source materials relevant to state and local history. The state established a regional repository system that placed many local government records in university and community repositories close to their point of creation. Any serious researcher of state and local history must consult multiple collections in order to access all potential resources.

Walter Romig's *Michigan Place Names*, published in 1973, and *Michigan: A History of the Wolverine State* written by Willis Dunbar (1965) and revised by George S. May (1980) remain standard references for Michigan history, but countless other scholarly volumes on urban development, mining, lumbering, immigration, race relations, the auto industry, labor, and other topics provide rich resources for state and local historians today.

In 1989, the Michigan Historical Center and the Library of Michigan moved into a new building, joining the state's library, archives, and museum collections and exhibits in a single facility. For eight years, 2001–2009, they were administratively linked in the Michigan Department of History, Arts, and Libraries. Today the Michigan Historical Center is part of the Department of Natural Resources. It is the steward of collections that include eleven historic sites and more than 130,000 artifacts, 50,000 maps, 4,000 manuscripts, and 550,000 photographs, plus the archival records that document state and local government. The Archives of Michigan serves genealogists with both documents and a research library. The center continues the historical marker program and in 2015 launched one program linking heritage to linear trails and another helping communities discover forgotten stories of racial minorities.

The Michigan State Historic Preservation Office and the State Archaeologist are part of the Michigan State Housing Development Authority. They work closely with the private Michigan Historic Preservation Network.

Michigan archives and libraries continue to place publications and primary sources on the Internet. Among the notable collections are the Archives of Michigan collections at www.seekingmichigan.org and the Michigan County Histories and Atlases Digitization Project.

SANDRA S. CLARK
MICHIGAN HISTORICAL CENTER

See historical markers; United States, local history in.

microblogging. Microblogging is part *blog and part instant messaging. Twitter, a free microblogging service, exploded onto the social media scene in 2007. It is attracting an ever-growing following of staff at cultural institutions who see its value as another way to build relationships and attract new audiences. It has been listed among the six social media tools that every business and professional should use.

Wikipedia offers a basic definition: "Tweets are text-based posts of up to 140 characters, displayed on the author's profile page and delivered to other users—known as followers—who have subscribed to them. Senders can restrict delivery to those in their circle of friends or, by default, allow open access. Users can send and receive tweets via the Twitter website, Short Message Service (SMS) or external applications." Microblog users categorize related content using hashtags, metadata tags preceded by the pound sign.

Most museums give two main reasons for joining Twitter: to foster good public relations and to make connections with people. In some ways, Twitter is like sitting at the feet of a teacher and waiting for him or her to spout words of wisdom or witty observations and then hearing the reaction of the gathered crowd. It's simply another way to receive communication, albeit in short bursts of text. Blogs tend to be one-way communication—almost no readers make use of the option to comment on blog posts. Tweeting encourages more group communication, due in part to the ease of responding. In other words, if you write a blog, you promote it and hope an audience will find you. Your audience expects you will update your blog with new information on a regular basis. But if you send a tweet, your message goes instantly to your network and your chances of getting a quick response are high.

Who is using Twitter and other microblogging services? According to a Pew Study (2015), 23 percent of online adults said they use a service like Twitter to share updates about themselves and see updates of others. Thirty-two percent of online adults ages eighteen to twenty-nine use it, with the percentage dropping off the older the age. No surprise there. Twenty-nine percent of online adults ages thirty to forty-nine use Twitter. Up in the fifty-to-sixty-four age range, only 13 percent use Twitter and by the time we reach the sixty-five-plus age range, only 6 percent use the platform. Twitter users are slightly more racially and ethnically diverse than the full United States population and slightly more likely to live in urban areas.

Nina Simon, who writes the Museum 2.0 blog, thinks that microblogging is more participatory than other social media because there is a smaller distinction between the content producer and consumer—few people sign up as a follower and sit back and do not send a tweet. And with only 140 characters per message, there is a level playing field—the verbose folks have no room to make a lengthy argument. Short and concise is what the game's about. Other benefits, according to Simon, are that the tweeter gets instant feedback,

and tweeting does not require a maintenance strategy. If you stop tweeting, nothing happens. You can choose how often to send messages. In the blogosphere, readers expect fresh updates on a regular basis.

One reason a history organization might actively tweet is that it wants to establish a relationship with an audience that it cannot successfully reach with other forms of communication. It may be an audience that is enthusiastic about your work and wants to have an ongoing conversation with others who share this enthusiasm. These "followers" want information beyond what's going on at your institution—beyond what they can find on your website. They really want bits of information that let them feel they have special access to your organization—information that fuels their enthusiasm. To make your organization's Twitter feed useful and effective, it is helpful to understand why users are attracted to the medium. They like its conversational quality and the challenge of communicating in a set number of characters. Many microblog users enjoy seeing tangible results to their interaction and appreciate feeling like an important resource. Museums can tap into this interest by posting favorite tweets on their website or on a digital display in an exhibition area.

The writing style for tweets is casual and conversational—creating a friendly tone that is entertaining and approachable. It's important to keep in mind that your Twitter audience will extend beyond your geographic area and may not be able to attend your organization's events. So a combination of types of tweets is the best strategy—invitations to events, fun facts, blog links, insider information, insights, and direct answers to questions.

History organizations can employ hashtags to curate streams of similar content. Through hashtags, history organizations can help followers find their content, foster engagement with existing followers, and cultivate new audiences. Some tweets specific to a field of history may include a hashtag such as #LocalHistory or #Preservation to bring in new followers searching through other tweets with the same hashtag. Because Twitter allows for easy conversation, hashtags like #AskACurator can connect a museum curator to curious followers who may never be able to visit the museum or meet staff in person. Museum visitors can also attach their own hashtags to the tweets they publish, which can serve as a personal reflection of their visit. Nina Simon suggested that this opens opportunities for cultural institutions to understand the meanings visitors attach to museum objects and experiences. The museum field has used hashtags to host online events such as #MuseumWeek, a yearly event on Twitter in which participating museums offer behind-the-scenes looks into their collections, exhibits, and projects. Twitter also offers engagement within the field itself. History professionals have also used hashtags such as #Twitterstorians to build their networks, while the #MuseJobs hashtag can link job seekers to an open position in a museum.

When employed carefully and strategically, microblogging offers history organizations, history professionals, and the public ways to share ideas across the world.

TIM GROVE
NATIONAL AIR AND SPACE MUSEUM,
SMITHSONIAN INSTITUTION

See blogs and local history; social media.

Middletown study. During the mid-1920s, sociologists Robert S. Lynd and his wife, Helen Merrell Lynd, selected Muncie, Indiana, as the locale for their study of social change in American society. Their work resulted in the landmark study *Middletown: A Study in American Culture*, first published in 1929. In 1935, Robert Lynd returned to Muncie to investigate the impact of the Great Depression on the city; *Middletown in Transition: A Study in Cultural Conflicts* (1937) was the result. The strengths of the Lynds' works are many, but of particular value to sociologists, historians, and those interested in the study of the United States at the local level is the depth and breadth of their investigations. Both works about Muncie are classics not only because they are lively and intensive, but particularly because the Lynds avoid the myopia to which authors of local investigations often succumb.

Robert and Helen Lynd selected Muncie (population 38,000) not because it was a particularly outstanding city, but rather because its unremarkability made it a fine specimen of American life and culture. In many respects "Middletown," as the Lynds dubbed it in an effort to conceal Muncie's identity, was a microcosm of national society. Between

January 1924 and June 1925, the Lynds and their research associates lived in Muncie and insinuated themselves into the small city's life. They attended community meetings and church services; researched documentary material and compiled statistics; conducted interviews; and distributed questionnaires. The Lynds did not embark upon the project to prove a thesis about life in the nation, but rather they armed themselves with the belief that, no matter the locale, there are a limited number of fundamental activities in which humans are engaged. They reduced these to six areas: work, home life, education, leisure, religion, and community life. Rather than arriving at broad conclusions, the Lynds sought to suggest "possible fresh points of departure in the study of group behavior." Technological change, and especially its positive and negative aspects, is a central theme in the initial Middletown study. And although they shied away from conclusions, the Lynds' study emphasizes ambivalence about progress. They paint a portrait of a city looking toward the future while embracing tradition. Upon returning to Muncie in the midst of the Depression, Robert Lynd discovered what investigators of localities found throughout the nation: that the federal government had become an imposing presence at the local level and that cities increasingly surrendered their autonomy to Washington.

The *Middletown* studies are valuable to social scientists investigating other localities because the Lynds effectively demonstrated that Muncie was, indeed, a typical American city.

The extensive quantitative and qualitative data provide useful reference points for comparison and furnish an intriguing glimpse of American life during the 1920s and 1930s. Today, the Center for Middletown Studies, located at Ball State University in Muncie, collects materials and supports further research about the city.

See Rutledge M. Dennis, *Finding the African Americans That Middletown Left Out* (2012); Rita Caccamo, *Back to Middletown: Three Generations of Sociological Reflections* (2000); Luke E. Lassiter, ed., *The Other Side of Middletown: Exploring Muncie's African American Community* (2004); Dan Rottenberg, ed., *Middletown Jews: The Tenuous Survival of an American Jewish Community* (1997); Dwight W. Hoover, *Middletown: The Making of a Documentary Film Series* (1992), and *Middletown Revisited* (1990); Theodore Caplow, *All Faithful People: Change and Continuity in Middletown's Religion* (1983), and Caplow et al., *Middletown Families: Fifty Years of Change and Continuity* (1982).

JEFFREY S. COLE
GENEVA COLLEGE

military records, Canada. Canada has dozens of founding indigenous, or aboriginal nations, and two founding European nations: France and Britain. The challenge is to understand how aboriginal nations and the two European entities viewed war, and shaped their unique military experiences. All knew that conflict was part of the human condition: at times intense, frequent, and decisive, and sometimes not. Everyone, moreover, learned that survival required adaptation to others' ways of war. Before and after European arrival, indigenous peoples recorded events using oral methods, artifacts, and architecture. Increasingly, historians grapple with multidisciplinary evidence to explain aboriginal experiences and their relationships with Europeans. For example, the Directorate of History and Heritage has produced the publication *A Commemorative History of Aboriginal People in the Canadian Military*, which is available online at: http://www.cmp-cpm.forces.gc.ca/dhh-dhp/pub/boo-bro/abo-aut/index-eng.asp. Also, the University of Saskatchewan has produced an online portal called the Indigenous Studies Portal Research Tool, or iPortal, which is a database of electronic resources related primarily to the indigenous peoples of Canada. The iPortal provides access to digitized full-text documents as well as photographs, maps, and archival resources and is available online at http://iportal.usask.ca. Resources related to military history can be found by searching for keywords such as "war," "military," "soldier," or "battle."

European written military records in Canada date from the early 1600s to confederation and nationhood in 1867, with the priorities and concerns of first French (until 1763) and thereafter British soldiers, sailors, and administrators. After confederation, the federal government increasingly came to see the Canadian military experience as an essential component of national sovereignty and of the national memory. Since that time Canadian archives have collected records ranging from the tactical level up to civil-military and allied relations, from limited conflicts like the Fenian Raids (1866, 1870), the North-West Rebellion (1885), and the South African War (1899–1902), to the First (1914–1918) and Second (1939–1945) World Wars, the Korean Conflict (1950–1954), peace-keeping and humanitarian operations (1948 to present including the Balkans), the First Gulf War, and operations in southwest Asia.

Military museums throughout Canada hold interesting artifacts and archives, but the vast majority of Canadian military records are deposited in three locations in Ottawa, Ontario: at *Library and Archives Canada (LAC) (www.collectionscanada.gc.ca); the Directorate of History and Heritage (DHH), part of the Canadian Department of National Defence (www.cmp-cpm.forces.gc.ca/dhh-dhp); and the Canadian War Museum's Military History Research Centre (www.warmuseum.ca/learn/research-collections/military-history-research-centre).

LAC has organized its military documents into two categories. Government records are divided into record groups (RG) for government departments, several of which include military documents. For example, RG 9 consists of nineteenth- and early-twentieth-century militia and defense records; RG 150 contains the records of the Ministry of Overseas Military Forces in the First World War; and RG 24, by far the largest, holds twentieth-century material including documents from the Second World War. The second category of LAC documents is manuscript group (MG), records acquired from the Canadian private sector. These records comprise original and personal collections of Canadian sailors, soldiers, and airmen in all media: letters, diaries, reports, maps, plans, photographs, film, paintings, and drawings.

LAC also holds service records for all past members of the Canadian military. These records may sometimes be consulted on site or copies may be ordered, depending on applicable privacy restrictions. The website offers a variety of digitized documents and databases related to the military, including soldiers' attestation papers and Canadian unit and headquarters War Diaries from the First World War. LAC holdings may be searched online, and many finding aids for different groups of documents are now available on the website. Staff have also prepared research aids and thematic guides on materials related to Canadian military heritage and posted them online. On site, the LAC staff are available by appointment to help visitors find research materials. Researchers can register for user cards and order material online in advance of their visit. This is recommended because there is a wait of about a day for document delivery.

The DHH collection supports the research and writing of official histories of the Royal Canadian Navy, the Canadian Army, the Royal Canadian Air Force, and, after 1968, the unified Canadian Armed Forces (CAF). Some of the items date from the First World War, but most date from the Second World War and later. These research materials, all on site, complement those held by LAC, and are divided into several different collections.

The Kardex and Document Collections contain mainly operational records as well as some private documents. They include information on peacekeeping, women in the Canadian military, and bilingualism in the CAF. Some materials have been transferred to LAC, but the DHH retains the original references and document transfer lists. Smaller collections include biographical material on Canadians involved with the military and various reference files on Canadian bases, stations, ships, and aircraft. The DHH also holds copies of British and German records related to the Canadian experience during the Second World War. Annual Historical Reports filed by each active unit of the Canadian military are held at the DHH, describing unit activities when not deployed overseas or on domestic operations. Also, the DHH offers a small, specialized library on Canadian military history and related subjects, comprising official and general histories, orders, reports, and periodicals.

Visitors may consult documents on site in the DHH Reading Room. The DHH website gives visitor information and explains the archival holdings in more detail. Certain primary sources are available online, as are numerous books written by the public historians at the DHH, including official and commemorative histories. These materials may all be downloaded free of charge. The website offers image galleries of Canadian military badges and colors, some honors and awards citations, and information on the identification of newly discovered remains of Canadian military personnel who went missing during the First or Second World Wars, or the Korean War. A list of accredited CAF museums, with contact information, may also be found on the website.

The Canadian War Museum's Military History Research Centre houses primary and secondary research material documenting Canada's military history from the colonial period to the present. These records complement the collections at LAC and the DHH. The archival collection includes original letters, diaries, scrapbooks, logbooks, maps, postcards, and sheet music. It also contains original photographic prints in black and white and color, negatives, glass slides, daguerreotypes, and various other visual materials. The library holds regimental histories, published personal memoirs, periodicals and newspapers, wartime pamphlets, military technical and field manuals, and five thousand rare books. The catalog for the complete collection is available online at http://catalogue.warmuseum.ca. Some finding aids and a database of 144,000 Second World War clippings from the *Hamilton Spectator* are also online. On-site access to archival material and rare books is by advance appointment only.

The Canadian Military History Gateway (www.cmhg-phmc.gc.ca) is an online portal providing free access to websites and digitized material on Canadian military history and heritage, from earliest times to the present day. The gateway is managed by Canada's Department of National Defence, and the data is drawn from the collective online holdings of Canadian museums, libraries, archives, and seven federal organizations. The information is quality-controlled and authoritative. Resources available include links to scholarly research as well as art, images, personal anecdotes, video, music, and interactive tools.

See also Owen A. Cooke, *The Canadian Military Experience, 1867–1995: A Bibliography*, 3rd ed. (1997).

LAC is located at 395 Wellington Street, Ottawa, Ontario, K1A 0N4, Canada; telephone (866) 578-7777 for general information (toll free in Canada and the United States); fax (613) 995-6274; e-mail via the Ask Us a Question page at www.bac-lac.gc.ca/eng/assistance-request-form. The DHH can be contacted by mail at National Defence Headquarters, Major-General George R. Pearkes Building, 101 Colonel By Drive, Ottawa, Ontario, K1A 0K2, Canada; fax (613) 990-8579; e-mail via the Contact Us page at www.cmp-cpm.forces.gc.ca/dhh-dhp/adh-sdh/cl-lc/index-eng.asp. The research facilities are located at the Charles P. Stacey Building, 2429 Holly Lane, Ottawa, Ontario, K1V 7P2, Canada. The Canadian War Museum Military History Research Centre is located within the museum at 1 Vimy Place, Ottawa, Ontario, K1A 0M8, Canada; telephone (819) 776-8652; e-mail vimy.biblio@warmuseum.ca for general inquiries or to book an appointment.

VALERIE CASBOURN
AND R. H. CALDWELL
DIRECTORATE OF HISTORY AND
HERITAGE, NATIONAL DEFENCE
HEADQUARTERS (CANADA)

military records, U.S. The National Archives Building in Washington, D.C., contains military service and pension records for veterans from the Revolutionary War through the early twentieth century.

Regular Army: Enlisted personnel: 1789–October 31, 1912; Officers: 1789–June 30, 1917

Volunteers: Service performed during an emergency, 1775–1902

Navy: Enlisted personnel: 1798–1885; Officers: 1798–1902

Marine Corps: Enlisted personnel: 1789–1895; some Officers: 1789–1895

Coast Guard (predecessor agencies): 1791–1919

Confederate States: 1861–1865

Veterans' Records: Claims files for pensions based on federal military service, 1775–1912 and bounty land warrant application files relating to claims based on wartime service, 1775–1848.

To request copies of any of these records, order online (http://eservices.archives.gov/orderonline) or submit NATF Form 85 (pensions and bounty land) and/or NATF Form 86 (military service). Obtain forms online through www.archives.gov/contact/inquire-form.html or write to the National Archives and Records Administration, Attn: RDT1R, 700 Pennsylvania Avenue, NW, Washington, D.C., 20408-0001. Provide your name and postal mailing address, e-mail address, specify the form number, and state the number of forms you need (limit six per order).

The National Personnel Records Center (NPRC) in St. Louis, Missouri, is the permanent home for Military Service Records for most of our nation's service members. The following is the approximate date range for the service records for each service branch:

Air Force: All members separated between September 24, 1947, and May 1, 1994

Army: Officers separated after June 29, 1917; Enlisted separated after October 31, 1912

Navy: Officers separated after December 1901; Enlisted separated after 1884

Marine Corps: Officers separated after 1904; Enlisted separated after 1905

Coast Guard: All members separated after 1897

NOTE: The most accurate and up-to-date holdings information for Military Service Records and service members' medical records can be found at http://archives.gov/veterans/military-service-records/locations/index.html.

A veteran, next of kin of a deceased veteran, or researcher may request copies of records by using eVetRecs http://vetrecs.archives.gov or by submitting a Standard Form 180, *Request Pertaining to Military Records*, to the corresponding addresses indicated on the form. To facilitate timely processing, the requester should provide as much information about the veteran as possible; this will aid in locating the correct record. Copies of the form are available by writing or visiting NPRC at 1 Archives Drive, St. Louis, Missouri, 63138, or via the NARA website at http://archives.gov/veterans/military-service-records/standard-form-180.html.

The July 12, 1973, fire at the National Personnel Records Center destroyed roughly 80 percent of the records for Army personnel discharged between November 1, 1912, and January 1, 1960, and 75 percent of the records for Air Force personnel discharged between September 25, 1947, and January 1, 1964 (with names alphabetically after Hubbard, James E.). However, not all records affected by the fire were completely destroyed; many records survived the ordeal and are being restored on an as-requested basis. Some records that have been completely destroyed are being reconstituted using information derived from other government sources. Requesters would need to submit a Standard Form 180 to determine whether a record was affected by the fire.

MARY RYAN
UPDATED BY STAFF OF THE
NATIONAL ARCHIVES AND
RECORDS ADMINISTRATION

Minnesota, local history in. Minnesota is home to more than five hundred local history organizations (including at least one in each of the state's eighty-nine counties) and a state historical society older than the state itself. In addition, Preservation Alliance of Minnesota, the Minnesota Alliance of History Museums, the Minnesota Association of Museums, the fifty-plus historic preservation commissions, the State Historic Preservation Office, the eight Tribal Historic Preservation Offices, and the Minnesota Historical Society (MNHS) both reflect and encourage widespread interest in the past. Historyopolis.com is only one of many websites doing good local history.

The local history resources are equally rich. The Jeffers Petroglyphs in southwestern Minnesota document a time rich in birds and animals and native artists. Louis Hennepin's 1670s published letters narrate his and Daniel Greysolon, Sieur du Lhut's explorations of the Mississippi River environs and demonstrate as well early European misreadings of native peoples. The rich records of the eighteenth- and nineteenth-century voyageurs—from songs to account books—tell another set of stories including portraits of varied relations among Europeans and natives, as does Joseph Nicollet's 1830s detailed map.

In 1849 Pennsylvanian Edward D. Neill led St. Paul's First Presbyterian Church and began a lifetime of writing Minnesota's history, beginning with *History of Minnesota* published in 1858. He drew deeply from his own observations, involvements, and acquaintance with many of the Territory's minor and major actors, so his book functions as both primary and secondary source.

Like Neill, William Watts Folwell (4 vols. 1923–1930) and Theodore Blegen (1963, rev. 1975) focus on growth and progress in their state histories. Even so, all three continue—in part, if not in total—to be useful. So is William Lass's *Minnesota* (1976, rev. 1991). Labor activist and writer Meridel Le Sueur's *North Star State* (1945) tells mostly a story of Minnesota workers. Clifford E. Clark, ed., *Minnesota in a Century of Change* (1989) contributes mightily to twentieth-century history in the state.

The Minnesota statehood sesquicentennial prompted another generation of state histories, the two most substantial being Mary Lethert Wingerd's *North Country* (2010) about Minnesota to 1865 and Annette Atkins' *Creating Minnesota* (2007), which takes a social history approach.

From 1849, too, the MNHS has collected, cataloged, and preserved objects, documents, maps, paintings, official and private records and papers, newspapers, and, later, photographs and recordings. The Minnesota History Center (St. Paul) also features imaginative exhibits, education and historic preser-

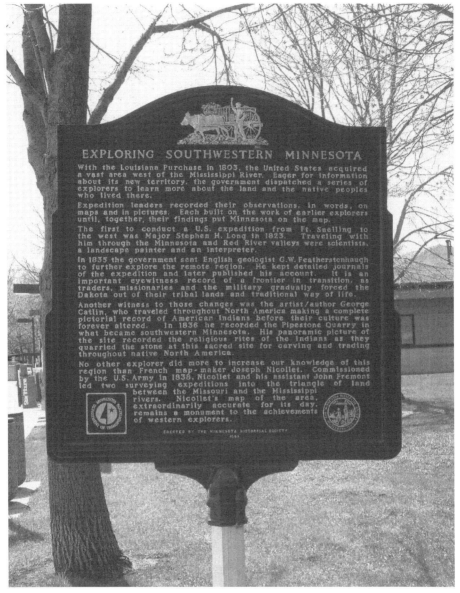

Early explorers of Southwestern Minnesota are commemorated in this historical marker near Blue Earth, Minnesota. CREDIT: MINNESOTA HISTORICAL SOCIETY.

vation offices, the largest historical society press in the country, and *Minnesota History*. The society's website—www.mnhs.org—offers photographs, birth and death records, maps, lesson plans, collection guides, and a fully digitalized run of *Minnesota History* and *Minnesota Collections*.

The Minnesota scholarship is strong. Janet Specter's *What This Awl Means* (1993), Scott Anfinson's *Southwestern Minnesota Archaeology* (1997), and Guy Gibbon's *Archaeology of Minnesota* (2014) analyze the region's physical remains. Marcia Anderson's forthcoming book examines Ojibwe bandolier bags (2016) and Colette Hyman also uses craft to understand *Dakota Women's Work* (2012). Many accounts focus on landscape: Chel Anderson and Adelheid Fischer's *The North Shore* (2015), Aaron Shapiro's *Lure of the North Woods* (2013), Sue Leaf's *Portage* (2015), Janet Timmerman's *Draining the Great Oasis* (2001), and David Lanegran's *Minnesota on the Map* (2004). Larry Millett concentrates on architecture. Afton Press specializes in fine arts. Peg Meier uses photographs and letters (*Bring Warm Clothes* [2009]) and Bruce White uses photographs (*We Are at Home* [2007]).

Brenda Child's *My Father's Knocking Sticks* (2014); Anton Treuer's *Warrior Nation* (2015); Diane Wilson, *Spirit Car* (2009); and Catherine Denial, *Making Marriage* (2013) add to the rich and growing literature by and about Native People in the twentieth and twenty-first centuries. William Green's two volumes on African Americans fill an important gap.

Not surprisingly, immigrants receive a lot of attention. Editor June Drenning Holmquist's *They Chose Minnesota* (1981) is still useful. Better, many of its essays have been revised, others commissioned, each published individually. Two dozen and counting, they include Ann Regan on the Irish, Chia Youyee Vang on Hmong, Dionicio Valdes on Mexicans, Kathleen Conzen on Germans, John Radzilowski on Poles, and Ahmed Yusuf on Somalis. The Norwegian-American Historical Association and strong Scandinavian interest has spurred much study: Jon Gjerde, *From Peasants to Farmers* (1989); Odd Lovoll, *Norwegians on the Prairie* (2007); Betty Bergland and Lori Lahlum, *Norwegian American Women* (2011); and Joy Lintelman, *I Go to America* (2012).

Books on the history of farming have given way to rural memoirs: Kevin Fenton, *Leaving Rollingstone* (2013), for example, and technological/business history: Thomas Misa, *Digital State* (2013); Donald Hall, *Generation of Wealth* (2014); Stephen George, *Enterprising Minnesotans* (2005); and Jeffrey Manuel, *Taconite Dreams* (2015).

Minnesota requires primary school students to learn state history. *Northern Lights* (1989) by Rhoda Gilman and Steve Sandell and its second and third editions by David Kinney (2003, 2013) offer thoughtful, interactive accounts of the state's past that reflect much of the best new scholarship in the field. The interactive version is especially popular with students.

MNHS is publicly funded. In addition, the state funds the Minnesota Digital Library, an online photo and primary documents goldmine; Minitex, a library lending service for books, articles, and microfilms. State budget cutbacks took a serious toll on the MNHS in the 2000s. Minnesota voters in 2008 amended the state constitution to raise the sales tax to support both outdoor and historical heritage. These funds have so far supported an online Minnesota History Encyclopedia (MNopedia.com), an Ojibwe language program, preservation of buildings and stabilization of collections, oral histories, public events, workshops, and cataloging by local history organizations. Minnesota Public Radio and Twin Cities Public Television are enthusiastic and quality creators of local history programming. Joe Amato has fiercely championed local history at the Center for Rural and Regional Studies at Southwest Minnesota State University and has supported the publication of many local studies.

The widespread interest in local history is encouraging and gratifying. Oh, yes, Garrison Keillor is one of ours, too, and although his stories aren't really "history" they have certainly engaged Minnesotans and others in the state's storied past.

ANNETTE ATKINS
SAINT JOHN'S UNIVERSITY/COLLEGE
OF SAINT BENEDICT

See field services; United States, local history in.

mission statement. A mission statement describes the purpose of an organization and directs the planning, implementation, and evaluation of its programs and activities. These statements can vary as seen in these two historic sites that are adjacent to each other in Hartford, Connecticut:

Mark Twain House and Museum: to foster an appreciation of the legacy of Mark Twain as one of our nation's defining cultural figures, and to demonstrate the continuing *relevance of his work, life, and times.

Harriet Beecher Stowe Center: to preserve and interpret Stowe's Hartford home and the Center's historic collections, promote vibrant discussion of her life and work, and inspire commitment to social justice and positive change.

Had Twain or Stowe heard the term "mission statement" in their lifetimes, they probably would have regarded it as one of the annual reports issued by Christian missionary associations on their work in another country (such as India), among a specific group of people (such as urban orphans), or to achieve a particular objective (such as building a school). Today's "mission statement" developed in the 1960s and has a significantly different purpose. The Ford and Carnegie foundations' scathing critiques of the lack of rigor in business schools in 1959 resulted in a growing emphasis on management, finances, and strategic planning informed by such diverse fields as economics, psychology, sociology, engineering, and mathematics. Mission statements became part of the toolkit for corporate success by codifying the company's ideals and providing a set of principles to guide its actions and decisions. Increased professionalization in the 1970s introduced mission statements to the museum field and by the 1990s, funders, government agencies, nonprofit organizations, and professional associations were expected to have a written mission describing their purpose to the public. By 2008, the standards of the *American Alliance of Museums include a mission "that states what the museum does, for whom, and why" and that "all aspects of the museum's operations are integrated and focused on meeting its mission" (AAM, *National Standards and Best Practices for U.S. Museums* [2008]).

The deployment of mission statements in thousands of businesses, government agencies, and nonprofit organizations prompted closer examinations of mission statements to determine whether they had strategic value or were an empty planning exercise. George McDaniel, executive director of Drayton Hall, observed that "One can always tell when a mission statement has been drafted by a committee whose members do not have a unified view because the statement consists of compromised wording and is too long, clumsily phrased, and difficult to repeat" ("At Historic Houses and Buildings: Connecting Past, Present, and Future," in *Public History: Essays from the Field*, ed. Gardner and LaPaglia [1999]). Management expert Peter Drucker complained that mission statements had become "a kind of hero sandwich of good intentions" and urged clarity and simplicity (*Managing the Nonprofit Organization* [1990]). Indeed, an analysis of twenty years of research on mission statements in business by Sebastian Desmidt, Anita Prinzie, and Adelien Decramer in 2011 showed that mission statements had very little positive influence on organizational performance unless they contained "no financial goals; identified an organization's values/beliefs; defined an organization's purpose(s), unique identity, distinctive competence/strength; and were relatively short" ("Looking for the Value of Mission Statements: A Meta-Analysis of 20 Years of Research," *Management Decision* 49, no. 3).

Although adoption of a mission statement continues to be regarded as a best practice by leaders in the field, its definition is continually evolving. The purpose of "preserving, collecting, and interpreting" among museums, archives, historical societies, and historic sites has become ubiquitous and obligatory, causing some organizations to either incorporate who they are serving and the change they hope to achieve to make their mission statements more distinctive and compelling, or to create a separate vision statement, code of ethics, or list of institutional values. Stephen Weil observed these changes in museums in 2002's *Making Museums Matter*: "Over three decades, what the museum might be envisioned as offering to the public has grown from mere refreshment (the museum as carbonated beverage) to education (the museum as a site for informal learning) to nothing short of communal empowerment (the museum as an instrument for social change)." If this trend continues, history organizations may soon be following the distinctions Peter Drucker saw between the purpose of nonprofit organizations and business or government:

Business supplies either goods or services. Government controls. A business has discharged its task when the customer buys the product, pays for it, and is satisfied with it. Government has discharged its function when its policies are effective. The nonprofit institution neither supplies goods or services nor controls. Its "product" is neither a pair of shoes nor an effective regulation. Its "product" is a changed human being. The nonprofit institutions are human-change agents. Their "product" is a cured patient, a child that learns, a young man or woman grown into a self-respecting adult; a changed human life altogether. (Managing the Nonprofit Organization [1990])

For further reading, see American Association of Museums, *Museums for a New Century* (1984); American Association of Museums, *National Standards and Best Practices for U.S. Museums* (2008); Sebastian Desmidt, Anita Prinzie, and Adelien Decramer, "Looking for the Value of Mission Statements: A Meta-Analysis of 20 Years of Research," *Management Decision* 49, no. 3 (2011): 468–83; Peter Drucker, *Managing the Nonprofit Organization* (1990); Walter Kiechel III, *The Lords of Strategy* (2010); George McDaniel, "At Historic Houses and Buildings: Connecting Past, Present, and Future" in *Public History: Essays from the Field* (1999); Lois Silverman, *The Social Work of Museums* (2010); Stephen Weil, *Making Museums Matter* (2002).

MAX A. VAN BALGOOY
ENGAGING PLACES LLC

See building bridges through local history; local historical societies and core purpose; values of history; vision.

Mississippi, local history in. In 2017 Mississippi will observe its bicentennial with celebrations across the state that will be highlighted by the planned opening on December 10 of the Museum of Mississippi History and Mississippi Civil Rights Museum in the capital city of Jackson.

Prior to statehood, Mississippi was controlled for a century by France, Britain, and Spain, but European domain ended when the Spanish evacuated Natchez on March 30, 1798. That year President John Adams approved an act of Congress that established the Territory of Mississippi bounded by Spanish West Florida on the south, Spanish Louisiana on the west and southwest, the state of Georgia on the east, and on

the north by lands that were occupied by the Choctaw and Chickasaw Indian confederacies but claimed by the U.S. government. By 1812, the Mississippi Territory had been expanded by Congress to encompass the boundaries of present-day Mississippi and Alabama, and on December 10, 1817, the western section of the Territory was admitted as the state of Mississippi, the nation's twentieth state, with Natchez as its capital.

By a succession of treaties with the U.S. government, the Choctaw and Chickasaw lost their native lands and were pushed west beyond the Mississippi River. The Choctaw tribe, which numbered more than 19,000, was the largest Indian group in Mississippi. By 1833, approximately 13,000 Choctaws were removed. Those who chose to stay in Mississippi are the ancestors of today's Mississippi Band of Choctaw Indians, which was formally recognized by the U.S. government in 1945 through the establishment of the 35,000-acre Choctaw Indian Reservation in Neshoba County and surrounding counties in east central Mississippi. The 1820 Treaty of Doak's Stand that provided for the cession of more than 5,000,000 acres of Choctaw land led to the relocation of the state capital to a site on the Pearl River near the geographic center of the state. The new capital was named in honor of Andrew Jackson who, later as president of the United States, would be the architect of Indian removal from the Southern states.

During the 1850s, Mississippians turned their attention to the past through the formation of a state historical society under the leadership of

This Mississippi Blues Commission marker in Holly Ridge honors blues legend Charley Patton. CREDIT: BROTHER ROGERS.

B. L. C. Wailes, a planter and naturalist of Washington, Mississippi, who had published a *Report on the Agriculture and Geology of Mississippi* in 1854. Believing that a brief history of Mississippi would interest the planters, for whom the report was designed, Wailes devoted the first 116 pages to a "Historical Outline" that covered the period from the DeSoto Expedition to the establishment of the Mississippi Territory.

In 1858 Wailes declined a request from Benjamin W. Sanders, state librarian, to aid in the preparation of a book on the history of Mississippi from 1798 to 1850, but instead developed a rough draft of the "Constitution and Act of Incorporation of the Histori-

cal Society of Mississippi," revising it with Sanders's assistance. Few attended the society's organizational meeting on November 9, 1858, when Wailes was elected president. A small room in the state capitol adjoining the state library was designated by the legislature for the collection of historical materials. Wailes devoted much time in the next twelve months to collecting historical documents, both manuscript and printed, but few people became paid members of the society and by 1860 it had dissolved.

Near the end of the nineteenth century, interest in Mississippi's history led to a revival of the Mississippi Historical Society. Reorganization efforts, beginning in 1890, were spearheaded by Franklin L. Riley, professor of history at the University of Mississippi, who led the society in urging the Mississippi legislature to create a state-funded agency to be responsible for the care and custody of the state's historical documents. Thus, the Mississippi Department of Archives and History (MDAH) was established in 1902. Riley also edited fourteen volumes of the valuable series, The Publications of the Mississippi Historical Society. Following Riley's departure from Ole Miss for another university in 1914, the society became dormant in the 1920s.

The society was reactivated in 1952 and joined with MDAH in the publication of *The Journal of Mississippi History*, a quarterly publication begun in 1939. The *Journal* remains a prime publishing outlet for academicians and interested lay historians. The society and MDAH have often joined forces on various historical programs and projects across the state.

The society has taken an active role in producing significant books on the history of the state. In the 1990s, the society initiated the Heritage of Mississippi Series that will include fifteen volumes, each covering an important subject or era related to the state's history. In 2000, the society launched its online publication, *Mississippi History Now*, to strengthen its educational and leadership role in generating a broader interest in Mississippi history, which is taught in Mississippi's public schools in the fourth and ninth grades.

Several marker programs recognize sites of unique historical significance throughout Mississippi. Since 1949,

the state *historical marker program, which is now administered by MDAH, has identified and interpreted historic sites across the state. At the beginning of the twenty-first century, Mississippi launched several heritage trails with markers placed around the state. The Mississippi Blues Trail and Mississippi Country Music Trail consist of markers that tell stories through words and images of blues and country musicians and of how the times and places influenced their music. The marker sites run the gamut from city streets to cotton fields, train depots to cemeteries, and juke joints to churches. Moreover, the Mississippi Arts Commission has developed a Mississippi Blues Trail Curriculum that brings blues into the classroom for students. The Delta Blues Museum is located in Clarksdale, Mississippi. Mississippi Freedom Trail markers commemorate civil rights events and Mississippi's pivotal role in the American Civil Rights Movement, whereas the Civil War Trail features markers, interpretive signage, and a driving tour of battlefields and significant sites. Mississippi has collaborated with Alabama and Georgia to create the Southern Literary Trail. The Mississippi Mound Trail will interpret Native American mounds with highway pull-offs and interpretive signage from the Grand Village of the Natchez Indians in present-day Natchez to the Winterville Mounds site north of Greenville.

In addition to the state historical society, Mississippi has more than one hundred local historical organizations within its eighty-two counties. The Marshall County Historical Society, the Natchez Historical Society, the Vicksburg and Warren County Historical Society, and the Jackson County Historical Society were among the first to be established. Generally begun after World War II, the local historical organizations operate museums, work toward preservation of local historical buildings, artifacts, and local records, produce and disseminate local history publications, sponsor historical markers, and promote genealogical research. In 1995, the Mississippi Historical Society, with MDAH assistance, established the Federation of Mississippi Historical Societies to provide a means by which local societies could exchange information and maintain contact to support projects and programs of mutual interest. The Mississippi Historical Society presents the Frank E. Everett, Jr. Award annually, as merited, to a local society that has done outstanding work in preserving and interpreting local history. There is also a statewide Junior Historical Society that operates under the auspices of the Mississippi Historical Society and the University of Southern Mississippi Department of History.

PEGGY W. JEANES
MISSISSIPPI HISTORICAL SOCIETY

See United States, local history in.

Missouri, local history in. The study of local history in Missouri has long been hampered by the fragmentation of cultural and historical organizations throughout the state. There is no one state agency in charge of all aspects of preserving and promoting the history of the Show-Me State.

The closest thing to such a centralized agency is the State Historical Society of Missouri (SHSMO), founded in 1898 by the Missouri Press Association with the goal of saving the state's historic newspapers. In 1899 the SHSMO was designated by the Missouri General Assembly as the trustee for the people of Missouri, charged with the responsibility of collecting and preserving the history of Missouri and the Midwest.

Headquartered in Columbia, on the campus of the University of Missouri, the SHSMO has research centers in St. Louis, Kansas City, Rolla, Springfield, and Cape Girardeau. True to its founders' intent, the SHSMO boasts the finest collection of Missouri newspapers available anywhere, with more than 50,000 reels of microfilmed papers dating to 1808, thirteen years before Missouri became a state. The SHSMO, in cooperation with the University of Missouri, also holds large manuscript collections that include documents dating to the late eighteenth and nineteenth centuries, such as Santa Fe Trail and Civil War era diaries, memoirs, and correspondence. Likewise, the SHSMO holds the papers of prominent Missouri politicians, including Champ Clark, Stuart Symington, John Danforth, and Thomas Eagleton. Inventories of manuscript collections held by the SHSMO can be accessed from the organization's website: http://shs.umsystem.edu/index.shtml.

In 1919, shortly after World War I ended, the Missouri legislature created a Soldiers and Sailors Memorial Hall, to be operated out of the state capitol. This institution soon expanded and changed its name to the Missouri State Museum. The State Museum is responsible for a

This marker in Kansas City, Missouri, high on a bluff overlooking the Missouri River, honors the assistance provided to the Lewis and Clark Expedition by local French community members. CREDIT: DEE A. HARRIS.

collection of approximately 50,000 artifacts that portray the state's cultural and natural history through a series of rotating, traveling, and permanent exhibits and educational programs.

In 1965, the Missouri legislature created the Missouri State Archives to serve as the repository for governmental records of permanent value. Located in the Missouri capital of Jefferson City

445

and operating under the direction of the Secretary of State, the Missouri State Archives is a rich repository of records ranging from the official papers of the state's governors to the records of state institutions, such as the Missouri State Penitentiary, and military records from the War of 1812 through World War I.

In 1989, the Missouri General Assembly established a Local Records Program, administered by the *state archives. Through this program, local records archivists have identified, preserved, and made accessible countless local historical records, such as wills and land records.

Founded in 1968, Missouri's State Historic Preservation Office operates out of the Missouri Department of Natural Resources. This state agency coordinates surveys statewide to identify historic, architectural, and archaeological resources. Significant properties identified in the surveys may be nominated to the *National Register of Historic Places.

The Missouri History Museum, formerly known as the Missouri Historical Society, is located in St. Louis, and is among the state's oldest historical organizations. Established in August 1866 by a group of St. Louisans to collect and preserve elements of the region's history, the museum's headquarters have been in the Jefferson Memorial in the city's Forest Park since 1913. This building was erected with funds from the Louisiana Purchase Exposition (the 1904 World's Fair). The Missouri History Museum became eligible for tax support in 1987, when the citizens of St. Louis City and County voted to include it in the Zoo-Museum Tax District. In

2000, the Missouri History Museum increased its space with a large addition to the original facility. The museum also has library, research, and conservation facilities nearby in a former Jewish temple renovated by the museum and opened in 1991.

The St. Louis Public Library's downtown facility, built in 1901 with the help of funds from Andrew Carnegie, also contains significant local history collections. The St. Louis Public Library system was created in 1865.

Likewise, the Kansas City Public Library houses the Missouri Valley Special Collections, a noncirculating library of local history and genealogy resources for the greater Kansas City area. This facility came into existence in 1960 and is a major resource for the history of Jackson County.

Similarly, the Mid-Continent Public Library in Independence is the largest library system in the Kansas City metropolitan area and houses many primary and secondary sources that are indispensable to an understanding of the region.

Students in Missouri study their state's history in the fourth grade. No other curriculum mandates the study of state history, although American history courses feature Missouri in the larger context of the history of the United States.

The following books are the top selections for general histories of Missouri: Carl H. Chapman and Eleanor F. Chapman, *Indians and Archaeology of Missouri* (1983); *Dictionary of Missouri Biography* (1999); William E. Foley, *The Genesis of Missouri: From Wilderness Outpost to Statehood* (1989); Lorenzo

Johnston Greene, Gary R. Kremer, and Antonio F. Holland, *Missouri's Black Heritage* (1993); William E. Parrish, gen. ed., *A History of Missouri*, six vols. (1971–1997); and Milton D. Rafferty, *Historical Atlas of Missouri* (1982). Likewise, *The WPA Guide to 1930s Missouri*, new foreword by Charles van Ravenswaay, new introduction by Howard W. Marshall and Walter A. Schroeder (1986), remains a valuable tool for understanding Missouri state and local history.

ROBERT ARCHIBALD
UPDATED BY GARY R. KREMER
STATE HISTORICAL SOCIETY OF
MISSOURI

See United States, local history in.

Montana, local history in. For most Montanans the "past" is only a few generations removed. Especially for tribal cultures, it is an integral part of everyday life. While there is a deep-seated interest in preserving Montana history, the boom-bust and natural resource economy of the state has been at times adverse to preservation. The number of local historical societies and museums is nearly 200; but most are small, volunteer-run, and still struggle to survive due to lack of funding and staff. There are tribal cultural committees, historical repositories, and historic preservation offices in many of the eight tribal governments and/ or seven tribal colleges in Montana. A handful of larger cultural institutions and support organizations in the state tend to and assist others in the preservation and dissemination of historical resources.

The Montana Historical Society (MHS) was founded in 1865 by forward-thinking pioneers in the territory's first capital, Bannack. The MHS is one of the oldest state historical societies west of the Mississippi. Today the MHS houses library, archives, museum, publications, education, and historic preservation functions. It is home to *Montana's Museum*, featuring western art and a wide array of magnificent artifacts representing the native and immigrant history of Montana's people. Its Research Center (historical library, archives, and photo archives) holds extensive collections of published material, manuscripts, *maps, photographs, *oral histories, and state records, making it a destination for researchers interested in Montana and Western American topics. MHS publications include the award-winning quarterly *Montana the Magazine of Western History*, and books covering a wide range of Montana and Northern Plains topics. Safeguarding of Montana's cultural resources, such as archeological sites and historic buildings, is promoted through initiatives of the *Historic Preservation Office*. There are over 1,150 Montana sites listed in the National Register of Historic Places; nearly 2,000 National Register signs relating the historic significance of a particular building or site are located in communities across Montana. The Outreach and Interpretation program offers educational programs of all types and for all ages—from an annual history conference to curriculum resources. Guided tours are provided at the state capitol building and at the Original Governor's Mansion, an 1888 Victorian home near downtown

447

This historical marker stands in front of the Original Governor's Mansion in Helena, Montana. CREDIT: MONTANA HISTORICAL SOCIETY.

Helena, which housed Montana's governors from 1919 to 1968. The Montana Historical Society is an agency of Montana state government; however, it receives only 60 percent funding from state appropriations. The MHS has increased public outreach through digital resources such as the online catalog, Montana history Wiki, JSTOR index of the quarterly magazine, resources for educators, and Montana newspapers on the *Chronicling America* website. *Social media outlets provide even more accessibility to MHS heritage resources. Plans for the future include the construction of a new building and renovation of the existing facility to result in a state-of-the-art heritage center.

The Western Heritage Center (WHC) founded in 1971 and serving Yellowstone County and the eastern part of Montana, features changing *exhibits, utilizes emerging technologies in programming, and focuses on community outreach to make the story of the Yellowstone River Valley engaging to audiences of all ages. The WHC is home to over 17,000 artifacts, historic photographs, and oral histories that document the history and development of eastern Montana.

In Bozeman, the Museum of the Rockies (MOR) is a multidimensional museum that serves the Yellowstone Region. Though best known for their paleontological collections, the MOR has superb collections that include historic photographs, homesteading artifacts, *decorative arts, Native American collections, and turn-of-the-twentieth-century textiles. The Tinsley House, a *living history farm, is located on the museum grounds and is a popular feature with school classes.

Focusing on western Montana, the Historical Museum at Fort Missoula showcases the military, forest industry, farming, and urban history of the region. The museum is located on the grounds of Fort Missoula, a late 1880s military post that later served as an internment camp for Italian and German detainees, and resident alien Japanese men during World War II. Many of the original buildings remain, including the Post Headquarters, Alien Detention Barracks, and Quartermaster's Storehouse.

Founded in 1967, the Museums Association of Montana (MAM) supports the museums in Montana through networking, advocacy, education, and promotion of cultural organizations in the state. With an all-volunteer board, the MAM serves Montana's museums by offering an annual conference with professional training opportunities, a quarterly newsletter, a *tourism map of Montana museums, and special projects like the statewide study, "The Impact of Museums on Montana's Economy and Community" (2011).

The Montana State Historical and Records Advisory Board assists local historical societies, museums, counties, tribal, or other historical records repositories in identifying and preserving historically valuable records and making them accessible to Montana citizens and other researchers. They provide a Local Records Re-grant Project, a Traveling Student Archivist Program (on-site assistance to underserved institutions), training workshops, and planning efforts for *digitization of collections.

The Butte-Silver Bow Public Archives, established in 1981, collects and preserves the archival history of the two-county area in southwest Montana. It is "the" resource for local history of the area. The Butte Archives expanded operations in 2011 into a beautifully renovated historic building, formerly the Butte Fire Department, built in 1900. Researchers, scholars, preservationists, and genealogists look to the professional staff of the archives for a wide array of reference services.

The Montana Preservation Alliance (MPA) is a statewide not-for-profit organization dedicated to providing Montanans with the resources necessary to preserve our state's unique history and culture. Since 1987, MPA has helped Montana citizens to achieve a diverse array of preservation initiatives ranging from roof repair and building stabilization to school education programs and cultural *landscape documentation. Through preservation team workshops, lobbying efforts, Preservation Excellence Awards, and annual publication of Montana's Most Endangered Places, MPA provides individuals and communities with the leadership and knowledge to preserve Montana's past.

The Montana Memory Project, a collection of digital collections and items relating to Montana's cultural heritage, documents the Montana experience through documents and images available free through the Internet. Many of the items are digitized copies of historic material; some items are contemporary. All serve as a resource for education, business, pleasure, and lifelong learning. Nearly twenty Montana libraries, museums, archives, and cultural institutions have contributed materials to this public collection administered by the Montana State Library.

Since 1972, Humanities Montana has served as Montana's independent nonprofit affiliate of the *National Endowment for the Humanities. Humanities Montana has benefited hundreds of Montana organizations and thousands of its citizens, providing support for public programs in the humanities throughout the state's communities. They offer grants, a speaker's bureau, community conversations, and other special initiatives.

The public schools of Montana have no regulations that mandate the teaching of local or state history. However, Montana history is taught primarily in middle school social studies classes or as an elective in high school. *Montana: Stories of the Land* (2008), a textbook directed to a middle school audience, provides a comprehensive history of Montana from the precontact period to the present, and incorporates the history of the state's native peoples throughout. The Montana Constitution (1972) outlines the state's responsibility to honor and teach the long view of history: "The state recognizes the distinct and unique cultural heritage of the American Indians and is committed in its educational goals to the preservation of their cultural integrity." Not until the 1999 legislature, however, did the government act on implementing these ideas: "Every Montanan, whether Indian or non-Indian, be encouraged to learn about the distinct and unique heritage of American Indians in a culturally responsive manner." Since then Montana's Office of Public Instruction added highly suc-

cessful Indian Education for All programs such as a tribal history initiative, Indian education curriculum, museum and school partnership grants, content standards, and teacher training.

SUSAN NEAR
MONTANA HISTORICAL SOCIETY

See American Indian history; United States, local history in.

monuments. See memorials and monuments.

Moorland-Spingarn Research Center (MSRC). This repository is located at Howard University in Washington, D.C., and is one of the largest and most comprehensive archives devoted to all aspects of the history and culture of African Americans and of graduates of the university. The collections include bound volumes, journals and periodicals, manuscripts, and images. The interim director and university archivist is Dr. Clifford L. Muse Jr. The phone number for the MSRC is (202) 806-4237. See online at www.howard.edu/msrc.

See African American history.

Mormons, sources for. See Appendix B.

mortality schedules. Mortality schedules are special census schedules that were used in censuses from 1850 through 1880 and in the special census of 1885. They provide a listing of persons who died in the year prior to the census. Information recorded on the schedules includes the name of the deceased, sex, age, color (white, black, or mulatto), place of birth, month in which the death occurred, occupation, disease or cause of death, and the number of days the person was ill. The schedules are an early attempt to provide a uniform reporting of *vital statistics. Deaths seem to have been significantly underreported, but the schedules provide unique access to records for individuals who wouldn't have appeared in the decennial census. The causes of death might also be useful for local historians.

*Ancestry.com provides an index to selected state mortality schedules over the range of years they were produced (subscription required). It is not an index to all the mortality schedules but certainly helpful. For a chart of locations for all the schedules and more information see the *Ancestry Wiki*, which features a *digitized version of *The Source: A Guidebook to American Genealogy*, ed. Szucs and Luebking, 3rd ed. (2006): https://www.ancestry.com/wiki/index.php?title=The_Source:_A_Guidebook_to_American_Genealogy. The mortality schedules can also be searched or browsed from microfilm from the *National Archives—see U.S. Census Bureau, "Measuring America," available online at http://usa.ipums.org/usa/resources/voliii/measuring_america.pdf for reel numbers.

ROBERT KIBBEE
THE HISTORY CENTER IN TOMPKINS
COUNTY (NY)

See census, United States; genealogical resources online.

mug books. Mug books are nineteenth-century compilations of photographs and biographies of prominent men. Most often, inclusion was determined by one's willingness to pay a fee to be included. The word "mug" came to refer to the face, probably from eighteenth-century drinking mugs that were made to represent a human face, such as Toby mugs. In time, "mug" meant an ugly or a criminal face. Photographs taken after an arrest are called mug shots. See Oscar Lewis, "Mug Books," *Colophon* 17 (1934).

See county histories.

municipal corporation. This term refers to a political body authorized under state law and created by local residents. It is also called a municipality. The municipal corporation has the power to tax, spend, borrow, regulate, and exercise the right of eminent domain.

municipal records. See local government records.

museum ethics. Ethics is a system of principles, standards, or values that guides conduct. Ethics is about how we *ought* to conduct ourselves—not about what we can do or get away with but rather what we ought to do. It is not intuitive or based simply on applying logic or common sense—ethics is based on established practices and shared recognition of responsibility.

What is a code of ethics? A code of ethics is simply a set of established principles, usually within a professional context or area of practice. It is a not a set of prescriptive rules that all must follow but rather an articulation of the expectations of peers regarding both individual and collective roles, duties, and responsibilities. A code sets standards of integrity and describes acceptable practice for all stakeholders.

Why is ethics important? Ethics makes clear to all that the public interest takes priority over personal interest. With a code of ethics in place to guide conduct and decision making, the need for external regulation diminishes. In *Museum Ethics* (1997), Gary Edson writes that ethics, by ensuring that others in the same situation would make the same decision, provides "predictability, consistency, and stability."

More specifically, why is ethics important for museums? Ethics establishes the fundamental premises on which the museum community is established, in juxtaposition with other groups and communities of practice. Ethics is critical in defining who we are and what we do, providing guidance as we address our responsibilities individually and collectively. Working within that framework, we know that the decisions we make are the same that other museums would make when facing the same situation. Ethics removes impulse or personal preference from the equation. As such, ethics is critical to public confidence and accountability, demonstrating that we recognize that we hold collections and operate in the public trust. That trust or confidence can be fragile—it can be undermined as much by the appearance of unethical behavior as by actual misconduct.

What's the difference between ethics and the law? We enact laws to clearly establish the minimum standards for avoiding civil or criminal liability, but ethics requires of us a higher level of conduct or practice. An action may be technically legal yet still be unethical. For example, *copyright violation or infringement is a legal problem—copy-

right restricts the use of others' exact words but not their larger arguments or content. You can operate within copyright law (by limiting use of specific wording to fair use and providing attribution for all quotations) but still be guilty of misusing others' ideas or concepts by presenting them as your own, a violation of ethical principles against plagiarism. There are legal penalties for copyright infringement, but none for plagiarism—but that does not excuse it. Similarly, we know there are various laws and controls that address trade in cultural property, but there are also many gaps in the law and in enforcement. Ethically, we cannot take advantage of such loopholes—we have to be self-limiting. Ethics sets a higher standard than the law.

What are the limitations of ethics? Codes of ethics are generally not enforced—there are no punishments or penalties for ethical lapses. Instead we depend on self-motivation and peer pressure to prevent or stop unethical behavior. Nor does ethics always provide easy answers. The choice is often not between "good" and "bad," but between competing "goods"—for example, some actions may be acceptable once but not over the long term. While many of the decisions we have to make involve risk, ethics provides guidance in making those decisions.

What's the difference between a professional code of ethics and an institutional code of ethics? Museums are most familiar with the codes of ethics that define us as a profession. But to whom do such codes apply? The broader ones adopted by the International Council of Museums and the *American Alliance of Museums (AAM) address the entire museum community—not just professionals but volunteers, trustees, and others involved in the work of the museum. But there are also codes for subsets of the museum profession. History museums follow the code established by the *American Association for State and Local History, and other sectors (for example, zoos and aquariums, youth museums, art museums) have their own special codes as well. One can also find codes of ethics for professional groups within the museum community (curators, conservators, interpreters, registrars, museum stores) as well as within related professions and disciplines (*historic preservation, libraries and special collections, and archives as well as disciplines such as history and sociology). AAM's *Codes of Ethics and Practice of Interest to Museums* provides the texts of sixty-one such codes or statements. Not only is there a sometimes bewildering array of professional codes, but the codes are often not as useful as one might hope. Many are too general to provide sufficient direction, are not well understood even within the profession, and, in the final analysis, are not enforceable.

While professional codes of ethics provide important context and establish the standards of the field, on a day-to-day basis institutional codes of ethics are more critical. An institutional code draws on pertinent professional codes but is tailored to the specifics of a museum. In developing such a code, a museum not only addresses the lack of specificity in the professional codes but also builds internal agreement about ethical standards and responsibilities,

reinforcing public perception of integrity. In other words, by raising consciousness about ethical conduct, the process or discussion can be as important as the document that is produced.

To develop an institutional code of ethics, you should bring together a diverse team of staff and other stakeholders—it should not be a top-down process nor should it be led by lawyers on your board. Remember that this is about ethics and not law, and your code should be rooted in the culture and values of your museum, not legalese. There are many different ways to get started—you can, for example, begin with one of the professional codes, looking at what you would need to add or revise to address your own particular circumstances, or you can find an example from another museum and adapt it. Whatever your process, the code you produce should be kept relatively short and user friendly and should be reviewed and discussed by all stakeholders before being adopted by your board and implemented.

For further reading, see Sally Yerkovich, *A Practical Guide to Museum Ethics* (2016); Marie C. Malaro, *Museum Governance: Mission, Ethics, Policy* (1994); Gary Edson, ed., *Museum Ethics* (1997); and *Writing a Museum Code of Ethics* (1993).

JAMES GARDNER
NATIONAL ARCHIVES
AND RECORDS ADMINISTRATION

See ethics and local history; museums and the matter of ethics.

museum theater. The past thirty years have seen an increase in the amount and variety of theater happening in museums and historic or heritage sites across the United States, Canada, the United Kingdom, and Europe, as well as the Asia Pacific region. This growth is reflected in the various networks of the International Museum Theatre Alliance (IMTAL), a membership organization dedicated to supporting the use of theater and theatrical techniques in museums, heritage sites, zoos, and aquaria. Theater is often one type of live or interpretive program a museum might offer visitors, in addition to planetarium shows, object theaters, demonstrations, or audio tours. Initially used by a few pioneering institutions, now innovative museum professionals around the world have turned to theater as a successful medium for educating visitors about a variety of subjects. Research and *evaluation studies have confirmed theater's potential efficacy, value, and reach.

Museum theater takes many forms, including first-person interpretation, *living history, science demonstration, puppetry, storytelling, creative drama, musical, simulation, and scripted play. It can be written or improvised. It can be an informal discussion between interpreter and visitor, or a formal presentation on a stage with a seated audience. While the primary style of museum theater employed by many museums remains the solo character monologue, scripted or improvised, there are always evolving styles and techniques being tried and tested. These programs can be directly connected or tangential to a museum's exhibitions and collection, but they are always in fulfillment of a museum's *mission.

While content and styles change by project, there are consistent aspects of museum theater: narrative/story, conflict, imaginative play, emotion, and learning. Whether to pique a visitor's interest in a subject or provide context for a historic moment, there are continual shifts in the kinds of learning goals underlying museum theater, often reflective of shifts in museum practice. For instance, theater offerings support the current trend in the museum field (the focus of the newly formed steering committee, Museums and Race, which held a sold-out series of programs at the AAM conference in 2016) to approach challenging issues like slavery, and invite controversy (see Rose 2016; Kidd, Cairns, Drago, Ryall, and Stearn 2016). In many ways, museum theater programs have been ahead of this curve, because theater has proved itself an effective and powerful method for approaching difficult or complex content.

Theater provides distancing that creates a safe space within which to explore topics that might be hard to broach otherwise in an exhibit. Since 1998, Conner Prairie, in Fishers, Indiana, has employed theater in its participatory theater experience *Follow the North Star* to demonstrate the wide-ranging social attitudes toward African Americans in pre–Civil War Indiana. Participants travel back to the year 1836 and assume the role of fugitive slaves seeking freedom on the *Underground Railroad through the state. Traveling as a group, they encounter a variety of characters, ranging from sympathetic allies to racist antagonists, and later dissect their experience in a facilitated conversation. It is a powerful experience that generates empathy, provokes discussion, and immerses visitors in an important part of the nation's history.

For a holiday program at the Atlanta History Center, an enslaved character was created in order to engage visitors in his dilemma of whether to use his one-day pass for Christmas to attempt an escape North with his newly pregnant wife. He did not want others to suffer should he try, but was distraught at the thought of his child being born into slavery. This program revealed a very different perspective on the holiday than had been done previously. In this way and others, theater can serve as a tool for critical thinking (Jones 2011). The conflict and dilemmas inherent in history make theater a natural choice of interpretive method. Across institutions, museum theater programs have been created to encourage visitors to question scientific positions and historians' stories, and to imagine another's perspective or alternative histories.

While museum theater has primarily focused on visitor interactions, it has also been used in staff trainings and youth development. The Missouri History Museum received the 2014 National Arts and Humanities Youth Program Award for its Teens Make History program, in which high school students research, write, and perform plays, and conduct exhibition projects, including *oral history interviews. These students from inner-city St. Louis have the opportunity to express their ideas about history through their performances in shows, such as #NextHashtag and #Sticks and Stones.

Museum theater has followed trends in theater as well as museums. Mirror-

ing the increase in participatory plays like Punch Drunk's *Sleep No More*, museums are creating similarly styled performances, like the Science Museum of Minnesota's *Mysteries at the Museum*, a forensic whodunit attended by over 1,200 in one performance. Punch Drunk has also created a museum theater piece for the National Maritime Museum at Greenwich (UK). Aimed at six-to-twelve-year-olds and their families, *Against Captain's Orders* involves the audience in a quest for several missing nautical objects. *Follow the North Star* is the veteran program in this style.

Historic sites that employ living history such as Colonial Williamsburg, Plimoth Plantation, and Conner Prairie are in essence stages on which historic drama and comedy can be realized. Done well, the visitor becomes a historic player, immersed in *historical thinking and context. As visitors explore 1836 Prairietown, Conner Prairie interpreters invite them to consider their position on gender equality or women's literacy. Lively conversations can ensue. Sovereign Hill, an outdoor museum interpreting Australia's discovery of gold, invites school groups to play historic characters in a theater program. Dressed in nineteenth-century-style clothing, and using classrooms and equipment typical of the era, students spend two days in one of four themed schools role-playing the lives of goldfields students to understand social conditions during the great Victorian Gold Rush.

Technology has expanded theatrical fare, as live actor/interpreters can interact with images of actors through effects like Pepper's Ghost, similar to a hologram, or perform in front of multimedia presentations, or incorporate innovative sound and lighting effects. Technology allows for larger spectacles and expanded casts than were generally possible or affordable in museum theater productions.

The professionals employed in museum theater are actors, writers, and directors, as well as historians and educators. The primary requisite is that anyone writing for or acting in museum theater be a skilled professional. The best outcomes often arise out of collaborations between theater artists, museum professionals, and historians or external experts. Everyone contributes their strengths to create a museum offering that engages visitors in critical thinking about a story that they can relate to their lives and existing knowledge of the world. It may be more questions than answers are the result, but that would be success for most practitioners. If this theater experience resonated in a visitor years later, firing a neuron, sparking a memory or connection, even better.

For further reading see D. Black and A. Goldowski, "Science Theater as an Interpretive Technique in a Science Museum," presented at the meeting of the National Association of Research in Science Teaching (March 1999); S. H. Cohn, "Evaluating the Effectiveness of the Science Museum of Minnesota's Traveling Theater Program" (2010); B. Goodacre and G. Baldwin, *Living the Past, Reconstruction, Recreation, Reenactment and Education at Museums and Historical Sites* (2002); C. Hughes, "Theater and Controversy in Museums," in *Journal of Museum Education* 23, no. 3 (1998); C. Hughes, *Performance for Learning: How Emotions Play a Part*, dissertation, Ohio State University (2008); A. Jackson and J. Kidd, eds., *Performing Heritage: Research, Practice and Innovation in Museum Theatre and Live Interpretation* (2011); A. Jackson and H. R. Leahy, "'Seeing It For Real?. . .?'—Authenticity, Theatre and Learning in Museums," *Research in Drama Education: The Journal of Applied Theatre and Performance* 10, no. 3 (2005); C. Jones, *An Illusion That Makes the Past Seem Real: The Potential of Living History for Developing the Historical Consciousness of Young People* (2001); J. S. Kidd, A. Cairns, A. Drago, A. Ryall, and M. Stearn, eds., *Challenging History in the Museum: International Perspectives* (2016); S. Magelssen, "'This is a Drama. You Are Characters': The Tourist as Fugitive Slave in Conner Prairie's 'Follow the North Star,'" *Theatre Topics* 16, no. 1 (2006); C. Oesterle, "Themed Environments—Performative Spaces: Performing Visitors in North American Living History Museums," in *Staging the Past: Themed Environments in Transcultural Perspectives*, ed. J. Schlehe, M. Uike-Bormann, and C. Oesterle (2014); and J. Rose, *Interpreting Difficult History at Museums and Historic Sites* (2016).

CATHERINE HUGHES
CONNER PRAIRIE

See building bridges through local history.

museums, public value of. "What's the public value of museums, anyway?" We are two colleagues who talk a lot about museums—what they do well to reach their audiences (real and potential) and what they need to work on.

We have both worked in Maryland; one of us is now working as a consultant and the other leads the Laurel Historical Society. Mary Alexander (MA) is a senior museum professional with more than forty years' experience. Lindsey Baker (LB) has been the director of a local historical society for the past eight years and has been in the field for fourteen years. MA has a master's degree in museum education; LB has a master's degree in history with a certificate in museum studies.

Here is a glimpse at our dialogue about the public value of museums— with some literary liberties—that perhaps you'd like to join.

LB: When I began working in museums, I did so because I thought it was a way for me to change the world. I think this is a common reason for entering the field for the younger generation of museum professionals. We are pretty idealistic and believe that our work is undertaken with this greater good in mind.

MA: I came to museum work from the classroom; I thought of museums as places for education in the company of friends and family. I also believed that museums were intended to "protect" objects—relics of the past, art of all kinds, and even entire venues of significance. My interests were less in the objects and more what "happens to people" while in the museums. But, my attitudes also are of museums as conservative institutions.

LB: In some ways I would argue that we have almost a generational split on the value or role of museums that we encounter every day as we interact with colleagues and visitors. We have people in my age cohort, let's say people aged twenty to forty-ish, who believe they are in the field of museums because of their public value and their potential to change the world. Meanwhile we work with and interact with people daily who have more traditional visions for museums.

MA: Would some basic definitions help?

The *American Alliance of Museums (AAM) accredit program defines a museum as "an organized and permanent non-profit institution, essentially educational or aesthetic in purpose, with professional staff, which owns and utilizes tangible objects, cares for them, and exhibits them to the public on some regular schedule."

The International Council of Museums in 1995 defined a museum as "a non-profit making, permanent institution in the service of society and of its development, and open to the public, which acquires, conserves, researches, communicates and exhibits for the purposes of study, education and enjoyment, material evidence of people and their environment."

This winter my students in Museum Scholarship and Material Culture at the University of Maryland created a museum definition that I find both creative and compelling: "A museum is an institution unbounded by physical space, which collects, researches, and exhibits the human condition for the purpose of engaging the local community and visitors from around the world in transformative experiences." It seems to me that "engagement" and "transformative" lie at the heart of our conversation.

LB: Exactly; your students give voice to why I went into museums.

I always think of AAM's *Excellence and Equity* report from 1992 as the most succinct explanation of potential public value. Not to be too generational, but I even have this quote on my Facebook profile that has been there since maybe 2006: "Guided by the spirit of excellence and equity, museums have the potential to nurture an enlightened, humane citizenry that appreciates the value of knowing about its past, is resourcefully and sensitively engaged in the present, and is determined to shape a future in which many experiences and many points of view are given voice."

457

museums, public value of

Excellence and Equity was really forward thinking, but I wonder other than inspiring a set of newbies into the field, what did it really accomplish?

MA: As we write (2016), both the American Alliance of Museums and the *American Association for State and Local History (AASLH) are leading national "conversations" about the public's role in and perception of museums. AAM is promoting a national discussion of Museum and Race that has emerged from the shocking attacks on young black men from Maryland to Missouri. The effort is not only to address the issue with visitors, but to force institutional changes that diversify the museum field itself. This initiative has roots in *Excellence and Equity* that addressed the questions: "How can museums, which have so much to contribute to the collective museum experience, welcome the broad spectrum of our society? How can they use the abundance of their collections and their scholarly resources to enrich and empower citizens from all backgrounds?"

At AASLH, the History Relevance Campaign serves as a catalyst for discovering, demonstrating, and promulgating the value of history for individuals, communities, and the nation. It argues that history can have more impact when it connects the people, events, places, stories, and ideas of the past with people, events, places, stories, and ideas that are important and meaningful to communities, people, and audiences today.

Both these initiatives build on the "expansive" definitions of the roles of museums.

LB: I think these are interesting attempts to get the field to think about the core of what museums do and can do in their communities. And I believe there are many other efforts going on that we might not even be aware of.

What I find so interesting is that the museum field is filled with people who have both opinions—those who believe museums are meant to protect culture and those who believe museums are meant to be active participants in change.

MA: Often *volunteers in museums, especially those focused on history, hold attitudes toward museums and their "service" to the public that are very traditional. This is part of the generational exchange you mentioned earlier.

LB: What I wonder is how the greater public views the value of museums?

I often reflect on an experience I had while traveling with non-museum friends. While in Trinidad with some very close friends, we decided to visit the National Museum and Art Gallery in Port of Spain. These are some of my best friends, but we had our biggest fight of the trip during our visit to the museum. You see, I spent much of my time taking pictures (without flash of course), debating the labels, and generally being a typical museum person in a museum—totally engaged with the museum as a museum with public spaces and opportunities rather than as a conveyer of information and protector of culture. My stance annoyed my traveling mates. They left the experience very upset with me. I had been told by a guard to stop taking pictures; I waited until he left the room and took another. My friends equated these actions with complete disrespect. I was dumbfounded—I had not hurt anyone by taking pictures.

What I realized was that my friends were a real-life example of non-museum folk reflecting the conservative view of museums. The museum was an institution meant to preserve materials, preserve culture, and as visitors our role was to honor the space and follow the rules. The visit exposed the rebel within me and my perceptions of the roles of museums. And in my friends' minds, I took liberties in a space that should have been respected.

MA: Your story for me reinforces the importance of museums as "conservative" institutions, seeking to protect *material culture for future generations. But that role is difficult to explain when some of the public feel either intimidated by museums or unwelcome.

LB: When I think about the current unrest in our country and how museums should be helping, I always think back to the Baltimore situation in 2015.

Following the unrest in Baltimore, I was profoundly disappointed in my profession. Although I was first able to really verbalize my feelings during the Baltimore Uprising, they are always with me when I think about the #BlackLivesMatter movement. Comments on *social media, news coverage, and general conversations have led me to see how museums have failed at helping people to critically analyze *primary and secondary sources, to see how unable people are to draw connections between the past and today, and to witness an utter lack of empathy for points of view and realities different from our own. This reflection has been personally painful. It's a wakeup call, not only for our country in relation to how we maintain savage inequality, but also to our profession.

What are we doing to better this world? These are the questions that guide my work and cause me to consider the public value of museums.

MARY ALEXANDER CAN BE REACHED AT ALEXANDER_SCHOU@MSN.COM. LINDSEY BAKER CAN BE REACHED AT LINDSEY.BAKER.22@GMAIL.COM.

See building bridges through local history; local historical societies and core purpose; mission statements; relevance; values of history; vision.

museums, small. In its November 2003 statement identifying strategic issues for the field, the American Association of Museums Board asserted, "The majority of museums in the United States are small institutions, many of them enjoying close ties with their communities. More needs to be done to understand and meet the special needs of this vital segment of the museum field." The issues facing small museums are many but equally, many resources are available for their development. Resources include the Small Museum Association (www.smallmuseum.org), the American Association for State and Local History (www.aaslh.org) with its StEPs graduated standards, and the American Alliance of Museums (www.aam-us. org) with the Museum Assessment Program. Many state field service or museum service organizations also offer training and technical assistance.

Almost three-quarters of collecting institutions in the United States could be considered small and these institutions hold 15 percent of the 4.8 billion collections items in the United States; 85 percent of small museums have no emergency plan, according to the Heritage Health Index published in 2005 by Heritage Preservation (https://www. imls.gov/publications/heritage-health-index-full-report).

Small museums often lack collections policies and clear collecting goals and as a result, often risk becoming the community attic, spending time and effort to catalog and care for unprovenanced collections. However, numerous small museums have made substantial progress in refining their collections to represent their community's entire history through new collecting efforts and deeper research into collections.

Many historical organizations have acquired historic buildings to house their operations. The restoration and maintenance of such a building requires a substantial commitment of both human and financial resources. Any such effort should be undertaken cautiously, with a clear understanding of both restoration and operating costs.

Small museums have many opportunities to connect directly with the communities they serve. Through lively programming, an active exhibits program, programs for schoolchildren, and collaborations with other community organizations, small history museums can make history at the center of many community efforts. In the last few years, many small museums have begun to use social media as a way to connect with audiences—small museums can be found on Facebook (www. facebook.com) and Twitter (www.twitter.com) sharing old photos, asking for memories, featuring collections items, and generally updating audiences on their work.

Small museums need to consider both the rationale for their existence and the ability of their own community to support their endeavors. Government grants and sugar daddies are rare and getting rarer. Support should come from a diverse base within the community. Those contemplating starting a museum should consult the Museum Association of New York's publication *What Comes First: Your Guide to Building a Strong, Sustainable Museum or Historical Organization (With Real Life Advice from Folks Who've Done It)*: http://manyonline.org/2010/10/manys-latest-publication-what-comes-first.

LINDA NORRIS
THE UNCATALOGED MUSEUM

See Small Museum Association.

museums and families. Research (and much anecdotal evidence) has shown that adult museum/historic site visiting habits are shaped by childhood experiences. For those working in museums

and historical organizations, attracting family audiences means audiences not for only today, but also for years to come. History museums lag far behind science centers and children's museums in attracting audiences; there is much room for history museums to expand their efforts in engaging family audiences and promoting intergenerational learning.

Making a museum family friendly begins even before the front door. First, it's important to consider that families come in all shapes and sizes. As you think about your audiences, make sure to use inclusive language. Designer Margaret Middleton's Family Inclusive Language chart gives words to avoid, such as mother or father, as not every adult with a child is necessarily a mom or dad, but could be grandparent or caregiver. The chart provides useful substitutions that can make everyone feel welcome, such as grown-up, adult, or caregiver.

A museum's website should have tips on visiting with children and feature family-friendly events. The most family-friendly museums have trained front desk staff or volunteers to be welcoming to all. They provide family restrooms, places to change diapers, breast feed, eat snacks, and sit down and relax. Family-friendly museums offer family ticketing and have rules that are "dos" such as "do explore, do respect others, do look for answers" rather than "don'ts."

Susie Wilkening, senior consultant and curator of museum audiences at Reach Advisors and lead author of *Life Stages of the Museum Visitor*, shared these tips for creating family-friendly museums at a family learning conference at the USS *Constitution* Museum:

- Create sticky memories. Given that children are more likely to remember seeing exceptional objects than any other museum experience, and remember them for decades, sticky memories can be created by ensuring that children experience the objects many museums want to share with them. "Sticky" objects tend to be large and narrative-based, such as dinosaurs, dioramas, suits of armor, and dollhouses.
- Combine them with hands-on activities. Hands-on activities are extremely popular and enjoyable for children, and are simply expected by most parents who bring their children to museums. Additionally, they have been proven to have positive learning outcomes, thus increasing the educational value of exhibitions and programs. A lack of hands-on activities signals to families that they are not welcome at a museum.
- Ditch the screens and buttons. While *some* parents and children enjoy interactive computer experiences, the majority of families do not come to museums for those types of experiences, and are more ambivalent about their presence in a museum setting. Indeed, many families come to museums for "real" experiences, and computers are secondary or even undesirable.
- Signal authenticity. Particularly at history organizations, visitors are looking for the real thing, the original stuff, if you will. Fortunately, history museums provide these in spades. Conveying this authenticity, this originality, is compelling to visitors. But don't say it explicitly! Saying it implies that someone has questioned the authenticity of a museum and its collections, and suddenly visitors wonder if a museum is as authentic as it proclaims, casting doubt on everything presented. Signal authenticity, don't say it!
- Engage the adults. Many adults visit museums in order to provide certain types of experiences for their children, whether they are fun, learning, or active. But their own intellectual and emotional stimulation as adults is often not considered, decreasing the quality of the visit for the entire family. Serve children well, but serve the adults just as well, and visits will be more positive.
- Create, and staff, natural photo spots. Most museums and historic sites have spots where the adults will pose their children for a picture. Adults thus end up with lots of pictures of their children, but few pictures of the entire family. Consider where those spots are at your museum, and then encourage staff and volunteers to observe that area carefully—and offer to take a picture of the *entire* family, for the family archives. It imprints a positive family memory and signals that the staff cares about their visitors.
- Don't neglect the amenities. A family can have an amazing museum visit, but if the restroom is dirty, guess what will be remembered? Amenities can positively make or break a visit. Ensure that restrooms are clean, changing areas are convenient and private, picnic areas prominent, and

461

benches prevalent. Parking should be convenient to the entrance of the museum and clearly marked.

- Tangible takeaway. Children love souvenirs and mementos, and will often keep them for years to come as a reminder of a visit. Consider what kind of (inexpensive) "gift" can be given to children that visit. It may be as simple as a snippet of hand-dyed yarn an interpreter is working with, or a wrought nail, but providing that tangible takeaway could be terrific investment in future visitation.
- Signal value. Families, more than any other audience segment, are thinking about the family budget. Fortunately, most museums are relatively affordable and provide a great value through fun and engaging programs and exhibitions. Make sure you are sharing that message to visitors, especially families, when they are weighing their options about what to do next weekend.
- Partner with complementary museums. Some museums serve families extremely well, while others struggle to attract them. To broaden an audience to include more families, consider working with local children's museums and science centers, who are already reaching families effectively.

Within exhibition spaces, family-friendly museums have inventive interactive elements, have real objects to inspire awe and wonder, and have ways for generations to engage in conversation with each other. Museums that engage with families talk to families through visitor surveys, conversations in exhibits, focus groups, and other feedback. Listening to what your audience wants provides the framework for creating engaging, memorable visitor experiences. Creating a family-friendly museum is not necessarily an expensive endeavor, but one that requires a commitment of time and energy from board, staff, and volunteers.

Resources for learning more about families in museums include the Family Learning Forum Project of the USS *Constitution* Museum (http://www.familylearningforum.org/index.htm); Nina Simon's Museum 2.0 blog (http://museumtwo.blogspot.com) and her book, *The Participatory Museum*; the British website, Kids in Museums (http://www.kidsinmuseums.org.uk); and the Family Inclusive Language Chart (https://incluseum.com/2014/07/07/including-the-21st-century-family).

Linda Norris
The Uncataloged Museum
Susie Wilkening
Reach Advisors

See evaluation.

museums and the matter of ethics. Ethics, or moral philosophy, deals with what is right or wrong, proper or improper, in human behavior and decision making. Although the formal study of ethics in Western society began with such ancient Greek philosophers as Aristotle, every society has developed its own standards of ethics. In our society, concepts of ethics are understood to apply only to those actions that persons or groups can make voluntarily—that is, where a choice is possible, and where the choice is based on knowledge. In other words, being forced to do something, or to act with inadequate information about the choices, is not an ethical situation. Ethics, then, refers to the classification of voluntary and informed actions or decisions as being either right or wrong in relation to some standard accepted by a society.

There are several kinds of standards and, and therefore, different approaches to the study of ethics. "Normative ethics" refers to any ethical system based on fixed rules or principles that apply to all actions and decisions. For example, the museum conservation ethic that all object treatments should be reversible is a fixed, or normative, principle. It is not subject to change, or even to special conditions—as we've seen in the debates over how best to stabilize and treat the Parthenon's ancient stones. Yet, challenges to this static idea have arisen and will continue to arise as debates continue about what is best for objects in the long term.

There are two types of normative ethical systems—teleological or consequentialist and deontological or nonconsequentialist. Nonconsequentialist (deontological) ethics are based upon an intrinsic rule or principle that universally applies in all cases regardless of what consequences might result from a given action or decision. One example is the ethical principle that one should not kill, no matter what the context might be. But consequentialist (teleological) ethics are not based on absolute principles per se, but also look at the consequences of an action. Thus, it may be wrong to kill, unless killing will save others. Most, if not all, museum ethics are consequentialist in nature. In the example given above, for instance, the ethical principle about reversibility of treatments is based on the idea that an irreversible treatment might ultimately cause harm to an object, an undesirable consequence.

Another approach is called "ethical relativism," which is based on the idea that there is no one set of ethical principles that applies in all societies at all times. In other words, ethics are particular to one society in one period, and may change. Ideas about what kinds of actions are ethically proper for curators in personal collecting, for example, have changed within our society through time, and ideas about the ethics of repatriation differ from country to country. We can also see that new ethical approaches in conservation that recognize Native American standards and treatments for sacred objects (which are based on a different approach to the idea of object integrity) are ethically relative.

Finally, there is also "situational ethics," which holds that ethical decisions may vary depending on the particular context, or situation, in which the decision must be made. Many classic, museum ethical debates over, for example, the use of funds from the sale of deaccessioned objects to repair a building, are based on this conceptual approach. Today, elements of many professional museum codes of ethics are situational in nature.

It is clear that the significant increase in professional museum concerns over ethics that began in the twentieth century are related to changing standards, changing working conditions, changing notions of professionalism, and even changes in laws. This continuing dynamic will undoubtedly lead to further issue-based ethical discussions. These are important for the profession as we confront new and challenging issues. Our understanding about the distinctions in the kinds of ethics, or ethical systems, that form the foundation of such discussions will therefore continue to be important for us.

JAMES NASON
UNIVERSITY OF WASHINGTON

See ethics and local history; museum ethics.

music. Music and musicians can be a valuable tool for local historians. Music often recounts events of local significance, it helps fashion local identity, and its style can yield important insights into local values. In addition, because musicians are often at the center of a community's social life they can be valuable repositories of its history.

For centuries, musicians have set local incidents to music. The music—ranging from the tale of murder in the North Carolina mountains like "Omie Wise," to a corrido ballad of Mexican heroes on the Texas-Mexico border in "Gregorio Cortez," to a song of catastrophe in the Pennsylvania mines in "The Avondale Disaster"—helped spread the word about local happenings in communities plagued by illiteracy or a lack of newspapers. Current events were as often sung about as read. Moreover, because these songs were frequently passed down, they became an essential part of the community's collective memory.

Music also helps mold a sense of local identity. Fabled musicians and the tunes they created are proudly claimed by the communities in which they grew up or lived. Even whole genres can become an important part of local identity, such as the blues in the Mississippi Delta, or polkas in the upper Midwest.

Historians should not overlook what values lie hidden in the music's style and performance. (See Alan Lomax, *Folk Song Style and Culture* [1968].) The transformation from congregational singing to church choirs, for example, is as important a shift in values as it is in musical practice. The historian, then, should ask a series of questions of the music: Who participates? When? How is it passed on? What skills are considered necessary to participate? What function does the music play in the community? These questions will uncover a host of closely held though often unarticulated beliefs and assumptions.

Finally, musicians can be important informants because their craft has traditionally played a vital role in community life. Musicians often travel extensively and meet many people. As a result, many come to know a great deal about a community's landmarks, history, and its people.

In short, music should not be viewed as simply entertainment. Instead, it can provide local historians with valuable insights into the community's history, sense of identity, and values.

The Society for American Music's web address is: www.american-music.org.

GAVIN JAMES CAMPBELL
DOSHISHA UNIVERSITY, KYOTO, JAPAN

muster roll. A list of those who have enlisted in a military effort. These are sometimes found in county courthouses, state archives, or in local historical societies.

myth. See folklore and folklife.

$\mathscr{N}$

National Archives and Records Administration (NARA), the. NARA is our national record keeper. By law, NARA is charged with safeguarding records of all three branches of the federal government. Its mission is to assure federal agencies and the American public of continuing access to essential documentation of the rights of citizens and the actions of their government. NARA preserves and provides access to such records through a national network of records services facilities from Boston to Southern California and Atlanta to Seattle, including thirteen presidential libraries. NARA currently holds more than 12 billion pages of textual records; 12 million maps, charts, and architectural and engineering drawings; 25 million still photographs and graphics; 24 million aerial photographs; 300,000 reels of motion-picture film, 400,000 video and sound recordings, and nearly 700 terabytes of electronic data. Much of the archival material, including special media such as still and motion pictures, sound recordings, maps, and electronic records, is housed in the National Archives at College Park, Maryland, and in the main National Archives Building in Washington, D.C. Twelve regional archives around the country house records from the federal courts and the regional offices of federal agencies in the geographic areas they serve. More material resides in NARA's records centers, where agency-owned records are held as long as needed before destruction or legal transfer to the National Archives.

In addition, NARA contains a unique resource in its thirteen *presidential libraries, one for each president from Herbert Hoover to George W. Bush. Presidential libraries may not be obvious sources of local history material, but researchers may find useful material among the records and papers from the office of the president, presidential commissions, the president, his family, associates, and members of his administration.

Another part of NARA, the Office of the Federal Register, publishes the daily *Federal Register*, a record of government proclamations, orders, and regulations; the weekly *Compilation of Presidential Documents*; and the annual *Code of Federal Regulations*, along with the *U.S. Government Manual and Public Papers of the Presidents*. It is also responsible for receiving and documenting Electoral College certificates for presidential elections and state ratifications of proposed constitutional amendments.

Anyone may use the National Archives. You do not need to be a U.S. citizen or present academic credentials or a letter of recommendation. To use original records, you must have a researcher card. Also, you must be at least fourteen years old, and you must show valid identification that includes a photograph to receive a card.

Records held by NARA are arranged by numbered "record groups." A record group comprises the records of a major government entity, such as a cabinet department, a bureau, or an independent agency. For example, Record Group 59 contains "General Records of the Department of State," and Record Group 29 holds "Records of the Bureau of the Census." Most record groups also contain records of predecessors of the organization named in the title. Records in all NARA locations across the country provide information on actions that affected everything from the entire nation to the individual home. While records in the Washington, D.C., area document actions at the national level, the holdings of NARA's regional archives document federal policies and programs at the local and regional level. The federal government documents people's lives in many ways, such as in census records and records of immigration, military service, and employment.

Examples of record groups useful for local history research cover many activities of the federal government. Records created by the Department of Agriculture and its agencies and the Bureau of the Census are rich resources for studies of rural America, documenting changes in farming practices, home life, and socioeconomic conditions. Through census enumeration district maps, one can trace urban growth. Important sources for the study of business history are censuses of manufactures and industry, patent records, court cases, and *Civil War–era tax records. (See *census records and *military records.)

Descriptions of the effects of and recovery from natural disasters may be found in several record groups, including records of the Weather Bureau, the Red Cross, the Federal Emergency Management Agency, the Office of the Chief of Engineers, District Courts, Naval Districts and Shore Establishments, and the U.S. Senate and House of Representatives.

The exploration and settlement of the West is documented in expedition records of the Geological Survey. Towns often sprang up around military installations; post returns and quartermaster records are valuable resources for tracing the interaction between civilian and military communities. Records relating to land claims may be found in records of the Bureau of Land Management, the Veterans Administration, and the U.S. Court of Claims.

The history of industrialization and urban living are well documented in U.S. District Court records. For example, a researcher studying auto manufacturing in Detroit will find a wealth of information in early bankruptcy and antitrust cases. Prohibition and gangsters are also well documented in Chicago, New York, and Philadelphia court records.

A local history study concentrating on the Civil War era will find valuable information in these records: census (population and nonpopulation schedules); Internal Revenue Service (assessment lists); Provost Marshal General's Bureau (draft records); Office of the Quartermaster General; Adjutant General's Office; Bureau of Refugees, Freedmen, and Abandoned Lands; District Courts of the United States; U.S. Army Continental Commands; Commissary General of Prisoners; War Department

Collection of Confederate Records; Southern Claims Commission, Accounting Officers of the Department of the Treasury; barred and disallowed Southern Claims, U.S. House of Representatives; U.S. Court of Claims; Civil War prize cases, U.S. District Courts; Civil War Special Agencies of the Treasury Department; and the Treasury Department Collection of Confederate Records.

Resources for studies of *Indian communities include records of the Bureau of Indian Affairs, the Indian Health Service, various army records, and records of the U.S. Congress. NARA facilities in the western states are exceptionally rich in records relating to Native Americans. Applications for enrollment and final rolls of the Five Civilized Tribes list thousands of citizens and freedmen in Indian Territory at the turn of the last century, and records of field offices allow the researcher to form a vivid picture of the daily interaction between federal agents and the native population.

Records relating to areas that were directly under federal jurisdiction are often found in their own record groups: Records of the Government of the District of Columbia, the Government of the Virgin Islands, the Government of American Samoa, the Panama Canal, the Puerto Rico Reconstruction Administration, and the Bureau of Insular Affairs (the Philippines, Cuba, and Puerto Rico).

The New Deal and the two world wars saw the creation of many new government agencies. The Works Progress Administration, Civilian Conservation Corps, Federal Theatre and Writers Projects, and Tennessee Valley Authority, among others, put people to work and changed the communities they lived in. During World Wars I and II, the government imposed controls on food, housing, and other resources to ensure ample supplies for soldiers at the battle front. These emergency measures are documented on the national and local levels in the records of the U.S. Food Administration, U.S. Housing Corporation, Office of the Housing Expediter, the War Industries Board, and Office of Price Administration, among others.

Although paper records make up the vast majority of NARA holdings, *photographs, motion pictures, sound recordings, *maps, architectural and engineering drawings, and computer datasets provide a wealth of opportunities for the researcher. Most records on these media will be found in the National Archives at College Park, but NARA facilities nationwide contain significant nontextual holdings. For example, in the regions you can find aerial photographs from the Soil and Conservation Service and the Bureau of Mines, maps and charts from the Bureau of Land Management and the Federal Highway Administration, architectural and engineering drawings from the General Services Administration and the War Assets Administration, motion pictures from the Office of Scientific Research and Development, and photographs from the U.S. District Courts Bureau and the *National Park Service.

Photographs from the Environmental Protection Agency's DOCUMERICA project of the 1970s record community life across America. Famous photographers such as Russell Lee and

Dorothea Lange and anonymous photographers in the local government bureaus documented the effects of the Great Depression and the New Deal. Maps and photographs from the western surveys trace national growth to the Pacific Coast. Aerial photographs give an exacting view of those same areas in the modern era. Census and economic statistics stored in electronic format reveal details about communities and industries. Architectural plans of public buildings are an invaluable source for *historic preservation projects. Films created by federal agencies, such as the Community Services Administration or the Extension Service, and donated collections, such as the Ford Film Collection, enable the viewer to see aspects of twentieth-century American life first-hand. No matter how large a list such as this grows, the diligent researcher is sure to uncover more resources and more ways to use them.

While these records may be found in NARA's facilities in the Washington, D.C., area and its regions, some bodies of records are concentrated in or are unique to the regional archives. Original records of U.S. district courts constitute the largest record group in all the regions and offer countless research opportunities. Commonly used *court records include *naturalization papers (declarations of intention and petitions for citizenship), bankruptcy case files, *copyright and patent files, and claims of various sorts. Eight locations (Atlanta, Chicago, Denver, Fort Worth, Kansas City, Riverside, San Francisco, and Seattle) hold records of the Bureau of Indian Affairs and the Bureau

of Land Management. Records relating to Chinese immigration and the impact of the Chinese Exclusion Acts may be found in nearly every location. Records unique to a single NARA facility include enrollment cards for the Five Civilized Tribes, in Fort Worth; World War I draft registration cards and Tennessee Valley Authority records, in Atlanta; records relating to the sinking of the *Titanic* and *Lusitania,* in New York; and records of the Government of American Samoa, 1900–1906, in San Francisco. All regional archives have extensive holdings of National Archives microfilm publications that reproduce, with introductions and annotations, some of the most frequently requested records in NARA custody. Every location that has microfilm has federal population censuses for all states, 1790–1940; Revolutionary War military service records; and passenger arrival and naturalization records. Additional microfilm publications usually reflect the special interest of the area served by the regional facility.

NARA is continually expanding the availability of its resources through the Internet. The NARA homepage (www.archives.gov) guides visitors to the main destinations of "Research Our Records," "Veterans Services," "Teachers' Resources," "Our Locations," and "Shop Online," as well as to *Prologue,* NARA's quarterly magazine, and information for records managers, preservation professionals, and visitors. The Federal Register page (www.archives.gov/federal-register) gives access to its publications, which include the daily Federal Register, the Code of Federal

Regulations, the United States Government Manual, Weekly Compilation of Presidential Documents, and the Public Papers of the Presidents.

The National Archives Catalog (https://catalog.archives.gov) is the online public portal for searching National Archives records and related resources. It searches descriptions of records, digital copies of records, Archives.gov web pages, and authority records. The catalog describes more than 94 percent of National Archives holdings at the series level and contains more than 12 million digital copies of records.

NARA Publications and Online Resources:

- NARA's homepage: www.archives. gov.
- NAC (NARA's search portal): www. archives.gov/research/search.
- Social media (blogs, Facebook, YouTube, Twitter, Flickr, Tumblr, Our Archives Wiki): www.archives. gov/social-media.
- Information about NARA's locations: www.archives.gov/locations.
- Information about the Presidential libraries: www.archives.gov/presidential-libraries.
- Information about NARA publications (both free and for sale): www. nara.gov/publications.
- *Prologue*: Quarterly of the National Archives and Records Administration: contains articles based on research in NARA records: www.archives.gov/ publications/prologue.
- Guide to Federal Records in the National Archives of the United States (1996): www.archives.gov/research/guide-fed-records.

Guides to Records in the Regional Archives

- Chinese Immigration and Chinese in the United States: Records in the Regional Archives of the National Archives and Records Administration, RIP 99: www.archives.gov/research/ chinese-americans/guide.html.
- Atlanta: Archival Holdings Guide: www.archives.gov/atlanta/holdings and www.archives.gov/atlanta/finding-aids.
- Boston: Archival Holdings Guide: www.archives.gov/boston/holdings and www.archives.gov/boston/finding-aids.
- Chicago: Archival Holdings Guide: www.archives.gov/chicago/holdings and www.archives.gov/chicago/finding-aids.
- Denver: Archival Holdings Guide: http://www.archives.gov/denver/ holdings and www.archives.gov/denver/finding-aids.
- Fort Worth: Archival Holdings Guide: www.archives.gov/fort-worth/ holdings and www.archives.gov/fort-worth/finding-aids.
- Kansas City: Archival Holdings Guide: www.archives.gov/kansas-city/holdings and www.archives.gov/ kansas-city/finding-aids.
- Riverside: Archival Holdings Guide: www.archives.gov/riverside/finding-aids/holdings.html.
- New York: Archival Holdings Guide: www.archives.gov/nyc/holdings and www.archives.gov/nyc/finding-aids.
- Philadelphia: Archival Holdings Guide: www.archives.gov/philadelphia/public/historical-research/html and www.archives.gov/philadelphia/ public/finding-aids.html.

- San Francisco: Archival Holdings Guide: www.archives.gov/san-francisco/finding-aids/holdings.html.
- Seattle: Archival Holdings Guide: www.archives.gov/seattle/holdings and www.archives.gov/seattle/finding-aids.
- National Archives Microfilm: http://www.archives.gov/research/microfilm.

Federal Register Online Publications: Federal Register publications, including the daily *Federal Register,* the *Code of Federal Regulations,* the *United States Government Manual,* and *Weekly Compilation of Presidential Documents*: www.archives.gov/federal-register.

To inquire about prices and order copies of publications other than Federal Register products, please contact: NARA Customer Service Center, 8601 Adelphi Road, College Park, MD, 20740-6001; (866) 272-6272; fax: (301) 837-0483.

MARY RYAN
UPDATED BY JAMES WORSHAM
NATIONAL ARCHIVES
AND RECORDS ADMINISTRATION

See Appendix D. Farm Security Adminstration Photos; Library of Congress.

National Association of Government Archives and Records Administrators. See state archives.

National Coalition for History. The National Coalition for History (NCH) is a consortium of over fifty organizations that advocates on federal, state, and local legislative and regulatory issues.

The coalition is made up of a diverse number of groups representing historians, archivists, researchers, teachers, students, documentary editors, preservationists, political scientists, museum professionals, and other stakeholders.

Since 1982, the NCH (formerly the National Coordinating Committee for the Promotion of History) has served as the voice for the historical community in Washington. The NCH seeks to encourage the study and appreciation of history by serving as a clearinghouse of information about the profession and as a facilitator on behalf of the interests of our diverse constituency.

The NCH is a nonprofit organization organized under Section 501(c)(3) of the Internal Revenue Code. NCH is solely supported by contributions from its member organizations and the general public.

In 2016, NCH's priority issues included:

- Federal funding for the *National Archives and Records Administration, including the *National Historical Publications and Records Commission (NHPRC); the *National Endowment for the Humanities (NEH); historical and preservation programs at the *National Park Service; the Department of Education; the *Institute of Museum and Library Services; and the *Library of Congress.
- Legislation and regulations affecting public access and the *digitization of federal records.
- Federal agency and regulatory issues such as the declassification of federal records as mandated by Executive Order 13526 and maximizing access

for historians and researchers to federal records and facilities.

For more information contact Lee White, Executive Director, National Coalition for History, 400 A St., SE, Washington, D.C., 20003; (202) 544-2422 x-116; lwhite@historycoalition.org.

LEE WHITE
NATIONAL COALITION FOR HISTORY

National Collaborative for Women's History Sites. See women's history at local history sites, interpreting.

National Council on Public History (NCPH) is a professional membership organization that inspires public engagement with the past and serves the needs of practitioners in putting history to work in the world. For more than thirty-five years, the NCPH has used its annual meeting, scholarly journal, print and electronic publications, numerous committees, and its members and alliances to build community among historians, expand their professional skills and tools, foster critical reflection on historical practice, and advocate for the interests of *public history practitioners and for connecting history to contemporary issues.

NCPH currently includes 1,600 individual members and nearly 400 institutional subscribers. Members include museum professionals, historical consultants, historians employed in government, archivists, historical administrators, preservationists, corporate and business historians, cultural resource managers, curators, film and media producers, oral historians, folklorists, anthropologists, digital historians, policy advisers, teachers, and pro-

fessors and students with public history interests. Increasingly, NCPH has been working to advance public history on an international scale and in 2010 helped form the International Federation for Public History. To build intellectual and professional community, the organization uses *social media and an online collaboration space, *Public History Commons. NCPH also advocates on behalf of the public history field, tracks new developments and statistics, and posts jobs and internships. Its awards program recognizes books, projects, articles, and other work within an expanding, interdisciplinary, and international field.

Each spring, the organization convenes a four-day annual meeting in a different city in the United States or Canada. Between 800 and 1,000 registrants participate in sessions, field trips, professional development workshops, seminar-like working groups, "Speed Networking," a mentoring program, a poster session, and an exhibit hall, as well as more experimental program elements. Member benefits include a discounted registration fee for the conference, as well as four issues of the quarterly journal, the *Public Historian;* four issues of the quarterly newsletter, *Public History News;* a weekly e-mail round-up of news stories related to public history; eligibility for certain NCPH awards; and access to discussion networks, discounts, and electronic resources.

NCPH was incorporated as a tax-exempt (501c3) educational organization in 1980 in Washington, D.C., culminating a period of ferment among PhD historians exploring employment options and the application of historical skills outside of colleges and universities in the late 1970s. In 1976, Robert Kelley and his colleagues began a program in public history at the University of California at Santa Barbara, while on the East Coast, the *American Historical Association and other organizations had formed the National Coordinating Committee on the Promotion of Historical Studies and the Employment of Historians (NCC). Assistance from the *National Endowment for the Humanities (NEH) and the Rockefeller Foundation helped bring historians to the Santa Barbara graduate program and connect those interested in the public history movement in California and Washington, D.C. In 1978, G. Wesley Johnson, also at UC Santa Barbara, launched a new journal, the *Public Historian*, with help from the Rockefeller Foundation. A national public history conference took place in spring 1979 in Montecito, California; this led to a meeting in September 1979 at the *National Archives in Washington, D.C., to form a council that would represent the various constituencies of public historians.

In its early form as an acting board of thirty-two directors, the NCPH was meant to be a council, more an organizational network and body of experts that would provide advice and issue reports than a membership organization. Nevertheless, the new nonprofit found that many public historians, working in a wide variety of jobs, wanted to join. When the council first met in 1980, it made the *Public Historian* the major publication of the organization. By 1984, the association was reconfigured to include as individual members anyone who subscribed to the journal, and until 2006

the University of California Press, which co-publishes the journal along with NCPH, handled NCPH memberships in combination with subscriptions. First located in Washington, D.C., the NCPH offices moved to West Virginia University in 1984, Northeastern University in 1987, and then to its current home, Indiana University–Purdue University Indianapolis, in 1990, where it receives the support of the IU School of Liberal Arts. In 1997, NCPH reincorporated as a nonprofit in the State of Indiana.

Cooperative relationships with other organizations and institutions have been crucial to magnifying the influence of NCPH over the years. The organization has collaborated with other groups for some annual meetings, and the University of California–Santa Barbara Department of History has hosted the editorial offices of the *Public Historian* for more than thirty years. During that time, the journal has remained the flagship publication in the burgeoning intellectual field and profession that is public history. The journal "emphasizes original research, fresh conceptualization, and new viewpoints" and encompasses "the considerable diversity of approaches to the definition and practice of public history" in its research articles, case studies, reports from the field, roundtables, special issues, and book, exhibit, and gray literature reviews. In 2013, the editorial team of the *Public Historian* expanded to include a coeditor and two international consulting editors. The coeditor is a public historian in residence housed within Rutgers University–Camden's Mid-Atlantic Regional Center for the Humanities (MARCH). A partnership with the University of Amsterdam supplies the two international consulting editors. A member of the National Coalition for History, American Council of Learned Societies, and supporter of the national History Relevance Campaign, NCPH also collaborates with other organizations to advocate for history.

NCPH's greatest strength has been its individual members, who provide leadership and expertise. Currently there are approximately thirty NCPH boards, task forces, and committees, including several awards committees, which harness the volunteer labor of around two hundred members of the organization. Through such *volunteers, the organization has been able to offer a wide variety of resources to the field and profession over the years.

NCPH's first major publication, *The Craft of Public History: An Annotated Bibliography*, appeared in 1983. In 1985, the organization began to take stock of public history training by publishing *Public History Education in America: A Guide*, which led to multiple editions of *A Guide to Graduate Programs in Public History*. The latter has taken new form today online as a free, international, and comprehensive resource, the *NCPH Guide to Public History Programs*. NCPH publications have also reflected a mission of guiding and explaining the professionalization of the public history community: the 1988 *Directory of Historical Consultants* and later related efforts, such as its current online consultants' directory, were aimed at solidifying the community of historians working for firms or offering their services for contract. *Ethics and Public History: An Anthology* was a collection of essays published in 1990 for NCPH

and used by many graduate programs and public history institutions for the next two decades. In 1990, NCPH produced a video, *Public History Today*, which aimed to introduce students and broader audiences to the field and profession of public history. In 1989 and 2002, NCPH collaborated with the American Historical Association (and the Public History Program at the University of South Carolina in 2002) in issuing *Careers for Students of History*. In 1986 and 2007, the NCPH *Code of Ethics and Professional Conduct* appeared. In 2010, the joint NCPH-AHA-OAH Working Group on Evaluating Public History Scholarship released a report on "Tenure, Promotion, and the Publicly Engaged Academic Historian."

More recently, the organization has been active in the digital realm. In 2012, NCPH began publishing a peer-edited blog, *History@Work*. This platform encourages a blend of scholarly, professional, and civic discussion arising from the practice of presenting history in public. *History@Work* is also the venue for digital publications of the *Public Historian*. Since 2008, the NCPH Curriculum and Training Committee has been developing "best practice" documents for public history curricula and programs. In association with a Summer 2014 special issue of the *Public Historian* and the theme "Sustainable Public History" at the 2014 NCPH annual meeting, the organization published a born-digital collection, *Public History in a Changing Climate*. In 2015, the New Professional and Graduate Student Committee published both in print and digitally the *Public History Navigator: How to Choose and Thrive in a Graduate Public History Program*, as a consumer's guide for students preparing for graduate school, with the intention of revising it regularly.

See Barbara J. Howe, "Reflections on an Idea: NCPH's First Decade," *Public Historian* 11, no. 3 (Summer 1989); G. Wesley Johnson, "Editor's Preface," *Public Historian* 1, no. 1 (Autumn 1978); Robert B. Townsend, "History in Those Hard Times: Looking for Jobs in The 1970s," *Perspectives on History* (September 2009), and the NCPH website, www.ncph.org.

JOHN DICHTL
UPDATED BY CHRISTINE CROSBY
AND STEPHANIE ROWE
NATIONAL COUNCIL ON PUBLIC HISTORY

See H-Local; H-Public; National Coalition for History; National Endowment for the Humanities.

National Endowment for the Humanities (NEH). Created by Congress in 1965, the National Foundation on the Arts and Humanities Act was to promote research, education, preservation, and public programming in the humanities. NEH grants typically go to cultural institutions, such as museums, archives, libraries, colleges, universities, and to individual scholars. The offices of the Endowment are located at 400 7th Street SW, Washington, D.C., 20506; (202) 606-8400. The website lists grant opportunities. See www.neh.fed.us.

National Historic Landmarks. See historic preservation; National Park Service; National Register of Historic Places.

National Historical Publications and Records Commission (NHPRC). The funding arm of the National Archives and Records Administration, the NHPRC is a federally funded program that assists with records management, archives, and documentary editing projects. See its varied grant programs at www.archives.gov/nhprc.

National History Day. This year-round program uses history to challenge sixth-to-twelfth-grade students to improve their research, analytical, and communication skills. Its origins date to 1974, when faculty at Case Western Reserve University sponsored a "History Day" for Cleveland schools. The program spread quickly: at the first national contest in 1980, nineteen states participated. Funding from the National Endowment for the Humanities stimulated further expansion over the next decade. Now funded by a variety of means, including contributions from corporate and individual donors, National History Day has become international: 600,000 students from all fifty states, the District of Columbia, Guam, American Samoa, the Department of Defense Schools in Europe, and International Schools in Asia and Central America participate. At the local and affiliate levels, History Day sponsors include museums, historical societies, archives, universities, and state humanities councils.

Each year, participants research topics related to a broad annual theme, such as "Innovation in History" or "Debate and Diplomacy in History." While students may choose national or world history topics, many choose to study local people and events. In seeking sources, some students visit historic sites, museums, or archives, while others conduct *oral history interviews. They present their findings in papers, exhibits, performances, documentaries, or websites. History educators, public historians, and others volunteer as judges at regional and affiliate contests, held in the spring. The year culminates with the national finals each June at the University of Maryland in College Park.

Annually, more than 40,000 teachers participate in National History Day. To support their efforts, the program provides pedagogical materials, including lesson plans, research guides, and tools to foster active learning and the use of primary sources. The national and affiliate programs sponsor summer institutes and workshops, allowing teachers opportunities for continuing professional development.

In February 2012, NHD received the prestigious National Humanities Medal from President Barack Obama. The effectiveness of the program on student achievement and interest in history is demonstrated in the findings of a formal external evaluation released in 2011. The findings conclude that students who participate in NHD are outperforming their peers in writing, reading, critical thinking, and across academic subjects.

The address for National History Day is 4511 Knox Road, Suite 205, College Park, MD, 20742; (301) 314-9739; www.nhd.org.

KIM FORTNEY
NATIONAL HISTORY DAY

See primary source analysis.

National Park Service. Concerned about America's receding Western wilderness on a trip to the Dakotas in 1832, artist George Catlin suggested that the government preserve some part of it in a "nation's park." Catlin's vision was partly realized when Congress granted Yosemite Valley to California for a state park in 1864. Eight years later, Congress reserved the spectacular Yellowstone country in the Wyoming and Montana territories "as a public park or pleasuring-ground" for the American people. With no state government yet to manage it, Yellowstone came under the U.S. Department of the Interior as a national park. As the first area designated a national park, its creation established a model for the rest of the world.

Other national parks followed in the 1890s and early 1900s, including Sequoia, Yosemite (to which California returned Yosemite Valley), Mount Rainier, Crater Lake, and Glacier. Meanwhile, recognizing a need to protect prehistoric Indian remains on federal lands, in 1906 Congress passed the Antiquities Act authorizing presidents to reserve significant cultural as well as natural features as national monuments. President Theodore Roosevelt proclaimed the first eighteen national monuments, including El Morro, New Mexico, containing ancient inscriptions, and Arizona's Petrified Forest and Grand Canyon.

The need to better manage these areas led Congress in 1916 to create a new bureau within the Interior Department— the National Park Service (NPS). The law made the NPS responsible for Interior's parks and monuments and directed it "to conserve the scenery and the natural and historic objects and the wildlife therein and to provide for the enjoyment of the same in such manner and by such means as will leave them unimpaired for the enjoyment of future Generations." This new agency oversaw fourteen parks, twenty-one monuments, and one reservation, together encompassing six million acres.

The first NPS director, Stephen T. Mather, vigorously promoted park *tourism and expansion of the park system, particularly in the east with Shenandoah and Great Smoky Mountains national parks in the Appalachians and other additions. His successor, Horace M. Albright, continued to expand the system in the early 1930s with the acquisition of Civil War battlefields, presidential sites, *memorials, and other historic properties, many transferred from the War Department and other federal agencies. With the Historic Sites Act in 1935, the NPS became deeply involved with *historic preservation. Its role in heritage preservation would expand even further with the passage of the National Historic Preservation Act of 1966.

Starting in the 1930s, the NPS also became involved with areas selected primarily for their recreational value. President Franklin Roosevelt challenged the NPS to be socially useful during the depression. It assumed management of hundreds of CCC camps and the construction of many state parks. The scenic Blue Ridge and Natchez Trace parkways were launched as Depression relief projects. Later the NPS was called on to manage recreation areas to serve urban populations. It assumed responsibility for Lake Mead National Recreation Area at the reservoir created by Hoover Dam in 1936, the first of a dozen reservoir-based additions. In 1972, Gateway and Golden Gate national recreation areas in New York City and San Francisco became the precedents for other urban recreation areas serving Cleveland, Atlanta, and Los Angeles. The expansion continued most dramatically when the Alaska National Interest Lands Conservation Act of 1980 more than doubled the size of the national park system by adding over 37 million wilderness acres in Alaska.

The NPS today is vastly different from the one that Mather and Albright envisioned some one hundred years ago. The national park system has swelled to 413 park units in every state and in the U.S. territories of American Samoa, *Guam, Puerto Rico, and the Virgin Islands and its units carry two dozen different designations. These areas include national parks, monuments, battlefields, military parks, historical parks, historic sites, lakeshores, seashores, recreation areas, scenic rivers and trails, and the White House. The service, with 22,000 permanent, temporary, and seasonal employees, and 221,000 volunteers, now administers over 84 million acres. This includes maintaining over 27,000 historic structures, nearly 70,000 archeological sites, 597 natural landmarks, 48 national heritage areas, and the largest system of museums in the world—holding more than 120 million objects, artifacts, and archives. Park visitation has climbed to roughly 307 million annually.

The NPS has evolved from an agency that managed a handful of natural parks and a small number of archeological elements in the Southwest to America's premier protector and preserver of places with nationally and internationally significant natural and cultural resources. The service now places greater emphasis on ecological integrity, civic engagement, and sustainable technologies and practices—concepts foreign to Albright and Mather. In recent years, the national park system has become increasingly complex and diverse. It encompasses wilderness areas, heritage sites, and national trails. It manages conservation and preservation programs beyond park boundaries such as Rivers and Trails; National Heritage Areas; *National Register of Historic Places; National Natural and Historic Landmarks; Heritage Documentation Programs (*Historic American Building Survey, *Historic American Engineering Record, and *Historic American Landscapes Survey); state, tribal, and local preservation programs; *Native American Graves Protection and Repatriation Act Program; American Battlefield Protection Program; Submerged Cultural Resources Program; National Historic Lighthouse Preservation Act Program; and National Maritime Heritage Grants Program, all to support preservation of natural and cultural resources throughout the country. The Land and Water Conservation Fund and the Federal Historic Preservation Tax incentives program provide additional ways for the NPS to give back to local communities in ways that will help sustain the nation's natural and cultural heritage.

More sites of challenging, painful, or neglected history have been added to the system, such as the Oklahoma City Memorial, the Hawaiian leper colony of *Klaupapa*, the African Burial Ground National Monument in New York City, the Sand Creek Massacre National Historic Site in Colorado, the Japanese-American detention camp at Manzanar, and the September 11th Memorial in Pennsylvania. The NPS has continued to grapple with changing demographics and technological advances. It has come to recognize that its approach to interpretation must change to reflect the more diverse demographics of the nation and use new technology to reach visitors. It now places new emphasis on its education role and increased its efforts to engage the public through striving to be more relevant, diverse, and inclusive. Yet, for all of its efforts and accomplishments, as the National Park Service celebrates its centennial, and looks forward to the next one hundred years, it continues to face critical challenges that will have a huge impact on the future of the national park system. The challenges for its second century include budget constraints, deteriorating infrastructure, degradation of archeological sites and historic structures, climate change, endangered species, invasive species, snowmobiles, bioprospecting, airborne contaminants, and a growing lack of interest in the nation's history.

Janet McDonnell
Updated by Anna Gibson Holloway
National Park Service

See National Register of Historic Places.

National Portrait Gallery. The National Portrait Gallery maintains the

477

Catalog of American Portraits (CAP), a collection of images and information on more than 200,000 portraits in public and private collections across the United States and abroad. Established in 1966, the CAP continues to acquire new material regularly, focusing on one-of-a-kind likenesses such as paintings, sculpture, drawings, miniatures, silhouettes, and daguerreotypes. CAP manual files contain a photograph of the portrait and standard cataloging information, such as medium, support, dimensions, condition, description, provenance, and bibliographic references, plus biographical sketches of the artist and sitter. Often, archival correspondence and primary research material is included as well. A searchable database of over 120,000 portraits is available on the National Portrait Gallery's website, at http://npg.si.edu/portraits/research. The search includes both the Catalog of American Portraits and National Portrait Gallery collections. Researchers can also write, phone, fax, or e-mail questions to the following address: Catalog of American Portraits, National Portrait Gallery, Smithsonian Institution, P.O. Box 37012, MRC 973, Washington, D.C., 20013-7012; telephone (202) 633-8260; fax (202) 633-8243; e-mail: NPGResearch@si.edu.

The National Portrait Gallery shares a library with the Smithsonian American Art Museum, which contains a collection of 180,000 books, exhibition catalogs, *catalogues raisonnes*, serials, and dissertations concentrated in the area of American art, history, and biography, with supportive materials on European art. The American Art/Portrait Gallery Library also contains an extensive collection of ephemeral materials and clippings, artists' books, auction catalogs, scrapbooks, and microform. Contact the library by telephone at: (202) 633-8240; e-mail: AAPGLibrary@si.edu; website: http://library.si.edu/libraries/aapg.

The National Portrait Gallery's research facilities are open to the public, preferably by appointment, weekdays 10:00 a.m.–5:00 p.m., except federal holidays. The facilities are located in the Victor Building at 750 9th Street, N.W., Washington, D.C., one block north of the museum.

Susan Garton
National Portrait Gallery

See portraiture.

National Register of Historic Places. Every state and community has places important to its past. In recognition of this, the National Park Service, within the U.S. Department of the Interior, expands and maintains the National Register of Historic Places. This is the nation's official list of districts, sites, buildings, structures, and objects significant in national, state, and local history, architecture, archeology, engineering, and culture. The register recognizes the value of places as diverse as a dugout shelter of an Oklahoma pioneer settler, the Breakers Mansion in Newport, and a 12,000-year-old prehistoric site. In addition to providing recognition of a property's historic significance, listing in the National Register brings other benefits. Listed properties must be considered in planning federal or federally assisted projects and in decisions about coal-mining permits. National Register properties also become eligible for federal tax benefits and federal preservation grants.

Places selected by Congress to be historical units of the National Park System and National Historic Landmarks designated by the Secretary of the Interior for their significance to all Americans are listed automatically in the National Register. Under the National Historic Preservation Act of 1966, as amended, states, federal agencies, and *American Indian tribes may nominate other places within their jurisdictions. State, federal, and tribal preservation offices run programs to look for and evaluate buildings, sites, and other physical remnants from the past. Then they nominate to the National Register of Historic Places those they decide are historically or culturally important. Most nominations come through state historic preservation officers. The professionals in state historic preservation offices work closely with local governments, historical organizations, and the public in locating, researching, and documenting places that might qualify for recognition in the National Register.

National Register criteria for evaluation are broad enough to accommodate the country's rich history. To qualify, places may: (a) be associated with events that have made a significant contribution to the broad patterns of our history; (b) be associated with the lives of persons significant in our past; (c) embody the distinctive characteristics of a type, period, or method of construction; represent the work of a master; possess high artistic values; or represent a significant and distinguishable entity whose components may lack individual distinction; or (d) have yielded or be likely to yield information important in prehistory or history. Places may meet one or more of the criteria; must possess integrity of historic location, design, workmanship, feeling, and association; and generally, though not always, be at least fifty years old.

Published guidance in National Register bulletins assists those evaluating properties for possible nomination to the National Register. In addition to bulletins explaining how to apply the criteria and how to fill out registration forms, there is guidance on identifying, evaluating, and documenting specific types of places found in many communities, such as cemeteries, battlefields, mining resources, archeological sites, landscapes, and lighthouses. All bulletins are now available online via the publications page, http://www.nps.gov/history/nr/publications/index.htm.

By 2014, the National Register had listed more than 90,000 historic properties. Because historic districts often include hundreds of significant buildings and other features, these listings represented about 1.7 million resources, approximately 90 percent of which are important at the state and local level. The National Register maintains a file on each listed property, with a physical description, geographical information, one or more maps, an explanation of historical significance, a bibliography, and at least one photograph. Frequently, files contain additional information such as correspondence or notes from the review process. *Digitization of the National Register files began in 2008, and the Register expects to complete digitization of all existing files by 2019.

Information about National Register properties can be found using NPGallery, the National Park Service's online database that provides access to its digital records. Accessing NPGallery through the website, http://npgallery. nps.gov/nrhp, researchers can search for properties by browsing or by employing the Basic or Advanced Search functions. Searches by resource name, geographic location, subject, keyword, or date range will yield PDF versions of nomination forms and accompanying images such as photographs. Additionally, from the page, https://www.nps. gov/nr/research, researchers can download files that include lists of properties listed in the National Register, spatial data for mapping applications, and files for database applications. Complex and customized searches require the assistance of National Register staff.

The National Park Service promotes awareness and use of historic places listed in the National Register in various ways. Through its Teaching with Historic Places (TwHP) program, it offers curriculum materials, workshops, and written guidance on using historic places effectively in the classroom and on forging productive partnerships between educators, historians, preservationists, and others. The centerpiece of the program is some 160 online lesson plans on themes throughout American history. Based on real historic places listed in the National Register, these lessons enhance instruction of history, social studies, geography, civics, and other subjects. Students experience the excitement of these special places and the stories they have to tell through hands-on investigation and analysis

of carefully selected written and visual materials. Teaching with Historic Places also has a professional development website: "Teaching Teachers the Power of Place." Teaching with Historic Places, including the lesson plans and other materials, is available on the National Park Service website at https:// www.nps.gov/subjects/teachingwith-historicplaces/index.htm.

The National Park Service has also created the ongoing Discover Our Shared Heritage Travel Itinerary Series, which helps people learn about and plan trips to thousands of special places included in the National Register of Historic Places. The travel itinerary website is at https://www.nps.gov/ subjects/heritagetravel/discover-our-shared-heritage.htm. Some itineraries feature historic places associated with themes in American history such as those on the American presidents, the Lewis and Clark Expedition, civil rights, the *Underground Railroad, aviation, women's history, Route 66, Mounds of the Mississippi, Florida shipwrecks, and World War II in the San Francisco Bay area. Other itineraries highlight historic places in communities such as Indianapolis, Chicago, Baltimore, Seattle, Detroit, and Washington, D.C.; or regions like the American Southwest. Many sites featured in itineraries have associated Teaching with Historic Places lesson plans.

The National Park Service's National Register of Historic Places website, a fundamental resource for information about the National Register program and related activities, is located at https://www.nps.gov/nr. The address and telephone number of the National

Register of Historic Places are National Park Service, 1201 I (Eye) Street, NW, Washington, D.C., 20005; (202) 354-2211.

CAROL D. SHULL AND BETH M. BOLAND
UPDATED BY JEFF JOECKEL
NATIONAL PARK SERVICE

See house museums in the twenty-first century.

National Trust for Historic Preservation. The National Trust for Historic Preservation is a private, nonprofit membership organization that works to save America's historic places and promote preservation as a tool to advance vibrant, sustainable communities. Chartered by Congress in 1949, today the organization is supported primarily by private contributions and is broadly recognized as the leader of the historic preservation movement in the country.

Headquartered in the historic Watergate complex in Washington, D.C., with 8 regional offices, 800,000 members and supporters, and 27 historic sites across the country, the National Trust works with preservation groups in all 50 states to save and interpret such nationally significant places as Lyndhurst, Drayton Hall, Farnsworth House, Hinchliffe Stadium, President Lincoln's Cottage, and Philip Johnson's Glass House.

Over the past sixty-seven years, the National Trust has established several influential initiatives. Its signature program is the National Treasures portfolio, a diverse and revolving list of over eighty of the most important and critically threatened historic places in America. Other important endeavors include Main Street America, which has brought new economic life to more than 2,000 historic downtowns; HOPE Crew, which helps young people of diverse backgrounds obtain valuable hands-on skills in preservation; Historic Hotels of America, which works to preserve the authenticity of noteworthy inns and lodges; and the annual list of America's 11 Most Endangered Historic Places, which garners national attention for places under threat of irreparable damage.

The National Trust also publishes a quarterly magazine entitled *Preservation*, and plays an instrumental role in upholding legal protections for historic buildings, such as the National Historic Preservation Act of 1966, *Penn Central Transportation Co. v. City of New York*, *National Trust v. U. S. Army Corps of Engineers*, and Section 4f of the Transportation Act.

In 1995, the National Trust for Historic Preservation decided to forgo an annual congressional appropriation (which had been in place for thirty years and would provide up to 20 percent of the organization's budget) in favor of full reliance on private-sector funding. Today, its $61 million operating budget is mostly supported by contributions, investment income, and contract services.

2600 Virginia Ave, NW Suite 1100; Washington, D.C., 20037; (202) 588-6000; www.SavingPlaces.org.

KEVIN MURPHY
NATIONAL TRUST FOR
HISTORIC PRESERVATION

See cultural heritage tourism; house museums in the twenty-first century.

Native American Graves Protection and Repatriation Act (NAGPRA). The Native American Graves Protection and Repatriation Act (NAGPRA) was enacted November 16, 1990, to address the rights of lineal descendants, Indian tribes, and Native Hawaiian organizations to Native American cultural items, including human remains, funerary objects, sacred objects, and objects of cultural patrimony, held in museum or federal agency collections and when there are new discoveries on federal or Indian land. The act is administered by the National NAGPRA Program within the National Park Service.

Museums that receive federal funds must comply with NAGPRA. This includes filing inventories and summaries of Native American cultural items in their collections, publishing notices of inventory completion and intent to repatriate in the Federal Register, and repatriation. Publication of notices is a barometer of NAGPRA activity by museums and federal agencies working with tribes to make decisions on transfer of control of Native American human remains and cultural items.

The National NAGPRA Program offers grants to museums (and federal agencies) to assist with documentation and repatriation efforts. For more information go to www.nps.gov/nagpra/ or contact nagpra_info@nps.gov.

See American Indian history; Hawai'i, local history in; National Park Service; patrimony; repatriation.

Native American history. See American Indian history.

nativism. The term nativism comes from the Native American Association, formed in 1837 in opposition to Irish immigration of that decade. The Native American Party began in Philadelphia in 1845 and the Know-Nothings (or American Party) rose in the 1850s. The Ku Klux Klan of the 1920s was a secret nativist organization opposing African Americans, Catholics, Jews, and immigrants. The term generally means opposition to immigration by ethnic or cultural groups that nativists assume are not capable of being assimilated.

See John Higham, *Strangers in the Land* ([1963] 1988), and *Send These to Me: Immigrants in Urban America* (1984). See also Juan F. Perea, ed., *Immigrants Out! The New Nativism and the Anti-Immigrant Impulse in the United States* (1997); Dale T. Knobel, *America for the Americans: The Nativist Movement in the United States* (1996); Walter Benn Michaels, *Our America: Nativism, Modernism and Pluralism* (1995); Martin Robin, *Shades of Right: Nativist and Fascist Politics in Canada 1920–1940* (1992); Ray Allen Billington, *The Origins of Nativism in the United States* (1974), and Jerome R. Adams, *Greasers and Gringos: The Historical Roots of Anglo-Hispanic Prejudice* (2006).

naturalization records. Naturalization is the process by which noncitizens (aliens) apply for and are granted citizenship. In England, in its American colonies, and in the United States, naturalization has been granted by special legislative act, or by court proceedings authorized by statute. During the early colonial period "denization" was used to grant an alien some of the rights (such as land ownership) of a native-born individual. A British statute of 1740 provided for naturalization of an alien who resided in a colony for at least seven years. (Immigrants from the British Isles were exempt because they were subjects of the crown.)

Since 1790 naturalization proceedings in the United States have occurred pursuant to federal law, under Art. 1, Sect. 8 of the Constitution. Until 1906 any state or federal court with a clerk and a seal could naturalize aliens. An immigrant wishing to be naturalized filed a declaration of intent to become a citizen (filing was voluntary after 1952). After residing in the United States for five years, the alien could petition the court to be naturalized. If the petition was satisfactory, the alien took the oath of allegiance, and the court clerk recorded the naturalization order or certificate. That gave the new citizen all the rights of a native-born citizen.

Major changes in the process were enacted in 1906. Naturalization proceedings were limited to the higher federal and state trial courts. The Bureau of Naturalization, after 1933 the Immigration and Naturalization Service, issued standard forms requiring a wealth of information from the petitioner. Literacy and citizenship tests were now required. The number of courts authorized to perform naturalizations was gradually reduced, and by the later twentieth century most naturalizations occurred in the U.S. District Courts. Starting in 1991 the Immigration and Naturalization Service, since 2003 called U.S. Citizenship and Immigration Services, granted citizenship to aliens under authority of the Attorney General. New citizens may take their oath before the judge of any federal or state court of record.

Between 1855 and 1922, an alien woman became a citizen if she married a native-born or naturalized citizen. Since 1922 a woman alien must be naturalized on her own. Nonnative minor children become citizens when their parents are naturalized. (All children born in the United States are automatically citizens.) Formerly enslaved African Americans became citizens when the Fourteenth Amendment was ratified in 1868. *American Indians became citizens by federal laws of 1887 and 1924. For many decades, aliens from East and South Asian countries were barred from becoming citizens. Expedited naturalization proceedings became available to aliens who are army veterans starting in 1862; navy veterans starting in 1894; and wartime enlistees since 1918. Currently expedited naturalization is available to noncitizen members of the armed forces and recent veterans, as well as their spouses.

Naturalization records are an important source of data on immigrants in a community, even though pre-1906 filings often give only the name of alien, country of origin, current residence, and filing date. There are pitfalls in using nineteenth-century naturalization records. Spellings of names of aliens from non-English-speaking countries were often inaccurate. In large cities many aliens were naturalized just before a general election, so that they could vote. Many older naturalization records have been microfilmed, and online digital versions through FamilySearch and Ancestry provide convenient access. Guides to the complexities of naturalization laws and forms are James C. Neagles and Lila Lee Neagles,

Locating Your Immigrant Ancestor: A Guide to Naturalization Records, rev. ed. (1986); John J. Newman, *American Naturalization Records, 1790–1990: What They Are and How to Use Them* (1998); and Christina K. Schaefer, *Guide to Naturalization Records of the United States* (1997). See also Marian L. Smith, "'Any woman who is now or may hereafter be married . . .': Women and Naturalization, ca. 1802–1940," *Prologue* 30 (1998): 146–53.

JAMES D. FOLTS
NEW YORK STATE ARCHIVES

See courts and court records; genealogical resources online.

Nearby History series. A collection of guides to local history research designed for students and others with an interest in exploring their own past. The series rests on the assumption that most historical research techniques can be mastered by any literate person, and furthermore, that local historians need to alert themselves to the full range of research possibilities, compare similar phenomena in different settings, and place developments in a broad historical context. The series originated in 1982 with *Nearby History: Exploring the Past Around You* by David E. Kyvig and Myron A. Marty, which itself grew out of an earlier collaboration, *Your Family History: A Handbook for Research and Writing* and has been followed by ten other books.

The first five volumes were initially published, as was Nearby History, by the *American Association of State and Local History (AASLH). Those books, appearing between 1986 and 1990, were *Local Schools: Exploring Their History* by Ronald Butchart; *Houses and Homes: Exploring Their History* by Barbara J. Howe, Dolores A. Fleming, Emory L. Kemp, and Ruth Ann Overbeck; *Public Places: Exploring Their History* by Gerald Danzer; *Places of Worship: Exploring Their History* by James P. Wind; and *Local Businesses: Exploring Their History* by K. Austin Kerr, Amos Loveday, and Mansel Blackford.

Krieger Publishing Company continued the series in 1994 as "Exploring Community History" with *Invisible Networks: Exploring the History of Local Utilities and Public Works* by Ann Durkin Keating. Four other volumes followed between 1996 and 2006: *American Farms: Exploring Their History* by R. Douglas Hurt; *Unlocking City Hall: Exploring the History of Local Government and Politics* by Michael W. Homely; *Getting Around: Exploring Transportation History* by H. Roger Grant; and *Joining In: Exploring the History of Voluntary Organizations* by Karen J. Blair.

Substantially updated editions of Nearby History appeared in 2000 and 2010 with, among other things, expanded bibliographies and discussions of the use of the Internet and other digital technologies for historical research. A fourth edition, with historian Larry Cebula joining the writing team, is currently under way.

DAVID E. KYVIG
UPDATED BY LARRY CEBULA
EASTERN WASHINGTON UNIVERSITY

Nebraska, local history in. In 1858, four years after Nebraska Territory's creation, a Nebraska Historical Society was founded in the capital city of

This interpretive sign marks the original route of the Lincoln Highway in Elkhorn, Nebraska. CREDIT:
NEBRASKA STATE HISTORICAL SOCIETY.

Omaha, but soon died for lack of support. With the coming of statehood in 1867, the legislature moved the capital to a small village renamed Lincoln and designated a "historical block" on the city's original plat for a State Historical and Library Association. The association subsequently incorporated but never used the property and disbanded after the legislature deeded the block to the city in 1875.

The Nebraska State Historical Society (NSHS), which is today the state's flagship historical organization, was incorporated as a private membership society in 1878, modeled after state historical societies previously established in Minnesota and Wisconsin. When the NSHS requested state funding in 1883, the legislature designated it a "state institution" and made the first modest appropriation for its support.

From 1893 until 1933, the University of Nebraska provided space for the society's offices and collections. The NSHS moved into the new Nebraska state capitol building in the latter year and in 1953 into its newly constructed Lincoln headquarters, where its administrative offices and library/state archives remain. The NSHS also administers the Nebraska History Museum in Lincoln, five historic sites, the state historic preservation office, the state archeology office, a publications office, and the Gerald R. Ford Conservation Center in Omaha. Two society-owned sites are managed by cooperating foundations under contract. Although a majority of the NSHS funding comes from the state, only in 1993 did the legislature formally designate it a state agency. Membership provisions remained intact, and the members elect three-quarters of the NSHS governing board (one-quarter are gubernatorial appointees). Legislative appropriations enabled major renovations of the NSHS headquarters (2009–2010) and the Nebraska History Museum (2014–2015).

Among the society's noteworthy superintendents (now called directors) were Addison E. Sheldon (1916–1943) and James C. Olson (1946–1956). Olson initiated several programs extending the society's reach, including lectures and films based on NSHS resources and delivered via the new medium of educational television. During his tenure the society opened its first facility outside of Lincoln, the Fort Robinson Museum, in 1956.

The earliest local history organizations in Nebraska were "old settlers" associations. Many transformed into county historical societies as the "pioneer" generation passed on. By 1931, Nebraska had at least thirty town and county historical organizations. The Nebraska State Centennial in 1967 and the American Revolution Bicentennial in 1976 sparked renewed interest in state and local history while, at the same time, many towns and counties were celebrating their own centennials, often publishing an accompanying history book. The Nebraska Statehood Sesquicentennial in 2017 will offer new opportunities. In 2015, more than 300 museums or historical organizations statewide were listed on the Nebraska Museums Association website.

The first general history of the state was *Johnson's History of Nebraska* (1880) by Harrison Johnson, followed by A. T. Andreas's *History of Nebraska* (1882), a trove of information on early counties and towns. The three-volume *Illustrated History of Nebraska* (1905–1913) by J. Sterling Morton, succeeded by Albert Watkins, marked the first such effort with scholarly pretensions. While not up to modern standards, Morton-Watkins includes copious annotation from primary sources, along with biographical data on prominent Nebraskans. In 1931, NSHS Superintendent Sheldon authored *Nebraska: The Land and the People.* James C. Olson's *History of Nebraska*, the first modern, one-volume text, was published in 1955. Revised editions followed in 1966, 1997, and 2015, the latter coauthored by Ronald C. Naugle and John J. Montag. Arcadia Publishing has issued numerous short histories of Nebraska towns, forts, and community organizations in its Images of America series. The Nebraska and Oklahoma university presses have published scholarly works addressing Nebraska history including Frederick C. Luebke, *Nebraska: An Illustrated History* (1995), David Wishart, ed., *Encyclopedia of the Great Plains* (2004), and James E. Potter, *Standing Firmly by the Flag: Nebraska Territory and the Civil War, 1861–1867* (2013).

Since 1918 the NSHS quarterly, *Nebraska History*, has published hundreds of articles about state and local history. An older publications series, originally featuring historical addresses and reminiscences, was continued to accommodate monographs on topics such as overland freighting, overland migration, and ranching. The society launched its imprint Nebraska State Historical Society Books in 2010, which has published four titles. Other historical content is delivered via the quarterly *Nebraska*

History News, NSHS website and blog, Facebook, YouTube, and a column for Nebraska's weekly newspapers. Since 1961 more than 500 historical markers have been installed statewide through a NSHS-administered program.

Nebraska has never had an official "state historian," although NSHS staff members have filled that role. Annually the NSHS recognizes individuals or organizations for exemplary research and writing, historic preservation, archeological investigations, or museum programs. The Nebraska Museums Association advocates for the state's museums, county historical societies, and other cultural institutions, holds an annual conference, and offers publications and workshops. The Nebraska State Genealogical Society is the principal organization for family historians.

Nebraska history is taught in the fourth grade, and the Nebraska Department of Education adopted state social studies/history standards for K–12 in 1998. That year the NSHS and Nebraska Wesleyan University inaugurated the "Nebraska Institute" summer workshop series to help social studies teachers learn how to incorporate historical documents, objects, and place in their curriculum. Annually the NSHS presents the James C. Olson Award to the K–12 teacher who best exemplifies the use of such teaching tools in the classroom.

JAMES E. POTTER
NEBRASKA STATE HISTORICAL SOCIETY

See United States, local history in.

Nevada, local history in. Nevada had been only sparsely settled thirteen years before it became a state in 1864. Its early history was marked by a boom-and-bust mining economy, and a very itinerant population that came from and went to neighboring states and territories with each discovery of gold or silver. Its university was not established until 1885, twenty-one years after statehood.

The first histories written in Nevada were not state histories, but histories of the Comstock Lode, the primary reason for Nevada's rapid settlement. Newspaper reporter William Wright, a.k.a. Dan De Quille, wrote *History of the Big Bonanza: An Authentic Account of the Discovery, History, and Working of the World Renowned Comstock Silver Lode of Nevada* in 1876 and *A History of the Comstock Silver Lode & Mines, Nevada and the Great Basin Region; Lake Tahoe and the High Sierras* in 1889.

The first state histories were written by Californians when Oakland publishers Thompson and West sent writers to compile the first Nevada history. Myron Angel edited the *History of Nevada, with Illustrations and Biographical Sketches of Its Prominent Men and Pioneers* in 1881. In 1890 Nevada was included in Hubert Howe Bancroft's *History of Nevada, Colorado and Wyoming, 1540–1888*.

The new century brought new mining booms and a new interest in Nevada history. Former congressman and attorney Thomas Wren edited *A History of the State of Nevada, Its Resources and People*, in 1904, followed in 1913 by newspaperman Samuel Post Davis's two-volume history of the state. Former governor and congressman James Graves Scrugham's three-volume history *Nevada, A Narrative of the Conquest*

This Nevada historical marker, shaped like the state itself, tells the story of Pyramid Lake, located about forty miles north of Reno. CREDIT: NEVADA STATE HISTORIC PRESERVATION OFFICE.

of a Frontier Land, Comprising the Story of Her People from the Dawn of History to the Present Time came in 1935. This was followed by Effie Mona Mack's Nevada, A History of the State from the Earliest Times through the Civil War. Mack's was the first history written by a historian.

Forty years after Nevada's statehood the Nevada Historical Society (NHS) was organized as part of the Social Sciences Section of the Nevada Academy of Sciences. History and Political Science Professor Jeanne Elizabeth Weir was in the forefront of this effort because Nevada's pioneers were dying and she believed work should not be delayed in collecting the state's history. Membership dues were not enough to sustain the new organization, however; it became the state's first official historical agency in 1907. The society published historical papers on towns and cities, first settlements, and pioneer biographies. It also published manuscripts from the society's collections. It organized pioneer celebrations and pageants. During World War I the legislature gave it the responsibility to preserve a full account of Nevada's contributions to the war. During the Great Depression, the society oversaw programs of the Federal Relief Agency (FERA) and the Works Progress Administration (WPA). Workers and volunteers from Nevada Federation of Women's Clubs organized the collections, wrote Nevada: A Guide to the Silver State in 1940 and made inventories of Nevada materials held by federal, state, and county governments. In 1957 the NHS began publishing the Nevada Historical Society Quarterly. At first it reproduced primary sources and reminiscences, but it became an academic journal in the mid-1970s.

In the early 1960s the state's two universities in Reno and Las Vegas began Special Collections departments in their libraries, collecting literature, photographs, manuscripts, and business records of Nevada's past. The University of Nevada–Reno (UNR) and the Nevada State Library began a thorough inventory of Nevada's newspapers and a twenty-year project to microfilm all of the existing issues and place them in libraries throughout the state. UNR also began the *Oral History Program under Mary Ellen Glass modeled after the program at Columbia University. The Division of State Archives was created in the Secretary of State's office in 1965—one year after the state celebrated its centennial.

Local historical societies emerged in the late 1950s and early 1960s. For the most part they are museums, housing a community's memories and relics, but a few publish historical journals, including Humboldt, Elko, Nye, Washoe, and Churchill Counties. In all, eleven of Nevada's seventeen counties have museums with few paid staff and many enthusiastic volunteers.

The study of Nevada's constitution is a requirement for graduation from high school and the universities, usually taught as part of a history or political science class. It can be offered in fourth grade and seventh or eighth grade depending on the school district. Eleanor Bushnell wrote the first study of Nevada's constitution, followed by Don W. Driggs, who also wrote Nevada Politics & Government: Conservatism *in an Open Society* (1996). Michael W. Bower's *The Sagebrush State: Nevada's History, Government, and Politics,* 3rd ed. (2006) has replaced the older texts.

Beginning with William Douglas in 1910, the Secretary of State's office has irregularly published a political history of Nevada. At first it listed state office holders, but it expanded to include the formation of the state, histories of the court system and state legislature, and essays on topics such as women in politics, political parties, ballots and voting systems, and minority office holders. The current edition (2006) was the first edition to be published simultaneously in print and online.

Richard Gordon Lillard's *Desert Challenge: An Interpretation of Nevada* (1942, rev. ed. 1979) and Gilman Ostrander's *Nevada, the Great Rotten Borough, 1858–1964* (1966) forced Nevadans to rethink their past. James Hulse's popular history *The Nevada Adventure* (1965) has remained in print for thirty-two years, through six editions. His *Forty Years in the Wilderness: Impressions of Nevada 1940–1980* (1986) is still read, quoted, and argued about. Russell Richard Elliott of the University of Nevada–Reno wrote the first real state history in 1973, revised by William D. Rowley in 1987, followed by a history of Nevada's twentieth-century mining booms. Sally Zanjani's books on Goldfield, the early organization of Nevada, and Sarah Winnemucca contributed greatly to the state's historical literature. Stanley Paher created an encyclopedic book on Nevada's ghost towns and mining camps, Mary Ellen Glass wrote about the politics of the 1890s and 1950s, Wilbur Shepperson

and Elmer Rusco wrote on Nevada's immigrants and minorities. Edna B. Patterson, Louise A. Ulph, and Victor Goodwin wrote *Nevada's Northeast Frontier* in 1966. Ralph Roske, Eugene Moehring, and Michael P. Green wrote several histories of Las Vegas. Green has just written *Nevada: A History of the Silver State* (2015), which provides a fresh look at Nevada's past.

The legislature created the Nevada State Museum in 1939 and the State Railroad Museum in 1981. In 1981 the museums were organized into the Department of Museums and History. Twelve years later the department was combined with the State Library and Archives, the Arts Council, and Division of Historic Preservation into a Department of Museums, Library and Arts, later renamed the Department of Cultural Affairs.

The start of the twenty-first century included new interest in local history when Arcadia Publishing began contacting potential local authors to write picture books of Nevada's communities. Since 2001, thirty-eight books have been written providing a visual history of many cities, counties, and locales. Local public libraries have undertaken local history projects to make local history sources online including oral histories, newspapers, and high school yearbooks.

Throughout the 1990s the Atomic Energy Commission was studying the feasibility of a nuclear waste repository in central Nevada and provided funds to those affected counties for planning and the study of their past. The available funding produced local history projects in Esmeralda, Nye, and Eureka

Counties, resulting in more than one hundred oral histories and a dozen histories of the towns and mining camps of central Nevada.

Nevada's local history has become digital in the new century with the development of historic site applications for Reno and Sparks, digital collections at both university library's digital collections websites and the Nevada State Library and Archives's digital collections website, which includes a complete searchable collection of the *Nevada Historical Society Quarterly* from 1957 to 2009.

As Nevada approached its 150th anniversary of statehood, the future of the past looked bleak. The 2009 Nevada State Legislature cut museum staff, including directors and curators. Two years later Governor Brian Sandoval and the State Legislature saved the state's five museums and the Nevada Historical Society from closing their doors. The celebration of 150 years of statehood renewed interest in state and local history with more than 500 celebratory events and projects held in every community in Nevada and created a fund that will be used to help state and local museums. As the state emerged from the recession, funding for state and local historical societies and museums is being restored. Nevada's history will continue to be preserved, interpreted, and written in the twenty-first century.

JEFFREY M. KINTOP
NEVADA STATE ARCHIVIST

See United States, local history in.

New Brunswick, local history in. The local history of New Brunswick is pursued by professional and amateur historians and members of the general public. Research is conducted at the province's four public and two private universities, the New Brunswick Museum, the Provincial Archives of New Brunswick (established 1968), at *living history museums, in local museums and archives, and in public libraries. Areas of research include First Nations history, the history of Acadia, the arrival of the Loyalists and the creation of the province, and the development of particular communities. Pioneer historians of these experiences include Peter Fisher, James Hannay, William O. Raymond, William F. Ganong, John C. Webster, Pascal Poirier, Placide Gaudet, Alfred G. Bailey, and W. Stewart MacNutt. Fisher's *Sketches of New-Brunswick* (1825) was the first published history of the province; the most recent remains MacNutt's *New Brunswick: A History, 1784–1867* (1963). *Acadiensis* (1971), the academic journal of the history of the Atlantic region, is produced at University of New Brunswick in Fredericton. The *Revue de la Société Historique du Madawaska* (1971) and *Revue d'histoire de la Société Historique Nicolas-Denys* (1970), supported by the Edmundston and Shippagan campuses of the Université de Moncton, offer particular insights into local history in the northwest and northeast. *Generations*, the quarterly of the New Brunswick Genealogical Society, publicizes family research. A new online *Journal of New Brunswick Studies* (2010) is sponsored by St. Thomas University.

Saint John had both the first museum and the first historical society. The New

Brunswick Museum of 1929 is a descendant of Abraham Gesner's natural history museum of 1842; its archives originated in significant donations by two early members of the Historical Society. The New Brunswick Historical Society, which first met in 1874 at the Mechanics' Institute, collected documents and publications on the early history of the province and published material designed to promote knowledge of the province and general history. Although its early collection was destroyed in the Saint John fire of 1877, the society persisted until the 1930s and was revived in the 1950s. Its regular publication, *Collections of the New Brunswick Historical Society* (1894–1930 and 1954–1984) originally included transcribed documents and other statistical and descriptive information on the history of the province. A monthly newsletter was initiated in 1965.

Regional historical societies came later. The York Sunbury Historical Society (established 1932), based in Fredericton, the capital, focuses on central New Brunswick. The Fredericton Region (formerly York Sunbury) Museum (founded 1934 by the society) possesses significant artifacts and some documents, the latter mainly housed in the provincial archives. Its publication, the *Officers' Quarters*, is available on the museum's website. The Société Historique du Madawaska (established 1953 by academics at the Université Saint Louis, now the Edmundston Campus of the Université de Moncton) took firm hold in the late 1960s, soon establishing its journal.

Local historical societies burgeoned in the 1960s, encouraged by the New Brunswick Historical Society, with which they affiliated. Many acquired and restored local historic properties for museums and archives. One of the first was the Carleton County Historical Society (1960). Some, such as the Queens County Historical Society, oversee several museums. Others, like the Charlotte County Historical Society, operate local archives; the collections of the Charlotte County Archives (1975), located in St. Andrews, include original eighteenth-century and later documents, as well as photographs, newspapers, maps, and architectural drawings. The archival collection is complemented by local eighteenth-century architecture, including houses moved from the American to the British side of the border.

With a population of 752,000, the province today supports over 30 local history associations. While each of New Brunswick's fifteen counties has a county or regional historical association, smaller local societies are also ubiquitous. Various heritage societies and cultural associations, the United Empire Loyalist Association, as well as the several branches of the New Brunswick Genealogical Society and local genealogical societies also promote the study of local history.

New Brunswick's living history museums complement its forty traditional museums. The best known, both originally Canadian centennial projects, are Kings Landing Historical Settlement in York County and the Village Historique Acadien at Caraquet in Gloucester County. Both house eighteenth- and nineteenth-century material history collections that draw researchers as well as tourists. New Brunswick's oldest continuously occupied village, also an archaeological site that includes the Augustine Mound, is part of the recently developed Metepenagiag Heritage Park on the Red Bank First Nation Reserve in Northumberland County.

The websites of regional and local historical societies, heritage groups, archival repositories, and museums introduce researchers to their collections, as well as to various aspects of local history through online finding aids. Besides extensive catalogs of their collections, the Provincial Archives of New Brunswick and the New Brunswick Museum offer sophisticated virtual exhibits with professionally researched essays and scanned documents.

The universities' collections are also extensive. The University of New Brunswick Archives website provides an online finding aid, digital collections, and searchable databases. It also includes links to the largest Loyalist collection in North America and to the Atlantic Canada Portal, which features several New Brunswick collections. The Centre d'études Acadiennes at the Université de Moncton, with its associated Musée Acadien, holds the most extensive collection on the Acadians of the Maritimes. The Centre's website provides comprehensive links to Acadian collections across borders. The Mount Allison University Archives also provide online information on collections as well as a number of virtual exhibits.

In both English and French sectors of the New Brunswick school systems, local history is included in the curriculum at the elementary and middle school levels. In high school, the English sector permits optional courses in local history, while the French offers a grade-twelve course in Acadian history. The history of the province is a substantial part of university courses on the history of the Atlantic region. Innumerable MA theses and PhD dissertations on New Brunswick history have been completed for the University of New Brunswick and the Université de Moncton.

GAIL CAMPBELL
UNIVERSITY OF NEW BRUNSWICK

See Canada, local history in.

New Hampshire, local history in. New Hampshire residents have a well-deserved reputation for preserving the state's history as a means of commemorating the uniqueness that is New Hampshire. While the impulse to preserve is ever-present, the natural frugality of the state's voters tends to channel the efforts into small local societies that struggle to survive through volunteer efforts and fundraising.

In 1823, the New Hampshire Historical Society was formed through the initiative of John Farmer, considered the founder of systematic genealogy in America, and Jacob B. Moore, a Concord printer and bookseller. Farmer's influence attracted a veritable who's who of nineteenth-century New Hampshire leaders to sign on as founders, including William Plumer, Levi Woodbury, and Jeremiah Mason. The society is the fifth oldest state historical society in the United States and remains today the repository of much of the state's history including the papers of Franklin Pierce, Daniel Webster, and Gen. John Stark and more than 5,000 genealogies.

This private not-for-profit institution maintains both a library and a museum in a historic building in downtown Concord, the state's capital.

Though founded on the 200th anniversary of the first settlement in New Hampshire in Dover in 1623, the New Hampshire Historical Society is not the oldest in the state. That distinction belongs to the Portsmouth Athenaeum, which has continued to preserve local history since 1817. There are currently more than two hundred local historical societies in existence in New Hampshire, nearly two-thirds of which were formed since 1960, largely the result of efforts to preserve historic houses or buildings. Proof of the importance of town government in New Hampshire history is the fact that there is only one county historical society in existence in the state, the Historical Society of Cheshire County in Keene. Since most local societies maintain archives or collections that are largely inaccessible to researchers, an effort was begun to create and maintain an online database of historical collections held by any institution in the state. Sponsored by a grant from the Institute of Museum and Library Services, five state institutions (New Hampshire State Library, New Hampshire State Council on the Arts, New Hampshire Division of Historic Resources, New Hampshire Division of Archives and Records Management, and the New Hampshire Historical Society) have compiled a database of historic archives and collections held anywhere in New Hampshire (available to the public at www.findnhhistory. org). The effort of these institutions also attests to the important role that state government currently plays in the preservation and dissemination of the state's history.

*Digitization of important state and local manuscripts is occurring slowly but surely. The New Hampshire Historical Society recently completed a major capital campaign with much of the money intended for digitization of its important collections. A significant initiative of the New Hampshire Historical Society is the launch of the *New Hampshire History Network.* This is a web-based platform that will allow collections from the society and those of New Hampshire's 206 local historical societies to be shared in digital form and made accessible to the public. The network will provide a new level of public access to historic collections including artifacts, fine art, documents, and photographs. It will host online exhibitions, a timeline of New Hampshire history, school lesson plans, and other valuable material—all in one place.

The first *History of New-Hampshire* was written by the Reverend Jeremy Belknap in 1792 with new editions in 1812 and 1831. While several popular illustrated state histories have been published in recent years, there is a need for a scholarly state history that covers the modern era. The publications of current New Hampshire historians Jere R. Daniell, R. Stuart Wallace, David Watters, Howard Mansfield, Mike Pride, and others contribute much to our understanding of state history. The official documents of the colonial province of New Hampshire and the early state records were in a thoroughly disorganized state until John Farmer responded to the call of Governor Bell and began to organize them in the 1830s. Farmer's efforts led to the publication of a forty-volume work now referred to as the *State Papers*, published between 1867 and 1943 under the direction of various editors including Nathaniel Bouton and Otis Hammond. County histories of all ten New Hampshire counties were published in the 1880s. Many local town histories were also published in the late nineteenth century. More than two hundred towns have published histories.

The New Hampshire Department of Education first began to require the teaching of New Hampshire history in the public schools in 1923. The more recent (1995) "NH Social Studies Framework" specifies that all public schools must teach local history in third grade and the state's history in fourth grade.

PETER WALLNER
NEW HAMPSHIRE HISTORICAL
SOCIETY, RETIRED

See United States, local history in.

New Jersey, local history in. The formal recording of the historical materials of New Jersey began during the middle of the eighteenth century with the Religious Society of Friends. In 1758, two Cape May County Quakers, Aaron Leaming and Jacob Spicer, published a compilation of grants, laws, and other material of the province up to 1702, when East and West Jersey were united as a Royal Colony. Their effort was followed in 1765 by another Quaker, Samuel Smith, whose *History of the Colony of Nova-Caesaria; or, New Jersey* begins with the "discovery of America" and

extends to 1721, though it also includes Smith's observations on the Stamp Act crisis. His work began the narration of New Jersey history.

In 1834 Thomas F. Gordon published *The History of New Jersey, from its Discovery by Europeans to the Adoption of the Federal Constitution*, a pedestrian account, subsidized by the state legislature. Gordon also compiled a gazetteer, the only one of its kind for many years. A decade later, it provided the starting point for John W. Barber and Henry Howe's illustrated compilation, *Historical Collections of the State of New Jersey*, for their popular series. It was reprinted a dozen times over the next quarter century, and lightly updated once or twice.

In 1845, a group of the state's leading men formed the New Jersey Historical Society "to discover, procure, and preserve" historical material. Its collections are the most important trove of archival materials about New Jersey. Yet the society has not prospered in the twenty-first century. Its collections are only open a few afternoons a week, and *New Jersey History*, the successor to the society's annual proceedings, which went digital in 2010, has not published since 2013.

One of the society's founding members, William A. Whitehead, can be considered the state's first scholarly historian. His 1846 *East Jersey under the Proprietary Governments* was the new society's first publication. Working with William Nelson, Whitehead also produced the first two dozen volumes of *Documents Relating to the Colonial History of New Jersey*, on which generations have relied.

This sign, placed in the 1960s by the New Jersey Tercentenary Commission, commemorates the Henry Guest House in New Brunswick, New Jersey. CREDIT: HOWARD GREEN.

The first professionals to turn their attention to New Jersey produced narrow political histories based on the earlier collected materials: Edwin F. Tanner's *The Province of New Jersey, 1664–1738* (1908) and Edgar J. Fisher's *New Jersey as a Royal Province, 1738–1776* (1911). In 1924, Charles M. Knapp produced *New Jersey Politics during the Period of the Civil War and Reconstruction*, which argued that New Jersey was a largely Copperhead state whose support was soft for the Union cause. Knapp's framework prevailed until William Gillette dismantled it in 1995 in *Jersey Blue: Civil War Politics in New Jersey, 1854–1865*. Knapp's work continues to exert a deleterious influence on textbooks and curriculum materials.

The first half of the twentieth century saw three multivolume, multi-author surveys. The first came from Francis Bazley Lee, an attorney, in 1902. His five-volume *New Jersey as a Colony and as a State* was followed in the early 1930s by the six-volume *New Jersey: A History* edited by Rutgers College historian Irving Kull, and by the five-volume *The Story of New Jersey* compiled in 1945 by William Starr Myers, a political scientist at Princeton University.

A fourth multivolume series produced volumes that had lasting influence. In 1929, a collector of memorabilia, Lloyd W. Smith, offered funds to the Princeton University history department for an exhaustive survey. Under the general editorship of Thomas J. Wertenbaker, Smith's funds led to three important volumes: Wheaton J. Lane's *From Indian Trail to Iron Horse: Travel and Transportation in New Jer-*

sey (1939), Donald Kemmerer's *Path to Freedom: the Struggle for Self-Government in Colonial New Jersey, 1703–1776* (1940), and Leonard Lundin's *Cockpit of the Revolution: The War for Independence in New Jersey* (1940). Lane, who recognized, without naming, a "transportation revolution" a dozen years before George Rogers Taylors's seminal work, is unsurpassed, and Lundin remains an influential account, though Larry R. Gerlach improved upon it in *Prologue to Independence: New Jersey in the Coming of the American Revolution* (1976).

The first monograph on *African American history in New Jersey was Marion Thompson Wright's *The Education of Negroes in New Jersey* (1941). A solid work, it did not lead to further study for decades.

Following World War II, the writing of New Jersey history improved in quantity and quality. Richard P. McCormick's *Experiment in Independence: New Jersey in the Critical Period, 1781–1789* (1950) helped the ongoing effort to include New Jersey in the larger search for synthetic interpretations of U.S. history.

In 1953 a former journalist, John T. Cunningham, published *This is New Jersey*, the first of over fifty books in which he strove to reach a broad audience with histories of New Jersey.

The state's 1963 tercentenary led to publication of a thirty-one-volume series of short monographs on a wide range of New Jersey history subjects, though it neglected race and gender.

The tercentenary also led to creation of a state agency, the New Jersey Historical Commission, which produced, or catalyzed, much important work both scholarly and popular. Documentary works the commission produced, or supported, include *New Jersey in the American Revolution, 1763–1787: A Documentary History*, the five-volume papers of William Livingston, the state's first governor, and the Thomas A. Edison papers. A project the historical commission cosponsored with the New Jersey Historical Society resulted in the first comprehensive work of African American history since Wright's work: *Freedom Not Far Distant: A Documentary History of Afro-Americans in New Jersey* (1980), edited by Clement Alexander Price.

Women's history in New Jersey got a slower start than black history. While some important monographs, such as Felice Gordon's *After Winning: The Legacy of the New Jersey Suffragists, 1920–1947* (1986), came earlier, the first comprehensive work on the history of women in New Jersey appeared in 1990: *Past and Promise: Lives of New Jersey Women.* This collection of biographical sketches was compiled by a collective of women scholars known as the Women's Project of New Jersey under the general editorship of Joan M. Burstyn.

The picture in 2015 is mixed. Monographs such as David Hackett Fischer's Pulitzer Prize–winning *Washington's Crossing* (2004), and Howard Gillette's *Camden After the Fall: Decline and Renewal in a Post-Industrial City* (2005) suggest that historians will continue to probe New Jersey's past for a window on America. *New Jersey: A History of the Garden State* edited by Maxine N. Lurie and Richard Veit was published in 2012, the first one-volume history of the state in forty-five years. To commemorate New Jersey's 350th anniversary in 2013, the New Jersey Historical Commission launched a publication series that includes a projected 10 scholarly volumes. An online journal, *New Jersey Studies*, debuted in 2015, hoping to publish twice a year.

The commission also launched a website it hopes will remain a statewide platform for the history community, featuring a *blog, calendar of events, and educators' resources section. A number of the many historic sites associated with the War for Independence are energized by their inclusion in the Crossroads of the American Revolution National Heritage Area. But attendance at historic sites and museums is declining, and the efforts to digitize historical materials and make them available is going slowly. It is too soon to tell how well the community will be able to interest the audiences of the digital age in the history of New Jersey.

HOWARD L. GREEN
INDEPENDENT CONSULTANT

See United States, local history in.

New Mexico, local history in. The first history of New Mexico was Gaspar Pérez de Villagrá's *Historia de la Nueva México* (1610), a verse epic about the exploits of Juan de Oñate. Several Spanish language histories followed: Fray Alonso de Benavides's *Memorial* in 1630; compilations by Franciscans fray Francisco Atanasio Domínguez in 1776 and fray Silvestre Vélez de Escalante between 1776 and 1779; and Pedro Baptista Pino published *Exposición sucinta y*

sencilla de la provincia del Nuevo Mexico in Cadiz, Spain, in 1812.

The first history of New Mexico in English was W. W. H. Davis's *El Gringo* (1857), followed by Elias Brevoort's *New Mexico: Her Natural Resources and Attractions* (1874); Governor L. Bradford Prince's *Historical Sketches of New Mexico* in 1883; Helen Haines's *History of New Mexico from the Spanish Conquest to the Present Time, 1530–1890* in 1891; and George B. Anderson's two-volume *History of New Mexico* in 1907. Other significant state histories include Benjamin Read's *Historia Ilustrada de Nuevo Mexico* (1911, with English translation the following year); the first of five volumes of Ralph Emerson Twitchell's *The Leading Facts of New Mexican History* (1911); Charles F. Coan's three-volume work, *A History of New Mexico* (1925); Frank D. Reeve's three-volume *History of New Mexico* (1961); Warren A. Beck's *New Mexico, A History of Four Centuries* (1962); and Ellis Arthur Davis edited *The Historical Encyclopedia of New Mexico* in two volumes in 1945. Marc Simmons published *New Mexico: A Bicentennial History* in 1977. Often reprinted, this volume is used in schools throughout the state.

Numerous regional, county, and community histories have been published through the years. Among the most noteworthy community studies are Simmons's *Albuquerque: A Narrative History* (1982) and Chris Wilson's *The Myth of Santa Fe* (1997). Because of the abiding interest in Billy the Kid, the historiography of Lincoln County is extensive and ever growing. Two recent state histories are *A History of*

An early alignment of famed Route 66 is commemorated in this New Mexico historical marker, placed in 2015, near Santa Fe. CREDIT: TOM DRAKE, NEW MEXICO, HISTORIC PRESERVATION DIVISION.

New Mexico Since Statehood by Richard Melzer, Robert J. Torrez, and Sandra K. Mathews (2011) and *New Mexico: A History* by Joseph P. Sanchez, Robert L. Spude, and Arthur R. Gomez (2013). There has been remarkable growth in the publication of local histories. Arcadia Publishing has ninety-six New Mexico titles, primarily collections of historic photographs. The History Press also has a smaller number of community histories.

The State Legislature created the position of State Historian in 1945, although it lapsed after 1948. In 1967, the post was reinstituted and was held by the senior archivist at the State Records Center and Archives. In 1971, increased demand for historical services led to the temporary separation of the State Historian from Archival Services for nine months. In 1981, the State Historian was again separated from Archival Services. New Mexico has no official municipal or regional historians, but there are historical societies in most of its thirty-three counties and many municipalities.

The Historical Society of New Mexico was organized on December 26, 1859. Founding members came from Santa Fe's elite: government officials, military officers, merchants, and clergy. The society was the only local organization where Anglos (including many Jews) and Hispanos came together because of common interests.

The approaching Civil War divided the society. The first president, John Breckenridge Grayson, resigned in 1861 to join the Confederacy, and others departed for war. On December 26, 1880 the society reestablished itself, based on its original constitution with only minor changes, and began to gather artifacts and documents relating to New Mexico history and culture for the society's museum housed in the east end of the Palace of the Governors. L. Bradford Prince was president of the Historical Society from 1883 until his death in 1922.

The territorial government created the Museum of New Mexico in 1909 and housed it in the west end of the Palace of the Governors. In the 1920s, the museum began to take over the operation of the society's collections, which were formally donated to the museum in 1977.

New Mexico joined the Union in 1912, and the following year, Ralph Emerson Twitchell's *Old Santa Fe* became the official bulletin of the society until it ceased publication in 1916. In 1926, Lansing B. Bloom and Paul A. F. Walter began the *New Mexico Historical Review* as the society's official publication. Since 1963, the University of New Mexico has published the quarterly journal.

The territory and then state of New Mexico provided funding to the Historical Society until 1959, when it reorganized and reincorporated as a nonprofit educational organization. Since 1974 it has hosted an annual history conference. It publishes *La Crónica de Nuevo México*, a quarterly bulletin that disseminates historical research, book reviews, and information about events around the state. The society makes grants to local historical societies and operates a speakers' bureau. The society supports research and publication on New Mexico history, with annual awards that recognize outstanding contributions.

In 2003, the New Mexico Legislature required the teaching of semester-long courses in New Mexico history in the fourth and seventh grades. The following year the legislature made a half-credit survey course in New Mexico history, taught in the ninth grade, a requirement for high school graduation. The impact of the adoption of Common Core standards on the teaching of New Mexico history is unclear at this time.

Genealogical research plays an important role in state and local history in New Mexico. Founded in 1960, the New Mexico Genealogical Society is the state's oldest. The explosion of interest in Hispanic genealogy led to the formation of new organizations, including the Hispanic Genealogical Research Center of New Mexico, founded in 1993. In addition to these statewide organizations, there are numerous county genealogical societies, most with a presence on the Internet.

Major themes in New Mexico local history involve land and water rights, immigration, ethnicity, economic development, and cultural persistence.

RICK HENDRICKS
STATE HISTORIAN OF NEW MEXICO

See United States, local history in.

new social history. Once upon a time, early in the twentieth century, most historical writing emphasized political, institutional, military, and diplomatic matters. When the realization dawned that many aspects of history were thereby being neglected, social history came to be defined as "history with the politics left out." In other words, social history was everything else. During the middle third of the twentieth century, therefore, social history tended to emphasize *material culture and the ways people lived in times past. (Note the concurrent appeal of museum "period rooms.") Consequently, social history paid considerable attention to such matters as urban transportation, firefighting, bathtubs, department stores, home appliances, and sanitation.

During the later 1960s, professional historians began to develop what is referred to as the "new social history," new because it stressed the history of society in a holistic way: the history of social structure and class, the history of mobility (social and physical), the history of intergroup relations, ethnicity, race, gender, and religion. For two pioneering works that proved to be especially influential, see Stephan Thernstrom, *Poverty and Progress: Social Mobility in a Nineteenth-Century City* (1964), a study of Newburyport, Massachusetts, in the later nineteenth century that used *census data in an innovative manner, and Thernstrom and Richard Sennett, eds., *Nineteenth-Century Cities: Essays in the New Urban History* (1969).

Two developments in historical scholarship in Europe were particularly seminal in stimulating the new social history. British historians, along with Scandinavian and French to a lesser degree at first, pioneered in using such demographic sources as tax lists; records of births, baptisms, marriages, and deaths; wills and parish and census records—all in an effort to investigate such matters as the distribution of wealth and the transmission of property, average age of marriage for males and females, premarital pregnancy, life expectancy, fluid versus static populations in communities, and so forth.

Second, the French and then others began to use the in-depth case study of particular communities or provinces as a way of testing broad generalizations that had been asserted without adequate attention to regional differences and variations. Influential French local studies tended to focus upon periods and places when conflict was especially prominent. They did so because the records can be very rich for times of crisis (such as the Inquisition or the French Revolution), and because an emphasis upon contestation tended to highlight unequal distributions of wealth and power. Therefore, even though these case studies concentrated on temporal "moments" such as a year, a decade, or a generation, they often illuminated long-standing resentments and related issues within a community.

Critics of the new social history became increasingly vocal from the mid- and later 1980s onward. They acknowledged that the new social history provided a much greater degree of precision, and opened whole new areas for investigation (especially what was called "history from the bottom up," meaning the history of ordinary people), yet offered very little of a qualitative nature concerning the history and role of human values. Therefore these critics pleaded for a closer alliance of social and cultural history, a marriage of quantitative with qualitative information and interpretive insight. For a striking comparison between a breakthrough book in relatively "pure" (i.e., quantitative) social history and a social/cultural study of the same locality, see Merle Curti, *The Making of an American Community: Democracy in a Frontier County* [Trempeleau County, Wisconsin] (1959), and Jane Marie Pederson, *Between Memory and Reality: Family and Community in Rural Wisconsin, 1870–1970* (1992).

The implications of these developments for local historians should be self-evident. For too long, historians have neglected nonliterary source materials that are abundant though frustratingly incomplete at times (and occasionally inaccurate), materials that make us realize that for centuries we perceived only the tip of the iceberg of the human past. Used with care, and especially in the context of case studies, such neglected data enable us to test the conventional wisdom about such significant subjects as the New England town as the seedbed of American democracy. (An important cluster of case studies in 1970–1971 helped us realize that we really needed a typology of the New England town, because it mattered a great deal whether the town was coastal and commercial or inland and agricultural, or who the initial settlers were and what expectations they had concerning optimal farm size or apprenticeship for artisanal training.)

The new social history has now spawned a very rich body of literature on such ethnic enclaves as Chinatown in San Francisco or Poles and parish life in Detroit. Combined with mobility studies, it has told us a great deal about the African American migration northward to Chicago, c. 1915–1945. Combined with biography it has illuminated life in a small town like Emporia, Kansas, home of William Allen White, who became famous as editor of the *Emporia Gazette*. And combined with ethnicity and the particularities of economic change, it has shaped our understanding of intergenerational change in a place like Whiting, Indiana.

See John Bodnar, "Moral Patriotism and Collective Memory in Whiting, Indiana, 1920–1992," in Bodnar, ed., *Bonds of Affection: Americans Define Their Patriotism* (1996), 290–304; and Michael Kammen, *Mystic Chords of Memory: The Transformation of Tradition in American Culture* (1991).

MICHAEL KAMMEN
AMERICAN HISTORIAN (1936–2013)

See Annales School; Cambridge Group for the History of Population and Social Structure.

New York, local history in. In 1804 merchant John Pintard organized the New-York Historical Society as a private member organization to host events and house a library and historical archive. By 1850, there were seven county historical societies within the state; a number of others were created after the Centennial of the American Revolution in 1876. For the most part, town historical societies date from the twentieth century, many created after 1950. Thinking that the New-York Historical Society paid too little atten-

The unveiling ceremony for the A.M.E. Zion Church historical marker in Elmira, New York. CREDIT: AMY H. WILSON.

tion to areas outside of Metropolitan New York, in 1899 a group founded the New York State Historical Association (NYSHA). NYSHA moved about the state until 1939, when it settled in Cooperstown. For many years, Dixon Ryan Fox was its dynamic director and Louis Jones shaped its impressive folk art collection. Interestingly, responding to the Bicentennial of the American Revolution, between 1970 and 1990, a number of new town historical societies formed, often as a desire to preserve a threatened building to provide archive or museum space. Some of these became strong societies; others were burdened by keeping up a building, or paying insurance, or with an aging membership unable to

continue, and while some thrive, others have already closed down.

The first state history was Washington Irving's *Knickerbocker's History* (1809), followed by William Smith's *History of New York* (1829; a 1973 modern edition edited by Michael Kammen). The state engaged Edwin O'Callaghan to collect pertinent documents from European archives; he issued his massive *Documentary History* between 1849 and 1851. Other state histories have followed: David Ellis et al., *A History of New York State* (1957; reprint 1967); Michael Kammen, *Colonial New York* (1975); and most recently Milton M. Klein, ed., *The Empire State: A History of New York* (2001). Prior to 1869, there were several town histories, including ones for Albany, Cooperstown, and Binghamton, written to promote the community and to capture knowledge before it was lost. Many more town histories appeared in the twentieth century, especially in the 1950s, and again after the celebration of the Bicentennial of the American Revolution. Up to 1968, these books can be tracked in Harold Nestler, *A Bibliography of New York State Communities: Counties, Town, Villages* (with an addendum issued in 1975).

A number of publishers issue books of local history, among them Syracuse University Press, Cornell University Press, the State University Press, and North Country Books. The WPA Guides were important in their day, and so are the *Encyclopedia of the City of New York*, which appeared in 1995, and the *Encyclopedia of New York State* in 2005. Both encyclopedias have become indispensable. For the past twenty years, Arcadia Publishing and the History Press (now combined) have published county, town, and village histories in some profusion, and also histories of ethnic groups, clubs, colleges, and athletic teams and more recently of lore, ghosts, and postcard collections.

New York established the position of State Historian in 1895, a position occupied by several distinguished historians who had significant influence in making state documents available and serving as a focal point for the doing of local history. In 1919 the state required the position of municipal historian be created for each community with a population larger than 400, in part to track veterans of the Great War. Later, county and borough historians were re-

quired by legislation, in all now numbering over 1,350 throughout the state. Appointed municipal historians formed the Association of Public Historians of New York State (APHNYS) in 1999, combining a 1971 Municipal Historians Association and a County Historians organization created in 1986. Two state history conferences, dating from the late 1980s, meet annually bringing academic and independent historians together. A New York Academy, to recognize those involved with state and local history and culture, was founded in 2007.

In the twentieth century, the State Education Department created a social studies curriculum for the public schools, requiring since 1942 that local history be taught. Today it is taught in the fourth grade. Teachers use materials and topics that come to hand, their success measured by the number of students who fondly recall their fourth-grade local history classes or their participation in the Yorker young historian group or in History Day activities. There are very few courses in New York State history taught at the college level.

Genealogy has long been popular and important, incorporated into the function of historical agencies and supported by separate organizations, especially those on the Internet. Notably, Genweb, available by county name, serves as a useful clearinghouse for genealogical information.

New York has been fortunate in its historians. Notable practitioners include Carl Carmer, who wrote about central New York; Alf Evers, historian of Woodstock; and Blake McKelvey, noted for his work on Rochester. There have been a number of academic historians who have contributed, including Sean Wilentz, Ken Jackson, Michael Kammen, Patricia Bonomi, Phyllis Field, and Eric Foner. Once significant, *New York History* is no longer issued in print form by NYSHA and many people regret the absence of the Cooperstown Summer Seminars that provided inspiring courses on state history and workshops on traditional crafts. The New York State Archives provides links to documents and helpfully answers researchers' questions (www.archives. nysed.gov). A number of state and local newspapers are available from the New York Public Library, from nyshistoric-newspapers.org, and from privately run www.fultonhistory.com.

Major themes in New York's local history concern community growth, demographic change over time, ethnicity, race, gender, and the changes brought about by technological advances, especially those concerning transportation and communication. The *Underground Railroad and the 1848 Seneca Falls Convention are popular subjects of interest.

The most vital connection today among historians and historical organizations in the state is the New York History blog (newyorkhistoryblog.org) run by John Warren, who regularly publishes notices of meetings, alerts to history in the news, promotes new books and essays of interest, and provides commentary about history people, events, and meetings around the state. Warren is supported, not at all well, by donations, while his service is greatly admired and is the best link within the state to our state and local history.

New York provides an excellent model for others of how local and state history can be organized to be educational, effective, and entertaining to the public and to engage the energy of local practitioners. That it falls short of its potential is a concern to many; it lacks leadership from the state, clearer goals, better coordination, and more resources to achieve its potential. The state's *Path Through History* website is promotional but does not fund the development of sites. For comments about the doing of history in New York State, see the essays offered by Bruce Dearstyne and Peter Feinman, published frequently on the New York History Blog.

CAROL KAMMEN
TOMPKINS COUNTY (NY) HISTORIAN

See United States, local history in.

new western history. See western history and local historians.

New Zealand, local history in. New Zealand is a South Pacific nation comprising two main islands, together slightly smaller in area than Italy, with a population of 4.4 million, about three-quarters of whom are British or Irish in ethnic origin. The indigenous Māori population comprises about 15 percent of the total, with smaller minorities of other Polynesians (7 percent), and Chinese and Indians together (9 percent). European colonization followed the Treaty of Waitangi (1840). Māori resistance was largely quelled in the wars of the 1860s, but remaining grievances are still being settled by the official Waitangi Tribunal, set up in 1975. This is a permanent commission of inquiry charged with making recommendations on claims brought by Māori relating to actions or omissions of the Crown that potentially breach the Treaty of Waitangi. The tribunal reports constitute a form of local history studies. Gold rushes attracted a wave of European settlers in the 1860s, as did assisted immigration schemes in the 1870s. The economy remains that of a primary producer, exporting dairy products, meat, wool, timber, wood products, fish, and horticultural products, but also some machinery. New Zealand has a highly literate population and per capita New Zealanders are among the world's most avid readers of books and users of the Internet.

Difficult communications for much of the nineteenth century made European settlement highly localized, and strong regional identities and loyalties persist to the present day. Early local histories were mostly celebratory and sentimental, applauding the achievements of the "pioneers." Jubilees of schools, churches, and small towns have always produced publications, but these are often small-scale and amateurish by modern academic standards.

Publishers began to show interest in more serious works of local history in the 1920s and 1930s, many of which first appeared in serial form in local newspapers. The centenary of the Treaty of Waitangi in 1940 and subsequent provincial centenaries aroused greater public interest in local history. In the South Island, the provinces of Otago and Canterbury have been particularly well represented. The Otago centennial in 1948 prompted an impressive series of local and regional volumes. A. H. McLintock's monumental *A History of Otago* (1949) provided a regional overview, while K. C. McDonald wrote *White Stone Country: The Story of North Otago* (1962). Canterbury followed with an impressive three-volume regional history by C. R. Straubel, W. J. Gardner, and W. H. Scotter that appeared between 1957 and 1972. Milestones in regional history were W. J. Gardner's *The Amuri* (1956) and J. M. Sherrard's *Kaikoura* (1966), which set high scholarly standards for all subsequent regional and local histories. These pioneering works were joined by Erik Olssen's *A History of Otago* (1984) and Stevan Eldred-Grigg's *A New History of Canterbury* (1982). On the other hand, the North Island was more patchily covered, notable exceptions being W. H. Oliver and Jane M. Thomson's *Challenge and Response: A Study of the Development of the Gisborne East Coast Region* (1971); A. J. Dreaver's *Horowhenua County and its People: A Centennial History* (1984); A. G. Bagnall's *Wairarapa: An Historical Excursion* (1976); Chris Maclean's *Kapiti* (1999); and Roberta McIntyre's *The Canoes of Kupe: A History of Martinborough District* (2002).

New Zealand has long had a predominately urban population, and this has been reflected recently by several major studies of cities. These include P. J. Gibbons' *Astride the River: A History of Hamilton* (1977); *The Making of Wellington, 1800–1914,* ed. David Hamer and Roberta Nicholls (1990); *Southern Capital: Christchurch: Towards a City Biography, 1850–2000,* ed. John Cookson and Graeme Dunstall (2000); and Russell C. J. Stone's

From Tāmaki-makau-rau to Auckland (2001). Suburbs have attracted attention in their own right with D. G. Pearson's *Johnsonville: Continuity and Change in a New Zealand Township* (1980) and Erik Olssen's study of the Dunedin suburb of Caversham, *Building the New World* (1995).

The inauguration of the J. M. Sherrard Award in 1972 as a biennial memorial prize in local and regional history has had a significant influence. It remains the only award of its kind in New Zealand, with a current value of NZ $1,000. In abeyance for a decade, the award was revived in 2012. Winners include Robert Peden's *Making Sheep Country: Mt Peel Station and the Transformation of the Tussock Lands* (2011); Rollo Arnold's *Settler Kaponga, 1881–1914: A Frontier Fragment of the Western World* (1997); Jim McAloon's *Nelson: A Regional History* (1997); and Peter Tremewen's *French Akaroa* (1990).

There are several excellent histories of Māori tribes (*iwi*), the best-known of which are Angela Ballara's *Iwi: The Dynamics of Māori Tribal Organisation from c.1769 to c.1945* (1998) and J. M. McEwen's *Rangitāne: A Tribal History* (2002).

Local and regional history is now a well-respected genre of New Zealand history. Several important works appear most years, almost all of them well up to professional scholarly standards. The Professional Historians' Association of New Zealand, founded in 1994, has done a great deal to promote the professionalization of local and institutional histories. It facilitates institutions and organizations wanting research carried out to make contact with professional historians, both within and outside the universities.

ALEX TRAPEZNIK
UNIVERSITY OF OTAGO, NEW ZEALAND

See Australia, local history in; England, local history in.

Newfoundland and Labrador, local history in. Interest in the history and heritage of the Province of Newfoundland and Labrador—simply "Newfoundland" until 2001—has grown and expanded significantly since 1950. It is an interest that encompasses the history of towns and outports, of buildings and families, of music and dance, of language and the visual arts, and of peoples of European and aboriginal descent.

The post-1950 growth was triggered initially by two related factors. Hitherto a separate political entity, Newfoundland became a Canadian province in 1949, with a local government that promoted both modernization (a "new Newfoundland") and the need to preserve something of the traditional society. One of the first acts of that government was to convert Memorial University College, founded in the 1920s, into a degree-granting institution. It saw the new university as the institution that could further its goals, and the university administration proved cooperative. It was certainly keen to promote academic research related to the province, and the result was a strong emphasis on Newfoundland studies in most Arts Faculty departments that lasted well into the 1980s. The university's role was all-important, even though it was, in a sense, reflecting a fear of cultural loss that still persists, given the economic and demographic fragility of rural Newfoundland and Labrador. This is expressed these days in the large number of local publications dealing with family and community history, and websites concerned with the Newfoundland past. In contrast, academic interest in local history has declined in recent years, and it is not the lively field that it once was.

The 1950s may mark the beginning of serious academic involvement with local history, but there had been interest long before. The first history of the island of Newfoundland was published by the Chief Justice, John Reeves, in 1793. At least five histories appeared during the nineteenth century, the most important and influential being Daniel W. Prowse's *History of Newfoundland from the English, Colonial and Foreign Records* (1895). The first history of Labrador (which was annexed to Newfoundland in 1763), by W. G. Gosling, appeared in 1910. Prowse and his circle were instrumental in the foundation of the *Newfoundland Quarterly* magazine (1901) and of the Newfoundland Historical Society (1905), both of which still exist and maintain websites. The *Quarterly*, now owned and published by the university, has always contained many articles on local history. The Historical Society organizes an annual lecture series, symposiums, and a publications series.

The university's initial commitment was demonstrated by the creation of a Centre for Newfoundland Studies as part of its library, which in turn published a *Bibliography of Newfoundland* (1986), and its role in creating an archival collection that eventually (1960) came under government control as the Provincial Archives of Newfoundland and Labrador. However, the university library still maintains its own separate and important archive division. Within the English Department, scholars published a *Dictionary of Newfoundland English* (1982), the result of many years of meticulous study, which was widely praised as a model of its kind. Separate departments of linguistics and folklore grew out of the English Department in the late 1960s, both with a strong local focus. The latter is the only such department in Anglophone Canada, and manages a substantial folklore archive. The History Department encouraged research that fundamentally altered hitherto accepted interpretations of the Newfoundland and Labrador past, and created a Maritime History Group, whose legacy is the current Maritime History Archive. The Geography Department until recently was strongly biased toward historical geography, which led to valuable work on settlement patterns, the urban morphology of St. John's, and striking plates in *The Historical Atlas of Canada* (1987).

In addition to the *Quarterly*, the university publishes the academic journal *Newfoundland and Labrador Studies* (available online). It also funds the extensive and heavily used Newfoundland and Labrador Heritage website (www.heritage.nf.ca). Courses on various aspects of the province's past remain on the books, and local research continues, resulting in some important recent publications on the province's history.

The provincial archive is now located in the cultural complex in St. John's called The Rooms, which also houses the provincial museum and art gallery. The archive is heavily used by genealogical researchers, many of them members of the Family History Society of Newfoundland and Labrador. The Association of Newfoundland and Labrador Archives represents archives large and small across the province, and there is also a Museum Association of Newfoundland and Labrador. The Newfoundland Historic Trust and the Heritage Foundation of Newfoundland and Labrador are primarily concerned with historic buildings, while federal historic sites in the province are promoted by the Historic Sites Association of Newfoundland and Labrador. In 1999, the Association of Heritage Industries was created as an umbrella organization. The provincial government provides vital assistance to these organizations, and administers its own network of local museums and historic sites through the Department of Tourism, Culture and Recreation. All of these institutions maintain websites. There are numerous local historical societies and locally owned museums both on the island of Newfoundland and in Labrador.

The most important Labrador publication for local historians is *Them Days*, based in Happy Valley–Goose Bay, which also maintains a substantial archive in cooperation with the Labrador Institute of Memorial University. *Them Days* began as a publication of the Labrador Heritage Society located in Northwest River, where it runs the Labrador Heritage Museum. Past and ongoing research into aboriginal land claims in Labrador by the provincial and federal governments and by aboriginal organizations themselves (Inuit,

Innu, and Métis) has generated a large amount of local historical data and new interpretations of the region's history. The same is true on the island with reference to Mi'kmaq land claims.

The history of Newfoundland and Labrador more or less disappeared from the provincial school curriculum during the 1980s. Thanks to pressure from heritage groups and their allies, a grade eight course on the province's history since 1800, and a locally focused social studies course at grade eleven, are now in place. Literature courses have always contained a significant amount of Newfoundland and Labrador material. In this connection, it is worth noting that a number of authors either based in the province or with connections to it have written historical novels set in Newfoundland and Labrador, some of them winning literary prizes.

Overall, the province and its inhabitants have, for the most part, come to see its history and heritage as a cultural and economic asset. It is a sector that depends on volunteer commitment and enthusiasm as much as on government support and, since there will always be those who think that bland office towers and anonymous housing developments are preferable to the imaginative reuse of older buildings, battles continue to be fought. But local history is alive and well in the community, even if the academic world now seems to have other priorities, one hopes temporarily.

JAMES K. HILLER
MEMORIAL UNIVERSITY
OF NEWFOUNDLAND

See Canada, local history in.

newspaper resources. See Library of Congress; local history resources online.

North Carolina, local history in. The first monograph devoted to the history of North Carolina was written by Dr. Hugh Williamson, signer of the Constitution, and was published in 1812. *The Colonial and State Records of North Carolina*, twenty-six volumes published between 1886 and 1907, has been an extraordinary resource for students of North Carolina's history. The books include documents and materials related to North Carolina from domestic and European repositories. The series comprises the earliest days of European settlement through the ratification of the federal Constitution. More recently, William S. Powell has written numerous books on the state's history and has edited three seminal reference works: the *North Carolina Gazetteer*, the six-volume *Dictionary of North Carolina Biography*, and the *Encyclopedia of North Carolina*. Powell's major reference works are now integrated into the North Carolina State Library's online encyclopedia, *NCPedia* (http://ncpedia. org).

The North Carolina Literary and Historical Association was founded in 1900 to promote the state's history and literature, recognizing leaders in those fields each year. A legislative mandate of March 7, 1903, established the North Carolina Historical Commission, predecessor to today's Office of Archives and History. Due to budgetary constraints and the inability to assemble the members, however, the historical commission languished until the 1907 legislature amended the original act, broadening the powers, increasing the budget, and allowing for the employment of R. D. W. Connor as full-time secretary. Initially, the historical commission's most important obligation to the state was to collect, edit, and publish documents—to make records available and to assure their preservation. Connor, who later served as first U.S. archivist, sought to build a historical commission that was public service oriented, in order to make North Carolina's history accessible to all citizens.

The historical commission issued its first two volumes in 1908. The commission's popular quarterly journal, the *North Carolina Historical Review*, was launched in 1924. Over the years the Historical Publications Section has offered pamphlets and books on a wide variety of topics, such as pirates and gold mining, as well as the time-honored county histories and documentaries.

In 1914, the General Assembly reassigned the Hall of History from the Department of Agriculture to the Historical Commission. That institution would change its name to the North Carolina Museum of History in 1965. Currently, the Division of State History Museums includes the North Carolina Museum of History in Raleigh and six divisional museums: the Museum of the Albemarle in Elizabeth City, the Museum of the Cape Fear Historical Complex in Fayetteville, the Mountain Gateway Museum in Old Fort, the North Carolina Maritime Museum in Beaufort and its branch in Southport, and the Graveyard of the Atlantic Museum in Hatteras. Together, the museums interpret

This historical marker in New Bern, North Carolina, commemorates a landmark court case. CREDIT: NORTH CAROLINA OFFICE OF ARCHIVES AND HISTORY.

the state's history through exhibits, educational programs, and publications.

The Highway Historical Marker Program was established in 1935 with the first marker being erected the following year. Over the years about 1,600 markers have been placed around the state. Subjects of markers range from Cherokee petroglyphs to Quaker meetinghouses, civil rights landmarks to iron furnaces. The markers are one of the most visible initiatives of the Office of Archives and History and one that clearly stimulates local enthusiasm. Although the markers do not contain much text, the agency maintains a website that supplies an essay to accompany each marker. The Internet has raised the visibility of the program and interest from the public continues to increase. Recent marker topics have included surfing activity in Wrightsville Beach in the early 1900s, astronaut training at Morehead Planetarium in the 1960s and 1970s, and movie star and Johnston County native Ava Gardner.

The State Archives instituted its local records program in 1959, assisting counties with records retention and accessioning records into the archives' collection. Today the Government Records Branch provides and administers records management services to state government agencies, local governments, and state-supported institutions of higher education.

Over the years the archives has continued to serve a growing number of genealogical and historical researchers. In all, the archives house over 55,000 cubic feet of permanently valuable records containing millions of individual items. The staff works to preserve the materials and to provide the public with access to the records through reference services and *digitization.

In 1955 the legislature transferred most state historic site projects to the Department of Archives and History, creating the Division of Historic Sites. Today the division oversees twenty-seven historic sites, interpreting centuries of history in all areas of the state from the mountains to the sea. Each represents an important period in our state's history and offers visitors an exceptional learning experience.

In 1939, staff members of the Historical Commission were instrumental in the formation of the Society for the Preservation of Antiquities, a private venture influential in the evolution of state historic preservation initiatives. The National Historic Preservation Act of 1966 authorized the creation of the *National Register for Historic Places

and charged individual states with conducting statewide surveys of historical properties. In North Carolina the survey was initiated in 1967; the first nominations to the National Register were made in 1969. Staff of the State Historic Preservation Office review federal- and state-funded projects to assess their potential impacts on historic properties and then take action to minimize negative impacts when possible.

Although the state had been involved in archaeological activities since the 1930s, it was not until 1973 that the Archaeology Section was created. Underwater Archaeology has had a visible presence in the state for many years, most recently with the *Queen Anne's Revenge* shipwreck. The Office of State Archaeology, capturing the imagination of the public, benefits from resourceful volunteer work throughout the state.

In 1941, Christopher Crittenden, director of the agency from 1935 to 1968 and founder of the American Association for State and Local History, wrote, "Our histories should be something of broad, general interest—not merely for the professional historians, not merely for the genealogists, not just for any other limited group, but instead for the people at large." Those words still ring true and inspire his successors at the Office of Archives and History.

Among the prominent local history museums are Wilmington's Cape Fear Museum, the Greensboro Historical Museum, and the Charlotte Museum of History. Old Salem Museums and Gardens is a privately operated restored Moravian town that interprets life in the eighteenth and nineteenth centuries.

Many more historical, genealogical, and preservation organizations operate throughout the state. The Federation of North Carolina Historical Societies was formed in 1976 to assist local organizations in carrying out their work. The federation offers professional development workshops, technical advice, and a quarterly newsletter. It operates an interest-free loan program for organizations wishing to publish local histories or to plan special events. Each year the federation recognizes outstanding local historical organizations.

The standard course of study in public schools includes North Carolina history in fourth and eighth grades.

ANSLEY HERRING WEGNER
NORTH CAROLINA OFFICE OF
ARCHIVES AND HISTORY

See historical markers; United States, local history in.

North Dakota, local history in. The Red River Valley Old Settlers Association was North Dakota's earliest historical association, formed in Grand Forks in 1879, ten years before statehood. Most local historical societies were formed in the 1960s and 1970s. Approximately 250 local historical associations exist in North Dakota. State law provides that county historical associations affiliated with the State Historical Society may receive a portion of a mill levy for support. With that assistance and additional community support, many local historical societies maintain museums and archives.

In 1889, the Ladies Historical Society of Bismarck and North Dakota was established. It was reorganized and incorporated as a statewide organization, the North Dakota Historical Society, in 1895 and renamed the State Historical Society of North Dakota in 1903. By 1905 the society was receiving state funding as well as offices and museum space in the state capitol, and was designated trustee of state historic sites. Many more historic sites were acquired during the 1920s and 1930s; the society now manages the North Dakota Heritage Center & State Museum in Bismarck, as well as the Pembina State Museum and an additional fifty-six state historic sites, the most recent being the Welk Homestead near Strasburg, acquired in 2015.

The North Dakota Heritage Center & State Museum, home of the state museum, archives, State Historic Preservation Office, and state historical society offices, completed an expansion project that nearly doubled the size of the building in 2014.

Many additional entities also tell the story of early life in North Dakota. Fort Union Trading Post National Historic Site marks one of the most important fur trade posts on the upper Missouri from 1828 to 1867. Knife River Indian Villages National Historic Site, historically the home of the Hidatsas, preserves archaeological sites dating back thousands of years. Fort Abraham Lincoln State Park is known as the home of Lt. Col. George Armstrong Custer and the Seventh U.S. Cavalry Regiment. Fort Abraham Lincoln State Park is also known for On-a-Slant Village, one of the seven to nine traditional Mandan villages at the Heart River occupied in

This North Dakota historical marker is located along the historic Bismarck to Deadwood stage trail on Highway 21 near Flasher, North Dakota. CREDIT: STATE HISTORICAL SOCIETY OF NORTH DAKOTA.

the 1500s to late 1700s. Fort Mandan and the Lewis and Clark Interpretive Center highlights the time the Lewis and Clark Expedition spent with the Mandan and Hidatsa people in 1803–1804, as well as changes brought by the fur trade.

A number of important publications also help keep alive North Dakota's academic record of history. The first *Collections of the State Historical Society of North Dakota* was published in 1905 under the direction of Orin G. Libby, professor of history at the University of North Dakota and secretary of the society from 1903 to 1944. His best-known work is *The Arikara Narrative of the Campaign Against the Hostile Dakotas, June, 1876*, the first American Indian account of the Battle of the Little Bighorn, published in 1920. In 1926 the first edition of *North Dakota*

Historical Quarterly appeared. Publication of the journal was suspended for a few years during the Great Depression. In 1945 the name was changed to the current *North Dakota History: Journal of the Northern Plains*, which continues to publish quarterly. A number of works combining a history of the state and biographies of early settlers were published in the first decades of the twentieth century: the *Compendium of History and Biography of North Dakota* was published in 1900, Clement A. Lounsberry published *Early History of North Dakota: Essential Outlines of American History* in 1917, and Lewis F. Crawford's *History of North Dakota* was published in 1931.

A significant history of North Dakota remains Elwyn B. Robinson's *History of North Dakota*, published in 1966. A 1995 reprint includes a preface and postscript by noted North Dakota historians D. Jerome Tweton and David B. Danbom and remains the standard today. Robinson's emphasis on the state's remoteness, economic dependence, and the early radical response, as well as the "Too-Much Mistake" and the continuing need to adapt to the environment remain major themes in interpreting the state's history. *Plains Folk: North Dakota's Ethnic History,* published in 1986 and edited by William C. Sherman and Playford V. Thorson, is also essential to an understanding of the state's history. *North Dakota: 1960 to the Millennium* by Kimberly Porter is the most recent history of the state continuing from Robinson's book. Mary Jane Schneider's *North Dakota Indians: An Introduction,* 2nd ed. (1994) provides information on the major contemporary tribal cultures of North Dakota: Arikara, Dakota, Hidatsa, Mandan, Lakota, and Turtle Mountain Chippewa.

Genealogical research is extremely popular, and many organizations assist those seeking information on their ancestors from North Dakota, such as the Germans from Russia Heritage Collection at North Dakota State University and the state archives at the North Dakota Heritage Center & State Museum.

North Dakota history has been part of the state-required curriculum for fourth and eighth graders for more than eighty years. Schools are also required to offer North Dakota studies at the high school level at least every other year. Most institutions of higher education in the state also offer a North Dakota history or regional studies course, and North Dakota State University offers a bachelor's degree in public his-

tory. A number of textbooks have been published for classroom use since 1910. For forty years, from 1942 until 1983, *Our State North Dakota* was used in eighth-grade classes. In 2006 North Dakota Studies, a program of the state historical society, published a series of fourth-grade textbooks, and in 2007 published *North Dakota Legendary* for eighth-grade students. *North Dakota Legendary* was replaced in 2014 with a rewritten online curriculum based on primary sources called *North Dakota: People Living on the Land.* An online version of the fourth-grade curriculum will be available in 2016. North Dakota Studies also prints *North Dakota History: Readings about the Northern Plains State.* This text is essentially for high school and college students.

A number of conferences are regularly held in the state relating to North Dakota's history. Preservation North Dakota, a grassroots organization dedicated to preserving our state's historic resources, hosts a yearly conference and workshops throughout the state. The state historical society's historic preservation programs and a Certified Local Government program encourage and support local governmental and private efforts to preserve, protect, and interpret historic properties through the marshaling of federal, state, and private monies and preservation expertise to preservation needs.

KATHY DAVISON
UPDATED BY PAM BERRETH SMOKEY
STATE HISTORICAL SOCIETY
OF NORTH DAKOTA

See American Indian history; United States, local history in.

Northwest Territories, local history in. For the 42,000 residents of thirty-two communities in Canada's Northwest Territories (NWT) today, managing escalating resource development and its impact on traditional lifeways and economies is a major concern. The transfer of federal authority (completed in April 2014), aboriginal land claims, and dealing with social stresses caused both by isolation and by accelerated change brought about by participation in the global economy, are also important current issues. In many ways, they serve as tropes for local history, recurring again and again since before the former Hudson's Bay Company territory entered Canadian Confederation in 1870. Between 1870 and 1999 the NWT focused on the establishment of local responsible government, development of its significant oil, gas, and mineral resources, and in negotiating aboriginal self-government and land claim agreements—processes that continue today. Morris Zaslow's *The Opening of the Canadian North: 1870–1914* (1971) and *The Northward Expansion of Canada: 1914–1967* (1988) provide the best capsulated history of this expansive period.

Early exploration literature, usually serving to inventory and document the NWT's peoples and resources, is extensive. Two excellent examples, both more biographical and reflective than most, are George Douglas's *Lands Forlorn: A Story of an Expedition to Hearne's Coppermine River* (1914) and Frederick Watts's *Great Bear: A Journey Remembered* (1980). Bern Will Brown's *Arctic Journal: A Fifty-Year Adventure in Canada's North* (2003) presents personal observations of dramatic change in the latter half of the twentieth century, while he served as a Catholic priest to numerous missions in the Mackenzie Valley.

The Mackenzie Valley Pipeline Inquiry (MVPI), commissioned in 1974 and headed by Justice Thomas Berger, conducted hearings in all NWT communities, providing aboriginal people a direct voice in setting the course of future development. Berger's report *Northern Frontier, Northern Homeland* (1977, 2 vols.) called for a ten-year moratorium on pipeline development. Published originally in 1975, Rene Fumoleau's *As Long as This Land Shall Last: A History of Treaty 8 and Treaty 11, 1870–1939* (2004) presented a controversial examination of Canada's efforts to clear title to land through treaty-making in the NWT. It inspired the Dene Nation, a polity representing the Athapaskan-speaking aboriginal people of the NWT, to issue the *Dene Declaration of Rights*, launching an extensive period of land claim and self-government negotiation that has involved both Dene and Inuit communities. In 1977, the Dene Nation presented its position on aboriginal rights in *Dene Nation: The Colony Within* (ed. M. Watkins [1977]), and more recently, John B. Zoe edited a volume that examines the role that culture and education played in negotiating a self-government agreement in *Trails of our Ancestors: Building a Nation* (Tłįchǫ Government [2007]; see www.tlicho.ca). Two other regional histories explore these themes extensively: Keith Crowe's *History of the Original Peoples of Northern Canada* (1991) and Kerry Abel's *Drum Songs: Glimpses of Dene History* (1993). Between 1974 and today, the geopolitical landscape of the NWT has undergone much change with land claims being settled with the Inuvialuit (1984), Gwich'in (1992), Sahtu (1993), and Tłįchǫ (2003). The Inuit of the Eastern Arctic signed their land claim in 1993, which called for the creation of a new territory and, on April 1, 1999, the new territory of Nunavut was created, changing the boundaries of the NWT dramatically.

Cultural organizations, like the Gwich'in Tribal Council's Department of Cultural Heritage (formerly Gwich'in Social and Cultural Institute; established in 1993; www.gwichin. ca), have also been making significant contributions in publishing local histories. *Gwichya Gwich'in Googwandak: The History and Stories of the Gwichya Gwich'in As Told By The Elders of Tsiigehtshik* by M. Heine, A. Andre, I. Kritsch, A. Cardinal, and the Elders of Tsiigehtchic GSCI, 2nd ed. (2007) is an excellent example. Local biographies recounting traditional practices have served to document past lifeways; John Tetso's *Trapping is My Life* (1970) documents one of the oldest traditional economic pursuits in the NWT. Mary Crnkovich edited an engaging volume of social, political, and cultural commentary in *"Gossip": A Spoken History of Women in the North* (1990), which documents the changing role of women in the NWT.

Both the Yellowknife Heritage Committee (established by city bylaw in 1985) and the Fort Simpson Historical Society (incorporated in 1990) have made significant advances in having local historical buildings recognized and designated by municipal authorities.

Museums with a regional focus—Fort Smith's Northern Life Museum (opened 1974) and the Norman Wells Historical Centre (opened in 1989)—have partnered with the NWT's only territorial museum, the Prince of Wales Northern Heritage Centre (PWNHC; opened 1979), in Yellowknife, to preserve and promote NWT's history. Due to its isolation, the NWT has taken advantage of web-based exhibits to promote local history; the historical timeline is a prime example (available at http://www.nwttimeline.ca). The PWNHC is also home to the NWT Archives which, since 1979, holds and collects both government and nongovernment records (www.nwtarchives.ca).

The Department of Education, Culture and Employment develops the curriculum for kindergarten to grade nine. At various points across these grades, students learn local or northern history, including: K: Stories and Celebrations; grade one: Connections to the Past; grade four: The NWT—Our Places, Stories, and Traditions; grade seven: The Northern Circumpolar World. For grades ten through twelve, the NWT follows Alberta's curriculum, with the exception of Northern Studies 10, which explores the history, peoples, and issues of the North. The NWT Heritage Fairs Society coordinates school participation in the popular national heritage fair program, currently sponsored by *Canada's History* magazine, formerly *The Beaver*. The Heritage Fair allows students to explore history in a variety of formats and the NWT stimulates an interest in local history by offering the Minister's NWT History Awards, given to the top three projects focused on local history. As well, under the tagline of "uncover the mystery of our history" the PWNHC posts teacher resources for heritage fairs on its website (http://www.pwnhc.ca/education-and-out-reach/heritage-fairs/#tab-id-6).

THOMAS D. ANDREWS
PRINCE OF WALES NORTHERN HERITAGE
CENTRE, YELLOWKNIFE,
NORTHWEST TERRITORIES

See Canada, local history in.

Norwegians in America, sources for. See Appendix A.

Nova Scotia, local history in. Nova Scotia was one of the founding provinces of Canadian Confederation, and the scene of some of the earliest French and English settlements in North America. It was a major battlefield in the imperial struggles of those powers until the cession of French claims in 1763. In 1758 Nova Scotia became the first region within today's Canada to elect a representative House of Assembly. The province has, then, a lengthy documentary heritage.

Thomas B. Akins was appointed Commissioner of Public Records in 1857, the first in English-speaking Canada. Akins's work was continued by Harry Piers and culminated in the opening of the Nova Scotia Archives in Halifax in 1930. Akins was a diligent collector and arranger of historical materials. By 1878 he had gathered and cataloged 450 bound folios of documents, plus dozens of boxes of papers that he considered worth saving, but of less value than those in the bound folios. The *Inventory of Manuscripts in the*

Public Archives of Nova Scotia (1976) gives some idea of what Akins and his successors accomplished.

Following abortive attempts at forming a historical society in 1850 and 1863, the Nova Scotia Historical Society was founded in 1878 due to the efforts of Judge John W. Ritchie and Reverend George W. Hill. This organization endured, changing its name to the Royal Nova Scotia Historical Society in 1978. It is the longest continuously functioning provincial historical society in Canada. The society produced forty-four volumes of its *Collections* (1878–1996). From 1971 until 1980 William McCurdy published the *Nova Scotia Historical Quarterly*, which was superseded by the *Nova Scotia Historical Review*, under the aegis of the provincial archives (1981–1996). The *Collections* and the *Review* were merged in the annual *Journal of the Royal Nova Scotia Historical Society* (1998 to the present). The growing interest in genealogical history led to the appointment of a genealogical committee, and in 1982 to the creation of a distinct Genealogical Association of Nova Scotia, which publishes the *Nova Scotia Genealogist* several times per year.

John Howe, King's Printer, published the prospectus of a proposed history of Nova Scotia in 1801. Rev. Dr. William Cochran attempted the project a decade afterward, but was thwarted by a lack of accessible materials upon which to carry out the necessary research. The first published history was prepared by Thomas C. Haliburton as a pamphlet of 150 pages that circulated in 1824. It was a precursor of Haliburton's more ambitious pair of volumes, *An Historical and Statistical Account of Nova-Scotia*

(1829). The narrative portion runs to 1763, with a brief chronological section extending to 1828. The second volume is statistical and is based on the census of 1827. Beamish Murdoch was next in the field with a three-volume history of the province published between 1865 and 1867. Then came Duncan Cameron's 500-page volume in 1873, which continued Haliburton's narrative account from 1763 to 1867, when Nova Scotia became part of the Dominion of Canada.

The Murdoch and Campbell histories, together with King's College's annual award of a cash prize for the best local history, excited sufficient interest that the first county or regional histories were written. A number found their way into print, some into a second or even a third edition. This early group includes Richard Brown's history of Cape Breton Island (1869), Mather B. DesBrisay's account of Lunenburg County (1870), Thomas Miller's historical and genealogical account of Colchester County (1873), James F. Moore's Queens County (1873), Rev. J. F. Campbell's Yarmouth County (1876), and Rev. George Patterson's history of Pictou County (1877). Another flurry of books appeared around the turn of the century: W. A. Calnek's Annapolis County (1897), Isaiah Wilson's Digby County (1900), Howard Trueman's Chignecto Isthmus (1902), and Arthur W. H. Eaton's Kings County (1910). The scholarship and reliability of these early works and of their more recent successors varies considerably.

A few scholarly histories of the Atlantic region have been written within the past generation—John G. Reid's *Six Crucial Decades: Times of Change in the History of the Maritimes* (1987) may be mentioned, as well as *The Atlantic Region to Confederation* (1994), *The Atlantic Provinces in Confederation* (1993), and *Atlantic Canada: A History* (2010). No documented provincial history exists. Works for the general reader include Lesley Choyce: *Nova Scotia: Shaped by the Sea* (1996, 2007) and Harry Bruce, *An Illustrated History of Nova Scotia* (1997).

In the 1970s, when a new generation of scholars questioned the traditional emphasis on *political history, Nova Scotian universities responded by taking more interest in local and regional studies than previously. Saint Mary's University has offered interdisciplinary courses in Atlantic Canada Studies since 1975, adding a graduate degree in 1983. Cape Breton University offers courses in Atlantic Canada Regional Studies, including two courses in Cape Breton history, one about Mi'kmaq history and culture, and another about the social history of Louisbourg. Mount St. Vincent has courses in the history of the Maritime Provinces and a half course on women's history in the region, while Dalhousie University more specifically has a course in Nova Scotia history. St. Francis Xavier University offers a course on the Maritime Provinces 1500–1950. For the French-speaking, Université Ste.-Anne supplies a baccalaureate in arts with a major in Canadian Studies. Cape Breton University is also home to the Beaton Institute (1957), a regional archives for Cape Breton Island, and Acadia University to the Planter Studies Centre (1983), which holds conferences and encourages research on the pre-Revolutionary New England settlers. The inclusion of provincial history within the formal public school curriculum is minimal, tending to be subsumed within more general offerings.

The Nova Scotia Museum (1868) operates twenty-seven museums across the province. These include Balmoral Grist Mill; Ross Farm; the Uniacke, Prescott, Haliburton, McCulloch, and Perkins houses; the Maritime Museum of the Atlantic; the Fisheries Museum of the Atlantic; and Acadian, Highland, and Sherbooke villages. A full list may be found at www.museum.gov.ns.ca.

The website http://novascotiaheritage.ca/en/home/default.aspx maintains a list of heritage institutions across the province. Other useful directories are on http://nsgna.ednet.ns.ca, www.rootsweb.com/~canns, and www.councilofnsarchives.ca. A valuable source for researchers is the Nova Scotia Archives site at www.gov.ns.ca/nsarm.

TERRENCE M. PUNCH, CM
INDEPENDENT SCHOLAR

See Canada, local history in.

Nunavut, local history in. Nunavut is the newest of Canada's thirteen provinces and territories. It was created in 1999 when one-fifth of Canada's territory was severed from the Northwest Territories, to fulfill a promise made to Inuit when they settled their land claim in 1993. The population is 85 percent Inuit, living in the capital city of Iqaluit and in twenty-six "hamlets." All the settled places except one are on salt water, and all rely on local game resources, air links to the south, and annual sealifts during the short season of open water.

For centuries, Inuit lived in multifamily hunting groups and their autonomy was rarely challenged. By 1923 British fur traders, explorers, and whalers had opened the entire area to commercial influences. While Canada had started taking over Great Britain's colonial claims in the Arctic as early as 1870, it was slow to extend Canadian institutions into the territory. After 1950, benign neglect was replaced with a more assertive though underfunded colonialism, and the people were gathered into their present-day communities.

Descriptions of northern Canada generally conceptualize Nunavut as either "homeland" or "frontier." Recent writing prefers the "homeland" perspective, focusing on millennia of occupancy and adaptation and commenting favorably on efforts by Inuit to reassert control of land and resources. The "frontier" perspective is largely the work of *Qallunaat* (non-Inuit) who treat Nunavut not as a frontier of settlement but as a frontier of exploitation, of science, or of adventure, especially the search for the fabled Northwest Passage. Outside views stereotype the Arctic as "harsh" and, while they cannot avoid issues of place and environment, they generally say little about community.

There are two main strands of "homeland" local history in Nunavut. First, there are the histories of individual communities, together with the surrounding hunting territories. Second, there are distinct histories of larger ecological or cultural regions. Because of Nunavut's size and despite its having just 32,000 inhabitants, particular areas have been occupied by groups—termed "-*miut* groups"—who may be distinguished from their neighbors by dialect, kinship, adaptation to specific hunting opportunities, and variable degrees and kinds of historic contact with outsiders. This regional diversity within a shared Inuit identity is reflected in a significant volume called *Uqalurait* by J. Bennett and S. Rowley (2004), which was compiled under direction from Inuit elders and other cultural leaders as an "Oral History of Nunavut."

Local history in Nunavut generally has a public purpose. A federal effort in the 1960s released a platoon of social scientists on the Arctic, either pursuing "urgent ethnology" or trying to mitigate colonialism's impact. Frank Vallee's *Kabloona and Eskimo in the Central Keewatin* (1962) and John and Irma Honigmann's *Eskimo Townsmen* (1965) stand out. In the same period, Area Economic Surveys foreshadowed the later practice of presenting historical material one modern-era community at a time.

A major achievement was the publication of Milton Freeman's *Inuit Land Use and Occupancy Project Report* in 1976. This pivotal document employed interviews in communities to provide a "comprehensive and verifiable record" of historic and recent Inuit use of the lands and waters, and their consequent legal title. Anthropological observation, individual memory, and modern mapping techniques combined in what is still a foundational document for understanding twentieth-century Nunavut history.

Thus local history in Nunavut benefited from growing concerns about Inuit rights and the resulting use of historical experience and traditional knowledge for cultural awareness and identity building. Regional magazines like *Inuit Today* and *Inuktitut* fostered social cohesion. For logistical reasons, academic fieldwork tends to be community-based, so many prestigious academic journals like *Polar Record* publish what is in effect local history.

The academic field of Nunavut local history is dominated by anthropologists, geographers, historians, journalists, and others with a knack for learning from elders and hunters. Some writers have exploited archives, starting with W. G. Ross's evocative books on whaling in Hudson Bay and Davis Strait. Work by Peter Kulchyski and Frank Tester showed the impact of southern decision making on northern peoples through studies of the 1950s relocations, events explicitly mentioned in the high school curriculum. Lyle Dick's *Musk-Ox Land* is an unrivaled history of one enormous island, Ellesmere Island, in the age of contact.

The historical character of much environmental inquiry also marks local works like *Inuit Qaujimaningit Nanurnut: Traditional Knowledge of Polar Bears* (Gjoa Haven Hunters and Trappers' Organization [2005]). Politics and society stimulate local history too: recently the Qikiqtani Truth Commission devoted two years to researching in archives and receiving statements from hunters and other witnesses to government actions during the disruptions of the 1950s and 1960s; nine thematic reports and thirteen community histories were published in 2015. Local history also draws opportunistically on the research interests of external researchers, and on the mandate of national parks to interpret Inuit history to visitors.

Works created in the "frontier" tradition are not without merit, despite limitations. Exploration narratives embraced geography but usually ignored communities; the sovereignty narrative was concerned with the symbolic occupation of spaces that were sometimes imagined to be empty. Late colonial writing includes numerous memoirs of fur traders and missionaries, whose hegemonic concern for the "outside" accompanied place-based stories that are still of interest.

Local history is fostered throughout Nunavut by the Department of Culture, Language, Elders and Youth (CLEY), and the Inuit Heritage Trust (IHT). The latter is an arm of Nunavut Tunngavik Incorporated (NTI), the birthright corporation that manages Inuit interests in Nunavut. These bodies have complementary mandates to support visitor centers and elders' centers, place-names research, *oral history, museums, and archives. Most communities have at least one institution promoting local and regional history, including multipurpose facilities at Cambridge Bay, Baker Lake, Iqaluit, and Pond Inlet, park offices in Kimmirut and Pangnirtung, and Nunavut Arctic College. There is no university in Nunavut; secondary schools generally follow the Alberta curriculum but incorporate Inuit culture and traditional knowledge wherever possible. They share with primary schools a foundational curriculum document, *Inuuqatigiit*, which links past to future. A central part of this is the strong encouragement given to involving elders in the classroom.

PHILIP GOLDRING
INDEPENDENT SCHOLAR

See Canada, local history in.

nurses, Civil War. During the American Civil War, some women, motivated by patriotism, religion, geographic proximity to a battle site, or by request from a family member, moved from the domestic sphere into military hospitals. Mistrusted by some surgeons and quartermasters, many were told war "was no place for a woman." The soldiers, however, tended to find their presence comforting as they nursed, offered food, prayed with them, wrote letters, and tended to those nearing death. Attention has been paid to these women in recent decades. See especially Jane Schultz, *Women at the Front: Hospital Workers in the Civil War in America* (2004); Drew Gilpin Faust, *Mothers of Invention: Women of the Slaveholding South in the American Civil War* (1996), and Jean Adie, *Patriotic Toil: Northern Women and the American Civil War* (1998). These books have full and helpful bibliographies including citations to record groups concerning these nurses held in the *National Archives.

Among the earliest books that touch on the subject of women nurses are Linus P. Brockett and Mary C. Vaughan, *Women's Work in the Civil War* (1867); Mary Gardner Holland, *Our Army Nurses* (1895); and George Barton, *Angels of the Battlefield: A History of the Labors of the Catholic Sisterhood in the Late Civil War* (1898). George W. Adams has written *Doctors in Blue: The Medical History of the Union Army in the Civil War* (1952) and *Doctors in Gray: The Confederate Medical Service* (1958). See also Mary Elizabeth Massey, *Bonnet Brigades: American Women and the Civil War* (1966) and the important article by Ann Douglas, "The War within a War: Women Nurses in the Union Army," *Civil War History* 18, no. 3 (September 1972): 197–212.

There are, in addition, a number of published first-person accounts by women who went to nurse. See S. A. Palmer, *Aunt Becky's Army-Life* (1867); Sophronia Bucklin, *In Hospital and Camp: A Woman's Record of Thrilling Incidents Among the Wounded in the Late War* (1869); Hanna L. Ropes, *Civil War Nurse: The Diary and Letters of Hannah L. Ropes* (1980) and Susie King Taylor's *Reminiscences of My Life in Camp* (1902;

reprint 1988) by an African American woman who nursed. Louisa May Alcott wrote about her weeks as a Civil War nurse in *Hospital Sketches* (1863).

These Civil War nurses raise interesting questions about gender and war and about medical knowledge, and they document the beginning of professional nursing in this country.

CAROL KAMMEN
TOMPKINS COUNTY (NY) HISTORIAN

nursing history. See health care as local history topic.

O

obituaries. An obituary is a published report of an individual's death. It generally supplies information about the death itself (the time, place, and cause), the funeral, and the disposition of the deceased's remains. An obituary, however, also includes details about the life of the departed. This can include alternate names (such as a married woman's maiden name), a birthplace, parents' names, places of residence, schools attended, places of employment, military history, names of spouses, names of children, names of siblings, religious affiliation, and membership in fraternal organizations, clubs, or other groups. Today it is not uncommon for obituaries to list hobbies along with other leisure time activities or interests. Names of pets may be detailed. Close friends and caretakers are included. A photograph often accompanies the text. An obituary is a miniature biography, and for many it is the only time that their life stories are presented in a public forum. Much of this information may not be easily attainable elsewhere, making obituaries invaluable to researchers. Also, the information presented in an obituary can supply ideas for other avenues of investigation.

Researchers interested in obituaries need to be aware of three other types of reports—the death notice, the funeral notice, and the memorial. The distinction between a death notice and an obituary can be slight. Some newspapers charge for the placement of obituaries, some for death notices. Death notices are sometimes administered by the advertising department. Obituaries are often considered news stories. Simply put, in most but not all instances, a death notice will be much shorter than an obituary; it provides very little information outside of the details of the death and perhaps the funeral. It is not a biography. It is a notification of a death. But it is possible to find death notices, especially in large newspapers, as lengthy and involved as an obituary. They often come from a funeral home and are not edited by the newspaper.

Of the four announcement types, the funeral notice is the least used today. Funeral notices appear after the primary death report, if there is one, and after the funeral. While the obituary or death notice may supply details about the funeral to encourage attendance, the funeral notice reports on the funeral as an event. Some funeral notices resemble wedding announcements more than they do obituaries. For example, details about the service are given, such as the hymns sung or scriptures read. A description of the floral tributes is not unusual. Perhaps, more importantly, the pallbearers, actual or honorary, may be included. These names can be a treasure trove of genealogical clues. Pallbearers are often "minor" relatives, such as cousins, nephews, and in-laws. Their surnames may not appear in the obituary. The family friends and colleagues listed as pallbearers can also open up new research doors.

Memorials appear in the newspaper at the time of an anniversary. This is usually the anniversary of the death, but could also be a birthday or wedding day. They are generally brief, providing life dates and a statement of grief, often a poem or Bible verse. They may include a photograph. Those left behind are listed, but not always fully identified, only first names given, or simply "Your husband" and "Mom." Memorials are two-dimensional headstones.

The information in an obituary usually goes through a variety of filters. The person writing the obituary, whether a reporter or funeral home employee, may not have known the subject personally. Also, the writer's informant, usually the bereaved, may not have been thinking clearly at the time of the interview. And the informant may not have firsthand knowledge of some of the details they are reporting. This is especially true if the deceased is elderly and the informant is a new member of the family, or not related at all. Only notables have their obituary data confirmed prior to their death. The writing of one's own obituary as a phenomenon began in the late twentieth century.

Over time, different individuals have been responsible for the composition of obituaries. In the late nineteenth century freelance writers could be commissioned by the deceased's loved ones to author the obituary. Today, in some newspapers obituaries are written by journalists. Some papers even supply the writers' bylines. There are two associations for obituary writers—the In-

ternational Association of Obituarists and the Society of Professional Obituary. Both hold conferences and present awards. There is a growing trend for major newspapers to write lengthy obituaries for noncelebrities, "Average Joes." *The Dead Beat*, by Marilyn Johnson, provides an entertaining discussion of the lives of professional obituary writers and their followers.

It is also not uncommon for obituaries to be submitted by family members and friends. Factors affecting an obituary's authorship include historical period, newspaper, locale, and the deceased's standing in the community. However, the length, or even existence, of a death notice or obituary, if a fee is involved, may not reflect the individual's standing in the community, but the solvency of the estate. Newspapers that charge fees can be found as far back as the nineteenth century.

When seeking an obituary, a researcher should consult all newspapers published where the death occurred, and also the areas where the deceased, or his immediate family, lived. Neighboring newspapers may supply differing amounts of information, as well as differing facts. Discrepancies increase the importance of locating all published reports in the hopes of being able to discern accuracy. If the deceased spent their final years in a community removed from where they grew up or spent the majority of their adult working life, the family may not have submitted an obituary to the paper in that area.

While the community newspaper is usually the most frequent source for the local historian to investigate, obituaries also appear in other types of serial publications, at the local, state, and national levels. For example, the publications of religious denominations can be very useful, even for nonclergy subjects. Historically, the obituaries in religious newspapers may appear quite different from those in the community press; emphasis is placed not on the facts of the individual's life, but on their spiritual character and their relationship with their God.

Newsletters and magazines published by schools, professional organizations, clubs, and fraternal organizations can also be sources for obituaries. They can supply insight into different aspects of a person's life. For instance, the *Confederate Veteran* is a historic national publication known for the usefulness of its obituaries. Newspapers published by minorities and foreign language papers can report on members of their communities who may have been ignored in the mainstream publications.

Comprehensive indexing is rare for local newspapers; however, the rise of genealogical publishing in the last quarter of the twentieth century has seen an increase in the production of books of abstracts and specialized indexes to such papers. Some of these publications focus exclusively on obituaries and death notices. Such tools can assist the local history scholar in locating obituaries when the date of death is unknown. It is, of course, a stroke of luck if the newspaper one is investigating has such a publication, and it covers the period needed. PERSI (PERiodical Source Index) is a very useful database that indexes references to obituaries, and obituary sources, that appear in a wide variety of genealogical and local history periodicals. PERSI is an index and does not include the full text of any obituaries.

PERSI is included in the family history product HeritageQuest available through many libraries. HeritageQuest includes PERSI entries up to 2009. Another subscription database, Findmypast, also includes PERSI. It can also be found in libraries, though in the United States it is not as widespread as HeritageQuest. Individuals can subscribe to Findmypast on their own; they cannot to HeritageQuest. Findmypast has the full run of PERSI and is working to include the full article cited.

Clipped obituaries can often be found in vertical, surname, family, genealogy, or obituary files compiled by, and/or held by, libraries and archival institutions. These files are usually arranged by the individual's last name. Unfortunately, it is common that the items in such files do not include complete citations, which can hinder some research. Obituaries can also be found in family Bibles and in scrapbooks, held in both institutions and in private hands. Such scrapbooks can be the products of family members or of community chroniclers. Scrapbooks can be useful, for they bring together a large number of obituaries, usually tied together by some theme, such as family name or time period, and often include clippings from a variety of sources. Other institution types that should be consulted for obituary files are funeral homes, churches, cemeteries, and newspapers.

While obituary publications with a national focus are not usually useful to the local history scholar, some can assist with community research. For example, both the *Avery Obituary Index to Architects* and the *Biographical Dictionary of American Architects (Deceased)* can lead to information on architects who may have worked in the community. Such sources could assist in confirming a commission, or aid in the evaluation of an architect's professional development and style. There are also a number of sources that document the deaths of U.S. doctors. Such national sources, however, tend to be expensive and are often only held by larger public or academic libraries.

The rise of the Internet has greatly facilitated the dissemination of obituary information worldwide. There are numerous sites where obituaries are posted, abstracted, indexed, and discussed. Funeral homes and cemeteries post obituaries. These sites often allow individuals to express sympathy to the family or discuss their own memories of the dead, creating separate unique documents with insights into the life and character of the departed.

Modern newspapers allow for access, from a distance, to contemporary obituaries through their web pages and online archives. Some of these are fee driven; some not. Some provide full-text obituaries, and some simply provide the citation. Some include death notices; some do not. Some sites take the obituaries down after a set time; others do not. The longevity of online obituary information, as it is with all electronic sources, is unknown.

Many newspapers and funeral homes have a relationship with Legacy.com. The largest obituary collection on the web, Legacy purports to publish "more than half of all newspaper obituaries

and death notices from the U.S. and Canada." Content goes back to 2001. It is a useful way to search for obituaries when the location of the death is not known or it is unclear what the most likely funeral home or newspaper might be. Legacy.com is also a useful tool for comparing an obituary's content in different papers. An interesting feature for genealogists and obituary aficionados is the site's Obituary Messenger. This provides researchers the opportunity to set up keyword alerts by name, phrase, and location.

Websites focusing on older obituaries are generally the product of genealogists and genealogical groups, as well as research institutions. Genealogy discussion lists and social networking sites often include the posting of obituaries discovered by their members. An excellent starting point for locating obituary sites on the web is the metasite *Cyndi's List of Genealogy Sites on the Internet.* As of April 24, 2011, her obituary page (http://www.cyndislist.com/obits.htm) contained links to over 400 sites. The links are arranged alphabetically by title and include sources for both contemporary and historic obituaries. Some sites are accessible only through subscription. While the vast majority of sites listed relate to the United States, there are some international links. Cyndi's List is updated regularly, and inactive links are removed in a timely manner.

More and more libraries are placing their own obituary indexes online. At times, these are products that have been maintained in paper form for years. Libraries have always played an active role in obituary research. It is wise to always consult the website for the public library in the area in which the death occurred when searching for an obituary or looking for research guidance.

There are also a growing number of newspaper databases, many commercial, that allow searching not only by name but also by such factors as town, occupation, or reported cause of death, thus easing the use of the obituary as a tool to evaluate social trends. The major library database companies often provide access to our country's primary newspapers, those of the big cities. Often separate databases cover the modern and historic papers. Individuals cannot subscribe to these databases on their own; they must be accessed through a library. Researchers should identify the subscription databases available to them in their own locale and in their investigative area of interest just as they would any other source type.

There are several products, however, for accessing obituaries that individuals can subscribe to on their own at generally reasonable rates. GenealogyBank (http://www.genealogybank.com) provides access to content from hundreds of newspapers. *Ancestry.com, perhaps the most well-known genealogy website, includes hundreds of databases with obituary content. While one needs to subscribe to truly perform an effective search in Ancestry, it is possible to consult the descriptions of the various databases without paying. The descriptions include such information as the number of obituaries in the database, the date range, and, in some cases, a brief publishing history of the newspaper in question, along with contact information, if appropriate. They are excellent research starting points. There

is also a library version of Ancestry, AncestryLibraryEdition. It includes most of the same content as Ancestry.com, although nearly all the newspaper data is lacking from LibraryEdition. Newspaper content alone can be obtained through Newspapers.com, an Ancestry product. A similar database is NewspaperArchives.com. Individuals can subscribe and it provides access to the digitized microfilm of many small city and town papers. Many libraries also have access to NewspaperArchives—often, however, only for their own town.

Obituaries are more than informational sources; they are also cultural documents reflecting the times in which they were written. While the number of people whose deaths are reported in the news has increased greatly since the eighteenth century, even in small local papers social factors influence what death is reported and at what length. Over time gender, race, and ethnicity have determined who warranted an obituary, at what length, and at what level of detail. Obituaries are a reflection of their community. They also can tell us a great deal about our changing attitudes toward death, how we report on this great eventuality, and how we mourn the passing of the various members of our community.

MARY K. MANNIX
FREDERICK COUNTY (MARYLAND)
PUBLIC LIBRARIES

See Ancestry.com; biographical dictionaries; genealogical resources online; genealogy, an archivist's view; HeritageQuest Online.

objects. See material culture.

Ohio, local history in. Local and state history is flourishing in Ohio and points to the truth that for Ohioans the parts of their history are greater than the sum of what we would call "Ohio history." Ohio's history is Ohio's histories.

Ohio and its local history is the subject of thousands of publications, ranging from Caleb Atwater's 1838 *A History of the State of Ohio: Natural and Civil* to a 2005 book of essays, *Ohio and the World, 1753–2053*, ed. Geoffrey Parker, Richard Sisson, and William Russell Coil. Besides the latter, three other works that students of the Buckeye State's history should read are George Knepper's *Ohio and Its People* (2003), Andrew R. L. Cayton's thought-provoking interpretation in his book, *Ohio: The History of a People*, and the ninth printing of Eugene H. Roseboom and Frances P. Weisenburger's profusely illustrated *A History of Ohio* (1953). These, along with *Timeline*, the quarterly popular history magazine of the Ohio History Connection, and the academic journal *Ohio History*, provide a fairly comprehensive overview of the state's history.

Prolific publishers of Ohio and its local history include the Kent State University Press, the Ohio State University Press, the Ohio University Press/Swallow Press, and the privately held Orange Frazer Press. Local historians in Ohio keep Arcadia and the History

Community members pose at the dedication of an Ohio historical marker honoring Mount Enon Missionary Baptist Church in Dayton, Ohio. CREDIT: OHIO HISTORY CONNECTION.

Press busy, too. The two have published approximately 550 works about the history of Ohio's communities (Arcadia, 513; History Press, 45). Local historians and historical societies have also published or reprinted earlier histories on their own with the help of local publishers and printers. These include many titles from the Ross County Historical Society in Ohio's first state capital of Chillicothe, many of them written by the society's archivist Patricia Medert. In the early 1990s, the Summit County Historical Society in Akron managed the Summit County Historical Society Press, which saw thirteen works published.

Often described as "a textbook of Ohio history with pages spread across the state," or humorously as "history on a stick," the Ohio Historical Markers program has since its inception in 1957 erected more than 1,500 free-standing markers, most of which describe local historical people, places, and events. A legacy of Ohio's sesquicentennial in 1953, markers are public history originated by the public. Staff from the Local History Office of the Ohio History Connection collaborate with local sponsors to identify the historical significance and accuracy of a marker's subject matter and then collaborate to write the marker text. Recently, the program has erected an average of twenty new makers per year. An up-to-date list of markers is online at www.remarkableohio.org.

The histories of Ohio's places have also inspired video and radio documentarians. The public television station (WBGU) operated by Bowling Green State University has produced more than twenty programs on local and regional historical topics. Independent producers affiliated with Ohio University's WOUB have produced documentaries about the founding of Marietta, Ohio's first official American settlement, and about Ohio's historical geography and settlement patterns. WOSU at the Ohio State University in Columbus has produced shows about landmark buildings in central Ohio, legendary (at least in Ohio) football coach Woody Hayes, and the Emmy-winning series *Columbus Neighborhoods*, among others.

Digital sources for Ohio's state and local history include Ohio History Central, at www.ohiohistorycentral.org, an online encyclopedia of Ohio history. While Ohio History Central strives to be interpretive and authoritative, the goal of the Ohio Memory Project, at www.ohiomemory.org, is to provide digital access to historical treasures and primary resources held by hundreds of local historical societies and museums, libraries, and archives around the state. At a local and regional level, sites like Toledo's Attic (www.toledosattic.org), the Encyclopedia of Cleveland History (http://ech.cwru.edu), the Akron area's Summit Memory (www.summitmemory.org) and the Greater Cincinnati Memory Project (www.cincinnatimemory.org) accomplish for those regions what Ohio History Central and Ohio Memory do for the state.

There are more than nine hundred historical organizations in Ohio. All of Ohio's eighty-eight counties have at least one—and usually many more—local historical societies. There are approximately 320 town or "area" oriented historical societies; approximately 240 organizations inspired by specific "topics," ninety genealogical societies, eighty county historical societies, seventy historic building or district preservation groups, sixty township level historical societies, fifty-three state memorials, museums, and sites that are part of the Ohio History Connection's network and administered by local partners, thirty public libraries that include historical museums or archives, and twelve regional, multi-county historical societies.

What is striking about Ohio's historical organizations is how relatively young most are compared to the two-hundred-year history of the state. Approximately half were founded between 1960 and 1989. The older organizations are the regional and county historical societies; all but seven of the eighty county-level groups were founded by 1971 and most of the regional societies were established by 1900.

The historical society with the oldest roots in the state is the Cincinnati Historical Society Library. The society's origins stretch back to the incorporation of the Historical and Philosophical Society of Ohio (HPSO) in 1831. The HPSO was formed in Columbus, the state's capital, then moved to Cincinnati in 1849. In 1963, the HPSO became the Cincinnati Historical Society and in 1990 it joined the Cincinnati Natural History Museum and Robert D. Linder Family Omnimax Theater in opening the Cincinnati Museum Center in the newly restored Union Terminal train station. In 1995, the museum operations at the terminal merged, creating the Cincinnati Historical Society Library.

The largest historical society in Ohio remains the Ohio History Connection, which until May 2014 was the Ohio Historical Society. The Ohio History Connection was founded in 1885 and is a private not-for-profit organization that receives a biannual subsidy from the state for carrying out history services mandated by the Ohio Revised Code. Some of these functions include operating the state museum and archives, the state historic preservation office, and a network of state historic sites and memorials, many of which are owned by the State of Ohio.

Another of the Ohio History Connection's state-mandated functions is to provide support and assistance to local historical societies. This effort dates back to 1954, following Ohio's 1953 sesquicentennial. High points in the decade that followed included the creation of the Ohio History Connection's Field Services Office in 1954 and the founding of the Association of Historical Societies of Ohio, a statewide professional association for local historical organizations, in 1960. After twenty years of a relationship that ebbed and flowed, the association, by this time known as the Ohio Association of Historical Societies and Museums (OAHSM), had renewed their mutually beneficial bonds in the early 1980s. In 2010, OAHSM changed its name to the Ohio Local History Alliance. As Ohio's local historical organizations move further into the twenty-first century, their relationship to the Ohio History Connection remains mutually beneficial. The Local History Office of Ohio History Connection (the successor of the Field Services Office) administers alliance programs under the direction of the alliance's board.

In the 2010s, the Ohio History Connection, through its Local History Office, began to address two long-standing issues raised by the local history community for decades: the need for more people and more funding. The Ohio History Service Corps began filling the former in 2010. In 2012, a new grant program, the History Fund, began to meet the latter. The Ohio History Service Corps, an AmeriCorps State & National program, places a group of between ten and twenty AmeriCorps members annually with local historical societies and historic preservation organizations. Across Ohio, members have completed projects in the areas of historic site survey, collections digitization, and capacity building projects at their host organizations and for others in regions surrounding their host sites. They have also leveraged over $160,000 of cash resources and over $444,000 of in-kind donations.

Made possible through a "check-off" on state income tax forms, the sales of Ohio History "mastodon" license plates, and donations, History Fund grants have supported, among others, collections care projects, the rehabilitation of buildings on the *National Register of Historic Places, public programs, and digitization initiatives intended to "strengthen Ohio history." The History Fund in its first three years has made thirty-three grants, totaling $348,000 and generating $548,000 in matching support, in twenty-two of Ohio's eighty-eight counties. The need for funding, however, is far greater than the grant program's donor-limited capacity. Since 2012, the History Fund has received more than $2 million in grant requests (and pledging $4.4 million in match) from more than half (forty-six) of the state's counties.

Following the sesquicentennial of 1953, Ohio's legislature required the teaching of state history in the schools. What was taught and how was the decision of local school districts. With the adoption of a uniform statewide model for local K–12 curricula in 1994, Ohio history moved to the fourth-grade social studies curriculum and local history to the third grade. Ohio's department of education introduced an even higher degree of standardization among local curricula with the implementation of fully formed standards for social studies beginning in 2002. Students were tested first against the model curriculum in the mid-1990s and then against "the standards" after they were implemented. Revised in 2010, "Communities: Past and Present, Near and Far" is addressed in third grade, with the study of local history focused on the examination of artifacts and documents. In the fourth grade, students learn about "Ohio in the United States."

Discovering a need for an authoritative text, as well as lesson plans and instruction strategies for teaching Ohio history, the Ohio History Connection launched its online textbook *Ohio as America* in 2011. It is aligned with Ohio's New Learning Standards in Social Studies, released in 2010. Because *Ohio as America* is published online, it is regularly updated, based on the feedback from users. In the 2014–2015 school year, *Ohio as America* had more than 220 subscribers in 650 grade-school buildings and was used by 28 percent of Ohio fourth-grade students. For the contents of Ohio's standards for history and social studies education, go to http://education.ohio.gov.

ANDY VERHOFF
OHIO HISTORY CONNECTION

See historical markers; United States, local history in.

Oklahoma, local history in. Although Oklahoma did not become a state until 1907, local history organizations began recording its history before that time. The Territorial Press Association met on May 16, 1893, in Kingfisher, Oklahoma Territory, and decided to preserve the newspapers of the territory. The first "Historical Custodian" was William P. Campbell, who collected not only newspapers but also government documents. The press association gained the support of the territorial governor and, in 1901, the collections of what was thereafter known as the Oklahoma Historical Society (OHS) were moved to Oklahoma City. The OHS began publishing *The Chronicles of Oklahoma*, a quarterly scholarly journal, in 1921. In 1930 the OHS moved to the Wiley Post Building on the State Capitol Complex grounds, its home for the next seventy-five years. The OHS began acquiring historic sites in 1957 and in 2015 the Museums and Historic Sites Division of the OHS encompassed some twenty-one museums, military sites, and historic homes across the state, with ten additional affiliated sites. In 1967 the society added the State Historic Preservation Office to protect historic places and aid in the naming of sites to the *National Register of His-

toric Places. In 2005 the OHS relocated to its current location in the Oklahoma History Center, a building that houses its Research Library, the Oklahoma Museum of History, the Museums and Sites Division, the State Historic Preservation Office, the Publications Division, and the administration. Today the OHS exists as the statewide center for collecting, preserving, and sharing the history and heritage of the diverse people of Oklahoma.

Oklahoma's historians reflect this diverse heritage. Muriel H. Wright was born in the Choctaw Nation before statehood and became one of its foremost historians. She, along with historian and OHS board member Joseph Thoburn, wrote the four-volume work *Oklahoma: A History of the State and Its People* (1929). She also wrote three textbooks on Oklahoma history used in the public schools: *The Story of Oklahoma* (1929), *Our Oklahoma* (1939), and *The Oklahoma History* (1955). Her *A Guide to the Indian Tribes of Oklahoma* (1951) remains a reference for the study of the American Indian tribes of Oklahoma. Wright also provided the research for the majority of the state's historical markers in the 1940s and 1950s. Her early collaborator, Joseph Thoburn, was a civic leader in Oklahoma City who published the first Oklahoma history textbook, *The History of Oklahoma* (1908). He also did the first archaeological excavations in Oklahoma and helped found the *Chronicles of Oklahoma*.

Angie Debo, a student of another important Oklahoma historian, Edward Everett Dale, was one of the first historians to integrate government records and

This historical marker in Kingfisher, Oklahoma, marks the birthplace of the Oklahoma Historical Society. CREDIT: OKLAHOMA HISTORICAL SOCIETY.

*oral histories when telling the story of American Indians in Oklahoma. Her *The Rise and Fall of the Choctaw Republic* (1934) is an early example of the ethno-historical approach to research. Debo's controversial book *And Still the Waters Run* (1940) discusses the termination of tribal governments and allotment of tribal lands. During the Great Depression, Debo worked as the editor of the Indian-Pioneer Papers and served as director of the project that resulted in *Oklahoma: A Guide to the Sooner State* (1941), both Works Progress Administration projects for the OHS. Another prominent Oklahoma historian, Grant Foreman, acted as director of the Historical Records Survey, which was the body that compiled the volumes that be-

came the Indian-Pioneer Papers. Foreman came to Indian Territory in 1899 as a fieldworker for the Dawes Commission. Foreman was elected to the OHS board of directors in 1924, where he lobbied for the building of the Wiley Post Building and for the purchase of the Fort Gibson Barracks. Five of his books appear in the University of Oklahoma Press's Civilization of the American Indian Series, including *Indian Removal* (1933) and *The Five Civilized Tribes* (1934). As a member of the OHS board of directors, he was instrumental in the acquisition of the OHS Research Library's Indian Archives.

Arrell M. Gibson, career history professor, served as curator of the Western History Collections at the University of Oklahoma from 1957 to 1970, and director of the Stovall Museum (now the Sam Noble Oklahoma Museum of Natural History) from 1960 to 1987. His works include such titles as *The Kickapoos* (1963), *The Chickasaws* (1971), and *Wilderness Bonanza* (1972). Gibson's Oklahoma history textbook, *Oklahoma: A History of Five Centuries* (1965), is still in use. Oklahoma historians Danney Goble and W. David Baird updated Oklahoma history textbooks when they wrote *The Story of Oklahoma* in 1994, with a second edition released in 2007.

Into the twenty-first century, Bob L. Blackburn has been a tireless advocate for the preservation and sharing of Oklahoma history. Blackburn is the author of more than fifteen books on various Oklahoma topics. He spent several years as the editor of the OHS's *Chronicles of Oklahoma* journal before stepping into the role of deputy director and then executive director of the OHS. During his tenure as executive director, the OHS published *The Encyclopedia of Oklahoma History and Culture* (2009), edited by Dianna Everett, a two-volume reference with 2,455 entries including major events, biographies, geographic features, and more. The OHS continues to add new entries to the online version of this encyclopedia.

Oklahoma history has been taught since 1971 in state's public schools. As of 2015, Oklahoma history is included in the curriculum for third-grade and high school students. Third-grade students are taught three "strands" of information. First, they are introduced to selected, historically important Oklahomans with the goal of developing an appreciation for the diversity of Oklahoma's population. The second strand includes the study of geographic features and natural resources. The third strand explores the economics of the use of natural resources. At the high school level, students study Oklahoma history and government with the goal of linking Oklahoma's history to local, national, and global contexts. The knowledge base broadens to include more specific events ranging from prehistoric American Indian settlement to modern cultural and political movements. Teachers expect students to understand the relationship between the geographic regions of Oklahoma, to identify the significance of the exploration expeditions through and territorial claims on the land that would become Oklahoma, and to know the impact that American Indians have had on the culture of Oklahoma from prehistory through modern times. Classes cover major events, including events prior to statehood such as the Civil War and cattle drives, and the development of constitutional government in Oklahoma. Students discover how economic cycles, such as the Great Depression and oil booms and busts, affected the people of the state and how political movements and race relations, such as Populism and the Tulsa Race Riot, shaped the culture of the state.

References: Bob L. Blackburn, "Battle Cry for History: The First Century of the Oklahoma Historical Society," in *The Encyclopedia of Oklahoma History and Culture*, ed. Dianna Everett (2009); the Oklahoma Historical Society website, www.okhistory.org; Oklahoma State Department of Education website, http://ok.gov/sde/sites/ok.gov.sde/files/documents/files/Social%20Studies%20OK%20Academic%20Standards.rev815pdf.pdf; Tom Lindley, "Executive Session: Bob Blackburn—Oklahoma's Official Timekeeper," *Journal Record*, April 2, 2010.

ELIZABETH M. B. BASS
OKLAHOMA HISTORICAL SOCIETY

See American Indian history; United States, local history in.

online encyclopedias. See Texas Online, Handbook of.

Ontario, local history in. One of the best-known and earliest works of local history in Ontario, based on the Scottish genre of Statistical Accounts, was Scottish-born Robert Gourlay's 1822 two-volume *A Statistical Account of Upper Canada*. It was followed by J. M. McMullen's 1855 survey, *The History of Canada from its Discovery to the Present Time*, regarded as the first reputable survey of the colony's history. In 1862 Charles Lindsey made a foundational contribution to the liberal reform political narrative with his two-volume biography of his father-in-law, reformer William Lyon Mackenzie, incorporating an account of the 1837 Rebellion. Other writers focused on different historical actors and events. Fugitive slave narratives published in 1855 by Boston abolitionist Benjamin Drew told readers about slavery in the American South and the escape to freedom in Canada, as well as details about individual, family, and community histories in the United States and in Canada West. While indigenous communities used oral narratives, ritual, and performance to transmit their histories, prominent Upper Canadian Ojibwas George Copway and Peter Jones published narratives of the Ojibwa people of the Great Lakes area: Copway's 1850 *Traditional History and Characteristic Sketches of the Ojibway Nation* and Jones's 1860 *History of the Ojebway Indians*. In the twentieth century, Gerald Craig's 1963 history of Upper Canada (1784–1841), reissued in 2013 with a new introduction by Jeffrey McNairn, and J. M. S. Careless's 1967 study of the union of Upper and Lower Canada or Ontario and Quebec (1841–1857) are central surveys. Peter Baskerville's 2005 *Sites of Power: A Concise History of Ontario* is an important work that incorporates a range of recent scholarship.

The War of 1812 became a key event in public commemorations of the colony's history, starting in the 1820s with the erection of monuments to British General Isaac Brock. In the 1850s and 1860s some two dozen local histories were published: the first history of an Ontario county was James Croil's 1861 study of Dundas. However, the "heyday" of local history in the province began in the 1880s, sparked by the desire to commemorate the hundredth anniversary of the Loyalist influx following the American War of Independence. Local history societies were founded across the southern part of the province and in Ottawa and tended to focus on the Loyalists, the War of 1812, and the "pioneer past." A small number of influential local history women's organizations wrote about and commemorated the same imperial nationalist subjects as their male counterparts, but were arguably less nostalgic about the drudgeries of pioneer life.

The year 1888 saw the founding of the Ontario Historical Society (OHS), a province-wide group that brought the local groups together for annual conferences and the publication of their work, followed by the formation in 1896 of the United Empire Loyalist Association. Today the OHS publishes a *Bulletin*, a scholarly journal, *Ontario History* (originally *Papers and Records* [1899]), and publications in Ontario history. OHS also promotes a wide range of historical initiatives across the province, honors a range of individuals and institutions with awards, including the Fred Landon Award for the best book on local or regional history, and lobbies government for the protection of the built heritage. The most prominent actors in the latter area, though, have been the Architectural Conservancy of Ontario (1933), academics such as University of Toronto professor Eric Arthur, and local advisory committees set up under the Ontario Heritage Act (1974).

Formed in 1961, the province-wide Ontario Genealogical Society remains very active because of widespread public interest in *family history. The 1970s saw the foundation of a number of new historical societies, sparked by the 1967 Canadian Centennial celebrations and by a desire to address a broader range of Ontario residents' history. In 1976 University of Toronto history professor Robert F. Harney was instrumental in forming with colleagues the Multicultural Historical Society of Ontario. Two years later the Ontario Black History Society was launched and has been influential in having Black History Month formally celebrated in the province. From 1918 to 1960 historian and

University of Western Ontario librarian Fred Landon pioneered this area by writing extensively on the history of African Canadians.

Until the establishment of the Royal Ontario Museum in Toronto in 1912, most museums in Ontario were organized by particular individuals or groups: Mechanics' Institutes, religious orders, colleges and universities, or scientific societies. In 1857 the Superintendent of Education, Egerton Ryerson, set up an Educational Museum in the Toronto Normal School that was used in teacher training. Niagara-on-the-Lake local historian and retired teacher Janet Carnochan was a central figure in the town's museum, which in 1907 opened in Memorial Hall, the first purpose-built museum in the province. Other institutions, of which the Lennox and Addington Historical Society (1907) and the Norfolk Historical Society (1900) are among the oldest, provide both interpretations of local history and research material. University and local libraries' special collections, most notably the University of Western Ontario's Regional Collection, also hold rich resources. Founded in 1903, the Archives of Ontario holds records from the provincial government, the private sector, individuals and voluntary organizations, as well as vital statistics, material pertaining to Native people, visual material, and sound and moving images. On the Six Nations reserve at the Grand River, the Woodland Cultural Centre, founded in 1972, collects and displays the histories of the Anishinaabe, the Whata Mohawks, Six Nations of the Grand River, and the Mohawks of the Bay of Quinte.

Ontario's university history departments have produced MA and PhD dissertations that have contributed to political, social, cultural, and economic history at the local, regional, and provincial levels. Over the last few decades, *public history programs, which frequently feature local history in their graduate students' research, have been established in universities such as Carleton, Waterloo, and the University of Western Ontario. At the elementary level, for at least forty years students have explored the province's pioneer history, often visiting local history museums and pioneer villages. As of 2005, Ontario's high school curriculum includes a course that focuses on local archives and trains students to explore local history topics.

CECILIA MORGAN
UNIVERSITY OF TORONTO

See Canada, local history in; historical markers.

oral history. There are two distinct sources for the widespread and growing interest in oral history in recent decades. Each has relevance for the practice of local history, and each has been intensified by rapidly unfolding new digital capacities for collecting, exploring, and sharing first-person testimonies and narratives bearing on local history.

The first source flows from the recognition that reliance on traditional written documentation is insufficient for more recent history because so much of significance in modern life is simply not captured by such documents. With telephones replacing letter writing, with few crucial meetings or events recorded or noted in detail, with the accelerating onslaught of paper matched by the shrinking number of truly substantive and meaningful documents, those interested in the history of any community, business organization, government agency, or family, need to go beyond the conventional record simply to find out what happened—much less to place it in any framework of understanding. Oral history—the generation, collection, and consequent study of historic documents generated through systematic, recorded interviews—has been one attractive response to this documentary challenge.

A second source of interest flows from the recognition that the traditional documentary record is, in the nature of things, biased toward those with the power, privilege, and the institutional or social standing that generates records in the first place. It is necessarily history from the top down, seen through the eyes of powerful institutions, the press, and those people whose memoirs and letters are more likely to be written, collected, preserved, and published. In this light, oral history has been attractive as a way to alter the historical record fundamentally, not just to supplement it. Oral history has appealed to many as a route to a more democratic history, often written "from the bottom up," by bringing into the historical record those whose experiences, memories, perspectives, and understandings have rarely been included at all as part of history.

Each of these perspectives inevitably comes into play in documenting a community, region, or local institution. But it is important to realize that these are not identical impulses, nor are they even necessarily harmonious. In many projects, significant choices and trade-offs may have to be made between the goals of deepening the historical record and of altering the angle of vision and inclusion more profoundly—that is, whether to use oral history to find better answers to older questions, or to use it to ask and answer very different questions altogether.

As this suggests, turning to oral history is no magic answer to the complex challenges facing local historians, no instant connection to "the voice of the people" or "the way it really was." It is, rather, a complex and powerful historical tool to be used with care and sensitivity.

In this light, even the inherent limitations and disadvantages of oral history offer corresponding opportunities of particular use in the local history setting. For instance, many see oral history as problematic because it necessarily relies so centrally on individual memory; because it involves, by definition, looking back at history and experience from a contemporary vantage; and because oral history is shaped by the questions, comments, and responses of the interviewer. The resulting document is not simply a record of what the interviewee had to say, since questions produce answers and those questions make the interviewer an integral part of the resulting document.

Oral historians respond that every type of historical document has its own peculiarities, problems, and capacities; one needs to be just as careful in assessing the historical meaning and reliability of a newspaper editorial, a government report, or a *diary entry. Just as these documents can be extremely valuable once their particular qualities are taken into consideration, so too oral history interviews become more historically meaningful, rather than less so, when seen as documents providing a unique window onto memory, individual and collective, or as a dialog about historical experience that shows its changing meaning over time and that joins a participant's experience and the perspective of the inquiring expert. Such insights help us see how people understand, represent, and make use of their own history. In this way, oral histories become revealing documents about culture, values, family, and community rather than simply records of facts and events.

In all these ways, oral history enriches the record for local history, and also the process by which this history is preserved, communicated across time and generations, and made a resource for community dialog in the present. But these very qualities suggest one important caveat: for the real value of oral history to flower, it is important to see it as an ongoing process. Interview projects have to be planned carefully, and the resulting documents have to be organized, listened to, studied, used, discussed, and brought into the broader process of historical interpretation. Far too many communities have embarked on oral history projects with great enthusiasm, but deflected or avoided decisions about the more complicated next steps—whether practical ones of organizing, indexing, and transcribing the tape collection so that it is usable, or more demanding ones of editing, selecting, and incorporating oral history documents in actual documentary products or community processes. The result, much too often, is shoeboxes of unorganized, unindexed cassettes and the rapid evaporation of a group's interest and enthusiasm, since first deciding what to do with an oral history collection, and then actually doing it, are so much more daunting, frustrating, and costly than the fun of plunging ahead with interviewing.

The digital age has widened considerably the potential for oral history. It is now much easier to make and preserve (with appropriate backup!) digital recordings; it is increasingly feasible to digitize older collections of analog tape recordings. Once oral histories are in digital formats, it becomes easier to access and work with the real primary source that the method is unique in capturing—voices and (in video) faces, expression, bodies, and home or community contexts. Simple and accessible multimedia tools for "doing something" with these sources bring voice and face and image into range for community presentation, classroom uses, and family engagement. Oral history recordings are rapidly changing from being archival resources only, usually accessed only through cumbersome text transcriptions, into true multimedia resources. Transcriptions themselves have taken on new life because of the power of rapid text and keyword searching, increasingly linkable by time stamps to particular passages of audio or video.

As a result, oral history in many communities is rapidly becoming the most accessible of resources, with samples, whole interviews, and searchable collections commonly reachable in local libraries, schools, community centers, and on the Internet. Even newer modes of access are coming rapidly into play, such as mobile *apps that can access oral histories keyed to GPS coordinates on a tour; smartphone and tablet multimedia e-publications linking interviews to photographs, documents, and other historical *primary sources, and the like. Oral history is playing a key role on an exploding range of modes and models for bringing local history into the life of a community and its schools.

But seemingly dramatic breakthroughs can also serve to intensify, rather than resolve, older, pervasive problems. If the fate of too much community-based oral history projects was disorganized and inaccessible shoeboxes of old cassettes, the fate of too many contemporary projects is likely to be, on the one hand, an overwhelming digital shoebox of recordings posted to websites where they can rarely be meaningfully explored, and, on the other, highly selective productions or presentations drawing from the multimedia power of a collection in ways that cannot begin to represent the range and potential of the content beyond the immediate purpose of the presentation.

The best advice for novice oral historians facing a widening range of choices at every stage in the process is to become more familiar with oral history as a tool and as a surprisingly rich ground for new insights and understandings. Novices should think carefully, from the start, about what to do with the oral history and how to see oral history as a broader process of local history making rather than only as narrow document collecting. And local projects should try to develop, from the start, some sense of how the collection can be made accessible and usable, through application of new digital capacities appropriate to the project and its resources (staff and financial) in scale and sophistication. The more these choices can be clarified up front (from the role of transcription to the extent of *digitization to the development of content-management annotation and indexing), the better the chance for the project to become supportable and self-sustaining, and to accomplish something more than the proliferation of a new generation of shoeboxes.

There are many, many resources available to assist the new oral historian in the local history setting, and to help more experienced ones see their work in a new and more powerful light. The best place to start is the *Oral History Association (www.oralhistory.org), which publishes the *Oral History Review* and a useful pamphlet series, and holds an annual convention that routinely brings together academic, media, educational, and community practitioners in a refreshing and stimulating meeting. Its recently adopted "Principles and Best Practices" document provides an invaluable checklist of basic criteria and suggestions useful in planning any local oral history project.

Two extremely useful anthologies of articles and essays on oral history are Willa Baum and David Dunaway, *Oral History: An Interdisciplinary Anthology*, 2nd ed. (1996); and Robert Perks and Alistair Thomson, *The Oral History Reader*, 3rd ed. (2015). More recent collections bring cutting-edge new digital dimensions into sharp focus: Donald Ritchie, *The Oxford Handbook of Oral History* (2011), and a spirited new collection that has a much broader orbit than oral history but speaks to local history potentials very directly: Bill Adair, Benjamin Filene, and Laura Koloski, eds., *Letting Go? Historical Authority in a User-Generated World* (2011). Willa Baum also wrote the still-useful *Oral History for the Local Historical Society*, 2nd ed. (1977). Among the best of the "manuals" on oral history are Donald Ritchie, *Doing Oral History*, 2nd ed. (2003); and Edward Ives, *The Tape-Recorded Interview: A Manual for Fieldworkers in Folklore and Oral History*, 2nd ed. (1995), which is technologically outdated but filled with the best kind of timeless wisdom and guidance from a master practitioner. Ives's book has also been rendered in a half-hour video, *An Oral Historian's Work*, which is particularly useful for introducing and training community oral historians (Northeast Historic Film, Blue Hills, ME, 04615; (207) 374-2736).

For useful broader reflections growing out of concrete oral history projects, see Paul Thomson and Hugo Slim, *Listening for a Change: Oral Testimony and Community Development* (1995); Paul Thomson, *The Voice of the Past* (1994); Alessandro Portelli, *The Death of Luigi Trastulli and Other Stories: Form and Meaning in Oral History* (1993); and Michael Frisch, *A Shared Authority: Essays on the Craft and Meaning of Oral and Public History* (1990).

Michael Frisch
University at Buffalo, SUNY

541

See Canada, local history in. Nunavut, local history in.

Oral History Association (OHA). Founded in 1966, the OHA works with policy makers, educators, and others to establish best practices and encourage support for oral history and oral historians. With an international membership, OHA serves a broad and diverse audience including teachers, students, community historians, archivists, librarians, and filmmakers. The OHA encourages standards of excellence in the collection, preservation, dissemination, and uses of oral testimony and has established a set of goals, guidelines, and evaluation standards for oral history interviews. The association also recognizes outstanding achievement in oral history through an awards program.

OHA publications include the *Oral History Review*, the U.S. journal of record for the theory and practice of oral history and related fields, published twice each year; the *OHA Newsletter*; and a series of pamphlets, including *Doing Veterans Oral History* (2015). Contact oha@gsu.edu; (404) 413-5751; www.oralhistory.org.

See oral history.

Oregon, local history in. The origins of local and state history institutions in Oregon come directly from the nineteenth-century pioneer settlement experience. Veterans of the overland trail emigration and others who arrived by ship during the 1840s and 1850s gathered as the Oregon Pioneer Association and began publishing annual *Transactions* that included reminiscences, diaries, speeches at pioneer meetings, and

documents in the early 1870s. By 1898, members of the pioneer group succeeded in chartering the Oregon Historical Society (OHS) as a private organization with state blessings. Among state historical societies in the American West, OHS is unusual because it is a private chartered corporation, rather than a state agency. The society headquarters in downtown Portland includes one of the premier historical libraries on the Pacific Coast that holds more than 25,000 maps, 30,000 books, 12,000 linear feet of documents, and 2.5 million images. OHS began publishing the *Oregon Historical Quarterly* in 1900, first as an extension of the *Transactions* but soon including researched articles about significant events in Oregon's past and stands as the journal of historical record for Oregon. OHS also established a book publishing program, which flourished from the early 1970s until it was abruptly discontinued in 2005. Among its most important publications is *Oregon Geographic Names*, perhaps the best state *place-names book in the country. First published in 1928, *OGN* is a fact-filled compendium about local places that includes unique details about place-name origins and the histories of small towns and out-of-the-way areas in the state. *OGN*'s first compiler, Lewis A. McArthur, was a utility industry businessman with a deep interest in local history. His son, Lewis L. McArthur, took up the challenge in 1974 and compilation of the fourth edition. *OGN* is currently in its seventh edition.

County and local historical societies and museums have long been at the center of collecting, preserving, and interpreting Oregon's history. The Or-

This interpretive sign in Courthouse Square Park in Dayton, Oregon, is dedicated to the city's founding fathers. CREDIT: OREGON TRAVEL EXPERIENCE.

egon Museums Association includes more than 200 institutions in its membership. These museums and libraries have substantial holdings of unique materials. County historical organizations have published local and county histories since the 1870s and several have supported local history journals, such as *Cumtux*, published by the Clatsop County Historical Society since 1980. The journal title, *Cumtux*, comes from the Chinook jargon word meaning "to know, to inform." The Southern Oregon Historical Society in Medford, for example, has been an active center for sixty-four years and includes research facilities that include the Peter Britt collection of five thousand glass plate negatives, plus hundreds of *maps and architectural drawings, and over one thousand *oral histories, business records, journals, and *diaries documenting life in southern Oregon. Among other local and regional historical societies are the Columbia River Maritime Museum in Astoria on the lower Columbia River, the Deschutes County Historical Society in Bend, the Lane County Historical Society in Eugene, the Shaw Historical Library in Klamath Falls, the Coos County Historical Society in Coos Bay on the southern Oregon coast, and the Three Rivers Historical Museum in Ontario. There are important caches of local history materials in museums, such as the Eloriaga Museum in Jordan Valley that collects information on Basque immigrants, the Claire McGill Luce History Collection at the Harney County Library in Burns that documents the history of ranching, the High Desert Museum near Bend that tells the history of Oregon's Great Basin

landscapes, and the state-operated Kam Wah Chung Museum in John Day that focuses on Chinese emigrants to the mining country in eastern Oregon.

Perhaps the most significant development in local and regional history collections and exhibits during the last two decades is the emergence of professional archival and museum projects at Oregon's Indian Reservations. The Museum at Warm Springs, a twenty-year project of the Confederated Tribes of Warm Springs Indian Reservation in Central Oregon, opened in 1991 in a stunning building built with local materials and set near the Deschutes River. The main exhibits set out the deep histories of the Wasco, Warm Springs, and Paiute people and focus on events and developments from the Columbia River south to the Deschutes River Basin in Central Oregon. In 1998, the Confederated Tribes of the Umatilla Indian Reservation opened Tamastslikt Cultural Institute, a 45,000-square-foot museum building that includes several exhibit spaces, archives and research library, and substantial artifact collection. Tamastslikt is the only Native American museum on the Oregon Trail.

Most histories of the state include descriptions and discussions of regions and special local areas that have been considered important to larger historical developments. The lesser-known local histories are included in Ralph Friedman's books, *Oregon for the Curious* (1966), *In Search of Western Oregon* (1990), and *The Other Side of Oregon* (1993). Local histories and people in eastern Oregon are the focus of *The Oregon Desert* (1964) by E. R. Jackman and R. A. Long. The stories associated with early Willamette Valley towns are detailed in Howard Corning's *Willamette Landings* (1973). Published encyclopedias of Oregon include the *Dictionary of Oregon* (1956), which was compiled from WPA files on local history research, and *The Oregon Encyclopedia of History and Culture* (2007), a continuing online publication of Portland State University, Oregon Historical Society, and Oregon Council of the Teachers of English. The *Oregon Encyclopedia* won the National Council of the Teachers of English Multicultural Award in 2009, the *American Association for State and Local History Leadership in History Award in 2011, and the Western History Association Autry Public History Prize in 2012. Oregon history is a required school subject in the fifth grade, although many middle and high schools in the state also include Oregon history courses that often include local history subjects.

Local history documentation, preservation, and interpretation through maintenance of historic sites, publications on historic districts, and public events are the work of the Historic Cemeteries Program, Oregon Heritage Commission, and State Historic Preservation Office, all part of Oregon's Department of Parks and Recreation. The Oregon Heritage Commission sponsors an annual Heritage Conference, where the local history advocates gather to present papers and further the preservation of the state's heritage. In 2015, multiple public and private entities launched the Willamette Falls Legacy Project to create a historical park at Willamette Falls in Oregon City, the second largest waterfall by volume in the United States and the site of Native habitation over ten millennia and modern industrial development since the nineteenth century.

WILLIAM L. LANG
PORTLAND STATE UNIVERSITY

See American Indian history; United States, local history in.

Organization of American Historians (OAH). Founded in 1907 as the Mississippi Valley Historical Association, and renamed Organization of American Historians in 1965, The OAH is the Organization of American Historians is the largest professional society dedicated to the teaching and study of American history. The mission of the organization is to promote excellence in the scholarship, teaching, and presentation of American history, and to encourage wide discussion of historical questions and equitable treatment of all practitioners of history. The OAH represents more than 7,800 historians working in the United States and abroad. Their members include college and university professors, precollegiate teachers, archivists, museum curators, public historians, students, and a variety of scholars employed in government and the private sector. The OAH advances the teaching and practice of American history through its numerous publications, programs, and initiatives. Publications include the *Journal of American History* (the leading scholarly journal in the field), the *Magazine of History*, and the *OAH Newsletter*. Contact the OAH at 112 N. Bryan St., Bloomington, IN, 47408; (812) 855-7311; oah@oah.org; www.oah.org.

organizational records, using local. Americans are joiners—always have been. Over time, we've formed organizations around all kinds of commonalities: military service, profession, philanthropic bent, the drive to serve, and dozens and dozens of organizations for youth.

Many of these groups are national: labor unions, veterans' organizations, service clubs, fraternal organizations, and youth organizations. But each of these national organizations relies on a network of fairly independent local chapters or affiliates. Rotary, the Benevolent Protective Order of the Elks, Veterans of Foreign Wars, Boy Scouts, and Girl Scouts all rely on volunteer community leadership to function and thrive. Each of these local chapters, affiliates, councils, or troops has its own local leadership. All keep some sort of records of meetings, membership lists, financial records, and often a visual or artifactual record of their activities in their communities.

The records of these organizations can be a local history bonanza, if you can locate and gain access to them. The Girl Scouts of the USA encourages their local councils to gather and care for their records through professional training offered to volunteer archivists. Most councils are happy to share these records with enterprising researchers. The Boy Scouts, while not having a formalized program of recordkeeping (beyond those legally required), also produce and use an abundance of records that can tell local stories. Supreme Court Chief Justice Warren Burger and Associate Justice Harry Blackmun were Scouts together in Troop 18 on the east side of St. Paul, Minnesota, when they were boys in the early 1920s. The chartering records for that troop reveal

a great deal about the leadership in the community. Troop newsletters, journals, or committee meeting records reveal both service and leisure activities, favorite gathering places, and touchstones of community importance. The lives of adolescents can be revealed in these records. Rotary, Lions, and other service organization records can reveal ongoing community needs.

These records are not always easy to find. Some organizations donate at least their monthly newsletter to a local historical organization. Chapters that have folded, or organizations that no longer exist, sometimes see to the preservation of their history through donation to historical societies or museums. And sometimes, the oldest living member of an organization can pull amazing things out of an upstairs closet. In Boy Scouting and Girl Scouting, there are council-level records that may or may not be available (these organizations take the privacy of living members seriously). However, much can be learned about community leadership through them. Rotary has districts (that sometimes cross state lines), but local clubs may also have long-term members who can tell you where the organization's records are.

Unlike government records, these records cannot be assumed to be open and are not required to be available to anyone outside the organization. But the time taken to locate and secure access to them can be well spent and provide you with information on your community that you might find nowhere else.

CLAUDIA J. NICHOLSON
NORTH STAR MUSEUM OF BOY SCOUTING
AND GIRL SCOUTING

P

pageants. For the first thirty years of the twentieth century, American communities large and small staged pageants, usually featuring large casts of townspeople. The themes of these extraordinary affairs were community development and progress, in which change was seen as a graceful transition that incorporated the values of the past. These pageants contained contradictory themes while stressing the unique identity of each place. David Glassberg has noted that these pageants were a blend of "progressivism and antimodernism." Advocates of pageants viewed them as instruments of "communal transformation, able to forge a renewed sense of citizenship out of the emotional ties generated" (Glassberg, 284). By the 1930s, however, the community pageantry popular in the progressive era was supplanted by more professional dramatic productions such as Paul Green's "The Lost Colony."

See David Glassberg, *American Historical Pageantry: The Uses of Tradition in the Early Twentieth Century* (1990); Michael Kammen, *Mystic Chords of Memory: The Transformation of Tradition in American Culture* (19991); and W. Lloyd Warner, *The Living and the Dead* (1959).

CAROL KAMMEN
TOMPKINS COUNTY (NY) HISTORIAN

See museum theater.

parks. Parks, including greenways, preserves, waysides, recreation areas, and amusement parks, can be windows to a rich past because the history, function, and design of parks typically are associated with some important aspect of local or regional history. Some parks contain one or more historic places that preserve, interpret, or commemorate important events or people. The history of a park's creation may be linked to important social, cultural, or environmental concerns of a particular period of time; oftentimes, pre-park history can tell us something about individuals or groups beyond the founding families or the local gentry. Parks are especially associated with past activities of local women's clubs and garden clubs, local chapters of conservation organizations such as the Izaak Walton League, and patriotic societies such as the *Daughters of the American Revolution. In addition, many parks contain outstanding examples of rustic architecture that link them, historically, to a nationwide movement in the 1920s and 1930s when *landscape architects across the country collectively created a distinctive naturalistic architectural style for parks. Others may be good examples of designed landscapes associated with individual landscape architects or civic planners. Recreation areas and amusement parks can tell us much about the leisure activities and cultural patterns of a local community. Because parks typically are public spaces, they offer abundant opportunities for interpreting local history as well as natural history; for this reason, parks often are components of heritage areas.

In addition to local libraries, historical society collections, regional repositories, and the recollections of long-time residents, researchers may find useful information in the respective state historic preservation offices: reports and surveys of historic buildings, structures, and objects (such as outdoor sculpture), and prehistoric sites. Many websites may contain facsimiles of documents and historical images that pertain to even the smallest communities; see, for instance, the "American Memory—*Library of Congress" website: http://memory.loc.gov. Keith Eggener's *Cemeteries* (2010), a Library of Congress Visual Sourcebook, includes an essay explaining the influence of the nineteenth-century rural cemetery movement on the landscape design of America's first urban parks. Karen R. Jones and John Wills explore the universality and adaptability of the "park" concept in *The Invention of the Park: Recreational Landscapes from the Garden of Eden to Disney's Magic Kingdom* (2005). Good contextual background on the American park movement and the influence of federal spending on parks in the 1930s may be found in Peter J. Schmitt, *Back to Nature: The Acadian Myth in Urban America* (1990), and Phoebe Cutler, *Public Landscape of the New Deal* (1985). On the history of urban parks, Galen Cranz, *The Politics of Park Design: A History of Urban Parks in America* (1982) is still valuable, as is William H. Wilson, *The City Beautiful Movement* (1989). *A Breath of Fresh Air: Chicago's Neighborhood Parks of the Progressive Reform Era,* *1900–1925*, ed. Constance Gordon and Kathy Hussey-Arnston (1989) explores the history of social-welfare campaigns and municipal parks, and *The Park and the People: A History of Central Park* (1992) by Roy Rosenzweig and Elizabeth Blackmar examines the meaning of "public" in public parks. More recent studies that examine urban parks through an environmental lens include Matthew W. Klingle, *Emerald City: An Environmental History of Seattle* (2007) and *Remaking Boston: An Environmental History of the City and Its Surroundings,* ed. Anthony N. Penna and Conrad Edick Wright (2009). William S. Collins, *The Emerging Metropolis: Phoenix, 1944–1973* (2005), a historic resource context study produced for the Arizona State Parks Board, includes a chapter devoted to the significance of parks in Phoenix's post–World War II growth and development. On the parks designed by Frederick Law Olmsted and Jens Jensen, two of America's most influential landscape architects, see Robert E. Grese, *Jens Jensen: Maker of Natural Parks and Gardens* (1992), Lee Hall, *Olmsted's America* (1995), Joan Hockaday, *Greenscapes: Olmsted's Pacific Northwest* (2009), Francis R. Kowsky, *The Best Planned City in the World: Olmsted, Vaux, and the Buffalo Park System* (2013), and Charles E. Beveridge at al., eds., *Frederick Law Olmsted: Plans and Views of Public Parks* (2015). Examples of the roles that local communities have played in establishing state parks may be found in Thomas R. Cox, *The Park Builders: A History of State Parks in the Pacific Northwest* (1988) and Rebecca Conard, *Places of Quiet Beauty: Parks, Preserves, and Environmentalism*

(1997). The social/cultural history of amusement parks as mass entertainment is the subject of Michael Immerson, *Coney Island: The People's Playground* (2002), Gary S. Cross and John K. Walton, *The Playful Crowd: Pleasure Places in the Twentieth Century* (2005), and LeRoy Ashby, *With Amusement for All: A History of American Popular Culture Since 1830* (2006). Daniel Rosensweig, *Retro Ball Parks: Instant History, Baseball, and the New American City* (2005) examines the recent phenomenon of revitalizing urban economies with publicly financed or subsidized ballparks.

REBECCA CONARD
MIDDLE TENNESSEE STATE UNIVERSITY

See Historic American Landscapes Survey; landscapes.

parish histories. See Catholic Church, Appendix B.

passenger lists. Passenger lists contain information about the millions of immigrants who arrived in the United States between 1820 and 1945. A vast majority of the available passenger lists are housed at the *National Archives in Record Group 36. These lists were compiled in compliance with an 1819 Act of Congress that required ships entering U.S. ports from foreign countries to file a list of passengers with the collector of customs. The lists contain name of ship, the master, the port of embarkation, date of arrival, and port of arrival. Included are names of each passenger, age, sex, occupation, name of country of origin, country of intended settlement, and information concerning the cause

of death if it occurred en route. Where the original list has not survived, there is often a copy or an abstract. These can also be found in Record Group 36.

In 1893, the information collected was standardized so that the reports from all ports were the same after that date. There was also increased information about immigrants, including their ability to read and write, marital status, nationality, last legal residence, destination beyond the port of entry, town, city, or country of birth, and previous U.S. residence for those returning to this country. Passenger lists also contain information regarding a passenger's self-reliance and moral character; if the passenger had bought his own ticket or if a contractor had paid for the passage; the amount of money under thirty dollars held by the passenger, what sort of luggage the passenger arrived with, name of relatives or friends that the immigrant hoped to join, if the passenger had been a public ward or had been in prison, and if the passenger was a polygamist. There is also information about the health of the immigrant.

The National Archives has published a *Guide to Genealogical Research in the National Archives* (1982) that includes an introduction to the use of ship passenger lists and a table of information about the availability of information. In addition, *Immigrant and Passenger Arrivals: A Select Catalogue of National Archives Microfilm Publications* (1983) provides more details about which lists are available. *Soundex is used to search the large name indexes.

While the name indexes contain important information, it is important to remember that the book indexes are even more complete and should not be passed by. They are arranged chronologically by date of arrival.

See Frank H. Serene, "American Immigrant Families: Ship Passenger Lists," in *Our Family, Our Town: Essays on Family and Local History Sources in the National Archives*, ed. Timothy Walch (1987). See also the National Archives Microfilm Publication M1066, *The Registers of Vessels Arriving at the Port of New York from Foreign Ports, 1789–1919*, and the *Mortan-Allan Directory of Ship Arrivals*.

RootsWeb has a searchable passenger list database available at http://userdb. rootsweb.ancestry.com/passenger. Searchable passenger list data is also available at *Ancestry.com, Cyndi's List (www.cyndislist.com), and *FamilySearch.org, among other online sites.

See genealogical resources online.

patrilineal. A society where descent is traced through the male line, claiming that descent from a common, often distant, ancestor. Patrilineal is not the same as patriarchies, where rule is centered in men, such as in families that followed biblical injunctions and where the patriarch's word was law, where religious, social, and political functions were often linked to land and possessions.

See clan; matrilineal.

patrimony. Patrimony is generally defined as property that is received as an inheritance or legacy from a father or other ancestors. In the museum context, it usually refers to objects that are associated with the heritage and identity of a people, group (e.g., a clan), community, or nation and that is seen by them as being inalienable, that is, its possession cannot be legally transferred without the express consent of all the people, group, community, or nation. Patrimony might specifically refer to a sacred object, a historical object associated with an event or person of note, a place, a body of knowledge, or anything else that is seen by those who possess or are responsible for it to be inseparable from them and that helps define who they are as a people. Patrimony is not a common concept in the United States, although our national parks, the Declaration of Independence, the Constitution, our flag, and other symbols of our national identity can be regarded as elements of our patrimony.

The patrimony of one group may not be seen as important by others, or its significance recognized by foreign people or governments. This may lead to the destruction or alienation of patrimony either without recognition of the impact of its loss to a group, or specifically because of such recognition. In the latter case we have historic cases of one group seizing the patrimony of another specifically as part of a military defeat, with the strategic intention of demoralizing the conquered (e.g., the English removal of the royal Scottish Stone of Scone to London). Second, patrimony can through time change its home. This refers to so-called new patrimony (e.g., the Mona Lisa being now seen as part of French and not Italian cultural patrimony). Third, some argue that important art works or artifacts should not be seen as primarily associated with one specific nation or people, but instead as works belonging to all humankind, and thus nonpatrimonial except in a universal sense. From this perspective, patrimony that is alienated by war, colonialism, or other mechanisms remains a part of a worldwide heritage, but no longer supports the original owner's identity and heritage since it lies beyond their access, use, and ultimate control. Repatriation restores the control of alienated patrimony to the people and community where it originated and with whom it is affiliated.

Wars, colonial disruptions of traditional indigenous societies, looting, smuggling, and thefts of significant cultural property of all kinds, including patrimony, have been a serious international problem over the past century. These losses, fueled by increasing market values for art and artifacts, have been widespread and massive. As a result, cultural property, repatriation, and preventive actions relating to illicit cultural property acquisition and trafficking have been at the forefront of national and international concerns and resulting conventions. The 1970 UNESCO Convention on the Means of Prohibiting and Preventing the Illicit Import, Export, and Transfer of Ownership of Cultural Property, for example, was one response. It urged countries to adopt laws to protect their heritage, mechanisms to prevent illicit acquisition, and international means to repatriate alienated material. The convention's extensive listing of cultural property that might be of concern included prehistoric, historic, scientific, literary, artistic, natural history, and ethnographic materials as well as others, with the understanding that any or all of these might be important for a na-

tion's heritage. Adopted by the United States in 1983, as well as by more than eighty other countries, the convention has been used to restrict the importation into the United States of archaeological materials from Mexico, El Salvador, Bolivia, Peru, Guatemala, and Mali.

International efforts to confront the illicit alienation of cultural property were also matched by growing national concerns over indigenous materials held by museums and other agencies. These concerns were originated by native peoples, and focused on the repatriation of significant cultural property and, in the United States, human remains. In the United States these concerns ultimately led to the 1990 passage of the *Native American Graves Protection and Repatriation Act (NAGPRA, Public Law 101-601, 25 U.S.C. 3001). Aside from being the most comprehensive cultural property law of its kind, this groundbreaking legislation also specifically addressed patrimony.

NAGPRA mandates the repatriation of Native American human remains to culturally affiliated tribes or individuals, identifies procedures to be followed when planned or inadvertent discoveries of human remains or cultural property are made, prohibits the illicit trafficking of human remains or cultural property, and requires the repatriation of four types of cultural property: associated and unassociated funerary objects, sacred objects, and objects of cultural patrimony. Patrimony is defined in the law as: "objects having ongoing historical, traditional, or cultural importance central to a group or culture as a whole and considered to be or have been inalienable by that group or culture."

Indigenous declarations and convention processes at the international level have also addressed cultural patrimony, including the 1993 Mataatua Declaration on Cultural and Intellectual Property Rights of Indigenous Peoples, which urged recognition of indigenous rights of identification, control, and use of their cultural property; the development of new mechanisms to protect such cultural property; and the repatriation from museums and other agencies of such cultural property as well as human remains. New protocols issued in 1995 for aboriginal and Torres Strait Islander materials in Australia, as well as the 2006 Protocols for Native American Archival Materials, specifically extend the focus on cultural property generally to intellectual property and seek the repatriation of such property. Finally, the adoption in 2010 by the United States of the 2007 United Nations Declaration on the Rights of Indigenous Peoples is an important recognition of the rights of indigenous people to "maintain, control, protect, and develop their cultural heritage" and its associated intellectual property, and to seek restitution of traditional resources that were alienated.

While patrimony, like beauty, may be in the eye of the beholder, its significance to its community cannot be overstated. Because of its nature, its identification and the recognition of its importance may be contentious once it is alienated. The resolution of issues about patrimony therefore requires consultation, patience, respect, and adherence to relevant laws and ethical codes. Museums should expect that there will be an increase in the scope of what is considered patrimony as well as in indigenous concerns across national boundaries about its repatriation.

JAMES NASON
UNIVERSITY OF WASHINGTON

See heritage; intellectual property rights; matriarchy; Native American Graves Protection and Repatriation Act (NAGPRA); repatriation.

pattern books. See architectural pattern books.

Pennsylvania, local history in. Pennsylvania played a pivotal role in the early history and development of the nation and is home to a number of major historical organizations. The Historical Society of Pennsylvania, founded in Philadelphia in 1824, is among the oldest historical societies in the United States. The Historical Society of Western Pennsylvania was formed in 1879 after several previous attempts beginning in 1834. A third of county historical societies date back to the nineteenth century and nearly half were founded between 1900 and 1940. Today, each of the state's sixty-seven counties has an official county historical society, many of which have formal relationships with local governments for funding and archival responsibilities. In addition, many communities have organized local historical societies, mostly dating from the mid-twentieth century, often inspired by interest in local history at the time of the American Revolution Bicentennial or efforts to preserve a local building or historic site.

The organization of the Presbyterian Church in the United States is commemorated in this historical marker at the corner of Arch and North 3rd streets in Philadelphia, Pennsylvania. CREDIT: MAX A. VAN BALGOOY.

A number of statewide nonprofit organizations have been created to support local and state history. The Pennsylvania Genealogical Society, formed in 1892, is now affiliated with the Historical Society of Pennsylvania. In 1905, twelve county historical societies formed the Pennsylvania Federation of Historical Organizations, which incorporated two years later. In 1989, the organization added "Museums" to its name, and more recently changed its name to PA Museums, to better reflect current membership and constituency. The Pennsylvania Historical Association, with a focus on academic studies, organized in 1933 and held its first conference in 1934. Preservation Pennsylvania was established by the Commonwealth's General Assembly in 1982 as a statewide revolving fund to assist in the acquisition and rehabilitation of historic properties. Since then, Preservation Pennsylvania has expanded its role as a private, nonprofit membership organization with a statewide mission to protect and preserve Pennsylvania's irreplaceable historic places.

Pennsylvania's government historical services are consolidated under the Pennsylvania Historical and Museum Commission. In 1903, the Public Records Division of the State Library was created to care for the state's government records and archival collections. A State Museum was established in 1905 as part of the Department of Education. In 1913, legislation was passed, at the request of the Pennsylvania Federation of Historical Organizations, authorizing the Pennsylvania Historical Commission to oversee historical markers, commemorations,

and archaeological investigations. In 1919 the commission acquired its first historic site, Old Economy Village, in Ambridge, last home of the Harmonists. In 1945, the State Archives, State Museum, and Historical Commission were brought together as an independent commission and renamed the Pennsylvania Historical and Museum Commission. Responsibility for *historic preservation was added in the 1960s with the passage of the National Historic Preservation Act.

One of the earliest publications was the state's printing of the first three volumes of colonial records in the *Pennsylvania Archives (1838–1840)*. William Mason Cornell published *The History of Pennsylvania From the Earliest Discovery to the Present Time: Including an Account of the First Settlement by the Dutch, Swedes and English and the Colony of William Penn, His Treaty and Pacific Measures with the Indians* (1876) and Albert Sidney Bolles published *Pennsylvania, Province and State: A History from 1609–1790* (1899). Philip S. Klein and Ari Hoogenboom's *A History of Pennsylvania* (1973) and Randall M. Miller and William Pencak's *Pennsylvania: A History of the Commonwealth* (2002) were both published by Penn State Press.

Pennsylvania has several outstanding journals and popular magazines of Pennsylvania history. The Historical Society of Pennsylvania publishes both a scholarly quarterly journal, *Pennsylvania Magazine of History and Biography* (since 1877) and a popular magazine, *Perspectives.* The magazine of the Historical Society of Western Pennsylvania is *Western Pennsylvania History* and the

Pennsylvania Historical Commission publishes *Pennsylvania Heritage* in partnership with the Pennsylvania Heritage Foundation, its membership organization. *Pennsylvania History: A Journal of Mid-Atlantic Studies* is a quarterly journal published by the Pennsylvania Historical Association (since 1934).

While public support and involvement with history projects tends to be more focused on independent efforts at the local level, one recent exception was a statewide effort to plan Pennsylvania commemorative activities during the 150th anniversary of the Civil War. A website, traveling exhibition, and publications resulted from a broad collaboration of large and small history organizations throughout the state. "The People's Contest," a digital archive project of the Penn State Richard's Civil War Era Center, linked to that statewide effort, continues to identify, digitize, and make available primary resources drawn from both small local historical societies and large major research repositories (http://peoplescontest.librar ies.psu.edu).

Other collaborative digital resources include access to Pennsylvania history *primary sources through the website www.ExplorePaHistory.com. The Philadelphia Encyclopedia project is a civic project of the Mid-Atlantic Regional Center of the Humanities to create a comprehensive history of the city as both a digital resource and print volume.

BARBARA FRANCO
INDEPENDENT SCHOLAR

See historical markers; United States, local history in.

pension records, military. Military pension records are a rich source of information about individual veterans. Several lists of pensioners have been produced. The U.S. Census took special counts of veterans of both the Revolutionary War and the Civil War. In the 1840 *census there were questions for identifying veterans of the Revolutionary War. The data was then extracted and compiled into a separate index. For the 1890 census an entire schedule was designed to capture information about Civil War pensioners or their widows. Although the U.S. Census was limited to Union veterans, some Southern states created pension lists of Confederate veterans for their own use. The schedules provide a useful index to the actual pension records, which can be ordered from the *National Archives. Because the 1890 census was lost, the 1890 Veterans Schedule can be used in its place to identify many heads of *households. In 1883 each state was required to produce a *List of Pensioners on the Roll*. The entire compilation for the country was published as a Senate document: *U.S. Congress Serial Set vol. 2081, Ex. Doc. 84, Part 4*. This list also can be useful in locating records or at least locating veterans. These three lists and many state lists have been *digitized and are searchable through *Ancestry.com (subscription required), but many have been digitized by state archives or historical societies and can be searched for free.

ROBERT KIBBEE
THE HISTORY CENTER IN TOMPKINS
COUNTY (NY)

Pentecost. Pentecost is celebrated by Jews seven weeks after the second day of Passover; it is called Shavuous. Christians celebrate Pentecost on the seventh Sunday after Easter. It commemorates the descent of the Holy Spirit on the Apostles and is also called Whitsunday.

perambulation. We associate the word "perambulation" with William Lambarde (1536–1601), author of *The Perambulation of Kent*, published first in 1570 with many editions thereafter, regarded as the first work of local history. This term came into common use in England, before the publication of Ordnance Survey maps in the later eighteenth century, to designate an annual walk around the boundaries of a parish with the rector, who would recite prayers at various points. Used today, the word means leisurely walking, during which one can gain a close knowledge of a geographic region, its botany, topography, and recorded history. See editorial, *History News* (Summer 1997).

PERSI. See HeritageQuest online; obituaries.

photography. Most local history institutions, regardless of size, level of professionalization, and degree of funding, maintain photograph collections. Museums, historical societies, archives, and libraries (academic, public, and special) all collect photographs. It is not uncommon for folklorists, oral historians, and historic preservationists to also own photograph collections. While documentary photographs dominate such collections, they may also include historic photographs, or copies of historic photographs. Many other offices, both in the government and the private sector, create photographs in the performance of their daily duties. Real estate developers, railroads, and utility companies are just three examples. Photographs are everywhere and can be produced by almost anyone. A large segment of the population now has the capability to take photographs with their phones. Due to this abundance, photographs are documents even the smallest, most poorly funded, local history institution can easily acquire.

These collections include many types of photographs as well as examples of many different photographic processes and formats. Common examples include cased photographs, *cartes-de-visite*, cabinet cards, stereographs, and postcards. They may represent a number of processes: daguerreotypes, ambrotypes, slides, negatives, Polaroids, and digital. They can all be useful. At times even a very "bad" photograph, with little to no aesthetic appeal, can serve a purpose. The only image left of a house long gone may have a thumb covering the top gable yet still be treasured.

The type of photograph, and the photographic process used, can often help date an image. If the photographer is known, details relating to their career, such as when a studio was located at a certain address, can often tentatively place an image in time. It may also be possible to track the history of the studio, using *city directories, phonebooks, the *census, and *advertisements. Images can also be dated by a careful examination of the subjects' *costumes or by other such clues in the photograph. Conventions that apply to painted *portraits also apply to photographs and can be useful in interpreting the image.

Photographs can be exceptional documentary devices. They supply a record of events, places, peoples, and things that may not be documented in any written record. Photographs can, however, be deceiving. A photographer can control what the viewer sees and may be recording with a bias or certain intent. The popularity of digital photography, scanners, and graphic editing software has greatly increased the possibility that an image may be altered. Even historic images can be changed. Convincing alterations that were once only possible in the darkroom, in the hands of a skilled artist, can now be easily accomplished on a home computer by almost anyone. As with any type of document, the photographer's intent should be confirmed with other source types, if possible.

While photographs may be easy to obtain, they require proper storage and care. To ensure longevity, they should be housed in a climate-controlled environment, in archival containers (boxes, folders), protected from light, dust, humidity, and severe temperature changes. How they are handled during research and exhibition is pivotal and a major preservation concern. Photographs are a very impermanent medium. Differing photograph types also have different storage and processing needs. This should be kept in mind when they are acquired.

Photographs can be found in scrapbooks of mixed media and, of course, a wide variety of photo albums. Some of these albums can be inherently destructive to the photos. Beautiful, unique historic images may have been placed in magnetic photo albums, permanently damaging the image and requiring a conservator, and a substantial fee, if it is ever to be removed, and it may never be removed. Yet, this image can still be tremendously valuable to the right researcher.

How a researcher gains access to the images in a photograph collection differs with each facility. Photographs have often not received the intensive cataloging necessary to make them easily available, because cataloging images can be very time consuming. Photographs are almost always unique; they therefore require original cataloging. Many photographs held in archives will be arranged by provenance, which emphasizes the office of origin and not the subject matter, making them difficult to access.

Cataloging, or in archival terms description, can be seen as a preservation measure. The more thoroughly an image is cataloged, or described, the less likely it will be handled for inappropriate reasons. If there is no detailed finding aid, a researcher may need to go through a large number of photographs to find what they need. Even if the researcher is wearing cotton gloves and is delicate in their approach, the potential for damage increases. Some institutions create surrogate images, either scans, photocopies, or copy photos, for researchers to consult in just such situations, thus reducing the physical handling of the original images.

A basic understanding of photographic history can be useful to anyone working with image collections. For example, photography was invented in 1839; therefore, it is impossible to locate photographs of anything that occurred prior to that time. Color photography did not reach true commercial success until after 1935. Nineteenth-century "color" photographs were hand tinted. It is not unusual for such a hand-colored portrait to be misidentified as a painting. Knowledge provides a greater understanding of the images under one's care and how they can meet the needs of researchers.

A strong photograph collection can be a wonderful public relations tool. Probably a more varied group of patrons are interested in pictures than in other types of *primary sources. When an image is reproduced for publication, particularly when it is used in a magazine or newspaper, the name of the institution is brought before a new and larger audience. It is very important when allowing the distribution of images, especially for commercial purposes, to always make the patron aware of any *copyright concerns. In an ideal situation, where the donor held the copyright, the rights were signed over to the institution in the deed of gift. But this does not always happen, and it is not unusual for a local history institution to be unaware of who holds the copyright for a sizable portion of their photograph collection. The importance of adhering to copyright law cannot be overemphasized.

The institution also needs to be aware of any changes, such as cropping or color alterations, that will be done to the image by a researcher. The institution will need to decide whether such alterations will be allowed. Some institutions do not even permit any changes to the image that may "fix" damage or deterioration.

If an image is to be used in a publication, a credit line should be required.

This should be specified in a written policy; it is also wise to request a copy of the final product. These can be very useful tools for tracking how a collection is being used. The sale of images for reproduction will bring the name of the institution into the public eye, but it can also serve as a money-making venture. Reproduction fees will probably not make an institution rich beyond all dreams, but it might finance a few archival boxes.

The rise of digital photography has, of course, impacted local history institutions. Institutions that collect "born digital" images need to consider whether they will keep them solely in an electronic format or if they will also print them. If kept electronically, the files will need to be housed on a secure site. They should also be backed up, preferably in another location. As time progresses and formats change, the files will need to be migrated and migrated again. This is a commitment that will never end. If printed, does the institution have the time and staff to do so? Will they be able to cover the cost of printing paper and toner?

Since digital photography does not require the expense of film and development, amateur photographers tend to take more digital images than they would if using a film camera. Many of the photographs donated to local history repositories are the product of amateur photographers. Digital donations, therefore, tend to be large. The size of such a gift should not scare curators faced with such a collection. These materials will, however, need to be appraised before being added to the holdings. Appraisal is the process by which archivists determine which items are of "enduring value" and should be saved. The value can be informational, evidential, associational, and\or artifactual. In library terms, the donation may need to be "weeded" for images that have no value to the institution and its mission. Even small computer files should not be saved if they have no enduring value.

The Internet has allowed an increasing number of people to access photographic collections. Digital Public Library of America (https://dp.la) is a useful site for research and serves as a gateway to many institutions. The best-known site is "American Memory," a product of the National Digital Library Project of The *Library of Congress (http://memory.loc.gov/ammem/amtitle.html); however, it is possible for many very small, poorly funded institutions to put a sampling of their collection on the web, increasing the visibility of their institutions and their holdings. Posting images on such social networking sites as Flickr and Facebook increases access and promotes the institution. It can also be a useful tool for gathering further details about an image or even assisting in the identification of an unknown photograph.

Digitizing a photo collection, or a portion of a collection, is a useful access tool, but it is not a permanent preservation measure, though it does potentially limit the need for handling the original photographs. If an institution creates digital copies of nondigital photographs in their collection, they also need to make decisions about the long-term care of these "new" images.

Before placing images online, an institution must determine how they want to control the photographs. For example, do they wish to put up high-quality images ready for publication—images that people can use without obtaining permission or paying fees if the institution charges for reproduction or copyright use? Watermarking images with the institution's name is a common practice to control unauthorized distribution.

Photography is also a way to promote contemporary documentation. It can be especially useful when working with children, but the idea of using adults, perhaps even amateur photographers, should not be overlooked. Sending these interested parties out to photograph vanishing houses, cemeteries, their own neighborhoods, and local events is a way to promote interest in your institution. It also gives the participants a sense of what history is and may get them to look at their own world in a new way. Further, it may add many useful images to the collection. It is hard to get people to write insightful *diaries and letters of value to future historians, but it is not hard to get them to take photographs.

A local history collection's finest photographs not only supply evidence and help to document another time or place, but they also make the viewer think. Thus, they not only assist with research; they also stimulate research. At times images can raise more questions than they answer. Photographs can be very powerful documents; they can move us in a way that most textual documents do not. This is why photographs are worth the time, effort, and expense needed to maintain them.

See Susan Sontag, *On Photography* ([1977] 1990); and Michael Lesy's books, *Dreamland: America at the Dawn of the Twentieth Century* (1997), *Time Frames: The Meaning of Family Pictures* (1980), and *Wisconsin Deathtrip* (1973). Also of interest is the genealogy-oriented work of Maureen Alice Taylor, such as *The Last Muster: Images of the Revolutionary War Generation* (2010), along with her guides to dating photographs. *Photographs: Archival Care and Management* by Mary Lynn Ritzenthaler and Diane Vogt-O'Connor (2006) is the definitive source on the care of photograph collections.

MARY K. MANNIX
FREDERICK COUNTY (MD)
PUBLIC LIBRARIES

See digitization; Farm Security Administration photographs; intellectual property rights; postcards; social media.

pietist. Originally this term referred to seventeenth-century German religious persons who emphasized repentance, faith, regeneration, and sanctification. In general, pietists are those who stress the devotional over the intellectual aspects of the Christian religious experience.

Pinterest. See social media.

Place-names. American place-names provide a deep repository of information about a place and those who named it. The majority of place naming in the United States happened in the last 300 years. These names are newer than their counterparts in the Old World, and so, many of their reasons for use are still accessible.

Place-names come in several types. George R. Stewart in his 1970 *American Place-Names* provides a classification scheme by "mechanism of origin" rather than motivation of the namer. There are ten classes in this system, ranging from simple descriptive names (such as Black Rock) to commemorative names (Lincoln City), from manufactured names (Texarkana) to transfer names (Cambridge, Massachusetts). This system helps in organizing large groups of names and in understanding why places may be named what they are when no other information is available.

The study of place-names—toponymy, a subdiscipline of onomastics—is embedded in such fields as geography, anthropology, history, and linguistics, among others. For the local historian, understanding the reason local places were named what they were can help in understanding what the place was like when first settled, what events occurred there, the attitudes of the folks living there to outside events, or what the place meant to the world outside of it. For example, there are several Moscows in the United States that were named because Napoleon was defeated by the residents of Moscow, Russia, in 1812. This event provided an example of courage and standing up for oneself that folks in their little towns thousands of miles away wanted to be a part of (an example of a commemorative name). Other Moscows were named because folks there had come from places that were already named Moscow (a transfer name). And then there was the Moscow that no longer wanted to be associated with the original one when the 1917 Revolution tainted the name, and so the village in New York became Leicester instead. Why Leicester? To conform with the post office and township already named for Leicester Phelps, the son of a prominent judge.

Much of the study of the origins of names has been done by a variety of researchers, some as graduate theses, and others as independent scholars curious to know why places were named what they were. An early compilation is that put out by the United States Geological Survey (USGS) of the Department of the Interior in 1902, *The Origin of Certain Place Names in the United States* by Henry Gannett (1978). Gannett used as his sources a variety of *gazetteers and histories to then put in dictionary form this collection of place-name origins. The New Deal agency, the Works Progress Administration, which published the wonderful American Guidebook series for each state in the 1930s and 1940s, had its researchers find the origins of many place-names. Much of this work has not been published, but that which has is very useful and comprehensive. See, for example, *Palmetto Place Names* (1941). Since these works appeared, there have been many place-name books published for most of the country. When using these, it is best to avoid the ones that restrict themselves to "The 1001 Names of . . ." These cannot tell the whole story. Compilations like Helen Carlson's *Nevada Place Names: A Geographical Dictionary* (1974) are much more useful because in-depth research has gone into the study of every name in the state. The USGS today provides the scholar of place-names with the Geographic Names Information System, a searchable database of all the names in the country, some with their name origins. GNIS can be accessed at http://geonames.usgs.gov.

People name where they live, first, simply as a matter of identification, but the name they give their place then usually means something more than the words themselves. And place naming continues. Today we see naming going on in suburban subdivisions, in street names, in naming or renaming of hills and mountains and streams. Each version of a place-name holds a story that provides an insight into us as we are when we participate in naming the land.

REN VASILIEV
SUNY COLLEGE AT GENESEO

Poles in North America, sources for. See Appendix A.

political history. "All politics is local," wrote former Speaker of the U.S. House of Representatives, Tip O'Neill. By that he meant that most of the time Americans are firmly rooted in their local traditions and concerns when they participate in the political arena. In his own political life, and in his suggestions to others, as he recounts in his autobiography, *Man of the House: The Life and Political Memoirs of Speaker Tip O'Neill* (1987), O'Neill never forgot to keep in close and constant contact with the local community from which he had come, the Irish neighborhoods of Boston and Cambridge, Massachusetts, never to lose touch with the friends and neighbors with whom he had grown up, and never to forget their concerns, large and small. The reward for him and others like him was electoral victory, and the reputation that they took to their graves: that they never forgot where they came from even as they rose to the highest positions within the American political nation.

The notion that all politics is local has more than a public relations element to it, or the demonstration of psychological bonding between leaders and those they lead. In O'Neill's statement lies a number of critical components of U.S. politics through the years. First, there are always local matters that take on political weight, for example, local planning decisions, taxation and development issues, as well as matters related to social concerns: schools, local behavioral ordinances, and the like. The U.S. governmental process has always vested much power in local governments about these matters, and local power struggles result in sharp disagreements when one person's or group's idea or requested action is unwelcome, useless, or devastating to another individual or group. Roads may connect people to markets, schools, and churches, but they also cut through someone's property or change the quality of life in another corner of a town. Where does one put necessary but intrusive community services? "Not in my backyard" is the familiar refrain of many, despite the general benefits gained by all. Such difficulties lead to extensive debate and battles at the electoral and administrative levels to resolve issues that affect people differentially. Robin Einhorn's study of the battles over taxation policy in nineteenth-century Chicago, *Property Rules: Political Economy in Chicago, 1833–1872* (1991), suggests the continuing *relevance and power of such local concerns.

O'Neill's claim that all politics is local has another dimension as well. More often than not, political perspectives and electoral choices at the state and national level have traditionally been set by the experiences of individuals in their original social nexus. A number of community studies—for example, Don Doyle's study of Jacksonville, Illinois, in the mid-nineteenth century, *The Social Order of a Frontier Community: Jacksonville, Illinois, 1825–1870* (1978)—examines how these small-scale socioeconomic dynamics led to political commitments and activity. It is in their formative experiences in home, neighborhoods, and school, that most Americans develop outlooks, commitments, and prejudices, which they then take into larger arenas. The nation's uneasy cultural diversity, often first encountered at home and among neighbors, promoted intense political conflict. Even future prominent political leaders, such as Abraham Lincoln, as Kenneth Winkle describes his background in *Young Eagle: The Rise of Abraham Lincoln* (2001), were rooted in the particular local social and political environment of which they were a part. Another very useful study by Jonathan Rieder, *Canarsie: The Jews and Italians of Brooklyn against Liberalism* (1985), demonstrates how much this remained true in the twentieth century when local battles over housing and schools continued to create searing political confrontations.

In particular, such local divisions led to one's choice of political party. Scholars of voting behavior, such as Paul Bourke and Donald DeBats in *Washington County: Politics and Com-*

munity in Antebellum America (1995), have discovered that amid the closeness of statewide and national elections, at the local level—in townships, wards, and precincts—electoral choice is not all that divided, but highly committed to one party or the other from unit to unit, depending on the ethnic, religious, and economic nature of the people who cluster together in such small-scale places. Different townships, often next to one another, populated by different ethnic and religious groups, have voted differently from one another and have persisted in such differential behavior over long periods of time.

In short, as Samuel P. Hays has effectively argued in his study of the late nineteenth and early twentieth centuries, *American Political History as Social Analysis* (1980), when people voted Democratic or Republican, for Abraham Lincoln, Grover Cleveland, Woodrow Wilson, or Theodore or Franklin Roosevelt, their choice was set less by the quality and nature of the arguments offered by the parties in their national campaigns than by how such arguments were refracted through prisms established in the local neighborhoods where voters had originally ingested their political understanding. It is also of some note how much such refraction was rooted in memories stretching far back in the history of different groups, in the persistent hatred between Irish and British, or Protestants and Catholics, of acts of oppression from long ago, still remembered and passed on from generation to generation. Similarly, Lee Benson's study of New York State in the 1830s and 1840s, *The Concept of Jacksonian Democracy: New York*

as a Test Case (1961), underscores how the tensions that developed between different groups in the New World—between New England "Yankees" and Dutch "Yorkers," for example, as they came in often unfriendly contact in colonial and early national New York over issues never subsequently forgotten—had enormous staying power on the political scene.

U.S. politics always has had a strong organizational component to it, particularly in the structures and actions of the political parties. Political life in the United States originated in local meetings of the party faithful in town, district, and county conventions, where issues were framed and articulated, resolutions passed, and delegates selected to take each locality's message to the next level of political organization such as state conventions. Local newspaper editors trumpeted their party's cause in a persistent drumbeat of demands, reminders, and exhortations addressed to the farmers, workers, and merchants of their neighborhood. Campaign rallies were held in local towns and county seats, addressed by local candidates and reminding everyone of their faith and commitment. Finally, on election day, local party organizers mobilized their followers to get them to the polls, watched over the count at the end of the day, and led celebrations of victory or lamentations about their defeat through the streets and pathways of thousands of local venues. Before the days of radio, movies, and television, such local focus was the heart of the political process and even in a more complicated and far-reaching communications age, many of these activities still occur, echoing moments when much political activity had strong local flavor.

That partisan commitment also worked upward to shape the stance of the national parties. Where should power lie in the American situation: primarily at the level of the national government? Or should power be left to state and local governments who are allegedly more attuned to local needs and wishes? Such arguments over the locus of power have remained a constant of U.S. political confrontation over two centuries as the champions of local control of one's destiny have never lost their force even as the power of the national government has grown beyond measure. In the early years of the republic, Jeffersonians championed state and local power against the national commitments of the Hamiltonian Federalists. As many scholars have demonstrated, throughout the nineteenth century Democrats persisted in that commitment to local control against Whig and then Republican efforts to expand the power of the national state. See, for example, my *The American Party Battle, 1828–1876* (1999).

Interestingly enough, these arguments between the national parties were always shaped by localist perspectives. Democrats firmly argued that the American nation was a wonderful coming together of distinct localities each of whose individual freedom and security within the nation could only be guaranteed by weak governmental power at the center. In contrast, their opponents argued that only the power of a strong national government could guarantee and advance the economic viability and social security of different communities. In the twentieth century, the positions of the two national parties shifted significantly, the Democrats becoming the party of national power, the Republicans that of state and local predominance, but the nature of the general arguments recognizing the vitality of localist commitments and outlooks remained potent even as the nation dramatically changed.

This persistent localist dimension to political choice, activity, and confrontation underscores the need for historians to work extensively in local research resources, in small town newspapers and village courthouse records that help us recapture the issues and events of interest in different places, while providing insight into the perspectives of the people living there. Political historians have learned that they have to reach beyond the large cosmopolitan newspapers, the *New York Times* and the *Washington Post*, to recapture the pith and flavor of what lies behind national outcomes and perspectives. In a research project concerning New York State politics before the Civil War, for example, the scholars involved made sure that they pored over local newspapers, at least one from each party, in every county of the state. These were filled with news of local meetings, of sharp confrontations over one matter or another, with letters and editorials of a highly focused nature, all of which captured, as expected, the localist dimension present, and its interaction with the larger perspectives and issues being argued far away that were shaped and enriched by their origins in the local venues of the state. Research in local historical societies also produced a great deal of biographical and other material about those politically involved, and the issues and actions that rarely made the larger newspapers or the manuscript collections of national figures. In local libraries, historical societies, and county courthouses lies much gold for students of U.S. political history.

JOEL H. SILBEY
CORNELL UNIVERSITY

poll tax. The term comes from poll, meaning "head," and is thus a head tax that is levied upon certain classes of citizens—such as adult males or voters. In this it is distinguished from an income tax, property tax, or sales tax, which is based on a person's income, property, or on a financial transaction. Such taxes were common throughout the United States before the Civil War, especially in the colonial period, but even as late as 1923, thirty-eight states still collected a poll tax. Beginning in 1877 the poll tax gained notoriety as the primary means by which Southern states in the aftermath of Reconstruction restricted access to the ballot. Though aimed primarily at ending African American political participation, the poll tax along with a number of other voter qualifications helped disfranchise many poor whites as well. The tax was usually fairly minimal—$1 was common—and was not collected unless the individual intended to vote. Nevertheless, the tax often involved inconveniences designed to limit the number of people who paid. In some states, for instance, voters had to pay the tax up to eighteen months ahead of time. When they went to cast their ballot, they then had to produce proof that they had paid the tax. Moreover, some states required those who paid to also pay for of all the previous years when they were eligible to vote, whether they had voted or not. Because most poor whites and blacks were deeply in debt, such sums proved impossible to pay. State officials did not prosecute those who never paid the tax if they did not attempt to vote, since the penalty for not paying the tax was loss of suffrage. Although upheld by the Supreme Court for over fifty years, poll taxes for federal elections were abolished after passage of the Twenty-fourth Amendment in 1964. Two years later, the Supreme Court struck down all poll taxes for state and local elections as well. See Michael Perlman, *Struggle for Mastery: Disfranchisement in the South, 1888–1908* (2001). Poll tax records are available online at *Ancestry. com and *FamilySearch.org.

CAROL KAMMEN
TOMPKINS COUNTY (NY) HISTORIAN

poormaster. This municipal official, usually elected and funded with tax monies, was in charge of dispensing the dole to those in need.

popular culture. Popular culture is a word concept often used rather casually and in various ways. It can best be understood in relation to what it is not: high or elite culture, folk or vernacular culture, or mass culture. The first, high culture, has existed for centuries, but received its clearest definition in the nineteenth century as the best that has been thought and said in the world. The second, folk culture, is as old as humankind and refers to a wide range of ordinary and local activities and products, from domestic architecture to the songs distinctive to a particular subculture. The third, mass culture, is a twentieth-century phenomenon made possible by mass communication, mass production, and new technologies of efficient distribution.

Popular culture is usually understood as reaching a much wider audience than folk culture but a smaller one than mass culture. It is associated with commercialized modes of creating and distributing products designed for edification or leisure, such as religious tracts written to disseminate the Protestant Reformation or household objects meant to appeal to the expanding middle class of the eighteenth and nineteenth centuries.

In the United States, popular culture is most closely manifest by and associated with the entrepreneurial desire to make a profit by filling the leisure needs of people in all social classes. Prime examples would be the minstrel show, the songs of Stephen Foster (and, subsequently, the sale of sheet music), dime novels, wild-west shows (associated with Buffalo Bill, especially), the circus (associated with P. T. Barnum, particularly), burlesque and vaudeville, and participatory sports.

Popular culture has been regarded as more interactive and participatory than mass culture. But there are phenomena that illustrate an era of historic overlap between the well-established existence of popular culture and the advent of mass culture. Silent film, comic strips, and comic books become mass culture when they become syndicated nationally. Radio became part of mass culture when local stations joined national networks during the 1930s. Baseball played

in small communities for the pleasure of the community is popular culture, whereas baseball broadcast on national television exemplifies mass culture. Mass culture is more likely to be spectatorial and often passive by comparison to the participatory aspect of popular culture.

MICHAEL KAMMEN
AMERICAN HISTORIAN (1936–2013)

See ephemera; material culture.

population statistics. See census, United States.

portraiture. Portraits are images of specific individuals created for those who knew them personally or admired them as public heroes, political figures, or popular personalities. Portraits were rare in the American colonial period; fewer than 1 percent of people in the American colonies commissioned painted or sculpted portraits, due to their expense and the scarcity of artists to create them. After the American Revolution, the heroes of the new republic were honored in celebratory paintings, sculpture, and prints and from this time forward the demand for public and private portraits increased steadily. Less expensive forms of portraiture, including miniatures, drawings, and silhouettes, became popular as artists responded to the demand, and thus more Americans could afford to have images made of themselves. With the invention of the daguerreotype in 1839 in France and its introduction to the United States, photography became a popular way to satisfy the growing demand for likenesses. At the same time political and cultural heroes continued to be depicted in paintings, sculptures, and prints. In terms of purpose and social role, painted or sculpted portraits made before the mid-nineteenth century differed little in purpose from these photographic portraits, although of course photographs are more easily created and duplicated, and are therefore usually less expensive. Once photography became widely available, painted, sculpted, and printed portraits frequently became expressions of the artist's creativity because the artist was freed from the constraints imposed by the commercial requirement of producing a likeness.

Individual portraits made during the heyday of formal American portraiture often seem distant, cold, and emotionless today. Portraits can become more accessible to viewers through the use of documentation on how the artist and the subject of the portrait, known as the sitter, came together, and when and why the portrait was made. These connections can be documented through detailed biographical information found in artists' records, personal letters and diaries, contemporary newspaper articles, or family histories. Regional portraits can be used in exhibitions and publications to personalize the history of an area or region: its growth, and changes over time; its social and political structures; and its economy. The selection of portraits should include images of political and social leaders as well as those of others whose names or lifestyles are recognizable to the visitor as markers of major milestones in the area's history. Displays of portraits are very successful if they include a variety of images, in terms of the age or ethnicity of the sitter, or a variety of clothing or poses represented, and if the portraits include specific objects, or have unusual settings or backgrounds that personalize the depictions. Unattributed portraits of unidentified sitters can be dated by the style of the clothing and exhibited or published as a visual timeline of fashion and local taste. Identifying and documenting the artists of the portraits can also convey aspects of the locale: were the artists from the area, or were they itinerants? Where were they trained? Is their work nationally or regionally known? Other issues in the study of American portraits include the importance of the taste of the sitter in determining the appearance of a portrait, and the recognition of the emotional aspects of portraiture, which is often the most easily overlooked aspect of a portrait's power to communicate.

Portraiture has often been an imitative, repetitive, and conservative art. The most creative American artists, including John Singleton Copley, Gilbert Stuart, Thomas Sully, and Thomas Eakins, invented new poses and characterizations, and influenced numerous less well-trained or less well-traveled artists. Until recently the history of American portraiture has been included in surveys of American art but the subject has not been the focus of a monographic study. A new publication, *American Faces: A Cultural History of Portraiture and Identity* by Richard H. Saunders (2016), addresses important issues in the history of American portraiture. Many other publications provide documentation on individual artists and portrait formats. These range from catalogs of the collections of portraits in a particular museum or historical society, such as *A Brush with History: Paintings from the National Portrait Gallery* by Ellen G. Miles and Carolyn Kinder Carr (2001), to studies of individual artists' works, and surveys of portraits in a particular state or region, including *Lessons in Likeness: Portrait Painters in Kentucky and the Ohio River Valley, 1802–1920* by Estill Curtis Pennington (2011), and the state-by-state surveys compiled and published by the National Society of the Colonial Dames of America. At times these studies focus on stylistic types of portraits, such as colonial, neoclassical, Romantic, and "folk" or "naïve," as for example *American Folk Portraits: Paintings and Drawings from the Abby Aldrich Rockefeller Folk Art Center* (1981). Many studies focus on portraits of single sitters, usually notable or frequently depicted public figures such as Benjamin Franklin, George Washington, and Abraham Lincoln. The most talented and influential portrait painters are well documented by single studies of their work in monographs or exhibition catalogs. And the work of regional artists who imitated them has also become well known through individual publications and exhibitions. Studies of patronage in certain cities or regions, such as Charleston, South Carolina, or New York City, include portraits, while some studies have been made exclusively of portraits of particular social groups, for example, Gwendolyn DuBois Shaw's *Portraits of a People: Picturing African Americans in the Nineteenth Century* (2006). Two databases at the Smithsonian Institution provide information on many painted and sculpted portraits

that are in American public and private collections: these can be consulted on the websites of the *National Portrait Gallery (www.npg.si.edu; see "The Portraits: Research-Catalog of American Portraits") or the National Museum of American Art (www.americanart.si.edu; see "Research"). Websites of other museums include reproductions of portraits in those collections and often offer extensive documentation or analysis of the images and the artists who made them.

ELLEN G. MILES
SMITHSONIAN NATIONAL
PORTRAIT GALLERY

See Archives of American Art; photography.

Portuguese in North America, sources for. See Appendix A.

post office records. While today the post office is usually overlooked, in the past it was one of the most important government agencies for bringing the nation together and disseminating information throughout the country. The local postmaster was the most visible representative of the federal government and he, or she, was an important political appointee during a great part of the nineteenth century. Records relating to the activities of the post office in individual communities can provide extremely detailed and valuable historical information about the economic activity in individual towns.

One of the most important documents in this regard is an obscure government publication known as the *Official Register* (OR). This was a list of every government employee that was published first in 1816 and then every two years from 1817 to 1911. It contained the salary of each employee. For present purposes, the most revealing information in the OR is the listing of the salaries of each postmaster. During the period of publication most postmasters' salaries were a direct function of the amount of business their post office did in a given year. For example, the Concord, New Hampshire, postmaster's compensation in the fiscal year ending 1859 was $1,783. The relevant compensation formula shows that the Concord office did $5,424 in business that year. The major components of this sum were the value of stamps canceled and mailbox rents. It should be noted that, until the middle of the nineteenth century, mailing a letter was an expensive proposition. From 1816 to 1845 postage on a letter going over 400 miles was twenty-five cents, a considerable sum at the time. The amount of business a post office did is a more accurate reflection of the economic activity of the locality than any other available index. Analyses of OR data can reveal changes in local economic trends over the years that would otherwise be harder to identify. Among such effects would be whether, or to what extent, the various nineteenth-century national recessions (e.g., 1837, 1857) affected an individual community. It is very important to note that, for reasons unknown, the 1843 OR reports compensation for a two-year period so those figures must be divided by two to be comparable with data from other years. It is also important to note that the spellings of names in the OR may occasionally be inaccurate. For ex-

ample, the ORs for 1895 and 1897 give the name of the Carmel, New York, postmaster as "J. A. Ziekle." However, his obituary on the front page of the February 17, 1949, issue of the *Putnam County Press*, presumably more accurately, spells the last name "Zickler."

The information in the OR is not only of interest regarding local history, but is also a valuable resource for genealogists since the publication lists the names of each postmaster. Using successive years of the OR can help reveal how long an individual remained in the position in the town. In larger cities and towns, the postmastership was an important political reward for party faithful and for much of the latter nineteenth century it changed hands when the party in power in Washington changed. These changes help explain the political aspects of local history at the town level. In smaller post offices, the postmastership was often passed down through family connections, as was the case in Etna, New Hampshire, where the Spencer/Elder family held the position from 1891 through 1991 with only a twenty-two-year gap from 1929 to 1951. The family association with the position in smaller towns probably reflects the fact that small-town post offices were very commonly in the general store, which itself was often a multigenerational family affair.

While this is not an entry on the OR per se, it is worth mentioning here that the OR lists *all* federal government employees, not just postmasters. Initially produced in one volume, by the 1870s it was big enough to be split into two separate volumes, with volume two covering only postal employees. An idea of the completeness of the lists can be seen from the fact that the 1885 volume two, for the postal service, measures about 7.5 inches by 11.25 inches and is 1,056 pages long. In addition to postmasters, it lists mail contractors, who carried the mail, mail messengers, and employees of the Railway Mail Service. For some of these positions the lists include where the individual was born. The listings in volume one cover all other government employees in the executive, legislative, and judicial branches and also, sometimes, list the state or country in which the individual was born. Such information will be of obvious interest to genealogists.

The Texas Postal History Society has provided links to online scanned copies of the ORs for individual years except 1853. To access these, go to www.texas covers.org, the group's website. Click on the "featured articles" button at the bottom of the page and then on the link labeled "Portal to Official Registrar of the United States." Unfortunately, the scanned copies of the OR online are not searchable. One has to go to the listing for each post office of interest for each year to view the information.

An excellent example of the use of the OR was published by Robert Dalton Harris in *P.S.: A Quarterly Journal of Postal History* (1977, 4, 913). He showed that changes in the figures reported in the OR for several small towns in central New York reflected decreases in the production of glass in the area in the early 1850s. In this way OR data may be used to show shifts in patterns of economic activity and industrialization.

The OR data is much more detailed than even decennial *census data. The OR data is available every two years. The census counted the population of legally defined geographical entities such as a town. But a town could have within it more than a single post office, each serving a different sociological clientele. The town of Hanover, New Hampshire, is a case in point. Hanover is considered one locality as far as the census is concerned. But during different periods of time there were three separate post offices within Hanover—Hanover, which served the town proper and the Dartmouth College community, while the Hanover Center and Etna post offices served more rural groups. Data for each one is listed separately in the OR, allowing for more specific studies of socioeconomic changes in rural areas.

Another valuable resource that the Texas Postal History Society has provided is a link to known scanned postal route maps available online. These maps, first produced by the Post Office Department from the mid-1800s through at least 1970, give detailed information on how mail was transported into, out of, and through individual communities. Following the same route as before, click on the link to "Portal to on-line Post Route Maps of the US." These postal route maps show changes in how a local community was integrated into the nationwide mail communication system over the years.

In addition to published postal records and *maps, actual artifacts of postal operations can reveal a great deal about local history. During the nineteenth and into the early part of the twentieth centuries the day-to-day operation of individual post offices required the use of several different types of financial recordkeeping forms and ledgers. These were designed for the use of the postmaster or clerks but did not have to be forwarded to higher authorities within the postal service. They were much like check records many people still keep. These ledgers are underappreciated as sources of local history. Since they were not designed to be kept permanently they are scarce, but when they turn up can be very informative.

The Putnam County (New York) historian's office has in its collection the *Record and Postal Account Book* of Mahopac Falls, New York, a small town in Putnam County. This lists the monthly value of stamps canceled for the period from April 1892 to December 1894. The value of canceled stamps was used to compute the postmaster's compensation and so these records are quite detailed. By the 1870s Putnam County was a popular summer resort destination where the well-to-do from New York City would vacation. This seasonal activity is reflected in the figures in the record book, which show a dramatic increase in the "value of stamps canceled" during the summer months, especially July and August when the "summer people" were in residence at the many local hotels and boarding houses.

In my personal collection I have the "Domestic Money Order Cash Book" (Post Office Department Form N) from Center Barnstead, New Hampshire, for the years 1895 to 1897. This book was used to record the value of all domestic postal money orders issued and paid each day. Center Barnstead was in an agricultural region. An analysis of the inflow and outflow of money via postal money orders shows a peak of inflow in April and outflow in the fall. These seasonal changes in agricultural income and payment most likely reflect the pattern of the local agricultural economy, although examination of additional such cash books is needed to confirm this idea.

The examples here show the importance and usefulness of examining documents and artifacts related to the post office for local history. Such items can be very informative about economic, political, and social aspects of the history of a locality. Genealogical researchers as well will find them an overlooked source of information on federal employees.

TERENCE HINES
PACE UNIVERSITY

postcards. Government-issued postcards began in Austria in 1869 with the Korrespondenz Karte. Some years earlier in the United States, John P. Charlton of Philadelphia obtained a copyright for a privately printed card decorated with a small pattern. In 1873, the U.S. government issued postal cards of its own, costing one penny each. These were stamped on one side where the address would be added, and plain on the reverse side. Picture postcards in the United States date from 1893. At first these cards carried a picture on one side, the stamp and address on the reverse, and the only space on which to write was around the border. These cards cost two cents to send until 1898, when all postcards could be mailed for one penny. In 1907, the U.S. Postal Service allowed writing on the card next to the address. Nearly one billion postcards traveled through the U.S. mail in 1913.

poverty

The subjects of these first postcards were either sentimental or of particular scenes or buildings, so early postcards are often useful for the local historian in seeing how buildings or streets once appeared. They are often used in "then-and-now books" that document the changes in a community from one time to another. There are a number of books devoted to the cards of a particular locality, and early postcards are sought by collectors. Arcadia Publishing produces a postcard history book series with more than 700 titles available (http://www.arcadiapublishing.com/series/postcard-history-series-books).

The Curt Teich Postcard Archives at the Lake County Discovery Museum at 27277 N. Forest Preserve Road, Wauconda, IL, 60084, houses over 365,000 cataloged postcards, constituting the largest public collection of postcards and related materials. Many of the archives' postcards are available online; links to digital images on their AgPix, Stock Index Online, and Flickr sites, as well as the Illinois Digital Archives, can be found at (http://www.lcfpd.org/museum/research/teich). The museum publishes several books on postcard history and sponsors the biennial Postcard Art Competition/Exhibition (PACE). E-mail teicharchives@lcfpd.org or tel. (847) 968-3381.

Postcrossing emerged in 2005 as a way to use social media to share postcards globally. Participants sign up online at (http://www.postcrossing.com) to send and receive printed postcards; members in over 200 nations exchange postcards at a rate of more than 1,000 postcards per hour.

For further information on postcards, visit the website of the Smithsonian National Postal Museum (postalmuseum.si.edu).

HEATHER A. WADE, CAE
INDEPENDENT SCHOLAR

See photography.

poverty. See failure and local history.

Presbyterian Church, sources for. See Presbyterian Church in America; Presbyterian Church U.S.A.; and Presbyterian Church in Canada in Appendix B.

presidential libraries. The papers of the presidents of the United States were managed in a disorderly fashion for the first century and a half of the nation's history. Some found excellent homes in places such as the Massachusetts Historical Society (John and John Quincy Adams) or in the Library of Congress (Washington, Jefferson, Theodore Roosevelt, and Woodrow Wilson, for example). The descendants of Rutherford B. Hayes built a library on the family's estate in Fremont, Ohio, to house his collection. Unfortunately, the papers of several presidents were scattered (Abraham Lincoln) or lost (John Tyler and Zachary Taylor). In 1939, President Franklin D. Roosevelt set a precedent, followed with modifications, when he placed his papers in a new structure he built with private funds on the grounds of his home at Hyde Park, New York. Roosevelt donated the building and his papers to the federal government for management by the National Archives and Records Administration (NARA).

There are now thirteen federal presidential libraries managed by NARA, spanning the administrations of Her-

572

bert Hoover through George W. Bush. These presidential libraries are built with private funding and ownership is then transferred to NARA when construction is completed. All are open to the public for researchers and visitors to museum exhibits and special events. The libraries are federal facilities, but all are supported to some extent by a private not-for-profit foundation which often assists in the partial funding of museum exhibits, public programs, and outreach to schools. Some of the private foundations operate public policy centers, conference facilities, and think tanks adjacent to presidential libraries.

While the holdings of the libraries vary, collections include the official documents of each president's administration as well as audiovisual materials, artifacts, and manuscripts related to the life and times of the president, his family, and close associates. Increasingly, electronic records comprise a major component of the presidential materials.

In addition to the thirteen federal (NARA) presidential libraries, several diverse institutions operated by state, local, or private entities hold collections related to certain presidents and use the name "presidential library."

NARA (FEDERAL) PRESIDENTIAL LIBRARIES

Herbert Hoover Presidential Library
210 Parkside Drive
PO Box 488
West Branch, IA 52358-0488
Ph: (319) 643-5301
Fx: (319) 643-6045
hoover.library@nara.gov
hoover.archives.gov

Franklin D. Roosevelt Presidential Library
4079 Albany Post Road
Hyde Park, NY 12538-1999
Ph: (845) 486-7770
Fx: (845) 486-1147
roosevelt.library@nara.gov
www.fdrlibrary.marist.edu

Harry S. Truman Presidential Library
500 West U.S. Hwy 24
Independence, MO 64050-1798
Ph: (816) 268-8200
Fx: (816) 268-8296
truman.library@nara.gov
www.trumanlibrary.org

Dwight D. Eisenhower Presidential Library
200 SE 4th Street
Abilene, KS 67410-2900
Ph: (785) 263-6700
Fx: (785) 263-6718
eisenhower.library@nara.gov
www.eisenhower.archives.gov

John F. Kennedy Presidential Library
Columbia Point
Boston, MA 02125-3398
Ph: (617) 514-1600
Fx: (617) 514-1652
kennedy.library@nara.gov
www.jfklibrary.org

Lyndon B. Johnson Presidential Library
2313 Red River Street
Austin, TX 78705-5702
Ph: (512) 721-0200
Fx: (512) 721-0170
johnson.library@nara.gov
www.lbjlibrary.org

presidential libraries

Richard Nixon Presidential Library
18001 Yorba Linda Boulevard
Yorba Linda, CA 92886
Ph: (714) 983-9120
nixon@nara.gov
www.nixonlibrary.gov

Gerald R. Ford Presidential Library
1000 Beal Avenue
Ann Arbor, MI 48109-2114
Ph: (734) 205-0555
Fx: (734) 205-0571
ford.library@nara.gov
www.fordlibrarymuseum.gov

Gerald R. Ford Presidential Museum
303 Pearl Street, NW
Grand Rapids, MI 49504-5353
Ph: (616) 254-0400
Fx: (616) 254-0386
ford.museum@nara.gov
www.fordlibrarymuseum.gov

Jimmy Carter Presidential Library
441 Freedom Parkway
Atlanta, GA 30307-1498
Ph: (404) 865-7100
Fx: (404) 865-7102
carter.library@nara.gov
www.jimmycarterlibrary.gov

Ronald Reagan Presidential Library
40 Presidential Drive
Simi Valley, CA 93065-0699
Ph: (800) 410-8354
Fx: (805) 577-4074
reagan.library@nara.gov
www.reaganlibrary.gov

George Bush Presidential Library
1000 George Bush Drive, West
College Station, TX 77845
Ph: (979) 691-4000

Fx: (979) 691-4050
bush.library@nara.gov
bush41.org
bushlibrary.tamu.edu

William J. Clinton Presidential Library
1200 President Clinton Avenue
Little Rock, AR 72201
Ph: (501) 374-4242
Fx: (501) 244-2883
clinton.library@nara.gov
clinton.library.gov

George W. Bush Presidential Library
2943 SMU Boulevard
Dallas, TX 75205-2300
Ph: (214) 346-1650
Fx: (214) 346-1699
gwbush.library@nara.gov
www.georgewbushlibrary.smu.edu

NON-FEDERAL PRESIDENTIAL LIBRARIES (NOT MANAGED BY NARA)

Rutherford B. Hayes Presidential Center
Spiegel Grove
Fremont, OH 43420

Abraham Lincoln Presidential Library
and Museum
212 N. Sixth Street
Springfield, IL 62701

William McKinley Presidential Library
& Museum
800 McKinley Monument Drive NW
Canton, OH 44708

Woodrow Wilson Presidential Library
20 N Coalter Street
Staunton, VA 24401

Michael J. Devine
Updated by Erin Williams
National Archives
and Records Administration

primary source analysis. The *Library of Congress calls primary sources "history's raw materials." If so, then history organizations are the forges where primary sources are analyzed and connected to broader historical narratives. We often think about visitors seeing the final products of historians' work: reading a published book, viewing a completed exhibit, or taking part in a program. The Information Age has changed how individuals document their own lives and how they access and distribute historical information. This presents opportunity for history organizations to provide the public with guidance on how to navigate this abundance of information both online and offline.

As history organizations work to become more transparent and collaborative institutions, they can harness these raw materials as tools for exploring both historical content and the process of research. Primary source analysis beckons inquiry, which emphasizes the *process* rather than the *conclusion.* Inviting the public to examine original records in exhibitions and programs can bring new perspectives to existing narratives, generate more personal connections with the past, and prompt further inquiry.

History organizations have people with the skills, experience, and knowledge the public will rely on as they learn to work with primary sources, including those found online. Some of the public may be unfamiliar with the concept of "primary sources" altogether or how they are both limited and limitless in what they can tell about the past. Engaging the public in this way transforms the expert into a teacher and the student into a scholar; as Kathleen McLean writes in *Letting Go: Sharing Historical Authority in a User-Generated World,* this approach "expands our definitions of expert and expertise."

Analyzing a primary source begins with fundamental questions such as:

- What kind of source is it?
- Who created it? What is their point of view?
- Who is the audience or user?
- When and why was it created?
- What story does it tell?

Who asks these questions? It can be text on exhibit labels, printed handouts, or digital *apps. It can also be a person, perhaps a museum docent or program facilitator, in dialogue with visitors. Together, history organizations and the public can construct historical narratives.

People today, as in the past, curate their own lives with writing, media, and *material culture. Writing, photos, and videos in particular have become standard digital communication tools, created and shared streams of posts and pictures. People who navigate the digital worlds in which this media circulates understand their power. How can audiences come to see this power as part of a longer story of media development? Words and writing make the qualities of a document multidimensional; the language, vocabulary, grammar, syntax, handwriting or typeface, or even doodles around the margins allow us to talk with people of the past, even when we won't be able to have all the answers. Analyzing media in historical settings can help bring out its relevance as a method of storytelling and source of information. One can ask what story was being told by creating this source, who was telling it, why this method was chosen to tell the story, how it was composed, and what technology was used. By asking these questions, the public may not only see their historical relevance but understand themselves as authors of their own historical record.

The Library of Congress suggests a method of inquiry that invites people to wonder, investigate, construct, express, reflect, and connect. Each phase of this method informs the others (www.loc.gov/teachers/primary-source-analysis-tool).

- *Observe*: What do you notice? What details emerge when you look closely? What did you notice that you didn't expect, cannot explain, and didn't notice earlier?
- *Reflect*: Where do you think this came from? Why do you think somebody made this? What do you think was happening when this was made? Who do you think was the audience? What tool was used to create this? Why do you think this item is important? If someone made this today, what would be different? What can you learn from examining this?
- *Question*: What do you wonder about who, what, when, where, why, and how?

The University of California at Irvine History Project identifies six "Cs" of primary source analysis:

- *Content*: what is the main idea?
- *Context*: what is going on when the source was created?
- *Communication*: what is the point of view or bias? Is the source reliable?
- *Citation*: who is the creator and when was it created?
- *Connections*: what is your prior knowledge about the source or its subject?
- *Conclusions*: how does the primary source contribute to our understanding of history?

These questioning strategies are especially useful in the Information Age, in which hundreds of billions of web pages must be critically examined before taken as quality content. History organizations can hone primary source analysis skills applicable in any place or field of study. Teachers trained in primary source analysis help prepare students for how to analyze information they encounter beyond the classroom, ranging from narratives on display in museums or popular culture. Primary source analysis accounts for 60 percent of *National History Day judging criteria, putting the most emphasis on accuracy, context, analysis and interpretation, how sources were used, and whether research was wide and balanced. Students who participate in National History Day also perform significantly better on standardized tests in multiple subjects including reading, science, math, and social studies. They walk away from the experience with stronger abilities to gather, analyze, and interpret information, skills they carry with them into the future.

The process of discovery through a variety of primary sources makes history more accessible. The National Museum of American History's *Engaging Students with Primary Sources* ties primary source analysis to different learning styles and the theory of multiple intelligences. Because every individual learns differently, having an assortment of primary sources available to examine helps reach more people. A single document or artifact can be a springboard for incorporating other primary sources, bridging more connections between the sources and the stories they each tell.

People also like to feel involved in the process of discovery and contributing to larger projects, as evidenced by the popularity of citizen science. The *National Archives' DocsTeach and Smithsonian Institution's Learning Lab allow users to curate collections of documents and artifacts to tell stories or create activities. A number of *crowdsourcing projects promote primary source analysis. Decoding the Civil War challenges volunteers to decipher coded Army telegrams, while the United States Holocaust Memorial Museum's History Unfolded asks volunteers to probe local newspapers for articles written about the Holocaust during World War II to study how events were reported in the American press. *Digitization projects such as the Smithsonian Transcription Center, in which thousands of volunteers transcribe primary sources such as field journals and business records,

also make documents more accessible for both professional researchers and the public.

At local history organizations, local residents may feel deeply connected to the history that surrounds them, tracing their genealogies back to the first settlers or to momentous historical touchstones. However, that is not always the case. As communities change, history organizations can bring in new perspectives of old stories. Primary source analysis also opens opportunity to view traditional narratives through a new lens. Engaging with primary sources can create not just new perspectives but enhanced relevance to local history. By giving the tools for primary source analysis, history organizations can help empower the public to make sense of both the past and present.

For further information see Library of Congress, "Teacher's Guides and Analysis Tool" and "Primary Source Analysis Tool," Teachers, Using Primary Sources, http://www.loc.gov/teachers/usingprimarysources/guides.html; George Mason University, "Making Sense of Evidence," *History Matters*, http://historymatters.gmu.edu/browse/makesense; National Archives and Records Administration, "Document Analysis Worksheets," Teachers' Resources, Teaching With Documents, https://www.archives.gov/education/lessons/worksheets; Reference and User Services Association, "Primary Sources on the Web: Finding, Evaluating, Using," Resources, http://www.ala.org/rusa/sections/history/resources/pubs/usingprimarysources; and Virginia Tech, "Evaluating Internet Information,"

Evaluating Webpages for Research, http://www.lib.vt.edu/instruct/evaluate.

PAMELA CURTIN
WEST VIRGINIA UNIVERSITY

See digitization; exhibits and local history; historical thinking; radical trust and voice of authority; relevance.

Prince Edward Island, local history in. Although an intense particularism has always characterized Canada's smallest province, the level of heritage awareness associated with it has been cyclical, waxing and waning according to the needs of the present. As in many places, local history activity began as a private initiative, but in recent decades the state has become the dominant partner in funding and directing the preservation and presentation of Prince Edward Island's past.

Organized heritage activity on Prince Edward Island (PEI) dates from the late nineteenth century, when the closure of the settlement period and concern over the province's declining prospects triggered a wave of historical awareness. In 1806, promoter John Stewart published the earliest history of the province, *An Account of Prince Edward Island*, and in 1857, journalist Thomas Kirwan issued a prospectus for a history of the colony, although the work never materialized. The first formal treatment was Duncan Campbell's *History of Prince Edward Island* (1875). Its popularity—it sold over 2,700 copies by subscription—was a harbinger of future developments. In 1880, J. H. Meacham's *Illustrated Historical Atlas of Prince Edward Island* prefaced its cadastral maps and detailed engravings with a substantial historical

sketch. A year later, in September 1881, a group of eminent local citizens established the Prince Edward Island Historical Society with Lt. Gov. T. H. Haviland Jr. as president. It was incorporated the following spring, but quickly lapsed into obscurity. The Prince Edward Island Natural History Society, which followed in March 1889, was also dominated by gentleman amateurs. In 1901, it reorganized as the Natural History and Antiquarian Society, but a slender membership and leadership base contributed to its demise in 1908. There would be no enduring natural history society again until 1969.

Despite such organizational struggles, and the refusal of provincial funding, the flowering of local history continued. *The Prince Edward Island Magazine*, 1899–1905, was weighted toward local history, and in 1906, a massive compendium of historical and genealogical essays, *Past and Present of Prince Edward Island*, appeared. Its coeditor, Judge A. B. Warburton, subsequently authored *A History of Prince Edward Island* in 1923. Five years later, the Cummins Map Company produced its *Atlas of Province of Prince Edward Island*, which included an account of the province's involvement in World War I as well as a rural directory for each island township.

War and depression stunted the subsequent development of local history organizations, but in the early postwar period, the Prince Edward Island Historical Society was revived, this time with a broader membership base, and remained active into the mid-1960s. Its heir was the Prince Edward Island Heritage Foundation, incorporated in

1970 amid a massive, state-led effort to transform the island's economy and society. Rapid change fed local fears that the island's heritage was slipping away, resulting in an unprecedented wave of heritage awareness during the 1970s. Using federal money provided for the 1973 centennial of the island's entry into confederation, the province created a network of small theme museums. These were entrusted to the Heritage Foundation, which in 1983 was reorganized as the Prince Edward Island Museum and Heritage Foundation, a decentralized provincial museum system with broad responsibility for the island's human and natural heritage. The organization today operates seven sites across the island, although the province still lacks a central museum facility.

Heritage developments in local communities have paralleled those at the provincial level. The Garden of the Gulf Museum, the island's first, opened in Montague in 1957. The island's Acadian community established its own historical society as early as 1955, and in 1964 began the Acadian Museum in Miscouche. The Alberton Museum opened the same year. Other constituencies soon followed, and the 1970s spawned dozens of local history societies and museums. Many began and ended with publication of a community history but among the most durable have been the Prince Edward Island Genealogical Society (1976), the Belfast Historical Society (1976), and the Malpeque Historical Society (1979). The Community Museums Association of PEI, founded in 1983, now links nearly forty local museums and societies. In recent years, island history has entered the digital age.

Each major heritage agency and organization has its own website with varying levels of content, but the largest and most eclectic source for local history is probably Dave Hunter's *Island Register*. Over 1,000 maps appear on *The Island Imagined*.

The writing of island history has also kept pace. While D. C. Harvey, Frank MacKinnon, and A. H. Clark each produced early classics, the number and range of publications dealing with provincial heritage has increased exponentially since the 1970s. Hundreds of articles have appeared in the *Island Magazine*, a semiannual popular history journal published since 1976 by the provincial museum. Meanwhile, the island's centennial in 1973 yielded F. W. P. Bolger's *Canada's Smallest Province*. A number of popular histories have followed, although a comprehensive, updated provincial history remains lacking. Bolger, Ian Ross Robertson, J. M. Bumsted, Georges Arsenault, and David Weale head the most recent generation of island historians.

The growing body of scholarship increasingly informs educational curricula in the province. Island history inserts were added to standard primers beginning in the early twentieth century, and in recent decades two grade six texts, Blakeley and Vernon's *The Story of Prince Edward Island* (1963) and *Abegweit: Land of the Red Soil* (1984) were commissioned, with supplemental materials periodically added by the Department of Education. Island history is a social studies option at most senior high schools, although there has been no purpose-written text since Harry Baglole, ed., *Exploring Island History*

579

(1977). Island history has been a staple offering on the curriculum at the University of Prince Edward Island since Bolger created the first survey course in 1970. As of 2016, four island history courses are offered at the university.

Since the 1970s, the island's heritage has increasingly been commodified for tourist consumption, while the local history movement has more or less institutionalized. Islanders' sense of particularism, however, remains and provides perhaps the best guarantee for the continued health of local and provincial heritage.

EDWARD MACDONALD
UNIVERSITY OF PRINCE EDWARD ISLAND

See Canada, local history in.

public health. See health care as local history topic.

public history. The term "public history" has been described by some as a historical field, by others as an approach to historical inquiry, and still others consider it a "movement" (Robert Weible, "The Blind Man and His Dog: The Public and Its Historians," *Public Historian* 28, no. 4 [Fall 2006]: 15). Most public historians credit the late Robert Kelley of the University of California at Santa Barbara with coining the phrase "public history" in 1976 and with creating the first graduate program to train historians in this new area. Kelley was a traditionally trained and academically employed historian who discovered that his particular knowledge of water policy in California interested attorneys and policy makers who wrestled with problems and dis-

putes over that limited commodity in the West. Kelley's experience working in the legal arena combined with the shrinking academic market for historians in the 1970s convinced him that historians were ignoring an opportunity to revitalize their profession.

Robert Kelley defined public history in the first issue of the *Public Historian* as "the employment of historians and the historical method outside of academia" (Robert Kelley, "Public History: Its Origins, Nature, and Prospects," *Public Historian* 1, no. 1 [Autumn 1978]: 16). However, it was clear at the First National Symposium on Public History, held in Montecito, California, in April 1979, that historians, who self-identified as public historians, saw this field of practice in much broader terms. Larry Tise traced the roots of public history to the early twentieth century when professional historians recognized that they needed to address how history was used at the local and state levels. Later, in the 1930s, historians worked to preserve and interpret the nation's historic sites (Larry Tise, "First National Symposium on Public History: A Report," *Public Historian* 2, no. 1 [Autumn 1979]: 60–61). Joel Tarr, who used the terms public and applied history interchangeably, argued that public history needed a theoretical approach to distinguish it from history undertaken in the academy (Joel Tarr, "First National Symposium on Public History: A Report," *Public Historian* 2, no. 1 [Autumn 1979]: 1011). Still, in the academic job crisis of the 1970s and early 1980s, many established historians saw the emergence of public history as a vehicle for the employment of graduate students in new venues. One of the best-known anthologies on public history, *Public History: An Introduction* (1986), acknowledges the vocational aspect of the field by illustrating the wide variety of jobs held by historians outside the university. The authors of *Public History* reflect the diversity of public historians, many of whom have worked for corporations, public and private museums and historical sites, as well as for federal, state, and local agencies.

Many introductory syllabi for public history courses still define the field as a function of employment. However, this definition is far too narrow for most practicing public historians. When not employed as academic historians, public historians gain very little commonality of purpose or perspective by using a definition of what they are not. The presence of a substantial number of directors of public history graduate programs in the *National Council on Public History (NCPH) also suggests that public historians cannot and should not dissociate themselves from their academic brethren. As public historians have engaged with their "publics" during the last thirty years and have honed their skills, they have increasingly recognized the importance of broadening the field's definition.

Methodological emphasis is one way to further define the nature of public history. Public historians are quick to note that they are professional historians first and public historians second. They are trained to employ the same methods and analytical approaches that all historians utilize. A reliance on primary source material, the critical comparison of documentary evidence, and a healthy dose of skepticism characterizes the work of the public historian. But a willingness to operate outside the sometimes-narrow focus of academic history has allowed public historians to experiment with sources and approaches not usually found in a traditional graduate program. Public historians have been quick to embrace the analytical techniques of other disciplines, such as archaeology, anthropology, geography, and numerous natural sciences. You are as likely to find a public historian working in the field with a hard hat or a GPS unit as you would locate one sitting in a library perusing a manuscript collection.

The method of public history also includes the way in which historical thought is communicated to various "publics." Public historians are sensitive to their audience and many would suggest that the way in which we define, work with, and learn from our audience differentiates public history from other fields of history. Borrowing from social science concepts, Rebecca Conard and others have explored the "reflective practice" of public historians and examined the ways in which they interact with others to solve contemporary problems (Rebecca Conard, "Public History As Reflective Practice: An Introduction," *Public Historian* 28, no. 1 [Winter 2006]: 1112). This methodological approach encourages the public historian to embrace the "team approach" to research. The use of historical or interdisciplinary research teams is one of the principal features that distinguish public history graduate programs from graduate training in other fields of history. It also encourages public historians to involve their audiences, patrons, and constituents in the historical process through "shared inquiry." Public historians often look to the users of history to "create a problem-definition that requires an explanation based in *historical thinking" (Noel J. Stowe, "Public History Curriculum: Illustrating Reflective Practice," *Public Historian* 28, no. 1 [Winter 2006]: 47).

All historians employ similar means to communicate their findings through reports, books, lectures, and displays in multimedia format. But the published monograph remains the principal means of disseminating historical knowledge in an academic setting. Public historians, of necessity, have been forced to abandon the traditional written monograph for more accessible modes of communication. Public historians look first to their nonhistorian audience when devising a scheme for what Leslie Fishel has called the "delivery" of history ("Public History and the Academy," in *Public History: An Introduction*, ed. Barbara J. Howe and Emory L. Kemp [1986], 11). They incorporate the oral record, the visual arts, and an interpretation of physical remains as often as they reduce their findings to a written report or a book. The emphasis is on ensuring that history reaches as wide a community as possible and public historians are not bound to a particular format to accomplish this goal.

Expanding on this idea that the public historian's toolbox is designed, in large part, to assist in reaching as broad an audience as possible, the past decade has produced an ever-increasing assortment of digital outlets available to practitioners. In the past decade, the online

availability of historical materials including archival documents, monographs, historic site descriptions, etc., has revolutionized historical research and enabled a wide segment of the public to engage in historical inquiry. Likewise, professional historians have seized on this opportunity to expand their own reach and further localize the nature of their work. Perhaps even more importantly, they have embraced these emerging mediums not merely as research tools but also as methods of reaching out to entirely new audiences in an effort to remain relevant in the twenty-first century. Public historians employ all manner of digital mediums ranging from websites, *blogs, podcasts, streaming video services, mobile *applications, video games, and many more. In short, the modern public historian adapts to whatever form of communication can ensure the widest public audience. In the next decade we will undoubtedly see public historians embracing emerging technological advances in virtual and augmented reality and further connecting with the public through social media outlets and whatever yet undeveloped digital interpretive platforms may arise.

Public history has distinguishable features that set it apart from other areas of history. However, as the field matures, fewer practitioners look to those aspects of their work that separate them from other historians. Rather, they focus on the skills and insights into the past that draw all historians together. Public historians are not confined to any particular topical or geographical area of history. Although it is true that many public historians have long-standing connections to local history—given the interest in employing public historians shown by local historical groups, museums, and interpretive sites—the field also has a growing international perspective. Public historians in the United States have forged strong links to their counterparts in Canada, Australia, and New Zealand, where public history is a definable feature of the historical landscape.

Although the term "public history" has only recently become part of a growing international vernacular, historians around the globe have been engaged with applied history activities for decades. Civilizations on every populated continent have representative museums, archives, and historic sites, and, over the last century, each of these entities has had profound and far-reaching interpretive influences. Further, the more recent applied historical approaches in television, film, and digital media transcend borders, and, through modern distribution methods, now reach a worldwide audience. Accordingly, it is essential to recognize that the practice of public history, as a discipline, was not exclusive to the United States and Canada, but rather a range of internationally defined methodological approaches that evolved simultaneously.

The major difference between international practitioners has been in the designation process, as practicing historians outside North America rarely self-identified as "public historians." Because of the efforts of Kelley and others in the 1970s, applied practitioners in the United States and Canada enjoyed the advantages of a distinctive set of definitions for public history processes, and a term for the practice as a whole. Without this disciplinary foundation, historians elsewhere who work outside of academic settings have faced challenges in receiving proper recognition for their efforts. Fortunately, these circumstances have begun to change. Emerging from efforts of public historians working in Europe, Australia, New Zealand, and elsewhere, collaborations with members of the National Council on Public History in North America have created cross-continental conversations about applied history practice. These early cooperative activities ultimately led to the creation of the International Federation of Public Historians (IFPH). Since then, the organization's membership has continued to grow and has held meetings in Amsterdam; Jinan, China; Bogota, Columbia; and elsewhere.

The combined efforts of the IFPH and the NCPH have actively encouraged the professional identification as a "public historian" to expand internationally. In turn, these cooperative efforts will enable global public historians to learn from each other's accomplishments and collaborate on moving disciplinary practices forward into the future.

Public history has evolved since the 1970s and public historians now see themselves as practitioners of history. They define themselves not by where they work, but by how the engagement of and investment by the users of history provides a unique texture to historical knowledge and makes the profession of history more visible and accessible to larger numbers of people. In this sense, public history may be characterized more as an attitude or perception about the use and value of history than as a distinct field of history.

See James B. Gardner and Peter S. LaPaglia, *Public History: Essays from the Field* (1999); Susan Porter Benson, Stephen Brier, and Roy Rosenweig, eds., *Presenting the Past: Essays on History and the Public* (1986); Barbara J. Howe and Emory L. Kemp, eds., *Public History: An Introduction* (1986); and David F. Trask and Robert W. Pomeroy III, eds., *The Craft of Public History: An Annotated Select Bibliography* (1983). For an international perspective on public history see Holger Hoock, "Professional Practices of Public History in Britain: An Introduction," *Public Historian* 32, no. 3, (Summer 2010): 724; and Lyle Dick, "Public History in Canada: An Introduction," *Public Historian*, 31, no. 1 (February 2009): 714.

ALAN S. NEWELL, PATRICK MOORE, AND TIM ROBERTS
THREE21 INNOVATIONS, LLC

See digital history; National Council on Public History.

public history commons. The Public History Commons is a project of the *National Council on Public History (NCPH), designed to "serve the field by providing a platform where practitioners, scholars, and others with an interest in the presentation and interpretation of history in public can share ideas and resources." Launched in 2012 with the help of the Roy Rosenzweig Center for History and New Media, the commons began as a sister site of the NCPH website and a platform for timely and changing content about the public history field. It housed the History@Work

*blog, the Public History News Feed, the Public History Commons Library, and digital publications from the *Public Historian* journal. In February of 2016, both the commons and History@Work moved to new homes on the National Council on Public History website, ncph.org.

History@Work was the first feature of the commons. It evolved from NCPH's inaugural blog, *Off the Wall*, which was launched in 2010, offering "critical reviews of history exhibit practice in an age of ubiquitous display." At the dawn of the second decade of the twenty-first century, blogging was becoming an increasingly accepted form of historical publishing, proffering an informal platform for historians to opine about their favorite subjects. Unlike journal articles, monographs, and conference papers, blog posts gave historians, museum curators, graduate students, consultants, and others an opportunity to develop their authorial voices, explore new ideas, go off on tangents, and to generally "humanize" their scholarly personas.

History@Work is a multi-authored, multi-interest blog with a lofty mission: "Like the field itself, the blog is designed to blend scholarly, professional, and civic discourse arising from the practice of presenting history in public." A team of lead editors works with topic-specific editors to recruit posts on timely topics in the field and to cover a broad spectrum of interests and constituents. The blog is "lightly peer-reviewed," meaning that every post is reviewed by its author, a topic editor, a lead editor, and a copy editor before being published to the site. Common topics covered include NCPH's annual conference, issues of interests to consulting historians, exhibits and projects (the new home of "Off the Wall"), perspectives of graduate students and new professionals, voices from within the academy, international perspectives, NCPH, and social and environmental issues. The blog is also the venue for digital publications from the *Public Historian*, the field's flagship journal.

History@Work, like other blogs, has the advantage of more rapid publication than traditional journals and makes an effort to "streamline" particularly timely posts in order to encourage lively discussions in the comments section. History@Work also relishes the cross-referencing and indexing capabilities of a system of "tags" that link posts together thematically and geographically. The blog's tag-cloud reveals preferences for "advocacy, *digital history, museums, public engagement, scholarship, and training" along with important forays into questions of "employment, entrepreneurialism, government, memory, methods, and preservation."

In addition to promoting History@Work, the Public History Commons maintains a "blog roll" of other pop-

ular blogs by public historians. The commons also strives to be the go-to place for public history information by sponsoring a news section (currently linked with the *H-Public listserv) and a library that houses stand-alone resources of value to public historians. These include grant-writing guides, recommended reading lists, and best practices documents. The library is also a place to hold a deeper archive of supporting literature for some of the *Public Historian*'s digital articles (for example, files related to the New-York Historical Society's award-winning "Slavery in New York" exhibit profiled in an essay by Richard Rabinowitz published in the August 2013 issue (35, no. 3) of the *Public Historian*. The contents of the commons will continue to evolve in response to the changing needs and interests of the public history community.

ADINA LANGER
KENNESAW STATE UNIVERSITY

See National Council on Public History.

Puerto Ricans in North America, sources for. See Appendix A.

Q

Quakers, sources for. See Society of Friends, Appendix B.

Quebec, local history in. Any overview of local history in Quebec must recognize that Quebec history is both national and local, reflecting Quebec's ambiguous status within Canada. Taken in its national sense, the writing of Quebec history dates back to the first decades of European colonization, with works such as Marc Lescarbot's *Histoire du Canada* (1636). Other works followed in the seventeenth and subsequent centuries, including pioneering nineteenth-century texts in English. From the mid-nineteenth century, French Canadian historians increasingly dominated. Up to the 1950s, while their general histories purported to focus on Canada as a whole, Quebec was typically the central concern. From the 1960s, with the rise of Quebec nationalism, these "national" histories became more overtly focused on Quebec, leading to works such as Paul-André Linteau et al.'s *Histoire du Québec contemporain* (1989) or John Dickinson and Brian Young's *A Short History of Quebec* (2008).

Reflecting both this "national" turn and the linguistic fracture within Canada, Quebec history has developed a distinct status within Canadian history. In 1947, Quebec historians founded their own scholarly society, the *Institut d'histoire de l'Amérique française*, which runs a major annual congress and publishes the *Revue d'histoire de l'Amérique française*. For many Quebec specialists, these are more important than their Canadian equivalents. Quebec also has its own national library and archives (BAnQ—*Bibliothèque et Archives nationales du Québec*—the archives founded in 1920 was merged with the 1967 library in 2004) and its own scholarly granting programs. Quebec history is at the core of the "national" history curriculum in the schools, nominally entitled Canada-Quebec but focusing on Quebec itself and its relations with the rest of Canada. Even in Quebec's francophone universities, "national" historians focus the bulk of their teaching and research on Quebec alone. Quebec's provincially run museums, such as the *Musées de la civilization* (1988) and the *Musée national des beaux-arts du Québec* (1933), also have national ambitions.

This conception of Quebec history as national rather than local has paradoxically led to a vibrant local history scene. Quebec is the only province with a systematic project of regional histories, published since the 1980s, under the aegis of the *Institut national de la recherche scientifique—Culture et Société*. The twenty-two substantial volumes adopt a resolutely local approach and reflect collaboration between academic researchers and more locally based historians.

With a few exceptions such as François Dollier de Casson's *Histoire de Montréal,* written 1672–1673 but not published until 1868, or Alfred Hawkins's *Picture of Quebec; With Historical Recollections* (1834), Quebec local history took off in the mid-nineteenth century, with works such as Louis-Philippe Turcotte's *Histoire de l'Île d'Orléans* (1867) and Cyrus Thomas's *Contributions to the History of the Eastern Townships* (1866). Given the strength of the Catholic church, it is perhaps unsurprising that most local histories were parish histories, a genre much in vogue from the late nineteenth to the mid-twentieth century. The development of a larger network of towns and cities in the twentieth century led to local urban histories, though scholarly work has focused on the larger centers of Montreal, Quebec, Trois-Rivières, and Sherbrooke.

Quebec also has a full complement of local history societies. One of the earliest was the Literary and Historical Society of Quebec, founded in 1824 for a largely Anglophone membership. On the francophone side, one might note the *Société historique de Montréal* (1858). Both are still in operation. Currently, the *Fédération des sociétés d'histoire du Québec* (founded in 1965) has some 200 members, both francophone and Anglophone, and also including local museums. There are also many local history journals, such as *Cap-aux-Diamants.* Strong interest in genealogy in Quebec, along with excellent preservation of sources such as parish records and notarial documents, has contributed to the development of resources that bring together the scholarly community, genealogists, and amateur historians. These include the online database of the *Programme de recherche en démographie historique,* which covers the entire Catholic population of Quebec up to the mid-nineteenth century, and various census *digitization projects.

Quebec has also been a pioneer in ethnology, often as a way of preserving regional cultures and traditions. This began in the first half of the twentieth century with the work of ethnologists such as Marius Barbeau and Luc Lacourcière. In 1922 Quebec also became the first Canadian province to provide legislative protection for its heritage. There is indeed a strong emphasis on *patrimoine,* a notion that has a deeper resonance than *"heritage" and encapsulates both material and immaterial culture, as can be seen in resources such as the *Encyclopédie du patrimoine culturel de l'Amérique française.* The 1972 Cultural Property Act covers documentary heritage, artwork, archaeological and ethnological artifacts, built heritage, and so on. It also regulates the Ministry of Culture's extensive *Répertoire du patrimoine culturel du Québec.*

Also contributing to the strength of local history has been the increasing availability of local sources. Most local Quebec newspapers were microfilmed by the *Société Canadienne du microfilm,* founded in the late 1940s by a Quebec entrepreneur. More recently, both BAnQ and Google embarked on systematic digitization of many Quebec local newspapers. In the 1970s, the archival holdings of BAnQ were decentralized to nine regional centers, providing easier access to local sources. Even older local histories have undergone a revival through projects such as Canadiana.

org, the Our Roots digital library, or archive.org's digitized versions of the Canadian Institute for Historical Microreproductions' comprehensive collection of pre-1920 Canadian imprints.

Local history in Quebec faces many of the same challenges as elsewhere. Minority or disadvantaged groups have generally been underrepresented or absent, as in the case of native peoples, of more recent immigrants, and of women. Even Anglophone heritage has been relatively marginalized, despite groups such as the Quebec Anglophone Heritage Network.

Broader analysis and contextualization are often lacking in amateur local histories, and interpretations are sometimes decades behind what is current in the scholarly community. However, the material exists in Quebec to facilitate building upon the mass of local histories to create a stronger and more nuanced national history of Quebec.

DONALD FYSON
UNIVERSITÉ LAVAL, QUEBEC

See Canada, local history in; patrimony.

R

radical trust and voice of authority. History organizations continue to confront the big challenge of tapping into the so-called Web 2.0 or social media revolution without compromising their expert voice. *Time* magazine's Person of the Year (December 25, 2006) for 2006 was "You"—the many Internet users in the world who are transforming the fabric of the web into personal social commentaries, online communities, and personal collections to share with fellow Internet users. Social media tools give users more opportunity to create their own web content and offer greater potential for them to interact with others in the digital world. Younger social media users have grown to expect that they will be part of the conversation and expect the ability to offer an opinion or contribute content in some form. Not surprisingly this is rightfully alarming to institutions seen by their constituents as a voice of authority. Yes, it offers great potential to engage new audiences, but it seems antithetical to the concept of museums as bastions of expertise and scholarship. However, to ignore social media is to risk alienating your organization from a large percentage of users, specifically the youngest generations, who use social media the most. Social media tools (such as Instagram, Pinterest, Facebook, Flickr, YouTube, wikis, blogs, and others) offer new types of marketing opportunities and new ways to engage young audiences.

But when public trust is involved, the fear of losing control of the message becomes understandable. A 2001 survey by the *American Association of Museums (AAM) found that "museums are the most trusted source of information, ahead of book and television news." (*Museums News*, July/August 2006, 31). Another survey concluded that Americans put more trust in history museums and historic sites as sources for learning about the past than in any other source, including personal accounts from family (Rosensweig and Thelen, *Presence of the Past*, 21).

The tension revolves around control—social media brings a fear that when users contribute, control is forfeited and anything could happen. The notion of "radical trust" springs from this tension. It suggests greater equality between museum and constituent.

According to Darlene Fichter, "Radical trust is about trusting the community. We know that abuse can happen, but we trust (radically) that the community and participation will work. In the real world, we know that vandalism happens but we still put art and sculpture up in our parks. As an online community we come up with safeguards or mechanisms that help keep open contribution and participation working" (http://library.usask.ca/~fichter/blog_on_the_side/2006/04/web-2.html).

There are no easy answers, but many history organizations have found successful ways to solicit and incorporate user generated content (see also crowdsourcing).

Perhaps the question we should be asking is how social media can help us expand our dialogue with the public. The *Library of Congress (LC) took a big step into the arena in January 2008 when they launched a pilot project on Flickr, the photo sharing website. They had three goals: (1) make more people aware that the library has photos to share, (2) gain a better understanding of how social tagging and community input could help both users of collections and the library, and (3) gain experience participating in Web 2.0 communities interested in the LC's collections—ultimately drive traffic to the LC website. The Minnesota Historical Society is another history organization that has experimented with social media. Their Minnesota's Greatest Generation *Share Your Story* website, www.mngreatest generation.org, launched in August 2005. Besides collecting *oral histories, it served to inform the development of an upcoming exhibition.

TIM GROVE
NATIONAL AIR AND SPACE MUSEUM,
SMITHSONIAN INSTITUTION

See blogs; building bridges through local history; crowdsourcing and crowdfunding; social media.

regionalism. Regionalism and the meaning of "place" have been persistent themes in American history, linking specific geographic locales with the people who have inhabited those spaces. "Place absorbs our earliest notice and attention," wrote Eudora Welty, "it be-

stows upon us our original awareness. . . . Sense of place gives us equilibrium; extended, it is sense of direction too." A nation always on the move, Americans crave roots; a nation shunning permanence, we dream of a "homeplace."

Lewis Mumford, one of America's most creative thinkers about cities, planning, technology, and the human condition, identified the "region" as one of the cures for the myriad problems of modern twentieth-century America. The region, he argued, with its small-scale patterns of life, ecological and human balance, and traditions of indigenous people, would counteract the ills associated with a stultifying national consolidation, rampant consumerism, economic centralization, and urban decadence. Central to this bulwark was Mumford's conception of the regional museum, which he described in *The Culture of Cities* (1938) as portraying "in compact and coherent form the actual environment . . . the place: the work: the people in all their ecological relations." The mission of such a museum was to give people a way of "coping with the past, of having significant intercourse with other periods and other modes of life, without confining [their] own activities to the molds created by the past."

Mumford's work on regionalism was written in the context of intense public, academic, and governmental interest in regions from the 1920s through the 1940s. There had always been nostalgic reexaminations of particular localities throughout American history, especially in areas undergoing economic modernization and dislocation. The historian Frederick Jackson Turner (see *frontier thesis) and others in the 1890s produced serious studies of the role of regions in American history and life. But the increasing bureaucratization of U.S. society after World War I, and the alarming deficiencies of the national economic system revealed by the Great Depression spurred renewed and widespread interest in the cultural roots of America, in the various regions that collectively defined the nation. Sociologists at the University of North Carolina, Southern Agrarians at Vanderbilt University, New Deal bureaucrats, artists such as Grant Wood and Ben Shahn, writers from William Faulkner to Sinclair Lewis, musicians and composers such as Woody Guthrie and Aaron Copeland, and many others all looked to the regions to find the meaning of America, according to the historian Richard Maxwell Brown. The objective of much of this examination was reform and renewal, with the implicit (and often explicit) assumption, similar to Mumford's analysis, that what was most vital and real about the United States could be located in the regions.

As relative prosperity returned to America in the 1950s and 1960s, as the Cold War encouraged a consensus interpretation of U.S. history, and as homogenizing influences such as the interstate highway system, television, and the jet airliner seemed to reduce the significance of regional identities, there was a quiescence in the study of regionalism. Since the 1970s, however, regionalism has again received considerable attention. The persistence of distinct regional traits, the increasing interest in local and *family history, the revitalization of the historic preservation movement, the academic interest in history "from the bottom up," efforts at decentralization, and ironically, a backlash from the pervasive homogenizing forces of modern society have all contributed to this "new" regional revival.

In addition to a plethora of academic studies of U.S. regions since the 1970s, and new governmental programs aimed at regional collaboration, many universities have established regional study centers such as the Center for Great Plains Studies at the University of Nebraska, the Center for the Study of Southern Culture at the University of Mississippi, and Appalachian State University's Center for Appalachian Studies. Local museums, historical societies, and other cultural agencies have also focused on region, often to contextualize local histories and experiences with a broader perspective. Under the rubric of "heritage tourism," more museums are turning to collaborations and partnerships to both fund their missions and to help instill in their patrons a more nuanced interpretation of regional identity. Continuing in the tradition of John Cotton Dana and his innovative Newark Museum, and in ways reminiscent of Mumford's concepts, many museums and historical societies have restyled themselves as "history centers," becoming virtual community centers for a wide and diverse range of regional educational programs.

Broader regional coalitions have been encouraged at the state and federal government level. National heritage areas and corridors, under the sponsorship of the *National Park Service, have sprouted since the 1980s, and represent regional collaborative efforts between historical and cultural organizations to define and interpret the distinctive traits of specific regions. As of 2011, forty-nine National Heritage Areas have been designated by Congress. Individual states, such as Pennsylvania, Maryland, and Oregon, have also started their own heritage area programs. All of these initiatives are focused on specific historical legacies of individual regions. But similar to the efforts of the New Deal period, they also include economic and social renewal as principal goals, and closely link *historic preservation, economic (re)development, and tourism. Various other regional humanities centers across the United States, such as the Mid-Atlantic Regional Center for the Humanities at Rutgers University–Camden, focus on the study of a region's history, people, and culture.

There is a certain contradiction, of course, in this interest in regionalism. At the same time that we Americans demand unfettered mobility, fast-food restaurants, and discount superstores, we also crave rootedness, a "sense of place," authenticity, and distinctiveness. We want Lake Wobegon, but we just hope there's a Walmart somewhere nearby. Michael Steiner and Clarence Mondale, in *Region and Regionalism in the United States*, suggest additionally that the very vastness of the United States creates a paradox, "that the larger and more expansive a nation, the more urgent is the need of its citizens for distinctive regional identities." As Nathaniel Hawthorne once confided to a friend, "New England is quite as large a lump of this earth as my heart can really take in."

This complexity and even ambivalence about regionalism and the "real" America, however, is the type of issue of immense interest to a new breed of regional scholar. Steeped in such fields as American studies, postmodernism, and cultural studies, these researchers study not only the "reality" of a region's past, but also more amorphous topics such as how regional identity and consciousness are formed, the "invention" of region, regional relationships of power, and the shifting and overlapping definitions of regions. Edward Ayers and Peter Onuf, in *All Over the Map: Rethinking American Regions*, remind us, for example, that U.S. regions "were never bounded and complete entities." Instead, regions "have always been complex and unstable constructions, generated by constantly evolving systems of government, economy, migration, event, and culture." Regions are not, and never were, static entities, and a certain measure of flexibility is thus required in their study.

Most of all, however, regional study requires an intimate knowledge of place. In *A Continuous Harmony*, Wendell Berry wrote of his understanding of regionalism:

The regionalism that I adhere to could be defined simply as local life aware of itself. It would tend to substitute for the myths and stereotypes of a region a particular knowledge of the life of the place one lives in and intends to continue to live in. It pertains to living as much as to writing, and it pertains to living before it pertains to writing. The motive of such regionalism is the awareness that local life is intricately dependent, for its quality but also for its continuance, upon local knowledge.

The search for local knowledge, for regional renewal, for answers to complex questions about region, for the identification and preservation of distinct regions, is "every American's search," according to the geographer Pierce Lewis, "for reassurance that there are places, however remote, that will survive our frenetic passion for mobility, places where we can go and find the genius loci, alive, healthy, and benevolent."

See Barbara Allen and Thomas J. Schlereth, eds., *Sense of Place: American Regional Cultures* (1990); Edward Ayers, Patricia Nelson Limerick, Stephen Nissenbaum, and Peter S. Onuf, *All Over the Map: Rethinking American Regions* (1996); Wendell Berry, *A Continuous Harmony* (1970); Richard Maxwell Brown, "The New Regionalism in America, 1970–1981," in *Regionalism and the Pacific Northwest*, ed. William G. Robbins, Robert J. Frank, and Richard E. Ross (1983), 37–96; Robert L. Dorman, *Revolt of the Provinces: The Regionalist Movement in America, 1920–1945* (2003); M. H. Dunlop, "Curiosities Too Numerous to Mention: Early Regionalism and Cincinnati's Western Museum," *American Quarterly* 36 (1984): 524–48; Merrill Jensen, *Regionalism in America* (1951); Pierce Lewis, "Defining a Sense of Place," *Southern Quarterly* 17 (Spring/Summer 1979): 24–46; Timothy R. Mahoney and Wendy J. Katz, eds., *Regionalism and the Humanities* (2009); Jay Mechling, "If They Can Build a Square Tomato: Notes Toward a Holistic Approach to Regional Studies," *Prospects* 4 (1979):

59–77; Lewis Mumford, *The Culture of Cities* (1938); Alvin Rosenbaum and Marcy Mermel, "Why Now is the Time to Rethink Regionalism," *Colloqui: Cornell Journal of Planning and Urban Issues* 10 (spring 1995): 31–37; Michael Steiner and Clarence Mondale, *Region and Regionalism in the United States* (1988); John L. Thomas, "Coping with the Past: Patrick Geddes, Lewis Mumford and the Regional Museum," *Environment and History* 3 (1997): 97–116; and Charles Reagan Wilson, ed., *The New Regionalism* (1998).

DEAN HERRIN
NATIONAL PARK SERVICE

See Appalachia.

regionalisms. Regionalisms are those words in a language whose use is restricted to a geographic area. A regionalism may be restricted to a multistate region of the country, a single state, part of a state, or even to an individual city or town. Even a word common to many parts of the country may be a regionalism as long as it is not common in the country as a whole. For instance, although the word "icing" is used across the country, it is a regionalism used less frequently in the northern and Pacific regions. The word's synonym, "frosting," also ranges across the country, but its use is infrequent in the southern half of the country and heavy in the northern and western regions. This example shows that a person from New England or California is much more likely to use the term "frosting" in cases where a person from the South would probably use "icing," though the synonymous term "filling" is found scattered across the Southern states. We can establish these facts because of the intensive work in linguistic geography that has taken place over the last several decades. Linguistic geography carefully plots the regional distribution of words, so that we can confidently state that someone using the term "Kaiser blade" (also called a swingblade) in casual conversation probably lived in the lower Mississippi Valley, and most likely in Mississippi itself.

People often portray regionalisms as quaint dialect terms, interesting only for their divergence from the standard dialect of a language. But such words do the important business of communicating and are valuable as an object of study because of the light they shed on the people using the words. Such words can show us interesting distributions of words, a region's solution to lacunae in the general vocabulary, and a region's interest in maintaining a separate identity. Regionalisms can serve as a way for a group to form a separate geographic identity, and as such they are common in both the rural and urban sections of the country.

As with any words, regionalisms do not maintain an immutable status within any speech community. Some escape the province of one region and become standard terms. For instance, "enchilada" was once considered a regionalism confined to California and the Southwest, but now it is a standard food term in American English. Also, these regional words do not remain in use indefinitely. With the change of generations, we add new words to our vocabularies as others slip away.

The Rhode Island term, "eaceworm," meaning "earthworm," is now obsolete, though it was once considered that state's most common term to describe that animal. "Elbedritsch," a Pennsylvanian term for the quarry of a snipe hunt, has almost dropped out of currency.

Increased mobility and the rise of the mass media over the course of the twentieth and twenty-first centuries have led to some diminution of regional differences in speech in the United States, but linguistic shibboleths endure. During President Clinton's first term in office, he used the term "Adam's off-ox" to the consternation and bemusement of much of the national media. Used chiefly west of the Appalachians and common in Arkansas, this term is usually used in phrases like "I don't know him from Adam's off-ox." Although everyone understood what Clinton meant by this term, few people in the media were familiar with it or even understood that an "off-ox" is the ox on the right-hand side (the far side from the point of view of the driver) of a yoke of oxen.

The range of some regional terms is determined by natural geography itself. For instance, the term "muscadine," a type of American grape, is confined primarily to the range of the fruit itself. A "blue northern" is a cold northern wind that signals a rapid decrease in temperatures and is restricted to Texas, which is where that wind occurs. Similarly, "chinook" is used in the Northwest to describe a wind in that part of the country. The range for the term "fox and geese" (a game designed to be played in the snow) is isolated to the northern, snowy states. The range of "Jersey mosquito" (any large mosquito) is limited almost entirely to New York, New Jersey, eastern Pennsylvania, and the southern New England states, where the word in fact appears to be common.

Some regionalisms arise because they describe an activity limited to or more common in one part of the country. For instance, the verb "fire-hunt" (to hunt animals by shining lights in their eyes at night) is found chiefly in the southern and midland parts of the country, indicating possibly that the activity is more common there than elsewhere. In North Carolina the synonymous term "fire-lighting" is the common term. The near-synonymous "headlighting" is used chiefly in Texas and northern Michigan. "Forty-two" is the name of a card game apparently invented and played almost exclusively in Texas. Although known in other parts of the country, the true range of "lutefisk" centers on Minnesota and its surrounding states and almost nowhere else, since this delicacy is common where Scandinavian immigration was common. The word "baga," a foreshortening of "rutabaga," is common in Michigan, Wisconsin, and Minnesota, probably in part because that is a region of the country where the vegetable is more commonly consumed.

Foreign languages are often the source of regionalisms, since different regions have had varying levels of contact with different languages. "Motte," restricted almost entirely to Texas, meant "a grove of trees, especially if in an open prairie." The source of this word is believed to be the Norman English word "motte," which Irish immigrants brought to Texas in the nineteenth century. "Haole" is a common Hawaiian-language word used in English to describe non-Polynesians, especially whites. The now archaic Dutch word "kill," meaning stream, is common in geographic names throughout the Hudson Valley of New York and other areas of Dutch settlement, and it is still understood by some in the region. "Lagniappe," with its myriad pronunciations, is found chiefly in the Gulf states and especially in Louisiana, since that is where the French language had the greatest effect on the language. The term "gumband" (derived from the German gummiband, meaning a rubber band) is now rare but was used chiefly in Pennsylvania, where the German language continues as a presence.

Many regionalisms serve as examples of a region's inventiveness in naming parts of their world. "Borrow pit" is used in the western part of the country, primarily the Rocky Mountains, for a ditch by the side of the road. Originally, the term was "barrow pit," in reference to the mound made by creating such a ditch, but now those who use the term believe, erroneously, that the term comes from the idea of borrowing the dirt from the ditch to build the adjacent roadway. "Darning needle" is a term for dragonfly that is most common, but now almost unknown, in New York and New Jersey. The use of the term "mall" meaning a highway median strip was almost entirely restricted to upstate New York, just as "maniportia" (delirium tremens) was restricted to Maryland. Similarly, the term "dropped egg," meaning "poached egg," is virtually restricted to New England. The word "duck," used to mean "cigarette butt," is confined to the southeastern United States.

With these examples in mind, it is important to remember that errors in identifying regionalisms are rife, even when carried out by professional language watchers making comparisons of national varieties of English, such as British and American English. Also, all speakers of a region will not necessarily use a particular regionalism even if it is common to that region. Absolutes are lacking. For these reasons, any decisions made about regional linguistic variation should be made only with adequate documentary proof and should probably still contain caveats ("used chiefly in Delmarva," "more common in western New York and the upper Midwest," "apparently restricted to the Ozarks," etc.). One of the best sources of information on regional American English is *The Dictionary of American Regional English*, which is now complete and available online. Although a well-respected and dependable dictionary, some of its conclusions are based primarily on data now decades old, so caution should be used even when using this valuable resource.

GEOFFREY A. HUTH
NEW YORK STATE UNIFIED
COURT SYSTEM

relevance. If something is relevant, it is related or useful to what is happening or being talked about. To assess the relevance of something, a person must know why it matters and how it relates to present activity. People value things that are relevant to them. Value and relevance are intertwined. If something loses its relevance, its value usually decreases (see values of history). The study of history and the lessons one can learn from the past are not automatically relevant to society. Many historic house tours, museum exhibitions, and classroom lectures, for example, can be filled with interesting content but demonstrate no relevance to the audience. Interesting content is not the same as relevance.

When society places less value on history education and practice, it is often because it fails to see them as relevant to current societal concerns, such as the economy, jobs, policy issues, family life, or challenges facing communities. While most people recognize that everything has a history, they don't always understand why they should care about the past.

History organizations that teach history to the public through exhibitions and programs want to be relevant to their communities. To accomplish this, they need to connect their content to their audiences. Whatever the content, good educators strive to make a personal connection to the audience. You can demonstrate why people should care about something when you show how it connects to and affects them: the choices they make in their daily life; the challenges and opportunities their neighborhood must deal with; the religious or political atmosphere in which they operate; the viability of public policies put forward by their leaders.

As national conversations change, so should content discussed at history museums and historical sites. History practitioners should be aware of how their collections and content areas relate to local, state, and national conversations and seize opportunities to participate in these conversations. For example, if a history-related topic such as Confederate monuments suddenly becomes a popular national topic, history organizations should be prepared to show connections between past and present. Or, if an issue with deep historical roots, such as immigration or drug policy, is a main topic of conversation, history organizations have an opportunity to be part of the conversation and provide needed historical context. The facts of a community's history may not change, but what a community considers important changes over time.

The themes of history evolve as well, and museums desiring to stay relevant will adapt. Where past focus was on biography of political leaders and major anniversaries of battles and other events, in recent decades history has broadened to include social history about people from many backgrounds. The topic of slavery has been evolving from something that was too uncomfortable for sites to discuss, to a topic that is increasingly interpreted from many angles and is eagerly sought by visitors. For example, in response to some reactions that ask why it is important to study historical slavery today, President Lincoln's Cottage, a site in Washington, D.C., associated with the *National Trust of Historic Preservation, tackled this head-on. At the site where President Lincoln spent time writing the Emancipation Proclamation, the staff decided to mount an exhibition about human trafficking today. They developed a concurrent student program titled Students Opposed to Slavery that

continued beyond the life of the exhibition and draws student participation from several nations. The National Museum of Civil War Medicine's Letterman Institute uses examples of Civil War medicinal practices to demonstrate the relevance of historical perspectives to modern medical challenges.

The International Coalition of Sites of Conscience attempts to connect past and present "in order to envision and shape a more just and humane future" (ICSC mission statement). The United States Holocaust Memorial Museum in Washington, D.C., offers various programs reaching teen audiences, law enforcement, military leaders, and the legal fields to discuss past and present connections related to political freedoms and civil rights.

Relevancy is not the same as advocacy. While most history organizations are cautious to advocate for issues, they can provide a platform for discussion of the issues without advocating for them. Helping the public to understand the history of issues, the decisions, and the attitudes that brought the past to the point of the present is a responsibility of any history organization.

The History Relevance Campaign is a grassroots effort of leaders in the history field to encourage history organizations to consider their own relevance and to find ways to demonstrate this relevance to their various stakeholders, including funders, community members, local leaders, and others. The more society views history education and practice as relevant, the more their value increases.

TIM GROVE
NATIONAL AIR AND SPACE MUSEUM,
SMITHSONIAN INSTITUTION

See building bridges through local history; slavery interpretation at museums and historic sites.

relics. See patrimony.

religion, history of. The latest edition of J. Gordon Melton's *Encyclopedia of American Religions* (2009) lists 2,300 independent groups placed within twenty-six large "families." Every world religion has multiple listings. Many of the listed organizations are tiny, scarcely more than moveable office addresses that will disappear before the next religious census. Once powerful national denominations are shrinking in size and have learned to value variety. In recent years there has been an astonishing growth in the number of independent megachurches as well as in the number of people who count themselves religious but who belong to no religious organization. The vast array and diversity of institutions suggest a reason that local historians are often the best recorders of what is most interesting about American religious life.

In studying American religion, local historians have sometimes focused on regions. Whitney Cross's *The Burned Over District* (1950) became a model, prompting studies of religion in the Hudson Valley, in southern California, and in *Appalachia. The geographical concentration of some important American religious groups—the Mormons, the Seventh-Day Adventists, the Amish—make them important subjects of local study. For the same reason, Native American religions lend themselves to the talents of the local historian.

From the region, local historians moved down to towns—the communitarians of Amana, Iowa; the Hasidic Jews of Sharon Springs, New York; the Swedenborgians of Bryn Athyn, Pennsylvania; the New Age groups of Sedona, Arizona. Some religious movements erupt for accidental reasons in a particular area and produce sensational headlines—as, for example, the Branch Davidians did in Waco, Texas, in 1993. Local historians more properly concentrate on connections between religion and place that develop over a long period of time.

Place can also be part of a large urban landscape. The shifting ethnic neighborhoods in New York, Boston, Baltimore, Chicago, New Orleans, Santa Fe, and Los Angeles have been sites where immigrants have reinvented the religious traditions of Europe, Asia, Africa, and Latin America. Studies of American Catholicism have long emphasized the local differences that separate ethnic parishes. Robert Orsi, with his studies of the Madonna shrine at Mount Carmel Church in New York City and the St. Jude statue at Our Lady of Guadalupe Church in Chicago, has demonstrated the important cultural issues that can be read from the ritual practices of a single church.

Local historians interested in American religions can make excellent use of interviews. A major challenge is to record oral testimony about the traditions of groups whose written documents are thin. The small African American churches of the South are an example. So are the many scattered Pentecostal churches whose local practices vary enormously. Local historians especially need to collect the written and oral records of recent immigrants to the United States—from

Latin America and the Caribbean, from Asia, and from the Near East. These will be enormously important later in understanding Islam in the United States, Catholic vernacular religions of refugees from Central America, and the practices of Asian churches that dot the neighborhoods of all major cities.

In their various endeavors, local historians share interests with sociologists and anthropologists who are often explicitly trained to focus on the local and particular. Their studies reveal how local history is not parochial history but a chance to interpret religion in concrete situations that reveal the connections between the lived experience of religion and large questions about public and private life. Local history has tied religion to family practices, to gender construction, to the creation of class, to nationalism, and to an immense range of other social and cultural issues.

See Catherine Albanese, *American Religion and Religions* (2006); Robert Orsi, *The Madonna of 115th Street: Faith and Community in Italian Harlem* (1985); Paul Johnson, *A Shopkeeper's Millennium: Society and Revivals in Rochester, New York. 1815–1837* (1978); Amanda Porterfield, *The Transformation of American Religion* (2001); and Robert Putnam and David Campbell, *American Grace: How Religion Divides Us and Unites Us* (2010).

R. LAURENCE MOORE
CORNELL UNIVERSITY

See Appenidix B; oral history

repatriation. In a museum or archive context, repatriation refers to the return of culturally significant property to its country, culture, or community of origin or its individual owner. Repatriation can result from laws that restore ownership rights to property that has been illicitly obtained or transferred, or where evidence is lacking about the circumstances of its original transfer of ownership from its community or nation. In other cases repatriation may be the result of a treaty ending a war or other binding agreements that correct historic wrongs. Whatever its foundation, the future of repatriation as an ethical concept, a legal requirement, and an operational issue for an institution is clearly embedded in its past.

While there are many examples of repatriation that predate World War II, contemporary issues of repatriation are a phenomenon of the last half of the twentieth century, when social, political, and economic forces led to concerns about the source and process of alienation of significant cultural property. During this period there was a sharp increase in the market value of objects of antiquity, ethnographic artifacts, and art pieces. This led to a dramatic and massive international acquisition of objects for personal and institutional (museum and corporation) collections. This collecting was accompanied by an ongoing, widespread, and intensive looting of archaeological sites, illicit object smuggling, collection thefts, and dealing in materials illegally taken from their places of origin. Nearly all of these materials came from poor Third World countries and went to rich Western countries, with the devastating loss of many traditional cultures' material heritage. The lack of protective laws or the means of enforcing such laws in

Third World countries were important contributing factors in this process, as were the disruptions caused by wars. During the same period concerns arose over the ownership of art works and other property taken from European Jews by the Nazi government, with many art works winding up in American and other museum collections, often with flawed provenance. Also, Native Americans and other indigenous peoples began to seek remedies to their historic loss of property during colonial and postcolonial periods.

By the 1960s, widespread public media exposures of the alienation of cultural property led to serious professional and political attention, with both nations and native communities alarmed and outraged by the loss of national treasures, including sacred objects and objects of *patrimony. The resulting 1970 UNESCO Convention on the Means of Prohibiting and Preventing the Illicit Import, Export and Transfer of Ownership of Cultural Property urged, among other provisions, that nations find better ways to protect their *heritage and to ensure the return of stolen cultural objects to other nations, including the passage of new laws. The convention was signed primarily by Third World governments. While the United States did not pass a law implementing certain aspects of the convention until 1983 (Public Law 97-447), it did implement a treaty with Mexico in 1970 for the repatriation of primarily pre-Columbian and colonial period cultural property brought to the United States in contravention of Mexican law. American museum organizations and individual

museums, recognizing the problem, also adopted resolutions and policies against suspect foreign acquisitions, with some also adopting a new Ethics of Acquisition policy proposed by the International Council of Museums in 1970. This policy asked that museums not accept new materials protected by source nation laws unless they were accompanied by legal export and ownership documents.

In the United States, national political attention has focused primarily on continuing Native American concerns over human remains and cultural objects held by museums and agencies, with calls for the repatriation of human remains and cultural property at both state and national levels. The serious ethical and legal issues for repatriation were debated for a number of years, although individual states continued to pass or consider their own repatriation legislation. Finally, in 1990, Congress unanimously passed the Native American Graves Protection and Repatriation Act (NAGPRA, Public Law 101-601, 25 U.S.C. 3001), the first and most comprehensive national law to deal with the repatriation and other disposition of indigenous cultural property and human remains. This law mandates that museums, schools, and government agencies provide detailed information on their Native American cultural property holdings and human remains to potentially affiliated American tribes that are federally recognized, and then engage in consultations with those tribes regarding repatriation or disposition actions. Cultural property, including funerary objects, sacred objects, and objects of cultural patrimony, are eligible for repatriation from institutions to individuals or tribes that establish their affiliation with those objects. NAGPRA's other provisions include penalties for illicit trafficking in restricted materials, procedures for returning human remains to affiliated tribes or individuals, and procedures to be followed when planned research or inadvertent discoveries of materials or human remains are made. While NAGPRA is not without flaws, attempts to provide for the repatriation of cultural heritage to indigenous communities have been made in Australia and Canada and elsewhere.

Unfortunately, looting, thefts, and smuggling continue to be major problems that must be addressed at national and international levels. This has been the focus of a series of international conventions and agreements in recent decades. There has been a corresponding sharp increase in the interest of many indigenous people, and their representatives in the United Nations, in seeking the voluntary international repatriation of culturally sensitive objects now in museums. In other words, the conditions and concerns that led to the 1970 Convention and to NAGPRA have not disappeared; if anything, they will continue to confront museums as major ethical and legal issues. The ethical issue is a human rights and heritage concern that centers on the presence of human remains, and sacred, patrimonial, or illicitly obtained specimens in museum collections. The legal issues are reflected by the international attempts to create new conventions and agreements, the reconciliation of common law versus civil law systems (the Unidroit Convention), as well as by special treaties and customs agreements such as those now in effect between the United States, Mexico, and other nations.

It is also clear that repatriation has sparked new interest on the part of indigenous peoples in other aspects of their traditional cultures, notably traditional intellectual property, which was also collected and placed in museums and libraries. The growing indigenous community movement to regain control over such property represents another, future repatriation issue that lies on the museum doorstep today. Several actions indicate the seriousness of this issue, including 2003 UN Convention for the Safeguarding of the Intangible Cultural Heritage, the 2006 Protocols for Native American Archival Materials, and the Pacific Model Law, among others.

Repatriation is such an important ethical and legal concept that, once under way, it is impossible to imagine that it could be stopped, deterred, reversed, or otherwise eliminated from our professional life. Instead, it is the kind of concept that is likely to lead to expanded perspectives of concern in areas that were not at all originally contemplated. Whether this process will fundamentally change the way in which museum staff and scholars conduct research, document and acquire collections, or even work autonomously all remains to be seen—but all of these are potential outcomes that we must as museum professionals consider when contemplating the volatile future of repatriation.

JAMES NASON
UNIVERSITY OF WASHINGTON

See intellectual property rights; museums, and the matter of ethics; Native American Graves Protection and Repatriation Act (NAGPRA); patrimony.

resorts, historic. Resort destinations have been a part of North American culture from the early days of European settlement. Adopting the practice of their European forebears to resort to spas, colonists visited hot springs in Virginia, Connecticut, and Pennsylvania. But the rise of the nineteenth-century resort hotel and cottage community was, as historians have noted, part and parcel of the modernization of U.S. society. Resorts developed as a result of what historian Jon Sterngrass has called the "general commodification of pleasure," which relied upon new means of transportation, boosters selling uniqueness of place, and all classes of Americans with some disposable income. Resort-going, common among the wealthy during the first half of the nineteenth century, became by the early twentieth century a more widespread pastime, but one stratified by class and separated by race and religion. By the twenty-first century,

Enterprising Americans developed nineteenth-century resorts near mineral springs and waterfalls, in mountainous valleys, and along the coastline. These destinations allowed mostly well-to-do Americans to jettison, in a limited way, the societal strictures of their home communities. Saratoga Springs, a backwater before the American Revolution, became by the 1820s a fashionable resort. At the same time, Newport, Rhode Island, once a thriving port city, was becoming a destination in its own right, with large hotels that hosted patrician clients. Early resorts were made up of hotels and boarding homes surrounded by semipublic and public spaces like promenades, parlors, or tea rooms—spaces where antebellum Americans could mingle, dance, gossip, be seen, and take in the salubrious (in the term of the day) benefits of the sea and mountain air or mineral springs. Resorts offered mobility and a certain amount of freedom, and visitors took part in a fluid transiency that might upset traditional societal mores (that applied to gender, for example). Going away became popular by mid-nineteenth century, as illuminated by an 1855 guidebook that chronicled the growth of eastern resorts: forty were located in the mountains; sixty-nine near waterfalls; eighty near watering places; and 103 in close proximity to mineral springs. And northeastern resort destinations did not draw only local elites; southerners burdened by summer heat found that prewar northern resorts were an attractive getaway.

American resorts changed in style and in geography because of the industrial boom of the Gilded Age. A new era of mass production led to the growth of *popular culture, of which leisure activities were an important part. Nickelodeons, Tin Pan Alley music, and Chautauqua lecture series were part of this growth, but so was leaving one's hometown or city for vacation, whether for the day, week, or entire season. As vacationing became more common, it also became a means for conspicuous consumption, a way for the wealthy to distance themselves from the growth of popular day resorts such as Coney Island (which transformed from an elite resort to one that served the working class in the late nineteenth century). In Newport, the wealthy insulated themselves in private "cottages," away from the hotels that had once been the center of life in the resort town.

Growing transportation networks of the industrial age opened up new vacationing frontiers. Northerners began traveling south as rail made inroads into the Carolinas, Georgia, and then to Florida. Florida towns on the coast—Boca Raton, St. Augustine, and Miami—became destinations for the elite. Many resorted to the South to escape the harsh northern winters and some, like the Welland family in Edith Wharton's *The Age of Innocence*, pointedly assumed that warm southern air was beneficial for respiratory ailments (they were aided by local boosters who touted a healthful southern climate). Other southern points, such as Thomasville, Georgia; Aiken, South Carolina; and areas around Beaufort and Georgetown, South Carolina, became winter retreats for wealthy sportsmen. In addition to the South, *tourism in the West grew in conjunction with the region's settlement by whites. By the turn of the twentieth century, hotels like the Stanley Hotel in Estes Park, Colorado (now the gateway to Rocky Mountain National Park), afforded majestic views of the Rocky Mountains. Even farther west, the "pleasure piers" of southern California drew eastern resort-goers as the "Coney Island of the West." Transportation revolutions also made vacationing easier for the working classes. The subway in New York City, for ex-

ample, made possible an afternoon on the beach at Coney Island.

The proliferation of automobile ownership by the second and third decades of the twentieth century also transformed the resort landscape. Resorts grew in places away from coastlines and mountain ranges, such as rural Michigan, but also began to cater to populations that had been excluded from older resorts. Destinations such as Oak Bluffs in Martha's Vineyard; American Beach near Jacksonville, Florida; and Highland Beach in Maryland catered to upper-class African Americans. The Idlewild community in Michigan began in 1912 as one of the only resorts where blacks could purchase property, and until the 1960s remained a vibrant middle-class resort. In the 1920s, affluent Jewish Americans resorted to the Catskills in New York state and to a number of hotels, including Grossinger's and the Concord, during the summer months. Gay men and women, too, sought places of leisure, particularly after World War II (the war, as has been documented by historians, catalyzed a new articulation of gay culture). Palm Springs, California; Fire Island, New York (and particularly the community of Cherry Grove); and Provincetown, Massachusetts, were popular resort destinations for gays and lesbians by the mid-twentieth century.

By the late twentieth century, and after the Civil Rights Act of 1964 that outlawed segregation, resorts for African Americans and, to a large extent, Jewish Americans dwindled in popularity. With the growing accessibility of air travel in the mid and late twentieth century, U.S. resorts faced competition from destinations across the globe. The result was a move toward a promise of luxury and all-inclusive stays. Mountain and ski resorts, spa resorts, and beachside resorts were and are still popular, but so too are mega-resorts like Walt Disney World in Orlando, Florida—the destination resort extraordinaire. Resort hotels around the country were also less likely to be built and run by local entrepreneurs and more likely to be owned by a corporate hotel chain or development conglomerate. In the twenty-first century, resort-going has not slowed; it is part of the booming tourism industry in the United States, which made up 2.7 percent of the U.S. GDP in 2014.

Scholarship on the history of resorts tends to focus on charting the development of specific resort locales, but there are good overviews of historical tourism and vacationing in the United States. See, for example, Cindy S. Aron's *Working at Play: A History of Vacations in the United States* (1999) and John Sears's *Sacred Places: American Tourist Attractions in the Nineteenth Century* (1999). Works that focus on specific resorts normally offer good overviews of resort-going in America in introductions or early chapters. Jon Sterngrass's *First Resorts: Pursuing Pleasure at Saratoga Springs, Newport, and Coney Island* (2001) compares the pre– and post–Civil War evolution of three well-known resorts. More recent scholarship has focused on resorts that catered to specific populations. Ronald J. Stephens charts the history and development of the Idlewild Resort in *Idlewild: The Rise, Decline and Rebirth of a Unique African American Town* (2013). Andrew Kahrl focuses on black

beachside resorts on the East Coast in *This Land Was Ours: African American Beaches from Jim Crow to the Sunbelt South* (2012). Alison Rose Jefferson also looks at beach resorts, though on the West Coast, in her dissertation, "Leisure's Race, Power, and Place: The Recreation and Remembrance in the California Dream" (2015). Karen Christel Kahulik's *Provincetown: From Pilgrim Landing to Gay Resort* (2007) charts the historical development of that destination, and anthropologist Esther Newton's *Cherry Grove, Fire Island: Sixty Years in America's First Gay and Lesbian Town* (repr. ed. 2014) offers a cultural history of the important mid-twentieth-century gay resort. There are numerous memoirs and a few *oral histories about the so-called Borscht Belt—Jewish resorts in the Catskills—including *It Happened in the Catskills: An Oral History in the Words of Busboys, Bellhops, Guests, Proprietors, Comedians, Agents, and Others Who Lived It,* by Myrna Katz Frommer and Harvey Frommer (2009).

Researching resorts in the United States might begin with period guidebooks. The earliest guidebooks for tourists were released in the early nineteenth century, but with the rise of diverse resort destinations by the 1840s, guidebooks came into increasing circulation. D. Appleton & Co. of New York began a travel series of guidebooks that served tourists traveling in different regions of the United States. Appleton guides targeted the average traveler, including those with families. These and other guides are accessible via the WorldCat catalog and online at HathiTrust digital library (http://hathitrust.org) by running a catalog search for "guidebooks."

The Digital Public Library of America (http://dp.la), which pulls from the collections of an array of institutions, is also a crucial resource in a search for guidebooks; use the site's general search function to locate guidebooks and then refine by location. Other helpful sources are *advertisements in national newspapers such as the *New York Times*; resort menus (which can also be found using the digital collections noted above); and *diaries and journals of travelers.

JULIA BROCK
UNIVERSITY OF WEST GEORGIA

See African American history; LGBT history, interpreting; travel literature.

Rhode Island, local history in. Although Rhode Island and Providence Plantations is the smallest state, it has an impressive number of historical societies, heritage and preservation societies, museum buildings, specialized museums, and National Landmark structures, many of which have archives, docents, and historical programs. These institutions and organizations are situated in every part of the state and often reflect an intense concern by local people to preserve elements of their town's history.

The oldest and most significant historical society is the Rhode Island Historical Society, which was founded in 1822, making it the fourth-oldest state historical society in the nation. Its Mary Elizabeth Robinson Research Center houses the society's manuscript, book, print, photographic, and film collections. It is also the largest genealogical resource in the state. The society also maintains two National Historic Landmark buildings: the Aldrich House (1822) and the John Brown House (1788), the latter as a museum. The society publishes *Rhode Island History*, a peer-reviewed scholarly journal, and maintains the Museum of Work and Culture in Woonsocket, a museum devoted to the ethnic and *labor history of northern Rhode Island. Also in Providence are the Providence Athenaeum, the Providence Public Library, the Special Collections at Rhode Island College and Providence College, and the collections of the library of Brown University. In addition to the private societies, museums, and libraries, the Rhode Island State Archives and the State Library have rich resources.

In 1854 the "Southern Cabinet" of the Rhode Island Historical Society was incorporated as the Newport Historical Society, whose emphasis is on Newport County and which publishes *Newport History*. Newport is also the home of the Preservation Society of Newport County, which has eleven (mostly Gilded Age) mansions and is Rhode Island's largest cultural organization. In addition, there are other privately owned and maintained mansion museums, including Rough Point, the mansion of Doris Duke. Newport's other specialized museums include the Tennis Hall of Fame and Museum, the Museum of Yachting, and the National Museum of American Illustration, which is housed in another Victorian mansion called Vernon Court. The Redwood Library and Athenaeum Museum, founded in 1747, is the oldest lending library in the nation, and it maintains impressive special collections.

A survey of the sector conducted in 2012 by the Rhode Island Historical Society indicated that there are 464 history and *heritage organizations in

Sissieretta Jones is honored by this historical marker in Providence, Rhode Island. CREDIT: SARAH ZURIER, RHODE ISLAND HISTORICAL PRESERVATION AND HERITAGE COMMISSION.

the state. A directory of many of these organizations is maintained by the Rhode Island Historical Society and can be accessed at http://www.rhodi. org. Indeed, most towns and cities in the state have each created either a historical society or a heritage and preservation society, devoted to preserving and presenting local history. The Providence Preservation Society, founded in 1956, brought about the creation of the College Hill Historic District, the first such district in the state. By 2004 all but four towns had historic districts, and Providence had thirty. In addition, the John H. Chafee Blackstone River Valley National Heritage Corridor, encompassing parts of eleven towns and cities in Rhode Island and another dozen in Massachusetts, seeks to preserve the history and artifacts of the river where the American industrial revolution began, and legislation was passed in 2014 that designates this area as a new national park. Other specialized organizations and museums include the Italian Historical Society, the American-French Genealogical Society, the Black Heritage Society, Rhode Island State Police Museum Foundation, the Rhode Island Jewish Historical Association, the Culinary Arts Museum of Johnson & Wales University, and Preserve Rhode Island, the state partner of the National Trust.

The first state history, written by John Callender in 1739, was entitled *An Historical Discourse on the Civil and Religious Affairs of the Colony of Rhode Island and Providence Plantations, from the First Settlement to the end of the First Century*. Reprinted in 1838 with Elton Romeo as editor, this remained the only history written until 1877. Edward Field produced *The State of Rhode Island and Providence Plantations at the End of the* Century (1902; 3 vols.). Then, Thomas W. Bicknell wrote *The History of the State of Rhode Island and Providence Plantations* (1920; 5 vols.), and Charles Carroll published *Rhode Island: The Centuries of a Democracy* (1932; 4 vols.). These last two were subscription financed, and each had two volumes of biographies paid for by the subscribers. William McLoughlin wrote *Rhode Island: A Bicentennial History* (1978) as part of the series on the states produced by W.W. Norton. Since then, only popular, illustrated histories have appeared, including Patrick Conley's *An Album of Rhode Island History, 1636–1986* (1986) and George H. Kellner and J. Stanley Lemons's *Rhode Island: The Ocean State* (2004). Rhode Island's colonial and early national eras have received the greatest scholarly attention, but increasingly scholars are examining the ethnic and labor histories of the late nineteenth and early twentieth centuries. The twentieth century is ripe for full investigation. In the late nineteenth century Richard Bayles compiled detailed histories of Rhode Island's two major counties: *History of Newport County* (1888) and *History of Providence County* (1891). In the past decade, numerous books by firms like the History Press and *Arcadia Press have tackled a variety of topics on Rhode Island history. Most towns and many villages have been treated in town histories, and the historical and architectural surveys of the Rhode Island Historical and Heritage Commission are important sources about the state's towns and neighborhoods.

The state's history continues to attract attention because Rhode Island was the first place in modern history that had full religious freedom, the first place in America where Jews and Quakers were free to worship, the place where the American industrial revolution began, the first urban, industrialized state, the first state to have a Roman Catholic majority, and the state considered the Queen of Resorts from the Gilded Age to World War I. From its origins as an agricultural economy in the seventeenth century, Rhode Island rode high in oceanic trade and commerce in the eighteenth century, including substantial involvement in the slave trade, became heavily industrialized and urbanized in the nineteenth century, and then experienced "de-industrialization" and the development of a postindustrial economy in the twentieth and twenty-first centuries.

The state has no specific requirement for teaching its history. If and when it is taught is up to individual school districts, and currently it is no more than a one-semester elective at the senior high school level.

J. STANLEY LEMONS
UPDATED BY ELYSSA TARDIF
RHODE ISLAND HISTORICAL SOCIETY

Roman Catholic Church, sources for. See Appendix B.

Romanians in North America, sources for. See Appendix A.

Roots: The Saga of an American Family. Alexander Haley's (1921–1992) book *Roots* was published in 1976 and made into a popular television miniseries in 1977. The book's influence was significant and believed by many to be true. Amid much discussion, however, the book was shown to be a largely fictional account with parts of it based on the work of others. *Roots* fueled an interest among many people who had not earlier considered searching for ancestors that coincided with the development of the Internet.

See Ancestry.com; genealogy, African Americas; genealogical resources online.

RootsWeb.com. RootsWeb.com (http://www.rootsweb.ancestry.com) is a volunteer site that depends on individual submissions of data, such as cemetery transcriptions, local tax lists, *census records, and *obituaries. Most of the data is submitted by individual researchers, but local historical societies also contribute. These records are then made accessible to researchers through several different kinds of search engines. Although the site is free, it is owned and managed by *Ancestry.com and to some extent acts as a portal to Ancestry.com.

RootsWeb is best known for its extensive tools for communication between researchers. These include surname research tools, in particular around 30,000 surname mailing lists and nearly 200,000 message boards that allow researchers working on particular families or topics to communicate with each other. It also has its own system for publishing submitted genealogies, the WorldConnect Project. WorldConnect provides an easy-to-use interface for searching over 300 million records. Submissions vary widely in accuracy and documentation, but the results are organized in a way that makes them easy to compare. The data is in the standard GEDCOM format that allows it to be exported into personal genealogical software such as FamilyTreeMaker and Legacy.

RootsWeb is a sprawling site with many features. The communication tools can be very rewarding for a committed researcher and WorldConnect is a valuable resource for users willing and able to evaluate the data presented there.

Robert Kibbee
The History Center in Tompkins
County (NY)

See genealogical resources online.

Russians in North America, sources for. See Appendix A.

S

Sabbatarian. A Sabbatarian is one who keeps the seventh day of the week as holy, as directed by the fourth commandment.

Sanborn fire insurance maps. See maps and atlases.

Saskatchewan, local history in. Saskatchewan, the iconic western Canadian province known for its agriculture and resources, has a varied and dynamic relationship with local history. Oral and written memory was first captured in 1913 by Norman Fergus Black in *Saskatchewan and the Old North West*, a mere eight years after the province, and a provincial museum, were created in 1905. Black used archival sources from the provincial Legislative Library (founded in 1876 when Saskatchewan was part of the Northwest Territories). To preserve and augment these sources, Black lobbied unsuccessfully for a provincial archivist. A second provincial history was published by Legislative Librarian John Hawkes in 1924, entitled *The Story of Saskatchewan and its People*. Both were multivolume hardcover books that offered extensive biographies and reprinted important documents from the library collection. Yet they differed in tone: Black wrote in romantic style, intent on a Eurocentric history of great men and events; Hawkes was a pragmatic journalist who liked first-person accounts and hoped his book would foster a "Saskatchewan tradition," a sense of place and pride.

The first lecture at University of Saskatchewan, established 1907, was in history. Professor and historian A. S. Morton soon became an advocate for provincial history. He established the Historical Public Records Office at the university and was named Provincial Archivist in 1937. In 1945, Morton convinced the socialist Co-operative Commonwealth Federation government to create a provincially funded Archives of Saskatchewan to secure the ongoing collection and preservation of public and private material. Among the first to utilize it were the Homemakers Clubs or Women's Institutes (WI), vying for the annual "Tweedsmuir Prize" for the best local history published by a Canadian WI. In 1948 the archives established its journal, *Saskatchewan History*. In 1949, the province founded the Western Development Museum, dedicated to preserving provincial *heritage artifacts and stories.

Excitement surrounding the 1955 provincial Golden Jubilee intensified historical activity. In 1954, the Department of Education altered the high school curriculum to allow students to research a school or community history. Hundreds of local histories were produced by schools, WIs, and other community groups to mark the anniversary. Other initiatives included a new provincial museum (now the Royal

Saskatchewan Museum), and a new provincial history book, Jim Wright's *Saskatchewan: The History of a Province.* Its idealized pioneer settlement mythology marginalized indigenous and ethnic history but it was enthusiastically embraced by a largely rural audience.

Building on jubilee enthusiasm, the Saskatchewan History and Folklore Society was established in 1957. It supports a variety of initiatives, including a heritage marker program, *oral history, funding assistance, and its popular *Folklore* magazine. *Folklore* publishes reminiscences, poetry, and photographs in contrast to the academic articles in *Saskatchewan History.*

Although a few graduate students wrote in-depth community studies between the 1940s and 1960s, by the late 1960s the split between popular and academic history became more apparent. Saskatchewan academics turned their attention to social movements, biographies, economic change, institutions, crisis moments, labor relations, ethnic studies, and gender history. While other academics across Canada and the United States subsumed local history into case studies, few such studies emerged in Saskatchewan. Place-based histories were relegated to amateur historians and genealogists.

Coinciding with Canada's centennial in 1967 and a provincial "homecoming" celebration in 1971, local initiatives toward artifact collection, museum creation, oral research, and written documentation continued to swell outside academia. During the 1970s, local history caught the attention of book printers such as Friesens of Manitoba and Turner-Warwick of Saskatchewan.

They offered local history groups an easy-to-use, step-by-step process to produce hardcover history books that were particularly good at reproducing photographs, enshrining a community's visual memory. With seed money from the federal seniors' New Horizons project and the Celebrate Saskatchewan committee, the province's seventy-fifth anniversary celebrations saw hundreds of communities join the "fad" to research and publish professionally printed local history books. Reprints, second editions, and new community histories have continued that trend. Most can be found in the Prairie History Room of Regina Public Library; some have been digitized on ourroots.ca.

The practice of commissioning provincial histories to coincide with anniversary celebrations also continued. For 1980 John Archer penned *Saskatchewan: A History* while provincial archivist Douglas Bocking selected photographs from the archives' extensive collection for *Saskatchewan: A Pictorial History.* For the 2005 provincial centennial, University of Saskatchewan historian Bill Waiser published *Saskatchewan: A New History.* While Archer and Bocking once again centralized the pioneer narrative, Waiser challenged that mythology by introducing extensive indigenous history and pointing out the tensions in the provincial story: north and south, rural and urban, native and newcomer, success and failure. His book topped the Saskatchewan best seller list, bridging the gap between academic and popular history. Released in 2016, Waiser's prequel, *A World We Have Lost*, aims to examine the pre-1905 provincial story.

By the millennium, Saskatchewan historians embraced computers, digital scanning, and website development, allowing publication in alternative media. Popular websites include Saskatchewan Settlement Experience (www.sasksettlement.com), the Indigenous Studies Portal (iportal.usask.ca), and the *Encyclopedia of Saskatchewan*. The Saskatchewan Heritage Foundation, a Crown corporation, supports built heritage and *archaeology. The Heritage Property Act, administered by the Department of Tourism, Parks, Culture and Sport, allows designation of both municipal and provincial properties.

In 2009, Heritage Saskatchewan, an advocacy group that supports heritage projects and groups, was formed. The Saskatchewan Museums Association boasts over 200 member museums, including four Western Development Museums and the RCMP Museum in Regina. Two National Parks and several Provincial and National Historic Sites welcome visitors, including Batoche, a battlefield of the 1885 Rebellion. Precontact First Nations history is enshrined at Wanuskewin Heritage Park near Saskatoon. Indeed, indigenous cultures lead historical investigation in the twenty-first century.

Under the current provincial curriculum, history is taught on an inverted pyramid, from a focus on "self" in grade one through world history in high school. "Saskatchewan" is the grade-four social studies unit. At both provincial universities, Saskatchewan content is usually included in broadly based "prairie" history courses. Neither university offers local history courses, but recent academic attention to "place

histories" and "memory studies" may yet bring local history back into entry-level university classrooms.

MERLE MASSIE
UNIVERSITY OF SASKATCHEWAN

See Canada, local history in.

Scandinavians in North America, sources for. See Appendix A.

Scotland, local history in. Where does national history end and local and regional history begin? In Scotland, historians deal with a legacy of past nationhood and institutions, such as the law, the kirk (church), schools, universities, and many offices of state, which survived the union with England and Wales in 1707, providing a framework for quite distinctive developments in a Scottish administrative state, largely independent of the United Kingdom. Since devolution and the reestablishment of the Scottish Parliament in 1999 it has been claimed that there is no longer any local history in Scotland, only national history. While this obviously fits the political discourse, local historians remain the foot soldiers of Scottish history, contributing to the enormous range of studies in recent decades. There are certainly many Scotlands, so apart from the Lowland-Highland divide, many areas, from Orkney and Shetland in the north to Dumfries and Galloway in the south, have varied and distinctive histories.

Modern scholarly work treats major developments, themes, and debates. Although slower to adopt new approaches than England, France, and the United States, Scotland caught up rapidly. The surge in scholarship from the 1960s, of which T. C. Smout remains a key representative, emphasized social and economic themes. Before this the great strengths lay in *political history and local studies, a situation reflected in the *Scottish Historical Review* and the journals of local scholarly societies. Before the appearance in 1981 of *Scottish Economic and Social History* (since 2003–2004, *Journal of Scottish Historical Studies*), some Scottish research was published in UK publications like the *Economic History Review*, *Social History*, *Past and Present*, and occasionally in U.S. journals.

The new scholarship unlocked afresh the vast resources of the National Archives of Scotland (www.nas.gov.uk), the National Library of Scotland (www.nls.uk), and university and local archives for studies of all periods of Scottish history. The theoretical underpinnings were weaker than in England, and much economic history remained for a while essentially descriptive. Economic research drew on the U.S. schools of capitalist/economic growth approaches, and concentrated on economic, entrepreneurial, industrial, labor, and ultimately "rust belt" (areas of former heavy industry) histories, when the old economy gradually collapsed. Many community-based industrial and labor histories (some researched and written by university adult classes) gave a strong local focus to this work.

By contrast, social history had more in common with the approaches of French scholars (history from below, and of ordinary folk), work by Smout and R. Houston being representative of the genre. Houston and R. Anderson both revisited the discourse about the purpose and impact of Scottish education and its class implications. Education and the democratic tradition remain hot topics in Scottish history. Class became a fashionable topic, as it had in England thanks to the work of E. P. Thompson on the English working class. The Scottish working class, long thought to be compliant and suppressed by the moral order imposed by kirk, elites, and industrialists, was soon shown to be nothing of the kind, particularly in the work of C. A. Whatley, who vigorously pursued some of Smout's earlier assumptions about the apparently quiescent lower orders. Much of the scholarship to the 1990s was summarized in the excellent People and Society series, followed more recently by that on the History of Everyday Life in Scotland, which will ultimately cover the period 1600–1800. There has been some impressive work on urban history with wide coverage in E. P. Dennison et al., *Painting the Scottish Town: Scottish Urban History in Art* and B. Harris and C. McKean, *The Scottish Town in the Age of the Enlightenment.* In the meantime political history experienced something of a resurgence, as have medieval studies (the latter rather constrained by sources for all but the more dogged or skilled in the local context).

Several reference works refer to local and regional issues, for example, G. Donaldson and R. Morpeth, *Dictionary of Scottish History*; M. Lynch, ed., *Oxford Companion to Scottish History*; and I. Donnachie and G. Hewitt, *Companion to Scottish History.* The first is mainly short entries, but nevertheless very comprehensive, while the other two works cover the *historiography generally and specifically (with appropriate bibliographies). The *Oxford Companion* (also available electronically) has well-annotated discussions of recent work. It is supplemented by T. M. Devine and J. Wormald, eds., *The Oxford Handbook of Modern Scottish History 1500–2010*, which provides more detailed coverage of themes and issues relevant to local studies. There are numerous other reference works on a wide range of specific topics, such as business biographies, church history, urban history, etc., that review the historical literature specific to their subject.

There are several serviceable guides. Among the best are D. Moody, *Scottish Local History* and C. Sinclair's *Tracing Local History*, the latter describing the potential of the National Archives of Scotland. Moody produced two further guides on Scottish towns and on Scottish family history. A. Adolph's *Tracing Your Scottish Family History* is comprehensive and provides useful material for community history as well as genealogy. The National Library of Scotland and many local history libraries have their own guides. Web-based versions from national and local institutions proliferate. More specialist aids, dealing with parliamentary papers and other official sources, newspapers, photographs, etc., are available. M. L. Cox, *Exploring Scottish History*, is an excellent guide to the historiography, libraries, archives, and their holdings. The Scottish Archive Network (www.scan.org.uk) provides one of the most comprehensive online guides to holdings, worth examining to get a sense of the rich resources waiting to be explored in national and local archives.

Bibliographies of recent work are regularly provided in such publications as *Scottish Historical Review*, *Scottish Economic and Social History*, *Scottish Local History Forum*, and local society publications, often incorporating source listings, lists of accessions in various archives, new websites, etc.

Web-based resources are now extensive: those covering *demography being accessible via www.scotlandspeople.gov. uk. The *Statistical Accounts of Scotland*, covering every locality in the country in the 1790s and 1830s to 1840s, are available online from a variety of portals, as is the multivolume *Ordnance Gazetteer of Scotland* (1890s), also much used by local historians. Other major national sites covering a wide range of historical and heritage materials include SCRAN (www.scran.ac.uk) and Canmore (www.canmore.org.uk). Most local authorities (the second tier of government in the country) provide local history portals via libraries and archives, detailing resources, holdings, and access arrangements. Two examples must suffice. In Fife, www.fifedirect.org.uk highlights archive holdings, searchable catalogs of records, bibliographies of secondary works, and a very useful facility providing searchable local history articles. Wider in scope perhaps is that of Highland, www.ambaile.org. uk, providing archive listings and access to a vast range of resources in both English and Gaelic covering many aspects of Highland history and culture. It is worth noting the many sources and works in Gaelic that English scholars have generally ignored.

Support structures for the subject include the Scottish Local History Forum (www.slhf.org), an umbrella organization to which many societies are affiliated. Its publication, one of the main outlets for local history articles, also provides reviews, bibliographies, and listings of current work. Local Studies Scotland (https://locscot. wordpress.com) is devoted to the care and dissemination of local and family history material. Most members are librarians working in the front line of local studies, but also a wide range of organizations and people form the history and *heritage sectors. There are several regional and specialist organizations that coordinate the work of societies, including archaeology and family history. Some long-established societies produce prestigious journals and publications. A number of specialist national societies, such as the Scottish Economic and Social History Society and the Scottish Labour History Society, publish useful journals.

The longest established journal is the *Scottish Historical Review*, which covers all periods and varied approaches. The successor to *Scottish Economic and Social History*, the *Journal of Scottish Historical Studies* is a forum for current research and general interest articles on all aspects of Scottish social and economic history. It includes business, labor, gender, urban, and cultural history. Another national publication of note is *History Scotland* magazine, a bimonthly, which publishes a wide range of material including local and regional history. Although not immediately obvious, English journals, such as *The Local Historian* and *Local Population*

Studies, occasionally publish Scottish articles, while *Northern History* regularly features cross-border history (as do Scottish journals from time to time). Is the border, then, the dog that does not bark in some of the current historical discourse?

Despite the large volume of work published in recent decades, there are many "black holes" in our knowledge of Scottish history, national and local, so the scope for interesting and original work genuinely contributing to knowledge is considerable. More and more sources are being unlocked, while *digitization and the Internet have opened up many of them to a global audience. It goes without saying that resources for Scottish studies in the other countries of the British Isles and many more beyond those shores cover every aspect of Scottish migration, settlement, enterprise, and culture touched by the diaspora.

IAN DONNACHIE
THE OPEN UNIVERSITY

See England, local history in; Ireland, local history in; Wales, local history in.

Scots in North America, sources for. See Appendix A.

Scots-Irish in North America, sources for. See Appendix A.

Serbs in North America, sources for. See Appendix A.

Seventh-Day Adventists, sources for. See Appendix B.

sites of conscience. See history museums and identity; tourism.

slang. Slang consists of those nonstandard words used in informal speech to mark social or regional identity or identity within a particular interest group. In this way, slang is related to jargon, which consists of the technical terms used by a particular group. Slang focuses instead on words basically used for fun, words used to show the difference between the speaker and the general population. What slang does is set the stage for the level of discourse in a conversation; it declares that a conversation will be informal. Slang also marks group solidarity. People do not use slang terms to hide information from outsiders, but people outside a group will be less likely to use slang terms from outside their own group. Thus, teenagers use teenage slang, either within or without their group, to exhibit solidarity with their peers. Although often the province of youth, many other types of groups use slang in this way: the military, sports players and aficionados, sailors, college students, doctors, cowboys, urban blacks, computer users, actors and other theater professionals, people living in particular cities, narcotics users, prisoners, etc.

Within some of these groups it is important to distinguish technical jargon from slang. Unlike jargon, slang is not the technical vocabulary of a group or profession, but is jocular, informal vocabulary. For instance, baseball has a large specialized vocabulary, many of whose words are technical terms of some kind ("hit," "error," "shortstop"), but many of which are actually slang ("bases drunk" to mean "bases loaded," "dinger" for "home run," "hot corner" for "third base," and "tools of

ignorance" for "catcher's gear"). Note that each slang term is a synonym for an apparently adequate term previously in use. For the most part, slang consists of inventive synonyms for standard words, and some slang terms are little more than manipulated versions of current words ("binocs" for "binoculars" or "spazz" as a derogatory term for "a pathetic person, a spastic").

Though sometimes restricted to one region, slang usually escapes the province of one area and moves by slang-railroad across broad speech communities. In New York State, there is a definite movement of youth slang from New York City to the cities of upstate New York. A slang term that is restricted regionally would be considered a *regionalism, but there remain significant differences between the terms. Whereas slang is a language of fun and abuse and invention, a regional dialect develops more slowly, generally remains longer in use, and is used for all colloquial conversations. Slang and regionalisms can both separate groups of people, but slang is not necessarily regional. Many slang terms used by the medical profession or teenagers are virtually as popular in all corners of the country.

Slang has long been thought to include nothing but ephemeral terms, but the *Random House Historical Dictionary of American Slang* has proved that some slang terms actually have had lifetimes that have lasted centuries, often without experiencing significant changes in meaning. The term "cool" meaning "suave" has been current slang since at least the early 1920s. The nautical word "barnacleback" for a seasoned seaman remained in circulation at least from

1846 to 1967, quite a long time for a term expected to be ephemeral. Jazz musicians of the 1930s invented the term "groovy," which we now generally associate exclusively with the psychedelic 1960s. Most people probably believe that the now-dated term "bad" (counterintuitively meaning "good") originated as a slang term in the 1980s, but they would be off by a century.

Most slang terms, however, are quickly replaced in the marketplace of words as the old slang loses its novelty and effect, becoming (in the now-defunct mid-1990s term of North American teenage slang) "played." Few people now would recognize the mid-1850s term "ipsydinxy," meaning whiskey, or the Civil War term "blenker," meaning "to plunder civilian possessions." The teenage term "dope" (meaning "cool") arrived on the scene in the 1980s and soon disappeared. Because of the well-known rapid obsolescence of many slang terms, Hollywood has occasionally taken the protective steps of developing a panoply of slang especially for a particular movie, so that the slang within it would not be outdated by the time the movie was released (see 1989's *Heathers* and 1995's *Clueless*). Although slang words often become archaic, many never quite become obsolete. We still understand them, though we rarely use them. The real problem with the history of slang is that many terms truly are fleeting, so many are never collected or remembered in any way.

Slang terms can also transform into standard words in the language, especially where the language has no other word to describe the idea. Examples include the very common words, "blizzard," "hijack," "jazz," and "quiz." More commonly, slang terms become the jargon of the professions or avocations that use such slang, just as sports slang occasionally becomes technical terms in the field.

Many slang terms function as terms of opprobrium, the mechanisms for heaping contempt upon others. Many of these terms are vulgar and avoided in polite conversation, but even a modest term like "bootlicker" is full of strong negative connotations. People often fear that this offensiveness is the only use of slang, and they consider this its defining element. Since slang is generally a collection of anti-establishment terms, such words are common, but vulgarity and contempt are not the major functions of slang. Principally, slang serves as an important social marker, separating one group from others as it brings the members of that group more closely together.

In local terms, slang is interesting for two reasons. First, there may be regional slang that is interesting to study. Many localities, for instance, have developed slang terms for geographical features, well-known buildings, and transportation systems in their area. One of the richest examples of this is Boontling, a slanguage that was used exclusively in the Anderson Valley of Mendocino County, California. Originally and consciously designed as a secret lingo—probably for the adults of the valley to speak of sensitive matters without their children understanding—Boontling eventually became a second language of the valley as people learned the language from context. This language probably began in the 1880s and persisted until the teens of the twentieth century, with its zenith occurring in the 1890s. Second, though it is much more difficult to track adequately, people can study the geographical sources and dates of appearance of slang terms used in a region. For instance, looking at cities in the state of New Jersey, which slang terms common there originated in New York City, which originated in Philadelphia, and which are indigenous to the Garden State? In California, is there a separate development of slang in San Francisco versus Los Angeles?

GEOFFREY A. HUTH
NEW YORK STATE UNIFIED
COURT SYSTEM

See regionalisms.

slave schedules. The first (1790) U.S. Census collected the names only of white heads of *households. Other male members of the household over sixteen years of age were simply enumerated as "free" or "slave." The distinction was critical: according to the Constitution slaves counted as only three-fifths of a person for purposes of apportioning Congress. In later censuses the heads of households were named and other members of the household, although still unidentified, were numbered in various sex/age classifications. Slaves of any age and sex were numbered together until 1820 when classifications (much broader than those used for free people) were also applied to the enslaved population. In 1850 all free members of the household including free blacks were named, although relationships among the household members were not recorded. Slaves, who in most cases did not have, or were

not allowed to have, family names, required a special enumeration. The census developed "slave schedules," which listed the slaves anonymously under their owner, with a separate line for each slave. Information included age, sex, color, whether deaf, dumb, or blind, and whether the slave had escaped within the last year or had been manumitted. The 1860 schedule was essentially the same with the addition of a line for "slave houses." For a good description of the schedules see U.S. Census Bureau, *Measuring America*, available online at https://www.census.gov/prod/2002pubs/pol02-ma.pdf.

The schedules are important cultural and historical documents, although of limited use for genealogical purposes. An African American family name might tentatively be traced back to a particular owner or plantation, if the name is distinctive and the general area the family is from is known. With some supporting information (age, sex, and color) or information from a later census, it might be possible to at least make a plausible identification of a slave described in the schedule with a known ancestor. For a discussion of the genealogical potential see Tony Burroughs, "Census Records in African American Research," at the *Ancestry Wiki*, a digitized version of *The Source: A Guidebook to American Genealogy*, ed. Szucs and Luebking, 3rd ed. (2007): http://www.ancestry.com/wiki/index.php?title=Census_Records_in_African_American_Research.

The Slave Schedules can be searched or browsed at *Ancestry.com (subscription required) or FamilySearch.com (free of charge) or from microfilm from the *National Archives—see *Measuring America* above for reel numbers.

ROBERT KIBBEE
THE HISTORY CENTER IN TOMPKINS
COUNTY (NY)

See census, United States; genealogy, African American.

slavery interpretation at museums and historic sites. Interpreting slavery, with its powerful resonances, is a privilege and a great responsibility. For many years, the museum field at large has neglected to interpret, interpreted incompletely, or perpetuated myths about the presence and lives of enslaved people at historic sites and museums across the country. As historic sites and museums position themselves to bear witness to the tragic history of U.S. slavery, they should ask about their interpretive experience, "What is *at stake* if visitors leave our site without an accurate, balanced, and sensitive understanding of slavery and its role in our history?"

Slavery played an essential role in the history interpreted at a multitude of historic sites throughout the nation, including historic homes, small family farms, commercial centers, and industrial sites, as well as at large-scale plantations. By interpreting this history, we can tell more comprehensive and balanced stories about our sites and of all who lived or worked there, bringing forth the voices of the marginalized. Just as importantly, we can expand visitors' understanding of the contributions of slavery, and of the lives of enslaved African Americans, to the political, economic, and social life of the entire nation. Finally, because slavery is a painful

chapter in our nation's history, and one fraught with implications for our society today, there is tremendous value in helping our visitors to understand that the institution of slavery wasn't merely the responsibility of the South or of a wealthy elite, but was a cornerstone of the nation's economy and society, and an engine of upward mobility for millions of American families.

Our distorted public memory of slavery contributes to making this a challenging history to interpret, as does the fact that history involves the painful invocation of episodes of trauma, violence, and oppression. There are two issues that make the interpretation of slavery, and similarly controversial histories, especially challenging for museums and historic sites: the ways in which this history invokes *contested narratives* and how *racial identity* influences the experience of interpreters and visitors.

All people, including site staff and visitors, have identities that define how they see themselves, how they make sense of the world, and how they interact with others. These identities, in turn, are largely based on narratives: "It is through narrativity that we come to know, understand, and make sense of the social world, and it is through narratives and narrativity that we constitute our social identities [and] come to be who we are" (Margaret R. Somers, "The Narrative Constitution of Identity: A Relational and Network Approach," *Theory and Society* 23 [1994]). These narratives include not just personal stories, but also broad historical narratives that are widely shared, such as narratives about how the United States came to be, how families have prospered here, and about the nation's defining values. People hold multiple identities at once, and thus they possess narratives about their families, their region, their racial or ethnic groups, their social class, and their nation, among others.

Interpreting slavery well means exposing staff and visitors to a narrative in which slavery played a much broader role in the history of the nation than our traditional public memory implies. As a result, staff and visitors will find themselves contending with a narrative that tells how slavery was an essential part of the successes of the northern colonies, and of the northeastern, midwestern, and western states, and therefore of many white families and institutions that do not see their histories as intertwined with those of slavery at all. This situation sets up a sharp clash between old and new narratives that can cut to the core of a person's sense of identity.

Dismantling old narratives and replacing them with new, and historically more accurate, alternatives may be healthy and productive. But this process can generate resistance, resentment, or outright disbelief, and requires careful thought and sensitive handling for a successful outcome. When people confront information that does not fit within the narratives that inform their identities, they tend to experience "serious mental confusion," "powerlessness, despair, victimization," and other cognitive and emotional difficulties (Somers, 617, 630). The process of integrating a new historical narrative into one's identity, and reconciling it with core beliefs and values, is a gradual one, involving fits and starts, and is mostly an unconscious process. It is therefore essential that an interpretive plan and staff training take this process, and its manifestations, into account, and that visitors be given plenty of opportunity to express their cognitive and emotional struggles as they absorb the interpretation.

The history of slavery in the United States is not merely a painful part of our shared past, evoking trauma, violence, and oppression. Slavery is also a living history that conjures powerful emotions for many Americans because it raises issues like racial justice, healing, or repair. Confronting this history invokes historical narratives at the core of how many Americans understand their identity—whether on the basis of race or ethnicity, or in terms of family, socioeconomic class, or regional affiliation.

No matter what race or ethnicity we belong to, Americans come with "racial baggage"—preconceived notions about others based on skin color, as well as a stew of emotions such as defensiveness, fear, anger, guilt, shame, or resentment. These emotions can be easily stirred up by the topic of slavery, especially if the topic is explored in depth, made personal, or presented in a way with which we are not already familiar. A site's interpretive plan must therefore take into account the cognitive and psychological challenges for staff and visitors as they encounter this history.

Historic sites and museums can apply the following framework to develop a comprehensive and conscientious interpretation of slavery.

- Comprehensive Content—A sound interpretation of slavery begins with historical research about the role of slavery that is both broad—covering not just your site, but also the role slavery played in the broader history of your community, state, and the nation—and deep—offering a well-rounded narrative informed by individual stories and, wherever possible, rich personal details to lend humanity to the enslaved and to highlight their broader role in history.

- Race and Identity Awareness—The racial identity of both staff and visitors play a role in how interpretation is offered and received. As professionals, we must be aware of, and comfortable with, our own knowledge and feelings about race and slavery, and we need to understand where our visitors are coming from in order to help them understand their own concerns surrounding race and identity when learning about slavery.

- Institutional Investment—All of an institution's core constituencies—board, management, staff, and volunteers—must be invested in and support the institution's interpretation of slavery. Board and management set the mission and vision for the site, make strategic decisions regarding the allocation of resources, and set the tone for how the institution approaches the subject affectively. Meanwhile, staff, and not just those directly involved in the interpretation of slavery, also play a major role in determining how the interpretive plan is implemented and whether it succeeds.

- Community Involvement—The (re-) interpretation of slavery provides opportunities to connect your institution with new community partners, including individuals and organizations

that might relate to, and find value in, the stories and perspectives of traditionally marginalized historical voices. Partners from the community around your site—descendants of slave owners and enslaved persons, neighbors, businesses, civic organizations, municipal government, social groups, churches, universities—should be actively involved in your site, helping to shape narratives, attending events, providing funding, donating objects and contributing research and stories, and advocating for your site.

- Visitor Experiences and Expectations—We don't "do" this ourselves—our visitors are equal partners in interpretation. We need to know what sorts of preconceptions visitors bring with them, what their expectations of the visit are, and how their actual experiences match up to their expectations.

- Staff Training—How staff members are trained is an integral part of an institution's commitment to interpreting slavery, and should be given considerable time and attention. This nation's pervasive public myths about the history of slavery, and the understandable sensitivities that both staff and visitors have in addressing this material, mean that sites can't just give employees the historical content and tell them to "go for it." Trainers and staff need to discuss the nuances of creating a content-balanced, affectively balanced narrative and how to help visitors scaffold their knowledge and fashion new historical narratives out of cognitive dissonance.

"That US slavery has both officially ended yet continues in many complex forms—most notably institutional-ized racism and the cultural deni-gration of blackness—makes its representation particularly burden-some in the United States. Slavery here is a ghost, both in the past and a living presence, and the problem of historical representation is how to represent that ghost, something that is and yet is not" (Michel-Rolph Trouillot, *Silencing the Past: Power and the Production of History* [1995], 146).

Presenting the history of slavery in a comprehensive and conscientious manner is difficult and requires dili-gence and compassion—for the his-tory itself, for those telling the story, and for those hearing the story—but it's a necessary part of the collective U.S. narrative about our past, present, and future.

Adapted from Kristin L. Gallas and James DeWolf Perry, "Developing Comprehensive and Conscientious In-terpretation of Slavery at Historic Sites and Museums," *History News* (Spring 2014).

See Kristin L. Gallas and James De-Wolf Perry, *Interpreting Slavery at Mu-seums and Historic Sites* (2015), www.interpretingslavery.com; Jennifer L. Eichstat and Stephen A. Small, *Rep-resentations of Slavery: Race and Ide-ology in Southern Plantation Museums* (2002); E. Arnold Modlin et al., "Tour Guides as Creators of Empathy: The Role of Affective Inequality in Mar-ginalizing the Enslaved Population at Plantation House Museums," *Tourist Studies* 11, no. 3 (2011): 3–19; Julia Rose, "Three Building Blocks for De-veloping Ethical Representations of

Difficult Histories," *AASLH Technical Leaflet #264* (2013).

KRISTIN L. GALLAS
INDEPENDENT CONSULTANT
JAMES DEWOLF PERRY
CENTER FOR RECONCILIATION

See building bridges through local history; slave schedules.

Slavs in North America, sources for. See Appendix A.

Slovenes in North America, sources for. See Appendix A.

small museums. See museums, small.

Small Museum Association (SMA). The Small Museum Association is an all-volunteer organization serving small museums in the mid-Atlantic region and beyond. SMA's mission is to de-velop and maintain a peer network among people who work for small mu-seums, giving them opportunities to learn, share knowledge, and support one another. SMA does this through annual conferences and by providing information on grants and professional development opportunities. Contact president@smallmuseum.org; www.smallmuseum.org.

See museums, public value of.

social class. When Americans speak colloquially of "the wrong side of the tracks," they acknowledge the salience of social-class differences in the histo-ries and on the townscapes of ordinary American communities. What has so long been inscribed in popular speech did not, however, find its way into the earliest written chronicles of town life. The nineteenth-century founders of American local history generally did not examine class differences, even while they established the distinctiveness of local elites through extended discussions of the "leading families," or the "bench and bar" of their towns, or by publishing separate biographical volumes devoted to sketches of wealthy and influential men.

Social class emerged as a significant theme of local history only much later, and then most frequently in scholarly analyses of community life rather than in town chronicles. Pointing the way were several notable sociological studies, the first and most influential being Robert S. Lynd and Helen Merrell Lynd's thorough study of Muncie, Indiana, published in 1929 as *Middletown: A Study in Modern American Culture*. This book, along with the *"Yankee City" series of studies published by W. Lloyd Warner and his associates (between 1941 and 1959), August Hollingshead's *Elmtown's Youth* (1975), and others, searched for methods through which the residents of a community, their living patterns and institutions, and even their belongings, could be made to speak of meaningful social divisions. All of these were contemporary studies that provided ideas about social class but few methodological insights for historians who necessarily rely on a written record, and on artifacts no longer in daily use. The historians who would eventually inject a class dimension into local history were, for the most part, those interested above all in the formation of a U.S. working class, and who, inspired by work in England

by E. P. Thompson and in America by Herbert Gutman, sought to explore the totality of working-class experience by examining the lives of working men and women in specific industrial and communal settings. Their studies of industrial towns in turn inspired historians interested in middle and upper classes as distinct social formations to turn their attention to local communities. By the 1980s the exploration of social class in specific local settings was an established and well-recognized practice of American academic historians.

Examining class in any community requires an understanding both of conceptual issues and of the relevance and use of specific sources. Concepts of social class are generally of two types: those that interpret class as a derivation of prevailing (in modern society, capitalist) "modes of production," and that, for the most part, stress the binary opposition of employers and employees in a categorically defined two-class society, or those that interpret class as a set of status clusters, or even as a continuum of status differences, as these manifest themselves in the living standards and styles, and in the perceptions and terminology, of any community or larger population. The first, Marxian type of class theory has had its greatest impact on historical studies of working-class formation in industrial communities; it is the organizing principle, for example, of Paul Faler's *Mechanics and Manufacturers in the Early Industrial Revolution: Lynn, Massachusetts, 1780–1860* (1981). The latter type has informed most sociological studies of American communities, and even where sociologists have stressed the divide between business proprietors and workers (as in *Middletown, where the authors found "the outstanding cleavage" in the community to be the "division into working class and business class"), they have insisted on a more comprehensive empirical validation of social differences of this sort in the day-to-day lives, the social perceptions, and the sensibilities and ambitions, of those who lived on both "sides of the tracks."

Apart from (but also deriving from) the question of what class means, is the further question of how to examine social differences through surviving and available historical sources. These may be plentiful or scarce in any given community, and the significance of the variation from one place to another is magnified by the fact that there are few national or state sources relevant to the study of local social structures. The most obvious and significant extra-local documents are the manuscript schedules of various national (and in some cases, state) population schedules, which identify the occupation, age, place of birth, race, and in a few censuses the (self-reported) value of real and personal property of each local inhabitant. For some American communities there is also an unusually informative tax register created in pursuance of a national direct tax levied in the year 1798. The types and quality of information recorded on these extra-community records vary, however, and are available only for specific years. The local historian must examine, for the most part, local records, of which the most useful are official tax, land, and probate records (the latter are especially important where they include detailed *inventories of decedents'

goods), local newspapers, records of churches and other local organizations, *maps and *photographs of the physical town and its inhabitants, and, perhaps above all, personal records such as diaries and correspondence, particularly those that name friends and associates, discuss social affinities and divisions, and express social assumptions in an identifiable language of status or class. Few communities, and few archives beyond the community's borders, can be expected to contain collections of sources that yield a comprehensive view of local social divisions and relations; in particular, documents written about and by the poorest and most transient inhabitants are few and far between. But in most, if not all, there are the materials for exploring at least some dimensions of inequality, some aspects of social status, and some of those local inhabitants of "the wrong side of the tracks" who were so frequently excluded from the first local histories.

STUART M. BLUMIN
CORNELL UNIVERSITY

social history. See labor history and the history of communities; new social history.

social media. Social media is constantly changing, and the use of it by local history organizations continues to evolve. Briefly, Wikipedia defines social media as "media for social interaction, using highly accessible and scalable communication techniques. Social media is the use of web-based and mobile technologies to turn communication into interactive dialogue." For local history organizations, it's a critically important way to engage audiences of all ages and contribute to your organization's reputation. The Pew Research Center's research confirms the importance of social media in American life (http://www.pewinternet.org/2015/08/19/the-demographics-of-social-media-users): 62 percent of the entire adult American population uses Facebook; 26 percent of the entire adult population uses Pinterest; 24 percent of that same population uses Instagram; and 20 percent of that population uses Twitter. (To read more about social media and museums, visit Colleen Dilen's blog, http://colleendilen.com.) Many museums now develop social media policies to ensure effective communication (for examples, see http://socialmediagovernance.com/policies.php#axzz1gL9a9MTQ). As of late 2016, many local history organizations use social media in some of the following ways:

Facebook (www.facebook.com)
To engage with fans in ways that include posting of historic photos, quizzes, giveaways, event announcements, and regular updates from all areas of museum work.

Pinterest (www.pinterest.com) and Instagram (www.instagram.com)
Pinterest and Instagram are visual tools. Pinterest is a way to both share and collect. Some museums use it as an inspiration board, collecting images that might inspire future work (for interest, entry desks, or interactive exhibitions); other museums use it to share their collections. Instagram, with hashtags, is a great way to highlight behind-the-scenes work, from collections management to getting ready for a big party.

Twitter (www.twitter.com)
Twitter is a form of social media shorthand—*micro blogging. It is an online program where real-time "tweets" of 140 characters or less are posted. You follow tweeters of interest to you, and others follow your tweets. Many tweeters post links to articles and information of interest, such as this December 12, 2011 post from Lisa Craig Brisson: "Reinventing the history museum field trip experience @mnhs. Lots of neat work going into this project" http://ht.ly/7WomD.

Blogs
A blog (shortened form of web log) is a website that's regularly updated with new content. Most blogs are hosted on either Google's Blogger or Wordpress. Bloggers interested in local history include local historians (see Ray LaFever, of Bovina, New York, where he presents "occasional tidbits about the history of this small town in the Northern Catskills of New York," http://bovinanyhistory.blogspot.com), libraries with local history collections (see the Kingston, Massachusetts, Public Library's blog, Pique of the Week, http://piqueoftheweek.wordpress.com), and local and county historical societies. Some organizations use it to promote events and activities, but others have a collections focus. For instance, the Montgomery County Historical Society's blog, A Fine Collection, takes one object per week, includes a photo, and explores the history and context of objects ranging from 1980s shopping bags to a Grecian sofa, circa 1820 (http://afinecollection.wordpress.com). While Historic Cherry Hill in Albany, New York, is closed for resto-

ration, they've established a restoration blog and a series of entertaining YouTube videos to connect their audience to the museum.

In addition, a number of independent history professionals and museum and archive staffers have their own blogs and Twitter feeds. Nina Simon of the Museum 2.0 blog writes passionately and effectively about using web 2.0 philosophy in designing exhibits and programs within the physical space of the museum.

Livestreaming has now become a part of museum life. Periscope or Snapchat (which vanishes in twenty-four hours) both are ways of sharing video content. And it's sure that new ways continue to emerge as now both Instagram and Facebook also encourage video content.

Expanding Our View

Increasingly, new websites provide ways for web users to share content, and local history museums can participate in this as well. *History Pin "is a way for millions of people to come together, from across different generations, cultures and places, to share small glimpses of the past and to build up the huge story of human history" (www.historypin. org). The site does this by encouraging the uploading of historic and contemporary photos, linked to Google maps.

Watch for Change

Five years ago, few people would have predicted that museums of all sizes and disciplines have active Facebook pages. Over a single weekend in 2016, the game Pokemon Go gained 9.5 million users, and many museums capitalized on the interest. It's sure that new plat-

forms and ways of using social media will emerge and local history museums can keep up by regular web surfing and keeping a careful eye on what larger museums are doing. The best part of most social media (and those listed above) is that most of it is free to use!

Have a Plan

Consider developing a social media plan. The Western Museums Association has a handy presentation on what to consider: http://www.westmuse.org/creating-successful-social-media-strategy.

Linda Norris
The Uncataloged Museum

See blogs; crowdsourcing and crowdfunding; History Pin; microblogging; radical trust and voice of authority.

social purity. The American social purity movement began as a response to two developments in the late eighteenth and early nineteenth centuries. One was a growing concern about the tendency of immigrants and native-born Americans to crowd together in impersonal cities where immoral enticements abounded but where community standards and social disapproval had little influence on behavior. The other was the growing belief that moral suasion could help to perfect society. Throughout the century, various theories about how to control urban temptations and how to monitor the experiences and behaviors of the morally vulnerable attracted reform-minded, middle-class Americans.

It became clear early that institutional religion alone did not have the power in cities that it did in small, intimate communities. Increasing numbers of Irish and German immigrants, most of whom were either Catholic or had no formal religious beliefs, could not be reached by sermons preached in Protestant churches. The social and cultural segregation imposed in ghettos isolated these newcomers from the moral influence engendered in smaller, more socially unified settlements. Ordinances to control behavior that did not appear to harm anyone were not popular in a country where the individual freedoms of its male electorate were considered inviolate. To change attitudes and behaviors, the reform groups used two approaches, subtle coercion and militancy.

Many of the earliest and more subtle efforts of these groups were variations of activities already practiced formally in Protestant churches. The Bible Society movement presented immigrants with gifts of Testaments, simultaneously engendering a sense of welcome and a feeling of indebtedness to the giver. The Tract Society movement freely distributed other publications that told stories centering on moral choices: heroes and heroines who chose rightly prospered or were comforted, and those who made immoral choices suffered. The Sunday School movement in its early years focused on the formation of moral attitudes in young, impressionable minds. Church members attempted to attract immigrant children to these classes. However, their goal of blending social classes so that the morality and social responsibility of middle-class children would become a model for poor street urchins was short-lived, and in many churches Sunday school attendance became an exclusively middle-class experience.

During the latter half of the nineteenth century, reform movements focused on controlling the urban environment, a more expensive proposition than publishing, preaching, and psalm singing, and social purity organizations adopted businesslike practices. Wealthy patrons supplied funding for facilities where middle-class values could be inculcated in selected groups. The YMCA movement, for example, established in 1851, gave young clerks, salesmen, and bank tellers places where they could develop wholesome interests and participate in healthful activities. Women's industrial unions offered single, female factory workers safe and temptation-free boarding, and monitored their social experiences. And the City Mission movement held derelict children as virtual captives by offering meals, beds, baths, and clothing and at the same time immersing their charges in sermons and hymn singing. In some extreme cases, children were sent to live with families in the nation's interior, where they might learn responsibility and embrace middle-American values.

Militant groups like the Female Reform Society, founded in 1834, took stands against the vices prevalent in cities. The society not only led public protests against houses of prostitution, but it also published the *Advocate of Moral Reform*, hoping to shame the evil-doers. This periodical published clients' names. Similar reform groups saw alcohol as the major factor in poverty, abuse, and indolence. The American Temperance Union, Washington Temperance Society, and Sons of Temperance conducted parades against alcohol consumption. Hoping to force innkeepers and other purveyors of spirituous liquors out of business, they pressured individuals to join abstinence campaigns.

Paralleling the temperance movement, equally active groups, like the New York Committee for the Prevention of State Regulation of Vice, moved against states' attempts to legalize prostitution so that it could be regulated. Spreading throughout the country and gaining the endorsements of physicians, clergymen, and women's rights advocates, the movement incorporated as the American Purity Alliance in 1895 and held the first National Purity Congress in Baltimore. Thereafter local vigilance organizations continued the work in individual communities, occasionally urged on by national gatherings in Boston and Chicago.

In 1912 the alliance merged with the National Vigilance Committee, and the following year with the American Federation for Sex Hygiene; the united groups adopted the title American Social Hygiene Association. In addition to reforming prostitutes and penalizing the men who engaged them, the reformers sought censorship of pornography in print and eventually in film, endorsed open discussions about sex in schools, and promoted the ideal of marital fidelity. Becoming the American Social Health Association in 1959, the group's focus has been on the prevention of STDs.

In the twentieth century, specially trained social workers and probation officers began to apply theories of urban sociologists and psychologists in their work with those judged socially impure. Liberalizing influences of publicized events, medical advances, and increasing professionalization early in the twentieth century replaced the grassroots movement for social purity.

Sources available online at Google Books: William D. Bliss et al., eds., *New Encyclopedia of Social Reform* (1908) and Aaron M. Powell, *The National Purity Congress: Its Papers, Addresses, Portraits* (1896). See also Paul Boyer, *Purity in Print* (1968), and *Urban Masses and Moral Order in America* (1978); David Pivar, *Purity and Hygiene: Women, Prostitution, and the "American Plan," 1900–1930* (2002) and *Purity Crusade: Sexual Morality and Social Control, 1868–1900* (1973).

Teresa Lehr
College at Brockport, SUNY

Social Security Death Index. The Social Security Death Index (SSDI) is a government-provided database used for genealogical research and epidemiological studies. This database is searchable from both major genealogical websites, *Ancestry.com and *FamilySearch (www.familysearch.org), both providing their own search interfaces. There is a comparison of the various interfaces as well as a good overview of what the index contains and techniques to search it effectively at www.searchforancestors.com/records/ssdi.html. SSDI contains partial social security records for most people who died after 1965 and who had contributed to social security. The database is updated slowly, usually lagging about three years. Various restrictions have been placed on the timing of data release due to concerns about identity theft. Earlier records exist; some can be found in the database, but currently pre-1965 records are not being added to the system in any regular way. Each record in the database contains only basic information. The full application form, which has valuable additional information (such as mother's maiden name, current address, spouse, etc.), can be ordered for a fee at http://www.ssa.gov/online/ssa-711.pdf.

ROBERT KIBBEE
THE HISTORY CENTER IN TOMPKINS
COUNTY (NY)

See genealogical resources online.

Society of American Archivists. The Society of American Archivists (SAA) was organized in 1936, shortly after the establishment in 1934 of the *National Archives and Records Administration. It is the principal professional organization for archivists in the United States and has a worldwide membership of more than 6,200 individuals and institutions. More than forty-five component groups provide members with opportunities to serve on a variety of committees and working groups that support the business of the association and help advance the profession, or for exchange of more specialized professional information relevant to their type of institution (business archives, government archives, college and university archives, museums, religious collections) or to the kind of work an archivist does (*digitization, preservation, visual materials, description). Forty-one universities host SAA student chapters around the country. SAA leaders represent the organization on the boards of nineteen affiliated institutions' committees and commissions in the United States and internationally.

SAA publishes a semiannual scholarly journal, *The American Archivist*, in print and online at americanarchivist. org. *Archival Outlook*, an award-winning bimonthly magazine, is published in print and online at http://www2. archivists.org/archival-outlook/back-issues. *In the Loop*, SAA's e-newsletter, is published biweekly for a circulation of more than 9,000 subscribers. *Word of the Week* is a weekly e-mail produced by SAA's Dictionary Working Group that defines new archives terms and updates existing dictionary entries. Almost all of this content is open access.

In addition, SAA has a robust book publishing program. Since the 1970s, SAA has published more than 150 monographs and e-books addressing a variety of topics and include the Archival Fundamentals Series and the Trends in Archives Practice series. These books are available for sale at http://www2. Archivists.org/bookstore. Some titles are open access at http://www2.archivists.org/publications/moreresources and, in 2010, SAA allowed the HathiTrust to publish eighty-two of its out-of-print titles on archives issues at http://www2.archivists.org/publications/freepublications.

SAA maintains a full catalog of educational opportunities for advanced as well as fundamental training in professional archival skills at http://www2.archivists.org/prof-education/catalog and also offers two certificate programs: Digital Archives Specialist (DAS) and Arrangement & Description (A&D). The *Guidelines for a Graduate Program in Archival Studies* are available at http://www2.archivists.org/prof education/graduate/gpas. SAA's annual meetings are held in late summer in different cities throughout the country and include a wide array of informative education sessions, pre-conference workshops, networking opportunities, special events, exhibits, and tours of local repositories. Under the auspices of SAA, an independent organization, the Academy of Certified Archivists (http://www.certifiedarchivists.org) was created in 1989 to administer a professional certification program.

SAA's mission is to promote the value and diversity of archives and archivists and their vital work in preserving records of enduring value. To that end, it advocates on behalf of members and their institutions to various audiences, including policy makers, resource allocators, and the general public (http://www2.archivists.org/advocacy). American Archives Month, held each October, and #AskAnArchivist Day on October 1 (a social media initiative) are two of its biggest public awareness programs.

SAA annually recognizes leaders and achievers in the field of archives through an awards competition, student scholarships, and the naming of Fellows (http://www2.archivists.org/aboutsaa/awardsandscholarships).

The Society of American Archivists is located at 17 North State Street, Suite 1425, Chicago, IL, 60602-4061; (312) 606-0722; toll free (866) SAA-7858; www2.archivists.org and servicecenter@archivists.org.

CONSTANCE SCHULTZ
AND HEATHER A. WADE
UPDATED BY ABIGAIL CHRISTIAN
SOCIETY OF AMERICAN ARCHIVISTS

See archives and local history.

Society of American Historians. See historical fiction.

Society of Friends, sources for. See Appendix B.

Soundex. To use the Soundex Indexing System to locate *census information about a person, you must know his or her full name and the state or territory in which he or she lived at the time of the census. It is also helpful to know the full name of the head of the *household in which the person lived, because census takers recorded information under that name.

The Soundex is a coded surname (last name) index based on the way a surname sounds rather than the way it is spelled. Surnames that sound the same, but are spelled differently, such as "Smith" and "Smyth," have the same code and are filed together. The Soundex coding system was developed so that a surname can be found even though it may have been recorded under various spellings.

To search for a particular surname, you must first work out its code. For help coding a surname, follow the link to a Soundex calculator on Archives.gov's Soundex page (http://www.archives.gov/research/census/soundex.html). The instructions below will help you code a name yourself and understand the Soundex process.

Basic Soundex Coding Rule: Every Soundex code consists of a letter and three numbers, such as W252. The letter is always the first letter of the surname. The numbers are assigned to the remaining letters of the surname according to the Soundex guide shown below. Zeroes are added at the end if necessary to produce a four-character code. Additional letters are disregarded. For example: Washington is coded W252 (W, 2 for the S, 5 for the N, 2 for the G, remaining letters disregarded). Lee is coded L000 (L, 000 added).

The Soundex Coding Guide

Number	Represents the Letters*
1	B, F, P, V
2	C, G, J, K, Q, S, X, Z
3	D, T
4	L
5	M, N
6	R

*Disregard the letters A, E, I, O, U, H, W, and Y.

Additional Soundex Coding Rules

1. Names with double letters: If the surname has any double letters, they should be treated as one letter. For example, Gutierrez is coded G362 (G, 3 for the T, 6 for the first R, second R ignored, 2 for the Z).
2. Names with letters side by side that have the same Soundex code number: If the surname has different letters side by side that have the same number in the Soundex coding guide, they should be treated as one letter. For example: Pfister is coded as P236 (P, F ignored, 2 for the S, 3 for the T, 6 for the R). Jackson is coded as J250 (J, 2 for the C, K ignored, S ignored, 5 for the N, 0 added).
3. Names with prefixes: If a surname has a prefix, such as Van, Con, De, Di, La, or Le, code both with and without the prefix because the surname might be listed under either

code. For example: Van Deusen might be coded two ways: V532 (V, 5 for N, 3 for D, 2 for S) or D250 (D, 2 for the S, 5 for the N, 0 added). (Note: Mc and Mac are not considered prefixes.)

This article is based on The Soundex Indexing System (http://www.archives.gov/research/census/soundex.html)

MARY RYAN
NATIONAL ARCHIVES
AND RECORDS ADMINISTRATION

South Carolina, local history in. South Carolinians are proud of their history as evidenced by the plethora of local and statewide organizations devoted to preserving and interpreting the past. Every county has at least one historical society that preserves it history through archives, museums, and historic sites. There are also several statewide organizations dedicated to preserving historical resources.

The oldest historical oriented organization in South Carolina is the Charleston Library Society. Founded in 1748, primarily as a circulating library, over the years the society has developed an important research collection of books and manuscripts about the state. In its original charter the Library Society envisioned itself as the initiator of a museum and a college, the present Charleston Museum and the College of Charleston.

The oldest museum in the country is located in Charleston, South Carolina. Founded in 1773, the Charleston Museum's primary focus during the nineteenth century was on studying and preserving the natural resources found along the coast. In the early twentieth century the museum opened

First African Baptist Church, the oldest church on Hilton Head Island, South Carolina, unveiled this historical marker for its sesquicentennial in 2012. Credit: South Carolina Department of Archives and History.

its South Carolina Hall and began collecting *material culture artifacts from across the state. The first organization to begin actively and purposefully collecting South Carolina material culture artifacts was the United Daughters of the Confederacy. In 1895 one of the earliest efforts of the Wade Hampton Chapter "was the establishment of the South Carolina Relic Room." Today the South Carolina Confederate Relic Room and Military Museum is an agency of state government and is ac-

credited by the American Association of Museums.

The founding of the South Carolina Historical Society in 1855 saw the establishment of the first organization specifically devoted to collecting and preserving South Carolina historical material. The Historical Society's purpose is "to collect information respecting every portion of our state, to preserve it, and when deemed advisable to publish it." The other major repository of nongovernment records in the state is the South

Caroliniana Library. Since the founding of the South Carolina College in 1801, the University of South Carolina collected and preserved Caroliniana. However it was not until 1940 when the university opened a new library that the oldest free-standing college library building in the country, the South Caroliniana Library, was dedicated to preserve the history and literature of the state.

The first effort by state government to preserve any of the state's history occurred in 1891 when the Public Records Commission was created primarily to obtain copies of the documents in the British Public Records Office relating to South Carolina. Subsequently it became apparent there was a need to consolidate the state's "scattered records." In 1894 the Historical Commission was established but it did not begin to receive an annual appropriation until 1905. Today the South Carolina Department of Archives and History is the repository for all state government records as well as overseeing the preservation of local government records throughout the state. In addition to operating the state archives the agency also houses the state historic preservation office.

South Carolina was one of the last states to develop a state museum. During the state's tercentennial celebration in 1970, a move began that resulted in the creation of the South Carolina Museum Commission in 1972. From 1972 until the opening of the museum in 1988 the commission developed three different master plans on three sites before successfully renovating an 1894 textile mill into a comprehensive state museum featuring cultural history, natural history, art and science, and technology. In the late 1990s the state museum began a campaign to add a planetarium, 4D theater, and observatory. However, the state's economy remained in the doldrums until after the recession and these additions were not completed until late 2014.

The first full state history was not written until 1920 when Yates Snowden's five-volume *History of South Carolina* was published. Snowden's work contained two volumes of history and three volumes of biographical sketches. David Duncan Wallace's four-volume *A History of South Carolina*, published in 1934, is generally regarded as the first comprehensive history of the state. In 1951 Wallace's four-volume work was condensed into a single volume, *South Carolina: A Short History* that served as the standard state history for the next fifty years. While a number of state histories followed Wallace's work, it was not until the publication of *South Carolina: A History* by Walter B. Edgar in 1998 that a comprehensive history of the state was written that incorporated the vast scholarly resources developed during the last half of the twentieth century.

In the 2005 standards adopted by the State Department of Education, South Carolina is studied by students in the third and eighth grades. The third-grade curriculum is "South Carolina Studies" with students exploring the state's varied geography and the diversity of its people. In the eighth grade "South Carolina: One of the United States" focuses on the history of South Carolina and the role the state played in the development of the United States as a nation.

RODGER STROUP
SOUTH CAROLINA DEPARTMENT OF
ARCHIVES AND HISTORY, RETIRED

See building bridges through local history; United States, local history in.

South Dakota, local history in. As America's fortieth state, South Dakota was late to join the Union. Long before the arrival of European settlers, American Indians populated the region's prairies, plains, and mountains. Early explorers such as the Verendrye brothers and Lewis and Clark were quickly followed by fur traders. A series of conflicts and treaties with the Dakota, Nakota, and Lakota peoples reduced Indian lands and led to the establishment of reservations. In 1861 Congress created Dakota Territory. The gold rush of 1876 brought speculators and miners to the Black Hills, and the Homestead Act helped to spark the Great Dakota Boom of the 1880s, boosting population, but partisan politics in Washington, D.C., delayed statehood for South Dakota until 1889.

The drought and depression of the 1920s and 1930s brought hard times for the agricultural state. Meanwhile, tourism gained a foothold with the carving of Mount Rushmore and President Calvin Coolidge's selection of the Black Hills for his summer White House in 1927. Later, four large multipurpose dams constructed on the Missouri River and the development of pheasant

A sandstone building is seen in the background of this historical marker honoring the sandstone architecture of Hot Springs, South Dakota. CREDIT: SOUTH DAKOTA STATE HISTORICAL SOCIETY.

hunting created new recreational opportunities, making *tourism the state's second-largest industry.

The preservation of South Dakota history rests with the State Historical Society and many local historical societies, historic houses, museums, interpretive centers, and archives. The majority of the state's collections are housed in small museums, often run by *volunteers. The State Historical Society traces its roots to 1862 with the formation of the Old Settlers Association of Dakota Territory. Privately chartered as the South Dakota State Historical Society in 1890, the society became "duly organized" by the state legislature in 1901 and was assigned to supervise the Department of History.

For nearly a quarter century, Director Jonah L. ("Doane") Robinson oversaw the society's collection of historical artifacts, records, and library materials. In 1902, he began producing the biennial South Dakota Historical Collections series as part of the state-mandated mission "to collect, preserve, exhibit and publish material for the study of history." Robinson also initiated the "State Museum," an assemblage of military, natural history, and aboriginal curios displayed in the state capitol in Pierre. While Robinson started the drive to construct a separate facility, the Soldiers' and Sailors' World War Memorial Building became a reality under successor Lawrence K. Fox in 1932.

Will G. Robinson, son of Doane, became director in 1945. He microfilmed the society's accumulation of newspapers and instituted the *historical marker program. A new level of professionalism arrived with Director Dayton W. Canaday in 1968. Canaday hired the first trained history specialists and focused on organization of primary research materials. In 1970 the society began its quarterly journal, *South Dakota History*. Governmental reorganization in 1972 put the functions of the society, *archaeology and *historic preservation programs, and four state university museums within a new Office of Cultural Preservation in the Department of Education and Cultural Affairs. In 1982 the South Dakota Heritage Fund was formed as a private, nonprofit support group for the society.

Fred W. Lillibridge succeeded Canaday as director in 1985 and oversaw the creation of an Office of History that unified the society's staff, funds, membership, and collections as an integral part of state government. To commemorate the centennial of South Dakota statehood, the State of South Dakota constructed a modern facility to safeguard the society's archival and museum collections. Director Junius R. Fishburne moved the society into the Cultural Heritage Center in Pierre for the 1989 celebration. The society's administrative offices, archives, museum, and publishing programs were the first to occupy the 63,000-square-foot building. The Heritage Fund raised money to design and install the permanent exhibition, *The South Dakota Experience.* Fishburne was succeeded as director in 1995 by former state legislator Mary B. Edelen. Jay D. Vogt, who headed the Heritage Fund, was named deputy director in 1999 and assumed management of the society. He was appointed director in 2003.

In recent years, the society has built on its past achievements. The historic preservation office was relocated to new quarters in the Cultural Heritage Center. State funding supported the compilation of American Indian records from federal repositories. The society established its own press to publish books on the state's heritage and history. An archaeological study of Fort Pierre Chouteau National Historic Landmark was conducted to prepare for interpreting the site. In 2003, the society became part of a new Department of Tourism and State Development. Since then, the society has renovated the Verendrye National Historic Landmark as part of its heritage tourism program and expanded its traveling exhibitions, classroom education kits, technical advice and assistance efforts, and publications. Reorganization of state government moved the society to the Department of Tourism for four years, and the Heritage Fund changed its name to the South Dakota Historical Society Foundation to better reflect its relationship with the society. By executive order in 2015, the South Dakota Codified Laws were updated to eliminate references to former agencies and structures and formalize the society as a division of the Department of Education, operating in five program areas: archaeology, archives, historic preservation, museum, and publishing.

In 2014–2015, the Great Sioux Horse Effigy, an artifact donated to the State Historical Society by missionary Mary C. Collins in 1920 and symbol of the society, was the central piece in *The Plains Indians: Artists of Earth and Sky* exhibition viewed by over 500,000 people in Paris, Kansas City, and New York. The State Historical Society published *Pioneer Girl: The Annotated Autobiography of Laura Ingalls Wilder*, edited by Pamela Smith Hill, in 2014. The never-before-published autobiography, authorized by the Little House Trust, received rave reviews and topped the best seller lists for weeks as a nonfiction title.

Important early histories of South Dakota include works by Doane Robinson in 1904 and 1930 and the five-volume *History of Dakota Territory* and *South Dakota: Its History and Its People* by George W. Kingsbury and George Martin Smith. Herbert S. Schell wrote the first comprehensive one-volume history of the state, *History of South Dakota* in 1961; the society published a revised fourth edition in 2004 with new chapters by John E. Miller. Other state histories include *Challenge: The South Dakota Story* by Robert F. Karolevitz and *The South Dakota Story* by David Miller and Nancy Veglahn. In 2005, the Center for Western Studies at Augustana College, Sioux Falls, published a compilation of essays entitled *A New South Dakota History*. Historians writing South Dakota history today include Jon K. Lauck, an independent scholar, Sioux Falls; Molly Rozum, University of South Dakota, Vermillion; and Brad Tennant, Presentation College, Aberdeen, among others. Working retired professors include John E. Miller, South Dakota State University, Brookings; James D. McLaird, Dakota Wesleyan University, Mitchell; and David A. Wolff, Black Hills State University, Spearfish. Communities often publish local histories to commemorate significant anniversaries, such as a town's centennial.

South Dakota history is taught at the fourth-grade level, and the Department of Education sets the standards for the teaching of social studies, which includes history. In 2002, the State Historical Society together with the Department of Education created the award-winning online South Dakota history curriculum and text, www.sd4history.com, which is still used throughout the state.

JAY D. VOGT
SOUTH DAKOTA STATE
HISTORICAL SOCIETY

See American Indian history; United States, local history in.

Southeast Asians in North America, sources for. See Appendix A.

Spanish in North America, sources for. See Appendix A.

state archives and records management programs. While many state constitutions and early statutes established requirements to make and keep records of government, the first state archives—those agencies whose primary charge is to preserve and protect state government records—were not established until the first decade of the twentieth century. While the states had been accumulating records since colonial and territorial times, often in great volume, the lack of a formally designated agency to care for these records had resulted in great disparities from state to state in their physical condition, accessibility, and prospects for continued survival.

Today all fifty states, the *District of Columbia, and most of the territories have formal archival programs and all but two have formal records management programs. The combined paper- and film-based holdings for all state archives in 2014 totaled approximately 2.8 million cubic feet, with another 5.1 million cubic/linear feet in the holdings of state records centers. Collectively, the state archives have accessioned about 447 terabytes of electronic records and hold another 244 terabytes that have not yet been accessioned. In addition to state government records, many state archives hold records from local governments and from nongovernmental organizations, institutions, and individuals. In other states, holdings of "private" papers comprise a substantial volume of the total holdings, especially in the state historical societies serving *Nebraska and *Wisconsin.

Good records management programs ensure that records are maintained in efficient and economical ways while they are still in active use. Tools like records retention and disposition schedules identify the small but critical body of records that are essential to current government operations and those that warrant permanent retention in the state archives, estimated to range between 2 and 5 percent of all records created. Records managers also ensure that the other 95 to 98 percent are retained only so long as they are needed and then disposed of according to properly enforced records disposition laws and regulations.

While wide variations among the states remain in terms of resources—financial, human, and administrative—substantial agreement now exists on the principles and policies essential to a sound program for state government records management and the care of archival records.

In 2014 more than one million people accessed information from their state archives by mail, e-mail, phone, in-person visits, and through web searches. Most state archives are working hard to make their holdings accessible via the web. At least thirty-nine now provide access to at least half or more of their holdings on their own. Most state archives create virtual exhibits or memory projects that focus on especially significant documents, collections, or topics and many place emphasis on facilitating use of documents in the classroom by providing teaching resources, including curricular packets, along with digital images of original documents.

The first state archives were created at the turn of the twentieth century, largely in response to an alarming report by the *American Historical Association (AHA) on primary source documentation in the United States. It detailed the sometimes "total neglect" of government records in the then forty-six states and spurred twenty-three states to create central repositories for their archives by 1910. Another wave of new state archives occurred during the middle third of the century prompted by two factors: the establishment of the *National Archives in 1934 and the paper explosion that all governments experienced during World War II. Seven states created official archival repositories between 1935 and 1950, and fourteen more were established in the next two decades. This period also saw the rise of records management at both the federal and state levels. At least thirty-five states made some move toward in-

stituting records management between 1945 and 1965.

The organizational structures that the states chose as they implemented these programs were as different as the states themselves. A few state archives were established as independent agencies; others were assigned to state libraries, historical societies, secretaries of state, or other government agencies. In some states, the archives and records management functions were assigned to the same agency; in others they were split. In addition, like all state officials, state archivists had to deal with the realities of operating in a political system. Every state archivist then and now has to wear, "in addition to an archivist's garb, the cloak of a diplomat, a politician, and, most of all, a missionary; for only through building personal and official relationships with members of the executive and legislative branches could he or she win the respect and funds necessary for the development of an adequate program" (H. G. Jones, "The Pink Elephant Revisited," *American Archivist* 43, no. 4 [Fall 1980]: 481).

Legislation establishing a state archives or records management program did not guarantee that it would actually become a functioning part of state government. In some states, many years elapsed between the creation of a state archives in law and the provision of adequate appropriations, staff, and facilities. This gap between legal responsibility and resources to adequately carry out that responsibility persists to this day in many state archives and records management programs.

The last of the state archives were created during the 1970s and 1980s. A number of these can trace their establishment to persistent efforts by archives and records professionals who leveraged funds provided by the *National Historical Publications and Records Commission (NHPRC), the funding arm of the National Archives, to assess conditions and provide strategic plans for implementation of effective programs. Several other existing but weak state archival programs also succeeded in using this NHPRC assessment and planning process to gain support from their legislators and agency heads to strengthen archives and records programs in their states.

It is possible to see real progress in state archives and records programs by comparing the conditions Ernst Posner described in his landmark study *American State Archives* with those of today. In 1962–1963, Posner's book "told an uncomplimentary story of archival lethargy or neglect in about three quarters of the states of the Union." At that time, twelve states had no state archivists, and nine of those had no program at all for the management of permanent government records. Change happened slowly at first, but some movement in the right direction began to occur in the decade immediately after Posner's report was published. Between 1963 and 1973, eight states established archival agencies for the first time and thirteen created records management programs. State archival programs in *Rhode Island and *Idaho were not firmly established until 1989 and 1990, respectively. By 1993, there was a functioning state archival program in every state in the union.

Major changes in the ways state archives worked, especially on collabora-tive initiatives, also began to occur in the mid-1970s. A significant number of long-term state archivists retired during this time, resulting in a generational turnover in the leadership of the state archives and records management programs. In retrospect, 1974 was an especially key year because it saw both the creation of a new professional association, the National Association of State Archives and Records Administrators (NASARA), and the establishment of the Records Program within the National Historical Publications Commission, which then became the National Historical Publications and Records Commission (NHPRC). Both of these have been critical to the advancement of sound practices and innovative programs for state government records.

NASARA was founded by state archivists, but became NAGARA in 1984 when the organization expanded its membership and mission to include local and federal interests and "Government" replaced "State" in the organization's name. Over the years, NAGARA has provided a focal point for collaborative activity across all three levels of government, promulgating best practices and providing important resources through its publications and conferences. Since the outset of the NHPRC Records Program in 1974, the state archivists have also functioned as state historical records coordinators, chairing state boards that evaluate applications to the commission from within their states. In this capacity, the state archivists came together as the Council of State Historical Records Coordinators (COSHRC) in the 1980s; in 2005 the organization changed its name to the Council of State Archivists (CoSA) to encompass all aspects of the work of state archivists.

As noted earlier, NHPRC's Records Program has had a substantial impact on the development of state archives and records programs, furnishing the resources and incentives to make real change possible. As the NHPRC Records Program developed, it focused ever greater attention on and vested significant responsibility with the fifty state archivists. In order to participate fully in the grant program, NHPRC required each state to establish a State Historical Records Advisory Board (SHRAB), appointed by the governor and headed by the state archivist acting as state coordinator. All but two of the fifty states now have authorized a SHRAB, although some are more active than others and levels of activity have waxed and waned over the years. Grant proposals from both public and private repositories are reviewed by their respective state boards and, in turn, the SHRABs are expected to foster archival activity within their states.

The first significant body of work generated by NHPRC through the State Historical Records Advisory Boards was the Statewide Historical Records Assessment and Planning Projects. The first round of grants for these projects was made in 1981 when the Reagan administration's downsizing initiatives threatened NHPRC with extinction. The commission "wanted to leave a legacy of assessment reports that the states themselves could use as central planning and action documents." Fortunately, NHPRC survived, but the state assessments proved to be a wise investment nonetheless. By the mid-1990s, all fifty states had completed at least one such project; several of the earliest had actually gone on to complete reassessments, in order to monitor either progress or strategic planning projects to carry progress forward.

To an extent even greater than Posner's *American State Archives*, these reports often became catalysts for change. Perhaps it was because the process itself—the surveys, analyses, and strategic planning—was ultimately as important as, or more important than, the written documents themselves. In completing the assessments, archivists from public and private repositories came together over many months with genealogists, attorneys, local government officials, librarians, and educators to identify needs and propose solutions. The process itself helped build networks and alliances and reinforced the leadership status of the state archivist/coordinator. With leadership from the state archivist in his or her role as state historical records coordinator, many of these alliances have been maintained and have prospered in the years since the assessment projects were conducted.

One of the areas that the NHPRC specifically asked each state to evaluate was state government records. There are numerous examples of concrete, positive actions taken as a result of recommendations made in the assessment reports. At least two states appointed their first professional state archivists as a result of NHPRC-sponsored studies (*Rhode Island and *Idaho). Several reports made successful arguments for new state archives buildings (*New Mexico, *South Carolina, and *Delaware). In *Pennsylvania, the records management function was transferred to the state archives. Many have since developed training and assistance programs for local governments and for private archival repositories.

Archives and records management (ARM) programs have actively sought ways to increase revenue outside of regular appropriations from the state legislatures. Many of the state ARM programs receive income from some combination of fees, revolving funds, and trust funds that provide substantial support for staff and programs.

Like many other sectors of government, state archives and records programs have had to become more entrepreneurial in their outlook. Resources can grow, but these programs will constantly be looking for new methods of generating revenue. The most desirable approaches will be those that generate substantial income without unduly restricting access by imposing prohibitive fees for reproductions or other use-related activities.

Going forward, the top priorities for state archives include securing and maintaining adequate funding and staffing to meet their legal charge, electronic records management, and digital preservation of an increasing number of holdings, keeping up with the demands for adequate physical space, and ongoing training and program development.

Excerpted and modified from the *State of State Records*, published by the Council of State Archivists, 2015.

ANNE W. ACKERSON
COUNCIL OF STATE ARCHIVISTS

state historians. In 1895 New York legislation created the office of state historian (Chapter 393, Laws of 1895) with the charge to compile the state's military records. New York State Historians have also overseen the publication of documentary volumes of the papers of governors; they have answered questions from the state government and the public, and have given some oversight to the many appointed local and municipal historians in the state and others. Until 1911, the governor appointed the state historian; after that date, the office of state historian fell under the aegis of Commissioner of Education.

In 1909 Maine appointed a state historian and Arizona did so in 1912. In 1919 Wyoming created a state historian, a position that was abolished during the Great Depression, the historian's duties distributed to other departments. Illinois named a state historian in 1943, New Mexico in 1945, although the position lapsed briefly and was only reinstated in 1967. In the 1970s Kentucky appointed a state historian. In 2005 Texas created a nonfunded position that has been held by a member of history departments at Texas State University and Austin College.

What did state historians do? In the case of New York, they contributed a number of documentary editions of the papers of governors; in Arizona the state historian has often authored histories of the state. In some cases, the job description for state historian has directed little beyond the traditional "collection, preservation, and dissemination of information," allowing each appointee to define the position as best suits individual interests and the state's needs. In Connecticut, the Regents of the University of Connecticut appoint the state historian from the department of history at the university. That individual is charged with providing information on "historical matters to the media, public, and legislature," and the state historian is to "maintain active programs of historical research & public outreach" by giving lectures, organizing programs, and providing teacher education throughout the state.

In some states without a designated state historian, these duties have been taken on and accomplished by the leader of the state historical society, heads and staff of an office of history or of preservation and culture, or from within the state archives. In the case of Idaho, in 1956 H. S. "Jerry" Swinney was the first professionally trained historian to head the Idaho State Historical Society; he became a significant leader collecting and preserving documents, exhibiting and interpreting state history, and promoting historic sites. In more recent times, much historical activity has also come from departments of cultural tourism.

What then, should a state historian do today? In the first place, the state historian should be an advocate for history, recognizing good practices, exemplary exhibits, articles, pamphlets, programs, and books. A state historian might also provide education to the many people who are involved with state and local history, from those in the academic world, museums, associations, genealogical groups, school educators, and independent historians. Conferences may provide a common meeting ground; seminars on special topics in state history and regional meetings could be used for training, and information about important history themes, sources, and historical questions can be taken home by participants to teach to others. The Internet provides an effective interactive means of delivering short courses on topics in state history and on the doing of local history and of keeping connected about projects, research interests, and activities.

The Internet is a powerful means of distributing source materials from central archives to those around the state. Documents can easily be scanned and then discussed, showing how they might have had an impact upon a locality or how to use similar documents located within a county courthouse, thereby contributing to a greater understanding of state and local history. The state historian is able to publicize research interests from around the state and to pose questions in order to create a community of state and local scholars.

A state or local historical organization has a mission to collect, preserve, and disseminate knowledge; few engage in history education, especially for those working on the local level. House museums and other history sites have particular goals. A state historian, on the other hand, could focus efforts on promoting the state's unique past, creating community among those who are involved in history that they might know of other good ideas, new uses for sources, methods, scholarship opportunities, etc. for preservationists, archivists, historians, genealogists, and environmentalists by means of the Internet, regional meetings, and special events. A state historian should provide needed educational opportunities by means of short courses or Internet instruction. A state historian can promote the past and help people find a relationship with the place in which they find themselves and understand how they or their forebears got there, in addition to giving direction and sometimes correction to the many ways in which states now use history in wayfinding signs, seeking tourists, and promoting the history of the state.

CAROL KAMMEN
TOMPKINS COUNTY (NY) HISTORIAN

See county historians; and local and state history by state name.

state historical societies. See individual state entries; United States, local history in.

state humanities councils. In 1965, Congress enacted legislation creating the National Foundation for the Arts and Humanities, composed of the National Endowment for the Humanities and the National Endowment for the Arts. The humanities councils trace their origin to the 1970 legislation that authorized both agencies for an additional five years and called for exploration of a structure for "state programs" as part of the National Endowment for the Humanities (NEH). In 1971, NEH organized the first volunteer "state committees" in a handful of states and granted funds to these quasi-autonomous boards for local regranting. Widely viewed as an experiment, these earliest programs flourished and found a niche in the mix of local programming and educational support. In rapid man-

ner, NEH facilitated the establishment of additional state committees. In 1976, with the intent of ensuring that the U.S. public enjoyed the benefits of the humanities, Congress set aside designated funds appropriated to NEH for the exclusive use of the new state-based programs. In operation today are fifty-six autonomous state humanities councils, one in each state and in American Samoa, the District of Columbia, Guam, the Northern Mariana Islands, Puerto Rico, and the U.S. Virgin Islands. A parallel structure of programs also exists within the National Endowment for the Arts. Unlike the humanities, however, state arts councils function as agencies of state government.

The mission and statutory rules governing humanities councils have evolved since the earliest legislation. Congress initially limited councils to making grants in support of thematic humanities and public policy programs. In 1976 these restrictions were lifted, enabling councils to make grants in all areas of humanities education such as NEH itself does.

The legislation also requires that councils be governed by elected boards made up of a broad and geographic representation of scholars and the public in each state. These boards rotate regularly and are self-perpetuating, though each council must publicly solicit new members. The governor of each state may appoint up to five board members depending on the size of the board, which varies.

Humanities councils undergo a formal NEH assessment each five years, after which they are authorized to receive funding for the next five-year cycle. Funding distribution for states is based on a formula that gives a base amount to all councils and an additional amount dependent on population. All federal funds must be matched by other sources of funding (private or state) on a one-to-one basis. Prior to 1996, councils followed a procedure not unlike any other applicant to NEH. Each council submitted a proposal that was evaluated by a review panel in Washington with the chairman making the final funding decision. Only one designated entity in each state is eligible to receive funds. In 1996, the chairman of NEH replaced this grantor-grantee model with the certification process now in place. Typically, the council's board and staff conduct a comprehensive internal assessment that culminates in a visiting team of external evaluators, including at least one member of NEH's staff. As part of the process, councils are required to develop a five-year strategic plan, which becomes the basis for future assessment.

The councils operate with an autonomy and flexibility unusual in federal-state partnerships. This is attributable to several factors. By incorporating as private, nonprofit organizations, councils avoid the bureaucratic impediments of public agencies. Careful management by NEH, council boards, and staff in the earliest years of the state program avoided embarrassments that might have triggered greater Washington control. The stipulation by Congress and the Office of Management and Budget of wise guidelines for the expenditure of funds (e.g., federal funds may not be used for lobbying), combined with requirements for annual audits and re-

ports, has helped establish a rigorous standard of accountability. Finally, and not least important, the effective advocacy and mediation of the Federation of State Humanities Councils, the councils' membership organization founded in 1977, has helped define the appropriate balance between national oversight and local control.

As partners, the NEH and state humanities councils help carry out the congressional mandate of strengthening scholarship and equitably disseminating the results to the American people. Not surprisingly, there is inevitable competing state-based and national perspectives that grow out of this unique relationship that are both challenging and fruitful. In the mid-1990s, strong congressional support for the kinds of grassroots programs that humanities councils favor helped shore up support for NEH at a time when NEH's existence was challenged by new forces in Congress. There have also been times when strong support for NEH benefited the states. Moreover, NEH has imported into its thinking and priorities some of the innovative concepts of council programming, such as library-based discussion programs and family literacy. Likewise, "blockbuster" NEH programs—and strong, popular NEH chairs—have helped reinforce council initiatives at the state level. What is clear is that the NEH and the councils are not simply mirror images of each other operating at different planes. While that is probably healthy pluralism, there is still an unrealized potential in this partnership. This may be changing. The past five chairs (Lynne Cheney, Sheldon Hackney, William Ferris, Bruce Cole, and James Leach) have worked directly with councils in undertaking national thematic programs, while the most recent chair, William "Bro" Adams, has pushed other divisions of NEH to adopt a more civic and public purpose in their core grant making. It is worth remembering that the councils, and NEH too, are relatively young organizations that have no precedent in U.S. history.

While each state receives federal formula funds, every year more state councils add "outside" funds to their basic federal grant. Councils now receive support from state government, private foundations, corporate foundations, and individual donors. The long-term trend is toward budgets that reflect a healthy and proportionate mix of public and private funding sources as councils explore innovative programs that respond to varieties of public need (public health, veterans, new readers, rural communities, and social equity).

Related to new funding priorities is the growing level of activism toward agencies of government and legislatures. Unlike their sister organizations, arts agencies, all of which are agencies of government, humanities councils enjoy wide latitude with regard to advocacy provided no federal funds are used for this purpose. *Volunteers serving on council boards are not restricted in their political activism as private citizens—nor are the grant recipients of council funds or the audiences who benefit directly from council-funded programs. These groups make up a powerful grassroots constituency that is one of the keys to public support for humanities funding at the state and national levels. The big question facing

councils is whether this growing base of constituent support can be converted into larger state and federal appropriations for the humanities. The trend was positive until 2009, when in successive years state legislatures confronted steep revenue declines that forced cuts in education and other areas of discretionary spending. The federal budget in 2011 faced similar pressures. Both cultural endowments experienced unprecedented 8 percent mid-year cuts that year, as did state councils. Indeed, few federal agencies and almost no earmarked programs that are part of discretionary spending were spared (defense is the major exception). This somewhat static trend in public funding certainly will continue through 2017 and perhaps well after, to the extent that reducing the national deficit remains a national priority. In response to the national debt, how deeply future cuts will go (or whether there are prospects for funding increases) depends on whether Congress makes cuts to entitlement programs which constitute the great bulk of federal expenditures.

Another important trend is in types of programs that councils fund and conduct. From the beginning, humanities councils made grants to community, civic, and cultural organizations, including colleges and universities, in order to promote greater public involvement in the humanities. Scholars usually are involved in council-funded programs as project directors, presenters, or consultants. As a rule, councils avoid funding projects that are intended exclusively for strictly student audiences, though programs for teacher enrichment are commonly funded. Some councils fund scholarly research; the majority do not. A typical council grant might range from several hundred dollars to $20,000 or more. Examples of projects are media programs (television and radio), the development of museum exhibitions, library-based programs, workshops for schoolteachers, speakers' bureaus, community symposia, conferences, and interpretation of archeological and historic sites. In most states, the councils have been the major statewide source of grant support (often, the only source) for local history programs for the public. This may also explain the strong support that humanities councils enjoy in Congress.

Increasingly, states are pursuing council-conducted opportunities that follow newer kinds of strategic thinking aimed at gaining greater public and private funding support, building audiences and constituencies, and deepening their impact. This is especially the case with unique commemorative events, such as the Lincoln bicentennial, state centennials, and the 150th anniversary of the Civil War. A byproduct is diminishing funds for grant making, in part a reflection of increased operating costs and near-stagnant federal support upon which the grant-making program depends. But grants will never be eliminated entirely because so many councils recognize that grants offer the ideal mechanism for responding to initiatives that bubble up from the community and not infrequently become a basis for new council initiatives.

Some of these new council initiatives in fact represent new models of programming for the future. In Virginia, the council has created a center and fellowship program that is attracting scholars and students of Virginia history and culture from around the world for a period of residency that entails research, writing, and public programs. Connecticut's council is partnering with the state legislature in helping to make local history the state's major cultural tourism industry. In Maine, the humanities council has become a national leader in medical humanities programs. Vermont and New Hampshire are known for their impressive statewide programs for authors and audiences. Louisiana's council is publishing *Cultural Vistas*, a statewide magazine that connects the state's citizens with their local history, folkways, culture, and history. The Tennessee council's Southern Festival of Books is pioneering a connection between writers and the public that typically features stories of a particular place. The Alaska, Washington, Kansas, and Florida councils are developing an entrepreneurial approach to programming that suggests an entirely new way of thinking about and carrying out programs on local history and culture as well as other topics. The Minnesota council has created a nationally unique center for teachers. The Texas council, with state support, has launched a major statewide initiative aimed at professional development in history for teachers in middle and high schools. The California council has made "stories" the centerpiece of its programs, which also enables it to form new relationships with immigrant communities. Massachusetts continues to support (often in partnership with media organizations and higher education) conferences and symposia that explore issues of democracy and change in the United States and the world. The North Carolina council is engaged in a nationally significant literacy program that is helping to instill nurturing values in new readers, families, and children. The Georgia council has developed an exclusively online state encyclopedia that highlights local culture and history and is linked with other digital resources in the state. These experiments can be multiplied around the states and suggest a new surge of creativity at work.

As the missions of councils become more focused and pragmatic, so too does their programming. We are witnessing a move away from the academic definition of the humanities and the reliance on traditional models of programming (the university-centered outreach approach that emphasizes humanities disciplines) toward a more informal definition, one that readily accommodates new audiences, formats, and diversity of experience and expertise. This trend is more gradual than sudden. It owes something to a more generalized change in philanthropy that looks at systemic problems. It also reflects a natural process of maturation whereby councils set new goals for themselves in response to opportunities and needs in local communities as well as obstacles.

The priorities of scholars and scholarship remain important in council programs, but the influence of each is complemented as newer types of leaders appear on council boards and staff, recruited precisely because of the "real-world" expertise they bring (corporate, organizational, philanthropic, political, fundraising). Inventive or "relevant"

programs that in former years would have been seen as outside the domain of the humanities disciplines are developing around new, local priorities. These include battling adult illiteracy, encouraging family reading programs, promoting community dialogues that clarify values and strengthen mutual respect, serving rural communities, forming partnerships with schools and teachers to strengthen humanities instruction, and reaching poor and underserved youth. Councils are also developing signature projects with a wide public appeal, such as traveling Chautauqua shows, book and humanities festivals, popular magazines, state encyclopedias, and cultural tourism. In its twentieth year of existence, the Smithsonian Institution's "Museum on Main Street" partnership with humanities councils continues to make high-quality exhibitions and programs available to rural and underserved communities. Such opportunities are often coupled with professional development for local cultural organizations.

The majority of the programs supported by councils involve literature, reading programs, history, and heritage; in many states, humanities councils have been the single most important source of program support (sometimes the sole source) for museums, historical societies, and libraries. The success of almost thirty years of funding efforts can perhaps best be measured by the geometric increase in public humanities and history programs that now take place in hundreds of communities on a weekly or even daily basis.

Paradoxically, as more of the public enjoys the humanities, within our institutions of higher education, the domain of the humanities is shrinking in the competition with more "practical" fields of study. Though it has not always been so obvious, the fact remains that the long-term health of history and the humanities, whether in the community, the classroom, or scholarship, are entwined. The hope is that all three can grow together in a spirit of shared civic purpose, lifelong learning, and organization partnership.

JAMIL S. ZAINALDIN
GEORGIA HUMANITIES COUNCIL

STEM education in history organizations. STEM is an acronym for Science, Technology, Engineering, and Mathematics. STEM education, both formal and informal, emphasizes interrelationships among the four fields. In the United States, STEM is a term that has been used in schools, educational policy, and curriculum development with increasing popularity since the 1990s. STEM initiatives work toward improving K–12 and postsecondary programs, increasing engagement and representation among women and minorities, and building an innovative, prosperous workforce.

Why discuss STEM in an encyclopedia of local history? The Department of Education says people equipped with STEM knowledge and skills "solve tough problems, gather and evaluate evidence, and make sense of information." The same could be said for historians. In response to the emphasis on STEM education, some history organizations have incorporated the ideas, themes, and skill sets of STEM into their existing historical content. As a result, these his-

tory organizations have illustrated their own contributions to STEM fields and affirmed their *relevance in a STEM-focused world. A STEM approach to historical interpretation is one that embraces science, technology, engineering, and math as interrelated and significant to the past.

STEM and history have a lot to offer one another. While today these fields appear to be separate, STEM and history can trace their genealogies back to the same patterns of deep, nuanced thinking about the world. All four components of STEM have pasts with lasting legacies. History organizations can provide social and cultural contexts to scientific, technological, engineering, or mathematical achievements. Historians can pose complicated questions about human decision making and problem solving that shape both the past and the present. In turn, historical interpretation can benefit from a deeper understanding of STEM topics. By explaining the processes behind how things work, stories of the past become more dynamic and relatable.

Presenting history through the lens of STEM can enrich the experience of today's public. For example, Jackson's Mill historic site in Weston, West Virginia, integrates STEM into its interpretation of the childhood farmstead of Stonewall Jackson. Interpreters at Jackson's Mill emphasize how people in the nineteenth century employed tools, knowledge, and skills to make a living on the frontier. At first, this appears to be purely historical information. But at the blacksmith shop, visitors learn about heat, fuel, and types of metal, all of which involve science, technology, engineering, and math. When visitors try their hand at candle making, they learn about the types of wax, chemical changes, and home production of goods. The cabins and surrounding *gardens tell stories of food, hunting, agriculture, weaving, and spinning, all cultural activities that rely on nature.

The Oliver Evans gristmill at Jackson's Mill offers the opportunity to address both the invention and its inventor. Oliver Evans applied scientific and mathematical knowledge of physics, machinery, and power to engineer a technology that solved age-old problems in grain processing. Like all inventors, he struggled with the design and applied critical thinking skills that today are considered essential to STEM education. By improving the quality and quantity of flour, the automatic gristmill was both a scientific feat and a historical moment with social and economic reverberations. Interpretation should clearly draw these connections and then allow visitors to think both historically and scientifically to make meanings of their own.

A growing number of history organizations are creating spaces for visitors, primarily children, to experiment with design, invention, and critical thinking within a historical context. These "STEM spaces" apply STEM skills to historical ideas, exhibition content, and museum collections.

At the National Museum of American History, children at the Spark!Lab create and test an invention that solves a problem just like inventors of the past. They can follow in the footsteps of Thomas Edison and create their own style of lamp, make music with an instrument all their own, or imagine ways to improve the grocery shopping cart. The laboratory displays historic artifacts that illustrate the diversity of invention and its broad influences on American history. By promoting STEM skills, Spark!Lab places the act of invention on a continuum that children are carrying forward at the museum.

The National Air and Space Museum's highly interactive *How Things Fly* exhibit includes a STEM space called the Design Hangar, in which visitors are challenged to design "aircraft" that accomplish a certain goal, such as flying steadily in a wind tunnel. However, the ultimate goal of the Design Hangar is not to have visitors create a perfectly functioning finished product, but to engage visitors in the process of design. To emphasize important STEM skills like experimentation and persistence, staff and *volunteers at the Design Hangar pull examples from history. Engineers, whether they worked on the first airplanes or on rockets to the Moon, used faulty designs to enhance their knowledge of manned flight and improve their machines.

Integrating STEM and history education can benefit both the organization and the audience. This is especially pertinent to schools that, like many history organizations, are suffering in the current economic climate. The recession slashed school budgets, eliminating half of planned field trips in 2010–2012, according to a survey by the American Association of School Administrators. Teachers and students alike are under pressure to deliver good scores on high-stakes tests. In 2015–2016, 12 percent of the administrators surveyed reported they had brought back their field trips to pre-recession levels and another 26 percent considered it. A history organization that integrates STEM in its interpretation can provide students with a well-rounded experience that covers multiple school subjects at once. With an assortment of learning opportunities available, teachers can make stronger arguments for choosing to visit a historic site for a field trip. History organizations should also align their field trips with state and national standards so that teachers can easily check off the standards they need to meet.

STEM can open new doors to collaborate with universities, science centers, nature reserves, *parks, a variety of clubs, and federal agencies such as the *National Park Service, Smithsonian Institution, and NASA. Collaboration can bring new resources, expertise, and perspectives. The National Museum of the American Indian and the National Air and Space Museum Planetarium have worked together on multiple programs, including a presentation on Hawaiian sailors' use of the stars to navigate the Pacific Ocean. Although their individual missions are different, the strengths of each institution complement one another.

Granting agencies and private donors are also expressing interest in projects that are at the intersection of STEM and history. Funders such as the National Science Foundation and *National Endowment for the Humanities have supported projects by history organizations for education, exhibits, and preservation. Conner Prairie Interactive History Park in Fishers, Indiana, established its STEM space, Create.Connect, with the help of the Science Museum of Minnesota and a $2.3 million grant from the National Science Foundation. The programs and activities at Create.Connect "bridge the subjects of science, technology, engineering and math and the people, places and events of history." Parents sought these blended experiences for their children, reporting in a 2014 visitor study that the top three goals they wished to achieve at Create. Connect were exploring STEM through inquiry-based learning, increasing knowledge of history, and preparing children for the future.

Finally, the conservation of historical artifacts and sites would not be possible without STEM fields. History organizations can discuss conservation efforts through the lens of STEM education. Back at Jackson's Mill historic site in West Virginia, the Oliver Evans gristmill was actually relocated from another site in order to preserve it. Each piece of wood and stone was marked with numbers, dismantled, and reassembled in its current location. The story arc of this gristmill is one of both past and present achievements in STEM. When made accessible to the public, these stories can represent the multiplicity and relevancy of history.

PAMELA CURTIN
WEST VIRGINIA UNIVERSITY

Swedes in North America, sources for. See Appendix A.

Swiss in North America, sources for. See Appendix A.

$\mathcal{T}$

teaching local history in the classroom: one perspective. Over the past several years, the history department at New Mexico State University has developed an introductory history course for entering freshmen. Designed as a broad overview of the craft of history, "Making History"—as we have titled it—introduces students to the discipline of history. The course builds on our use of local history in a number of courses including "Time Traveling through New Mexico's Past," "Interpreting Historic Places," and "Historic Preservation" as well as in several of our U.S. history survey courses. Learning goals include (among others) understanding the differences and similarities between history and memory, analyzing *primary sources, and appreciating how historical experiences and memories have shaped contemporary societies. The course was designed with an international component to address a New Mexico state requirement encouraging curricula to enhance "respect for other people and cultures," but a strong component of "Making History" is its emphasis on local history.

In thinking about how we wanted to begin a conversation with our students about the nature of "history making" we eventually settled on an approach built around the idea that all history is local. To elaborate on this point, we selected two texts that illustrate connections between place and memory: Carol Kam-men's *On Doing Local History* (2014) and Eric Foner's *Who Owns History: Rethinking the Past in a Changing World* (2002). These books reinforce the major themes of the course that revolve around history in our everyday lives, the representation and misrepresentation of the past, and the importance of history to informed and responsible citizenship. Most of all, we wanted our students to explore the nature of the past and consider the place of history in their everyday lives.

Throughout the semester, we reflect on the usefulness of local history markers and landmarks to stress that primary source evidence can come in the form of artifacts, landscapes and buildings, film and photographs, newspapers and directories, government documents, and cemetery markers. Las Cruces, New Mexico, located in the south-central portion of the state, just north of El Paso, offers numerous local stories and remnants that capture, we hope, the historical imagination of the students. The campus itself has a number of buildings listed in the *National Register of Historic Places that reveal the original architectural interest of the founders and later New Deal influence in the form of plaques, WPA sidewalk impressions, and building murals. The taming of the lower Rio Grande provides local history lessons and examples as the town is crisscrossed with an intricate system of major, minor, and lateral

teaching local history in the classroom: one perspective

irrigation canals (called *acequias* in this corner of the state) that document the economic/agricultural history of the community as well as its connections to federal government water policy.

One of the most important aspects of the course, as our students tell us, are the class trips to local places of interest and history. Las Cruces is fortunate to have a state-operated farm and ranch museum that captures the ranching and farming history of the Mesilla Valley. The local railroad museum allows our students to better understand the role of the railroad in developing not only Las Cruces itself, but all of the southwestern part of the state. The Branigan Cultural Center, creatively managed by the city, features a rotating series of exhibits on the arts and local history. The most unexpected (for the students) and rewarding (for me) visit outside the classroom is to a local cemetery. We visit the graves and recount the biographies of New Mexico State University's first president, Mexican and Japanese pioneers in developing crops in this part of the state, a man who was killed in Pancho Villa's famous 1916 raid on Columbus, New Mexico, and Patrick Floyd Garrett, who gained fame in killing Billy the Kid. Most of our students have studiously avoided cemeteries but find the stories associated with them compelling. They tell us that after taking this course, they view them as windows into the past. To personalize the cemetery visit, one of the requirements of the class is to add two family members to the *Find a Grave* website.

By illuminating the range and diversity of local history, we hope our students will begin to understand that

history does not just happen in other places, but that history—that is the relationship of people to each other and to the land—has shaped, physically and psychologically, this corner of the country. That shaping has influenced the present society of the Mesilla Valley, the forty-mile stretch of the Rio Grande north of the Mexican border. If it is true that we are who we have been, then this valley's past speaks eloquently about the present nature of our existence.

The community here is heavily Hispanic because Las Cruces is located on the historic El Camino Real—the King's Highway—between Mexico City and Santa Fe. Before 1848, of course, the valley was part of Mexico. After 1848, west of the river belonged to Mexico while the east bank was ceded to the United States as a result of the Treaty of Guadalupe Hidalgo. The 1853 Gadsden Purchase relocated the boundary with Mexico south to its present location in El Paso. The ceremony transferring the western side of the valley to the United States took place in Mesilla, located just west of Las Cruces, and is reenacted annually. The bandstand in Mesilla Plaza (a National Historic Landmark) bears the date 1854.

It is through an engagement with these places and events (and many others) that we encourage our students to appreciate their own history and the nature of history making. The purpose of the course is to encourage an understanding of the ethereal relationship between remembering and forgetting, between history and memory, between place and placelessness, and, most of all, to appreciate the colorful and complex journey from then to now. It is our be-

lief that this introductory exposure to the structure of the historian's craft will lead to greater historical comprehension among our students as well as an appreciation for their own unique pasts.
DWIGHT PITCAITHLEY
NEW MEXICO STATE UNIVERSITY

See relevance; values of history.

Teaching with Historic Places. See National Register of Historic Places.

technology and local history. It is quite natural for those of us who live in wealthy and developed Western nations to take technology and its place in our lives for granted. Historians are not immune to this tendency. While we all recognize the importance of certain momentous events—the invention of the printing press or the steam engine or the completion of the first transcontinental railway—we often fail to examine the more mundane but no less important story of how technology has shaped our communities and our individual lives. The evidence of technology's pervasiveness is all around us—from the buildings we live and work in to the cars we drive and the roads we drive on—yet it seems as if most of us seldom notice it. We have grown accustomed to its benefits and have learned to expect it to work well, which it usually does. We are so utterly dependent on technology that we are sometimes inclined not to examine it too closely.

But examine it we must. Because technology permeates every aspect of our lives, no historian can create an accurate picture of the past without dealing with it. So if we really want to understand our communities and how they have changed over time we need to know something about the technologies that have been part of that transformation. We need to know, for example, what impact the introduction of the telephone had on small towns, how the construction of streetcar lines changed the urban landscape of a city, and what rural electrification meant to farm families.

So, the question then becomes how best to approach what can be an intimidating subject. It's important to recognize that you don't have to be an expert or even technologically inclined to explore the history of technology. It isn't necessary to understand every minute detail of how a machine or system works or to grasp all the intricacies of the inventive process in order to write about technology. What you do need is a few basic principles, a good chronology of events, and some advice on where to look for reliable information on the technology you want to explore.

Broadly speaking, there are three basic principles that you should keep in mind when researching the history of any technology. First, people create technology. Scientists, inventors, mechanics, and engineers develop tools to solve problems, to enhance our ability to do work, to win professional acclaim, to achieve fame, and even just to make money. Remember that, once introduced, technology is shaped by society and by wider social, political, and economic forces. Inventors may have one idea about how their device should be used but people may adapt it and apply it in completely different ways. The inventors of radio saw it as a means of mobile and long-distance communication. After 1918, amateur enthusiasts turned it into an entertainment medium and broadcasting was born. Moreover, technologies can be rejected by a society—nuclear-power reactors are one example—that doesn't believe the benefits are sufficient to justify the risks and costs involved. A related point that is also worth noting is the impetus that war provides for technological development. Many of the devices and systems we use in our daily lives either began as military research projects or benefited from massive military investment.

We should also remember that technology is a tool; it is neither inherently good nor inherently bad. In North America and the West generally, we have tended to stress the positive attributes and accomplishments of technology, associating it with progress and prosperity. Yet every invention has costs as well as benefits and a careful historian will look at both when exploring the impact of a given technology on a community.

Finally, there is much more to the history of technology than invention. It is only one stage in the long, complex, cumulative process by which people transform experience, ideas, and abstract scientific principles into working technologies. A patent record will tell you who holds the legal claim to an invention, but it will not tell you how many other people contributed to the process of invention or how much effort it took to turn a patentable device into a usable appliance. Nor does it tell us anything about the application and adaptation of technology that may be every bit as important as invention, particularly in a local history context.

There are many different ways to approach the history of technology. The most familiar is probably that which focuses on the history of a particular machine or system and explores local use or impact. This is a straightforward method that allows researchers to look at any number of technologies from the telegraph to the washing machine. For residents of industrial towns, it is also possible to research a local factory, mine, or other worksite by looking at the machines the workers used or the products they were making. This approach can highlight the ways in which business has applied technology to improve productivity and how this has changed many people's working lives and the character of the communities in which they lived. There are also more abstract ways to look at the influence of technology. Local historians can explore the social and cultural relationships that people have had with technologies. What did it mean to own a bicycle in the 1890s or a car in early twentieth century? How did families incorporate the new entertainment medium of broadcasting into their homes and their lives? Researchers can also look at how technology has changed our perceptions of time, speed, distance, and efficiency. Did rapid transportation and communication really broaden our horizons and enhance our understanding of the world? Another abstract approach would be to examine the impact electronic communication systems (telegraph, telephone, radio, television, the Internet) have had on our sense of local and regional identity and on our ability to preserve them.

To get started exploring the history of technology, it is important to find a good general overview of the history that will provide a good foundation for understanding technology. There are many such works available, all of which take a slightly different approach to explaining and interpreting technological change. Three recent books worth noting are *A Culture of Improvement: Technology and the Western Millennium* (2007) by Robert Friedel; *Technology Matters: Questions to Live With* (2006) by David E. Nye; and *Human-Built World: How to Think About Technology and Culture* (2004) by Thomas P. Hughes. Other useful works include *The Norton History of Technology* by Donald Cardwell (1995); *The Machine in America: A Social History of Technology* by Carroll Pursell (1995); and *A Social History of American Technology* by Ruth Schwartz Cowan (1997). These are just a few examples of the many good general histories available.

For looking up information on specific technologies or inventions, there are a number of general reference guides, dictionaries, and encyclopedias that list and describe important innovations. Most cover a wide range of devices and developments, from the everyday to the exotic—one even has an entry for gas-chamber execution—and are popular in style and format. *Eureka! How and When the Greatest Inventions Were Made* (1974) edited by Edward de Bono, is large-format book with plenty of images to support the text. Divided into sections by broad themes, it provides a fairly comprehensive survey of

developments up to the 1970s, with entries that are at least three paragraphs long and yet manage to convey the main points as well as some of the complexity of technological change. This book also has a chronological table placing technological breakthroughs in the context of other important events. Gerald Messadié has produced three handbook guides (1991): *Great Modern Inventions*; *Great Scientific Discoveries*; and *Great Inventions Through History*. These have entries that begin with a description of how the process or device works and then provide a sketch of its development. Other quick reference guides include *Science and Technology Desk Reference* compiled by James E. Bobick and Magery Peffer, which has a fifteen-page chronology and an extensive bibliography, and the *Biographical Dictionary of the History of Technology*, edited by Lance Day and Ian McNeil. The McGraw-Hill *Concise Encyclopedia of Science and Technology* (2004) is also a useful source.

For more detailed information and analysis on specific technologies, researchers can turn to *A History of Technology* (1979), a seven-volume compilation of essays on the development of technology from ancient times until about 1950. These volumes are especially strong in "big" technologies such as power generation and distribution; industrial processes and machinery; mining; building and construction, including bridges, railways, and roads; and water supply and treatment systems. Essays average about twenty pages and each is followed by a list of references that will guide the truly tireless researcher to even more specialized works on the topic. As with all works that try to cover a lot of historical and technological ground, these books do not always get the details right. The popular books seldom reflect the latest specialist research, and they all tend to concentrate on the achievements of great world powers and major international companies, often neglecting the contributions of the less well known. Also, most overviews seem to celebrate technological change and only rarely point out its negative consequences, consequences that we sometimes see all too vividly in our local communities when companies close local factories or mines, abandon rail or other transportation infrastructure, or move or scale back their operations.

Those researchers who want more critical and current analysis of technological developments can also search library catalogs and online resources by subject, and in most fields they will find at least a few useful works. This is especially true in the United States and Great Britain, where the history of technology is a large and well-developed academic and public history field. Though some of these works may be a little complex or theoretical, they do offer a more detailed and subtle picture of technology and society and can lead readers to a wealth of other sources on the subject, including artifact and archival collections, *oral history interviews, and other useful records.

Museums, historic sites agencies, and historical societies can also be very good sources of information. In the United States, the *National Park Service is responsible for a wide range of technology-themed sites and staff histori-

ans have produced research reports on many of these. The National Museum of American History has a large and impressive collection of technological objects and the curators responsible for these collections have also conducted an enormous amount of research on both the objects and the fields they represent. State museums and historical societies will also often have collections of objects and documents that relate to the history of technology.

In the United Kingdom, the Science Museum and its affiliates provide equally rich and reliable resources relating to many topics in the history of technology. There are also many regional museums like the Ironbridge Gorge Museum at Coalbrookdale that have documented the history of industry in Britain. Specialized institutions, like the many maritime museums around the United Kingdom, also provide a wealth of primary sources—objects, images, and documents—as well as research reports and publications on many topics.

For Canadians, Parks Canada and the Canada Science and Technology Museum are responsible for preserving industrial, scientific, and technological objects and sites of national importance, while regional museums like the Reynolds-Alberta Museum and the Marine Museum of the Atlantic do the same for the provinces and regions. Like their counterparts in other countries, the historians and curators at these institutions have carried out research on many topics related to the history of technology. Some of it is available in published form but most can be viewed in libraries and even online in some cases.

University departments can also be a good source of information and collections. Many science and engineering schools have extensive collections of historical objects like instruments, test equipment, and models. Also, researchers at these institutions often needed access to a supply of precision equipment, devices, and infrastructure and the skilled workers who made and repaired these objects. This demand might have encouraged the development of a skilled workforce in the nearby communities.

The research conducted by the larger institutions and agencies is a useful starting point for anyone interested in the history of technology. The national and regional perspectives can provide important context for local events and developments. The more comprehensive reports will also explain the history of the technology in some detail: who invented a device or system, how it works, who contributed to its evolution over time, what social, cultural, and economic forces informed that evolution, and what impact the technology has had on society.

With this as a foundation, local historians can establish a framework for their own research. At the community level, resources may be less plentiful or obvious so historians will have to use their instincts and their imagination in tracking down material. *City and business directories, insurance maps, and newspaper ads can provide some basic information about what types of businesses existed at different times and where they were located. Old catalogs, trade magazines, and manuals contain valuable technical and production information as well as the names of lo-cal dealers. Large construction projects such as the installation of street lighting, power and water service, and public transit systems were often topics of heated debate in towns and cities and are thus likely to be recorded in political debates, election materials, and local newspaper articles.

In those fields where governments played a direct role in the adoption, application, or regulation of technology, the official government record can be very useful. In Canada, for example, the annual reports of federal departments like Marine and Fisheries and Transport record the locations and dates of construction of all kinds of technical infrastructure. They also contain detailed technical information on everything from lighthouse construction and life-saving equipment to radio communication, air navigation, and the licensing of broadcasting stations.

Business records can be harder to track down and, where they have survived, are often devoted to administrative and financial matters rather than manufacturing processes, machinery, products, and personnel. Some large companies with national networks, often regulated by government—telephone and railway companies are obvious examples—have kept detailed records and will sometimes have information relating to local infrastructure. The most historically conscious may also have photo and artifact collections. Researchers can fill some of the gaps in local business records by locating and interviewing former employees who can sometimes provide personal accounts of how a factory evolved over time and what impact retooling and automation had on the conditions and quality of work there. All of these sources, though, should be used carefully and corroborated wherever possible.

*Photographs can also be a valuable and interesting source of information. Streetscapes are especially useful since they often depict modes of transportation, road surfaces and buildings, public lighting and signage, and trolley, telegraph, telephone, or electrical wiring. The alert researcher may also notice parking meters, gas stations, broadcast antennas, and countless other technological details that might normally escape our notice. Interior images can also reveal a great deal about the technological past. Does the room have a fireplace? Is it fueled by wood, coal, or gas? Or is the room heated by a radiator? Are there any electrical outlets or appliances visible? What kind of lamps are in use?

Like most subject areas, the history of technology has a significant presence on the Internet but researchers should use these resources with care. Anyone can "publish" their research online and much of what has been posted is not reliable. Most of the old myths and legends (and a great many new ones) make the rounds and all kinds of alleged experts add their voices to the testimony until even the most far-fetched tales develop of kind of popular authenticity. The best approach is to stick with reputable sites, that is, those that are affiliated with respected institutions and agencies (those that do research) or those set up and monitored by groups of retired professionals or serious enthusiasts. Also, look for references that tell you where the information provided came from and don't be afraid to contact the site managers if you have questions about the content. Always be skeptical and critical of the sites you visit.

Last but not least, look closely at the technology that interests you. Go to your local museum or historic site, to a flea market or antiques fair, or even to your grandparents' attic or garage and examine the actual objects. Look for information about the item. What is it and what was it used for? How old is it? Does it have a make or model label? Can you find a serial number? What is it made of and what are its dimensions? Does it have ornamentation and is there an aesthetic element to its design? Is it hand- or factory-made? Was it modified by the user?

Once you have answered some of these basic questions you can move on to more interpretive concerns. What does the object tell you about the people who created it, used it, or preserved it? Why did they make, acquire, or cherish it? What, if anything, does this tell you about their values and ideals, hopes and desires? What does it suggest about our relationship with technology? Can it help to inform the choices we make today? If you need help framing the right questions to ask about a device, you can consult any number of books on material history or material culture studies. One very useful source is "Artifact Study: A Proposed Model," by E. McClung Fleming, published in Thomas. J. Schlereth, ed., *Material Culture Studies in America* (1982). This brief article lays out a basic framework for looking at and exploring history through objects.

Once you start thinking about technology, you will begin to see it everywhere and will understand the many meanings and stories that it contains. Its history is as varied and complex as the history of the people who for centuries have created and used it. And thinking about the history of technology not only helps us to understand the central role it has played in the evolution of our communities; it also enhances our ability to understand and make decisions about the role of technology in our lives today and in the future.

SHARON BABAIAN
CANADA SCIENCE AND TECHNOLOGY
MUSEUM

SOME IMPORTANT DATES IN THE HISTORY OF TECHNOLOGY

1800—Alessandro Volta invents the voltaic pile, the first source of continuous electrical current.

1814—George Stephenson introduces the first practical steam locomotive.

1834—Charles Wheatstone and William Cooke patent and demonstrate the first practical electromagnetic telegraph.

1844—Friedrich Gottlob Keller invents wood-pulp paper.

1856—William H. Perkin prepares the first aniline dye.

1857—E. G. Otis installs the first safety elevator.

1866—Britain and North America linked by the first viable trans-Atlantic submarine telegraph cable. (First attempts made in 1857–1858 and 1865.)

1872—Brooklyn Bridge opened but not to traffic until 1883.

1874—H. Solomon introduces pressure-cooking methods for canning foods, which begin to appear in stores around 1880.

1876—Alexander Graham Bell registers his phone patent just hours ahead of fellow inventor Elisha Gray.

1880—Swan and Edison independently develop the first practical electric lights.

1885—Karl Benz builds a single-cylinder engine for motor cars.

1888—English bicycle makers Starley and Sutton introduce the third version of their Rover bicycle. This leads directly to the development of the modern safety bicycle, which soon eclipses the high-wheeled ordinary and gives rise to a bicycle craze across the Western world.

1906—R. A. Fessenden broadcasts the human voice via radio waves to ships at sea.

1908—L. H. Baekland introduces Bakelite. With its commercial manufacture the following year, the "Age of Plastic" begins.

1909—Charles Saunders distributes Marquis wheat, a revolutionary early-ripening hard spring wheat, to farmers on the northern Great Plains.

1913—Ford introduces assembly line techniques that revolutionize automobile production.

1920—First scheduled radio broadcasts take place in North America. By 1924 there are 2.5 million radio receiving sets in the United States, and by 1925 there are 1.65 million in Great Britain.

1928—John Logie Baird demonstrates color television, while George Eastman exhibits the first color motion pictures. The following year Kodak introduces 16mm movie film.

1931—The Empire State building, started in 1929, is completed.

1936—The Boulder (Hoover) Dam is completed, creating the largest reservoir in the world.

1938—Eli Franklin Burton and his students demonstrate the first practical electron microscope at the University of Toronto.

1938—Lajos Biró invents the ballpoint pen.

1940—Howard Florey develops penicillin as a practical antibiotic. It is used successfully to treat chronic diseases in 1943.

1942—Magnetic recording tape is invented. The first magnetic recording of sound had been accomplished in 1899.

1946—Bell Labs in the United States introduces public automobile-based radiotelephone service. Bell Canada begins testing a similar system. The following year a Bell Labs researcher demonstrates the cellular concept for mobile telephone delivery but the technology to support it did not exist.

1947—Researchers at Bell Labs invent the transistor. Its first widespread commercial use is in transistor radios introduced in 1954. By the 1970s, engineers have developed a method of putting multiple circuits on one piece of semiconductor material and the microprocessor is born.

1955—Nuclear-generated power is used in the United States for the first time. Other Western countries join the nuclear club soon after.

1958—Using equipment he had developed himself, Charles David (Dave) Keeling begins systematic measurements of atmospheric CO_2 at Mauna Loa in Hawai'i and in Antarctica. Within four years, the project—which continues today—provides the first unequivocal proof that CO_2 concentrations are rising.

1959—The St. Lawrence Seaway is opened, making the Great Lakes accessible to ocean-going vessels.

1962—Rachel Carson's environmental exposé *Silent Spring* and revelations about the effects of Thalidomide begin to undermine society's confidence in science and technology. Seven years later, the U.S. government takes steps to ban DDT and removes cyclamates from the market.

1966—Color television, introduced to U.S. viewers in 1951, is finally becoming more popular.

1971—The largest ship built to date, the 372,400-ton tanker Nisseki Maru, is launched in Japan. With the dramatic rise of oil prices after 1973, builders begin to construct even larger supertankers that put increasing stress on port facilities and pose huge risks for the environment.

1975—The CN (Canadian National) tower, begun in 1973, is completed. At just over 1,815 feet (553 meters) it is the tallest free-standing structure in the world.

1977—The Apple II personal computer is introduced. IBM introduces its own DOS-based system in 1981. By the later 1980s, the computer has become a fixture in most of our lives.

1981—Binning and Rohrer conduct the first scanning tunneling microscope experiment demonstrating the imaging of surfaces at the atomic level.

1982—Barney Clark lives 112 days after receiving an artificial heart to replace his own failing heart.

1983—The first cellular phone system begins operation in Chicago and European nations discuss technical standards for cellular systems that will apply to all of Europe. By 1984 twenty-five U.S. cities have cellular service.

1986—The first module of the *Mir* space station is launched. The space shuttle *Challenger* explodes shortly after takeoff; and the largest nuclear accident in the world takes place at the Chernobyl power reactor, spreading radioactive fallout across much of Europe.

1987—The U.S. Department of Agriculture approves Calgene's genetically modified Flavr Savr tomato for commercial production in the United States.

1987—Researchers demonstrate real-time magnetic resonance imaging of the heart. Functional imaging of the brain follows in 1993.

1988—The smallest portable telephone on the U.S. market weighs about one pound (450 grams), costs about $2,000, and offers forty-five minutes of talk time.

1990—Logitech introduces the first fully digital camera aimed at the mass market. The Dycam model I costs about $1,000 and has a capacity of thirty-two black-and-white images. The NAVSTAR Global Positioning System becomes operational.

1990—NASA and the European Space Agency launch the Hubble telescope.

1992—At the first Earth Summit in Rio de Janeiro, governments agree the United Framework Convention on Climate Change. Its key objective is "stabilization of greenhouse gas concentrations in the atmosphere at a level that would prevent dangerous anthropogenic interference with the climate system." Developed countries agree to return their emissions to 1990 levels.

1993—The World Wide Web, which began operating in Switzerland in 1990, becomes freely accessible to anyone with a modem and a personal computer.

1995—The DVD is introduced.

1995–1997—With the introduction of the first pesticide-producing crop (Bt corn 1995) and the first herbicide-resistant plant (Roundup Ready soybean 1996), genetically modified organisms become a fact of life. Opposition to these developments in Europe leads the EU to initiate mandatory labeling in 1997.

1998—Construction begins on the International Space Station.

1998—Swatch and Daimler-Benz launch the Smart Car (**S**watch **Mer**cedes **Art**) in nine European countries.

2000—There are just over ten cellular or mobile telephone subscriptions per one hundred inhabitants worldwide. By 2009 there are more than sixty-seven subscriptions per one hundred inhabitants for a total of about 4.6 billion subscriptions.

2001—American surgeons Gray and Dowling implant the first self-contained artificial heart in Robert Tools.

2001—Apple introduces the first iPod just months after the debut of iTunes, but it does not gain a strong foothold in the market until 2004. By 2007, Apple has sold over 100 million of the devices.

2003—Researchers announce the official completion of the human genome project.

2004—The social media revolution begins with the launching of Facebook. The following year, Hurley, Chen, and Karim introduce YouTube and in 2006 Twitter debuts. In 2014 Facebook had over 1.3 billion active users while Twitter had 310 million in 2016.

2006—Researchers and engineers install the first in-stream tidal current generator in North America at Race Rocks, British Columbia. It is the first phase of a multiphase project.

2008—Half a century after beginning observations at Mauna Loa, the Keeling project shows that CO_2 concentrations have risen from 315 parts per million (ppm) in 1958 to 380 ppm in 2008. In 2013, researchers determine that the daily mean concentration has surpassed 400 ppm.

2009—Statoil inaugurates the world's first operational deep-water, large capacity floating wind turbine in the North Sea off the coast of Norway. In 2011, Japan announces plans to develop a large floating turbine installation to supply energy to the Fukushima region, which has had a shortage of electrical power since the tsunami destroyed the nuclear plant there in March 2011.

2010—Major car makers Nissan and Chevrolet introduce mass-production plug-in electric cars in December. They join a small but growing club of electric car manufacturers. Worldwide plug-in car sales grow from just under 12,000 in 2007 to over 315,000 in 2014.

2014—China Shipping Container Lines (CSCL) launches the first of five gigantic container ships intended for the Asia-Europe trade routes. *CSCL Globe* was the largest container ship in the world at the time of its launch in November 2014, with a maximum capacity of 19,100 twenty-foot containers or TEUs.

2014—Toyota announces the first mass market hydrogen-powered car, the Mirai, and Google introduces a new concept for their driverless car without steering wheel or control pedals and unveils a prototype the same year.

2014—Hitchbot, the hitchhiking robot, travels across Canada from Nova Scotia to British Columbia, recording its experiences along the way.

2015—Researchers at the École Polytechnique Fédérale de Lausanne photograph the quantum wave-particle duality of light. This will help researchers better understand the fundamental nature of light, and could even assist in the development of quantum computing and a number of other technologies.

2015—New Horizons probe reaches Pluto, sending back invaluable and beautiful images of the distant planet.

2015—Renewable energy overtakes coal in the energy mix of the United Kingdom.

temperance. See social purity.

Tennessee, local history in. Settled by colonists in the 1770s and entering the Union as the sixteenth state in 1796, Tennessee's first organized historical society appeared in 1820. The founders of the Tennessee Antiquarian Society (later reorganized into the Tennessee Historical Society in 1849) felt part of a dynamic time in the creation of American history. A commitment to the guardianship of the experiences of the first settlers and heroes of the American Revolution drew the society's

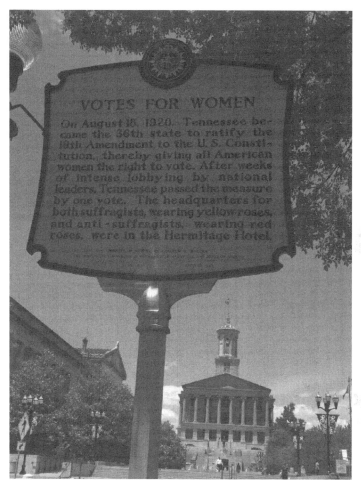

This marker, in front of the Tennessee state capitol in Nashville, commemorates the state's ratification of the nineteenth amendment to the U.S. Constitution. CREDIT: ANN TOPLOVICH, TENNESSEE HISTORICAL SOCIETY.

organizers together to preserve this past and to assert Tennessee's pride among the states. By 1834, the East Tennessee Historical and Antiquarian Society was founded in Knoxville. In 1857, the Old Folks of Shelby County formed in Memphis. The current East Tennessee and West Tennessee Historical Societies respectively trace their origins to these organizations.

The Tennessee Antiquarian Society served as an important resource for its president, John Haywood, who wrote the first histories of the state. *The Natural and Aboriginal History of Tennessee* and *The Civil and Political History of the State of Tennessee* appeared in 1823. J. G. M. Ramsey's *The Annals of Tennessee to the End of the Eighteenth Century* appeared in 1853. The most recent comprehensive history of the state is *Tennesseans and Their History* (1999), while *The Tennessee Encyclopedia of History and Culture* (1998, 2003, 2011) provides a free web-based resource that includes entries on all ninety-five Tennessee counties and cities over 100,000 in population. The Tennessee Historical Society has published the *Tennessee Historical Quarterly* since 1942, a peer-reviewed scholarly journal on all aspects of Tennessee history, and annual papers are published by regional historical societies. Many county and local history books and journals are published as well. The best source for up-to-date information on these titles is the catalog of the Tennessee State Library and Archives (TSLA).

In addition to printed histories, the Internet is increasingly rich in resources for local history in Tennessee. Guides to manuscript collections are available online for the major collecting institutions of the state, such as the TSLA, McClung Collection of the Knox County Public Library, and the Mississippi Valley Collection at the University of Memphis. *Digitization of collections through cooperative arrangements among these and other collecting institutions has progressed rapidly in the twenty-first century and many primary documents related to local history are now available online. Other web-based projects, such as Google Books, are making once hard-to-find local publications available to researchers, while many public libraries now allow free access to patrons to U.S. *Census and other records for Tennessee. A good (and constantly updated) general resource on local history is the TnGenWeb project website, which has links for the state's ninety-five counties. These county sites in turn have detailed information on available records, publications, and local history organizations.

In 2004, *A Directory of Tennessee Agencies* (available at the TSLA website) identified approximately 950 private and public history organizations in Tennessee. These range from house museums and community historical societies to state agencies such as the Tennessee Historical Commission (THC). The THC manages the state *historical markers program, as well as historic preservation programs; the almost two thousand markers provide a visible reminder of the state's local history. The Tennessee Civil War Trails program, under the Tennessee Department of Tourism Development, has erected more than 1,000 local history markers as part of Tennessee's Civil War sesquicentenary.

The Tennessee State Historian, a position created in 1955, is appointed by the governor. Carroll Van West, PhD, has served in the post since 2013. He is author of a dozen books on local history and is director of the Center for Historic Preservation (CHP) at Middle Tennessee State University. The CHP works on local history projects across the state.

In the early 2000s, the Tennessee Department of Education implemented social studies curriculum standards for public K–12 schools that integrated Tennessee history into American and world social studies. Until the late 1980s, Tennessee history was required to be taught in Tennessee classrooms but had later become elective. The issue of whether state and local history should be taught to Tennessee students continues to be debated, but actual instruction now depends on whether the individual teacher deems it important. Local history projects by students are among the most successful in Tennessee's competition for *National History Day. About 7,000 students participated in History Day in 2015.

Despite the reduction in emphasis on local history in the schools, interest in Tennessee local history has increased among the general population with the commemoration of the 150th anniversary of the Civil War. The state commission's projects emphasized local experiences in the Volunteer State, which was engulfed in its entirety by battles and Union and Confederate occupation. The African American story from the Civil War, especially its contributions of U.S. Colored Troops, through the civil rights movement, is especially important in Tennessee's local history. The bicentennial of the War of 1812 had similar success, while the centennial of World War I will also draw attention to local contributions to Tennessee's role in the development of U.S. history.

ANN TOPLOVICH
TENNESSEE HISTORICAL SOCIETY

See United States, local history in.

Texas, local history in. Public interest in local history is high in Texas, given the effectiveness of time-honored programs and the development of new initiatives that focus resources and address new perspectives on the past. The interest remains underpinned by strong grassroots efforts complemented by partnerships with both private and public entities. There is also promising new support from the university level, where local history is increasingly viewed as a viable means of promoting public history, more diverse research projects, and community involvement.

A key player in the promotion of local history has long been the Texas Historical Commission (THC). Beginning in 1953 as the Texas State Historical Survey Committee, the THC has evolved through the years due to federal and state legislation and funding, but also because the agency's early leaders established a foundation of county historical commissions. The network of *volunteers serving each of the 254 counties ensures a standard program of service, *heritage education, teamwork, and shared visions. As a result, local history benefits from the unique partnership in such diverse areas as historical designations, archeological stewardship, downtown revitalization, museum training, cemetery preservation (50,000+), military history, historic site interpretation (the THC administers twenty sites), and architectural assistance. Two particularly successful efforts are the Texas Historic Courthouse Preservation Program (THCPP) and the Official Texas Historical Marker Program. Under the former, established in 1998, the state has provided significant financial and technical assistance to counties for full courthouse restorations and emergency grants. As legislative funding continues, other counties prepare for participation by raising matching funds and developing master plans. To date, the THCPP remains the largest state-county preservation partnership in the nation's

ST. PETER'S CATHOLIC CHURCH
IN 1866 BISHOP CLAUDE M. DUBUIS
OF GALVESTON SENT A YOUNG FRENCH
IMMIGRANT, EMIL L. J. R. FLEURY, TO
ORGANIZE A CONGREGATION AND BUILD
A CHURCH TO SERVE BOERNE AND THE
OUTLYING TOWNS AND ARMY POSTS.
THIS STONE STRUCTURE WAS COM-
PLETED IN 1867. FEATURES INCLUDE
AN ENTRY PORTICO WITH SHINGLED
GABLE END, A SMALL BELFRY, AND
SEGMENTAL—ARCH WINDOWS. FLEURY,
WHO LEFT BOERNE IN 1869, RETURNED
IN 1923 TO HELP LAY THE CORNER-
STONE FOR A NEW SANCTUARY.
RECORDED TEXAS HISTORIC LANDMARK — 1987

This Texas Historical Commission marker commemorates the founding of the first Catholic Church in Boerne, Texas. CREDIT: KATHY NICHOLS.

history. Equally effective in terms of generating interest in local history, the marker program relies on applications from county commissions and now boasts more than 16,000 historical markers, far more than any other state.

To ensure the continued viability of its various programs, the THC provides general local assistance through its website and *social media, webinars, newsletter (*The Medallion*), and the County Historical Commission Outreach Program. It also maintains a searchable online database of detailed information on markers, *National Register properties, State Antiquities Landmarks, military sites, and museums, and oversees the Texas Preservation Trust Fund, providing critical financial assistance to local preservation projects.

Other state-level leaders in the promotion of local history include the Texas Parks and Wildlife Department, which oversees several historical parks, as well as a unique collection of recreational parks built by the Civilian Conservation Corps of the New Deal era. There is also the General Land Office, which maintains an archive of county maps and land records, and promotes history through publications, teacher aids, and symposia, and the Texas State Library and Archives Commission, which provides assistance to local libraries and resource centers on such matters as genealogy, records retention, *digitization, research databases, and archival conservation. Additionally, in 2005, the legislature created the position of State Historian, tasked with promoting Texas history in communities and schools, and functioning as special liaison to the governor on historical matters.

Significant nonprofit promoters of local history are such long-standing regional organizations as the West Texas Historical Association and East Texas Historical Association. There are also more than 900 history-related museums in the state, representing a wide range of culture and geography. Among the many examples in that regard are the Panhandle-Plains Historical Museum (Canyon), Museum of the Big Bend (Alpine), Museum of the Coastal Bend (Victoria), and Texas Forestry Museum (Lufkin). The premier statewide historical organization and a leading promoter of local history is the Texas State Historical Association (TSHA), the state's oldest learned society. Headquartered at the University of Texas at Austin, TSHA promotes the appreciation of Texas history through various educational programs, such as the Junior Historians (K–12) and Walter Prescott Webb Society (college level). Other programs include an annual meeting for researchers, writers, and enthusiasts; the *Texas Almanac*, a compendium of state and local data; the *Southwestern Historical Quarterly*; and the *Handbook of Texas Online*, an authoritative historical encyclopedia of more than 25,000 entries.

Increasingly, the study of local history is finding a home with institutions of higher education, as evidenced by such programs as the Baylor University Institute for Oral History and Texas State University's Center for Texas Public History, which recently completed a grant-funded initiative to assist county commissions and nonprofit groups on local projects, from museums and cemeteries to markers and *oral history. In

Denton, the University of North Texas maintains the Portal to Texas History, providing access to an expansive online collection of photographs, *maps, documents, newspapers, publications, and artifacts.

Given its ample geography and richly diverse past, as well as the success of myriad public and private efforts to promote heritage *tourism and education, Texas provides a vast backdrop for the study of history. There have been many important accomplishments in the preservation and promotion of history in recent years, and there are significant indicators that perhaps the best in that regard is yet to be. Texas history presents its challenges, no doubt, but it is still good business and remains dynamic, viable, relevant, grounded in local history, and prepared for the future.

DAN K. UTLEY
TEXAS STATE UNIVERSITY

See historical markers; United States, local history in.

Texas Online, Handbook of. In 1897, the Texas State Historical Association (TSHA) was founded by ten individuals on the University of Texas campus. Their mission was to "foster the appreciation, understanding, and teaching of the rich and unique history of Texas." For almost 120 years, the association has played a vital leadership role in Texas history research and education, helping to identify, collect, preserve, and tell the stories of Texas. TSHA's *Handbook of Texas* is the embodiment of the association's mission and remains the most comprehensive and widely viewed state encyclopedia in the country.

As early as 1939, TSHA Director Walter Prescott Webb encouraged a project to develop a state encyclopedia. The original *Handbook of Texas* was published in 1952, and its popularity was immediate. Over the next sixty years, the association updated and expanded the *Handbook* with the help of dedicated professors, graduate students, and lay historians. In 1996, TSHA printed a new six-volume set of the *Handbook* with more than 20,000 entries by nearly 3,000 authors, and made it available to the public for purchase.

With the onset of the digital age, TSHA decided to launch the *Handbook of Texas Online* in 1999. The online version boasts more than 27,000 authoritative entries on Texas and annually reaches more than six million people from more than two hundred countries. It is constantly used by authors for references and facts for Texas history books and articles and is a valued source for students of all ages.

The *Handbook* is a multidisciplinary collection of articles about Texas history and culture, including geographical and biographical information. TSHA has a dedicated staff who manage, research, edit, and assign entries for the *Handbook*. Developing a project of this magnitude required support from numerous colleges, universities, research centers, historical associations, sponsors, staff, and the public. Most notably is TSHA's partnership with the University of North Texas Portal to Texas History, which provides a home for TSHA's digitized publications, and allows global access to the *Handbook*.

The *Handbook* is available free of charge to the public. Google Analytics reveals that the *Handbook* is accessed most on weekdays during the school year from general Internet searches. The *Handbook* is unique in that the entries are written by qualified authors under the supervision of TSHA staff, while other digital encyclopedias allow users to contribute content with little to no oversight. Entries are continually updated and are internally cross-referenced to allow users to learn more about the topic. Furthermore, there are over 700 illustrations and audio clips to supplement the entries. Several spinoffs of the *Handbook* are now available through TSHA, including the *Handbook of Texas Music, Handbook of Civil War Texas,* and *Handbook of African American Texas.* The most recent projects under way are the *Handbook of Tejano History* and the *Handbook of Houston.*

The *Handbook of Texas* is dedicated to preserving the rich and diverse history of the Lone Star State and will continue to succeed in its mission thanks to local, state, and national support, as well as the financial and intellectual sponsors who make the project possible. The global reach of the *Handbook of Texas* shows that interest in Texas history extends far beyond the geographic borders of the state.

BRIAN BOLINGER
TEXAS STATE HISTORICAL ASSOCIATION

See digital history.

tourism. "Heritage tourism," often interchangeable with "cultural tourism," is a term that refers to the promotion and marketing of the history of a particular locality, environment, nation, or cultural or ethnic heritage in order to attract visitors and tourists. There is nothing new about the fusion of history-based pilgrimage and commerce. The earliest religious pilgrimages to sacred sites and landscapes and ancestral homelands were a form of heritage tourism. Vendors, moneychangers, and mendicants have always existed at those sites.

In the United States, the tourism that developed with the rise of a middle class in the nineteenth century featured sites important to the evolving national story of European, especially English, settlement and the founding of the American republic. George Washington's home, Mount Vernon, was an early destination for the curious and patriotic, despite the fact that Washington's heirs still lived there. Mount Vernon became a shrine and an icon for American identity even before the national patriotic narrative was attached to places on the land, objects, or memorials. In general, Americans were careless of the structures, landscapes, and artifacts related to their history until after the Civil War.

The 1876 centennial and World War I (1914–1918) framed an era of great activity in the collection, preservation, and memorialization of American history. Urban museums, historic houses, monuments, statuary, markers, and parks proliferated, primarily through the efforts of local history societies and national patriotic and commemorative organizations. These sites related most frequently to a national identity based on military, diplomatic, political, and pioneer history. Often they evidenced pride in a local story connected to the dominant national narrative. The interpretation offered a limited, but coherent, story of American triumph over nature's adversity, indigenous savages, and foreign enemies.

The nature of heritage tourism changed when the automobile became an important means of transportation in the 1920s. Now sites far from the railroad line had only to pave their roads and perhaps advertise to attract both the casual visitor and the intentional tourist who organized an excursion around a particular theme. Interrupted by the Depression and World War II, tourism rebounded with postwar prosperity, interstate highway construction, and longer family vacations in large Detroit-built automobiles. Heritage or cultural tourism became an activity characteristic of a great mass of Americans, and there were few sections of the United States that did not respond to the possibility of acquiring a few tourist dollars. In these local efforts, items for sale usually referenced a commonly understood history and geography. Rubber alligators, papoose dolls, and sketches of Ichabod Crane in flight had common *popular-cultural meanings and settings for most Americans.

The founding of the *National Endowment for the Humanities in 1965 marked the beginning of federal grants for the public presentation of well-researched history. Heritage or cultural tourism has also had the attention and support of the *American Alliance of Museums, the *National Trust for Historic Preservation, and the *Institute for Museum and Library Services, often in partnership with *state humanities councils, the National Council of State Historic Preservation Officers, and others. This has had a beneficial effect on scholarship and Americans have, in recent decades, revised their history to include more voices and more perspectives on the American past. Heritage narratives have frequently been modified to be more inclusive, often evoking local controversy and a defense of the once-dominant narratives.

Concurrent to investment in scholarship, local governments allied with local historical societies to produce economic-development plans that typically made optimistic claims for the profitability of heritage tourism. By the 1980s, "heritage tourism" was a more organized and commercialized effort to attract the tourist dollar. In a variety of publications, heritage tourism was touted as the answer to postindustrial America's local-economy blues. The blighted urban downtowns, depleted county seats, and bankrupt family farms could thrive again through the fiscal magic of heritage tourism. Heritage tourism promised clean industry, local jobs, and a general sprucing up of neighborhoods in decline since a global economy took the factories and brought box chain stores.

While some communities have successfully developed a heritage tourism program, others have foundered. In order for a community to support heritage tourism, the community must be part of the process of determining the meaning and value of local cultural resources. Community planning should take primacy over economic planning, and the community must do comprehensive and accurate research and data collection. If local historians have been part of the process of cultural inventory and have made their research methods known and accepted, there will be community benefits beyond tourism revenue. Issues of cultural resources and site integrity must be negotiated and mediated. The community should be an informed and discerning "first tourist."

Many sites continued to attract the public by reinforcing commonly held beliefs and understandings about American history. But these sites, now more driven by economics than national ideology, had their own inherent difficulties as once-standard interpretations of sites were challenged by new research and by groups previously excluded or denigrated. State and federal heritage site interpretations were often contested, with the extended controversy over interpreting *slavery in the first federal executive mansion, part of Independence National Park in Philadelphia, as a primary example. But representations based on the perceived needs of the tourism industry remained the standard for many sites.

Heritage tourism has been essentially commercial, seeking both to entertain and educate its audiences. The issue of cultural resource management for heritage tourism involves such problems as restoring sites to a grandeur, cleanliness, or historic importance that they never had, and attempting to "preserve" traditions. Cultural traditions are never static and attempts to revive them in an earlier, purer form always reflect contemporary culture more than the past. But several developments in heritage tourism have expanded its reach and its meaning. One develop-ment is the expansion of *environmental heritage tourism, which stresses the American natural heritage and species diversity and gives more attention to the sustainability and viability of the attraction that draws tourists. Another recent development is that of "sites of conscience," places associated with the dark and painful side of local and national histories. Such sites as the Lower East Side Tenement Museum in New York City and the District Six Museum in Cape Town, South Africa tell stories of local history that exploited, divided, and limited residents. These sites are linked internationally at www.sitesof conscience.org.

Just as existing sites may be reinterpreted, some sites of memory are spontaneous and, as with Mount Vernon, are sacralized by the visitation of the public over time until they are made official. The 1994 Oklahoma City bombing site may be an example. The Internet has encouraged heritage group formation and facilitated "reunions" of admirers or descendants of any ethnic, occupational, or religious group who return to a meaningful place with regularity, creating new sacred sites. There is the further complex question of the role of digital sites and *social media. Heritage tourism sites welcomed the ability to put their attractions online, thus enabling those with small budgets to promote themselves nationally. With the advent of social media, these sites are assessed and reviewed online by visitors as well. A site in *Indiana or *North Dakota may have a national audience, but it also has national online reviews of its value to the visitor. How are these assessments to be negotiated?

Several books review the process by which U.S. towns and cities have become sites for heritage tourism. Among the best is Dennis R. Judd and Susan S. Fainstein, eds., *The Tourist City* (1999). A book of essays by scholars, it describes the evolution of towns and cities from centers of trade and production through eras of abandonment to current efforts to market them as centers of historical *landscapes, structures, and services. They divide these efforts into three categories: (1) the resort city, such as Las Vegas; (2) the traditionally historic city, such as Boston; and (3) the converted city that has purposely developed a tourist section, such as Seattle. The latter may be the most problematic for local historians because it is often set apart from the "real" city, depends on a Disneyesque version of the American past, and succeeds in driving out whatever was unique in an area. Yet the authors understand the importance of tourism in a postindustrial world with a global economy. Good chronicles of the recent woes of cities, towns, and even suburbs are Richard Moe and Carter Wilkie, *Changing Places: Rebuilding Community in the Age of Sprawl* (1997), and Jon C. Teaford, *The Rough Road to Renaissance* (1990). A theoretical but very useful account of changes in U.S. neighborhoods and cities is Michael Sorkin, ed., *Variations on a Theme Park: The New American City and the End of Public Space* (1994).

Outside the American city, Hal Rothman's *Devil's Bargain: Tourism in the American West* and *See America First: Tourism and National Identity* by Marguerite S. Shaffer (2001) explore roadside attractions and Cynthia Aron,

Working at Play: A History of Vacations in the United States (2001) shows Americans connecting vacations with self-improvement and health.

A brief article in *History News* by Roy C. Turnbaugh, "Myths and Realities: The Uses and Misuses of History" (54, no. 1 [Winter 1999]: 18–21), succinctly notes the origins of much local legend in popular culture, citing the need such fictions fill, and notes the power of "toxic historical myths" in an age of mass communication. Another brief article, with a good bibliography, is Michelle J. Dorgan's "Why Heritage Is Not a Bad Word: The Role of Historians in the Heritage Industry," *Public History News* 18, no. 1 (Fall 1997). The article focuses primarily on the development of heritage areas.

For a general background to the subject of heritage tourism, start with Eric Hobsbawn and Terence Ranger, *The Invention of Tradition* (1974), one of the first books to examine the origins of traditions. David Whisnant's *All That Is Native and Fine* (1981) is an excellent chronicle of how well-meaning outsiders "helped" *Appalachians, in the early years of the twentieth century, to rediscover and market their past. For the origins of tourism, see John F. Sears, *Sacred Places: American Tourist Attractions in the Nineteenth Century*, 2nd ed. (1989).

National context for local issues may be found in John Bodnar, *Remaking America: Public Memory, Commemoration, and Patriotism in the Twentieth Century* (1992); Michael Kammen, *Mystic Chords of Memory: The Transformation of Tradition in American Culture* (1991); Edward Linenthal,

Sacred Ground: Americans and Their Battlefields (1991); and *The Unfinished Bombing: Oklahoma City in American Memory* (2001). International (primarily European and North American) context may be found in David Lowenthal, *Possessed by the Past: The Heritage Crusade and the Spoils of History* (1996).

A useful survey is David Thelen and Roy Rosenszweig, *The Presence of the Past: Popular Uses of History in American Life* (1998). The fourth edition of Freeman Tilden's *Interpreting Our Heritage* (2008) offers the most popular and long-lived interpretation of the natural and manmade environment of the National Parks. A growing academic interest in cultural or heritage tourism may be sampled in Emma Waterton and Steve Watson, eds., *Culture, Heritage and Representation: Perspectives on Visuality and the Past* (2010).

MARIE TYLER-MCGRAW
INDEPENDENT SCHOLAR

See cultural heritage tourism; heritage; resorts, historic; travel literature.

town. A town is bigger than a village or hamlet, but smaller than a city. In New England, a town is a unit of local government, a political subdivision of the state—such as a county or city government. It may also be called a township.

transcript. A modern rendering of a document; a copy or representation.

travel literature. The genre of travel writing poses a particular dilemma for the local historian. By definition the traveler is alien, the original outsider; the travel narrative itself is inevitably a form of colonialism, an effort by that traveler to filter the local story through his own lens of order and structure. Travel writing thus becomes something for the local historian to challenge, resist, correct. Aside from the occasional collaborator, no self-respecting Canaanite would turn to the Book of Genesis to learn the history of her people and place. Likewise, those living in the cedar forests outside of the Sumerian city of Uruk would have resented their characterization as howling beasts by the hero of the Epic of Gilgamesh. From the earliest entries in the field, travel writing serves as a record of what they think of us (or what we think of them), a record that is tarnished by all the sins for which such colonial ventures have become known.

Yet historians know that they can ill afford to discard an available source. If the accounts of even sympathetic outsiders can be faulted for their narrowly selective vision (think of Margaret Mead in New Guinea or Carl Van Vechten in Harlem), then the record produced by loyal insiders might be equally tainted by parochialism and a kind of xenophobic *boosterism. Mark Twain's biting skepticism went a long way toward deflating the pretensions of self-styled local aristocrats, both in the American South and in Europe. By his own account, Richard Wright might never have escaped the South had he not encountered H. L. Mencken's sustained outsider's assault on Southern manners and mores. If the mirror the outsider holds up is always a bit distorted, it is also true that such distortion is often informed by a kind of truth that might otherwise be missed.

Travel writing is thus both a bane and a boon for the local historian. Nowhere has this duality been more obvious than in the United States. Americans have long received the views of outsiders with both wary skepticism and an almost indiscriminate enthusiasm. Glance at any nineteenth-century newspaper and chances are good that you will find a report of some visiting dignitary's observations upon the local scene. Of course, the tactful visitor was always prepared with, well, some tactful observations, for many a traveler has learned the hard way that hell hath no fury like local pride scorned. Those same American citizens who yearned to hear such worldly authorities as Matthew Arnold, Charles Dickens, or Mrs. Trollope praise their local institutions and manners were quick to dismiss those observers as ignorant if they were unduly judgmental of those institutions and manners. Indeed, so obsessed were these Americans with the views of the outsider that they granted alien status to one of their own: Henry James might well be said to have made his career as an insider on the outside looking back in at the American scene.

Of course, historians have been generally cautious in using such accounts. James's pose as an almost disembodied outsider is particularly easy to dismantle, and while his account does tell us a good deal about the manners and customs of the America he visits, it ultimately tells us more about Henry James than it does about Boston or New York in 1904. A notable and significant exception to this legacy of benign skepticism involves the mother of all travel books, Alexis de Tocqueville's *Democracy in America*. Nearly 185 years after the travels it depicts, de Tocqueville's text still exercises a hold on the American imagination that can exceed that of such secondary documents as the Constitution and the Declaration of Independence. In some circles—academic, congressional, cultural—de Tocqueville's observations about the essence of the United States are revered with a kind of fundamentalism that would impress William Jennings Bryan. Indeed, de Tocqueville has so thoroughly influenced the study of U.S. culture and politics that debate over his legacy has focused less on whether he got it right than on whether the United States should be the kind of country he described.

If the mark of a successful travel book is its thorough absorption into the culture it purports to describe, then de Tocqueville's two-volume opus is peerless in its achievement. The exhaustive detail with which the Frenchman regales his audience threatens to crush any instinct to treat his account with a skeptical eye. The sheer weight of his work lends it an authority that has proven difficult to resist. Several new editions have been issued since the turn of the millennium, including one by the Ur-canonical Library of America series, and de Tocqueville's journey continues to serve as a model for those in search of a gimmick around which to structure their own cross-country wanderings, a kind of pseudo-intellectual's *On the Road*. Among the many lessons his book and its legacy offer is one about the perils of relying too heavily on the presumably detached outsider to tell us who we are. This is a different but no less serious peril than rejecting that outsider as having nothing to tell us that we need to hear. While the learned outsider's account might provide an antidote to parochialism, it also might erase those features that are distinctively local and vulnerable to assimilation.

Much of the older tradition of travel writing sought to locate a sense of national identity at the local level. Nineteenth- and early twentieth-century observers of the American scene generally aimed to uncover a cohesiveness and unity within the myriad parts that made up the (as opposed to "these") United States or—much the same thing—to expose local variations as grotesques that invited gawking on the part of the observer and embarrassment on the part of the observed. Such accounts neatly served the purposes of those working to keep the Union from fraying in the years before the Civil War and those working to swiftly heal old wounds and get back to business in the years after. It was the same impulse that elevated Muncie, Indiana, to the national norm of *"Middletown, USA." This emphasis on what different American places held in common persisted through the middle of the twentieth century, when increasing mobility put millions of Americans on the road in search of the comforts of home. Popular travel writing mixed just enough of the exotic with a healthy dose of the familiar, allowing the mobile consumer to enjoy an authentic experience with minimal risk. Not coincidentally this brought great joy to chambers of commerce around the country, where efforts to accommodate local conditions to the expectations of the traveler mirrored the efforts of those who sought to bring American history into agreement with de Tocqueville's observations. One charmingly absurd relic of this trend is the authentic adobe McDonald's restaurant in Taos, New Mexico.

While this trend is far from played out, the demystification and distillation of the local in service to the traveler has spawned several counter-traditions in travel narrative. In academic, cultural, and tourism circles, Americans have rediscovered "sense of place," that amorphous quality that is presumed to distinguish Portsmouth, New Hampshire, from Portsmouth, Virginia. Whether in the *New York Times* Travel Section, the "Local Scene" chapter of the ubiquitous Frommer's guide, or on one of the seemingly endless variations of the Travel Channel/Food Network road show, the putative goal is the same: to articulate, in a tone of reverent discovery tinged with insider privilege, that which makes a place unique, worth visiting or living in, worth learning about. Rather than finding the familiar within the strange, the emphasis has turned to highlighting the strange as a kind of pure essence concealed within the dross of all that is familiar.

This strain of travel narrative has achieved its most compelling—and revealing—expression in the explosion of food writing that has marked the past decade or so, during which eating one's way across the world, or at least across the country, has emerged as the most reliable of the savvy traveler's motifs. Sharing some important characteristics with the expanding academic interest in foodways, these efforts to entice the epicurious traveler have enabled a recognition and celebration of quantifiably local traits and traditions. To explore what people eat, how, and why, is to take seriously the distinctive ethnic and cultural traditions, geography, and climate that do as much to shape the identity of a place as any carefully managed branding campaign. Rather than "where can you get good sushi or a decent bagel in Bloomington" the focus instead is on local foods and their specific cultural context. At its best, the emergence of the gastronomical tourist and the travel narrative industry that caters to him can enable a place to speak in its own voice rather than through the imperial lens of its interpreter.

Yet even the most earnest and understated quests for the unique and idiosyncratic—the sine qua non of the genre—can too easily lead to caricature, thereby revealing the devil's bargain that travel and tourism inevitably imposes upon all of its objects. Guy Fieri's approach in "Diners, Drive-Ins and Dives" is emblematic. While on the surface an unrestrained love song to regionally distinct food traditions, Fieri's method is not far removed from the colonial tradition he would presumably scorn. Like Bobby Flay and his "Throwdown," Fieri roars into town ready to bless the locals with his presence, to put them on the map (where, of course, they were not located before) and bestow upon them the national acclaim and recognition only he (and the dozens of his competitors) can bestow before riding off into the sunset. For their part, the locals welcome the attention as well-earned validation for their hard work and perseverance and hope fervently to be included in the next edition of *500 Things to Eat Before It's Too Late: And the Very Best Places to Eat Them*. The short and slippery slope between Fieri's gonzo celebration of America's vernacular dining destinations and Andrew Zimmern's nearly pornographic *Bizarre Foods* suggests the irresistible pull of the sensationalist and exploitative: Look at what those weird people eat, while I alone have made it out alive to tell you.

Zimmern, of course—along with Rachael Ray and Fieri and Anthony Bourdain—presents himself as the detached enthusiast, the global traveler opening himself to any and all manner of local custom for the edification of his audience and a dose of self-improvement on the side. In this he follows fully in the tradition of such explorers as Mungo Park, Alexander von Humboldt, George Catlin, and J. N. Reynolds, those erstwhile pursuers of knowledge for knowledge's sake whose service to imperial and colonial ventures was the unintended consequence of their excursions. The sheer range of names and histories represented here reflects how flexible—and opportunistic—that pose can be. But it also suggests that, at least when it comes to the troubled relationship between traveler and local destination, the post-modernists might have something to teach us. Perhaps the problem is not one of finding the appropriate method for representing the local to the world—the right attitude, the proper level of detachment and neutrality, the erasure of the subject—but a frank acknowledgment of the Heisenberg Uncertainty Principle: that the act of observing changes not only what is being observed but the observer herself or himself. The local is not a static, unchanging entity to be protected from outside influence but, everywhere and anywhere, a dynamic product of that influence.

Such a perspective is what the foodways approach could offer at its best. It is also at the heart of another tradition of travel narrative that has coalesced in the past few years, both as a model for contemporary efforts in the field and a way of reimagining the historical tradition: the travel meta-narrative, propelled by the mildly ironic, keenly self-aware subject who, rather than affecting an invisible neutrality, openly includes herself or himself as an actor in the tale, a co-protagonist with the place being visited. At the risk of provoking howls of outrage, I would suggest that Anthony Bourdain achieves this much more successfully than his competitors in the food travel industry, acknowledging his larger-than-life presence and the privilege that enables him to indulge his tastes for "natural fusion" while opening himself to the experience of place without reservation. Bourdain aims for—and more often than not hits—somewhere between the imperious appropriation of place for his own ends and the romantic delusion of leave-no-trace travel. Writers as diverse as Aaron Sachs, Sarah Bakewell, and Ryszard Kapuscinski have reimagined their subjects (Humboldt, Montaigne, and Herodotus, respectively) along much the same lines: as travelers

who address the otherness of their own selves as well as that of the places and people they have visited. In his delightful *The Art of Travel*, Alain de Botton provides what amounts to a taxonomy of the self-aware traveler. If, as Emerson suggested, travel risks being a "fool's paradise" that proves to us only the "indifference of places," then de Botton's exploration of the "importance of having the right question to ask of the world"—a dynamic that highlights the organic relationship between asker and asked—may be the only honest path to the wisdom that sits in places.

CHARLES MITCHELL
ELMIRA COLLEGE

See culinary history and the local historian; cultural heritage tourism; resorts, historic; tourism.

Turks in North America, sources for. See Appendix A.

Turner, Frederick Jackson. See frontier thesis; Western history and local historians.

Tweedsmuir History Prize. See Canada local history in; Saskatchewan, local history in.

Twitter. See microblogging; social media.

𝒰

Ukranians in North America, sources for. See Appendix A.

Underground Railroad. The Underground Railroad—the resistance to enslavement through escape and flight, through the end of the Civil War—refers to the efforts of enslaved African Americans to gain their freedom by escaping bondage. Wherever slavery existed, there were efforts to escape, at first, to maroon communities in rugged terrain away from settled areas, and later across state and international borders. While most began and completed their journeys unassisted, each subsequent decade in which slavery was legal in the United States saw an increase in active efforts to assist escape. As a series of local and individual stories, collectively these acts of self-liberation aggregated as a nationally significant movement. The decision by an enslaved individual to escape was intensely personal and their journeys, whether alone or in small groups, generally traversed through the countryside unnoticed. For those who provided assistance, the decision was sometimes spontaneous. Often, however, they were part of local networks of extended families and church associates resisting the Fugitive Slave laws to help free a people.

Until the end of the Civil War, enslavement was legal in the United States. In contrast to Revolutionary War era rhetoric about freedom, the new U.S. Constitution protected the rights of individuals to own and enslave other people. The Fugitive Slave Law of 1793 also enforced these slaveholding rights, providing for the return to enslavement of any African American accused or even suspected of being a freedom seeker. Denied access to an attorney or a jury trial, a freedom seeker faced any white person making an oral claim of ownership to a magistrate. Those who assisted the freedom seeker, or merely interfered with an arrest, faced a $500 fine, a clear acknowledgment of the impact of the Underground Railroad phenomenon decades before it was given its name.

The increasing incidence of escapes caused enactment of a tougher law, the Fugitive Slave Act of 1850, which compelled all citizens to participate in the capture and return of freedom seekers, or risk fines and prison sentences. The spectacle of African American re-enslavement on the slightest pretext and the sale of kidnapped free African Americans south into slavery brought home the moral dilemma to individuals in the North. Some opponents to slavery opted to change laws, while some recognized a higher moral law.

Wherever there were enslaved African Americans, there were people eager to escape. There was slavery in all original thirteen colonies, in Spanish California, Louisiana, and Florida, and on all of the Caribbean islands until the

Haitian Revolution (1791–1804) and British abolition of slavery (1834). The Underground Railroad started at the place of enslavement. The routes followed natural and manmade modes of transportation—rivers, canals, bays, Atlantic Coast, ferries and river crossings, roads and trails. Location close to ports, free territories, and international boundaries prompted many escapes.

Using ingenuity, freedom seekers drew on courage and intelligence to concoct disguises, forgeries, and other strategies. Slave catchers and enslavers watched for runaways on the expected routes of escape and used the stimulus of advertised rewards to encourage public complicity in apprehension.

There is probably no subject more challenging to local historians than that of the Underground Railroad. Despite years of claims that Underground Railroad history was secret, local historians, genealogists, oral historians, and other researchers today find that there are *primary sources describing the flight to freedom of many enslaved African Americans. Court records, memoirs of conductors and freedom seekers, letters, runaway ads in newspapers, church and military records all testify to the determination of the enslaved to seek freedom for themselves and their families.

Documents from before 1865 are found in the *National Archives, in state archives and historical society libraries, in special collections in local libraries, and in private hands. Often no one has put together the pieces of the stories of freedom seekers by looking at their starting and end points, much less points in between. Once a freedom seeker is identified in a runaway ad or

letter belonging to a slave master, newspaper accounts, *diaries, or so-called slave narratives may fill in the story.

In addition to official archives and historical societies, some families still retain journals, letters, and other documents. Tracing family connections—both historically and to descendants—often sheds new light on the Underground Railroad movement. Oral traditions can provide important clues to past Underground Railroad activity. Generally discounted by historians, this information can help unlock the mysteries of the Underground Railroad. Like written sources, it should be analyzed for its origin, specificity, and reliability, and used along with other pieces of evidence.

The Underground Railroad is a way to approach slavery through the lens of agency for the enslaved person and through the hopeful inspiration of people of all backgrounds working together. The overriding reason for a revival of history of underground activity is surely that in this nation where race has been a pressing national concern, accounts of Underground Railroad heroes inspire the hearers. Thus, Underground Railroad activity becomes a symbol of positive behavior in our long national history of racial anguish and has been recognized as the beginning of the civil rights movement.

In 1998, the National Underground Railroad Network to Freedom Act was passed, directing the *National Park Service to implement a program to preserve and commemorate this history. The National Underground Railroad Network to Freedom (NTF) stimulates and facilitates the work of local historians by promoting their efforts, connecting those in different countries, counties, states, and regions, and connecting them with tourist entities and local planning and preservation agencies. There are now 582 members in thirty-seven states plus the Virgin Islands and the District of Columbia, all with well-documented local stories to tell.

The story of the Underground Railroad that has emerged from this public history project is more complicated than one of freedom seekers and those who aided their progress north, west, and south. The story has the added nuance of community conflict, of moral decision making, of the law abiding—those who, after 1850, did not aid runaways, even if they might have wanted to. The story is also of communities known as safe and those that were decidedly unsafe. It is the story of a shifting network of routes that changed with times and local attitudes, one particular route used on one day, a different way the only sure path on another. It is the story of churches that split apart over this issue and of ministers finding ways to justify the return of those escaping. All this makes the Underground Railroad interesting and important because, in context, it becomes an episode in courage and moral character.

Increasing records and data available to local historians through the Internet and the Network to Freedom's local and national leadership has enabled researchers to network with one another. As they develop their local stories, they are able to piece together bits of information to better understand Underground Railroad routes, strategies, and, sometimes, individual biographies of

freedom seekers. For example, a slave inventory or a runaway *advertisement in the South might be matched with a letter, newspaper article, or *obituary in the North that reveals a story of escape and even later activism helping others obtain freedom.

To become a part of this national story, visit the Network to Freedom website at http://www.nps.gov/ugrr.

DIANE MILLER
NATIONAL UNDERGROUND RAILROAD
NETWORK TO FREEDOM

See African American history; slavery interpretation at historic sites; slave schedules.

unions. See labor history and the history of communities.

Unitarian Universalist Association, sources for. See Appendix B.

United States, local history in. It is difficult to overemphasize the role of tradition in thinking about and in the doing of local history in the United States. American interest and contributions to local history began with colonizers and settlers who recorded their observations of the New World and of what they were accomplishing—some even as events were in progress following the English tradition that dates from the sixteenth century. Those early books recorded information about localities, shire, parish, and estate lines, about ecclesiastical descent, great families, and the military in particular.

That tradition carried over. Americans, as had the English, documented and celebrated history, with collections of manuscripts and the creation of state historical associations, in some places even before statehood. Swelling arcs of interest in local history followed and these pivotal times engendered greater—and at times lesser—interest and activity in the history of localities. The doing of local history, over time, became a curious and interesting mirror of traits—of vigorous organizational zeal and an overzealous promotion of place with an inflation of patriotic feeling for the local often without regard for context—traits frequently identified as typically American.

The Western tradition of documenting local history came to these shores with the earliest European settlers who generally ignored Native American systems of accounting for the past. In the south and west, local accounts by the Spanish were about the land from which the Native Americans were driven, about explorers, priests and missions, and the development of spiritual and commercial centers. In the East, in the English tradition, local history focused on institutions of stability and of community growth, on land, and early settling families. Local history in the colonies appeared in the form of state papers, lectures, and sometimes even sermons. The urge to record was strong, yet local history existed in the shadow of the growing national story as citizens created historical accounts to suit the emerging country.

It is difficult, however, in this country's very federated nation to write of one tradition, of one way of doing things for the entire nation. There are regional differences and there are differences in time, for some places developed political and historical consciousness earlier than others. Some mirrored those already established, some differed. And all changed over time, pushed by events and historical fashions, many constrained by that very tradition or financial exigencies. From all of this interesting patterns emerge.

In the face of writing that extolled and explained the uniqueness of the United States, histories in various forms described the local, promoting attachment to and often the enhancement of place. Those early histories recounted tales of early settlers, the founding of places, local industry, the creation of schools, governments, and churches—and of those who led them. They boosted their communities in the face of competition from other nearby growing towns or the lure of "elsewhere." They gathered what was known and rushed to do so before the voices of the town's founders were lost to time. Many reprinted early documents, listed municipal officers, promoted the idea of collecting local artifacts and in doing so, created a distinct antiquarian tradition that lasted within local history through the nineteenth and in some places into the twentieth-first century. At the same time, the earliest local histories established the characters in a community worthy of remembering: the preacher, newspaper publisher, local politicians, founding families: in general, those who were healthy, wealthy, wise—and male.

An even stronger urge by those interested in local history was that of creating organizations, the earliest of which depended on the generosity and industry of founders who donated collections and provided funds for buildings, libraries, and further collecting. These private state associations (Massachusetts Historical Society [1791]; New-York Historical Society [1804]; Pennsylvania Historical Association [1824]) first functioned as men's clubs, with membership by invitation. These organizations hosted lectures, collected books into a useful library, and amassed artifacts and manuscripts. The Massachusetts Historical Society even proposed that a member upon admission "engage to use his utmost endeavors to collect and communicate to the society—Manuscripts, printed books and pamphlets, historical facts biographical anecdotes, observations in natural history, specimens of natural and artificial curiosities, and any other matters that may elucidate the natural and political history of America." The results of all this were eclectic collections and serial publications of early colonial and state documents and the correspondence of the prominent or politically powerful that would ensure that these papers were "beyond the reach of accident."

In Maine, "49 prominent men" incorporated the historical society in 1822; in New Hampshire in 1823 a "who's who" of state leaders created a society; in Virginia the historical society was created in 1831 by a group of "white men." For the most part, throughout the nineteenth century and well into the twentieth, these private, independent eastern historical societies maintained themselves by means of contributions from their members without public funds or grants. It was not, of course, all smooth sailing. Some associations began, disappeared, and were later reconstituted. For example, Indiana's first state association, founded in 1831 as a "state archival agency," "went dark" and was revitalized in a somewhat different form only in 1886. Some history organizations wrestled over location or finances—or lack thereof—or who would lead. Any number of state historical societies collapsed over differences caused by the Civil War, only to reappear in a new form later in the nineteenth century.

It was during the celebration of the American Centennial in 1876 that the arc of local history swung sharply upward as interest in the local expanded. The Centennial spurred the writing of local history, resulting in the publication of documents, essays about community origins, civic lists, and the names of soldiers who had fought in the Civil War. This activity attracted the attention of commercial publishers who sent compilers to collect information and solicit prepaid subscriptions, resulting in large books, some of one county, often of several. These commercial publishers in Philadelphia, Syracuse, and Chicago and (later in the century) in San Francisco and elsewhere, broadened the spectrum of those included in local history by offering anyone with a sum of money to have an engraved portrait included in the book. This was an opportunity that many men took up, and often, for a larger fee, included wife, house, and sometimes carriages and livestock.

The centennial also ignited interest in the creation of new historical organizations in both states and counties. Some of these, such as those in trans-Mississippi states (Nebraska, Oklahoma, South Dakota, Colorado, and

Idaho to name a few) began as old settler or pioneer associations. While males founded the predominant number of these, North Dakota provides an interesting exception as it began as the Ladies Historical Society of Bismarck and North Dakota, founded in 1889, then became the North Dakota Historical Society in 1895, and in 1903 was renamed the State Historical Society of North Dakota. Many of these later organizations, especially those west of the original colonies, were promoted by and partially supported by the state, which saw historical activity important to current residents and to those of the future—a form of honor for pioneers who braved to enter land considered by those who pioneered there to be new. Historical organizations helped create an established culture in places where little yet existed, other than the culture already on the land, that of various Indian tribes, which was in general discounted. They promoted a reverence for first families. A number of these new organizations consciously modeled themselves on the Wisconsin Historical Society, which had been founded in 1846.

Another nineteenth-century innovation was New York's 1895 establishment of the position of state historian. Today, any number of other states have since designated a state historian. Arizona appointed its first in 1901, while Texas did so in 2007. In some cases the state historian is a governor's appointment and a state employee, whereas in the states of Connecticut and Texas, the position of state historian is awarded to a member of a state university faculty. In some states there is a close connection between the historical society and the state university: for example, in Wisconsin the state historical society is located on the University of Wisconsin, Madison campus and many state university presses include books about state or local history among their offerings.

Local history's appeal changed little from its origin to the middle of the twentieth century. Although women's names appear more frequently as historians, professors, and organizers, they were also, in many cases, the keepers of local documents and often a small organization's main curator. Local history's audience was primarily the middle class; it remained largely concerned with the collection and preservation of artifacts and information. During the Great Depression, the New Deal Works Progress Administration commissioned writers to delve into local and state history; some of those WPA guides are still in print and useful.

In the 1930s, academic history enlarged its focus to include urban history and there was a dramatic shift in the 1960s with the emergence of the *New Social History changing academic and state and local history alike. This departure was due in part to the influence of the French *Annales School of history and to the interesting uses of population data by the *Cambridge Group, but it also bubbled up through the reading of anthropological theory. Historians and their graduate students turned to questions about community, generational influences, mobility, ethnicity, race, and gender. Responding to the social concerns of the civil rights era, and to a perceived shortage of employment in the academy, the public history movement began in the 1970s and thereafter sent trained graduates to state and local historical societies, into industry, and to positions with government.

The arc of state and local history soared during and after the celebration of the Bicentennial of the American Revolution in 1976. Rather than a giant fair as held 100 years earlier, the Bicentennial was mostly celebrated in America's localities that were already gaining new attention from movements that looked away from major sites to the treasures in America's hometowns. *Roots*, the fictionalized genealogical saga of an African American family, became a television mini-series in 1977 and unleashed a torrent of genealogical searches from people once thought to be without a documentable family line. Soon, people from a variety of ethnic backgrounds became involved in family searches. With the advent of the Internet, genealogical activity has increased, it now being considered the second most popular "hobby," the first being gardening. The visibility and activity of those involved in the preservation movement also brought new interest and energy to the pursuit of local history.

Over the course of the twentieth century, many states instituted courses in local history, set primarily in the fourth grade, though a few have programs for older students. In 2009 Colorado mandated that local history be taught in the fourth grade, which spurred the teaching of Colorado history in the state's colleges, whereas, once vibrant, the teaching of state history has all but disappeared at the college level in Illi-

nois. The content of these public school courses ranges from civics preparation, to study of the state constitution, to student community projects. Some colleges have offered state history courses, and some made it a requirement so that its graduates would be prepared to teach state history in the public schools.

Tourism or cultural heritage tourism turned to state and local history in the latter decades of the twentieth century, leading to interesting and sometimes disturbing emphases. Local history sites were viewed as bankable community assets. This emphasis on value led some history organizations into curious enterprises, enabled and enhanced by electronic technology. Historical organizations hired trained professionals who brought with them an interest in testing the New Social History in localities. Often, traditional topics were replaced by programs and exhibits featuring African American history, the history of ethnic groups, women's history, philanthropy, and the development of public services. Local historians scoured communities for sources of untapped information and researchers turned to older documents, such as the state and federal census, to use in new ways. The biggest shift of emphasis today might be the attention paid to Native Americans, especially pronounced in states with large Indian populations, such as Utah, New Mexico, and Alaska, and mirrored in a number of Canadian provinces. The influence of the National Endowment for the Humanities has been significant, as in Guam where local history is promoted by its humanities council.

The nature of local history writing in many instances featured focused studies that rested on new questions. Commercial publishers, such as Arcadia, which merged with the History Press, and others came onto the scene. Acquisition editors sought people to write town histories and the history of sports or local organizations, and they encouraged the publication of "then and now" books, postcard histories, and images culled from the community. They offered authors formats that promoted some chronological balance, editing services, and royalties. These historians continue to be source-based, mostly without an interest in a theoretical underpinning. The public has responded enthusiastically, quickly becoming familiar with the lively brown paperback books that have been the result and can be found in bookstores, groceries, and even filling stations.

Another important consequence of this dramatic rise in the popularity of local history has been the creation of new historical organizations. There are many causes of this surge. In some ways, it was a reaction to changes in larger organizations bringing on professional staff, with the enthusiasm for local history generated by the Bicentennial and the buzz around history in the years that followed. But in large part, this increase was the result of aging local buildings and the attention brought by the preservation movement to save what could be salvaged. People all over looked at unused or shabby schoolhouses or religious structures or old homes and created organizations to take on their care. The logical next step was often the incorporation of a historical society.

This has led to a tremendous growth in the number of history organizations in the country, especially those created between the years 1970 and 1990. According to AASLH, in 1936 there were 583 history organizations in the United States, which is most probably something of an undercount. That meant, on average, twelve organizations per state, although they were certainly not spread out in such a mathematical fashion. The situation today is quite different and somewhat alarming. Today, there are nearly 200 historical organizations in the state of Montana, mostly small, volunteer-run, and struggling to survive because of lack of funding. There are 200 in New Hampshire, two-thirds having been created since 1960—most to preserve old houses that struggle today to survive. There are more than 300 in Nebraska, 400 in Wisconsin, 600 in Georgia, and more than 820 in Texas. In Ohio there are "approximately 320 town or area historical societies; approximately 240 organizations inspired by specific topics, ninety genealogical societies, eighty county historical societies, seventy historic building or district preservation groups, sixty township level historical societies, fifty-eight state memorial sites" administered by local organizations, thirty public libraries that include historical museums or archives, and twelve regional, multi-county historical societies: more than 1,000 historical organizations in the Buckeye State alone!

All this indicates a great deal of historical interest, but the founders of many of these new organizations are aging and few have generated much interest among younger folks. The buildings they maintain need to be retrofitted for safety and to comply with laws about disability access. They need insurance and upkeep and many, especially since 2000, have gone dormant or even out of business. An organization needs to attract necessary resources to achieve its goals and to survive; it needs also to offer incentives to its members or audience to promote enthusiasm and to align them to its purpose. An organization needs to give or show purpose by clearly stating its ideals and goals. The organizational enthusiasm of the last quarter of the twentieth century is something about which we have all become concerned. There are solutions but they might require a medicine that tastes bitter to some.

Larger state historical societies are not immune from the problems of our day, either. In a less than rosy economic situation, a number of state historical societies over the past decade have experienced downsizing of staff and an inability to meet high public expectation. In Kentucky, there is a check-off box on the state income tax form that directs a bit of tax money to support state museums. In 2008 Minnesota passed an impressive and history-friendly Clean Water, Land and Legacy Amendment directing a portion of a sales tax to support outdoor and historical heritage. Yet, when the state closed for several days in 2011 because of an inability to meet its financial responsibilities, the Historical Society of Minnesota also shut down. In Nevada, a state with a rising population, the situation is slightly different. Because so many newcomers moving to Nevada have little interest in or connection to Nevada history, "they tend to look at those agencies that preserve the state's history as a luxury the state cannot afford." In 2003 in South Dakota, the State Office of History became part of the Department of Tourism and State Development, as happened in Nevada that same year, although in 2015 the History Office was placed into the state Department of Education. The combination of history and tourism has happened in other states as well.

In the name of local history Americans exhibited and perhaps magnified traits that have been associated with our national character. Americans promoted their communities and became local boosters and even chauvinistic. Moreover, Americans have approached local history as they have other public endeavors, as Alexis de Tocqueville noted, "they form a society [and] with skill," he wrote, "inhabitants of the United States succeed in proposing a common object for the exertions of a great many men and in inducing them voluntarily to pursue it" (*Democracy in America*, vol. 1, 1835).

This enthusiasm for history organizations cannot be taken to mean that across the country historical knowledge has increased or even been sharpened, for many in the United States know little history and are rather careless about accuracy, although vigilant when historians veer from a known narrative. We are a perplexing and sometimes paradoxical people.

Local history has been alert to the need for change. It has enlarged the scope of who and what is discussed, and thus democratized the characters involved. Today written local history paints on a broadened canvas, creating a more complete picture of who has lived in our towns and cities. A look at current historical journals shows that local history has been taken up by a variety of writers on local topics that range from environmental change to the development of local institutions, such as libraries. Wallace Stegner remarked that along with Americans buried in the local cemetery, long rooted in place, there are the bare root people who also need to be accounted for; those people who move about, who try one thing and then another, whose lives do not end up local legends. They too are part of American local history.

The Internet has brought new challenges to local history but also opportunities that some history organizations have embraced speedily, others with more reluctance. A number of states have created online encyclopedias and others have posted digitized *primary source material on the web, extending its reach considerably. Florida has turned to an older technology, radio, to deliver history to a wide audience in its *Florida Frontiers* series, weekly radio broadcasts created in conjunction with the public radio station. Montana has created an online wiki; Alabama has created an online repository of images called *Alabama Mosaics* drawing from archives located around the state; and *Maine Memory* is very popular. Some online technology has led to issues for organizations that must grapple with a balance between their own scholarly authoritative voice and a trust in user-generated content.

American historical organizations have modernized to become more open to new subjects, members, and platforms and to a greater degree of cooperation with other cultural institu-

tions than ever before. Local history has gained, not lost its audience. Today's economic challenges, while difficult to live through, could possibly—through reflection, adaptation, cooperation, new endeavors in terms of venue, media use, and publication possibilities in all formats—see the various ways of doing local history continue to be a keen reflection of America's hometowns and those of us who live in them.

CAROL KAMMEN
TOMPKINS COUNTY (NY) HISTORIAN

See Annales School; Arcadia Publishing; boosterism; Cambridge Group for the History of Population and Social Structure; cultural heritage tourism; mug books; new social history; public history; *Roots*; social media; tourism; and the local history as it has developed in individual states, by name. See also Canada, local history in; and England, local history in, for comparative views.

U.S. Geological Survey. See maps and atlases.

U.S. military records. See military records, U.S.; pension records, military.

U.S. GenWeb Project. The U.S. GenWeb Project (usgenweb.org) is a website devoted to genealogical research. It is an all-volunteer site, organized by geographical hierarchy (state-county). The county sites host databases of local information and maintain message boards through which researchers can contact each other. A related project is U.S. GenWeb Archives (usgwarchives.net), which provides access to a variety of user-submitted documents and records. The GenWeb Project and the archives are valuable sources for local historians and many are supported or hosted by local historical societies.

ROBERT KIBBEE
THE HISTORY CENTER IN TOMPKINS
COUNTY (NY)

See genealogical resources online.

Utah, local history in. In the year 1897 Utahns celebrated the fiftieth anniversary of the arrival and settlement of the first Mormon pioneers in the Great Salt Lake Valley. The year 1897 also marked the one-year anniversary of statehood. Sixty leading citizens of Utah of the day, including Governor Heber M. Wells; bank president W. S. McCornick; women's leader, suffrage activist, and editor Emmeline B. Wells; Judge C. C. Goodwin; and local attorney and political activist Jerrold R. Letcher decided the time was right to organize a state historical society. The founders set the society's tasks as "the encouragement of historical research and inquiry by the exploration and investigation of aboriginal monuments and remains, the collection of such materials as may serve to illustrate the growth of Utah and the intermountain west, the preservation in a permanent depository of manuscripts, documents, papers and tracts of value; [and] the dissemination of information and the holding of meetings." Membership was open to "any person of good moral character who has an interest in the work of the Historical Society." In 1917 the Utah State legislature made the Utah State Historical Society (USHS) a state agency and gave it a budget of $200. It is now part of the Utah Division of State History.

Because Utah is a state very much aware of the importance of history, much of the funding for history has come from the state legislature. For instance, in 2014 the legislature put Utah's History Day program on solid footing by housing it at the Division of State History and providing an ongoing appropriation for it. Other history funding has come from grants and enthusiastic citizens.

In 1929, USHS began publication of the *Utah Historical Quarterly (UHQ)*, the state's official historical record. Since then, *UHQ* has become a valuable repository for primary sources and scholarship on diverse Utah history. As part of the state centennial in 1997, the legislature funded the writing and publishing of 300-page histories of all twenty-nine counties. USHS has published the county histories and *UHQ* in print and, as part of ongoing *digitization efforts, online. These publications and other historical resources, including web supplements to the journal, are available at uhq.utah.gov.

The Utah State Historical Society also developed a research library that has grown into a significant historical resource. Today, the Research Center for Utah State History and Utah State Archives provides access to manuscripts, books, pamphlets, images, and records from state and local governments. Many of these resources have been digitized and made available online.

The Mountain West Digital Library (MWDL) was founded at the University of Utah in 2001, bringing together partners from universities and colleges, museums, libraries, communities, and institutions to provide a common portal for digital research resources, including photographs and documents of many kinds. The MWDL now includes partners from states surrounding Utah. In addition to gaining access to digital collections through MWDL, researchers can search through the finding aids of contributing institutions; see mwdl.org. Through another partnership, the Utah Digital Newspapers project has digitized more than one million pages from historical newspapers from cities and towns throughout the state, and digitization is ongoing. This searchable database is available at digitalnewspapers.org.

Very early, local chapters of the Daughters of Utah Pioneers (DUP) began to establish "relic halls," small local museums displaying Mormon pioneer and local artifacts. The majority of the 150 history museums in the state are still managed by the Daughters of Utah Pioneers, which was organized in 1901. The DUP and the Sons of Utah Pioneers, established in 1933, focus on the pioneer heritage of the state, and each operates a research library and publishes history books and magazines.

Several history museums were established to focus on specific themes. For instance, the Hellenic Cultural Museum in Salt Lake City relates the story of the Greeks in Utah. The Topaz Museum, working with the Japanese American community in Utah and partnering with the Great Basin Museum of Delta, tells the story of the 8,000 Japanese Americans who were interned during World War II on a desolate 640-acre patch of ground called Topaz. The Fort Douglas Military Museum, located in Salt Lake City, the Hill Air Force Museum, near Ogden, and the Historic Wendover Airfield Museum show the important roles of Utah's military bases. Many communities run museums highlighting specialized subjects or local history. For instance, the Park City Museum has exhibits on silver mining and the development of skiing.

Prehistoric and historic Native American cultures are important to Utah's history, and several museums focus on these topics. In the early years of the twenty-first century, a consortium of cultural and historical interests under the general guidance of the state's Division of Indian Affairs produced educational resources for students in fourth and seventh grades, the grades in which students are taught Utah history. The consortium also produced a website of digitized articles, books, documents, *oral histories, *photographs, and *maps regarding Utah's Native American tribes (utahindians.org) and the book *A History of Utah's American Indians* (2000).

The *National Park Service operates historic sites and visitor centers throughout the state. Each site or visitor center displays and interprets local history for visitors, and many have archives available to researchers. The State of Utah operates several heritage parks and museums, each focusing on a specific theme, such as territorial government or prehistory, for example. As yet, the state does not maintain a statewide history museum to showcase the Utah State Historical Society collections and tell the inclusive story of Utah history, but efforts are now being made to plan and construct one.

The Church of Jesus Christ of Latter-day Saints (Mormons) has developed and operates historical sites in the state, as well as a church history museum in Salt Lake City. In 2009 it opened in Salt Lake City a state-of-the-art facility housing its research collections, which are largely open to the public. Many documents have been digitized and are online. Other churches—the Catholic Diocese, for instance—also provide access to historical documents.

Due to the influence of the Mormon church, *genealogy has become a major thread in the history of Utah's history. The church has run a genealogy library since 1894, with the current library now located west of Temple Square. The church's storage vaults for some 35 billion images of genealogical information, carved into solid granite in Little Cottonwood Canyon, are legendary. Many of the companies and organizations that provide *family history resources to the world had their beginnings in Utah and are still located here.

Geographically, Utah is the center of the American West and has been called the "Crossroads of the West." Several locally and nationally recognized historical trails traverse the state—among them the Old Spanish Trail, the Mormon Pioneer Trail, the Pony Express Trail, the California Trail, the Hole-in-the-Rock Trail, and the Lincoln Highway. Working hand in hand with several federal government agencies, local trail organizations have identified, marked, and interpreted these trails.

During the twentieth century, citizens became increasingly aware of the value of historic buildings. Preservation efforts resulted in the formation of the Utah Heritage Foundation in 1966. Working with the State Historic Preservation Office, as many as ninety communities throughout the state are devoting resources to documenting and preserving their historic buildings. A number of *historic preservation organizations, history organizations, and communities have organized to form heritage alliances in order to share regional history with tourists.

For decades, history organizations have erected markers and monuments to tell the story of the past. Found throughout the state, some of these monuments have been inaccurate or biased, but as historical awareness has evolved, so has the purpose and text of markers. In 2016, for instance, a diverse coalition erected a marker at the site of a little-remembered massacre of Paiutes in the town of Circleville.

Since Hubert Howe Bancroft published the *History of Utah* in 1889, Utah scholarship has evolved, and books have addressed diverse issues. Seminal monographs and works of Utah history include Juanita Brooks, *The Mountain Meadows Massacre* (1950), a topic recently revisited by scholars, most notably Will Bagley, Glen M. Leonard, Richard E. Turley Jr., and Ronald W. Walker; Dale Morgan, *The Great Salt Lake* (1947); Wallace Stegner, *Beyond the Hundredth Meridian: John Wesley Powell and the Second Opening of the West* (1954); Leonard J. Arrington, *Great Basin Kingdom: An Economic History of the Latter-day Saints* (1958); Helen Papanikolas, ed., *The Peoples of Utah* (1976); Jeffrey Nichols, *Polygamy, Prostitution, and Power: Salt Lake City, 1847–1918* (2002); Nancy

J. Taniguchi, *Castle Valley, America: Hard Land, Hard-Won Home* (2004); and Jared Farmer, *On Zion's Mount: Mormons, Indians, and the American Landscape* (2008). While these offer various examples of local history, they are significant for placing state and local history in a regional or national context. Influential general histories of the state include Richard D. Poll et al., eds., *Utah's History* (1978); Dean L. May, *Utah: A People's History* (1988); Allan Kent Powell, ed., *Utah History Encyclopedia* (1994); Thomas G. Alexander, *Utah: The Right Place* (1995);

Brian Q. Cannon and Jessie Embry, eds., *Utah in the Twentieth Century* (2009); and Charles S. Peterson and Brian Q. Cannon, *The Awkward State of Utah: Coming of Age in the Nation, 1896–1945* (2014).

CRAIG FULLER
UPDATED BY KRISTEN ROGERS-IVERSEN
UTAH STATE HISTORICAL SOCIETY

See historical markers; United States, local history in.

utopianism. See failure and local history.

$\mathcal{V}$

Valley of the Shadow, the. A project of the Virginia Center for Digital History, http://valley.lib.virginia.edu is an interactive digital archive of two counties, one Northern and one Southern, aligned at opposite ends of the Shenandoah Valley during the American Civil War era. The archive contains thousands of records including official documents, *census records, letters, *diaries, newspaper articles, and images from Augusta County, Virginia, and Franklin County, Pennsylvania. A unique organization of the material allows creative exploration of the political and social environment of the time. "Valley" is a convincing example of how local history can be brought to life on the web through the integration of digitized archival resources.

ROBERT KIBBEE
THE HISTORY CENTER IN TOMPKINS
COUNTY (NY)

See digital history; genealogy resources online; local history resources online.

values of history. Values are beliefs shared by an individual or a community about what is important or valuable. Although *values* and *ethics* are terms used interchangeably at times, ethics are the action and manifestation of values. In addition to a mission and vision, some history organizations have adopted a statement of values or a code of ethics to clarify their identity and guide decisions. For example, the Society for Historical Archaeology includes in its code of ethics that members "shall not sell, buy, trade, or barter items from archaeological contexts," an action based in part from their belief that "historical and underwater cultural resources" are a "valued resource for knowledge exchange." The importance of values was underscored nearly a generation ago in *Museums for a New Century* (1984): "An effective museum leader—whether scholar or M.B.A. or both—must first understand, believe in, and speak for the values of the institution."

A common challenge for state and local history organizations is explaining the values of their institutions or history to the public. Too often the reason is internally focused or simply a variant of George Santayana's quote that "those who cannot remember the past are condemned to repeat it," which does little to adequately explain its impact or relevance in a manner that's meaningful to nonhistorians. As professors Roy Rosenzweig and David Thelen confirmed in a national survey on the popular uses of history, most Americans associate "history" with their most unpleasant experiences in school: the forced regurgitation of boring facts. The perception that history is merely the mindless memorization of meaningless myths has pushed history out of the classroom, reduced funding by foundations and government, and worn away at attendance and membership. Nevertheless, Rosenzweig and Thelen noted that Americans are "already quite involved with the past—through formal activities like going to museums as well as informal pursuits like talking with their families" and that "the most powerful meanings of the past come out of the dialogue between the past and the present, out of the ways the past can be used to answer pressing current-day questions about relationships, identity, immortality, and agency" (*The Presence of the Past* [1998]). The public and historians both value history, but seem to define and use it differently.

To help national, state, and local history organizations speak more clearly and develop consensus about the relevance and meaning of history, the History Relevance Campaign, a grassroots effort formed by several leaders in the history field, produced "The Values of History: Seven Ways it is Essential." Shaped by hundreds of organizations and individuals, both professional and amateur, in 2013–2014, these Values of History are:

1. Identity. History nurtures personal identity in an intercultural world. History enables people to discover their own place in the stories of their families, communities, and nation. They learn the stories of the many individuals and groups that have come before them and shaped the world in which they live. There are stories of freedom and equality, injustice and struggle, loss and achievement, and courage and triumph. Through these varied stories, they create systems of personal values that guide their approach to life and relationships with others.

2. Critical Skills. History teaches critical twenty-first-century skills and independent thinking. The practice of history teaches research, judgment of the accuracy and reliability of sources, validation of facts, awareness of multiple perspectives and biases, analysis of conflicting evidence, sequencing to discern causes, synthesis to present a coherent interpretation, clear and persuasive written and oral communication, and other skills that have been identified as critical to a successful and productive life in the twenty-first century.

3. Vital Places to Live and Work. History lays the groundwork for strong, resilient communities. No place really becomes a community until it is wrapped in human memory: family stories, tribal traditions, civic commemorations. No place is a community until it has awareness of its history. Our connections and commitment to one another are strengthened when we share stories and experiences.

4. Economic Development. History is a catalyst for economic growth. People are drawn to communities that have preserved a strong sense of historical identity and character. *Cultural heritage is a demonstrated economic asset and an essential component of any vibrant local economy, providing an infrastructure that attracts talent and enhances business development.

5. Engaged Citizens. History helps people craft better solutions. At the heart of democracy is the practice

of individuals coming together to express views and take action. By bringing history into discussions about contemporary issues, we can better understand the origins of and multiple perspectives on the challenges facing our communities and nation. This can clarify misperceptions, reveal complexities, temper volatile viewpoints, open people to new possibilities, and lead to more effective solutions for today's challenges.

6. Leadership. History inspires local and global leaders. History provides leaders with inspiration and role models for meeting the complex challenges that face our communities, nation, and the world. It may be a parent, grandparent, or distant ancestor, a local or national hero, or someone famous or someone little known. Their stories reveal how they met the challenges of their day, which can give new leaders the courage and wisdom to confront the challenges of our time.

7. Legacy. History, saved and preserved, is the foundation for future generations. History is crucial to preserving democracy for the future by explaining our shared past. Through the preservation of authentic, meaningful places, documents, artifacts, images, and stories, we leave a foundation upon which future Americans can build. Without the preservation of our histories, future citizens will have no grounding in what it means to be an American.

History organizations rank these values differently; however, as a combination they have been endorsed by more than 130 diverse local, state, and national organizations, including the *American Association for State and Local History, *National Coalition for History, *National Council on Public History, National Conference of State Historic Preservation Officers, *National History Day, *Society of American Archivists, and the National Society of the Colonial Dames of America.

For further reading, see *American Association of Museums, *Museums for a New Century* (1984); History Relevance Campaign at HistoryRelevance.com; and Roy Rosenzweig and David Thelen, *The Presence of the Past* (1998).

MAX A. VAN BALGOOY
ENGAGING PLACES LLC

See building bridges through local history; mission statements; museum ethics; museums and the matter of ethics; relevance.

Vermont, local history in. The interesting and often curious history of the Green Mountain State is preserved and shared through a network of organizations and agencies, both statewide and at the community level. The state's premiere heritage organization, the Vermont Historical Society (VHS), was chartered by the State of Vermont in 1838 under the leadership of the organization's first president, Henry Stevens. Throughout its history VHS has been steadfast in its mission to collect, preserve, and present artifacts, documents, and information about the state's history. Once considered a "scholars only" institution, VHS is today a dynamic partner with schools, local historical

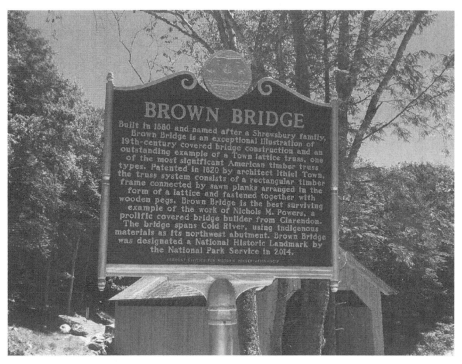

Brown Bridge, a National Historic Landmark in Shrewsbury, Vermont, is honored in this historical marker. CREDIT: VERMONT DIVISION FOR HISTORIC PRESERVATION.

societies, and other organizations concerned with preserving the cultural heritage of the state.

Although it is a private nonprofit organization, the Vermont Historical Society serves as an instrument of state government, performing functions defined in statute. The Vermont History Center in Barre serves as the repository for museum and archival collections and hosts the Leahy Library, a facility promoting research and study in all aspects of Vermont history, including genealogy. Since 2012 the center has also featured exhibition galleries and is the home of the state's archaeology resources.

The Vermont History Museum, located next to the State House in Montpelier, presents three hundred years of Vermont history through the dynamic exhibition, *Freedom and Unity*. VHS also presents a variety of educational and public programming throughout the state. The VHS website provides many resources that support the exploration of Vermont history at www.vermonthistory.org.

At the community level, over 200 town-based historical societies and museums serve as the stewards of local history in Vermont. Most are volunteer-run organizations with seasonal hours, but with rich collections. These organizations are provided coordination and support through the Vermont Historical Society's League of Local Historical Societies and Museums. League programs and services include an annual conference, workshops and related learning opportunities, mentoring programs, weekly e-newsletters, and technical assistance.

Since 1999, the state's local historical societies have shared their stories through exhibits and presentations at the Vermont History Expo. Now presented biannually, History Expo is a two-day event on the grounds of the Tunbridge World's Fair. Called "Vermont's Family Reunion," Expo features demonstrations, lectures, music, food, games, reenactments, and other exciting activities that explore and celebrate the rich heritage of Vermont. A common theme for each Expo provides a focal point for the exhibits and programs.

The Vermont Historical Society is joined by statewide agencies and organizations that are primarily concerned with preserving the state's cultural heritage. The Vermont Division for Historic Preservation (DHP) is a state agency that serves as the State Historic Preservation Office and administers and operates Vermont's state-owned historic sites, state and federal registers, the statewide archeology program, and various other programs that promote the preservation of the state's historic resources. The Preservation Trust of Vermont is a private, nonprofit organization that partners with the DHP to promote and advocate for preservation statewide.

The Vermont State Archives and Records Administration (VSARA), a Division of the Vermont Office of the Secretary of State, serves as the official repository for state documents and promotes research on the state's history. At their state-of-the-art facility in Middlesex, VSARA provides seamless integration of state government records management and archives functions. Overseeing the restoration and interpretation of the Vermont State House, as well as the care and use of the state's sizable collection of artwork, is the Office of the State Curator. The Vermont Humanities Council supports programming throughout the state on all of the disciplines of the humanities, with a particular emphasis upon Vermont history. Through ongoing field research, a multimedia archive, and an apprenticeship program, the Vermont Folklife Center in Middlebury preserves the folk arts and cultural traditions of Vermont and the surrounding region.

Among the notable published works on Vermont history is the five-volume *Vermont Historical Gazetteer* by Abby Maria Hemenway. Published in serialized form between 1867 and 1891, this seminal work is still used today. Walter Hill Crockett's *Vermont, The Green Mountain State* is a five-volume set published between 1921 and 1923. *Freedom and Unity: A History of Vermont* was a collaboration between Michael Sherman, Gene Sessions, and J. Jeffrey Potash. Published by the Vermont Historical Society in 2004, *Freedom and Unity* is considered the most comprehensive single-volume publication on the state's history and is used as a textbook for Vermont history courses throughout the state. In addition, the VHS semiannual journal, *Vermont History*, features contemporary scholarly research.

In recent years the personalities behind some of the state's major heritage organizations have changed with the departure of several long-serving leaders who collectively had over 100 years of service to their respective organizations. The recent retirements of the first state archivist, Gregory Sanford; the first state archaeologist, Giovanna Peebles; and the first chief of operations of state-owned historic sites, John Dumville has signaled that a new generation of leaders is coming forth to build upon the impressive efforts of these pioneers.

MARK HUDSON
VERMONT HISTORICAL SOCIETY

See historical markers; United States, local history in.

vernacular architecture. Vernacular architecture refers to common, everyday, or ordinary building that helps define the character of a region, time, or place. All building types technically could be considered vernacular, but that which traditionally has been characterized as vernacular architecture includes those buildings, spaces, or collections of buildings generally absent from the annals of architectural history. This includes many company towns, barns, mills, commercial strips, apartment buildings, warehouses, parking structures, fairgrounds, water towers, office parks, factories, rest stops, trailer parks, and single-family housing of all types which—all told—comprise far more of the world's *built environment than has traditionally captured the attention of architectural historians. Despite lingering beliefs to the contrary, vernacular architecture is not anonymous or un-self-conscious; regardless of aesthetics, vernacular builders make very conscious choices about their built environment, typically paying close attention to costs, materials, and function. Vernacular architecture may be professionally designed, as well, and—depending upon the availability of materials, fashion, and the common practice of building in a locality—may incorporate details drawn from long-standing architectural traditions.

Because the subject encompasses such a vast range of building types, vernacular architecture is perhaps better identified with the process that created it than the product that resulted—although both are part of its meaning. It is not an architectural "style" or single type but rather a physical embodiment of practices that shape a common, often local, built environment—much as the language or dialect spoken by the people of a community is considered the "vernacular." Vernacular architecture is ordinary *building* as much as it delineates ordinary *buildings,* for the practice of construction often incorporates building traditions and materials common to the locality or region rather than more extravagant processes requiring skilled craftspeople or multinational construction companies.

Scholars of vernacular architecture seek to uncover the cultural ideas and labor that went into producing the *built environment as much as they attempt to read culture and context through the finished work, whether at the scale of the neighborhood, town, countryside, state, or nation. Rather than restricting their focus to the architect, scholars of vernacular architecture investigate the role of bricklayers, carpenters, electricians, farmers, contractors, real estate agents, community leaders, policy makers, and developers in trying to understand how a building or space came to be. They also attempt to uncover users' perceptions of space in order to understand how a building has resonated over time. Because an understanding of vernacular architecture must delve into issues of culture, studies of the vernacular draw regularly from fields such as folklore, anthropology, sociology, cultural history, and American studies as well as geography, archaeology, *historic preservation, and *architectural history. Without as much existing documentation and/or literature regarding their subject, scholars of vernacular architecture frequently engage in fieldwork prior to issuing reports or making conclusions. Their methods are difficult to untangle from those who study the cultural landscape—the difference might be only a matter of scale (vernacular architecture scholars more frequently examine single buildings; those studying the cultural landscape more commonly look to entire regions, *parks, or *landscapes where the human and natural have intersected).

The methods and practices of vernacular architecture studies have been long championed by the Vernacular Architecture Foundation, founded in 1979 (www.vafweb.org), and highlighted in their now biannual journal, *Buildings & Landscapes*. Ideas and methods of the vernacular have influenced the field of architectural history to such an extent that all aspects of the built environment are today deemed worthy of study.

See Howard Davis and Louis P. Nelson, "Editors' Introduction," *Buildings & Landscapes* 14 (Fall 2007): iv-vi; Paul Groth, "Frameworks for Cultural Landscape Study," in Groth and Todd W. Bressi, eds., *Understanding Ordinary Landscapes* (1997): Thomas Carter, ed., *Images of An American Land: Vernacular Architecture in the Western United States* (1997); Dell Upton and John Michael Vlach, eds., *Common Places: Readings in American Vernacular Architecture* (1986); Dell Upton, "Vernacular Buildings," in *Built in the U.S.A.: American Buildings from Airports to Zoos* (1985), 167-71; Amos Rapaport, *House Form and Culture* (1969).

J. PHILIP GRUEN
WASHINGTON STATE UNIVERSITY

See architectural history.

Victoria County History. See England, local history in.

village. From the Latin villaticus, meaning a collection of dwellings, a village is larger than a hamlet but smaller than a town. It is not an urban area and usually has a population of 2,500 inhabitants or fewer.

Virginia, local history in. Virginia's largest business is history. The first permanent English settlement was founded at Jamestown in 1607. The British surrendered to American and French forces at Yorktown to end the American Revolution. As the "Mother of Presidents," Virginia produced four of the first six presidents of the United

The birthplace of Powhatan is commemorated in this historical marker in Henrico, Virginia. CREDIT: VIRGINIA DEPARTMENT OF HISTORIC RESOURCES

States. More battles during the Civil War were fought on Virginia soil than in any other state. Much of Virginia's historical memory has concentrated on the history of white Virginians, particularly white Virginia men. Virginia women participated in the founding of the Mount Vernon Ladies' Association and established the Association for the Preservation of Virginia Antiquities, one of the oldest preservation organizations in the country. The first efforts to preserve and interpret Virginia's history were accomplished by private individuals and organizations, and that remains the pattern to the present day. Virginians' desire to preserve the commonwealth's colorful and complex history has resulted in the proliferation of independent local historical societies, museums, and archives that rely on private endowments and annual fundraising campaigns with little or no financial support from the state government.

Virginia is home to two of the earliest organizations—the Mount Vernon Ladies' Association and the Association for the Preservation of Virginia Antiquities—that sought to preserve the commonwealth's built past. Both organizations were founded before 1900 by women who, denied open access to politics and many public venues, embraced preservation as part of their responsibilities as nurturers. Preserving historic places, they reasoned, enabled

Virginia, local history in

them to educate the next generation with the virtues of past Virginians. In 1858 the Mount Vernon Ladies' Association, founded by Ann Pamela Cunningham, of South Carolina, bought Mount Vernon to preserve it as a shrine to George Washington. Organized in 1889, the Association for the Preservation of Virginia Antiquities (APVA, now Preservation Virginia) was the nation's first statewide *historic preservation organization. It reflected a deeply rooted localism as it established branch chapters, mostly in eastern and Tidewater Virginia. The APVA enshrined old buildings, graveyards, and historical sites—many of which were forlorn, if not forgotten—and exhibited them as symbols of Virginia's identity. Today, Preservation Virginia has branches throughout the Commonwealth and is dedicated to preserving and promoting the Commonwealth's historic places.

In addition to local historical societies and libraries with archival collections, there are two major institutions whose collections reflect a statewide interest in documenting Virginia's people and history. In 1831 a group of white men founded the Virginia Historical Society, electing Chief Justice John Marshall its president and former U.S. president James Madison its first honorary member. Throughout its history, the society has amassed an impressive collection of manuscripts, books, and artifacts that document generally the thoughts and lives of white Virginians. In recent years, the society has collected more aggressively materials related to and has expanded its interpretation of *African American history. The society remains a private not-for-profit institution with collections that increasingly document the diversity of Virginia.

The Commonwealth of Virginia has demonstrated its keen awareness of Virginia's history in creative ways. Established in 1823 by the General Assembly, the Library of Virginia collects state records and archival materials that document the history of Virginia from its founding in 1607. The library holds records for three other government-based history projects—the World War History Commission, the Historical Highway Marker Program, and the Virginia Writers' Project. In 1919 the Virginia General Assembly established the World War History Commission to document the role of Virginians in the "Great War" and to record its impact on the commonwealth's economy and politics. In addition to encouraging localities to gather newspaper clippings, the Commission issued questionnaires to returning veterans, black and white, men and women, that included questions about their feeling about military service generally and what their service had meant to them personally. The Commission published seven volumes of material culled from the local histories and questionnaires. In 1926 the State Commission on Conservation and Development established a historical highway marker program to encourage tourism through a uniform system to mark historic places and events and to foster interest nationwide in Virginia's history. Today, more than 2,200 silver signs with black lettering dot Virginia's roadsides. The state library managed the program from 1950 until 1966 when it was transferred to the newly created Virginia Historic Landmarks

Commission (now the Department of Historic Resources) that still manages the program. Since 1976, private organizations, local governments, and individuals pay for the markers. During the Great Depression, Virginia writers, historians, and archivists gathered life histories of Virginians living through the depression, interviewed former enslaved African Americans, documented historic sites and events, and compiled guidebooks of state, local, and specialized histories. The major publication, *Virginia: A Guide to the Old Dominion*, was a 700-page volume that included fifteen interpretive essays (one of them by Douglas Southall Freeman on the spirit of Virginia), fifteen chapters on the commonwealth's largest cities, and twenty-four detailed tours of the state's major regions and points of interest.

Published histories of Virginia have been sources of controversy for decades. Traditionally these histories, from Robert Beverly's *History of Virginia* (1705) to Virginius Dabney's *Virginia: the New Dominion* (1971), emphasized the influence of wealthy white men to the exclusion of women, Virginia Indians, and African Americans. During the decades after the American Civil War, organizations, such as Confederate veterans groups and the United Daughters of the Confederacy, complained loudly about improper depictions of the South. Writers who compiled histories for the commonwealth's schoolchildren dispatched the post-Civil War period with a few brief paragraphs that lamented Reconstruction and the subsequent failure of Virginia to regain a place on the national stage. In 1948, the Virginia General Assembly created a state textbook commission to counter the perceived slight of Virginia's role in the founding of the nation and misrepresentation of its part in the Civil War. The commission sponsored new textbooks on Virginia history, geography, and government for use in the fourth and seventh grades and in high school. By 1972 dissatisfaction with the textbooks resulted in their removal from the curriculum. Adoption in the 1990s of uniform statewide Standards of Learning for social studies education in Virginia led to the publication of a new generation of textbooks that included more social and cultural history and enhanced treatment of economic and demographic history, women, African Americans, and Indians. Educators increasingly turn to the Internet for resources to complement print and electronic editions of instructional materials. Institutions such as the Library of Virginia and the Virginia Historical Society are answering the need for reliable resources by digitizing their collections and creating searchable databases that combine text and images.

BARBARA BATSON
LIBRARY OF VIRGINIA

See historical markers; United States, local history in.

vision statement. A vision statement describes a business's or nonprofit organization's long-term major goal or desired end state and directs the planning, implementation, and evaluation of its programs and activities. There are many definitions for vision statements, some that conflict with each other, but the consensus is that they describe an ambitious but achievable long-term goal (ten to thirty years ahead, beyond the term of the current board or tenure of the executive director); that the statement is clear, compelling, and short (about twenty-five to fifty words); and yet is sufficiently vague and abstract to be unaffected by typical economic cycles or social fads.

An often-cited example of a vision statement is found in John F. Kennedy's address to Congress in 1961 on urgent national needs:

I believe that this nation should commit itself to achieving the goal, before this decade is out, of landing a man on the moon and returning him safely to earth. No single space project in this period will be more impressive to mankind, or more important for the long-range exploration of space.

Kennedy, however, would not have identified this as a "vision statement," a term that would become popular in the 1980s when businesses sought success through visionary leadership and an entrepreneurial spirit. Discovering the ingredients of an effective vision was elusive, however, because there was little agreement about its essential qualities and how it affects strategy. In the 1990s, the value of visionary leadership and vision statements came under increasing scrutiny, especially in *Built to Last: Successful Habits of Visionary Companies* (1994) by Jim Collins and Jerry Porras. They questioned the belief that vision statements by themselves made companies visionary and instead claimed that "creating a statement can be a helpful step in building a visionary company, but it is only one of thousands of steps in a never-ending process." As an alternative, they recommended a Big Hairy Audacious Goal, which they nicknamed BHAG (pronounced *be-hag*). This specific type of goal is intended to drive momentum because it manifests the company's ideology, requires a high level of commitment, and is clear and compelling.

During this same time, the *mission statement, one of the key governing documents of nonprofit organizations, also came under increased scrutiny. The core functions of collecting, preserving, and interpreting seemed to be an insufficient response to questions raised by funders and the public about the social impact and contributions of museums and historical societies. Laura Roberts, Lois Silverman, Harold Skramstad, Stephen Weil, and other leaders in the museum and history field began to question the adequacy of mission statements in providing strategic direction or addressing community needs. Roberts felt that the mission of education was being neglected, Silverman suggested that museums could play a role in therapy and social work, Skramstad urged that mission statements needed to answer "so what?," and Weil predicted a new relationship between museums and the public, which will have "revolved a full 180 degrees" with the public in the superior position. Some museums and historical societies responded to these critiques by either expanding their mission statements to incorporate an ultimate goal (e.g., to encourage appreciation, to inspire commitment, to be a vital resource) or crafting a separate vision statement.

By 2001, Jim Collins refined his ideas in his bestseller *Good to Great*, introducing the Hedgehog Concept to identify the three elements that must be addressed in effective vision statements: what are your deepest passions (which includes mission and values), what will make you the best in the world, and what drives your economic engine. When the three elements overlap, they form the Big Hairy Audacious Goal. Evaluation consultant Randi Korn adapted the Hedgehog Concept to the museum field by encouraging the practice of holistic intentionality, which clarifies what the museum wants to achieve and results in a "genuine, shared vision held by everyone because it passionately expresses the impact the museum hopes to attain." At the core is an "impact statement," which is a form of vision statement that integrates personal passion, the organization's strengths and capabilities (which includes the collections and staff), and the audience's interests and needs (*relevance). Indeed, this follows a shift throughout the field from *inward*-looking vision statements (goals that are primarily important to or cause a change within the institution, such as becoming the region's best museum, having the finest collections, reaching one million visitors) toward versions that are *outward*-focused (goals that are primarily important to or cause a change in external audiences, such as creating connections across neighborhoods, providing a common place to discuss contemporary issues, ensuring students develop critical skills for employment).

For further reading, see Jim Collins, *Good to Great* (2001); Jim Collins, *Good to Great and the Social Sectors* (2005); Randi Korn, "The Case for Holistic Intentionality," *Curator* 50, no. 2 (April 2007): 255–64; Robert Putnam and Lewis Feldstein, *Better Together: Restoring the American Community* (2003); Stephen Weil, "The Museum and the Public," *Curator* 16, no. 3 (1997): 257–71.

MAX A. VAN BALGOOY
ENGAGING PLACES LLC

See building bridges through local history; evaluation; mission statements; relevance; values of history.

vital records and vital statistics. Vital records document major life events, in particular, birth, marriage, and death. They provide a documented framework for the life of an individual and are critically important to genealogists and local historians. The care and comprehensiveness with which life events have been registered has varied considerably over time and place. Government involvement is a recent phenomenon; early records in America were almost always kept by local religious establishments, mirroring the practice of most European countries. These records were uneven at best, both in content and coverage. There is no single source for research in early vital records; researchers will need to consult church records, newspapers, cemetery records, and family records such as Bibles and genealogies to establish dates and places for vital events. The variety of records, jurisdictions, and sources is described in Johni Cerny, "Vital Records," in *The Source: A Guidebook to American Genealogy*, 3rd ed. (2010), 603ff. Another source is the FamilySearch Wiki and particularly this handout for an online genealogy class: https://familysearch.org/wiki/en/U.S._Vital_Records_Class_Handout.

Many early vital records have been digitized into searchable databases, but coverage is still haphazard. One important source is *Ancestry.com, a subscription service, which provides a consistent search interface to millions of birth, marriage, and death records for the United States, Canada, and many European countries. Most of these records have been transcribed from microfilm. Another source, *FamilySearch (http://www.familysearch.com), free and publicly available, is provided by the LDS (Mormons). FamilySearch provides an interface to the *International Genealogical Index (IGI), an enormous index, originally of birth and marriage records, but now supplemented with death, burial, and *naturalization records as well. The construction of the index began in 1969, but records go back to the fifteenth century.

Many state governments began to require registration of vital events late in the nineteenth century, although some New England towns began much earlier. Colorado did not require records until 1968. Most vital records are available from states for a small processing fee. There is no overall index but there are guides to coverage and access for individual states both online: *Where to Write for Vital Records* from the Centers for Disease Control and Prevention, http://www.cdc.gov/nchs/w2w. htm; and in print: Alice Eichholz, ed., *Red Book: American State, County, and Town Sources*, 3rd. ed. (2004).

The closest thing to a national index of information about the deaths of individuals is the *Social Security Death Index (SSDI), which provides an index to over 77 million Social Security records, including the original application form, which can be ordered for a fee. Coverage is strongest for deaths or applications for benefits from 1962 onward, but there are many earlier records. There are numerous portals to the SSDI. A meta-search engine with helpful tips for searching is available from about. com: http://genealogy.about.com/od/ free_genealogy/a/ssdi.htm.

Vital records are compiled into vital statistics. The impetus for collecting vital statistics is partly for general demographic analysis and partly for understanding public health trends. A local historian might use the compilations to understand long-term demographic trends in her area, changes in birth rates by race, for example, or causes of death. States and some large cities have the primary responsibility for compiling the statistics from their records. A uniform national standard allows the Division of Vital Statistics of the National Center for Health Statistics to use the information from the states as part of the National Vital Statistics System. The results are published by the Centers for Disease Control in *Vital Statistics of the U.S.* and available online at http://www. cdc.gov/nchs/data_access/vitalstatsonline.htm. These statistics are presented at the national and state levels and occasionally at the county level. Most states publish their own compilations of data; these analyze the data at the county or city level or even school district level (for births). A local historian would be more likely to use one of these state compilations. County health departments may have their own compilations that may predate state collections. An example of a state compilation (for New York) is http://www.health.state.ny.us/nysdoh/vital_statistics.

ROBERT KIBBEE
THE HISTORY CENTER IN TOMPKINS COUNTY (NY)

See local government records; mortality schedules.

volunteers. "Volunteer, *noun*—from the *perspective of the doer.* Someone who gives time, effort and talent to a need or cause without profiting monetarily" (*By the People: A History of Americans as Volunteers* by Susan J. Ellis and Katherine H. Campbell via www.energizeinc.com).

At local history organizations, volunteer jobs are as diverse as the organizations they serve. Boards of directors volunteer their time and talents to shape the future and provide support for the organization. Volunteers may also catalog collections, give guided tours, work with school groups, tend gardens, plan special events, repair buildings, and even mow the lawn! Volunteer staff members should be treated with the same professionalism as paid staff members.

This includes a job description and regular evaluations. A volunteer job description can include the training available for the volunteer position, the time commitment required, and a list of basic responsibilities. For instance, the Dunbarton House docent volunteer description (http://dumbartonhouse.org/wp-content/uploads/2015/07/Docent-Fall-2015-Training-edit.pdf) includes these responsibilities:

- Welcome and introduce visitors to Dumbarton House;
- Provide guided tours;
- Introduce and assist with self-guided tours;
- Collect admission fees and sell gift shop items;
- Maintain the security of the collection during tours and when staffing the Visitor Center;
- Maintain all aspects of the Visitor Center during shift; and
- Represent Dumbarton House in a professional and courteous manner to members and the visiting public.

At the same time, volunteers must understand that individual needs and desires are secondary to the overall organizational goals.

Local history organizations should track volunteer hours because some sources of funding allow the use of volunteer hours as a match. In addition, it helps to demonstrate to supporters and governmental agencies the many ways in which your local community supports the organization.

Many organizations recognize and celebrate their volunteers through special volunteer efforts, service pins, or installations in the museum recognizing the commitment of time. Overall, in the United States, volunteerism is declining due to a number of factors including a changing American family. Local history organizations often find themselves unable to attract new volunteers. But with effective planning and recruitment, organizations can find energetic new volunteers. Consider both national trends and those in your community when designing your volunteer program and always, always, look outside the group of people you know.

Seeking a diversity of volunteers, making your organization is representative of your community is an important strategy. This will ensure that everyone feels welcome at your organization.

The American Association of Museum Volunteers (AAMV) provides Standards and Best Practices for Museum Volunteer Programs. The standards are easily scalable to different size institutions (http://www.aamv. org/resources/standards-and-best-practices).

The Stanford Innovation Social Review (http://www.ssireview.org/articles/ entry/the_new_volunteer_workforce) provides these suggestions for finding and retaining volunteers:

- Rethink work roles
- Assign appropriate tasks
- Create bonding experiences
- Support and train volunteers
- Use new technologies
- Develop strategic plans

LINDA NORRIS
THE UNCATALOGED MUSEUM

$\mathcal{W}$

Wales, local history in. It is easy to overlook the most obvious Welsh historical *primary sources: those revealed in the patterns of the physical landscape of the country and its material structures. Much of the history of Wales, its economic, social, and even cultural development, has been fashioned by its physical nature and its location in the main island of Britain. It is also one of the key determining factors that have shaped the idea of the "local" in Welsh history. Wales occupies 8,016 square miles in the west of the main UK landmass. Its eastern border joins it with England, but it is otherwise surrounded by sea. Much of its terrain is mountainous and the patterns of its *demography—both historical and modern—show that the most hospitable areas for settlement have straggled along the northern and southern coasts, with urbanization creeping inland to those areas where natural resources once provided the focus of the country's heavy industry. In central Wales there is a great hinterland fit for various types of farming, but a large proportion of it is mountainous and has only limited agricultural use.

Many of the documentary sources for Welsh history and local history, particularly the earliest written sources, are in the Welsh language. The Welsh Language Act of 1993 formalized and protected the status of the language. It remains the language of high and *pop-ular culture, of broadcasting, music, and film, and is spoken by a fifth of the population of Wales. The administration of the country is entirely bilingual. The Welsh language is crucial to the history and identity of Wales, and while many Welsh historians have worked in the medium of English, it is important for historians to be aware of the voices that may be omitted without recourse to Welsh-language sources.

History and *local history* in Wales are all but indivisible, and there are times when the same can be said about the division between Welsh and British history. While the history of the administration of Wales is an important subject that has occupied historians of Wales, the cultural history of the country has been characterized by a tapestry of events, movements, and characters that were revealed and are best understood at a local level. However, Welsh history is not *synonymous* with local history, from either a historiographical or a factual perspective. Long before Wales possessed any administrative autonomy, it was widely recognized as a country and the Welsh as a nation. The network of communities contributing to this shared sense of nationhood makes the study of local history in Wales such an interesting and rewarding pursuit.

Distinguishing between those elements that separate Welsh local history from the broader orbits of interest of Welsh historians—what Glanmor

Williams wrote in a famous essay, "Local and national history in Wales," that appeared in D. H. Owen, ed., *Settlement and Society in Wales* (1989)—is thus not always easy. Indeed, in that essay, Williams suggests that "Up to a point it would be perfectly feasible to argue that the history of Wales consists of the sum of its local histories. . . . [Though not entirely true] it would be truer of Wales than of many other countries because the forces of its geography, economics and politics have always been centrifugal and not centripetal." At its most basic and mundane level it can be said that Welsh local history is essentially concerned with events, themes, and topics that are focused on narrow and contained geographical areas that can be defined by a unitary identity (such as a town, valley, or county). But the themes that have occupied local historians almost always reflect themes that have been developed at the national level. In addition to its intrinsic value and as has so often been the case, local history has been an important tributary for wider historical interests.

The relationship between Welsh history and Welsh local history stretches back at least into the nineteenth century. Many of the interests of nineteenth-century Welsh historians were rooted in local history, and the period saw a flourishing of local and county history societies and publications. This identification with locality and community has persisted into the twentieth century and beyond—a network of county record offices and local studies libraries continues to support the work of local historians. The publication of journals and county record series, and the impetus for the study of local history has been strengthened with the founding of societies such as Llafur (Labour), the Society for the Study of Welsh Labour History, founded in 1970 and since renamed the Welsh People's History Society.

The late nineteenth and early twentieth centuries were also hugely significant to the development of Welsh historical studies in that they saw the foundation of the major Welsh academic and scholarly institutions—the University of Wales (the first university college opened in Aberystwyth in 1872), the National Museum of Wales, and the National Library of Wales (both 1907). While the National Archives in London is in fact the official archive for Wales as well as England, the National Library of Wales has increasingly assumed a similar de facto status. These national institutions of Wales have established a body of Welsh historical scholarship and built up large and impressive Welsh historical collections. In the twenty-first century, the digitization of such collections has become a significant activity.

Both Welsh history and local history form part of the national curriculum specified by the Welsh government. From the age of seven, all children in Welsh schools study topics in local history. The individual university colleges in Wales teach Welsh history as a major in history programs, while the Open University has a postgraduate (master's) program that puts local history in the foreground. Furthermore, the countrywide network of *labor history, county history, and local history associations bring local historians together with the county archive services for educational activities that may be unaccredited and informal but are no less powerful. The intensity of this endeavor has increased since about 2006, as digitization projects, especially those of the National Library of Wales, have come to fruition.

TREVOR HERBERT AND HELEN BARLOW
OPEN UNIVERSITY

See England, local history in.

Washington, local history in. Geography and population have been the chief influences on state and local history in the Evergreen State. In the late 1800s, Washington's population exploded, more than tripling in less than a decade. As the pioneer era faded, concern about losing historical memory led to the 1891 creation of the Washington State Historical Society (WSHS) in Tacoma. The choice of Tacoma was significant: the city lost the transcontinental railroad terminus to Seattle, and building a museum helped it stay competitive.

Although the young organization struggled with inadequate finances and sluggish collection building, the society became a trustee of the state in 1903. This new status ostensibly made it easier to get state funding and made the society an unusual hybrid of state agency and nonprofit organization. After an attempt to move the organization to Seattle failed, support for the society solidified, eventually leading to the construction of the Washington State History Museum in 1911. Consolidation with a local art museum in 1930 augmented its collection, including an important assemblage of Northwest Indian basketry. The Public Works Administration funded a major addition

to the museum in 1937. A new Washington State History Museum opened in downtown Tacoma in 1996, sparking an economic and cultural renaissance in a deteriorating city. Today, the museum anchors a revitalized urban neighborhood with two other museums and a branch of the state's largest university.

For much of the twentieth century, Washington had three historical societies claiming statewide influence. The Eastern Washington State Historical Society organized in 1916 as the Spokane Historical Society, focusing principally on the arid Inland Northwest region that includes much of the state east of the Cascade Range. Now the Northwest Museum of Arts and Culture, it highlights regional history, fine arts, and Native American culture. In 1941 the State Capital Museum opened in Olympia, housed in an impressive mansion donated to the state and run by the volunteer State Capital Historical Association. In 1993, WSHS assumed management of the museum. Lack of funds forced its closure in 2015, leaving the state capital without a bricks-and-mortar home for interpreting state history.

In the 1950s and 1960s, wartime industrial development increased the state's population by nearly half. At the same time, interest in preserving the *built environment surged (Washington's Senator Scoop Jackson sponsored the 1966 National Historic Preservation Act), and most of the state's thirty-nine counties established historical societies between midcentury and the state's 1989 centennial. Regional groups, such as the League of Snohomish County Heritage Organizations and the Heritage Network, promote their members'

This historical marker in front of the old state capitol building in Olympia commemorates the date when women in Washington won the right to vote, which energized the national women's suffrage movement. CREDIT: HEATHER LOCKMAN.

interests, reflecting major historical influences, tribal, maritime, and railroad history museums are found throughout Washington. The Heritage Capital Grants Fund provides millions of dollars to capitalize *heritage infrastructure, while the Heritage Barn Register and Historic County Courthouses programs focus on specific types of buildings.

Each year historians and enthusiasts gather at the Pacific Northwest History Conference (since 1947) and the Pacific Northwest Historians Guild conference. They also meet during the state legislative session to discuss policy issues with lawmakers in the weekly Heritage Caucus, one of the only gatherings of its kind in the country. As befits the home of important technology companies, innovative digital resources include *HistoryLink* (an online encyclopedia of Washington history) and the Washington Women's History Consortium (an online portal to aggregated women's history resources from the state's universities, libraries, and archives).

The University of Washington and Washington State University presses are known for their offerings in regional history. UW's Center for the Study of Pacific Northwest History offers *Pacific Northwest Quarterly*, the chief academic journal of regional history. WSHS publishes *Columbia*, a full-color Northwest history magazine. Many local history organizations have brought forth histories of a specific geographic area, town, person, or building.

An excellent history of the region before statehood is *Washington Territory*, by Robert E. Ficken. The first comprehensive state history was 1909's *History of the State of Washington* by pioneer Edmond Meany, an indefatigable promoter of state history. Norman Clark's *Washington: A Bicentennial History* (1976) uses a social history theoretical approach. *Washington: A Centennial History* (1989) is a comprehensive overview cowritten by Ficken and Charles LeWarne, author of the preeminent K–12 state history textbook. In keeping with Washington's regional perspective, excellent regional histories include Carlos Schwantes's *The Pacific Northwest: An Interpretive History* (2000); Gordon B. Dodds's *The American Northwest: A History of Oregon and Washington* (1986); and Dorothy Johansen's *Empire of the Columbia: A History of the Pacific Northwest* (1967). Other histories have examined exploration and settlement; economic diversification and atomic development during World War II; the natural environment; various social groups including American Indians, African Americans, and women; and Pacific Northwest regionalism. Notable contemporary historians working in these areas include Paula Becker, John Findlay, Alexandra Harmon, Bruce Hevly, Ruth Kirk, Lorraine McConaghy, Esther Mumford, and Quintard Taylor.

Each of Washington's 295 school districts must meet state standards for social studies education. Students complete one semester of state history during primary school, usually in fourth grade, generally centering on tribes and treaties, exploration (particularly the Lewis and Clark Expedition), and immigration and settlement. Many students revisit state history in seventh grade, when U.S. history (statehood to the present) is required. High school graduation requirements include one semester of state or regional history, typically taught during the eleventh grade. State legislation passed in 2015 requires the teaching of tribal history as part of state history studies.

At the college level, the University of Washington and Western Washington University have stand-alone programs dedicated to the study of the Pacific Northwest. Every state and major private college offers at least one course in Pacific Northwest history, and several require it for history majors. Many also offer classes in Pacific Northwest anthropology, *archaeology, arts, environmental studies, and natural history. One semester of instruction in Washington State history is required for all graduate degrees in education.

LAUREN DANNER
INDEPENDENT HISTORIAN

See United States, local history in.

web history. The World Wide Web, or web, is a system of interlinked hypertext documents accessed using the Internet, a global system of interconnected computer networks. Many history organizations started building websites in the mid-1990s and today no organization can afford to be without a presence on the web. Younger generations link an organization's reality with whether it exists online. The first Museums and the Web conference, an annual international conference for cultural institutions, was held in 1997. Most organizations started out by establishing a presence online, posting general marketing and visitor information—hours, location, exhibitions. The next general phase was digitizing collections and allowing website users to access images and descriptions of the collections. Early fears that putting collections online or creating online versions of exhibitions would severely affect visitor attendance to the physical space proved unfounded. It increased access to collections and exhibitions. The next phase included providing tools to encourage researchers, educators, and other professionals to use the online materials. As websites begin to reflect the broader functions of an entire organization, there is an increase in online stores and online fundraising and other functions.

Web 2.0 refers to a second iteration of the web that does not refer to technical change but to emphasis on user-generated content and various tools to share content easily among a community of users. The term was popularized in late 2004. The rise of this social media, such as wikis, *blogs, mashups and folksonomies in the last ten years has stimulated the growth of new marketing and communication tools to help history organizations stay connected to their audiences. It is important to remember that with a website, the audience reaches around the globe. With an increasingly transient society, people with connections to a particular community may live anywhere in the world. Social media has also fostered the expectation of a more participatory nature for websites; history organizations are struggling with what it means to share authority and allow users to contribute content to websites. Another issue has been whether to charge for images from collections. There is a growing movement toward providing all materials without charge. However, many institutions rely on revenue from permission fees and copies of images for income.

With the permanence of the web medium established, history organizations have struggled with where to locate the responsibility for the website within an organization's hierarchy. A website should be considered a digital partner that complements the brick-and-mortar institution. Function varies by institution—for some the website is primarily a marketing tool, for others it is a research or education tool. Larger institutions have staff devoted to maintaining the website, while smaller ones hire an outside company for this job. It is important to keep a website maintained and up to date with the latest information about your organization.

The web is still a relatively new medium representing a combination of written word, photo, audio, and video, along with its own design style. Some people have said it is most similar in format to an exhibition. Writing for an online audience is different from writing for other mediums. Online users have different expectations than exhibition visitors or book readers. Just as with other mediums, it is important to understand who uses the medium and how they use it.

The web medium may actually offer a richer format for presenting the past than other mediums.

On the scale of interpretation to facts, history websites fall under "more interpretation needed" while art websites are at the other end with very little interpretation necessary to enjoy works of art. One does not need to know about the artist and her reasons behind a piece in order to enjoy it. Science seems to fall somewhere in the middle, with some explanation of the facts necessary to bring understanding. History, asking the "why" and "what if" questions, requires a context in order to understand. History is all about interpretation and the web format offers content developers and designers various ways that allow the user to draw conclusions and compare interpretations with scholars. Careful use of language on a website can guide a user to engage actively with the content, transforming a static collection of *primary sources, for example, into new interpretations. Websites can also offer digital spaces for users to share their thoughts or converse with others.

As we all know, any event can be seen from multiple perspectives, and a historical presentation is richer when it encourages its audience to consider several perspectives. This multiple-perspective approach can get tedious in other mediums, like books or exhibitions, especially if many perspectives are presented. Multiple perspectives can also be a challenge online, but the web format is especially suited to layering. A good site that illustrates this is the award-winning "Raid on Deerfield" website, http://1704.deerfield.history. museum. Subtitled "the many stories of 1704," the site does an excellent job of presenting the facts of an event through many different lenses.

More than other disciplines, history is about story and narrative is at its core. And we all know that a good story told well can be a captivating force. This narrative does not always need to be linear. Websites are full of nonlinear stories of people, objects, and places. The web medium can magnify features of stories, offer sidebars, and pose questions with links that subtly guide the user along. When a story is told through layering, users can uncover it at their own pace and go as deep as they want.

The web can layer maps and photos to demonstrate movement through time in ways that other mediums simply cannot. Ultimately it seems to be about the power of layering. The richness of history is well suited to the web's dynamism. The more we continue to think critically about the technology, the stronger our websites will become.

TIM GROVE
NATIONAL AIR AND SPACE MUSEUM,
SMITHSONIAN INSTITUTION

See radical trust and voice of authority; social media.

Welsh in North America, sources for. See Appendix A.

West Indians in North America, sources for. See Appendix A.

West Virginia, local history in. West Virginia, the thirty-fifth state, was created in 1863 at the height of the Civil War. An organized effort to collect and preserve records and artifacts of the

This marker tells this history of Grave Creek Mound in Moundsville, West Virginia. Credit: West Virginia State Archives.

new state began in 1869 when the West Virginia Legislature authorized the formation of the first of several statewide historical societies that existed for various lengths of time between 1869 and 1929. Each of the failed societies was charged with the collection and preservation of documents and artifacts important to the state's history, but that proved a happenstance effort until the creation of a State Department of Archives and History in 1905 and the appointment of Virgil A. Lewis as the first director. With legislative backing, Lewis quickly created a library of state documents and reports and a museum containing important artifacts and other items of the state's history. The invaluable collections were located in the capitol annex building and escaped damage when the state capitol building burned in 1921.

The current West Virginia Historical Society was organized in 1940. The society has a close connection with the Archives and History Section of the West Virginia Division of Culture and History. County and local historical organizations have been critical partners in the collection and preservation of local and state history. As of March 2015 there were 115 such groups according to the Archives and History website.

West Virginia History was published as the official state history journal by Archives and History from 1939 until

2006. Responsibility for the journal was transferred to West Virginia University, which published the first number of a new series in fall 2007. The *West Virginia Historical Society Magazine* is published semiannually and a number of county and special interest history societies publish journals or newsletters and maintain libraries of genealogical and local historical materials.

The Archives and History Section is the state's major repository of official records, manuscripts, genealogical materials, and other documents and maintains an excellent library and research facility at the state capitol complex in Charleston. Collections include materials related to the John Brown raid at Harpers Ferry and the Granville B. Hall verbatim transcriptions of the debates leading to West Virginia's first constitution. The archives maintains an extensive collection of online materials for research including records for genealogists; Civil War letters, documents, and pictures; a John Brown exhibit; and photos and documents relating to the 1960 John F. Kennedy presidential campaign. Large regional collections at West Virginia University's West Virginia and Regional History Center and Marshall University's Morrow Library Special Collections, which includes the unique Rosanna Blake Collection of Confederate memorabilia, are important local history resources.

Public school standards require one year of instruction in West Virginia's history and culture and either West Virginia History or an Appalachian studies course is available in the colleges and universities. West Virginia eighth graders are tested in state history, gov-ernment, and politics with the winners being awarded the honor of becoming a knight or lady of the Golden Horseshoe Society, named for the golden horseshoes that Governor Alexander Spotswood awarded in 1716 to explorers of Virginia's western regions.

Authors of county and military histories, biographies, and a few state histories stimulated interest in West Virginia history. Examples include Governor George W. Atkinson, Hu Maxwell, Thomas C. Miller, Virgil A. Lewis, James M. Callahan, Boyd B. Stutler, and Phil Conley. The first historians concentrated on topics arising from the Civil War and the creation of the state. Early interpretations that western Virginians were largely Unionists were challenged by Richard O. Curry and others, who wrote at a more remote period from the actual events. Later historians, John A. Williams, Ronald L. Lewis, David Corbin, John Hennen, Ronald Eller, and others focused on the impact of capitalists, political power, and immigration on the development of the state.

Charles H. Ambler and Otis K. Rice were the dominant West Virginia historians of the twentieth century. Ambler, at West Virginia University and Rice, at West Virginia Institute of Technology published extensively on topics relating to the state. Rice was named West Virginia Historian Laureate in 2003 and was followed by Ronald L. Lewis who was named to that post in 2010.

In 2009, the West Virginia Legislature created the West Virginia Sesquicentennial Commission to observe the 150th anniversary of the Civil War and the creation of West Virginia. Reenactments and historical presentations from

2011 to 2015 told the story of the war and West Virginia's birth.

A number of ongoing efforts to promote interest in local and state history include funding from the West Virginia Humanities Council for local history proposals and for *The West Virginia Encyclopedia*, an important resource for state history, which is available in print and in an online version. The West Virginia Humanities Council is also cooperating with West Virginia University Press to bring back rare and out-of-print books dealing with the state's history and literature. Archives and History has an ongoing project to digitize county and state records for online access and is in the process of assisting counties in preserving their records in digital form. Archives and History also sponsors an annual History Day at the legislature, awards to History Heroes who have performed exemplary work for their local historical societies, a History Bowl competition to stimulate interest from public school students in the state's heritage, and strong support for local history and genealogical societies.

KENNETH R. BAILEY
WEST VIRGINIA UNIVERSITY INSTITUTE
OF TECHNOLOGY, RETIRED

See United States, local history in.

Western history and local historians. When most Americans hear the term "the West," they think of a land inhabited by cowboys, pioneers, gunfighters, and "wild Indians," images crafted by a complex but curious blend of Jeffersonian agrarianism, Free Soil ideology, John Wayne, the Marlboro Man, and *Dances with Wolves*. For historians, this image is associated with the historical model crafted by Frederick Jackson Turner. Arguably the most influential U.S. historian in the twentieth century, Turner intellectualized the link between a place loosely defined as "the West" and an equally vague concept known as "the frontier" (see *frontier thesis). Presenting his theory at the World's Columbian Exposition in Chicago in 1893, Turner held that the key to understanding the history of the United States was the frontier experience. For him, the frontier was a constantly moving line of demarcation where "savagery" met "civilization," and successive waves of European infiltration drove civilization's advance irresistibly forward. Trappers and traders heralded the decline of wilderness barbarism. Permanent settlers soon followed, bringing with them increasingly intensive modes of agricultural production. Finally, the appearance of "manufacturing organization with city and factory system" represented the ultimate triumph of American nationalism (see Frederick Jackson Turner, "The Significance of the Frontier in American History," reprinted in *History, Frontier, and Section: Three Essays by Frederick Jackson Turner* [1993], 59–91).

A native of Wisconsin, Turner was determined to make the West the focal point of U.S. history. When Turner wrote the frontier thesis, the "germ theory" then prevalent in scholarly circles established the roots of American culture within the tribal antecedents of medieval Teutonic civilization. Such a view suggested that the American experience was a mere footnote to historical processes long since past. The implication of Turner's hypothesis was the complete reverse. The frontier was the cradle of American values. The distance of the wilderness from established institutions and, hence, European origins produced a spirit of individualism, spurred the growth of democratic traditions, and "Americanized, liberated, and fused" a diverse stock of immigrants "into a mixed race, English in neither nationality nor characteristics." (Turner, *History, Frontier, and Section*, 1–7, 75–76). The taming of the frontier then represented a process, a mechanism by which Europeans could craft a new, homogenous, and democratic culture. The "West" was merely the incidental direction people headed in the course of becoming American.

Whatever the merits of the frontier thesis, Turner's story was not an inclusive history. Turner never talked about Mexicans, or African Americans, Asians, or women. The frontier thesis assumed, if not celebrated, the destruction of the Indians, not the possibility that Native Americans might have adapted and even survived with much of their cultures intact. Turner spent little time on the influence of the federal government on frontier development, although many westerners were certainly aware of the importance of Washington on regional development. He gave a nod to the rise of the city, but only as an end point in his historical process, not as a concurrent method of conquest and settlement. There is a passing note to the development of the factory system, but the egalitarian qualities of the frontier supposedly suppressed any aspect of class. There are no mining companies, no railroad strikes, no water wars.

Turner's developed West was a region full of farmers, not of oil derricks busily extracting irreplaceable resources from the land.

Many of these omissions were understandable in so short an essay. Some of Turner's exclusions stem from his nineteenth-century convictions. Turner himself moved on to refine his view of history. Many in the profession did not. Whatever the difficulties inherent in the frontier thesis, now so apparent in hindsight, much of the unwillingness of historians to challenge Turner came from the fact that the frontier thesis in so many ways spoke to them. Turner's America looked much like the small towns from which numerous historians originated. The frontier thesis meant that America was special, that it was energetic, triumphant, and democratic. It also gave them a benchmark from which to view their own rapidly changing world, filled with anxiety about the "closing of the frontier" and the nation's rapid industrialization and urbanization, a sense of loss that Turner himself seems to have felt. Professionally, local historians could now weave their provincial subjects into a wider historical narrative (Turner, *History, Frontier, and Section*, 1–26).

Although the frontier thesis dominated historians' view of the West for more than a half century, challenges to its basic assumptions appeared sporadically, only to reach a torrent in the past two decades. These new approaches to the history of the West, gathered today under the general banner of the "New Western History," suggest the range of lenses through which local historians can view their subjects as examples or products of Western localities. Patricia Nelson Limerick's *The Legacy of Conquest: The Unbroken Past of the American West* (1987) is rightly seen as one of the most important attempts to give the New Western History a broad conceptual framework. Synthesizing the work of many scholars, Limerick openly rejected Turner's concept of the frontier as a social process. Beyond such ethnocentric demarcations as "civilization" and "savagery," one of the problems with the Turnerian view is that it really says little about the West. The frontier moves over time, from Puritan New England to the Dominguez Rancho, so to speak. The frontier therefore is as much the domain of a historian of Colonial Williamsburg as a historian of Albuquerque. Contrasting social structures, technologies, cultures, and environmental conditions makes little difference it seems, as long as the localities sit somewhere on the frontier.

Instead of seeing the West as a process, New Western Historians see the region as a place. Now just where the West is has been open to debate. Limerick equivocated on the subject, but many accept Donald Worster's assertion that it is the region of diminishing rainfall west of the 100th meridian. (See Limerick, *The Legacy of Conquest*, 26. For Worster's opinion on just where the West is, see Donald Worster, *Under Western Skies: Nature and History in the American West* [1992], 25.) Yes, it is arbitrary, but you have to start somewhere. If your locality happens to be on the ninety-ninth meridian and you consider it to be a western place, feel free to move the West, but only just a little.

In regard to the particulars of that place, New Western Historians generally accept the notion that the West is a region that has undergone conquest. Unfortunately for the pioneers, when they arrived in the West, people were already living there. All of North America is such a place, but the conquest took place after the United States gained the status of a fully formed nation-state, and the conquest of the region challenged the nation's commitment to democratic ideals and constitutional supremacy. Moreover, the West's position as a global crossroads between indigenous America, Anglo-European America, Spanish America, and Asian America made the conquest more complex. Once the pioneers settled their farms, they may have been surprised that the Indians and Mexicans did not go away. In fact, they may have been surprised that other groups kept coming. The West may not have had the teeming immigrant neighborhoods of Brooklyn, but the region did and does have its Chinatowns, its Japan Towns, its Little Saigons, and its South-Central Los Angeles.

As a cultural crossroads, scholars now focus on those left out of Turner's story. Women are now major players in the history of the West. The "pioneer woman" challenges old myths about the "minimal" role of frontier women and the ability of the "democratic frontier" to subsume traditional gender roles. More recent studies highlight women's role as cultural intermediaries between the men in their lives, an insight that fits nicely into the theme of the West as global crossroads. The decade of the 1960s likewise saw an increase in interest in the history of the Spanish-speaking peoples of the West, reminding historians of the region that when they speak of the "frontier," they must address the question of just whose frontier they are talking about. Borderland studies are now a major component of any serious examination of the West. Native Americans were not simply on the anterior side of those multiple frontiers, but they continued to dwell within those lines long after their passage. Rather than portraying native peoples as passive victims, historians in the post-Turnerian era point to Indians as engaged historical actors, and emphasize indigenous societal structures and cultural forms as well as postcontact resistance, adaptation, and survival. And when we address aspects of "European settlement," we must be careful of old generalizations. The Mormon appearance in Utah led to a short-lived military conflict with the United States and a longer struggle over statehood and religious practice. The West was full of small African American farming communities like Kansas's Nicodemus and California's Allensworth, and black enclaves could be found in almost every Western city. If one chanced upon a clash between Native Americans and U.S. Army units in the West, there was a good chance that the latter were also composed of men of African descent, and even natives of other tribes.

As problematic was the fact that Western people inhabited a region that was rich in natural resources but less than hospitable to human occupation. Whatever the accomplishments of the rugged individualists of Western lore, they could not have conquered and settled the region without the help of large institutions. Not only did the U.S. Army and the state militias fight a series of wars against native bands, but they secured original access to those lands by engaging in a major war against Mexico. The federal government divided the land and distributed it to homesteaders, railroads, and miners. Federal and state water projects brought water to the desert, and nurtured agricultural and industrial development in many ways. Land companies subdivided the towns, and corporate mining quickly replaced the forty-niners of lore. This conquest of nature may have appeared to Turner's generation as the triumph of civilization, but New Western Historians recognize that such changes in the land brought a heavy price in environmental damage and a constant debate on the proper distribution of resources, particularly water.

However, local historians, like Western historians in general, should not lose sight of the qualities their topics share, no matter how nearby and personal they may appear, with wider aspects of national, or even global history (Limerick, *The Legacy of Conquest*, 26). The New Western History not only explores new perspectives on the development of the region, but the school's themes also lend themselves readily to comparative and interdisciplinary approaches. Comparative studies can prevent the field from becoming too narrowly focused, and can allow local historians to engage their specific subjects while addressing the question of *American exceptionalism and a host of other topics. The American West is ripe for comparative studies of such topics as colonialism and white-native relations. What were the differences between the American subjugation of native peoples in the Southwest and the British conquest of Canada's Indians, or Australian aborigines? How did conquest transform such features as status, religion, gender roles, and even ecological systems in African, Asian, and American settings? Comparative thinking can be an effective tool in promoting local history in a world that is becoming increasingly global, particularly among younger generations instantaneously connected to people and events through *social media and other digital sources of information.

Over a quarter-century has passed since the publication of *The Legacy of Conquest*, and today New Western History themes permeate, if not dominate, university classrooms. Standard college texts like Richard White's *Its Your Misfortune and None of My Own*, and Robert Hine and John Faragher's *The American West: A New Interpretive History*, engage Western topics from multiple ethnic and racial perspectives, shatter the old view of the settlers as a monolithic group, deal at great length with environmental issues, and highlight the prominent role of the federal government and corporations in regional development.

Yet New Western History themes are also moving beyond limited scholarly audiences and are penetrating the realm of *public history, the field in which many local historians work. The popularity of the Autry National Center in Los Angeles attests to this. Although in some ways clinging to the singing cowboy mythologies of the past, the museum is also a superb storyteller when

it comes to the relationships between different racial and ethnic groups, the role of women, and the despoliation of western resources. The New Mexico History Museum engages Borderlands history and the Native American experience in the Southwest. The California Room of the Oakland Museum traces the history of the Golden State through such interactive exhibits as "Before the Other People Came," "Creative Hollywood," and "Negotiating the Border," where visitors are invited to examine immigration from multiple perspectives. Even the federal government has felt the mark of new historical interpretations, changing the name of the "Custer Battlefield National Monument" to the "Little Big Horn National Monument" in 1991, and constructing a memorial there to specifically address "the Plains Indians Legacy" (see Karen R. Jones and John Wills, *The American West: Competing Visions* [2009], 5).

Where is Western historiography headed? A perusal of articles written in the last five years in the Western History Association's *Western Historical Quarterly* reveals the continued dominance of New Western History themes. Borderland, environmental, and ethnic histories, perhaps rightfully, continue to fill its pages. The *Pacific Historical Review*, the quarterly journal published by the Pacific Coast Branch of the *American Historical Association, demonstrates a similar persistent focus. For the future, increasing trends toward globalization and the stark prospect of climate change may prompt some scholars to search for antecedents in the regional past. Yet such "new" topics, focusing on interconnectedness and environmental challenge as they do, still fit squarely in the Western historiographic tradition.

Regardless of specific focus, it is through such topics that local historians may cast their subjects as definitively "Western" while engaging audiences in this increasingly global society. However, local historians have not completely abandoned traditional conceptions of the frontier. The rugged pioneer and the lonely cowboy were very real parts of the Western experience, and should be examined where they are pertinent. As many historians have found, institutions will be hard pressed to expunge John Wayne from the American consciousness, even if they wanted to. Even Hine and Faragher's "New Interpretive History" cannot seem to escape from the power of Turner's notion of directional movement as the centerpiece of American history, for the authors reserve a good deal of space for the European colonization of America east of the Mississippi.

Public historians in particular must find a delicate balance between teaching the complex, multiple viewpoints of the New Western History and the mythical West that many audiences crave. In a symposium on the teaching of the history of the American West held at the annual conference of the Western History Association January 1999, William Cronon presented what might be an effective means for dealing with the frontier of tradition:

The frontier is such a powerful mythic force in American culture that it's usually best not to act as if one can assault it frontally in the classroom and thereby expunge its influence on the minds of students. The myth is in fact more power-ful than we are, and usually wins. The better course of action is teach as if one were practicing Judo, using the weight and energy of the myth to move the students forward by first engaging them with it and then shifting its momentum in the more historical directions we hope to carry them. Better to try to shift and reshape the myth, acknowledging its partial truths while denying its distortions, than to claim that it has no real-ity whatsoever. (William Cronon to the author, January 28, 1999)

By introducing audiences to frontier concepts and then asking questions about their relationship to historical realities, historians can negotiate the powerful divide between New and Old Western histories. This endeavor is not as difficult as it seems as we move beyond the dominance of Baby Boomer America. As Pixar's Sheriff Woody discovers, the advent of the Space Race and the march of technology decimated his popularity, leading to the ascendancy of Buzz Lightyear. Outside parts of the interior west, where powerful Western icons, *landscapes, and even politics survive in some form, an increasing number of Americans never grew up with John Wayne, *Gunsmoke*, or *Howdy Doody*. Although the Hollywood gunslinger may always be with us, the resilience of the John Wayne myth may indeed be weakening, allowing for a popularization of the academic trends crafted by the pioneers of the New Western History some thirty years ago.

For in-depth discussions of these themes, see William Cronon, George Miles, and Jay Gitlin, eds., *Under an Open Sky: Rethinking America's Western Past* (1992); Patricia Limerick, Clyde A. Milner III, and Charles E. Rankin, eds., *Trails: Towards a New Western*

History (1991); Gerald D. Nash, *Creating the West: Historical Interpretations, 1890–1990* (1991); Gerald D. Nash and Richard Etulain, *The Twentieth Century West: Historical Interpretations* (1989); Patricia Nelson Limerick, *The Legacy of Conquest: The Unbroken Past of the American West* (1987), 26; Robert Hine and John Faragher, *The American West: A New Interpretive History* (2000); Richard White, *It's Your Misfortune and None of My Own: A History of the American West* (1991); Patricia Limerick, "Going West and Ending Up Global," *Western Historical Quarterly* 32 (Spring 2001), 4–23; Douglas W. Dodd, "Legacy of Conquest and Trails: Twenty Years Later: Public Historians and the New Western History—Introduction"; Louise Pubols, "The Singing Cowboy and the Professor: The New West at the Autry Center"; Jay M. Price, "Still Facing John Wayne After All These Years: Bringing New Western History to Larger Audiences"; Gregory E. Smoak, "Beyond the Academy: Making the New Western History Matter in Local Communities," *Public Historian* 31 (Fall 2009): 67–89; and Karen R. Jones and John Wills, *The American West: Competing Visions* (2009), 5; Donald Worster, "The American West in the Age of Vulnerability," *Western Historical Quarterly* 45 (February 2014): 5–16.

ROBERT PHELPS
CALIFORNIA STATE
UNIVERSITY–EAST BAY

See frontier thesis.

wiki. See crowdsourcing and crowdfunding; social media.

Wisconsin, local history in. Successes in collecting, preserving, and sharing the history of Wisconsin have been the result of democratic and progressive themes that run through the state's history. The Wisconsin Historical Society, nearly 400 affiliated local historical societies, regional Area Research Centers, and numerous local historic preservation commissions and advocacy groups still reflect the original programmatic aims of several remarkably visionary leaders. For more than 160 years, the state has operated under the leadership of a strong central agency, while maintaining a large degree of local control and access.

An awareness of the need "to preserve the materials for a complete history of Wisconsin" was in the minds of the members of the state constitutional convention of 1846, which after finishing their work, reconvened at a nearby hotel and formed the Wisconsin Historical Society. Although statehood would have to wait until 1848, the Wisconsin Historical Society continued, and today's efforts to collect, preserve, and share stories of the state and its local communities stem from those original efforts.

Seven years after its founding, the society reorganized in 1853 and received a charter that created a membership organization called the State Historical Society of Wisconsin, a name that at times it used concurrently with Wisconsin Historical Society. That same year, Wisconsin became the first state to make a continuing annual appropriation to the work of a historical society and Lyman Draper was hired as its director. Draper envisioned a democratic

This historical marker near Black River Falls, Wisconsin, honors Congressional Medal of Honor winner Mitchell Red Cloud, Jr. CREDIT: WISCONSIN HISTORICAL SOCIETY.

society, open to anyone willing to pay annual dues and preserving the stories of people from all walks of life. Draper collected widely, immediately shaping the society to be not only a national repository of North American interests, but also a publisher in earnest, with the first volume of the *Wisconsin Historical Collections* appearing in 1855. Another nineteen volumes followed over the next fifty years, containing thousands of documents, including *diaries, interviews, and pioneer recollections, as well as Indian and archaeological lore.

Beginning in 1887, Draper's successor, Reuben Gold Thwaites, continued publishing and collecting, emphasizing materials with specific reference to Wisconsin. In concert with the Progressive spirit that imbued civic life in the state during his twenty-six-year tenure, Thwaites further democratized the society—enlisting the aid of anyone interested in *historic preservation, local history, and public education writ large. He promoted the founding of local societies and the reinvigoration of Old Settlers' societies to enhance historical presentation (in exhibits) as well as documentation and commemoration of historic events with appropriate markers and fanfare. His efforts helped the society erect the impressive structure on the University of Wisconsin–Madison campus that still houses its headquarters, library, and archives as he simultaneously built collections and public support. He encouraged and offered on-site support for county and local historical societies to duplicate such a model at the local level.

Legislation passed in 1897 allowed local historical groups to incorporate and affiliate with the Wisconsin Historical Society. Groups in Brown County and Ripon were the first two local societies to affiliate with the state society under the new law. By 2015, nearly 400 local societies achieved that status. While there are some significant exceptions, most of these groups are small, having fewer than 100 members, no professional staff, and receiving little to no government funding. Affiliation gave the Wisconsin Historical Society no programmatic authority over the local societies, but it did create a formal structure to ensure networking among the local societies and communications between the state society and the local groups. The Wisconsin Council for Local History, a group made up of all affiliates, was created in 1961 to further promote communication. The Wisconsin Historical Society continues to assist local societies through specialized workshops, regional conventions, and an annual convention. Local society members have opportunities to learn from one another and from the expertise of archivists, preservationists, museum personnel, and other professional staff at the Wisconsin Historical Society.

Starting in the 1960s, a number of communities created local historical preservation commissions, a process that was accelerated in 1980 with the creation of the federal certified local government program. Like the affiliated local historical societies, these entities have a formalized relationship with the State Historic Preservation Office at the Wisconsin Historical Society.

Since the early 1950s the Wisconsin Historical Society makes its extensive collection of archival materials available through its Area Research Center system, a network of fourteen archival repositories. Records created by local governments and manuscript collections of regional interest are housed at these centers. Most centers also hold additional local collections, all of which can be transferred from one center to another through a courier system.

The Wisconsin Historical Society Press has continued to publish broadly, including a definitive six-volume History of Wisconsin series, covering topics from exploration through the 1960s and many monographs accessible to interested readers as well as scholars. Since 1917, the society has also published the *Wisconsin Magazine of History*, a quarterly journal for members. Another key aspect of the society's mission has focused and continues to provide materials on state and local history for K–12 classrooms. The most significant of these has been the award-winning textbook for fourth grade, *Wisconsin: Our State, Our Story*.

The Wisconsin Historical Society of the twenty-first century is one of the largest, most active, and most diversified state historical societies in the nation, with extensive collections, ten historic sites around the state, and a museum in Madison. As the Internet has transformed the possibilities for outreach, the society's virtual presence has developed apace at www.wisconsinhistory.org. Key online collections include more than eighty Wisconsin County Histories; Wisconsin Local History & Biography Articles (thousands of historical newspaper articles on Wisconsin people and communities); tens of thousands of *digitized historical photographs, *maps and other images in the Visual Materials and Film Collection (formerly known as Wisconsin Historical Images); and the Dictionary of Wisconsin History (searchable by place, event, or people). The website also includes a directory of affiliated local historical societies with links to their websites.

Presently, the Wisconsin Historical Society carries on the same progressive tradition in which the society and hundreds of local organizations work together to collect, preserve, and share the stories of the state and its communities.

BOBBIE S. MALONE
UPDATED BY JOHN ZIMM
WISCONSIN HISTORICAL SOCIETY

See field services; United States, local history in.

women's history at local history sites, interpreting.

In the past forty years historians have amassed an astounding amount of research and writing on women's history, and historic site interpretation has increased and improved. In 1971 when many colleges first offered women's history courses, there were limited texts with women's history defined as the history of suffrage. There was no systematic survey of *primary sources. Women at historic sites gave ladylike tours and performed living history activities like spinning and candle dipping, but did little else. While some sites worked hard to dress interpreters accurately, others dressed them in polyester and cotton costumes. Since then, writings, including memoirs and biographies, extensive surveys, and advancements in theory for history, anthropology, geography, *vernacular architecture, and *material culture, have produced countless resources and publications. Research has built upon research, finding new sources and creatively reusing old ones. However, this wealth of knowledge remains unevenly incorporated into the interpretation of historic sites, many of which still focus on a few great men or include stories about women told derisively or as part of belittling myths. At Jamestown, Virginia, interpreters have claimed "the women came in 1618" ignoring the Native American women who had lived there for thousands of years; at a Civil War battlefield, with documented civilian deaths and an extended free black family living there, interpreters assured visitors that "there's no women's history here." As long as such misconceptions and distortions continue, a need exists for greatly increased awareness of the roles and experiences of women in our history.

Fortunately, there have been many improvements in historic site interpretation. Now, at Andrew Jackson's home, The Hermitage, the enslaved Hannah Jackson greets visitors who still learn about Jackson and his wife Rachel; the Otis House in Boston now interprets many of its female residents, with a bedroom from its boarding house era, as well as the lives of Harrison Gray and Sally Foster Otis. These examples illustrate that inclusion of women's experiences at historic sites often widens visitors' encounters with various socioeconomic groups. They also show how integral women were to families even as custom, legal requirements, and practical considerations limited their experiences and visibility. It is known that women were also to be found at Civil War battlefields, as nearby residents, as wives and sisters of soldiers, as nurses, and as soldiers who had served under disguise. After years of searching, historians have concluded that no historic site is void of women's history—even Alcatraz Island in San Francisco Bay housed wardens' families, and women from the American Indian Movement participated in the occupation of the island from 1969–1971.

By beginning with the assumption that women were present at or at least affected by every historic site, many otherwise invisible women soon become apparent and many previously ignored connections become clear. Once one becomes aware of these women, their lives become visible. Native American men's hunting practice is now understood to supplement native women's corn-beans-squash agriculture. Enslaved women grew the crops that made Martha and George Washington wealthy. John Adams and Ben Franklin benefited by their hardworking wives Abigail and Deborah, who kept the respective family farm and printing businesses going as their husbands served the young nation. Mid-Atlantic women's butter and eggs, which they sold to colonial city dwellers, provided their families much-needed currency; Italian tenement women ran informal boarding houses; and black single women sent money to their sharecropping families from their meager incomes as domestic workers—all these women played crucial roles in their family economies. Stephanie McCurry's new *political history, *Confederate Reckoning* (2010), shows the importance Confederate soldiers' wives played in that government's fall as women demanded better treatment, straining already scarce resources, and asked their soldiers to come home (i.e., desert) before the war was over. These studies show the amazing variety of American women's lives and why we should reconsider stories once assumed too well known to be examined again. They also revisit places such as seaports where women played important roles when their husbands were at sea and where a surprising number of ships sailed with the captain's wife onboard. Cape Cod National Seashore preserves the Penniman house, home to a whaling family whose wife rescued her captain-husband after she sailed through a major storm.

We need to place more emphasis on linking the stories of local history sites to academic scholarship. Too often sites are interpreted using basic biographical information rather than setting the story in its wider historical context. In addition to assuming that women (and girls) were present, it's important to ask different questions of old legal sources as Lea Vandervelde did so well in realizing that Harriet Robinson had a key role in suing for her own freedom and also getting her famous husband, Dred Scott, to do so (their cases were combined). Marla Miller's *Betsy Ross & the Making of America* (2010) shows how working-class women affected the successful American Revolution and illustrates a newer scholarship tied to historic sites. Here a biography lures readers into the social history of revolutionary Philadelphia with all the uncertainties and contingencies involved. Here women too

often lose husbands, children, and economic security. Greater research in material culture and the vernacular *landscape as practiced by Laurel Thatcher Ulrich in *The Age of Homespun: Myths and Objects and Stories in the Creation of an American Myth* (2001) and Jessica Sewell, in *Women and the Everyday City: Public Space in San Francisco, 1890–1915* (2011) provides insights and templates. Much more research in demographic, spatial, process-oriented (rather than major events), and ethnic history will enhance historic site interpretation and preservation.

Some historic sites still want to celebrate women's history with tea parties; others face difficult economic times, cutting back staff, hours, and programming. Still others have focused their resources on specific programs and audiences, working to identify ways to encourage repeat visitation. They use small armies of dedicated *volunteers and equally dedicated staff to keep the doors open and visitors coming. Some sites dress for different occasions— such as in Richmond, Virginia, where Maymont exhibits mourning to illustrate Victorian death customs and to show different objects from their collections. Many offer Christmas-themed and women's history month events. The challenge remains finding ways to share quality women's history with the public while keeping doors open and bills paid. Various organizations help historic sites with both administrative and programmatic issues—the *American Association for State and Local History (see *Great Tours!* [2002]) has long been exemplary in giving sites guidance and support, as have the *American Alliance of Museums and the *National Trust for Historic Preservation. Various ethnic and regional organizations offer help. The *Organization of American Historians publishes *The Magazine of History*; the National Collaborative for Women's History Sites offers training, publications such as *Women's History: Sites and Resources* (2008) and *Integrating Women's History into Historic Sites*, and a website, www.ncwhs.org.

Meanwhile, many younger academic historians have shifted from women's history to gender history, accepting the claim that women's history has been "done" and gender history is more exciting. More established women's historians remain skeptical. They consider the past forty years of research remedial rather than exhaustive and fear that "gender history" will again obscure still-undiscovered histories of women and girls. Given how much is still being learned about women's lives, it's clear there's much more to be learned.

Continuing growth of web resources, *social media, and other electronically based communication will offer greater access to historic places even as they challenge the notion of experiencing places—that virtual visits can replace in-person visits. The challenge to the long-standing business model of few paid staff, many volunteers, and much local support will continue to force historic sites to find new resources. New websites, social media, and online exhibits, from the Martha's Vineyard Museum's "Girl on a Whaling Ship" to the Autry Museum's "There Are No Renters Here" exhibit on women homesteaders, simultaneously provide challenges and opportunities. Because many academic websites are gated, access for local history sites and public historians to digital primary sources and relevant academic sources (footnotes never killed anyone) is difficult. Bringing together historic sites and academic research will enhance both. Several important changes have come during the past few years:

- Greater recognition of varieties of female sexuality, as seen in Susan Ferentino's book *Interpreting LGBT History at Museums and Historic Sites* (2014), which documents many previously unappreciated women;
- A generational shift as the first large academic cohort of women historians retire;
- The insight that "intersectionality" brings—that gender, race, class, sexuality, etc., do not exist separately in people but interact with and reinforce each other (for better and for worse).

Women traveling west in wagon trains marveled at their own accomplishments as they crossed the plains and sighted the Rocky Mountains ahead. Some women then grew faint; the stories of those who kept going continue to encourage us. May we honor them by telling "the whole story"—one that fully incorporates the lives of women.

See Darlene Clark Hine: *A Shining Thread of Hope: The History of Black Women in America* (1999) and *Black Women in America*, 3 vols. (1994); Sara Evans, *Born for Liberty: A History of Women in America* (1997); Anne M. Derousie and Susan Ferentinos, *Exploring a Common Past: Researching and Interpreting Women's History for Historic Sites* (2003); Vicki L. Ruiz, *From Out of the Shadows: Mexican Women in Twen-*

tieth-Century America (1999); Daphne Spain, *Gendered Spaces* (1992); Barbara Abramhof Levy, Sandra Mackenzie Lloyd, and Susan Porter Schreiber, *Great Tours!: Thematic Tours and Guide Training for Historic Sites* (2002); Polly Welts Kaufman and Katherine T. Corbett, *Her Past Around Us: Interpreting Sites for Women's History* (2003); Vicki L. Ruiz and Virginia Sanchez Korrol, *Latina Legacies: Identity, Biography and Community* (2005); Susan Ware and Stacy Braukman, eds., *Notable American Women: A Biographical Dictionary*, 5 vols. (2005); Page Putnam Miller, *Reclaiming the Past: Landmarks of Women's History* (1992); Gail Lee Dubrow and Jennifer B. Goodman, eds., *Restoring Women's History Through Historic Preservation* (2002); Heather A. Huyck and Peg Strobel, eds., *Revealing Women's History: Best Practices at Historic Sites* (2011); Ellen Carol DuBois and Lynn Dumenil, *Through Women's Eyes: An American History* (2008); Vicki L. Ruiz, ed., *Unequal Sisters: An Inclusive Reader in US Women's History*, 4th ed. (2007); Barbara Handy-Marchello, *Women of the Northern Plains: Gender & Settlement on the Homestead Frontier, 1870–1930* (2005); Virginia K. Bartlett, *Keeping House: Women's Lives in Western Pennsylvania, 1790–1850* (1994); Shirley Hune and Gail M. Nomura, *Asian/Pacific Islander American Women: A Historical Anthology* (2003); Susan Ferentinos, *Interpreting LGBT History at Museums and Historic Sites* (2014); Linda K. Kerber, Jane Sherron De Hart, and Cornelia H. Dayton, *Women's America: Refocusing the Past*, 7th ed. (2010); Heather A. Huyck, ed., *Women's History: Sites and Resources,*

2nd ed. (2010); Elizabeth Jameson Susan Armitage, eds., *Writing the Range: Race, Class, and Culture in the Women's West* (1997).

HEATHER HUYCK
NATIONAL COLLABORATIVE FOR
WOMEN'S HISTORY SITES

See clans; family history; house museums; household; new social history; United States, local history in.

Worldconnect Project. See RootsWeb.

WPA Historical Records Survey. The Historical Records Survey was a project of the Works Progress Administration (WPA) begun by President Franklin D. Roosevelt as one his New Deal programs. Beginning in 1935, the purpose of the project was to survey and index historically significant records in archives, libraries, historical societies, and town halls across the country. The result was the creation of bibliographies, inventories, indexes, and other records that continue to benefit historians and genealogists today. For a detailed inventory of records generated by the WPA Historical Records Survey, see Bryan L. Mulcahy, *Works Progress Administration (WPA) Historical Records Survey* (2011) at: http://www.rootsweb.ancestry.com/~flmgs/articles/Works_Projects_Ad ministrationMarch2011_BM.pdf.

writ. A writ is an order from a court that either requires an act be carried out or gives the authority to someone to have the thing done. There are many kinds of writs.

Wyoming, local history in. The original Wyoming State Historical Society was founded by legislative action in 1895, but not as a membership organization. In essence, it was the state agency charged with maintaining the state collections and promoting interest in the history of the five-year-old state. The first director of the new agency was Robert Morris, the son of Esther Hobart Morris, pioneer woman justice of the peace.

In 1919 the legislature established a state historical board, composed of the governor, the secretary of state, and the state librarian. The board hired the state historian and the collections, previously held in the state library, were transferred to the custody of the state historian. Collections were displayed in various locations, including the top floor of the state capitol. No provision was made for a membership society until two years later when the legislature charged the state historian with forming a "society."

Volunteers, many affiliated with the society, marked pioneer trails and sites with various monuments beginning in the 1890s. Dr. Grace Raymond Hebard, a University of Wyoming professor, was instrumental in organizing many of these marking efforts, in conjunction with the Daughters of the American Revolution and the Wyoming Pioneer Association, which formed in the early 1900s. In 1927, the state established the Historical Landmarks Commission that oversaw such activities and also purchased historic properties for preservation. Fort Bridger, a state historic site, was purchased in 1929; Fort Laramie, a

This "Dinosaur Graveyard" historical marker is located along U.S. Highway 30 near Medicine Bow, Wyoming. CREDIT: PHIL ROBERTS.

national historic site, in 1937. The state acquired South Pass City State Historic Site in 1965 and several other sites followed, including Trail End State Historic Site in Sheridan in the early 1980s and the Wyoming Pioneer Museum on the grounds of the State Fair Grounds in Douglas, originally established by the Pioneer Association.

The first course in state history was taught at the University of Wyoming by Dr. Hebard in 1909 and has been part of the curriculum at most of the state's seven community colleges since they were established after World War II. Hebard was instrumental in the legislative act passed in 1927 requiring the teaching of the state constitution. The state has not mandated instruction in state history, but the history of Wyoming is commonly taught to students in fourth grade and in eighth grade.

The state historian post was abolished during the Great Depression and the duties were reassigned to the state librarian. Various county and local historical societies continued to meet and provide historical advice and direction to their local communities. In 1951, the legislature created the Wyoming State Archives and Historical Department. It assumed the duties of archiving public records, preserving historical collections and promoting historical interest. The historical division became the home of *Annals of Wyoming* (published twice annually) and Lola Homsher, the director of the newly formed Wyoming State Archives and Historical Department, became its editor.

Consistent with the legislative charge, Homsher helped organize the present Wyoming State Historical Society. The membership paid state and local dues, a portion of which went to pay for production and distribution of *Annals of Wyoming* and the newsletter known as *Wyoming History News*, both fulfilling the state agency's statutory charge of promoting and fostering Wyoming history.

The format of *Annals*, since its beginning in 1923, was a lightly illustrated six-by-nine-inch perfect-bound book. It changed to its present magazine-style in 1979. *Annals* remains a journal dedicated to furthering historical interest and scholarship, the only scholarly historical journal published in Wyoming. About the same time, *History News* moved from a bimonthly newsletter to publication ten times annually.

Because of state government reorganization during the administration of Gov. Mike Sullivan, the State Archives, Museums and Historical Department was abolished and the existing duties and personnel became part of the Wyoming Department of Commerce. The new department was a patchwork of state agencies ranging from the Wyoming Recreation Commission (home of the State Historic Preservation Office [SHPO] since the SHPO was federally created in 1966) to the Board of Architects, the Department of Economic Planning and Development, and the Board of Barber Examiners.

Before reorganization, Dr. David Kathka headed the State Archives, Museums and Historical Department and remained director after the merger. Following the appointment of Celeste Colgan to the post, the state cut off support to the society. The organization, for the first time, became wholly independent.

The state turned over publication of *Annals of Wyoming* and *Wyoming History News*, the society's newsletter, to the State Historical Society. Meanwhile, the state retained the state archives, historical collections, state museum, and historical sites.

In Laramie, the American Heritage Center (AHC) at the University of Wyoming, established in the 1920s, has become one of the largest university archives in the United States. The editorial office of *Annals of Wyoming* is now housed at the AHC in Laramie. *Annals* has been produced and edited by volunteer historians at the University of Wyoming since the society became independent in 1995.

In 2002, the society and the state once again began cooperative programs, but the society continues to be independent of state control with a paid executive secretary and a board elected from four regions of the state. Nineteen of the twenty-three counties have chapters of the state society with two others operating independent organizations. The society sponsors a summer trek along with annual meetings. It has been primary sponsor for Wyoming History Day since the program's inception in the early 1980s.

The society sponsored creation of a website, WyoHistory.org, in 2010. Project director Tom Rea was a founder of the site that went online for the first time in May 2011 and remains (2016) its director.

PHIL ROBERTS
UNIVERSITY OF WYOMING

See United States, local history in.

Y

Yankee. The origin of this word is murky. In 1683, according to the *Oxford English Dictionary*, *Yankee* was in use in England as a surname, possibly of Dutch origin. British soldiers in the New World colonies used it as a term of contempt, and thereafter it came to mean a New Englander. After the Battle of Lexington, New Englanders began to use the word themselves, even making up a mythical band of Indians, the Yankos (meaning "invincibles"), from which they claimed the word came. The word was often used by Southerners about those north of the Mason-Dixon Line, often with negative overtones. *Yankee* was often preceded by epithets, especially "damned." In addition, during the two world wars the term *Yanks* was used by Europeans to describe all Americans. For a more detailed discussion of the word, see *Yankee* in Stephen Thernstrom, ed., *Harvard Encyclopedia of American Ethnic Groups* (1980).

youth culture. The concept of a youth culture has undergone interesting transformations during the past century. Although the concept has existed almost continuously throughout the twentieth century, it has meant different things at different times, and even meant different things to diverse people at the same time. Early in the century, for example, a journal such as *Youth's Companion* was respectable and nationalistic, but simultaneously so-called Muckrakers caused concern about "street arabs," children who appeared to be homeless, antisocial, and a threat to decent communities.

During the 1920s the phrase "youth culture" invoked young people of college age and slightly older, partying extravagantly in raccoon coats and swallowing goldfish. A decade later, when swing bands enjoyed immense popularity, youth culture usually referred to intensely active dancers, jitterbugging wildly to boisterous music and perhaps, because of body contact, stimulating lascivious behavior. By the early 1940s, "crooners" like Frank Sinatra created hysterical adoration from young fans, mainly female, and set a pattern that persisted through the eras of Elvis Presley, rock and roll, and the Beatles.

The most important phase in the history of youth culture, however, occurred after World War II, and especially during the early and mid-1950s when a variety of authorities decided that comic books, films, and television were inciting juvenile delinquency, primarily in the form of violence and premature sexuality. Senator Estes Kefauver held televised hearings that caused a national stir as one expert after another testified that a "generation gap" existed and that young people felt misunderstood and responded with rebellion, aimed at society in general but family in particular. It was common to hear that family values were in jeopardy.

Less familiar but more important because it was more enduring, advertising began to target young people as a separate market that had disposable income and needed to be attracted with different kinds of ads than the ones that appealed to adults. Eugene Gilbert was the immensely influential pioneer who became a pied piper of marketing techniques for a distinct youth culture. His syndicated columns, books, journal articles, and speeches paved the way for a permanent revolution in the promotion of goods directed to teenagers and eventually even preteens. By the end of the 1950s, for example, blue jeans had become the universal mode of dress for young people—and eventually for those not so young. But while disputes raged over wearing jeans to school (1950s and 1960s), jeans became a prime symbol of the newly entrenched youth culture.

During the later 1960s and 1970s, the concept of youth culture became intensely politicized because of bitter opposition to the war in Vietnam, because of young people experimenting with drugs and openly acknowledged sexual activity, burning draft cards, and rejecting the lifestyle and values of people over the age of thirty. Free speech and the desire for a less authoritarian, more democratic society also moved many young people to activism—much of it constructive, some of it destructive and even self-destructive.

By the 1980s many of those "young people" had reentered the mainstream of American society, but a recurrence persisted of concern about the impact of television and film upon the antisocial behavior of youth. In addition, a diminution of job opportunities during the 1980s and early 1990s caused a sense of despair among many young people—a feeling that they would not have the same opportunities in life that their parents had enjoyed.

See James Gilbert, *A Cycle of Outrage: America's Reaction to the Juvenile Delinquent in the 1950s* (1986); Paula Fass, *The Damned and the Beautiful: American Youth in the 1920's* (1977); Joseph F. Kett, *Rites of Passage: Adolescence in America, 1790 to the Present* (1977); and Joan Jacobs Brumberg, *The Body Project: An Intimate History of American Girls* (1997).

MICHAEL KAMMEN
AMERICAN HISTORIAN (1936–2013)

Yukon Territory, local history in. The Yukon Territory is home to two main cultural groupings each with a distinctive expression of local history. Indigenous peoples maintain a land-based oral tradition speaking to their origin and their relationships with the human and nonhuman inhabitants in this land. In contrast, a Western pioneering story, expressed in documentary as well as oral sources, describes discovery, settlement, and the building of communities. In the mid-twentieth century both traditions of local history were disrupted and sometimes overwhelmed by a national narrative that ignored the indigenous tradition and subsumed the pioneer chronicle into a modernist tale of northern resource development and national economic progress. More recently, Yukon people have expressed their diverse local histories in new and evolving contexts. Especially important has been the acknowledgment of the plural character of the territory's history and the associated respect for the different futures advanced by these various narratives of belonging.

The oral traditions, the literature of Yukon indigenous peoples, include the exploits of the trickster Raven; the story cycle of the Traveler, a mythic hero who traveled downriver establishing the finely balanced order of the world; and many more narratives describing the compact between the human, natural, and spiritual worlds. These stories, attached to the physical features of the cultural landscape as though it were a history book, create a sense of both personal and community identities and document their origins belief that "we have always been here." The annual round of hunting and gathering through this land of storied locales frames a moral order binding communities together, evokes a set of ethics describing responsible approaches to the resources of their homeland, provides information on the effective use of those resources, and highlights their interest in and rights on these lands. *My Stories are My Wealth* (1977) limns this indigenous local history tradition.

The Western pioneer approach to local history is exemplified by Discovery Day, the founding day of the newcomer society. First celebrated in 1911, it emphasized the individual prospector/miner discovering and opening up the territory. The associated parade, celebrating community building and the establishment of a self-governing part of Canada, continues in Dawson City today. The Yukon Order of Pioneers, a mutual aid group of men predating the Klondike gold rush (1896–1898), was recognized as a prime carrier of this

non-aboriginal history. In addition to promoting the celebration of Discovery Day, the members produced booklets such as Jack McQuesten's *Recollections* (1952) describing the early history of the region. The Imperial Order Daughters of the Empire likewise celebrated British-Canadian traditions with Dominion Day tea parties and promoted the writing of local history in schools. From the gold rush onward a continuous trickle of reminiscences has appeared. Margaret Shand's *The Summit and Beyond* (1959) stands out among these because of her thirty-year stay in the territory.

Through the first half of the twentieth century the people of these two cultures generally lived their separate realities, with a mutual acceptance of the other. Increasingly family interconnections and shared economic interests engendered more intertwined, local, usually oral narratives, some recorded in local newspapers, photos, and other documentary sources such as Chief Isaac's reports in the *Dawson Daily News*. These narratives focused on skill and survival in the Yukon landscape, with the prowess of First Nations hunters, trappers, river pilots, and woodcutters paralleling and sometimes attached to stories of non-aboriginal mail carriers, Mounted Police, missionaries, and miners.

From the late 1940s the Canadian government with its modernist colonial northern agenda increasingly limited indigenous access to and use of their land, instead promoting industrial development that overwhelmed the existing non-aboriginal settlements. Both the indigenous oral tradition and the local non-aboriginal pioneer stories were denied in the telling and documenting of a new northern history. The metropolitan thesis in its Yukon version, Harold Innis's *Settlement and the Mining Frontier* (1936) reinterpreted the gold rush within a national narrative of economic expansion focused on the major urban centers of the St. Lawrence Valley. With the expansion of government, military, and business interests after the Second World War, Canada's interests in the North overtook Yukon peoples' capacity and power to express local history themes. The national commemoration of the Klondike gold rush, beginning in the mid-1950s, had more to do with celebrating contemporary northern resource exploitation and national economic development than the local stories of settlement, community, hunting, and belonging. Most of the published history in this period, now by nonresident experts, was about "Canada's North."

Countering, and more recently shaping, these "outside" stories are a growing number of indigenous cultural centers, festivals, and community history societies, museums, regional government agencies and, latterly, ethnic cultural communities, all fostering local Yukon history. Early examples of this resurgence are the Skookum Jim Friendship Society (1960), which documented traditional indigenous practices, and the McBride Museum (1952) in Whitehorse. Subsequent works grounding these local stories include *A History of the Settlement of Teslin* (1972), *Edge of the River, Heart of the City* (1994), and *Hammerstones: History of the Tr'ondëk Hwëch'in* (2003). Nonprofit and government bodies established in the 1970s, primarily the Yukon Historical and Museums Association, the Association franco-yukonnaise, the Yukon Archives, and the Yukon's Cultural Services Branch, all work to celebrate the diverse narratives of contemporary Yukon society. The Yukon's archaeology publication series is a model for accessible statements of local history (http://www.tc.gov.yk.ca/yukon_community_booklets.html). The forerunners of today's First Nation governments in the Yukon expressed their modern history in *Together Today for Our Children Tomorrow* (1973), which was the basis for their treaty with Canada (1993). New threads are being added to the complex multicultural fabric of Yukon history as local immigrant groups prepare their stories of being Yukoners. Finally, the rise of community-based research, as practiced by anthropologist Julie Cruikshank and demonstrated in the Mayo Historical Society's *Gold and Galena* (1990), has allowed local history to "push back" into national narratives. Over the past century the products of local history in a broad range of mediums have evolved from mutually exclusive stories into a richly textured pluralistic set of interwoven narratives of belonging.

DAVID NEUFELD
PARKS CANADA
LINDA JOHNSON
ADÄKA CULTURAL SOCIETY,
WHITEHORSE

See Canada, local history in.

Z

Zouaves. A special unit of the French army, made up of Algerian soldiers, was known as Zouaves. The regiment wore a brilliantly colored uniform with baggy trousers, gaiters, a short open jacket, and a turban or fez. They were popularized in the United States by Elmer Ellsworth (1837–1861) who, before the Civil War, organized the Chicago Zouaves into a spectacular drill team that he toured about the country giving exhibitions. At the outbreak of war, Ellsworth raised a company called the Fire Zouaves (the 11th New York Volunteer Infantry). In Alexandria, Virginia, while removing a Confederate flag from the roof of a tavern, Ellsworth was killed by the inn's proprietor. The tavern owner, in turn, was shot by a member of the regiment. The incident received a great deal of publicity, and the Zouaves became widely known and admired.

APPENDIX A

Ethnic Groups

For research concerning ethnic groups, we suggest consulting any of the recent guides to ethnicity. Two very useful titles are *American Immigrant Cultures: Builders of a Nation*, ed. David Levinson and Melvin Ember (1997); *Encyclopedia of Race, Ethnicity, and Society*, ed. Richard T. Schaefer (2008); *Gale Encyclopedia of Multicultural America*, cont. ed. Robert von Dassanowsky; ed. Jeffrey Lehman (1999); *Encyclopedia of Immigration and Migration in the American West*, ed. Gordon Morris Bakken and Alexandra Kindell (c. 2006); *Encyclopedia of American Immigration*, ed. James Ciment (2001); and the *Harvard Encyclopedia of American Ethnic Groups*, ed. Stephan Thernstrom (1980). These books include detailed essays on most ethnic and many religious groups with ethnic backgrounds. Articles relate history, origins, periods of greatest emigration, social composition, settlement patterns, occupations, churches and schools, organizations, politics and culture, folk customs, ties with the homeland, and assimilation patterns. There are useful bibliographies. These books also contain exceedingly informative essays that deal with questions of American identity, *folklore, intermarriage, labor, prejudice, and religion.

What appears below, by ethnic group, is the most recent scholarship. Not every national group is included—only those with a substantial representation in the 2000 census. Periodical literature, for the most part, is also not included. The recent literature will lead to that which is older and the encyclopedias, noted above, will give a fuller list. The Internet is another source of information, full in some cases, spotty in others. The major study centers concerning immigration and ethnicity should be consulted; each has a presence on the web. See also the entry above for *Immigration History Research Center.

African immigrants. The Balch Institute for Ethnic Studies merged with the Historical Society of Pennsylvania, but its materials are still available: https://hsp.org/collections/catalogs-research-tools/subject-guides/african-american-collections. The African American Museum of Philadelphia also has collections useful for the researcher, www.aampmuseum.org. For the immigration of Africans to the United States, see Marilyn Halter, *Between Race and Ethnicity: Cape Verdean American Immigrants, 1860–1965* (1993), especially the useful bibliography. Also see J. Rollings, ed., *Hidden Minorities* (1981); Carole Boyce Davies, ed., *Encyclopedia of the African Diaspora: Origins, Experiences, and Culture* (2008); Emmanuel Yewah and 'Dimeji Togunde, eds., *Across the Atlantic: African Immigrants in the United States Diaspora* (2010). Isidore Okpewho and Nkiru Nzegwu, ed., *The New African Diaspora* (2009); Yoku Shaw-Taylor and Steven A. Tuch, eds. *The Other African Americans: Contemporary African and Caribbean Immigrants in the United States* (2007); Kwado, Konadu-Agyemang, Baffour K. Takyi, and John Arthur, eds., *The New African Diaspora in North America: Trends, Community Building, and Adaptation* (2006); John A. Arthur, *Invisible Sojourners: African Immigrant Diaspora in the United States* (2000).

Albanians. The major archive for Albanian Americans is the Fan S. Noli Library established in 1973 at St. George Albanian Orthodox Cathedral, 523 East Broadway, South Boston, MA 02127; (617) 482-2002. See *The Albanian Struggle in the Old World and New* (1939), a WPA project, and Constantine A. Demo, *The Albanians in America: The First Arrivals* (1960).

Arabs. The Arab American Ethnic Studies Foundation was founded in 1972. It is located at 4367 Beverly Blvd., Los Angeles, CA 90004; (213) 666-1212. The Arab American National Museum features a history of the immigrant experience, www.arabamericanmuseum.org. Arab Americans appear in the archives of the *Immigration History Research Center at the University of Minnesota, cla.umn.edu/ihrc. See Mohammed Sawaie, *Arabic-Speaking Immigrants in the United States and Canada: A Bibliographical Guide* (1985); Alixa Naff, *Becoming American: The Early Arab Immigrant Experience* (1993); Angela Brittingham and Patricia de la Cruz, *We the People of Arab Ancestry in the United States* (2005), http://www.census.gov/prod/2005pubs/censr-21.pdf; Gregory Orfalea, *The Arab Americans: A History* (2006).

Armenians. The Armenian Library and Museum of America is located at 380 Concord Ave., Belmont, MA 02478-3032; (617) 489-2284; www.almainc.org. See Robert Mirak, *Torn Between Two Lands: Armenians in America, 1890 to World War I* (1983); Michael J. Arlen, *Passage to Ararat* (1975); Aram Serkis Yeretzian, *A History of Armenian Immigration to America with Special Reference to Conditions in Los Angeles* (1974); and M. Vartan Malcom's *Armenians in America* ([1919] 1969).

Austrians. See Franz A. J. Szabo, *Austrian Immigration to Canada* (1996); E.

Appendix A

Wilder Spaulding, *The Quiet Invaders: The Story of the Austrian Impact upon America* (1968); and Wilhelm Schlag, "A Survey of Austrian Emigration to the United States," in *Ostreich und die angelsächsische Welt*, ed. Otto von Hietsch, 2 vols. (1961); John M. Spalek and Sandra H. Hawrylchak, *Guide to the Archival Materials of the German-speaking Emigration to the United States after 1933* (1997); Frederick C. Engelmann, Manfred Prokop, and Franz A. J. Szabo, *A History of the Austrian Migration to Canada* (1996).

Basques. There is a Basque Studies Program at the University of Nevada in Reno, with some additional Basque materials at the University of Idaho in Moscow; at the Newberry Library; and at the New York Public Library. The Basque Memorial Museum is located at 301 S. Ave Q, Bosque, TX 76634; (817) 675-3845; www.basquemuseum.com. There was a Basque-language newspaper, published in Los Angeles in 1885, another that lasted from 1893 to 1898, and none until 1974 when *Voice of the Basques* was issued in English from Boise, Idaho. See Grant Edwin McCall, *Basque-Americans and a Sequential Theory of Migration and Adaptation* (1973); Flavia M. McCullough, *The Basques in the Northwest* (1974); and the writings of Robert Laxalt, including "Lonely Sentinels of the American West: Basque Sheepherders," *National Geographic Magazine* 129 (1966): 870–88; Gloria P. Totoricaguena, *Basque Diaspora: Migration and Transnational Identity* (2005); Nancy Zubiri, *A Travel Guide to Basque America: Families, Feasts, and Festivals* (2006).

Belgians. There is a Belgian American Resource Collection at the Cofren Library, University of Wisconsin at Green Bay, uwdc.library.wisc.edu/collections/wi/belgamrcol. See Luc Sante, *The Factory of Facts* (1998); Henry Verslype, *The Belgians of Indiana* (1987); Henry Lucas, *Netherlanders in America* (1955); and Henry G. Bayer, *The Belgians: First Settlers in New York* (1925). Also, Joseph A. Amato, *Servants of the Land: God, Family, and Farm: The Trinity of Belgian Economic Folkways in Southern Minnesota* (1990) and Bernard A. Cook, *Belgians in Michigan* (2007).

Bosnian Muslims. There is a Slavic American Collection at the Louisa H. Bowen University Archives and Special Collections, Lovejoy Library, Southern Illinois University at Edwardsville, Edwardsville, IL, 62026-1063; (618) 650-2665; fax (618) 650-2717; www.siue.edu/~skerber/Historical_Materials2.html. See George J. Prpic, *The Croatian Immigrants in America* (1971); Gerald G. Govorchin, *Americans from Yugoslavia* (1961); and Senad Agic, *Immigration & Assimilation: the Bosnian Muslim experience in Chicago* (2004).

Bulgarians. There is a Slavic American Collection at the Louisa H. Bowen University Archives and Special Collections, Lovejoy Library, Southern Illinois University at Edwardsville, Edwardsville, IL, 62026-1063; (618) 650-2665; fax (618) 650-2717; www.siue.edu/~skerber/Historical_Materials2.html. See Nikolay Altankov, *The Bulgarian Americans* (1979).

Caribbeans. See Miguel Gonzalez-Pando, *The Cuban Americans* (1998); Catherine A. Sunchine and Keith Q. Warner, *Caribbean Connections: Moving North* (1998); Roy Bryce-Laporte and Delores Mortimer, *Caribbean Immigration to the United States* (1976); Richard S. Dunn, *Sugar and Slaves* (1972); Gilbert S. Osofsky, *Harlem: The Making of a Ghetto* (1971); and Constance R. Sutton and Elsa Chaney, *Caribbean Life in New York City* (1987).

Central and South Americans. See A. J. Jaffee et al., *Spanish Americans in the United States: Changing Demographic Characteristics* (1976). For a local study, see Carlos U. Lopez, *Chilenos in California: A Study of the 1850, 1852, and 1860 Censuses* (1973). Also, Juan González, *Harvest of Empire: a history of Latinos in America* (2000); Lee V. Douglas, comp., *Hispanic Local History and Genealogy in the United States: selected titles at the Library of Congress* (2002).

Chinese. The Chinese Historical Society of America is located at 650 Commercial Street, San Francisco, CA 94133; (415) 391-1188; www.chsa.org. The Southern California Chinese Historical Society is located at 969 N. Broadway, Los Angeles, CA 90012; (213) 621-3171. There is a Museum of Chinese in America at 215 Centre Street, New York, NY 10013; (212) 619-4785; mocanyc.org. See also the Hawai'i Chinese History Center at 111 N. King St., Suite 410, Honolulu, HI 96817; (808) 521-5948. See Arthur Bonner, *Alas! What Brought Thee Hither: The Chinese in New York, 1800–1950* (1997) and Shih-Shan Henry Tsai, *China and the Overseas Chinese in the United States, 1868–1911* (1983).

Cubans. Cuban Studies is published by the Center for Latin American Studies at the University of Pittsburgh. University of Miami's Cuban Heritage Collection includes digital materials and archival material; library.miami.edu/chc. See Felix Roberto Masud-Pilato, *From Welcomed Exiles to Illegal Immigrants: Cuban Migration to the United States, 1959–1995* (1996); Maria Cristina Garcia, *Havana USA: Cuban Exiles and Cuban Americans in South Florida* (1996); Eleanor Meyer Rogg, *The Assimilation of Cuban Exiles: The Role of Community and Class* (1974); Richard R. Fagen, Richard A. Brody, and Thomas J. O'Leary, *Cubans in Exile: Disaffection and the Revolution* (1968); Alex Antón and Roger E. Hernández, *Cubans in America: A Vibrant History of a People in Exile* (2002); and Miguel A. Bretos, *Cuba & Florida: Exploration of an Historic Connection, 1539–1991* (1991).

Czechs and Slovaks. Materials can be consulted at the Archives of Czechs and Slovaks Abroad at the University of Chicago, 1100 E. 57th St., Chicago, IL 60637; (312) 753-2856; www.lib. uchicago.edu/e/su/slavic/acasa.html. Also consult the *Immigration History Research Center. See also the Czech Heritage Collection at the University of Nebraska, in Lincoln; libraries.unl.edu/ czech-american-collections. There is a Czechoslovak Heritage Museum and Library at 2701 South Harlem Ave., Berwyn, IL 60402; (312) 795-5800. The Czechoslovak Genealogical Society

International can be contacted at (CGSI) P.O. Box 16225, St. Paul, MN 55116-0225; (612) 595-7799; www.cgsi.org. For Slovaks, see the collection of materials at the Jankola Library & Slovak Museum in Danville, PA; jankolalibrary.sscm.org and the *Immigration History Research Center of the University of Minnesota; cla.umn.edu/ihrc. See Esther Jerabek, Czechs and Slovaks in North America (1977); Vera Laska's chronology, The Czechs in America, 1633–1977: A Chronology & Fact Book (1977); Emily Greene Balch, Our Slovic Fellow-Citizens ([1910] 1969); and R. W. Seton-Watson, A History of the Czechs and Slovaks ([1943] 1965). Also, Jan Habenicht, History of Czechs in America (1996); Miloslav Rechcígl, Czechs and Slovaks in America (2005); Konstantin Culen, History of Slovaks in America (2007); Ján Pankuch, History of the Slovaks of Cleveland and Lakewood (2001); and Robert Zecker, Streetcar Parishes: Slovak Immigrants Build Their Nonlocal Communities, 1890–1945 (2010).

Danes. The Danish American Heritage Society, organized in 1977 is located at 29672 Dane Lane, Junction City, OR 97448; (503) 998-6725; www.danish-heritage.org. See Henning Bender and Birgit Flemming Larsen, eds., Danish Emigration to the U.S.A. (1992), and Danish Emigration to Canada (1991); Peter L. Petersen, The Danes in America (1987); Frederick Hale, Danes in North America (1984); Kristian Hvidt, Danes Go West: A Book about the Emigration to America (1976), and Flight to America: The Social Background of 300,000 Danish Emigrants (1975); and John H.

Bille, A History of the Danes in America (1971). Also, Frederick Hale, Danes in Wisconsin (2005); and Gerald Rasmussen and Otto N. Larsen, Oregon Danish Colony: Ethnic Assimilation in Junction City, 1902–1952 (1998).

Dutch. The Association for the Advancement of Dutch American Studies, www.aadas.nl, founded in 1979, is at 3207 Burton SE, Grand Rapids, MI 49506; (616) 957-6310; the Holland Society of New York Library, www.hollandsociety.com, is located at 122 E. 58th St., New York, NY 10022; (212) 758-1675. There is a Netherlands Museum, www.hollandmuseum.org, at 8 E. 12th St., Holland, MI 49423; (616) 392-3129. See Henry S. Lucas, Dutch Immigrant Memoirs and Related Writings (1997); Rob Kroes and Henk-Otto Neuschafer, The Dutch in North-America: Their Immigration and Cultural Continuity (1991); Gerald F. De Jong, The Dutch in America, 1609–1974 (1975); and Henry S. Lucas, Netherlanders in America: Dutch Immigration to the United States and Canada, 1789–1950 (1955). Also, Robert P. Swierenga, Faith and Family: Dutch Immigration and Settlement in the United States, 1820–1920 (2000); Joyce D. Goodfriend, Benjamin Schmidt, and Annette Stott, Going Dutch: the Dutch Presence in America, 1609–2009 (2008); and Hans Krabbendam, Freedom on the Horizon: Dutch Immigration to America, 1840–1940 (2009).

East Asians. See Katy Gardner, Global Migrants/Local Lives: Travel and Transformation in Rural Bangladesh (1995); Johanna Lessinger, From the Ganges to the Hudson: Indian Immigrants in New

York City (1995); Niaz Zaman and Kamal Uddin Ahmed, *Migration, Migrants and the United States* (1992); Hugh Tinker, *The Banyan Tree: Overseas Emigrants from India, Pakistan and Bangladesh* (1977); Norris Hundley, ed., *The Asian Americans* (1976); Leona B. Bagai, *The East Indians and the Pakistanis in America* (1972); and Arthur Wesley Helweg, *Strangers in a Not-So-Strange Land: Indian American Immigrants in the Global Age* (2004). See also *Division of Hearts*, a video recording by Satti Khanna and Peter Chappell (1987).

English. See Charlotte J. Erickson, *Invisible Immigrants* (1972); Stanley C. Johnson, *A History of Emigration from the United Kingdom to North America, 1762–1912* (1966); Wilbur S. Shepperson, *British Emigration to North America* (1957); and Bernard Bailyn, *Voyagers to the West: A Passage in the Peopling of America on the Eve of the Revolution* (1986). See also Allen G. Noble, ed., *To Build a New Land: Ethnic Landscapes in North America* (1992); William Dollarhide, *British Origins of American Colonists, 1629–1775* (1997); David A. Gerber, *Authors of Their Lives: The Personal Correspondence of British Immigrants to North America in the Nineteenth Century* (2006); William E. Van Vugt, *British Buckeyes: the English, Scots, and Welsh in Ohio, 1700–1900* (2006); and Faren Rhea Siminoff, *Crossing the Sound: The Rise of Atlantic American Communities in Seventeenth-Century Eastern Long Island* (2004).

Estonians. There is Estonian material at the *Immigration History Research Center at the University of Minnesota, a collection of materials at Estonian House (Eesti Maja), cla.umn.edu/ihrc, at 243 East 34th Street, New York, NY 10016; (212) 684-0336; and at Kent State University in Ohio. See Jaan Pennar, *The Estonians in America, 1627–1975: A Chronology and Fact Book* (1975); Eevi Truumees and Emmi Bajars, *Estonian Americans, Seabrook, New Jersey* (1999); and Helmuth Kalmann and Thomas Palm, *The West Coast Estonian Days, 1953–1999: A Pictorial Overview: The Origins and Evolution of the Festival Over the Last 46 Years, with Data on the Events, Participation and Leadership* (2000).

Filipinos. See Joyce Yukawa, *Migration from the Philippines, 1975–1995: An Annotated Bibliography* (1996); Frank H. Winter, *The Filipinos in America* (1988); Jonathan Okamura, *Imagining the Filipino American Diaspora: Transnational Relations, Identities and Communities* (1998); Maria Root, ed., *Filipino Americans: Transformation and Identity* (1997); E. San Juan Jr., *From Exile to Diaspora: Versions of the Filipino Experience in the United States* (1998); and Rick Baldoz, *The Third Asiatic Invasion: Empire and Migration in Filipino America, 1898–1946* (2011).

Finns. The Finnish American Historical Archive, created in 1932, houses the largest collection of Finnish–North American materials in the world. It is located at the Finnish American Historical Archive at Finlandia University, 435 Quincy Street, Hancock, MI 49930; www.finlandia.edu/faham.html. A second collection of materials about

Appendix A

Finns in America is located at the *Immigration History Research Center of the University of Minnesota, cla.umn. edu/ihrc. See Philip J. Anderson, Dag Blanck, and Peter Kivisto, eds., *Scandinavian Immigrants and Education in North America* (1995); Reino Kero, *The Finns in North America: Destinations and Composition of Immigrant Societies in North America before World War I* (1980); John I. Kolehmainen's *Finns in America: A Bibliographical Guide to Their History* (1947) is the standard guide to source material; see A. William Hoglund's *Finnish Immigrants in America, 1880–1920* (1979). Also see Armas Kustaa Ensio Holmio, *History of the Finns in Michigan* (2001); Gary Kaunonen, *Finns in Michigan* (2009); Art Jura, *Fenni: the Finns among Us: A History of the Finns in New England and Beyond* (2001), and his *Fenni-2: More Finns among Us: A History of the Finns in America* (2005).

French. See Jean-Louis Houde, *French Migration to North America, 1600–1900* (1994); Hubert Charbonneau, *The First French Canadians: Pioneers in the St. Lawrence Valley* (1993); James S. Pula, *The French in America, 1488–1974: A Chronology and Factbook* (1975). See also Mason Wade, *The French Canadians, 1760–1976* (1968); Robert Rumilly, *Histoire des Franco Américans* (1972); Jay Gitlin, *The Bourgeois Frontier: French Towns, French Traders, and American Expansion* (2010); Carl J. Ekberg, *French Roots in the Illinois Country: The Mississippi Frontier in Colonial Times* (1998); and Jacqueline Lindenfeld, *The French in the United States: An Ethnographic Study* (2000).

Germans. The major archive is held by the German Society of Pennsylvania located at 611 Spring Garden St., Philadelphia, PA 19123; (215) 627-4365; fax (215) 627-5297; www.germansociety. org. There is material also at the Max Kade German-American Research Institute, www.maxkade.la.psu.edu/links. html. See Andreas Lehmann, *Go West! Ostdeutsche in Amerika* (1998); Dirk Hoerder and Jöeg Nagler, eds., *People in Transit: German Migrations in Comparative Perspective, 1820–1930* (1995); Timothy Walch, *Immigrant America: European Ethnicity in the United States* (1994); Eberhard Reichmann, La Vern J. Rippley, and Jörg Nagler, eds., *Emigration and Settlement Patterns of German Communities in North America* (1995); Heinz Kloss, *Atlas of German-American Settlements* (1974); and Tomas Jaehn, *Germans in the Southwest, 1850–1920* (2005).

Greeks. There is an archive devoted to Greeks in this country at the University of Utah, www.lib.utah.edu/collections/special-collections/index.php. There are also materials about Greek immigration at the New York Public Library and in various university collections around the country; see pahh.com (Preservation of American Hellenic History) for a fuller list. See Thomas Burgess, *Greeks in America* (1970); Michael N. Cutsumbis, *A Bibliographic Guide to Materials on Greeks in the United States, 1890–1960* (1970); and Theodore Saloutos, *Greeks in the United States* (1964). Also, Stavros Frangos, *Greeks in Michigan* (2004); Marios Christou Stephanides, *The History of the Greeks in Kentucky, 1900–1950* (2001); Paul

Koken, Theodore N. Constant, and S. G. Canoutas, *A History of the Greeks in the Americas, 1453–1938* (1995).

Gypsies. There is a Gypsy Lore Society at the Victor Weybright Archives of Gypsy Studies, Cheverly, MD 20785; (301) 341-1261; www.gypsyloresociety.org. See Marlene Sway, *Familiar Strangers: Gypsy Life in America* (1988); Gabrielle Tyrnauer, *The Gypsy in Northwest America* (1977); and Rena C. Gropper, *Gypsies in the City: Culture, Patterns and Survival* (1975). Also, Angus Fraser, *The Gypsies* (1992); and William G. Lockwood and Sheila Salo, comps., *Gypsies and Travelers in North America: An Annotated Bibliography* (1994).

Haitians. See Michel S. Laguerre, *Ethnicity as Dependence: The Haitian Community in New York City* (1978); Roy Bryce-Laporte and Dolores Mortimer, eds., *Caribbean Immigration to the United States* (1976); and Jervis Anderson, "The Haitians of New York," *New Yorker* (1975); Flore Zephir, by Nathalie Dessens, *The Haitian Americans (2004); From Saint-Domingue to New Orleans: Migration and Influences* (2007); and Michel S. Laguerre, *American Odyssey: Haitians in New York City* (1984).

Hungarians. The *Immigration History Research Center of the University of Minnesota has a significant collection of material, cla.umn.edu/ihrc. In addition, there is the American Hungarian Foundation Library, 177 Somerset St., New Brunswick, NJ 08903; (201) 846-5777; libraries.rutgers.edu/

hungarian. See Joseph D. Dwyer, ed., *Hungarians in the United States and Canada: A Bibliography: Holdings of the Immigration Research Center* (1977); and Joseph Széplaki, ed., *The Hungarians in America, 1583–1974: A Chronology and Fact Book* (1975). Also, Julianna Puskás, *Ties That Bind, Ties That Divide: 100 Years of Hungarian Experience in the United States* (2000); Éva V. Huseby-Darvas, *Hungarians in Michigan* (2003); and Albert Tezla, *The Hazardous Quest: Hungarian immigrants in the United States, 1895–1920: A Documentary* (1993).

Indians, East. See East Asians.

Indochinese. There is a Vietnamese Immigration Collection, 1975–1976, at the State University of New York at Buffalo, libweb.lib.buffalo.edu/archives/collections/detail.asp?ID=508. See Darrel Moutero and Marsha I. Weber, *Vietnamese Americans: Patterns of Resettlement and Socioeconomic Adaptation in the United States* (1979); and Gail B. Kelly, *From Vietnam to America: A Chronicle of Vietnamese Immigration to the United States* (1977). Also, James M. Freeman, *Changing Identities: Vietnamese Americans, 1975–1995* (1995); and Michelle Houle, *The Vietnamese* (2006).

Irish. The American Irish Historical Society is located at 991 Fifth Avenue, New York, NY 10029; (212) 288-2263. It includes newspapers, records of Irish-American organizations, letters and documents of important Irish Americans, and a popular culture collection containing playbills, sheet music, flyers, photographs, programs, and other ephemera. Consult aihs.org/library. See Frank D'Arcy, *The Story of Irish Emigration* (1999); Arthur Gribben, ed., *The Great Famine and the Irish Diaspora in America* (1999); Edward Laxton, *The Famine Ships: The Irish Exodus to America* (1997); Noel Ignatiev, *How the Irish Became White* (1995); John Duffy Ibson, *Will the World Break Your Heart? Dimensions and Consequences of Irish American Assimilation* (1990); Carl Wittke, *The Irish in America* ([1956] 1970); and William V. Shannon, *The American Irish* (1966). Also, David T. Gleeson, *The Irish in the South, 1815–1877* (2001); Ronald H. Bayor and Timothy J. Meagher, *The New York Irish* (1996) and *The Columbia Guide to Irish American History* (2005); Charles Fanning, *New Perspectives on the Irish Diaspora* (2000); David M. Emmons, *Beyond the American Pale: the Irish in the West, 1845-1910* (2010); William Barnaby Faherty, *The St. Louis Irish: An Unmatched Celtic Community* (2001); and James Rogers and Matthew J. O'Brien, *After the Flood: Irish America, 1945–1960* (2009).

Italians. The Italian Historical Association is a commemorative society organized in 1949, located at 209 Flagg Ave., Staten Island, NY 10304. There is also information on Italians in America at the Center for Migration Studies, Staten Island, NY; archives.cmsny.org/tag/italian-americans; (718) 351-8800. In addition, there is the Urban History Collection at the University of Illinois at Chicago Circle; *Immigration History Research Center (IHRC). The University of Minnesota has col-

lections representing a wide cross-section of Italian American life, 826 Berry Street, St. Paul, MN 55114; cla.umn.edu/ihrc. See S. M. Tomasi and M. H. Engel, *The Italian Americans* (1971); and Joseph Lopreato, *Italian Americans* (1970). Also, Lydio Tomasi, ed., *Italian Americans: New Perspectives in Italian Immigration and Ethnicity* (1985); and there are many regional studies about Italian Americans: C. J. Shane, *The Italians* (2005); Jordan Stanger-Ross, *Staying Italian: Urban Change and Ethnic Life in Postwar Toronto and Philadelphia* (2010); and Jerre Mangione and Ben Morreale, *La Storia: Five Centuries of the Italian American Experience* (1992).

Japanese. The Japanese American National Museum is located at 369 East First Street, Los Angeles, CA 90012; (213) 625-0414; fax (213) 625-1770; www.janm.org. The National Japanese American Historical Society is located at 1885 Folsom St., San Francisco, CA 94103; (415) 431-5007; fax (415) 431-0311; www.njahs.org. See Ronald Takaki, *Issei and Nisei: The Settling of Japanese America* (1994); Roger Daniels, *Asian America: Chinese and Japanese in the United States since 1850* (1988); H. Brett Melendy, *Chinese and Japanese Americans* (1984); and Robert A. Wilson and Bill Hosokawa, *East to America: A History of the Japanese in the United States* (1980). Also, Brian Niiya, ed., *Encyclopedia of Japanese American History: An A-to-Z Reference from 1868 to the Present* (2001); Jere Takahashi, *Nisei/Sansei: Shifting Japanese American Identities and Politics* (1997); Paul Spickard, *Japanese Americans: The For-

mation and Transformations of an Ethnic Group, rev. ed. (2009).

Jews. The American Jewish Historical Society has headquarters at 2 Thornton Road, Waltham, MA 02453-7711; (716) 891-8110; www.ajhs.org. The most important archives are at the Jacob Rader Marcus Center of the American Jewish Archives, 3101 Clifton Ave., Cincinnati, OH 45220; (513) 221-1875; americanjewisharchives.org; and YIVO: The Institute for Jewish Research, located at 15 West 16th Street, New York, NY 10019; (212) 246-6080; fax (212) 292-1891; www.yivo.org. The Jewish Museum has a large collection of materials related to Jewish life, 1109 Fifth Avenue, New York, NY 10128; (212) 423-3200; www.thejewishmuseum.org. See Jeffrey S. Gurock, ed., *American Jewish History: The Colonial and Early National Periods, 1654–1840* (1997); Stephen H. Norwood and Eunice G. Pollack, eds., *Encyclopedia of American Jewish History* (2008); Roberta Rosenberg Farber and Chaim I. Waxman, *Jews in America: A Contemporary Reader* (1999); Jeffrey S. Gurock, *American Jewish History* (1998); Howard M. Sachar, *A History of Jews in America* (1992); Abraham J. Karp, *Haven and Home: A History of Jews in America* (1985); Irving Howe, *World of Our Fathers* (1976); Henry Feingold, *Zion in America* (1974); and Nathan Glazer, *American Judaism*, rev. ed. (1972).

See also Appendix B, Jews.

Koreans. The Korean American Historical Society is located at 10303 Meridian Ave. N., Suite 20, Seattle, WA 98133-9483; (206) 528-5784; fax (206) 523-4340; www.kahs.org. There is a Center for Korean Studies at the University of Hawai'i, located at 1882 East-West Road, Honolulu, HI 96822; (808) 956-7041; www.hawaii.edu/korea. See Pyong Gap Min, *Koreans in North America: Their Twenty-First Century Experiences* (2013); Ilpyong J. Kim, ed., *Korean-Americans: Past, Present, and Future* (2004); Jenny Ryun Foster, Frank Stewart, and Heinz Insu Fenkl, eds., *Century of the Tiger: One Hundred Years of Korean Culture in America, 1903–2003* (2003); Elaine H. Kim, *East to America: Korean-American Life Stories* (1996); Pyong Gap Min, *Caught in the Middle: Korean Merchants in America's Multiethnic Cities* (1996); Ronald Takaki, *From the Land of Morning Calm: The Koreans in America* (1994); Hyung-chan Kim and Wayne Patterson, eds., *The Koreans in America* (1977). For Hawai'i, see Arthur L. Gardner, *The Koreans in Hawaii: An Annotated Bibliography* (1970).

Latvians. The best collection of materials can be found at the Latvian Association, 400 Hurley Avenue, Rockville, MD 20850-3121; www.alausa.org; at the Jewish Family Research Institute, 15 West 16th St., New York, NY 10011; (202) 294-8318; www.cjh.org/p/pdfs/Latvia07.pdf; the *Immigration History Research Center at the University of Minnesota, cla.umn.edu/ihrc; and the Hoover Institution on War, Revolution, and Peace, Stanford University, Stanford, California; www.hoover.org/library-archives/collections/latvia. See Maruta Kārklis, *The Latvians in America, 1640–1973: A Chronology and Fact*

Book (1974) and Silvija D. Meija, *Latvians in Michigan* (2005).

Lithuanians. Archival collections can be found at the World Lithuanian Archives, 5620 S. Claremont Ave., Chicago, IL 60636; hwww.lithuanianresearch.org/eng/plaeng/plaenghome.htm; the American Lithuanian Cultural Archives are on Thurber Road, Putnam, CT 06206; (203) 928-9317; lkma.org. There is also material in the University of Pennsylvania Library in Philadelphia, www.library.upenn.edu/collections; and in the New York Public Library. See David Fainhauz, *Lithuanians in the USA: Aspects of Ethnic Identity* (1990); Antanas J. van Reerian, *Lithuanian Diaspora: Königsberg to Chicago* (1990); Milda Danys, DP, *Lithuanian Immigration to Canada after the Second World War* (1986); Leo Alilunas, *Lithuanians in the United States* (1978); and Algirdas M. Budreckis, *The Lithuanians in America, 1651–1975: A Chronology and Fact Book* (1976). Also, David Fainhauz, *Lithuanians in the USA: Aspects of Ethnic Identity* (1991); Marius K. Grazulis, *Lithuanians in Michigan* (2009); and Algimantas Kezys, *Faces of Two Worlds: A Study in Portraits of the Lithuanian Immigrant Experience: Photographs*, with notes by the photographer, 2 vols. (1986).

Macedonians. See George J. Prpic, *South Slavic Immigration in America* (1978); Stoyan Christowe, *My American Pilgrimage* (1947), *This Is My Country* (1938); and Robert D. Kaplan, *Balkan Ghosts: A Journey through History* (1993).

Mexicans. The rich materials of the Balch Institute now are held at Historical Society of Pennsylvania, www.hsp.org. Research collections on the Mexican American experience can be found at Stanford University library. stanford.edu/areas/mexican-american-collections and the University of Texas at Austin, https://www.lib.utexas.edu/benson/collections/rare-books-and-manuscripts/mexican-american-latino-manuscripts. See Neil Foley, *Mexicans in the Making of America* (2014); Timothy J. Henderson, *Beyond Borders: A History of Mexican Migration to the United States* (2011); Mark Overmyer-Velázquez, *Beyond la Frontera: The History of Mexico-U.S. Migration* (2011); Manuel G. Gonzales, *Mexicanos: A History of Mexicans in the United States* (2009); Alma M. García, *The Mexican Americans* (2002); Oscar J. Martínez, *Mexican-origin People in the United States: A Topical History* (2001); Monica Perales and Raúl A. Ramos, eds., *Recovering the Hispanic History of Texas* (2010); Zaragosa Vargas, *Crucible of Struggle: A History of Mexican Americans from Colonial Times to the Present Era* (2010); and Carlos M. Fernández-Shaw, *The Hispanic Presence in North America from 1492 to Today* (1999).

Norwegians. The Norwegian American Historical Association, established in 1925, is located at 1520 St. Olaf Ave., Northfield, MN 55057; (507) 646-2222; www.naha.stolaf.edu. It publishes works about the Norwegian-American experience. There is a Scandinavian Studies program at Luther College, Decorah, IA, where Vesterheim, a museum devoted to Norwegians in the United States, is located, vesterheim. org. There is additional material at the Sons of Norway in Minneapolis, www. sofn.com, and at the historical societies in Wisconsin and Minnesota. There is a Nordic Heritage Museum at 3014 NW 67th St., Seattle, WA 98117; (206) 789-5707. See Odd Sverre Lovoll, *Across the Deep Blue Sea: the Saga of Early Norwegian Immigrants* (2015); Daron Olson, *Vikings across the Atlantic: Emigration and the Building of a greater Norway, 1860–1945* (2013); David C. Mauk, *The Colony That Rose from the Sea: Norwegian Maritime Migration and Community in Brooklyn 1850–1910* (1997); John E. Bodnar, *Collective Memory and Ethnic Groups: The Case of Swedes, Mennonites, and Norwegians* (1991); Ingrid Semmingsen, *Norway to America: A History of the Migration* (1978); Arlow W. Anderson, *The Norwegian Americans* (1974); Theodore C. Blegan, *Norwegian Migration to America, 1825–1860* ([1931] 1969); Carlton C. Qualey, *Norwegian Settlement in the United States* (1968); Richard J. Fapso, *Norwegians in Wisconsin* (2001); and Jon Gjerde and Carlton C. Qualey, *Norwegians in Minnesota* (2002).

Pakistanis. See East Asians.

Poles. There is an archive at the Polish Museum of America, 984 N. Milwaukee Ave., Chicago, IL 60622; (773) 384-3352; www.polishmuseumofamerica. org and also at the *Immigration History Research Center at the University of Minnesota, cla.umn.edu/ihrc. The Central Council of Polish Organizations, established in 1930 by the Polish

Historical Society, is located at 4291 Stanton Ave., Pittsburgh, PA 15201; (412) 782-2166. The Polish American Historical Society is located at 984 N. Milwaukee Ave., Chicago, IL 60622; (312) 384-3352; www.polishamericanstudies.org. See William J. Galush, *For More than Bread: Community and Identity in American Polonia, 1880–1940* (2006); Dennis Badaczewski, *Poles in Michigan* (2002); John Radzilowski, *Poles in Minnesota* (2005); John J. Bukowczyk, *A History of the Polish Americans* (2008); James S. Pula and Mieczyslaw B. Biskupski, eds., *The Polish American Encyclopedia* (2011). Also James S. Pula, *Polish Americans: An Ethnic Community* (1995); Waclaw Kruszka, *A History of the Poles in America to 1908* (1993); John J. Bukowczyk, *And My Children Did Not Know Me: A History of the Polish Americans* (1987); Frank Renkiewicz, ed., *The Polish Presence in Canada and America* (1982); Joseph Anthony Wytrwal, *Behold! The Polish-Americans* (1977); Caroline Golab, *Immigrant Destinations* (1977); Helena Z. Lopata, *Polish Americans: Status Competition in an Ethnic Community* (1976); and Victor Greene, *For God and Country: The Rise of Polish and Lithuanian Ethnic Consciousness in America, 1860–1910* (1975).

Portuguese. The Oliveira Lima Library at The Catholic University of America in Washington, D.C. is a repository of materials on the history and culture of the Portuguese-speaking peoples: cohent@cua.edu; (202) 319-5059; libraries.cua.edu/oliveiralima. See also David J. Viera, *The Portuguese in the United States: A Bibliography* (1989); Frederic

A. Silva, *"All Our Yesterdays . . ."*: *The Sons of Macao—Their History and Heritage* (1979); Carlos Almeida, *Portuguese Immigrants: The Centennial Story of the Portuguese Union of the State of California* (1978); Leo Pap, *The Portuguese in the United States: A Bibliography* (1976); Manoel da Silveria Cardozo, ed., *The Portuguese in America, 590 B.C.–1974: A Chronology and Fact Book* (1976). See also Maria José Lagos Trindade, "Portuguese Emigration from the Azores to the United States during the 19th Century," in *Portugal and America: Studies in Honor of the Bicentennial of American Independence* (1976); Donald Warrin and Geoffrey L. Gomes, *Land, as Far as the Eye Can See: Portuguese in the Old West* (2001); Kimberly DaCosta Holton and Andrea Klimt, *Community, Culture and the Makings of Identity: Portuguese-Americans along the Eastern Seaboard* (2009); Alvin Ray Graves, *The Portuguese Californians: Immigrants in Agriculture* (2004); and Jerry R. Williams, *In Pursuit of Their Dreams: A History of Azorean Immigration to the United States* (2005).

Puerto Ricans. El Museo del Barrio is located at 1945 Third Ave., New York, NY 10029; (212) 831-7272; www.elmuseo.org. See María Pérez y González, *Puerto Ricans in the United States* (2000). Also Carmen Teresa Whalen and Víctor Vázquez-Hernández, *The Puerto Rican Diaspora: Historical Perspectives* (2005); and Lisa Pierce Flores, *The History of Puerto Rico* (2010).

Romanians. The Romanian Cultural Institute includes a Library located at 200 E 38th St., New York, NY 10016; (212) 687-0181; www.icrny.org. The Romanian-American Heritage Center houses materials relating to Romanian immigrants in the United States; it is located at 2540 Grey Tower Road, Jackson, MI 49201; (517) 522-8260; studiiromanoamericane.wordpress.com. See Gerald Bobango, *The Romanian Orthodox Episcopate of America: The First Half-Century, 1929–1979* (1979); Mary Leuca and Peter Georgeoff, *Romanian Americans in Lake County, Indiana: Resource Guide* (1977); Joseph J. Barton, *Peasants and Strangers: Italians, Rumanians, and Slovaks in an American City, 1890–1950* (1975); and Christine A. Galitzi, *A Study of Assimilation among the Roumanians of the United States* ([1929]1968). Also, Vasile Hategan, *Romanian Culture in America* (1985); Arthur Diamond, Romanian Americans (1988); Vladimir Wertsman, *The Romanians in America, 1748–1974: A Chronology and Factbook* (1975); and Vladimir Wertsman, *Romanians in the United States and Canada: A Guide to Ancestry and Heritage Research* (2002).

Russians. There is material about Russian Americans in the Bakhmeteff Archive of Russian & Eastern European History and Civilization at Columbia University: (212) 854-3986; library.columbia.edu/indiv/rbml/units/bakhmeteff.html. Other materials can be found at the History of Russia/Commonwealth of Independent States Collection, Hoover Institution Library and Archives at Stanford University. The address is H. Hoover Memorial Building, Courtyard, Stanford, CA 94305;

(650) 723-3563; fax (650) 725-3445; www.hoover.org/regions/russia. The Museum of Russian Culture, which contains a library and archive, is located at 2450 Sutter St., San Francisco, CA 94115; (415) 751-1572; www.mrcsf.org/home. There are additional materials at the *Library of Congress and a large and useful bibliography of Internet resources at the University of Pittsburgh at www.ucis.pitt.edu/reesweb. See Ira A. Glazer, ed., *Migration from the Russian Empire: Lists of Passengers Arriving at the Port of New York* (1995); Susan Wiley Hardwick, *Russian Refuge: Religion, Migration, and Settlement on the North American Pacific Rim* (1993); and Vladimir Wertsman, *The Russians in America: A Chronology and Fact Book* (1977). Also, Vera Kishinevsky, *Russian Immigrants in the United States Adapting to American Culture* (2004); Gerald Gilbert Govorchin, *From Russia to America with Love: A Study of the Russian Immigrants in the United States* (1993); and Lydia B. Zaverukha and Nina Bogdan, *Russian San Francisco*, (2010).

Scandinavians. The American Scandinavian Foundation is located at 127 E. 73rd St., New York, NY 10021; (212) 879-9779; www.amscan.org. The foundation issues *Scandinavian Review* (1913–). See Gerald D. Anderson, *Prairie Voices: An Oral History of Scandinavian Americans in the Upper Midwest* (2014). See also Danes; Finns; Norwegians; Swedes.

Scots. Archival records can be found at the Presbyterian Historical Society

history.pcusa.org and the Historical Society of Pennsylvania, in Philadelphia, www.hsp.org; at the New-York Historical Society, www.nyhistory.org; the North Carolina State Department of Archives and History in Raleigh, www.history.ncdcr.gov; the University of North Carolina Library in Chapel Hill, library.unc.edu/wilson; and the *Library of Congress. See Ian Adams, *Cargoes of Despair and Hope: Scottish Emigration to North America, 1603–1803* (1993); George F. Black, *Scotland's Mark on America* ([1921] 1972); David Dobson, *Scottish Emigration to Colonial America, 1607–1785* (1994); Carlton Jackson, *A Social History of the Scotch-Irish* (1993); Michael Fry, *How the Scots made America* (2005); R. Celeste Ray, *Highland Heritage: Scottish Americans in the American South* (2001); Ferenc Morton Szasz, *Scots in the North American West, 1790–1917* (2000); David Dobson, *Scots in Georgia and the Deep South, 1735–1845* (2000) and his *Scots in New England, 1623–1873* (2002), *Scots in the Mid-Atlantic Colonies, 1635–1783* (2002), and *Scottish Emigration to Colonial America, 1607–1785* (2004). Also Alan T. Forrester, *Scots in Michigan* (2003); and Allan I. Macinnes and Marjory Harper, *Scotland and the Americas, c. 1650–c. 1939: A Documentary Source Book* (2002).

Scots-Irish. See William Kelly and John R. Young, eds., *Ulster and Scotland, 1600-2000: History, Language and Identity* (2004); Tyler Blethen and Curtis Wood, *Ulster and North America: Transatlantic Perspectives on the Scotch-Irish* (1997). Also Edward R. R. Greed, ed., *Essays in Scotch-Irish History* (1969); and James G. Leyburn, The Scotch-Irish: A Social History (1962).

Serbs. The Slavic American Collection at the Louisa H. Bowen University Archives and Special Collections, Lovejoy Library, Southern Illinois University at Edwardsville, Edwardsville, IL 62026-1063; (618) 650-2665; fax (618) 650-2717; www.siue.edu/lovejoylibrary/archives. See Robert P. Gakovich and Milan M. Radovich, eds., *Serbs in the United States and Canada: A Comprehensive Bibliography* (1976); J. Kisslinger, *The Serbian Americans* (1990); and Adam S. Eterovich, *Croations from Dalmatia and Montenegrin Serbs in the West and South, 1800–1900* (1971).

Slavs. There is a Slavic American Collection at the Louisa H. Bowen University Archives and Special Collections, Lovejoy Library, Southern Illinois University at Edwardsville, Edwardsville, IL 62026-1063; (618) 650-2665; fax (618) 650-2717; www.siue.edu/lovejoylibrary/archives.

Slovaks. See Czechs.

Slovenes. The largest collection of materials on the Slovenes is at the *Immigration History Research Center, University of Minnesota, Minneapolis, cla.umn.edu/ihrc. See George J. Prpic, *South Slavic Immigration in America* (1978); Marie Prisland, *From Slovenia to America: Recollections and Collections* (1968); Gerald Gilbert Govorchin, *Americans from Yugoslavia* (1961); and Jay Sedmak, *An Inspired Journey: The SNPJ Story: The First One Hundred*

Years of the Slovene National Benefit Society (2004).

Spaniards. See James D Fernández and Luis Argeo, *Invisible Immigrants: Spaniards in the US (1868–1945)* (2014); Carlos M. Fernández-Shaw, *The Hispanic Presence in North America from 1492 to Today* (1999); A. J. Jaffe, Ruth M. Cullen, and Thomas D. Boswell, *Spanish Americans in the United States: Changing Demographic Characteristics* (1976); and John M. Nieto-Phillips, *The Language of Blood: The Making of Spanish-American Identity in New Mexico, 1880s–1930s* (2004). See also Basques.

South Asians. See East Indians.

Southeast Asians. See Cathleen Jo Faruque, *Migration of Hmong to the Midwestern United States* (2002); Norma Murphy, *A Hmong Family* (1997); Kalsuyo Howard, *Passages: An Anthology of the Southeast Asian Refugee Experience* (1990); James H. Jafner, Jeannine Muldoon, and Elizabeth Bower, *Southeast Asian Refugees in Western Massachusetts* (1989); and Franklin Ng, *The History and Immigration of Asian Americans* (1985). Also, Kaarin Alisa, *The Hmong* (2007); and Jeremy Hein, *Ethnic Origins: The Adaptation of Cambodian and Hmong Refugees in Four American Cities* (2006). See also Indochinese.

Swedes. The Swedish American Historical Society, at 5125 N. Spaulding St., Chicago, IL 60626; (773) 583-5722; www.swedishamericanhist.org. There is also a Swedish-American Historical Museum, founded in 1926, located at 190 Patterson Ave., Philadelphia, PA 19145;

(215) 389-1776; www.americanswedish. org. The Swenson Swedish Immigration Research Center at Augustana College Library holds a collection of books and archival materials; Rock Island, IL 61201; (309) 794-7266; www.augustana. edu/general-information/swenson-center. The American Swedish Institute is located at 2600 Park Ave., Minneapolis, MN 55407; (612) 871-9907; www. asimn.org. See Axel Friman, George M. Stephenson, and H. Arnold Barton, eds., *America, Reality & Dream: The Freeman Letters from America & Sweden, 1841–1862* (1996); Philip J. Anderson, Dag Blanck, and Peter Kivisto, eds., *Scandinavian Immigrants and Education in North America* (1995); H. Arnold Barton, *A Folk Divided: Homeland Swedes and Swedish Americans, 1840–1940* (1994); and Ulf Beijbom, *Swedes in America: Intercultural and Interethnic Perspectives on Contemporary Research* (1993). Also, Philip J. Anderson and Dag Blanck, *Swedes in the Twin Cities: Immigrant Life and Minnesota's Urban Frontier* (2001); Jennifer Eastman Attebery, *Up in the Rocky Mountains: Writing the Swedish Immigrant Experience* (2007); and H. Arnold Barton, *The Old Country and the New: Essays on Swedes and America* (2007).

Swiss. The Swiss American Historical Society is located at Old Dominion University, Norfolk, VA 23508; swissamericanhistoricalsoc.org. See Heinz K. Meier, *The Swiss American Historical Society, 1927–1977* (1977); Konrad Basler, *The Dorlikon Emigrants: Swiss Settlers and Cultural Founders in the United States* (1996); Leo Schelbert, *America Experienced: Eighteenth and Nineteenth Century Accounts of Swiss Emigrants to the United States* (1996), *Swiss in North America* (1974), and *New Glaus, 1845–1970: The Making of a Swiss American Town* (1970). See also Frederick Hale, *Swiss in Wisconsin* (2007); David H. Sutton, *Helvetia: The History of a Swiss Village in the Mountains of West Virginia* (2010); Charles R. Haller, *Across the Atlantic and Beyond: The Migration of German and Swiss Immigrants to America* (2008); and Leo Schelbert and Christine de Graffenried, *Three Hundred Years New Bern, North Carolina* (2009).

Turks. See Rifat N. Bali and Michael D. McGaha, *From Anatolia to the New World: Life Stories of the First Turkish Immigrants to America* (2013); Joseph M. Scolnick and N. Brent Kennedy, *From Anatolia to Appalachia: a Turkish-American Dialogue* (2003). Also, Lisa DiCarlo, *Migrating to America: Transnational Social Networks and Regional Identity among Turkish Migrants* (2008); and A. Deniz Balgamis and Kemal H. Karpat, *Turkish Migration to the United States: From Ottoman Times to the Present* (2008).

Ukranians. There are several Ukranian cultural centers in the United States and Canada. The Ukranian Museum, founded in 1978, is located at 203 Second Ave., New York, NY 10003; (212) 228-0110; www.ukrainianmuseum.org. It contains primarily ethnographic and photographic materials. The Ukranian American Archive and Library is at 11756 Charest St., Detroit, MI 48212; (313) 366-9764; www.ukrainianmuseumdetroit.org. The Ukrainian Museum-Archive in Cleveland seeks to preserve the immigrant experience; http://www.umacleveland.org. See Thomas M Prymak, *Gathering a Heritage: Ukrainian, Slavonic, and Ethnic Canada and the USA* (2015); Myron Kuropas, *The Ukrainian Americans: Roots and Aspirations 1884–1954* (1991), *To Preserve a Heritage: The Story of the Ukrainian Immigration to the United States* (1984), *The Ukrainians in America* (1972), and *Ukrainians of Chicagoland* (2006); Alexander Lushnycky, *Ukrainians of Greater Philadelphia* (2007); Stephen P. Haluszczak, *Ukrainians of Western Pennsylvania* (2009); Nancy Karen Wichar, Ukrainians of Metropolitan Detroit (2009); and Agnes Palanuk, *Ukrainians in North Dakota: In Their Voices* (2011).

Welsh. See William D. Jones, *Wales in America: Scranton and the Welsh, 1860–1920* (1993); Rowland Berthoff, *British Immigrants in Industrial America 1790–1950* (1968); Alan Conway, ed., *The Welsh in America* (1961); Arthur H. Dodd, *The Character of Early Welsh Emigration to the United States* (1957); Ronald L. Lewis, *Welsh Americans: A History of Assimilation in the Coalfields* (2008); William E. Van Vugt, *British Buckeyes: the English, Scots, and Welsh in Ohio, 1700–1900* (2006); and Phillips G. Davies, Welsh in Wisconsin (2006).

West Indians. See Ransford W. Palmer, *Pilgrims from the Sun: West Indian Migration to America* (1995); Holger Henke, *The West Indian Americans* (2001); Nancy Foner, *Islands in the City: West Indian Migration to New York* (2001); Guy T. Westmoreland, *West Indian Americans: A Research Guide* (2001); and Alwyn D. Gilkes, *The West Indian Diaspora: Experiences in the United States and Canada* (2007). See also Caribbeans.

Virginia Cole
Cornell University

Religion in North America and Its Communities

DIRECTORIES AND HANDBOOKS

North America is the most religious, and religiously diverse, place on earth. Historians seeking to understand a community's religious groups may start with J. Gordon Melton, comp., *Religious Bodies in the United States: A Directory* (1992) (includes not only Christian but also Jewish, Islamic, Hindu, Buddhist, other Asian, and "Metaphysical-Ancient Wisdom-New Age" groups). Local congregations are usually part of larger religious bodies, whose publications and archives often contain useful historical and statistical data. Addresses and summary data are found in the annual *Handbook of Denominations in the United States* (1951+) (includes Judaism and Islam but not south and east Asian religions) and *Yearbook of American and Canadian Churches* (1916+) (lists religious archives; see selective list below).

ENCYCLOPEDIAS

Encyclopedias have proliferated in recent decades, conveniently presenting a wealth of factual information but usually downplaying historical debates. Encyclopedias of American religion can help the community historian understand the doctrinal, cultural, and social background of local congregations. General works include Stephen J. Stein, *The Cambridge History of Religions in America*, 3 vols. (2012); Edward L. Queen II, Stephen R. Prothero, and Gardiner H. Shattuck Jr., *Encyclopedia of American Religious History*, 2 vols., rev. ed. (2000) (introductory articles with brief bibliographies); J. Gordon Melton et al., eds., *Encyclopedia of American*

Religions, 8th ed. (2009) (huge compendium, categorizing every religious body in the United States in twenty-four religious "families"); Charles H. Lippy and Peter W. Williams, eds., *Encyclopedia of the American Religious Experience: Studies of Traditions and Movements*, 3 vols. (1988) (covers all traditions but fullest on Christianity; good bibliographies); and Wade Clark Roof, ed., *Contemporary American Religion*, 2 vols. (2000) (surveys myriad aspects of "popular religious culture").

More specialized encyclopedias are Daniel G. Reid, ed., *Dictionary of Christianity in America* (1990) (concise, readable essays; covers United States and Canada); Rosemary Skinner Keller and Rosemary Radford Ruether, *Encyclopedia of Women and Religion in North America*, 3 vols. (2006) (topical and biographical entries); Michael Glazier and Thomas J. Shelley, eds., *The Encyclopedia of American Catholic History* (1997) (includes articles and bibliographies on each state); Larry G. Murphy, J. Gordon Melton, and Gary L. Ward, eds., *Encyclopedia of African American Religions* (1993); and Jocelyne Cesari, ed., *Encyclopedia of Islam in the United States*, 2 vols. (2007). Stephan Thernstrom, ed., *Harvard Encyclopedia of American Ethnic Groups* (1980) contains much information on religion.

ATLASES

Most religious groups are strongly regional in their distribution, as is shown in Edwin S. Gaustad and Philip L. Barlow, *New Historical Atlas of Religion in America* (2001; first pub. 1962) and William M. Newman and Peter L. Halvorson, *Atlas of American Religion: The Denominational Era 1776–1990* (2000).

GENERAL HISTORIES

Surveys—A huge scholarly literature underlies several masterly surveys: Sydney E. Ahlstrom, *A Religious History of the American People*, 2nd ed. (2004; first pub. 1972); Edwin W. Gaustad, *A Religious History of America*, rev. ed. (1990; first pub. 1966); Winthrop S. Hudson and John Corrigan, *Religion in America: An Historical Account of the Development of American Religious Life*, 6th ed. (1998; first pub. 1965); Martin E. Marty, *Pilgrims in Their Own Land: 500 Years of Religion in America* (1984); and Mark A. Noll et al., eds., *Eerdman's Handbook to Christianity in America* (1983) (readable and well illustrated).

Judaism—The rich tradition of Judaism in America is explored by Norman H. Finkelstein, *American Jewish History* (2007) (accessible text, well illustrated); Howard M. Sachar, *A History of the Jews in America* (1992) (comprehensive survey); Abraham J. Karp, *A History of the Jews in America*, rev. ed. (1997) (balanced treatment of Judaism, "which is simultaneously religious, cultural and ethnic"; many quotes from community sources); and Nathan Glazer, *American Judaism*, 2nd ed. (1989) (brief, lucid overview).

Catholicism—The Catholic Church is by far the largest religious body in North America, organized hierarchically but distinguished by its ethnic and cultural diversity. Accessible general works are Patrick W. Carey, *Catholics in America: A History*, rev. ed. (2008) (has a lengthy bibliography) and James J. Hennessey, *American Catholics: A History of the Roman Catholic Community in the United States* (1981). Jay P. Dolan, ed., *The American Catholic Parish: A History from 1850 to the Present*, 2 vols. (1987) is a unique work, presenting studies of parish-level Catholic life in all regions of the United States.

Protestantism—American Protestantism has a complex history characterized by denominationalism, revivalism, and contending liberalism and fundamentalism. Exploring one or more of those themes are Patricia U. Bonomi, *Under the Cope of Heaven: Religion, Society, and Politics in Colonial America* (1986); Jon Butler, *Awash in a Sea of Faith: Christianizing the American People* (1990) (American Protestantism as a distinctive culture with multiple origins); Nathan O. Hatch, *The Democratization of American Christianity* (1989) (studies the Methodists, Baptists, "Christians," Mormons, and black churches, early nineteenth century); Timothy L. Smith, *Revivalism and Social Reform: American Protestantism on the Eve of the Civil War* (1980; first pub. 1957); George M. Marsden, *Fundamentalism and American Culture: The Shaping of Twentieth-Century Evangelicalism, 1870–1925*, 2nd ed. (2006); and Robert Wuthnow, *The Restructuring of American Religion: Society and Faith Since World War II* (1980).

DENOMINATIONAL STUDIES

Protestant denominations remain very numerous, despite many mergers during the twentieth century. Good overviews of several major traditions are found in the Denominations in America series, edited by Henry W. Bowden (1985–2004) (11 vols., on the Baptists, Churches of Christ, Congregationalists, Episcopalians, Lutherans, Methodists, Presbyterians, Quakers, and Unitarians and Universalists, as well as the Catholic and Orthodox churches; each includes a biographical section and bibliography). Other general surveys include E. Clifford Nelson, ed., *The Lutherans in North America* (1975) (discusses all branches of Lutheranism; attentive to regional developments); Frederick A. Norwood, *The Story of American Methodism* (1974) (includes merged bodies and still separate black Methodist churches).

Good books about religious movements originating in America have been written by committed adherents as well as disillusioned critics; community historians should consider both perspectives. Examples of such strongly argued works are Ellen MacGilvra Rosenberg, *The Southern Baptists: Subculture in Transition* (1989) (sociological perspective, often critical); Leonard J. Arrington, *The Mormon Experience: A History of the Latter-Day Saints* (1979) (LDS author; readable, comprehensive);

Malcolm Bull and Keith Lockhart, *Seeking a Sanctuary: Seventh-Day Adventism and the American Dream*, 2nd ed. (2007) (emphasizes theology and lifestyle); and M. James Penton, *Apocalypse Delayed: The Story of Jehovah's Witnesses*, 3rd ed. (2015) (by a former Witness). Utopian communities of the antebellum period were surveyed by John Humphrey Noyes, *History of American Socialisms*, introduction by Mark Holloway (1966; first pub. 1870).

SELECTED ARCHIVES

The following list is organized alphabetically. It includes religious groups of over 100,000 adherents that have organized archives, and some archives of smaller groups.

United States
African Methodist Episcopal Church—Department of Research and Scholarship, 500 8th Ave. South, Nashville, TN 37203; archive.ame-church.com.

African Methodist Episcopal Zion Church—Department of Records & Research, 701 West Monroe St., Salisbury, NC 28144; www.livingstone.edu/heritage_hall.htm.

American Baptist Churches in the U.S.A.—American Baptist Historical Society, 3001 Mercer University Dr., Atlanta, GA 30341; abhsarchives.org.

American Jewish Archives—Jacob Rader Marcus Center, Hebrew Union College, 3101 Clifton Ave., Cincinnati, OH 45220; americanjewisharchives.org.

American Jewish Historical Society—Center for Jewish History, 15 West 16th St., New York, NY 10011; www.ajhs.org.

Assemblies of God—Flower Pentecostal Heritage Center, 1445 Boonville Ave., Springfield, MO 65802; www.ifphc.org.

Catholic Church—American Catholic History Research Center, Catholic University of America, 101 Aquinas Hall, Washington, D.C. 20064; archives.lib.cua.edu. Catholic archives are decentralized. *The Official Catholic Directory* (1913+) has addresses for each archdiocese, diocese, and parish, and for eastern rite churches and religious orders.

Christian Church (Disciples of Christ) in the U.S. and Canada—Disciples of Christ Historical Society, 1101 19th Ave. South, Nashville, TN 37212; www.discipleshistory.org.

Christian Reformed Church in North America—Heritage Hall, Calvin College, 1855 Knollcrest Circle SE, Grand Rapids, MI 49546; www.calvin.edu/hh.

Church of God (Cleveland, Tenn.)—Dixon Pentecostal Research Center, 260 11th St. NE, Cleveland, TN 37311; www.cogheritage.org.

Church of Jesus Christ of Latter-day Saints (Mormons)—Church History Library, 15 East North Temple St., Salt Lake City, UT 84150; churchhistorylibrary.lds.org.

Church of the Nazarene—Nazarene Archives, 17001 Prairie Star Parkway,

Lenexa, KS 66220; www.nazarene.org/ organization/general-secretary/archives.

Episcopal Church—Archives, PO Box 2247, Austin, TX 78768; www.episcopalarchives.org.

Evangelical Lutheran Church in America—Archives, 321 Bonnie Lane, Elk Grove Village, IL 60007; www.elca.org/ archives (also nine regional archives).

International Pentecostal Holiness Church—Archives and Research Center, PO Box 12609, Oklahoma City, OK 73157; iphc.org/gso/archives.

Lutheran Church, Missouri Synod—Concordia Historical Institute, Concordia Seminary, 804 Seminary Pl., St. Louis, MO 63105; www.lutheranhistory.org.

Mennonite Church U.S.A.—Archives, 1700 South Main St., Goshen, IN 46526; www.MennoniteUSA.org/history; Library and Archives, Bethel College, 300 East 27th St., North Newton, KS 67117; www.bethelks.edu.

Presbyterian Church in America—Historical Center, 12330 Conway Rd., St. Louis, MO 63141; pcahistory.org.

Presbyterian Church, U.S.A.—Presbyterian Historical Society, 425 Lombard St., Philadelphia, PA 19147; www.history.pcusa.org.

Reformed Church in America—Archives, 21 Seminary Place, New Brunswick, NJ 08901; www.rca.org/rca-basics/archives.

Salvation Army—Archives and Research Center, 615 Slaters Lane, P.O. Box 269, Alexandria, VA 22313; www.salvationarmy.org.

Seventh-Day Adventist Church—Office of Archives, Statistics, and Research, 12501 Old Columbia Pike, Silver Spring, MD 20904; ast.gc.adventist.org.

Society of Friends (Quakers)—Friends Historical Library, Swarthmore College, 500 College Ave., Swarthmore, PA 19081; www.swarthmore.edu/library/ friends.

Southern Baptist Convention—Southern Baptists Historical Library and Archives, 901 Commerce St., Suite 400, Nashville, TN 37203; www.sbhla.org.

Unitarian Universalist Association—Andover-Harvard Theological Library, Harvard Divinity School, 45 Francis Ave., Cambridge, MA 02138; www.hds.harvard.edu/library.

United Church of Christ—Archives, 700 Prospect Ave., Cleveland, OH 44115; www.ucc.org/about-us/archives; Congregational Library and Archives, 14 Beacon St., Boston, MA 02108; www.congregationallibrary.org; Evangelical and Reformed Historical Society, Lancaster Theological Seminary, 555 West James St., Lancaster, PA 17603; foerhs.info; Amistad Research Center, Tilton Hall, Tulane University, 6823 St. Charles Ave., New Orleans, LA 70118; www.amistadresearchcenter. org (American Missionary Assoc. archives, documenting aid to new Congregational churches and to freedmen after the Civil War; available on microfilm).

United Methodist Church—General Commission on Archives and History, 38 Madison Ave., PO Box 127, Madison, NJ 07940; www.gcah.org; Center for the Evangelical United Brethren Heritage, United Theological Seminary, 4501 Denlinger Rd., Dayton, OH 45426.

Canada

Anglican Church of Canada—General Synod Archives, 80 Hayden St., Toronto, ON M4Y 3G2; www.anglican.ca/archives.

Canadian National Baptist Convention—Canadian Baptist Archives, McMaster Divinity College, 1280 Main St. West, Hamilton, ON L8S 4K1; www.mcmasterdivinity.ca.

Evangelical Lutheran Church in Canada—Archives, Lutheran Theological Seminary, 114 Seminary Crescent, Saskatoon, SK S7N 0X3; www.elcic.ca.

Pentecostal Assembles of Canada—Archives, 2450 Milltower Ct., Mississauga, ON L5N 5Z6; www.paoc.org.

Presbyterian Church in Canada—Archives and Records Office, 50 Wynford Dr., Toronto, ON M3C 1J7; www.presbyterianarchives.ca.

United Church of Canada—Archives, 40 Oak St., Toronto, ON M5A 2C6; archives.united-church.ca.

JAMES D. FOLTS
NEW YORK STATE ARCHIVES

State Historical Organizations

The following is a list of state historical organizations, state archives, or libraries. Included for each organization, where available, are its mailing address, telephone and fax numbers, and web addresses. Heads of these organizations are not listed. Also included at the top of the list is the address for the *American Association of State and Local History (AASLH) .

AASLH
2021 21st Avenue
Nashville, TN 37212
(615) 320-3203; fax (615) 327-9013
www.aaslh.org

Alabama Department of History and Archives
P.O. Box 300100
Montgomery, AL 36130-0100
(334) 242-4435
archives.alabama.gov
State archives and history museum

Alabama Historical Commission
468 South Perry Street
Montgomery, AL 36104
(334) 242-3184
www.preserveala.org
State historic preservation agency

Alaska Historical Society
P.O. Box 100299
Anchorage, AK 99510-0299
(907) 276-1596
www.alaskahistoricalsociety.org
Private historical society

Arizona Historical Society
949 E. Second Street
Tucson, AZ 85719
(520) 628-5774
www.arizonahistoricalsociety.org
State historical society

Arizona State Museum
P.O. Box 210026
University of Arizona
Tucson, AZ 85721-0026
(520) 621-6302; fax (520) 621-2976
www.statemuseum.arizona.edu
State museum

Appendix C

Arkansas History Commission and State Archives
One Capitol Mall
Little Rock, AR 72201
(501) 682-6900
www.ark-ives.com
State archives

California Historical Society
678 Mission Street
San Francisco, CA 94105
(415) 357-1848; fax (415) 357-1850
www.californiahistoricalsociety.org
State historical society

California State Archives
1020 O Street
Sacramento, CA 95814
(916) 653–7715; fax (916) 653-7363
www.sos.ca.gov/archives
State archives

California State Library
Box 942837
Sacramento, CA 94237-0001
(916) 654-0261
www.library.ca.gov
State library

Colorado Historical Society
1200 Broadway
Denver, CO 80203
(303) 447-8679
www.historycolorado.org
State historical society and museum

Connecticut Historical Society
1 Elizabeth Street
Hartford, CT 06105
(860) 236-5621; fax (860) 236-2664
www.chs.org
Private historical society

Connecticut Commission on Culture and Tourism
One Constitution Plaza, 2nd floor
Hartford, CT 06103
(860) 256-2800; fax (860) 256-2811
www.cultureandtourism.org

Delaware Division of Historical and Cultural Affairs
Hall of Records
21 The Green
Dover, DE 19901
(302) 736-7400
www.history.delaware.gov
State preservation agency, archives, and museum

Delaware Historical Society
505 Market Street
Wilmington, DE 19801
(302) 655-7161
www.dehistory.org
Private historical society and museum

Historical Society of Washington, D.C.
801 K Street, NW
Washington, D.C. 20001
(202) 249-3955
www.dchistory.org
District historical society

Florida Historical Society
435 Brevard Ave.
Cocoa, FL 32922
(321) 690-1971
www.myfloridahistory.org
Private historical society

Museum of Florida History
500 South Bronough Street
Tallahassee, FL 32399-0250
(850) 245-6400
www.museumoffloridahistory.com
State museum

Georgia Department of Archives and History
5800 Jonesboro Road
Morrow, GA 30260
(678) 364-3710
www.georgiaarchives.org
State historical society and archives

Georgia Historical Society
501 Whitaker Street
Savannah, GA 31401
(912) 651-2125; fax (912) 651-2831
www.georgiahistory.com
Private historical society

Bishop Museum
1525 Bernice Street
Honolulu, HI 96817-0916
(808) 847-3511
www.bishopmuseum.org

Hawaiian Historical Society
560 Kawaiahao Street
Honolulu, HI 96813
(808) 537-6271
www.hawaiianhistory.org
Private historical society

Idaho State Historical Society
2205 Old Penitentiary Rd.
Boise, ID 83712
(208) 334-3356
http://history.idaho.gov
State historical society

Illinois State Historical Society
521 E. Washington Street
Springfield, IL 62701
(217) 525-2781
www.historyillinois.org
Private historical society

Illinois State Museum
502 South Spring Street
Springfield, IL 62706
(217) 782-7386
www.museum.state.il.us
State museum

Indiana Historical Bureau
140 North Senate Avenue Room 130
Indianapolis, IN 46204
(317) 232-2535; fax (317) 232-1659
www.in.gov/history
State historical commission

Indiana Historical Society
450 West Ohio Street
Indianapolis, IN 46202-3269
(317) 232-1882
www.indianahistory.org
Private historical society

Indiana State Museum
650 W. Washington St.
Indianapolis, IN 46204
(317) 232-1637
www.indianamuseum.org
State museum

State Historical Society of Iowa
600 East Locust
Des Moines IA 50319
(512) 281-5111
www.iowaculture.gov/history
State historical society

Kansas State Historical Society
6425 SW Sixth Avenue
Topeka, KS 66615
(785) 272-8681
www.kshs.org
State historical society and museum

Appendix C

The Filson Historical Society
1310 S. Third Street
Louisville, KY 40208
(502) 635-5083
http://www.filsonhistorical.org
Private historical society

Kentucky Historical Society
100 W. Broadway
Frankfort, KY 40601-1931
(502) 564-1792; fax (502) 564-4701
history.ky.gov
State historical society and museum

Louisiana State Museum
660 North 4th Street
Baton Rouge, LA 70802
(225) 342-5428
www.louisianastatemuseum.org
State historical society and museum

Maine Historical Society / Center for Maine History
489 Congress Street
Portland, ME 04101
(207) 774-1822
www.mainehistory.org
Private historical society

Maine State Museum
83 State House Station
Augusta, ME 04333-0083
(207) 287-2301
http://mainestatemuseum.org
State museum

State Archivist Maine
State Archives
84 State House Station
Augusta, ME 04333-0084
(207) 287-5790
www.maine.gov/sos/arc
State archives

Maryland Historical Society
201 W. Monument Street
Baltimore, MD 21201
(410) 685-3750
www.mdhs.org
Private historical society

Massachusetts Historical Society
1154 Boylston Street
Boston, MA 02215
(617) 536-1608
http://www.masshist.org
Private historical society

Historical Society of Michigan
5815 Executive Drive
Lansing, MI 48911
(517) 324-1828
http://www.hsmichigan.org
Private historical society

Michigan History Center
702 W. Kalamazoo St.
Lansing, MI 48915
(517) 373-3559
www.michigan.gov/mhc
State historical agency (museums, archives, historic preservation, archaeology)

Minnesota Historical Society
345 W. Kellogg Boulevard
St. Paul, MN 55102-1906
(651) 259-3000
www.mnhs.org
State historical society and museum

Mississippi Department of Archives and History
200 North Street
Jackson, MS 39201
(601) 576-6850
www.mdah.state.ms.us
State archives, museum, historic properties, and SHPO

Missouri Historical Society
P.O. Box 11940
St. Louis, MO 63112
(314) 746-4599
www.mohistory.org
Private history museum and library and research center

State Historical Society of Missouri
1020 Lowry Street
Columbia, MO 65201
(800) 747-6366
www.shsmo.org
State historical society

Montana Historical Society
225 N. Roberts Street
Helena, MT 59620
(406) 444-2694; fax (406) 444-2696
www.mhs.mt.gov
State historical society

Nebraska State Historical Society
1500 R Street
P.O. Box 82554
Lincoln, NE 68501-2554
(402) 471-3270
www.nebraskahistory.org
State historical society and museum

Nevada Historical Society
1650 N. Virginia Street
Reno, NV 89503
(702) 688-1190
www.museums.nevadaculture.org/nhs-home
State historical society

New Hampshire Historical Society
30 Park Street
Concord, NH 03301
(603) 228-6688
www.nhhistory.org
Private historical society

New Jersey Historical Commission
225 West State St.
P.O. Box 305
Trenton, NJ 08625-0305
(609) 292-6062
http://nj.gov/state/historical

New Jersey Historical Society
52 Park Place
Newark, NJ 07102
(973) 596-8500
http://www.jerseyhistory.org
Private historical society

New Jersey State Museum
205 West State Street
P.O. Box 530
Trenton, NJ 08625-0530
(609) 292-6300
http://www.state.nj.us/state/museum
State museum

Museum of New Mexico
P.O. Box 2087
Santa Fe, NM 87504
(505) 476-5200; fax (505) 476-5104
www.museumofnewmexico.org
State museum

New-York Historical Society
170 Central Park West
Manhattan, NY 10024-5194
(212) 873-3400
www.nyhistory.org
Private historical society

New York State Historical Association/The Farmer's Museum/Fenimore House Museum
P.O. Box 800
Cooperstown, NY 13326
(607) 547-1400; fax (607) 547-1404
www.nysha.org
Private historical society

Appendix C

New York State Museum
222 Madison Avenue
Albany, NY 12230
(518) 474-5877
www.nysm.nysed.gov
State museum

North Carolina Division of Archives and History
4610 Mail Service Center
Raleigh, NC 27699-4610
(919) 807-7280; fax (919) 733-8807
www.history.ncdcr.gov
State historical society and archives

North Carolina Museum of History
5 E. Edenton Street
Raleigh, NC 27601-1011
(919) 807-7900
http://ncmuseumofhistory.org
State history museum division

State Historical Society of North Dakota
612 E. Boulevard Avenue
Bismarck, ND 58505
(701) 328-2666
http://history.nd.gov
State historical society

Ohio Historical Society
800 E.17th Ave.
Columbus, OH 43211
(614) 297-2300
www.ohiohistory.org
Private historical society

Oklahoma Historical Society
800 Nazih Zuhdi Drive
Oklahoma City, OK 73105
(405) 521-2491
www.okhistory.org
State historical society

Oregon Historical Society
1200 SW Park Avenue
Portland, OR 97205
(503) 222-1741
www.ohs.org
Private historical society

Pennsylvania Heritage Foundation
400 North Street
Harrisburg, PA 17120
(717) 787-2407
www.paheritage.org

Pennsylvania Historical and Museum Commission
300 North Street
Harrisburg, PA 17120
(717) 787-3362
www.phmc.pa.gov
State historical society

Historical Society of Pennsylvania
1300 Locust Street
Philadelphia, PA 19107-5699
(215) 732-6200; fax (215) 732-2680
http://hsp.org
Private historical society

Rhode Island Historical Society
110 Benevolent Street
Providence, RI 02906
(401) 331-8575
www.rihs.org
Private historical society

South Carolina Department of Archives and History
8301 Parklane Road
Columbia, SC 29223-4905
(803) 896-6196
http://scdah.sc.gov
State SHPO and archives

South Carolina Historical Society
100 Meeting Street
Charleston, SC 29401
(803) 723-3225
www.schistory.org
Private historical society

South Carolina State Museum
301 Gervais Street
Columbia, SC 29214
(803) 898-4291
www.scmuseum.org
State museum

South Dakota State Historical Society
900 Governors Drive
Pierre, SD 57501
(605) 773-3458; fax (605) 773-6041
http://history.sd.gov
State historical society

Tennessee Historical Commission
2941 Lebanon Road
Nashville, TN 37243-0442
(615) 770-1097
https://tn.gov/environment/section/
thc-tennessee-historical-commission
State historical commission

Tennessee Historical Society
305 6th Avenue North
Nashville, TN 37243
(615) 741-8934
www.tennesseehistory.org
Private historical society

Tennessee State Museum
505 Deaderick Street
Nashville, TN 37423
(615) 741-2692
www.tnmuseum.org
State museum

Texas Historical Commission
108 West 16th Street
Austin, TX 78701
(512) 463-6096
www.thc.state.tx.us

Texas State Historical Association
3001 Lake Austin Boulevard #3.116
Austin, TX 78703
(512) 471-2600; fax (512) 473-8691
www.tshaonline.org
State historical society

Utah State Historical Society
300 Rio Grande Street
Salt Lake City, UT 84101
(801) 245-7225
https://heritage.utah.gov/history/his-
torical-society
State historical society

Vermont Historical Society
60 Washington Street
Barre, VT 05641
(802) 479-8500
www.vermonthistory.org
Private historical society

Library of Virginia
800 East Broad Street
Richmond, VA 23219-1905
(804) 692-3500
www.lva.virginia.gov
State library

Virginia Historical Society
428 North Boulevard
P.O. Box 7311
Richmond, VA 23221-0311
(804) 358-4901
www.vahistorical.org
Private historical society and museum

Washington State Historical Society
1911 Pacific Avenue
Tacoma, WA 98402
(888) 238-4373
www.washingtonhistory.org
State historical society

West Virginia State Museum
1900 Kanawha Boulevard East
Charleston, WV 25305
(304) 558-0220
www.wvculture.org/museum/State-
Museum-Index.html
State museum

State Historical Society of Wisconsin
816 State Street
Madison, WI 53706
(608) 264-6400

www.wisconsinhistory.org
State historical society, museum, and archives

Wyoming State Historical Society
602 9th Street
P.O. Box 247
Wheatland, WY 82201
(307) 322-3014
http://wyshs.org
State historical society

Wyoming State Museum
Barrett Building
2301 Central Avenue
Cheyenne, WY 82002
(307) 777-7022
http://wyomuseum.state.wy.us
State museum

APPENDIX D

$\mathcal{NARA}$ $\mathcal{Facilities}$

The addresses of the National Archives and Records Administration (NARA) regional facilities are listed below. The main National Archives in Washington, D.C., and College Park, Maryland, and Field Offices around the country hold permanently valuable records of federal agencies and the courts. The Federal Records Centers, including the National Records Center in Suitland, Maryland, hold records still active from federal agencies and courts. The hours are as follows: The National Archives Building in Washington, D.C., and the National Archives at College Park are open for research Monday–Saturday, 9:00 a.m. to 5:00 p.m. Field Offices are open Monday through Friday. Visit the website: www.archives.gov/locations or call for specific hours. All facilities are closed on federal holidays.

Appendix D

National Archives and Records Administration
700 Pennsylvania Avenue, NW
Washington, D.C. 20408
(202) 357-5000

National Archives at College Park, MD
8601 Adelphi Road
College Park, MD 20740-6701
(301) 837-2000

Washington National Records Center
4205 Suitland Road
Suitland, MD 20746
(301) 778-1510

National Archives at Atlanta, GA
5780 Jonesboro Road
Morrow, Georgia 30260
(770) 968-2100

Atlanta Federal Records Center
4712 Southpark Blvd.
Ellenwood, GA 30294
(404) 736-2820
These facilities serve Alabama, Florida, Georgia, Kentucky, Mississippi, North Carolina, South Carolina, and Tennessee.

National Archives at Boston, MA
Boston Federal Records Center
380 Trapelo Road
Waltham, MA 02452-6399
(781) 663-0130

Pittsfield Federal Records Center
10 Conte Drive
Pittsfield, MA 01201-8230
These facilities serve Connecticut, Maine, Massachusetts, New Hampshire, Rhode Island, and Vermont.

National Archives at Chicago, IL
Chicago Federal Records Center
7358 South Pulaski Road
Chicago, IL 60629-5898
(773) 948-9001

Dayton Federal Records Center
3150 Springboro Road
Dayton, OH 45439
(937) 425-0600

Dayton-Kingsridge Federal Records Center
8801 Kingsridge Drive
Dayton, OH 45458
(937) 425-0690
These facilities provide storage and other services for active and inactive historical records created or received by federal agencies in Illinois, Minnesota, and Wisconsin, and federal courts in Illinois, Indiana, Michigan, Minnesota, Ohio, and Wisconsin.

National Archives at Denver, CO
Denver Federal Records Center
17101 Huron Street
Broomfield, CO 80023-8909
(303) 604-4760
This facility serves Colorado, Montana, New Mexico, North Dakota, South Dakota, Utah, and Wyoming.

National Archives at Fort Worth, TX
Fort Worth Federal Records Center
1400 John Burgess Drive
Fort Worth, Texas 76140
(817) 551-2000
This facility serves Arkansas, Louisiana, Oklahoma, and Texas.

National Archives at Kansas City, MO
400 West Pershing Road
Kansas City, MO 64108
(816) 268-8000

Lenexa Federal Records Center
17501 W. 98th, Suites 3150 & 4748
Lenexa, KS 66219
(913) 563-7600
These facilities serve Iowa, Kansas, Missouri, and Nebraska. They also retain records for Minnesota, North Dakota, and South Dakota up to the 1960s.

Lee's Summit Federal Records Center
200 Space Center Drive
Lee's Summit, MO 64064-1182
(816) 268-8100
This facility serves New York, New Jersey, Puerto Rico, and the U.S. Virgin Islands.

Kansas City Federal Records Center
8600 NE Underground Drive, Pillar 300-G
Kansas City, MO 64161
(816) 994-1700

National Archives at New York City, NY
One Bowling Green, 3rd Floor
New York, NY 10014
(212) 401-1620
This facility serves New Jersey, New York, Puerto Rico, and the U.S. Virgin Islands.

National Archives at Philadelphia, PA
Philadelphia Federal Records Center
14700 Townsend Road
Philadelphia, PA 19154-1096
(215) 305-2044
This facility serves Delaware, Maryland, Pennsylvania, Virginia, and West Virginia.

National Archives at Riverside, CA
Riverside Federal Records Center
23123 Cajalco Road
Perris, CA 92570-7298
(951) 956-2000
This facility serves Arizona, Southern California, and Clark County, Nevada.

National Archives at San Francisco, CA
San Francisco Federal Records Center
1000 Commodore Drive
San Bruno, CA 94066-2350
(650) 238-3501
This facility serves Northern and Central California, Hawai'i, Nevada (except Clark County), American Samoa, and the Trust Territory of the Pacific.

National Archives at Seattle, WA
Seattle Federal Records Center
6125 Sand Point Way NE
Seattle, WA 98115-7999
(206) 336-5115
This facility serves Alaska, Idaho, Oregon, Washington, Hawai'i (all agencies except Courts and Justice), and the Pacific Ocean Area.

National Archives at St. Louis, MO
National Personnel Records Center
1 Archives Drive
St. Louis, MO 63138
(314) 801-0800
This facility is the central repository of personnel-related records for both the military and civil services of the U.S. government.

State Archivists

Alabama Department of Archives and History
Steve Murray, State Archivist
(334) 242-4441

Alaska State Archives
State Archivist, *vacant*
(907) 465-2241

American Samoa Office of Archives and Records Management
James Himphill, Territorial Archivist
(684) 699-6848

Arizona History and Archives Division
Melanie Sturgeon, State Archivist
(602) 926-3720

Arkansas History Commission
Lisa Speer, State Archivist
(501) 682-6900

California State Archives
Nancy Zimmelman Lenoil, State Archivist
(916) 653-7715

Colorado State Archives
State Archivist, *vacant*
(303) 866-2329

Connecticut State Library
Lizette Pelletier, State Archivist
(860) 566-1100

Delaware Public Archives
Stephen Marz, State Archivist
(302) 744-5049

District of Columbia Office of Public Records
Rebecca Katz, Public Records Administrator
(202) 671-1105

Florida Archives and Records Management
Gerard Clark, State Archivist
(825) 245-6639

The Georgia Archives
Christopher Davidson, State Archivist
(678) 364-3710

Hawaii State Archives
Adam Jansen, State Archivist
(808) 586-0310

Idaho State Archives
David Matte, State Archivist
(208) 514-2328

Illinois State Archives
David Joens, State Archivist
(217) 782-1083

Indiana Archives and Records Administration
Jim Corridan, State Archivist
(317) 232-7191

State Archives of Iowa
Anthony Jahn, State Archivist
(515) 281-4895

Kansas Historical Society
Matt Veatch, State Archivist
(785) 272-8681

Kentucky Department for Libraries and Archives
State Archivist, *vacant*
(502) 564-8300

Louisiana State Archives
Florent Hardy, Jr., State Archivist
(225) 922-1200

Maine State Archives
David Cheever, State Archivist
(207) 287-5793

Maryland State Archives
Timothy Baker, State Archivist
(410) 260-6402

Massachusetts Archives
John D. (Jack) Warner, State Archivist
(617) 727-2816

Michigan Historical Society
Mark Harvey, State Archivist
(517) 373-1415

Minnesota Historical Society
Shawn Rounds, State Archivist
(651) 259-3265

Mississippi Department of Archives and History
Julia Marks Young, State Archivist
(601) 576-6991

Missouri State Archives
John Dougan, State Archivist
(573) 751-4717

Montana Historical Society
Jodie Foley, State Archivist
(406) 444-7482

Nebraska State Historical Society
Gayla Koerting, State Archivist
(402) 471-4783

Nevada State Library and Archives
Jeffrey Kintop, State Archivist
(775) 684-3410

New Hampshire Division of Archives and Records Management
Brian Burford, State Archivist
(603) 271-2236

New Jersey State Archives
Joseph Klett, State Archivist
(609) 292-9507

New Mexico Commission of Public Records
Linda Trujillo, State Archivist
(505) 476-7911

New York State Archives
Thomas Ruller, State Archivist
(518) 473-7091

North Carolina State Archives
Sarah Koonts, State Archivist
(919) 807-7339

State Historical Society of North Dakota
Ann Jenks, State Archivist
(701) 328-2090

Northern Marianas College Library Programs & Services
Territorial Archivist, *vacant*
(670) 237-6797

Ohio History Connection
Fred Previts, State Archivist
(614) 297-2536

Oklahoma Department of Libraries
Jan Davis, State Archivist
(405) 522-3191

Oregon Archives Division, Office of the Secretary of State
Mary Beth Herkert, State Archivist
(503) 373-0701

Pennsylvania State Archives
David Carmichael, State Archivist
(717) 783-5796

Instituto de Cultura Puertorriquena
Territorial Archivist, *vacant*
(787) 725-1060

Rhode Island State Archives
Gwenn Stearn, State Archivist
(401) 222-2353

South Carolina Department of Archives and History
Eric Emerson, State Archivist
(803) 896-6185

South Dakota State Historical Society
Chelle Somsen, State Archivist
(605) 773-5521

Tennessee State Library and Archives
Wayne Moore, State Archivist
(615) 253-3458

Texas State Library and Archives Commission
Jelain Chubb, State Archivist
(512) 463-5455

U.S. Virgin Islands Division of Libraries, Archives, and Museums
Susan Lugo, Territorial Archivist
(340) 774-0630

Utah State Archives and Records Services
Patricia Smith-Mansfield, State Archivist
(801) 531-3850

Vermont State Archives and Records Administration
Tanya Marshall, State Archivist
(802) 828-0405

Library of Virginia
Sandra Treadway, State Archivist
(804) 692-3535

Washington State Archives
Steve Excell, State Archivist
(360) 586-2664

West Virginia Archives and History
Joe Geiger, State Archivist
(304) 558-0230

Wisconsin Historical Society
Matt Blessing, State Archivist
(608) 264-6480

Wyoming State Archives
Michael Strom, State Archivist
(307) 777-7020

ABOUT THE CONTRIBUTORS

Anne W. Ackerson serves as executive director of the Council of State Archivists and is the former director of the Museum Association of New York (MANY). Prior to her tenure at MANY, Anne served as director of several historic house museums and historical societies in central and eastern New York. She is the coauthor of *Leadership Matters* (2013),which examines the leadership needs of twenty-first-century history museums, and is working on a new book about women in the museum workplace. Entries: deaccessioning; local historical societies and core purpose; state archives and records management programs.

Mary Alexander directed the Museum Advancement Program at the Maryland Historical Trust from 1999 to 2014. She has worked in the Washington, D.C. area since 1970, primarily focusing on museum education. From 1987 to 1991 she led the national "Common Agenda for History Museums" program for the American Association for State and Local History. She revised her father, Edward Alexander's *Museums in Motion: An Introduction to the History and Functions of Museums*, published in 2008. Entry: museums, public value of.

Patricia Dockman Anderson is editor of the *Maryland Historical Magazine* and director of Publications and Library Services of the Maryland Historical Society and adjunct professor of history at Towson University. Entry: local history in Maryland.

Jenny Andrews is an editor and writer specializing in landscape design, botany, horticulture, and garden history. Her previous include horticulturist at Cheekwood Botanical Garden in Nashville, education director for the Garden Conservancy, and editor for garden-oriented publications, including executive editor for *Garden Design* magazine. Currently she is pursuing a master's degree in Public History at Middle Tennessee State University. Entries: gardens; gardens and landscapes, researching historic; garden history, interpreting at history sites.

Thomas D. Andrews (PhD, University of Dundee) is territorial archaeologist with the Prince of Wales Northern Heritage Centre in Yellowknife, Northwest Territories, Canada. Entry: local history in Northwest Territories.

Joan (Jo) Antonson is the deputy state historic preservation officer and state historian for the State of Alaska. She is an associate editor of *Alaska History*, the scholarly journal of the Alaska Historical Society. She has been researching, writing, interpreting, and promoting Alaska's history since 1975. Entry: local history in Alaska.

Douglas Armstrong is professor of anthropology at the Maxwell School, Syracuse University. Entry: archaeology.

Robert W. Arnold III is a career public historian now retired from the New York State Archives. He taught American Revolution, colonial America, Civil War, and New York state histories for thirty-two years at the College of Saint Rose and Excelsior College in Albany, New York. Arnold received a number of local, state, and national awards in the course of his career. Entries: local government records; local government research topics.

Chris Myers Asch is the editor of *Washington History, a Publication of the Historical Society of Washington, D.C.* and the author of the forthcoming book, *Chocolate City: Race and Democracy in the Nation's Capital*. Entry: local history in the District of Columbia.

Annette Atkins has her BA from Southwest Minnesota State University and her MA and PhD from Indiana University. She is currently Professor Emerita of History at Saint John's University and the College of Saint Benedict. She has spent her career teaching U.S. history to undergraduates and taking a special interest in reaching out-of-school groups from high school teachers to Road Scholars to historical society members to Rotary Clubs. She is currently officed at the Minnesota Historical Society. Her publications include *Creating Minnesota* (2007); and articles in *Minnesota History, Western Historical Quarterly*; Madison, ed., *Heartland*; and Grabowski, ed., *Minnesota Real and Imagined*. Entry: local history in Minnesota.

Sharon Babaian is curator of transport (land and marine) at the Canada Science and Technology Museums Corporation in Ottawa, Canada. Prior to this, she was a historian at the museum with interest in a wide variety of topics in the history of science and technology in Canada. She has also written a history of the museum. Entry: technology and local history.

Kenneth R. Bailey (PhD Ohio State University) is the author of four books and numerous articles on West Virginia history and former two-time president of the West Virginia Historical Society. He retired as dean of the College of Business, Humanities and Sciences at West Virginia University Institute of Technology, Montgomery, West Virginia. Entry: local history in West Virginia.

Lindsey Baker is the executive director of the Laurel Historical Society a small community organization located in Laurel, Maryland. She attended Goucher College for her undergraduate degree and the University of Delaware for her graduate degree in history with a concentration in museum studies. Entry: museums, public value of.

Helen Barlow is a research associate in the arts faculty at the Open University (UK). She is a contributor to the *Oxford Dictionary of National Biography* and the *Dictionary of Nineteenth-Century Journalism*, and the editor of the anthology *Small Country, Big History: Themes in the History of Wales* (2009). Entry: local history in Wales.

William David Barry is an author, historian, and reference assistant at the Maine Historical Society in Portland, Maine. He has a BA in American history and a MA in American cultural history from the University of Vermont. Entry: local history in Maine.

Elizabeth M. B. Bass is the director of publications for the Oklahoma Historical Society and the editor of the *Chronicles of Oklahoma*. She was a contributing author to *Inspired to Lead: The Governors and First Families of Oklahoma* (2007) and *Another Hot Oklahoma Night: A Rock and Roll Story* (2009). Entry: local history in Oklahoma.

Barbara C. Batson has worked at Old Salem Museum, the Museum of Early Southern Decorative Arts, Historic Deerfield, the Valentine Museum, and the Library of Virginia. She is the author of *Freeing Art from Wood: The Sculpture of Leslie Garland Bolling* (2006) and coauthor of *A Capitol Collection: Virginia's Artistic Inheritance* (2005). Entries: house museums; local history in Virginia.

Bob Beatty is chief of engagement for the American Association for State and Local History and CEO of the Lyndhurst Group, LLC. From 1999 to 2007 he directed the education department at the Orange County (Florida) Regional History Center. Entry: *History News* and *Dispatch*.

Kay Bland was the K–12 education coordinator at the Butler Center for Arkansas Studies, part of the Central Arkansas Library System. She prepared free online lesson plans and other free educator resources utilizing entries in the online *Encyclopedia of Arkansas History & Culture*, Butler Center Books, and other Butler Center resources. Now retired, she lives in Colorado. Entry: local history in Arkansas.

Jody Blankenship has been the CEO of the Connecticut Historical Society since 2013. Prior to this appointment he has served in various capacities at the Kentucky Historical Society and the Ohio Historical Society. Jody holds a BA in history from Ohio Northern University and an MA in history museum studies from the Cooperstown Graduate Program, and he is an alumnus of the Seminar for Historical Administration. Entry: local history in Connecticut.

Stuart M. Blumin is professor of American History emeritus at Cornell University. His most recent books include *The Encompassing City: Streetscapes in Early Modern Art and Culture*, and (with Glenn C. Altschuler) *The GI Bill: A New Deal for Veterans*. Entry: social class.

Brian Bolinger is chief executive officer of the Texas State Historical Association. Entry: Texas Online, Handbook of.

Ray E. Boomhower is interim senior director of the Indiana Historical Society Press. He has written extensively on Indiana history, including biographies of Guss Grissom, Lew Wallace, Ernie Pyle, and May Wright Sewell. Entry: local history in Indiana.

Janelle Carter Brevard is director of communications and government affairs for the Institute of Museum and Library Services, where she is responsible for public and legislative affairs, strategic planning and messaging, and media relations. Entry: Institute of Museum and Library Services.

Julia Brock is assistant professor of history and codirector of the Center for Public History at the University of West Georgia. She received her PhD in public history from the University of California, Santa Barbara. Entry: resorts, historic.

Simon J. Bronner is distinguished professor of American studies and folklore and chair of the American Studies program at the Pennsylvania State University–Harrisburg. Author or editor of over thirty-five books, he also serves as director of the Center for Pennsylvania Culture Studies. Entries: fakelore; folklore and folklife.

Ben Brotemarkle is executive director of the Florida Historical Society and professor of humanities at East Florida State College. His books include *Beyond the Theme Parks: Exploring Central Florida* (1999) and *Crossing Division Street: An Oral*

About the Contributors

History of the African American Community in Orlando (2005). Brotemarkle is producer and host of the weekly public radio magazine and public television series "Florida Frontiers," archived at www.myfloridahistory.org. Entry: local history in Florida.

G. David Brumberg is the former director of the New York Historical Resources Center and the history bibliographer at Cornell University. Entries: Dun & Bradstreet credit reports; failure and local history.

Robert G. Buss is executive director of the Hawai'i Council for the Humanities; before that he served from 1983 to 2003 as its program officer and was the founding coordinator of its Hawai'i History Day program in 1991. Entry: local history in Hawai'i.

R. H. Caldwell has been a historian at the Directorate of History and Heritage, National Defence Headquarters in Ottawa, Canada, since 1992. In 2006 he began preparations for an official history of the Canadian Armed Forces in Afghanistan. He has worked with Canadian soldiers as well as allied forces overseas. Entry: military records, Canada.

Gail G. Campbell, professor emeritus of history, University of New Brunswick, specializes in the sociopolitical history and historical demography of nineteenth-century New Brunswick. Her major publications include studies of political engagement in nineteenth-century New Brunswick and Ontario; her monograph on nineteenth-century New Brunswick women diarists will be published in 2017. Entry: local history in New Brunswick.

Gavin James Campbell is a professor at Doshisha University (Kyoto, Japan) and author of *Music and the Making of a New South* (2004). Entries: Appalachia; music.

Valerie Casbourn worked as the assistant archivist at the Directorate of History and Heritage, National Defence Headquarters in Ottawa, Canada from 2007 to 2014. She is pursuing a master of library and information science degree at the University of Western Ontario. Entry: military records, Canada.

Abigail Christian is the editorial and production coordinator for the Society of American Archivists. She lives in Chicago. Entry: Archives Week; Society of American Archivists.

Sandra Clark has a BA and MA in history from Michigan State University. Her work has included teaching Canadian and American history; serving as an editor and speechwriter for the Canadian Embassy in Washington; and editing *Michigan History* magazine. Clark became director of the Michigan Historical Center in September 1991. She is a past president of the Michigan Museums Association and the American Association for State and Local History. Entry: local history in Michigan.

Jeffrey S. Cole is professor of history at Geneva College in Beaver Falls, Pennsylvania. Entry: Middletown Study.

Virginia Cole has a PhD in history from the State University of New York at Binghamton. She is currently Archaeology, Classics, History, and Medieval Studies Librarian at Cornell University. Entries: local history resources online; Appendix A.

Rebecca Conard is professor of history emerita and former director of public history at Middle Tennessee State University. She has written extensively on the history of parks and protected areas, historical/cultural landscapes, and the history of public history. Entry: parks.

Lauren Coodley retired after a career teaching history at the Napa Community College. She is most recently the author of *Napa Valley Chronicles* (2013) and *Upton Sinclair: California Socialist, Celebrity Intellectual* (2013). All of her books and articles are at www.laurencoodley.com. Entry: agricultural history, problems documenting.

Sheila McIsaac Cooper is emerita from Indiana University, where she was associate dean of the graduate school and taught British history. Often a visiting scholar at the Cambridge Group for the History of Population and Social Structure, her publications include articles and chapters on early-modern mobility, servants, family, and kin. Entry: demography.

Christine Crosby joined the National Council on Public History as membership coordinator in 2015. A graduate of Taylor University (2012) in Indiana, she graduated in 2015 from the Indiana University-Purdue University Indianapolis public history master's program. Entry: National Council on Public History.

David Crosson has directed history organizations and museums throughout the country for over thirty years, including a decade as administrator of the State Historical Society of Iowa. As president and CEO of History San Jose and executive director of the California Historical Society, he was intensely involved with California's state and local history and history education for fifteen years. He retired from the California Historical Society in 2011 and currently is senior associate with Bryan and Jordan Consulting LLC. Entry: local history in California.

Pamela Curtin is an MA student of public history at West Virginia University. She holds a BA in history from Saint Vincent College and has worked at the Smithsonian National Air and Space Museum, Powdermill Nature Reserve of the Carnegie

About the Contributors

Museum of Natural History, and the McCarl Coverlet Gallery at Saint Vincent College. Entries: apps; primary source analysis; STEM education in history organizations.

Lauren Danner became fascinated by Pacific Northwest history during graduate school, and worked for the Washington State Historical Society coordinating multiple statewide outreach programs from 2003 to 2010. She is working on a book about North Cascades National Park. Entry: local history in Washington.

Virgil W. Dean received his PhD in U.S. history from the University of Kansas in 1991, and has been researching and writing about Kansas and regional history for almost thirty years. He is the consulting editor of *Kansas History: A Journal of the Central Plains*, published quarterly by Kansas State University and the Kansas Historical Foundation, and the author or editor of numerous books and articles including *John Brown to Bob Dole: Movers and Shakers in Kansas History* (2006) and *Lawrence: Images of America*, released in 2015. Entry: local history in Kansas.

John Dichtl, president and CEO of the American Association for State and Local History, earned his PhD in early American history at Indiana University and has worked for the National Council on Public History and the Organization of American Historians. Entry: American Association for State and Local History.

Paul Dolinsky, a graduate of Penn State's Landscape Architecture program, is chief of the Historic American Landscapes Survey, National Park Service. Until 2006, he directed the Historic American Buildings Survey. Entry: Historic American Landscapes Survey.

David Donath is president of the Woodstock Foundation, which owns and operates the Billings Farm & Museum. He is a former chair of the American Association for State and Local History and a longtime member of the Vermont Advisory Council on Historic Preservation. He has over thirty years of experience directing historic sites and outdoor museums. Entry: living history museums.

Ian Donnachie is professor emeritus in history, The Open University, where he latterly chaired a Taught Masters in Local and Regional History in Britain and Ireland. He is the author of numerous studies including a history of New Lanark, and a biography, *Robert Owen: Social Visionary*. He is chair of Friends of New Lanark World Heritage Site and also involved in historical and heritage promotion more widely. Entry: local history in Scotland.

Ellen S. Dunlap has been president of the American Antiquarian Society since 1992. Entry: American Antiquarian Society.

Bruce S. Elliott is a graduate of the Centre for English Local History at the University of Leicester (UK) and of the Department of History at Carleton University in Ottawa, Canada, where he is the former departmental graduate chair and teaches, among other things, local, urban, rural, and public history and a seminar on gravestones and cemeteries. Entry: local history in Canada.

Cynthia G. Falk is a professor of material culture at the Cooperstown Graduate Program, a master's degree program in museum studies sponsored by the State University of New York College at Oneonta. Falk is the author of the books *Barns of New York: Rural Architecture of the Empire State* (2012) and *Architecture and Artifacts of the Pennsylvania Germans: Constructing Identity in Early America* (2008) and coeditor of *Buildings & Landscapes: The Journal of the Vernacular Architecture Forum.* Entry: material culture.

Benjamin Filene is professor of history and director of the public history program at the University of North Carolina, Greensboro. His publications include *Letting Go? Historical Authority in a User-Generated World* (2011). Entry: history museums and identity.

Monaeka Flores is the coordinator of Marketing and Programs at the Guam Humanities Council (dba Humanities Guåhan). She has a BA in visual arts from the University of Guam and is currently a graduate student in Micronesian Studies also at the University of Guam. Entry: local history in Guam.

James D. Folts is head of reference services, New York State Archives, where he has worked since 1980. He holds a PhD in history from the University of Rochester and has publications in New York State legal, local, religious, and Native American history. Entries: Civil War tax records; courts and court records; Freedom of Information Act; naturalization records; Appendix B.

Jeff Fortney is a post-doctoral fellow at Central Michigan University. His research examines race, slavery, and the Civil War in Indian Territory. Entry: American Indian history.

Kim Fortney, deputy director of National History Day (NHD) since 2009, directs the National Contest and is the primary liaison with the fifty-seven affiliate programs. Previously she worked in museum education and administration. She served as president of the board of the Mid-Atlantic Association of Museums (2008–2010). Kim coedited *An Alliance of Spirit: Museum and School Partnerships*, published in 2010. Currently she is a member of the executive committee of the History Relevance Campaign, a coalition of professionals seeking to elevate the value of history among stakeholders and the general public. Entry: National History Day.

About the Contributors

Barbara Franco is a graduate of Bryn Mawr College and the Cooperstown Graduate Program in Museum Studies and has had a long career working in museums and historical organizations. She served as executive director of the Pennsylvania Historical and Museum Commission and founding executive director of the Gettysburg Seminary Ridge Museum. She is currently an independent scholar and museum consultant. Entry: local history in Pennsylvania.

Gerald Friesen is Distinguished Professor Emeritus at the University of Manitoba, where he taught for forty years, and a past president of the Canadian Historical Association. Entry: local history in Manitoba.

Michael Frisch, former editor of the *Oral History Review* and president of the Oral History Association (2010), is professor/senior research scholar in American studies and history, emeritus, University at Buffalo, SUNY. He now directs the Randforce Associates, a digital/multimedia oral history consulting office originating in the university's Technology Incubator, and Talking Pictures, LLC, developer of the multimedia oral history mobile app, PixStori. Entry: oral history.

Donald Fyson, full professor at the Département des sciences historiques of Université Laval, is a specialist in eighteenth-, nineteenth-, and twentieth-century Quebec history, notably its social, sociolegal, and sociopolitical aspects. He is particularly interested in the relationship between state, law, and society, especially as seen through the criminal and civil justice system, the police, and local administration. Entry: local history in Quebec.

Kristin L. Gallas is the coeditor of *Interpreting Slavery at Museums and Historic Sites* (2015). She facilitates workshops for public history professionals on interpreting slavery and helps sites develop comprehensive and conscientious interpretive plans. Entry: slavery interpretation at museums and historic sites.

James B. Gardner is executive (retired) for legislative archives, presidential libraries, and museum services at the National Archives. He was formerly Associate Director for Curatorial Affairs at the National Museum of American History, Smithsonian Institution. Gardner's publications include *The Oxford Handbook of Public History*. Entry: museum ethics.

Susan Garton has worked for twenty-five years at the National Portrait Gallery, Smithsonian Institution, where she is currently acting head of Collections Information and Research. She has an MA from the Williams College Graduate Program in the history of art and a BA in American studies from Yale University. Entry: National Portrait Gallery.

Matthew Gilmore is founder-editor of H-DC (for Washington, D.C. history) and edits H-DC and H-Local; he served as H-Net's Vice President for Networks 2005–2011. Entry: H-Local.

David Glassberg teaches American environmental and public history at the University of Massachusetts–Amherst. He is the author of *American Historical Pageantry: The Uses of Tradition in the Early 20th Century* (1990) and *Sense of History: The Place of the Past in American Life* (2001). Entry: landscape.

Philip Goldring is a public historian and consultant based in Ottawa, Ontario. A graduate of Dalhousie University and the University of London, and formerly a research manager with Parks Canada, he currently specializes in the history of northern Canada, and in applied toponymy. Entry: local history in Nunavut.

Gordon Goldsborough serves several roles with the Manitoba Historical Society, being a past president, webmaster, and an editor for the journal *Manitoba History*. Entry: local history in Manitoba.

David M. Grabitske, DBA, grew up in Maryland during the national bicentennial. Today he cheers on about 500 local history organizations in Minnesota as manager of state history services for the Minnesota Historical Society. Entries: field services; Field Services Alliance.

Conny Graft is located in Williamsburg, Virginia and is a consultant in interpretive planning, research, and evaluation for nonprofits including museums, parks, zoos, and health care organizations. Entry: evaluation.

Paul Grebinger is emeritus professor of anthropology in the College of Liberal Arts, Rochester Institute of Technology. He has written on local historical topics including, with Corinne Guntzel, the domestic economy of Elizabeth Cady Stanton in Seneca Falls, New York, on technological change in button manufacture in the Rochester garment industry and, with his wife Ellen, on the efflorescence of nursery industries in Rochester and Geneva, New York. Entry: horticulture and local history.

Howard Green is a public history consultant. His clients have included the Army Corps of Engineers, the Union League of Philadelphia, Save Ellis Island, Inc., the VNA Health Group, and other public and private organizations. Entry: local history in New Jersey.

Emily Greenwald is a shareholder and vice president of Historical Research Associates, Inc., a history, archaeology, and historic preservation consulting firm based in Missoula, Montana. She holds a PhD in history from Yale University. Entry: fees, consulting.

Tim Grove is chief of museum learning at the Smithsonian National Air and Space Museum in Washington, D.C., where he develops exhibitions and web and new media projects. He originated and wrote the History Bytes column in *History News* for thirteen years. He serves on the leadership team for the History Relevance Campaign. Entries: blogs; crowdsourcing and crowdfunding; historical thinking; microblogging; radical trust and voice of authority; relevance; web history.

J. Philip Gruen is associate professor and director of the School of Design and Construction at Washington State University. He is the author of *Manifest Destinations: Cities and Tourists in the Nineteenth-Century American West*. Entries: architectural history; vernacular architecture.

Kristen Gwinn-Becker, PhD is an accomplished scholar, published author, and thought leader in the field of digital heritage collections and content. She currently serves as the chief executive officer of HistoryIT, a technology company that supports institutions as they embrace innovative digital approaches in order to secure meaningful access to our history for generations to come. Entry: digitization.

James L. Hansen, FASG. Reference librarian and genealogical specialist at the Wisconsin Historical Society, 1974–2014. Author, editor, teacher, and lecturer on a wide range of genealogical topics. Entry: genealogy, an archivist's view.

Rick Hendricks, author of numerous works on Spanish colonial history, is the State Historian of New Mexico. Entry: local history in New Mexico.

Trevor Herbert is professor of music at the Open University (UK). He has worked extensively on cultural and musical aspects related to brass instruments, with publications including *The British Brass Band: A Musical and Social History* (2000) and *The Trombone* (2006), and is also coeditor with Professor Gareth Elwyn Jones of the seven volumes of the University of Wales Press series "Welsh History and its Sources" (1988–1995). Entry: local history in Wales.

Dean Herrin is chief historian of the National Capital Region, National Park Service, Washington, D.C. Entry: regionalism.

Terence Hines is a cognitive neuroscientist at Pace University in Pleasantville, New York. He became interested in the importance of the post office in local history both as a philatelist and while writing a book on the history of the postal service in his hometown of Hanover, New Hampshire. Entry: post office records.

Anna Gibson Holloway is the maritime historian for the Park History Program of the National Park Service. She is the former curator of the award-winning USS *Monitor* Center in Newport News, Virginia and has written extensively about the Union ironclad and nineteenth-century maritime history. Entry: National Park Service.

Andrew Horrall is a senior archivist at Library and Archives Canada. He holds a doctorate in history from the University of Cambridge. Entry: Canada, Library and Archives.

Mark Hudson has served as the executive director Tudor Place Historic House and Garden since 2015. Previously he served as executive director for the Vermont Historical Society and the Historical Society of Frederick County, Maryland and as curator for the Boone County Historical Society in Missouri. He holds a master of historical administration and museum studies degree from the University of Kansas and a master of arts degree in library science from the University of Missouri. Entry: local history in Vermont.

Catherine Hughes is a hybrid theatre practitioner, museum professional, educator, researcher, and author of *Museum Theatre: Communicating with Visitors through Drama*. She is director of interpretation and evaluation at Conner Prairie History Museum, overseeing daily operations of seven interpretive areas. Entry: museum theater.

Rebecca Hunt is a historian teaching at the University of Colorado, Denver, where she specializes in social history of the American West and public history. She writes on community, gender, and ethnic history. Her most recent book is *Natrona County: People, Place and Time* (2011). Entry: local history in Colorado.

G. Howard Hunter is the academic dean at Metairie Park Country Day School in Metairie, Louisiana. He has taught history for over thirty years and has published articles in *Newsweek*, *Louisiana History*, *Louisiana Cultural Vistas*, and the *Times Picayune*. He is the past president of the Louisiana Historical Society. Entry: local history in Louisiana.

Geof Huth is the chief records officer and chief law librarian of the New York State Unified Court System. Previously, he had served for nearly twenty-four years at the New York State Archives, lastly as the director of Government Records Services. Entries: regionalisms; slang.

Heather A. Huyck has been a historian for forty years for the National Park Service, the U.S. House of Representatives Subcommittee on National Parks, and the College of William & Mary, specializing in women's and public history. She has visited 321 national park sites and many other historic sites and is past president, National Collaborative for Women's History Sites. Huyck is writing a book on interpreting women's history at museums and historic sites. Entry: women's history at local history sites, interpreting.

Peggy W. Jeanes, founding editor of *Mississippi History Now*, is now editor emerita. She is currently serving a three-year term on the Mississippi Historical Society Board of Directors. Entry: local history in Mississippi.

Jeff Joeckel is an archivist in the office of the National Register of Historic Places at the National Park Service. Entry: National Register of Historic Places.

Linda Johnson has lived and worked in the Yukon since 1974 as an archivist, researcher, and writer for Yukon government, Yukon College and several Yukon First Nations and cultural organizations. Her publications include *The Kandik Map* (2009), *With the People Who Live Here: A History of the Yukon Legislature, 1909-2009* (2009), *A History of the Yukon Commissioners 1898-2010* (2012), *Whitehorse: An Illustrated History* (2013), and numerous articles and conference papers. She is currently employed as Researcher/Writer for the Adäka Cultural Society in Whitehorse, Yukon. Entry: local history in Yukon Territory.

Mitch Kachun is professor of history at Western Michigan University in Kalamazoo, Michigan. His teaching specialties are African American history and collective memory. Kachun's publications include *Festivals of Freedom: Memory and Meaning in African American Emancipation Celebrations, 1808–1915* (2003) and *First Martyr of Liberty: Crispus Attucks in American Memory* (2017). Entries: African American history; emancipation celebrations.

Carol Kammen is the Tompkins County (New York) historian and author of several books, including *On Doing Local History* (2003); *Ithaca: A Brief History* (2008); *Cornell: Glorious to View* (2005), *First Person Cornell: Student Diaries, Letters, Email & Blogs* (2006), *Part & Apart: The Black Experience at Cornell* (2008), and *Zen and the Art of Local History* (2014), and has written the "On Doing Local History" column for *History News* since 1995. She coedited the first and second editions of the *Encyclopedia of Local History*. Entries: advertisements; censorship; county histories; local historian as public intellectual; manifest destiny; New York, local history in; poll tax; state historians; United States, local history in.

Michael Kammen, who died in 2013, was a Pulitzer Prize–winning professor of history at Cornell University. He wrote more than two dozen books including the monumental *Mystic Chords of Memory: The Transformation of Tradition in American Culture, In the Past Lane: Historical Perspectives on American Culture*, and others detailing American memory and our concern for the past. Entries: American exceptionalism; Annales School; heritage; historiography; memorials and monuments; popular culture; new social history; and youth culture.

Robert J. Kibbee is a trustee at the History Center in Tompkins County (New York). He retired from Cornell University, where he was the map and geospatial information librarian. He specializes in historical cartography and web-based cartography. Entries: adoption; Ancestry.com; census, United States; city directories; FamilySearch; GIS in local history; genealogical resources online; genealogy, African American; household; inflation and local history; maps and atlases; mortality schedules; pension records; RootsWeb.com; slave schedules; Social Security Death Index; Valley of the Shadow; vital records and vital statistics.

Kimberlee Kihleng has served as the executive director of the Guam Humanities Council (dba Humanities Guåhan) since 2005. She holds a PhD in anthropology from the University of Hawai'i at Manoa and throughout her career has held both academic and applied positions focused on the arts, culture, and history of the Pacific Islands. Entry: local history in Guam.

Jeffrey M. Kintop is the Nevada State Archivist and has worked in Nevada history for thirty-six years. He has coauthored several books and contributes to collective works on Nevada History. Entry: local history in Nevada.

Liza Kirwin is the deputy director of the Archives of American Art, Smithsonian Institution. She holds a PhD in American studies from the University of Maryland–College Park, a master's degree in library science from the Catholic University of America, and a bachelor's degree in art history from the Johns Hopkins University. She has managed the archives' exhibition, acquisition, and oral history programs and is the author of numerous articles and books about the archives' holdings. Her most recent publication is *Lists: To-dos, Illustrated Inventories, Collected Thoughts, and Other Artists' Enumerations from the Smithsonian's Archives of American Art* (2010). Entry: Archives of American Art.

Mary-Jo Kline. Holding a PhD in American history from Columbia University and a degree in Library and Information Science from Catholic University, Mary-Jo Kline boasted a long career as a documentary editor before preparing *A Guide to Documentary Editing* ([1987, 1998] 2008). Onetime staff member of the Library of Congress's "American Memory" project and the former American history librarian at Brown University, she has proudly donated the records of her own family to the Chemung Valley History Museum in her hometown, Elmira, New York. Entry: documentary editing.

Harry Klinkhamer is a public historian and researcher from the greater Chicagoland area. Entry: Conference of State and Local Historical Societies.

About the Contributors

Gary R. Kremer is the executive director of the State Historical Society of Missouri and the author of twelve books and dozens of articles on the history of Missouri. Entry: local history in Missouri.

Guy Lancaster is the editor of the *Encyclopedia of Arkansas History & Culture*. He holds a PhD in heritage studies from Arkansas State University and is the author of the award-winning *Racial Cleansing in Arkansas, 1883–1924: Politics, Land, Labor, and Criminality* (2014). Entry: local history in Arkansas.

William L. Lang is emeritus professor of history at Portland State University. He is author or editor of eight books on environmental and Pacific Northwest history, including *Explorers of the Maritime Pacific Northwest: Mapping the World through Primary Documents* (2016), and is the founder of the Center for Columbia River History and executive editor of *Oregon Encyclopedia*. Entry: local history in Oregon.

Adina Langer is a public historian based in Atlanta, Georgia, where she is the curator of the Museum of History and Holocaust Education at Kennesaw State University. In the past she taught exhibition development and digital history courses at Georgia State University, consulted on projects in Lansing, Michigan, Chicago, Illinois, and New York City, and managed the development of the memorial exhibition at the 9/11 Memorial Museum in New York. She has an MA in archives and public history from New York University and a BA in history and creative writing from Oberlin College. Entries: digital history projects; public history commons.

Gabrielle M. Lanier is professor and interim head of the department of history at James Madison University, where she also directs the public history program. She is the author of *The Delaware Valley in the Early Republic: Architecture, Landscape, and Regional Identity* (2005), and, with Bernard L. Herman, *Everyday Architecture of the Mid-Atlantic: Looking at Buildings and Landscapes* (1997). She is the subject editor for the North America section of *The Encyclopedia of Vernacular Architecture of the World*, 2nd ed., Marcel Vellinga, ed. (forthcoming). Entry: architectural pattern books.

Catherine Lavoie has a master's degree in American Studies from the University of Maryland. She began work with the Historic American Buildings Survey, National Park Service, in 1985, becoming senior historian in 1994 and HABS Chief in 2006. She was the 2003 recipient of the Vernacular Architecture Forum's Buchanan Award for excellence in fieldwork and interpretation for the documentation for HABS of the Friends Meeting Houses of the Delaware Valley. Entry: Historic American Buildings Survey.

Herbert I. Lazerow, AB Pennsylvania, JD Harvard, LLM George Washington, DESS Paris I Panthèon-Sorbonne, is professor of law at the University of San Diego. He is the author of *Mastering Art Law* (2015) and numerous articles on tax law, property law, art law, and genealogy. Entry: Jewish genealogy.

Erika Lee is the Rudolph J. Vecoli Chair in Immigration History and the Director of the Immigration History Research Center at the University of Minnesota. She is also the author of several books and articles on immigration and Asian American history, including *The Making of Asian America: A History*. Entry: Immigration Research History Center.

Teresa K. Lehr, MA in history and English, has retired from teaching research and nonfiction writing at the College at Brockport, SUNY. She has researched and written seven books, five of which are about the history of local health care. Her most recent publication, *The Great Tonsil Massacre*, is a historical novella about a public health initiative that took place in Rochester, New York in 1920 and 1921. Entries: crime, history of; gravestones; health care as local history topic; social purity.

Jane Freundel Levey is managing editor of *Washington History, a Publication of the Historical Society of Washington, D.C.*, and a consulting curator at the George Washington University Museum. Entry: local history in the District of Columbia.

Edward MacDonald is an associate professor of history at the University of Prince Edward Island. For thirteen years he was curator of history at the Prince Edward Island Museum & Heritage Foundation, where he edited its popular history journal, *The Island Magazine*. Entry: local history in Prince Edward Island.

Esther Mackintosh is the president of the Federation of State Humanities Councils. She has a PhD in American literature from Kansas State University and worked in magazine publishing for several years before joining the federation. Entry: Federation of State Humanities Councils.

Mary K. Mannix is the Maryland room manager of the C. Burr Artz Public Library, Frederick County Public Libraries (FCPL) in Frederick, Maryland. She also oversees the FCPL Thurmont Center for Agricultural History and the Brunswick Branch History Room. Entries: obituaries; photography.

Merle Massie is a specialist in the local, agricultural, and environmental history of western Canada. Entry: local history in Saskatchewan.

Deidre McCarthy is chief of CRGIS for the National Park Service. Entry: Cultural Resources Geographic Information Systems (CRGIS).

About the Contributors

George W. McDaniel is executive director emeritus of Drayton Hall, a historic site in Charleston, South Carolina, owned by the National Trust for Historic Preservation, after serving as its executive director for twenty-five years. He is now a museum consultant and president of McDaniel Consulting, LLC. Entry: building bridges through local history.

Lauris McKee is an associate professor emerita at Franklin and Marshall College. Her research projects in the Ecuadorian Andes were funded by the National Institutes of Health, the Fulbright Foundation, and the National Science Foundation. Entries: clan; ethnography; ethnohistory and local history; family.

Ellen Miles retired in 2010 from the Smithsonian National Portrait Gallery, where she had been on the curatorial staff for forty years and was responsible for numerous exhibitions and publications. Miles received the Smithsonian Distinguished Scholar Award in 2004. Entry: portraiture.

Diane Miller began her career with the National Park Service in 1984, and has served as the national program manager for the National Underground Railroad Network to Freedom since 1999. Currently she is a PhD candidate at the University of Nebraska–Lincoln working on a dissertation about the role of the Wyandot and other Ohio Emigrant Tribes in the Underground Railroad in Ohio and Kansas. Entry: Underground Railroad.

Charles Mitchell is professor of American studies at Elmira College in Elmira, New York. Many years ago he published a book on the afterlife of Ralph Waldo Emerson that several of his friends and family read. His essays—on a narrow range of disconnected subjects—have appeared in *Isle, Terrain.org*, the *Bloomsbury Review*, and *Isotope*. The IRS has yet to question his tax deduction for hiking boots. Entry: travel literature.

Patrick Moore is director of the New Mexico Historic Sites Division, a senior historian with Historical Research Associates, Inc., a partner with Three21 Innovations, LLC, and a founder of NextExitHistory™. Moore is the past president of the National Council on Public History (NCPH) and was the 2007 Carnegie Foundation-CASE U.S. Professor of the Year for the State of Florida. Entry: public history.

R. Laurence Moore has written widely on the subject of American religion and culture. He received his degree from Yale University and joined the Cornell faculty in 1972. He is the Howard A. Newman Professor Emeritus of American studies and history. Entry: history of religion.

Tom Morain, an author and popular speaker, served as director of Historians for Living History Farms in Des Moines and head of the State Historical Society of

Iowa. He currently teaches and writes at Graceland University in Lamoni, Iowa. Entry: local history in Iowa.

Cecilia Morgan is a professor in the department of Curriculum, Teaching and Learning, University of Toronto and is also cross-appointed to the department of History. Her latest books are *Creating Colonial Pasts: History, Memory, and Commemoration in Southern Ontario, 1860–1980* (2015) and *Commemorating Canada: History, Heritage, and Memory, 1850s–1990s* (2016). Her latest book, *Building Better Britains? Settler Societies Within the British Empire, 1783–1920*, was published by University of Toronto Press, fall 2016. Entry: local history in Ontario.

Fred Muratori is a reference librarian and the bibliographer for English-language literature, theater, and film at Cornell University's John M. Olin Library. Entry: biographical dictionaries.

Kevin Murphy is the speechwriter at the National Trust for Historic Preservation. He holds a PhD in history from Columbia University and lives in Washington, D.C. Entry: National Trust for Historic Preservation.

James D. Nason is professor emeritus, American Indian Studies, anthropology; director emeritus, museology; and emeritus curator of Pacific and American ethnology, Burke Museum of Natural History and Culture, University of Washington. An anthropologist and museum specialist, Nason's research and publications on legal, ethnohistorical, social change, and museological work in Micronesia, Canada, and the United States include extensive applied work and currently focus on indigenous intellectual property rights. Entries: intellectual property rights; museums and the matter of ethics; patrimony; repatriation.

Susan Near is a development and marketing officer at the Montana Historical Society and has held various positions there since 1982. Near holds an MA in American history from the University of Delaware; has served on a number of professional boards including those of the American Association of Museums, the Museums Association of Montana, and Humanities Montana; and teaches museum management for the Northern States Conservation Center's online museum classes. Entry: local history in Montana.

David Neufeld retired after thirty years as the Yukon and western Arctic historian with Parks Canada, continues his work with both Yukon aboriginal and non-aboriginal communities on their local histories. The resulting community-driven projects have informed school curricula; supported content for local museums, culture centers, and historic sites; strengthened intergenerational ties; and fostered more respectful and meaningful relationships between communities and regional and national governments. Entry: local history in Yukon Territory.

About the Contributors

Alan S. Newell is the founder of Historical Research Associates, Inc., a national public history consulting firm established in 1974. He currently serves as managing partner of Three21 Innovations, LLC, a digital technology company. Newell has been a long-term member of the National Council on Public History where he has served on the board of directors and as president in 2000. In 2008, he was awarded the Robert Kelley Memorial Award for his service to the field of public history. Entry: public history.

Claudia J. Nicholson is a thirty-eight-year veteran of history museums and historical agencies. She has written and taught on museum collections, establishing small museums, and has spent the last eleven years as executive director of the North Star Museum of Boy Scouting and Girl Scouting, where she has enjoyed learning the stories of Boy Scouting and Girl Scouting. Entry: organizational records, using local.

Linda Norris is an independent museum professional working with museums and history organizations to develop compelling narratives, connect with communities, and build professional capabilities. She blogs at the Uncataloged Museum (http://uncatalogedmuseum.blogspot.com) and has worked with museums ranging from western Saskatchewan to eastern Ukraine. Entries: deaccessioning; docent; exhibits and local history; museums, small; museums and families; social media; volunteers.

Richard O'Connor is chief of the Historic American Engineering Record and oversees the Heritage Documentation programs at the National Park Service. He earned his PhD in history from the University of Pittsburgh and has researched and written on glass, iron, and brick making, among other topics in the history of technology. Entry: Historic American Engineering Record.

Kara T. Olidge is executive director of the Amistad Research Center at Tulane University, New Orleans, Louisiana. Entry: Amistad Research Center.

Sandra Oliver is a freelance food writer and food historian. In 1971 she developed a fireplace cooking program at Mystic Seaport Museum. She was the editor of *Food History News* for twenty years from 1989 to 2009, and the author of *Saltwater Foodways: New Englanders and Their Food at Sea and Ashore in the 19th Century* (1995) and *Food in Colonial and Federal America* (2005). She continues to write about food history and lectures and teaches across the country. Entry: culinary history and local history.

Susan M. Ouellette, professor, department of history at Saint Michael's College (Colchester, Vermont), received her PhD from the University of Massachusetts, Amherst. Her teaching and research interests encompass early America to the Civil

War, and includes local history. Her enthusiasm for local topics has translated into a number of published scholarly articles, book chapters on the Lake Champlain region, and a new book based on the journal of an early nineteenth-century farmwife in upstate New York. Entry: family history.

Natalie Panther has a PhD in American Western history and is the program officer at the Helmerich Center for American Research at Gilcrease Museum. Entry: Frontier Thesis.

Leslie Paris is associate professor of history at the University of British Columbia, where her research examines the history of American childhood. Entry: children's history.

Randall L. Patton is the Shaw Industries Professor of History, Kennesaw State University. His publications include *Carpet Capital: The Rise of a New South Industry* and *Working for Equality: The Narrative of Harry Hudson*. Entry: business and industrial history.

Phillip Payne is a professor of history at St. Bonaventure University. He teaches United States and public history. He is the author of *Dead Last: The Public Memory of Warren G. Harding's Scandalous Legacy* (2009) and *Crash! How the Boom and Bust of the 1920s Economy Worked* (2015). He previously worked in public history. Entry: boosterism.

James DeWolf Perry, coeditor of *Interpreting Slavery at Museums and Historic Sites* (2015), is the executive director of the Center for Reconciliation in Providence, Rhode Island and the former executive director of the Tracing Center on Histories and Legacies of Slavery. Entry: slavery interpretation at museums and historic sites.

Keith Petersen is retired from the Idaho State Historical Society. He is the author of several books and articles about the history of Idaho and the Northwest. Entry: local history in Idaho.

Robert Phelps is an associate professor of history at California State University–East Bay, where he specializes in the history of California and the American West, as well as public history. Entry: western history and local historians.

Joshua Piker is the editor of the *William and Mary Quarterly* at the Omohundro Institute of Early American History and Culture and professor of history at the College of William & Mary. He is the author of two monographs, *Okfuskee: A Creek Town in Colonial America* and *The Four Deaths of Acorn Whistler: Telling Stories in Colonia America*. Entry: American Indian history.

About the Contributors

Dwight T. Pitcaithley is a professor of history at New Mexico State University and served as chief historian of the National Park Service from 1995 to 2005. Entry: teaching local history in the classroom.

Mike Polston is a longtime educator and serves as the staff historian of the *Encyclopedia of Arkansas History & Culture*. He has published extensively in a variety of newspapers and state historical journals and helped to found the Museum of American History in Cabot, Arkansas. In addition, he is the coeditor of *To Can the Kaiser: Arkansas and the Great War* (2015). Entry: local history in Arkansas.

James E. Potter has been on the staff of the Nebraska State Historical Society since 1967, formerly serving as state archivist and editor of *Nebraska History*. Currently he is the society's senior research historian. Entry: local history in Nebraska.

Norma Prendergast received her PhD in art history from Cornell University and was coeditor of the first edition of the *Encyclopedia of Local History* (2000). Entries: bird's eye view; Farm Security Administration photographs; historicism.

Stephanie Przybylek, owner/artist, Creative Animal Fine and Decorative Arts, was executive director, Delaware Military Heritage & Education Foundation. She holds a BA from Gettysburg College and an MA in art history from the University of Delaware. She worked in the museum field for more than fifteen years, including positions as curator of the Cayuga Museum & Case Research Lab Museum in Auburn, New York; director of collections and interpretation for the Schenectady Museum in Schenectady, New York; and director of collections and museum programs for the Delaware Historical Society. Entry: local history in Delaware.

Terrence M. Punch, CM, D Litt, is former president of the Royal Nova Scotia Historical Society and of the Genealogical Institute of the Maritimes. He is the author of nine books about early Irish, Scots, and Montbéliardais arrivals in Atlantic Canada before Canadian Confederation. Entry: local history in Nova Scotia.

Phil Roberts holds a PhD in history from the University of Washington and a JD in law from the University of Wyoming College of Law. He has taught the history of Wyoming and the American West at the University of Wyoming since 1990. Entry: local history in Wyoming.

Tim Roberts is a practicing public historian trained at the University of West Florida. Tim currently works as a project historian with Historical Research Associates and is a founding partner of the digital humanities consulting company, Three21 Innovations, LLC. Entry: public history.

Alan Rogers has been engaged in local community history in the United Kingdom and internationally since 1957; he is visiting professor at the universities of Nottingham and East Anglia, and author of a number of local studies and books and many articles about local history sources and methods. Entry: local history workshops.

Kristen Rogers-Iverson is the former associate editor of the *Utah Historical Quarterly* and associate director of the Utah Division of State History. Entry: local history in Utah.

Stephanie Rowe became executive director of the National Council on Public History in 2016 after working for the organization since 2012 in the roles of program manager, associate director, and interim executive director. She earned her BA in social studies (2006) from Ithaca College and MA in history museum studies (2008) from the Cooperstown Graduate Program. Entry: National Council on Public History.

Mary C. Ryan is a writer-editor on the Strategy and Communications Staff of the National Archives and Records Administration. She is also managing editor of *Prologue* magazine, the quarterly of the National Archives. Entries: military records, U.S.; National Archives and Records Administration (NARA); Soundex.

Stuart W. Sanders is the outreach services manager for the Kentucky Historical Society. He is the former executive director of the Perryville Battlefield Preservation Association and is the author of three books and a number of articles and essays. Entry: local history in Kentucky.

Philip V. Scarpino is professor of history and director of the graduate program in public history at Indiana University/Purdue University, Indianapolis. His is director of oral history for Indiana University's Randall L. Tobias Center for Leadership Excellence. His areas of expertise include public history, environmental history, oral history, and historic preservation. Recent, related publications: "Addressing Cross-Border Pollution of the Great Lakes," in Michael Behiels and Reginald Stuart, eds., *Transnationalism in Canada-United States History into the Twenty First Century* (2010), 146–67; "Isle Royale National Park: Balancing Human and Natural History in a Maritime Park," *George Wright Forum* 28, no. 2 (2011): 182–98; and "A Historian's Perspective on Rivers of the Anthropocene" in Janos Bogardi et al., eds., *The Global Water System in the Anthropocene: Challenges for Science and Governance* (2014). Entries: borders and boundaries; environmental history.

Thomas F. Schwartz worked in special collections at the Illinois State Historical Library, now the Abraham Lincoln Presidential Library, from 1985 to 2011. He was Illinois state historian from 1993 to 2011 and is now the director of the Herbert

About the Contributors

Hoover Presidential Library-Museum in West Branch, Iowa. Entry: local history in Illinois.

Leigh Shaw-Taylor is director of the Cambridge Group for the History of Population and Social Structure. He is a senior lecturer in eighteenth- and nineteenth-century British economic and social history at Cambridge University. Entry: Cambridge Group for the History of Population and Social Structure.

Joel Silbey is professor emeritus of history at Cornell University. He is author of several books and articles about the history of American politics. Entry: political history.

Patrizia Sione is the reference archivist at the Kheel Center for Labor-Management Documentation & Archives at Cornell University. She has studied the community of radical Italian immigrants in Paterson, New Jersey, at the turn of the twentieth century, for her dissertation at Binghamton University. Entry: labor history and the history of communities.

Pam Berreth Smokey is editor for the State Historical Society of North Dakota. She has been employed with the society since 2012. Entry: local history in North Dakota.

Bonnie Stacy is chief curator at the Martha's Vineyard Museum. She received her master's degree in the history of decorative arts from the Bard Graduate Center and is the author of two books on Martha's Vineyard history. Entry: decorative arts.

Cathy Stanton is a cultural anthropologist and public historian whose work focuses on the social, political, and economic functions of commemorative projects of all kinds. She teaches at Tufts University and currently serves as the digital media editor for the National Council on Public History. Entry: H-Public.

Rodger Stroup retired in 2009 as the director of the South Carolina Department of Archives and History after working for more than forty years in the public history field in South Carolina. He currently serves as superintendent of railway operations for the South Carolina Railroad Museum in Winnsboro, South Carolina. He is currently working on a book on the history of the South Carolina State Fair to be published in 2019, the 150th anniversary of the fair. Entry: local history in South Carolina.

James Sweany has worked at the Library of Congress for more than twenty years. He presently serves as head of the library's Local History & Genealogy Reading Room. Entry: Library of Congress.

Steven Teske is an archival assistant at the Butler Center for Arkansas Studies, part of the Central Arkansas Library System. He has fact-checked and written entries for the online *Encyclopedia of Arkansas History & Culture*, a project of the Butler Center, and is the author of *Unvarnished Arkansas: The Naked Truth about Nine Famous Arkansans* (2012), among other books. Entry: local history in Arkansas.

Kate Tiller is reader emerita in English local history, University of Oxford, a fellow of Kellogg College, Oxford, and a visiting fellow in English local history at the University of Leicester. She is a former editor of *The Local Historian* and her *English Local History: An introduction* (2002) is a widely used textbook. Her research interests center on rural change, and on religion and community post-1750. Entries: British Association for Local History; local history in England; local history in Ireland.

Ann Toplovich is executive director of the Tennessee Historical Society. Her career of over thirty-five years in public history has allowed her to work with communities in every county across the state of Tennessee. Entry: local history in Tennessee.

Kenneth C. Turino is manager of Community Engagement and Exhibitions at Historic New England, the oldest, largest, and most comprehensive regional heritage organization in the country. Mr. Turino holds a master of arts degree in Teaching, Museum Education, from the George Washington University and is an adjunct professor in the Tufts University Museum Studies Program. Entry: local history in Massachusetts.

Marie Tyler-McGraw, author of several books, is retired from the National Park Service and continues to research and write local history from her home in Shepherdstown, West Virginia. Entry: tourism.

Dan K. Utley, a longtime employee of the Texas Historical Commission, is now chief historian with the Center for Texas Public History at Texas State University. Entry: local history in Texas.

Max A. van Balgooy is president of Engaging Places LLC, a design and strategy firm that connects people and historic places. He works with a wide range of historic sites on interpretive planning and business strategy, from James Madison's Montpelier to Frank Lloyd Wright's Taliesin West. These experiences provide a rich source of ideas for EngagingPlaces.net, where he blogs regularly about the opportunities and challenges facing historic sites and house museums. Entries: house museums in the twenty-first century; mission statement; values of history; vision.

David G. Vanderstel, PhD, is an independent historian and consultant living in Bloomington, Indiana. He served as senior historian at Conner Prairie Museum, adjunct assistant professor of history at IUPUI, senior research associate at the

About the Contributors

Polis Center at IUPUI where he was assistant editor of *The Encyclopedia of Indianapolis*, and executive director of the National Council on Public History for more than eleven years. He remains active in state and local history as well as historic preservation initiatives in Indianapolis and Monroe County, Indiana.

Ren Vasiliev is a professor of geography at the State University of New York College at Geneseo and author of *From Abbotts to Zurich: New York State Placenames* (2004). Entry: placenames.

Kierra Verdun is an intern for Historypin. She is a student at Kalamazoo College currently pursuing a bachelor of arts degree in history, and was connected to Historypin through the campus's Arcus Center for Social Justice Leadership. Entry: Historypin.

Andy Verhoff has worked, over his twenty-plus-year career, with more than 220 local history organizations and hundreds of local historians in Ohio's eighty-eight counties. He is currently the coordinator of the History Fund grant program at the Ohio History Connection in Columbus and, in general, a local history jack-of-all trades (and master of some). Entry: local history in Ohio.

Jay D. Vogt is director of the South Dakota State Historical Society located in the Cultural Heritage Center in Pierre, South Dakota. Vogt is active in the American Association for State and Local History and the National Conference of State Historic Preservation Officers. Entry: local history in South Dakota.

Heather A. Wade, CAE, independent scholar and contractor in archives, earned an MA in applied history from George Mason University in 2002. She is a Certified Archivist Emerita, and serves on the editorial board of *Collections: A Journal for Museum and Archives Professionals.* She has administered archives and museums in a variety of public and private settings, and is an archives educator. Entries: archives and local history; DAR Library; diaries; postcards.

Peter Wallner has a PhD in U.S. history from Pennsylvania State University. His experience includes thirty-plus years of teaching and he is the author of a two-volume biography of the fourteenth president of the United States, Franklin Pierce. Wallner recently retired as library director of the New Hampshire Historical Society. Entry: local history in New Hampshire.

Amy Jordan Webb is a senior field director at the National Trust for Historic Preservation. She joined the National Trust for Historic Preservation's Heritage Tourism Program in 1993 and served as the program's director from 1995 to 2011. Entry: cultural heritage tourism.

Margaret Webster is a visual resources consultant who lives in Ithaca, New York. For many years she was the director of the Knight Visual Resources Facility in the College of Architecture, Art & Planning at Cornell University. She is the chair of the VRA Foundation; she also served a term as president of the Art Libraries Society of North America. Entry: Buildings of the United States.

Robert Weible served as New York State Historian and the chief curator at the New York State Museum from 2008 to 2015. As chief of the Division of History for the Pennsylvania Historical and Museum Commission (1989–2004), he managed—and modernized—that state's historical marker program. Weible is a past president of the National Council on Public History. Entry: historical markers.

Lee White is currently the executive director of the National Coalition for History (NCH) in Washington, D.C. He is an attorney with over thirty years' experience in government relations with membership associations, as well as several years with the federal government as a legislative specialist. White holds a law degree from the Catholic University of America and an MA in American history from George Mason University. Entry: National Coalition for History.

Kent Whitworth serves as the executive director of the Kentucky Historical Society and is a founding member of the History Relevance Campaign steering committee. Entry: local history in Kentucky.

Susie Wilkening is a senior consultant and curator of museum audiences with Reach Advisors' Museums R+D division. In that work she helps museums understand the impact they are capable of having in the lives of their visitors and their communities, and, as a field, the impact museums have on society. Prior to joining Reach Advisors in 2006, Susie worked for ten years in museums, including tenures as the executive director of the Saratoga County Historical Society and as the development director of Historic Huguenot Street. Entry: museums and families.

Erin Williams is a program analyst in the Office of Presidential Libraries of the National Archives and Records Administration. Entry: presidential libraries.

Roger L. Williams is retired executive director of the Penn State Alumni Association and affiliate associate professor of higher education at Penn State. Entry: agricultural and mechanical colleges.

Amy H. Wilson is an independent museum consultant and editor of this volume. She was first curator, then director of the Chemung County Historical Society in Elmira, New York, for thirteen years. Her independently curated exhibits include *Atlanta in 50 Objects* for the Atlanta History Center and *1968 in America* for Exhibits USA. Wilson coedited the *Encyclopedia of Local History*, second editon. She received her MA in public history from Indiana University/Purdue University, Indianapolis.

Janis Wilton is a public and oral historian based at the University of New England in Australia, where she coordinates and teaches in the university's undergraduate and postgraduate awards in local, family, and applied history. Her website is www.une.edu.au/staff/jwilton.php. Entry: local history in Australia.

James Worsham is editorial team leader and editor of *Prologue* magazine on the Creative Services Staff of the National Archives and Records Administration. Entry: National Archives and Records administration.

Kerri Young is a Historypin engagement manager in San Francisco. She has worked on a number of projects including the crowdsourced-based Year of the Bay, and is currently working with the National Archives and Records Administration (NARA) on a WWI and WWII moving image engagement project. Kerri is responsible for building and managing community relationships, helping implement and experiment with new audience participation strategies to promote dynamic and engaging programs within the cultural heritage sector. Entry: Historypin.

Jamil Zainaldin is an American historian and president of the Georgia Humanities Council. Entries: local history in Georgia; state humanities councils.

John Zimm received a BA in history from the University of Wisconsin–Madison in 2003. He has worked at the Wisconsin Historical Society Press since 2002. Entry: local history in Wisconsin.